Literature Criticism from 1400 to 1800

Guide to Thomson Gale Literary Criticism Series

For criticism on	Consult these Thomson Gale series
Authors now living or who died after December 31, 1999	*CONTEMPORARY LITERARY CRITICISM (CLC)*
Authors who died between 1900 and 1999	*TWENTIETH-CENTURY LITERARY CRITICISM (TCLC)*
Authors who died between 1800 and 1899	*NINETEENTH-CENTURY LITERATURE CRITICISM (NCLC)*
Authors who died between 1400 and 1799	*LITERATURE CRITICISM FROM 1400 TO 1800 (LC)* *SHAKESPEAREAN CRITICISM (SC)*
Authors who died before 1400	*CLASSICAL AND MEDIEVAL LITERATURE CRITICISM (CMLC)*
Authors of books for children and young adults	*CHILDREN'S LITERATURE REVIEW (CLR)*
Dramatists	*DRAMA CRITICISM (DC)*
Poets	*POETRY CRITICISM (PC)*
Short story writers	*SHORT STORY CRITICISM (SSC)*
Literary topics and movements	*HARLEM RENAISSANCE: A GALE CRITICAL COMPANION (HR)* *THE BEAT GENERATION: A GALE CRITICAL COMPANION (BG)* *FEMINISM IN LITERATURE: A GALE CRITICAL COMPANION (FL)* *GOTHIC LITERATURE: A GALE CRITICAL COMPANION (GL)*
Asian American writers of the last two hundred years	*ASIAN AMERICAN LITERATURE (AAL)*
Black writers of the past two hundred years	*BLACK LITERATURE CRITICISM (BLC)* *BLACK LITERATURE CRITICISM SUPPLEMENT (BLCS)*
Hispanic writers of the late nineteenth and twentieth centuries	*HISPANIC LITERATURE CRITICISM (HLC)* *HISPANIC LITERATURE CRITICISM SUPPLEMENT (HLCS)*
Native North American writers and orators of the eighteenth, nineteenth, and twentieth centuries	*NATIVE NORTH AMERICAN LITERATURE (NNAL)*
Major authors from the Renaissance to the present	*WORLD LITERATURE CRITICISM, 1500 TO THE PRESENT (WLC)* *WORLD LITERATURE CRITICISM SUPPLEMENT (WLCS)*

ISSN 0740-2880

Volume 125

Literature Criticism from 1400 to 1800

Critical Discussion of the Works
of Fifteenth-, Sixteenth-, Seventeenth-, and
Eighteenth-Century Novelists, Poets, Playwrights,
Philosophers, and Other Creative Writers

Thomas J. Schoenberg
Lawrence J. Trudeau
Project Editors

THOMSON
━━━━★━━━━ ™
GALE

Detroit • New York • San Francisco • San Diego • New Haven, Conn. • Waterville, Maine • London • Munich

THOMSON

GALE

Literature Criticism from 1400 to 1800, Vol. 125

Project Editors
Thomas J. Schoenberg and Lawrence J. Trudeau

Editorial
Jessica Bomarito, Kathy D. Darrow, Jeffrey W. Hunter, Jelena O. Krstović, Michelle Lee, Russel Whitaker

Data Capture
Frances Monroe, Gwen Tucker

Indexing Services
Factiva®, a Dow Jones and Reuters Company

Rights and Acquisitions
Margaret Abendroth, Timothy Sisler, Jessica Stitt

Imaging and Multimedia
Dean Dauphinais, Leitha Etheridge-Sims, Lezlie Light, Mike Logusz, Dan Newell, Christine O'Bryan, Kelly A. Quin, Denay Wilding, Robyn Young

Composition and Electronic Capture
Gary Oudersluys

Manufacturing
Rhonda Dover

Associate Product Manager
Marc Cormier

LIBRARY OF CONGRESS CATALOG CARD NUMBER 94-29718

ISBN 0-7876-8742-1
ISSN 0740-2880

Printed in the United States of America
10 9 8 7 6 5 4 3 2 1

Contents

Preface vii

Acknowledgments xi

Literary Criticism Series Advisory Board xxx

Preface

*L*iterature Criticism from 1400 to 1800 (*LC*) presents critical discussion of world literature from the fifteenth through the eighteenth centuries. The literature of this period is especially vital: the years 1400 to 1800 saw the rise of modern European drama, the birth of the novel and personal essay forms, the emergence of newspapers and periodicals, and major achievements in poetry and philosophy. *LC* provides valuable insight into the art, life, thought, and cultural transformations that took place during these centuries.

Scope of the Series

LC provides an introduction to the great poets, dramatists, novelists, essayists, and philosophers of the fifteenth through eighteenth centuries, and to the most significant interpretations of these authors' works. Because criticism of this literature spans six hundred years, an overwhelming amount of scholarship confronts the student. *LC* organizes this material concisely and logically. Every attempt is made to reprint the most noteworthy, relevant, and educationally valuable essays available.

A separate Thomson Gale reference series, *Shakespearean Criticism,* is devoted exclusively to Shakespearean studies. Although properly belonging to the period covered in *LC,* William Shakespeare has inspired such a tremendous and ever-growing body of secondary material that a separate series was deemed essential.

Each entry in *LC* presents a representative selection of critical responses to an author, a literary topic, or to a single important work of literature. Early commentary is offered to indicate initial responses, later selections document changes in literary reputations, and retrospective analyses provide the reader with modern views. The size of each author entry is a relative reflection of the scope of the criticism available in English. Every attempt has been made to identify and include the seminal essays on each author's work and to include recent commentary providing modern perspectives.

Volumes 1 through 12 of the series feature author entries arranged alphabetically by author. Volumes 13-47 of the series feature a thematic arrangement. Each volume includes an entry devoted to the general study of a specific literary or philosophical movement, writings surrounding important political and historical events, the philosophy and art associated with eras of cultural transformation, or the literature of specific social or ethnic groups. Each of these volumes also includes several author entries devoted to major representatives of the featured period, genre, or national literature. With volume 48, the series returns to a standard author approach, with some entries devoted to a single important work of world literature and others devoted to literary topics.

Organization of the Book

An *LC* entry consists of the following elements:

- The **Author Heading** cites the name under which the author most commonly wrote, followed by birth and death dates. Also located here are any name variations under which an author wrote, including transliterated forms for authors whose native languages use nonroman alphabets. If the author wrote consistently under a pseudonym, the pseudonym will be listed in the author heading and the author's actual name given in parenthesis on the first line of the biographical and critical information. Uncertain birth or death dates are indicated by question marks. Topic entries are preceded by a **Thematic Heading,** which simply states the subject of the entry. Single-work entries are preceded by the title of the work and the name of its author.

- A **Portrait of the Author** is included, when available.

- The **Introduction** contains background information that introduces the reader to the author, work, or topic that is the subject of the entry.

- The list of **Principal Works** is ordered chronologically by date of first publication and lists the most important works by the author. The genre and publication date of each work is given. In the case of foreign authors whose works have been translated into English, the title and date (if available) of the first English-language edition is given in brackets following the original title. Unless otherwise indicated, dramas are dated by first performance, not first publication. Lists of **Representative Works** by different authors appear with topic entries.

- Reprinted **Criticism** is arranged chronologically in each entry to provide a useful perspective on changes in critical evaluation over time. The critic's name and the date of composition or publication of the critical work are given at the beginning of each piece of criticism. Unsigned criticism is preceded by the title of the source in which it originally appeared. All titles by the author featured in the text are printed in boldface type. Footnotes are reprinted at the end of each essay or excerpt. In the case of excerpted criticism, only those footnotes that pertain to the excerpted texts are included. Criticism in topic entries is arranged chronologically under a variety of subheadings to facilitate the study of different aspects of the topic.

- A complete **Bibliographical Citation** of the original essay or book precedes each piece of criticism. Source citations in the Literary Criticism Series follow University of Chicago Press style, as outlined in *The Chicago Manual of Style,* 15th ed. (Chicago: The University of Chicago Press, 2003).

- Critical essays are prefaced by brief **Annotations** explicating each piece.

- An annotated bibliography of **Further Reading** appears at the end of each entry and suggests resources for additional study. In some cases, significant essays for which the editors could not obtain reprint rights are included here. Boxed material following the further reading list provides references to other biographical and critical sources on the author in series published by Thomson Gale.

Indexes

A **Cumulative Author Index** lists all of the authors that appear in a wide variety of reference sources published by Thomson Gale, including *LC.* A complete list of these sources is found facing the first page of the Author Index. The index also includes birth and death dates and cross references between pseudonyms and actual names.

A **Cumulative Topic Index** lists the literary themes and topics treated in *LC* as well as other Literature Criticism series.

A **Cumulative Nationality Index** lists all authors featured in *LC* by nationality, followed by the numbers of the *LC* volumes in which their entries appear.

An alphabetical **Title Index** accompanies each volume of *LC.* Listings of titles by authors covered in the given volume are followed by the author's name and the corresponding page numbers on which the titles are discussed. English translations of foreign titles and variations of titles are cross-referenced to the title under which a work was originally published. Titles of novels, dramas, nonfiction books, and poetry, short story, or essay collections are printed in italics, while individual poems, short stories, and essays are printed in roman type within quotation marks.

In response to numerous suggestions from librarians, Thomson Gale also produces an annual paperbound edition of the *LC* cumulative title index. This annual cumulation, which alphabetically lists all titles reviewed in the series, is available to all customers. Additional copies of this index are available upon request. Librarians and patrons will welcome this separate index; it saves shelf space, is easy to use, and is recyclable upon receipt of the next edition.

Citing *Literature Criticism from 1400 to 1800*

When citing criticism reprinted in the Literary Criticism Series, students should provide complete bibliographic information so that the cited essay can be located in the original print or electronic source. Students who quote directly from reprinted criticism may use any accepted bibliographic format, such as University of Chicago Press style or Modern Language Association (MLA) style. Both the MLA and the University of Chicago formats are acceptable and recognized as being the current standards for citations. It is important, however, to choose one format for all citations; do not mix the two formats within a list of citations.

The examples below follow recommendations for preparing a bibliography set forth in *The Chicago Manual of Style,* 15th ed. (Chicago: The University of Chicago Press, 2003); the first example pertains to material drawn from periodicals, the second to material reprinted from books:

Morrison, Jago. "Narration and Unease in Ian McEwan's Later Fiction." *Critique* 42, no. 3 (spring 2001): 253-68. Reprinted in *Literary Criticism from 1400 to 1800.* Vol. 76, edited by Michael L. LaBlanc, 212-20. Detroit: Thomson Gale, 2003.

Brossard, Nicole. "Poetic Politics." In *The Politics of Poetic Form: Poetry and Public Policy,* edited by Charles Bernstein, 73-82. New York: Roof Books, 1990. Reprinted in *Literary Criticism from 1400 to 1800.* Vol. 82, edited by Michael L. La-Blanc, 3-8. Detroit: Thomson Gale, 2003.

The examples below follow recommendations for preparing a works cited list set forth in the *MLA Handbook for Writers of Research Papers,* 5th ed. (New York: The Modern Language Association of America, 1999); the first example pertains to material drawn from periodicals, the second to material reprinted from books:

Morrison, Jago. "Narration and Unease in Ian McEwan's Later Fiction." *Critique* 42.3 (spring 2001): 253-68. Reprinted in *Literary Criticism from 1400 to 1800.* Ed. Michael L. LaBlanc. Vol. 76. Detroit: Thomson Gale, 2003. 212-20.

Brossard, Nicole. "Poetic Politics." *The Politics of Poetic Form: Poetry and Public Policy.* Ed. Charles Bernstein. New York: Roof Books, 1990. 73-82. Reprinted in *Literary Criticism from 1400 to 1800.* Ed. Michael L. LaBlanc. Vol. 82. Detroit: Thomson Gale, 2003. 3-8.

Suggestions are Welcome

Readers who wish to suggest new features, topics, or authors to appear in future volumes, or who have other suggestions or comments are cordially invited to call, write, or fax the Associate Product Manager:

Associate Product Manager, Literary Criticism Series
Thomson Gale
27500 Drake Road
Farmington Hills, MI 48331-3535
1-800-347-4253 (GALE)
Fax: 248-699-8054

Acknowledgments

The editors wish to thank the copyright holders of the excerpted criticism included in this volume and the permissions managers of many book and magazine publishing companies for assisting us in securing reproduction rights. Following is a list of the copyright holders who have granted us permission to reproduce material in this volume of *LC*. Every effort has been made to trace copyright, but if omissions have been made, please let us know.

COPYRIGHTED MATERIAL IN *LC*, VOLUME 125, WAS REPRODUCED FROM THE FOLLOWING PERIODICALS:

Comparative Drama, v. 34, summer, 2000. Copyright © 2000, by the Editors of *Comparative Drama.* Reproduced by permission.—*English Literary Renaissance,* v. 31, spring, 2001. Copyright © 2001 by *English Literary Renaissance.* Reproduced by permission of the editors.—*French Studies,* v. 47, January, 1993 for "The Play of Words and Music in Molière-Charpentier's *Le Malade Imaginaire,*" by Nicholas Cronk. Copyright © 1993 Oxford University Press. Reproduced by permission of Oxford University Press and the author.—*Medieval & Renaissance Drama in England,* v. 3, 1986; v. 11, 1999. Copyright © 1986, 1999 by Rosemont Publishing & Printing Corp. All rights reserved. Both reproduced by permission.—*Modern Languages,* v. 64, March, 1983. Reproduced by permission.—*Renaissance Drama,* v. 22, 1991. Copyright © 1992 by Northwestern University Press. Reproduced by permission.—*Renaissance Quarterly,* v. 30, 1977; v. 39, 1986. Copyright © 1978, 1986 by The Renaissance Society of America, Inc. Both reproduced by permission.—*South Central Review,* v. 3, spring, 1986. Copyright © 1986 The Johns Hopkins University Press. Reproduced by permission.—*Speculum,* v. 42, January, 1967. Copyright © 1967 by the Medieval Academy of America. Reproduced by permission.—*Studies in English Literature 1500-1900,* v. 32, spring, 1992; v. 38, spring, 1998. Copyright © 1992, 1998, The Johns Hopkins University Press. All reproduced by permission.—*Word & Image,* v. 3, January-March, 1987 for "Native English Emblem Books and their Catholic Manifestations" by Anthony Raspa. Copyright © 1987 Anthony Raspa. Reproduced by permission of Taylor & Francis, Ltd., http//:www.tandf.co.uk/journals and the author.

COPYRIGHTED MATERIAL IN *LC*, VOLUME 125, WAS REPRODUCED FROM THE FOLLOWING BOOKS:

Barnwell, H. T. From *Molière: Le Malade imaginaire.* Grant & Cutler, 1982. Copyright © Grant & Cutler Ltd. 1982. Reproduced by permission.—Calder, Andrew. From *Molière: The Theory and Practice of Comedy.* The Athlone Press, 1993. Copyright © by Andrew Calder 1993. All rights reserved. Reproduced by permission of The Continuum International Publishing Group.—Camporeale, Salvatore I. From "Poggio Bracciolini versus Lorenzo Valla: The *Orationes in Laurentium Vallam,*" in *Perspectives on Early Modern and Modern Intellectual History: Essays in Honor of Nancy S. Struever.* Edited by Joseph Marino and Melinda W. Schlitt. University of Rochester Press, 2001. Copyright © Salvatore I. Camporeale. Reproduced by permission.—Daly, Peter M. From "England and the Emblem: The Cultural Context of English Emblem Books," in *The English Emblem and the Continental Tradition.* Edited by Peter M. Daly. AMS Press, 1988. Copyright © 1988 by AMS Press, Inc. All rights reserved. Reproduced by permission.—Daly, Peter M. From "The Arbitrariness of George Wither's Emblems: A Reconsideration," in *The Art of the Emblem: Essays in Honor of Karl Josef Höltgen.* Edited by Michael Bath, John Manning, and Alan R. Young. AMS Press, 1993. Copyright © 1993 by AMS Press, Inc. All rights reserved. Reproduced by permission.—Erne, Lukas. From *Beyond* **The Spanish Tragedy:** *A Study of the Works of Thomas Kyd.* Manchester University Press, 2001. Copyright © 2001 Lukas Erne. Reproduced by permission of Manchester University Press, Manchester, UK.—Fowler, Alastair. From "The Emblem as a Literary Genre," in *Deviceful Settings: The English Renaissance Emblem and Its Contexts.* Edited by Michael Bath and Daniel Russell. AMS Press, 1999. Copyright © 1999 by AMS Press, Inc. All rights reserved. Reproduced by permission.—Freeman, Rosemary. From *English Emblem Books.* Chatto & Windus, 1948. Reproduced by permission of the Literary Estate of the author.—Giamatti, A. Bartlett. From "Hippolytus among the Exiles: The Romance of Early Humanism," in *Poetic Traditions of the English Renaissance.* Edited by Maynard Mack and George deForest Lord. Yale University Press, 1982. Copyright © 1982 by Yale University. All rights reserved. Reproduced by permission.—Greenberg, Mitchell. From *Baroque Bodies: Psychoanalysis and the Culture of French Absolutism.* Cornell University Press, 2001. Copyright © 2001 by Cornell University. Used by permission of the publisher, Cornell University Press.—Grene, Nicholas. From *Shakespeare, Jonson, Molière: The Comic Contract.* Barnes & Noble Books, 1980. Copyright © by Nicholas Grene 1980. Reproduced by permission of the author.—Koppisch, Michael S. From *Rivalry and the Disruption of Order in Molière's Theater.* Fair-

PHOTOGRAPHS AND ILLUSTRATIONS APPEARING IN *LC*, VOLUME 125, WERE RECEIVED FROM THE FOLLOWING SOURCES:

Thomson Gale Literature Product Advisory Board

English Emblem Books

Collections of symbolic images paired with verse, which were popular in England during the sixteenth and seventeenth centuries.

INTRODUCTION

The emblem book has long been a curiosity of English literature, studied by few and generally categorized as a minor genre in a time when major modes of writing were flowering. Renewed attention to methods of book production, to the social function of art, and to the relationship between word and image has brought modern readers back to the emblem book as a revealing and historically particular expression of Renaissance culture.

Although the definition of the emblem book is somewhat amorphous, the strictest definition calls for a three-part form consisting of the motto, or title; the picture; and the epigram, or short verse. This is the model introduced in Italy by Andrea Alciato (sometimes spelled Alciati) in *Emblematum Liber* (1531), which is considered the first emblem book. Peter M. Daly has suggested at least three variations within the tradition of emblem literature: expanded forms, including longer commentary; more parts, meditations, or other works illustrated by emblems, which take a secondary role; and theoretical discussions of the emblem. Emblem books were generally moral in theme and tone, with the author providing an instructive interpretation of the image. The influence of the emblem in the culture of the sixteenth and seventeenth centuries also extended to other forms of art—Daly has called the motto a "mode of thought" that was reflected in painting, weaving, embroidery, and even silversmithing.

The first emblem literature published in English was Samuel Daniel's *The Worthy Tract* (1585), a translation of Paolo Giovio's *Dialogo dell'imprese militari et amorose.* Giovio's work was not an emblem book itself, but a commentary on the genre. Perhaps more significant to the development of the native English emblem book was the publication in 1586 of Geoffrey Whitney's *A Choice of Emblemes.* Whitney's book followed the pattern of Alciato and provided a model for later English emblem writers. As Whitney's emblems demonstrate, originality was not considered a requirement or even a virtue in the early emblem book: of 248 images, 204 were printed from the same woodcuts used for ear-

lier Continental works. Likewise, the epigrams attached to the pictures were widely known classical stories related in verse, drawn from other poets. The art of the emblem writer was thus one of combining words and images, using the motto to direct the reader's interpretation of the new creation.

The emblem later became a more prominent part of Renaissance culture, influencing the poetry of William Shakespeare and Edmund Spenser and finding a niche in courtly society. In 1612 Henry Peacham published *Minerva Britanna, or A Garden of Heroical Devises.* Peacham distinguished his work with his own illustrations, though these were based upon images from earlier emblem books. The genre reached its peak with Francis Quarles, whose *Emblemes* (1635) and *Hieroglyphikes of the Life of Man* (1638) enjoyed a great deal of popular success.

Though critics tend to devalue the poetical merit of emblem writing, many have offered the qualified praise that Quarles's poetry was among the best the genre had to offer. Like his predecessors, Quarles drew heavily from earlier works, though the illustrations for his *Hieroglyphikes* were likely created expressly for the book, which was an uncommon practice. Quarles's popularity has tended to overshadow the work of the other major English emblem writer of his time, George Wither. Wither's *A Collection of Emblemes Ancient and Modern* (1635) took its images from the works of Gabriel Rollenhagen, adding Wither's own mottos and poetry, along with several verse dedications throughout the work to members of the court of Charles I. Wither and Quarles were among the last authors to treat the emblem book as a serious genre. In 1686 John Bunyan published the emblem-based *A Book for Boys and Girls,* whose title reveals the fallen status of the emblem book by the time of the Restoration.

Scholarship on the emblem has tended to focus on generic definition and the typology of images. Pioneers in this field include Rosemary Freeman and Mario Praz, whose work stressed the origins and variations of emblem books, as well as the aesthetic and intellectual culture from which they arose, both in England and on the Continent. Later critics, in particular Daly, have suggested that, despite their scholarly achievements, Freeman and Praz took too narrow a view of the emblem. Daly has contended that the emblem was a more widespread phenomenon than earlier research had implied, and that the interpretation of emblems required a broad understanding of how meaning is created. Daly, Michael Bath, and Alan R. Young are among the leading scholars reconsidering the analysis of the emblem and its varied functions in society. These critics and others have emphasized the question of the stability of the image and of figurative language, both for the reader and for emblem writers themselves. While critics differ in their conclusions, concern for the connection between the sign and what it signifies is a repeated theme in critical interpretations of the emblem book, one that reflects both the Reformation theological concern for the power and use of images, and the Renaissance uncertainty about the origins of authority.

REPRESENTATIVE WORKS

Philip Ayres
Emblemata Amatoria (emblem book) 1683

Thomas Blount
The Art of Making Devises: Treating of Hieroglyphics, Symboles, Emblemes, Aenigmas, Sentences, Parables, Reverses of Medals, Armes, Blazons, Cimiers, Cyphres and Rebus [translator; from Henri Estienne's *Art de Faire les Devises*] (nonfiction) 1646

John Bunyan
A Book for Boys and Girls (emblem book) 1686

Thomas Coombe
The Theatre of Fine Devises [translator; from Guillaume de la Perrière's *Le Théâtre des Bons Engins*] (emblem book) 1614

Samuel Daniel
The Worthy Tract of Paulus Iovius Contayning a Discourse of rare inventions, both Militarie and Amorous, called Imprese. Whereunto is added a Preface containing the Arte of composing them, with many other notable devises [translator; from Paolo Giovio's *Dialogo dell'imprese militari et amorose*] (nonfiction) 1585

Jeremias Drexel
The Christian Zodiak: or Twelve Signes First Written in Latin (emblem book) 1633; republished with pictures, 1647

Abraham Fraunce
Insignium, Armorum, Emblematum, Hieroglyphicorum, et Symbolorum (nonfiction) 1588

Christopher Harvey
Schola Cordis, or The Heart of itself gone away from God [translator; from Benedict van Haeften's *Schola Cordis*] (emblem book) 1647; republished as *The School of the Heart*, 1676

Henry Hawkins
Partheneia Sacra (emblem book) 1633
The Devout Heart [translator; from Etienne Luzvic's *Le Coeur Devot*] (emblem book) 1634

Thomas Heywood
Pleasant Dialogues and Drammas Selected out of Lucian, Erasmus, Textor, Ovid, etc., With sundry Emblems extracted from the most elegant Jacobus Catsius (dialogues, plays, emblems) 1637

Edward Manning
Ashrea; or, The Grove of Beatitudes (emblem book) 1665

P. S.
The Heroicall Devises of M. Claudius Paradin . . . Whereunto are added the Lord Gabriel Symeons and others; translated out of Latin [translator; from Claude Paradin's *Devises Heroiques* and other works] (emblem book) 1591

Henry Peacham
Minerva Britanna, or A Garden of Heroical Devises (emblem book) 1612

Francis Quarles
Emblemes (emblem book) 1635
Hieroglyphikes of the Life of Man (emblem book) 1638

Geoffrey Whitney
A Choice of Emblemes (emblem book) 1586

Andrew Willet
Sacrorum Emblematum Centuria Una (emblem book) c. 1592

George Wither
A Collection of Emblemes Ancient and Modern (emblem book) 1635

OVERVIEWS

Rosemary Freeman (essay date 1948)

SOURCE: Freeman, Rosemary. "The Methods of the Emblem Writers." In *English Emblem Books*, pp. 9-36. London: Chatto & Windus, 1948.

[*In the following essay, Freeman provides a foundation for understanding emblem books, describing the relationship between word and image, and the concept of allegorical thinking—the intellectual milieu from which the emblem arose. Freeman also discusses the limitations and capabilities of the emblem as a means of imaginative expression.*]

I

Emblem books are picture books made up of emblematic pictures and explanatory words. Some of the words will probably be familiar enough to readers of seventeenth century literature, for they are the constantly repeated tags of Elizabethan morality such as *Festina Lente*, and *Vincit qui patitur*; others will be strange only because they were not so constantly repeated. The pictures, however, present more serious difficulties: they appear curious, if not uncouth, to an unaccustomed eye, and they demand an inspection perhaps too prolonged for so meagre a reward. They rarely, in fact, achieve any great merit as art. Since, therefore, a part of this study presupposes serious consideration of a number of them, some explanation of their purpose and character is needed, both as an apology and as an apparatus of approach.

[Two] engravings . . . define to the eye the scope of this book. They are contrasted as different methods of solving the same problem; together they establish the province and limits of the term 'emblematic'. The first, drawn from George Wither's *A Collection of Emblemes* has affinities sometimes quite obvious, sometimes more remote, with all the reproductions which are to follow in this study. It is, in fact, a representative emblem. The second, drawn from Lord Shaftesbury's unfinished *Second Characters or the Language of Forms* (1713) shows what an emblem was *not*.[1] It was designed with the conscious aim of proving that certain subjects could be represented in painting 'without necessary recourse to what is absolutely of the emblem kind', and in the very acute discussion which accompanies it, Shaftesbury fastens immediately on the points at issue and clearly distinguishes between the principles underlying the two methods. That he is led finally to dismiss all that is represented by Wither's picture as 'magical, mystical, monkish and Gothic', does not diminish the penetration of his analysis and, since he stood outside the emblem tradition, he was able to look back to it and could be more articulate about it than those who were within. It is, therefore, useful to be able to compare the two pictures and to set beside a plate engraved when the emblem literature was at its height, criticism written when it was meaningless.

The two pictures are divided by exactly a century. Wither's *A Collection of Emblemes* was printed in 1635 but its plates were all drawn from Gabriel Rollenhagen's *Nucleus Emblematum Selectissimorum* which had appeared in 1611-13. Emblem books were then already popular both in England and on the Continent; a hundred years later the interests of both reader and writer had changed, as Shaftesbury's categorical condemnation of their previous tastes must show. The original picture for his *Second Characters* was painted by an Italian working in France, Paolo de Matteis. Shaftesbury accompanied the commission with a little treatise in French for the painter's better understanding of the principles of his art. This theoretical discussion, entitled 'A Notion of the Historical Draught of Hercules', was published first in the *Journal des Sçavans* in 1712, and translated into English in the following year. Its author had intended that the essay, together with an engraving of the finished picture, should form one section of the projected work, *Second Characters,* but this he never lived to complete.[2] Enough, however, of the book exists in notes and brief treatises to indicate its direction, and the 'Notion' itself is complete.

The theme of the two pictures is the same. It was one familiar in various guises to contemporary readers, and Rollenhagen found no occasion to go to the original source but clings to a current conception of Virtue as an old man. The exact story, however, is recorded by Xenophon, and Shaftesbury's picture is based on that. The fable describes the meeting of Hercules and two goddesses, Virtue and Pleasure, their conflicting invitations to him, the long debate which follows, and the final decision of the hero.

The story offers an opportunity for what Shaftesbury calls 'history painting', that is, painting where 'not only men, but manners, and human passions are represented', and not only human passions but human actions. The artist is asked to set before the eye struggles which are agitating only within the mind and to transfix in one instant events which take place in time. Shaftesbury and Wither have different methods of solving this problem. In the engraving of Hercules Shaftesbury has appointed his time carefully: he rejects three possible alternatives and finally chooses the moment when Pleasure has ceased to plead and Virtue is still speaking. Hercules is leaning towards her with the memory of Pleasure's inducements still in his mind, and the ensuing conflict is conveyed by his attitude and expression. In Wither's picture none of the three characters has any particular interest in the others: it is a tableau in which each is posed in an attitude appropriate to his own nature. There is no sense of dramatic moment.

These two opinions as to the importance of the element of time in pictures of this kind are part of a wider issue which resolved itself finally into the eighteenth century critical battle over the exact interpretation of the Horatian formula, *Ut pictura pœsis*. Both pictures are expressly based on this formula, but it bears a wholly different interpretation in each. Shaftesbury often anticipates Lessing in his determination of the proper spheres of poetry and painting, and his conclusions are always abruptly at variance with the practice of the emblem artists.[3] Aiming at 'a just conformity with historical truth, and with the unity of time and action', he can only represent the fable 'by setting in view such passages or events as have actually subsisted, or according to nature might well subsist, or happen together in one and the same instant. And this is what we may properly call the rule of consistency.'[4] The emblem writers had no such rule of consistency; often several events which could not by any chance have subsisted together in one time are found side by side within the single frame of an emblem from Wither or Whitney. The encroachments of the painter upon the domain of the poet occur everywhere in the emblem books.[5] Whitney's Arion, for example, is cast into the waves and is seen simultaneously riding away upon the dolphin in another corner of the picture.

Divergence upon the question of time is, however, only one side of the difference. Shaftesbury next transfers his attention to the posture and form of the three figures. In Wither these are represented with small regard for those 'living appearances' which constituted for Shaftesbury the chief province and the true criterion of painting. The characters of Vice and Virtue are indicated in their outward form, but they are made even more distinct by the collection of objects which surround them. Vice holds a whip in her hand, at her feet is a lute, and beside her a vase of flowers;[6] the mask which she holds in front of her face barely conceals her real nature. Virtue, a sober old man, bears a book in his hand, and the rod of Mercury, the symbol of wisdom, lies at his feet. Behind is a sunflower, the emblem of constancy in the pursuit of an ideal, which is balanced on Vice's side by crossed bones and a skull. Shaftesbury will have none of this; he insists on the visual, not the symbolical:

> By the word moral are understood, in this place, all sorts of judicious representations of the human passions. . . . As the moral part is differently treated in a poem from what it is in history, or in a philosophical work; so must it, of right, in painting be far differently treated from what it naturally is, either in the history, or poem. . . . For the completely imitative and illusive art of painting, whose character it is to employ in her works the united force of different colours; and who, surpassing by so many degrees, and so many privileges, all other human fiction, or imitative art, aspires in a directer manner towards deceit, and a command over our very sense; she must of necessity abandon whatever is over-learned, humourous, or witty; to maintain herself in what is natural, credible, and winning of our assent: that she may thus acquit herself of what is her chief province, the specious appearance of the object she represents.[7]

Even where it seems to him advisable to add what he calls 'some exterior marks more declaratory and determinative of these two personages, Virtue and Pleasure', the claims of the probable must be respected. The two attributes of Virtue, forbearance and endurance, may be indicated by a bit or bridle placed somewhere by her side, and a helmet, 'especially since they are each of them appurtenances essential to heroes (who in the quality of warriors, were also subduers and managers of horses), and that at the same time these are really portable instruments such as the martial dame who represents virtue, may be well supposed to have brought along with her'.[8]

From such a contrast as this some of the principles of the emblem writer begin to emerge more plainly. For him, all objects have an allegorical significance. Both in their patterned arrangement and in the fact of their being present at all, the claims of verisimilitude are ignored. The vase of lilies and the death's head cannot be numbered among 'portable instruments', nor has Vice any plausible reason for having brought them along with her; the reader is not even required to suppose that she did. Shaftesbury's criterion of the natural and credible is irrelevant here since in such pictures objects are introduced not for their 'specious appearance' but for their significance. Dryden raised the same issue when he criticised the symbolic representation of the theatrical army: 'What is more ridiculous than to represent an army with a drum and five men behind it?'[9] The emblem writer dispenses even with the five men; he entrusts his meaning to the drum alone, and relies upon the reader's ability to accept a symbolical connection between things. His pictures are, in fact, allegorical, and allegorical in certain specific ways. Shaftesbury's strictures are of a piece with the kind of criticism implied in Dryden's rewriting of Shakespeare's plays; they mark the first appearance of the standards by which Quarles's and Whitney's Victorian editors were to judge their emblems, and in distinguishing Wither's methods from those of Shaftesbury it is possible to disentangle the conceptions of the seventeenth century emblem writers from those which have been since current almost to the present time.

The apologists of the emblem books, both the writers in their prefaces and the critics, unite in one common critical formula. It is the phrase quoted by Plutarch from Simonides that poetry is a speaking picture and painting dumb poetry; Henry Hawkins, for instance, prefaces his translation of a French emblem book with the injunction: 'If you eye wel and marke these silent Poesies, give eare to these speaking pictures.'[10] The chief end of an emblem, according to a French handbook on the subject, is 'to instruct us, by subjecting the figure to our view, and the sense to our understanding'.[11] Wither describes the process in greater detail:

> When you have heeded, by your *Eyes* of *sense*,
> This *Helmet,* hiving of a Swarme of *Bees,*
> Consider, what may gather'd be from thence,
> And, what your *Eye* of *Understanding* sees.[12]

He calls the pictures without their mottoes 'dumb figures' or, 'dumb showes'; indeed the dumb show of the stage is in both form and function only a much more elaborate version of the pictures in an emblem book. Harington makes the same point when he explains the purpose of the engravings which he had made for his translation of *Orlando Furioso,* the merits of which he, 'though partial', does not hesitate to describe:

> The use of the picture is evident, which is, that (having read over the booke) you may read it (as it were againe) in the very picture.[13]

This conception of the double medium was one which was assumed rather than explored by the seventeenth century critics; it was frequently invoked as a ready-made critical tag to be introduced whenever necessity arose, and it was rarely elaborated. Further comment was added merely to prove the inferiority of painting since that can speak only to the sense. 'The conceits of the mind are pictures of Things and the tongue is the interpreter of those pictures.' Henri Estienne, speaking of a related mode, the device, says:

> Moreover, the invention is pleasing and efficacious, since to the contentment of the sight, it adds a ravishing of the mind, and that to the satisfaction both of the one and the other; it brings also some profit and utility, which is the perfection of a work; wherefore it surpasseth not onely all other Arts, but also Painting, since this onely representeth the body and exquisite features of the face, when as a Device exposeth the rare conceipts, and gallant resolutions of its Author, far more perspicuously, and with more certainty, then Physiognomy can, by the proportions and lineaments of the face.[14]

This is a questionable contention, but it holds good if painting is conceived as no more than dumb poetry. It is relevant here, too, to recall that contemporary pictures sometimes closely resembled devices. Drummond of Hawthornden in a letter to Sir George Keith describes the pictures at the Fair at St. Germains in terms not unlike those of Estienne:

> I was much taken with the daintiness of the many Portraicts there to be seen. The devices, Posies, Ideas, Shapes, Draughts, of the Artificers were various, nice, and pleasant. Scarce could the wandering thought light upon the Storie, Fable, Gayetie which was not here represented to the view. If *Cebes* the *Theban* Philosopher made a Table hung in the Temple of *Saturn,* the Argument of his rare *Moralities,* and *Jovius* and *Marini,* the Portraicts in their *Galleries* and *Libraries* the subject of some books; I was brought to think I should not commit a great fault, if I sent you for a token, from this Mart a Scantling of this Ware which affordeth a like contentment to the Beholder and possessor.

He then lists the pictures, which consisted mainly of classical subjects—'on this Table *Flora* her bewitching Twins, on that not far from these *Mars* is surprized by

the *Lemnian,* and the Senate of the Gods are all laughing; near by *Jupiter* is comming down in a Golden Showre in his *Danaes'* lap'. In another the painter had drawn Venus 'lying on a Bed with stretched out arms, in the hand she presented to a young man (who was adoring her, and at whom little Love was directing a Dart) a fair face, which with much ceremony he was receiving, but on the other side, which should have been the hinder part of that head, was the Image of death; by which *mortality* he surpassed the others more than they did him by *Art*'. Emblems were, of course, a special interest for Drummond, but even if it was his choice to isolate those particular pictures they were none the less there. Finally, there were the double pictures or perspectives which were so fascinating to his contemporaries. He describes several:

> Here were many double Pictures, the first view shew old men and young Misers gathering carefully, the second view shew young men and prodigals spending riotously with *stultitiam patiuntur opes.* Churchmen and grave Senatours consulting and seriously deliberating, the one face of the Picture represented, the other Fools dancing, Souldiers dicing and fighting.[15]

In these one image was super-imposed upon the other, so that as Cleopatra said of Antony, the figure was painted 'one way like a Gorgon, the other way a Mars' and a moral lesson could be drawn from the contrast between the two.

All these pictures stand somewhere between the painted sign and the written word. They verge on the emblematic, and it remained for Shaftesbury in the detachment of the succeeding century to establish a schematic account of them. He distinguishes precisely between what he terms the true, or 'emblematic', in pictures, and the false or 'enigmatic'; and this distinction corresponds to the difference between his Hercules and that of Wither. Everything that characterises the seventeenth-century emblem book belongs, for him, to the region of the enigmatic: the true emblematic is constituted by 'the relief works and inwrought of the polite ancients' (presumably coins stamped with Athena's owl, etc.). He, therefore, divides those representations which cannot be classified with painting proper into two types:

1. *True, natural and simple*: Emblematical designs: whether graphical or plastical. The Greek and Roman anaglyphs of this narrative, historical and didactic, with what answers to the same in drawings, prints, etc. Paintings or full colours have hardly place here: because of wrong situation, loss of distances, and confusion of perspective.

2. *False, barbarous and mixed*: Enigmatical, preposterous, disproportionable, gouty and lame forms. False imitation, lie, impotence, pretending. Egyptian hieroglyphics. Magical, mystical, monkish and Gothic emblems.[16]

Wherever Shaftesbury grants his Hercules any share of the emblematic it is always of the first order.[17] Virtue and Pleasure are themselves of this category: if the strength of Virtue is to be conveyed the painter may do so by designing her to stand firmly on one foot, the other raised upon a piece of rocky ground; there is no need for her to be poised triumphant upon a globe. Literal translation of the conceits of the mind into pictures is no longer the basis of historical painting:

> The moral part in painting lies but little in the forms . . . but is expressed in the air, attitude, feature, action, motion; and is therefore wholly lodged in that part of painting called the movements, where action, passion, the affections are shown.[18]

In the 'enigmatical' emblems which are to be the concern of this book it is an axiom that the moral part does lie in the forms. The illustrations to this and the succeeding chapters will show how frequently and easily the meaning was externalised. Occasion, for instance, conveys little by her 'air, attitude, feature, action, motion', spirited though these are: the razor, the winged feet and the long forelock were what made her recognisable to contemporaries. In the same way, in the 'Hercules', all the factors which are involved in the decision the hero has to make are projected into pictorial form; and the sense of the picture lies in the total effect of these pictorial details.

II

This assumption that the meaning of the picture was to be conveyed in allegorical rather than naturalistic terms remained a constant factor in the constitution of emblems although the range of subject matter and the manner of its presentation in the books themselves changed as the century progressed. The picture and the word or poem were to be very closely interrelated: in the words of Bargagli, one of the Italian exponents of the science of emblem writing, they were to be 'so strictly united together, that being considered apart, they cannot explicate themselves distinctly the one without the other',[19] and one of the means by which this close interrelation was achieved was to be found in the use in the picture itself of detail which had a literary rather than a visual significance. It was taken for granted that the allegory in the picture as well as in the poem should assume a literary form. It is, of course, not necessarily of the nature of things that this should be so: Shaftesbury was at pains to point out that an allegorical meaning could be bestowed on pictures through other means, and Blake's paintings prove how successfully it could be conveyed in the visual forms, in the shape and placing of the figures, and in the pattern of the picture as a whole. But for the emblem writers it was a first principle. The essence of the term 'emblematic' lies in such a detailed pictorial and allegorical presentation of ideas, and the pleasure of the reader lay in identifying the significant details and correlating them with the moral doctrines taught in the accompanying poem.

Emblematic ways of perception in this sense were widely current in all forms of art in the sixteenth and seventeenth centuries. Shaftesbury in his rejection of the whole method as enigmatical, monkish and Gothic is voicing the prejudice of a classical age against anything which appears to be mediaeval. In reality, however, the emblems are not so much mediaeval in their interests as renaissance: they draw upon stock mediaeval symbols for some of their material, but some of it is also classical, and is derived from Greek and Roman legends, from classical history, and from Ovid. In Italy, where they first appeared, their classical affinities were at least as important as their mediaeval, and through the epigram and pithy moral saying which accompany the picture they are related to the Greek anthology. It is, indeed, this epigrammatic element and their use of classical themes that make them peculiarly characteristic of Renaissance literature. Furthermore, although the fashion is linked through its allegorical material with the surviving interests of the Middle Ages, the way in which the themes are treated is not mediaeval at all. The mediaeval conception of the world was disappearing and with it the mediaeval genius for allegorical presentation of people and ideas. Sidney makes an illuminating comment on the intellectual state of his own age when in writing to Languet in 1574 he says:

> . . . in your letters I fancy I see a picture of the age in which we live: an age that resembles a bow too long bent; it must be unstrung or it will break. . . .[20]

His image of the bow symbolises the nature of much Elizabethan literature. Ideas are held together by tension and no longer by the interlocking of a system. For the mediaeval man the whole world had been symbolic, and all the details of experience had formed part of one unified allegorical conception of the meaning of life:

> Omnis mundi creatura
> quasi liber et pictura
>   nobis est in speculum,
> nostrae vitae, nostrae sortis,
> nostri status, nostrae mortis
>   fidele signaculum.[21]

For the Elizabethans this great framework no longer existed as a single unity: it had not completely vanished but it had broken up, leaving fragments of the old allegorical ways of thinking still present in men's minds, but present only as fragments and not co-ordinated.

Inevitably the disappearance of a unified framework into which each small detail was known to fit had distinct effects upon the way in which allegorical ideas were presented. The change is not reflected only in emblem books: it is clearly marked in all forms of allegorical expression in the sixteenth century, and it constitutes the great difference in method between Spenser's presentation of an allegorical theme and that of his predecessors. The new technique is perhaps best seen in the treatment of personification where the distance from a naturalistic conception is always most clearly apparent. In the first place a much greater freedom of presentation was possible when a unified allegorical picture of the world existed. The personified figures of the later Middle Ages were often accorded a treatment far more realistic than that which the Elizabethans were able to provide. They could move and act naturally because their place in the symbolised world was assured. They derived their meaning from, and were always referred back to, an established and integrated scheme. The Elizabethan symbol is isolated, and partly perhaps for that reason, is treated statically and quite unrealistically. Dunbar's Seven Deadly Sins dance by their own vitality:

> Me thocht, amangis the feyndis fell,
> Mahoun gart cry ane dance
> Off schrewis that wer nevir schrevin . . .
> 'Lat se', quod he, 'Now quha begynnis;'
> With that the fowll Sevin Deidly Synnis
> Begowth to leip at anis.
> And first of all in dance wes Pryd,
> With hair wyld bak and bonet on syd,
> Lyk to mak waistie wanis.[22]

The figures in the emblem books, however, are turned about by their authors to show off their symbolical properties; and in Spenser, too, the personifications which constitute most of the minor figures in *The Faerie Queene*, such as those of the Seven Deadly Sins in the House of Pride, or the figures in the Masque of Cupid, do not move freely and naturally with their own life but are made to move by the author, and to move more for the sake of display than of action. Secondly, this stiffness and lack of freedom in presentation is accompanied by a passion for allegorical detail for its own sake. The emblem writers, however familiar their material might be, never wearied of explaining its significance: over and over again the points of likeness between the picture and what it stands for are elaborated. They are not taken for granted and made a part of the living human being as they are by Dunbar or by Skelton in the *Bouge of Court* or by Chaucer in his list of personifications in the *Knight's Tale*. Instead, the details are laboriously enumerated and attached to a figure that is, and remains, lifeless.

These two characteristics are perhaps rather unexpected as results of the disintegration of a unified allegorical conception of the world: it might have been supposed that the effects would be a greater, and not a diminished, freedom in the presentation of the isolated parts. But in practice when the validity of any relationship ceases to be taken for granted, the free and unselfconscious movement which is based upon it is no longer possible: and this is what happened to allegory in the sixteenth century. Whereas the mediaeval personification could spring spontaneously into being and carry its meaning lightly with it, the Elizabethan personification had to be established, and made intelligible by careful analogy; hence the stiffness of the figures and the long lists of parallels between the image and the idea it expresses. Because the relationship between symbol and thing symbolised had changed, the method had to be one of manipulation rather than exploration. Spenser cannot penetrate into the nature of his symbolical figures as Chaucer or Dunbar can, absorbing the allegorical into the human: he has to impose their significance upon them by external means. The emblem books themselves, indeed, provided a peculiarly suitable form for this kind of symbolisation, and this may account in part for their popularity in the late sixteenth century. In them the personifications, and the other forms of symbolic representation too, were required only to exist, not to function; they had not to live and move credibly, and consequently those elements in the mediaeval scheme which still had meaning locally could be preserved in them without reference to, or need for, a coherent framework. In *The Faerie Queene* the lack of vitality in such figures as Occasion, Ignaro, or the ladies and the servants in the House of Alma, weakens the force of the allegory and remains one of the great defects of the poem.

Personification is, of course, only one of the forms through which allegorical thinking is expressed but what holds true for it, holds true for the others also. All differ from the mediaeval type of allegory in this way. The forms which occur most frequently in the emblem books apart from the personified figures are the short anecdote and the abstract symbol. The first, the anecdote, was drawn from classical myth and legend, from historical incidents, from jest books, collections of fables and other sources of that kind. 'The Choice of Hercules' is a representative example of this sort of emblem, and it is characterised by the same stiffness of presentation and love of allegorical detail as is found in the personifications. The abstract symbol was more widely used still. It formed the staple of the emblem writer's stock-in-trade and was employed both as part of a composite picture, where it contributed one more significant detail to the personification or the anecdote, and also by itself as the single subject of an emblem: the sunflower, for instance, which adds something to the allegorical conception of the 'Choice of Hercules', was elsewhere treated independently. These symbols are emblematic in just the same way as are the personifications and the moral anecdotes, but because their makeup is considerably simpler, they reflect more plainly the virtues and the limitations of the whole method. For that reason it is useful to consider them more fully than the other two.

Symbols have been used so variously and with such complex effect in poetry at different periods that it is necessary to elucidate the sense in which the term is here applied. They were included, as one of the descendants of the Hieroglyphic, among devices and other related forms by critics who discussed the nature of the emblem and its kin in the sixteenth and seventeenth centuries, and the word 'symbol' is therefore used in a special and limited sense in that connection.[23] It has, however, acquired a much wider significance for the modern critic, and to cling to this limited sense would be to ignore the difficulties that must be encountered in using the word at all. A poetic symbol in the modern sense is a concrete image, complete in itself, which stands for some abstract idea or series of ideas in the poetic mind. By this definition all emblems are symbols: they present an ethical concept in the form of a picture, real or imagined, and the picture is not to be interpreted literally but figuratively. The picture itself may be of various different types: Shaftesbury's ideal emblematic picture is very different from Wither's: but both have some kind of symbolic purpose. Since, however, the symbols used by poets often bear a very rich and complex meaning, the term is sometimes used in a qualitative as well as in a merely explanatory sense. Thus, although Blake and Herbert both wrote poetry in which concrete images stand for abstract ideas those images are described without hesitation as 'symbols' in Blake's poems, whereas in Herbert's there may be some doubt as to the propriety of the term and something a little less laudatory such as 'conceits' may be used instead. In this narrower sense no emblem could be called a symbol since no emblem ever achieved the fulness and richness of the emotional content of one of Blake's symbols. When, therefore, the term is used in connection with the images in the emblem books it is used in a purely factual way, and no standard of value is implied. It remains to be considered, however, whether the failure of the emblem writers to create in their poetry symbols of the richest kind is inherent in the method they chose, and follows inevitably from the kind of symbol they adopted and from the way they related it to the ideas they wished it to convey.

The critics who discussed the theory of emblem writing did, of course, realise to some extent how highly involved the question was. They saw that the relationship between the symbol and the thing symbolised could vary greatly in kind and complexity. Henri Estienne, the French critic, who had read widely in the theories of the Italians and usefully summarises their views in his book, tried to get to the root of the matter through the actual nature of the symbol itself. He distinguishes between two kinds of resemblances between things—the 'intrinsicall, occult, naturall and essentiall' on the one side, and on the other the 'extrinsicall, manifest, artificall, knowne and accidentall'. The example he takes to illustrate the distinction is somewhat absurd, but it makes his point. The Egyptian hieroglyphic of an enfranchised slave is a hat:

> As if you consider a hat, as it is an instrument invented to keep off the sunne and raine, you consider it purely

according to its nature; but if you take it for a figure of liberty, you suppose then that either God or man have already imposed this signification upon it.[24]

It is, in that case, a symbol of the accidental kind, and the relation between the image and its significance is purely arbitrary. Estienne then goes on to insist, quite rightly, that the best symbols are intrinsic, and he maintains that these are to be found in those similitudes and relations which we discover 'walking in the spacious fields of the wonderful secrets of nature and qualities of things'. In this, too, he is probably right, for only in nature and human nature are to be found symbols of permanent validity: the penny-farthing was soon superseded as a symbol of speed whereas a winged foot is unlikely ever to lose its significance. But his distinction breaks down in the end because it ascribes everything to the kind of symbol chosen and nothing to the method by which this is related to the ideas for which it stands: his theory will hold good for the very simple type of pictorial symbol, which is most effective when its relation to what it represents is both self-evident and fundamental—the hammer and sickle is a better symbol than the stars and stripes—but in literature, where it must be used in a context, other factors come into play and something more than an intrinsic image is needed before a successful symbol can be produced. Indeed, it may even be true that a good symbol can be made out of an apparently external and accidental image provided that it is adequately related to the ideas within the poem.

The limitation of Estienne's classification is seen if it is applied to the emblem books themselves. There the symbols are largely of the kind which he deprecates and the correspondence between idea and image is mainly arbitrary. But there are some which he would have called intrinsic. The skull and crossed bones, for instance, which was frequently used by emblem writers, has a connection with death which is by no means arbitrary, and it is a self-evident and intrinsic symbol of mortality; the sunflower or the marigold, which was commonly supposed to turn about on its stalk in accordance with the movement of the sun, is a perfectly just image of faithfulness. There is no question in either emblem of forcing a significance upon an unsuitable image. Yet in the hands of the emblem writers these images appear not to have any greater degree of plausibility than Estienne's hat. It is the method which matters, and it must be admitted that even when they are based on images which do bear a fundamental resemblance to the idea which is to be expressed, the emblems are unsatisfactory as poetic symbols. In spite of the accumulation of parallels which he can produce, the emblem writer fails in the end to provide any convincing reason for his choice of that particular image. It remains arbitrary. Wither, for instance, takes the symbol of the Marigold and gives it a religious significance:

When, with a serious musing, I behold
The gratefull, and obsequious *Marigold,*
How duely, ev'ry morning, she displayes
Her open brest, when *Titan* spreads his Rayes;
How she observes him in his daily walke,
Still bending towards him, her tender stalke;
How, when he downe declines, she droopes and
    mournes,
Bedew'd (as 'twere) with teares, till he returnes;
And, how she vailes her *Flow'rs,* when he is gone,
As if she scorned to be looked on
By an inferiour *Eye;* or, did contemne
To wayt upon a meaner *Light,* then Him.
When this I meditate, methinkes, the *Flowers*
Have *spirits,* farre more generous, then ours;
And, give us faire Examples, to despise
The servile Fawnings, and Idolatries,
Wherewith, we court these earthly things below,
Which merit not the service we bestow.
    But, oh my God! though groveling I appeare
Vpon the Ground, (and have a rooting here,
Which hales me downward) yet in my desire,
To that, which is above mee, I aspire:
And, all my best *Affections* I professe
To *Him,* that is the *Sunne of Righteousnesse.*
Oh! keepe the *Morning* of his *Incarnation,*
The burning *Noone* tide of his bitter *Passion,*
The *Night* of his *Descending* and the *Height*
Of his *Ascension,* ever in my sight:
    That imitating him, in what I may
    I never follow an inferiour *Way.*[25]

There are plenty of likenesses yet the Marigold carries no conviction as a symbol of religious life in the poem, and Wither might multiply his points of resemblance indefinitely without ever being able to persuade the reader that they are anything more than accidental. The fault does not lie in the Marigold but in what Wither does with it. Blake will take the same image, draw no explicit comparisons and yet invest the flower with the whole meaning of his poem:

Ah, Sun-flower! weary of time,
Who countest the steps of the Sun,
Seeking after that sweet golden clime
Where the traveller's journey is done:

Where the Youth pined away with desire,
And the pale Virgin shrouded in snow
Arise from their graves, and aspire
Where my Sun-flower wishes to go.[26]

It is perhaps unfair to contrast so good a poem with one so poor, but the difference in method cannot otherwise be defined. Wither's Marigold behaves towards the sun as a man should behave towards God, fixes its eye upon him, laments his absence when he is gone, and follows no lesser light: the actions of the flower and of man are equated at each point. But Blake does not equate, he identifies. His poem is about time and about aspiration: the Sunflower which follows, and grows weary of following, the sun, and which, in following, seeks for some unattained golden world associated with it, com-

bines in itself those two themes. Everything in the poem enriches the meaning of the symbol; the movement of the sun marks the passage of time, 'weary', 'countest', 'steps' build up the impression of the gradualness and tedium of the process, and at the same time contribute to the idea of aspiration, linking up with the traveller in the fourth line. The 'sweet golden clime' is the world to which the sun retreats or it may be the world which the sun represents; in its general associations with Paradise it has an application for all humanity which is carried on in the next line by the 'traveller's journey' with its suggestion of pilgrimage and the journey of human life. In the second stanza these ideas are developed further: the conception of the 'sweet golden clime' is further defined by the extremes of heat and cold, of passion and frigidity which have destroyed the Youth and the pale Virgin; and when they rise from their graves, the 'time' of the opening lines is shown to be not only time as it is in itself, wearisome, slow and yet a condition of human life, but also as it is in contrast to eternity. The more the vocabulary is explored the fuller and richer the meaning of the whole poem becomes; and this meaning is strengthened by the actual structure of the poem with its curious circular movement. Both the incomplete syntax and the way in which the ideas are developed lead back again to the beginning: the movement of the Sunflower is embodied in the movement of the poem. The symbol is an entirely valid one because it is made so within the poem.

Such an achievement would have been impossible for an emblem writer because his method really precludes it. He chooses his image and imposes some significance upon it: in practice the image was generally ready to hand in the emblematic plate, but even poets who made their own plates, like Peacham, always begin with the picture and then make an interpretation for it. Blake, on the other hand, begins with his ideas and concentrates them into the single image of the Sunflower, which then becomes their symbol invested with all the richness of a complex meaning. The existence or non-existence of an essential connection between the symbol and what it stands for has little to do with its success: what matters is whether it is established as essential, and so made wholly convincing within the poem. In Blake the connection is recognised to be intrinsic, in Wither it remains arbitrary.

In this imposition of meaning upon a predetermined image lies the essential weakness of the emblem writer's method. The point by point comparison which they adopted to explain the likeness could not, in the nature of things, be fruitful because the symbol always remained detached from what it stood for. The fact that the images of the emblem writers were almost wholly visual may also have contributed something to their lack of success as symbols: each detail in them is a pictured detail, to be seen by the eye, and this inevitably limits the scope of the comparison. The weakness of the technique is that although the symbol is plausibly and persistently equated with the idea or ideas it represents, it is never actually identified with them: it does not become the idea itself, wholly inseparable from it, as Blake's Sunflower is inseparable from the ideas of time and aspiration. There may be nothing wrong with the emblem writer's symbol as such, yet it fails to convince the reader. For his method, with its detailed equation of picture and meaning, is the method of fancy rather than of imagination, as Wordsworth and Coleridge were later to define the distinction. He deals in fixities and definites, establishing parallel after parallel in a purely objective way. His symbol is a matter of choice not of necessity, and because he deduces his ideas from it instead of concentrating them in it, it remains the arbitrary product of a fanciful rather than an imaginative experience.

This limitation within the emblem technique itself must be admitted at the outset, although since the emblem writers were never poets of much merit the ultimate value of their symbols was rarely tested. Their methods were, however, used to better purpose by better men, and the issue becomes important when the work of those contemporary poets who made use of their technique is considered. The one among these who owes most to it is George Herbert, and the connections between his poetry and the emblem books will be indicated in a later chapter. As has already been suggested, Herbert's images can only doubtfully be called symbols. They almost always belong to the second group of connections indicated by Estienne—those which are artificial and accidental by nature—and they are largely visual. In both these ways they resemble the images of the emblem writers. They are to some degree like emblems also in the manner of their presentation. Herbert does not labour his parallels point by point as Wither and Quarles do, but his method is nevertheless that of equation rather than of identification. The image remains independent of the ideas it conveys, and does not wholly embody them as Blake's does. Yet within the poem the parallel is convincing: the pulley and the church floor can be accepted as credible symbols even though they are arbitrary. Herbert succeeds in making them the focus for complex ideas and emotions, and so combines in his poems something of the richness of meaning which Blake's symbols have with the detachment which characterises the emblem writer's treatment of them. His images are symbols in precisely the same sense as the images of the emblem writers, and yet they are the means by which he achieves his success as a poet. The degree of success varies from poem to poem according to the quality of the meaning concentrated in them, but it is always achieved through, and not in spite of, the emblem method. The emblematic image remains the basis upon which the poem is built, and if it appears fanciful in itself it is nevertheless made valid by the use to which Herbert puts it.

The poems of Herbert show that there were potentialities of success within the emblematists' use of symbol. Some modifications of method were necessary even then, but these were not fundamental, and the connections between his poems and those of the emblem writers are close enough to prove that their arbitrary and largely visual symbols had a value for poetry. They were, indeed, employed widely by seventeenth century poets as a form of imagery and as an incidental element in their poems, but it is only rarely that they constitute the basic principle of construction as they do for Herbert. Although its introduction in a poem is no guarantee of success, the intrinsic symbol undoubtedly has certain advantages over the arbitrary type: inasmuch as it has a significance outside its context and is part of general human experience, it is more accessible and more immediately productive of emotional response and therefore helps the poet in his task. Similarly the symbol that is not purely pictorial has also more in its favour at the outset than one which appeals only to the eye, for it is less clearly defined and so more elastic and capable of wider application. The emblem writer's type of symbol was probably, therefore, by nature less open to imaginative treatment, and, poor poets as they were, they were never able to make much of it. But in more competent hands it could be used successfully and although, with the single exception of Herbert, no poet of distinction was willing to entrust the responsibility for the whole of his poem to it, many were content to make it a part. The extent to which the imagery of seventeenth century poetry is visual and clearly outlined yet at the same time rich with meaning is proof of the fruitful way in which it penetrated contemporary habits of thought.

The emblematic image, then, had potentialities as a medium for poetry. In all its forms it remains unlike the earlier type of allegory: in the emblem books the treatment of the abstract symbol, the stiffness of the personified figures, the imposition of moral significance upon straightforward unallegorical stories, the introduction of purely figurative detail in the plates and the interpretation of realistic detail there in a figurative way, all bear witness to the forced and arbitrary nature of Elizabethan and Jacobean symbolism. And yet the allegorical way of thinking was pervasive and habitual; if it had not been, the emblem books would not have existed at all. It had, however, ceased to be pervasive and habitual in the mediaeval fashion: allegory had become an interest for its own sake instead of a means of interpreting the universe. For the emblem writers, the establishment of likenesses is an end in itself rather than a means to an end, and even for poets like Spenser and Herbert, who are still using allegory and symbol for a purpose, there is a new selfconsciousness in the handling of the medium. Spenser shows it in his elaboration of allegorical detail and his lack of freedom in the treatment of his characters, Herbert in his search for unusual and unexpected analogies. Yet, although this selfconsciousness is a sign of the decline of allegory as a mode of thought and reflects the disintegration of the old mediaeval framework, the emblematic image nevertheless had great vitality. Not until the Restoration was it dismissed altogether as a needless obscurity. In eighteenth century poetry symbolism apart from personification has small place: with Blake it returns to English poetry as a mode of thought, but this is individual and personal thought, not the collective experience of everyone that it had been in the Middle Ages.

III

The emblematic image, as reflected in the emblem books, underwent some changes during the hundred years of its popularity in English literature. It did not change in its fundamentals; but the material with which the emblem writers deal and, in some degree, their manner of dealing with it, altered in accordance with changes in contemporary taste. The first emblem book introduced into England, Whitney's *A Choice of Emblemes* which appeared in 1586, was introduced in response to a demand already well established, and others which were published in imitation of it continued to satisfy the same taste in much the same way for about forty years. In 1635, however, Quarles brought a wholly new type of emblem book to England and this replaced the by now outworn formulas of the older variety.[27] Finally the fashion began to decay, and when in 1683 Philip Ayres published a third version of the form, the interests of English poets had gone elsewhere and his emblem book had none of the seriousness and the vitality which mark the two previous types.[28] These three authors all found their models abroad: their books are translations or adaptations of foreign emblem books. But in importing them, they and their successors made them a part of English literature, and although the impulse came originally from abroad, it remains none the less true that each type is closely related to a particular phase of English literary taste.

Of the three groups it is only the first two which can be said to have a serious bearing on English literature: the third merely marks the departure of poetic energy into other channels. The first group, that introduced by Whitney in 1586, is characterised by a wide range of content but complete unity of method and intention; whereas the second, whose most representative figure is Quarles, is more limited in its field but far more elastic in its applications. As might be expected, the first is accompanied by a compact and consistent body of criticism, whereas the second, although it may provoke some interesting speculation from contemporary poets,

has no commonly accepted rules or definition. The differences of method and intention are reflected in various ways. The same emblematic characteristics—the persistently literary nature of the symbolisation and the arbitrary way in which the significance is imposed—lie behind both, but they find different forms of expression in each. There is, in the first place, a change in theme, a shift in the later emblems from what is impersonal, to more individual and subjective types of material. If, for instance, [two illustrations, one from each group,] are contrasted the difference can easily be seen: both treat the theme of shipwreck: but for H. G. this symbolises the errors of the Catholic Church, for Quarles, the state of the soul alienated from God: his interest is psychological where H. G.'s is wholly objective. As a consequence of this new interest, the later emblem writers preferred to invent their own images or to adapt familiar ones and apply them in their own way, whereas the earlier writers were content very often with the conventional symbols and personifications or with traditional episodes from history, legend, or fable. Secondly, and corresponding to the difference of theme, there is a difference in the handling of the material. The earlier type of emblem is much less complicated in its nature and its treatment. The words and the picture in it each formed self-contained statements of the author's conception and they were equally appropriate carved in jewels, blazoned on shields, embroidered on hangings or engraved in books. The author indeed needed a certain kind of wit rather than any poetic ability. The presentation of a single image or episode, with its appropriate moral significance indicated briefly in the motto and the poem, was enough. The emblem was then considered complete.

In the second type of emblem, however, literature claims what had been regarded as no more than a 'sweet moral symbol', and it becomes no longer sufficient in itself, but something that must be made use of, and turned to all kinds of literary purposes. It was made into verse by Quarles, and transformed in poetry by George Herbert; it was made an element of refreshment in a manual of devotion by the Jesuit, Henry Hawkins, and the basis of a series of meditations by another religious writer. Consequently emblems of this later kind are differently conceived; original in design, they are considerably more complicated, and often include a far wider range of ideas than did the earlier ones. They could not be used outside literature as the earlier ones so often are: and, whereas in such books as those of Peacham and Whitney the personifications, abstract symbols and episodes are all indiscriminately classed as emblems, these later authors adopt the principle of one type to one volume, and it is the narrative type which is commonly assumed to constitute the true emblem. Hawkins, in fact, makes a clear division between a 'device' and an 'emblem' in his book, the one being the representation of a single object with an interpretative

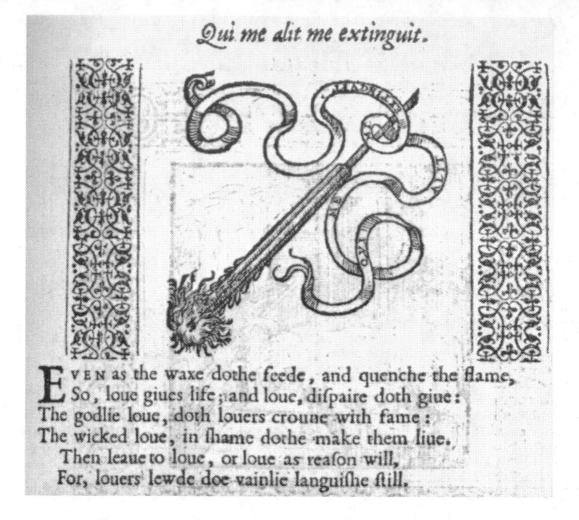

"Qui me alit me extinguit" ("Who feeds me extinguishes me"), from Geoffrey Whitney's A Choice of Emblemes *(1586).*

motto, the other a highly complicated allegorical picture accompanied by an explanatory poem. Such a distinction cannot in practice be made in the earlier emblems, though both the critics and the authors of the emblem books make attempts to draw one. In one sense their narrative emblems are much less emblematic than the later type: they are not full of symbolical detail and do not include abstract symbols and personifications in the elaborate way the later books do. That is because they are still close to the device, still seen as single moral symbols, where Quarles's emblems are complex and the picture needs to be explored in detail.

The second group of emblem books has then a different province and requires a different mode of approach. Briefly, the first group is the production of the men whom R. L. Stevenson in a frivolous little rhyme about the *ars emblematica* characterised as the 'ambidextrous Kings of Art', men who were equally at home with the engraving tool and the pen, and whose interests lay as much in the decorative and pictorial aspects of their work as in its verse. The second group is primarily lit-

erary. The emblem books in it need to be considered individually and for their literary merit rather than collectively and in relation to the other arts as the first type must be.

Towards the end of the century the form was banished from serious literature as a childish toy. At best it could survive in the nursery through a conscious didacticism; at worst in the drawing room archly 'dedicated to the Ladyes'. Philip Ayres's emblem book *Emblemata Amatoria* is an elegant volume containing verses written in copper-plate in four languages and pictures representing the amorous adventures of Cupid. It had considerable popularity, for it appeared in two editions in 1683, and was reprinted at least twice; but its province is made clear in the sub-title *Cupids Addresse to the Ladies*. The days of serious emblem writing were over; and this volume bears much the same relation to Whitney's and Quarles's conception of the emblem book as do Lady Mary Wortley Montagu's shooting activities to the tournaments in *Arcadia*:

The next day I was to wait on the empress Amelia, who is now at her palace of retirement half a mile from the town. I had there the pleasure of seeing a diversion wholly new to me, but which is the common amusement of this Court. The empress herself was seated on a little throne at the end of a fine alley in the garden, and on each side of her were ranged two parties of her ladies of honour with other young ladies of quality, headed by two young archduchesses, all dressed in their hair full of jewels, with fine light guns in their hands; and at proper distances were placed three oval pictures, which were the marks to be shot at. The first was that of a CUPID, filling a bumper of Burgundy, and the motto, *'Tis easy to be valiant here.* The second a FORTUNE, holding a garland in her hand, the motto, *For her whom Fortune favours.* The third was a SWORD with a laurel wreath on the point, the motto, *Here is no shame to be vanquished.*[29]

Heraldry and chivalry have become a civil game and such an account burlesques the solemn ritual that a Tournament once was:

But by and by, even when the Sunne (like a noble harte) began to shew his greatest countenaunce in his lowest estate, there came in a Knight called *Phebilius,* a Gentleman of that country, for whom hatefull fortune had borrowed the dart of Love, to make him miserable by the sight of *Philoclea.* For he had even from her infancie loved her, and was striken by her, before she was able to knowe what quiver of arrowes her eyes caried; but he loved and despaired; and the more he despaired, the more he loved. He sawe his own unworthines, and thereby made her excellencie have more terrible aspect upon him: he was so secrete therein, as not daring to be open, that to no creature he ever spake of it, but his harte made such silent complaints within it selfe, that while his senses were attentive thereto, cunning judges might perceave his minde: so that he was knowne to love though he denied, or rather was the better knowne, because he denied it. His armour and his attire was of a Sea couler, his *Impresa,* the fishe called *Sepia,* which being in the nette castes a blacke inke about it selfe, that in the darknesse thereof it may escape: his worde was, *Not so. Philocleas* picture with almost an idolatrous magnificence was borne in by him.[30]

Symbols had become frivolous, and emblem books became frivolous too: the only alternative to frivolity was childishness, and so the fashion ends, charmingly in the nursery with Bunyan's *Country Rhymes for Children,* or lightly in the drawing-room with graceful picture books like Ayres's. Indeed it must have been hard for the reader of the 1680's to understand how it had ever been an adult taste at all.

Notes

1. The term *Character* is here used by Shaftesbury in a sense in which it obtained throughout the seventeenth century. He means signs or symbols of any kind. A chart is appended to the book, in which Characters are divided into three groups, FIRST CHARACTERS or linguistic symbols, SECOND CHARACTERS or statuary and painting, and THIRD CHARACTERS or emblematical designs which group he also terms MIDDLE as falling somewhere between the first and second. See Appendix 2. p. 241.

2. It has been edited from the MSS. by Benjamin Rand: *Second Characters or the Language of Forms,* by the third Earl of Shaftesbury. Harvard 1914. All references are to this edition.

3. The treatise was translated into German and did have considerable influence on German thinkers. See Benjamin Rand's introduction to his edition, p. xxii.

4. Shaftesbury, op. cit. p. 36.

5. This encroachment was exemplified for Lessing by Titian's Prodigal Son. 'His dissolute life, his misery and repentance are all represented on one canvas.' *Laokoon.* Ch. 18.

6. The flowers are lilies. Cp. John Webster, *The White Devil.* V. 4. 118, where Brachiano's ghost appears to Flamineo bearing 'a pot of Jilly-flowers with a skull in it'. For the association of lilies with corruption cp. Shakespeare's 'lilies that fester smell far worse than weeds'.

7. Shaftesbury, op. cit. pp. 53-5.

8. Ibid. p. 58.

9. Dryden, Essay of Dramatic Poesy. *Works.* Ed. Scott. 1892. Vol. XV. p. 323.

10. *The Devout Hart or Royal Throne of the Pacifical Salomon.* 1634. pp. 4-5.

11. *L'Art de faire les Devises,* by Henri Estienne. Paris. 1645. Translated from the French by Thomas Blount, *The Art of Making Devises.* London. 1646. All quotations are from the edition of 1650.

12. George Wither, *A Collection of Emblemes.* 1635. p. 90.

13. Ariosto, *Orlando Furioso,* in English Heroical verse by John Harington. 1591.

14. Estienne, op cit. p. 14.

15. William Drummond of Hawthornden, 'Letter to S. G. K.' in *The History of Scotland.* 1655. pp. 249-52.

16. Shaftesbury, op. cit. p. 91.

17. In a letter to Sir John Cropley (Feb. 16, 1712) he says that his own designs 'run all on moral emblems', and the minute instructions which he sent to Micklethwayte for the emblematic engravings in *Characteristicks* show his principles in practice.

18. Shaftesbury, op. cit. p. 98.

19. Quoted in H. Estienne, op. cit. p. 10.

20. Translated from the Latin by Steuart A. Pears, *The Correspondence of Philip Sidney and Hubert Languet.* London. 1845. The original letter is printed by Feuillerat, *Works of Sidney,* C.U.P. 1923. Vol. III. p. 86: . . . ex tuis enim litteris quasi imaginem nostrum temporum videor mihi videre, quae iam sane ut arcum nimis diu intensum, aut relaxari aut frangi oportet . . .

21. Alan of Lille. Quoted by F. J. E. Raby, as an example of the mediaeval symbolical outlook in *A History of Christian-Latin Poetry.* 1927. p. 355.

22. Dunbar, 'The Dance of the Sevin Deadly Synnis.' *The Poems of William Dunbar,* ed. W. Mackay Mackenzie. 1932. p. 120. The poem was written some time between 1496 and 1507.

23. e.g. by Henri Estienne, op. cit. p. 4; Abraham Fraunce, *Insignium, Armorum, Emblematum, Hieroglyphicarum, et Symbolorum . . . explicatio.* London, 1588. Book III. passim; and Claude Mignault in the preface to his edition of Alciati.

24. Op. cit. p. 41.

25. George Wither, op. cit. p. 109. The Marigold, Sunflower, Heliotrope and Girasole were regarded as interchangeable terms in the seventeenth century.

26. Blake, *Songs of Experience.* 1794. *The Poetry and Prose of William Blake,* ed. Geoffrey Keynes. 1941.

27. Francis Quarles, *Emblemes.* 1635.

28. Philip Ayres, *Cupids Addresse to the Ladies. Emblemata Amatoria.* 1683.

29. Lady Mary Wortley Montagu, 'Letter to the Countess of Mar.' 14 Sept. 1716. *Letters and Works,* ed. Lord Wharncliffe. London. 1893. Vol. I. p. 243.

30. Sidney, *Arcadia.* 1590. Bk. I. Ch. 17. ed. A. Feuillerat. C.U.P. 1912. p. 107.

Alastair Fowler (essay date 1999)

SOURCE: Fowler, Alastair. "The Emblem as a Literary Genre." In *Deviceful Settings: The English Renaissance Emblem and Its Contexts,* edited by Michael Bath and Daniel Russell, pp. 1-31. New York: AMS Press, 1999.

[*In the following essay, Fowler discusses the variety of forms in which emblem writing appeared in England, tracing the innovations and elements that made emblems appear to be a new genre during the Renaissance. Fowler also addresses the relation of the emblem to better-known Renaissance literature.*]

Modern emblem studies may be said to begin with Henry Green's paper of 1865, read to the Architectural, Archaeological, and Historical Society of Chester, calling for a facsimile edition of Geoffrey Whitney's *A Choice of Emblems.*[1] After Mario Praz's learned bibliography of 1947, development was rapid. About two thousand emblem collections have now been rediscovered—twice the number listed in Praz's second edition of 1964. Since the first planting of Green's and Howard Bayley's seminal ideas, sizable forests have been consumed in emblem criticism. Emblems, once dismissed as popular, trivial, and visually second-rate, have become the object of an independent specialism. Yet there is still little agreement as to what constitutes the emblem as a genre.[2] And, now that literary criticism threatens to merge into media studies, the emblem is increasingly treated from a visual viewpoint, with consequent neglect of its literary aspects. This paper discusses how far emblems belong to literature, and constitute, indeed, a literary genre.

I do not mean to renew the search for defining characteristics of the emblem as a fixed class of literary works. To define "the emblem" is to make a rope of sand.[3] A definition that worked for the late Middle Ages, when *imprese* and rebuses predominated, would hardly fit the sixteenth-century device and contrasting emblem—let alone their conflated form in France the century after. Besides, the emblem's chronological *termini* are elusive. Was its origin ancient, as Claude-François Menestrier thought? Or late fifteenth-century, as Daniel Russell? Or did it originate in 1531? Its decline has been variously dated to the seventeenth, eighteenth, and nineteenth centuries, or denied to have taken place at all. Emblem motifs persisted in baroque and rococo decoration; in Victorian picture books; in Robert Louis Stevenson's *Moral Fables.* And they still figure in conceptual art like Ian Hamilton Finlay's, to say nothing of TV commercials, where slogan, visual, and poetic prose often recapitulate the emblem's classic three-part form. The emblem's own emblem is Proteus. As with any literary genre, we are faced with the diversifications of historical existence. Literary kinds have a diachronic dimension: change discloses, fashion fashions them.[4] It is precisely innovation, in fact, that makes generic form apparent. And the emblem is no exception. It, too, came about through gradual transformation of earlier genres, and went on changing.

RELATION OF PARTS

Pre-Wittgensteinian theorists tried to define the emblem in terms of an essential relation between its picture and epigram. That relation being changeable, conflicting theories inevitably resulted. In one, the picture dominated: emblem history was traced back through *impresa* and *devise* to misunderstood Egyptian hieroglyphics, or those of nature. Were not *imprese* in common (or at least, noble) use, long before Alciato? The dolphin-and-anchor motif appeared on an *aureus* of the Emperor Titus in 80 A. D., possibly before a motto was linked with it, whether FESTINA LENTE or SEMPER FESTINA TARDE, or SPEUDE BRADEOS.[5] Non-verbal *imprese,* fulfilling their heraldic function, helped to elucidate medieval Europe. From the thirteenth century onwards, however, mottos began to appear on seals, crests, and shields. (At least a score of British families share the motto FESTINA LENTE.) When the *impresa* had a text, it was of the briefest. Even so, this had genre characteristics or rules, including special rhetorical features—ellipsis, enigma, and (as in FESTINA LENTE) paradox.[6] Early theorists restricted the topics, too, of the visual device. Hearts and human figures were out; while Henri Estienne disapproved of the dolphin and anchor as insufficiently natural.[7] *Imprese* came to resemble emblems in attracting explanatory commentary, as in Paolo Giovio's *Dialogo dell' Imprese* (1555). Works like Girolamo Ruscelli's *Le Imprese Illustri* (1566) go from vignettes and descriptions to explanations and digressions not unlike Claude Mignault's, say, in Andrea Alciato's *Emblemata* beginning in the 1570s.[8] There are obvious grounds for considering the *impresa* a precursor of the emblem.

Nevertheless the theory of pictorial origin meets with formidable difficulties. Not least of these are the many emblems without pictures. Andrew Willet did not mean his *Sacrorum Emblematum Centuria Una* (1592?) to have any; he was content with what he calls "naked emblems."[9] Notice the double articulation Willet's words imply: a conceit clothed in language may be further clothed (or not clothed) in picture, just as soul is clothed in flesh. (John Peacock has admirably shown how, in such contexts, "soul" and "body" shifted in meaning, according to which side the writer belonged to, in the *paragone* of literature and visual art.[10]) Jacob Cats's emblems similarly displayed their nudity in Heywood's *Pleasant Dialogues.* Surely the nude emblem printers cannot all have been unable to afford clothing?

According to the other main hypothesis, Hessel Miedema's, emblems are primarily verbal: the *picturae* merely illustrate what can exist perfectly well without illustration. Emblem history is traced to literary origins, in Philostratus's *Imagines* and the ekphrastic or descriptive epigrams of the Greek Anthology. (As it happens, Greek Anthology epigrams are found illustrated at Pompeii; but this was unknown in the Renaissance.[11]) Epigrams undoubtedly made a major contribution to the emblem. And proponents of the literary hypothesis can claim the support of Alciato himself, who from his letter to Francesco Calvi was quite clear that emblems—as he conceived them in 1523—were epigrams.[12] They can make something, too, of the emblem's unrestricted topics; for, alone of genres, epigram enjoyed complete freedom of subject. And they can point, of course, to the nude emblem collections; not forgetting Alciato's Lyons edition of 1548, and perhaps also his ghostly project of 1523.

Yet the theory of a purely literary origin has not carried conviction either. For one thing, it depends heavily on the fortuity of many printers simultaneously opting for catchpenny illustrations. If print was decisive, it can hardly have been so quite in the way Miedema suggests.[13] A more serious objection is that many emblems had pictures, but no early publishing history. I am thinking of such cases as Moritz Tilo's additions to Alciato; and (to mention British examples only) the manuscript collections of Thomas Palmer, Abraham Fraunce, Andrew Willet, and Patrick Cary. Palmer actually bypassed the printer by cannibalizing *picturae* from earlier emblem books. Tilo's sketches may have served some private operation of *inventio,* rather than have been meant for publication. Still, they hardly show the emblemist thinking along lexical lines. The epigram theory thus has its difficulties; although, as we shall see, it has much to tell about the origin, and particularly the chronology, of the emblem vogue.

In the Renaissance, visual and literary theories competed wordily. Ernest Gilman (1989, 63) has suggested that "logocentric bias" led seventeenth-century critics to prefer voice to the "ekphrastic structures" of the sixteenth century. But the later emblems were no less pictorially conceived than the earlier. And the conception of the emblem as syllogistic goes back before Dominique Bouhours (1628-1702) and Fr. Pierre Le Moyne (1602-1672) to Henri Estienne's *L'Art de faire des devises* (1645).[14] Confusion is, after all, to be expected in early theories of rapidly developing genres. *Impresa,* epigram and emblem seem each in turn to have exerted generative pressure. One may venture the hypothesis that the complete emblem first arose as a modal transformation of epigram by *impresa.*[15] (Unless the imperialistic epigram incorporated the *impresa* as one of its many conquered subjects.) Subsequently, the emblem vogue became influential enough for its collective form to be sometimes transferred to the *impresa* and *devise.*

Synchronic relations between structural parts cannot by themselves provide an adequate basis for describing a genre. One has to take into account both diachronic evolutions and social settings. Thus, *imprese* might be wordless (especially when used in ornament); or consist of picture and word (the common two-part form); or be accompanied by explanatory commentary—perhaps even by a short verse. *Imprese* and *devises* appeared at first singly, for the most part outside literature. Only later, after the emblem vogue was well under way, did they congregate in printed collections like Ruscelli's. Emblems, by contrast, from the first came typically in collections, and usually printed collections.[16] Occasionally, they had a two-part format of epigram and *pictura.* More often, they had the familiar three-part format of Alciato's *Emblematum Liber* (Augsburg 1531). That is to say: an epigraphic or allusive motto; a picture; and an epigram—usually ekphrastic, but sometimes independent. Commentary or quotations might be added, to make four or five parts, as in Alciato's *Emblemata cum Commentariis* of 1621.

LABELS

Allowance must be made for regional differences. The emblem was popular in early seventeenth-century Britain, but almost out of fashion in France until it fused there with the *devise*—something that happened much less in Britain, where honour was valued differently.[17] Yet national preferences could also be overridden by the traffic of international mannerism—not only exchange of ideas and copying of pictures, but polyglot macaronicisms and the ubiquitous Latin *koine.* Everywhere device and emblem overlapped, until they were only distinguished by social function. The same picture might appear in tournament *impresa,* mural decoration, printer's device, or emblem. The Vespasian dolphin and anchor, which was reintroduced in Francesco Colonna's *Hypnerotomachia* (1499) and adopted by the printer Aldo Manuzio as his device, appeared also as an emblem *pictura,* for example in Alciato's *Emblematum Liber* of 1531. In a similar way, virtually every Roman coin reverse was reused in some Renaissance emblem. Considering these multifarious continuities, it is striking that early theorists were so certain about the emblem's being new. The emblem label identified, clearly, what was felt to be a distinct novelty.

Modern genre study starts by clearing away confusions between *res* and *verba,* between actual distinctions of genre and mere variation in labelling. All Renaissance critical terms were ambiguous, if not positively misleading—not least *devise,* which in Marot could mean "motto."[18] Moreover, the motto might also be termed "mot"; "word"; "*sententia*"; "*inscriptio*"; "*elogium*" or picture label; and "emblem" (as in *The Shepheardes Calender*). The figure, similarly, could be "*pictura*"; "*eikon*"; "*imago*"; and (of course) "emblem."[19] Finally, the epigram answered to "epigraph"; "*subscriptio*"; "emblem" again (as in Alciato); and "*elogium*"—the last a usage Richard Lovelace plays on in "Amyntor's Grove," which he presents as a blown-up inscription for a group portrait of the Endymion Porters.[20] Some termed the epigram a *descriptio* or *explicatio* of the figure; others denied it to be anything of the sort, or referred to figure and epigram together as "emblem."[21] Mason

Tung's advice to be sceptical about all early emblem terminology is amply justified.

Interpreted sympathetically, however, the early labels contain useful suggestions. "Emblem" itself, Greek and Latin *emblema,* could refer to mosaic, appliqué, or inlaid ornament—as in Milton's paradise, "the ground more coloured than with stone / Of costliest emblem."[22] Daniello Bartoli (1608-1685), interestingly, likens the emblem to an intarsia of metaphorical analogy.[23] Were an emblem's parts thought of as composing the intarsia? Or were whole emblems collectively inlaid like tessarets? Another interesting label is Palmer's title *Two Hundred Poosees.* The term "posy" goes back before 1530, when Jehan Palsgrave's French dictionary listed "poysy, devyse, or worde, devise."[24] Earlier, the posy was a ring motto; but Palmer clearly intends "emblem." His title puns on "posy" of flowers, and hence of poems with their flowers of rhetoric. His book is an anthology. "Posy" regularly had this collective implication; as when Andrew Kingsmill called *Comfort in Affliction* (1585, written ca. 1569) his "poor posy." However vaguely framed, Palmer's title lets one glimpse his sense of a collective form.

THINKING IN EMBLEMS

Confusions in the Renaissance terminology imply more than failure to resolve differences of opinion about the emblem. The genre was also bafflingly elusive, because the semiotic relations of words to images were altering profoundly, so that different concepts, old and new, existed simultaneously.[25] Nevertheless, intelligible explanations were constructed. On one model, *picturae* worked syllogistically, like hieroglyphs or rebuses. *Pictura* and epigram combined to function as terms in quasi-logical propositions, or to formulate more complex ideas.[26] Here one needs to recall that rebus discourse, widespread in earlier heraldic devices, was still available in the seventeenth century. A striking example is the 1618 Antwerp painting for the Violieren or Chamber of Rhetoricians, by Jan Brueghel I and others, in which four consecutive complicated phrases can be deciphered by suitably combining the eleven human figures, five animals and birds, and other attributes.[27] Thinking in rebuses and emblems was more feasible when the superstructural *picturae* and ekphrastic epigrams accompanied familiar mental images. Iconographic symbols, in particular, seem to have informed the substrate of dreams, fantasies, and imaginative thought. Bringing this to the theoretical light of day, however, entailed—and still entails—very difficult abstraction.

Renaissance processes of thought will not have been like ours. All the same, scholastic hypotheses like the "soul" and "body" of emblems give the impression of awareness of associative processes. One may conjecture an emblematic mind-set, in keeping with the shared analogical world-picture (if not quite with Albrecht Schöne's monolithic consensus). An important factor, probably, was the memory-art tradition, with its regular associating of words and mental images. Emblems seem to have had close interconnection with mnemonic images (a link still to be examined); declining as they did when memory-art was generally abandoned in the late seventeenth century.[28]

Medieval memory-art assisted the devout in contemplating interpreted imagery, so as to edify, or construct, their souls.[29] A similar purpose clearly governed the English mural emblem series in Lady Drury's Oratory, a closet for private meditation that has amazingly survived intact (although now removed to Christ Church Mansion, Ipswich).[30] Associative habits can also be inferred in Palmer's *Poosees,* from his juxtaposition of emblems with *picturae* sharing the same natural object. Here, as in Tilo, groups of *picturae* with a common element bring together parallels, opposites, qualifications, variations. Alciato already followed the practice when he gave Titus's dolphin and anchor the motto A PRINCE WHO SEEKS HIS SUBJECTS' SAFETY, implying something distinct from FESTINA LENTE.[31] And Palmer gave the same *pictura* religious associations by substituting the motto GOD IS OUR REFUGE IN ADVERSITY.[32] Conversely, FESTINA LENTE was attached to many different *picturae,* copiously varied.[33] This associative play finds modern analogies in manipulative reapplications of political symbols and commercial logos, as well as in travesties of classic images, like Marcel Duchamp's moustached Mona Lisa, and Edvard Munch's *The Scream* as a tie or pop-up doll.

Just as the visual images of memory-art often served to call up associated texts, so did emblem pictures and mottos. It is because the motto signals a relevant context that emblem theorists sometimes call it a *lemma.*[34] Brief mottos can cue verses, chapters, passages—even whole books—and so bring to bear complex ideas.[35] In fact, emblem-art was an art of allusion. Hence, perhaps, the genre's strange label. For Greek *emblema* meant an appliquéed insertion, such as an inset ornament or label motif on a *krater.* And the Renaissance emblem was also an insertion: its ideas, extracted from classical literature, the Bible, or the Fathers, were designed to be reinserted in the modern setting, enhancing, ennobling, reforming. Allusion could substitute for the absent situation of utterance, by cuing a familiar context. As with radio fixes in position-finding, epigram and picture might offer an *embarras de richesses* of meanings separately, but together with the motto they focussed an optimally relevant composite meaning.[36] This is particularly obvious when familiar sayings are involved, as in Cats's proverb emblem collection *Spiegel van de Oude en de Niewe Tyt* (The Hague, 1632).

Not that maxims and *sententiae* were univocal. Desiderius Erasmus's *Adagia* would be enough in itself to prove the contrary. Indeed, it was precisely the complexity of the motto in relation to the other emblem elements that often enabled the ensemble to be a suitable channel for classical ideas. Brief as the mottos were, trifling as the emblems seemed, they constituted nothing less than a conduit for the transfer of ancient wisdom. In this transfer and reassimilation—this *translatio studii*—Erasmus's friend Alciato played a not inconsiderable role.[37] In so vital an enterprise of the Renaissance there was no place for glib obviousness. It called rather for indirection and subtle elusiveness—a depth inviting scholarly commentary, or public elaboration in masques, mural paintings, and the like.

ASSEMBLY OF THE EMBLEM ELEMENTS

Associative manipulation of visual images pervaded Renaissance classicism, but for that very reason cannot explain the emblem's novelty. Yet something was new. If anything is certain about Alciato's 1523 letter to Calvi, it is that he is describing a novelty. He has to explain everything from scratch:

> I give in each separate epigram a description of something, such that it signifies something pleasant taken from history or from nature, after which painters, goldsmiths and founders can fashion objects which we call badges and which we fasten on our hats, or else bear as trade-marks . . .[38]

Yet *imprese* for shields were as ancient as the hills, and hat badges were old hat. For example, the pelican in her piety (soon to appear in emblems by Whitney, George Wither and others) had been a charge in medieval heraldry, and went back before that to Philostratus. Could the novelty be the individual, secular application, by contrast with religious medieval images? No; for the fifteenth century abounded in compelling secular images like the imperial iconography, or the countless *imprese* ornamenting the Palazzo Ducale at Urbino, with their challenges to respect, admire, or fear. Alciato's tree and plant emblems may have reflected the voguish interest in conceptual garden-art, which often figured mythologically appropriate trees;[39] but philosophical gardens were hardly new either. As for the motto, it was often indistinguishable from that of an *impresa,* say, or from a *sententia* in a tapestry or mural.[40] In fact, the separate elements of the emblem were ubiquitous, in poetry and masque, painting and graphic art, city signboards and house names, ecclesiastical murals and alchemical treatises. Novelty lay solely in their assembly into a multimedia genre combining epigraph, pictural device, and epigram.

New literary genres seldom (perhaps never) appear out of the blue. Instead, they combine or adapt the formal repertoires of existing genres.[41] One of the contributory repertoires will quite often be extra-literary. A structural armature, perhaps, will be imported: examples might include the literary inventory, the testament, and the interview. Regarding the emblem from this point of view, one can see that its immediate literary antecedent was the ekphrastic epigram. That is to say, a short poem describing, explaining, possibly troping, a natural object or work of art. But it is almost as obvious that, whereas the motto by itself had complex antecedents, the structural idea of combining motto and *pictura* derived, simply enough, from the earlier *impresa* or *devise*. It was taken over, that is, from an extra-literary genre. And one particular group of devices, I wish to suggest, may well have been decisive: namely, the trademarks of printers. (These are omitted, oddly, from the otherwise full list of emblem applications in Daly [1979].)

In his letter to Calvi linking his projected epigram-emblems to trademarks, Alciato himself instances printers' devices. Many of the early printers used these—perhaps to suggest, if not claim, social status. They were thus in a strict sense *devises,* boasting personal or professional ideals.[42] Alciato's first example is Aldo Manuzio's dolphin and anchor. In the context of printing, one may suppose, its FESTINA LENTE motto implied productivity combined with care—"I can certainly affirm that I have as my constant companions the dolphin and the anchor. I have accomplished much by holding fast and much by pressing on."[43] In this practical, self-advertising implication, the Aldine anchor resembles the elephant device of another printer, Calvi himself. For, as Alciato teased him, the elephant "carries its young for a long time and produces nothing."[44] More seriously, the elephant device would imply unhurried labour combined with impressive output. Many other printers adopted familiar devices, often rebuses: for example Guy Marchant (1483-1502),[45] whose musical notes sol and fa, clasped hands of Faith, and FIDES with FICIT "underneath"—*sous,* making *sufficit*—together make up SOLA FIDES SUFFICIT. Sometimes printers' devices would incorporate a verse epigram, whether in title-page or colophon: an example is the 1497 *devise* of Felix Balligault.[46] The elements of emblem thus occur all together in fifteenth-century title-pages and colophons. The printer's device seems to have been the prototype of emblem, just as colophon typography was, of shape poetry.[47]

In this, we can see one possible reason why the coming of print was a precondition for the emblem genre, and why the emblem should be so bound up with typographic culture. Another reason, perhaps more fundamental, is that the epigram craze itself depended on print. The epigram's ancient models, the Planudean and Palatine Anthologies, had existed for centuries in manuscript—the former since 1300. But only with the *editio princeps* of the Planudean Anthology in 1494, Estienne's edition in 1566, and Salmasius's rediscovery of the

Palatine Anthology in 1606, did the vogue of the epigram really take off. Further impetus was given by Latin translations like Alciato's in Jan Cornarius's *Selecta Epigrammata* (Basel, 1529), and especially Hugo Grotius's *Poematum Collecta* (1617),[48] besides such vernacular versions as Timothy Kendall's (1577).

The contribution of print was not only to facilitate rapid dissemination of epigrams and emblems. It also fixed the classic emblem format—motto, *pictura,* epigram, in that order—as manuscript circulation could never have done.[49] From the first, the emblem was a literary genre, primarily realized in book form; whereas the radical of presentation of the extraliterary device was mainly heraldic or decorative. This is not to endorse Clark Hulse's contrast of noble *impresa* and popular emblem.[50] The rules of the *impresa* were designed for mass spectator sport; brevity ensuring visibility in the tournament lists. If the difficulty of the *impresa* held the people at lance length, the emblem was not less élitist, with its Latin epigrams and polyglot mottos—to say nothing of its framing cartouches, which were often strapwork, a type of ornament suggesting equestrian leather and nobility.

EMBLEM COLLECTIONS AS "SILVAE"

Almost invariably the emblem was a collective genre: a salient feature that has received surprisingly little attention. *Imprese* often occurred singly; but emblems typically came in series, or at least in book-length collections. This, too accorded with the medium of print; only manuscript items circulated singly or in small groups.

If emblems belonged to collections, one may reasonably ask what sort of collections. Since the Greek Anthology was a model, one answer might be that the early emblem books resembled anthologies. I say early, because the more specialist collections—alchemical, erotic, pious, academic—tended to come later, in the seventeenth century, when systematic or encyclopedic summas were produced, sometimes with prefaces explicitly announcing their method. (A similar tendency is observable in visual art; as witness the gallery paintings of Antwerp.[51]) The earlier collections, on the contrary, usually addressed miscellaneous topics. Palmer's *Poosees* are mixed bunches—"a florilege for all," as it were, "That have not time for studies general."[52]

Focussing more specifically on the emblem's epigram component, one can add that miscellanies of epigrams were identified as *silvae.* This ancient kind was treated rather sarcastically by Quintilian, who described a fashion for ostentatiously impromptu, disparate effusions, apparently disordered but really contrived as coherent sequences, varied on purpose. So long as classical concepts of art and nature prevailed, the *silva* genre continued current. Sometimes it was clearly labelled. Statius; Augustino Mascardi (1622); Abraham Cowley (1637);

John Dryden (1685): all these and many others composed *silvae,* titled as such.[53] Pierre de Ronsard, moreover, had his *Bocage* (1554); Ben Jonson his *Forest* (1616) and *Underwood* (1640); and Francis Bacon his prose *Sylva Sylvarum* (1627).[54] For exploring the genre's metaphorics naturally led to associated syntagms of *silva* itself. Undoubtedly the emblem-epigram collections also would be regarded as *silvae.*

Emblems characteristically exploited figurative relations between their pictures and epigrams; so that it is unlikely to have been accidental that plant emblems were common in emblem *silvae.* Alciato's collections include many. His *Emblematum Libellus* (Venice, 1546) introduced no less than fourteen tree emblems (a continuous group, CXCIX-CCXII, in the synoptic numbering). Here and in the 1548 Lyons edition these and other plant emblems are seeded throughout, as if to make *silvae* in substance as well as form. And still other emblems include subsidiary representations of shade trees suitable for retired meditation. Palmer's *Two Hundred Poosees,* similarly, has a high proportion of plant emblems—twenty-four; while his *Sprite of Trees and Herbes* concentrates on plants exclusively. Georgette de Montenay's *Emblemes ou Devises Chrestiennes* (1571), an influential book in England, has eleven plant emblems out of a hundred. And an earlier French emblem book recently discovered by John Manning (1993), Charles Jourdain's *Le Blason des Fleurs* (Paris, 1555), draws its diverse moral and therapeutic lessons entirely from plants. Early realizing metaphorical possibilities in the genre label, Jourdain's collection anticipated many later emblem gardens. These include Joachim Camerarius's *Symbolorum et Emblematum ex Re Herbaria* (Nuremberg, 1593), Daniel Stolcius's *Hortulus Hermeticus Flosculis Philosophorum* (Frankfurt, 1627), and Henry Hawkins's *Partheneia Sacra* (Rouen, 1633)—the last a monastery rather than a neo-Stoic garden.

One implication of being *silvae* is that emblem collections may have structural arrangements like those found in non-emblem *silvae,* for example Jonson's *The Forest.*[55] So far, only Quarles's emblems seem to have received much structural analysis.[56] Other collections merit it; not least Alciato's *Emblematum Liber* (Augsburg, 1531) and *Emblematum Libellus* (Paris, 1534). Both are structured according to the pattern of embedded pairs known as ring composition. Such patterns were common in mannerist architecture, and are not unexpected, therefore, in the multimedia emblem, itself an interface between spatial and literary art.[57] In the 1531 edition, the first six and last six emblems correspond in order, each to each. The lineage of Massimiliano Sforza in the first emblem matches *optimus civis* in the last; while both feature Athena, goddess of wisdom and of war. In the second and second last emblems, Massimiliano is addressed (ostensibly, but really the next Duke of Milan, Francesco II): one advises Italian alliances; the other, domination of the moribund nation. The third and third last consider silence: fools' silence passing for wisdom, and silence that refuses to flatter. The fourth and fourth last address rhetoric's power to subdue ferocious political beasts. Next comes a pair on patronage (Emblems V and C); the nurturing stork's reward contrasting with the impositions of harpies. Finally, crows (VI) match pigeons (XCIX), in such a way as to compare the precariousness of prestige gained through consensus government to the fragility of a woman's reputation.[58] The structure seems designed to facilitate discreetly implicit admonition. The ineffectual Massimiliano and his successor Duke Francesco (who tried to dispense with imperial support) are reminded who placed them in power, and counselled to a wiser course. One recalls Fr. Juan Nieremberg's example of Porphyry's encomium with its hidden patterns.[59] An outwardly naive form may be the Silenus mask disguising profundities—like nature (says Nieremberg), the panegyric of God. The comicality of early emblem *picturae,* in the same way, probably had as much to do with the *iocosa seriosa* tradition as with artistic shortcomings.[60]

Earlier and later emblem collections seem to have relied on somewhat different conceptions of "silva." Besides meaning "forest" and implying profuse variety, the word also corresponded to Greek *hyle,* "stuff," material to be interpreted. The early, humanist collections were conceived rhetorically, as didactic or even monitory miscellanies, hopefully instructing princes through witty indirection. But the great majority of later collections were religious, and either pursued divine love, or attended to the hidden meanings or "signatures" of the natural world. Bartoli saw the emblems' intarsia of various woods as analogous to nature's enciphered precepts. The *silva* of nature turned out to be composed of Trees of Life, or of Science—or Porphyrian Trees of ramifying distinctions.[61]

If the emblem collection was partly a literary genre, the individual emblem had a place in literature too. For one thing, emblems were continually quarried for metaphors. Praz hardly exaggerates when he writes that in the seventeenth century "every poetical image contains a potential emblem."[62] Obvious instances of inset emblems include the *imprese* in Shakespeare's *Pericles* and Donne's notorious compasses in "A Valediction: Forbidding Mourning." Critics have tended to treat such borrowed emblems as intertextualities like any others. But emblems came ready glossed, so that they probably had a special function. From being already interpreted, if not overinterpreted, they could facilitate immediacy of uptake, while promoting complexity and compression.

Emblems contributed differently, according to how completely, and directly, they were realized. One possibility was the emblematic title-page, which historically preceded the emblem collection itself.[63] One might almost think of the frontispiece as an emblem *pictura,* with the title as motto. (For Renaissance authors appear to have discovered the complexity of titles at much the same time as that of fictionality itself.) On the same analogy, an epigraph might supply the epigram, or the text itself be the *explicatio.* The relation of frontispiece to text was consciously considered: George Wither desiderated a title-page "that's emblematical"; and the emblematic frontispiece was often described as the "soul" or "ratio" (meaning) of the book. Or, by a compound ratio, soul was to body as title-page to book as motto to *pictura.*[64] An epigraphic epigram, on the other hand, might be "the mind, or soul, of the frontispiece," or (as in Walter Ralegh's *History of the World*) "the mind of the front." After all, it often summarized the frontispiece's themes, and hence those of the book itself.[65] Alternatively, as Richard Wendorf has observed, a frontispiece portrait might constitute the *pictura* (for portraits sometimes had their mottos), with multiple epigrams to follow.[66]

Margery Corbett, R. W. Lightbown and others have discussed many frontispieces presenting emblematic *picturae* of the book's contents. A good example is Burton's *Anatomy of Melancholy* in early editions, whose much-divided title-page has many little cuts figuring the subdivisions, or *cuts,* of the book itself.[67] And in the 1726 edition of Cats's *Philogami et Sophronisci Dialogus* the crowded titlepage anticipates the contents so minutely that interpreting it would take longer than reading the dialogue itself.[68]

Title-pages sometimes incorporated tree emblems or devices. Often these were the printer's device—perhaps a rebus like Grafton's of a tun with a grafted tree.[69] Many printers had tree devices, whether from a connection with woodblock printing (continued later with wooden display type), or from their wooden presses' requiring woodworking skills for maintenance.[70] Some of the devices featured the *arbor scientiae* or Tree of Knowledge—for example Joannes Theodore's, Abraham Wolfgang's and Robert Roger's, combining the tree with the fox-and-honey fable to imply the book's wholesome edification; or Robert Estienne's NOLI ALTUM SAPERE device, a wood-cut of cut wood, which was used in England, perhaps under licence.[71] We cannot know how often arboreal frontispieces carried associations of *silva* or *hyle*; but such a decorum would have been anything but foreign to the ethos of Renaissance humanism.

Later frontispieces ran more to architectural frames. These might claim to furnish the "porch" or entrance,[72] or else to figure the book's "frame" or structure. This type featured paired columns, pyramids, or obelisks, often surmounted by globes, or symbols of sun and moon, or the Tetragrammaton. Janet Levarie Smarr (1984) has analysed several instances;[73] one may add the frontispiece of Richard Brathwait's *A Survey of History* (1638), with its obelisks, and that of John Gerard's *The Herball or General History of Plants* (1636), combining obelisks and plants.[74] Sometimes obelisks or columns supported a sun and a moon (day and night), as in Richard Haydocke's *Spare Minutes,*[75] symbolizing heaven and Earth, or implying the book's comprehensive coverage. Comprehensiveness and cosmic authority is particularly clear in the frontispiece of Petrus Peña and Matthias de Lonbel's *Stirpium Adversaria Nova* (1570), with its map below and celestial spheres above. Smarr draws on neo-Platonism to explain the ubiquitous suns as enlightening sources of wisdom; later examples combined ascent to heaven with signatures in nature.

By setting out the contents in a visual, memorable form, emblematic title-pages perpetuated mnemonic habits.[76] But their pre-expounded emblems served also to prompt an appropriate mind-set for the text to follow. They might even guide uptake by supplying relevant associations. In *Paradise Lost,* the description of heaven-gate's architectural "frontispiece" or portico includes a Jacob's ladder: "The stairs were such as whereon Jacob saw / Angels ascending and descending" (III.510-11). This emblem was so familiar, from its use in frontispieces of books,[77] that Milton was able to use it in a highly compressed way. He contrasts Satan's moral crossroads with that of Jacob (also a fugitive, but repentant), for whom the ladder meant spiritual ascent. And the emblem had further implications, of nature's contemplative value. Here, Milton's inset emblem is complete with its motto, the italicized quotation from Genesis: "This is the gate of heaven."

INSET EMBLEMS

One group of poems that came particularly close to being complete emblems were shape or figure poems such as Robert Herrick's "The Pillar of Fame" and George Herbert's "The Altar." Shape poems figured prominently in Renaissance *silvae*: a typical British example is Richard Willes's *Poematum Liber* (1573), designed for imitation by Winchester schoolboys. Useful shapes (column, wings and the like) were also listed among epigram subtypes in poetics such as Julius Caesar Scaligero's *Poetices Libri Septem* (Lyons, 1561), with examples from Simmias, and George Puttenham's *The Art of English Poesy* (1589).[78] In all such cases, typographic patterning supplied the equivalent of an emblem *pictura.*[79]

These are far from being the only emblematic poems of the Renaissance. As Rosalie Colie and others have shown, a great many epigrams and short lyrics may be regarded as effectually constituting nude emblems. It is hardly necessary to elaborate on how often this is true with George Herbert, Henry Vaughan and Edward Taylor. Taylor's imagery, in particular, even when it seems perfunctory—"bran, a chaff, a very barley yawn [husk]"[80]—covers a wonderfully rich emblematic pith, copious in biblical and world-picture associations. Emblematic allusiveness was second nature to him. Here, the husks associate and contrast with the equally insignificant seed in the parable, that grows mightily when it dies. In such nude emblems, the title often functions as a motto; especially when it is a biblical quotation. The emblem-inspired George Herbert was the first English poet to use titles imaginatively in an enigmatic or allusive way.[81]

As fully emblematic, and similarly multimedia, was the masque. For, what is the action of a masque but animated emblem *picturae*?[82] The masque as a whole can either be seen as dramatized emblem or as modulation of comedy by emblem. Such ideas may be found in Inigo Jones (who described the masque as "nothing else but pictures with light and motion").[83] And Jonson writes of pairs of masquers presenting fans on one of which is a "mute hieroglyphic, expressing their mixed qualities."[84] Perhaps, on the same analogy, masque dialogue presented hieroglyphics not mute—emblem *subscriptiones*. On the City pageants or "devices," Jonson goes into more detail:

> The symbols used are not, neither ought to be, simply hieroglyphics, emblems, or *impreses,* but a mixed character, partaking somewhat of all, and peculiarly apted to these more magnificent inventions, wherein the garments and ensigns [symbolic attributes] deliver the nature of the person, and the word the present office.[85]

The emblem has a yet further, but less obvious, claim on our interest: its implicit contribution to several literary masterpieces. The symbolism of Shakespeare's late romances—to mention one group of instances—could be described as a series of emblems writ large. For the inset masque in *The Tempest* is by no means the only emblematic element. From the initial shipwreck, the action unfolds emblem after emblem of moral shipwreck and spiritual repentance.[86] An even more striking example is *A Winter's Tale,* where the visual focus of the dénouement is an enigmatic emblem figure, Hermione's stony-hearted, softened, moved and moving "statue."

Such deeply implicit emblems were possible only after lengthy development. The Hellenistic emblem was revived, after many centuries, in the minute and deeply significant descriptions of the *Hypnerotomachia.* Later, Colonna's reputation extended to England, and his compelling work exerted a profound influence on Spenser.[87] *The Faerie Queene* is certainly the most emblematic long poem in our literature. Critics debate its

characterization in the "Letter to Ralegh" as "a continued allegory or dark conceit." But perhaps Spenser simply means that its *concetti,* like those of emblems, are intended as matter for meditation. And, indeed, many of its descriptive passages can be seen as nude emblems. As for the narrative, it sometimes moves consecutively from virtual emblem to virtual emblem, almost in the manner of Jan Brueghel's continued rebus. The emblematic material of Part I ranges from Ponsonby's anchor device on the 1590 title-page and iconographic descriptions of Redcrosse, Una and the Monster Errour (I.i.1-27), to the Hermaphrodite emblem (III.xii.45-46)—Holzwart's Emblem XXV, AMOR CONIUGALIS[88]—and the *pictura* of St George and the dragon. This dragon is one of several: earlier, Arthur's dragon crest; the dragon under Lucifera's feet; the one under Cupid's statue; and the Old Dragon defeated by Redcrosse; later, Geryoneo's monster; the crocodile-dragon at Isis Church; and Echidna's hind-quarters.[89] To each of these descriptions, familiar dragon emblems make substantial contributions. And this is but one strand of many. Every sort of emblem imagery is to be found in the poem: religious emblems in Book I; moral emblems and the Tablet of Cebes in II; Petrarchan *trionfi* and chivalric *imprese* in III and IV; and, in V, political emblems like that of Geryon, recalling Thomas Palmer's (nude) Emblem CXLIV, CONCORDE UNVINCIBLE. Most prominent of all, the masque-like dance of the Graces in VI.x effectually sets in motion Alciato's Emblem CLXIII, GRATIAE.

A characteristic instance, surely worth further study, is the powerful image of Amoret in the masque of Cupid at the House of Busyrane, carrying her everted heart in a silver basin:

> At that wide orifice her trembling hart
> Was drawne forth, and in silver basin layd,
> Quite through transfixèd with a deadly dart,
> And in her bloud yet steeming fresh embayd . . .[90]

—which may at first recall Georgette de Montenay's 1571 Emblem LXXXI, BEATI MUNDO CORDE [Blessed are the pure in heart], with its heart in a chalice or laver. This is surely a relevant association; but is it optimally relevant? The Spenserian episode contains many evocations of jealousy, and also of "envious desire" (III.xi.26). Perhaps, then, a more appropriate association may be emblems of envy. These sometimes had *picturae* portraying, with horrible literalism, the action of "eating one's heart out."[91] Emblem collections are far from being dictionaries of meanings; but they frequently offer relevant fields of association that orient criticism usefully.

We may ask what concealed such emblematic pictorialism, until recently, from all but a few good readers, such as Alexander Pope's mother, John Ruskin,

C. S. Lewis and Rosemond Tuve.[92] Ignorance of emblems is only part of the answer. Another factor may well be that Spenser generally blends or synthesizes emblems into composite descriptions. A single *ekphrasis* is liable to correspond to parts of several emblems; and even a complete nude emblem will finesse on its source.[93] This method has a counterpart in Renaissance visual art, where symbolic images may be composite in extremely subtle ways—as, indeed, iconography exists to explain. Spenser critics have tended to be hesitant in addressing this interface with art history. But fortunately, encouraging progress has recently been made in this direction by John Manning, Ruth Luborsky and others.

However intuitive a work of Renaissance literature may seem, it should be regarded as challenging the combined resources of emblem scholarship and traditional art history. Between these two approaches, I see no necessary division. After all, as Adrien Delen pointed out, some of the finest graphic artists of the Renaissance—Albrecht Dürer, Hans Holbein II, Arnold Nicolai, Wenceslaus Hollar among them—were happy to practise emblem-art.[94] An emblem's raison d'être, however, lay in its ideas and wit rather than in independent picturing. Indeed, the emblem collections were among other things, as I have argued, collective literary works. On this depended the strategic position of emblem-art as a third Grace between the Sister Arts of *Poesia* and *Disegno*. And on this, too, depended the potential of emblems for rearrangement and reapplication.

Notes

1. *On the Emblems of Geoffrey Whitney . . . A Paper Read before the Architectural, Archaeological, and Historical Society of Chester.* 1865 (Bodleian Lib. 21998. e. 10).

2. See Stegemeier (1946); Praz (1964); Jöns (1966); Heckscher and Wirth (1967); Schöne (1968); Hill (1970); Daly (1972); and the classified bibliography in Dees (1986). For recent discussions of the emblem genre, see Daly (1979a); Russell (1985); Bath (1988) and (1990).

3. Cf. Russell (1985) 15-16; Hill (1970).

4. See Fowler (1985).

5. BM cat. II, 234, Pl. 45, Nos. 19, 20 (no motto); Aulus Gellius and Suetonius, *Divus Augustus* II. xxv. 4: "he thought nothing less becoming in a well-trained leader than haste and rashness, and, accordingly, favourite sayings of his were: 'More haste, less speed' [Greek, *speude bradeos*]." There are opposite examples, however, like the golden shield with a verbal inscription listing Octavianus's four virtues (clemency, valour, justice, piety), voted by the Senate in 27 B. C.; see Syme (1960) 313.

6. Cf. Russell (1985) 59.

7. Ibid. 53. Cf. Contile's strict rules for the motto: see Fraunce (1991) 25.

8. E.g., *Emblemata cum Commentariis Claudii Minois* (Padua, 1621).

9. Other examples are listed in Young (1988). See also Fraunce (1991) 21. For a medieval instance of *ekphrasis* by Robert Holcot, see Gent (1981) 31 n. 118.

10. Peacock (1990) 155.

11. See Praz (1964) 25, 31.

12. Miedema (1968) 236. For a meticulous account of Alciato's earliest emblem projects, see Scholz (1991).

13. Nor is there an adequate explanation on the basis of Fr. Walter Ong's suggestion that allegorical tableaux resulted from the introduction of print; see Praz (1964) 15n.

14. Cf. Russell (1985) 44.

15. For a fuller explanation of the term "modal transformation," see Fowler (1985), chaps. 9 and 10.

16. The earliest collection known seems to be Du Moulin's, in a manuscript of 1515-1526. For an account of its three-part emblems with prose *subscriptiones,* see Massing (1987).

17. Cf. Russell (1985) 74.

18. Russell (1985) 34.

19. Ibid. 80.

20. See Fowler (1994).

21. Russell (1985) 81.

22. *Paradise Lost* iv.703; the reference may be to broderie composed of coloured earth and stones.

23. Praz (1964) 13, 19.

24. See *OED,* s. v. Posy.

25. On this aspect of the early development of the emblem, see Russell (1985); Bath (1989).

26. Russell (1985) 52.

27. Hendrik van Balen and Frans Francken II; see Filipczak (1987) 25, and Fig. 59.

28. See Engel (1991). Cf. Russell (1985) 83; Gilman (1989) 66; Carruthers (1990) Index, s. v. Sight.

29. See Carruthers (1990) chap. 5 and passim.

30. See Farmer (1984) chap. 7. On emblematic motifs in painted ceilings, see Bath (1994).

31. Andrea Alciato, *Emblemata* (Padua, 1621) Embl. CXLIV. On the associative function of emblems, see Goedde (1989) 134 and passim.

32. Emblem LXVI; see Palmer (1988) pp. xxiv-xxv: a theme returned to more than once.

33. Wind (1968) 98.

34. Miedema (1968); Goedde (1989) 131.

35. Russell (1985) 81.

36. Cf. Goedde (1989) 76; Fraunce (1991) 37.

37. Daly (1979) 11.

38. Letter to Calvi, cit. Miedema (1968) 236.

39. E.g. Thorpe Castle, as Mildmay Fane describes it in the 1640s: "Thorp Palace: A Miracle" 10-12: Fowler (1994) 220. Cf. the garden statue in Philipott (1950) 24, "On a Nymph," which relates to many emblems of weeping nymphs by Hugo and others.

40. E.g., in the Munich Antiquarium of Duke Albrecht V of Bavaria: Haskell (1993) 21; and, in Tudor England, Sir Nicholas Bacon's *sententiae*: McCutcheon (1977); Bath (1993) 16n.

41. See Fowler (1985) 156-58.

42. Russell (1985) 65, 66, 67, 70, 71-72.

43. Bayley (1909) 145; Moseley (1989) 5, 30 n. 10; Wind (1968) 98.

44. Letter to Calvi, cit. Miedema (1968) 236.

45. Céard and Margolin (1986) Fig. 73.

46. De Vinne (1902) 11-12, 26, 44. Johnson (1934) Loggan No. 4 has both verse and emblematic figures.

47. See Fowler (1995).

48. *Poematum Collecta et Magnam Partem Nunc Primum Edita . . .* , ed. G. Grotius (Leiden, 1617).

49. Steyner's Augsburg 1531 Alciato already has the "classic" sequence; although, to save paper (which accounted for more than 60% of production costs) he did not begin each emblem on a new page. That refinement was added by Wechel in his Paris 1534 edition. See Scholz (1993).

50. Hulse (1990) 164.

51. See Filipczak (1987).

52. Complimentary verses before Thomas Philipott's *Poems* (1646), in Philipott (1950).

53. E.g., Augustino Mascardi, *Silvarum Libri IV* (Antwerp, 1622).

54. The term was so fashionable that reference books were called *silvae*; see, e.g., Simon Pelegromius, *Synonymorum Sylva* (1632).

55. See Fowler (1982).

56. Gilman (1989) 95; Lewalski (1979). Both are now corrected in Höltgen (1993).

57. Emblems are sometimes found visibly linked in pairs. See an example of 1549, Butsch (1969) No. 131. On the relation between ring composition in architecture and in poetry, see Fowler (1970); Fenoaltea (1990).

58. In the authorized edition by Wechel (Paris, 1534), the pattern remains unchanged; except that the emblem matching that on silence is omitted—possible in mimetic decorum.

59. Praz (1964) 19-20.

60. See Bowen (1985); Barolsky (1978). Thus, the jolly dolphin in *Emblematum Liber* (1531) XXII may not altogether be an effect of the crudity of the woodcut. It contrasts strikingly with Palmer's upright, religiously symbolic dolphin and anchor.

61. For the Tree of Science, see, e.g., Stephanus's device in Davies (1935) 125; Scholz (1988) 67.

62. Praz (1964) 15. Much the same is true of Renaissance visual art, as, e.g., E. de Jongh (1967), Lawrence Goedde (1989) and Linda Bauer (1988) have effectively shown.

63. See Höltgen (1986) chap. 3.

64. Russell (1985) 41, 43, etc. The latter analogy, however, is rejected in Fraunce (1991) 5-7, 21, 37.

65. Höltgen (1986) 93.

66. Wendorf (1990) 48-50, referring to Walton's account of portraits of Donne.

67. Corbett and Lightbown (1979); Idol (1980); David H. Radcliffe (private information); Frank (1968) Nos. 71, 76, 124.

68. *Alle de Wercken* (Amsterdam, 1726).

69. McKerrow (1949) Nos. 104, 114.

70. See Moxon (1683). A glance through collections of printers' devices turns up more trees than any other single *motif*: e.g. McKerrow (1949) 29, 36, 38-39, 60, 65, 102, 104, 114, 128, 146, 348-52 etc.; Davies (1935) 58, 63, 69, 77, 82-85, 88, 92a, 93, 94, 96, 97 etc.; de Vinne (1902); Butsch (1969).

71. E.g. Stephanus's *Maximus Tyrius* of 1557. Cf. Davies (1935) Nos. 84, 125.

72. The proscenium arch, in the case of printed masques; see Limon (1991).

73. E.g., de Jode, 1578; Valeriano, 1615.

74. Johnson (1934) Marshall, No. 48; Payne, No. 9. See also Marshall, No. 12, illus in Farmer (1984) Fig. 34 from Henry Isaacson's Saturni *Ephemerides* (1633).

75. Höltgen (1986) 132.

76. On the mnemonic background of columnar title-pages and diagrams, see Doob (1990) 121, Figs. 3, 4, 15; and Index, s. v. Bookcase.

77. Davies (1970).

78. Cf. Abraham Fraunce's examples in *The Arcadian Rhetoric* (1588). The pattern poems of Hrabanus Maurus (ca. 780-856) were printed in near-facsimile editions early in the sixteenth century: e.g. *De Laudibus Sancte Crucis Opus Erudicione Versu, Prosaque Mirificium,* ed. J. Wimpheling (Phorcheim, 1600).

79. For a contrary view, emphasizing the difference between shape poems and emblems, see Westerweel (1992).

80. Meditation II.xviii: Heb. 13.10, "We Have an Altar"; Fowler (1991) 734. Alan Howard's criticism of Taylor, that the emblem habit led him to skim the Book of Nature perfunctorily, is rejected in Gilman (1989) 59-60.

81. On epigraphic and postscriptive procedures in the seventeenth-century religious poem, see Chambers (1992) 43-44. On titles, see Gardner (1966); Levin (1977); Fowler (1982) 92-98.

82. Emblems are sometimes said to have entered the masque *via* its scenery. A source at least as likely was the title-pages of printed realizations; see, e.g., Corbett and Lightbown (1979) 4-6.

83. Orgel and Strong (1973) II, 480.

84. Jonson, *The Masque of Blackness* 267-69. Cf. Russell (1985) 86, and see Young (1992).

85. Discussing *The King's Entertainment in Passing to His Coronation.* See Gilbert (1969) 16.

86. On Renaissance symbolisms of shipwreck, see Goedde (1989). For an excellent account of the emblematic basis of Shakespeare's earlier plays, see Abraham (1991).

87. The *Hypnerotomachia* was translated by Sir R. Dallington as *The Strife of Love in a Dream* (1592).

88. Daly (1979a) Fig. 1.

89. I.vii.31; I.iv.10; III.i.48; I.xi.8-15; V.xi.24; V.vii.15; VI.vi.10. Mercilla's suppressed crocodile had several emblem associations, especially Camerarius's NUSQUAM TUTA TYRANNIS; see Henkel and Schöne, cols. 668, 670, 674, 675.

90. *The Faerie Queene* III.xii.21.1-4.

91. As in Jan van der Straet's design, engraved by Philip Galle; see Harvey-Lee (1992) No. 10.

92. Lewis (1967); cf. his study of the emblem source of "Spenser's Cruel Cupid," Lewis (1966); Tuve (1966) and (1970).

93. See Fowler and Manning (1976).

94. Delen (1935) II, 107.

References

Abraham, Lyndy (1991). "'The Lovers and the Tomb': Alchemical Emblems in Shakespeare, Donne and Marvell." *Emblematica,* 5: 301-20.

Barolsky, Paul (1978). *Infinite Jest: Wit and Humor in Italian Renaissance Art.* Columbia: University of Missouri Press.

Bath, Michael (1989). "Honey and Gall or: Cupid and the Bees. A Case of Iconographic Slippage." In *Andrea Alciato and the Emblem Tradition: Essays in Honor of Virginia Woods Callahan.* Ed. Peter M. Daly. New York: AMS Press. Pp. 59-94.

———(1990). "What is the Corpus?" In *The Index of Emblem Art Symposium.* Ed. Peter M. Daly. New York: AMS Press. Pp. 5-20.

———(1993). "Applied Emblematics in Scotland: Painted Ceilings, 1550-1650." *Emblematica,* 7: 259-305.

Bath, Michael, Manning, John, and Young, Alan R. (1993). *The Art of the Emblem: Essays in Honor of Karl Josef Höltgen.* New York: AMS Press.

Bauer, Linda Freeman (1988). "Seventeenth-Century Naturalism and the Emblematic Interpretation of Paintings." *Emblematica,* 3: 209-28.

Bayley, Harold (1909). *A New Light on the Renaissance Displayed in Contemporary Emblems.* London: Dent.

Bowen, Barbara C. (1985). "Two Literary Genres: the Emblem and the Joke." *Journal of Medieval and Renaissance Studies,* 15: 29-35.

Butsch, Albert Fidelis (1969). *Handbook of Renaissance Ornament.* Ed. Alfred Werner. New York: Dover.

Carruthers, Mary (1990). *The Book of Memory: A Study of Memory in Medieval Culture.* Cambridge: Cambridge University Press.

Céard, Jean, and Margolin, Jean-Claude (1986). *Rebus de la Renaissance: Des Images qui Parlent.* 2 vols. Paris: Maisonneuve et Larose.

Chambers, Alexander B. (1992). *Transfigured Rites in Seventeenth-Century English Poetry.* Columbia, Mo.: University of Missouri Press.

Corbett, Margery, and Lightbown, Ronald (1979). *The Comely Frontispiece: The Emblematic Title-Page in England 1550-1560.* London: Routledge and Kegan Paul.

Daly, Peter M. (1972). "Trends and Problems in the Study of Emblematic Literature." *Mosaic,* 5: 53-68.

———(1979). *Literature in the Light of the Emblem.* Toronto: Toronto University Press.

———(1979a). *Emblem Theory: Recent German Contributions to the Characterization of the Emblem Genre.* Nendeln: Liechtenstein: KTO.

———, ed. (1988). *The English Emblem and the Continental Tradition.* New York: AMS Press.

Davies, H. Neville (1970). "The First English Translations of Bellarmine's *De Ascensione Mentis.*" *The Library,* 25: 49-52.

Davies, Hugh William (1935). *Devices of the Early Printers 1457-1560.* London: Grafton.

Dees, Jerome S. (1986). "Recent Studies in the English Emblem." *English Literary Renaissance,* 16: 391-420.

Delen, Adrien Jean (1935). *Histoire de la Gravure.* Paris.

Doob, Penelope Reed (1990). *The Idea of the Labyrinth from Classical Antiquity through the Middle Ages.* Ithaca: Cornell University Press.

Engel, William E. (1991). "Mnemonic Criticism and Renaissance Literature." *Connotations,* 1: 12-33.

Farmer, Norman K., Jr. (1984). *Poets and the Visual Arts in Renaissance England.* Austin: University of Texas Press.

Fenoaltea, Doranne (1990). *Du Palais au Jardin: L'Architecture des Odes de Ronsard.* Geneva: Droz.

Filipczak, Zirka Zaremba (1987). *Picturing Art in Antwerp 1550-1700.* Princeton: Princeton University Press.

Fowler, Alastair (1970). *Triumphal Forms: Structural Patterns in Elizabethan Poetry.* Cambridge: Cambridge University Press.

———(1982). "The '*Silva*' Tradition in Jonson's *The Forrest.*" In *Poetic Traditions of the English Renaissance.* Ed. Maynard Mack and George de Forest Lord. New Haven: Yale University Press. Pp. 163-80.

———(1985). *Kinds of Literature.* Cambridge, Mass.: Harvard University Press; Oxford: Clarendon Press.

———(1991). *The New Oxford Book of Seventeenth Century Verse.* Oxford: Oxford University Press.

———(1994). *The Country House Poem: A Cabinet of Seventeenth-Century Estate Poems and Related Items.* Edinburgh: Edinburgh University Press.

———(1995). "'Cut Without Hands': Herbert's Christian Altar." In *Presenting Poetry: Composition, Publication, Reception.* Ed. Howard Erskine-Hill and Richard A. McCabe. Cambridge: Cambridge University Press. Pp. 41-51.

Fowler, Alastair, and Manning, John (1976). "The Iconography of Spenser's Occasion." *Journal of the Warburg and Courtauld Institutes,* 39: 263-66.

Frank, Joseph (1968). *Hobbled Pegasus.* Albuquerque, N. Mex.: University of New Mexico.

Fraunce, Abraham (1991). *Symbolicae Philosophiae Liber Quartus et Ultimus.* Ed. John Manning, trans. Estelle Haan. New York: AMS Press.

Gardner, Helen (1966). "The Titles of Donne's Poems." In *Friendship's Garland: Essays Presented to Mario Praz.* Ed. Vittorio Gabrieli. 2 vols. Rome: Edizioni di Storia e Letteratura. I, 189-208.

Gilbert, Allan H. (1948). *The Symbolic Persons in the Masques of Ben Jonson.* Durham, NC: Duke University Press.

Gilman, Ernest B. (1989). "Word and Image in Quarles's *Emblemes.*" In *The Language of Images.* Ed. W. J. T. Mitchell. Chicago: University of Chicago Press. Pp. 59-84.

Goedde, Lawrence Otto (1989). *Tempest and Shipwreck in Dutch and Flemish Art: Convention, Rhetoric, and Interpretation.* University Park, Pa.: Pennsylvania State University Press.

Harvey-Lee, Elizabeth (1992). *Eve: Women as Models; Women as Printmakers.* Print catalogue. London: Harvey-Lee.

Haskell, Francis (1993). History and its Images: Art and the Interpretation of the Past. New Haven: Yale University Press.

Hawkins, Henry (1993). *Partheneia Sacra.* Ed. K. J. Höltgen. Aldershot: Scolar.

Heckscher, William S., and Wirth, Karl-August (1967). "Emblem, Emblembuch." In *Reallexikon zur Deutschen Kunstgeschichte* (1937-), ed. Otto Schmitt et al., rev. K.-A. Wirth, vol. 5. Stuttgart: Druckemüller. Cols. 85-228.

Hill, Elizabeth K. (1970). "What is an Emblem?" *Journal of Aesthetics and Art Criticism,* 29: 261-65.

Höltgen, Karl Josef (1986). *Aspects of the Emblem.* Kassel: Reichenberger.

Horden, John (1988). "Renaissance Emblem Books: A Comment on Terminology." In *Literature and the Art of Creation: Essays and Poems in Honour of A. Norman Jeffares.* Ed. Robert Welch and Suheil Badi Bushrui. Totowa, NJ: Barnes and Noble. Pp. 61-70.

Hulse, Clark (1990). *The Rule of Art: Literature and Painting in the Renaissance.* Chicago: Chicago University Press.

Idol, John L., Jr. (1980). "Burton's Illustrative Use of Emblems." *Renaissance Papers,* vol. for 1979. Pp. 19-28.

Johnson, Alred Forbes (1934). *A Catalogue of Engraved and Etched English Title-Pages Down to the Death of William Faithorne, 1691.* London: Oxford University Press for the Bibliographical Society.

Jongh, E. de (1967). *Zinne- en Minnebeelden in de Schilderkunst van de Zeventiende Eeuw.* Amsterdam: n. p.

Jöns, Dietrich (1966). *Das Sinnen-Bild: Studien zur Allegorischen Bildlichkeit bei Andreas Gruphius.* Stuttgart: Metzler.

Levin, Harry (1977). "The Title as a Literary Genre." *Modern Language Review,* 72: xxiii-xxxvi.

Lewalski, Barbara Kiefer (1979). *Protestant Poetics and the Seventeenth-Century Religious Lyric.* Princeton: Princeton University Press.

Lewis, C. S. (1966). "Spenser's Cruel Cupid." *Studies in Medieval and Renaissance Literature.* Cambridge: Cambridge University Press. Pp. 164-68.

Limon, Jerzy (1991). "The Masque of Stuart Culture." In *The Mental World of the Jacobean Court.* Ed. Linda Levy Peck. Cambridge: Cambridge University Press. Pp. 209-29, 333-36.

Manning, John (1993). "An Unlisted and Unrecorded Sixteenth-Century French Emblem Book: Charles Jourdain's 'Le Blason des Fleurs.'" *Emblematica,* 6: 195-99.

McCutcheon, Elizabeth (1977). *Sir Nicholas Bacon's Great House Sententiae.* English Literary Renaissance Supplements, vol. 3. Honolulu: University of Hawaii Press.

McKerrow, R. B. (1949). *Printers' and Publishers' Devices in England and Scotland, 1485-1640.* Rev. ed. London: The Bibliographical Society.

Massing, Jean Michel (1987). "A New Work by François du Moulin and the Problem of Pre-Emblematic Traditions." *Emblematica,* 2: 249-71.

Miedema, Hessel (1968). "The Term *Emblema* in Alciati." *Journal of the Warburg and Courtauld Institutes,* 31: 234-50.

Moseley, Charles (1989). *A Century of Emblems: An Introductory Anthology.* Aldershot: Scolar.

Moxon, J. (1683). *Mechanic Exercises.* London: J. Moxon.

Orgel, Stephen, and Strong, Roy (1973). *Inigo Jones: The Theatre of the Stuart Court.* 2 vols. London: Sotheby/Parke-Bernet; Berkeley: University of California Press.

Palmer, Thomas (1988). *The Emblems of Thomas Palmer: 'Two Hundred Poosees': Sloane MS 3794.* Ed. John Manning. New York: AMS Press.

Peacock, John (1990). "Inigo Jones as a Figurative Artist." In *Renaissance Bodies: The Human Figure in English Culture c. 1540-1660.* Ed. Lucy Gent and Nigel Llewellyn. London: Reaktion. Pp. 154-79.

Philipott, Thomas (1950). *Poems (1646).* Ed. L. C. Martin. Liverpool: Liverpool University Press.

Praz, Mario (1964). *Studies in Seventeenth-Century Imagery.* Rev. edn. Rome: Edizione di Storia e Letteratura.

Russell, Daniel (1985). *The Emblem and Device in France.* Lexington, Ky: French Forum.

Scholz, Bernhard F. (1988). "Jacob Cats' *Silenus Alcibiadis* in 1618 and in 1816: Changes in Word-Image Relations from the 17th to the 19th Century." *Word and Image,* 4: 67-80.

———(1991). "The 1531 Augsburg Edition of Alciato's *Emblemata*: A Survey of Research." *Emblematica,* 5: 213-54.

———(1993). "From Illustrated Epigram to Emblem: The Canonization of a Typographical Arrangement." In W. Speed Hill, ed., *New Ways of Looking at Old Texts. Papers of the Renaissance English Text Society 1895-1991.* Binghampton, NY: Renaissance English Text Society. Pp. 149-157.

Schone, Albrecht (1968). *Emblematik und Drama im Zeitalter des Barock.* Rev. ed. Munich: Beck.

Smarr, Janet Levarie (1984). "The Pyramid and the Circle: 'Ovid's Banquet of Sense.'" *Philological Quarterly,* 63: 369-86.

Stegemeir, Henri (1946). "Problems in Emblem Literature." *Journal of English and Germanic Philology,* 45: 26-37.

Syme, Ronald (1960). *The Roman Revolution.* Oxford: Oxford University Press.

Tuve, Rosemond (1966). *Allegorical Imagery: Some Medieval Books and their Posterity.* Ed. Thomas P. Roche, Jr. Princeton: Princeton University Press.

———(1970). *Essays by Rosemond Tuve: Spenser; Herbert; Milton.* Princeton: Princeton University Press.

Vinne, Theodore Low de (1902). *A Treatise on Title-Pages.* New York: Century.

Wind, Edgar (1968). *Pagan Mysteries in the Renaissance.* Rev. ed. London: Faber.

BACKGROUND AND CONTEXTS

Rosemary Freeman (essay date 1948)

SOURCE: Freeman, Rosemary. "The Beginnings of Emblem Writing in England." In *English Emblem Books,* pp. 37-55. London: Chatto & Windus, 1948.

[*In the following essay, Freeman considers European influences on the development of the emblem book in England, suggesting that English emblem writers were more imitative than innovative. Freeman also notes the technical limitations that obstructed the production and popularity of illustrated books in England.*]

I

Emblem writers in England did not create the taste which they satisfied; they imported the fashion from abroad when a marked interest in it had already shown itself in various ways. The word 'emblem' according to Geoffrey Whitney, the first serious exponent of the fashion in England, had indeed existed in the language well before the beginning of the sixteenth century:

> . . . thoughe it be borrowed of others, & not proper in the Englishe tonge, yet that which it signifieth: Is, and hathe bin alwaies in use amongst us, which worde being in Greeke ἐπεμβάλλεσθαι, vel ἐμβλῆσθαι is as muche to saye in Englishe as *To set in, or to put in*: properlie ment by suche figures, or workes, as are wroughte in plate, or in stones in the pavements, or on the waules, or suche like, for the adorning of the place.[1]

In this sense it continued to be used through the seventeenth century, and Milton so uses it.[2] But however familiar it may have been before the Renaissance, it was newly established in the vocabulary in the mid-sixteenth century to mark a distinct literary form—strictly the contents of a book of emblems. This consisted of a collection of pictures, of the kind already illustrated from Wither, each accompanied by a motto and a moral exposition usually in verse. In seventeenth century terminology it was generally the picture alone that was the 'Emblem', the motto was called the 'Word', and the poet added verses or 'moralised the emblem'. Thus Georgette de Montenay's *A Booke of Armes* is represented on the title page as containing 'one Hundred Godly Emblemata, in peeces of brasse very fine graven,

and adorned pleasant to be seen'; and *The Mirrour of Maiestie* has 'emblemes annexed, poetically unfolded'. This same distinction between the different parts occurs also in single emblems outside the collections; the poem called 'Wither's Motto', for example, had an engraved emblematic frontispiece matched by a set of verses called 'The Explanation of the Emblem', which begins:

> This little Emblem here doth represent
> The blest condition of a man Content.

The parts of the picture are then listed and are each regarded as 'expressing' the author's meaning. These explanatory poems were often designated *The Meaning of the Emblem,* or *The Mind of the Frontispiece.* Another example of a complex emblematic frontispiece was that published in *Eikon Basilike* in which Charles I is represented surrounded by the symbols of his fate. Single emblems of this kind were a later extension of the method of the emblem book proper and became enormously popular in the mid-seventeenth century; often a number of small pictures would be engraved within the main frame of the frontispiece to indicate the general drift of the text. In Burton's *Anatomy of Melancholy,* for instance, there are emblematic pictures representing the different forms of melancholy.

The word 'emblem' had then in the sixteenth century acquired an entirely new sense; and even though it was already familiar in the language there is no question of any actual continuity from mediaeval usage. It was imported into England along with the literary form it described.[3]

The first emblem book made its appearance in Italy in 1531. It was the work of a distinguished Italian lawyer, Andrea Alciati, who was responsible for both the form and its name. The name he derived from G. Budé's *Annotationes in Pandectas* where the word 'emblem' is used in the old sense of mosaic.[4] The form is less easily traceable, being an amalgamation of several different influences. The question of origins is not of any historical importance for English literature since the emblems reached this country in the shape in which Alciati had formed them and were not re-created out of their sources, but it has a certain critical interest as it helps to emphasise the distinctive features of the convention.

Henri Estienne in *L'Art de faire les Devises* gives his subject its due importance by placing the first emblem in the Garden of Eden:

> Those (whose scrutiny into the Origin of Devises soares highest) doe derive them from God himselfe, and affirme that he is the first Author of them, since he planted the Tree of Life, or rather the Tree of Knowledg of Good and Evil in the terrestrial Paradise, explaining himself by these words, Ne Comedas.[5]

He then suggests more helpfully that 'if the sense of devises have not so noble and ancient an origin it must at least be derived from the hieroglyphics of the Egyptians'. This was a derivation much favoured by Italian theorists and was generally accepted in England whenever origins were considered; Quarles, in fact, called his second emblem book *Hieroglyphikes of the Life of Man* and offered it as an 'Ægyptian dish'. The connection between the two is obviously close, and the affinity grows more marked when direct reference is made by contemporary critics to a book of Egyptian Hieroglyphics which was circulating in the sixteenth century. This was the collection made by Horapollo, a Greek Grammarian of Phonebethis in Egypt, who was teaching in Constantinople in A.D. 408-50. It was supposedly written in Coptic and was translated into Greek by a certain Philipus, the only form in which it is extant.[6] In 1505 Aldus issued an edition of it at Venice under the title of *Hieroglyphica,* and other editions and translations of it into Latin, French, Italian and German were published during the sixteenth century. There was no contemporary English version, but it was certainly known in the foreign texts, for references to 'Orus Apollo' are frequent among English authors and critics. The other main source of the convention was the Greek epigram. The emblems were pictures, but they were also 'pithy moral sayings'. Professor Praz has stressed the importance of the *Planudean Anthology* as an influence upon Alciati. Forty-four out of the whole two hundred and twelve emblems he finds to be directly derived from the Greek Anthology, and the remainder are, in his view, conceived in the same spirit, so that, granting the Hieroglyphics their share of influence, Alciati's real model was the Greek epigram.[7] This account gives greater weight to the verbal, the 'witty' side of the emblem form than to the pictorial and consequently minimises its significance as a branch of symbolism. But the apologists fastened upon the hieroglyphics as the prototype of the emblems and of all other symbolical writing, and appealed directly to Horapollo because his collection best exemplified that mode of expression in which word and picture are completely united. In Estienne's opinion, every branch of symbolical writing, the 'Enigma, Emblem, Fable and Parable', depended upon and had an affinity with the science of Hieroglyphics; they are all, as Shaftesbury later observed, forms half way between pictures and words.[8] Furthermore, interest in hieroglyphics was bound up with a wider issue, with the view of nature held by such writers as Sir Thomas Browne in the early part of the seventeenth century. Nature was for him a 'Universal and publick Manuscript' written in hieroglyphics:

> The Finger of God hath left an Inscription upon all his works, not graphical or composed of Letters, but of their several forms, constitutions, parts and operations, which, aptly joyned together, do make one word that doth express their natures. By these Letters God calls the Stars by their names; and by this Alphabet Adam assigned to every creature a name peculiar to its Nature.[9]

Quarles prefaces his *Emblemes* with a statement which explicitly links this doctrine with the emblem method:

> Before the knowledge of letters GOD was knowne by *Hierogliphicks*. And, indeed, what are the Heavens, the Earth, nay every Creature, but Hierogliphicks and *Emblemes* of his Glory?

Besides acknowledgements to the Egyptians, the critics produced several pictorial parallels from the Classics. Abraham Fraunce, in a critical work on emblems and devices, refers to the description of Achilles' shield in the *Iliad,* and Estienne to the devices on the shields carried in the *Seven Against Thebes.*[10] The seals and coins of the Roman Emperors are also included among the early forms of the device, and two pages of examples were engraved for *The Art of Making Devises*. All these references tend to emphasise the pictorial aspects of the emblem books, and it is evident that this is what constituted their chief interest in contemporary eyes. The emblems do clearly have affinities with the epigram, 'that fag end of poetry', as Edward Phillips called it; Alciati's emblems come within the category of 'flourishes of wit' in Hoole's list of useful models for children in schools, and they were also discussed by English critics among the figures of rhetoric;[11] but it was for their pictures that they were read and remembered in their own time and afterwards.

Alciati's particular contribution consisted in taking over a familiar method, and often familiar themes, and translating them into literary terms. The result was a book the popularity of which was so great as to be almost inconceivable to the modern reader. It went into ninety editions in the sixteenth century alone, was wedged between solemn and cumbrous annotations, translated into French, Italian, English and Spanish, and finally modified and imitated all over Europe. Its popularity had in no measure decreased in the seventeenth century; it was commented upon at even greater length than before by John Thuilius, a professor of Latin in Germany, and even in the eighteenth century when the impulse behind the allegorical method had altogether vanished, five editions of his work are known, and the fashion which he had set on foot reached even to Russia.[12]

Some account of Alciati's book as the begetter of offspring so numerous and so various may be given here. It originally appeared in manuscript and had been in circulation for ten years before Steyner printed the first edition in 1531. This contained a hundred and four emblems with ninety-eight cuts. Three years later Wechel issued another edition from Paris with eleven new emblems, and in subsequent editions the numbers were gradually increased to a total of two hundred and twelve—a hundred and ninety-eight emblems and fourteen trees. New sets of cuts were made by the various presses and they were often surrounded by elaborate borders. In 1549 Aneau rearranged the emblems according to subjects; in 1571 Claude Mignault embedded them in copious notes; and from the presses of Roville and Bonhomme at Lyons came a whole series of translations in French, Italian and Spanish. This ceaseless labour of expansion and editing offers a surprising contrast to conditions in England where there is no evidence of any emblem books having been enlarged. They rarely attained even a second edition. The salient exception is Quarles, for whose work there was a continual demand, and several other writers of his type such as Edmund Arwaker and Christopher Harvey reprinted their books at least once. The early emblem writers emulated the continental model but they did not oust it, and therefore it is not to Whitney but to Alciati that reference is always made by English writers. Whitney, Combe and P. S. and those who wrote like them, wrote to prove that 'as the Latins have these emblematists . . . so we have these . . .' but they wrote for a literate and articulate class to whom the language of the originals presented no difficulty. The emblem book was a developing mode in Italy, still tentative and exploratory; by the time it reached England its scope had been defined and its exponents could proceed along familiar lines.

Alciati's emblems are drawn chiefly from natural history, fable and mythology; the verses are in Latin, sometimes only of two lines and rarely of any great length. . . . The emblem of the ass which thought that the homage of the crowd was directed towards itself and not to the shrine on its back, was used again by Whitney. A few of Alciati's emblems were dedicated to friends or patrons—a gesture which became popular later in England. The 'arbores', which appear all together at the end of the book, are interesting as a collection of those trees which had fixed and formalised associations arising from mythology or from their natural properties, but they were not adopted by Whitney and have small bearing upon the one English emblem book which does contain trees alone—a little devotional work called *Ashrea; or, The Grove of Beatitudes* (1665), in which eight trees are made pivots for a scheme of meditation.[13] The reproduction from Alciati . . . shows 'Alcides' speckled poplar tree', which, along with the vine and the oak, is one of those specially connected with a god; among others are the lemon tree bearing the golden apples of Venus—golden, but γλυκυπικρος—the box, the tree of lovers, for 'Pallor inest illi, pallet et omnis amans', the victorious laurel which was also memorable for its remarkable property that 'Subdita pulvillo somnia vera facit'. They probably owe their inclusion to the classical tradition of the tree lists which came down from Vergil and Ovid and made their way to England in the fourteenth century. There is one in the *Parliament of Foules* as well as that at the burial of Arcite: they appear again in *The Faerie Queene,* in Drayton's *Endymion and Phoebe*, in Matthew Royden's *Elegy on Sidney,* and there is a last remnant of the same tradition in Dyer's *Grongar Hill*.

The *Emblematum Liber* was rapidly imitated by Alciati's contemporaries and by the time it reached England it was accompanied by a train of imitations and apologies. For Francis Meres, Reusner and Sambucus had already begun to share the platform with Alciati; and the French writers too were acquiring authority.[14] Alciati was translated into French by J. Le Fèvre as early as 1536, and again by Aneau in 1549, who then set out to produce a similar book of his own; de la Perrière's *Le Theatre des bons Engins* appeared in 1539, Corrozet's *Hécatomgraphie* a year later, and Paradin's *Devises Heroiques* in 1557. Although the output was not comparable with that in Italy, it is evident that the fashion was widespread in France as at least eight independent books of emblems apart from translations of Alciati, Hadrian Junius, and Sambucus had appeared there before 1586.

France was not the only country in which the fashion took root. In Spain it was given fresh impetus by the way in which the Jesuits took the emblem books over for educational and missionary purposes; one Spanish emblem book of this kind, a treatise on the education and conduct of princes, written, however, by a layman, was translated into English by Sir James Astry in 1700.[15] In Holland it was adapted to suit the tastes of a democratic middle class. The tournament devices, which had filled the pages of the Italian and French books and which became popular in England too, were replaced for Dutch readers partly by emblems of love representing the adventures of the young Cupid, and partly by emblems of a more realistic kind upon domestic subjects. The emblems of love drew their material chiefly from Ovid; they had already appeared among others in the work of Alciati and his imitators, but it remained for the Dutch to develop them into an elaborate convention. An example of this type of work can be seen in the plate from Philip Ayres. Ayres was an English writer but most of his plates are copied from those of Cornelius Boel in Otho Vaenius's *Amorum Emblemata* and are characteristic both of the matter and the manner of the Dutch emblems.[16] The success of the emblem fashion in the Low Countries was to a considerable extent an engraver's success. While in England the art was still only slowly being developed, goldsmiths on the Continent had from the middle of the fifteenth century been working at copper plates, and by the end of the sixteenth a flourishing trade of engraving and printselling had sprung up, in which whole families were often engaged. From Antwerp especially the output was enormous: engravings of paintings and of maps, portraits, illustrations and decorative borders for books were turned out in huge quantities; Flemish books of patterns were used by English craftsmen and Flemish plates by English printers. Some engravers such as

Simon van de Passe, and later his brother Willem, and Marten Droeshout to whom we owe the portrait of Shakespeare in the first folio, migrated to London where they had no difficulty in finding employment. Others were invited over by patrons who were interested in their work: the Earl of Arundel, for instance, brought Lucas Vorsterman to England after his quarrel with Rubens and found him employment.[17] The emblem books offered yet another field in which the Dutch and Flemish engravers could excel and the standard of their plates is high. The pictures of Jacob Cats's emblems formed one of the early models of Sir Joshua Reynolds, who owned a copy of Vaenius's emblems from Horace as well—presumably also for the sake of their engravings.[18] Cats's emblems gave much more scope to the artist than did those of other Dutch writers like Heinsius and Vaenius because they were not concerned with the Ovidian theme of Cupid but with aspects of social and domestic life. 'Father Cats' as he was called, shared the interests of the Dutch interior painters: his emblems show scenes of family life, a housewife in the kitchen with her maid, illustrating the English proverb: 'A little pot is soon hot', a man and a woman playing battledore and shuttlecock, with the motto, *Amor, ut pila, vices exigit,* incidents in the streets or in the country. The central figure is often highly emblematic but the pictures still have carefully detailed naturalistic backgrounds. Cats's work was known in England and there was an attempt to translate some of it by Thomas Heywood in *Pleasant Dialogues and Drammas,* a hotchpotch of verse dialogues, elegies, emblems and epitaphs drawn from various sources and translated.[19]

II

It is clear from any consideration of the development of emblem books on the Continent that their counterparts in England must be regarded as dependent on, rather than contributory to, the general European movement. Not only were they not a native invention, but nothing very new was added to them by their English adaptors in the course of the hundred years during which they were a vital interest, nor was their popularity, though considerable, in any degree comparable with the emblem-mania which overtook Italy, and to a lesser extent France. The works of Alciati and Ruscelli and some of the French emblematists had long been familiar to English readers before Whitney's collection made its appearance. Travellers on the Grand Tour had certainly read and had probably brought back with them some of the books and works of criticism from abroad. Sidney, for instance, writing to Languet in 1573 from Venice offered to send him a copy of Ruscelli's *Imprese,* which he recommended among various other 'elegantes libri'.[20] Edward VI owned Giovanni Marquale's Italian version of Alciati printed in 1549,[21] and Whitney had a copy of the 1562 edition of Paradin.[22] The introduction of emblems into the vernacular did not diminish the

popularity of Alciati: a painstaking reader would even annotate an edition of Whitney with page references to his source,[23] and the frequent quotations from the *Emblematum Liber* rather than from Whitney show that the *Collection* in no way superseded it. Before any emblem book was published in England Samuel Daniel had translated the *Dialogo dell'Imprese Militari et Amorose* of Paolo Giovio, adding certain devices of his own choice which he had collected in Italy and, as a preface, a long letter written by a certain N. W. which bears witness to wide reading in French and Italian emblems. N. W.'s account is interesting as a statement of the current notion of what constituted a device. He sets out with customary bashfulness:

> But concerning the arte of Imprese I neede not draw the petigree of it, sith it is knowne that it descended from the auncient *Aegiptians* and *Chaldeans,* in the Schoole of *Memphis:* who devised meanes before Charecters were founde out, to utter their conceiptes by formes of Beastes, Starres, Hearbes, (as you have declared) and these notes were called ἱερογλήφικα i.e. sacrae notae . . .

> But to what end served this? to shadow suerly their intents and purposes by figures. So counsayled *Plato:* so practised the first parents of Philosophie. As by the picture of a Stork they signified Αντιπελαργια. By a Serpent pollicie. By an Olive peace. By a Gote lust: drawing these Charecters from the world, as from a volume wherein was written the wonders of nature. Thus was the first foundations layd of *Imprese:* From hence were derived by succession of pregnant wittes *Stemmata* Coates of Armes, *Insignia* Ensignes, and the olde Images which the *Romanes* used as witnesses of their Auncestors, *Emblemes* and *Devises.* Then what was the intent of these Ensigns and *Devises*? What cause can bee pretended for them? What did they import? *Iamblicus* saieth that they were conceiptes by an externall forme representing an inward purpose: so *Fergusus* the first Scottishe King did beare in his Standard a *Lion geules,* to bewray his courage, testifie his stomache, and dismaie his adversarie, which being well marshalled, is borne for the achievement of the Kings ever since. So did the *Athenians* beare their Owle; the *Thebans* their *Sphinx*; the *Switzers* their *Beare.* But among all inventions surpasse for witt and art your *Imprese*: neither less renowned, than the *Insegnes,* nor less heroicall than the Armes called by *Paradin, Symbola Heroica,* by *Symeon, devises illustres.*[24]

Only two years after the appearance of Whitney's collection of emblems, Abraham Fraunce issued a treatise on Insignia in which he drew freely upon the criticism of continental theorists. There is no doubt that interest in emblems was widespread in the 1580's, and even though the direct literary expressions of it were still few the taste was well established in other fields. A sense of the emblematic was so much a part of the disposition of the age that it asserted itself on every side. The devices for tournaments which occupied a prominent place in Elizabethan court life gave it full scope: 'things worthy of observation' in Whitehall were for a visitor, Paul

Hentzner, 'a variety of emblems on paper cut in the shape of shields, with mottoes, used by the nobility in tilts and tournaments, hung up here for a memorial'. The Progresses of Elizabeth provided another opportunity: the usual mode of greeting in Oxford, for example, was a 'banket' and 'thousands of verses and emblematical poetries' hung upon the outer walls of the colleges. The Queen herself delighted in them and in one of her visitations she 'casting her eyes on the walls of St. Mary's Church, All Souls, University and Magdalen Colleges . . . was often seen to give gracious nods to the Scholars'.[25] In her first public procession through London she found emblematical tableaux and verses set up at various points in the City representing the qualities of good government. At Cheapside there were two hills, each with a tree on it, one withered to represent a 'decayed commonweale', the other green to represent a 'flourishing commonweale', and between the two came forth Truth and Time. The point of this was not lost on Elizabeth who is said to have cried, 'And Time hath brought me hither!'[26] A smaller and more personal form of the same interest is seen in jewelry. Among the New Year gifts presented to Elizabeth are many, the designs of which were to become familiar themes in the emblem books later. Some needed only verses to turn them into emblems proper: there was for instance among the presents 'a juell of golde, being a woman ennamuled called VIRTUTE, a pair of compasses in one hand and a green garlande in the other, standing upon a rainbow';[27] and her suitor, Anjou, gave her 'a shakyll of golde with these words graven, SERVIET ETERNUM DULCIS QUEM TORQUET ELIZA, and a padlocke of golde hanging by a little chayne of golde'. The Darnley Jewel which Lady Margaret Douglas had made in memory of her husband, the Earl of Lennox, comes perhaps most close to the literary form. It has figures of Faith, Hope, Victory and Truth, each with their emblems, enamelled on the front, and the crowned salamander in flames and the pelican in her piety on the back. Inside are emblematic pictures including Truth, the daughter of Time, with the motto TYM GARES AL LEIR.[28] This was made at least fifteen years before the publication of Whitney's book.

The same tendencies can be seen also in sixteenth-century domestic architecture and household decoration. The Tudor rose, for instance, that decorated the bedchamber of Wolsey, the heraldic beasts on the ceiling of Plas Mawr in Wales built in 1577, the Wheel of Fortune in Little Morton Hall all have their counterparts in the engravings of Whitney. Personified figures peopled the tapestries and embroidered hangings on Elizabethan walls, though these again are clearly a legacy from the Middle Ages and cannot be confined to any single period. One specifically emblematic piece of decoration which was made prior to 1586 was the bedspread embroidered by Mary Queen of Scots which William Drummond saw and described in detail to Ben Jonson.[29] Drummond's interest in emblems and devices led him to make a list of those he had seen and he tells Jonson that it 'will embellish greatly some pages of your book and is worthy your remembrance'. The emblems are all accompanied by mottoes and many were derived from Paradin and other French emblematists whose work Mary would have known at the French Court. There are imprese of the outstanding French, English, and Italian noblemen and churchmen in the late sixteenth century—the crowned Salamander in flames, the Phoenix, the Palm-tree, the Portcullis of Henry VIII, the bird in the cage with the hawk above, all of which became the commonplaces of emblematic decoration and of the emblem books themselves. Some reappeared in Whitney, coming direct from Paradin,—'the *Impressa* of the Cardinal of *Lorrain* her Uncle, a *Pyramide* overgrown with *Ivy,* the vulgar word, *Te Stante Virebo*', for example. There was also on the bedspread an emblem of two women upon the Wheel of Fortune, one holding a lance, the other a cornucopia, 'which *Impressa* seemeth to glaunce at Queen *Elizabeth* and her self', as Drummond said. Mary referred again to her own fortunes in another emblem which she wore on her signet ring and which she also embroidered on a cushion; it had this sentence: VIRESCIT VULNERE VIRTUS, 'and a hand with a knife cutting down the vines as they use in the spring time'.

Emblems had, too, appeared tentatively in literary form before Whitney made his collection. One work, *A Theatre for Worldlings,* has more than once been described as the first emblem book printed in England.[30] It is known now chiefly because Spenser is reputed to have been the translator of some of its verses. Originally written in Flemish, it was translated into French the same year, and in 1569 Henry Bynneman brought out an English version with woodcuts copied from the engravings of the original.[31] Its full description is 'A Theatre wherein be represented as wel the miseries & calamities that follow the voluptuous Worldlings, as also the great ioyes and pleasures which the faithful do enioy', and its main object is an attack on the Pope, who is represented as the Beast of Revelation and the 'begetter of the Mysterie of iniquitie'. The text consists of six poems translated from Petrarch, eleven from Du Bellay, and four sonnets, based on the Apocalypse, composed by van der Noot himself; these are interpreted at length in prose. Spenser's hand in the book is not acknowledged, and the translation of the prose is ascribed at the beginning to Theodore Roest. But when the *Complaints* were published in 1591 Spenser included in them the 'Visions of Petrarch and the Visions of Bellay', which are revised versions of the translations in the *Theatre*. It is more than probable, therefore, that they were the early work of Spenser. Something even closer to the work of Alciati was produced by Gascoigne, who included three unmistakable emblems in his *Hermit's Tale,* a story told three times over in three languages and presented in manuscript with many professions of the author's worthiness, to the Queen.[32] The pictures are drawn in pen and ink and set in scroll-work frames. The first represents a foot, trampling upon a snake, the motto being *Spretaque sic vivunt, sic concultata resurgunt.* Alciati would, of course, have added a poem enlarging upon the theme, but, though lacking this, the design has both the matter and the manner of the emblem proper. Ownerless legs or arms stretching from the sky are as common in the emblem books as they are in the Castle of Otranto. The motto explains the picture, the picture particularises the motto, each depends on the other. A poem to bring home a point which was without doubt perfectly clear to the Queen is all that is needed to complete it. In the other two emblems, one of which was copied from Alciati, poems are supplied in place of the motto.[33] All three treat of the same subject—Gascoigne's plea for royal favour. They bear no immediate relation to the story and were obviously intended to be an additional attraction to catch the eye of the Queen. A book full of them would have constituted an emblem book. Doubtless there were other appearances of single emblems such as those of Gascoigne; but it was not till 1586 that a complete emblem book in the English language was published.

III

There were various reasons why, despite this background of knowledge and interest, emblem books themselves were so late in appearing in the vernacular in England and so relatively few when they did come. In the first place these early emblem books are inseparably related to devices and heraldry—the prerogative of a limited class—and their readers would have been those for whom French and Italian presented no difficulties and to whom English was still an insular rather than a European language. But this is not an altogether sufficient explanation; for in France the first, at least, of these conditions existed and yet French emblematists sprang up as soon as the fashion reached the country. But England was still conscious of inferiority to the Continent in respect of the polite arts, and the ever increasing number of these publications while offering a wide selection to a man like Whitney and awakening the desire for emulation in a man like Henry Peacham, had also an inhibiting effect. One English emblem writer, Andrew Willet, for instance, is articulate over his hesitation where others may have remained quite mute. Willet was famous for his immense learning and huge literary output; he produced two theological works a year, provoking an astonished contemporary to describe him as one that 'must write as he sleeps it being impossible he should do so much waking'. He had apparently read widely in the emblem books of France and Italy, and he criticises a previous emblematist, unnamed but from all appearances Whitney, for thinking it enough to have translated old material drawn from

abroad or to have added new merely of the same kind. He then continues:

> Ego, ne actum (quod aiunt) agerem, vel in alienam messem falcem immitterem, ad sacrum tantum fontem digitum intendens et intingens pedem, tentare volui, an in eodem genere, sed alia incedens via nostris placere possem.[34]

The size of the foreign harvest may have been the least of reasons, but it did seem to set up a standard which the English found hard to attain. Whitney's emblems appeared in 1586 at a time when there clearly was room for them; this was followed by Willet's little volume,—remarkable historically perhaps for its attempt to do something new, but otherwise only for the feebleness of its verse,—and two translations from the French. After this no more was published in England until Peacham's *Minerva Britanna* in 1612; Peacham does, it is true, comment on the slender collection of emblemata in the vernacular:

> I have heere (kind Reader), sent abroad unto thy view, this volume of *Emblemes,* whether for greatnes of the chardge, or that the Invention is not ordinarie: a Subiect very rare. For, except the collections of Master *Whitney,* and the translations of some one or two else beside, I know not an *Englishman* in our age, that hath published any work of this kind: they being (I doubt not) as ingenious, and happy in their inventions, as the best French or Italian of them all. Hence perhaps they term us *Tramontani Sempii,* Simple and of dull conceipt, when the fault is neither in the Climate, nor as they would have it, in the constitution of our bodies, but truely in the cold and frozen respect of Learning, and artes, generally amongst us: comeing far shorte of them in the iust valewing of well deserving qualities.

Compared with Italy, there was doubtless a cold and frozen respect of learning and the arts generally in England, but it can hardly be said that the invention was not by this time ordinary. The explanation is more nearly to be found in the practical difficulties of producing picture books in England. The cost of printing was a continual cause of complaint among the emblematists; and not only were the plates expensive to print, they had also to be acquired. The backward state of engraving in England compared with that on the Continent effectively checked the publication of illustrated books. John Harington, advertising the engravings in his translation of *Orlando Furioso* in 1591, for instance, emphasises both their singularity and their costliness:

> I will not praise them too much, because I gave direction for their making, and in regard thereof, I may be thought partiall, but this I may truely say, that (for mine owne part) I have not seen anie made in England better, nor (in deede) anie of his kinde, in any booke, except it were in a treatise, set foorth by that profound man, maister Broughton the last yeare, upon the Revelation, in which there are some 3 or 4 pretie figures (in octavo) cut in brasse verie workemanly. As for other

books that I have seene in this realme, either in Latin or English, with picturs, as Livy, Gesner, Alciats emblemes, a booke de Spectris, in Latin, & (in our tong) the Chronicles, the booke of Martyrs, the book of hawking and hunting, and M. Whitneys excellent Emblems, yet all their figures are cut in wood, and none in metall, and in that respect inferior to these, at least (by the old proverbe) the more cost, the more worship.

Harington's account is not strictly accurate in detail but the general truth of his statement is unquestioned; the first appearance of copper-plates for illustration of an English book was in 1540,[35] but there was no real demand for them until the beginning of the seventeenth century. Nor was woodcutting in a much better state. The emblem writers met the difficulty in various ways. Willet solved the problem by publishing 'naked emblems', or emblems without pictures. Whitney's *Choice* was published by Plantin and illustrated with woodcuts already in the printer's stock. Peacham made his own. Wither imported Rollenhagen's plates from Holland, which he admired though they were prefixed with verses 'so meane' that he cut them off.[36] In general, however, it seems that the production of emblem books in England was much retarded by the practical difficulties which their makeup presented.

Notes

1. Geoffrey Whitney, *A Choice of Emblemes*. Leyden. 1586.

2. *Paradise Lost*. IV. 700-3:

> Underfoot the Violet,
> Crocus, and Hyacinth with rich inlay
> Broider'd the ground, more colour'd then with stone
> Of costliest Emblem:

3. The term 'emblem' was current in three senses in the late sixteenth and the seventeenth centuries. It was used in connection with decoration to describe certain kinds of inlaid work, in connection with rhetoric to describe a particular rhetorical figure (see below, Chapter 4. pp. 86 ff.) and thirdly as a name for a particular literary form. The best contemporary set of definitions is that of Maximilian Sandaeus in *Theologia Symbolica*. 1626. pp. 169-70. who expands the number of senses to five:

> (1) Ipsum illud opus ex tessellis insititiis aptatum, atque consertum, dictum est *Emblema*.

> (2) Oratio culta, rerum verborumque luminibus, ut totidem flosculis, aut gemmulis nitens, *Emblema* vocari potest.

> (3) Florente Republica, vocabantur *Emblemata* in vasis aureis, argenteis, Corinthiis ornamenta quaedam exemptilia.

> (4) *Emblema*, pro ornatu quolibet temporario & exemptili ponitur.

> (5) Poetis, *Emblemata*, sunt *Carmina*, seu *Epigrammata*, quibus imagines, ἀγάλματα, *Symbola*, simulachra, pegmata, atque alia id genus scite adinventa, varie, atque erudite explicantur, ut post Claudium Mynoen in Syntagmate de *Symbolis*, docet Iacob. Pontan. . . . Itaque *Emblema* ab illis vocatur *Epigramma*, quod *Emblema complectitur* μετωνυμικῶς, ut fatentur.

> Requirunt autem Poeticae Magistri ad *Emblema* tria quaedam: *Epigraphen*, id est, sententiolam aliquam scitam & concinnam, tanquam rei totius animam: *Picturam* seu *Imaginem*, & *Poesin*, quae se ita explicent, ut altera alteri sit interpres. Et *Pictura*, tanquam corpus, *Poesis* habetur ut animus (*sic*).

4. Mario Praz, *Studies in Seventeenth Century Imagery*. 1939. p. 18. The history of the form is discussed in detail by Professor Praz in his first chapter.

5. Op. cit. p. 16.

6. See Samuel Sharpe, 'Notes on the Hieroglyphics of Horapollo Nilous'. *Original Papers read before the Syro-Egyptian Society of London*. 1845. Vol. I. Part I. pp. 45-62. Mr. Sharpe argues on the grounds that the author always spoke of the Egyptians as 'they', attempted to explain Egyptian words by the Greek language, and clearly had a very imperfect knowledge of the hieroglyphics he was interpreting, that it was a Greek work written by Philipus from Horapollo's explanations which he did not fully understand.

7. 'Between an emblem of Alciati and an epigram of the Anthology there is a difference only in name.' Op. cit. p. 21. See also p. 26.

8. See Shaftesbury's classification of Characters in Appendix 2. p. 241.

9. Sir Thomas Browne, *Religio Medici*. 1635. *Works*, ed. G. Keynes. 1928. Vol. I. p. 75.

10. Estienne, op. cit. p. 18.

11. Charles Hoole, *A New Discovery of the Old Art of Teaching Schoole*. 1660. p. 159.

12. H. Thomas, *The Emblemata Amatoria of Philip Ayres*. 1910. p. 22. A bibliography of Alciati's emblem book was made by Henry Green, *Andrea Alciati and his Book of Emblems*. 1872.

13. See below, Chapter 7.

14. Francis Meres, *Palladis Tamia*. 1598. p. 285v. 'As the Latines have these *Emblematists*, Andreas Alciatus, *Reusnerus*, and *Sambucus*: so we have these, *Geffrey Whitney, Andrew Willet*, and *Thomas Combe*.'

15. *Idea de un Principe politico cristiano.* By Diego Fajardo. 1640. Translated by Sir James Astry, *The Royal Politician.* 1700.

16. See below, Chapter 5, p. 116.

17. Sidney Colvin, *Early Engravings and Engravers in England.* 1905. p. 73.

18. C. R. Leslie and T. Taylor, *Sir Joshua Reynolds.* 1865. Vol. I. p. 13. See also F. W. Hilles, *The Literary Career of Sir Joshua Reynolds.* 1936. p. 119.

19. 'Monita Amoris Virginei . . . 1622', translated by Thomas Heywood in *Pleasant Dialogues and Drammas.* 1637. pp. 203-30.

20. Sidney, op. cit. p. 81.

21. Now in the British Museum. See 'A Collection of the Emblem Books of Andrea Alciati in the Library of G. E. Sears'. Pr. printed, New York. 1888.

22. See Sotheby's *Catalogue of Emblems sold in 1884.* Item 108: Paradin's *Devises Heroiques.* 1562. 'With motto and autograph of G. Whitney . . . *Constanter et syncere* Galfridus Whytney. Cestreshire.'

23. The Folger Library copy has notes in a contemporary hand.

24. *The Worthy Tract of Paulus Iovius . . . of Rare Inventions . . . called Imprese,* by Samuel Daniel. London. 1585.

25. J. Nichols, *Progresses of Queen Elizabeth.* 1823. Vol. III. p. 148.

26. For an interesting account of this emblem see F. Saxl, 'Veritas Filia Temporis' in *Philosophy and History,* ed. R. Klibansky and H. J. Paton. 1936. pp. 197-222. Dr. Saxl traces its development and use as a political symbol during the Tudor period and after. Another example of its use which is not, however, mentioned by Saxl is the Darnley Jewel.

27. The compasses represented Constancy, the garland and rainbow Victory and Peace. See below, p. 146.

28. See Joan Evans, *English Jewellery.* 1921. pp. 88-91. for an account and picture of the Darnley Jewel.

29. Letter to Ben Jonson dated July 1, 1619. The book referred to is Jonson's projected verse account of his journey to Scotland. For a full text of the letter see Herford and Simpson, *Ben Jonson.* Oxford. 1925. Vol. I. pp. 208-10.

30. C. H. Herford, *Literary Relations between England and Germany in the Sixteenth Century.* 1886. p. 369. Harold Stein, *Studies in Spenser's Complaints.* 1934. p. 111.

31. *A Theatre wherein be represented as wel the miseries & calamities that follow the voluptuous Worldlings, as also the great ioyes and plesures which the faithful do enioy . . .* Devised by S. Iohn vander Noods. London. Henry Bynneman. 1569.

32. B. M. Royal MSS. 18.A. XLVIII. Printed in Gascoigne, *Complete Works,* ed. J. W. Cunliffe. 1910. Vol. II. pp. 473-509. where the pictures are also reproduced.

33. Alciati. Emblem 192. This is one of the emblems woven in the borders of the Hatfield Tapestries. See below. p. 95.

34. Andrew Willet, *Sacrorum Emblematum Centuria Una.* Cambridge. n.d. sig.A.2^r.

35. *The Byrth of Mankynde,* a book on midwifery.

36. See below, p. 142.

Mario Praz (essay date 1964)

SOURCE: Praz, Mario. "Emblem, Device, Epigram, Conceit." In *Studies in Seventeenth-Century Imagery,* pp. 11-54. Rome: Edizioni di Storia e Letteratura, 1964.

[*In the following excerpt, Praz examines the peculiar fit between emblem literature and the seventeenth-century zeitgeist. Praz's history of the emblem emphasizes the influence of humanist interest in Egyptian hieroglyphics.*]

There lies asleep in old European libraries, chiefly in those of ecclesiastical origin, a vast literature of illustrated books which are very seldom and only cursorily consulted nowadays—the emblem literature. Although "emblems" form a permanent item in all second-hand booksellers' catalogues, I suppose that most people jump (or jumped, until recently) over it with the same expression of unconcern with which they meet Americana, Erotica, or Occultism. And as for the happy few whose eyes kindle at the sight of the magic word "emblems"—alas! their attention might as well be dedicated to collecting stamps or cigarette-cards, for their interest very seldom strays beyond the material possession of a rare thing and the pleasure, at best, of looking at fine plates[1]. True, they have the books sumptuously bound, in full levant morocco, gilt edges, inside dentelles, etc., but as for reading them, that does not seem to be their affair.

Does this literature deserve such oblivion? Is it unworthy of study, were it only as a document of a perversion of taste in bygone ages[2]? And above all, are emblems really such dead things?

On the contrary, they are alive and very much so, as they have always been, even if not under that particular name. You open the account of the solemn obsequies of a great seventeenth-century personage and smile at the numerous plates of emblems and devices. "An odd century!" you exclaim. But there is no need to make a special journey to visit D'Annunzio's Vittoriale to become aware that those people of the seventeenth century, even if they went a little too far, were not after all very different from ourselves. Italians may remember the stamps issued for the tenth anniversary of the Fascist regime. One used to give those stamps to child collectors. But that series could with equal right have been bound in a little volume to be placed next to those dusty folios of seventeenth-century pomps. Because each one of those stamps, with its figure and motto, is a perfect emblem or a perfect device.

* * *

All human things exist in every period of history, and it is only their proportion which makes one speak of fashions. Attic vase painters represented the heroes of the Trojan war with symbols of prophylactic intention upon their targes: Æschylus describes some of them in his *Seven Against Thebes*; a famous coin of Titus had on its reverse the dolphin twisted round the anchor; but one cannot define the Greece of Æschylus, or even the Rome of the Flavii, as an emblematic age, though the latter saw a great vogue for epigrams, a genre akin to the emblem as we shall see later on. But the Alexandrian was certainly an emblematic age with its *technopaegnia* and its formula "Ut Pictura Poesis"[3]; and emblematic was the mentality of the early Christians, with their well-known symbols, and that of the Middle Ages with their bestiaries, lapidaries and allegories. The author of the *Ovide Moralisé* who, having paraphrased the fable of Pyramus and Thisbe, proceeds to illustrate it symbolically:

> Or vous dirai l'alegorie
> Que ceste fable signefie . . .[4]

and Daniello Bartoli with his *Simboli trasportati al morale* and his *Geografia trasportata al morale* (Rome, 1664) are exponents of the same taste. And Professor Ferdinando Neri observed that[5]:

> Carducci, apropos of this canzone [*Qual più diversa* of Petrarch], has spoken of "fantastic, quaint, symbolical, winged" poetry, sprung from the ignorance and superstition of the Middle Ages . . . The fact is that allegory with its formality was always crossing Petrarch's path; he persisted in it from the early *Nel dolce tempo de la prima etade,* down to *Standomi un giorno* and *Tacer non posso,* and the late vision of the *Trionfi*; but he never made an art of it. And his "mediævalism" has an Alexandrine feeling.

He might have added to "Alexandrine" also "Baroque". Neri calls the *Trionfi* a vision of time and eternity through emblems. In fact every stanza of "Standomi un

giorno" needs only a figure to become an emblem proper, and what could be imagined nearer to the taste of the seventeenth century than the "strange phœnix" of one of those stanzas?

Petrarch's use of emblems must be considered in the light of the mediæval theory which saw in the fables of the poets foreshadowings of scientific and philosophic mysteries, regarding them, in a word, from a point of view akin to that from which hieroglyphics were afterwards to be interpreted, as I shall point out later. Petrarch proclaims this theory several times over; for instance, in the fourth book of his *Rerum Senilium Libri* (*De quibusdam fictionibus Virgilii*) and in the second volume of the *Epistolae Metricae* (epistle to Zoilus, p. 1351, col. 2 of the Henricpetri edition, 1554):

> quædam diuina Poetis
> Vis animi est ueloque tegunt pulcherrima rerum
> Ambiguum quod non acies, nisi lyncea rumpat—

where the *acies lyncea* seems almost to forestall the *agudeza* of the seventeenth-century writers.

After all the emblematists took it upon themselves later to supply with figures some of Petrarch's potential emblems. Thus one can see in Ruscelli's *Imprese illustri* and in Pittoni's *Imprese di diversi Principi,* the device of Lucrezia Gonzaga which shows a white doe under a laurel with the motto *Nessun mi tocchi* (Let no one touch me), taken from the sonnet: "Una candida cerva sopra l'erba". And Palazzi in the third of his *Discorsi sopra l'Imprese* mentions the device derived from a stanza of the canzone "Qual più diversa e nova" where the catoblepas is described ("Nell'estremo occidente . . ."), although the author of the device fitted the motto: *Pur che gli occhi non miri* (Provided you do not look into its eyes) to the basilisk instead of the catoblepas. And the canzone "Standomi un giorno", Englished presumably by Spenser (see Appendix), appeared in van der Noodt's *Theatre for Worldlings* (1569) illustrated with woodcuts[6].

Therefore one can safely assume that Petrarch was a forerunner of the Seicento not only because of his taste for conceits but also because of his emblematic bias. But emblems and conceits are fruits of the same tree, and the periods which were fond of conceits were also periods of emblems.

In the seventeenth century we watch the acute stages of a tendency of the imagination which Diderot attempts to explain in this way[7]:

> Il passe alors dans le discours du poëte un esprit qui en meut et vivifie toutes les syllabes. Qu'est-ce que cet esprit? J'en ai quelquefois senti la présence; mais tout ce que j'en sais, c'est que c'est lui qui fait que les choses sont dites et représentées tout à la fois; que dans le

même temps que l'entendement les saisit, l'âme en est émue, l'imagination les voit et l'oreille les entend, et que le discours n'est plus seulement un enchaînement de termes énergiques qui exposent la pensée avec force et noblesse, mais que c'est encore un tissu d'hiéroglyphes entassés les uns sur les autres qui la peignent. Je pourrais dire, en ce sens, que toute poésie est emblématique.

A passage from Schopenhauer[8] may be set beside this:

> The name of "emblems" is usually given to simple allegorical designs accompanied by an explanatory motto and destined to teach in an intuitive form a moral truth . . . they form a transition to poetical allegory . . . Quite different is the value of allegory in poetry; thoroughly inadmissible as it is in the plastic arts, one has to recognize that in literature it is perfectly admissible and useful . . . Since in poetical allegory a datum always results in a concept which one tries to make apprehensible by intuition through an image, one can well allow that a painted figure may sometimes be introduced either to accompany or support the expression; but such an image should not be considered as a work of representational art, but rather as a hieroglyphic sign; and it cannot have any value as a picture, but only as a poetic creation.

Since every poetical image contains a potential emblem, one can understand why emblems were the characteristic of that century in which the tendency to images reached its climax, the seventeenth century. In need as he was of certainties of the senses, the seventeenth-century man did not stop at the purely fantastic cherishing of the image: he wanted to externalize it, to transpose it into a hieroglyph, an emblem. He took delight in driving home the word by the addition of a plastic representation. The method of teaching through images was launched by a seventeenth-century man, J. A. Comenius (*Orbis Sensualium Pictus,* 1658) who anticipated Locke's psychology ("There is nothing in the understanding which was not before in the sense"). One must remember that this is the age of the opera, which carries out Diderot's saying: "les choses sont dites et représentées tout à la fois; dans le même temps que l'entendement les saisit, l'âme en est émue, l'imagination les voit et l'oreille les entend". If considered from a philosophical angle, the opera as a fusing together of various arts is purely an illusion; but from the psychological point of view it witnesses to a kind of imagination which tries to overreach itself, an appetite of the intellect as uncontrolled as an appetite of the senses: in a word, it argues a process of materialization rather than of sublimation.

The century which produced the great mystics produced also the emblematists: they seem opposites, and frequently these opposites are found united in the same person. Perhaps because their imagination was too vivid they sought shelter in a world emptied of perception, in the ineffable. "It seemed to happen to me that I saw the devils playing tennis with my soul". This image of St. Teresa (*Vida,* XXX) finds a counterpart in emblems, for instance in the fourth plate of Solórzano Pereira's *Emblemata* (Madrid, 1651), where one sees illustrated the image of God who deals with kings as with tennis-balls. In this case, as with emblems in general, some will think it absurd that one should speak of incontinency of the imagination, and will rather call this device a didactic trick calculated to teach in an intuitive form a moral truth, and we shall in fact see that this is the reason why the Jesuits made so much of the emblem. But it is not, however, at all easy to discriminate between the two tendencies, the sensuous and the didactic, which in the seventeenth century are combined in emblematic literature[9]. Are not both these aspects mentioned together by Erasmus[10] apropos of that mother of the emblem, the metaphor?

> Sic enim augurabar, quod . . . intelligerem non nitorem modo, sed universam prope sermonis dignitatem a metaphoris proficisci. Nihil autem aliud est παραβολή, quam Cicero collationem vocat, quam explicata metaphora . . . Metaphora sola cumulatius præstat universa quam exornationes reliquæ singula. Delectare vis? Nulla plus habet festivitatis. Docere studes? Non alia probat vel efficacius vel apertius.

Brief is the transition from this praise of metaphor, or from the praise of the *acutezza recondita* which one reads in Castiglione's *Cortegiano* (XXX):

> If the words used by a writer bear with them a little, I will not say difficulty, but recondite wit (*acutezza recondita*) . . . they give a somewhat greater authority to the writing, and cause the reader to be more wary and attentive and to ponder more, and to delight in the ingenuity and learning of the writer—

to the following praise of emblems in Gracián's *Agudeza y arte de ingenio*[11]; "Emblems, Hieroglyphs, Apologues, and Devices, are like precious stones to the gold of elegant discourse". Therefore it has been observed with reason that the foundation of *secentismo* is to be found in the poetics of the Renaissance. The same Emanuele Tesauro who said of the metaphor[12]:

> Metaphor packs tightly all objects into one word: and makes you see them one inside the other in an almost miraculous way. Hence your delight is the greater, because it is a more curious and pleasant thing to watch many objects from a perspective angle than if the originals themselves were to pass successively before one's eyes—

saw the sky as "a vast cerulean Shield, on which skilful Nature draws what she meditates: forming heroical Devices, and mysterious and witty Symbols of her secrets", saw the thunderbolts as "formidable witticisms (*Arguzie*) and Symbolical Ciphers of Nature, both dumb and at the same time vocal: having the Bolt for their body and the Thunder for their motto", and imagined

God as a "witty speaker, who talking in riddles to Men and Angels, clothed his most exalted concepts with various heroical Devices, and pictorial Symbols". In this passage one sees the extreme practical consequences (a system of universal emblematics) of an ancient opinion which Plutarch formulated thus[13]:

> Nature herself has put before us sensible images and visible representations: the sun and the stars, of the gods; sudden lightnings, comets and meteors, of mortals—

an opinion which was widespread in the Middle Ages, when Alanus de Insulis[14] sang:

> Omnis mundi creatura
> quasi liber et pictura
> 　　　nobis est et speculum:
> nostrae vitae, nostrae mortis,
> nostri status, nostrae sortis
> 　　　fidele signaculum.

And Daniello Bartoli (*De' Simboli trasportati al morale*) enlarged thus on the etymological definition of the emblem (i. e. a work of mosaic, of inlay):

> In many places have I seen works and wonderful samples of the ancient and now almost discontinued art of inlay . . . It is all skill of the intelligence and of the hand, working the one to select, the other to weld together those different slices of wood, having a certain colour, a certain grain, a certain pattern, and alternatively so light and clear and so shaded and dark, that when joined together, whatever one intended comes out as an effect of their union: but with a shading from one leaf to another, with such mingling of colours, that it does not seem to be a grouping of many slices of various trees and of various woods artistically put together, but a work born of a piece in one tree-trunk, which quite by chance appeared when splitting it . . . In such works of inlay, one wishes to make it appear as if nature had imitated art, contriving in such a way that art may not be distinguished from nature. Is not the source of wonder, and therefore of delight in such works, the fact that one sees one thing used to express another? the deception being all the more innocent in that in the whole composition of a false thing there is yet no element which is not true. The same happens when we use anything taken from history, from fables, from nature and art, to represent something in the moral order which it is not: in such a way that there should be so much appropriateness and correspondence of reciprocal proportion between truth and its likeness that the whole, so to speak, should not seem to be an artifice of the brain but the *philosophy of nature, as if nature had written, almost in cipher, her precepts everywhere.*

The link with the Alexandrians is expressly stressed by Father Juan Eusebio Nieremberg, a Jesuit (author, among other books, of a *Gnomoglyphica*), in his *Oculta Filosofia*[15]:

> Plotinus called the world the Poetry of God. I add, that this Poem is like a labyrinth, which is read in every direction, and gives intimation of, and points to, its Au-

thor. Among the poetical devices of antiquity were celebrated Theocritus' flute, the egg, wings and hatchet of Simias of Rhodes. But above all the Panegyric which the Poet Porphyrius addressed to the Emperor Constantine is most cunning and incomparable, and was celebrated by St. Jerome, Fulgentius and Bede . . . All this Panegyric consists of seventeen most artfully contrived labyrinths, where one verse joins and is knitted together with another in different manners, and the praises of Cæsar are celebrated in all parts, by the beginnings, the middles and the ends of the lines, and crosswise, from the first letter of the first line to the last letter of the last line, and then, by combining crosswise the remaining letters of the lines between the first and the last, the second letter of the second line, the third of the third, etc., so as to form a thousand other sentiments in the praise of Cæsar. So do I imagine the world to be a Panegyric of God.

But the most prodigious *technopaegnion* was elaborated by Erycius Puteanus upon a line by the Jesuit poet Bernard Van Bauhuysen (Bernardus Bauhusius):

> Tot tibi sunt dotes, Virgo, quot sidera cælo.

Puteanus showed that the words of that line could be combined in 1022 different ways, as many as was the number of the stars then known, so that one could say with reason that the sky was a perfect emblem of the Virgin's virtues: "Omnia in Deo et Natura θαυμάσια. Imago Virginis cœlo, cœlum versu adumbratum". This line was called "starry Proteus", "Homeric wonder", after the words of Pollux the Sophist related by Philostratus (*Vitæ Sophistarum*), and was also called "Periclymenus multiformis", after Euphorion and the Scholiast of Apollonius[16]. In such cases the Alexandrine age, the Middle Ages and the Baroque age reveal the same peculiarity of taste, which, considered beside other analogies (we shall see, for example, a similar taste for the epigram and conceit in the Alexandrians and the writers of the seventeenth century, and on the other hand attention has often been drawn to the affinities between the Gothic and the Baroque), allows us to survey the history of taste on broader lines than has hitherto been done. Therefore we shall not turn away from the emblem-books as from an idle study, and little does it matter if from an essentially modern ethical point of view emblems and conceits may appear to be "fantastic analogies which under the cloak of instilling love and fear of God and the light of truth into the soul, deceived it with an idle pastime"[17]. Even those which to us nowadays seem aberrations of taste deserve dispassionate attention, rather than Croce's attitude of scorn and contempt[18]:

> It was the need of feeding the eye as well as the other senses, of stirring the imagination in default of nourishing the heart, the intellect and the fancy, that led to all the kinds of pageants, both sacred and profane, which were then so frequent—such as processions, catafalques, illuminations, arches, cardboard statues, de-

vices, emblems. And a similar need gave rise to the academies, which re-echoed with baroque verse, and trifled with futile and ridiculous themes.

One will hesitate to believe that emblems and devices were incapable of nourishing the heart, the intellect and the fancy, when one considers the effect they had on certain mystics, and when one reads what the Jesuit Louis Richeome wrote of religious images which teach "profitablement, vivement et délicieusement les vertus, les fruits et les délices" of the mysteries of the Faith:

> Il n'y a rien qui plus délecte et qui fasse glisser plus suavement une chose dans l'âme que la peinture, ni qui plus profondément la grave en la mémoire, ni qui plus efficacement pousse la volonté pour lui donner branle et l'émouvoir avec énergie.[19]

Either I am much mistaken or this passage speaks actually of heart, fancy and intellect receiving nourishment from those symbolical images which at first one would feel tempted to call, with Croce, "trifles". But I shall have to return to this point in more detail later.

> Every power has a King among its acts and another among its objects: among those of the mind the Conceit reigns and Wit (*agudeza*) triumphs . . . Understanding without Wit or Conceits is a Sun without light or rays . . . This need for the conceit is common to prose and verse. What would Augustine be without his subtleties, and Ambrose without his ponderings? Martial without his salt and Horace without his maxims? . . . If perceiving Wit gives one the reputation of being an Eagle, producing it will make one into an Angel: for the latter is an office of Cherubs, and an exaltation of mankind, which elevates us to an extravagant Hierarchy . . . What beauty is to the eyes and harmony is to the ears, the Conceit is to the Understanding.

Thus Gracián[20], who illustrates the various aspects of *agudeza* chiefly by epigrams from Martial and emblems from Alciati. And Tesauro enriched his *Cannocchiale Aristotelico, o sia Idea delle Argutezze Eroiche* with two treatises, one on the conceits for the use of preachers (*concetti predicabili*) and another on emblems, and separately compiled a volume of *Inscriptiones*[21], that is "epigrams" according to the original meaning of the word. Now the emblem, if we bear in mind the value which Alciati gives to this term, is exactly the reverse of the epigram. He declared in fact in his commentary upon *De Verborum significatione* (second paragraph): "verba significant, res significantur. Tametsi et res quandoque significant, ut hieroglyphica apud Horum et Chæremonem, cuius argumenti et nos carmine libellum composuimus, cui titulus est Emblemata"[22]. Emblems are therefore things (representations of objects) which illustrate a conceit; epigrams are words (a conceit) which illustrate objects (such as a work of art, a votive offering, a tomb). The two are therefore complementary, so much so that many epigrams in the *Greek Anthology*

written for statues are emblems in all but name. The name was devised by Alciati who derived it from F. Budé's *Annotationes ad Pandectas* where it signified "mosaic work": in this very sense the term *emblematura* had been used by F. Colonna in his *Hypnerotomachia,* which had a great influence on the origin and fashion of emblems. The emblem and the epigram represent, therefore, two different ways of envisaging the same *technopaegnion*; and the representational point of view implied by the word *emblem* (a counterpart of the literary point of view implied by *epigram*) was adopted by Andrea Alciati under the influence of Egyptian hieroglyphics.

Emblems originate, in fact, as Ludwig Volkmann has demonstrated[23], as a humanistic attempt to give a modern equivalent of the hieroglyphs as they were wrongly interpreted on the strength of the accounts given by Pliny, Tacitus, Plutarch, Apuleius, Clemens Alexandrinus, Plotinus, etc. It was thought that the hieroglyphs were a purely ideographical form of writing, that with them the Egyptian priests foreshadowed divine ideas, and that the Greek philosophers had drawn upon hieroglyphic wisdom. Cassiodorus and Rufinus saw in them also prefigurations of Christian doctrine. The fashion for hieroglyphs among the humanists was started by the *Hieroglyphica* (of the enigmatic character) by Horapollo or Horus (Orus) Apollo, an author supposedly Egyptian (he calls himself Nilous) of the IV or II century A. D., not better identified, and perhaps fictitious: neither has the Greek translator Philippus been identified. A Greek manuscript of the *Hieroglyphica* was purchased in 1419 in Andros by the Florentine priest Cristoforo de' Buondelmonti, and awakened great interest among the Florentine humanists, chiefly Marsilio Ficino.

The artists were not slow in making use of the new pseudo-science. L. B. Alberti speaks of it in his *Architettura* (Book VIII, Ch. 4); it suggested themes for medals, coins, decorations of columns, of triumphal arches, suites of rooms. The influence of Alberti is noticeable in the *Hypnerotomachia* (which was already written by 1467 and was published by Aldus in 1499) where we find several modern hieroglyphic inventions and symbolical figures, among which the famous one of Titus's coin, the dolphin twisted round the anchor with the motto *Semper festina tarde,* which was adopted for the Aldine editions. In the poem *Delphini Somnium* attributed to Francesco Colonna, the author of the *Hypnerotomachia*[24], we find the recurring device *Sacer est ignis credite laesis,* called 'impresa amorosa' on line 341. Aldus also printed the first edition of Orapollo (1505) which Filippo Fasanini translated into Latin (1517). Fasanini already speaks of the practical and decorative applications of the hieroglyphs, and of the advantage which will accrue from his translation to the writers of epithalamiums and to those "curiosi homines" who desire to decorate with symbols and mottoes such things as swords, rings, bells, beds, doors, ceilings. It is of this decorative use of emblems that Alciati speaks in his 1551 edition of the *Emblemata,* and he had already hinted at it in the dedication of the 1531 edition and in a letter dated 1522 to his friend Calvi. It is likely that Alciati got the first idea of his booklet of emblems from Fasanini who was professor in Bologna in those years in which Alciati was a student there. He obtained his doctorate in law in 1514.

The diffusion of hieroglyphs was also helped by the activity of Fra Urbano Valeriano Bolzanio (c. 1443-1524) who was in contact with, among others, F. Colonna and Giovanni de' Medici (afterwards Leo X). His nephew Pierio Valeriano in 1556 published in Basle a weighty treatise upon the *Hieroglyphica sive de sacris Ægyptiorum aliarumque gentium literis.* In Valeriano's book hieroglyphs are wedded to the symbolism of mediæval lapidaries and bestiaries, and of the *Physiologus* ascribed to Epiphanius, a collection of symbols suggested by animals (the stork, the pelican, the phœnix, etc.), which was itself of Alexandrine provenance. Among the painters who drew *motifs* from hieroglyphs were Pinturicchio (Stanze Borgia), Leonardo (several sketches), Mantegna (Triumphs of Cæsar), Giovanni Bellini (Allegories)[25], Dürer (Ehrenpforte of the Emperor Maximilian), Giorgio Vasari[26]. The origin of the emblem not only goes back to the hieroglyphs, but is to be traced, for the motto, to the devices, the fashion for which was fostered in Italy when the French occupied Milan in 1499, as we shall show later. Another impulse to the spreading of emblems came from the crystallization of ancient ethics in those collections of proverbs and maxims (chiefly Cato's *Moral Distichs,* Erasmus's *Adagia,* and Stobæus's *Anthology*) which enjoyed such a vogue in the sixteenth century[27].

The first edition of Alciati's *Emblematum Liber* appeared in Augsburg from the Heinrich Steyner press in 1531, and was significantly dedicated to the Imperial counsellor Konrad Peutinger, who had bought in Greece a manuscript of Orapollo, the translation of which, the work of B. Trebatius (Augsburg, 1515), had also been dedicated to him. Alciati writes thus in the dedication:

> Hæc nos festiuis emblemata cudimus horis,
>   Artificum illustri signaque facta manu.
> Vestibus ut torulos, petasis ut figere parmas,
>   Et ualeat tacitis scribere quisque notis.

Alciati draws on ancient historians, on Aulus Gellius, Pliny, Athenæius, Ælianus, Stobæus, Pausanias, on the apologues and proverbs, and utilizes the hieroglyphs, but above all he translates the epigrams of the *Planudean Anthology.* In this latter case he merely translates from Greek into Latin, and adds the illustra-

tion; but this was presupposed by the original. In fact, vestiges of three epigrams now in the *Anthology* have been discovered on the walls of a *cubiculum* in a Pompeian house, each illustrated by a painting[28]. It follows that between an emblem of Alciati and an epigram of the *Anthology* there is a difference only in name. Translated or imitated from the Greek epigrams, according to the commentator's explanations[29], are the following emblems, to which I add in brackets the source according to the numbering adopted in the *Anthologia Palatina cum Planudeis:*

> 5 (XVI. 115); 11 (X. 98); 23 (XVI. 183); 24 (IX. 130); 27 (XVI. 223); 28 (IX. 115); 33 (VII. 161); 42 (IX. 291); 46 (IX. 146); 48 (VII. 145); 51 (VII. 71); 54 (IX. 346 and XVI. 141); 59 (XI. 428); 64 (IX. 47); 86 (XI. 397); 90 (IX. 308); 95 (IX. 86); 104 (XVI. 107); 105 (VII. 172); 106 (IX. 221); 107 (XVI. 207); 108 (XVI. 250); 109 (V. 234); 110 (XVI. 201); 111 (XVI. 251); 112 (IX. 548 and IX. 302); 122 (XVI. 275); 130 (IX. 158); 134 (VII. 73); 136 (VII. 225); 152 (IX. 148); 160 (IX. 231); 161 (IX. 12); 162 (IX. 42); 167 (VII. 216); 168 (VII. 152); 173 (IX. 339); 177 (IX. 285); 180 (IX. 122); 185 (VI. 54); 187 (IX. 366); 193 (IX. 3); 194 (IX. 95); 195 (IX. 163).

Altogether about fifty emblems out of two hundred and twenty[30]. To be noticed for the influence it was destined to have is the group of love emblems 105 ff. Number 114 of 32 lines, *In statuam Amoris,* deals with one of the most familiar themes of the academies of the Renaissance: why love is naked, blind, winged, etc.[31]. Its direct source, however, is not in the *Anthology*[32], whereas emblems 105-113 are translated from it. The emblem entitled *Vis Amoris* shows the god in the act of breaking a thunderbolt:

> Aligerum fulmen fregit Deus aliger, igne
>   Dum demonstrat uti fortior ignis amor.

It is the following epigram of the *Planudean Anthology:*

> Ὁ πτανὸς τὸν πτανὸν ἰδὼν ἄγνυσι κεραυνὸν,
> δεικνὺς ὡς κρεῖσσον πῦρ πυρός ἐστιν Ἔρως.

Gracián goes into ecstasies over this emblem[33]: "Alciati, who did not weary of exercising his great Genius in any kind of subtlety, in order to measure the great strength of love . . .". Elsewhere, in the eleventh Discourse which treats "de las semejanças por ponderación misteriosa, dificultad, y reparo", he quotes emblem 112 taken from Theocritus, as Alciati himself declares (he means the Κηριοκλέπτης wrongly ascribed to Theocritus):

> Alveolis dum mella legit, percussit Amorem
> Furacem mala apes, et summis spicula liquit
> In digitis: tumido gemit at puer anxius ungue,
> Et quatit errabundus humum, Venerique dolorem
> Indicat et graviter queritur, quod apicula parvum
> Ipsa inferre animal tam noxia vulnera possit.

Cui ridens Venus, Hanc imitaris tu quoque, dixit,
Nate feram, qui das tot noxia vulnera parvus.

It will appear to us rather extravagant that Gracián should give to this somewhat platitudinous moral the name of *ponderación misteriosa*. But the seventeenth-century brain delighted in that comparison between the little bee and the little god, both causing burning wounds, since of what else did the essence of the conceit consist if not of comparisons of this kind? "It is an act of the understanding which expresses the correspondence which is found between objects": thus Gracián defined the conceit[34]. A similar conceit was contained in the other Planudean epigram which becomes the fifty-fourth emblem of Alciati, the swallow which makes its nest in the bosom of a statue of Medea:

Colchidos in gremio nidum quid congeris? eheu
Nescia cur pullos tam male credis avis?
Dira parens Medæa suos sævissima natos
Perdidit, et speras parcat ut illa tuis?

Gracián quotes this too[35], which can be put beside the series of astonishing occurrences exemplified elsewhere in the *Anthology,* and by Martial[36]. And in connexion with emblem 167, *In eum qui truculentia suorum perierit,* derived from an epigram in the third book of the *Planudean Anthology* on the dolphin washed ashore by the waves and buried by compassionate men—

Delphinum invitum me in littora compulit æstus,
Exemplum infido quanta pericla mari.
Nam si nec propriis Neptunus parcit alumnis,
Quis tutos homines navibus esse putet?

(. . . νῦν δὲ τεκοῦσα θάλαττα, διώλεσε· τίς παρὰ πόντῳ πίστις, ὃς ἰδίης φείσατο συντροφίης;)—

Gracián remarks, "Above all, when the Similitude is enhanced by mystery, and is given point by a weighty and sententious consideration, it is the triumph of Wit"[37].

All this was, therefore, much older than Alciati. It was, actually, Alexandrian, as Tesauro acknowledges in the *Trattato degli Emblemi* in an appendix to the *Cannocchiale* (ed. of Venice, 1678, p. 462): "And therefore if you read the collections of Greek writers [the *Anthology*], you will come across very many epigrams of various either fabulous or historical images, which forming, as they do, true and witty emblems, will show you that this art is not new, but rather that modern wits have drunk at the fountain of the old masters". Moreover the emblems which have no source in the *Anthology* are conceived in the same spirit; so that, allowing for the influence of the hieroglyphics (which had also, as we have seen, been transmitted through an Alexandrian deformation), Alciati's model remains, first of all, the Greek epigram. The influence of the epigram, on the other hand, was at the same time profoundly transforming poetry: it modelled the sonnet in its own image by making the tercets end in a conceit[38], and by supplying the sonneteers with a whole set of finicky and witty Alexandrian themes, it created the fashion for madrigals. Finally it broke up the long poems into groups of witty pictures, of which a typical example is offered by Marino's stanzas, each with its epigrammatic point.

Thus emblem and conceit are recognisably of the same epigrammatic origin, and the type of epigram which had a paramount influence is that brought to perfection by Martial. Therefore Gracián was not mistaken in calling Martial "Primogénito de la Agudeza"[39], and in seeing in Spain, his birthplace, the natural nursery of wit[40]:

There was ever in Spain freedom of Wit, either through gravity or through the native fire of the Nation, rather than through lack of invention of plan. Her two first geniuses, Seneca in the judicious, and Martial in the witty genre, established this opinion, gave credit to this taste.

Our Bilbilis contributed to the great Empress of the world, not monsters as did Africa, but him who was a monster of Wit. Martial went to Rome intending to become an orator: but his extreme readiness, which refused to tolerate the restraints of chained Eloquence, broke forth freely, in every kind and manner of Wit, such as is made eternal in his epigrams.

This taste (for I do not give it a definite name) remained tied to this ingenious Province, this beautiful face of the world; and it was never more flourishing than in this fertile century, in which its Wits have blossomed with the spreading of its Monarchy. All discourse is made with freedom, in sacred as well as in profane compositions.

Let reason back up authority. A Mind unfettered by rules has always been greater, because it lets itself be carried away by inborn fire in discourse, and by its ability in argument; because it would feel embarrassed and limited if it had to be bound by the prolixity of a discourse or be dependent on a certain line. Mark the difference there is between a sermon of St. Augustine or of the elegant Ambrose, and a wearisome allegory of Origen and his like. The subtlety and ornate style of St. Chrysologus, although it does not follow the invention of a scheme, does not for that cease to be greatly pleasing, and if it were more ordered, it would not be so impressive.

The illustration Gracián gives on the following page of *buen gusto* in the field of the conceit, deserves to be quoted because it concerns emblematics nearly:

That does not deserve the name of taste which abandons ornate for disorderly and disconnected Wit, when its very name condemns on the one hands its disorder and on the other approves its artfully contrived comeliness . . . Even an Epigram is adequately perfect when the conceits join and form a whole which is held together in a plan, as one sees in that great sonnet by Don Luys de Góngora to the Marques de Castel Rodrigo, which begins *Arbol de cuyos ramos fortunados*; and this other, in every way remarkable for the plurality of conceits, the singularity of each one of them, but much more so for the way they are joined and knit together; I found it among the manuscript works of the Bilbilis doctor and canon Francisco Antonio Fuser, a man excelling in both taste and wit. It runs thus:

Longino hiere a Dios tres vezes ciego,
  ciego del cuerpo, como se vé claro,
  ciego del alma, sin buscar reparo,
  y ciego de la colera, y su fuego.
Llegó a la cruz con gran desasossiego
  para acabar un hecho feo, y raro,
  el qual aunque costar le pudo caro
  le dió la vida, y le causó sossiego.
El hierro de la lança, que llevaba,
  le sirvió de eslabon, Christo de piedra,
  la Cruz de yesca para sus enojos.
Hirió en el pedernal con furia braba,
  sacó fuego de amor y tanto medra,
  que vino a ser la lumbre de sus ojos.

(Longinus wounds God, he being three times blind, blind in the body as is clearly seen, blind in the soul, without seeking remedy, and blind with anger and its fire. He came to the cross in great tribulation in order to perform a rare and ugly deed, which might have cost him dear, but on the contrary gave him life and peace. The iron of the lance he bore served him as steel, Christ as flint, the Cross as tinder for his ills. He struck the flint with fierce fury, drew forth fire of love and healing which became the light of his eyes.)

This sonnet (which, as we have seen, Gracián does not differentiate from an epigram) lacks only an illustration in order to become a perfect emblem like those which Alciati derives from the *Greek Anthology*.

Notes

1. Emblem books are often illustrated with plates by well-known artists. See A. J. J. Delen, *Histoire de la gravure dans les anciens Pays-Bas et dans les provinces belges des origines jusqu'à la fin du XVIIIe siècle,* Paris, Les Editions d'Art et d'Histoire, 1935.

2. The importance of emblem literature as a source of information on daily life and thought in the Renaissance has been stressed by R. J. Clements in *The Cult of the Poet in Renaissance Emblem Literature, PMLA,* LIX, 3, September 1944.

3. See the works quoted in the notes on pp. 170-171 of the *Greek Romances in Elizabethan Prose Fiction* by S. L. Wolff, Columbia University Press, 1912. Wolff remarks, however, that considering the fondness of the Greek romancers for representing all things to the eye, one is surprised to find them making such small use of emblems. He finds none in Longus, he recalls but one in Heliodorus ("Why is Cupid painted with two wings?"); but he finds a fair sprinkling of em-

blems in Achilles Tatius. The Byzantine romancers are richer in emblems, but they were under the influence of mediæval allegory.

4. On Ovid's allegories see L. K. Born, *Ovid and Allegory,* in "Speculum", IX (1934), pp. 362-79.

5. "La Cultura" Nuova Serie, Vol. I, no. 7 (July 1929), pp. 401 and 404.

6. See the chapter on "Petrarca e gli emblematisti" in my *Ricerche anglo-italiane,* Rome, Edizioni di Storia e Letteratura, 1944, pp. 303-19.

7. *Lettre sur les sourds et les muets,* in *Œuvres complètes,* ed. Assézat et Tourneux, vol. I, p. 374.

8. *Die Welt, etc.,* Vol. I, Book III, par. 50.

A very original point of view on the significance of the allegorical tableau is offered by W. J. Ong in the essay *From Allegory to the Diagram in the Renaissance Mind,* in "The Journal of Aesthetics and Art Criticism", XVII, 4 (June 1959). According to Ong the sixteenth- and seventeenth-century addiction to the allegorical tableau is closely related to addiction to new habits of communication of thought introduced by printing, such as the development of tables of dichotomies or bracketed 'outlines' of subjects: such outlines represent a kind of ultimate in the reduction of the verbal to the spatial: words are made 'intelligible' by being diagrammatically related to one another. The allegorical tableau occupies a kind of intermediate position between the aural and the visual worlds because of its special interaction of words and design. The peculiar dependence of visual symbol on verbalization which marks the great age of the allegorical tableau is testimony to the fact that it was a marginal age—an age when a verbal culture was being transmuted into a visual culture.

9. The case of the mystic, Marie de Valence, mentioned by H. Bremond, *Histoire littéraire du sentiment religieux en France,* Paris, 1925, Vol. II, pp. 55 ff., is typical enough: "On peut étudier l'activité spirituelle de cette ignorante, dans les élévations et dans les souvenirs qu'elle a dicté à son disciple émerveillé, Louis de la Rivière . . . Plus que d'autres, Marie s'attarde dans la région des objets sensibles, d'où il suit que chez elle le dépouillement progressif des images, leur sublimation, si l'on peut dire, est plus facile à suivre. Elle commence avec sainte Gertrude, et finit avec sainte Thérèse. 'Dieu lui donna un beau château spirituel qui lui représente la glorieuse Vierge Marie', ou bien 'on lui fait voir en vision que la glorieuse Vierge était un beau verger'; ou encore 'elle se voit entre les mains un vase plein d'une précieuse liqueur et entend ce que cela signifiait'. Une fois 'les vertus en forme de jeunes dames' se

présentèrent à elle et lui firent fête". In 1614 she listens to a sermon in which the moral and theological virtues are represented on triumphal chariots. Marie remarked that the preacher had succeeded better in representing the moral virtues, and showed in detail how the symbols should be corrected. In 1613 Marie visited the magnificent garden of the Sieur de la Buisse at Voyron. "Or, ainsi qu'elle se promenait par le jardin, elle arriva en un lieu fait en forme de grotte, où on lui donna la récréation d'une fontaine artificielle qui jetait, par divers tuyaux, les eaux, en haut, en bas, de ça, de là et de tous côtés. Là aussi étaient disposés plusieurs gentils artifices, comme d'oiseaux qui semblaient gazouiller, d'un ermite qui sonnait la cloche, et tout plein d'autres inventions qui faisaient la merveille par le lapse et la chute des eaux. Quand voilà qu'à l'instant, elle vit en l'esprit Jésus-Christ à l'instar d'une fontaine limpide . . . De là, on la mena voir une autre belle fontaine au sommet de laquelle il y avait un tuyau dans lequel on mit une chandelle allumée. A même temps on desserra certains ressorts, et l'eau sortant de dessous le tuyau, elle se forma en vase autour de la chandelle . . . Cette eau montait et descendait sans cesse autour de la chandelle, et en montant et descendant, le vase d'eau demeurait toujours parfaitement formé en ovale avec la chandelle en dedans et si pourtant ne s'éteignait pas . . . Mais voilà que tout à coup le Saint-Esprit lui fit voir intérieurement que l'âme bien fondée en charité était un chef-d'œuvre de Dieu où l'on voyait tout à la fois l'eau de vie de la grâce et le feu du divin amour". Similar representations are to be found, as we shall see, in the religions emblems of the period. For instance Christ in the aspect of a fountain (a *motif* which goes back to the Middle Ages, see E. Mâle, *L'Art religieux de la fin du moyen âge en France*, Paris, 1925, pp. 108 ff.: *La Fontaine de vie*) appears in *Emblèmes, ou devises chrestiennes* by Georgette de Montenay, Lyons, 1571 (plate 9), in H. Hugo's *Pia Desideria* (1624), in *Amoris divini et humani effectus* (1626).

10. Epistle to Petrus Ægidius, Ides of October 1514, *Opera Omnia,* Lugd. Batav., 1703, Vol. I, p. 559.

11. Page 357 of the Huesca edition 1649.

12. *Il Cannocchiale Aristotelico,* Venice, 1655, pp. 310, 77, 61.

13. *Moralia,* 416 D, *De oraculorum defectu.* This opinion became a commonplace with preachers and philosophers; see e.g. Berkeley: "The whole sensible universe is a system of signs".

14. Migne, CCX, 579.

15. *Oculta Filosofia de la Sympatia, y Antipatia de las cosas, artificio de la naturaleza, noticia natural del mundo, y segunda parte de la Curiosa Filosofia,* Barcelona, 1645, Ch. XI: *El mundo es un laberinto poetico. Tratase de los laberintos de Porphyrio poeta,* p. 106, first edition Madrid, 1633.

16. Ericj Puteani *Pietatis Thaumata in Bernardi Baubusj è Soc. Iesu Protheum Parthenium, unius Libri Versum, unius Versus Librum, Stellarum numero, sive formis MXXII variatum* [emblem], Antwerp, 1617. J. Addison quotes the composition inspired by this famous line as an instance of false wit in "The Spectator", no. 60. For another marvellous line, though in lesser proportions, by S. Pierre Fourier, see *La Vie du T. R. P. Pierre Fourier,* by R. P. Jean Bedel (1670), pp. 26, 27; and Bremond, *op. cit.,* Vol. I, pp. 317-18, note.

17. B. Croce, *Storia della Età Barocca in Italia,* Bari, 1929, p. 438. A remarkable attempt to see the connexion between emblems and conceits is made by T. O. Beachcroft in *Quarles—and the Emblem Habit,* in "The Dublin Review" Jan. 1931. But the author knows too little of the history of the emblem, to the point of mistaking Alciati for a Dutchman.

18. *Idem,* p. 489.

19. *Tableaux sacrés des figures mystiques du très auguste sacrifice et sacrement de l' Eucharistie dédiés à la très chrétienne reine de France et de Navarre,* Paris, 1601.

20. *Agudeza, cit.,* pp. 3-4.

21. *Il Cannocchiale Aristotelico . . . Accresciuto dall'Autore di due nuovi trattati, cioè de' Concetti predicabili, e degli Emblemi,* Venice, 1678. *Inscriptiones,* editio secunda, Taurini, 1666.

22. For the history of the word 'emblem' see further details in W. S. Heckscher's excellent essay on Emblem, Emblembuch (in collaboration with K.-A. Wirth) in *Reallexikon zur deutschen Kulturgeschichte,* Alfred Druckenmüller Verlag in Stuttgart. This long essay (covering about 70 closely printed pages in double column) contains much valuable information on the technical features of emblem literature and its application to the fine arts, on sources and antecedents and on the related field of heraldry; finally a classification of emblem-books according to various types or categories (thus providing a full list of short titles).

23. *Bilderschriften der Renaissance, Hieroglyphik and Emblematik in ihren Beziehungen und Fortwirkungen,* Leipzig, 1923. Volkmann followed the lead of Karl Gielhow, *Die Hieroglyphenkunde des Humanismus in der Allegorie der Renaissance,* "Jahrbuch der kunsthistorischen Sammlungen des allerh. Kaiserhauses", XXXII, 1 (1915).

24. See M. T. Casella and G. Pozzi, *Francesco Colonna, Biografia e opere,* Padova, Editrice Antenore, 1959, vol. II, p. 218.

25. G. F. Hartlaub, *Die Spiegel-Bilder des Giovanni Bellini,* in "Pantheon", 1942, 11 Heft, November, pp. 235-41.

26. See p. 52.

27. See P. Villey, *Les Sources et l'évolution des Essais de Montaigne,* Paris 1908, Vol. II, ch. 1, pp. 9 ff. Montaigne "inscrivait des sentences sur les travées de sa bibliothèque tant elles avaient de vie et d'efficace à ses yeux" (p. 57).

28. Dilthey, *Epigrammatum Pompeis repertorum trias* (Programm), Zurich, 1876.

29. See the Paduan text edited by Thuilius in 1621 which collects preceding commentaries and adds new ones: the numbering of emblems in this edition differs from Plantin's edition of 1573 and 1574 because of the addition of the emblem *Adversus naturam peccantes,* which formerly had been expurgated, so that the eightieth emblem of Plantin's edition becomes the eighty-first in the Paduan one, and so on.

30. Prof. J. Hutton, *The Greek Anthology in Italy to the year 1800,* Cornell Univ. Press, 1935 (Cornell Studies in English, XXIII), p. 204, has a slightly longer list, including some less evident imitations. However, he repeats twice the emblem on sign. E 8vo of the 1531 edition, giving to it in one case as a source IX. 122, in the other IX. 346. Also, VII. 225 has not inspired leaf 1, but leaf 11 of the 1549 ed.

31. See E. Panofsky, "Blind Cupid", in *Studies in Iconology,* New York, 1939, and the studies of J. G. Fucilla on similar Love themes in "Philological Quarterly", XIV, 2, April 1935 (*De Morte et Amore*), and in "Classical Philology", XXVI, 2, April 1931 (*Materials for the History of a popular classical Theme—Fleeing Love*).

32. Alciati's emblem *In statuam Amoris:*

> Quis sit amor, plures cecinere Poetæ,
>   Eius qui vario nomine gesta ferunt.
> Convenit hoc, quod veste caret, quod corpore parvus,
>   Tela alasque ferens, lumina nulla tenet.
> Hæc ora, hic habitusque Dei est, sed dicere tantos
>   Si licet in vates, falsa subesse reor.
> Eccur nudus agat? divo quasi pallia desint,
>   Qui cunctas domiti possidet orbis opes.
> Aut qui quæso nives boreamque evadere nudus,
>   Alpinum potuit, strictaque prata gelu?
> Si puer est, puerumne vocas qui Nestora vincit,
>   An nostri Ascræi carmina docta senis?
> Inconstans puer, hic pervicax [1531; obdurans 1551], pectora quæ iam
>   Trans adijt, nunquam linquere sponte potest.
> At pharetras et tela gerit, quid inutile pondus?

> An curvare infans cornua dura valet?
> Alas curve tenet quas nescit in æthera ferre?
>   Inscius in volucrum flectere tela iecur.
> Serpit humi, semperque virum mortalia corda
>   Lædit, et haud alas saxeus inde movet.
> Si cæcus vittamque gerit, quid tænia cæco
>   Utilis est? ideo num minus ille videt?
> Quis ne sagittiferum credat, qui lumine captus?
>   Hic certa, ast cæci spicula vana movent.
> Igneus est aiunt versatque in pectore flammas.
>   Cur age vivit adhuc? omnia flamma vorat.
> Quinetiam tumidis cur non extinguitur undis,
>   Naiadum quoties mollia corda subit?
> At tu ne tantis capiare erroribus audi,
>   Verus quid sit amor carmina nostra ferent.
> Iucundus labor est, lasciva per ocia, signum
>   Illius est nigro punica glans clypeo.

Compare the following sonnet of the fourteenth century, ascribed to Andrea Orcagna, publ. by Trucchi in *Poesie italiane inedite di dugento autori,* Prato, 1847:

> Molti poeti han già descritto Amore,
>   Fanciul nudo, coll'arco faretrato
>   . . . . .
> Ma come tutti quanti abbiano errato,
>   Mostrar lo intende l'Orcagna pittore.
>
> Sed egli è cieco, come fa gli inganni?
>   Sed egli è nudo, chi lo manda a spasso?
>   Se porta l'arco tiralo un fanciullo?
>
> S'egli è sì tener, dove son tanti anni?
>   E s'egli ha l'ale, come va sì basso?
>   Così le lor ragioni tutte annullo.
>
>   L'amore è un trastullo:
>   Non è composto di legno né d'osso,
>   E a molte gente fa rompere il dosso.

(Similar also is Nicolò da Correggio's sonnet, wrongly ascribed to Serafino Aquilano: "Pensato ho già tra me che cosa è Amore". Compare also the epigram of Hieronymus Angerianus (in *Erotopaignion,* 1512): "In tabula primus terrenum qui pinxit amorem . . .").

33. *Op. cit.,* p. 142.

34. *Op. cit.,* p. 7.

35. *Op. cit.,* p. 252.

36. Cf. in the *Anthology,* the epigrams: Σήν, Παφίη Κυθέρεια, παρ' ἠϊόν' εἶδε Κλέανδρος (*Palatina,* V. 208); 'Ανέρα θήρ, χερσαῖον ὁ πόντιος, ἄπνοον ἔμπνους (IX. 222); 'Αγγελίην πὰρ Ζηνὸς ἐπεὶ φέρεν ἠεροδίνης (IX. 223); 'Ακταίην παρὰ θῖνα διαυγέος ἔνδοθεν ἄλμας (IX. 227); Κρῆσσα κύων ἐλάφοιο κατ' ἴχνιον ἔδραμε Γοργώ (IX. 268); Λάρνακα πατρῴων ἔτι λείψανα κοιμίζουσαν (IX. 278); Παίδων ὃν μὲν ἔκαιεν 'Αρίστιον, ὃν δ'ἐσάκουσε (IX,

290); Γριπεύς τις μογέεσκεν ἐπ' ἰχθύσι· τὸν δ'ἐσιδοῦσα (IX. 442); Martial, IV. 18: "Qua vicina pluit Vipsanis porta columnis".

37. *Op. cit.,* p. 81.

38. This was facilitated by the affinity between sonnet and epigram: "Le Sonnet suit l'epigramme de bien près, et de matière et de mesure; et quand tout est dit, le sonnet n'est autre chose que le parfait epigramme de l'Italien, comme le dizain du François", wrote Sebillet (*Art poétique françois,* 1548, II, 2, ed. Gaiffe, p. 115). Already the popular form of epigram, which is the *strambotto,* born in Greek Sicily, had had a transitory but overwhelming influence on the lyrics of the end of the Quattrocento, chiefly on Cariteo and Serafino.

39. *Op. cit.,* p. 31.

40. *Op. cit.,* pp. 318-19.

Peter M. Daly (essay date 1988)

SOURCE: Daly, Peter M. "England and the Emblem: The Cultural Context of English Emblem Books." In *The English Emblem and the Continental Tradition,* edited by Peter M. Daly, pp. 1-60. New York: AMS Press, 1988.

[*In the following essay, Daly offers a survey of the history and theory of the emblem in England. His study of cultural context emphasizes concurrent movements in visual and tactile arts, as well as in printing.*]

During the reigns of Elizabeth and James, Englishmen were far more aware of emblems than some earlier historians of English literature would have us believe, especially those historians whose knowledge of the emblem was confined to the printed book, and often to those in English. The fact that the number of surviving English emblem books is small in no way reflects the pervasiveness of the phenomenon. It is a curious circumstance that it should have taken over half a century after the appearance of Alciato's *Emblematum liber* (Augsburg, 1531) for an Englishman[1] to publish a book of emblems. It is equally odd that only six[2] emblematic works were printed in English during the sixteenth century. However, we should neither overlook, nor underestimate the influence of Continental emblem books in England. There is still much work to be done on this subject.

Emblem Books

English literary historians tend to see the emblem largely through the eyes of Mario Praz and Rosemary Freeman.[3] To these writers we owe what has become a traditional conception of the emblem, as well as certain aesthetic and value judgements about the phenomenon and a general sense of the pervasiveness of emblematic modes in the various art forms of the sixteenth and seventeenth centuries. It is unnecessary to rehearse the achievements of Praz and Freeman here, nor do I wish to elaborate on those areas where modern theories of the emblem differ, a subject on which I have written elsewhere.[4] Suffice it to say that scholarship never stands still, and earlier theories and accounts will always stand in need of revision and correction as knowledge increases and as perspectives change. For my purposes here it is enough to note that Freeman's conception of the emblem is narrower than that of Praz and therefore her bibliography of English emblem books is smaller, thereby creating the impression that especially in England the emblem is a "secondary cultural phenomenon," Joseph Mazzeo's term,[5] or even a "fad" in the view of Lisolette Dieckmann.[6] Freeman's narrow, literary theory of the emblem restricts the term to the three-part combination of text and picture introduced by Alciato, and that is an oversimplification that can falsify our view of the workings of the emblematic mode. In order to gain an overview of these related forms and to avoid pedantic distinctions, I also include imprese and iconographic allegorizations under the general heading of emblem.

The emblem, both as an art form and as a mode of thought, played a greater role in book making and printing in England than Freeman's study suggests. Her bibliography, based on a restrictive conception of the emblem, lists only twenty-four books in a total of forty-six printings. According to my bibliography, which covers the same time period but is based on a broader conception of the emblem, some fifty books were published in English in at least 130 editions and printings up to the year 1700. Of these titles, eight also appeared in at least 111 editions and printings after 1700, and this does not include modern reprints and microforms. The eight titles include one love, two moral, and five religious emblem books. These emblematic publications may be divided into four groups:

1. emblem books in the strict sense, i.e. the tight three-part form introduced by Alciato;

2. expanded forms: e.g. van der Noot, who adds a book-length prose commentary to his collection of emblems, or Hawkins who employs a complex nine-part structure;

3. emblematically illustrated works such as meditations where the plate becomes an integral part, e.g. Drexel;

4. theoretical discussions of emblem and impresa which provide many examples of actual imprese, e.g. Giovio and Estienne.

Although this larger number of English emblem books is still small in comparison with the approximately one thousand emblem books published on the Continent during the same period, the English contribution is more significant than hitherto realized. Furthermore, I have omitted manuscript collections and those many illustrated, book-length descriptions of coronations, royal entries, progresses and pageants, which were so often emblematic in character.[7]

English emblem books were, then, more numerous and more important than has been thought. However, we still have lamentably little information on the details of book production and distribution. How large were the editions produced at the time? Who bought them, and who read them, and how influential were they for writers and artists? The only statistics that I have come across derive from the archives of the Plantin Press, which have miraculously survived to the present day. In a fascinating study based on the accounts of the Plantin Press in Antwerp, Leon Voet has unearthed details of costing and numbers of copies printed.[8] Plantin printed an Alciato edition in 1565 in 1,250 copies, and a further edition in 1567 of 1,000 copies. There was an edition of Faerno fables in 1566 of 1,600 copies, and a year later another printing of 1,250 copies. Plantin also published Junius' emblems into French in 1565 in 1,250 copies, in 1566 a further 850 copies, and a translation in 1567 in 1,000 copies. It is rare to have such accurate information, but from it we can see that during a three-year period one publisher printed no fewer than 8,200 copies of three emblem books, an eloquent witness to the popularity of this kind of book.

POETICS AND CULTURAL HANDBOOKS

It is evident that educated Englishmen were aware of Continental emblems and imprese long before any emblem book had been published in England, or in English. Thomas Palmer compiled an emblematic manuscript entitled *Two hundred poosees,* which he dedicated to Robert Dudley as Earl of Leicester and Chancellor of the University of Oxford, which allows us to date the manuscript to the year 1565. Palmer's unpublished manuscript may thus lay claim to being the earliest known English emblem book. It also documents the reception of Continental emblem books in England. John Manning[9] has recently shown that Palmer drew upon Aneau's *Picta poesis* (1552) for thirteen emblems, Wechel's bilingual Latin-German edition of Alciato (Paris, 1542) for thirty-two emblems, de Tournes's edition of Alciato (Lyons, 1547, frequently reprinted) for a further five emblems, Coustau's *Pegma* (Lyons, 1555) for nine emblems and Paradin's *Heroica symbola* (Antwerp, 1562) for seven more emblems. Furthermore, Palmer used Valeriano's *Hieroglyphica,* two editions of Aesop and two printers' devices.

George Puttenham wrote on the subject of emblematics in *The Arte of English Poesie,* which, although published in 1589, was apparently written between 1565

and 1585. Scholars disagree as to the dating of Puttenham's section "Of the device or embleme." Puttenham's editors, Willcock and Walker, suggest that the passage was added in 1589, whereas John F. Leisher[10] argues convincingly that it was part of the 1585 manuscript, which was published in 1589. Puttenham's five page discussion of the emblem is a little masterpiece of condensed information and argumentation. He aptly concludes his discussion with the following summary of the "vse and intent" (p. 107) of "liueries, cognizances, emblemes, enseigns and impreses" as follows:

> . . . the vse and intent . . . is to insinuat some secret, wittie, morall and braue purpose presented to the beholder, either to recreate his eye, or please his phantasie, or examine his judgement, or occupie his braine or to manage his will either by hope or by dread, euery of which respectes be of no litle moment to the interest and ornament of the ciuill life: and therefore giue them no litle commendation.
>
> (p. 107)

Leisher dispells the myth that George Puttenham held emblems in contempt, a notion that derives from Friedrich Brie's misunderstanding of Elizabethan English. Leisher concludes that interest in emblem and impresa "has passed beyond the stage of the courtly novelty and had by 1585 become a serious, well-known genre commanding the attention of the sober literary critic." (p. 3)

A year before Puttenham's poetics appeared, Abraham Fraunce published an important work in Latin on things emblematic, entitled *Insignium, Armorum, Emblematum, Hieroglyphicorum, et Symbolorum, quae ab Italis Imprese nominantur* (London, 1588). In the third book Fraunce reviews at some length impresa theory and the five rules for the creation of the perfect impresa, naming amongst others Giovio, Ruscelli, Fara, Contile, Bargagli and Paradin. Reviewing the most important emblem writers, Fraunce enumerates Alciato, Sambucus, de Bèze, Aneau, Reusner, Faerno and Junius. There is no reason to regard this as mere name-dropping. More concerned with practice than theory, Fraunce provides lists of imprese, giving the name of the bearer, describing the *figura* or picture, naming the *vox* or motto, and indicating the source where known. Fraunce himself wrote an emblem book, *Emblemata varia,* which exists in an undated manuscript version in the Bodleian. The forty oval emblems have mottoes, Latin epigrams, and are accompanied by notes on facing pages.

In 1598 Frances Meres published his *Palladis Tamia* where amongst other things he praises the English emblem writers Whitney, Willet and Combe, whom he associates with the Continental writers Alciato, Reusner and Sambucus. Thomas Combe's translation of La Perrière's *Theatre des bons engins* doubtless dates from

1593.[11] Although the unique complete copy belongs to the 1614 edition, the work was entered in the Stationer's Register on May 9, 1593. Meres writes of the English emblematists as though they were household names. The interest in emblems and imprese continued under the Stuarts. The English nobility was much given to the fashion for imprese, as we know from portraits, accounts of tournaments, and personal possessions which have survived. William Camden's book, first published in 1605, *The Remaines concerning Britaine* contains lengthy descriptions of the imprese of the English aristocracy (pp. 158-176). Judging by its ten printings, this must have been a popular work.

In 1612 Henry Peacham incorporated sections of Ripa's *Iconologia* in his popular *Gentleman's Exercise,* as Alan Young has established.[12] Peacham's cultural and educational handbook thus provides further evidence of the general and serious acceptance of the emblem.

THE CULTURAL CONTEXT OF ENGLISH EMBLEM BOOKS

I wish to leave the printed emblem book in order to review the role of the emblem in art as the broader cultural context of emblem books. The importance of the emblem as an expression of the cultural life of the Renaissance and Baroque is no longer in question. The combination of motto, picture and epigram is best regarded both as an art form and as a mode of thought.[13] It finds expression in illustrated books, but perhaps even more importantly it helped to shape all the visual arts. Combinations of mottoes and pictures, as well as emblematic motifs with their implied meanings, are to be found in paintings and portraits, wall and ceiling decorations of all kinds, carving, stained glass and jewelry. Ephemeral and fragile, but equally significant, were the emblematic designs etched on to glass, embroidered on to cushions and bed valances, and woven into table carpets and tapestry wall hangings. The public was further made aware of emblems by the preacher in his sermon.[14] They saw and heard emblems on the stage, in pageants, entries, and street processions. Perhaps it is not an exaggeration to suggest that emblems were as immediately and graphically present in this period as illustrated advertising is today.

In the following I shall review briefly the role of emblem and impresa in art, i.e. portraiture, wall and ceiling decoration, wood carving, tapestry and painted cloths, embroidery and jewelry. Space does not allow for a consideration of the use of emblem and impresa in drama, pageants and tilts, although much work has been done on the subject.[15] The second general area I wish to review might be called the emblem and book production, which will include title-pages, frontispieces, printers' devices and illustrations, and lastly illustrated broadsides.

PAINTING AND PORTRAITURE

Elizabethan painting and portraiture aimed at the stylized, heroic and allegorical representation of its subjects. The flattery inherent in portraits often took the form of hierarchical, political and symbolic allusion. Portraits of Elizabeth I were thus endowed with the qualities associated with icons, and Roy Strong's choice of the terms "icon" and "cult" in the titles of his studies[16] is particularly appropriate. He shows how two decades of destruction of religious art and artifacts led to the impoverishment of all English art, not only by virtue of the destruction of existing art, but because it also discouraged the production of new art. Just as the Byzantine icon emerged after a period of iconoclasm, so too the flowering of Elizabethan art followed the Protestant-inspired destruction of religious art in England.

Elizabethan painting harks back to the symbolic modes of the Middle Ages, but it is enriched with Renaissance hieroglyphs, imprese and emblems to produce a style that is essentially anti-naturalistic, strangely unlike the realism and psychological individualization that characterizes much Dutch art of the same period. The sitter was just as concerned to project his conception of himself and his role in society, as he was with the re-creation of his physical likeness. To fulfil this purpose artists resorted to the use of costume, accoutrements and symbols, even verbal statements, to translate into visual and external terms notions of self and the social and political status of the sitter. The way of thinking that produced imprese and emblems thus shaped the art of portraiture during the period.[17]

Whereas art historians increasingly recognize the emblematic quality of Elizabethan painting, literary scholars appear, perhaps understandably, less aware of the fact, and yet painting forms part of the cultural context of printed emblems. This emblematic quality resides in the use of mottoes, even explanatory poems or statements, inserted emblem or impresa pictures, and isolated emblematic motifs. Perhaps the best known motto on a portrait of Elizabeth is the famous NON SINE SOLE IRIS [No rainbow (Iris) without the sun], which accompanies the celebrated Rainbow Portrait[18] of the queen as the royal Astraea, variously attributed to Marcus Gheeraerts, the Younger and Isaac Oliver. Holding the rainbow in her left hand, Elizabeth is associated with the sun, without which there can be no rainbow. This is as much a political statement, underscoring the divine right of the sovereign, as it is a promise of peace for the realm. There is more than an echo of the Old Testament, where the rainbow is a sign of the covenant between God and his people, thereby reinforcing the notion of the divinely sanctioned monarch. Elizabeth had always insisted that England would enjoy peace and prosperity as long as a united people obediently followed the dictates of its sovereign, who was ultimately responsible to God alone. As a motto NON SINE SOLE IRIS is a many faceted political statement, which captures in words the significance of the portrait.

Elizabeth's servants, suitors, and courtiers frequently chose to incorporate mottoes, indeed impresa-like statements, in their portraits, which were often intended as a compliment, or tribute, or a plea, to their sovereign. Thus Sir Walter Raleigh stresses both his love and his personal excellence in the motto "Amor et virtute" [Love and by virtue] in a portrait, attributed to the monogrammatist H, which abounds with visual, symbolic references to the queen.[19] Similarly, Robert Cecil, 1st Earl of Salisbury, included in his portrait the motto SERO, SED SERIO [Late, but serious] as an impresa-like statement of his own high seriousness. Evidently Cecil, delayed for an important meeting of the Council, excused himself wittily with these words.[20] Sir Henry Lee, long time Queen's champion at the Accession Day Tilts, liked to have his portrait rendered the more significant by the inclusion of his impresa-like motto "Fide et constantia" [By faith and constancy].[21] These few examples are typical of the Elizabethan use of mottoes in portraits, the significance of which is not always obvious at first sight.

In structural terms a portrait becomes most obviously emblematic when the pictured subject, as an icon, is accompanied not only by a motto but also by an explanatory poem, usually placed in a cartouche towards the bottom of a painting. The poem, like the *subscriptio* of an emblem, explicates the picture by both describing and interpreting individual motifs.

A picture by Marcus Gheeraerts, the Younger, which is known as either "The Lady in Fancy Dress" or "The Persian Lady"[22] shows a woman in rich floral dress, standing next to a stag. Above her head a swallow sits on the branch of a tree, which is inscribed with three mottoes. Although it is difficult to decipher them from the black and white photograph provided by Roy Strong in his *Icon,* I suggest the following alternative readings: "Iniusti iusta querela" [The just complaint of the unjust]; "Mea sic mihi" [What is mine is mine], and finally "Dolor est medecina amori[s]" [Grief is the remedy for love].[23] A sonnet explaining the lady's love-lorn situation is inscribed in the cartouche, bottom right. The first quatrain equates the "restless swallow," shown in the picture, with the speaker's "restless minde," reviving "renewing wronges" and expressing her "Just complaintes of cruelly vnkinde." The second quatrain directs attention to the stag: "With pensive thoughtes my weeping Stagg I crowne." In fact, she crowns the stag with a garland of pansies, while a long bracelet of pearls, themselves emblematic of sadness, hangs from her wrist over the stag's head.

The proverbial association of the stag and melancholy finds expression in the second line of the second quatrain: "Whose Melancholy teares my cares Expresse." The stag's famous tears, together with the speaker's sighs, are said to be the only "physicke that my harmes redresse." The concluding sestet speaks of the "goodly tree" that the speaker "did plant in love," but to no avail, for "the shales be mine, the kernels others are." The "love tree" is not identified in the sonnet, as were stag and swallow, but it appears to be a peach tree, a fruit often associated with love in the emblematic tradition.[24] At least since the Egyptian hieroglyphics, the peach fruit had been associated with the heart, and during the Renaissance by extension and perhaps by conflation with the apple also with notions of love. It became enshrined in the hieroglyphics of Valeriano. Both Plutarch and Valeriano note that the heart-shaped fruit of the peach is sacred to Isis, the goddess of fertility associated by the Greeks with Demeter.[25] In this highly emblematic and literary picture the three mottoes and the three motifs of swallow, peach tree and stag serve to explain the pensiveness of the standing woman. Although the sonnet offers a fuller elucidation, somewhat in the manner of an emblematic *subscriptio,* much of the meaning is implied by the visual motifs rather than stated in the verse.

Finally, we might return to Sir Henry Lee, whom Marcus Gheeraerts the Younger once painted (ca. 1590-1600) together with his dog, Bevis, with the motto "More faithfull then favoured."[26] The dog was, of course, proverbial for trust and faithfulness, and this aspect is emphasized by Lee's gesture of placing his left hand on the dog's head. The poem, comprising ten iambic pentameters, expounds on the nature of "love and faith," contrasting Lee's own undivided loyalty and the "very scante" faithful friends; Lee's dog is compared with Ulysses' dog, which proved "true and kinde." It is interesting to note that this poem is said to commemorate an incident in which Lee was rescued by his dog. However, as in the emblem proper, which generalizes the particular in order to make valid statements, there is no reference in the picture or poem to the biographical incident.

Some portraits contain complete emblem pictures set into the top corner. In his study *The English Icon* Roy Strong reproduces four examples: ". . . a queen issues from a castle to view weapons enmeshed . . . , a Cupid aims his dart at a chaste unicorn . . . , a man stands in the midst of a circular maze . . . , [and] a lady sits unharmed amidst reptiles. . . ."[27] In many instances a Latin motto appears in or beneath this inset emblem picture. Although the references are now frequently lost to us, it is evident that these emblematic pictures were meant to convey something of importance about the sitter.

The relationship of inset picture to sitter is usually clear in the case of an impresa. A miniature portrait by Nicholas Hilliard shows the Duke of Cumberland wearing his armour; in the background we see his impresa of a fork of lightning and the motto "Fulmen acquasque fero" [I bear lightning and the waters].[28] Another full length portrait of Cumberland as the queen's Champion and Knight of Pendragon Castle, also by Hilliard, shows his impresa shield on a tree behind him. The device features a centred earth, above it the sun and beneath it the moon; it is accompanied by the motto "Hasta quan[do]" [When the spear], indicating as Roy Strong suggests that "Cumberland would wield the lance (hasta) as Champion until the sun, moon and earth went into eclipse."[29]

Equally emblematic is the use in portraits of isolated motifs, which are intended to make allegorical statements about the sitter. The Ermine Portrait of the Queen (1585), variously attributed to Sir William Segar and Nicholas Hilliard, shows Elizabeth with a small ermine, a gold coronet around its neck, looking up at the queen and placed above her left wrist. The ermine was a common emblem of purity, but in this case the golden coronet directly associates the purity of the ermine with the queen. Elizabeth holds in her right hand an olive branch, while the handle of the massive sword of state can be seen close to her left hand. The sword and olive branch are emblems of justice and peace, which she embodies just as the ermine alludes to her personal moral virtue.[30] Examples could be multiplied. There is the famous Sieve portrait (ca. 1580), attributed to Cornelius Ketel, which celebrates the queen as the Roman vestal virgin Tuccia, by virtue of the sieve she carries in her hand. There are layers of significance here. Educated Elizabethans might well have recognized in the sieve an emblem or impresa of discerning knowledge and virtue, for such was its meaning in Paradin's collection of *Heroicall Devices* (p. 184), published in English translation by P. S. in 1591.

Pearls, emblematic of purity, were so much the favoured jewel of the queen that many of her courtiers had themselves portrayed wearing not only the queen's colours of black and white but also pearls as a compliment to the monarch. In Nicholas Hilliard's portraits of a "Young Man amongst Roses"[31] and of Sir Walter Raleigh (1588)[32] both men wear pearl-embroidered garments. Raleigh also wears a pair of pearl earrings in one ear. To make the reference even clearer, there is in the top left corner of the portrait the crescent moon of Cynthia, an allusion to Elizabeth as the moon-goddess. This crescent moon stands directly above the motto "Amor et virtute" [Love and by virtue], indicating emblematically the object of his love. In the portrait of the "Young Man amongst Roses" it is the eglantine, Elizabeth's favourite flower symbol, which emblematically identifies the royal object of love.

Colours could also be emblematic, conveying precise meanings. Elizabeth's preferred colours were white for purity and black for constancy, and this was well known to courtiers and commoners alike. Reference has been made to the portraits of rival courtiers in which the subjects wear black and white, but the colours were also worn by Elizabeth's champions at the tilt, and by her dancers at court. Leaving the court for the cities, the town of Sandwich was decked out in black and white to greet Her Majesty in 1573 and 200 men, dressed in white doublets, black hose and white garters came out to greet her.[33] Generally speaking, emblematic language, i.e. specific motifs and colours and their meanings, was well understood in the sixteenth and seventeenth centuries. It is only the more riddling use of certain impresa that was exclusive and recondite. Copies of emblematic portraits of Elizabeth I, or icons as Roy Strong prefers to call them, circulated widely. Both the queen and Council tried on several occasions to control the production of portraits for propaganda purposes to ensure a certain kind of uniformity.

WALL AND CEILING PAINTING

As emblematic structures and motifs played such an important part in Tudor and Jacobean painting, it comes as no surprise to find something similar in the decoration of secular and ecclesiastical buildings. Just how important emblems and imprese were is difficult to ascertain, since so many buildings have disappeared, and in the cases of those that remain changes in taste led to the replacement of one set of decorations by another. I am not aware of any inventory that draws together the information that is available in a scattered form. Our knowledge tends to be rather accidental.

Even in its day, Blickling Hall in Norfolk, was an exceptionally fine, although still characteristic example of contemporary decoration. The ceiling of the Long Gallery, some 123 feet long, is an elaborate example of Jacobean plaster work. The eleven central panels are dedicated to five heraldic patterns and allegories of the Five Senses and of Learning. The sense of hearing carries the motto "Auditus" and shows a man playing a lute sitting next to an amply bodied female singer holding a large book.[34] The side rows on the ceiling contain virtues and assorted emblems, largely deriving from Peacham's *Minerva Britanna* (London, 1612). Two examples must suffice: "Pulchritudo foeminea" [Feminine beauty] shows a naked virgin sitting on dragon, taken from Peacham, p. 58; the motto "Non invicta recedo" [Not unconquered—I retire] accompanies a rhinoceros that derives from Peacham, p. 106.

The great Gallery at Lanhydroc House near Bodmin, Cornwall, 116 feet long, is all that remains of the original house built 1630-40. The impressive plasterwork on the barrel-vaulted ceiling is presumed to have been finished before the outbreak of Civil War in 1642. It is made up of some twenty-four panels illustrating Old Testament scenes from the Creation to the Burial of Isaac.[35] These panels are arranged twelve on each side and are interspersed with other smaller circular panels depicting various birds and beasts, many of them as in nature but others of heraldic, mythological and emblematic provenance. In the centre of each half ceiling and making up a sequence of large circles are panels depicting birds which appear to have thematic significance. For instance, a crane clutching a stone separates the scene showing the sacrifice of Cain and Abel from the next panel which illustrates Cain killing Abel. The crane was, of course, a common emblem of prudence and watchfulness, virtues that Abel apparently lacked. Among the other birds one can recognize a dragon-tailed bird holding a mirror, which may represent prudence. There is also an ostrich with a horseshoe in its mouth, emblematic of fortitude[36] and fortitude in adversity,[37] an eagle with crown and sceptre, and the pelican in her piety. The left-hand side of the half barrel ceiling repeats what is to be found on the right-hand side, thus all the beasts and birds of the one side are reflected in the patterns of the other. Although there are no mottoes or inscriptions on the ceiling, the birds clearly embody an abstract meaning that makes them emblematic rather than merely decorative.

The Palace of Whitehall, which had played such a central role in the cultural and political life of Elizabethan England, was ravaged by fire in the year 1619. The impresa shields used in the Accession Day Tilts were on permanent display in the Waterside Gallery for all to see. Writing in 1598, the German visitor Paul Hentzner alludes briefly to them.[38] However, the published information available is scanty, although uniquely interesting manuscripts exist. Reference is occasionally made to the lengthy descriptions recorded by another German traveller, probably Johannes Georg Dehn Rotfelser, a member in the entourage of Otto of Hesse who visited London in 1611. His account has never been translated into English, and only briefly excerpted in German.[39]

After the great fire, the Banqueting House at Whitehall was rebuilt by Inigo Jones and finished in 1622. Peter Paul Rubens was commissioned to decorate the ceiling, and as this room was the principal room of state, decorations were a matter of political importance. The paintings celebrate the absolute monarch from whom peace and plenty flow. This is the burden of Rubens's iconographic decorations, which are mythological in the main, but frequently employ emblematic pictorial language. Art historians have pointed to the influence of Ripa (Liberty), Alciato (Cupid driving a lion-drawn chariot), and van Veen (Hermathena), reflecting the emblematic and iconographical tradition.[40]

Windsor Castle must also have had its share of emblematic embellishment. Paul Hentzner mentions a "gallery everywhere ornamented with emblems and figures" (p. 134) that caught his eye when visiting the third court at Windsor.

The taste for emblem and impresa was not confined to the monarchy and aristocracy. Landed gentry and the rising middle class liked to decorate their homes with emblems. Hawstead Hall in Suffolk, the home of Sir Robert Drury, had a painted wainscoted closet, often referred to as the oratory of Lady Drury.[41] The emblematic panels are now preserved in the Branch Museum, Christchurch Mansion, Ipswich. The four walls are decorated with a total of sixty-one painted panels and seven thematic statements set in cartouches. No fewer than forty-three are emblematic combinations of motto and symbolic picture, for which Norman K. Farmer, Jr. has established sources or analogues in the works of Continental writers such as Camerarius, Paradin, Reusner, Valeriano and Ripa, as well as the Englishman Whitney. The oratory is a kind of emblem theatre—the phrase was often used in the titles of emblem books—a theatre for spiritual contemplation. The subjects of meditation are introduced by general statements, e.g. "Frustra nisi Dominus" [In vain without the Lord], which appear just below the ceiling. These thoughts are then focussed by the single emblems beneath. As Farmer observes, the emblems "take the thinker directly into the heart of the meditation on such subjects as the relation of the individual to the world, the desirability of living within one's own center, the psychology of assertiveness, fear, anxiety, and the mysteries of the world itself" (pp. 104f.).

CARVING

From Gabriel Harvey's *Marginalia* we know that his father's house in Saffron Walden boasted a fine chimney mantle, carved in clunch, which may be seen in the Museum at Saffron Walden.[42] The three panels and certain individual motifs derive from Alciato emblems: the bee hive and the laden ass flank the much larger central panel depicting Ocnus in contemporary dress making rope. Since John Harvey was a farmer who apparently made much of his wealth from rope-making, it was natural that he should choose the motif of Ocnus. But it is even more understandable that he should replace Alciato's original motto warning against wasting money on harlots[43] with a new riddling motto NEC ALIIS NEC NOBIS [Neither for others nor ourselves], which only makes sense when one recognises that the ass is eating the rope laboriously produced by Ocnus. The rope is destined neither for Ocnus nor his clients. Each of the Alciato emblem pictures is given a new moralising motto, so that together they form a series of related statements on the value of labour. ALIIS ET NOBIS [For others and ourselves] is illustrated by bees returning to their beehive; NEC ALIIS NEC NOBIS [Neither for others nor ourselves] shows the work of the rope maker Ocnus destroyed by the ass; and ALIIS NON NOBIS [For others not ourselves], is exemplified by the ass, which though laden with food stuffs, eats thistles. While there is no doubt that Alciato is the source for the emblematic motifs on the Harvey chimney mantle, they convey quite different meanings in the Italian's emblem book. Alciato's beehive stands for the clemency of the prince, and the laden ass eating thistles connotes greed. There is nothing capricious about this re-interpretation. Whoever designed the mantle piece re-interpreted the Alciato emblems within the spectrum of possible meanings established by tradition for each of the dominant motifs. The educated Elizabethan visitor to Harvey's house would have had little difficulty in "reading" the meaning of the emblematic panels as he warmed himself before the fire.

During the second half of the sixteenth century wood panelling, often embellished with carving, was increasingly used for interior decoration. Such panelling frequently replaced or covered up earlier wall painting. Emblems, indeed, programmes involving emblematic designs were probably not uncommon, if the examples preserved in University College, Oxford are any indication. The Summer Room is decorated with twenty-eight carved oak panels that were moved to the College from a house built in 1572. Peter C. Bayley[44] has shown that twenty of these carved pictures derive from the emblems of Alciato. They include Ganymede and the eagle, Tantalus, Prometheus and the eagle, the ass bearing Isis on its back, the three girls playing at dice, the lame man carrying the blind man, and the figure of constrained genius whose hand is weighted down by a stone.

Wood, no less than silver and gold, was used to embody emblematic compliments to the queen and impresa-like statements of a subject's loyalty. On occasions the carver was instructed to cut a verbal motto into the wood, the words of which replace actual emblem pictures. Without knowing the heraldic and emblematic meanings of certain flowers and animals, the visitor to Hardwick Hall would be hard pressed to understand the following inscription carved deep into a table:

> The redolent smell of Eglantine
> We stags exalt to the Divine.[45]

The stag was, however, the heraldic animal of the Cavendish family and the eglantine was one of the most important floral emblems of Elizabeth. Bess of Hardwick was giving expression to the loyalty of the Cavendish family to the crown.

TAPESTRIES

From the early sixteenth century onwards wealthy Englishmen began adorning their manors and mansions with tapestries from the Continent. By the time of his death, Henry VIII had collected over 2,000 pieces of tapestry, which are listed in the inventory made at the time. By the end of the century, however, tapestry had ceased to be a collector's item for the very wealthy. Visiting London in 1598 Hentzner noted that Englishmen's "beds are covered with tapestry, even those of farmers."[46] In 1611 Johannes Georg Dehn Rotfelser filled two sides of his diary with a description of the "emblems worked into the old tapestry," which he observed in the great hall at Richmond.[47] In 1638 the historiographer of France, Sieur de la Serre, recorded the visit of Mary de Medicis, the Queen Mother of France to England. Like earlier Continental visitors he, too, was struck by the richness of the tapestries hanging at the Palace of Whitehall. Of the tapestries in the bed chamber he writes that it was a "new tapestry, all of silk, just new from the hands of the workman, representing the Twelve Worthies; and certainly this work was so rare and precious, that Europe cannot boast anything similar. . . ."[48] The Frenchman admits that "to express to you the great number of chambers, all covered with tapestry . . . would be impossible."[49]

While the major themes of these tapestries derive largely from Biblical, classical and mythological sources, as well as from contemporary Elizabethan life, the borders are frequently embellished with heraldic, allegorical and emblematic devices. There are also armorial tapestries,[50] and yet others in which emblematic and allegorical representations play a significant role. This fact was not always recognized by scholars and antiquarians who described these tapestries in the early decades of this century. Art historians and literary scholars today still have insufficient information to allow them to know just how pervasive the emblem tradition was in this particular art form. Such tapestries are rare and frequently belong to private collections, inaccessible to most of us.

One of the greatest examples of Jacobean tapestry to have survived is the set of "Four Seasons" tapestries, originally made in 1611 for Sir John Tracy of Toddington, and now hanging in Hatfield House.[51] The designer, Francis Hyckes, had enjoyed a classical education at Oxford and retained a life-long interest in Latin and especially Greek. He was also very knowledgeable about Continental emblems and imprese.

Francis Hyckes based his designs for the "Four Seasons" upon engravings by Martin de Vos, but he added wide borders containing no fewer than 170 emblems, each comprising a Latin motto and a circular picture, nine inches in diameter.

The first attempts undertaken in this century to identify and interpret the emblem borders of the "Four Seasons" tapestries were made by writers who pursued the subject with much devotion but little knowledge of em-

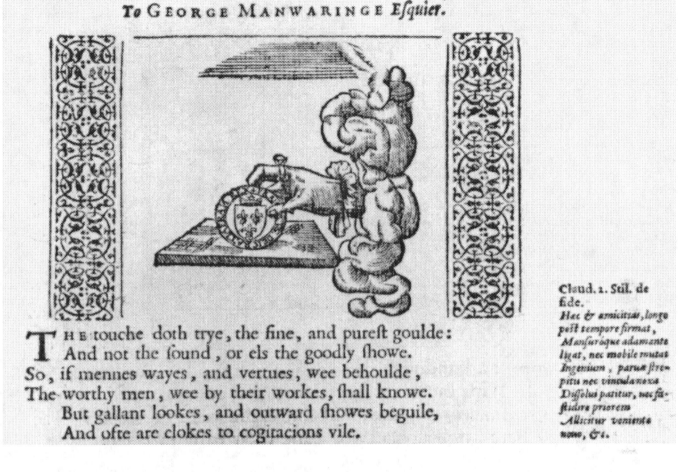

"Sic spectanda fides" ("Thus is faithfulness to be tested"), from Geoffrey Whitney's A Choice of Emblemes *(1586).*

blematic traditions or iconographical conventions. Consequently, these writers frequently failed to identify correctly the iconographical motifs, and this in turn must lead to a misinterpretation of the tapestry. Thus W. G. Thomson in his study *Tapestry Weaving in England. From the Earliest Times to the End of the XVIIIth Century* (London [1915]) describes Spring emblem 37 "Consilium" [Counsel] as a "figure holding a horn-book" (p. 61). One may well wonder what a "horn-book" is, and what kind of "counsel" might derive from it. On close examination the "horn-book" turns out to be the tables of the law, surmounted by a cornucopia. The picture and text together suggest that the "counsel" is the law of God, which, if observed, will result in the abundance and prosperity denotated by the cornucopia.

A comparison of the tapestry emblems with the emblem books reveals that there are three apparent sources for the forty-two emblems that frame the "Spring" panel. These are: Geffrey Whitney's *A Choice of Emblemes* (Leyden, 1586), as A. F. Kendrick[52] had suggested earlier, but even more importantly, Joannes Sambucus'

Emblemata, in the Antwerp edition of 1566,[53] and Andrea Alciato's *Emblemata,* in all likelihood a Plantin edition.[54] There is some doubt whether Whitney was a source at all since all of the fifteen Whitney emblems that Kendrick regarded as sources derive either from Alciato or Sambucus. Furthermore, I have discovered that twenty of the emblems derive from Alciato and twenty-one from Sambucus, the remaining emblem being a traditional representation of justice. Since all the "Spring" emblems derive directly or indirectly from Alciato and Sambucus, and none is an original creation of Whitney, it seems reasonable to conclude that Hyckes drew on these two Continental sources. Interestingly enough, Plantin was the publisher of Sambucus and the some of the most influential Alciato editions, probably the one used by Hyckes. Plantin also issued the Whitney compilation, which drew heavily on plates already used for Alciato, Sambucus and others.

Although my research into the sources of the emblems in the borders of the other three tapestries is not yet concluded, it is evident that Francis Hyckes utilised at the very least the following Continental emblem writers: Andrea Alciato, Joannes Sambucus, Guillaume de la Perrière, Georgette de Montenay, Gabriello Faerno and others in addition to the collection made by Geffrey Whitney. All this indicates how influential the Continental tradition was in Jacobean England.

The "Four Seasons" tapestries are not unusual in including emblematic and iconographic materials in larger designs. Another Sheldon tapestry, measuring 16' 3" by 6' 2" and depicting the Expulsion from Paradise, hangs in the library at Sudeley Castle in Gloucestershire. Mr Dudley B. Sidgwick, the Curator at Sudeley Castle, informs me[55] that John Humphreys visited the castle in 1923 to make the description of the tapestry that appeared in his book on *Elizabethan Sheldon Tapestries*.[56] Humphreys provides a full account of the rich background of Elizabethan flowers and assorted animals together with the border depicting the hunt. But the description of the eight medallions is iconographically inaccurate and incomplete. By virtue of their mottoes, one Latin and six English, and iconographically significant details, these medallions must be considered emblematic. I offer here my description of the medallions, the panels and two other allegorical figures.

Starting from the left, we observe a trinity of Christian virtues. There is first the figure of Hope, a woman standing before an anchor and wearing a blue dress inscribed with the word "Hope." Beneath stands the figure of Faith holding a cross, whose dress bears the inscription "Faithe." To the right and centred between Hope and Faith is Charity holding a baby in her arms and surrounded by three other children. This medallion is inscribed "Charatie" at the top. To the right of Charity stands Judith, holding a sword in her right hand and the head of Holofernes in her left hand. This figure is not placed within a medallion, but rather stands in the background of English flowers and animals. To the right of Judith are the two central panels dedicated to the Expulsion and Justice.[57] The top panel depicts Adam and Eve being expelled from Paradise by the angel brandishing a flaming sword; the apple tree is featured in the background. Directly beneath this is a medallion inscribed IVDICES [Judges]. To the left under the inscription is a pair of scales beneath which there is an open book bearing the words SECVND LEGEM, which means either "according to the law," i.e. "Secund[um] legem" or "second law," i.e. "Secund[am] legem." Under the inscription we see a robed judge standing on a pedestal or cube, denoting constancy. At the top right is situated a two-headed bust, a Janus figure, representing prudence,[58] and below to the right of the judge there is a seated lion which is frequently associated with power,[59] vengeance[60] and revenge.[61] I shall return to this panel and its Latin motto later.

To the right and centred stands another female figure holding a bag. She may be the maid who frequently accompanies Judith in paintings and tapestries, including a piece by Sheldon now in the Metropolitan Museum of Art in New York (No. 42.27). There follows a trinity of moral virtues, Temperance, Justice and Prudence,[62] that balance the Christian virtues on the left of the panel. In the centre is a medallion inscribed "Temperance," depicting a woman who pours water from a jug into a wine goblet. She also wears a blue dress. To the right again, and placed on a level with the Expulsion from Paradise is a medallion inscribed IVSTICE. This features a woman holding an upright sword in her right hand, from which a pair of scales hangs down. Her left hand holds the tables of the law, lightly balanced against her left knee. Her right foot is placed squarely on a cube. This figure of Justice is similar to that in the "Spring" panel (emblem 27) of the "Four Seasons" tapestries. Beneath Justice is a medallion inscribed PROVIDENC, which depicts a woman holding a mirror in her right hand and a snake encircling her left arm.

The central panels deserve closer attention. The Expulsion from Paradise, IVDICES, and Judith embody the themes of justice and retribution. Whereas God punishes the disobedient Adam and Eve, and Judith is Jehovah's agent of retribution, the IVDICES panel is a hieroglyphic combination of motifs illustrating justice. The motto IVDICES suggests not only judges, but also the Old Testament book of Judges. The motif of the open book with its inscription SECVND LEGEM may hold a clue to the central meaning of the whole tapestry, a meaning that seems to have eluded earlier commentators. One must first decide whether SECVND is an abbreviation of "secundum" [according to] or "secundam" [second]. If "secundum," then the open book is the book of the law. But the phrase may also be construed as referring to the second law or commandment: "Thou shalt not make unto thee any graven image" (Exodus 20,4). The two panels can be regarded as embodying in pictorial form the first two commandments brought down by Moses. The transgression of Adam and Eve was in two ways a sin against what would later be established as the first commandment: "Thou shalt have no other gods before me" (Exodus 20,3). Firstly, they had followed the advice of the serpent thereby rejecting the will of God, an act that set the serpent "before" the Lord. Secondly, in disobeying Jehovah's ordinance not to eat of the tree of the knowledge of good and evil, they were assuming a God-like prerogative, for the Lord had reserved the knowledge of good and evil to himself. Although not depicted in the Expulsion from Paradise, the serpent is none the less an implied link to the IVDICES picture beneath. The association becomes the more significant when we recall that the children of Israel worshipped a graven image in the form of the brasen serpent, which the Lord charged Moses to create in order to cure the repentant people from the plague of fiery serpents. We read in II Kings that during the reign of Hezekiah the king "did that which was right in the sight of the Lord" by breaking into pieces the "brasen serpent that Moses had made: for unto those days the children of Israel did burn incense to it. . . ." (II Kings 18,4). Furthermore, the book of Judges (IVDICES) is a history of the Israelites' "whoring after other gods" (Judges 2,11f.), and of God's punishment and subsequent deliverance of his people. If, then, the reference to SECVND LEGEM, is an allusion to the second commandment, then the whole tapestry is, quite literally, centered on the first two of the ten commandments, which enshrine the worship of God as laid out in the Old Testament.

PAINTED CLOTHS

Whereas the wealthy purchased, or commissioned, expensive tapestries, the less well-to-do bought the ubiquitous substitute of painted cloths. Done in oil on canvas or cloth, they depicted classical, mythological and Biblical themes, as well as scenes from Elizabethan life. The pictorial subjects were often supported by proverbs and mottoes, and presumably emblems. Painted cloths were sufficiently important to be listed in inventories and wills. In 1558 a French visitor wrote: "The English make great use of Tapestries, and of painted linens . . . for you can enter but few houses where you do not find these tapestries."[63] Harrison informs us: "In the days of Elizabeth, the walls of our houses on the inner side are either hanged with tapestry, arras work, painted cloths, wherein either divers histories, or herbs, beasts, knots, and such like are stained."[64] Such painted cloths were used in homes, inns and taverns, and temporary buildings of all kinds; they functioned as a backdrop on stage and for other entertainments. Unfortunately, only a very few examples have withstood the ravages of time, the earliest dating from the end of the seventeenth century. From the brief description available it is impossible to determine to what extent painted cloths were emblematic. But it is inconceivable that the emblem, popular for its decorative beauty as well as its moral seriousness, should not have been influential.[65]

EMBROIDERY

Emblems, impress and allegories also contribute to the designs in embroidery,[66] whether used as cushion covers, table carpets, decorative panels for wall hangings, or simply to embellish garments. One set of Hardwick embroideries depicts Penelope and other worthies of antiquity flanked by the iconographically represented virtues of Sapientia and Prudentia.[67] Roy Strong suggests that Bess of Hardwick was celebrating herself through Penelope as the exemplary wife and widow both in this embroidery and in the painting "Ulysses and Penelope."[68] In such cases the emblem or iconograph takes on the function associated with impresa.

Mary Queen of Scots[69] has gone down in history as, amongst other things, a great needlewoman. Destined to become Queen of France, she was brought up from the age of six in France by her grandmother, the Duchess Antoinette de Guise, and her powerful uncles. In her carefully supervised education, languages played a significant role: French, Italian, Latin, Spanish and some Greek. She also learned the social graces and activities prized at a Renaissance court: horse riding, dancing, singing, playing the lute, sewing and embroidery. The Continental tradition of imprese, augmented by the growing emblem literature—Wechel in Paris took the lead in publishing the first translations of Alciato into French and German—was imprinting its stamp on the cultural life of the French court. Henry II chose as his personal impresa three crescent moons, which symbolize the goddess Diana and her namesake his mistress Diane de Poitiers, with the motto "Donec totum impleat orbem" [Till he fills the whole world]. Mary's mother, Marie de Guise, took the phoenix rising from the flames, with the motto "En ma fin git ma commencement" [In my end lies my beginning], an appropriate impresa for a woman who had suffered widowhood twice. Marguerite, the sister of Francis, had chosen for herself an impresa which can either be construed as spiritually lofty or aristocratically superior: the marigold which always follows the sun, accompanied by the motto "Non inferiora secutus" [Not following lower things]. The flower actually depicted in the picture is not the marigold but the marguerite, a pun on the bearer's name. Mary later was to take this same emblem and attach to it a French motto "Sa virtu m'atire" [Its strength draws me]. If the letters of the motto are transposed it will be noted that they produce the name Marie Stvart. The emblem and impresa would later play a significant role in the embroidery of the Queen of Scots.

Within an eighteen month period death took off Henry II of France, Mary's mother, the Queen of Scotland and finally Mary's husband, Francis, who had succeeded to the French throne. Rather than become a second dowager Queen of France she returned to Scotland in August 1561 to claim the throne. Mary brought with her not only hangings and tapestries, beds and cushions, but two professional embroiderers and three upholsterers to improve her Scottish residences.

It is probably to this period that the embroidered royal bed belonged, which William Drummond saw in Edinburgh in 1619. Its embroideries were attributed to Mary. Since the bed no longer exists, Drummond's description in a letter to Ben Jonson, dated July 1, 1619, is the only surviving evidence. That he should have described and interpreted the imprese in such detail reveals not only his own knowledge and interest, but also the importance of emblems and imprese in the cultural life of the times. The thirty-two imprese include those of the French court mentioned earlier, as well as the imprese of Francis II, her uncle, the Cardinal of Lorrain, Henry VIII, and the Duke of Savoy. Drummond gives

Mary's own impresa pride of place in his description, perhaps because it was indeed the central element in the political and moral programme of emblematic embellishments, but also, one assumes, because the Queen of Scots was no longer the enemy of Elizabeth's England, but in Drummond's words "the late Queen mother to our sacred Soveraign."[70] Mary's impresa was a loadstone turned towards the pole, its motto her name and its anagram: "Maria Stuart, sa vertue m'attire" [Its strength draws me]. Drummond comments on the political implications of two imprese which appear to allude to Elizabeth. "Two Women upon the Wheels of Fortune, the one holding a Lance, the other a Cornucopia; which *Impressa* seemeth to glaunce at Queen *Elizabeth* and her self, the word [i.e. motto] *Fortunae Comites* [Companions of Fortune]." The other impresa features an eclipse of the sun and moon.

Mary's marriage to Lord Darnley, son of the Earl of Lennox, a Catholic claimant to the throne of England, infuriated Queen Elizabeth. The birth of Mary's son, James, who would later unite the kingdoms of Scotland and England, dashed Darnley's ambitions to become the ruler of Scotland. The murders of Mary's Italian secretary, David Rizzio, and later of Darnley himself, and Mary's subsequent marriage to Bothwell, who was widely suspected of having initiated Darnley's murder, all added to the notoriety of the Scottish Queen. Her subjects rose against her. Bothwell fled the field of battle, leaving Mary to be taken back to Edinburgh as a prisoner. She remained a captive in the castle on Lochleven for the next ten and a half months, during which time it is presumed she produced a number of large pieces of embroidery subsequently attributed to her. In her captivity she asked, amongst other things, for an embroiderer who would "drawe forth such worke as she would be occupied about."[71]

Mary escaped, but defeated in her attempt to regain the Scottish throne, she was forced to seek sanctuary in Elizabeth's England. Her uninvited presence in England was both an embarrassment and a source of danger to Elizabeth, who had little choice but to keep the Catholic Queen and heir to England's throne in near regal captivity. Nearly eighteen years later, execution ended her imprisonment.

From the beginning of 1569 Mary was in the custody of George Talbot, sixth Earl of Shrewsbury, and his second wife Elizabeth, Bess of Hardwick. Mary and Bess would spend a great deal of time together devising and executing various embroideries: Bess for her Cavendish home that she was re-building, and Mary to pass the time. The two women signed their creations with ciphers and monograms. Continental imprese and emblems frequently served as models for their work.

Mary was an intelligent and scheming woman: she used her needle as well as her pen to communicate with would-be allies. The Queen of Scots had a distinct purpose in mind when in 1570 she sent to the Duke of Norfolk a cushion embroidered by her own hand, depicting a hand holding a pruning knife, cutting away the unfruitful branch of green vine in the foreground. The emblem bears the motto "Virescit vulnere virtus" [Virtue flourishes by wounding].

Mary signed the design by placing directly beneath the first word of the motto her cipher, made up of the letters MA within the Greek letter Θ for her first husband, Francis. While the motif of the pruning of the vine could be understood as a religious emblem, admonishing patience and pious resignation, or a personal impresa, witnessing the stoic fortitude of the bearer, Mary's intention was different. Norfolk understood the message, which encouraged him to cut down the unfruitful branch, Elizabeth, to make way for the flourishing of the fruitful branch, Mary. The Queen of Scots had already indicated her willingness to share her matrimonial bed and the crown of England with the ambitious earl who in 1572 paid for his treachery with his head.

Even when Mary's use of emblem and impresa was not subversive, it was frequently allusive, conveying a hidden meaning to the alert and sympathetic observer. The story is told that she received an English envoy sitting under her cloth of estate which was decorated with Marie de Guise's impresa of the phoenix (see above). The envoy, Nicholas White, did not understand the "riddle,"[72] but it was presumably intended as a statement of personal commitment, to make a new beginning herself when she had arisen from the ashes of her captivity.

Mary continued to take a genuine interest in the children of the Duke of Norfolk after his death. His eldest son Philip Howard had been married during childhood to Ann Dacre, to whom the condemned Duke entrusted all his young children before his death. When it appeared that the marriage of Ann and Philip was endangered by Philip's ambitions at Elizabeth's court, Mary "devised a cryptic embroidery for Ann Dacre."[73] It showed two turtle doves in a tree, the right side leafy, the left leafless. The motto "Amoris sorte pares" [Equals by the fortune of love] referred as much to Mary's own mourning for the executed Duke as it expressed sympathy with Ann. Later in 1585 Philip, who had become a Catholic, was apprehended attempting to leave the country. He died in the tower six years later.

A piece of emblematic embroidery exists which it is thought was made for the ill-fated Philip Howard. It depicts an armillary sphere above a stormy sea with sea monsters and ships. The Spanish motto reads "Las pennas passan y queda la speranza" [Sorrows pass but hopes arise]. A series of imprese fills the border urging fortitude and apparently expressing the hope for succour or reward. The borders also contain the arms of France, Spain, England and Scotland. Some of the emblems derive from Paradin's collection of imprese, although Marguerite Swain does not note this.[74] One picture shows a hand to which is attached a snake above a fire with the motto "Quis contra nos" [Who is against us (if God be for us)?], which was taken from Paradin, p. 187. Similarly, the sword cutting through the Gordian knots with the motto "Nodos virtute resoluo" [I resolve the knots through virtue] also derives from Paradin (p. 214). The remaining imprese are too faint to identify from photographs, but they may also derive from Continental sources.[75]

A particularly interesting and complicated example of emblematic embroidery is the coverlet depicting "The Shepheard Buss."[76] The love-sick shepherd, whose name is embroidered above his head, strikes a languishing pose in a stylized arbor. A Latin motto surrounds the picture, accompanied by four impresa pictures which make visual statements on the dangers of love. A rectangular outside border explains the meaning of the whole design in a statement made up of words and rebus devices:

> False *Cupid* with misfortunes *wheel* hath wounded *hand* and *heart*.
> Who *siren* like did *lure* me with *lute* and charmed *harp*.
> The *cup* of care and sorrow's *cross* do clips my *star* and *sun*
> My *rose* is blasted and my *bones,* lo, *death* inters in urn.[77]

The four impresa pictures derive from Paradin's *Devises*: a snake in a strawberry plant, the sunflower drawn to the sun, a dog jumping from a sinking ship and a hand holding a fan of peacock's feathers with bees. These imprese lack mottoes, which suggests knowledgeable observers were able to decipher them without the aid of textual elucidation. Whether they derive from the translation of Paradin published in 1591, as Roy Strong asserts, or from the earlier original is not clear.[78]

Ladies used their embroidery needles not only to decorate cushions and covers, but also to embellish articles of clothing. In his essay on the Hatfield tapestries, A. F. Kendrick refers to an embroidered tunic, which is said to have belonged to Queen Elizabeth herself. It is a linen tunic embroidered in black silk and adorned with flowers, birds, animals and mythical beasts, as well as "a few emblematical subjects, and three of these are found in Whitney's book."[79] Unfortunately, neither Kendrick nor Nevinson[80] identifies the emblems and their precise sources.

Although very few garments have survived from the Elizabethan period, contemporary paintings and portraits give us a lively impression of what embroidered garments looked like. In the Rainbow Portrait the left sleeve of Elizabeth's dress is embroidered with a curled snake from the mouth of which hangs what appears to be a jewelled heart, red in colour, indicating that wisdom governs the heart or emotions of the monarch. Elizabeth is also wearing a cloak embroidered with eyes and ears, signifying either the constant watchfulness or the omniscience of the sovereign.

EMBLEMATIC JEWELRY AND SILVERWARE

Jewelry, like every other art form, was influenced by the Renaissance delight in emblem and impresa. Unfortunately, the Civil War destroyed much of the art of the English Renaissance, just as the Reformation had earlier destroyed many of the treasures of the Middle Ages. Many of the surviving pieces of Tudor and Jacobean jewelry were reset in the course of time as taste changed. As Lesley Parker has observed, settings "were modified to comply with the demands of fashion, fortune and felony."[81] Although relatively little remains, contemporary portraits and inventories are an additional source of valuable information.

Two famous examples from Elizabeth's collection will illustrate emblematic jewelry: the Phoenix Jewel and the Pelican Jewel. The Phoenix Jewel shows the profile image of the queen cut from a gold medal struck in 1574 while the obverse depicts the mythical bird in a flaming fire, signifying legendary uniqueness and solitariness. The queen's heraldic flowers, Tudor roses and eglantine, surround the royal portrait in translucent red and green enamel.[82] The Pelican Jewel, prominent in the Pelican Portrait and attributed to Nicholas Hilliard, features the pelican in her piety, thereby associating the monarch with Christ, and underscoring not only the divine right of the king, but perhaps more importantly, the notion that the good king lives out a kind of *imitatio Christi*.[83]

Household silverware was often embellished with emblematic designs. One of the rare pieces to have survived is the Vyvyan Salt, once owned by the Vyvyan family of Trelowarren in Cornwall and now in the Victoria and Albert Museum. The verre-eglomisé panels are decorated with designs, which, as Joan Evans notes,[84] were probably copied from Whitney. There are: a vine encircling a tree, "Prudente[s] vino abstinent" [Prudent men abstain from wine]; a snake hiding in strawberry plants, "Latet anguis in herba" [The snake lurks in the grass]; crowned Tantalus, trapped in a lake, unable to pluck fruit from a near-by tree, "Avaritiae stipendium" [The reward of avarice], and roses, from which spiders and flies draw nourishment, "Vitae aut morti" [For life and for death]. If Whitney was the source, the Vyvyan Salt is no slavish copy. Whereas Whitney entitles the Tantalus emblem simply "Avaritia," the artist, or the person who commissioned the Salt, improved on the original motto by adding the interpretational key word "stipendium."

PRINTING AND BOOK MAKING

TITLE-PAGES AND FRONTISPIECES

No history of emblematic forms would be complete that ignored the influence of emblem in the creation of title-pages and frontispieces for books in general. With the exception of some comments on individual works by McKerrow and Ferguson in their collection of title-page borders,[85] some references by Johnson in his catalogue of English title-pages,[86] the methodologically important study of twenty frontispieces by Corbett and Lightbown[87] and relevant essays by Farmer and Höltgen little has been done on the subject to my knowledge.[88] And yet it is also here that one could expect to trace the influence of emblematic and hieroglyphic forms in the art of the woodcut and engraving during the period.

Emblematic frontispieces and title-pages were carefully devised by authors in order to make visual statements about the books they introduced. Virtually every motif carries significance; little if anything is purely decorative. Thus the relationship between frontispiece and book is closer than many a modern reader would imagine. Corbett and Lightbown discuss the frontispiece to Sidney's *Arcadia,* which is typical in most ways. At the top, a cartouche frames Sidney's crest of a porcupine passant. A shepherd and an amazon, dressed in costumes that correspond closely with descriptions in the romance, stand to the left and right of the frontispiece. At the bottom there is an emblem, which depicts a boar backing away from a marjoram bush. The motto NON TIBI SPIRO [I breathe (sweet scents) but not for you] captures the meaning of the scene. In Sanford's foreword "To The Reader" the marjoram bush is explained as the ethical treasures of the *Arcadia,* which are presumably enjoyed only by the virtuous-minded. This emblem can be traced to Camerarius, and even further to Horapollo. A single title-page was frequently re-used by the printer for several different works. Thus one emblematic design was often more significant in terms of its distribution than it might at first appear. A case in point is the edition of *The Psalmes of David,* which H. Bynneman published in 1571. The emblem which interests us is found at the base of an arch. The motto "Non vi sed virtute" [Not by strength but by virtue] is printed at the top of an oval, which shows a dragon sprawled on its back on the ground with a panther (?) at its throat.[89] The printer used this title-page with its emblem for at least twenty-six different works that appeared in thirty-one editions between 1570 and 1629.

Some of the emblematic combinations of motto and picture found on title-pages are in fact printer's devices. One of the emblematic panels of the title-page introducing *A shorte introduction of grammar* (London, 1574) depicts three sweet williams growing out of a cask or tun, which is inscribed with the letters NOR. At the root of the sweet william plant a "W" may be detected. This was the punning emblem or rebus for the printer William Norton.[90]

These illustrated title-pages and frontispieces are deeply indebted to allegorical, emblematic and hieroglyphical traditions, which are to be understood both as an art form and a symbolic mode of thought. While the emblematic mode is clearly important, frontispieces should not be simply regarded as emblems. Corbett and Lightbown point out that no matter how similar, the frontispiece does not exist in its own right, as does an emblem, nor does it make a self-contained philosophical or moral statement. Rather it introduces, even epitomizes, the book that follows. The term "frontispiece" can mean both the entrance to a book and to a building; as Höltgen points out, there are also close links between emblematic title-pages and architectural allegories such as triumphal arches for state entries. Höltgen also describes and illustrates for the first time the subgenre of emblematic brasses: they are monumental mural brasses, engraved in a shallow technique, and for the most part executed during the first half of the seventeenth century.[91]

PRINTERS' DEVICES

In the early sixteenth century, printers' devices tended to be uncomplicated signs associating the printer with his place of work. For instance, James Gaver's colophon informs us that he was "dwellynge at the sygne of the Sonne,"[92] hence his choice of the sun as a device. During the later sixteenth century, however, emblematic forms greatly influenced the creation of printers' devices, which frequently assumed the function of an impresa rather than a geographic sign. Thus William Leake who lived at the Crane, the White Greyhound and the Holy Ghost used none of these as his sign, but took the emblematic combination of a globe of the world surmounted by a winged death's head, which in turn was topped by a small hourglass before a larger open book inscribed with the motto "I live to dy. I dy to live".[93] This printer's device derives from the emblem "In morte vita" [Life in death] in Sambucus' collection (p. 99 of the 1566 ed.).

Several of Alciato's emblems re-appear with minor modifications as printers' devices. During the years 1571-4 William Williamson used a device showing Triton on a dolphin encircled by the snake of eternity, accompanied by the motto "Immortality is gotten by the study of letters." This derives ultimately from Alciato's emblem 133, but since it was used earlier by Jean Waesbergh of Antwerp and Rotterdam (1557-88) Williamson may have simply adopted the device of the Continental printer. Maurice Sabbe has written a brief study of the relation of Alciato emblems to some Continental printers' devices.[94]

John Wolfe adapted a Whitney emblem, which derives ultimately from Hadrianus Junius, for his Italian books with their fictitious imprints. The device portrays a palm tree with serpents and toads scrambling around its base, with the motto "Il vostro malignare non jiova nulla" [Your maligning is of no avail].[95]

On the basis of his study of hundreds of printers' and publishers' devices used in England and Scotland between 1485 and 1640 Ronald B. McKerrow concluded that "perhaps the majority [of such devices] are based ultimately on emblems. But it does not follow that they were in all cases taken directly from emblem books. Many came to England through the medium of the device of a foreign printer" (p. xxv). Thus the Plantin device of a pair of compasses with the motto "Labore et Constantia" [Through labour and constancy] was used by John Harrison and Nicholas Oakes; Wechel's Pegasus surmounting a caduceus over crossed cornucopias was copied by John Nicholas III from about 1660 to 1684.

In our enthusiasm for the emblem and impresa we should guard against the temptation to exaggerate the importance of some of our discoveries. The fact that printers and publishers employed emblems so readily does not necessarily imply that they were avid readers or collectors of emblem books. However, since each title published was sold in the hundreds of copies, it does mean that the emblematic device on title-pages, frontispieces and colophons appeared many thousands of times. In terms of distribution and frequency, then, the emblematic printer's device played a small and yet significant role. Precisely how significant we do not yet know, since much of the earlier research was done without the knowledge of emblem books available to us today. McKerrow does not notice that R. Wolfe's device showing three boys throwing sticks at a tree in order to obtain the fruit derives from Alciato's emblem 193, and the early date of 1549 precludes any reliance on Whitney. A fuller knowledge of the emblem tradition will in fact contribute to the correct interpretation of printer's devices. McKerrow (p. xxiv) admits being unable to decipher the meaning of the complex hieroglyphic device which Islip used in 1598 and 1613 and which derives from Sambucus (1566, p. 97) "Quibus respublica conservetur" [By means of these the state may be kept safe]. When Thomas Scarlet and Richard Bradick use Camerarius' emblem 9 from his collection *Symbolorum et emblematum ex volatilibus et insectis* (1596) showing an eagle holding up its young to the sun with the motto "Sic crede" [You must believe in this] the printer is not merely referring to his "first class work" as McKerrow remarks (p. xxiv), but rather the printer is claiming the truth, in some instances perhaps the divine inspiration for the books he publishes.

It would appear that the Continental emblem writers from whom English printers most frequently borrowed emblems were Alciato, Sambucus, Camerarius and Junius. Frequently, Whitney was an intermediary.

ILLUSTRATED INITIALS

The illustrated initial, which dates back to early medieval illustrated manuscripts, has never completely disappeared; from time to time it makes a minor comeback. The smallest form of book illustration, it is perhaps hardly surprising to find the omnipresent emblem incorporated into illustrated initials. The title-pages for the domestic accounts of Elizabeth's household were illustrated with line drawings of emblematic and heraldic motifs and imprese. Michael Bath reproduces and discusses the cerf volant,[96] which with its crown and motto "Hoc Caesar me donavit" [Caesar gave me this] embellishes the accounts for the year 1580. The cerf volant was one of the badges of the kings of France, borrowed by Elizabeth I in keeping with her title of Queen of England, France and Ireland, as the title-page of the account states. Elizabeth's household accounts and other royal papers will doubtless yield further evidence of the pervasive emblematic mode, and a study of sources is likely to underscore yet again the importance of Continental traditions in England.[97]

BROADSIDES

Broadsides, being ephemeral and fugitive material, are notoriously difficult to study. They are dispersed throughout the libraries of the world and usually inadequately catalogued. This makes it doubly difficult to make any reliable pronouncements. There are a few printed collections and catalogues.[98] The British Library probably has the largest, if scattered collection, accompanied by information on some holdings at other libraries. The University of Texas possesses an important collection of seventy-four illustrated broadsides; however, only five are in English.[99]

From an examination of the 516 broadsides collected by the Society of Antiquaries of London, and described in their catalogue[100] it would appear that emblematically illustrated broadsides were something of a rarity in England. There seem to be broadly two kinds of emblematic illustration, the portrait and the hieroglyphic combination of motifs.

No. 101 is described as "The Rare Print of the Portrait of Queen Elizabeth in the Clouds." The whole broadside has a perfectly emblematic structure. At the top we read the motto PER TAL VARIAR SON QUI [The world may change but I am here]. Beneath is the portrait of Elizabeth who holds a fan of ostrich feathers in her right hand; above her head is a circle of stars. Beneath the print we read the following epigram:

Lo here her Type who was of late The Prop of Belgia,
    Stay of France,

> Spaines Foyle, Faiths Shield, and Queen of State, of
> Armes and Learning, Fate and Chance,
> in briefe, of women, nere was seene, so greate a
> Prince, so good a Queen.

We are not surprised to find that Nicholas Hilliard designed the portrait. There are other similar broadside portraits of the Earl of Cumberland, Robert Cecil, and Prince Henry.

Perhaps the most impressive of these emblematic and hieroglyphic portraits is the broadside, dated March 4th, 1619, which marks the death of Queen Anne.

The closest relative of the printed emblem is the illustrated broadside, which introduces its emblematic design with the self-conscious use of the term "emblem." The year 1647 saw the appearance of an illustrated broadside entitled "An Embleme of the Times,"[101] setting out God's gracious dealings with England. The large picture graphically sets out instances of "legall punishments" in the shape of a soldier identified as "war," a two-headed woman identified as "hypocrisy" and an angel, sword in hand, identified as "pestilence." Biblical texts frame the picture on both sides, while beneath the illustration rhyming pentameters develop the themes of peace and religion, which are the subject of the broadside.

THE ENGLISH EMBLEM AND THE CONTINENTAL TRADITION

Whereas we know of the translation and borrowing done by English writers, we still have but the vaguest notion of the role Continental emblem books played in the original. Some information is available on the use to which Ben Jonson and Inigo Jones put Ripa's *Iconologia* in the creation and production of court masques. The emblematic interpretation of literature and drama, especially studies of source and influence, has remained largely speculative. Such literary criticism is likely to remain speculative until more accurate information on the emblems themselves is available.

Leaving aside translations and borrowings, we need to establish which Continental emblem books were available in their original languages in England, and how widely they were distributed, read and used. What is required is the compilation of an inventory of Continental emblem books in England and references to Continental emblem writers in English during the sixteenth and seventeenth centuries. One could start with public and private libraries where careful research would be required to collect the information that will begin to provide a more accurate picture. However, the mere fact that a sixteenth-century emblem book exists in an old library does not necessarily prove that it was there in the sixteenth century. Happily, some libraries, such as the Bodleian, possess catalogues dating back to the pe-

riod.[102] Some of the colleges at Oxford[103] and Cambridge, the Inns of Court, and various of the great houses in England possess catalogues from the period. A catalogue of Robert Cecil's library, dating from 1615, is preserved at Hatfield House. It will be interesting to see which emblem books, if any, Elizabeth's first minister possessed.[104] We know that Thomas Palmer dedicated a manuscript emblem book to him in 1598 as a new year's gift.[105] The library of Sir Thomas Knyvett of Ashwellthorpe (ca. 1539-1618) is known to have included two Alciato editions (Lyons, 1551 and Lyons, 1573), the Altdorf emblems, Bargagli, Camden, Camerarius, Canisius, Contile, Giovio, Junius, Ruscelli, Sambucus, Strada, Typotius, Van Veen (*Moralia Horatiana*) and Valeriano.[106] There are some printed records of private libraries of the period in existence, such as that of Sir Thomas Browne, Ben Jonson, Henry Pyne,[107] and the list of the books owned by William Drummond and others read by him during the years 1604-14.[108]

Proof of ownership, whether indicated by name, initials or an ex libris, occasionally allows us to date the presence of an emblem book in a given place. Princeton University Library possesses a copy of Sambucus' *Emblemata,* printed with blank pages as an album amicorum, and which had been owned by the influential German baroque writer Georg Philip Harsdröffer. The British Library has a copy of Hawkin's *The Devout Hart* with the entry "Anne Fortescue her Book 1683, given mee by my Cosin . . ."[109]

In addition to the evidence provided by libraries and by translators of Continental emblems, English writers and artists occasionally refer to emblem writers in letters, diaries and published works. In a letter to Edmund Spenser, Gabriel Harvey writes of "Jouios and Rassellis Emblemes in Italian, Paradines in Frenche. . . ."[110] John Harington had evidently seen an Alciato in England in the late 1580's. In an "Advertisement to the Reader," which prefaces his *Orlando Furioso* (London, 1591) he comments somewhat disparagingly on the use of woodcuts in Alciato and Whitney whereas his illustrations, which he himself designed, "are all cut in brasse" (sig. A).[111] William Drummond, who in 1619 described in detail the imprese adorning the state bed of Mary Queen of Scots for Ben Jonson, also wrote "A short Discourse upon Impresa's" in the form of a letter to the Earl of Perth.[112] He provided the Earl with a succinct review of imprese theory expressed in thirteen points, demonstrating his mastery of the subject. The undated letter was evidently written between 1611 and 1633.

CONTINENTAL EMBLEMS AS SOURCES

While it was not uncommon for German Baroque dramatists to annotate printed editions of their plays with references to emblem writers, this was much less the case with men of the Elizabethan and Jacobean theatre. As far as I am aware, painters did not follow any such practice, either in England or on the Continent, although it is possible that some artists' notebooks may contain references to emblem writers. It is, then, to modern scholarship that we must look for information on emblem books, and especially Continental emblem books as the sources for both writers and artists. Source hunting is, of course, a precarious activity, because emblems are highly derivative in two senses of the word. Firstly, later emblem writers re-use, one might almost say recycle, the emblems of earlier authors. Secondly, the emblem itself is a repository for the knowledge and lore, the traditions and attitudes of its time. A. F. Kendrick suggests that the embroidery known as "The Shepheard Buss" has "emblems worked upon it which are to be found in Whitney's volume" (p. 97), but he gives neither descriptions nor evidence for the statement; Roy Strong states the same emblems "are from the 1591 translation of Paradin's Devises."[113] But Strong does not tell us why the Paradin imprese derive from the English translation rather than one of the earlier original versions. Paradin's imprese were known to English devisers of tournament imprese as early as 1560, as Alan R. Young has demonstrated.[114]

While it is often impossible to identify sources, we can at least point to a Continental tradition. Peter Bayley has established Alciato as the source for the wood carvings that now decorate the Summer Room in University College, Oxford. Kendrick and others have demonstrated that Richard Hyckes drew extensively on the emblem books of such Continental writers as Alciato, Sambucus, La Perrière and de Montenay for the borders of his "Four Seasons" tapestries. Michael Bath has been able to establish Paradin as a source for the illustrated initials in Elizabeth's account book for 1580, and since no English translation of Paradin was made before 1591, the illustrator must have used an earlier Continental version such as that published in 1567. However, in order to ascertain precise sources or even an emblematic tradition deriving from the Continent, we need much more accurate information on the reception of European emblems in England.

Notes

1. Whitney's is the first English emblem book in the strict sense that it is modelled on Alciato's volume. It is predated by Daniel's translation of Giovio in 1585 and the English version of van der Noot's *Theatre for worldlings* that appeared in 1569.

2. The six titles are: Jan van der Noot, *Theatre for worldlings* (London, 1569); Samuel Daniel's translation of *The Worthy Tract of Paulus Jovius* (London, 1585); Geffrey Whitney, *A Choice of Emblemes and other Devises* (Leyden, 1586);

P. S.'s translation of *The Heroicall Devises of M. Claudius Paradin* (London, 1591); Andrew Willet, *Sacrorum emblematum centuria una* [London, 1592?]; and Thomas Combe, *Theater of Fine Devices* [London, 1593?]. However, since Daniel's volume contains an unacknowledged selection from the imprese of Ludovico Domenichi, and P. S's translation includes imprese by Gabriel Simeoni, a total of eight separate works are represented by these six English titles.

3. One of the few exceptions is the article by Jerome Dees on "Studies in the English Emblem," *English Literary Renaissance,* 16 (1986), 391-420.

4. Peter M. Daly, *Emblem Theory. Recent German Contributions to the Characterization of the Emblem Genre* (Nendeln: Kraus-Thompson Organization, 1979).

5. Joseph Mazzeo, "A Critique of Some Modern Theories of Metaphysical Poetry," *Modern Philology,* 50 (1952), 93.

6. Liselotte Dieckmann, *Hieroglyphics. The History of a Literary Symbol* (St. Louis, Mo.: Washington University Press, 1970), p. 45.

7. For example, John Ogilvy, *The Entertainment of . . . Charles II* (London, 1662); *A Description of General Solemnities* (London, 1675); Francis Sanford, *The History of the Coronation of James II* (London, 1687); and *An exact Relation of the Entertainment of . . . William III* (London, 1691).

8. Leon Voet, *The Plantin Press (1555-1589). A Bibliography of Works Printed and Published by Christopher Plantin at Antwerp and Leyden,* 6 vols. (Antwerp: Van Hoeve, 1980-83).

9. John Manning, "Continental Emblem Books in Sixteenth-Century England: The Evidence of Sloane MS 3794," *Emblematica* 1 (1986), 1-11.

10. John F. Leisher, "George Puttenham and Emblemata," *Boston University Studies in English,* I (1955-6), 1-8.

11. Peter M. Daly, "The Case for the 1593 Edition of Combe's *Theater of Fine Devices,*" *Journal of the Warburg and Courtauld Institutes,* 49 (1986), 255-257.

12. Alan Young, "Henry Peacham, Ripa's *Iconologia,* and Vasari's *Lives,*" *Renaissance and Reformation,* 9 (1985), 177-188.

13. Albrecht Schöne, *Emblematik und Drama im Zeitalter des Barock,* (Munich: Beck, 1964; 2nd ed. 1968); Dietrich Walter Jöns, *Das 'Sinnen-Bild'. Studien zur allegorischen Bildlichkeit bei Andreas Gryphius* (Stuttgart: Metzler, 1966); Daly, *Em-*

blem Theory. Peter M. Daly, *Literature in the Light of the Emblem. Structural Parallels between the Emblem and Literature in the Sixteenth and Seventeenth Centuries* (Toronto: University of Toronto Press, 1979).

14. Jenner informs us that he based his emblem book *The Soules Solace* on sermons that he heard in London. It is known that certain preachers employed emblems in their sermons and in fact preached emblematically. See Dietrich Walter Jöns, "Die emblematische Predigtweise Johann Sauberts" in *Rezeption und Produktion zwischen 1570 und 1730.* Festschrift für Günther Weydt zum 65. Geburtstag, ed. Wolf Dietrich Rasch, Hans Geulen und Klaus Haberkamm (Bern and Munich: Francke, 1972), pp. 137-158.

15. For a review of the emblematic aspects of various forms of drama, see Daly, *Literature in the Light of the Emblem,* ch. 4, pp. 134-167.

16. Roy Strong, *The English Icon: Elizabethan and Jacobean Portraiture* (London: Paul Mellon Foundation in association with Routledge & Kegan Paul; New York: Pantheon Books, 1969); Roy Strong, *The Cult of Elizabeth. Elizabethan Portraiture and Pageantry* (London: Thames and Hudson, 1977).

17. Leslie Duer, "The Painter and the Poet: Visual Design in *The Duchess of Malfi,*" *Emblematica* I (1986), 293-316.

18. Reproduced in colour in Strong, *Cult,* plate 1 [p. 9].

19. Reproduced in Strong, *Cult,* p. 74.

20. Strong, *Icon* p. 260 and Roy Strong, *Tudor and Jacobean Portraits,* (1969), p. 275.

21. Marcus Gheeraerts, The Younger's portrait is reproduced and discussed by Strong in *Icon,* p. 281; see also pp. 282 and 290.

22. Reproduced in Strong, *Icon,* p. 288.

23. Strong reads the first motto as "Iniusti Iusta querela"; the second word seems to me to be "iusta," which also appears to make more sense; and in the third motto "Dolor est medicina ed lori (?)" the last two words are probably "amori[s]," which suits the grammar of the motto, expresses the theme of the painting, and harmonizes with the sonnet in the cartouche.

24. A characteristic example may be found in Otto van Veen's *Amorum emblemata* (Antwerp, 1608), p. 70, where a Cupid holds a branch with peach leaves and fruit, gesturing silence. The emblem is reproduced and discussed in Daly, *Emblem Theory,* pp. 103-107.

25. Piero Valeriano, *Hieroglyphica,* Bk 54 "De persico": Cor; see also "De Malo" Bk. 54. The edition used is Lyons, 1602, pp. 573-578.

26. Reproduced in Strong, *Icon,* p. 290.

27. Strong, *Icon,* p. 31.

28. Reproduced in Strong, *Cult,* p. 142.

29. Reproduced in Strong, *Cult,* pp. 156f. The motto, previously thought to be Spanish, eluded explanation until it was discovered that the miniature had been trimmed, resulting in the loss of the letters "do." See *Artists of the Tudor Court. The Portrait Miniature Rediscovered 1520-1620,* by Roy Strong with contributions from V. J. Murrell (London: Victoria and Albert Museum, 1983), p. 134.

30. Reproduced in colour in Strong, *Cult,* pp. 148f.

31. Reproduced in Strong, *Cult,* plate 2 [p. 10]. See also pp. 56-83.

32. Reproduced in Strong, *Cult,* p. 74.

33. Strong, *Cult,* p. 71.

34. The panel "Auditus" is reproduced in the National Trust guide.

35. The panel depicting Adam and Eve is reproduced in Arthur Foss, *Country House Treasures* (London: The National Trust / Weidenfeld and Nicolson, 1980), p. 208.

36. Joachim Camerarius, *Symbolorum et emblematum ex volatilibus et insectis* (1596), No. 19.

37. Juan de Boria, *Empresas morales* (1581), No. 89.

38. Paul Hentzner, *Travels in England during the Reign of Queen Elizabeth* in James Beeverell, *The Pleasures of London* (London: Witherby & Co, 1940), p. 117. This volume is translated and annotated by W. H. Quarrell who added Walpole's translation (1797) of Hentzner from the French. Hentzner (1558-1628) was a Silesian whose travels were published as *Itinearium Germaniae, Galliae; Angliae; Italiae* (Nuremberg, 1612); another edition Nuremberg, 1629; under a somewhat different title another edition Breslau 1617.

39. The manuscripts, 4 Ms. Hass. 68, belong to the Kassel Landesbibliothek and Murhardschee Bibliothek.

40. *The Renaissance Imagination.* Essays and Lectures by D. G. Gordon, collected and edited by Stephen Orgel, (Berkeley: University of California Press, 1975) pp. 24-50; Pamela Wachna, "Rubens at Whitehall," M.A. Thesis, McGill University, 1979.

41. Norman K. Farmer, Jr., *Poets and the Visual Arts in Renaissance England* (Austin: University of Texas Press, 1984).

42. G. C. Moore Smith (ed), *Gabriel Harvey's Marginalia* (Stratford upon Avon: Shakespeare Head Press, 1913), pp. 7-8.

43. The motto to Alciato's Ocnus emblem (Padua 1621, no. 92) reads "Ocni effigies, de iis qui meretricibus donant, quod in bonos usus verti debeat" [A picture of Ocnus; on those who give to harlots what should be turned to better use]. I am indebted to Mr. Bari Hooper of Saffron Walden for sending me his description of the mantlepiece, which has suffered some damage, making it difficult to identify all the details from the photograph. Mr. Hooper had also recognised Alciato as the source for the main panels.

44. Peter C. Bayley's articles "The Summer Room Carvings" appeared in *The University College Record,* 3 (1958), pp. 192-201; 4 (1950), pp. 252-256; 5 (1960), pp. 341-346.

45. Strong, *Cult,* p. 70.

46. Paul Hentzner, "Travels in England" in James Beeverell, *The Pleasures of London,* p. 139.

47. 40 MS. Hass. 68, fol. 79ᵛ.

48. Sieur de la Serre, "History of the Entry of Mary de Medicis, the Queen Mother of France, into England, anno 1638" in James Beeverell, *The Pleasures of London,* p. 89.

49. Cit. from Beeverell, p. 90

50. John Humphreys, *Elizabethan Sheldon Tapestries* (Oxford: Oxford University Press, 1929), pp. 19, and 24f.

51. Peter M. Daly, "'The Four Seasons' Tapestries (1611) made for Sir John Tracy of Toddington," forthcoming in the *Proceedings of the Manorial Society of Great Britain.*

52. A. F. Kendrick, "The Hatfield Tapestries of the Seasons," *Walpole Society,* 2 (1913), pp. 89-97.

53. A comparison of the motto of Spring no. 35 "Animi sub vulpe laetentes" with Sambucus texts shows that the source is not the first edition of 1564, where the same emblem (p. 124) bears the motto "Fictus amicus" but the edition of 1566, or perhaps one of even later date, with the identical motto "Animi sub vulpe laetentes" (p. 171). Whitney could not have been the source since he modified the 1564 motto to read "Amicitia fucata vitanda" (p. 124).

54. "Spring" emblem 10 may be taken as evidence of Hyckes's use of the Plantin edition of Alciato. Whereas the earlier Wechel Paris editions (emblem 5), and the Roville/Bonhomme Lyons printings (emblem 30) had depicted a stork in flight carrying another on its back, the Plantin editions and the tapestry depict a stork flying with food in its beak to its nest where three young birds are waiting.

55. Letter from Dudley B. Sidgwick dated August 25, 1982.

56. Humphreys, pp. 20-2.

57. These panels and Judith are reproduced in colour in *Sudeley Castle. An Illustrated Guide.*

58. Alciato, *Emblemata* (Padua: Tozzi, 1621), emblem 18.

59. Ripa, Hertel ed., p. 31.

60. Ripa, Hertel ed., p. 47.

61. Ripa, Hertel ed., pp. 60, 169.

62. These three are reproduced in Humphreys, plate VII.

63. Quoted from Humphreys, p. 9.

64. Quoted from Humphreys, p. 9.

65. For further information on painted cloths and Shakespeare, see Arthur H. R. Fairchild, "Shakespeare and the Arts of Design," *The University of Missouri Studies,* 12 (1937), pp. 1-191.

66. George Wingfield Digby, *Elizabethan Embroidery* (London: Faber & Faber, 1963); A. F. Kendrick, *English Needlework,* 2nd ed. revised by Patricia Wardle (London: Black, 1967); John L. Nevinson, *Catalogue of English Domestic Embroidery of the Sixteenth and Seventeenth Centuries,* 2nd ed. (London: H. M. Stationary Office, 1950); Patricia Wardle, *Guide to English Embroidery* (London: H. M. Stationary Office, 1970).

67. Reproduced in Strong, *Icon,* p. 41.

68. Strong, *Icon,* p. 41.

69. The fullest account of the embroidery done by Mary Queen of Scots during her captivity in Scotland and in England is found in Marguerite Swain's book, *The Needlework of Mary Queen of Scots* (London and New York: Nostrand-Reinhold, 1973). This study describes and reproduces all the work bearing her monogram or cipher, as well as pieces attributed to her.

70. Quoted from Wingfield Digby, p. 49, where the letter is cited in its entirety.

71. Quoted from Swain, p. 42.

72. Quoted from Swain, p. 63.

73. Quoted from Swain, p. 78.

74. Quoted from Swain, p. 87.

75. This armilliary embroidery is also reproduced in Wardle, *Guide,* plate 28C. For a full account of the Oxburgh hangings, see Swain, pp. 95-120.

76. The coverlet belongs to the Victoria and Albert Museum and is reproduced by Strong, *Cult,* p. 76, and Wardle, *Guide,* plate 29.

77. I have underlined the rebus.

78. Strong, *Cult,* p. 76.

79. Kendrick, "The Hatfield Tapestries of the Seasons," p. 97. Kendrick, *English Needlework,* p. 75.

80. Nevinson, p. 78.

81. Lesley Parker, *Renaissance Jewels and Jeweled Objects* (Baltimore: The Baltimore Museum of Art, 1968), p. 15.

82. Reproduced by Strong, *Cult,* p. 73, and Joan Evans, *English Jewelry,* plate 19.

83. Reproduced by Strong, *Icon,* p. 161.

84. Joan Evans, *Pattern. A Study of Ornament in Western Europe from 1180 to 1900.* (New York: Hacker Art Books, 1975), first published Oxford, at the Clarendon Press, 1931.

85. R. B. McKerrow and F. S. Ferguson, *Title-Page Borders used in England & Scotland 1485-1640* (London: Bibliographical Society at the Oxford University Press, 1932). This represents a collection of over 300 titlepages described and reproduced in facsimile.

86. Alfred Forbes Johnson, *A Catalogue of Engraved and Etched English Title-pages down to the Death of William Fairthorne, 1691* (London: Bibliographical Society at the Oxford University Press, 1934).

87. Margery Corbett and R. W. Lightbown, *The Comely Frontispiece. The Emblematic Title-Page in England 1550-1660* (London: Routledge & Kegan Paul, 1979).

88. Most recently, Norman K. Farmer, Jr., "Renaissance English Title-Pages and Frontispieces: Visual Introductions to Verbal Texts," in *Proceedings of the IXth Congress of the International Comparative Literature Association,* vol. 3 (Innsbruck, 1981), pp. 61-5. See Karl Josef Höltgen. "Emblematic Title-Pages and Brasses," in his *Aspects of the Emblem. Studies in the English Emblem Tradition and the European Context.* With a foreword by Sir Roy Strong. (Kassel: Reichenberger, 1986).

89. McKerrow, No. 133.

90. McKerrow, Nos. 143, 144, also R. B. McKerrow, *Printers' Devices* (1913), No. 174.

91. Höltgen, "Emblematic Title-Pages and Brasses," *Aspects of the Emblem,* pp. 122-131, 135-140.

92. McKerrow, No. 90.

93. McKerrow, No. 341.

94. Maurice Sabbe, "Le symbolisme des margues typographiques," *De Gulden Passer. Le Compas d'Or* N.S. 10 (1932), 93-119.

95. McKerrow, No. 278 (Whitney, p. 118 and Junius [1569], No. 9).

96. Michael Bath, "The legend of Caesar's deer," *Medievalia et Humanistica,* N.S. 9 (1979), 53-66, and "The white hart, the *cerf volant,* and the Wilton Diptych," *Third International Beast Epic, Fable and Fabliau Colloquium.* Münster 1979. Proceedings (Cologne and Vienna: Bohlau, 1981), pp. 25-42.

97. See below, Michael Bath, "Collared Stags and Bridled Lions: Queen Elizabeth's Household Accounts."

98. Many German illustrated broadsides were collected and published in two volumes by William A. Coupe, *The German Illustrated Broadsheet in the Seventeenth Century* (Baden-Baden: Heitz, 1966). Wolfgang Harms is currently editing the collection in the Herzog August Bibliothek, Wolfenbüttel. See Wolfgang Harms (ed), *Deutsche Illustrierte Flugblätter des 16. und 17. Jahrhunderts,* Band I: *Die Sammlung der Herzog August Bibliothek in Wolfenbüttel,* Kommentierte Ausgabe, Teil 1: Ethica, Physica. Herausgegeben von Wolfgang Harms und Michael Schilling zusammen mit Barbara Bauer und Cornelia Kemp (Tübingen: Niemeyer, 1985). Band II: *Die Sammlung der Herzog August Bibliothek,* Teil 2: Historica. Herausgegeben von Wolfgang Harms zusammen mit Michael Schilling und Andreas Wang (Munich: Kraus International Publications, 1980), now available from Niemeyer (Tübingen). Three further volumes are in preparation.

99. The collection is described in *Emblem Books at the Humanities Research Center. A Checklist with Selected Emblematic Broadsides,* introduced by Norman K. Farmer, Jr., (Texas, Austin, [1979]). The broadsides are described in a little more detail in Norman K. Farmer, J., "Popular Imagery," *The Library Chronicle,* N.S. 4 (1972), 48-57.

100. *Catalogue of a Collection of Printed Broadsides,* compiled by Robert Lemon (London, 1866).

101. Wing E-703.

102. The Thomas James Catalogue of 1605, and 1620; a list of books donated by Robert Burton, 1639; the catalogue of Thomas Hyde, 1674; the donation

of books made by the second earl of Essex in 1600. See also Lucy Gent, *Picture and Poetry 1560-1620: Relations between literature and the visual arts in the English Renaissance* (Leamington Spa: James Hall, 1981), which also contains an inventory of library catalogues.

103. For instance, N. R. Ker, *Records of All Souls College Library 1437-1600* (London: for the Oxford Bibliographic Society, by the Oxford University Press, 1971).

104. Karl Josef Höltgen has now examined the manuscript catalogues of 1615 and 1637 at Hatfield House. He informs me that he has found only one entry for a book of emblems or imprese, *Cent. imprese d'huomini d'arme 4* (Cecil Papers, FP 5/22, fol. 37ᵛ).

105. The MS. is I. Bod. Ashmole MS 767. See Rosemary Freeman, p. 235. Palmer produced two other MS collections: BL Sloane 3797 (see Note 8) and BL Additional MS 18040.

106. The British Library has several seventeenth-century catalogues of the libraries of "eminent persons" whose books were put up for auction: "A Catalogue of the Libraries of 2 Eminent Persons (1684)" (BL 821.i.4[4]) and many others. There is also the list of English books printed not later than 1600; "Part II History [Library of Henry Pyne]" (London 1847; BL 011904.h.45). The BL catalogues of special purchases from great houses might also yield information (See Reader's Guide 9).

107. D. J. McKitterick (ed.), *The Library of Sir Thomas Knyvett of Ashwellthorpe, c. 1539-1618* (Cambridge: Cambridge University Library, 1978).

108. The list is printed by French Rowe Fogle in his *A Critical Study of William Drummond of Hawthornden* (New York: King's Crown Press, Columbia University Press, 1952), pp. 179-186.

109. Robert Burton's name, or initials, often accompanied by his own mark of three dog's heads (derived from his coat-of-arms), adorn the books that he donated to the Bodleian and Christ Church. From the list of Burton's books (see *Oxford Bibliographical Society, Proceedings and Papers,* vol. 1, 1922-26, pp. 222-246) Karl Josef Höltgen reports the following items: Abraham Fraunce, *Insignium Explicatio* (London, 1588), Horapollo, *De Hieroglyphicis Notis* (Basel, 1518), Hadrianus Junius, *Emblemata* (Antwerp, 1566) and Joannes Sambucus, *Emblemata* (Antwerp, 1566).

110. Edward J. L. Scott (ed.), *Letter-book of Gabriel Harvey, A.D. 1573-1580,* Camden Society Publications, new series, vol. 33 (Westminster: Camden Society, 1884), pp. 78-79.

111. John Harington, *Orlando Furioso in English Heroical Verse* (London: Richard Field, 1591).

112. The "Discourse" was printed in John Sage and Thomas Ruddiman (ed.) *The Works of William Drummond, of Hawthornden* (Edinburgh: James Watson, 1711); rpt Hildesheim and New York: Olms, 1970

113. Strong, *Cult,* p. 76.

114. See below Alan R. Young, "The English Tournament Imprese."

MAJOR EMBLEM WRITERS

Peter M. Daly (essay date 1993)

SOURCE: Daly, Peter M. "The Arbitrariness of George Wither's Emblems: A Reconsideration." In *The Art of the Emblem: Essays in Honor of Karl Josef Höltgen,* edited by Michael Bath, John Manning, and Alan R. Young, pp. 201-23. New York: AMS Press, 1993.

[*In the following essay, Daly revisits earlier interpretations of Wither's work, suggesting that critics have mistaken the purpose of Wither's commentary. Daly contends that Wither understood the symbols of his emblems to have specific and recognizable meanings.*]

Critics from Rosemary Freeman (1948) to Michael Bath (1989), Charles Moseley (1989) and Richard Cavell (1990)[1] have tended to lend credence, if in differing measure, to George Wither's comments about his emblems. Authorial statement has thus coloured the critical reception of the emblems. Wither's comments have been seen as suggesting an arbitrary relationship between word and image, or thing and meaning, which, in Bath's view "comes close to sabotaging the credibility of the whole emblematic enterprise."[2]

In assessing Wither's emblems, Rosemary Freeman[3] seems to take too literally both the author's criticism of the emblems he appropriates from Gabriel Rollenhagen, whose name he never mentions, and Wither's critical comments on the illustrations and the meanings implied by, or attributable to, some of the symbolic motifs. But, as Irma Tramer[4] had already demonstrated in the 1930's, Wither often read the original texts more closely than he acknowledged, incorporating or adapting some important interpretational suggestions from his sources. In other words, Wither understates, for whatever reason, his indebtedness to his Continental emblem sources.

And he also evidently understood better than he pretended the meaning and complexity of the material with which he was working.

Freeman argues that Wither was more interested in "driving home the moral lesson" than "in the meaning of the pictures, and these he often treats in a highly cavalier fashion" (p. 144). She suggests:

> The reason for this airy dismissal of the original sense lies partly in the fact that the pictures were imported from Holland and some of them seemed to him exceptionally obscure, but it is mainly due to Wither's consciousness that his material belongs to a tradition now obsolete.
>
> (p. 144)[5]

But, the evidence she adduces in support of this statement is unconvincing. It is true that Wither introduces some emblems by phrases such as "in former times," "earlier," or such statements as the following:

> Our Elders, when their meaning was to shew
> A *native-speedinesse* (in Emblem wise)
> A picture of a *Dolphin-Fish* they drew . . .
>
> (2,10)

But this does not prove the material obsolete. Such iconographic materials were, of course, current among a courtly and learned audience. One has only to think of the masques of Ben Jonson, Thomas Heywood's allegorical pageants for Lord Mayors' Pageants, and his emblematic decorations for Charles I's ship *The Sovereign of the Seas*.[6] Thomas Blount published the first edition of his translation of Henri Estienne's *The Art of Making of Devises* in 1646. This occurred during the Civil War, when, as Blount was aware, the Royalists and Parliamentarians drew upon the tradition of the emblem and impresa for the creation of hundreds of cornets under which they fought and died. The printing history of English emblem books in the seventeenth century also shows that the tradition was far from obsolete.[7]

In addition, it is important to note that some of Wither's remarks are better understood as reader-oriented; he is explaining traditional, at times learned, allusions to a mixed readership. Phrases such as "in former times" (1,39), "in former Ages" (1,45), "Our Elders" (2,10), "The Sages old" (2,26), "old *Emblem* (worthy veneration)" (2,42), and "wise *Antiquitie*" (2,47) are also rhetorical strategies designed to lend authority to symbols and their meanings that may be unfamiliar to some readers.[8] That Wither is conscious of his reader is clear from the manner in which he constantly addresses those who take his book in their hands as though he is engaging in an interpretative process in which he is the interpretative authority and the reader the recipient. This is the context for his continual use of such forms of ad-

dress as "you" (1,40, 1,46, 3,42), "thee" (1,50, 3,34, 4,3) and "Reader" (2,33, 2,41, 3,12), and the extensive use of imperatives such as "mark well" (2,34, 3,24, 4,5), "looke here" (3,20) and "consider this" (3,34).

The received opinion in English scholarship is that Wither was by turns perplexed by the subtleties of the originals, impatient with their obscurity, and critical of their obsolescence. Certain of Wither's authorial statements have been taken as supporting the view that his emblems are arbitrary. As yet, however, no-one has studied the two hundred emblems carefully enough to test this received wisdom, nor has anyone compared authorial statement with actual practice. From his general Introduction to *A Century of Emblems* (Aldershot: Scolar Press, 1989), it would appear that Charles Moseley subscribes to this general view. He tells us that "Wither seems in some ways to look back to earlier conceptions and applications of the emblem even while he is explicitly uneasy about the value of its complexity . . ." (p. 23); his verses are "comments—sometimes puzzled—on and responses to what the 'author' of the emblem intended" (p. 24); he "used the picture as a starting point for ingenious analysis of its possible meaning" (p. 24) with the result that in his epigrams Wither "expounds ideas that can be attached to the illustration" (p. 24). Moseley's conclusion, carefully worded though it is, is ultimately a misrepresentation of Wither's emblem book. He writes:

> But he was aware from his own occasional difficulty in explaining and using the picture by which he was bound that visual symbols must not be too complicated—as well as the possibility of one symbol quite legitimately carrying several independent meanings . . . This implies that in the very act of using picture plus verse to suggest a general and universal truth in a special and particular application, Wither must have been uneasily aware of the doubtfulness of the emblem's status. His book thus becomes, indeed, a sort of lottery of meaning: the wheel design and the moveable pointers at the end suggest that he recognized that its significance is ultimately determined by its reader.
>
> (p. 25)

In fact, as I shall demonstrate, Wither accurately identifies, names and describes the symbolic motifs in virtually all of the two hundred engravings, providing the correct general meaning and only thereafter specifying more narrowly their application according to the themes and maxims that he wishes to express. The meaning of any given Wither emblem comprising his English couplet motto, engraving and epigram is not "a lottery of meaning" (p. 25). The lottery was used as a way of applying the fixed meaning of the emblems, but it does not "unfix" that meaning.

It has become something of topos when writing about Wither to note the Englishman's impatience with his learned Continental source. Moseley, albeit in a footnote, asserts that Wither was "exasperated" with the "multi-valency" in a Rollenhagen emblem.[9] It seems to me that it is not the multi-valency but rather the obscurity of the *pictura* featuring three interlocking crescent moons surmounted by a crown that Wither objects to when he begins his *subscriptio*:

> What in this *Emblem,* that mans meanings were,
> Who made it first, I neither know nor care;
> For, whatsoe'er, he purposed, or thought,
> to serve my *purpose,* now it shall be told;
> Who, many times, before this Taske is ended,
> Must picke out *Moralls,* where was none intended.

(2,49)

Since this is a hieroglyphically stylized configuration, indeed an impresa probably deriving from Paradin,[10] one can understand Wither's difficulties. An impresa is always allusive and often esoteric; without knowing the identity of the bearer and the circumstances of its use, the impresa virtually defies interpretation. Paradin informs us that this is the device of Henri II in his role as defender of the Church. In his commentary Paradin refers to the scriptural use of the moon as a prefiguration of the Church. It is this meaning that Wither explicates. But obscurity not multivalency is the problem. In fact, Wither can recognise and use multivalency when its suits his purpose, as is demonstrated by his interpretation of the owl as "night," "studious Watchfulnesse," and the "Bird of Athens" (1,9).

Michael Bath[11] is the first modern scholar since Irma Tramer to attempt a serious re-evaluation of Wither's emblems. He begins by considering the relation of text and image, noting that the precisely ruled pages of Wither's emblems create a strong impression of a discrete unity, which is reinforced in the four-book structure with its separate title-pages and dedications. However, Bath finds that certain features "argue against the unity of form and purpose which this apparently orderly structure suggests" (p. 4). These include Wither's apparent indifference to the originally intended meaning in his sources. It is important to recognize that Wither's source emblems were tripartite, but his own emblems have four parts: in addition to epigram, *pictura* and Latin motto encircling the engraving, Wither places an English couplet above the *pictura* which for the English reader replaces or augments the original Latin motto. Wither often explicitly signals the relationship of picture to text by the use of deictic phrase or comment. Such *deixis* may lend authority to interpretation, but Bath suggests it may also paradoxically indicate its abitrariness. He finds that Wither thus often deconstructs the unity of the emblem.

According to Bath, the 30-line epigrams are usually divided tidily into representation or description and interpretation, with a Puritan emphasis on "bringing home the moral to life of the individual reader, a process which the Lottery reinforces" (p. 9). When prayer concludes the epigram, the emblem shows a certain affinity with the three stages of Ignation meditation.

Bath also pays close attention to the composition of de Passe's "finely-drawn and intelligently-designed engravings" (p. 5), which, as Wolfgang Harms[12] has shown, are characterized by inner-pictorial comment and symbolic statement. Many a single motif, cluster, or scene in the middle or background adds to the meaning of the motif in the foreground. Although Wither's texts seldom specify those meanings, they remain available for the knowing reader. Bath refers to a convincing example in his discussion of the emblem of the stricken deer (4,6), enriched by two other stag and eagle motifs. Although Wither does not comment on these visual motifs and their meanings, his concluding verse suggests that he was not unaware of some of this meaning: "And, therefore, from my *Selfe,* I flie to *Thee.*" Bath summarizes:

> Such an emblem will stand as a model of semiological consistency and closure: all its elements contributing to a complex unitary significance, underwritten by the authority of received meanings which had been sanctioned by previous, indeed Biblical, usage.

(p. 12)

Bath believes that many other emblems, however, betray Wither's scepticism about ascribing meaning to image, his "impatience at allegorical subtlety," and an insistence on arbitrariness that in Bath's view "comes close to sabotaging the credibility of the whole emblematic enterprise" (p. 12). While Bath presents a well argued case, Wither's actual practice still needs to be compared with authorial statements. Further careful analysis is required to establish to what extent Wither actually builds on the inherited significance implied by his emblem sources. In this regard Wither's intended readership and his own purposes—religious, moral, social, and political—in the earlier 1630's will need to be taken into account.

The need for such a re-evaluation is supported by Bath's far-reaching interpretation of the architectural and cosmic structuring of the book, which was Wither's creation. In his "Writ of Prevention," Wither uses an architectural metaphor for the four books, thus associating them with architectural space used as memory-places in the *ars memorativa*. To this Bath adds the idea of the book as microcosm, invoked perhaps through the final lottery with its four compass points, which effectively squares the circle. To what extent Wither intended the values inherent in these symbolic schemes cannot be determined. At least they bespeak the "survival of a largely instinctive and conservative desire for a fitting correspondence between the ordered universe and the microcosm of the book" (p. 14). Such a sense of order, whether instinctive or conscious, is anything but arbitrary, and this brings Bath to consider the lottery. In the final analysis the lottery "is not determined by 'Chance' but 'divinely sent'" (p. 16).

Wither's alleged arbitrariness must also be seen in the light of a scholarly tradition and set of generic assumptions associated with the names Rosemary Freeman and Mario Praz who see arbitrariness as characteristic of the emblem genre. However, since 1964 other voices, if largely German-speaking, and therefore not always heard in English circles—Albrecht Schöne,[13] Dietrich Walter Jöns,[14] Wolfgang Harms,[15] and most recently Carsten-Peter Warncke[16] to name but the most influential—have pointed to the role played in the emblem by inherited modes of Christian exegesis and allegory, which must modify our assumptions about arbitrariness.[17]

It is time, I believe, to re-consider the "arbitrariness" of word-image relationships in Wither's emblems. To do this, I propose first to re-examine authorial statement, then consider Wither's actual practice by comparing a number of his English emblems with their sources. In the process I shall concentrate on Wither's treatment of foregrounded symbolic clusters.[18]

What are we to make of Wither's famous and almost denigratory statements? Consider this: *"To seeke out the Author of every particular Emblem were a labour without profit; and, I have beene so far from endeavouring it, that, I have not so much as cared to find out their meanings in any of the Figures; but, applied them, rather, to such purposes, as I could thinke of, at first sight"* (A2). This has been taken as proof of Wither's indifference to his source and to the original meanings in the emblems, and as a "frank confession of the arbitrary nature of the sign" (Bath, p. 6). But is Wither referring only to his Rollenhagen source, and should we take his statement at face value? Irma Tramer, writing her German dissertation in the 1930's, was not deterred by such authorial assertions. She investigated the possibility that Wither, in spite of his off-handed statements, had actually read Rollenhagen closely and consulted his sources. She shows that Wither "knew and in part used" Rollenhagen's texts,[19] and that he in fact incorporated general ideas and even key words from Rollenhagen's Latin epigrams into his English mottoes. Indeed, it is evident that virtually all of Wither's mottoes are accurate renderings, if longer, of Rollenhagen's Latin mottoes, which invariably encapsulate the meaning of the emblem. In other words, Wither did in fact "find out" Rollenhagen's "meaning." I would suggest that Wither's comment—so often taken as a proof of his arbitrariness—makes little sense if taken as referring to the two hundred emblems by the one author Gabriel Rollenhagen, and that the plural "their meanings" sug-

gests that Wither is aware that the Rollenhagen emblems with their couplet *subscriptiones* often ultimately derive from others, and it is "their [original authors'] meanings" that he refuses to pursue. We may believe that Wither did not consult Sambucus, Simeoni, and Alciato, but he certainly understood in virtually every case the meaning of the emblematic *pictura,* which he almost always describes and interprets with care and precision, as I shall show. Against this apparent confession of carelessness must also be set the more sober statement of intention in one of the dedications. Writing in the dedication to Francis, Duchess Dowager of Richmond and Lennox in Book 3, he recommends his emblems to her as "A *Treasury* of Golden *Sentences*":

> . . . this humble *Offring,* here,
> Within your gracious presence, doth appeare.
> And, that it may the more content your eye,
> Well-graven *Figures,* help to beautifie
> My lowly *Gift*: And, vailed are in these,
> A *Treasury* of Golden *Sentences*;
> By my well-meaning Muse, interpreted.

Then there is the following apparently impatient statement in emblem 2,5:

> . . . little care I take
> Precisely to unfold our *Authors* mind;
> Or, on his meaning, *Comments* here to make.
> It is the scope of my Intention, rather
> From such perplext *Inventions* (which have nought
> Of Ancient *Hieroglyphick*) sense to gather
> Whereby some usefull *Morall* may be taught.

Freeman quotes this statement in support of her assertion that Wither "often treats [the meaning of the pictures] in a highly cavalier fashion" (p. 144). But Freeman offers a partial quotation shorn of its context. If we look carefully at the full statement, it would appear that Wither is saying something different. Wither makes this comment in the *subscriptio* to the emblem on the need for unity in the kingdom with its hieroglyphically stylized *pictura* of birds supporting a sceptre.[20] The statement follows his accurate description of the symbolic cluster, a description not present in the original:

> A *Crowned Sceptre,* here is fixt upright,
> Betwixt foure *Fowles,* whose postures may declare,
> They came from *Coasts,* or *Climats* opposite,
> And, that, they diffring in their natures are.

In her quotation, Freeman omits the next line and a half:

> In which, (as in some others, that we find
> Amongst these *Emblems*) . . .

This indicates that Wither is speaking of the present emblem and only "some others" i.e. not all the emblems. He is neither generalising, nor is he giving expression to the "airy dismissal of the original sense" of the emblem (Freeman, p. 144), but is addressing the question of the precise meaning of the "diffring . . . natures" of the four birds in this emblem. When Wither observes:

> . . . little care I take
> Precisely to unfold our *Authors* minde

he is referring to the meaning of the "diffring . . . natures" of the birds, about which he refuses to speculate. In fact, this is not unreasonable. By comparison with the original by Alciato, Rollenhagen, or his artist Crispin de Passe, had introduced significant alterations into the picture. Alciato created a complex motif using not birds of different kinds but one species, the crow, and Alciato did indeed base his emblem on a meaning regarded as inherent in these birds, namely their unity and harmony.[21] Although the engraving by Crispin de Passe is more elegant, it is inaccurate, however, if intended as a copy of the Alciato emblem. For whatever reason, de Passe replaced Alciato's crows with birds of different species[22] thus weakening the original symbolic meaning, and requiring a slightly different interpretation. For his part, Wither refuses "*Comments* here to make," but he is careful to apply the four different birds to four different kinds of citizens: "The *Rich*, the *Poore*, the *Swaine*, the *Gentleman*," summarized as "men of all Degrees."

Emblem 2,49, discussed earlier, featuring three interlocking crescent moons surmounted by a crown elicits from Wither the impatient comment:

> What in this *Emblem*, that mans meanings were,
> Who made it first, I neither know nor care;
> For, whatsoere, he purposed, or thought,
> To serve my *purpose*, now it shall be taught;

Rollenhagen's motto "Donec totu[m] impleat orbe[m]" [Till he replenish the whole world[23]] is a typically incomplete impresa motto, designed to be enigmatic, which is only partially explained in the epigram with its brief mention of the moon and the fame of the King of France. The motif is, in fact, an impresa for Henri II in his role as defender of the faith, as recorded in the impresa collections of Paradin and Typotius.[24] Unless one knows the identity of the bearer of an impresa and the occasion of its use, the meaning is usually obscure. It is hardly surprising that Wither, who evidently did not know the Paradin or Typotius collections, can make little sense of this. But then Wither looks more closely at the "knot of *Moones* (or *Crescents*)" and observes that it may illustrate a "Mystery"

> Of pious use (and, peradventure, such,
> As from old *Hieroglyphicks*, erres not much)

In sound biblical tradition he interprets the moon as the church, and in so doing converts an impresa into a religious emblem. Wither has, in fact, remained within a tradition of religious imagery, and the resulting emblem is anything but arbitrary.[25]

Elsewhere in *A Collection of Emblemes,* it is at times difficult for the modern reader to understand Wither's objection to the symbolic picture. Emblem 2,29, for example, features an open book surmounted by a winged heart from which smoke ascends towards a sun inscribed with the tetragrammaton. It is of a kind with many similar hieroglyphic combinations in the collection. Although Wither considers it mean, "vulgar" and defective, he none the less decides that it can "yield some *Fruit,* and shew a good *Intention.*" Once again, his interpretation is serious and reasonable.

The figure of Geryon, the three-bodied giant of Greek mythology, is represented in the Rollenhagen's emblem 2,45 by a crowned warrior with six arms, each bearing a different weapon. Wither does not seem to recognise the provenance of the figure, which he condemns as a "*Monster*" rather than a "*Hieroglyphicke*." He complains that he received

> These *Figures* (as you see them) ready made
> By others; and, I meane to *morallize*
> Their Fancies; not to mend what they devise.
>
> (3,45)

Wither then offers two plausible interpretations. The first focusses on the "*unconquerable strength*" of him who holds "*Faculties, or Friends*" together. The second is a moral statement urging that affections and sense obey reason. Wither then concludes with the observation that, although other readings are possible, his are certainly "good":

> If others thinke this *Figure,* here inferres
> A better sense; let those *Interpreters*
> Vnriddle it; and, preach it where they please:
> Their *Meanings* may be good, and so are these.

My final example has to do with Wither's doubts about what might be called the factual basis for emblem 3,49 which shows two men sawing through a tree against which an elephant leans. Wither explains that this was thought to be the means whereby elephants were trapped, but, he observes "on what grounds, I cannot tell." Although he evidently does not believe the fable, he is prepared to find a useful truth in it:

> Now, though the part *Historicall,* may erre,
> The *Morall,* which this *Emblem* doth inferre,
> Is overtrue . . .

He interprets the motif as meaning that the world is full of treachery, and he applies this general notion to the city, court and church.

These, then, are the critical comments that Wither makes in the preliminary matter and the two hundred emblems. As I hope to have shown, very few of these observations show a writer perplexed or exasperated; taken in context these comments do not introduce "ingenious analysis . . . [or] ideas that can be attached to the illustrations" (Moseley, p. 24), which would suggest an arbitrary treatment of the source emblems. It now remains to be seen whether Wither's actual practice is arbitrary.

Wither treated his Rollenhagen source emblems with considerable respect and attention, providing close, if expanded, translations of the Latin mottoes, and almost invariably incorporating into his epigrams an accurate description of the *pictura*. Rarely does he interpret the illustration without describing it.[26] Wither's normal procedure is to combine description with a general interpretation of meaning before making specific his application of the emblem to a particular theme or concern. This is normal emblematic practice. In his descriptions he invariably shows that he is aware of the Christian and classical traditions, sometimes erudite, which inform his source emblems. His identification of pictorial motif is especially careful when that complex is of classical origin. Emblem 2,10 features the dolphin entwined about an anchor for which Wither composed an interpretative motto:

> *If* safely, *thou desire to goe,*
> *Bee nor too* swift, *nor* overslow.

He describes and interprets the picture, providing a general authority for the motif combination in his opening lines:

> Ovr *Elders,* when their meaning was to shew
> A *native-speedinesse* (in Emblem wise)
> The picture of a *Dolphin-Fish* they drew;
> Which, through the waters, with great swiftnesse, flies.
> An *Anchor,* they did figure, to declare
> *Hope, stayednesse,* or a *grave-deliberation*:

Wither discusses the application of this in the rest of the epigram, leading up to a final couplet which sums up the meaning of the whole emblem echoing the motto and thereby effecting an impressive closure of the whole emblem:

> By *Speedinesse,* our works are timely wrought;
> By *Staydnesse,* they, to passe are, safely, brought.

A similar situation is encountered in the cornucopia emblem (2,26). The notion that "Good-fortune" will accompany "True-vertue" (motto of 2,26) is illustrated by two cornucopias encircling a caduceus. This complex might not have been readily understood by all of Wither's readers, but rather than displaying impatience or condescension, he explains the motifs, their meanings and even the technical terms with all the concern of a dedicated teacher:

> Marke, how the *Cornucopias,* here, apply
> Their *Plenties,* to the *Rod of Mercury*;

And (if it seeme not needlesse) learne, to know
This *Hieroglyphick's* meaning, ere you goe.
The *Sages* old, by this *Mercurian-wand*
(*Caduceus* nam'd) were wont to understand
Art, Wisdome, Vertue and what else we finde,
Reputed for endowments of the *Minde.*
The *Cornucopias,* well-knowne *Emblems,* are,
By which, great *wealth,* and *plenties,* figur'd were;
And (if you joyne together, what they spell)
It will, to ev'ry Vnderstanding, tell,
That, where *Internall-Graces* may be found,
Eternall-blessings, ever, will abound.

A further example of Wither's concern to offer the reader a helpful exegesis is found in the griffin emblem (3,5). The theme of virtue and fortune is the embodied in the difficult and complicated picture of a griffin with wings outstretched, surmounting a stone block chained to a winged sphere. Wither knows that he cannot appeal to the Book of Nature for the meaning of the griffin, and his observation shows an understanding of both allegorical and exegetical procedures:

> The *Griphon,* is the figure of a creature,
> Not found within the Catalogues of *Nature*:
> But, by those Wits created, who, to shew
> *Internall* things, *externall Figures* drew

The combination of bird and beast signifies "The *Vertues,* both of *Body,* and of *minde.*" After this general introduction Wither specifies the meanings of the individual motifs: the stone expresses the "firme abiding, and the solidnesse" of true virtues; the winged ball is "the gifts of changing *Fortune.*" But he knows that in fact material fortune is not always attendant upon virtue, and he concludes:

> But if we bide content, our worth is more;
> And rich we are, though others think us poore.

Wither bestows the same interpretative care on the theme of virtue and fortune endangered by envy, which in 2,39 is illustrated by the complex *pictura* of an eagle with outstretched wings surmounting a winged sphere set on a square altar and flanked on each side by a snake poised to strike. The confidant motto reads:

> *He needs not feare, what spight can doe,*
> *Whom* Vertue *friends, and* Fortune, *too.*

Wither's epigram opens with a general description of the "*Eaglet,*" "*Winged-ball,*" and "*Altar,*" and their meaning as representing wealth and virtue. He then makes those meanings more specific:

> My Iudgement, by that *Altar-stone,* conceives
> The sollidnesse, which, true *Religion* gives;
> And, that fast-grounded *goodnesse,* which, we see,
> In grave, and sound *Morality,* to be.
> The *Flying-ball,* doth, very well, expresse
> All *Outward-blessings,* and, their *fickleness.*
> Our *Eaglet,* meaneth such *Contemplatives,*

. . .

> The *Snakes,* may well resemble those, among them,
> Who, meerely out of *envie,* seek to wrong them;

Wither treats an emblem on wisdom in Book three with the same interpretative precision. Wisdom is embodied in the hieroglyphic combination of two snakes encircling a laurel tree (3,8). Again Wither describes and identifies the general meaning of laurel as "Glory," "renowne" and "*Wreaths* of *Honour,*" while the serpents are "WISDOME'S *Emblems.*" Their combination declares:

> That, *Wisdome* is the surest meanes to save
> Our Names and Actions, from *Oblivion*'s Grave.

Wither then suggests two more specific meanings for the wisdom of the snake, i.e. "*Morall-wit*" and "*Christian-policie,*" which again is not an arbitrary imposition of meaning on image, but rather represents a narrowing of the application of the general notion of wisdom:

> The *Snakes* are *two,* perhaps, to signifie
> That *Morall-wit,* and *Christian-policie*
> (Vnited both together) doe contrive
> The safest *guard,* and best *preservative.*

A spade surmounting a winged sphere set on a stone altar (4,31) bodies forth the notion encapsulated in the motto:

> A Fortune *is ordain'd for thee,*
> *According as thy* Labours *bee.*

Wither begins the epigram by identifying the spade with labour, the sphere with "*flitting-rowling-worldy-things*" and the altar with "Things firmer, sollid, and of greater worth." He expands on the application of the motif cluster to various situations in life and concludes with a prayer which implicitly activates the religious significance of the altar:

> To *worke-aright,* oh *Lord,* istruct thou mee;
> And, ground my *Workes,* and *buildings* all on thee:
> That, by the fiery *Test,* when they are tride,
> My *Worke* may stand, and I may *safe* abide.

This, then, is the final and specific application of the emblem which Wither has taken over from Rollenhagen, and again there is nothing arbitrary in his treatment of the material.

Wither's treatment of Fortuna (3,40) reveals the same concern to identify and interpret for his reader all her relevant attributes, including her blindness, nakedness, forelock, winged sphere and, hand-held moon. The only subjective or innovative comment is reserved for Fortuna's scarf blown back like a sail. He writes:

> A *Skarfe display'd by the wind,* she beares,
> (And, on her *naked Body,* nothing weares)

To shew, that what her *Favorite* injoyes,
Is not so much for *Vsefulnesse,* as *toyes.*

But there is no reason to label this arbitrary or a cavalier disregard for the source emblem.

One final emblem must stand for the scores of other examples that could be cited.[27] Emblem 4,40 depicts a notched wheel of Fortune with two cornucopias chained to a stone block. Both the Latin and English mottoes indicate that fate is the restraining influence. In the first line of his epigram Wither identifies the wheel with "*Fate,*" which he later insists is a function of "*God*'s Providence"; the movement of the wheel shows "That, some *waxe Poore,* as others *Wealthy* grow." The notches or "stops," as Wither calls them, are the obstacles "Which barre all those that unto *Wealth* aspire" such as "want of wit," sloth, pleasure, pride, and "Conscience."

The perception that Wither's interpretation of the Rollenhagen emblems is arbitrary is implied in the statement that he "used the picture as a starting point for ingenious analysis of its possible meaning . . . [and] expounds ideas that can be attached to the illustration" (Moseley, p. 24). And this mistaken view may derive from the fact that Wither not infrequently provides two or more different interpretations or applications of the general meaning associated with the visual symbols in the engraving. In Emblem 3,8 two snakes entwined about a laurel tree signifies the idea that wisdom secures lasting honour of noble deeds, which is the notion conveyed by Rollenhagen's couplet *subscriptio.* The fact that Wither suggests that the two snakes may signify "*Morall-wit,* and *Christian-policie*" is certainly the Englishman's addition, but since in *bonam partem* the snake can mean prudence and wisdom, Wither's specifications are hardly arbitrary.

Rollenhagen's emblem of Virtue strengthened through Unity, "Virtus unita fortior" (2,43) is illustrated by a bound sheaf of arrows which a bear cannot break apart. Wither likewise interprets the general sense as "That Safeguard, which is found in *Vnity,*" but he applies it firstly to "*Children of one Sire*" whose strife will be their undoing, and secondly more broadly to all humankind in a spiritual sense:

> For, wee are *Brethren* all; and (by a *Bloud*
> More precious, then our nat'rall *Brother-hood*).

The one application is a natural extension of the other, which has its authority in Scripture as Wither reminds the reader:

> The *Psalmist,* numerous *Off-springs,* doth compare
> To *Quivers,* that with *Shafts* replenish'd are.

In Rollenhagen's collection the leaky barrel is a warning against the untrustworthiness of the whore (2,88). Wither writes a new English motto which makes a more general statement:

The Tongue, *which every secret speakes,*
Is like a Barrell *full of leakes.*

(4,38)

Wither begins his epigram with a reiteration of that general message about the "babling *Tongue*" and later narrows its application to the "trustlesse nature of a *whorish woman,*" which can hardly be considered arbitrary or something he attached to the original since it in fact derives from Rollenhagen's epigram.

In several cases Wither applies a general emblematic meaning to three or more situations. Emblem 1,15 depicts branches consumed by fire and smoke on an altar. In feeding the flame the wood, i.e. the "*Nourisher,*" is consumed. Wither applies this to parents who support "thriftlesse *Children* in unlawfull *Pleasures,*" to "such *Wantons* as doe feede / Vnchaste Desires," and to those who and further the careers of ungrateful men, to good statesmen who secure a thankless commonwealth, and to those who devote their life and health to study only to become "helps to other men." The fact that Rollenhagen does not make the application of the emblematic motif precise beyond the notion of self-sacrifice does not make Wither's interpretation in any sense arbitrary.

A similar situation is encountered in many emblems and one last example must stand for many.[28] Emblem 2,6 showing the wind enflaming a lighted torch embodies a similar warning, which is expressed in Wither's English motto as follows:

From that, by which I somewhat *am,*
The Cause of my Destruction *came.*

Self-inflicted destruction is the general interpretation which Wither firstly applies broadly:

Thus fares it, in a Thousand other things,
As soone as they the *golden Meane* exceed; . . .

He then refers this to successful men who leave virtue behind in the climb upwards; secondly to those who grow wealthy and whose riches then make them uncharitable and "hard-hearted"; then finally to those whose love becomes a physical obsession. I can see no reason to label "arbitrary" such an exercise in the application of a general statement to specific situations.

Wither's treatment of the classical content of Rollenhagen's *picturæ* bespeaks both care and understanding. He takes pains to explain to his readers some of the classical stories alluded to by a symbolic motif. A case in point is the Ixion emblem (2,7) used as a warning to "*Guilty men.*" In a few lines Wither refers to the myth according to which the ungrateful Ixion coveted Zeus' wife Hera (Wither refers to her as "Juno") and thought to possess her, only to find that Zeus had

tested his intentions by creating a cloud in the likeness of Hera (Juno). For his treacherous and attempted adultery Ixion was perpetually bound to a flaming wheel. Wither writes:

To gaine a lawlesse favour he desired,
And, in his wicked hopes beguiled was:
For, when to claspe with *Iuno,* he aspired,
Instead of her, a *Clowd,* he did embrace.
He, likewise, did incurre a dreadfull *Doome,* . . .

In similar manner Wither briefly recounts the story of Ganymede in the opening lines of emblem 3,22, insisting that although this is a fable it none the less contains a "*Reall truth,*" which he interprets in terms of the Christian doctrine of the purification and regeneration of the soul through baptism:

Though this be but a *Fable,* of their ["Poets"] feigning,
The *Morall* is a *Reall truth,* pertayning
To ev'ry one . . .
By *Ganymed,* the *Soule* is understood,
That's washed in the *Purifying flood*
Of sacred *Baptisme* (which doth make her seem
Both pure and beautifull, in *God*'s esteeme).
The *Ægle,* meanes that Heav'nly *Contemplation,*
Which, after Washings of *Regeneration,*
Lifts up the *Minde,* from things that earthly bee,
To view those *Objects,* which *Faith*'s Eyes doe see.

Wither treats certain other fables in a similar manner.[29]

His understanding of the Rollenhagen emblems and his acquaintance with classical traditions is also evidenced by the references he makes to classical figures and motifs which are never mentioned in his sources. Wither expands on the motif of Diana the huntress by renaming her Cynthia (1,24). As noted above, he tells the story of Ixion's attempted rape of Juno which was never alluded to in the source (2,7). In an emblem on royal power Wither refers to Alexander and Caesar (2,16). The importance of learning is demonstrated by an owl which Wither names "the Bird of *Athens*" and in this context he discusses knowledge, studies and the "Academ" (2,17). Learning is also the subject of 2,25 where Wither calls the moon "horned *Cynthia*" and holds up Cato as exemplary. Wither names Mars and Pallas in his English motto and epigram to 2,18, Pegasus and Bucephalus in 2,43, Janus in 3,4, Appelles' table in 3,14, Styx and Acheron in 3,18, Phoebus in 3,25, Titan in 4,1 Alexander and, by implication, Diogenes in 4,14, and Apollo in 4,26. None of these is particularly erudite, but none the less they can hardly be regarded as household terms for the uneducated London reader who is often thought to constitute the audience for the book.

Wither evidently has some readers in mind who will understand these classical references, and such technical terms as "tetragrammaton" (2,29 and 4,33). In some emblems he appears to expect the reader to understand Latin. With such phrases as "words inclosing" (4,31)[30] he also occasionally refers to the engraved Latin mottoes, which presupposes that some readers would be able to understand them.

The perception that Wither's emblems are arbitrary, and often self-consciously so, appears related to some assumptions about his intended readership. Again Wither's comments in the introduction have supported the view that he had an uneducated, lower middle class reader in mind. In his dedication to King Charles and Queen Henrietta Maria he says that his emblems will profit "vulgar Iudgements" (fol *3r) and "common Readers" ("To the Reader," A1r, A2r). These phrases also re-appear in some emblem epigrams.

There is, however, an economic consideration that argues against the assumption that the lower middle class of London merchants are the prospective purchasers. With its large folio format, 200 copperplate engravings on finely ruled pages, and final lottery with volvelles, *A Collection of Emblemes* was the most costly emblem book ever produced to that date in England. It would have been beyond the means of members of the lower middle class. That this expensive book was something of a collector's piece is suggested by the fact that over 70 copies are known to have survived. It was evidently a prized possession.

But what was the audience for this book?[31] This is a complex question which I can only begin to address here. Perhaps the most useful approach is to look for different kinds of evidence in the text. As I have shown, Wither's use of classical allusion, often with no parallel in his source and at times exceeding the requirements of the *picturae*, suggests an educated, though not erudite readership, as does the occasional reference to the Latin mottoes, which the reader is assumed to understand. The mere fact that Wither carefully identifies the symbolic motifs in the engravings does not of itself prove that the author had a classically illiterate readership in mind. Even Alciato has some epigrams with descriptions of motifs. We must always bear in mind that, unlike an Alciato, Wither proceeded from the complete tripartite emblem which included an engraving. But this is not to say that *A Collection of Emblemes* is an academic book aiming to impress with its erudition court and intelligentsia. There are no scholarly marginalia and apparatus, no name dropping as with Ben Jonson and Thomas Heywood,[32] who both parade their learning.

Although he makes no display of learning, Wither is clearly in touch with the humanistic and Christian traditions that inform the emblems that he appropriated from Rollenhagen. This becomes evident in the manner in which he identifies and describes accurately the motifs, their uses and properties, and attendant meanings.

Wither was certainly courting the influential albeit not through the parade of erudition. He dedicated the first of the four books to the King Charles and Queen Henrietta Maria, the second to Charles, Prince of Wales and his brother James, Duke of York, the third to Frances, Duchess-Dowager of Richmond and Lennox and her nephew, James, Duke of Lennox, and the fourth to Philip, Earl of Pembroke and Henry, Earl of Holland. In one emblem Wither expresses the hope that the king will "shine" upon him:

> Vouchsafe to shine on Mee, my Gracious King,
> And then my Wither'd Leaves, will freshly spring.
>
> (3,25)

This and other evidence suggests that Wither had a broader readership in mind than has been recognised so far, a socially and educationally mixed audience.

This reconsideration of the arbitrariness of Wither's emblems, although based on an analysis of Wither's use Rollenhagen's texts and engravings, has also touched on questions of author intention as well as reader reception. These are large and complex issues that await a fuller treatment, and that holds true for most emblem books not only Wither's.

By way of summary, I would say that Wither does very occasionally show some impatience with the source emblems, and he even criticizes the factual basis for one or two motifs. He can show also a certain independence of mind with regard to the sources. But, as I hope to have shown, these are rare occurrences that have been exaggerated by some critics and misinterpreted by others. The closer one reads Wither's emblems, especially in conjunction with their direct and indirect sources, the less one is prepared to accept Freeman's judgements, and the more skeptical one becomes about taking Wither's authorial pronouncements at face value. Authorial statements must always be compared with actual practice, and emblem writers are no exception to this rule. It is clear from his accurate identification and interpretation of complex emblematic and hieroglyphic motifs that Wither knew and understood the tradition in which the Rollenhagen emblems stand. His ready citation of classical names, where these are absent in the originals, bespeaks a comfortable acquaintance with classical traditions. Some of the formulations and apparently off-hand remarks in his epigrams must be seen as rhetorical and educational strategies. It must always remembered that Wither had a mixed readership in mind, as well as a moral and religious purpose.

Notes

1. See, Richard Cavell, "Representative Writing: The Emblem as (Hiero)glyph" in *The European Emblem: Selected Papers from the Glasgow Confer-*

ence, 11-14 August, 1987, ed. Bernhard F. Scholz, Michael Bath and David Weston (Leiden, New York, Copenhagen and Cologne: Brill, 1990), pp. 167-185. I tend to agree with the reviewer who wrote that Cavell's "post-Derridean musings . . . seem to me to add very little to the insights of the numerous authors he quotes. I would have been more interested in an expansion of his remarks on what Wither does with Rollenhagen's emblem pictures" (*Emblematica,* 5 forthcoming). He only devotes two pages to Wither's practise as emblem writer.

2. See Michael Bath's "Introduction" to the new facsimile reprint edition of Wither's *A Choice of Emblemes* (Aldershot: Scolar Press, 1989).

3. Rosemary Freeman, *English Emblem Books* (1948; rpt. London: Chatto & Windus, 1967), pp. 235-236.

4. Irma Tramer, *Studien zu den Anfängen der puritanischen Emblem-literatur in England: Andrew Willet—George Wither.* Diss. Berlin, 1934.

5. Elsewhere Freeman refers to the Rollenhagen emblems as "old fashioned" (p. 142).

6. Alan R. Young, "Thomas Heywood's Pageants: New Forms of Evidence," *RORD,* 30 (1988), 129-148, and *His Majesty's Royal Ship. A Critical Edition of Thomas Heywood's "A True Description" (1637)* (New York: AMS Press, 1990).

7. Peter M. Daly and Mary V. Silcox, *The English Emblem: Bibliography of Secondary Literature,* Corpus Librorum Emblematum (Munich, London, New York, Paris: K. G. Saur, 1990), and Peter M. Daly and Mary V. Silcox, *The Modern Critical Reception of the English Emblem,* Corpus Librorum Emblematum (Munich, London, New York, Paris: K. G. Saur), forthcoming.

8. See also 1,43.

9. "George Wither suggests just this multivalency, in his flat footed way, in the exasperated response to the cut he took over from Rollenhagen as No. XLIX of Book 2 . . ." Charles Moseley, "Introduction" to *A Century of Emblems. An Introductory Anthology* (Aldershot: Scolar Press, 1989), n. 22. However, in the same book Moseley offers quite a different interpretation of the same comment by Wither: "His comments on the difficulty of interpretation illustrate one aspect of the intellectual appeal of the emblem, and his reference to 'Hieroglyphicks' . . . reminds us of its authority" (p. 225). Moseley's comment applies more to the humanistically-schooled reader of Rollenhagen than it does to Wither's epigram.

10. Claude Paradin, *Devises heroiques* (first ed. Lyons, 1551).

11. See his "Introduction" to the new facsimile reprint edition by Scolar Press, 1989.

12. "Der Fragmentcharakter emblematischer Auslegungen und die Rolle des Lesers. Gabriel Rollenhagens Epigramme," in *Deutsche Barocklyrik,* ed. Martin Bircher and Alois M. Haas (Bern & Munich: Francke, 1973), pp. 49-64.

13. Albrecht Schöne, *Emblematik und Drama im Zeitalter des Barock* (Stuttgart: Beck, 1964, 2nd ed. 1968).

14. Dietrich Walter Jöns, *Das "Sinnen-Bild." Studien zur allegorischen Bildlichkeit bei Andreas Gryphius* (Stuttgart: Metzler, 1966).

15. See especially Wolfgang Harms' overview article "Emblem / Emblemtik" in *Theologische Realenzyklopädie,* vol. 9 (Berlin and New York: de Gruyter, 1982), 552-58.

16. Carsten-Peter Warncke, *Sprechende Bilder—sichtbare Worte,* "Wolfenbüttler Forschungen," vol. 33 (Wiesbaden: Otto Harrassowitz, 1987).

17. See Peter M. Daly, *Emblem Theory. Recent German Contributions to the Characterization of the Emblem Genre* (Nendeln: Kraus Thomson Organization, 1979) and *Literature in the Light of the Emblem. Structural Parallels between the Emblem and Literature in the Sixteenth and Seventeenth Centuries* (Toronto: University of Toronto Press, 1979).

18. The whole question of background scenes, which could also contribute to this re-assessment of arbitrariness, deserves separate treatment.

19. "Es läßt sich jedoch beweisen, daß Wither Rollenhagens Text, obwohl er ihn verschweigt, gekannt und zum Teil benutzt hat" (p. 34).

20. For a discussion of the Alciato emblem on which Rollenhagen's emblem is based, see Peter M. Daly, "Alciato's Emblem 'Concordiae symbolum': A Medusa's Mirror for Rulers?" *German Life and Letters,* 44 (1988), 349-362.

21. An indication of the many editions carrying this motif forward will be found in Daly, "Alciato's Emblem 'Concordiae symbolum': A Medusa's Mirror for Rulers?" (see note 20 above).

22. Curiously, the art historian Carsten-Peter Warncke misidentifies the four birds as crows, although one has a long beak foreign to the crow family. See his facsimile edition of Rollenhagen, p. 120. Also discussing the pre-history of the motif, he fails to

mention the most immediate Alciato source, which is one of the editions printed by Christian Wechel in Paris or his imitators.

23. The translation is by P. S. as it appears in his edition *The Heroicall Devises of M. Claudius Paradin* (London, 1591).

24. Claude Paradin, *Devises heroiques* (first ed. Lyons, 1551), translated by P. S. as *The Heroicall Devises of M. Claudius Paradin* (London, 1591) and Jacob Typotius *Symbola divina et humana* (Prague, 1601-1603).

25. A similar situation will be encountered in 4,40 where Wither appears to complain impatiently of the original meaning intended for the motif of two cornucopias tied to a wheel of fortune:

> For, whatsoere their *Autors* understood,
> These *Emblems,* now, shall speake as I thinke good.

But the resulting descriptions and interpretations are not arbitrary.

26. Among the rare instances are the following: 3,36 and 4,15,

27. The following epigrams identify and interpret the visual motifs: 1,2 1,5, 1,6, 1,9, 1,24, 1,30, 1,39, 1,43, 1,45, 1,47, 2,4, 2,5, 2,6, 2,7, 2,20, 2,21, 2,24, 2,29, 2,32, 2,33, 2,35, 2,37, 2,38, 2,41, 2,43, 2,47, 2,48, 2,49, 3,1, 3,2, 3,3, 3,4, 3,6, 3,10, 3,11, 3,12, 3,13, 3,14, 3,15, 3,16, 3,17, 3,18, 3,20, 3,21, 3,23, 3,25, 3,27, 3,29, 3,30, 3,32, 3,34, 3,35, 3,41, 3,42, 3,43, 3,48, 3,49, 4,1, 4,2, 4,5, 4,6, 4,7, 4,11, 4,12, 4,13, 4,16, 4,18, 4,19, 4,20, 4,21, 4,24, 4,25, 4,27, 4,28, 4,32, 4,33, 4,35, 4,36, 4,37, 4,40, 4,41, 4,46.

28. See also 1,11, 1,18, 1,20, 3,31, 3,41, 4,3, 4,11, 4,21, 4,28, 4,44, 4,45.

29. For instance, he narrates the story of a crow putting stones in water pot to get water (2,2) and a fool with goslings (4,17).

30. See also 4,27: "And, by the *Words* about it, wee are taught / *To keep our latter ending still in thought.*"

31. The only attempt to investigate Wither's emblems in the light of his intended readership was undertaken by Wolfgang Harms in an essay which contrasts Rollenhagen's brief epigrams with Wither's 30-line "illustrations." Unlike Joachim Camerarius and Jan David, Rollenhagen does not provide full information on the tradition of the emblem and its intended meaning; rather, the knowledgeable reader receives but an indication through some key words ["Stichworte"]. Wither has a different reader in mind and a different purpose. Harms notes that the brevity of Rollenhagen's epigrams

is striking when one considers that they appeared at a time when the tendency was to expand the textual parts of the emblem. Rather than interpreting this brevity as an indication of enigmatic intention, Harms argues convincingly that Rollenhagen counted on the intellectual activity of the reader. His mottoes and epigrams are closely interwoven, but more importantly, the background scenes in the *picturae* provide clues, one might say glosses, on the meaning of the emblem as a whole.

32. Heywood's *Hierarchie of Blessed Angels* is likewise a large, illustrated, folio work but full of allusions and references to learned authorities, which include Alciato and Valeriano.

Alan R. Young (essay date 1999)

SOURCE: Young, Alan R. "Jacobean Authority and Peacham's Manuscript Emblems." In *Deviceful Settings: The English Renaissance Emblem and Its Contexts,* edited by Michael Bath and Daniel Russell, pp. 33-53. New York: AMS Press, 1999.

[*In the following essay, Young considers how Peacham's emblems for James I reveal the monarch's use of the image to establish authority. Young contends that Peacham's emblematic treatment of James's* Basilikon Doron *played a role in furthering the absolutist ideology from which the king drew his power.*]

Jonathan Goldberg recently argued that with the accession of King James I of England a significant change occurred in the nature of regal authority in England. Though delayed by an outbreak of plague, James I's first triumphal entry into London on 15 March 1604 established a new order. The new king offered "not simply an image of his power, but," as Goldberg puts it, "the power of himself as image," all within an absolutist context. Where Queen Elizabeth at her entry in 1559, some forty-five years earlier, had participated in the event by making impromptu speeches, smiling, offering courteous gestures, studying the devices, and reacting to their meaning, James remained distant and silent and displayed no apparent response to the pageants. As one of James's early biographers explained, the king "endured the days brunt with *patience,* being assured he should never have such another. . . . But afterwards in his *publick* appearances . . . the accesses of the people made him so impatient, that he often dispersed them with *frowns,* that we may not say with *curses.*"[1]

This was a new order, a new relationship between monarch and people and a new version of regal authority, one based upon an absolutist ideology that was expressed in many details of the seven highly emblematic triumphal arches created for James's entry. Goldberg's controversial but much-praised book examines, among other things, some of the visual media through which the absolutist image was disseminated during James's reign: triumphal arches, portraits, painted ceilings, masques, engraved title pages, architecture, and coins.[2] Though recognizing the role of the emblematic in representations of authority and in the establishment of that authority, Goldberg does not examine emblems *per se*. This is perhaps a pity since, as Wolfgang Harms has so effectively argued, the emblem carried its own special version of literary authority during the Renaissance: "Emblems contained truth, revealed truth or promised to make truth understandable." Since, according to the Divine Plan (or so the Renaissance view would have it), "all things and all events had been given their meaning which then had only to be revealed . . . understanding the meaning of the world is also the basis of the authority of emblematics from the late sixteenth century to the early eighteenth century."[3] As Daniel Russell has suggested, emblems derived further authority from their supposed relationship with hieroglyphics, these latter being, according to Ficino's reading of Plotinus's discussion of them, "symbolic entities that mediated between the human intellect and divine ideas, providing insight into the very essence of things and illustrating the dynamic process of divine thought."[4] Though, in practice, hieroglyphics may have had little influence on the actual making of emblems, "the ideal that they represented to the Renaissance humanists," as Russell points out, "did have an impact on the justification of the emblem."[5] The insistence of humanists on equating their emblems with ancient hieroglyphs derived from that general desire to seek for classical antecedents as part of a quest for imagined origins.[6] However, another way for us to understand this phenomenon would be to perceive the importance attached to hieroglyphics as being a means of establishing authority by implying a relationship of the emblem with an inherited form of expression and with an established tradition of meaning. The emblem, then, may be considered as an obvious choice—a double-barrelled one, if you like—for an artist wishing to secure regal authority for the new king through a medium that itself is imbued with authority.[7]

In what follows, I wish to explore Goldberg's general hypothesis concerning James I (and indirectly that of Harms concerning emblems) by examining some selected emblems of Henry Peacham that were composed very early in James's reign and were designed to be presented to the newly-crowned King.

Best known to emblem scholars for his printed emblem book (*Minerva Britanna*, 1612), Peacham was a schoolmaster in Kimbolton, Huntingdonshire, when James VI of Scotland began his spectacular progress south to be crowned James I of England in July 1603. In the course of his journey, James stayed at Hinchingbrooke Priory, Sir Oliver Cromwell's residence in Huntingdon. There, he was given an extravagant welcome and was also addressed by the heads of Cambridge University, from which Peacham had recently graduated. During James's two-day stay at Hinchingbrooke, Peacham presented one or two of his emblems to the King, and it was probably on this occasion that James Montagu, first Master of the newly-founded Sidney Sussex College, encouraged Peacham to turn James's recently-published *Basilikon Doron* into emblems.

James's book had been written and privately published (in an edition of only seven copies) as an educational treatise for his young son Prince Henry in 1599. It was reissued in a public version "within an hour" of his becoming King of England, and its re-publication so quickly after Queen Elizabeth's death was reported by Giovanni Carlo Scaramelli, Venetian Secretary in England, in a dispatch dated 24 April 1603.[8] James stayed at Hinchingbrooke from 27 to 29 April, so copies of *Basilikon Doron* may well have reached Huntingdon before him. Peacham mentions his first meeting with James I and the encouragement he received from Montagu in the dedication to James in the manuscript emblem book to be discussed below (p. 38). Not only did the Edinburgh printer Robert Waldegrave bring out a new edition, but half a dozen or so editions appeared in London, the book having been entered on the Stationers' Register on 28 March. In addition, there were editions in Latin, French, German, and Dutch that same year. Peacham clearly had access to an edition in English (probably not that of Waldegrave) but which is uncertain.[9] Whether he knew it at the time or not, Peacham's choice of the emblem as a medium was an apt one; James himself had been "in his yonger years" a composer of emblems, had taken "great delight, and pleasure" in the art.[10] In his preface "To the Reader" in *Minerva Britanna* (1612) Peacham recalled some of the emblems of James's Scottish forebears but then remarked: "Many and very excellent have I seene of his *Maiesties* owne Invention, who hath taken therein in his yonger years great delight, and pleasure, . . ."[11] It is also known that James was himself the owner of a number of emblem books.[12]

In enthusiastic pursuit of Montagu's suggestion, Peacham first composed a manuscript emblem book of fifty-six emblems,[13] divided into three books corresponding to the three-part division of *Basilikon Doron*. This latter had been addressed by James to his son, Prince Henry, offering him advice on religion, politics, and moral behaviour. In his emblem book, Peacham placed a quotation from James's work at the foot of each page.[14] Above this appeared a four-line Latin epigram, a pen-and-ink drawing, and a Latin motto. Often, relevant

"Fowling for partridges," from Henry Peacham's Minerva Britanna *(1612).*

quotations from the Bible, the Church Fathers, or the Classics were added.[15] Though dedicated to Prince Henry, this version seems not to have been presented to the Prince,[16] but later, in 1610, a revised and expanded version with coloured drawings did reach the Prince's hands.[17] My concern here, however, is with a third manuscript, one dedicated to James and dating, as far as one can tell, from shortly after 20 October 1604.[18] It is now in the British Library and is known as MS. Harleian 6855, Art. 13. From internal evidence, it would appear that this work is a draft of another now lost manuscript that Peacham did indeed present to the King.[19] Though it employs many of the same emblems to be found in the earlier draft manuscript for Prince Henry (Bodleian Library, MS. Rawlinson poetry 146) it departs from its predecessor in placing great emphasis upon the theme of Anglo-Scottish union, a matter dear to the King's heart from the very beginning of his reign,[20] and one very much in people's minds late in 1604 when the matter was under vigorous discussion by a rather sceptical Parliament.[21] That, through James, Great Britain could come into being and the fabled sov-

ereign unity of ancient times could be restored was a key aspect of his authority, and one he himself nourished. Cautious not to stress his descent from the Catholic Mary Queen of Scots, whom his predecessor had executed as a traitor, James preferred his new subjects to look back in the direction of his great-great-grandfather, the Tudor Henry VII.[22] The Tudors, furthermore, had encouraged the myth that their dynasty could claim descent from the supposed original British, the Trojans, and when James made his official entry into London (Troynovant) in 1604, he was hailed as a second Trojan Brutus. By uniting Britain, he was also helping to bring about the fulfilment of the myth of a new Roman empire rising in the West. His would be a new age that would, like that of Augustus and in keeping with the prophecies in Virgil, lead to a time of untold peace and prosperity.[23]

Peacham's emblematic symbolism, together with the ways in which it contributes to James's authority, often appears to echo that employed on the various triumphal arches erected for James's 1604 entry on March 15. Inevitably, one wonders whether Peacham was present in London for the occasion, or whether he purchased or had access to any of the three publications memorializing the event: Stephen Harrison's *Arches of Triumph* (1604) Thomas Dekker's *The Magnificent Entertainment Given to King James* (1604) and Ben Jonson's *His Part of King James his Royall and Magnificent Entertainment* (1604).[24] MS. Harleian 6855, Art 13, for example, contained a number of emblems that are largely heraldic in nature and thereby make use of yet another mode of authority—the official, sanctioned symbolism of the armorial code. The visual language of heraldry is a means of establishing identity and status, as well as a pedigree of descent, dynastic alliances achieved through marriage, and inherited ancestral marks of honour. Through heraldry, James's claim to sovereignty could be asserted, and his role in the creation of British unity could be clearly expressed, something very evident in the seven triumphal entry arches, which employed a great deal of heraldic symbolism. The first arch at Fenchurch, for example, contained the new royal arms. These added the harp of Ireland to the third quarter,[25] placed the old Tudor arms (i. e. the lions of England and the fleurs-de-lys of France quartered) in the first and fourth quarters, and added the red lion of Scotland in the second quarter.[26] On the arch these arms were situated to the right (the viewer's left) of the figure of Monarchia Britannica, who occupied the highest position on the arch. On the Gracechurch Street arch above the royal arms, which have James's new heraldic supporters, a lion for England and a unicorn for Scotland,[27] was depicted the seated figure of Henry VII passing his sceptre to a mounted James, thereby signifying the latter's Tudor ancestral link and his consequent claim to the English throne.[28] On the arch at Fleet Street were personifications of James's four kingdoms (England, Scotland, Ireland, France) each personification holding the appropriate heraldic shield, and on the final arch at Temple Bar in a prominent position at the top, were once more displayed the royal arms. Less overt was the central conceit employed in the design of another arch. Referring to the heraldic badge of the phoenix, so favoured by Elizabeth,[29] the Nova Faelix Arabia arch at Cheapside was designed to welcome James as the emergent phoenix that had arisen from the pyre of the former phoenix (Elizabeth). James's arrival now made Britain the New Arabia Felix.[30]

If this seems a somewhat prolonged prelude to a discussion of the manuscript emblem book that Peacham dedicated to James I, it is because Peacham's version of James's *Basilikon Doron* is closely related not only to its most direct source, James's book for his son, but also (though not exclusively) to the iconography and themes of James's triumphal entry. The heraldic symbolism and the prominence given to the theme of British unity provide the most obvious examples of the relationship (coincidental or deliberate) between Peacham's presentation gift to James,[31] and the 1604 triumphal arches. It is therefore with some examples of Peacham's heraldic emblems that I begin.

Most of the heraldic emblems in Peacham's gift to James occur at the beginning of Book II of the three Books that make up the manuscript, and they appear to have no direct source in James's *Basilikon Doron*.[32] They are anticipated by the emblem that separates Books I and II. This has no motto and, unique to his manuscript, its verses are in English (they are entitled "An Epigramme vpon this union"). The *pictura* consists of James's royal arms surmounted by a crown, on either side of which sit winged *putti* who each hold a rose and a thistle, heraldic devices representing England and Scotland respectively. The epigram below comments upon the origin and significance of each detail of the arms. Of the fleurs-de-lys, for example, Peacham says, "France showes the armes but wee ye King," while all the quarters of the armorial shield combine "the full confort to make." Not mentioned, however, are the *putti*'s flowers, the rose/thistle combination being an heraldic device that from the first was frequently used as an expression of the new unity of the two kingdoms and was developed further by Peacham in the sixth emblem of Book II, which depicts a rather incongruous clump of thistles and roses growing together and being watered by a hand extended from Heaven above. The accompanying motto, "Quem plantavi irrigabo" [That which I planted I will water] derives from 1 Corinthians 3.6 ("I have planted, Apollo's watered; but God gave the increase"). The epigram for II.6 makes clear the theme of unity and the divinely sanctioned role James plays in its achievement:

> Cyprigenae, agrorum decus ille, haec sacra puellae,
> Carduus unanimes & rosa verna virent;
> Quae gelidus coelo foecundans imber ab alto,
> Vult omen regnis (summe Iacobe) tuis.[33]

The eight heraldic emblems that appear at the beginning of Book II depict the English and Scottish lions jointly supporting an imperial crown; the phoenix; the portcullis; the fleurs-de-lys; the crowned lion with sword and sceptre; the thistles and roses; the Scottish unicorn with banner of St. Andrew; and the arms of the Duke of Lennox, because they show an example of another unification of separate kingdoms. Book II, Emblem II, may suffice as an example of Peacham's method. It has the motto "Omine meliore renascor" [I rise again with a better omen] and its *pictura* shows a crowned phoenix upon a tree stump, from which sprouts a sprig of what may be red and white roses.[34] The bird holds a sceptre in its right claw. The epigram speaks of the sad loss of the British phoenix (Elizabeth) and of the sudden rising again of the newborn phoenix (James) and its grasping of the sceptre, while proud Rome with its eagles lies prostrate:

Ut fato est visus Phoenix cessise Britannus
Angliaq[ue] infando victa dolore gemit;
Arripit enascens subito, novus iste favillis
Sceptra, iaces aquilis Roma superba tuis.[35]

As already pointed out, the heraldic significance of the phoenix was employed for the Nova Arabia Felix arch to assert James's claim to sovereignty in succession to Elizabeth and, more forcefully, to allude to the authority that derived from the King's uniqueness. At the foot of Peacham's page is a note which acknowledges that both Anne Boleyn and her daughter, Queen Elizabeth, used the symbol of the phoenix. The emblem also alludes to the Protestant triumph of James's accession, the Roman eagles being the frustrated hopes of the Roman church.[36] However, a pervasive image throughout James's entry to London and other literature and art designed to glorify him is that of James as a second Caesar Augustus, whose arrival heralds a new age of peace and plenty. Peacham's epigram is ambiguous in that it may also be read as suggesting that the stature of James as ruler is even greater than that of the rulers of ancient Rome.

The final heraldic emblem I wish to mention here is that which has pride of place at the conclusion of Book III of Peacham's manuscript. It occurs in neither of the other *Basilikon Doron* emblem books, nor does it appear in an anglicized form in *Minerva Britanna*. Based on a device Peacham found in Paradin's *Devises heroiques* (first published in 1551) the emblem has the special dedication "Ad Angliam de foedere & unione Britannica" [To England on the occasion of the British Agreement and Union]. Beneath the motto ("Tutissima inter pares unitas" [A union of equals is safest]) Peacham depicted the chivalric insignia of the French Order of St. Michael. This consists of a circular collar or chain made up of sea-shells interspersed with knots. From this is suspended a pendant depicting St. Michael. The connection with the theme of unity is supplied by Paradin, who explains that the invincible and indissoluble union among members of the order is signified by the double lacing that joins the shells together,[37] a point alluded to in Peacham's marginal note. In Peacham's epigram, there is a plea for unity following James's accession. An appended distich is even stronger, stating that under the auspices of the godlike James the golden age will return to British lands.[38] But this is no mere pious wish of the emblematist, since the entire concept is shown to have derived directly from the words of the "godlike James" himself, whose *Basilikon Doron* is quoted below:

So that even as in the times of our auncestors the long warres and many bloody battles betwixt these twoo Countries bred a natural and haereditary hatred in every of them, against ye other, the vniting and welding of them heereafter into one, by all sort of frendship commerce and alliaunce, will by the contrary produce, and maintaine a naturall and inseperable vnity of loue amongst them.

(*Basilikon Doron,* Book 3, p. 149, as quoted by Peacham)

A quite different type of emblem, though it employs an adaptation of a heraldic device, is that which begins the Harleian manuscript as well as both the other manuscript emblem books and *Minerva Britanna*.[39] Beneath the motto "Nisi desuper" [Only from above] is depicted a hand reaching down from the heavens and holding a chain which supports a crown. The epigram reveals that the chain is what links James to the right hand of God, who made James both a king and a man with authority ("imperio").[40] The idea of the double chain attached to the crown ("en duplici vinctum diadema catena") in part derives from the "double obligation" described as owed to God by a king in the quotation from *Basilikon Doron* (Book I, p. 2) that Peacham provides below. The King has a double obligation to God, "first for that hee made you a man, next for that hee made you a little God to sit on his throne, and rule over other men." Peacham thus in his first emblem establishes James's authority by signifying that James's crown is held by divine right and derives from divine will.[41] Furthermore, however, that authority in relationship to James's subjects is that of "a little God," who, according to the epigram, is aloft and far from the world of man ("procul a nostro").[42] That James did indeed see himself in this way and spoke as *verbum dei,* employing the style of gods (see Goldberg [1983] 26) is tellingly illustrated in James's sonnet that prefaces his *Basilikon Doron*. The opening lines state:

God giues not Kings the stile of *Gods* in vaine,
For on his throne his Scepter doe they swey:
And as their subiects ought them to obey,
So Kings should feare and serue their God againe.

After detailing the virtues required in a king, the final couplet says:

And so ye shall in Princely vertues shine
Resembling right your mightie King Diuine.[43]

In *The Trve Lawe of Free Monarchies* (Edinburgh, 1598) James had maintained that "Kings are called *Gods* by the propheticall King DAVID, because they sit vpon his throane in the earth" (sig. B3^r).[44] Peacham's rhetoric and iconography may thus be seen as carefully constructed to mirror this self-image of authority.

In parallel with motifs in the triumphal entry that presented James as a new Brutus, or (if only by implication) as a second Augustus, are a number of other emblems in Peacham's manuscript. Book II, Emblem XI, is one example. The emblem is specifically dedicated as a sacred gift to the most upright King James ("Iacobo piissimo Regi sacrum"). Beneath the motto ("Ex utroque immortalitas" [Immortality in both directions]) is portrayed a tomb upon which is a sceptre and branches of laurel and olive.[45] The inscription on the tomb clearly alludes to James: "D:I:S:A: BB M:" ("Dis ac bonis bene merentibus" [To the gods and good persons deserving well]).[46] The epigram addressed to James states that his upright qualities, memorable through all the ages, will carry him as far as the star of immortal Caesar.[47] Even before death, then, James's immortality is to be celebrated alongside that of Caesar. What is more, as the epigram explains, with his death will die justice, devotion to country, and the peace that is now enjoyed in distant places.[48] Here, Peacham provides a vision of even higher authority than that provided by James's original *Basilikon Doron*, which merely states:

> . . . a good King (after a happie and a famous reigne) dieth in peace lamented by his subiectes & admired by his neighbours and leaving a reverent renowne behind him on death, obtaineth ye Crowne of eternal foelicity in heaven.
>
> (*Basilikon Doron*, Book II, p. 26, as quoted by Peacham)

Elsewhere, James is urged not to follow Nero in being lax about the law but to use as his model the period in Roman history when law was strictly enforced (see Book II, Emblem XIII) and somewhat later in the manuscript he is referred to as "Caesar" when the idea of the king tempering justice with magnanimity is urged by Peacham (Book II, Emblem XXXII). Both these emblems are reminders of the power of the king in making and enforcing law, a concept that James himself felt strongly about. In his *Trve Lawe of Free Monarchies*, James had offered a forceful expression of his own concept of regal authority when he stated that "Kings were the authors & makers of the lawes, and not the lawes of the Kings" (sig. C7[r]) and that "the King is aboue the law, as both the author, and giuer of strength thereto" (sig. D1[r]). Commenting upon the authority James derived from allusions to Rome and the additional authority he achieved through being an author, Goldberg has aptly commented:

> The style James adopted, and which marks his writing, is the key to the symbolics of his power. "*Caesars* works shall iustly *Caesar* crowne." "Works" are opera, writing; discourse reigns supreme, its might is right, the sole truth: the acts of the king are crowned in words. There is an implicit politics in language: the root of author is *auctor*, originator, warrant of the truth, supporter of a law.
>
> (1983, 27)

As Goldberg reminds us elsewhere, John Florio told James in the preface to his 1603 translation of *Basilikon Doron* into Italian that James was "Cesare," and his writing followed the precedents established by such

works as the *Cyropaedia* or Caesar's *Commentaries* (1983, 42-44). By invoking the image of Caesar and the historical power of Rome and its foundation in law, as James's entry had done,[49] Peacham's emblem book shared in the establishment of James's authority, which is further enforced because Peacham's manuscript is based upon the already established authority of the King's own printed words. Peacham in effect magnifies and reflects that authority back towards the King, a process symbolized and made tangible when the emblematist eventually presented the King with the finished version of his manuscript. As if consciously aware of this point, in his printed emblem book, *Minerva Britanna* (1612), which is dedicated to Prince Henry and contains many re-workings of Peacham's *Basilikon Doron* emblems, Peacham suggested that his emblems were in many instances "royally descended":

> For in truth they are of right youre owne, and no other then the substance of those divine instructions, his Maiestie your royall father [i. e. King James] praescribed unto you.[50]

My final example of how Peacham's manuscript emblem book participates in the establishment of Jacobean authority concerns the manner in which Peacham, like the author/designer of the triumphal arches for James's entry, peoples his creation with allusions to kingly virtues. These are often ostensibly addressed in the manner of James's *Basilikon Doron* to Prince Henry. The assumption that the reader inevitably accepts is that the royal voice is that of the teacher who possesses those things that the pupil (Prince Henry) is asked to emulate.

There is, of course, a difference here between the way in which the emblems work and the way in which the triumphal arches function. These latter generally define the relationship between the monarch and the personified virtues represented on each arch through spacial symbolism. The virtues portrayed on the arches are often, for example, visually parallel to, or subservient to, the royal image or the heraldic arms or insignia symbolic of it. Thus, for the Fenchurch arch Theosophia (or Divine Wisdom) was seated *below* Monarchia Britannica,[51] and on the Gracechurch Street arch the figures of Peace and Hope are *below* the royal arms and the picture of James and Henry VII. For the Nova Faelix Arabia arch there was a crown placed upon the highest pinnacle. Below this was Arabia Britannica, her head bowed (see above) until the arrival of James, who is thus "superior" to her in status. Below her (and hence "below" James) are the figures of Fame, the Five Senses, the Fountain of Virtue, the three Graces, Love, Justice, and Peace. Finally, on the Temple of Janus arch although the four-faced Janus is at the highest point, its four faces "not enough, to behold the greatnesse and glorie of that day . . . ," (lines 407-08) the dominant

"The country swains at football," from Henry Peacham's Minerva Britanna *(1612).*

visual device at the top is the royal arms. Below the royal arms are represented Peace, Liberty, Safety, and Felicity. In Peacham's emblem book, a similar array of virtues are associated with the royal person. For the most part, these virtues provide the subject-matter of individual emblems, which, as one might expect, include below their epigrams quotations from James's *Basilikon Doron*. We are not dealing with actual personifications here, but with such emblematic concepts as the ermine to represent a clear conscience (see Book I, Emblem XII).[52] In two cases, however, Peacham creates personifications, and it is with these that I wish to conclude.

In Book I, Emblem V below the motto "Cuique et nemine" [To everyone and to no one], Peacham portrays Religious Faith, a woman leaning upon a cross.[53] In her right hand she displays some writings, but she holds something in her left hand hidden behind her back. As the epigram explains, the cross is her peace

and her only trust is heaven. Her teachings are revealed to all, but her pious works are concealed behind her back, an allusion, as the quotation from James's *Basilikon Doron* makes clear, to the Protestant concern about the relationship of faith and works, something that would have pleased James, who saw himself as very much the defender of Protestantism. In the way in which I read this emblem, the figure in the *pictura* offers a model to the reader (originally Prince Henry) for emulation, but at the same time that model is James himself. This process also characterizes my final example, Book II, Emblem XXXIV. Here, the motto is "Regum constantia" [The constancy of kings], and the *pictura* shows Atlas standing upon a square stone, itself symbolising constancy. Upon his shoulder Atlas bears the globe. As the epigram explains, a king is also an Atlas because he must shoulder the weight of the earth. The quotation from James's *Basilikon Doron* (Book II, p. 97) then adds a further dimension by saying that the king should be constant in his kindness towards honest men and invulnerable against all adversities. The emblem invites the reader, I would contend, to equate Atlas and James, Peacham's technique being yet another way in which the new king is invested with authority.

As I have tried to show, the emblem book that Peacham designed as a gift to James at the very beginning of that monarch's reign in England plays its own small part in the redefinition of kingly authority that so characterized Jacobean culture. Peacham's grasp of the tenets that lay behind the iconography of the triumphal entry into London provided for James permitted him to create a gift that, by using a similar type of iconography, was at one with some of the central concepts of Jacobean authority. By using James's own published writings as the basis for his emblem book, Peacham was also furnishing his gift with the authority already possessed by James as author and kingly voice. Finally, by choosing to use the emblem as his medium, Peacham invested his work with that added authority (described by Wolfgang Harms and others) which is provided by the emblem itself.

Notes

1. Wilson (1653) 13. Modern commentators have also noted James's silence upon this and other such occasions. Parry (1981), though he stresses the contrast between James's behaviour at his entry and that of Elizabeth, attributes to James a "haughty self-concern" and a dislike of crowds that "caused him to hasten tactlessly along the ceremonial way with a minimum of appreciation" (p. 21). David Bergeron (1971, 75) also comments on the contrast: "There are no references to any impromptu speeches which he [James] might have given along the way; James's role was much more passive" and hence a different type of theatrical experience at which "the spectators had to settle for the mute presence of their sovereign." Goldberg's interpretation, however, suggests another possible reading of James's behaviour.

2. Parry's earlier work (1981) is also important for its study of the role of visual media in the establishment of a distinctly Stuart culture and in the establishment of James's authority (though this is not the term Parry uses). Of particular relevance to my argument is Parry's valuable opening chapter on "The Iconography of James I."

3. Harms (1991) 6, 7.

4. Russell (1986) 230. The commonplace idea contained in Marsilio Ficino's translation of Plotinus provided the underlying principle behind Pierio Valeriano's *Hieroglyphica* (first publ. Basel, 1556).

5. Russell (1986) 236.

6. Russell (1986) 236. Russell (1988) adds further complexities to this issue by arguing that as the emblem genre developed, there was always a po-

tential for tension between authority derived from elsewhere (usually the past) and new uses to which "the traditional materials were put in the emblem" (p. 83).

7. As Harms puts it, ". . . emblematics could be used to secure authority for important people, that is for Authorities themselves" (1991, 10).

8. *CSP, Venetian 1603-07,* vol. X, 10, item 22.

9. For convenience, quotations here (unless otherwise stated) are from James Craigie's edition of *The Basilicon Doron of King James VI* for The Scottish Text Society (Edinburgh & London: Blackwood, 1944 and 1950). Craigie reprints the Waldegrave edition.

10. Peacham's choice of the emblem was also apt in another way. As Graham Parry pointed out, James's *Basilikon Doron* is itself coloured by numerous verbal illustrations of an emblematic nature (1981, 7).

11. Sig. A3^v. Perhaps, emblems were "in his blood." Inevitably, one recalls that his mother, Mary Queen of Scots, is credited with embroidering a large number of emblematic devices, some of which derive from Paradin, see Daly (1988) 21-24.

12. While Peter Young was James's tutor in Scotland, he drew up a list of the books in the young king's library. These included copies of Alciato, Giovio, and Montanus, and several copies of Paradin. For details concerning these, see Warner (1893), xxxiii-iv, xl, l, lx, lxi, lxv, lxvi.

13. Bodleian Library, MS. Rawlinson poetry 146. Because the title-page describes Prince Henry as "Regis Iacobi, Angliae[,] Scotiae, Franciae, et Hiberniae filij," the manuscript can be dated as having been composed between James I's accession and 20 October 1604 when James issued a proclamation changing his title to "King of Great Britain, France, and Ireland, Defender of the Faith, etc." For the record of James's change of title, see Tanner (1930) 34.

14. On occasion the passages from *Basilikon Doron* are omitted but the relevant volume and page numbers are provided.

15. Although James himself employed marginalia (mostly biblical), Peacham seems to have created his own, usually from Classical sources.

16. For a discussion of this point and a more detailed description of this manuscript, see Young (1979) 38-39, and 86-97.

17. For a discussion of the 1610 manuscript emblem book (British Library, MS. Royal 12A LXVI) see Young (1979) 40-41. Two years later, Peacham dedicated *Minerva Britanna* to Prince Henry.

18. The dedication is addressed "Piissimo ac Serenissimo IACOBO Magnae huius BRITANNIAE Monarchae primo," thus employing the title introduced by James in October 1604 (see above Note 13). For a discussion of this manuscript (British Library, MS. Harleian 6855, Art. 13) see Young (1979) 39-40 and 305-11.

19. Evidence that MS. Harleian 6855, Art 13, was never given to James occurs on folio 36^v where there is a rough draft for the dedication to Prince Henry that eventually appeared at the head of sig. A2^r in *Minerva Britanna*, while the blank folio 37^r was used as a scribbler for anagrams on "Henricus Vualliae princeps," "Sir Thomas Parrie," and "Sir Thomas Howard." That Peacham did present a version of his *Basilikon Doron* manuscript to the King is confirmed by the dedicatory epistle in another manuscript emblem book, Peacham's "Emblemata varia" (Folger Shakespeare Library, V. b. 45), in which he states that seventeen years previously the King had kindly accepted an emblematized version of *Basilikon Doron*.

20. See *The Proclamation for the Union of the Kingdoms of England and Scotland,* 19 May 1603, reprinted in Thomas Rymer's *Foedera,* xvi (1715) 506-07. Cf. also James's first address to the English Parliament in which he spoke at length about the advantages of the union of the "two ancient and famous Kingdoms" (*The Kings Maiesties Speech* [London, 1604], sigs. B1^v-B3^v).

21. *Calendar of State Papers, Domestic, 1603-1610* (London, 1857) x, items 15-1, 39-41, 55-56.

22. Given the various allusions to Henry VII during the 1604 entry, it would appear that James's subjects shared his view. James was the great grandson of the eldest daughter of Henry VII, Margaret Tudor, who married James IV of Scotland. In his first speech before Parliament, for example, James said: "by my descent lineally out of the loynes of *Henry* the seuenth is reunited and confirmed in me the Vnion of the two princely Roses of the two Houses of LANCASTER and YORKE, whereof that King of happy memorie was the first Vniter, . . ." (*The Kings Maiesties Speech* [London, 1604], sig. B1^r).

23. On this point, and for a discussion of how this mythology was integrated into James's triumphal entry, see Parry (1981), 4, 8-9, 16-20 *et passim.* Cf. Bergeron (1971) 81-82. As Parry points out in another context, Jacobean political ideology also appropriated the Tudor mythology of Arthurian ancestry, James being a second Arthur (p. 70).

24. These latter two have appeared in modern editions, which for convenience provide the source for any citations that follow here. See, Thomas Dekker, *The Magnificent Entertainment* (London, 1604) in Dekker (1955) II, 229-309; and Ben Jonson, *His Part of King James his Royall and Magnificent Entertainment* (London, 1604) in Jonson (1941) VII, 83-109.

25. Henry VIII was styled King of Ireland from 1542 but had not incorporated the harp into his arms.

26. The three lions of England (Gules, three lions passant guardant in pale or) were first used by Richard I and then by all subsequent English monarchs. In 1340 Edward III quartered the arms of England with those of France, a blue shield with gold fleurs-de-lys (azure, semy of fleurs-de-lys or). When Charles V reduced the number of fleurs-de-lys to three, this innovation was followed by Henry IV of England in 1405. The title King of France was employed by English kings until 1801. The claim to the Kingdom of France went back to the reign of Edward III. In the case of James, the claim was also derived through the person of his grandmother, Mary of Guise, the mother of Mary Queen of Scots.

27. These two heraldic beasts appear in prominent positions on the New World arch in Fleet Street.

28. As Bergeron points out (1971, 78) Henry was also an apt figure because he was another unifier, having united the warring houses of York and Lancaster.

29. See, for example, the examples cited by Strong (1977) 54, 73. One of Elizabeth's mottoes had been "Foelicior Phoenice." See, too, the so-called "Phoenix" Portrait of Elizabeth by Nicholas Hilliard, now in the National Portrait Gallery, which depicts the Queen wearing the Phoenix jewel at her breast, the 1596 engraving of Elizabeth by Crispin de Passe I, the full-length engraving of her (ca. 1595-1600) by William Rogers, and the "Phoenix Medal" of ca. 1574.

30. At James's approach, the figure of Arabia Britannica, her eyes downcast until this moment, upon hearing the trumpet of Fame, finally raised her head; see Thomas Dekker, *The Magnificent Entertainment* (1604) in Dekker (1955) lines 742-48 and 814-32.

31. In as much as we know it from the surviving draft.

32. For a discussion of certain aspects of Peacham's heraldic emblems, see Tung (1987) 86-94; and cf. Young (1979) 47-49.

33. This is the ornament of the fields, and these are the sacred rites of the Cyprian maiden. The wild thistle and the spring rose bloom together in harmony and the cold rain nourishing them from high heaven wants this to be a sign, great James, for your kingdoms.

34. As Tung points out (1987, 92) Anne Boleyn's device was, according to William Camden (a source Peacham knew well), "a white crowned Faulcon, holding a Scepter in her right talon, standing upon a golden truncke, out of the which sprowted both white and red roses, with MIHI, ET MEAE" (1984, 182). Peacham's emblem appears to conflate the properties of both the Boleyn falcon and Elizabeth's phoenix. In speculating as to why Peacham transformed the falcon into a phoenix, Tung concentrates his attention upon the phoenix emblem in *Minerva Britanna,* which is dedicated to Sir Robert Cecil and in my view is quite unrelated to the earlier *Basilikon Doron* versions. These last are surely primarily influenced by the pervasive phoenix symbolism that was associated with James in the years 1603-04.

35. [As the British Phoenix has appeared to yield through fate, England groans, overcome with unspeakable grief. But then, suddenly, rising again, the newborn Phoenix grasps the sceptre, while you, Rome, proud with your eagles, lie prostrate.]

36. In the earlier manuscript emblem book, MS. Rawlinson, poetry 146, Peacham included a similar phoenix emblem. However, the final line of his epigram referred to the eagles of the Spaniard (rather than those of Rome). The allusion is clearly to the threat of Catholic imperialism.

37. ". . . par la double laçure d'icelles ensemble, leur inuincible & indissoluble union" (*Devises heroiques,* 1557 ed., p. 23). Paradin also makes the point, though it is not exploited by Peacham, that the similarity of one shell with another signifies the equality which prevails among the members of the order, a meaning intended by those Roman senators who wore the device of a shell on their arms: ". . . par la similitude ou semblance de ses Coquilles, leur equalité, ou egale fraternité d'Ordre, (en ensuiuant les Senateurs Rommeins, qui portoient aussi des Coquilles es bras pour enseigne, ou Deuise,) . . ." (*Devises heroiques,* 1557 ed., p. 23).

38. "Auspiciis, propera, Divi coalesce Iacobi / Et terris redeunt aurea secla tuis" [Hasten and unite under the auspices of the godlike James, and the golden age will return to your lands]. See *Basilikon Doron,* Book III, Emblem XII.

39. In *Minerva Britanna* the emblem is dedicated "*to my dread Soveraigne* IAMES, *King of great* BRITAINE" (p. 1).

40. "Dextra Iacobe Dei te compede nectit eadem / Quem Regem imperio fecit et esse virum."

41. The same quotation from *Basilikon Doron* referring to James as a little God recurs in Book I,

Emblem III, thereby reinforcing the effect of the first emblem.

42. In the later version of the emblem that Peacham incorporated into *Minerva Britanna,* Peacham worked in the theme of union by describing the crown as a circlet that "boundes, the greater BRITANNIE, / From conquered FRAVNCE, to THVLE sung of old" (p. 1).

43. James VI (1944 and 1950) I, 5.

44. In the marginal note accompanying this statement, James inserted a reference to Psalm 82.6 "I have said, Ye are gods; and all of you are children of the most high." In a speech to the English Parliament in 1605, James stated: "Kings are in the word of GOD it selfe called Gods, as being his Lieutenants and Vice-regents on earth" (*Works* [1616] 500).

45. A marginal note explains that the laurel and the olive are symbols belonging to Florence.

46. I am indebted to my colleague Beert Verstraete, Department of Classics (Acadia University) for the translation of this inscription.

47. "Te tua sed pietas omni memorabilis aevo / Sidus ad eterni Caesaris usque feret." In the earlier version of this emblem in the Rawlinson manuscript, Caesar is specifically identified by a marginal annotation as Augustus.

48. "Iustitia occumbet tecum quie misa fidesque / In patriam raris pax et habenda locis."

49. See Goldberg's detailed discussion of this process, (1983) 43-54.

50. *Minerva Britanna,* sig. A2. Cf. Bath (1994) in which this same passage is quoted to suggest that Peacham is attempting to gain authority for his compositions by suggesting that their "real author" is King James (p. 98).

51. Ben Jonson in his account explains that Theosophia's motto was "Per me reges regnant" [It is through me that kings rule], thereby "Intimating, how by her, all kings doe gouverne, and that she is the foundation and strength of kingdomes, to which end, shee was here placed, vpon a cube, at the foot of the Monarchie, as her base and stay" (lines 64-67). Though Jonson's point is to show that the king's power is dependent upon divine wisdom, there is nonetheless an implied statement of the absolute authority of James conveyed by the vertical relationship involved. The Royal Exchange arch is something of an exception to this pattern in that Divine Providence was placed upon the highest pinnacle. Below her sat James, with Fortitude and Justice to either side, slightly above him.

52. The following are other examples of the subject-matter of this type of emblem: piety and religion (Book I, Emblem III); a sanctified and chaste heart (Book I, Emblem VII); the bearing of adversity (Book I, Emblem XI); vigilance (Book I, Emblem XVII); the king as a light for his people (Book II, Emblem IX); mercy (Book II, Emblem XIV); the helping of the oppressed (Book II, Emblem XVI); the king as physician to his country (Book II, Emblem XVII); the active pursuit of virtue (Book II, Emblem XXIV); magnanimity (Book II, Emblem XXXII).

53. The figure of religion first seems to have been presented in this fashion in Theodore de Beza's *Icones* (1580), Emblem 39. Another version may be found in Cesare Ripa's *Iconologia* (1603 edition), p. 429. It is not clear what Peacham's precise source was.

References

Bath, Michael (1994). *Speaking Pictures: English Emblem Books and Renaissance Culture*. London: Longman.

Bergeron, David (1971). *English Civic Pageantry 1558-1642*. London: Edward Arnold.

Camden, William (1984). *Remains Concerning Britain*. Ed. R. D. Dunn. Toronto: University of Toronto Press.

Daly, Peter M. (1988). "England and the Emblem: The Cultural Context of English Emblem Books," In *The English Emblem and the Continental Tradition*. Ed. Peter M. Daly. New York: AMS Press. Pp. 1-60.

Dekker, Thomas (1955). *The Magnificent Entertainment* (London, 1604). In *The Dramatic Works of Thomas Dekker*. Ed. Fredson Bowers. Cambridge: Cambridge University Press, II, 229-309.

Goldberg, Jonathan (1983). *James I and the Politics of Literature: Jonson, Shakespeare, Donne, and Their Contemporaries*. Stanford: Stanford University Press.

Harms, Wolfgang (1991). "The Authority of the Emblem." *Emblematica*, 5: 3-21.

James VI, King (1944 and 1950). *The Basilicon Doron of King James VI*. Ed. James Craigie for The Scottish Text Society. 2 vols. Edinburgh & London: Blackwood.

Jonson, Ben (1941). *His Part of King James his Royall and Magnificent Entertainment* (London, 1604). In *Ben Jonson*. Ed. C. H. Herford and Percy and Evelyn Simpson. Oxford: Clarendon Press. VII, 83-109.

Parry, Graham (1981). *The Golden Age Restor'd: The Culture of the Stuart Court, 1603-42*. New York: St. Martin's Press.

Russell, Daniel (1986). "Emblems and Hieroglyphics: Some Observations on the Beginnings and the Nature of Emblematic Forms." *Emblematica*, 1: 227-44.

Russell, Daniel (1988). "The Emblem and Authority." *Word & Image*, 4: 81-87.

Strong, Roy (1977). *The Cult of Elizabeth: Elizabethan Portraiture and Pageantry*. London: Thames and Hudson.

Tanner, Joseph R. (1930). *Constitutional Documents of the Reign of James I*. Cambridge: Cambridge University Press.

Tung, Mason (1987). "From Heraldry to Emblem: A Study of Peacham's Use of Heraldic Arms in *Minerva Britanna*." *Word and Image*, 3: 86-94.

Warner, George F. (1893). "The Library of James VI. 1573-1583 from a Manuscript in the Hand of Peter Young." *Miscellany of The Scottish Historical Society*, vol. 1. Edinburgh: Edinburgh University Press.

Wilson, Arthur (1653). *The History of Great Britain, being the Life and Reign of King James the First*. London: Printed for Richard Lowndes.

Young, Alan R. (1979). *Henry Peacham*. Boston: Twayne.

Young, Alan R. (1979a). "Henry Peacham's First Emblem Book: MS. Rawlinson Poetry 146." *Bodleian Library Record*, 10: 86-97.

Young, Alan R. (1979b). "Henry Peacham, Ben Jonson and the Cult of Elizabeth-Oriana." *Music and Letters*, 60: 305-11.

RELIGION AND EMBLEM BOOKS

Huston Diehl (essay date 1986)

SOURCE: Diehl, Huston. "Graven Images: Protestant Emblem Books in England." *Renaissance Quarterly* 39 (1986): 49-66.

[*In the following essay, Diehl questions the assumption that emblem books reflect a Catholic sensibility, suggesting that the genre's exploration of symbolic meaning resonated with the concerns of Protestant theology. Diehl observes that the most significant European influences on the English emblem book came from northern centers of Protestant reform.*]

European emblem books were enormously popular in the sixteenth and seventeenth centuries. One hundred and forty editions of a single emblem book by Alciati were printed in the sixteenth century alone and, by 1616—only eighty-five years after the first emblem appeared—seven hundred different editions of emblem books had been published. The vogue was so strong in England, Gabriel Harvey protested that the students of Cambridge neglected Aristotle and the classics for emblem writers like Claude Paradin.[1] A product of the printing press, as well as of Renaissance humanism, the emblem book flourished in an age when, for the first time, literary texts were printed commercially and made available to the reading public, rather than recited to a select, aristocratic audience. As a literary form with wide appeal, the emblem book may provide contemporary students with valuable insights into Renaissance culture—its beliefs, attitudes, and concerns.

Many students of the genre today, however, associate emblems with the medieval, even though the genre originated in the sixteenth century and continued to flourish in the seventeenth century. They compare emblem books to the bestiaries, herbals, and lapidaries of the Latin middle ages, liken emblematic techniques to those of medieval allegory and personification, and trace the myths and symbols of Renaissance emblems to their medieval sources. In general, these scholars view the genre of emblem as a profoundly conservative one, a genre which collects and preserves images of the past. The emblem, Henri Stegemeir asserts, is a "depository for many earlier literary and artistic traditions, themes, and opinions." Wolfgang Lottes concurs, arguing that "Although a Renaissance product, it [the emblem] was deeply rooted in the homogeneous medieval world picture in which each part had its place assigned and harmoniously corresponded to all other parts." Scholars see in the emblem genre "the vulgarization and liquidization of a mode of thinking which had its heyday in the Middle Ages." They consider the emblem book an art form based in "Christian, medieval belief," functioning "as reaffirmations of the desired, if threatened order."[2]

Because they believe the emblem's spirit is medieval, its impulse conservative, even reactionary, these scholars usually assume that emblem books are primarily Roman Catholic, that books of sacred emblems are, as Rosalie Colie asserts, "almost uniformly Roman Catholic." Equating emblems with Renaissance hieroglyphs, Frances Yates, for one, argues that hieroglyphs and emblems "became one with Catholic symbolism."[3] The assumption that emblems are aligned with Catholicism is further supported by the fact that the Jesuits adopted the form in the last decade of the sixteenth century and produced scores of seventeenth-century Catholic emblem books. This Jesuit interest in emblem books, especially, seems to color many scholarly assumptions about the emblem. Emblems, according to Praz, "seem calculated to further the Ignatian technique of the application of the senses to help the imagination . . . picture to itself . . . circumstances of religious impact."[4]

Even Ernest B. Gilman, when he discusses the Protestant bias of Francis Quarles' *Emblemes,* assumes that the emblem tradition on the continent is Roman Catholic. The "ideal bond" between emblematic picture and word, he writes, "was forged principally in Italy," which was Roman Catholic and therefore, unlike England, not hostile to the senses or to pictures. Gilman assumes that English Protestant emblem writers like Quarles significantly alter the original and dominant conception of the emblem, which he believes to be Roman Catholic.[5]

Although these assumptions about the nature and spirit of the emblem are prevalent, they fail to explain some of the most intriguing questions about the emblem genre. Why did the emblem book originate in 1531, in the early years of the Protestant reform movement, and in Northern European centers of reform? Why did the genre of the emblem book flourish during the years of religious controversy, then die out at the end of the seventeenth century? What accounts for the extraordinary popularity of the emblem books in the Protestant countries of northern Europe during the sixteenth and seventeenth centuries? Why, if the genre were fundamentally Catholic, did the Jesuits come so late to it, nearly sixty-five years after the first emblem book was published?

In fact, emblems were written by men and women who were actively engaged with the central controversies of their age. Originating with the humanist Andrea Alciati, a man also remembered for his legal reforms, the emblem soon became popular not only with other humanists, but with Protestants, who used it to advance their reformed theology, and Jesuits, who adopted it as a weapon in the counter-reformation. Emblems, I would like to argue, are important expressions of their own age, a period of reformation and counter-reformation. Even though emblem books use standard images and stories of the past, they reinterpret these received traditions. Indeed the very nature of the form—with its combination of pictures and words, classical and vernacular languages, enigmatic mottoes and didactic explanations, traditional iconography and original interpretations—reflects the central conflicts of the sixteenth and seventeenth centuries. Rather than hearkening back to earlier beliefs, these emblem books question and challenge the inherited ideas of the Latin Middle Ages.

From its inception the emblem genre appealed to men and women with Protestant sympathies. Many of the early emblem writers had important ties with the Protestant reform movement that have for the most part gone unobserved. Although he was Italian, Andrea Alciati, the first emblem writer, lived for a while in France where he taught legal jurisprudence at the University of Bourges, a major center of reform activity at the time. Alciati's most famous pupil at Bourges was none other than John Calvin. According to a recent legal historian, Calvin was one of a number of Bourges students who "constituted the intellectual posterity . . . of Alciato." Although he himself never broke with the Roman Catholic church, Alciati did, at least for a time, support the cause of religious reform. Furthermore, Alciati's emblem book was published first in Augsburg, then in Paris, both centers of early Protestant agitation. The publication dates of these early editions of Alciati (1531, 1536) coincide with periods of major reform activity in Augsburg and Paris.[6] The early publication of Alciati's emblems in Augsburg and Paris does not, of course, prove a Protestant bias. It does, however, undercut the assumption that the emblem book is, in essence, a product of Roman Catholic Italy. In fact, Alciati's emblem book was never published in Rome.

Many other early emblem books—as opposed to the early books of *imprese* that were especially popular in Italy—were similarly published in northern Europe, in Protestant centers like Geneva, Basel, Lyons, Leiden, Nuremburg, Frankfort, by printers known to be sympathetic to the Reformation. The authors of these emblems frequently dedicate their books to men and women who support religious reform: Marguerite of Angoulême, protector of French reformers and patroness of the reform leader Lefèvre d'Etaples; Marguerite de Valois, who married the Huguenot leader Henry of Navarre; Queen Elizabeth, the great Protestant monarch of the sixteenth century.[7]

A number of sixteenth-century emblem writers were actively engaged in reform activity. Barthelemy Aneau, translator of Alciati, author of *Picta Poesis,* and "a pioneer in the French emblem movement," was suspected of Protestantism and, as a consequence, murdered in a people's uprising in 1565. Théodore Bèze, author of *Icones* (1580), was Calvin's closest collaborator; he directed the Geneva Academy, which trained reformed clergy, and became the leader of the Protestant movement in Switzerland and France after Calvin's death. Guillaume Gerroult, whose *Emblemes* were published in 1550, has been called "one of the most fearless and independent thinkers of the non-Calvinist Reformation." Joachim Camerarius, the younger, author of a four-volume book of emblems, was the son of an important German reformer. While in school at the Lutheran University of Wittenberg, Camerarius lived with his father's close friend Philip Melanchthon, the German reform theologian. Dirck Coornhert, the Dutch humanist whose emblem book was published in 1585, was, according to a Reformation historian, "in close contact with the Baptists"; he "read all the tracts of the Reformers," and in his theological writings rejected completely the ceremonies, rituals, and external ornaments of the Roman Catholic Church. In addition, the first book of sacred emblems was written in 1571 by a French Protestant, Georgette de Montenay. Other early emblem writers, too, were associated with Protestantism, many were avowed and active reformers, and some

were censored and even persecuted for their anti-Catholic beliefs.[8]

It is this northern Protestant emblem tradition, not a southern Catholic one, that is imported to a receptive England. The earliest English emblem books are translations and adaptations of these works, or original works with their own Protestant bias. Jan van der Noot's *Theater for Voluptuous Worldlings,* if it is, as some scholars believe, an emblem book, is the first such work published in English, and it is explicitly anti-Catholic. Geoffrey Whitney published his emblem book, officially the first English emblem book, in Leiden, a Protestant intellectual center, with the Plantin Press, directed at the time by Plantin's Protestant son-in-law, Raphelengius. And Andrew Willet, another early English emblem writer, was a Protestant minister.

It is my contention that English emblem writers, from Jan van der Noot and Geoffrey Whitney to John Bunyan, express, either directly or indirectly, Protestant attitudes toward word and image. Their emblems, even those that are explicitly secular and predominantly humanist, reflect the new Protestant tenets of faith that spread through England in the sixteenth and seventeenth centuries. Some, like Andrew Willet and Thomas Jenner, create religious emblem books with a strong anti-Catholic bias and doctrinal bent. Others, like Geoffrey Whitney and Henry Peacham, focus on more secular and humanist topics. Still others, like Francis Quarles and Christopher Harvey, adapt Catholic emblem books to Protestant beliefs. As Barbara Lewalski and Ernest Gilman have carefully argued, such emblem writers alter their sources in significant ways, inverting the Catholic emblem books' values, reinterpreting the Catholic originals to conform to Protestant beliefs.[9] With the exception of the English Jesuit Henry Hawkins, all these English emblem writers express in their emblems a fundamentally Protestant view of the world and the relation of human beings to the visible creation.

How did the emblems suit the purposes of these Protestant writers? Why were Protestant readers in England and northern Europe attracted to a literary genre that collects the images of a medieval, Roman Catholic world and an ancient, pagan world? Even more puzzling, why would men and women active in the Protestant reform movement be involved with the publication of books of images, including sacred images, even as they vehemently attack the images of the Roman Catholic Church and endorse iconoclasm? Why would Protestants simultaneously be making and breaking images? Protestant attitudes toward images may illuminate these apparent contradictions and provide insights into the emblematic image as it was conceived by northern European, Protestant writers.

When the reformers condemn the images of the Roman Catholic Church, they focus their attack not on images *per se,* but on the misuse of images. They define "abused" images as those images which inspire worship or reverence or are believed to be efficacious or magical, and those which externalize religion "to please men" or "become ends in themselves."[10] In their support of iconoclasm, the reform theologians are concerned that the people will confuse the ecclesiastical image with what it represents, and thus idolize it. Leo Jud, the Zurich reformer, for example, objects that people "accord such images great honour, and entreat them with ornaments, silver, gold, precious stones, with sacrifices and with reverence, that is, by taking off their hats, bowing, and kneeling before them, all of which, however, God has forbidden."[11] He and others oppose the images of Roman Catholicism because they think these images seduce men into believing in what is visible and corporeal, rather than in the spiritual, which can never be seen or touched. "Against the express commandment of God," the Catholics, writes a Dutch reformer, have "erected an infinity of beautiful images, paintings and statues, gilded, like whores."[12] The reformers reject images which attract men to their physical and material qualities. The Roman Catholics, of course, also condemned the idolatrous worship of images and taught that an image should point beyond itself to spiritual things. They believed, however, that the physical qualities of an image could help the worshiper arrive at the spiritual, and, as a consequence, they did not distrust the sensuous aspects of the image.

Although they attack these abused images and the Catholic Church for encouraging such abuses, most Protestant theologians do not reject all images or even all sacred images. They repeatedly approve of images that serve as "memorials unto men, and a remembrance of the testament," "remind us of heavenly things," and "put us in remembrance that there is a Father in heaven," even as they condemn images that inspire worship, idolatry, or superstition. The Reformers allow the use of images as "commemorative aids."[13] Images, according to these theologians, are appropriate if they function as vehicles that remind the viewer of what he cannot see, rather than become ends in themselves. The viewer may properly use a visible image to recall something else, something spiritual, invisible, and incorporeal.

In their discussions of ecclesiastical art and iconoclasm, Protestant theologians attempt to demystify images. Acceptable images awaken the memory, enabling the viewer to recollect spiritual things through a process of association. Images are not efficacious; they do not pass the honor done them on to their prototypes; they should not be venerated. They may, however, serve as an aid to memory, helping the viewer to recall invisible spiritual truths. The memory stores images for future recollection and meditation, becoming "the Gallery of the soul" as John Donne describes it, "hang'd with so many, and

so lively pictures of the goodness and mercies of thy God to thee, as that everyone of them shall be a catechism to thee."[14] Images may thus serve an important function in the spiritual life of the Protestant, but not as external devotional images. Instead of inspiring veneration, images become internalized as the vehicles of spiritual recollection, a process that leads man to the invisible and incorporeal divinity. Images, properly used, are commemorative aids.

When English emblem writers justify and explain their emblems, they frequently define emblematic images as memorials and remembrances and describe the process of reading emblems as an act of recollection. Their language echoes the language of the reformers when they define unabused images. P. S., the English translator of Claude Paradin, says his emblematic images create "a perpetuall memorie" and calls the emblems in his book "most memorable." George Wither expresses the hope that his emblems may be "Teachers and Remembrances of profitable things," that they may "help the Memory" and "bring . . . into remembrance," significant truths; in his dedicatory poems he repeatedly claims that the emblem image "assisteth memory." Similarly, Christopher Harvey concludes his emblem book with the verse: "Then here I rest / From taking out new lessons, till I see / How I retaine the old in memory." And E. M., who appends a treatise on the art of memory to his short emblem book, refers to emblematic pictures as images which "call to mind," "remember," "revive and rub up the memory." The emblematic image, for E. M., serves as "a certain memento," as "our Remembrancer."[15]

I would like to suggest that these English emblem writers consciously define the images in their books as unabused or approved images, according to the tenets of the new Protestant faith. In a period of iconoclastic sentiment, in a country anxious about the Catholic threats from abroad, these writers justify emblematic images as memory images and thus align them with the only kind of image approved by the Protestant reformers. As memory images, the pictures in emblem books stimulate the reader to recollect spiritual truths, to remember what is not present or visible. Rather than eliciting veneration or reverence, they function as signs, motivating the reader to seek beyond the literal, to recall and contemplate what they represent. English emblem writers thus adapt the rhetorical tradition of the art of memory to Protestant concerns. By presenting their images as remembrances, they encourage their readers to use the images in a way approved by the reform theologians.

Furthermore, emblem writers do not instruct their readers in the formal memory systems of the past, even though they refer to the tradition of the art of memory. Instead, they invert the memory process. Unlike the classical art of memory which teaches men to project images in order to recall specifics accurately, or the medieval memory systems which teach men "to invent . . . images" in order to retain religious doctrine,[16] Protestant emblem books depict images that invite the reader to imagine or remember unseen truths. The emblem reader does not invent images so that he can retain his intentions and beliefs; rather he deconstructs images so that he can recollect moral and spiritual truths. The classical and medieval process of projecting images is reversed.[17] Since he moves from the image to a recollection of its significance, the reader of the emblem is no danger of overvaluing the picture before him.

It is, perhaps, significant that the emblem writer's interest in memory images occurs at the very moment when the need for artificial memory systems has almost disappeared. With the expansion of printing and the increasing availability of books, men no longer had to rely on their memories to retain ideas: books preserved ideas in print for them.[18] Emblem books are products of this revolution in printing; they destroy the need for an artificial memory even as they allude to it. No longer needed as an aid to the orator or worshiper, the art of memory is thus adapted to the book form where printing provides the image that the reader then uses as a stimulus to recollect the unseen. As a memento or remembrancer, the emblematic picture thus discourages abuse: it does not exist for its own sake, it does not stimulate readers to delight in the physical, and it does not inspire veneration.

English emblem writers share the reformers' concern for the abuse of images, even as they create images, and they frequently examine in their emblems the uses of images. Two such emblem writers depict an identical image—the brass serpent erected by Moses—in order to consider the uses of images. One, however, uses the brass serpent to illustrate the misuse of an image, the other to show the proper use of an image. Andrew Willet shows how the people of Israel misinterpreted the brass serpent, believing it was a God, and uses the image to teach that idols cannot be tolerated.[19] P. S., on the other hand, presents the same image, but focuses instead on it as a sign that prefigures Christ (sig. A4). The image of the brass serpent, these two emblems suggest, is neither inherently good or bad. Rather, what the viewer makes of the image, how he uses it, determines whether it is an idol to be condemned or a sign to be remembered.

As memorials and remembrances of spiritual things, unabused images as defined by the Protestant theologians reflect the new covenant theology and most Protestant reinterpretations of the sacraments. Calvin, for example, believes that God expresses his covenant with men visually, in "signs," "as a reminder" of his promises, and he defines a sacrament as an "outward sign,"

"to exercise us in the remembrance of" Christ.[20] When he rejects the Catholic belief in transubstantiation, Calvin substitutes instead the idea that the eucharist is a visible sign that reminds man of Christ's sacrifice. "From the physical things set forth in the Sacraments," he writes, "we ought to be led by a sort of analogy to spiritual things. Thus, when we see bread set forth to us as a sign of Christ's body, we must at once grasp this comparison: as bread nourishes, sustains, and keeps the life of our body, so Christ's body is the food and protection of our spiritual life" (pp. 118, 140). To experience fully the sacrament of communion as Calvin reinterprets it, man must "grasp this comparison" between bread and Christ's body; he must, in other words, recognize the resemblance between bread and Christ and "be led by a sort of analogy to spiritual things." The terms "comparison" and "analogy" are significant, since with them Calvin rejects the Catholic belief in transubstantiation and substitutes instead the idea of resemblance. Through its analogical relationship to Christ's body, the bread is a reminder to the communicant, a memorial of Christ's sacrifice. Literal bread may thus function as a visible sign which enables the communicant to apprehend the divine, or that which is incorporeal and invisible. Man knows the spiritual, according to reform theology, through resemblance and analogy.

In contrast to Thomist theology, which cited the mystery of the incarnation to justify the use of the visible as sensuous aids to devotion, Protestant reformers mistrusted the physical image and emphasized instead the metaphorical relationship between the image and the thing itself. As a consequence, the viewer could no longer venerate, honor, imitate, or trust in images; instead, he must interpret them. Images, for Protestants, remind the viewer of something else, something they are not. Protestantism teaches men to recognize an absolute distinction between the sign and thing it represents. It encourages men to see in the visible world, signs of the divine, but it insists on the disparity between visible and invisible. The image thus serves as a necessary but inadequate sign of the invisible.

English emblem writers are aware of how the Protestant reinterpretation of the sacraments redefines the nature and function of images. Thomas Jenner, for example, attacks the Catholic belief in transubstantiation in *The Soul's Solace* and, in doing so, he illustrates the Protestant attitude toward visible images. He depicts the facade of a tavern in an icon of an emblem titled, "The foolishness of Transubstantiation." A commercial sign displaying an image of grapes hangs above the tavern door to advertise the spirits sold within. A human figure climbs a ladder to this tavern sign and futilely attempts to eat the image of the grapes. This man, the accompanying verse explains, represents the Roman Catholic who, in his belief in the doctrine of transubstantiation, is a fool, because he mistakes the sign for the thing itself. "In *Christ* alone stands that *spiritual food*," writes Jenner:

> Which must not of these signs be understood.
> For *bread* is *bread*, even after *consecration*:
> The *worke* being done for Christ's *Commemoration*.
> If to remember *Him*, then hee's not there.
> Thus Rings for absent friends we use to weare.

Clearly, Jenner attacks here the identification or confusion of the image with the thing it signifies, not the use of the visual image. As the viewer must interpret the image of grapes, recognizing that it is a sign for the wine sold within, so the worshipper must interpret the communion wafer, recognizing that it is a sign or reminder of Christ. "The bush" of grapes, explains Jenner, "doth shew within are Wines to sell, / So shewes the bread in Christ doth fulnes dwell."[21] In this emblem Jenner stresses the importance of interpretation and comparison. Man knows not through immediate apprehension of the thing itself, but indirectly, through analogy and resemblance.

In another intriguing illustration of the Protestant sacrament and its redefinition of the nature of images, P. S. presents an image of bread on a cross. He substitutes, in other words, the communion wafer for the body of Christ, and thus forces the viewer to see that the image is a sign, not to be confused with the thing it represents. The image of bread on a cross reminds the viewer of what he cannot see through analogy. It is, P. S. explains in his accompanying epigram, a remembrance of Christ and his redemption of man (A6).

English emblem books thus reinforce the Protestant belief in the necessity of interpretation and speak to the new concern for the epistemological process. They force their readers to confront the disparity between signifier and signified and at the same time to pursue the analogous relationship between disparate things, between image and the invisible thing it signifies. The emblematic image stimulates the reader to seek what is absent and invisible; it thus serves as an intermediary between the physical and the spiritual worlds. The enigmatic quality of the emblem enhances its function as a sign. The reader at first confronts picture and motto which seem unrelated; as he works through the emblem he discovers a rhetorical relationship. In the process of discovery, he moves from the apprehension of the visual image to a recognition of an unseen truth. As he interprets the emblem, he relinquishes the external image itself and internalizes its significance. "My Rhetorick" writes Harvey, "is not so much an art, / As an infused habit in mine heart" (sig. K). The emblematic image insists on being translated and transformed.

This transformation may account for the appearance of standard Catholic images in the English emblem books of Protestant England. The Protestant preacher Andrew Willet, for example, describes the garments of a Roman Catholic priest in his anti-Catholic emblem book, but he neither attacks the image nor endorses Catholic doctrine. Instead, he acknowledges the traditional symbolic significance of the priest's garments, then concludes that the Protestant minister wears these clothes not on his body but in his heart (sig. C2). The reader of Willet's emblem is thus encouraged to transform or reform the traditional image, discarding the external thing and internalizing its meaning. In contrast, Henry Peacham presents the garments and ornaments of the Roman Catholic clergy to examine the misuse of images. He depicts the image of a man dressed in a cleric's robe and holding a pilgrim's staff and rosary to represent the hypocrite who displays external images of piety to hide an impure heart.[22] The image of the priest's clothes, these emblems suggest, may be properly or improperly used. As an external assertion of piety, the clothes are empty, meaningless, deceptive. As an internalized reminder of the minister's spiritual duty, the clothes are meaningful and worthwhile. Protestant emblems repeatedly urge readers to reject what is visible for what is invisible, to transfer their attention from external to internal things.

In another emblem Willet makes the precious oils and spices of Catholic ecclesiastical ceremony the subject of an emblem, but instead of encouraging his readers to imagine the sensuous appeal of an external thing like balsam, he exchanges the external thing for the spiritual. As precious balsam cures the body, he writes, so God's word comforts the heart. Willet makes the material object into a sign for the invisible and spiritual so that the reader turns away from the object and the physical world. His technique differs in significant ways from Jesuit emblems that elaborate on the sensuous qualities of the image and encourage their readers to imagine the sight, sound, taste, smell, and feel of the object depicted in order to apprehend the spiritual. Henry Hawkins, in his translation of the Jesuit emblem book by Stephanus Luzvic, invites his readers to use his emblems to contemplate "this great rich magazin of the treasures of Nature," and he explores the physical aspects of the image of a garden. "Here," he writes, "the sweet smelling balme exhales an odoriforous breath, here amid the snowes of lillyes, the roses grow al purple; here Cinamon with safron, cassia mixed with mirrh, have a fragrant odour with them."[23] Hawkins asks his readers to imagine in vivid detail the physical and sensuous qualities of the emblematic image, to experience the image as if it were a reality in the external world. Only after the reader has so imagined the image in all its sensuousness does Hawkins develop its moral and theological significance. For Hawkins the physicality of the image enhances its effectiveness.

In contrast, Willet and the other Protestant emblem writers deemphasize the sensuous qualities of the image, devalue the visual appeal, and concentrate solely on the moral or spiritual significance. The fig tree in Georgette de Montenay's emblem book, for example, does not appeal to the physical sense or invite a rhapsodic celebration of God's created world (sig. Dd^v). It becomes instead a sign of summer which in turn is analogous to charitable acts, a sign of Christ's presence in the world. Montenay's emblem of a fig tree is primarily intellectual, with little sensuous appeal. It demands that its readers see the visible things of the world as signs that must be interpreted, and it requires him to distance himself from the material thing, to translate the image.

Whereas the Jesuits use emblematic images to stimulate the reader to imagine a sensuous experience that leads him to God and to celebrate the beauty of God's creation, Protestant emblem writers express a far greater distrust of the corporeal and physical. Christopher Harvey speaks of "the dark night of error" which has "dimm'd thy sight," he confesses that he himself is "blind," and he urges his reader to "Turne in," "to bend thine eye / Inward." He asks God not to reveal the splendor of creation, but rather to "Teach me to know mine heart" (sigs. B^v, B, B2). Harvey clearly distrusts the material world, suspects his own ability to see, and turns from external to internal things. He emphasizes the mind's intellectual search for what is absent, not the physical presence of the image, and he encourages the reader to exchange physical sight for spiritual insight.

Thomas Jenner similarly distrusts earthly things. Like the Jesuit Hawkins, he presents an image of a garden, but he acknowledges its physical beauty only to reject it for God's superior truth that is like a blinding light. "The grasse, and hearbs, to looke on chears the sight," writes Jenner, "So doe the flowers, and fruits; t'is man's delight":

> But when
> He views the sunne, the case is altered then; . . .
> When one shall wisely see what God desires, . . .
> What himselfe wants, and what the law requires,
> Hee's strucken blind.
>
> (sig. C4^v)

In contrast to the Hawkins' emblem which urges the reader to respond to the intoxicating physical beauty of the flowers, Jenner here suspects and repudiates the visual appeal of the garden. God's word and law obliterate the physical, blinding men to the material splendor of earthly things and moving him from the allure of the earthly to a recognition of more important, spiritual reality. The reader stops seeing with his eyes and sees instead with his mind. In a way, the reader of this emblem engages in an iconoclastic act, destroying the image of the garden in order to embrace God's word and law.

Other English emblem writers convey a similar ambivalence toward the visual images they feature in their books. Even as they stress the primacy of sight over the other senses, they acknowledge the inadequacy of the senses and the superiority of word over image. As Barbara Lewalski has shown, the theoretical relationship between image and word in the emblem, in which the image resembles the body, the word the soul, conforms to the relationship between sign and word in Calvin's sacramental theology. Image and word are interdependent, but, in both emblem theory and Calvinistic doctrine, the word is primary and the image contributes to the apprehension of the word (Lewalski, pp. 186-87). Calvin envisions God using physical images to lead childlike humans to the spiritual, "to instruct us according to our dull capacity, and to lead us by the hand as tutors lead children" (p. 119). Likewise, English emblem writers imagine their readers as children who need external images to engage them and lead them to the serious and significant matter. George Wither, for example, writes in his Preface that "when levitie, or a childish delight, in trifling objects, hath allured them to locate on the *Pictures*; curiositie may urge them to peepe further, that they might seeke out also their *MEANINGS,* in our annexed Illustrations" (sig. #A2), and John Bunyan equates his adult readers to children, then writes:

> . . . by their Play-things, I would them entice,
> To mount their Thoughts from what are childish Toys,
> To Heav'n, for that's prepar'd for Girls and Boys.[24]

Protestant theologians and English emblem writers thus both consider the visible image as a necessary concession to the weakness of human nature. As physical beings, humans must rely, in part, on external things to lead them to the spiritual. "But as our faith is slight and feeble unless propped on all sides and sustained by every means, it trembles, waivers, totters," writes Calvin. "Here our merciful Lord so tempers himself to our capacity that (since we are creatures who always creep on the ground, cleave to the flesh, and do not think about or even conceive of anything spiritual) he leads us to himself even by these earthly elements, and in the flesh itself causes us to contemplate the things that are of his Spirit" (p. 118). Using a similar argument, Thomas Combe defends his use of pictures in terms of the limited capacity of humans to understand: "where oftentimes feeling and effectuall words, though never so sensible, do passe the Reader without due consideration," he writes, "pictures that especially are discerned by the sense, are such helps to the weakness of common understandings, that they make words as it were deedes, and set the whole substance of that which is offered, before the sight and conceipt of the Reader."[25]

In addition, emblem writers justify their use of images by likening them to the visible things God uses as divine signs and therefore arguing that God himself is an emblem writer. "And, indeed," writes Francis Quarles, "what are the Heavens, the Earth, nay every thing in nature, but *Hierogliphicks* and *Emblems* of His Glory?"[26] Sir James Astry takes a similar position when he defends his translation of a Spanish emblem book, reasoning that "Nor should any one be disgusted at the use of emblems, since God himself is the Author of them. The Brazen-Serpent (2), The Flaming-Bush (3), Gideon's Fleece (4), Sampson's Lion (5), The Priest's Garments (6), The Amours of the Kind Spouse (7), what are they else but Emblems?"[27] In casting God in the role of emblem writer, Quarles and Astry echo Calvin who interprets Biblical images like the rainbow and manna as visual signs created by God for the benefit of mankind.

The Protestant emblem technique thus conforms to the reformers' belief that the external things of the material world exist as God-made signs of invisible, spiritual truths. Emblems, as defined by Protestant writers like Montenay, Willet, Jenner, Harvey, and Quarles, reenact for the reader the ideal Protestant experience of the physical world as it is described by Joseph Hall. "Every action, every occurance shall remind me of those hidden and better things," writes Hall, "and I shall so admit of all material objects, as if they were so altogether transparent, that through them I might see the wonderful prospects of another world. And certainly, if we shall be able to withdraw our selves from our senses, we shall see, not what we see, but what we think . . . and shall make earthly things, not as lunets, to shut up our sight, but Spectacles to transmit it to spiritual objects."[28] For Hall, images and earthly things, properly used, function like spectacles or eyeglasses, redirecting the viewer from the external world of senses to the interior world of the mind, focusing the sight on the invisible and spiritual. Protestant emblems work in precisely the same way. By reminding the viewer of what he cannot see, the emblematic image points away from itself. When the reader sees the image, uses it properly, he sees through or beyond the material image and remembers "another world." Although the image is apprehended by the eye, it stimulates men to "withdraw" from the senses, to substitute spiritual for physical sight. In this way, Protestant emblem books reform the inherited images of medieval Catholicism, internalizing and personalizing them, altering forever the person's relation to them.

Notes

1. Robert J. Clements, *Picta Poesis: Literary and Humanistic Theory in Renaissance Emblem Books* (Rome, 1960), pp. 33, 127, 220; *Renaissance Letters: Revelations of a World Reborn,* ed. Robert J. Clements and Lorna Levant (New York, 1976), pp. 40-42.

2. "Problems in Emblem Literature," *Journal of English and Germanic Philology,* 45 (1946), 33; "Henry Hawkins and *Partheneia Sacra," Review of English Studies,* n.s. 26 (1975), 276; Mario Praz, *Studies in Seventeenth-Century Imagery* (Rome, 1964), p. 207; Peter M. Daly, *Literature in the Light of the Emblem* (Toronto, 1979), p. 52 who paraphrases Dietrich Jons, *Das "Sinnen-Bild." Studien zur allegorischen Bildlichkeit bei Andreas Gryphius* (Stuttgart, 1966), p. 56; Daly, *Literature,* p. 50.

3. *The Resources of Kind: Genre-Theory in the Renaissance* (Berkeley, 1973), p. 50; Frances Yates, "The Emblematic Conceit in Giordano Bruno's *De Gli Eroici Furori* and in the Elizabethan Sonnet Sequences," *The Journal of Warburg and Courtland Institutes,* 6 (1943), 105.

4. Praz, *Studies,* p. 170.

5. "Word and Image in Quarles' *Emblemes," Critical Inquiry,* 6 (1980), 385-410; reprinted in *The Language of Images,* ed. W. J. T. Mitchell (Chicago, 1980), p. 63.

6. Donald Kelley, *Foundations of Modern Scholarship: Language, Law, and History in the French Renaissance* (New York, 1970), pp. 102, 93.

7. See, for example, Guillaume de La Perrière, *Le Theatre des bons engins* (Paris, 1539); Georgette de Montenay, *Emblemes ou Devises Chrestiennes* (Lyons, 1571); Jan van der Noot, *A Theatre for Voluptuous Worldlings* (London, 1569). Leon Voet, *The Golden Compasses* (Amsterdam, 1969) identifies Christopher Plantin, a major publisher of emblem texts, as a member of the secret anabaptist sect called The Family of Love (1, pp. 21-30) and supports the theory of H. de la Fontaine Verwey that Plantin secretly "published the heretical writings of his own spiritual mentors—Hendrik Niclaes in 1555-56 and Hendrik Janssen Barrefelt in 1579-80" (2, p. 277). In addition to documenting Plantin's connections with Niclaes, Barrefelt, and The Family of Love, his "indifference towards the outward forms of religion," and the conversion to the reformed religion of his son-in-law Raphelengius, Voet argues that "Plantin's career as a printer undoubtedly has its origin in his religious convictions" (2, p. 24). Plantin never formally broke with the Roman Catholic Church, however, and, although his most intimate friends were also members of The Family of Love, he included supporters of both the Roman Catholic and Protestant positions in his circle.

8. Clements, *Picta Poesis,* p. 31; James Hutton, *The Greek Anthology in France* (Ithaca, 1946), p. 321; Henry Martyn Baird, *Theodore Beza: The Counsellor of the French Reformation* (New York, 1899) and G. A. Rothrock, *The Huguenots* (Chicago, 1979), p. 33; Clements, *Picta Poesis,* pp.

200-201; Karl H. Dannenfeldt, "Wittenberg Botanists during the Sixteenth Century," *The Social History of the Reformation,* ed. Lawrence P. Buck and Jonathan W. Zophy (Columbus, 1972), pp. 240-41; H. A. Enno Van Gelder, *The Two Reformations in the Sixteenth Century* (The Hague, 1961), pp. 312-18.

9. *Protestant Poetics and the Seventeenth-Century Religious Lyric* (Princeton, 1979), pp. 185-97 and Gilman, "Word and Image." Lewalski considers Quarles' emblem book "a thorough Protestant reworking of Hugo," p. 192. Both Lewalski and Gilman contradict Karl Joseph Höltgen's assertion that "One hardly finds any alterations of the pictorial sources of Quarles' emblem book for doctrinal reasons": *Francis Quarles 1592-1644* (Tubingen, 1978), p. 342.

10. John Phillips, *The Reformation of Images: Destruction of Art in England, 1535-1660* (Berkeley, 1973), p. 46. Phillips is here quoting William Tyndale, *An Answer to Sir Thomas More's Dialogue.* I present a similar argument and use some of the same quotations in my essay, "'To Put Us in Remembrance': The Protestant Transformation of Images of Judgment in English Renaissance Drama," *Homo, Memento Finis,* ed. David Bevington (Kalamazoo, 1985), pp. 179-208.

11. Charles Garside Jr., *Zwingli and the Arts* (New Haven, 1966), p. 134.

12. Phyllis Mack Crew, *Calvinist Preaching and Iconoclasm in the Netherlands 1544-1569* (Cambridge, 1978), p. 23.

13. Phillips, *Reformation of Images,* p. 45, from Tyndale, *Answer to More's Dialogue*; p. 54, from *Ten Articles*; p. 57, from Thomas Cranmer, *Bishop's Book*; p. 56.

14. *The Sermons of John Donne,* ed. George R. Potter and Evelyn M. Simpson (Berkeley, 1955), 2: sermon 11, 237.

15. *The Heroicall Devises of M. Claudius Paradin* (London, 1591), ¶5, ¶6; *A Collection of Emblemes, Ancient and Modern* (London, 1635), sigs. A2, A, K^v, K2; *Schola cordis or the heart of it selfe* (London, 1647), sig. K; *Ashrea* (London, 1665), sigs. b2, bs^v.

16. Frances A. Yates, *The Art of Memory* (Chicago, 1966), p. 74.

17. Barbara Lewalski similarly argues that "the typical Protestant procedure [of meditation] is very nearly the reverse" of Catholic meditation; "instead of the application of the self to the subject," she writes, Protestant meditation "calls for the application of the subject to the self": *Protestant Poetics,* p. 150.

18. Elizabeth L. Eisenstein, *The Printing Press as an Agent of Change* (Cambridge, 1979), pp. 129, 69; Yates, *Art of Memory,* p. 127.

19. *Sacorum emblematum centuria una* (Cambridge, 1591), sig. G2. Lewalski distinguishes between Catholic and Protestant theories of typology: *Protestant Poetics,* pp. 123-26.

20. *Institution of the Christian Religion,* trans. Ford Lewis Battles (Atlanta, 1975), pp. 123, 125, 118, 148.

21. *The Soules Solace, or thirtie and one spirituall emblems* (London, 1626), sig. F6^v.

22. *Minerva Britanna,* (London, 1612), sig. b3^v.

23. *The devout hart or royal throne of the pacifical Salomon* (Rouen, 1634), sig. G9^v.

24. *A Book for Boys and Girls, or, Country Rhymes for Children* (London, 1686), "To the Reader," no sig.

25. *The Theater of Fine Devices,* (London, 1614), sigs. A5, A5^v.

26. *Emblemes* (London, 1634), sig. A3.

27. *The Royal Politician* (London, 1700), sig. A3^v.

28. *The Invisible World, Discovered to spiritual eyes, and Reduced to useful Meditation* (London, 1652), pp. 335-56.

Anthony Raspa (essay date January-March 1987)

SOURCE: Raspa, Anthony. "Native English Emblem Books and Their Catholic Manifestations." *Word & Image* 3, no. 1 (January-March 1987): 104-10.

[*In the following essay, Raspa reviews the origins of English Catholic emblem books to argue that they do not differ significantly from the more common and prominent Protestant books. Raspa emphasizes the specifically English character of the Catholic emblem writers.*]

The Counter-Reformation emblem book in English in the seventeenth century, which Freeman, Lewalski and Daly have studied in the general contexts of emblem history, deserves to be considered in its own right.[1] English Catholic emblem books had distinctive characteristics that justify their consideration as a separate group. There were only five such books: the Jesuit Henry Hawkins' *Partheneia Sacra* published in Rouen in 1633; his translation of the French Jesuit Etienne Luzvic's *Le Coeur Devot* as *The Devout Heart* published in the following year, again in Rouen; the Protestant Christopher Harvey's verse translation of the last three of the four books of the Benedictine Benedict van Haeften's *Schola Cordis* as *The School of the Heart,* printed in London in 1647; *Ashrea: or, The Grove of Beatitudes* (London, 1665) by 'E. M.', who is held to be either the Jesuit Edward Mico or else Edward Manning; and, finally, Jeremias Drexel's *The Christian Zodiak: or Twelve Signes First Written in Latin. Zodiak* appeared without emblem pictures from the hand of an unidentified English translator in Rouen in 1633, and it reappeared in 1647 in a new edition with emblem pictures.[2]

Freeman and Lewalski have identified *Partheneia, The Devout Heart* and *Ashrea* as Catholic emblem books.[3] To these must be added *The School of the Heart,* because the Protestant Harvey's translation does not alter the aesthetics of the original, as, for example, the Protestant Arwaker's version of the Jesuit Hugo's *Pia Desideria* does some years later.[4] The anonymous translation of Drexel's *Christian Zodiak* must also be included, and Freeman and Lewalski seem simply to have overlooked it. The 1633, pictureless edition of *Zodiak* is not in the old *Short Title Catalogue of English Books* printed before 1640, but there is a copy in the British Library in London.[5]

The discussion of these five so-called English Catholic emblem books as a group, even if it only shows that the basis for their grouping is limited, is a logical step in the light of the contemporary scholarly criticism of the English emblem. The English Catholic emblem book of the Renaissance has been generally declared to be Jesuit. This statement is more or less correct. However, it may mistakenly suggest that the character of Jesuit Renaissance writings was homogeneous and that nothing can really be added to what we know of it. The statement also ignores the fact that Freeman and Lewalski wrongly identify *The School of the Heart* and van Haeften as Jesuit when they were Benedictine.[6] The English Catholic emblem book has otherwise been largely unexplored, with the exception of general references to its Jesuit character and of the articles on *Partheneia* by Wolfgang Lottes suggesting a source.[7] The Jesuit character of English emblem literature has otherwise been left uninvestigated. The references to Jesuit influences have been mostly limited to observations, such as those by Bush, that it is sensory and baroque and therefore alien to the mainstream of English literature.[8]

The current obscure context of Catholic emblem books deserves correction in the light of the considerable body of Catholic Renaissance literature because the latter's republication in several facsimile series in recent years has reminded scholars of its extent, importance and proximity to the centre of cultural life at this time. Counter-Reformation writings in England and in English, as these facsimile books have revealed, were much more distinctively English, complex and numerous than was previously assumed. These writings also include emblem literature. English Catholic emblem literature was as indigenous to its native writers and translators as English Protestant emblem books were to theirs. Both English Catholics and English Protestants, when they translated or borrowed continental material, picked from the same store of writings. When they dealt originally with the emblem, they partook equally in the joys and shortcomings related to the native origins of their tradition.

The opinions of Renaissance Englishmen about the emblem throw light on its Catholic manifestations. Moreover, the history of these opinions and the arguments they inspired are a different story from that of English emblem books *per se.* The emblem books on which modern critics have tended to concentrate were usually collections of graphic pictures. Each of these pictures, as is well known, was normally accompanied by a motto and sometimes by a prefatory quotation or both; each picture was invariably followed by a moralistic poem repeating in poetic imagery the symbols and figures in the picture; this was occasionally also followed by a prose passage or two explaining the meaning of part or of the whole of the picture or of the poem or both; and, finally, another quotation could serve as epilogue. The history of such books marked by these conventions is one which Freeman has already written, but it does not necessarily tell the story of what the emblem meant to its times.[9] In the sixteenth and seventeenth centuries the emblem suggested to English readers certain things which had an influence on the five Catholic emblem books in question. English Catholic emblem books were part of the general phenomenon of emblem literature in England, although at the same time they had their own characteristics.

The English emblem phenomenon manifested itself in two ways. Its history was divided not into kinds of emblem books but, rather, into the writing of emblem books themselves, and into the theory and criticism of emblem literature that modern critics have tended to dismiss as importations from the French and the Italians.[10] To look at English emblem literature in the light of this division helps greatly to clarify the nature of the Catholic books. It avoids the grouping of English emblem books into types and kinds based on modern critical principles, that have tended to obscure both the communal nature of all English emblem writings and the specific characteristics of its branches. There were only in fact a handful of English emblem books that did not borrow extensively, so far as we know, for either picture or text from any Catholic continental work. Of these ironically, two books, Hawkins' *Partheneia* and E. M.'s *Ashrea,* are Catholic, Counter-Reformation and most likely both Jesuit. They are also among the most native and the most elaborate of English emblem books along with Peacham's *Minerva Brittana* and Quarles'

Hieroglyphics of the Life of Man. By contrast to the Catholic *Partheneia* and *Ashrea*, Anglican or Calvinist books such as Quarles' *Emblems* and Whitney's *Choice of Emblems* borrowed liberally from continental Catholic sources. Therefore the grouping of English emblem books into the Catholic continental and the native Protestant British does not appear viable as a standard of what English emblem literature meant to its times.[11]

As a coherent cultural phenomenon capable of being treated independently of the European emblem tradition, English emblem literature began with Samuel Daniel's published translation of Giovio in 1585, and ended with Bunyan's *Book For Boys and Girls* in 1686 almost exactly a century later. In this period, the movement of English emblem literature appears to have had four fairly distinct characteristics. Firstly, throughout its history, discussions on the nature of the emblem and the production of emblem books occurred side by side. Secondly, these discussions concluded nothing final about the nature of the emblem as text or picture or both. Thirdly, the purpose of the emblem was understood as moral in the sense of the statement of an idealistic principle. Fourthly, two-level typology and four-level anagogy distinguished English Protestant and English Catholic emblem books respectively. The appearance of these four characteristics in part or even in the whole of the continental emblem tradition is not in question here.

As far as evidences of practice and theory are concerned, English emblem books and commentaries on the genre began at about the same time, although the commentaries were first on the published scene by one year. The Italian, Alciati, produced in Latin on an Augsburg press the first emblem book ever in any language in 1531, and a half century after him, in 1585, Daniel published the first commentary on the genre of the emblem in English.[12] Daniel translated the Italian Paolo Giovio's, or Paulus Jovius' *The Worthy Tract [. . .] Contayning a Discourse of rare inventions, both Militarie and Amorous, called Imprese. Whereunto is added a Preface contayning the Arte of composing them, with many other notable devises.* In the very next year, 1586, the first English emblem book appeared, Geoffrey Whitney's *A Choice of Emblemes.* Then, two years later, 1588, amid what was evidently a rapidly-growing English interest in emblem literature, yet a second English tract on the emblem appeared, this time in Latin. This was Abraham Fraunce's *Insignium, Armorum, Emblematum, Hieroglyphicorum, et Symbolorum,* published in London. Fraunce's tract relies on French and Italian commentators and quotes them, but is an otherwise original composition. Yet about another two years later, in 1590 or shortly thereafter, the second English emblem book, *Sacrorum Emblematum Centuria Una,*

by Andrew Willet appeared. Each of the verse emblems of Willet's book is printed in Latin and is followed by its English translation.[13]

A year or so later, in 1591, the numbers of emblem books and of commentaries on emblem books again kept pace with each other with the London publication by an anonymous 'P. S.' of *The Heroicall Devises of Claudius Paradin* containing a commentary and emblems. P. S.'s translation significantly altered Paradin's prefatory text on devises by introducing the word 'emblem' to distinguish emblem from devise. P. S. coped with the obscurity surrounding devise and emblem by translating Paradin's use of 'devise' by 'devise' for the art form which used only pictures and mottoes (Sigs. 5ᵛ, 6ʳ), and 'devise' by 'emblem' in the case of the art form that added passages of prose and poetry to picture and motto (Paradin, Sigs. a2ᵛ, a3ʳ). Two years later, in 1593, the appearance in manuscript of Thomas Coombe's translation of Guillaume de la Perrière's *Le Théâtre des Bons Engins* of 1536, as *The Theatre of Fine Devises,* duly entered in the Stationer's Register, again contained emblems and commentaries. Coombe's translation, however, was not published until 1614.[14]

These six books by Daniel, Whitney, Fraunce, Willet, P. S., and Coombe, constitute the history of the English emblem in the sixteenth century. They maintain a balance between theory and practice perceptible in the English emblem tradition in the next century as well. Notably, most of them are also inspired heavily by continental works, none of them, though they may have Anglican or Calvinist asides, is written consistently in an openly Protestant cause,[15] none is concerned formatively with the theological and political causes of what is considered as the Counter-Reformation, and the six works suggest the critical and historical marks of the English emblem tradition in the seventeenth century as well as in the sixteenth.

By contrast to the broad historical lines of theory and practice in the development of English emblem literature, contemporary discussions about the nature of the emblem touched on specific matters. These discussions centred on the question of what made up an emblem, and they gave to the history of the English emblem its second general characteristic. Commentators and emblem writers argued extensively and most consistently about whether the emblem was a text, or picture, or both. Concerns about the relative aesthetic, pictorial and poetic values of the emblem, which are a major issue with modern critics, were not a fundamental problem to its time. For Renaissance Englishmen, the issue of the nature of the emblem was concentrated largely on its constituent parts of picture and text, and it dominated their discussion in the history of the English emblem. First, in his preface to the reader in his translation of Giovio (1585), there is Daniel's description of an impresa as 'some figure and mot' (Sig. A6ʳ), and of a 'mot' as a short sentence or poesie normally of less than three major words (Sig. Aij,ʳᵛ). Daniel did not mention the word emblem, but his prefacer, who signed himself N. W., both introduced and tried to define it. The emblem, N. W. wrote, had more parts than the impresa, but of the same kind, namely, poetry and picture (Sig. viᵛ). As though answering Daniel by prefatory letter, N. W. attacked his definition of impresa and the absence of emblem in his discussion as evidence of narrowness. N. W. distinguished the impresa from the emblem on the grounds of length, and then associated the impresa anew with the emblem on the grounds of genre. He wrote:

> *Emblems* are generall conceiptes rather of moral matters then perticular deliberations: rather to give credit to the wit, then to reveale the secretes of the mind. What should I say more. This *Impresa,* is that perfect *Symbolum:* for antiquitie to be reverenced; for worthiness admired: for pleasure embraced. Pardon me (I pray you) if I rainge a little and chase a discorse in this so wide a Forrest.

(Sig. viiʳ)

With this, N. W. concluded his argument on the note that the emblem had picture and poetry as the source of its perfection.

Emblem is picture and poetry also in Fraunce's tract three years after that mock dispute between Daniel and N. W. In his section on symbol, emblem and hieroglyphic, Fraunce wrote that 'Emblems are said to be sententious images of a sort', and, a few lines later, he added that 'Metaphorically speaking, those emblems are called poetry by which images . . . are eruditely explained' (Sigs. N1, N2ʳ). At the height of its popularity in the period that stretched from Wither to Arwaker, the emblem was also understood to be made up in practice of picture and text. There are the examples of *Minerva Britanna* (1612) by Peacham the Younger who spoke of 'picture' and 'verse'; of *Emblemes* (1635) in which Quarles described the purpose of emblem as to please both eye and ear; of *A Collection of Emblemes* (1635) in which Wither speaks of the 'Collector of the said [his] Emblems' as either 'the Versifier or the Graver', and of emblem as 'Picture' and 'Verse' (Sig. A1ᵛ); of *Partheneia* in which Hawkins described his 'Devises' as 'consisting of Impreses, and Mottoes, Characters, Essayes, Emblemes, and Poesies' (Sig. Aiiᵛ, Aiiiʳ); and of *The Devout Heart* in which Hawkins speaks again of 'Pictures' and 'Poesies' (p. 4).[16]

However, in the middle of the seventeenth century at the height of its popularity in England, the attribution of picture to emblem was not always as clear as the above quotations suggest. A consensus as to what constituted an emblem was far from complete, and generally indecisive theoretical discussions of emblem as

picture or text prevailed. The lack of reference to picture is particularly true of the earlier and of the later stages of the emblem tradition, that is, of certain sixteenth-century texts and of the later commentators and emblem books in the seventeenth century. But the absence of references to picture occurs in the intervening period as well. For example, in 1637, in Thomas Heywood's *Pleasant Dialogues and Drammas,* which contains translations of Jacob Cats' *amatoria* emblems of 1618, the emblem is not a picture but a 'rich conceit, and excellent expression' (Sig. A4ᵛ);[17] and the discrepancy between the first translated edition of Drexel's *Christian Zodiac* published without pictures in 1633 and republished with pictures in 1647 has already been pointed out. Even later, as the century wore on, the uncertainty persisted. In 1686, Arwaker referred to emblem as picture alone. In his preface to his translation of the Jesuit Hugo's *Pia Desideria,* Arwaker complained that Quarles, in his earlier English translation of the work, had 'only borrow'd his [Hugo's] Emblems, to prefix them to much inferiour sense' (Sig. A5ʳ). In the same year, 1686, Bunyan's *A Book for Boys and Girls* contained 74 emblems. Yet, it was published without pictures until another hand than Bunyan's added them to the second edition in 1701. The title was then changed to *Divine Emblems . . . Fitted for the Use of Boys and Girls.*[18]

The difficult question of what constituted an emblem book—picture, prose, poetry, or a mixture of the three—was therefore a major mark of both English Catholic and Protestant emblem books. The importance of the question, moreover, was not diminished by the uncertainty that it spread over contemporary evaluations of the emblem. The issue of picture and text in both contemporary discussions and practice was an integral part of the English emblem tradition, and it gave birth to the even more important comments about its ideals.

The ideals of the emblem, which were the third quality to mark its history in England, encompassed the question of intention and moral. In discussions about the emblem, intention and moral were associated words and they were constantly applied to its purpose. They were also related to other words in the vocabulary of literary theory such as 'invention', 'decoration' and 'elaboration', and naturally to 'metaphor' and 'symbol'. Moral here was understood to signify what the Renaissance person should be, and contrasted with the later use of the moralistic in emblem literature suggesting what he should do. From the very beginning of the English emblem tradition, many emblems were moralistic. But the moral in the sense of an ideal state of being rather than the occasional appearance of moralistic emblems, marked the tradition as a whole.

The first theoretical English work on the emblem illustrates well the importance for it of the issue of moral and ideal. In the prefatory material of Daniel's translation of Giovio's *Discourse,* although Daniel and his friend N. W. jousted over the meanings of devise, emblem and impresa, they agreed as to their common significance. In his preface to the reader, Daniel grouped the impresa under the devise, and wrote that the purpose of the devise was 'to signifie our intentions by these formes or figures of creatures' (Sig. Ai^v). Moreover, 'intention' was present in all written and pictorial parts of devise and unified them; 'by adding mots and posies to their figures', Daniel wrote, the creators of devises 'disclose their intent by a more perfect order'. Then, he added, 'we may discover our secret intentions by colours and figures', through 'the figuring of things corporall and of visible forme' and of 'things incorporal' as well (Sigs. Aij^rv). Such an 'intention' in picture and word was a moral in the sense of a statement of any kind of truth or reality—theological, natural or political—as the Renaissance emblematist perceived it. The purpose of the devise was to figure forth that truth to suggest the proper dimension of the Renaissance reader's existence, and, when speaking of the impresa, Daniel described its 'figure and mot together' as signifying 'an enterprise, wherat a noble mind leveling with the aime of a deepe desire, strives with a stedy interest to gaine the prise of his purpose' (Sig. A^7r).

N. W., who agreed with Daniel about the ideal moral purpose of the devise, grouped the emblem as well as the impresa under it. However, the emblem was longer than the impresa, and its moral scope was therefore larger. Emblems, N. W. wrote, were 'general conceipts rather of moral matters then perticulare deliberations' (Sig. vi^r). Moreover, because of the 'moral matters' concerned, N. W. found that the 'sole word *Symbolum* every way is to large and generall a term' for the impresa. N. W. described symbol as 'that note by which we know or can conjecture any thing', and he wished to use a word with narrower applications than symbol to describe impresa. But he nevertheless spoke of impresa and of its practice as emblem as 'that perfect *Symbolum*' (Sigs. vi^r, vii^r). As N. W.'s argument moved uncertainly between emblem and impresa, the latter form, the impresa, he said, fell or was 'restrayned' within its own 'scope and generalitie', and in this way conformed to the usual metaphoric standards of symbol. By contrast, the emblem's purpose was more 'to give credit to the wit, than to reveal the secrets of the minde', but, like the impresa it too was symbolic. Constituted of such parts as picture, motto, verse, prose and quotation, the emblem was one complex symbol. The significance of these parts of the emblematic symbol for N. W. was its moral and intention.

In that early current of interest in the emblem in England marked by N. W. and Daniel, Abraham Fraunce's view of the emblem conformed much to the approach of his compatriots. The symbol, Fraunce wrote, 'is that by which we come to conjecture and know anything'

(*Symbolum . . . est id quo aliquid coniectamus et cognoscimus*) (Sig. M2), and it was with this understanding of the symbol that he discussed its influence on, and its similarities with, the emblem. However, as Fraunce was quick to point out, the emblem had many parts, through which it made its statement of precept and doctrine, and so differed from the usual concept of symbol as a single image. The intention, moral, precept or doctrine was transmitted to the reader by the relationship of one part of the emblem to the other, whereas normally the meaning of a symbol was communicated to a beholder by one image. Fraunce wrote: 'In an emblem, speech explains a figure and this is considered the greatest of vices in symbol where neither the speech should explain the figure nor the figure the speech; whereas in the emblem the figure with the speech explains the notions of the mind. An emblem is therefore so constituted that it states a certain general precept and doctrine' (Sig. N3).[19]

Many years later in his preface to his translation of Luzvic' work, in 1634, Hawkins continued faithfully the Protestant Daniel's, N. W.'s and Fraunce's tradition of emblem as a statement of intention. Hawkins discussed the now traditional intention of emblem in terms of idea and image. He presented to his reader, he wrote, 'the image of a Heart', not 'in idea, but lively deciphered with devout Embleames' (p. 4). To grasp the nature of human existence in statements of universal import in 'Poesies' and 'speaking pictures', and not the correction of behaviour, was the aim of the emblem (pp. 4-5). A little more than a decade after Hawkins' work appeared, Blount's translation from the French of Henri Estienne's *The Art of making Devises Treating of Hieroglyphics, Symboles, Emblemes,* aptly summarized the emblem's moral, symbolic and universal concerns. Blount's text reads, 'the Embleme is properly a sweet and morall Symbole, which consists of picture and words, by which some weighty sentence is declared' (p. 7); and Blount adds later, 'the words of the *Embleme* may demonstrate things universall, and hold the rank of morall precepts, which may as wel serve for all the wor[l]d, as for the proper author of the Emblem' (p. 25). The idealistic character of the English emblem tradition described by Hawkins and Blount persisted for many years, for it is found also in Philip Ayres' treatment of love in *Emblemata Amatoria* in 1683.[20]

English emblem writers therefore generally understood the emblem to be a complex symbol even if they disagreed over the details of the symbol's constituent parts. In the writings of Daniel, N. W., Fraunce, Hawkins and Blount, the emblem is discussed consistently as a symbolic structure, and this structure is viewed as typological with levels of meaning. Each emblem had a single meaning of universal importance underlying its prose or poetry or picture or all three, and the whole was to be understood by grasping the significance of its levels of meaning. As such, the emblem fulfilled the general Renaissance criterion that art should instruct, and its instruction appealed to the understanding rather than governed conduct. When the purpose of this instruction grew synonymous with moralistic conduct, the English emblem tradition came to an end. Bunyan's book for boys and girls, for instance, was a series of didactic, sententious poems. The emblem pictures added to them in the edition of 1701 were illustrations rather than an integral part of a symbolic unit. The view that emblem was a universal statement made in a typological structure of words and picture had receded, in spite of, and perhaps even because of, Bunyan's catechetical purpose.

The typological dimension of the emblem explored by English writers constituted its fourth characteristic. The emblem appeared to be understandable in terms of the principles of analogy and typology that the emblematist brought to bear on the historical material with which he dealt. Made up of poetry, prose, and picture, the emblem had levels of meaning in each one of its parts, held together by typological principles. English Catholic and Protestant emblem writers in the seventeenth century shared these principles, even though their approaches to typology differed, and even though their differences ultimately distinguished them.

As modern critics have shown, Renaissance typology had two general branches. The first of these was Catholic and continued with variations the medieval approach to typology which had four levels. The second of these branches was Protestant and put the accent on typology as the science for the examination of only two levels in things.[21] Four-level typology suggested that its science was based on the existential nature of things. That is, four-level typology held that things were knowable according to their literal or historical level, to their allegorical or figurative level, to their tropological or moral level, and to their anagogic or mystical level. Such levels of meaning could be pursued without the immediate interference of biblical types. For its part, two-level typology suggested that things possessed literal and mystical levels of meaning, and that such levels of meaning were immediately circumscribed by the prototypes of the Bible and by the copies of these prototypes in human history.

These concerns with four-level and two-level typology mark none of the sixteenth-century emblem books and their theories. When these early books were written, typology in contemporary thought had not assumed a prominence that required its expression in emblem literature. Sixteenth-century English emblem books therefore are characterized only by the first three marks of the four suggested here for their tradition in England. No strict division is possible among sixteenth-century English emblem books on Catholic or Protestant

grounds in spite of the anti-Catholic character of a few of Willet's emblems. Such books were concerned principally with introducing the emblem into English literature and with developing a working concept of it, irrespective of Anglican, Calvinist and Catholic traditions. The same may not be said of English emblem books in the following century.

Among the later five so-called Catholic emblem books, the development of four of them, *Partheneia Sacra, Ashrea, The Devout Heart,* and *The Christian Zodiak,* follow the model of the four-level typological science. The anonymous author E. M. of *Ashrea* described the role of what he called 'objects' and of 'mystical sense' in his emblem book in both his dedicatory letter and in his preface, then proceeded to give 'a particular account of the Design and Title of this little Work' (Sigs. a[3], a[4], a[5]), and finally he described the role of four-level typology using the Biblical story of Jonas and the whale.

A little later in his preface, E. M. gave another example of the typological forces at work in his volume. He wrote, describing the first of the four levels of meaning:

> *The Rain-bow shall be in the Clouds,* saith the Text, as spoken by God himself, *And I will look upon it, that I may* remember *the everlasting covenant.* Here we may say, the place consign'd was the Rain-bow, on which the Covenant, to be remembred, was placed; and [second or figurative level of meaning] by that Rain-bow was prefigured Christ, on the Cross, whom his Father beholding is moved to mercy, and compassion towards sinners.

> And [third or moral level of meaning] why should not we wretched sinners, whenever we behold, or represent to our selves this Rain-bow (to wit, Christ crucifi'd and fasten'd to the Cross) diversifi'd with the several colours of red, and white, and black, and blew, etc. immediately call to mind what he suffred, and for whom he suffred? And [fourth or mystical level of meaning], why may we not, upon that representation, according to the foresaid Art, assign eight several places, at certain distances, for our better remembrance and practice of the *Eight Beatitudes?*

E. M. concludes his prefatory remark with a reference to the tenth Book of *Confessions* which was the first of the last four books of Augustine's work to deal with creation, typology and human memory (Sigs. b[v], b2[rv]).

In *Ashrea, Partheneia Sacra, The Devout Heart* and *The Christian Zodiak,* such typology as E. M. described functioned roughly in this manner. In the second emblem, 'The Rose', in *Partheneia,* the picture of the rose was the object of four-level scientific investigation. The first text, 'The Character', which followed the picture, described the flower's historical or literal level, the 'glorie and delight' of flowers; the second text, 'The Morals', described its allegorical or figurative level, its 'blush'; the third text, 'The Essay', described its moral level, its 'hidden vertues'; and the fourth text, 'The Discourse', describes the flower's mystical level: Hawkins calls the flower the 'Mystical Rose' prefiguring Mary (pp. 17-24). Hawkins' *Partheneia* was united by these elements, first, that all his emblem pictures were drawn from the central prefatory emblem of a garden, and, second, that the fourth level of meaning of all of his emblems referred to Mary. The subsequent four-part structure of 'Embleme', 'Poesie', 'Theories' and 'Apostrophe' in each of Hawkins' emblematic units repeated the typological investigation of the first part. Such a description of the typological forces in English Catholic emblem literature tends to ignore the presence of other Counter-Reformation influences, like meditative techniques and Ignatian aesthetics. Consequently, the description may mistakenly be taken to suggest that nothing remains to be said. It nevertheless reveals an interesting truth.

In *Ashrea,* the object of each part of every one of E. M.'s eight emblems which is to be investigated is a Biblical citation of the beatitudes. The four levels of meaning of each beatitude are found first in the emblem picture, secondly in the little poem that follows, thirdly in the subsequent prose passage, and fourthly in the 'Considerations or the . . . Beatitude' that conclude every one of E. M.'s eight emblems. In *The Devout Heart,* the emblem picture is once more the object to be investigated by the four levels of Catholic typology, and the process closely resembles that of *Partheneia,* except that the four parts are called 'The Hymne', 'The Incentive', 'The Preamble to the Meditation' and 'The Meditation'. In Drexel's *Christian Zodiak,* the pattern is looser, but nevertheless its spirit prevails. In both 1633 and 1647 versions, the motto, Biblical quotation and picture of each of the twelve emblems are followed almost invariably by four, and much less often by three or five explanatory prose passages developing levels of significance.

In the last so-called Catholic emblem book of the seventeenth century, *The School of the Heart,* the Protestant translator Harvey omitted the first book of van Haeften's Latin text. He also versified his prose passages in the subsequent three books, and added an epigram between the Biblical quotation and the prose passage of each emblem. However, he maintained van Haeften's sense of typological study. He even wrote a verse epilogue on the four levels of meaning based on van Haeften's ideas in the omitted first book.[22]

By contrast to what we have been considering as English Catholic four-level typology, Anglican and Calvinist typology, with its preference for attributing two levels of meaning to things, had corresponding effects on emblem literature. In his translation of Hugo's *Pia Desideria,* for example, Arwaker eliminated all images, emblem pictures and textual illustrations that could not

be immediately related to Biblical type. He excised what he described as Hugo's 'severall fictitious stories', and he replaced them where possible with 'apposite example out of the Scriptures'. Arwaker also eliminated what he called the 'severall historical passages taken from the Legend of the Saints and Martyrologies' because of what he considered to be their questionable 'relations' (Sigs. A5^{r,v}, A6^r). Arwaker interpreted the mystical sense of his emblems immediately according to their historical suggestions, and he confirmed the meaning of that mystical sense according to Biblical type.

By the time that Arwaker wrote his translation, this concern with two-level typology in the field of emblem literature had already long been clearly enunciated. In 1634, in his preface 'To the Reader' in *Emblemes,* Quarles had defined emblem according to Biblical parable. 'An Embleme', he wrote, 'is but a silent Parable. Let not the tender Eye check, to see the allusion to our blessed Saviour figured in these Types. In holy Scripture, he is sometimes called a Sower; sometimes, a Fisher; sometimes a Physician: And why not presented so as well to the eye as to the eare?' (Sig. A3^r). In 1635, Wither, for his part, found the prototype for his artistic role in the figure of the Biblical David. He wrote that 'some Bookes conceitedly composed' had instructed him to 'knowledge' much as David had been enlightened by his own heart about his fallen nature. He took, Wither said, 'little pleasures in Rymes, Fictions, or conceited Compositions, for their owne sakes', but he approved of them for the 'good purposes' of 'instruction' (Sig. A^r).

Even if the number of English emblem books in the sixteenth and seventeenth centuries was large enough to produce many overtly different types, a common purpose underlay them all. The differences between so-called Protestant and Catholic emblem books were differences of degree and of emphases on shared interests rather than differences of native origin.

Notes

1. Rosemary Freeman, *English Emblem Books* (London: Chatto, 1948); Peter M. Daly, *Emblem Theory: Recent German Contributions to the Characterization of the Emblem Genre* (Nendeln/Liechtenstein: KTO Press, 1979); *Literature in the Light of the Emblem: Structural Parallels between the Emblem and Literature in the Sixteenth and Seventeenth Centuries* (Toronto: Toronto University Press, 1979); Barbara Kieffer Lewalski, *Protestant Poetics and the Seventeenth Century Religious Lyric* (Princeton: Princeton University Press, 1979), pp. 179-212.

2. Henry Hawkins, *Partheneia Sacra. Or the Mysterious and delicious garden of the Sacred Parthenes; Symbolically set forth and enriched*

With Pious Devises and emblemes (Rouen, 1633), of which the Scolar Press Facsimile copy, with an introduction by K. J. Höltgen (Menston: Scolar Press: 1971), is used here; Henry Hawkins, trans., *The Devout Heart* (Rouen, 1634), in *English Recusant Literature*, Vol. 119, of *Scolar Press Facsimiles* (Menston: Scolar Press, 1975); Christopher Harvey, trans., *The School of the Heart . . . In 47. Emblems* (London, 1647 [Cambridge University Library Shelf Mark: Yorke, e. 19]), from Benedict van Haeften, *Schola Cordis* (Antwerp, 1635); *Ashrea: or the Grove of Beatitudes, Represented in Emblems* (London, 1665), in *English Emblem Books,* no. 18, *Scolar Press Facsimiles,* with note by John Horden (Menston: Scolar Press, 1970); and Jeremias Drexel, *The Christian Zodiak: or Twelve Signes First Written in Latin by Fa. Ier. Drexel of the Societie of Iesus Newly Englished* (Rouen, 1633, printed without emblem pictures; printed in 1647 with emblem pictures).

3. Freeman, *English Emblem Books,* p. 174; Lewalski, *Protestant Poetics,* pp. 197, 469.

4. Edmund Arwaker, trans., *Pia Desideria: Or, Divine Addresses In Three Books* (London, 1686); Herman Hugo, *Pia Desideria Emblematis, Elegiis & affectibus* (Antwerp, 1624).

5. The British Library Shelf Mark of the 1633 English edition of *Zodiac* is C.111.d.23.

6. Freeman, *English Emblem Books,* pp. 132, 153, 173; Lewalski, *Protestant Poetics,* p. 193.

7. Wolfgang Lottes, 'Henry Hawkins and *Partheneia Sacra*', *Review of English Studies,* N.S. 26 (1975), Nos. 102 and 103, pp. 144-153, 271-286.

8. Douglas Bush, *English Literature in the Earlier Seventeenth Century,* in *Oxford History of English Literature* (Oxford; Clarendon Press, 1954), pp. 90, 148; Freeman, *English Emblem Books,* p. 43.

9. Other notable examples of books on the history of the emblem are by Alan Young, *Henry Peacham* (New York: Twayne, 1979); and Karl Josef Höltgen, *Francis Quarles 1592-1644. Meditativer Dichter, Emblematiker, Royalist. Eine biographische und kritische Studie* (Tübingen: Niemayer, 1978).

10. Freeman, *English Emblem Books,* pp. 43, 47.

11. Freeman, *English Emblem Books,* p. 233; Henry Green, ed., 'Introductory Dissertation', in Geoffrey Whitney, *A Choice of Emblemes* (New York: B. Blom, 1967), pp. lix-lx.

12. However, some critics consider that Puttenham wrote about five pages of criticism on the emblem in *The Arte of English Poesie,* which was published in 1589, between 1565 and 1585. The present paper considers that Puttenham restricted the meaning of emblem synonymously to that of the devise, and that he considered the devise to signify armorial ensignas and not literary forms; Puttenham, *The Arte of English Poesie* (Cambridge, 1936), pp. 102-108, and G. D. Willcock and A. Walker, 'Introduction', pp. xlv-liii.

13. Daniel's translation of Giovio's *Tract* appeared in London in 1585. Whitney's *Choice of Emblemes* in the following year is the first English emblem book, while Jan van der Noot's *Theatre for Worldlings* (London, 1569) forms part of the literary background to the English emblem, as Freeman says in *English Emblem Books* (p. 51), and is not an emblem book. Fraunce's tract was published in London. Willet's *Emblematum* was published in Cambridge by the university printer John Legate the Elder between 1590 when Sir Francis Walsingham died and 1598 when Francis Meres mentioned it in *Palladis Tamia* (J. Payne Collier, *A Bibliographical and Critical Account of the Rarest Books in the English Language* [London, 1865], Vol. II, p. 524). The old Cambridge University Library Catalogue, probably basing itself on the list of books printed by the University Press between 1521 and 1650, compiled by F. J. H. Jenkinson (S. C. Roberts, *A History of the Cambridge University Press,* 1521-1921 [Cambridge, 1921], p. 154), gives the date of the publication of Willet's book as 1588 when Legate the Elder took office as university printer (p. 152). However, this date is impossible because Willet's third emblem is a eulogy to Francis Walsingham who died in 1590. The British Museum Catalogue lists 1596, the old *STC* the same year, and the new *STC* 1592, as possible publication dates.

14. P. S.'s translation of Paradin appeared in London in 1591; Combe's *Theatre* would appear to date from 1593 when it was entered in the Stationer's Register; de la Perrière's *Théâtre* was published in Paris in 1539 with emblem pictures (in *Scolars Facsimiles and Reprints* [Gainesville, Florida, 1964]).

15. Of the one hundred emblems in Willett's *Sacrorum,* only five appear to bear overt anti-Catholic messages. There are passing derogatory references to papists in Nos. 3 and 6 and to Jesuits in No. 83, and a description of the eternal hell awaiting English Catholics in the ten lines of No. 19, and of Rome as anti-Christ in the 25 lines of No. 22.

16. Henry Peacham, *Minerva Britanna,* London, 1612, in Facsimile Reproduction by *Theatrum Orbis Terrarum,* Amsterdam, 1971; Francis Quarles, *Emblemes,* Sig. A3[r], second edition, 1643.

17. Thomas Heywood, *Pleasant Dialogues and Drammas Selected out of Lucian, Erasmus, Textor, Ovid, etc., With sundry Emblems extracted from the most elegant Iacobus Catsius* (London, 1637).

18. John Bunyan, *A Book For Boys and Girls: OR, Country Rhimes For Children* (London, 1686), in facsimile edition of 1689, later published (1701) in London as *Divine Emblems: OR, Temporal Things Spiritualized. Fitted for the Use of Boys and Girls.*

19. Fraunce's Latin passage reads: 'In emblemate vox figuram exponit, quod in symbolo vitium vel maximum esse solet, in quo, non vox figuram, nec figura vocem: sed figura cum voce, animi notionem explicat. Emblema ita constituitur, ut generalis sit illius praeceptio et doctrina.'

20. Henri Estienne, *The Art of Making Devises: Treating of Hieroglyphics, Symboles, Emblemes, Aenigmas, Sentences, Parables, Reverses, of Medals, Armes, Blazons, Cimiers, Cyphres and Rebus,* trans. by Thomas Blount (London, 1646), from the first edition in French, *L'Art de Faire les Devises* (Paris 1645).

21. For example, Lewalski, *Protestant Poetics,* pp. 111-144.

22. Harvey's translation begins with the second book of *Schola Cordis,* and its epilogue, called 'The Learning of the Heart', is a rhymed version of the first book of van Haeften's work. The first book of the Latin original contained no emblems, and the last three did. The four poems that make up Harvey's epilogue are entitled 'The Preface', 'The Grammar of the Heart', 'The Rhetorick of the Heart', and 'The Logick of the Heart' (pp. 191-196), and are based on ideas of the first book of *Schola Cordis* (principally on pp. 17, 20-22, 41-42, 57-59 of the Antwerp edition of 1635). Harvey's prefatory poem to his epilogue, called 'The Conclusion' (p. 190), is a re-working of van Haeften's original prefatory address, 'In Scholam Cordis'.

FURTHER READING

Bibliographies

Daly, Peter M., and Mary V. Silcox. *The English Emblem: Bibliography of Secondary Literature.* Munchen, Germany: K. G. Saur, 1990, 179 p.

Thorough listing organized by visual themes as well as authors; also includes general studies of the emblem in Europe.

Dees, Jerome S. "Recent Studies in the English Emblem." *English Literary Renaissance* 16 (1986): 391-420.

Surveys criticism on English emblems, covering the years 1945 to 1985.

Simonds, Peggy Muñoz. *Iconographic Research in English Renaissance Literature: A Critical Guide.* New York: Garland Publishing, 1995, 539 p.

A bibliography of primary and secondary literature, followed by an extensive index of imagery, motifs, legends, and personages.

Criticism

Bath, Michael. *Speaking Pictures: English Emblem Books and Renaissance Culture.* London: Longman, 1994, 311 p.

Surveys the theory and context of the genre before examining specific authors; an update to the standard texts by Freeman and Praz.

Daly, Peter M. *The English Emblem Tradition.* 5 vols. Toronto: University of Toronto Press, 1988-98.

Collects books of emblems and provides concordances and a general introduction on the art of the emblem.

Diehl, Huston. "Into the Maze of the Self: The Protestant Transformation of the Image of the Labyrinth." *Journal of Medieval and Renaissance Studies* 16, no. 2 (fall 1986): 281-301.

Looks at emblem representations of the labyrinth to establish a connection between Reformation culture and postmodern culture.

Horden, John. "Renaissance Emblem Books: A Comment on Terminology." In *Literature and the Art of Creation,* edited by Robert Welch and Suheil Badi Bushrui, pp. 61-70. Gerrards Cross, Buckinghamshire, England: Colin Smythe, 1988.

Suggests vocabulary for describing the methods by which emblems produce meaning, and discusses standards for legitimate interpretation of emblems.

Lawson, Bruce. "The Body as a Political Construct: Oliver Cromwell's Image in William Faithorne's 1658 Emblematic Engraving." In *Deviceful Settings: The English Renaissance Emblem and Its Contexts,* edited by Michael Bath and Daniel Russell, pp. 113-37. New York: AMS Press, 1999.

Discusses the symbolism of the emblem and its ability to convey several levels of meaning.

Thomas Kyd
1558-1594

English playwright, poet, and translator.

The following entry presents criticism on Kyd's works from 1986 to 2005. For criticism prior to 1986, see *LC*, Volume 22.

INTRODUCTION

Thomas Kyd is considered a major Elizabethan playwright, even though only two extant works have been positively attributed to him. A highly successful play in its time, Kyd's *Spanish Tragedy* is considered the first revenge tragedy, the forerunner to plays including William Shakespeare's *Hamlet* and John Webster's *Duchess of Malfi.*

BIOGRAPHICAL INFORMATION

Kyd's biography is the product of careful conjecture. Likely the son of Francis Kyd, a scrivener, Thomas was baptized November 6, 1558, in London. In 1565 he was enrolled at the Merchant Taylors' School. Fellow playwright Thomas Dekker mentioned Kyd's association with the Queen's Men between 1583 and 1585. According to some scholars, between 1585 and 1588 Kyd may have written the play now known as *Ur-Hamlet,* to which Shakespeare's *Hamlet* is believed to owe its beginnings. Kyd's *Spanish Tragedy* was performed sometime between 1582 and 1592, with its first recorded production and publication in 1592. Despite the play's popularity, Kyd published it anonymously. Kyd is believed to have also composed the anonymously published Turkish play *Soliman and Perseda* (1592).

The most significant public record of Kyd's life concerns his 1593 arrest by the Privy Council on the charge of atheism, which was a capital offense in Elizabethan England. The accusation was based on letters found in Kyd's possession, letters that Kyd later attributed to playwright Christopher Marlowe, with whom he shared quarters for a time. Kyd was tortured and interrogated but was eventually released. Some biographers have hypothesized that Kyd may have arranged Marlowe's murder in revenge for his arrest. Kyd found himself in desperate circumstances after his imprisonment. A letter to Sir John Puckering pleading his innocence suggests that an unnamed patron had abandoned him as a result of his arrest. Kyd urged Puckering to intercede on his behalf, describing himself as "utterly undone."

Kyd's translation of Robert Garnier's tragedy *Cornelia* (1594), dedicated to the Countess of Sussex, was an apparent attempt to revive his reputation. *Cornelia* is the only work aside from *The Spanish Tragedy* that has been positively attributed to Kyd. In his dedication to the play, Kyd declares his intent to translate another of Garnier's plays, presumably to capitalize on the courtly fashion for neoclassical French drama, but *Cornelia* was likely his last play. He died in August 1594, at age thirty-five. His death is believed to have been precipitated by the abuse and penury brought on by the Privy Council investigation. Kyd's parents refused to administer his estate, possibly because of the scandal associated with their son's name or to avoid taking responsibility for his debts.

MAJOR WORKS

Modern scholarship on Kyd focuses almost entirely on *The Spanish Tragedy*; *Cornelia* and *Soliman and Perseda* are minor afterthoughts in the study of his works. *Cornelia* is particularly far removed from those qualities of spectacle and mass appeal that distinguish *The Spanish Tragedy*; it is a closet drama, likely never intended to be performed, translated from the French in an academic style for a coterie audience. *Soliman and Perseda* is often attributed to Kyd because it was written in a similar style and has a similar plot to the play-within-a-play in *The Spanish Tragedy,* but Kyd's authorship cannot be confirmed.

The Spanish Tragedy, along with works by Marlowe and by Shakespeare, heralded the dawn of great Elizabethan tragedy and played a significant role in shaping the theater of the time. *The Spanish Tragedy* draws heavily from Senecan tragedy in its use of grand rhetoric and its themes of revenge and the relentlessness of fate, but Kyd added innovations such as intense visual representations of violence, intrigue plots influenced by Roman comedy, and concern for contemporary politics. The result was a new form of theater uniquely suited to its historical moment, and a model for even greater plays to come.

The Spanish Tragedy centers on Hieronimo's attempt to avenge the death of his son, Horatio, who died at the hands of a jealous rival, Balthazar, and his co-

conspirator, Lorenzo. The murder of Horatio sets in motion a complex revenge plot, finally realized when Hieronimo presents a play at the wedding ceremony between Bel-Imperia, Horatio's former lover, and Balthazar. Hieronimo convinces Lorenzo and Balthazar to participate in the play, along with Bel-Imperia, who is by now in league with Hieronimo. During the course of the enactment, Hieronimo's character stabs Lorenzo's character, and Bel-Imperia's character stabs Balthazar's character before stabbing herself. When the play is over, Hieronimo reveals that the deaths the audience witnessed were real. He then attempts to escape, in order to hang himself. When he is captured, he bites off his tongue rather than reveal that Bel-Imperia was a co-conspirator. Using a pen, Hieronimo then kills Lorenzo's father and himself.

Marking *The Spanish Tragedy*'s connection with medieval morality plays, all the action of the tragedy is viewed by a personified Revenge figure and by the Spanish courtier Don Andrea, whom Balthazar had killed in battle. Don Andrea angrily waits for justice throughout the play, as Revenge urges patience. The numerous murders achieved by the final scene gratify the two, and Don Andrea suggests that Horatio, Hieronimo, and his wife, Isabella (who killed herself in grief prior to the wedding ceremony between Bel-Imperia and Balthazar), will receive their final vindication in death, as they pass on to eternal rest while the villains Balthazar and Lorenzo face punishment in Hades.

CRITICAL RECEPTION

Recent scholarship on Kyd can be classified in three broad, sometimes overlapping, categories: performance studies, socio-political interpretations, and religious interpretations. With its highly visual style and its vivid depiction of violence, *The Spanish Tragedy* has given scholars insight into what Elizabethan performance may have looked like. Richard Kohler has suggested that the dialogue of the play gives strong evidence for potential staging methods that can illuminate both the play and the experience of theatergoing in Elizabethan England. Several scholars have also noted a parallel between public executions in sixteenth-century London and the violence that takes place in the play. Molly Smith has observed that Kyd's adaptation of the spectacle of public justice is a central factor in the play's growth beyond its Senecan roots. Like much historicist scholarship on Kyd, Smith's study draws upon the work of Stephen Greenblatt and Michel Foucault in its theoretical assumptions, in order to consider the theatrical nature of power in the Renaissance. James Shapiro, however, has suggested that *The Spanish Tragedy* has a unique ability to test those assumptions and to illustrate with greater complexity the power relationships that have interested historicist scholars.

Commentators focusing on the political context of *The Spanish Tragedy* have often observed the nationalism of the play, formed around its anti-Spanish and anti-Catholic undercurrents. Its nationalist bent is directly portrayed in the masque staged by Hieronimo in Act I, which represents England's triumph over Spain and Portugal. More recent interpretations of the play have highlighted its reflection of the anxiety and ambiguity that accompany nation formation. Scholars including Carla Mazzio and Eric Griffin have pointed to the ways the play relates to the contested arenas of language, empire, and religion, which would have resonated with Kyd's audiences, revealing discontinuities in national identity.

Religious tensions also inform *The Spanish Tragedy*'s place in the development of English drama. The beginnings of modern English theater run parallel to the end of the "old religion," Catholicism, and the rise of Protestantism. Thus a mode of interpreting signs in the theater began to develop in the context of a very public revision of the function of signs in religious worship. Huston Diehl has argued that the self-reflexive aspects of such plays as *The Spanish Tragedy*—the play-within-a-play, the "audience" commentary of Don Andrea, the heavily theatrical language—confirm the distance between the sign and the thing it represents. In so doing, Diehl has concluded, *The Spanish Tragedy* laid the groundwork for a mode of theatrical representation that was specifically Protestant. Responding to Diehl, Andrew Sofer has maintained that Kyd's use of visual spectacle was powerful because it exploited its connection to the visceral Catholic Eucharist, in which bread and wine become the real presence of body and blood. Beyond the doctrinal controversies over transubstantiation and idolatry, Robert Watson describes revenge tragedy as an expression of both humanity's anger at God for the curse of mortality, and the troubling suspicion that God's offer of redemption by substituting his son is an inadequate response to the injustice of death.

PRINCIPAL WORKS

The Spanish Tragedy (play) c. 1582-92

*Ur-Hamlet (play) c. 1585-88

The Housholders Philosophie [translator; from Torquato Tasso's *Il Padre di Famiglia*] (poetry) 1588

Soliman and Perseda (play) c. 1592

Cornelia [translator; from Robert Garnier's *Cornélie*] (play) 1594

The Works of Thomas Kyd [edited by Frederick S. Boas] (plays, poetry) 1901, revised edition, 1955

*The existence of this work is conjectural, as is Kyd's authorship.

CRITICISM

Richard C. Kohler (essay date 1986)

SOURCE: Kohler, Richard C. "Kyd's Ordered Spectacle: 'Behold . . . / What 'tis to be subject to destiny.'" *Medieval & Renaissance Drama in England* 3 (1986): 27-49.

[*In the following essay, Kohler attempts to recreate the staging of* The Spanish Tragedy, *including its original blocking, use of props and scenery, and means of entrance and exit. Kohler emphasizes the symmetry of staging, plot, and language to create a sense of order.*]

The reconstruction of original staging promises to be a useful tool of critical analysis, and few plays seem as productive of such results as Thomas Kyd's **The Spanish Tragedy.** Perhaps it was the marked appeal of the play's spectacle that kept it on the stage so long. The dramaturgy, as we know, is primarily an achievement in synthesis, a blend of the academic and popular, the classical and the contemporary. But a pronounced symmetry in its theatrical effects, as not only a method of underscoring plot development but also as an expression of theme, is only now becoming fully appreciated.[1] Kyd's achievement is perhaps too synthetic, but the obvious artifice of balanced proportion and ordered inevitability serves well his concept of destiny working through the desire for revenge. Such mechanical principles were probably those most congenial to his talent, but they resulted in a happy combination of means and ends, of challenge and capability.

Perceptive critical comment on the play's staging has appeared in recent years. Scott McMillin in his discussion of the Old Man as a "figure of silence" ranges well beyond that brief episode to comment on a number of staging parallels I will discuss, especially in the use of objects.[2] D. F. Rowan offers incisive comment on two of the major staging issues, the use or non-use of the "above" and the arbor.[3] Eleanor M. Tweedie provides a more extended study of particulars, including much on which we agree.[4] The most complete appreciation of the play's effect on stage, including "the bold architectural symmetry of its dramatic form," is found in Michael Hattaway's *Elizabethan Popular Theatre: Plays in Performance.*[5] I will confine my discussion here, first, to analysis of Act One, scene by scene, to reveal how the spectacle is symmetrically arranged to clarify Kyd's exposition; a second section will show in a general way how these techniques are exploited in the remainder of the play.[6] The study of staging is admittedly in large part an exercise in sustained conjecture, but surely there is value in evidence that on the one hand seems to assert its presence on the platform and on the other hand

gains some credence from reflecting coherently upon recognized, though debated, critical issues. This then is a suggestive supplement to our developing appreciation of the effect on stage that Kyd seems to have wanted.[7]

Our close visualization of the staging should be preceded by a brief statement of the evidence for symmetrical tendencies in the "stage pictures" of the Elizabethan theaters in general. For example, Bernard Beckerman concludes that at the Globe there was nearly always a central focus with the organizing principle "ceremony or duty,"[8] and George R. Kernodle emphasizes the use of a "center accent" with a scenic device such as a throne at the nucleus.[9] Beckerman observes that the principles of order that guided such arrangements are those of Elizabethan graphic art, simple and derivative, characteristic of the "massive and symmetrical" theater itself. These principles, he argues, were probably determined to some extent by the necessities of the repertory system, symmetrical balance being the simplest order in art, an order probably more evident in the earlier plays of the period where the dramatic material made balance more natural (pp. 164-165, 168). David M. Bevington's examination of doubling patterns demonstrates that the dramatic structure of popular drama was developed in terms of alternation and suppression of characters and thus had a symmetry that was also "unquestionably a vital structural principle of late medieval art."[10] H. B. Charlton asserts that Senecan influence led to "the heresy that there are no dramatic gods but form."[11] Kyd seems to some degree to have been a captive of just such concern. Which came first, the dual and serial relationships provided in the narratives, or the symmetrical orders of Renaissance art and classical drama—and possibly of Renaissance theaters? It may be true that plays are written for theaters, but when new capital is invested, the playhouses built provide facilities for the kinds of plays that people have been paying to see. For this reason, I assume that the Rose and **The Spanish Tragedy** complemented each other and that both were vital parts of the literary and theatrical conventions of the time.[12]

What may have been the first performance of **The Spanish Tragedy** at the Rose took place on Tuesday, 14 March 1592—the sixteenth play of the first twenty-five days. The day before the "spanes commodye donne oracio" had been acted,[13] and regulars at the Rose, of course, might already have seen or at least heard of **The Spanish Tragedy,** since it had been written and produced (at Burbage's Theater?) probably as long as seven to ten years before.[14] The production of the play at the Rose that I will attempt to reconstruct therefore may not have been as it was originally presented or as Kyd first intended it. However, the text, the "octavo in fours" of 1592, probably contains evidence of how the play *might* have been presented, at least in part, at the one theater where we know that it was, in fact, produced and where it was quite successful at the time of publication. That afternoon Henslowe took in 71s as half his share of the gallery receipts.[15] Never again would he record quite so successful a performance of the play.

I

Before the play began, a chair of state may have been placed at the center of the platform on a low dais, in anticipation of the entrance of the Spanish King in the second scene. The "state" or throne was, we know, among the most frequently employed scenic devices.[16] It is the almost certain use of a throne in the third scene that suggests its parallel presence in the second:[17] the Spanish army is directed in the second scene to march twice around "these walls" (121)[18] of what the General terms the "royal seat" (104); perhaps this reference is only figurative, but it is one that could also have been "contextually applied to the chair set apart for . . . the throne of a king" (*OED, seat,* 8). George F. Reynolds concludes that these "formal seats" were usually placed at front center, adding that "the unvarying feature . . . is the dais with two or more steps on which the seat stood," a structure not easily moved about: "when the throne recurs in two or more scenes in the same play, it seems likely it remained wherever it was, at least as long as there was use for it"[19]—exactly my view of the second and third scenes here. The chair could later be shoved back or removed entirely to free up space on what was nevertheless a rather large platform. Otherwise the stage would probably have been empty as the audience first heard and then, I think, located the source of a voice declaiming:

> When this eternal substance of my soul
> Did live imprison'd in my wanton flesh,
> Each in their function serving other's need,
> I was a courtier in the Spanish court.
> My name was Don Andrea.

(I.i.1-5)

I assume that throughout the play Andrea and Revenge were positioned in the gallery, above and behind the platform, perhaps at one side of the façade, or even further to the side in the second gallery adjacent to the façade. Such a placement, "above," however, is thoroughly controversial and must be discussed at length. It matches the traditional position for "presenters," whose function Andrea and Revenge perform; it also would not have interfered either with the action on the platform or sight-lines to that action.[19] Oseas the Prophet in *A Looking-Glass for London and England,*[20] performed at the Rose the previous week, was "set doune ouer the Stage in a Throne" (160) to "see the wrath of God that paies reuenge" (177), apparently remaining above (until the end of Act Four) to watch and comment on the events. His throne may have been lowered by machinery, but that would seem to have involved rather ex-

tended "hovering." It is true that the "above" also provided seats, and expensive ones, for the audience; it is equally true that the area was employed for theatrical action when appropriate. Later in the play, Pedringano, Balthazar, and Lorenzo are certainly placed above (II.ii), and Bel-imperia is "at a window" in III.ix; if Kyd's theater could sacrifice some space in these instances for dramatic effect, and do so perhaps yet again in the last act for those who watch the play-within-the-play, it seems likely that two more seats might be available for Andrea and Revenge to join the audience. Furthermore, the play concludes with Revenge declaring,

> Then haste we down to meet thy friends and foes,
> To place thy friends at ease, the rest in woes:
> For here though death hath end their misery,
> I'll there begin their endless tragedy. *Exeunt.*

Obviously "down" refers to some kind of descent, actual or imagined. Rowan, who places Andrea and Revenge on stage throughout, suggests that they exit through the platform trap, out of which he believes they emerged (p. 117), an emergence Hattaway also suggests although he has them later ascend to the gallery, at least in the Rose production (pp. 114-115). The references by Revenge to "here" and "there" provide an appropriate distinction between the surface of the platform, as it has been used, and the traditional hell beneath. But are we to imagine that the actors portraying the dead arise and then descend through the trap with Andrea and Revenge following, or are we to conclude that Revenge is describing only what is to come in an imagined future beyond the play itself? Neither possibility, however, seems conclusively to resolve the question of where Revenge is situated when he makes that final statement.[21]

Further support for assuming a position above for Andrea and Revenge may be found in the importance to the play of the metaphor of the world as a stage, a convention according to which the presence of the audience is acknowledged and the world of the audience is set against the world of the play.[22] The placement of Andrea and Revenge in an adjacent box in the gallery, on a level that continues around the inner circle, would have contributed directly to what is paradoxically a disjunctive and yet intense relationship between stage and audience that continues until the end.[23] Andrea and Revenge, as "presenters," may speak for the poet directly to the audience in the sense that their first speeches are a Prologue, but they are also derived from the "truchman" of the dumb shows and the "expositour in doctorys wede" of the miracle plays and moralities.[24] When Andrea declares that Revenge has led him "here, / I wot not how, in twinkling of an eye" (I.i.84-85), "here" could mean "at the Rose," with that audience that day, as they watched the play that Andrea and Revenge watch and comment upon. Revenge declares:

> Here sit we down to see the mystery,
> And serve for Chorus in this tragedy.
>
> (I.i.90-91)

Dream and drama are mixed with the present and the past, and the events to come are already determined, as they must be in a play, with the implication that life as well as art is a directed experience.[25]

> *Enter Spanish* KING, GENERAL, CASTILE, HIERONIMO.
>
> (I.ii)

The foregoing stage direction brings the players (perhaps including attendants) onto the platform; they would likely take customary ceremonial positions on either side of the King, who sits, in this reconstruction, on the throne at center. If Castile and the General are at one side of the central focus, Hieronimo could be somewhat isolated at the other, perhaps in significant violation of the persistent symmetry that we will find elsewhere. The General delivers a long descriptive speech about the recent victory in battle, to which the King responds by giving the General a "chain," the first in a series of hand properties that are used in parallel, while receiving from him "a paper" on which the Viceroy of Portugal has agreed to pay tribute. The King then turns to Hieronimo, addressing him only by his official title, Knight Marshall, asserting his function as chief magistrate of the court, and asking him to be cheerful since his son has won the prize of the battle just fought. Hieronimo responds by wishing a long life for his son in the service of the King, upon which the sound of "*A tucket afar off*" is heard (99), serving perhaps to accent the old man's first speech as well as to suggest danger, coupled as it is with the King's reply, "Nor thou nor he shall die without reward." These trumpets herald the arrival of the captive Balthazar, whose presence will ultimately bring about the deaths of both father and son. The King continues appropriately, "What means the warning of this trumpet's sound?" (101), and the General responds by introducing the first of the several pageants in the play—a "demonstration," as the General refers to it (107)—the passing of the army. The stage direction then calls for the entrance of the army with "*BALTHAZAR between LORENZO and HORATIO, captive.*" They enter at one door and march across carrying banners and spears and probably extra armor and equipment in an enhanced display, since they have been "by their foes enrich'd" (109).[26] In *1 Henry VI,* one of the most popular of the plays at the Rose at this time, such exhibitions were repeatedly used: the marching with drum and soldiers of I.ii, the marching of both the French and English to the sound of the drum and trumpets to sound a parley in III.iii, to say nothing of the numerous battles. Although Kyd is by comparison rather conservative, he provides a second and parallel exhibition when the King requests that the army march "once more about these walls" (121).

After the departure of the troops, Lorenzo and Horatio continue to hold Balthazar captive between them, presumably on one side of the stage, while Castile (Lorenzo's father), the General, and Hieronimo may be positioned opposite. Balthazar and his captors must stand together at least until line 159, when the King says, "Let go his arm," and the stage direction reads, "*Let him go.*" The stage is balanced, three performers on each side of the King, two fathers opposite two sons, Lorenzo and Horatio in opposition over Balthazar, a visual presentation of the first conflict in the main action of the play, the debate over who holds the right to the prisoner. Tweedie observes that a comparable image occurs in the next scene as part of the Portuguese subplot when "the innocent Alexandro is similarly held by attendants" (p. 226), an early example in the play of matching stage pictures.

As the scene continues, Hieronimo must identify his son for the King (116), because, as Tweedie observes, "It is a world in which class lines are so stringently drawn" (p. 226) that the King is later ignorant even of Horatio's death. The initial identification of characters in a theater without programs can be significant and should be considered in such critical controversies as the debate over the King's treatment of Horatio.[27] The King, already thinking of the triumph achieved by Lorenzo, refers to him now—and throughout the scene—only as "nephew" (132), underscoring his membership in the royal family. The King then turns to Hieronimo's son with, "And thou, Horatio, thou art welcome too"—as well Horatio should be welcomed having won the battle and the war. This the audience knows, as do Horatio and Revenge, from having heard the description of the battle by both Andrea and the General. To Balthazar, still in the grasp of his captors, the King declares,

> Meanwhile, live thou, though not in liberty,
> Yet free from bearing any servile yoke,
> For in our hearing thy deserts were great,
> And in our sight thyself are gracious.
>
> (I.i.147-150)

The King then asks to which man Balthazar is prisoner. A stichomythic debate follows between Lorenzo and Horatio, in which Kyd could surely have constructed a far better case, had he wished to do so, to justify Lorenzo's claim; instead, a careful balance is struck between the two sides—something that occurs often in the play. All that Lorenzo offers in his behalf is that he took the reins and seized the lance *after* Horatio had defeated Balthazar, certainly and in Lorenzo's own testimony no substantial claim. Balthazar refers repeatedly to Horatio as "this other," while stating plainly that his only reasons for surrendering to Lorenzo were "courtesy," recognition of rank, fair speaking, and the promise of "life" that Lorenzo offered. Perhaps the audience is to believe, in retrospect, that Lorenzo stepped in to prevent Horatio from taking immediate revenge, but Horatio says nothing to acknowledge such action when he offers his "authentic" report of the battle (I.iv). Again one must evaluate what the first-time audience may be presumed to have understood, and it seems clear at this point that from the General, from Lorenzo, and from Balthazar as well, Horatio deserves full credit for the Prince's capture, the issue clouded only by the question of rank. Precisely this issue contributes to sympathy for Horatio and eventually for his father. The fact that prejudice is chipping away at Horatio's just reward, as the Knight Marshall realizes, both as a father and as a judge, is confirmed in his next speech with its marked distinction between his son's achievement and Lorenzo's. Hieronimo states his confidence in the King's justice:

> My tongue should plead for young Horatio's right,
> He hunted well that was a lion's death,
> Not he that in a garment wore his skin:
> So hares may pull dead lions by the beard.

> (I.ii.169-172)

Perhaps the King's decision is unavoidable given the social circumstances:

> But nephew, thou shalt have the prince in guard,
> For thine estate best fitteth such a guest:
> Horatio's house were small for all his train.
> Yet in regard thy substance passeth his,
> And that just guerdon may befall desert,
> To him we yield the armour of the prince.

> (I.ii.185-190)

The next scene also closes with a reference to "guerdon" by Villuppo in the last line, a term that should emphasize proper recompense and requital, neither of which occurs here; Villuppo hopes for another distortion of justice: reward for his villainy.

Thus the main action of the play has begun with a ceremonious entrance of the court, the possible isolation of Hieronimo, a balanced exchange of properties, and the introduction of Balthazar and Lorenzo in tangency with the crown, while Hieronimo and Horatio have been separated from it, not greatly but distinctly. Though the King does give Horatio the "battle's prize" and in II.iii.32-36 reaffirms the award of ransom, Horatio's *full* rights are surely slighted and only because of social rank; this injustice, as we have seen, could well have been emphasized by the positioning of the actors on stage. It is of course those aligned with the King whom Hieronimo must eventually challenge when he seeks justice for his son's death.

> *Enter VICEROY, ALEXANDRO, VILLUPPO* [, Attendants].

> (I.iii)

Presumably, to avoid congestion if nothing else, these characters would enter by the door opposite the one just used for the exit of the Spanish court, and again my assumption is that the Viceroy proceeds to occupy the *same* throne. The throne must either be rushed on stage with the Viceroy's entrance to permit him to sit as indicated in the fifth line, or the throne must already be on stage and thus available in the preceding scene. Given the evidence that will be developed for symmetry in other staging effects, it seems unlikely that Kyd would overlook the opportunity of having the throne conveniently on stage from the beginning of the play and using it. Why have a throne at all for the one and not for the other? The Viceroy is seated for only seven lines, however, when he declares:

> But wherefore sit I in a regal throne?
> This better fits a wretch's endless moan.
> *Falls to the ground.*

The visual contrast is obvious: where the Spanish King sat in triumph and distributed rewards, the Portuguese monarch stretches himself on the platform before the throne to stress both defeat and sorrow over "loss" of his son (and the reference to "ground" surely suggests the direction is authorial, as has often been noted). In one of the productive recent studies of iconography in Elizabethan drama, Huston Diehl has emphasized the emblematic function of this action, viewing it as a "significant stage picture" that "makes thematic sense, for it resembles traditional depictions of men flung to the bottom of fortune's wheel and thus links the individual with the concept of fortune ruling him"—an observation confirmed by the Viceroy's complaint, "Fortune is blind and sees not my deserts" (23).[28] Instead of giving rewards, as the Spanish King did, the Viceroy gives up his crown, handing it to Alexandro, presumably at one side, while Villuppo may balance the stage at the other as he kneels to offer the Viceroy "the fortune" of his son. The Viceroy replies, "Stand up I say, and tell thy tale at large" (58), the third version of the battle (and a total fabrication) in which Villuppo accuses Alexandro.

Arthur Freeman considers the Portuguese scenes as providing an "emblem of too-hasty judgement" (p. 85), an emblem that is prepared for when, following the Viceroy's physical prostration and lament, Alexandro offers only slightly qualified assurance: "No doubt, my liege, but still the prince survives" (I.iii.43). Notice the ambiguity, the care taken not to present absolute certainty, that allows doubt while also establishing the Viceroy's unreasonable state of mind. Since the audience has seen Balthazar alive, well, and prospering in the enemy camp, they know Alexandro tells the truth, in whatever way he may have arrived at his opinion, and therefore are favorably disposed toward him. In another parallel with the preceding scene, a stichomythic exchange serves to accent the conflict between the truth, represented by Alexandro, and the Viceroy's inclination to believe the false, so long as it fits his disposition to despair. The Viceroy demands that Alexandro tell him "no more of news," but when Villuppo offers "ill news," the Viceroy readily responds:

> Speak on, I'll guerdon thee whate'er it be:
> Mine ear is ready to receive ill news,
> My heart grown hard 'gainst mischief's battery.

> (I.iii.55-57)

At the end of the scene, when the Viceroy is convinced that Alexandro has murdered Balthazar, the crown again is used when it catches his eye, "this diadem" (83), and confirms his suspicions: "Ay, this was it that made thee spill his blood," followed by *Take the crown and put it on again*" (86). Villuppo then remains for a soliloquy stating plainly that he is a villain who considers Alexandro an enemy:

> Thus have I with an envious forged tale
> Deceiv'd the king, betray'd mine enemy,
> And hope for guerdon of my villainy. *Exit.*

> (I.iii.93-95)

His self-disclosure permits the harsh and total condemnation of him in Act Two in the scene that just precedes Hieronimo's decision not to accuse Lorenzo of Horatio's murder; this juxtaposition helps the audience to share in Hieronimo's cautious delay when he receives Bel-imperia's letter.

> *Enter HORATIO and BEL-IMPERIA.*

> (I.iv)

By the time this entrance occurs, the audience has seen Spanish victory contrasted with Portuguese defeat in multiple parallels to which they may have been alerted by the possible use of the throne: both of the previous scenes began with brief questions and answers (and a three-line Latin declaration in both in nearly the same textual position, 12-14, 15-17); properties were passed back and forth (the chain and papers, the crown); the battle was described by the General and by Villuppo; Balthazar was prisoner in the one and Alexandro was taken into custody in the other, with sympathy created for Alexandro in much the same way that it was fostered for Horatio, two soldiers involved in the same battle, both judged by kings—one in triumph, the other in defeat—and both deprived of their rights through the statements of their fellow soldiers. Now the audience is to have the fourth description of the battle and another "exchange" of properties, this time to define the relationship between Bel-imperia and Horatio.

Immediately upon their entrance, Bel-imperia declares "this is the place and hour" to learn how Andrea was killed, a reference comparable to that voiced by Andrea

and Revenge at the beginning of the play on the immediacy of the whole theatrical experience. Horatio's extended narrative of the battle concludes with a comment on a scarf that Bel-imperia had given Andrea; Horatio possesses it now, "pluck'd from off [Andrea's] liveless arm" (42). She gives the scarf to Horatio; when he leaves, Bel-imperia is left alone and, as Villuppo did at the end of the previous scene, she defines her function in what is to come: she will love Horatio and seek revenge for Andrea.

The emphasis placed on Bel-imperia's reasons for revenge also indicates where sympathy is to be directed: three times she refers to Andrea's death as murder—a "murd'rous deed" committed out of "murd'rous cowardice" by Balthazar, who "murder'd my delight"; it was a dishonorable act to take advantage of "So many to oppress one valiant knight" (I.iv.72-76). It is then necessary for Kyd only to confirm the connection between Balthazar and Bel-imperia's brother. For that purpose, in a technique that Kyd uses consistently, he immediately provides a stage picture of opposition: Balthazar and Lorenzo promptly enter and confront Bel-imperia in a third stichomythic exchange.

Bel-imperia and the Portuguese Prince could well stand on either side of Lorenzo at center, before Horatio again appears and she deliberately "lets fall" her glove. Her brother and the Prince notice Horatio recover it, and this second property connecting Bel-imperia with her new love sets in motion the process of revenge that eventually will satisfy Andrea's desires.[29] Lorenzo at once assures Balthazar that he will "scatter" these clouds (107) of female humors. The audience's approval of Bel-imperia, and consequently their approval of her support for Hieronimo's revenge in the last act, are dependent upon sympathy for Andrea and Horatio and upon Kyd's skill in making her new love credible, or at least acceptable, as an instrument for *just* revenge. Why would an audience believe Horatio's version of the battle if it is not because their sympathy for him has already been established by the "frame"—the action of the play, after all, is to be Andrea's revenge—as well as by the treatment accorded Horatio in the second scene?[30] And Kyd has also heightened antipathy for Balthazar by having him indulge in the "ambages" with which even Lorenzo is impatient, just before Horatio comes back and "takes up" the glove.

For the banquet that follows, chairs and a table are no doubt brought out and placed in front of the throne that could remain at center. Edwards compares this entry of the court to that of the King and "all the State" in *Hamlet*, V.ii. Kyd will again use a pageantlike display, here synthesized with an appeal to the patriotic sentiments, when the play was probably written and first produced, of an audience soon to be faced with an attempted invasion from Spain. Kyd certainly may have felt a need to make some reference to relations between the two countries in a play located in Spain. His solution is multiple and complex, ingeniously making use of a long and familiar tradition, the masques that were so often presented in the Tudor court as entertainment for ambassadors and that normally took place in the banqueting-house, in which a "state" such as that which may still occupy the platform would likely be present.[31] It is recorded that the ambassadors on such occasions were seated at the right hand of the throne in carefully graded dignity, "not right out, but byas forward,"[32] as the King of Spain seems in fact to arrange things: if the Ambassador is to his right at the banquet table, the Prince would be to his left, followed on either side by Castile and Lorenzo:

> Sit down young prince, you are our second guest:
> Brother sit down, and nephew take your place:
> Signior Horatio, wait thou upon our cup,
> For well thou hast deserved to be honour'd.
>
> (I.iv.128-131)

This "honor" is presumably the greatest the King could grant on such an occasion—for someone of Horatio's rank. The *OED* lists the phrase "to wait on the cup" as "to attend as or in the manner of a servant to the personal requirements of" (*wait*, on or upon, v. 14.j), using as an instance Hieronimo's bitterly ironic comment to Isabella after Horatio's death:

> His majesty the other day did grace him
> With waiting on his cup: these be favours
> Which do assure he cannot be short-liv'd.
>
> (First Addition: II.v.11-13)

Horatio's responsibility for the cup was in behalf of the King, yes, but conspicuously as a servant. Thus, as Tweedie has also taken care to notice (p. 226), Horatio—and Hieronimo as well—stand while the rest sit and eat, for Hieronimo acts as "truchman" or interpreter[33] for his masque, the "pompous jest," as the King says (137), with which Hieronimo graces the banquet.

As Hieronimo leads each knight onto the platform, each passes across the front between the two audiences in the theater. Each knight is fully armed and carries a scutcheon that is then hung somewhere, possibly on the façade, perhaps on one of the pillars on either side of the banquet table, or on the front of the table itself.[34]

The three kings now enter, the knights one by one taking the kings' crowns and holding them captive, a stylized symmetrical display of "silent and therefore particularly intensive acting," as Deiter Mehl describes it,[35] designed to contrast with the actual play and to raise the interest of the audience to a peak before the required interpretation. Freeman effectively demonstrates that the events depicted in the masque, victories by

England over Portugal and Spain, are not as Frederick S. Boas thought "mainly fanciful"[36] but are derived from English popular history (pp. 55-56). Freeman further believes that the tone of the masque is comparable to that found in plays about Spain written before the Armada, a tone of defiance that had an "invective almost too violent"; he contrasts this mood with that of plays after 1588, where in referring to the Spanish, "deliberate bravado is replaced by calm self-confidence" (pp. 75-76). Although Kyd's masque seems to contain no "invective," it is certainly a patriotic appeal that would have been appropriate to the pre-Armada situation. Frank R. Ardolino has recently endorsed this view, arguing that "by means of the masque, Kyd reveals to his English audience its destiny as conqueror of Catholic Spain."[37] In this appeal we can find an interesting relationship to the use often made of the *tableaux vivants* from which the dumb shows seem partially, at least, to have derived. Kernodle shows that the *tableaux* were used to make special appeals to a prince and that "the whole range of literary and popular lore was searched for examples which could be made to resemble him or the deeds he had done, or the deeds the citizens wanted him to do." In such presentations, the principle of prefiguration was an important and familiar element (p. 68).

Kyd has therefore managed to present an essentially English pageant celebrating English victory, produced in a Spanish court. I suggest that in viewing this masque, the first audiences occupied the position usually reserved for the prince for whom such masques were staged; the events depict what Englishmen thought they had done and suggest what they then earnestly hoped they yet could do. All this is achieved while securing the isolation of both Hieronimo and Horatio and establishing Hieronimo as "master of revels," a position that he will occupy in presenting his play in the last act. Kyd's theatrical consciousness and sense of popular appeal are perhaps nowhere better revealed than in this adaptation of tradition to current events.

After Hieronimo's interpretation, the King declares, "I drink to thee for this device," asks, "Pledge me Hieronimo, if thou love the king," and then *Takes the cup of Horatio* (172-174). If, as it seems likely, Hieronimo also drinks, another parallel is offered, the two men raising their cups together, before the court leaves the stage and Andrea and Revenge conclude the act. It might be added that it is on the occasion of this masque that Hieronimo's name is first used in the play: before he is known only as the Knight Marshall and Horatio's father.

II

Kyd has established a symmetrical pattern of visual appeal in the first act that he continues to use in the balance of the play to clarify his plot and to manifest a theme of relentless necessity. A variety of theatrical elements preserve symmetry: scenic devices, the probably balanced doors of the façade, hand properties, blocking (the movement and positioning of actors on stage), the "above," and the device of the play-within-the-play. The scenic devices, thus far, have included (in this reconstruction) the throne for antithetical displays of Spanish victory and Portuguese defeat. The banquet has provided for the distribution of the characters in formal ceremony for the presentation of the celebratory masque, which in turn prepares the audience for Hieronimo's catastrophic "play" in the last act. The arbor in Act Two also contributes to the pattern of antitheses: it is initially a place of peace, safety, and love—and becomes a gibbet (II.iv). Thus it serves for the murder of Horatio and later, on the occasion of Isabella's suicide (IV.ii), acts as an emblem (whether actually exhibited or not) of both "life" and "love," eventually destroyed by her in a representation of fruitlessness and death.

Perhaps even the executioner's gibbet is used in two scenes: first to hang Pedringano in Act Three, at Hieronimo's order, and then very nearly to provide for Hieronimo's suicide in the last act.[38] Since *gibbet* was synonymous with *gallows* as well as signifying "A short beam projecting from a wall, having a pulley fixed at the end" (*OED*, 3a), such a beam combined with a ladder would have been enough for the action and would have occupied very little space at the rear of the stage. The Hangman is ordered to "turn him off" when Pedringano is executed. To "turn off" seems to have been standard reference to hanging, originally meaning "to turn off the ladder."[39] When Hieronimo *"runs to hang himself"* in Act Four, this direction clearly indicates the presence, and probably the obvious presence, of a hangman's rope, the "goodly noose" to which the Fifth Addition does not hesitate to refer (6). Might this be the rope still suspended from the gibbet used for Pedringano's execution? Surely Hieronimo does not get a rope, form a noose, and tie it somewhere above him; he must run *to* some such arrangement and be in the process of climbing up and putting his head in the noose when the court breaks in.[40]

Hieronimo's attempt to see the King in order to obtain justice (III.xii) is preceded and followed by a parallel pattern of scenes employing the doors of the façade. First he meets the two Portuguese and displays madness in going out one door and entering immediately through another (III.xi); in a second mad scene, he is chased through the doors by the three citizens (III.xiii).

Another feature of Kyd's symmetry, as we found in the first act, is the insistent coordinate use of hand properties: the chain of reward and the papers of tribute, and at a comparable point in the second scene, the Portuguese King's giving up his crown and then taking it

back. In Act Three he again surrenders it to "solemnize" the marriage of Bel-imperia to Balthazar: "I give it her and thee" (xiv.31). Two properties link Bel-imperia with Horatio, the scarf and the glove. McMillin has developed such use of objects in terms of a "scorn for language" in the play (p. 33) when Lorenzo applies a sword and bag of gold in Act Two to motivate Pedringano to inform on Bel-imperia: "Where words prevail not, violence prevails: / But gold doth more than either of them both" (i.108-109). McMillin includes the parallel use of the poniard and halter to kill Horatio (p. 42) and Hieronimo's debate between the latter properties in Act Three;[41] I would add Pedringano's "balancing" the gold in one hand and the pistol in the other (III.iii. 1, 5), and the "purse" that is sent by Lorenzo to Pedringano, paired with the empty box (III.iv.61); subsequently Pedringano matches the letter that he carries to the box and the pardon that he thinks it contains, believing he no longer needs the former now that he "has" the latter (III.vi.19-22). Then Pedringano jokes with the Hangman about the executioner's customary reward of the victim's clothes: "so I should go out of this gear, my raiment, into that gear, the rope" (45-46). When Isabella enters in III.viii, she speaks of having with her two herbs, one for the eye and the other for the head—but none for the heart. And there is also McMillin's suggestion of a pairing in the last act between dagger and rope (p. 42), the first used by Hieronimo to stab Lorenzo and the second in Hieronimo's attempt to hang himself. The number of daggers needed in this scene, however, may be a reflection of textual problems: Bel-imperia uses one to kill Balthazar and herself; Hieronimo has one to kill Lorenzo but appears to lose track of it, since he later *"makes signs"* for a knife to mend his pen (198), a knife he uses to kill Castile and himself.

Bel-imperia's letter of Act Three, "bloody writ" (III.ii.26), is matched by Pedringano's (III.vii), both serving the same purpose, to identify the murderers.[42] While the first is too much of an "accident" for Hieronimo to believe, the second confirms the truth of Bel-imperia's accusation, and the second "accident" is itself represented as renewing Hieronimo's faith in the justice of heaven (III.vii.56). In each scene the arrival of the letter is followed by speeches of analysis and calculation. Hieronimo's direct comparison of the accidents indicates that the parallel is not merely coincidental for him or for Kyd (III.vii.53). There are even two batches of letters delivered to the Viceroy: the first assures him that his son lives (III.i.68-69), and the second, presumably, contains the articles of the impending marriage between Balthazar and Bel-imperia, "his highness' farther articles" (III.i.74).

Whether or not the scarf that Bel-imperia gives to Horatio is identical with the "handkercher" that Hieronimo finds on Horatio's body, the first links Bel-imperia with Horatio, the second Horatio with Hieronimo.[43] McMillin points out that the "handkercher" dipped in Horatio's blood is "held in contrast to the inked document of legal supplication" from the Old Man (p. 45). The 1615 woodcut illustrates an emphatic final example of paired properties: Hieronimo holding the sword in one hand and the torch in the other when he finds his son.[44]

Because the Elizabethan repertory system, with its frequency of production, probably encouraged, if it did not require, simple symmetrical blocking, I have imagined in Act One the positioning of characters in balanced opposition: in Act Two, two groups of observers, both perhaps in the above, could watch the liaison between Bel-imperia and Horatio: Andrea and Revenge, and Balthazar and Lorenzo (II.ii).[45] In Act Three, the Ambassador, in saving Alexandro, may balance the stage when he enters with his attendants (III.i); and one can suppose a central focus on Pedringano and the executioner at the gibbet, the boy with the box at one extreme of the platform and Hieronimo at another (III.vi) .[46] Also in Act Three, when Lorenzo's suspicions are aroused and he arranges the murder of Serberine and the execution of Pedringano, Lorenzo seems to remain in a central position (III.ii). One by one he sends Pedringano, the Page, the Messenger, and even Balthazar to do his bidding. In III.iii Pedringano must conceal himself in a position separate from the Watch: he is surely unaware of their arrival and subsequent presence when he shoots Serberine, from whom he must also be separated, initially, since he declares, "Here comes the bird that I must seize upon" (III.iii.28); then the Watch must cross to find Serberine and take Pedringano prisoner. All this business strongly suggests a tripartite arrangement, perhaps Pedringano and the Watch at extremes, Serberine moving to center.

After Pedringano shoots Serberine, the boy with the box describes in soliloquy the "scurvy jest" of concealing that the box is empty (III.v). It is a jest that is actually on Lorenzo, since carrying out the plot to let Pedringano assume to the end he will be saved brings about the delivery of the letter that begins Lorenzo's fall. This nineteen-line prose scene occupies a position at the center of the play, occurring on both sides of the twenty-first leaf of a total of forty-two leaves in the 1592 quarto (Scolar facsimile), the turning point coming as the specific result of ironic reversal, treated in the comic mode. And, of course, in III.xiii there is the obvious comparison made between Hieronimo's loss and that of old Bazulto, the two leaving the stage leaning on each other—and, I suggest, it would be both appropriate and effective for the actor who played Horatio to double as old Bazulto, in whom Hieronimo sees his "Sweet boy" (146).[47]

Coming where some have believed an act break might have occurred, Bel-imperia's brief scene "*at a window*"

(III.ix) may be played opposite Andrea and Revenge above at the other extreme. If it is possible here to have her above, as surely is indicated, the letter that falls to Hieronimo could have been dropped by her, in view of the audience, from that position (III.ii); it is the place she was "sequester'd from the court" (III.ix.2) all this while. Hieronimo declares in the earlier scene that he is "heark'ning near the Duke of Castile's house" (III.ii.50), the place near which the Watch also appears in the next scene (III.iii.21). And does not Bel-imperia serve here as something of a chorus, asking, as Andrea does, why revenge has not yet been performed and then deciding upon patience, the advice we hear at the close of each act?

Finally, we have the play-within-the-play, viewed by two stage audiences, Andrea and Revenge as well as the court, conceivably opposite to each other in the "above." In the scene in which Hieronimo assigns roles, he specifies that his "strange and wondrous show besides" will be "*there* behind a curtain" (IV.i.185-186, italics mine), seemingly a place on stage that can later be covered when he "*knocks up the curtain*" (IV.iii). The curtain serves presumably to conceal something that is visible or that would otherwise become visible before he is ready. Just before he provides the curtain, Isabella has destroyed the arbor and raved about seeing the ghost of her son (IV.ii). As others have asked, does she see Horatio's body, and does Hieronimo place a curtain over or in front of it? Is the body on display for an extended period, as is suggested by the parody in *Antonio's Revenge* where the corpse of Feliche remains hanging for 147 lines? Hieronimo's play seems also sure to include some symmetry in blocking: Balthazar as Soliman and Hieronimo as the Bashaw must hold a private conversation about murdering Lorenzo as Erasto while Erasto is onstage with Bel-imperia; and thus Erasto is likely to have been in a separate position. Then Hieronimo must, it seems, cross the stage to kill Lorenzo, as Bel-imperia crosses to Balthazar to pretend submission before she stabs him (IV.iv.39-67).

Especially convincing evidence for deliberate symmetry in blocking is found at the beginning of III.xiv when the two monarchs greet each other, obviously from opposite sides of the stage, with their brothers and trains. The character of Don Pedro seems invented simply to provide the Viceroy with a brother to match Castile, at least for appropriate balance in royal ceremony and consequently in the balance of the staging. (Does Balthazar enter with his father, who has "followers," [24], with him, to match the Spanish King's party of four, with attendants unmentioned?) In any case, the King declaims, "Go brother . . . / Salute the Viceroy in our name," and Castile responds, "I go" (III.xiv.1-2). This statement is matched by, "Go forth, Don Pedro, for thy nephew's sake, / And greet the Duke of Castile" (3-4). Don Pedro's only line follows, "It shall be so."

He may not appear again: there is a request by the Viceroy at the end of the play for Don Pedro to carry off the body of the Viceroy's son, which serves, as before, to match the King's request of Castile; but, as Edwards notes, the stage direction that follows is inconsistent: the Viceroy bears the body off (IV.iv.205-217). Although textual corruption is likely in the last act, Don Pedro seems to be onstage, if he is there at all, again only to create balance. (Kyd does not give him an entrance, nor does Edwards.)

The creation of other characters for the purpose of "pairing" may include the maid provided for Isabella, who expresses sympathy but does little else (III.viii), and, in the scene immediately following, Christophil to lead off Bel-imperia. Neither appears elsewhere in the play (although Christophil is mentioned as the one to whom Lorenzo sends his ring to have Bel-imperia "enlarg'd" [III.x.6-7]). If the Fourth and Fifth Additions to the play in 1602 indicate any contemporary recognition of Kyd's symmetrical tendencies, we can observe the creation of two servants for Hieronimo, Jaques and Pedro, who enter with the two torches, and later the seating of the Painter and Hieronimo together, perhaps in the arbor where Horatio and Bel-imperia sat.

Opportunities for symmetry in staging may, of course, have resulted structurally from the invention of parallel incidents, a familiar element in Kyd's dramaturgy and unnecessary to discuss here. These are more evident in the first rather than the second half of the play, that is, in the part identified by some scholars as more academic or traditional.[48] While it is also unnecessary to summarize Kyd's well-recognized use of rhetorical patterns, such as the balanced sentences with insistent antithesis and alliteration, it is revealing to be reminded how Puttenham and others considered art as "a certaine order of rules," an approach advocated by Mulcaster, Kyd's headmaster at the Merchant Taylors' School.[49] Puttenham considered the use of figures as a technique to be noticed, not concealed, yet not to be strained or made absurd.[50] The obviousness of Kyd's figures—and perhaps of the other techniques noticed here—might then be considered as a demonstration of skill, as long as they are effective. It is also appropriate to remind ourselves that such techniques as anadiplosis lend themselves, through connecting repetition, to expressing the idea of an inevitable course of events; as a specific example, there is Balthazar's extended description of Horatio as his "destin'd plague" in II.i.118-133, the Prince resolving at the end to "tempt the destinies." No further evidence should be necessary to establish the use of dual and serial relationships in the staging of the play; and the symmetry in dramatic and linguistic techniques tends to endorse the significance of what has been found in the staging.

III

By way of conclusion, I wish to focus on two episodes in the play that may seem to a modern audience particularly clumsy and intrusive: Hieronimo's masque and the dumb show provided by Revenge, each serving to conclude one of the acts. I argued earlier that the first may not have appeared awkward to a contemporary audience, and I suggest now that the second directly expresses a central idea of the play. Furthermore, these episodes are parallel in manifesting concern over delay in the achievement of revenge, and, I believe, in effectively addressing that concern. Returning to the end of Act One, following Hieronimo's "pompous jest" (iv.137), one finds Andrea complaining:

> Come we for this from depth of underground,
> To see him feast that gave me my death's wound?
> These pleasant sights are sorrow to my soul,
> Nothing but league, and love, and banqueting!
>
> (I.v.1-4)

In this speech, Kyd displays his theatrical self-consciousness in a technique well-suited to the overall "idea of a play" that is so fundamental to this work. The festive occasion and the dumb show with its appeal to contemporary jingoism are condemned as a digression by a character who is observing this "inner" play from a position comparable to that of the audience at the Rose. The character's declaration serves to assert this sequence of delay to be an intentional part of the dramatic fabric, making it more credible.[51] Revenge then proceeds to promise what he will do, reassuring both Andrea and the audience that, "ere we go from hence" (5), the central purpose of the action will be achieved.

Revenge makes this promise again at the close of Act Three, assuring Andrea—and the audience—that, although Revenge may be asleep, his "mood" is "soliciting" the souls of men, and declaring as an introduction to the dumb show:

> Behold, Andrea, for an instance how
> Revenge hath slept, and then imagine thou
> What 'tis to be subject to destiny.
>
> (III.xv.26-28)

Apparently, Revenge then falls asleep once more, since after the show, Andrea calls for him to awake and "reveal this mystery" (29), upon which Revenge serves as "truchman" (as Hieronimo did in Act One), describing Hymen as hurrying after two nuptial torch-bearers to blow out the flames *and* quench them with blood (34), a curious straining after another dual effect. Revenge concludes that Hymen was "discontent that things continue so" (35), a reflection on the situation similar to Andrea's comment following Hieronimo's masque, and an inducement to the audience to join with Andrea, who says he is content "to sit and see the rest" (39). We have found here, therefore, a proleptic display in which Kyd has again used spectacle both to distance and to involve, to create sympathy for the revenger's impatience and to assert more directly than before the existence of a system within which revenge inexorably works itself out.

As suggested earlier, the contribution that ordered spectacle makes to the first act and to the play as a whole is also appropriate to and perhaps developed from the physical structure of the Elizabethan outdoor theater (as we now understand its design), as well as from earlier drama and art. The theater seems surely to have been symmetrical in its proportions and perhaps classical in its decor, from the encompassing galleries to the platform that probably extended to the middle of the yard.[52] It offered, as we know, at least two balanced entrances and probably a central opening or discovery space (or a "pavilion" or "house" as needed). Even the columns that supported the "heavens" served to frame the customary central focus.

Although some of Kyd's effects are stiffly contrived, many are ingenious and appropriate to the circumstances. That it was produced in theaters that reflected the dominant Renaissance concern—at least temporarily—for order expressed in terms of symmetry, is most appropriate. During much of the play the physical structure complemented the dramatic form as well as the literary content—the severe, clear, regulated pattern of Kyd's visual and aural effect. Thus, the play should be understood as neither a celebration nor a condemnation of the desire for revenge but as a wry if not bitter demonstration of its absolute existence and inevitable effect.

Notes

1. But see Barry B. Adams, "The Audiences of *The Spanish Tragedy*," *Journal of English and Germanic Philology,* 68 (1969), 221-236, for an early and valuable appreciation of the esthetic issues involved in this theatricality.

2. "The Figure of Silence in *The Spanish Tragedy*," *ELH: Journal of English Literary History,* 39 (1972), 27-48.

3. "The Staging of *The Spanish Tragedy*," in *The Elizabethan Theatre* V, ed. G. R. Hibbard (Hamden, Conn.: Archon, 1975), pp. 112-123.

4. "'Action is Eloquence': The Staging of Thomas Kyd's *Spanish Tragedy*," *SEL: Studies in English Literature, 1500-1900,* 16 (1976), 223-239.

5. (London: Routledge, 1982), pp. 101-128. He observes that scenes "repeat situations or gests" and that "Kyd's method of composition . . . is based

on analogy, on the creation of *figurae,* and the architectonic arrangement of these gives the play its strong dramatic rhythm" (p. 106).

6. For my study of the theatrical effect of the whole play, please see "The Dramatic Artistry of Thomas Kyd's *Spanish Tragedy*: A Study in Context, Meaning, and Effect," Diss. University of California, Los Angeles 1969.

7. T. W. Craik has provided a valuable summary of principles for such analysis: "The Reconstruction of Stage Action from Early Dramatic Texts," in *The Elizabethan Theatre* V, ed. G. R. Hibbard (Hamden, Conn.: Archon, 1975), pp. 76-91, observing that "one must be excited by the plays and wish to visualize them in action" and concluding that "although we can hardly hope to find conclusive proof, we can reasonably hope to find corroboration" through study of all the plays (p. 91). Such corroboration would only indirectly respond to the question, frequently raised, as to whether what is called for in stage directions was necessarily performed. Alan Dessen reminds us: "I find it chastening to remember that whoever annotated the manuscript of Heywood's *The Captives* for the theatre let stand the marginal stage direction for a murderous assault: '*Either strikes him with a staff or casts a stone*' (ll. 2432-34)": *Elizabethan Stage Conventions and Modern Interpreters* (Cambridge: Cambridge University Press, 1984), pp. 20-21. We are, of course, also uncertain in many cases whether or not the texts were always or ever performed exactly as they appear in print, but that does not prevent appropriate appreciation of what we have.

8. *Shakespeare at the Globe: 1599-1609* (New York: Macmillan, 1962), pp. 171-172.

9. *From Art to Theatre: Form and Convention in the Renaissance* (Chicago, Ill.: University of Chicago Press, 1944).

10. *From "Mankind" to Marlowe* (Cambridge, Mass.: Harvard University Press, 1962), pp. 114-119.

11. Introduction to *The Poetical Works of Sir William Alexander,* ed. L. E. Kastner and H. B. Charlton (Manchester: University of Manchester Press, 1921), pp. xx-xxi.

12. See Hattaway for especially useful insights into Kyd's manipulation of "spatial relationship between players and spectators," contrasting the empty stages of Renaissance drama, where time and change could be displayed, with "timeless" Medieval drama (pp. 101-102).

13. Arthur Freeman, *Thomas Kyd: Facts and Problems* (Oxford: Clarendon Press, 1967); Freeman

infers that the "spanes commodye" was based on the tragedy, possibly slapstick, not truly a "first part," and not necessarily by Kyd (pp. 174-177).

14. The traditional early limit has been 1582; Freeman prefers 1584-85, with a late limit of 1587-88 (p. 79).

15. R. A. Foakes and R. T. Rickert, eds. *Henslowe's Diary* (Cambridge: Cambridge University Press, 1961), pp. 16-20.

16. For a list of plays using a "state" in hall scenes, see E. K. Chambers, *The Elizabethan Stage*, 4 vols. (Oxford: Clarendon Press, 1923), III, 64, n. 5.

17. Hattaway observes that, if on stage throughout, "an empty throne would have been a good emblem of the vanity of human power" (p. 116). Although Tweedie assumes that the throne is used throughout (p. 233), I do not agree with her that the chair brought in by Balthazar in the last act (iii.15-16) is for the Spanish King. It may well be provided for Balthazar in his role as Soliman in the playlet.

18. Citations will be to the Revels edition, ed. Philip Edwards (London: Methuen, 1959).

19. *The Staging of Elizabethan Plays at the Red Bull Theater 1605-1625* (1940; rpt. New York: Kraus Reprint Corporation, 1966), pp. 56-57. Walter W. Greg, however, conjectured the carrying on by "2" of a "chair of state" in III.i of *The Plott of the Battell of Alcazar,* perhaps a Rose play: *Dramatic Documents from the Elizabethan Playhouses: Stage Plots, Actors' Parts, Prompt Books,* 2 vols. (Oxford: Clarendon Press, 1931), II, line 66.

20. Thomas Lodge and Robert Greene, *A Looking-Glass for London and England,* ed. W. W. Greg, Malone Society Reprints (London: Malone Society, 1932).

21. Tweedie believes they are not above because Revenge says, "Here sit we down to see the mystery" (I.i.90; pp. 224-225n.); no seats in the gallery? Adams places them onstage throughout, where, as an important reflection of his thesis, "they become part of the playwright's cosmos, even though they are not at its center" (p. 230). Edwards considers the "Enter" directions for Acts Three and Four (and the *"Exeunt"* at the end of Act Three) "palpable mistakes" (pp. xxxiii-xxxiv).

22. See Anne Righter's discussion of *The Spanish Tragedy* in *Shakespeare and the Idea of the Play* (Baltimore, Md.: Penguin, 1962), pp. 71-78. Righter accepts these characters as "part of the action," unlike Eleanor Prosser and Fredson Bowers, who do not fully acknowledge the effect that may have been produced by the "frame." For example, Bowers does not mention the epilogue (*Elizabethan Revenge Tragedy* [Princeton, N.J.: Princeton University Press, 1940]), and Prosser believes that Andrea and Revenge "take no active role in the play at all" and that the epilogue merely points to the "moral" that the villains will be tormented (*Hamlet and Revenge,* 2nd ed. [Stanford, Calif.: Stanford University Press, 1971], pp. 266-267, n. 2). In the Swan drawing the gallery seems divided into "rooms"; a similar arrangement at the Rose would lend itself to the appropriate separation of the watchers from the watched. Righter's discussion of Oseas watching from the throne in *A Looking-Glass for London and England* is on pp. 69-70.

23. Adams believes that Righter's views oversimplify "the relation between the aesthetic and nonaesthetic" and neglect to see Revenge as "author"; he perceptively points out that Andrea does not seek revenge at first and thus is curious, as the audience is, about the play they see together (pp. 230, n. 16, and 226).

24. Chambers, II, 547, n. 1.

25. Prosser observes that of thirty-six ghosts in English revenge plays, "or serving a similar function in other genres," more than one-third appear as prologues or choruses or both, the ghosts of Elizabethan drama customarily "establishing the playwright's theme of the inevitability of nemesis" (pp. 259-260).

26. Hattaway considers this entrance and passage as "the first of the play's dumbshows, almost certainly given to lavish musical accompaniment" and believes that the movements were from the "cave" of the yard (between the stage and side galleries), up a set of stairs to the stage, and after crossing, down and out the "cave" on the other side (p. 117), an action that might involve wending through the groundlings who would likely crowd as close as possible on all sides. Chambers observed that symbolic battles would often be followed by a "triumphant train" marching across (III, 53).

27. For a different view from mine see Charles A. Hallett and Elaine S. Hallett, *The Revenger's Madness: A Study of Revenge Tragedy Motifs* (Lincoln: University of Nebraska Press, 1980); they interpret the King's situation in this scene as having been made deliberately difficult by Kyd in order to show the wisdom of the magistrate, in that "the King administers justice conscientiously"; in Portugal, on the other hand, human error prevails, requiring a "wise subject" in Alexandro, who turns to divine power: "'Tis heaven is my hope" (II.i.35)

(pp. 134-135); this argument is offered in support of a more Christian reading than seems appropriate, but it accepts that "the destiny to which Hieronimo's passion subjected him had its roots in the order of nature" (p. 160).

28. "Iconography and Characterization in English Tragedy 1585-1642," *Comparative Drama,* 12 (1978), 120, in which a number of other examples are also identified. In a different article, Diehl discusses this fall in terms of the irony of the conventional image, since it is caused by "a lying counselor, not fortune": "Inversion, Parody, and Irony: The Visual Rhetoric of Renaissance English Tragedy," *SEL: Studies in English Literature 1500-1900,* 22 (1982), 206. Jonas A. Barish has compared this gesture to that of Shakespeare's Richard II, who also refuses "to be consoled for a loss that has not yet occurred": "*The Spanish Tragedy,* or the Pleasures and Perils of Rhetoric," *Elizabethan Theatre,* ed. John Russell Brown and Bernard Harris, Stratford-upon-Avon Studies 9 (New York: St. Martin's, 1967), p. 84. Falling to the ground is exploited, if not satirized, in *Antonio and Mellida,* Antonio engaging in the gesture some six times: see Ronald J. Palumbo, "From Melodrama to Burlesque: A Theatrical Gesture in Kyd, Shakespeare, and Marston," *Theatre Survey,* 17 (1976), 220-223.

29. Tweedie observes this use of the glove as "a visual image for the shift in her affections" (p. 232). Hattaway describes it as a figurative casting down of the gauntlet, "a bold gesture accessible to a boy player of feminine will subverting Balthazar's masculine assumption of superiority" (pp. 119-120).

30. For a recent opposite view see Barbara J. Baines, "Kyd's Silenus Box and the Limits of Perception," *The Journal of Medieval and Renaissance Studies,* 10 (1980), 41-51, where it is assumed that the audience would be suspicious of Belimperia's view and of Horatio's motives (p. 42). This discussion is developed from an analysis of the multiple perspectives of the play and considers the empty box as "a metaphor for the play's complex structure" (p. 41), finding Kyd's source as probably the figurative use of Silenus' box by Erasmus (pp. 45-47).

31. Chambers, I, 202-205.

32. John Finett's record, quoted by Chambers, I, 203-204. P. W. Biesterfeldt calls attention to the way each participant is seated by name as an instance of careful identification in a theater that did not provide programs, *Die Dramatische Technik Thomas Kyd's* (Halle: N. Niemeyer, 1936), p. 96.

33. Chambers, I, 190-191.

34. Such shields were used as part of Elizabethan pageantry at tournaments and were hung on posts below the Queen's window in the tiltyard of 1565 to celebrate a wedding. These bore *imprese* or emblems that required interpretation by the squires or pages who carried them: Chambers, I, 142-143, and 143, n. 1.

35. *The Elizabethan Dumb Show* (London: Methuen, 1965), pp. 66-68. As Mehl asserts, the London audience may have seen for the first time with this action a "play" introduced into the plot itself, the first modern play-within-a-play, suitably balancing the playlet to come (p. 66). For a summary of the analogies between Hieronimo's "Soliman and Perseda" and the love-triangle that leads to Horatio's death, see McMillin (p. 46).

36. *The Works of Thomas Kyd,* ed. Frederick S. Boas (1901; rpt. Oxford: Clarendon Press, 1955), p. 397.

37. "*Corrida* of Blood in *The Spanish Tragedy*: Kyd's Use of Revenge as National Destiny," *Medieval & Renaissance Drama in England,* I (1984), 41. Ardolino offers, as further reason to accept the royal parties as placed above the stage when Hieronimo performs his play, a parallel to the ceremonious dropping of the key at the Spanish bullfight (p. 43).

38. It was a standard scenic device: Chambers cites the *Wagner Book* description (1594): "the Gibbet, the Posts, the Ladders, the tiring house, there everything which in the like houses either use or necessity makes common" (III, 72).

39. Nashe in *The Unfortunate Traveler* (1594) wrote, "A fidler cannot turne his pin so soone, as he would turn a man of the ladder" (*OED,* 73d).

40. Tweedie favors a "gallows" or "hanging tree" that might have been "somewhere at center stage" above the trap for rapid introduction and removal and therefore used for both Horatio and Pedringano (pp. 234-235); Rowan accepts a "property arbour" on stage "from first to last, an emblem of the womb of destiny, of life and death," that might serve as a stake for Alexandro's intended execution, for Pedringano, and again as an arbor to reveal Horatio's body in the "grande finale" (p. 120). It is referred to as a "bower" or "bowers" six times, as a "garden plot" twice, and as a "garden" three times, but never as an "arbour" except in the stage directions. Perhaps this is a clue: as Rowan has also observed (pp. 119-120), the *OED* lists *bower* as "a place closed in or overarched with branches of trees, shrubs, or other plants; a shady recess, leafy covert, arbour" (3), while *arbour* includes mention of "framework,"

"trellis-work" (4), and "lattice work" (5), on which vines or shrubs were trained. Perhaps Kyd imagined a bower while the production facilities provided an arbor, such as that used in the Rose for *A Looking-Glass for London,* just six days before the performance we now are imagining. That arbor rose from a trap, as is indicated in the text, "By Magicke frame an Arbour out of hand" (l. 517) as well as in the stage directions, *"The Magi with their rods beate the ground, and from vnder the same riseth a braue Arbour"* (ll. 521-522). And, of course, the woodcut on the title-page of the 1615 edition of Kyd's play shows a small leaf-covered lattice-work structure that might easily have fitted into the trap, as nearly everyone has noticed.

41. The symbolism of the repeated use of rope and poniard is briefly discussed by Henry E. Jacobs, "Kyd's *The Spanish Tragedy* III.xii.s.d.," *The Explicator,* 34 (1976), Item 63: these properties are seen as representing "the two ends of the play's action: Horatio's death and Hieronimo's revenge," with Hieronimo "the causal link"; and also "the two sides of an ethical dilemma . . . emblems of justice and revenge."

42. Tweedie carries this a step further, connecting the writing with Horatio's blood on the handkerchief (p. 228).

43. It is difficult not to accept it as identical, and Ejner J. Jensen believes the terms were interchangeable: "Kyd's *Spanish Tragedy*: The Play Explains Itself," *Journal of English and Germanic Philology,* 64 (1965), 13-14. However, this assumption is not supported by the *OED: scarf* appears to be most often used to designate a broad band of cloth such as a military sash; *handkercher,* nevertheless, would be the appropriate name for Hieronimo to give it; we cannot expect that he would have known of the scarf and called it that, and handkerchiefs have been worn about the neck, as have scarfs. Given Kyd's skill in using properties, it seems unlikely that he would have passed over this opportunity to use one throughout the play as a symbol. Hieronimo will not put it from him, nor will he bury his son, until he obtains revenge.

44. Hattaway offers an appealing suggestion that Revenge in his first entrance might have carried both a sword and a torch (p. 113). If so, the emblematic parallel later when Hieronimo does so would have been immediately apparent. Hattaway cites the stage direction in *Locrine* (1591?) calling for Ate (or Revenge) to enter *"with a burning torch in one hand, and a bloody sword in the other hand"* (sig. A3ʳ).

45. Edwards believes that both the direction *"Pedringano showeth all to the Prince and* *Lorenzo, placing them in secret"* and the later *"Balthazar above"* (following l. 17) are authorial and adds "above" to the first direction while eliminating the second (pp. 34-35). I suggest, however, that the second direction serves to *remind* us of Balthazar's location (whether we are readers or actors readying a production).

46. Tweedie focuses here, as she also does with the liaison and the watch scene, upon what she terms "three-fold" grouping (p. 236).

47. McMillin offers an extended discussion of the parallels between these figures, Bazulto as mirror of Horatio and then of Hieronimo himself, especially when the corpse is revealed (IV.iv.96-97) (pp. 39-40).

48. For example, Boas, *Works,* and C. F. Tucker Brooke, *The Tudor Drama* (Boston: Houghton Mifflin, 1911). The dramatic effectiveness of the parallels of the Portuguese subplot to the main action has been most fully examined by Ken C. Burrows, who describes Kyd's "device of giving double value to the same event" (p. 28): "The Dramatic and Structural Significance of the Portuguese Sub-plot in *The Spanish Tragedy,"* *Renaissance Papers* (1969), 25-35. Also see William H. Wiatt, "The Dramatic Function of the Alexandro-Villuppo Episode in *The Spanish Tragedy,"* *Notes and Queries,* 203 (1958), 327-329, and G. K. Hunter, "Ironies of Justice in *The Spanish Tragedy,"* *Renaissance Drama,* 8 (1965), 89-104. Hattaway especially recognizes the symmetry in the scenes in terms of contrast, suggesting that I.iv can be matched with II.ii: Bel-imperia first attracts Horatio to confess love and loyalty and then "holds back, oppressed by a sense of danger" (pp. 120-121). Similarly, he finds the first two scenes of Act Four symmetrical "as usual" because of the contrast between Hieronimo's calm preparation for his revenge play and Isabella's "pathos and frenetic suicide" (pp. 125-126).

49. As Sister Miriam Joseph has pointed out, the ideal was, in Gabriel Harvey's description, "to imitate the excellentest artificiality of the most renowned workemasters that antiquity affourdeth": *Rhetoric in Shakespeare's Time: Literary Theory of Renaissance Europe* (New York: Harcourt, 1962), pp. 5-7. Barish has identified the symmetrical character of Kyd's rhetoric as well as its relationship to the plot and to the staging (pp. 59-85); Samuel J. Mitchell provides a very useful tabulation and analysis in "Rhetoric as a Dramatic Element in the Plays of Thomas Kyd" (Thesis, University of Texas 1951); and Thomas W. Ross has included in his old-spelling edition of the play a discussion of Kyd's rhetorical "flourishes" as functional, "not simply for decoration" (Fountainwell Drama Texts,

6 [Berkeley: University of California, 1968], pp. 6-9). Hattaway emphasizes Kyd's employment of "the boldest and simplest of the figures of sound": isocolon, parison, and paromoion, all involving repetition and parallelism (p. 107).

50. *The Arte of English Poesie*, ed. Gladys D. Willock and Alice Walker (Cambridge: Cambridge University Press, 1936), p. 159.

51. Adams describes this as "playwright-audience dialectic": "An audience's expectations have not been satisfied, but they have been validated by an authoritative spokesman" (p. 227).

52. There is the familiar argument from the Swan drawing with de Witt's accompanying comment about its resemblance to a Roman amphitheater with pillars painted to look like marble. This has been supplemented by evidence of symmetrical design, although without agreement on the source of that design: see John Orrell, *The Quest for Shakespeare's Globe* (Cambridge: Cambridge University Press, 1983), esp. pp. 139-157, and my "Vitruvian Proportions in Theater Design in the Sixteenth and Early Seventeenth Centuries in Italy and England," *Shakespeare Studies,* 16 (1983), esp. pp. 265-269, 314-318. Scott McMillin provides a very sensible appraisal of the physical circumstances at the Rose in "The Staging of Elizabethan Plays at the Rose Theatre," Diss. Stanford University 1965.

Huston Diehl (essay date 1991)

SOURCE: Diehl, Huston. "Observing the Lord's Supper and the Lord Chamberlain's Men: The Visual Rhetoric of Ritual and Play in Early Modern England." *Renaissance Drama* 22 (1991): 147-74.

[*In the following essay, Diehl examines* The Spanish Tragedy *and* Hamlet, *proposing an analogous relationship between the substance of visual signs in Renaissance drama and signs in Protestant Eucharistic ritual.*]

Recent scholarship has begun to engage provocative questions about the relation between the reformed religion and Tudor and Stuart drama.[1] Many of these studies focus on the antitheatrical biases and iconoclastic impulses of early English Protestantism. In an influential essay, Louis Adrian Montrose hypothesizes that the commercial stage serves as an important substitute for the rituals and images of the medieval church that the reformers denounce and forbid. Noting how easily the distinction between drama and ritual can become blurred in performance, Montrose argues that Renaissance English drama appropriates and transforms the forbidden Catholic rituals, rituals he associates with "the material efficacy of magic" (62). He suggests that the drama that emerged soon after Elizabeth reestablished the reformed religion may provide "another form of compensation" (60) for the suppressed Roman Catholic rituals and ceremonies, offering an eager populace what the new religion deprived them of: mystery, magic, spectacle, theatricality.

Although Montrose explores the relation between religious rituals and secular plays from the perspective of cultural anthropology, he denies the *reformed* sacraments the power anthropologists attribute to religious rituals to shape the way their participants experience and interpret their world "by inducing in the worshipper a certain distinctive set of dispositions (tendencies, capacities, propensities, skills, habits, liabilities, pronenesses) which lend a chronic character to the flow of his activity and the quality of his experience" (Geertz 95). Interested in how the suppression of the Roman Catholic Mass might have contributed to the emergence of the commercial stage, he fails to ask how the institution of the Protestant Lord's Supper might have shaped—in a constructive way—the new drama and its audiences.

Nevertheless, his thesis that Elizabethan drama replaces the lost medieval religious rituals presumably because the reformed religion fails to create viable ritual forms in place of the ones it destroys has gained wide acceptance.[2] Martha Tuck Rozett, in her book on the relation between the doctrine of election and the emergence of Elizabethan tragedy, comments that "[i]ronically, the reformers drove their audiences to seek in the theatre what the Church no longer provided" (21-22). Michael O'Connell even argues in his essay on spectacle in the church and the theater that Elizabethan drama "could be viewed as a competing—idolatrous—religious structure" (307). All these critics imagine a reformed religion essentially devoid of meaningful rituals, ceremonies, images, and communal experiences. And they imply that sixteenth-century Londoners, or at least the ten thousand or so who flock weekly to the theaters, are hostile to, and deeply dissatisfied by, the reformed religion they are required by law to worship.

Certainly, many experience the eventual suppression of the Roman Mass as a profound loss. Many others, however, are as profoundly affected by the power of the revised Protestant sacrament. That power is too often unacknowledged by literary critics who view the Reformation from the perspective of four centuries of continued demystification of the sacred, four hundred years of greater and greater rationalization of religion. The beginning of that process is all too often confused with the end—that modern moment that declares God absent, rituals empty, signs meaningless, community dead. But if the reformers, in their denunciation of the

Catholic Mass, anticipate, and set in motion, the anxieties of modernism, they do not empty the sacrament of the Lord's Supper of its meaning or deprive it of its ritual status.

In fact, many people in sixteenth-century England experience the Lord's Supper as meaningful, mysterious, and deeply satisfying. During the reign of the Catholic Queen Mary, numerous men and women—lay people as well as ministers and theologians, the illiterate as well as the educated—risk their lives in defense of the Lord's Supper. They openly defy authorities who require them to attend the Catholic Mass and submit to rigorous inquisitions in which Catholic clerics attempt to coerce them into renouncing their reformed faith. Many, many more are profoundly influenced by the Marian persecutions of such Protestants. Their martyrdoms had the effect of turning Londoners—"[t]he vast majority" of whom at the time "were wavering, uncertain and ignorant" about these religious upheavals—against Queen Mary and the Roman church (Alexander 175). Narrative accounts of these martyrdoms, particularly those recorded by John Foxe in his popular *Actes and Monuments,* a book required to be chained alongside the Bible in every parish church in England (King 435), assure that the Protestant martyrs continue to influence others throughout the latter part of the sixteenth century. The extent to which these people resist their monarch's attempt to reinstate the old Mass, and the sophistication with which they mount theological arguments in support of the reformed sacraments suggest how passionately they embrace the new religion, how fully they have—by the mid-1500s—internalized the teachings of the reformers.

This is *particularly* true in London and its surrounding parishes, where the influence of the Continental Reformation is felt most strongly and the conditions of urban life predispose citizens to embrace the new reformed ideology. Recent historical studies of the local reception of Protestantism in England reveal that the citizens of London accepted the reformed religion earlier and with far less resistance than people in rural and northern parts of England.[3] "Nowhere in the kingdom," Gina Alexander writes, "had there been a greater circulation of Protestant ideas of many varieties, nowhere had Protestant modes of worship taken firmer root than in the [London] diocese to which Bonner was restored in September 1553" (166).

If we grant that the reformed Lord's Supper is a viable and widely practiced religious ritual in late sixteenth-century London, one that shares with other such sacred rituals the capacity to alter, "often radically, the whole landscape presented to common sense" (Geertz 122), how might its regular observance affect the way its worshippers see, interpret, and interact with the visible world? More specifically, how might the practice of this ritual shape the way London playwrights imagine and London playgoers experience the spectacle and theatrics of Elizabethan and Jacobean drama?

Although the sacred space of the Anglican church may seem very far removed from the secular space of the London theater in Shakespeare's time, both the religious ritual and the popular play function, I suggest, as "cultural performances," those powerful cultural forms that symbolic anthropologists believe have the capacity to shape human consciousness.[4] Both are public and performative genres. Both occupy a communal space specifically designed for them, one that is marked off and set apart from the everyday world. Both are "central and recurrent" events in the lives of the citizens of London (Turner 23). Both are "orchestrations of media"—images, words, music—"not expressions in a single medium" (Turner 23). And both are reflexive forms that create what Victor Turner has described as a "'discontinuum' of action" during which their spectators "become conscious, through witnessing and often participating in such performances, of the nature, texture, style, and given meanings of their own lives as members of a sociocultural community" (22). Observing (celebrating) the Lord's Supper and observing (watching) the Lord Chamberlain's Men are, from this perspective, related cultural activities that help to structure the way Elizabethans and Jacobeans know and understand their world.

Rather than honor the distinctions between sacred and secular—distinctions that are themselves early Protestant constructions[5]—I therefore propose to treat both ritual and play as reflexive cultural forms that have the capacity not only to mirror but also to shape the lived experience of their participants. In observing the reformed Lord's Supper in the late sixteenth-century Anglican church, worshippers must acknowledge that the sacramental bread and wine are signs, and not the transubstantiated body and blood of Christ. They must consciously repudiate the old religion's belief that *viewing* the Host is salvific, and yet, in the absence of any such miraculous spectacle, attend to the figurative power of the communal bread and wine. And, they must cultivate a receptivity to the spoken word rather than worship the image. In observing the Lord Chamberlain's Men, the spectators must recognize (as the Mechanicals in *A Midsummer Night's Dream* are so anxious to demonstrate) that what they see is a representation, and not the literal presence of what is represented. They must consciously accept the illusory nature of theatrical images and yet believe in the figurative truth of those very images. And they must attend closely to the oral recitation of poetic verse while being careful not to overvalue spectacle.

In this essay, I will explore the relation between these two experiences, focusing on one aspect of the Protestant sacrament and the Renaissance play: the use of visible signs. Both Protestant ritual and Renaissance play, I will argue, destabilize their spectators, denying them any unmediated experience of visible things and fostering a distrust of externals. Nevertheless, both also insist on the figurative power of the visible sign, inculcating a new mode of seeing that, while it requires people to be skeptical about what they see and self-reflexive about their own looking, also encourages them to be receptive to the capacity of signs, in conjunction with spoken words, to move, persuade, and transform.

II

The iconoclastic impulses of the early Protestant reformers are in part a response to the iconophilia that pervades late medieval popular culture. Nowhere is this dialectic more fully articulated than in the eucharistic controversy of the sixteenth century. Because the early Protestants believe that the most heinous and blasphemous idol of the Roman Catholic church is the Mass itself, a ritual that many Catholics had come to view as a "mysterious spectacle" (Davies 139), the reformation debate over images necessarily addresses that central sacrament in both faiths, what the Catholics call the Mass and the reformed Protestants the Lord's Supper.[6] Rejecting the sacrament of the altar as "an abominable idol" and a "foul idol" (Foxe 8: 492, 498), English reformers condemn the emphasis in popular devotion on *viewing* the sacred Host, an experience that for many had become "the principal, if not the exclusive, concern of the worshippers" (Davies 140), so much so that "people frequently left the church after the elevation" (Miles 97). The Roman Mass deeply offends these reformers because the priest, in elevating the Host, presumes to offer a salvific vision of God, a God the reformers insist is invisible. How to see, what it is possible to see, and the power of what one sees are thus central issues in any interpretation of this sacrament.

In their condemnation of the Roman Catholic Mass, the English reformers explicitly call into question—and repudiate—the devotional gaze. Dismissing the adoration of the elevated Host as mere gaping, John Foxe, for example, ridicules "our mass-men" for "gazing, peeping, pixing, boxing, carrying, re-carrying, worshipping, stooping, kneeling, knocking, with 'stoop down before,' 'hold up higher,' 'I thank God I see my Maker to-day'" (Foxe 7: 198; 6: 361). Reformed Protestants object to the Mass because it deflects the worshipper's attention away from an invisible God and focuses it instead on "man-made" images. In a typical anecdote in a Protestant sermon, a Catholic priest offers a dying goldsmith "a cross of fine silver being double gilted" and tells him it is "your maker, your saviour, and redeemer, look upon hym." The goldsmith gazes silently at the cross before replying, unmoved and unrepentant, "what is the price of an ounce?" In an attempt to demystify such images, the preacher asks sarcastically, "Was not thys manne well edified by the sight of this goodly cross?" (Veron 102).

Such attacks on the images and rituals of the Roman Catholic church disrupt the way ordinary people understand what they see during the most sacred ritual of the Christian religion. Foxe documents this disruption. For example, he relates a conversation between two friends, a man named William Rivelay who believes he has "seen his Lord God in form of bread and wine over the priest's head," and a man named John Southwick who impatiently corrects him, exclaiming, "Nay, William! thou saw'st not the Lord God, thou sawest bread, wine, and the chalice." This anecdote illustrates how the reformed interpretation of the Lord's Supper challenges lay people's assumptions about the visible world and its relation to the divine. When Rivelay persists in his belief that he sees God, stubbornly asserting that "I trust verily that I saw my Lord God in form of bread and wine, and this I doubt not," Southwick attempts to teach his friend to see in a more analytical, self-conscious, and mediated way: "Nay, I tell thee thou sawest but only a figure or sacrament of him, which is in substance bread and wine" (Foxe 4: 206-07). In Foxe's polemical work, William Rivelay's way of seeing—one informed by what we might identify as a late medieval belief in the "sanctifying presence of God's image in the world"—is ridiculed as carnal and idolatrous while his friend John Southwick's, which carefully distinguishes between the visible sign and the invisible God it signifies, is repeatedly depicted as enlightened, indeed, heroic.

The Catholic authorities portrayed in *Actes and Monuments* ruthlessly attempt to impose a way of seeing on these martyrs who courageously resist their persecutors, denying, even under threat of torture and death, that they see Christ "flesh, blood, and bone" in the pyx (Foxe 8: 242). "I see nothing but a few clouts hanging together on a heap" (8: 158), Roger Bernard insists when a bishop points to the pyx over the altar and asks, "whom seest thou yonder?" In an effort to break the habit of "seeing and adoring the body in the form of bread," Foxe ridicules worshippers who "imagine a body where they see no body" and condemns the Mass as "altogether corporeal and extern" because it encourages "the outward seeing and touching of him, of itself, without faith" (Foxe 1: 528).

His rhetoric aggressively attempts to de-naturalize a mode of seeing that characterizes late medieval spirituality and, if Foxe can be trusted, still pervades the popular culture of sixteenth-century England. Adopting rhetorical strategies found in the polemical works of almost all the early English reformers and preachers, he attempts to shock his readers into confronting what he believes is the "corporeal" nature of the old religion and the "carnal understanding" of the eucharist (Foxe 1: 528; 8: 309). Because he believes that the doctrine of transubstantiation is an absurd literalization of a trope, he explores the implications of a literal understanding of the Host. He accuses Roman Catholics of worshipping a "bready God" who is "grated with the tooth," "conveyed into the belly," even vomited overboard by seasick sailors. He ridicules them for shutting God up in a box where it "breed[s] worms" and becomes "mouldy and overgrown with vermin" (Foxe 8: 498, 6: 345, 5: 511, 6: 341). His own literalizations, exaggerated, ridiculous, outrageous, attempt to undermine belief in the Mass by foregrounding its literalism and mocking its mystery.

In an emblem book that draws its images from Protestant sermons, Thomas Jenner employs a similar technique to satirize the papists' literalist interpretation of the Mass. Under the title "The foolishnes of Transubstantiation," he features a picture of a tavern with a sign on which a cluster of grapes is painted. High on a ladder, a man foolishly attempts to drink the image of the grapes. "Suche mad men *Papists* are," Jenner explains:

> which verefie
> That in a *little Wafer (hid)* doth lye
> *Christs very flesh*; While th'*elements* (there) be
> Hung out to Commers in, that they might see,
> In *Christ* alone stands that *spiritual food*;
> Which must not of these *signes* be understood.
>
> (sig. F7v)

Through such strategies, Foxe and Jenner attempt to shock and disrupt their readers, forcing them to become self-conscious about how they see and interpret the visible elements of the Lord's Supper.

According to the reformers, those elements, in the hands of the priests, are perversely turned into theatrical props that beguile the devout with dazzling spectacle and meaningless ceremonies. They sarcastically refer to the sacred images of the Roman church as theatrical properties—"puppets, maumats, and elfes" (Foxe 5: 409)—that the priests, like evil playwrights, use to stage illusory and empty visions. If, in this construction, the Host is nothing more than a "patched monster, a disguised puppet" (Foxe 8: 464), the priests who elevate it are "false theves and Juglers" who cunningly "bewitch the mindes of the simple people," seducing them "from the true worship of god unto pernicious Idolatry" by making them see Christ in "the creature of breade and wine" (Ridley, "Farewell" sigs. Bii, Bii.v). By means of such theatricality, the priests, so one popular song laments, fool the eyes of a credulous populace:

> Thus were we poor soules
> Begyled with idolles,
> With fayned myricles and lyes,

> By the devyel and his doctors,
> The pope and his procters;
> That, with such, have blerid our eyes.
>
> (Qtd. in Foxe 5: 409)

The reformers thus accuse the Roman Catholic authorities of fraudulently and tyrannically manipulating the sight of the lay people by turning mystery "into a blind mist of mere accidents, to blear the people's eyes, making them believe they see that they see not, and not to see that which they see" (Foxe 1: 83). And they imagine themselves liberating the people by removing the obstacles to clear seeing. Sight thus becomes a contested site on which these theological controversies are waged.

Although they are contemptuous of the devotional gaze, however, Calvin and the English reformers he influences do *not* eliminate the visible from the Lord's Supper. Rather, they identify the visible images of bread and wine as divine signs and repeatedly call attention to their *power.* Rather than forbid images, they distinguish between idols—images that tempt people to worship them—and figures—images that enable people to remember, and experience, what is absent. In reaction against popular devotional practices that encourage people to see and touch an incarnate God, these early Protestants teach worshippers to see the visible elements of the sacraments as divine signs that can lead them to an invisible God. If, for the reformers, any human attempt to render God visible is by definition idolatrous, God nevertheless chooses to represent himself in images, so that he "may after a sort be sene and felt of us" and the faithful may "behold and see him" in the sacraments "as it were in the face" (Calvin, *Four sermons* sigs. Kiii, Kiii.v). To Calvin, the sacraments are "the true pictures" and "the good images that God hath set before us" (*Galathians* sig. 114v), and reformed Christians are encouraged to discover God in "such tokens and sygnes" and to "turne our eyes to that countenance . . . that we should behold it with great heade, care and diligence" (*Four sermons* sig. Kii.v).[8]

According to Calvin, God uses these "earthly and visible signs" because he deems them "fitteth for us" (*Galathians* sig. 118) as "souls engrafted in bodies" (*Institutes* 4.14.3). Accommodating "our feeble capacity" (*Institutes* 4.17.11), God "condescends to lead us to himself even by these earthly elements, and to set before us in the flesh a mirror of spiritual blessings"; he thus "imparts spiritual things under visible ones" (*Institutes* 4.14.3). The sacraments—those "physical signs . . . thrust before our eyes" (*Institutes* 4.17.11)—thus represent "God's promises as painted in a picture" which God "sets . . . before our sight, portrayed graphically and in the manner of images" (*Institutes* 4.14.6; see also 4.17.11). Although they must not be confused with the things they signify, these images are thus vehicles that are essential to faith, God-given tokens and signs the believer is encouraged to contemplate, interpret, and, above all, experience.

Rather than eradicating the visual from the sacrament, or merely arousing mistrust of it, Calvin thus conceives of the visible element as a necessary rhetorical tool by which God "exhorteth us to come unto him," making "him selfe lowe, too the ende wee shoulde not have any excuse, to say wee were not able to mount up to such a heighth" (*Galathians* sig. 118). Images like the bread and wine of the Lord's Supper or the water of baptism are the "ladders and stayres" by which humans, creatures of the flesh, may climb to God (*Four sermons* sig. Kii.v). Worshippers are admonished not to "pluck down Christ from heaven, and put him in your faith, as in a visible place," but instead to "rise and spring up to him" by means of these images (Foxe 6: 339).

Analogy is therefore crucial to the Calvinist reinterpretation of the Lord's Supper. Because the sacrament depends on the correspondence between earthly bread and Christ's body, physical eating and spiritual nourishment, Calvin declares it meaningless *unless* the bread is literal bread, a sign of something it is not:

> The nature of the Sacrament is therefore canceled, unless, in the mode of signifying, the earthly sign corresponds to the heavenly thing. And the truth of this mystery accordingly perishes for us unless true bread represents the true body of Christ. Again I repeat: since the Supper is nothing but a visible witnessing of that promise contained in the sixth chapter of John, namely, that Christ is the bread of life come down from heaven [John 6:51], visible bread must serve as an intermediary to represent that spiritual bread—unless we are willing to lose all the benefit which God, to sustain our weakness, confers upon us.
>
> (*Institutes* 4.17.14)

In the words of Peter Martyr, "The analogy and resemblance between the sacrament, and the thing signified, must ever be kept in all sacraments" (qtd. in Foxe 6: 300).

When reformed theologians insist that the sacramental bread is a figure—"one thing spoken, and another meant; as Christ saith, 'I am a vine, I am a door, I am a stone,' etc. Is he therefore a material stone, a vine, a door?" (Foxe 8: 244)—they therefore also assert the potency of that figure. Emphasizing the memorial nature of the Lord's Supper, rather than the sacrificial, they grant images an important, indeed essential, mnemonic function. It is, for them, the *remembrance* of Christ's sacrifice, not the carnal presence of Christ, that enables the worshipper to benefit from the sacrament. Christ's words, "Do this in remembrance of me" (Luke 22:19), are thus the "key" to the sacrament that "opened and revealed" its meaning, and transubstantiation violates

Christ's words by turning "commemoration" into "adoration."[9] As a "perpetual memorie" (Bucer sig. Dviii.v), the Lord's Supper calls to mind a past event, renewing an understanding of its significance. It also helps its participants recall their own unworthiness. Only by remembering their own sins can they fully grasp the meaning of the sacrament as a promise of the redemption of sins.[10]

To stir the memory, the reformers advocate the use of a simple table like the one that might have been used at the original supper, and a whole loaf of bread, like the one Christ might have broken.[11] They thus propose the use of visible objects to create a representational scene, much as stage properties do on the bare Elizabethan stage. The communion table is in this way demystified, its symbolic nature emphasized in striking contrast to the sacred altar of the Roman church, which is shrouded in mystery. The Lord's Supper, the reformers insist, is a sacrament, a promise, a memorial, not a sacrifice or a miracle. In opposition to the Mass, which encourages its worshippers to see, ingest, and adore an incarnate God, the sight of whom is salvific, its worshippers are therefore invited to remember, receive, and rise up to a transcendent God who cannot be seen, eaten, or touched. But if God is invisible, the Protestant devout are "lifted up to heaven with our eyes and minds" (*Institutes* 4.17.18) by means of visible signs.[12]

That transcendent moment when "the divine essence infuseth itself unspeakably into the faithful receiver of the sacrament" (Foxe 6: 312) cannot be achieved by means of the visible image alone; Calvin accuses the Catholics of emptying the sacramental signs of meaning by divorcing them from words, thereby mystifying them (*Institutes* 4.17.39). He is especially contemptuous of the use of Latin in the Roman Catholic Mass, so that words are "whispered without meaning" (*Institutes* 4.14.4), and he ridicules the Mass for its primary emphasis on spectacle devoid of any explanatory words:

> [N]othing more preposterous could happen in the Supper than for it to be turned into a silent action, as has happened under the pope's tyranny. . . . Here we should not imagine some magic incantation, supposing it enough to have mumbled the words, as if they were to be heard by the elements; but let us understand that these words are living preaching which edifies its hearers, penetrates into their very minds, impresses itself upon their hearts and settles there, and reveals its effectiveness in the fulfillment of what it promises.
>
> (*Institutes* 4.17.39)

For Calvin and the English reformers he influences, then, the Mass is an abuse of God's sacrament not because it is dramatic or visual (in fact, in important ways the Lord's Supper is both) but because it is performed in "silence" or with "a mere noise"; they repeatedly insist that without words that "make us understand what the visible sign means," the eucharistic bread and wine are "utterly meaningless signs" (*Institutes* 4.17.39, 4.14.4, 4.10.15). Although literary scholars often assume that when Protestants condemn the theatricality and spectacle of the Mass, they condemn theater and image, *per se,* early Protestants use these words pejoratively almost exclusively to refer to the silent actions, gestures, and visual displays of the Mass, that is, to images and ceremonies that are *divorced from words.*

The poetic drama of the English Renaissance stage, with its rich and powerful verbal and vernacular texts, it hardly what Calvin has (or could have) in mind when he ridicules Catholic sacraments and ceremonies as "lifeless and theatrical trifles" that "draw the eyes of the common people to wonderment by a new spectacle," "theatrical props . . . where nothing appears but the mask of useless elegance and fruitless extravagance" (*Institutes* 4.17.43, 4.10.29). These sacraments are lifeless, useless, and fruitless because "there is no woorde that sanctifyeth them" (*Ephesians* sig. 85); they are nothing more than "bare sign[s]" because "the sacrament requires preaching to beget faith" (*Institutes* 4.14.4).

If Calvin creates distrust for theatrical actions and spectacular images unaccompanied by explanatory words, mystified by unintelligible incantations, or divorced from the divine Word, he imagines the Lord's Supper as a dramatic representation in which the spoken word has the capacity to render fully what the visible signs symbolize, thereby creating the felt experience of the original event and communicating its meaning: the sacrament of the Lord's Supper, he writes, "does not feed our eyes with a mere appearance only, but leads us to the present reality and effectively performs what it symbolizes" (*Institutes* 4.15.14). God's use of visible signs to represent himself endows that representation with mystery, those signs with the power to effect an inner, spiritual transformation.

III

Although Elizabethan and Jacobean plays frequently present wondrous spectacles, silent actions, mystified images, and cunning theatricality, they typically do so in order to scrutinize and demystify these visual displays.[13] Exploring the problematics of sight in a world made uncertain, even dangerous, by the intentional, often malicious manipulation of images, they manifest and produce an anxiety that people are prone to "believe they see what they see not, and not see what they see" (Foxe 1: 83). Surely these plays do not hark back to a late medieval spirituality in which concrete images make God accessible to their viewers and sight *relieves* doubt (Gibson 157). Far from being a compensatory cultural genre that appropriates the magic and spectacle of the suppressed medieval religious rituals, the plays

of the Elizabethan and Jacobean theater may well serve as "active agencies of change" (Turner 24) that challenge and disrupt older, medieval ways of seeing. Rather than functioning as "a competing—idolatrous—religious structure" (O'Connell 307), this drama may well foster a habit of mind that is distinctly Protestant.

Writers who defend plays against the Puritans' antitheatrical attacks, in fact, consciously align this drama with Protestantism despite their opposition to more radical Puritans. Thomas Heywood, for one, mocks the grounds on which Puritans object to boy actors playing women, comparing their citation of the biblical injunction against sodomy to the papists' literal interpretation of Christ's words "This is my body" (sig. C3). Thomas Nashe, for another, articulates rather than critiques Protestantism's deep distrust of spectacle and role-playing. Instead of praising the artifice of the stage, he argues that drama reveals and holds up for examination a dangerous and duplicitous artfulness that pervades human affairs. "In plays," he observes, "all cozenages, all cunning drifts overgilded with outward holiness . . . are most lively anatomized" (65). It is, Nashe's statement suggests, a Protestant-induced fear that authorities, institutions, demons, villains, and artists can manipulate the sight of the unsuspecting—and not the return of the repressed Roman Catholic spectacle—that energizes the theater of Renaissance England. Far from dazzling the eyes of its spectators, theater, Nashe claims, *exposes* the very agents of bedazzlement.

If playwrights are themselves sometimes accused of such manipulation and dazzlement, they neither deny the potential of their theater to fool the eye nor celebrate the capacity of their plays to enthrall spectators with wondrous spectacle. Instead, they use theater to interrogate theatricality. Through metadramatic devices like the play-within-a-play, they self-reflexively examine the nature, function, and power of their own visible signs. In so doing, these plays engage the very theological controversies (about the efficacy of visible signs and the danger of spectacle) that rage outside the walls of the theater. By exploring the relation between image and word, sign and thing signified, action and representation, plays-within-plays force spectators to become self-conscious about how they see and interpret theater and spectacle. Whether characters pervert, abuse, and exploit theater for their own dark purposes as in Kyd's **The Spanish Tragedy** or employ drama as a powerful tool in their quest for the truth as in Shakespeare's *Hamlet,* these plays address the Protestant inquiry into their own legitimacy and reflect upon their own use of visible signs.

Although the plays within both **The Spanish Tragedy** and *Hamlet* are the creations of protagonists motivated by revenge, they work upon their stage audiences in opposite ways. Hieronimo uses the play of "Soliman and

Perseda" as a cunning vehicle to kill the men who murdered his son while their fathers watch, unaware that the fictional story is being literally enacted in their presence. Hamlet presents "The Murder of Gonzago" in an attempt to discover whether Claudius is guilty of murdering his father. His play reenacts the ghost's narrative, reminding Claudius of his evil deed so effectively that he starts from his chair and, when he is alone, kneels in prayer and examines his guilty conscience.

It is surely significant that Hieronimo's play exhibits the very qualities that the reformers condemn in the Roman Mass and Hamlet's play, those they commend in the reformed Lord's Supper. Might not Kyd, who sets his play in Roman Catholic Spain (a country that, in the 1580s, not only attempted to invade England but sought as well to return it to Roman Catholicism), be exploring the danger of certain kinds of theater and spectacle associated with the Roman church? And might not Shakespeare, who links his hero to Protestant Wittenberg (a German university associated in Shakespeare's day not only with Luther, but with Melanchthon and his followers, the "Phillipists," and with a late-sixteenth-century group of "crypto-Calvinists") be demonstrating the power of a new kind of theater associated with the reformed church?[14]

In his staging of "Soliman and Perseda," Kyd emphasizes the spectacular and visual dimension of drama at the expense of the verbal. As both the playwright bent on revenge and the actor cast in the role of murderer, Hieronimo cunningly and duplicitously fools the eyes of his spectators who assume they are watching their sons "fabulously counterfeit" (4.4.77) death when, in fact, they are witnessing them die. He mystifies his spectacle of blood by having his actors perform their parts in various "unknown languages" (4.1.172)—Greek, Latin, Italian, and French—despite their objections that "this will be a mere confusion, / And hardly shall we all be understood" (4.1.179-80). Although he promises to interpret the play at its conclusion, his final oration relies heavily on visual images, becoming the occasion for the theatrical display of the body of Horatio, that "strange and wondrous show" (4.1.184) to which Hieronimo directs his audience's attention: "See here my show, look on this spectacle" (4.4.89).[15]

He also displays a handkerchief "dyed" in the "dearest blood" of his son (3.13.87). Calling it a "propitious" object that he has faithfully preserved, like a holy relic, near his "bloody heart," he commands his stage audience to "behold" it as well (4.4.125, 126, 122). For Hieronimo, the *sight* of the handkerchief has explanatory power, and the visual display of his son's body and blood renders his violent act (and his play) both understandable and justifiable. Preparing to "end my play" with his own suicide while asserting that he has "no more to say" (4.4.150-51), he attempts to display him-

self, hanging by his own rope, as a culminating spectacle: "Behold Hieronimo, / Author and actor in this tragedy" (4.4.146-47). Initially prevented from killing himself, he vows to remain silent and, to make good on that vow, bites out his tongue, creating by this willful and ultimate rejection of language another corporeal image. Pressured further to "reveal" the mystery of his drama, to explain himself in language ("Yet can he write," 4.4.244), he gestures for a knife to sharpen his pen and uses it instead to kill the duke of Castile and himself, again substituting dead bodies for explanatory words. Although students of this play often puzzle over what it is, exactly, that Hieronimo thinks he is refusing to reveal, since he explains his motives before he bites out his tongue, I suggest that his stubborn insistence on silence, like his polyglot play, assures that the spectacle of bodies and blood he has so elaborately staged will retain its primacy over the interpreting word.

In that spectacle Hieronimo substitutes actual killing for the reenactment of a killing and literalizes, in a grotesque manner, the action he purports to represent. His play blatantly violates the distinction between visible sign and the thing it signifies, turning the analogous into the identical, the symbolic into the literal, the represented into the real. Rather than reenacting past deaths, it stages actual deaths, creating for its on-stage audience the direct and unmediated experience of murder. If Hieronimo uses theater to kill, he exhibits on his stage the corpses and blood of the dead as the stuff of theater. Kyd expresses in a startling and unsettling way a profound anxiety about the very theatricality **The Spanish Tragedy** everywhere displays. Its reiteration of the issues surrounding the doctrine of transubstantiation—that is, whether the eucharist is an actual sacrifice or a remembrance of a past killing, and whether the communicants see the body of Christ or only a figure of that body—should not be obscured by its secular content. By mystifying and privileging spectacle, literalizing mimetic action, and displaying "real" bodies and blood, the play-within-the-play manifests the very qualities of the Roman Mass that the Calvinist reformers condemn when they complain that "of the sacrament" the papists "make an idol; of commemoration make adoration; instead of receiving, make a deceiving; in place of showing forth Christ's death, make new oblations of his death" (Foxe 5: 303). It thus uses the popular stage to address, examine, and articulate one of the most disruptive theological crises of its age, functioning like one of those "magical mirrors of social reality," that, according to Victor Turner, "exaggerate, invert, reform, magnify, minimize, dis-color, re-color, even deliberately falsify" the dominant conflicts and central events of a culture in order to reflect upon them (42).

If, by foregrounding the very issues that lie at the heart of the eucharistic controversy, **The Spanish Tragedy** explores—"anatomizes"—a dangerous and duplicitous theatricality, an abuse of theater that sixteenth-century Protestants attribute to Roman Catholicism, it fosters in its spectators a reflexive awareness of their own seeing. As audience members, they find themselves uncomfortably aligned with a series of on-stage audiences. They watch the king of Spain and viceroy of Portugal naively watch Hieronimo's play without understanding that their sons are being killed before their very eyes. They watch the king and ambassador watch a masque that, according to the king, "contents mine eye, / Although I sound not well the mystery" (1.4.138-39). That masque portrays three separate conquests of Portugal or Spain by Englishmen, but the Spanish king inexplicably (and surely, to an English audience, foolishly) finds these spectacles comforting, rather than disturbing. And they watch the ghost of Andrea watch the action of the larger play, as well as these interior dramas, while imposing narrow, naive, and perverse interpretations onto what he sees. This play thus invites its spectators to evaluate the flawed and unselfconscious looking of on-stage audiences even as they, with them, "sit . . . down to see the mystery" (1.1.90).

Even minor characters in this play focus the audience's attention on acts of seeing. Arrested for murder, Pedringano, for example, gazes upon an empty box, so confident it contains his pardon that he "flout[s] the gallows, scorn[s] the audience, and descant[s] on the hangman, and all presuming of his pardon from hence" (3.5.12-14). Critical efforts to identify sources for Pedringano's box in classical myths about Pandora's or Silenus's box (Ardolino, "Hangman's Noose"; Baines) ignore contemporary Protestant polemics ridiculing priests who claim to carry God in a box or pyx and mocking the Mass as a "Jacke of the boxe" (Davies 238). Pedringano's presumption that the physical presence of the box guarantees his pardon even though he is guilty and flagrantly disregards the law reiterates precisely the error Protestants believe Roman Catholics make when they presume that the sight of the Host will save them, regardless of their behavior. Kyd juxtaposes Pedringano's execution with the last-minute reprieve of Alexandro. In striking contrast to Pedringano, who trusts in externals while refusing to repent, the wronged Alexandro renounces all earthly things, puts his faith in "heaven" (3.1.35), and prepares to die. Whereas Pedringano is executed, still believing that "in that box is balm for both" his body and soul (3.6.81), Alexandro is miraculously saved from death and acquitted.

At the end of the play, the ghost of Andrea announces that "these were spectacles to please my soul" (4.5.12), but Kyd's audiences have learned to distrust spectacles of blood, strange shows in sundry languages, deliberately staged displays of boxed pardons, silent mysteries. Hieronimo effectively turns its uncritical delight in spectacle and theatrics back against this society, exposing its violence and corruption by displaying them on

the stage. He participates in its abuse of images as well. Although his play demonstrates—in a grotesque, graphic, and outrageously literal way—how "a letter (meaning a literal sense) . . . killeth" (Ridley, "Lord's Supper" 31-32), it does so by exhibiting the very qualities of the Mass that so offend the Protestant reformers and by creating the confusion that baffles and ruins those who behold it.

However disaffected from the Spanish court, Hieronimo is as knight marshal closely identified with its legal practices and aesthetic forms. Hamlet, in contrast, is identified in Shakespeare's play not with the Danish court, though he is its prince, but with the university from which he has been summoned: Wittenberg. He returns to Denmark from the cradle of the Protestant Reformation alienated from its monarch, critical of its customs and ceremonies, and exhibiting many of the traits associated with the new religion: interiority, skepticism, guilt, and a philosophical melancholy believed in the sixteenth century to have afflicted St. Paul and Luther as well (Waddington).

Hamlet's Wittenberg education is clearly pertinent to this play's exploration of theological questions about authority and patriarchy, faith and knowledge, judgment and retribution. It is, I believe, also relevant to Hamlet's distrust of theatrical posturing and interest in the dramatic arts. Although literary scholars usually associate Wittenberg with Lutheranism, it was, at the end of the sixteenth century, the site of a divisive conflict between orthodox Lutherans who advanced the doctrine of consubstantiation and Calvinists who, having gained control of the university, advocated a symbolic interpretation of the sacrament (Holborn 256-62, Strauss 34). Shakespeare may very well wish to allude to this historical conflict, which is roughly contemporary with his play of *Hamlet,* in order to foreground his own examination of theatrical role-playing and dramatic representation.

Hamlet articulates a dramatic theory that, on the one hand, critiques spectacle, theatricality, and artifice, and, on the other hand, affirms the power of representation. When he urges the Players to avoid the abuses and excesses of the stage, he singles out spectacle and a theatricality associated with histrionics, melodrama, and artificiality for particular scorn and exclaims "O, reform it altogether!" (3.2.35). His desire to reform the stage in accordance with Protestant reforms of the church suggests that, by the beginning of the seventeenth century, the theological concerns of the reformers have been appropriated by English playwrights who articulate an emerging Protestant aesthetics.

In contrast to Hieronimo, who creates a theater that intentionally mystifies images and decenters words, Hamlet distrusts the spectacular dimension of theater and scorns playgoers who unthinkingly allow themselves to be dazzled by it. His contempt for people who love spectacle for its own sake, for example, is strikingly similar to Calvin's scorn for "the untutored crowd [which] . . . is marvelously captivated by ceremonial pomp" and those "hypocrites and light-headed women [who] think that nothing [can be] more beautiful" than theatrical "trifles" (*Institutes* 4.10.12). In mocking the "barren spectators" for their love of "inexplicable dumb shows and noise" (*Hamlet* 3.2.39-41, 11-12), Shakespeare destabilizes his own spectators, requiring them to become self-reflexive about how they respond to theatrical spectacles, dumb shows, and other images divorced from words.

While Hamlet teaches his viewers to distrust certain kinds of theater, however, he imagines a profitable way of seeing, commending—again in words that are reminiscent of Calvin, who prizes those few who "more deeply investigate" the matter (*Institutes* 4.10.12)—the "judicious" few (*Hamlet* 3.2.25) who are not blinded by the spectacular or deluded by the mystified and can therefore attend to what is significant. His ideal playgoers concentrate on interpreting the meaning of what they see, considering "some necessary question of the play" (3.2.40) rather than taking pleasure in the superficial, the spectacular, or the trivial. By theorizing about drama in a play that features a play-within-a-play, Shakespeare drives his own audiences into a deeper investigation of theatrical signs. His protagonist imagines a theater in which word and image (the action represented on the stage) agree and reinforce each other, advising the players to "suit the action to the word, the word to the action" (3.2.17-18). Rather than exhibit or glorify the spectacular or artificial, he proposes a drama whose purpose is "to hold, as 'twere, the mirror up to nature, to show virtue her own feature, scorn her own image, and the very age and body of the time his form and pressure" (3.2.20-23). For him, theatrical images are reflections (shadows, figures) of a world beyond the stage and viewing a play is not an idolatrous, but an ethical act that drives the spectator inward.

If he frets about the tendency of spectators to overvalue spectacle, Hamlet does not therefore reject the theater because so many abuse it, but rather chooses it as his instrument. Deeply cognizant of the capacity of drama to stir its spectators, he believes, in fact, that plays can elicit self-recognition, confession, even repentance:

> I have heard that guilty creatures sitting at a play
> Have by the very cunning of the scene
> Been struck so to the soul that presently
> They have proclaimed their malefactions.
>
> (2.2.575-78)

Although we should not necessarily assume that the character of Hamlet voices Shakespeare's own beliefs about the theater,[16] Hamlet cites a familiar argument about the benefits of drama that is often invoked by Elizabethan playwrights when they defend theater against Puritan attacks. Thomas Heywood, for instance, narrates numerous examples about audience members who, upon seeing a dramatic representation of a crime they themselves have committed, are so overwhelmed by guilt that they confess. Hamlet here thus reiterates a widespread belief, articulated by Heywood, among others, that plays have the "power to new mold the harts of the spectators."[17] Although Heywood is addressing Puritan antagonists of the stage, his defense does not, as many have assumed, align him and his drama with Roman Catholicism or constitute a rejection of the Protestant religion as it was widely practiced in London in 1600. to the contrary, his belief in the efficacy of representation is fully in keeping with a reformed theology that teaches people to interpret the sacrament of the Lord's Supper as a representation of a past action, one which has the capacity to awaken memory, arouse guilt, elicit self-reflection, and remake hearts.

Hamlet's play, "The Murder of Gonzago," functions precisely in this way. Presenting a narrative about the murder of a king, it reconstructs the circumstances surrounding the murder of Hamlet's father as reported by the ghost. Unlike Hieronimo, Hamlet is careful in his play to preserve the distinction between the dramatic narrative and the "real" events it mirrors: the setting is Vienna, not Denmark; the murderer is a nephew, not a brother of the king (creating, of course, another powerful analogy); and Hamlet describes the play's action as being "something like the murder of my father" and a story that "comes near the circumstance" of that murder (2.2.581, 3.2.73). Hamlet's play nevertheless arouses Claudius from his moral stupor, overwhelming him with guilt and sending him to his knees in prayer. Although he struggles mightily against the potential of this scene to remold his heart (like Calvin's hardened sinners he "furiously repel[s] all remembrance" and therefore "in seeing see[s] not," *Institutes* 1.4.2), his intense response to watching his crime reenacted and his subsequent attempt to pray exemplify the extraordinary power Shakespeare attributes to theatrical representation and analogy.

That power, Shakespeare makes clear, does not reside primarily in the visual images of the theater, but rather in the words that interpret and enliven them. Indeed, throughout the performance of "The Murder of Gonzago," Shakespeare explores the relation between the visual and verbal elements of the drama. After the Prologue, whose brief speech, unaccompanied by theatrical images, focuses the audience's attention on the act of hearing (3.2.142), the Players present a dumb show that presents their play's entire story in mime. *Viewing* a reenactment of his crime and his courtship without *hearing* explanatory words, however, neither unsettles nor moves Claudius. Nor does the continuous verbal commentary of Hamlet, who, Ophelia observes, is "as good as a chorus" (3.2.236), alone have the power to stir Claudius. Yet, as soon as the character of Lucianus enters the garden prepared to kill the king and begins to speak, Claudius bolts from his chair, "struck so to the soul" by this combination of dramatic image, poetic text, and choral commentary, that he can no longer repress or conceal his guilt. Hamlet's play, in striking contrast to Hieronimo's, does not privilege spectacle but rather emphasizes the capacity of language to realize, or bring into being, what the images signify, (in Calvin's words) edifying the audiences, penetrating their minds, impressing upon their hearts, and settling there (*Institutes* 4.17.39).

Although the playlets in *Hamlet* and *The Spanish Tragedy* both call attention to the visual rhetoric of the stage, each examines the aesthetic experience of a markedly different kind of theater. "Soliman and Perseda" features a carnal spectacle of literal deaths, mystified by strange languages and silence. Kyd creates and sustains an ironic distance between his spectators, English playgoers in the public theater, and the on-stage spectators, the Spanish and Portuguese courtiers who are credulous and confused, and he dramatizes the abuse of theater even as he invents a drama that self-consciously avoids replicating that abuse. "The Murder of Gonzago," in contrast, represents a past murder that, through a union of theatrical signs and spoken words, has the capacity to reveal truths, profoundly affecting its spectators and eliciting painful self-examination. Shakespeare's own spectators watch as Hamlet and Horatio "observe"—indeed, "rivet" their eyes on—Claudius, who in turn watches first a dumb show and then a fully realized dramatic scene that reenacts a ghost's tale of murder, represents a killing he himself has committed (3.2.77, 82, 130-260). How they see all this watching and mirroring, especially in the context of the troubling vision of the ghost, the orchestrated spectacle of the monarchy, and the duplicitous role-playing of the courtiers, is integrally related to the way the reformed religion structures the experience of the Lord's Supper. Shakespeare fosters a mode of sight that is skeptical, mediated, self-relfexive, analogical, and, I submit, distinctly Protestant.

Notes

1. Scholars who consider the relation between this drama and the antitheatrical and iconoclastic dimensions of English Protestantism include: Barish, Davidson, Montrose, O'Connell, and Siemon. Scholars who examine the relation between this drama and some aspect of Protestant theology or the reformed faith include: Bryant, Cohen, Dollimore, Hunter, Kaula, Klinck, Rozett, Sinfield, and Waddington. See also Rose, who explores the relation between representations of women, love,

and marriage on the Renaissance English stage and English Protestant sexual discourse, and Breitenberg, who examines what he identifies as a collapse of "verbal and visual modes" in mid-sixteenth-century reform writing and drama.

2. Two scholars who do *not* agree with Montrose are Robert Knapp and C. L. Barber. In his recent book Knapp writes:

> Surely there is truth to the hunch that a philosophical doctrine of exemplarism and a theological doctrine of real presence sort better with metaphors of readability [and the Corpus Christi plays], while notions of God's unsearchable grandeur, the spiritually defective reason of human beings, and the superiority of historical types to other kinds of allegory better suit the image of the Globe, that *theatrum mundi* in which divine intentions are not so visible as divine magnificence and vengeance.

(20)

Barber speculates that there is a relation between "the Communion and the drama, the [Protestant] church and the [Renaissance English] theater" (13), but he does not fully develop this insight, turning instead to psychoanalytical analyses of plays by Marlowe and Kyd.

3. For historical studies of the local reception of Protestantism in England, see Palliser, Hutton, and Alexander. Davies also confirms that Londoners embraced Protestantism earlier and with less resistance than people living in northern and rural regions of England (162).

4. For a detailed discussion of the anthropological term "cultural performance," see Turner 23-27, 81-82.

5. In a concerted effort to counter popular belief in the magical power of images, for example, Protestant reformers repeatedly insist that images are material (as opposed to divine) objects, made of wood and marble, "stock or stone," and are human artifacts (as opposed to sacred objects), the work of "man's hands" (Foxe 8: 143 and 501). Furthermore, although they condemn "abused" images that elicit worship, inspire awe and reverence, perpetuate superstition, or are believed to have magical properties, the reformers allow "unabused" images. These approved images function in ways that we might recognize as secular: they may represent a historical event or person, portray the virtues and vices of individuals, depict the monarch and appropriate symbols of the state, and commemorate the dead (Phillips 89-91, 114-17).

6. For a comprehensive analysis of the various Protestant eucharistic theories, and their relative importance in English theology, see Davies, particu-

larly 76-123. Davies describes the three main theories developed as alternatives to transubstantiation—Consubstantiation or the Real Presence, Virtualism, and Memorialism—and he shows how the major English reformers adopted, interpreted, combined, and subtly altered all three of these theories. My discussion here is necessarily more general than Davies', and therefore cannot attend to all the distinctions among the various theologians and sects, but I have tried to concentrate on what I believe are the dominant features of the reformed Lord's Supper as understood by most early English Protestants and to emphasize the central issues that separated Roman Catholics from almost all early English Protestants. The scope of my paper also prevents me from distinguishing between Anglican and Puritan worship services, a distinction that became much more fully developed, and far more divisive, in the seventeenth century. In relying closely on Calvin, and citing extensively from Foxe, I accept the arguments of recent historians that early English Protestantism was most strongly influenced by Calvin and therefore that English theories of the eucharist tended toward Virtualism (Davies 111-20, Collinson 213-44, Dickens 197-201).

7. Gibson 14; see also Scribner, who quotes A. L. Meyer on medieval ways of seeing (4), and Bynum, who demonstrates how in late medieval spirituality, the physical was often inseparable from the spiritual (407-23).

8. In his recent biography of the French reformer, William Bouwsma notes how Calvin "often seemed much impressed by the special value of sight" (72). Calvin relies heavily on the visual mode of perception, favors metaphors of sight, and even likens the work of God to a corrective lens, a pair of spectacles for "bleary-eyed men and those with weak vision" (*Institutes* 1.6.1).

9. Ridley, "Lord's Supper" 22; Foxe quotes John Philpot, who accuses the Roman Catholics of taking "away the substantial parts of the sacrament, as, 'Take ye, eate ye, Drink ye all of this; Do ye this in remembrance of me:'" and replacing them with "'hear ye, gaze ye, knock ye, worship ye, offer ye, sacrifice ye for the quick and the dead'" (7: 654).

10. See, for examples, Calvin, *Institutes* 4.17.40; Calvin, *Ephesians* sigs. 76v-77; Perkins 126; Scultetus sig. C3; Ridley, "Lord's Supper" 15; Foxe 5: 163 and 7: 654.

11. For a discussion of the communion tables in Anglican churches, see Davies 204, 355, 363-65. Davies cites Protestants calling for the communion table to be "'an honest table, decently cov-

ered'" (364) and Catholics ridiculing Protestant communion tables as being "oyster boards" (238). It is perhaps also relevant that the early Protestants advocate a simple, unadorned sanctuary that places the minister in the midst of his congregation, very much like actors on the thrust stage of the Elizabethan theaters, rather than separating him from the lay worshippers as does the Roman church (363).

12. Calvin thus notes that "the apostle condemns as blind and accursed those who, content with present shadows, did not stretch their minds to Christ" (*Institutes* 2.11.10); and Bucer asks rhetorically if Roman Catholic worshippers "do beleve that god and the sayntes are in heven, why do they not rather lyft up their eyes to that place than to the deed ymages?" (sig. Eii.r).

13. Consider Iago's malicious manipulation of the handkerchief, that erroneous "ocular proof" that convinces Othello his wife is unfaithful (*Othello* 3.3.360), and Beatrice-Joanna's skillful histrionics, those falsified, visible responses to the virginity test that convince Alsemero his wife is chaste (*The Changeling* 4.2); the witches' emblematic and enigmatic apparitions that persuade Macbeth he is safe (*Macbeth* 4.1), and the sheeted figure of Charlemont that convinces D'Amville it is a threatening ghost from hell (*The Atheist's Tragedy* 4.3); the seductive succubus that appears as the beautiful Helen to a bedazzled Faustus (*Doctor Faustus* 5.1), and the disguised Margaret who appears as a promiscuous Hero to a confused Claudio (*Much Ado about Nothing* 3.2, 3.3, 4.1); the marvelous statue of Hermione that is revealed to be not stone, but the living woman herself, after its spectators stand in awe of its redemptive likeness (*The Winter's Tale* 5.3), and the ornamented courtesan who is revealed to be not a living woman, but the poisoned skull of Gloriana, after the lecherous duke kisses its fatal image (*The Revenger's Tragedy* 3.5).

14. "In the 1580's," Ronald Broude writes, "England was facing a religious and political crisis of the utmost gravity. 'The Enterprise,' the grandiose Catholic scheme for the invasion of England and the extirpation of English Protestantism, was being implemented by Spain, encouraged by Rome and France, while England was responding with a wave of nationalism and prayer" (130). See also Ardolino, "In Paris," and Justice 274. For discussions of the religious conflict in late-sixteenth-century Wittenberg, see Holborn and Strauss.

15. Surprisingly, many critical discussions of Hieronimo's play praise its spectacle. Asserting that "[o]nly recently . . . have dramatic critics been able to react without condescension or em-

barrassment to the basic satisfaction this kind of popular show can provide" (111), Michael Hattaway defends Hieronimo's use of sundry languages as the playwright's means of communicating with the illiterate: "it is possible," he speculates, "that he [Kyd] was trying to see whether he could employ a theatre language that would, to the unlettered at least, communicate by its mere sound" (110). Of Hieronimo's show, Carol McGinnis Kay asserts that "it is clear that this is not spectacle for spectacle's sake alone" (37). Donna Hamilton goes so far as to suggest the bloody spectacle approaches the Renaissance ideal of a speaking picture: "Hieronimo's playlet goes beyond his other attempts by being truly a speaking picture" (215).

16. I disagree with Annabel Patterson, who argues that Hamlet's scorn for the groundlings' love of dumb shows and his praise of the "judicious few" reveal elitist assumptions that would not be shared by his author. Hamlet delivers here a harsh critique of playgoers and their attachment to spectacle, but his desire to reform the theater suggests a firm belief in the public's capacity to change, a belief ardently shared by the reformers, who, while they ridicule popular piety, are also committed to reaching, educating, and thereby "saving" the masses. Shakespeare's own position on this issue should therefore not be inferred from the popularity of his plays, but rather from the nature of his drama. His plays do not rely primarily on spectacle, but rather on the power and sophistication of their verbal texts.

17. Heywood sig. B4. Montrose misidentifies the author of this passage as Thomas Nashe (62).

Works Cited

Alexander, Gina. "Bonner and the Marian Persecutions." *The English Reformation Revised.* Ed. Christopher Haigh. Cambridge: Cambridge UP, 1987. 157-75.

Ardolino, Frank. "The Hangman's Noose and the Empty Box: Kyd's Use of Dramatic and Mythological Sources in *The Spanish Tragedy* (III.iv-vii)." *Renaissance Quarterly* 30 (1977): 334-40.

———. "'In Paris? Mass, and Well Remembered!': Kyd's *The Spanish Tragedy* and the English Reaction to the St. Bartholomew's Day's Massacre." *Sixteenth-Century Journal* 21 (1990): 401-09.

Baines, Barbara J. "Kyd's Silenus Box and the Limits of Perception." *Journal of Medieval and Renaissance Studies* 10 (1980): 41-51.

Barber, C. L. *Creating Elizabethan Tragedy: The Theater of Marlowe and Kyd.* Ed. Richard P. Wheeler. Chicago: U of Chicago P, 1988.

Barish, Jonas. *The Antitheatrical Prejudice.* Berkeley: U of California P, 1981.

Bouwsma, William J. *John Calvin: A Sixteenth-Century Portrait.* Oxford: Oxford UP, 1988.

Breitenberg, Mark. "Reading Elizabethan Iconicity: *Gorboduc* and the Semiotics of Reform." *English Literary Renaissance* 18 (1988): 194-217.

Broude, Ronald. "Time, Truth, and Right in *The Spanish Tragedy*." *Studies in Philology* 68 (1971): 130-45.

Bryant, James C. *Tudor Drama and Religious Controversy.* Macon, GA: Mercer, 1984.

Bucer, Martin. *A treatise declaring . . . that pictures and other images which were wont to be worshipped are in no wise to be suffered in the temples or churches of Christien men.* London, 1537.

Bynum, Caroline Walker. "The Body of Christ in the Later Middle Ages: A Reply to Leo Steinberg." *Renaissance Quarterly* 39 (1986): 399-439.

Calvin, Jean. *Four godlye sermons against the pollution of idolatries.* London, 1561.

———. *Institutes of the Christian Religion.* Trans. Ford Lewis Battles. Ed. John T. McNeill. Philadelphia: Westminster, 1960.

———. *The Sermons of M. John Calvin upon the Epistle of S. Paule too the Ephesians.* Trans. Arthur Golding. London, 1577.

———. *Sermons of M. John Calvin upon the Epistle of Saincte Paule to the Galathians.* Trans. Arthur Golding. London, 1574.

Cohen, Walter. "The Reformation and Elizabethan Drama." *Shakespeare Jahrbuch* 120 (1984): 45-52.

Collinson, Patrick. *Godly People: Essays on English Protestantism and Puritanism.* London: Hambledon, 1983.

Davidson, Clifford. "The Anti-Visual Prejudice." *Iconoclasm vs. Art and Drama.* Ed. Clifford Davidson and Ann Eljenholm Nichols. Kalamazoo: Medieval Institute, 1988. 33-46.

———. "'The Devil's Guts': Allegations of Superstition and Fraud in Religious Drama and Art during the Reformation." *Iconoclasm vs. Art and Drama.* Ed. Clifford Davidson and Ann Eljenholm Nichols. Kalamazoo: Medieval Institute, 1988. 92-144.

Davies, Horton. *Worship and Theology in England.* Vol. 1: 1534-1603. Princeton: Princeton UP, 1970.

Dickens, A. G. *The English Reformation.* New York: Norton, 1964.

Dollimore, Jonathan. *Radical Tragedy: Religion, Ideology and Power in the Drama of Shakespeare and His Contemporaries.* Chicago: U of Chicago P, 1984.

Foxe, John. *The Acts and Monuments of John Foxe.* Ed. Stephen Reed Cattley. Intro. George Townsend. 8 vols. London, 1837-41.

Geertz, Clifford. *The Interpretation of Cultures.* New York: Basic, 1973.

Gibson, Gail. *The Theater of Devotion: East Anglian Drama and Society in the Late Middle Ages.* Chicago: U of Chicago P, 1989.

Hamilton, Donna B. "*The Spanish Tragedy*: A Speaking Picture." *English Literary Renaissance* 4 (1974): 203-17.

Hattaway, Michael. *Elizabethan Popular Theatre: Plays in Performance.* London: Routledge & Kegan Paul, 1982.

Heywood, Thomas. *An Apology for Actors.* Ed. Richard H. Perkinson. New York: Scholars' Facsimiles, 1941.

Holborn, Hajo. *A History of Modern Germany.* Vol. 1. *The Reformation.* New York: Knopf, 1959.

Hunter, G. K. "Tyrant and Martyr: Religious Heroisms in Elizabethan Tragedy." *Poetic Traditions of the English Renaissance.* Ed. Maynard Mack and George deForest Lord. New Haven: Yale UP, 1982. 85-102.

Hutton, Ronald. "The Local Impact of the Tudor Reformations." *The English Reformation Revised.* Ed. Christopher Haigh. Cambridge: Cambridge UP, 1987. 114-38.

Jenner, Thomas. *The Soules Solace: or Thirtie and one Spiritual Emblems.* London, 1626.

Justice, Steven. "Spain, Tragedy, and *The Spanish Tragedy*." *Studies in English Literature, 1500-1900* 25 (1985): 271-88.

Kaula, David. "*Hamlet* and the Image of Both Churches." *Studies in English Literature, 1500-1900* 24 (1984): 241-55.

Kay, Carol McGinnis. "Deception through Words: A Reading of *The Spanish Tragedy*." *Studies in Philology* 74 (1977): 20-38.

King, John N. *English Reformation Literature: The Tudor Origins of the Protestant Tradition.* Princeton: Princeton UP, 1982.

Klinck, Dennis R. "Calvinism and Jacobean Tragedy." *Genre* 11 (1978): 333-58.

Knapp, Robert S. *Shakespeare—The Theater and the Book.* Princeton: Princeton UP, 1989.

Kyd, Thomas. *The Spanish Tragedy. Drama of the English Renaissance.* Ed. Russell A. Fraser and Norman Rabkin. 2 vols. New York: Macmillan, 1976. 1: 169-203.

Marlowe, Christopher. *Doctor Faustus. Drama of the English Renaissance.* Ed. Russell A. Fraser and Norman Rabkin. 2 vols. New York: Macmillan, 1976. 1: 297-322.

Middleton, Thomas, and William Rowley. *The Changeling.* Ed. George Walton Williams. Lincoln: U of Nebraska P, 1966.

Miles, Margaret R. *Image as Insight: Visual Understanding in Western Christianity and Secular Culture.* Boston: Beacon, 1985.

Montrose, Louis Adrian. "The Purpose of Playing: Reflections on a Shakespearean Anthropology." *Helios* 7 (1980): 51-74.

Nashe, Thomas. *Pierce Penniless his Supplication to the Devil . . . and Selected Writings.* Ed. Stanley Wells. London: Arnold, 1964.

O'Connell, Michael. "The Idolatrous Eye: Iconoclasm, Anti-Theatricalism, and the Image of the Elizabethan Theater." *ELH* 52 (1985): 279-310.

Palliser, D. M. "Popular Reactions to the Reformation During the Years of Uncertainty, 1530-70." *The English Reformation Revised.* Ed. Christopher Haigh. Cambridge: Cambridge UP, 1987. 94-113.

Patterson, Annabel M. *Shakespeare and the Popular Voice.* Cambridge, MA: Blackwell, 1989.

Perkins, William. *A Warning against the idolatrie of the last times.* Cambridge, 1601.

Phillips, John. *The Reformation of Images: Destruction of Art in England, 1535-1600.* Berkeley: U of California P, 1973.

Ridley, Nicholas. "A Brief Declaration of the Lord's Supper, or, A Treatise against the Error of Transubstantiation." *The Works of Nicholas Ridley.* Ed. Henry Christmas. Cambridge: Cambridge UP, 1843. 1-45.

———. "A friendly Farewell." London, 1559.

Rose, Mary Beth. *The Expense of Spirit: Love and Sexuality in English Renaissance Drama.* Ithaca: Cornell UP, 1988.

Rozett, Martha Tuck. *The Doctrine of Election and the Emergence of Elizabethan Tragedy.* Princeton: Princeton UP, 1984.

Scribner, R. W. *For the Sake of Simple Folk: Popular Propaganda for the German Reformation.* Cambridge: Cambridge UP, 1981.

Scultetus, Abraham. *A Short Information, but agreeable unto Scripture: of Idol-Image.* Trans. Gotthard Voegehu. London, 1620.

Shakespeare, William. *The Complete Works.* Ed. Alfred Harbage. Baltimore: Penguin, 1969.

Siemon, James R. *Shakespearean Iconoclasm.* Berkeley: U of California P, 1985.

Sinfield, Alan. *Literature in Protestant England, 1560-1660.* Totowa, NJ: Barnes & Noble, 1983.

Strauss, Gerald. "How to Read a *Volksbuch*: The *Faust Book* of 1587." *Faust through Four Centuries.* Ed. Peter Boerner and Sidney Johnson. Tübingen: Niemeyer, 1989. 27-39.

Tourneur, Cyril. *The Atheist's Tragedy.* Ed. Irving Ribner. Revels Plays. Cambridge: Harvard UP, 1964.

———. *The Revenger's Tragedy.* Ed. R. A. Foakes. Revels Plays. Cambridge: Harvard UP, 1966.

Turner, Victor. *The Anthropology of Performance.* New York: PAJ, 1987.

Veron, John. *A stronge battery against the idolatrous invocation of the dead Saintes, and against the having or Setting by of Images in the house of prayer . . .* London, 1562.

Waddington, Raymond B. "Lutheran Hamlet." *English Language Notes* 27.2 (1989): 27-42.

James Shapiro (essay date 1991)

SOURCE: Shapiro, James. "'Tragedies naturally performed': Kyd's Representation of Violence, *The Spanish Tragedy* (c. 1587)." In *Staging the Renaissance: Reinterpretations of Elizabethan and Jacobean Drama,* edited by David Scott Kastan and Peter Stallybrass, pp. 99-113. New York: Routledge, 1991.

[*In the following essay, Shapiro places the spectacles of state justice in* The Spanish Tragedy *on the boundary between the authority of the absolutist state and the revolutionary potential of the theater.*]

According to Stephen Greenblatt's by now familiar formulation, there "is subversion, no end of subversion [in Elizabethan drama], only not for us." Nor, seemingly, for the Elizabethans either, since for Greenblatt subversion is always and necessarily contained: the "apparent production of subversion" is "the very condition of [royal] power."[1] It is a depressing conclusion, especially for those who want to see the theater as an agent of social change. Perhaps the vicious cycle of "subversion contained" is not quite as grim as Greenblatt would have us believe: he himself acknowledges that plays like *King Lear* strain this process to "the breaking point,"[2] while other new historicists, working backwards from the political and social dislocations that followed the closing of the theaters in 1642, have located the source of these revolutionary impulses in the earlier drama.

Nevertheless, both those who would argue for containment and those who insist that the drama is ultimately subversive tend to speak of *state power* and (to an even greater extent) *theatrical representation* as stable, fixed entities. Invariably, these critics "demonize" the absolutist state while "valorizing" the transgressive theater that would seek to challenge it. Evidence suggests, however, that the Elizabethan theater's relationship to political and judicial authority was more complex than either subverting or confirming state power; the theater's boundaries as a judicial institution were especially problematic. As a result of new historicism's totalizing view of antagonistic state and theater, the fluidity of the borders marking the respective domains of the theater and the state has generated little interest. Although scholars like Steven Mullaney have helped us identify "the place of the stage" geographically in Shakespeare's London,[3] its boundaries in relationship to competing sources of social and political authority in Elizabethan England remain largely uncharted.[4]

This essay examines the overlapping of authority that occurred at the site of one such boundary: staged violence. Since both the public theaters and the public authorities enacted high drama on scaffolds before crowds of spectators, it is easy to understand the need to keep these two kinds of performances distinct. Official forms of capital punishment were taboo in the theater no doubt because, as Foucault has argued, the scaffold of the state functioned not only as a "judicial" but also a "political" ritual in which a "momentarily injured sovereignty is reconstituted" and restored "by manifesting it at its most spectacular." Accordingly, the "public execution did not [merely] reestablish justice; it reactivated power." For the Renaissance ruler, then, the "ceremony of the public torture and execution displayed for all to see the power relation that gave his force to the law."[5] To permit the theater to imitate state spectacle could undermine the terrible power of officially sanctioned violence by showing it often enough to make it familiar or by resituating it within ethically and politically ambiguous contexts.

Consequently, though Tudor and Stuart drama was an extraordinarily bloody affair, playwrights steered clear of trespassing on this royal prerogative: characters are stabbed or poisoned, have their throats slit, or are shot while hanging chained from the upper stage, but only on the rarest occasions do we see them hanged from a noose, decapitated, or tied to a stake and then burned, or punished in the other ways carefully prescribed by the state.[6] We can search the canons of Marlowe, Shakespeare, Jonson, Webster, and others in vain for instances where characters are put to death the same way that convicted felons were in Elizabethan England.[7]

Thomas Kyd's *The Spanish Tragedy* (c. 1587)[8] stands as a striking exception. Its audience watches as Pedringano is tried, condemned, and "turned off" by a hangman, and witnesses as well the preparations for the torture and execution of Alexandro, who is bound "to the stake" onstage and prepared to be burned to death. It would also seem to offer the paradigmatic example of how drama can be a powerful agent of social change: the staging of Hieronimo's play results in the death of a royal heir and destroys the political accommodation between Spain and Portugal. Yet Hieronimo's court spectacle only attains this power when it oversteps the bounds of what we would ordinarily consider theater. The lines separating official and theatrical violence are blurred, as Kyd's play insistently seeks out representational no-man's-land, testing the boundaries between the prerogatives of the state and those of the theater. In so doing the play raises the possibility that it is not the opposition between state and theater, but their potential confusion and indistinguishability, that makes theater powerful and (to the political authorities) dangerous.

In exploring this possibility, this essay questions whether the terms and categories of thought that dominate current historicist and materialist discourse (e.g., "opposition," "containment," "subversion," "resistance,") are simply too inflexible, or themselves too ideologically bound (however "retheorized") to admit the possibility that the changes that may occur in individuals or societies through the mediation of theater can be quite random, subject to all kinds of unexpected and unpredictable forces. Theater, this essay argues, can be "subversive," but it is usually so in ways that are unforeseen by author, censor, or functionalist historicist.[9] Hieronimo's old play, "long forgot" (4.1.80), only becomes subversive within the context of a situation unimaginable when Hieronimo first wrote it; so too does Kyd's *The Spanish Tragedy*: in its afterlife upon the Jacobean and Caroline stages it was identified with the transgressive behavior of Englishwomen in ways unimaginable at the time of its composition. It is theater's unpredictability, then, that makes it so dangerous and at the same time so difficult to suppress or censor effectively.

The Privy Council knew exactly what subversive writing it was looking for in the spring of 1593: someone had posted a "lewd and vyle ticket or placarde" inciting London's apprentices "to attempt some vyolence" upon the city's foreign workers.[10] In the course of the investigation Kyd's lodgings were searched and atheistical tracts were found in his possession. Atheism was a capital offense. Kyd desperately maintained that the tracts were Marlowe's and had been accidentally shuffled among his papers when they had shared chambers two years before. He was imprisoned in Bridewell, where he was tortured by strappado.[11] In his written confession addressed to Sir Thomas Puckering, Kyd protested that

> [I]f I knewe eny whom I co[u]ld justlie accuse of that damnable offence to the awefull Ma[jes]tie of god or of

that other mutinous sedition tow[a]rd the state I wo[u]ld as willinglie reveale them as I wo[u]ld request yo[u]r L[ordshi]ps better thoughtes of me that never have offended you.[12]

Life, cruelly, was imitating art: five years before, Kyd had written a comparable declaration in *The Spanish Tragedy,* when Alexandro, falsely accused of treason, protests that he is innocent:

> But this, O this, torments my labouring soul,
> That thus I die suspected of a sin,
> Whereof, as heavens have known my secret thoughts,
> So am I free from this suggestion.
>
> (3.1.43-4)

The Viceroy's response—"No more, I say! to the tortures!" (3.1.47)—was apparently echoed by the Bridewell authorities. In Kyd's play Alexandro was spared from torture at the last moment. Kyd himself was not so lucky. He wrote shortly after his release of "bitter times and privie broken passions"[13] and was dead by the following August. In one of the darker ironies of the period, a playwright who explored so insightfully the workings of state violence had become, through unforeseen circumstances, its victim. It is likely that even as Kyd suffered in prison his play was being performed to admiring spectators.[14]

The same authorities who had so rigorously suppressed materials "lately published by some disordered and factious persons in and about the cittie of London"[15] nonetheless allowed a different kind of writing, Kyd's *Spanish Tragedy,* to circulate freely throughout England, both in print and on stage. Unlike atheistical tracts or racist placards, Kyd's play did not contain lines or passages whose potential subversiveness could be easily identified. Kyd and his fellow playwrights were careful enough to avoid writing that would lead to violent social disturbances. When they did not, the Master of the Revels was responsible for identifying and censoring such passages. But neither he nor the Bishop of London and Archbishop of Canterbury (who censored printed texts) were equipped to deal with the kind of subversion that occurred when the boundary between the domains of theater and the state was transgressed.

The action of Kyd's play repeatedly returns to the site of this contested boundary. The appearance of Alexandro, tied "to the stake" (SD 3.1.49), provides an intimation, though not a fully realized example, of state violence enacted onstage. The most obvious example is Pedringano's lengthy trial and public execution in Act 3, scene 6, which conforms closely in its outward features to the spectacle of public execution with which Londoners would have been familiar.[16] Pedringano enters "bound" to the "court," is asked to "[c]onfess [his] folly and repent [his] fault," and does so: "First I confess, nor fear I death therefore, / I am the man 'twas I slew Serberine" (3.6.29-30). As Foucault observes, such a confession "for satisfaction of the world" (3.6.25) was a crucial part of the ceremony of state execution, as was the condemned individual's relationship with the executioner, also elaborated upon in this scene.[17] Pedringano even partakes of the obligatory prayers and address to the spectators who have come to witness his execution. He asks the hangman to "request this good company to pray with me" (3.6.84), before reversing himself: "now I remember me, let them alone till some other time, for now I have no great need" (3.6.86-87). Hieronimo, as Knight Marshall overseeing this ceremony, is appalled to see "a wretch so impudent." He exits, ordering that the execution take place. The stage direction indicates that Pedringano's hanging occurs in full view, as the hangman *"turns him off"* (SD 3.6.104).

Yet the execution fails both judicially and politically. The judicial failure is underscored when the hangman, having learned of Lorenzo's role in Horatio's murder, approaches Hieronimo, admits that "we have done [Pedringano] wrong," and asks that the Knight Marshall stand between him and "the gallows" (3.7.26). It fails politically because Pedringano thinks that he is only playing his part in Lorenzo's plot, in which disaster will be averted with the reading of the King's pardon. For him the execution is just good theater. As a result, the representation of state violence undermines the authority of the state, since the symbolic meaning of a public execution, that which gives it sufficient integrity to reinscribe and reactivate the power of the sovereign, never occurs. Rather than confirming state justice, Pedringano's death merely parodies and demystifies it, as it parodically recalls the unceremonious execution (and perhaps even token disembowelment) of Horatio, who had been hanged from an arbor, then stabbed, in Act 2, scene 4.

Pedringano's mistaken belief that his execution is merely theater points to something particularly disturbing about theatrical representations of violence: neither the actor to be executed nor the spectators who witness the execution can be entirely sure that the violence is not real. We tend to speak of theater as a place where violence is merely represented, but it is well to remember that the Elizabethan stage doubled as a site of actual violent spectacle. Bear and bull baiting, for example, alternated with play production at the Hope Theater, while fencing was popular at others. Around the time of the first production of Kyd's play there was even a notorious incident in which spectators were accidently killed: Philip Gawdy writes in a letter to his father on 16 November 1587 that:

> My L[ord] Admyrall his men and players having a devyse in ther playe to tye one of their fellowes to a poste and so to shoote him to deathe, having borrowed their callyvers one of the players handes swerved his

peece being charged with bullett missed the fellowe he aymed at and killed a chyld, and a woman great with chyld forthwith, and hurt an other man in the head very soore.[18]

The state might resort to what Greenblatt (borrowing from Thomas Hariot) refers to as "invisible bullets";[19] the actors fired real ones. It is also worth remarking that the theaters were identified as a place for violent riots, and that they were situated nearby—and perhaps in the minds of Londoners identified with—the other sites of theatrical violence: London's prisons. Even more remarkably, the theaters served not only as sites of theatrical executions, but, on occasion, a place where individuals were put to death. Stow reports in his *Annales* (1615) that around the time of the earliest production of ***The Spanish Tragedy*** hangings took place at the Theatre. W. Gunter, a foreign priest, was hung "at the Theater" on August 28, 1588, and on October 1, of that same year, another priest, William Hartley, was also executed "nigh the Theator."[20]

Elizabethans were aware that the practice of using the playhouse for public executions had a predecent in the theater of ancient Rome. Thomas Heywood, for example, in his *Apology for Actors* (written c. 1607), describes the Roman practice of executing capital offenders in the theater. Heywood substantiates his account by citing a passage from Kyd's ***Spanish Tragedy***:

> It was the manner of their Emperours, in those dayes in their publicke Tragedies to choose out the fittest amongst such, as for capital offences were condemned to dye, and imploy them in such parts as were to be kil'd in the Tragedy, who of themselves would make suit rather so to dye with resolution, and by the hands of such princely Actors, then otherwise to suffer a shamefull & most detestable end. *And these were Tragedies naturally performed.* And such Caius Caligula, Claudius Nero, Vitellius, Domitianus, Comodus, & other Emperours of Rome, upon their festivals and holy daies of greatest consecration, used to act. Therefore M. Kid in the ***Spanish Tragedy,*** upon occasion presenting it selfe, thus writes.
>
> Why Nero thought it no disparagement,
> And Kings and Emperours have tane delight,
> To make experience of their wits in playes.[21]
>
> [4.1.87-89]

In Foucault's terms, the actions of these "princely Actors" displays, without the mediation of a public executioner, "the dissymmetry between the subject who has dared to violate the law and the all-powerful sovereign who displays his strength."[22] Such action would have placed an Elizabethan ruler in a double bind, since, as scholars like Stephen Orgel, Jonathan Goldberg, and Stephen Greenblatt have urged, royal power was manifested theatrically;[23] the sovereign had a considerable interest in not being represented in the public theater.

Heywood's quotation from *The Spanish Tragedy* is taken from a scene in which precisely this issue is at stake. When Hieronimo invites the Portuguese prince to perform in his play, Balthazar is shocked at the very idea—"What, would you have us play a tragedy?" (4.1.86), He knows that princes do not act in tragedies for good reason: since rulers are *de facto* actors, a prince would only expose the foundations of his power by performing onstage. Although he wishes to humor Hieronimo, Balthazar knows that the stage is potentially subversive in that it can easily collapse carefully circumscribed social roles by confusing two kinds of performances.[24] Notably, in the example Heywood offers, the tyrants, the victims, and the audiences were all aware that this was tragedy "naturally performed"; there is no pretence or deception. The question that remains is what distinguishes these executions from official ones, except that these take place in the theater (or, for that matter, what distinguishes this production from another, except that the actor is killed)?

The possibility of theatrical performances in which people were actually killed onstage without their (or the audience's) knowledge was seized upon by the antitheatrical writers, who warned that the kind of bloody spectacle supervised by Hieronimo was one of the dark secrets of the Elizabethan stage. I. G., the author of *A Refutation of the Apology for Actors* (1615), insinuates that Elizabethan actors took advantage of this confusion of theater and real life to kill unwitting actors onstage in front of unwitting spectators. Responding to Heywood's "memorable example of Julius Caesar, that slew his own servant whiles he acted *Hercules furens* on the Stage," I. G. finds in the same anecdote evidence against the players:

> Which example indeed greatly doth make against their Playes. *For it's not unlikely but a Player might doe the like now, as often they have done.* And then what a lamentable project would there be for the Spectators to behold: As many times it happens when their supposed nocent persons are falsely hanged, and divers of them ready to be strangld.[25]

I. G. conflates a number of disturbing scenarios. The first is one in which, like Heywood's "princely Actors," a ruler acting in a play kills a subject. The story of Julius Caesar killing his servant differs from the ones quoted above in that Caesar's actions were not premeditated, nor were they intended as a display and confirmation of royal power. Rather, Caesar, caught up in the part he was playing, forgot that he was only acting. I. G. then implies that this is a common danger of theatrical practice—that it is not unlikely that a player may forget himself, or, he then suggests more cynically, that players may capitalize on the audience's inability to distinguish between a real and a fake onstage murder, permitting actors to hang their victims "falsely." After all, given the sophistication of Elizabethan stagecraft,

how can we be sure that, in Hieronimo's ambiguous phrase, the "wondrous plausible" (4.1.85) violence is merely represented?

All this might be dismissed as the fantasy or nightmare of an empowered theater out of control, appropriating the prerogative of the state by taking justice into its own hands. But according to an account by Will Kempe, the famous comic actor for Lord Strange's Men and subsequently the Chamberlain's Men, the public theater did on occasion usurp the state's role in punishing criminals. Kempe recounts in his travelogue, *Kempe's Nine Daies Wonder* (1600), that while passing through Burnt-wood, on market day,

> two Cut-purses were taken, that with other two of their companions followed mee from London (as many better disposed persons did:) but these two dy-doppers gave out when they were apprehended, that they had laid wagers and betted about my journey. Whereupon the Officers bringing them to my Inne, I justly denyed their acquaintance, saving that I remembred one of them to be a noted Cut-purse, *such a one as we tye to a poast on our stage, for all people to wonder at, when at a play, they are taken pilfring.*[26]

Apparently, cutpurses caught in the act in the public theater were haled onstage, and tied to one of the posts of the stage. What makes all this even more confusing is that cutpurses are busily playing a role, masquerading as members of an audience and preying on their unsuspecting fellows. They are unmasked by revealing their true identity onstage, where, like criminals, they are forced to perform a different kind of role. Just as the state freely appropriates theatricality, so too (at least in such instances) the theater took upon itself the prerogative of the state, and in a kind of publicly authorized theatrical display, acted very much as the state did.

What would have happened to our conception of theatrical representation, one is tempted to ask, if a cutpurse had been caught and dragged onstage at that moment in a production of *The Spanish Tragedy* when Pedringano was bound to "the stake" (or, for that matter, during the anonymous Admiral's Men's play of 1587, when the actor about to be shot at is tied to the stage post)? Would the actor have been cut down and the cutpurse put up in his place? Has that stage post taken on the symbolic identity as the site of a criminal's punishment (and in a regular production, when an actor rather than a cutpurse was tied to it, would it have retained that symbolic force)? What distinguishes the punishment of an actor playing a criminal from the punishment of a criminal brought onstage and turned into a kind of actor? For that matter, when actors punish cutpurses onstage, is it still theater? Theater within theater? A state within theater?[27]

Kyd's exploration of the potential indistinguishability of theatrical and state violence reaches its climax in the denouement of *The Spanish Tragedy*. In his role as Knight Marshal, Hieronimo is called upon to fulfill a double function: both to "punish such as do transgress" (3.6.12) within the verge of the court, and to provide royal entertainment. In Act 4, scene 4, these roles coincide in the "tragedy" in which Hieronimo is both "Author and actor" (4.4.147). Kyd fully exploits in this scene the representational no-man's-land between official and theatrical violence. The result is a drama that serves as an immediate and unqualified agent of social change: Hieronimo's entertainment results in the death of Lorenzo, nephew to the King of Spain (and his apparent heir), as well as Balthazar, son and heir to the Viceroy of Portugal.[28] Hieronimo achieves justice by inverting the practice of "kings and emperors" like Nero who "have ta'en delight / To make experience [i.e., trial] of their wits in plays" (4.1.88-89).

Hieronimo's revenge drama depends upon a blurring of representational boundaries. Not only the onstage audience, comprising the "Spanish King, [the] Viceroy, the Duke of Castile, and their train" (4.4.1 SD), but the audience in the London theater is unaware that the murders they witness in the play are "permanent." Hieronimo triumphantly explains that their expectations are misplaced:

> Haply you think, but bootless are your thoughts,
> That this is fabulously counterfeit,
> And that we do as all tragedians do:
> To die today, for fashioning our scene,
> The death of Ajax, or some Roman peer,
> And in a minute starting up again,
> Revive to please tomorrow's audience.
> No, princes.
>
> (4.4.76-83)

Drama is empowered, but only when Hieronimo's play becomes more than imitation of action. A play written in another time and place turns out to be politically transgressive by accident. Hieronimo had "by chance" (4.1.78) written it in his university days at Toledo, when he was "young" and "plied [himself] to fruitless poetry" (4.1.71-72). The playbook, "long forgot," was, he says, "found this other day" (4.1.80). There may be an additional level of irony at work here, if in fact the subject of Hieronimo's play—the tragedy of "Soliman and Perseda"—was taken from an extant play of that title attributed to Kyd himself.

Kyd goes to considerable lengths to show that it is not the words by themselves which are transgressive; in fact, for no apparent reason Hieronimo insists that his play be spoken in sundry languages, which Balthazar fears will be "a mere confusion, / And hardly shall . . . be understood" (4.1.180-1). It is not what Jerzy Limon has called "dangerous matter"[29] that is politically subversive, but the theatrical use to which those words and actions could be put. The anxieties of Elizabethan antitheatrical writers were not entirely misplaced.

The Spanish Tragedy's own transgressive potential, like that of Hieronimo's revived play, would be realized in a historical moment unimaginable at the time of its composition, when Kyd's play became identified as a site of female resistance to patriarchal constraints. This identification first appears in Richard Braithwait's conduct book, *The English Gentlewoman* (1631), in the chapter on female "behaviour," where Braithwait holds up for "reproofe" those women who "give too easy raines to liberty" (53). He offers as an example a woman who was so enamored of the theater, which she frequented regularly, that on her deathbed she still cried out for Kyd's play. Going to the theater both to see and be seen

> is her daily taske, till death enter the Stage and play his part; whom shee entertaines with such unpreparednesse, as her *extreme act* presents objects of infinite unhappinesse: "As it sometimes fared with a Gentlewoman of our owne Nation, who so fairly bestowed the expence of her best houres upon the Stage, as being surprized by sicknesse, even unto death, she became so deafe to such as admonished her of her end, as shee clozed her *dying scene* with a vehement calling on *Hieronimo*."
>
> (53-54)

The anonymous (and probably fictitious) Englishwoman's obsessive attendance at the theater has so stripped her of reason that she dies confusing life with theater, calling not on her Maker but "on Hieronimo."

Braithwait's anecdote clearly appealed to the antitheatricalist William Prynne, who offered an embellished version of the story in his *Histriomastix* (1633). In Prynne's account the woman dies crying out "*Hieronimo, Hieronimo*; O let me see *Hieronimo* acted" (556). Prynne tries to make the story more plausible by insisting that Braithwait, his source, was "then present at her departure" (556). A decade later, when Braithwait "revised, corrected, and enlarged" *The English Gentlewoman* (1641), he retells the story in greater detail, and changes the ending to make her transgression even more shocking. Here, the woman "who so daily bestowed the expence of her best houres upon the Stage" (199) thinks, in her maddened state, that she actually *is* Hieronimo:

> when her Physician was to minister a Receipt unto her, which hee had prepared to allay the extremity of that agonizing fit wherewith shee was then assailed, putting aside the Receipt with her hand, as if shee rejected it, in the very height and heate of her distemper, with an active resolution used these words unto her Doctor: ["]Thankes good Horatio, take it for thy paines.["]
>
> (299)

In this version her actions are made to seem even more horrifying, as the dying woman's reflexive theatricality condemns her soul: she turns her deathbed into theater, projecting onto her physician the role of Horatio, retaining for herself Hieronimo's (or is this the dying Hamlet speaking?). Her soul is lost even as she loses her own identity by assuming that of the male actor's, and reverses (and mirrors) *The Spanish Tragedy*'s blurring of theatrical and real death.

The various versions of the anecdote suggest that Kyd's play, having entered the cultural vocabulary, becomes the means of expressing transgressive social attitudes: the play becomes the symbol of a dying woman's refusal to conform to cultural norms, even as the public theater, in Braithwait's account, becomes one of the few places where a woman could transgress the constraints placed on where she can go and what she can do. It may well be that Kyd's Belimperia provides a model for Braithwait's transgressive Englishwoman: only in the theater, after all, in her role as Perseda, was Belimperia sufficiently empowered and "able" (4.4.65) to revenge the wrongs done to her.[30] Kyd's great insight, though one that he did not live to see realized (if, indeed, he really saw it at all), was that theater's most serious threat to rival cultural practices and institutions derives from its unactivated potential, making dormant transgressive possibilities difficult to predict and even more difficult to control. As more archival material on theatrical practice becomes available in projects like the Records of Early English Drama (evidence that will no doubt qualify the largely anecdotal history that characterizes my own and many other historicist studies) the complex relationship between theater and state in Elizabethan culture will have to be rewritten. At this juncture the best that can be said is that there is no end of subversion, even for us; it just may not be the subversion we had been looking for.[31]

Notes

1. *Shakespearean Negotiations* (Berkeley: Univ. of California Press, 1988), p. 65.

2. Greenblatt, *Shakespearean Negotiations,* p. 65.

3. *The Place of the Stage: License, Play, and Power in Renaissance England* (Chicago: Univ. of Chicago Press, 1988).

4. There are some important recent exceptions: see *The Violence of Representation,* ed. Nancy Armstrong and Leonard Tennenhouse (New York and London: Routledge, 1989), especially Peter Stallybrass, "'Drunk with the Cup of Liberty': Robin Hood, the carnivalesque, and the rhetoric of violence in early modern England" (pp. 45-76); and Leonard Tennenhouse, "Violence done to women on the Renaissance stage" (pp. 77-97). Also see Pieter Spierenburg, *The Spectacle of Suffering* (Cambridge: Cambridge Univ. Press, 1984); J. A. Sharpe, "'Last Dying Speeches': Religion, Ideology and Public Execution in Seventeenth Century England," *Past and Present* 107 (1985),

144-67; David Nicholls, "The Theatre of Martyrdom in the French Reformation," *Past and Present* 121 (1988), 49-73; and Samuel Y. Edgerton, Jr., *Pictures and Punishment: Art and Criminal Punishment during the Florentine Renaissance* (Ithaca and London: Cornell Univ. Press, 1985).

5. Michel Foucault, *Discipline and Punish: The Birth of the Prison,* trans. Alan Sheridan (New York: Pantheon Books, 1977), pp. 47-50.

6. J. H. Baker, "Criminal Courts and Procedure at Common Law, 1550-1800" in *Crimes in England, 1550-1800,* ed. J. S. Cockburn (Princeton: Princeton Univ. Press, 1977), provides a useful summary of official punishment of commoners in England. Until 1790 the judgment read to convicted male traitors and felons was as follows:

> You are to be drawn upon a hurdle to the place of execution, and there you are to be hanged by the neck, and being alive cut down, and your privy-members to be cut off, and your bowels to be taken out of your belly and there burned, you being alive; and your head to be cut off, and your body to be divided into four quarters, and that your head and quarters be disposed of where his majesty shall think fit.

> (p. 42)

Playgoers crossing the bridge to Southwark would pass under those heads on their way to and from the theaters. The judgment for male petty-traitors was to be "drawn and hanged," while capital felons like Pedringano were "to be hanged by [the] neck . . . until dead." See, too: John Bellamy, "To the gallows and after," in *The Tudor Law of Treason* (London: Routledge & Kegan Paul, 1979), pp. 182-227.

7. The Admiral's Men's stage property for a lost play—"i frame for the heading in Black Jone"—indicates that beheadings could be represented onstage (see E. K. Chambers, *The Elizabethan Stage,* 4 vols. [Oxford: Oxford Univ. Press, 1923], 3:97). In addition, an episode in Marlowe's *The Massacre at Paris* in which a dead man is hung "upon this tree" (line 493) suggests that there was some sort of convention for hanging individuals onstage. There is the further possibility that Barabas's fate in Marlowe's *The Jew of Malta* (death by boiling in a cauldron) recalls the punishment for poisoning decreed by Henry VIII (though repealed in 1547). Barabas brags of poisoning wells (2.3.178) and subsequently poisons the nuns who have occupied his house. (For a brief account of this legislation, see Penry Williams, *The Tudor Regime* [Oxford: Oxford Univ. Press, 1979], p. 225). For a discussion of Marlowe and state violence see Karen Cunningham's "Re-

naissance Execution and Marlovian Elocution: The Drama of Death," *PMLA* 105.2 (1990), 209-22.

8. Quotations from the play are cited from Philip Edwards, ed., *The Spanish Tragedy,* The Revels Plays (Cambridge: Harvard Univ. Press, 1959).

9. Foucault (unlike many of his followers) is careful to acknowledge the unpredictable and improbable basis of much resistance: "there is a plurality of resistances, each of them a special case: resistances that are possible, necessary, improbable; others that are spontaneous savage, solitary, concerted, rampant, or violent; still others that are quick to compromise, interested, or sacrificial." Foucault further urges that the search "for the headquarters that presides over" the "rationality" of power is misguided; "neither the caste which governs, nor the groups which control the state apparatus, nor those who make the most important economic decision direct the entire network of power that functions in a society." *The History of Sexuality,* Volume I: An Introduction, trans. Robert Hurley (New York: Vintage Books, 1980), pp. 95-96.

10. *Acts of the Privy Council,* ed. J. R. Dasent, n.s. 24, 1592-1593 (London: 1901), p. 187. The Council was aware of the potential danger of such writing: "oftentymes it doth fall out of suche lewde beginninges that further mischiefe doth ensue" (187).

11. For an account of the modes of torture in Elizabethan England see John H. Langbein, *Torture and the Laws of Proof: Europe and England in the Ancien Régime* (Chicago: Univ. of Chicago Press, 1977), esp. pp. 73-90. That Kyd was not racked (as many have assumed) is made clear by Langbein's findings that after 1588 Bridewell replaced the Tower as the regular venue for torture; unlike the Tower, Bridewell was apparently not equipped with a rack. Under the Stuarts, the Tower regained its former prominence, and both rack and manacles were used in torture (84). Langbein also notes that the "reign of Elizabeth was the age when torture was most used in England" (82).

12. Quoted from the transcription of the letter provided in Arthur Freeman, *Thomas Kyd: Facts and Problems* (Oxford: Clarendon Press, 1967), p. 182. Sir Thomas Puckering had recently helped prosecute in the "Arraignment of Sir Richard Knightly, and other persons, in the Star-Chamber, for maintaining seditious Persons, Books, and Libels: 31 Eliz. Feb. 31, A.D. 1588." Knightly and fellow defendants were accused of publishing Puritan material described as "a most seditious and libellous pamphlet, *fit for a vice in a play*—and no other" (Howell, *State Trials* 1:1265 [italics mine]).

13. In his dedicatory epistle to the Countess of Sussex prefacing *Cornelia,* in F. S. Boas, ed., *The Works of Thomas Kyd* (Oxford: Clarendon Press, 1955), p. 102.

14. The play had a very strong run at Henslowe's Rose from the early months of 1592 through December-January 1593. The theaters were closed because of plague during the time of Kyd's imprisonment, but the players toured the provinces, and if we take Thomas Dekker's account of Ben Jonson's early career as an actor playing Hieronimo as indicative, Kyd's popular play was no doubt performed in the countryside at this time (see Ben Jonson, *Works,* 12 vols., ed. C. H. Herford and Percy and Evelyn Simpson [Oxford: Clarendon Press, 1925-52], 1:13). *The Spanish Tragedy* may well hold the record for performances at different theaters: Michael Hattaway lists (in addition to the Rose) the Cross Keys Inn; the Theatre; Newington Butts; the Fortune; the Curtain; the Globe; and even Second Blackfriars; in addition to provincial and foreign tours (*Elizabethan Popular Theatre* [London: Routledge & Kegan Paul, 1982], p. 103). By 1633 the play had gone through eleven editions.

15. As quoted in Freeman, *Thomas Kyd,* p. 25.

16. Members of Kyd's audience could recently have witnessed the public executions of Anthony Babington and his co-conspirators for treason, in late September 1586. The account of their execution should give some idea of the spectacle of the scaffold:

> Ballard was first executed. He was cut down and bowelled with great cruelty while he was alive. . . . Savage broke the rope, and fell down from the gallows, and was presently seized on by the executioner, his privities cut off, and his bowells taken out while he was alive. Barnwell, Tichbourne, Tilney, and Abington were executed with equal cruelty.

The other executions took place the next day. Queen Elizabeth,

> being informed of the severity used in the Executions the day before, and detesting such cruelty, gave express orders that these should be used more favourably; and accordingly they were permitted to hang till they were quite dead, before they were cut down and bowelled.

(Howell, *State Trials* 1:1158, 1160-61)

17. See Foucault, *Discipline and Punish,* esp. pp. 51-59.

18. Chambers, *The Elizabethan Stage,* 2:135.

19. See the chapter with that title in Greenblatt, *Shakespearean Negotiations,* pp. 21-65.

20. See Chambers, *Elizabethan Stage,* 2:396, n. 2. Also see: *A True Report of the Inditement, Arraignment, Conviction, Condemnation, and Execution of John Weldon, William Hartley, and Robert Sutton, who Suffred for High Treason* (1588); and "Unpublished Documents relating to the English Martyres, 1584-1603," ed. J. H. Pollen (Catholic Record Society, 5, 1908), p. 327.

21. Richard Perkinson, ed., Thomas Heywood, *An Apology for Actors* and I. G., *A Refutation of The Apology for Actors* (New York: Scholars' Facsimiles and Reprints, 1941), sig. E3ʳ, E3ᵛ [italics mine].

22. Foucault, *Discipline and Punish,* p. 49.

23. See Orgel, *The Illusion of Power: Political Theater in the English Renaissance* (Berkeley: Univ. of California Press, 1975); Goldberg, *James I and the Politics of Literature* (Baltimore: The Johns Hopkins Univ. Press, 1983); and Greenblatt, *Shakespearean Negotiations,* esp. pp. 63-65.

24. A Caroline parodic recollection of *The Spanish Tragedy* makes this point clearly. Thomas Rawlins's *The Rebellion* (1641) includes a scene in which a group of tailors (descendents of *A Midsummer Night's Dream*'s rude mechanicals) have rehearsed Kyd's play and prepare to entertain the king of Spain. The lead tailor, Vermine, like Shakespeare's Botton the Weaver, greedily wants to play all the parts, but will "Leave all to play the King," so that, as he declares in the real King's presence, "I *Vermine* / The King will act before the King." The syntax is ambiguous: is there a pause after his name or does he introduce himself as "Vermine the King"? Is he a king who will act before the king, or is he to act the king before the King? Theater's capacity to confuse and elide social difference—a favorite subject of antitheatrical tracts in the period—proved disturbing to a society that sought through institutional constraints to maintain these distinctions.

25. Perkinson, *A Refutation,* p. 28 [italics mine].

26. G. B. Harrison, ed., William Kempe, *Kempe's Nine Daies Wonder* (1600) (London: the Bodley Head, Ltd., 1923), p. 9 [italics mine].

27. Even after the closing of the theaters the slippery relationship between theatrical violence and political theatrics was recalled: "For when the Stage at *Westminster,* where the two Houses now Act, is once more restored back againe to *Black-Fryers,* they have hope they shall returne to their old harmlesse profession of killing Men in Tragedies without Man-slaughter" (from *Mercurius Anti-Britanicus* [11 August 1645], p. 20, rpt. in *The English Revolution III: Newsbooks I, Oxford Royalist,* Vol. 4, [London: Cornmarket Press, 1971], p. 322). I am indebted to William Sherman for this reference.

28. For an outstanding and groundbreaking discussion of the political implications of Hieronimo's play, see S. F. Johnson, "*The Spanish Tragedy,* or Babylon Revisited," in *Essays on Shakespeare and Elizabethan Drama in Honor of Hardin Craig,* ed. Richard Hosley (Columbia: Univ. of Missouri Press, 1962), pp. 23-36.

29. See Limon's *Dangerous Matter* (Cambridge: Cambridge Univ. Press, 1987).

30. Alternatively, Hieronimo's self-silencing may have offered itself as an appropriate model of resistance to dominant authority. For a discussion of silencing, subjectivity, and *The Spanish Tragedy,* see Catherine Belsey, *The Subject of Tragedy* (New York and London: Methuen, 1985), esp. pp. 75-78.

31. I am indebted to Jean Howard, David Scott Kastan, Stuart Kurland, William Sherman, Edward W. Tayler, and René Weis for their criticism of various drafts of this essay.

Molly Smith (essay date spring 1992)

SOURCE: Smith, Molly. "The Theater and the Scaffold: Death as Spectacle in *The Spanish Tragedy.*" *Studies in English Literature 1500-1900* 32, no. 2 (spring 1992): 217-32.

[*In the following essay, Smith suggests that Kyd's approach to staging executions evokes several aspects of contemporary public hangings.*]

I

Traditional criticism regards Kyd's **Spanish Tragedy** as important primarily for its historical position at the head of the revenge tradition. Its violence has frequently been attributed to Senecan models, and its dramatic deaths, including the spectacular *coup de theatre* in the closing scene, analyzed primarily for their influence on Shakespeare's dramaturgy. And yet, though the Senecan influence has been well documented, critics have paid little attention to contemporary cultural practices such as public executions and hangings at Tyburn to explain the play's particular fascination with the hanged man and the mutilated and dismembered corpse. No other play of the Renaissance stage dwells on the spectacle of hanging as Kyd's does, and the Senecan influence will not in itself account for the spectacular on-stage hangings and near-hangings in the play.[1]

During Elizabeth's reign, 6160 victims were hanged at Tyburn, and though this represents a somewhat smaller figure than those hanged during Henry VIII's reign,

Elizabethans were certainly quite familiar with the spectacle of the hanged body and the disemboweled and quartered corpse. In Kyd's treatment of the body as spectacle, we witness most vividly the earliest coalescence of the theatrical and punitive modes in Elizabethan England. Kyd also heightens the ambivalence inherent in the public hanging as spectacle and deliberately weakens the frames that separated spectators from the spectacle.

Kyd's merger of the spectacles of punishment and enacted tragedy was perhaps inevitable in light of the remarkable similarities in the format and ends of these popular events in early modern England. Indeed, the stage and the scaffold seem to have been closely related historically.[2] The famous Triple Tree, the first permanent structure for hangings in London, was erected at Tyburn in 1571, during the same decade which saw the construction of the first public theater.[3] At Tyburn, seats were available for those who could pay, and rooms could be hired in houses overlooking the scene; the majority of spectators, however, stood in a semi-circle around the event, while hawkers sold fruits and pies, and ballads and pamphlets detailing the various crimes committed by the man being hanged. Other kinds of peripheral entertainment also occurred simultaneously. In short, hangings functioned as spectacles not unlike tragedies staged in the public theaters.[4] The organization of spectators around hangings and executions and in the theaters, and the simultaneous localization of these entertainments through the construction of permanent structures, suggest the close alliance between these communal worlds in early modern England. Evidence also suggests that theater and public punishment provided entertainment to upper and lower classes and that both events were generally well attended. Contemporary letters abound in accounts of executions and hangings, details of which are interspersed among court gossip and descriptions of Parliament sessions. In a letter to Dudley Carleton, for example, John Chamberlain describes the hanging of four priests on Whitsun eve in 1612, noting with mild surprise the large number of people, among them "divers ladies and gentlemen," who had gathered to witness the event which took place early in the morning between six and seven.[5]

I am not alone in suggesting links between these modes of popular public spectacle in Renaissance England. Stephen Greenblatt argues for the implicit presence of the scaffold in certain kinds of theater when he writes:

> the ratio between the theater and the world, even at its most stable and unchallenged moments, was never *perfectly* taken for granted, that is, experienced as something wholly natural and self-evident. . . . Similarly, the playwrights themselves frequently called attention in the midst of their plays to alternative theatrical practices. Thus, for example, the denouement of Massinger's *Roman Actor* (like that of Kyd's *Spanish*

Tragedy) turns upon the staging of a mode of theater in which princes and nobles take part in plays and in which the killing turns out to be real. It required no major act of imagination for a Renaissance audience to conceive of either of these alternatives to the conventions of the public playhouse: both were fully operative in the period itself, in the form of masques and courtly entertainments, on the one hand, and public maimings and executions on the other.[6]

Presumably, the relationship between theater and the scaffold worked both ways: if dramatic deaths could suggest public maimings and executions, the latter could as easily and as vividly evoke its theatrical counterparts.

Indeed, contemporary narratives about public hangings and executions frequently insist on the theatrical analogy. Carleton, for example, in a letter to Chamberlain, details in vividly theatrical terms the trial and executions of several conspirators, including two priests, implicated in the plot to harm King James I shortly after his ascension to the throne in 1603. The letter moves from a casual narrative to a concentrated exposition of the drama as it unfolded. Carleton begins his account with the hangings of two papist priests: "The two priests that led the way to the execution were very bloodily handled; for they were cut down alive; and Clark to whom more favour was intended, had the worse luck; for he both strove to help himself, and spake after he was cut down. . . . Their quarters were set on Winchester gates, and their heads on the first tower of the castle." This was followed by the execution of George Brooke, whose death, Carleton notes wryly, was "witnessed by no greater an assembly than at ordinary executions," the only men of quality present being the Lord of Arundel and Lord Somerset.[7] Three others, Markham, Grey, and Cobham, were scheduled to be executed on Friday; Carleton narrates the sequence of events as it occurred, retaining information about their narrow escape from the gallows until the very end:

> A fouler day could hardly have been picked out, or fitter for such a tragedy. Markham being brought to the scaffold, was much dismayed, and complained much of his hard hap, to be deluded with hopes, and brought to that place unprepared. . . . The sheriff in the mean time was secretly withdrawn by one John Gill, Scotch groom of the bedchamber. . . . The sheriff, at his return, told him [Markham] that since he was so ill prepared, he should have two hours respite, so led him from the scaffold, without giving him any more comfort.[8]

Lord Grey's turn followed, and he spent considerable time repenting for his crimes and praying to be forgiven, all of which, Carleton points out, "held us in the rain more than half an hour." As in the case of Markham, however, the execution was halted, the prisoner being told only that the sequence of executions had been altered by express orders from the King, and that Cobham would die before him. Grey was also led to Prince Arthur's Hall and asked to await his turn with Markham. Lord Cobham then arrived on the scaffold, but unlike the other two, came "with good assurance and contempt of death." The sheriff halted this execution as well, telling Cobham only that he had to first face a few other prisoners. Carleton then describes the arrival of Grey and Markham on the scaffold, and the bewildered looks on the three prisoners who "nothing acquainted with what had passed, no more than the lookers on with what should follow looked strange one upon another, like men beheaded, and met again in the other world." "Now," Carleton continues, "all the actors being together on the stage, as use is at the end of the play," the sheriff announced that the King had pardoned all three. Carleton concludes his account by noting that this happy play had very nearly been marred "for John Gill could not go so near the scaffold that he could speak to the sherrif, . . . but was fain to call out to Sir James Hayes, or else Markham might have lost his neck."[9]

The metaphoric alliance between theater and public punishment, which permeates Carleton's narrative, might be regarded as fundamental in Renaissance England. The theater and the scaffold provided occasions for communal festivities whose format and ends emerge as remarkably similar; early plays such as Kyd's *Spanish Tragedy* register the close alliance between these popular activities especially vividly. But the influence of the scaffold may also account for a general dramatic fascination with the spectacle of death evident throughout the late sixteenth and early seventeenth centuries. In fact, the close alliance between theater and public punishment frames the great age of drama in England; after all, the period culminates with the greatest theatrical spectacle of all, the public execution of King Charles I.

Despite my collapse of the theatrical and punitive modes, however, an important distinction needs to be made between the festivity of theater and the spectacle of the scaffold. Theater establishes distance between spectacle and spectators, and festivity implicitly or explicitly invokes the frame to separate itself from everyday living. Indeed, distance in the theater and framing in festivity perform similar functions. However, the authenticity in the enactment of public punishment makes its distance considerably more nebulous. In fact, participants in public executions and hangings remained acutely aware of their profound relevance both to the authorities who orchestrated the performance and to the spectators who viewed it. Such awareness frequently resulted in conscious attempts by victims to manipulate and modify the distance that separated criminals from onlookers. In such circumstances, the formal efficacy of the execution diminished considerably and events could easily transform into celebration of the condemned vic-

tim's role as a defier of repressive authority. As Michel Foucault illustrates:

> the public execution allowed the luxury of these momentary saturnalia, when nothing remained to prohibit or punish. Under the protection of imminent death, the criminal could say everything and the crowd cheered. . . . In these executions, which ought to show only the terrorizing power of the prince, there was the whole aspect of the carnival, in which the rules were inverted, authority mocked and criminals transformed into heroes.[10]

Executions where the margins remained tenuous and where festivity merged so fully with the enactment of terror may be especially important to an understanding of the drama of death on the Renaissance stage. In early plays such as Kyd's, in the concluding representation of theater within theater, for example, we witness a conscious manipulation of distance and framing, dramatic exposition of the precarious nature of public spectacle itself as an illustration of royal and state power. The inner play's exposition of the shallowness of state authority gains added potency from the composition of its audience, the royal houses of Spain and Portugal. Hieronimo, the author of the inner play, even taunts his audience's reliance on the framed nature of theatrical tragedy:

> Haply, you think, but bootless are your thoughts,
> That this is fabulously counterfeit,
> And that we do as all tragedians do:
> To die today, for fashioning our scene,
> The death of Ajax or some Roman peer
> And in a minute, starting up again,
> Revive to please tommorow's audience.
>
>   (IV.iv.76-82)[11]

At this, its most clearly self-reflexive moment, Kyd's tragedy simultaneously indulges and exposes its reliance on the drama of terror, and, through the mixed reactions of its stage audience who at first applaud the tragedy for its realistic enactment and then condemn it for its gory authenticity, invites a reevaluation of the spectacle of terror itself.[12]

II

The Spanish Tragedy was staged within a decade after the construction of both the Triple Tree and the Theatre, and this perhaps accounts for the hangings, murders, and near deaths which abound in the play.[13] Lorenzo and Balthazar hang Horatio in the arbor in a spectacularly gruesome scene, Pedringano's death by hanging occurs on stage, Alexandro narrowly escapes being burnt at the stake, Villuppo exits the play presumably to be tortured and hanged, and Hieronimo tries unsuccessfully to hang himself in the last scene, though he duplicates the effects of a hanging by biting his tongue out. Of all these, however, Horatio's gruesome murder in the arbor remains the centerpiece; we come back to it again and again through Hieronimo's recounting of it, and as if to reiterate its centrality, the playwright exploits the value of the mutilated body as spectacle by holding Horatio's body up to view either literally or metaphorically several times in the course of the play.

Kyd thus exploits thoroughly the audience's voyeuristic interest in the hanged and mutilated corpse, but he prepares us for his centerpiece, Horatio's murder in the arbor, even from the opening scene through promises of torture, mutilation, and death. Repeated promises of more blood and gore, in fact, distinguish Kyd's version of the revenge play from Shakespeare's later rendering in *Hamlet*. While in the later play, Hamlet Senior insists that the torments of the netherworld are too horrible to be recounted (he is also forbidden to reveal its secrets), in the opening scene of Kyd's tragedy, Don Andrea's ghost provides with relish a vivid and detailed account of his sojourn through the underworld:

> Through dreadful shades of ever glooming night,
> I saw more sights than a thousand tongues can tell,
> Or pens can write, or mortal hearts can think.
> Three ways there were: . . .
>
> . . . . .
>
> The left-hand path, declining fearfully,
> Was ready downfall to the deepest hell,
> Where bloody Furies shake their whips of steel,
> And poor Ixion turns an endless wheel;
> Where usurers are choked with melting gold,
> And wantons are embraced with ugly snakes,
> And murderers groan with never killing wounds,
> And perjured wights scalded in boiling lead,
> And all foul sins with torments overwhelmed.
>
> (I.i.56-70)

The underworld, not constrained by economic considerations, retains ancient methods of public deaths such as boiling and drowning, punishments long abandoned in England as too costly and troublesome; indeed, at the end of the play, Don Andrea's ghost envisions similar elaborate deaths for his murdered enemies in the afterworld. The opening and concluding accounts of the underworld which frame the play emphasize the tragedy's links with the spectacle of public punishment, the primary purpose of which was to replicate torments awaiting the victim after death. The opening scene even concludes with Revenge promising us better entertainment than that detailed by Don Andrea, more blood and gore through the murder of the princely Balthazar by Don Andrea's "sweet" Bel-imperia.

Indeed, the very next scene provides more elaborate fare; the king's request for a "brief discourse" concerning the battle between Spain and Portugal elicits from his general a detailed description complete with similes and accounts of mutilated and dismembered bodies:

> On every side drop captains to the ground,
> And soldiers, some ill maimed, some slain outright:

> Here falls a body sundered from his head,
> There legs and arms lie bleeding on the grass,
> Mingled with weapons and unbowelled steeds,
> That scattering overspread the purple plain.
>
> (I.ii.57-62)

The king's satisfied response to this narrative, which ultimately details Spain's success in battle, captures the value of death as entertainment, an idea emphasized throughout the play in a variety of ways.

The audience hears four different versions of the battle in succession in these opening scenes—by Don Andrea, the Spanish general, Horatio, and Villuppo in the Portuguese court—and each account either elicits pleasure from the listener as in the scene just described or reveals the delight and ingenuity of the speaker.[14] The latter seems true of Villuppo's account of Balthazar's death to the viceroy in the scene which follows. Jealous of Alexandro's success at court, Villuppo fabricates a tale about Balthazar's treacherous betrayal by Alexandro in the midst of battle. The temperamental and fickle viceroy responds to the tale of his son's death with "Ay, ay, my nightly dreams have told me this" (I.iii.76) and immediately has Alexandro imprisoned. Villuppo closes this scene with an aside in which he revels in the ingenuity of his "forged tale." However, Villuppo's fantastic narrative must remind the audience of the uncanny way in which art mirrors life, for we have already been promised Balthazar's death by Revenge; when his murder occurs later in the play, its sequence mimics Villuppo's account, for the unsuspecting Balthazar is killed by his supposed wife-to-be, Bel-imperia, at what appears to be the height of his success. Even the viceroy's claim about his prophetic dreams gains ironic accuracy as the scene provides a narrative account of events yet to occur.

We arrive thus, via numerous accounts of death and mutilation, to the scene in the arbor where Bel-imperia and Horatio meet. Already aware of Pedringano's betrayal, however, the audience would view the images of war and love in the opening section of this scene as ominous. Interestingly, Pedringano, like the hangman who sometimes remained masked and hooded, conducts the ceremony of the hanging in disguise with the aid of his assistant Serebrine, while Lorenzo gives orders and joins in the stabbing after Horatio has been hanged. Though stage directions remain unclear, we can assume that Balthazar and Bel-imperia witness the stabbing, for Bel-imperia responds immediately to the horrible crime. Their function as spectators parallels our own and underscores Kyd's exploitation of the event as public spectacle. Foucault's argument that in early modern Europe, "in the ceremonies of the public execution, the main character was the people, whose real presence was required for the performance" proves especially appropriate to this hanging performed on a raised stage for an audience whose arrangement in "the pit" and the balconies above recalls the scaffold, and which certainly indulges the spectators' voyeuristic interest in death as spectacle.[15] The double framing of this event- the audience as spectators watching an already framed event-also anticipates the play within the play in Act IV which more explicitly raises questions about the value of death as entertainment.

A few scenes later, we are treated to a review of this event and later to another hanging (Pedringano's), whose format, however, remains remarkably different from the one we have just witnessed. Before turning to the later hanging, I would like to consider briefly the play's uncanny reliance hereafter on the spectacle of Horatio's mutilated body.

We are never allowed to forget this spectacle, and characters keep reminding us of this event in various ways. In fact, after the staging of this gory death, the earlier revenge plot associated with Don Andrea is all but forgotten; Horatio's murder and the collusive revenge orchestrated by Bel-imperia and Hieronimo on his behalf take center stage. Horatio's body, hanged and mutilated before a full house, thus takes precedence over Don Andrea, whose death has been narrated rather than witnessed. Interestingly, Don Andrea's funeral rites were conducted by Horatio in a private ceremony, and all that remains of him is a bloody scarf; it might even be argued that the complete obliteration of Don Andrea's corpse and the repeated emphasis on Horatio's symbolically reiterates the precedence of the second revenge plot over the first. Even Don Andrea's bloody scarf is duplicated through the rest of the play by Horatio's handkerchief which Hieronimo dips in his son's blood and presents on stage several times as a reminder of his unavenged death. This token of death also recalls a conventional practice at hangings and executions; onlookers frequently dipped their handkerchiefs in the blood of the victim which was believed to carry curative and divine powers.[16]

Unlike in *Hamlet* where murdered corpses remain hidden behind curtains or stuffed under the stairwell, Kyd's play thus presents death in vivid detail and follows this up with an elaborate scene of discovery in which both Hieronimo and Isabella identify Horatio's corpse. The ghost, perhaps echoing the audience's reaction to these events, expresses dismay at witnessing Horatio's murder rather than Balthazar's as promised, but Revenge, relishing the bloody detour, insists on the relevance of these events as preambles to more cunning deaths yet to occur: "The end is crown of every work well done; / The sickle comes not till the corn be ripe" (II.v.8-9).

After this murder, the focus of the play shifts to the psychological dilemma faced by Hieronimo as he plans revenge. The most interesting aspect of his character

hereafter becomes his mental absorption with duplicating his son's murder. At first, he tries to duplicate bodies by reenacting the event with himself as victim; in a vividly dramatic scene which takes place at court, he enters with a poniard in one hand and a rope in the other and debates his route to death:

> Turn down this path—thou shalt be with him [Horatio] straight—
> Or this, and then thou need'st not take thy breath.
> This way or that way?
>
> (III.xii.14-16)

Tormented by his inability to accomplish revenge, he spends most of his time wandering in the arbor looking for his son; here, near the very tree on which Horatio was hanged, the painter Bazulto, seeking justice for his own son's murder, visits him. In a psychologically revealing moment explored in one of the "additions," Hieronimo requests Bazulto to paint the scene of Horatio's murder, complete with the victim's doleful cry and his own emotional frenzy at discovering his son's body. In language, Hieronimo re-creates the event for us yet again: "Well sir, paint me a youth run through and through with villains' swords hanging upon this tree"; and later, describing his discovery of the body, he wishes to "behold a man hanging: and tottering and tottering, as you know the wind will weave a man" (Addition, III.xiii.131-32, 151-53). His desire to re-create events through painting at first and later through the drama at court contrasts sharply with Isabella's desire a few scenes later to destroy the arbor and the tree on which her son was murdered. Both scenes, however, serve to keep the gruesome murder firmly in our minds.

The play even provides a semi-comic version of this murder in another hanging a few scenes later. Pedringano's hanging also takes place on stage and provides a semi-comic and officially authorized spectacle, a direct contrast to Horatio's base and treacherous murder committed in secret and under cover of night. Through the attitudes of Pedringano who reaches his death with a merry jest, and the clown who cannot resist the event despite his sympathy for the deluded victim, the scene simultaneously exploits and satirizes the value of the public hanging as a reiteration of justice.

Commenting on the propensity for travesty inherent in the format of the public execution, Foucault illustrates that because the ritual of torture was sustained "by a policy of terror" which made everyone aware "through the body of the criminal of the unrestrained presence of the sovereign," it was especially susceptible to manipulation by its participants.[17] As I suggested earlier, the public execution's social relevance depended so fully on its proper enactment through the collusion of all participants, including the hangman as an instrument of the law, the criminal as a defier of divine and sovereign authority, and spectators as witnesses to the efficacy of royal power and justice, and the slightest deviation could lead to redefinitions and reinterpretations of power relations between subjects and the sovereign. Indeed, this happened frequently enough to cause some concern to the authorities.[18] The speech delivered on the scaffold by the victim provided an especially suitable opportunity for such manipulation; intended to reinforce the power of justice, it frequently questioned rather than emphasized legal efficacy. Chamberlain, for example, bemoans the custom of allowing the condemned to address the audience and cautions about the inherent danger of this practice; describing the bravely rendered speech by a priest who was hanged at Tyburn, he notes that "the matter is not well handled in mine opinion, to suffer them [condemned prisoners] to brave and talk so liberally at their execution."[19]

Pedringano's defiant attitude when faced with death reiterates the carnivalesque possibilities of the public execution. Duped by Lorenzo into thinking that he will be pardoned, Pedringano insists on mocking the authorities who sentence him. Even the hangman expresses shock at his callous indifference to death: "Well, thou art even the merriest piece of man's flesh that e'er groaned at my office door" (III.vi.81-82). Indeed, it might even be argued that despite his role as victim, Pedringano has the final say on this travesty of justice, for he exposes Lorenzo's crimes in a letter, and thus forces Hieronimo to confront the inadequacy of the judicial system. In his mockery from beyond the grave, Pedringano becomes a version of the grinning skeleton in the *danse macabre* as he exposes the futility of human endeavor. The clown's attitude also reiterates the inherent irony of this grotesque enactment of state justice. Having opened the empty box which supposedly contains a pardon sent by Lorenzo, the clown reacts to the trick with infinite glee; his reaction parodies similar responses towards death voiced throughout the play by many characters, among them Balthazar, Lorenzo, Villuppo, and Pedringano himself:

> I cannot choose but smile to think how the villain will flout the gallows, scorn the audience, and descant on the hangman, and all presuming of his pardon from hence. Will't not be an odd jest for me to stand and grace every jest he makes, pointing my finger at this box, as who would say, "Mock on; here's thy warrant." Is't not a scurvy jest that a man should jest himself to death?
>
> (III.v.10-18)

Indeed, he expedites Pedringano's death by playing his part to perfection.

In effect, the clown's attitude in this scene parallels the court's applause for the **"Tragedy of Soliman and Perseda"** staged as part of Bel-imperia's nuptial ceremony. After the tragedy, Hieronimo holds up his son's

body to the bewildered court as justification for the multiple deaths that have occurred: "See here my show; look on this spectacle" (IV.iv.89). The court's reaction as the truth unfolds changes from applause to anger and condemnation. Implicitly, Kyd invites the audience to reevaluate its response to the tragedy of evil so cunningly staged, for Hieronimo's theatrical production necessarily draws attention to the nebulous nature of the boundary that separates spectators from the spectacle.

Kyd's conscious exposition of this fragile distance may be best understood perhaps through Gregory Bateson's theory about frames in "play" and "fantasy" activities.[20] Bateson argues that in metacommunicative statements such as "This is play," "the subject of discourse is the relationship between speakers," and participants recognize the paradox generated by the statement which is "a negative statement containing an implicit negative metastatement." As he insists, "Expanded, the statement . . . looks something like this: 'These actions in which we now engage do not denote what those actions *for which they stand* would denote.'"[21] The idea holds also for specific forms of play such as the theater. Communication such as the above "This is play," in which participants recognize the metacommunicative implications of the statement, involves a complex set of rules, as Bateson notes, and "language bears to the objects which it denotes a relationship comparable to that which a map bears to territory."[22] But as Bateson insists, "the discrimination between map and territory is always liable to break down," and we frequently encounter situations which involve a more complex form of play where the game is constructed "not upon the premise 'This is play' but rather around the question 'Is this play?'"[23] Certainly, **The Spanish Tragedy** concludes by posing this question. Indeed, in problematizing boundaries, Kyd's tragedy imitates the scaffold most vividly; it also begins a trend in theatrical experimentation with framing that culminates in radical realignments considerably later, in the tragedies of Middleton, Ford, and Shirley.

Kyd's tragedy, in fact, closes by reminding us of yet another frame, that provided by Don Andrea and the ghost who have witnessed events with the theatrical audience, and whose pleased reactions underscore the value of death as entertainment. The ghost, in fact, catalogues the list of deaths with obvious relish:

> Aye, now my hopes have end in their effects,
> When blood and sorrow finish my desires:
> Horatio murdered in his father's bower,
> Vild Serebrine by Pedringano slain,
> False Pedringano hanged by quaint device,
> Fair Isabella by herself misdone,
> Prince Balthazar by Bel-imperia stabbed,
> The Duke of Castile and his wicked son
> Both done to death by old Hieronimo,

My Bel-imperia fall'n as Dido fell,
And good Hieronimo slain by himself.
Ay, these were spectacles to please my soul.

(IV.v.1-12)

His response reminds us of several such reactions to death in the course of the play: the court witnessing the **"Tragedy of Soliman and Perseda"** had commended the actors; Villuppo had reveled in anticipation as he plotted the death of Alexandro; the clown had marveled at the plot to send Pedringano to his "merry" death. Revenge even concludes the play with promises of further torments for the villains in the underworld. Thus, the play blatantly presents its multiple deaths as dramatic entertainment, but through Hieronimo's taunting condemnation of his audience's expectations, it also raises questions about theater's very status as a framed spectacle and about the value of death as public entertainment.

In short, the spectacular success of Kyd's play might be attributed in part to the author's ingenious transference of the spectacle of public execution with all its ambiguities from the socio-political to the cultural worlds. Greenblatt has suggested that traces of similar transference and appropriation are evident throughout the early modern period; "the textual traces that have survived from the Renaissance," he writes, "are products of extended borrowings. They were made by moving certain things—principally ordinary language, but also metaphors, ceremonies, dances, emblems, items of clothing, well-worn stories, and so forth—from one culturally demarcated zone to another." He goes on to insist that "we need to understand not only the construction of these zones but also the process of movement across the shifting boundaries between them."[24] In Kyd's early revenge tragedy, we witness the process of movement between social and cultural boundaries perhaps more vividly than in plays by his contemporaries. Like Greenblatt, Michel de Certeau in his arguments concerning the practice of daily living focuses on infinite borrowings among socio-cultural practices, the "tactics" of consumption and appropriation that "lend a political dimension to everyday practices."[25] "Everyday life," he insists, "invents itself by *poaching* in countless ways on the property of others."[26] The same might be said about the dramatic mode in particular in early modern England as it transferred, questioned, and modified elements from popular public institutions; certainly, Kyd's tragedy of death and evil bears testimony to this ingenious transference of the spectacle of death from the punitive to the dramatic modes.[27]

Notes

1. Frank Ardolino has recently argued for a more specific connection between the play's depictions of death and the St. Bartholomew's Day Massacre in Paris in 1572; see "'In Paris? Mass, and Well Remembered!': Kyd's *The Spanish Tragedy* and the English Reaction to the St. Bartholomew's Day Massacre," *The Sixteenth Century Journal* 21, 3 (Fall 1990): 401-409. For a discussion of relationships between public executions and Marlowe's dramaturgy, see Karen Cunningham, "Renaissance Execution and Marlovian Elocution: The Drama of Death," *PMLA* 105, 2 (March 1990): 209-222.

2. I include both executions and hangings under the term scaffold, but the distinction between these two forms of punishment is important. Executions were reserved for the upper classes and important criminals, while criminals of the lower classes were hanged. When William Laud appealed his death sentence, for example, the only concession made was to revise the sentence from hanging to execution in recognition of the prisoner's social stature.

3. Whether James Burbage's Theatre in Shoreditch was the first public playhouse is a matter of some dispute. See for example, Herbert Berry's "The First Public Playhouses, especially the Red Lion," *SQ* 40, 2 (Summer 1989): 133-148, where he argues that the Red Lion (which critics such as Chambers have regarded as an inn) was an earlier playhouse deliberately ignored by Cuthbert Burbage because of a falling out between his father, James Burbage, and Brayne, the owner of the Red Lion. But as Berry himself acknowledges, the Red Lion "must have been a very pale shadow of the Theatre. . . . So far as one can see, it had no walls or roofs, and the turret was to rest on the plates on the ground rather than on secure footings, along with, one might guess, the stage and galleries" (p. 145). The "secure footing" at least was provided only with the erection of the Theatre in 1576.

4. For descriptions of public executions and hangings in early modern England, especially at Tyburn, see Alfred Marks, *Tyburn Tree* (London: Brown, n.d.), and John Laurence, *A History of Capital Punishment* (Port Washington: Kennikat, 1932). See also *Albion's Fatal Tree,* ed. Douglas Hay, Peter Linebaugh, et al. (New York: Random House, 1967), though it deals primarily with the eighteenth century.

5. Thomas Birch, *The Court and Times of James the First,* ed. R. F. Williams, 2 vols. (London: Henry Colburn, 1849), 1:173.

6. Stephen Greenblatt, *Shakespearean Negotiations: The Circulation of Social Energy in Renaissance England* (Berkeley and Los Angeles: Univ. of California Press, 1988), p. 15.

7. Thomas Birch, 1:27.

8. Ibid., 1:29.

9. Ibid., 1:31-32.

10. Michel Foucault, *Discipline and Punish: The Birth of the Prison*, trans. Alan Sheridan (New York: Vintage Books, 1977), p. 61.

11. Thomas Kyd, *The Spanish Tragedy*, ed. Philip Edwards (Cambridge, MA: Harvard Univ. Press, 1959). All further citations from the play are taken from this edition.

12. Recent Renaissance criticism has shown particular interest in the self-reflexive and subversive aspects of drama in the sixteenth and seventeenth centuries and established the fragility of distance between spectacle and spectator especially in Shakespeare's plays. Greenblatt, for example, redefines this sense of distance in the dramaturgy of successful playwrights such as Marlowe and Shakespeare as the creation of anxiety. Anxiety in the theater also accompanies the evocation of delight: "the whole point of anxiety in the theater is to make it give such delight that the audience will pay for it again and again. And this delight seems bound up with the marking out of theatrical anxiety as represented anxiety—not wholly real, either in the characters onstage or in the audience" (*Shakespearean Negotiations*, p. 135). In characteristic privileging of the Shakespearean text, he goes on to describe "a kind of perfection" in the manipulation of anxiety, "a startling increase in the level of represented and aroused anxiety" in Shakespeare (*Shakespearean Negotiations*, p. 133). I would like to suggest that despite the heightening of what he terms as "delight" in the best plays of Shakespeare, the manipulation of anxiety in Shakespeare's works moves entirely in one direction, that is, to reiterate and rearticulate the distance between theater and spectator. Indeed, I will suggest that despite the sometimes fragile nature of this distance, Shakespeare's plays reveal an ultimately conservative tendency towards the demarcation rather than destruction of clear boundaries. In the work of other dramatists such as Kyd and Marlowe, and later, Shirley and Ford, however, one encounters the highly problematic staging of such anxiety and delight that Greenblatt celebrates in Shakespeare. Mary Beth Rose seems to be making a similar point when she argues that "given the variety of conceptual options in Jacobean culture, he [Shakespeare] often chooses the conservative ones, a pattern that becomes obvious when we view him not on his own, but in relation to his fellow playwrights" (*The Expense of Spirit: Love and Sexuality in English Renaissance Drama* [Ithaca: Cornell Univ. Press, 1988], p. 173).

13. The earliest and latest possible dates for the play are 1582 and 1592, respectively. I have gone by the generally accepted date of 1586-87. For a discussion of the problems in dating the play accurately, see Philip Edwards's introduction to his edition, pp. xxi-xxvii.

14. The exception to this might be Horatio's account of Don Andrea's death to Bel-imperia, though it also raises questions of authenticity by modifying two earlier accounts we have heard, the first by Don Andrea's ghost and the other by the Spanish general. Discrepancies among the earlier narratives should caution us, however, that the scene provides yet another tale glossed by the teller to satisfy Bel-imperia, a listener with different allegiances from the king and viceroy.

15. Foucault, p. 57.

16. Peter Linebaugh, "The Tyburn Riot Against the Surgeons," *Albion's Fatal Tree*, pp. 65-118, 109-110.

17. Foucault, p. 49.

18. In the eighteenth century, official concern about the efficacy of public executions and hangings in reinforcing royal and social authority became especially acute as these occasions increasingly provided excuses for rioting and general merrymaking (Foucault, p. 68).

19. Birch, 1:215.

20. Gregory Bateson, "A Theory of Play and Fantasy," *Semiotics: An Introductory Anthology*, ed. Robert E. Innis (Bloomington: Indiana Univ. Press, 1985), pp. 129-144.

21. Bateson, p. 133.

22. Bateson, p. 134.

23. Bateson, p. 135.

24. Greenblatt, p. 7.

25. Michel de Certeau, *The Practice of Everyday Life*, trans. Steven Rendall (Berkeley, Los Angeles, and London: Univ. of California Press, 1984), p. xvii.

26. Michel de Certeau, p. xii.

27. Research for this essay began during an NEH summer seminar at Berkeley in 1989 directed by Stephen Greenblatt. I am grateful to Professor Greenblatt for useful comments on the chapter from which this essay is taken. I am also grateful to the Cornell University Humanities Center for a fellowship in the summer of 1990 which enabled me to revise and prepare my manuscript for publication.

Robert N. Watson (essay date 1994)

SOURCE: Watson, Robert N. "*Religio Vindicis*: Substitution and Immortality in *The Spanish Tragedy*." In *The*

Rest Is Silence: Death as Annihilation in the English Renaissance, pp. 55-73. Berkeley: University of California Press, 1994.

[*In the following essay, Watson reads* The Spanish Tragedy *as a pagan rendering of the Christian narrative of overcoming death in which Kyd questions the justice of man's mortal condition.*]

> 'Tis not onely the mischiefe of diseases, and the villanie of poysons that make an end of us, we vainly accuse the fury of Gunnes, and the new inventions of death. . . . There is therefore but one comfort left, that though it be in the power of the weakest arme to take away life, it is not in the strongest to deprive us of death: God would not exempt himselfe from that. . . .
>
> —Sir Thomas Browne, *Religio Medici* (p. 115)

As a reliable end to mortal suffering, death may sometimes be a "comfort," but not even Browne can confront its inevitability without a hint of vengefulness against its "villanie." As Renaissance Christians called their own mortality God's benign justice rather than His brutal retaliation, so they interpreted Christ's mortality as voluntary. Like Shakespeare's Othello preparing to throw away a pearl richer than all his tribe, they could not bear to call a murder what they had thought a sacrifice (5.2.247-48, 64-65). But revenge against the God who imposed death would have been a natural impulse; killing His son would have been an apt expression of it; and guilt-ridden worship of that son would have been the predictable aftermath. Construing Christ's death as our redemption into eternal life performs the classic delusional function of revenge. Revenge commonly proposes to repeal a loss by imposing an equivalent loss on the entity that caused it, and blood-revenge implies that life can be restored like stolen property.

By displacing it into an earthly political crisis, Thomas Kyd can expose the retaliatory feud between humanity and God. And by displacing the pious rituals of his culture into pagan analogues, he can threaten to expose the emptiness of the consolations they offer, the lack of any ultimate stable referent behind the signifiers of immortality. As the Renaissance church divides and falters in its assurances concerning personal immortality, and as personal identity acquires its own kind of sacredness, English literature struggles to provide a system of compensation for the loss of each human life. Famous as a kind of prop-room for later Renaissance tragedy, *The Spanish Tragedy* is a similarly compendious collection of these anxious experiments in substitution, partly consoling the audience by enacting the compensatory formulas, and partly exposing the delusive aspects of those formulas.

All the permutations that will prove crucial in sustaining the morale of English Renaissance culture are here prominently displayed: parents (such as Hieronimo) whose immortality is precariously located in a child, whose death they can only mimic to sustain the identification; mourning symbols (such as the bloody scarf) that conjure the dead into a synecdochic presence; lovers whose exchanges boast of a timeless transcendence; art that can erect and resurrect representations of life; above all, revengers who convert the villain into a scapegoat for mortality itself, and imagine that relegating the villain into death will somehow liberate his victim back into life. Kyd pioneers, on the English stage, this absurd version of homeopathic medicine—death curing death—which I believe lies near the heart of the drama of blood-revenge.[1]

Revenge-tragedy has in common with marriage-comedy—and with orthodox Christianity—the function of figuratively curing mortality. As marriage promises to replace us with our progeny in the realm of life, so blood-revenge promises to replace us with our killers in the realm of death. No wonder blood-revenge often becomes black-comically hyperbolic in Jacobean tragedy, as revengers seek a dosage adequate to achieve the desired cure; and no wonder audiences tend to sympathize with even these sadistic excesses. A spectator need not have a murdered relative, only a dead one, to share the sense of betrayal and futility that generates dramatic avengers.

The Spanish Tragedy invites us to join an embittered ghost in watching a series of plays-within-plays, staged by personifications of revenge, that tell the ultimate villain, "Death, thou shalt die." Mortality becomes a game of tag, played with swords, in which only one person is "it" at a time; and the loser is the person who dies with no one left alive on whom his death can be avenged. This agon becomes particularly urgent when the procreative alternative has failed. Indeed, the ultimate punishment of the King and Viceroy seems to be precisely that they are left without the means to resist mortality: not only without progeny, but also with no one living on whom they can enact the sort of revenge that gives Hieronimo such satisfaction. The afterlife of lovers and the afterlife of soldiers—the two heavens of *The Spanish Tragedy*—are equally lost to them.

In both the play and the plays within it, death seems only too prominent. But exaggeration can be a tool of denial, and death here is systematically unwritten—or overwritten, so that it remains legible only in palimpsest, only in its living legacies. Revenge promises Don Andrea that in subsequent scenes "thou shalt see the author of thy death, / Don Balthazar, the prince of Portingale, / Depriv'd of life by Bel-imperia" (1.1.87-89). When Isabella finds her husband lamenting over their murdered son's body, she exclaims, "What world of grief—My son Horatio! / O where's the author of this endless woe?" Hieronimo replies in the vocabulary of Revenge: "To know the author were some ease of grief, / For in revenge my heart would find relief" (2.5.38-41).² Nothing could be a clearer ad hominem fallacy than the claim that death can be corrected by eliminating its "author." What is written in blood can hardly be erased. But more blood can perhaps render it comfortably illegible: the blood of an enemy, or the blood of the dying Christ effacing our mortal sins, including the Original Sin by which the first "author of our woe" made this "world of grief"—this world of death.

If the trespass that initiates the fatal cycle can be isolated in a villain, rather than universally transmitted like Adam's sin, then the human tragedy ceases to look like divine justice. If Helen Gardner is correct that the Renaissance revenger is characteristically placed "in a situation which is horrible, and felt by him and the audience to be intolerable, but for which he has no responsibility," and if the typical revenge-tragedy "does not display the hero taking a fatal step, but the hero confronted with appalling facts,"³ then the genre was always a potential medium for a theologically subversive analysis of the problem of mortality. If J. R. Mulryne is correct that each character in *The Spanish Tragedy* "attempts to clear a little space for himself, to impose his will a little, without being able to escape the pattern of consequence established by Revenge,"⁴ then the action of this play (as of *Macbeth*) is a potential allegory for the futility of all mortal strivings, an allegory that the verbal details repeatedly evoke and enrich.

THE VENGEFUL GHOST: A SYMPTOM OF ANXIETY

Revenge-tragedy commonly suggests that death is preventable as well as curable; it helps us regulate mortality-anxiety as well as mourning. By its long litanies of universally unnatural perishings, Kyd's play—like modern newscasts—implies that death is an avoidable accident of violence, not an inevitable result of decay. Mortality appears as the contingent history of Cain and Abel, not the universal legacy of Adam and Eve.⁵ In the closing Chorus, Don Andrea summarizes the action:

> Horatio murder'd in his father's bower,
> Vild Serberine by Pedringano slain,
> False Pedringano hang'd by quaint device,
> Fair Isabella by herself misdone,
> Prince Balthazar by Bel-imperia stabb'd,
> The Duke of Castile and his wicked son
> Both done to death by old Hieronimo,
> My Bel-imperia fall'n as Dido fell,
> And good Hieronimo slain by himself:
> Ay, these were spectacles to please my soul.

> (4.5.3-12)

Didn't anyone die of age or disease in those days? Perhaps it pleased the universally doomed souls in the audience to believe not.⁶

By making death the work of murderous brothers, Kyd spares us from recognizing it as the work of Mother Nature and Father Time, who together impose the consequences of Original Sin. In the opening speech of the play, the Ghost of Don Andrea reminds us of the process of biological decay that carries us all from spring toward winter, yet describes his own death as an abrogation of that system: "But in the harvest of my summer joys / Death's winter nipp'd the blossoms of my bliss" (1.1.12-13). This could perhaps be dismissed as a random rhetorical gesture, except that Hieronimo invokes exactly the same model to lament the death of Horatio:

> Had Proserpine no pity on thy youth?
> But suffer'd thy fair crimson-colour'd spring
> With wither'd winter to be blasted thus?
> Horatio, thou art older than thy father:
> Ah ruthless fate, that favour thus transforms!

> (3.13.147-51)

Violence thus repeatedly—perhaps, in an odd way, consolingly—appropriates the sovereignty of mortality. For mortal beings, in other words, violence is time compressed. Tragedy abets denial by disguising time as violence.

This is Hieronimo's second explicit reference to Proserpine in less than thirty lines, and the previous act implicitly invoked her several times more. In fact, the entire play is framed as Proserpine's plot—an odd choice, unless it derives from her identity, in Renaissance mythography, as a figure of the cyclical replacement of life on earth, and hence of compromise with mortality.⁷ The death of Horatio, repeatedly compared to an unseasonable destruction of spring vegetation, stands for mortality in general, and condemns it as a violation. Carried off to Hades, under-age and under protest, Proserpine, like revenge, marks death as both temporary and permanent, both a narrative contingency and a physical inevitability. As Kyd removes his story as a whole from a Christian to a pagan culture, so he specifically translates the Eden myth into the Demeter myth, further developing—and further disguising—his blasphemous critique of the orthodox interpretation of Original Sin.⁸ In Kyd's garden, the ordinary person is more sinned against than sinning.

Even violent, premature deaths must be marked as aberrations, if they are as threateningly commonplace as a fatal wound in battle.⁹ The murder of Horatio systematically re-enacts the death of Don Andrea, in order to reconceive it as a crime. Don Andrea appears to have died within the ordinary rules of combat, yet we find him in a vengeful rage, and his reasons are not so hard to fathom. The opening conversations among the living reflect our worst fears about how little our deaths will affect the world. The General reports a "Victory . . .

with little loss" that left "All well . . . except some few / That are deceas'd by fortune of the war." But, oh, the difference to me, the Ghost of Andrea might comment. The "cheerful countenance" of this messenger would surely have bruised his ego, a fact that could have been staged quite effectively (1.2.1-7; cf. the parenthetical containment of the dead at 1.2.108). No wonder Don Andrea is so determined to have a destructive impact from beyond, and no wonder audiences have responded to him so powerfully. Our guilt about the dead we have forgotten, and our anger at those who will forget us after we die, might easily be projected together into a vengeful ghost. If it is true that in early modern Europe "The dead were widely conceived of as anxious about the neglect of the living, and on occasion menacing towards those they feared would neglect them," and if it is true that the Elizabethans as a group "dreaded nothing so much as the possibility that future generations might not know they had lived,"[10] then it is not surprising that their literature features ghosts so prominently and so ambivalently.

The Ghost of Don Andrea and the figure of Revenge conspire to punish the world of the living and thereby redeem the world of the dead. The story-frame thus indulges two fantasies common in tribal belief-systems: it portrays every death as a crime susceptible to talionic punishment among the living, and it portrays the envious dead as more volitional and more fully conscious than the living, who become merely actors in a play the dead can frame. Death hardly appears a desirable alternative to life—the pagan Club Dead, with its "slimy strond" and "ugly waves," is no threat to put Club Med out of business—yet through revenge the will of Don Andrea continues to thrive beyond his death (much as Castiza's skull in *The Revenger's Tragedy* applies the kiss of death to her murderer). Don Andrea becomes a visible agent in the drama of denial the living act out on his behalf—that is, on their own behalf, prospectively. We kill others to combat our own mortality, and war—like most other forms of hunting—is partly a ritual enabling us to disguise this symbolic project as practical competition. By highlighting the psychological underpinnings of blood-revenge, *The Spanish Tragedy* removes that disguise.

In *The Spanish Tragedy,* metonymy is the master-trope of immortality; but perhaps it makes the merely figurative status of that trope dangerously visible. In a sense the play is itself a metonymic substitution, replacing the rituals of death erased by the Reformation. The essential passivity of the Protestant soul in its own salvation, the doctrine of soul-sleeping maintained for a time by Calvin and other reformers, and the colorlessness of many Protestant burials, all threaten to associate death with mere oblivion. Kyd responds to that threat by offering the spectacle of Don Andrea struggling toward a vividly drawn afterworld, and (in the Chorus following

act 3) by overcoming Don Andrea's horror at the inert figure of Revenge with an assurance that revenge can surmount mortality, despite appearances to the contrary: "Nor dies Revenge although he sleep awhile." Don Andrea can then relax: "Rest thee, for I will sit to see the rest." The play on the two meanings of rest—one associated with an ending, the other with a remainder—serves here (as it does in George Herbert's lyrics) to redeem the notion of death as restful sleep from the fear that the rest will be silence, that this sleep will never yield to a restored volitional consciousness.

Don Andrea's posthumous journey is full of Dantesque sound and fury, but subsumed by significant nothings:

> Through dreadful shades of ever-glooming night,
> I saw more sights than thousand tongues can tell,
> Or pens can write, or mortal hearts can think.
>
> (1.1.56-58)

This *praeteritio* is an anxiety-producing device, and it mimics in the audience Don Andrea's own experience of delay and uncertainty:

> When I was slain, my soul descended straight
> To pass the flowing stream of Acheron:
> But churlish Charon, only boatman there,
> Said that my rites of burial not perform'd,
> I might not sit amongst his passengers,
> Ere Sol had slept three nights in Thetis' lap,
> And slak'd his smoking chariot in her flood,
> By Don Horatio, our Knight Marshal's son,
> My funerals and obsequies were done.
> Then was the ferryman of hell content
> To pass me over to the slimy strond
> That leads to fell Avernus' ugly waves.
>
> (1.1.18-29)

The three-day wait associates Don Andrea's obstructed journey into the pagan afterlife with an Elizabethan anxiety that the path to Christian resurrection might prove similarly impassable, and an answering hope that this can occur only when a religious ceremony has been neglected. The two rituals Horatio performs for Don Andrea, funeral and vendetta, reflect the same need: the need to convert mourning into an active and efficacious condition, and to conceal the indifference and powerlessness of the dead. Burial thus serves very much the same purpose as prayers for the dead in purgatory, which the Reformation had suppressed in Kyd's audience; so does revenge, which provided an alternate outlet for the compulsion to redeem the beloved into eternal life.

The Spanish Tragedy puts revenge very much in the place of purgatory: a third course between heaven and hell that appeals to our need for models of retribution that carry over from life to death. The spirit of Don Andrea "trod a middle path" between the heavens of lovers and soldiers on his right, and "deepest hell" on his left. The only other road leads him directly to Proserpine and Revenge (1.1.59-85), whose stories, however violent or tragic, provide a navigable narrative track through the deserts of a vast annihilationist eternity.

Life learns from art the trick of making closure a triumph rather than a defeat. Hieronimo's life is done when his play is, his play when his task is, his task when revenge has symbolically reversed the death that deprived him of immortality by killing his only offspring. Hieronimo then violently seeks his own quietus by biting off his tongue, and by refusing to write anything but his own death scene, to assure that the rest will indeed be silence. The burden of closure thus passes to the audience—specifically, to the fathers of the new victims, who desperately seek a new revenge plot. The playing out of poetic justice is Hieronimo's equivalent of Jonson's epitaph "On My First Son," a "best piece of poetrie" that serves as a metonymic surrogate for the lost life it seeks forlornly to reconstruct.[11] Hieronimo is quite willing to die for his art, even without the proper burial craved by Don Andrea:

> If destiny deny thee life, Hieronimo,
> Yet shalt thou be assured of a tomb:
> If neither, yet let this thy comfort be,
> Heaven covereth him that hath no burial.
> And to conclude, I will revenge his death!

> (3.13.16-20)

Revenge, and the model of justice it artfully proposes, is a satisfactory alternative to the other rituals by which death and mourning—not merely the corpse—are safely contained.

Where revenge proves impossible, however, it becomes dangerously difficult to disguise mortality in the black robes of justice. That way madness lies, roused by the pain of futility in its most extreme form:

HIERONIMO:

> Justice, O justice! O my son, my son,
> My son, whom naught can ransom or redeem!

LORENZO:

> Hieronimo, you are not well-advis'd.

HIERONIMO:

> Away Lorenzo, hinder me no more,
> For thou hast made me bankrupt of my bliss.
> Give me my son! You shall not ransom him.
> Away! I'll rip the bowels of the earth
> [*He diggeth with his dagger*]
> And ferry over to th'Elysian plains,
> And bring my son to show his deadly wounds.

> (3.12.65-73)

It is simply too far to dig; Hieronimo can try to retrieve Horatio with that dagger, but only symbolically, through the wounds of Lorenzo, who thus must ransom Horatio after all. Hieronimo will eventually enact precisely this deadly substitution in the masque, by making Lorenzo take Horatio's role in the displaced re-enactment of Horatio's murder.

Horatio's parents make gestures of desperate protest comparable to the devastation Tamburlaine visits on the landscape for the death of Zenocrate, and to King Lear's anguished questioning over the body of Cordelia: "Why should a dog, a horse, a rat, have life, / And thou no breath at all?" (5.3.307-8). Kyd momentarily allows Isabella a consoling vision of her son in bliss—"To heaven, ay, there sits my Horatio, / Back'd with a troop of fiery cherubins" (3.8.17-18)—but this vision is surrounded with outbursts of evasive madness, as if perhaps the Christian response to death were just one more. She chops down the tree where her son was hanged, as if in symbolic retribution against "that Forbidden Tree, whose mortal taste / Brought death into the world" (*Paradise Lost,* I, 2-3). Hieronimo exclaims that

> The blust'ring winds, conspiring with my words,
> At my lament have mov'd the leaveless trees,
> Disrob'd the meadows of their flower'd green,
> Made mountains marsh with spring-tides of my tears,
> And broken through the brazen gates of hell.

> (3.7.5-9)

Such self-conscious enforcement of the pathetic fallacy encourages us to recognize the way we insist on, even hallucinate, the importance of our individual lives, clinging to a Ptolemaic astronomy of the domestic sphere. Like Don Andrea (and like John Donne, I will argue), we would far rather be at war with our universe than ignored by it. If the supposition that Elizabethans all complacently assumed a benevolently ordered universe needs any further refutation, here are characters of considerable appeal who plainly—and vengefully—recognize Mother Nature as an indiscriminate killer. To accuse indifferent biology of complicity in murder is (as Starbuck warns Ahab in *Moby-Dick*) at once an utter absurdity and a dangerous insight. Such an accusation could be framed only by a mind that—having lost the life it cares about most—needs death to seem explicable even more desperately than it needs death to seem contingent.

After struggling vainly to revive his murdered son with accusatory and consolatory mythologies, Hieronimo contemplates suicide (2.5.17-23-67). In the next act, he tosses aside the dagger and halter as instruments of self-destruction, only to take them immediately up again as weapons against Horatio's killers (3.12.19-21). Here as in *Hamlet,* suicide seems a plausible alternative to revenge because each offers reunion, either by joining the deceased in death or by incorporating his death as a living cause. In one of his final speeches, Hieronimo insists that, by his bloody actions, he has "offered to my son . . . my life" (4.4.159-60), as if somehow by being willing to die in this revenge, he could invest his vitality in his son's body as well as his son's cause.[12]

Amid all the windings of the plot and the whirling words, Hieronimo's speeches always return us to the simple recognitions at the core of tragedy through many of its historical phases: the brutal fact of death that awaits men and women, for all their love and imagination; and the futility of hoping to alter or transcend it through love, honor, progeny, justice, art, or even religion. This thematic focus, more deeply than the shared points of plot, is what *The Spanish Tragedy* bequeaths to Shakespeare's *Hamlet*. It is also a signature concern of Renaissance culture in general, as the relentlessness of physical mortality (and its avatars in error, mutability, and betrayal) erased each dreamer of glory, each aspiringly fashioned self.

THE BLOODY SCARF: A FLAG OF IMMORTALITY

From the opening lines, *The Spanish Tragedy* defines its story as a struggle between mortality and personal identity:

> When this eternal substance of my soul
> Did live imprison'd in my wanton flesh,
> Each in their function serving other's need,
> I was a courtier in the Spanish Court.
> My name was Don Andrea. . . .

> (1.1.1-5)

The principal action of the play that follows is violent murder, and its leading motive is revenge, but its primary psychological condition is mourning. The Viceroy mourns once for Bel-imperia and twice (once prematurely, later correctly) for Balthazar. Bel-imperia, Horatio, and Don Andrea himself mourn for Don Andrea; Don Andrea, Bel-imperia, Isabella, and Hieronimo mourn for Horatio; the Painter and the Senex mourn for their sons; the King mourns for his son, Lorenzo, and his borther, Castile. The resulting violence offers the audience an equivocal lesson about resisting the idea of annihilation—instructions for writing on that blankness. Hieronimo's final revenge allows the audience to participate in powerful action on behalf of the deceased; it also reminds the audience that such actions must be performed on the level of fantasy, whether by viewing a play like *The Spanish Tragedy,* or by performing some other metonymous act, some other act of substitution, upon one's own psychic stage.

After discovering and recovering Andrea's corpse, Horatio

> dew'd him with my tears,
> And sigh'd and sorrow'd as became a friend.

> But neither friendly sorrow, sighs nor tears,
> Could win pale death from his usurped right.
> Yet this I did, and less I could not do,
> I saw him honour'd with due funeral:
> This scarf I pluck'd from off his liveless arm,
> And wear it in remembrance of my friend.

> (1.4.36-43)

When Horatio determines to save something about Don Andrea, he settles on this bloody scarf; when Hieronimo memorializes Horatio, he seizes on the same artifact. The exchanges of this token—a sort of flag of the Human Immortality Party—reflect the way we pass along the painful legacy of love for mortal beings, the way each human life becomes devoted to the preservation of another, in an essentially circular argument of life-justification. "Our lives we borrow from each other," writes the atheistical Lucretius in a passage quoted by Montaigne, "And men like runners pass along the torch of life."[13]

By wearing this bright scarf in defiance of "pale death," Horatio becomes the reincarnation as well as the savior of Don Andrea—so thoroughly, in fact, that Bel-imperia becomes his lover, as she was Don Andrea's, to whom she originally gave the scarf. It is the visible legacy of their original erotic sin, re-enacted when her allure again brings death into the garden in 2.4. Her efforts to seize immortality by an infinite regress of substitutions (falling in love with Horatio in recompense for his love for her previous love) necessarily lead to a replication of death as well:

> how can love find harbour in my breast,
> Till I revenge the death of my beloved?
> Yes, second love shall further my revenge.
> I'll love Horatio, my Andrea's friend. . . .

> (1.4.64-67)

Bel-imperia is instinctively devoted to the power of metonymy. In both love and battle—a pairing prominent throughout the play—she can undo Don Andrea's deadly defeat by construing Horatio as his resurrected alter ego. Her assertion that she "So lov'd his life, as still I wish their deaths" betrays an assumption that the killing of his killers will somehow revive Don Andrea (4.1.22).

If substitution can promise a kind of immortality, if metonymy as a trope promises that there is something beyond the immediate identity to be signified, these symbolic tactics (like Derridean signifiers) also threaten to reveal the abysmal absences they serve to fill. Social replacements and generational replications are the only hope for sustaining human life, yet they are also the plainest reminders of human death. Each saving substitution in *The Spanish Tragedy* has a dark side. In resurrecting Don Andrea, whom Balthazar killed, Horatio necessarily undertakes the killing of Balthazar. Long before Balthazar actually dies, he perceives Horatio as his "destin'd plague," a mortal enemy threatening not only his immediate survival, but also his hopes for transcending death through honor or dynastic procreation:[14]

> by those wounds he forced me to yield,
> And by my yielding I became his slave.
> Now in his mouth he carries pleasing words,
> Which . . .
>
> in her heart set him where I should stand.
> Thus hath he ta'en my body by his force,
> And now by sleight would captivate my soul
>
> (2.1.118-31)

Bel-imperia's "favor must be won by [Horatio's] remove," Lorenzo tells Balthazar, and therefore Balthazar must seek "revenge." The markers change, but the transaction remains remarkably similar: "revenge" incorporates all the ways of retrieving one's immortality from whoever seems to have stolen it. This is particularly true in a scarcity economy such as *The Spanish Tragedy* depicts, where there is only one royal Balthazar to be claimed as a prisoner and only one royal Bel-imperia to be married, where parents have only a single son to carry their legacies into the future—and where each person has only one life to lose, a life that can often be saved only by taking someone else's.

This zero-sum game—something like musical chairs—connects the Portuguese subplot to the main plot. Like aristocrats in time of war, characters who wish to survive in revenge-tragedy must commonly induce someone to die in their place. Revenge stands in for salvation: an enemy's death becomes a miraculous escape from one's own mortality. "If Balthazar be dead, [Alexandro] shall not live," declares the Viceroy (1.3.91). Once Balthazar is revealed to be alive after all, the very ropes that were to hold Alexandro for execution are unwrapped and put around Villuppo, who had plotted Alexandro's death.

THE EMPTY BOX: A TERMINAL BETRAYAL

The master version of this pattern of substitution in Renaissance culture is Christ's willingness to die in order to redeem humanity from its mortal failings. In Pedringano's execution, even this transcendent instance of surrogacy comes under cynical interrogation. Lorenzo invokes the basic principles of immortality-by-metonymy to provoke Pedringano to murder Serberine: "For die he must, if we do mean to live."[15] When Pedringano is condemned for this murder; Lorenzo falsely promises a last-minute pardon to guarantee that his own complicity will not be revealed. Like Horatio's martyrdom on a special tree (after harrowing hell to redeem Don Andrea), this execution awkwardly recalls Christ mounted and mocked on the cross. Indeed,

Pedringano dies wondering why his lord has forsaken him, haunted by that lord's false promise that faith will disarm mortality. The stratagem by which Lorenzo keeps Pedringano silent about their conspiracy right up to the instant of that hanging bears disquieting resemblances to the entire Christian strategy of consolation. Like an Elizabethan clergyman, Lorenzo's messenger-boy is not exactly required to lie about these glad tidings, only to take their substance and truth on pure faith, and to urge Pedringano to do the same:

> Bid him not doubt of his delivery.
> Tell him his pardon is already sign'd,
> And thereon bid him boldly be resolv'd:
> For were he ready to be turned off
> (As 'tis my will the uttermost be tried),
> Thou with his pardon shalt attend him still:
> Show him this box, tell him his pardon's in't,
> But open't not, and if thou lov'st thy life.
>
> (3.4.66-73)

The boy—like a Shakespearean clown, assigned to carry the grimmest message in the lightest character, the better to ambush the audience and protect the playwright—cannot resist knowledge of this "forbidden" treasure. What he discovers is that the officially proffered hopes of salvation lack any real basis: "By my bare honesty, here's nothing but the bare empty box" (3.5.6-7). In a twist on St. Paul's formula, the absent letter kills, but by the time a man realizes he has been betrayed, his voice has been strangled and can never warn others of the treachery in high places. As the boy observes, it is a cruel if practical joke to give a condemned man such absurd encouragement. The last laugh is on Pedringano—unless it is on us. "Forgive, O Lord, my little jokes on Thee," writes Robert Frost, "And I'll forgive Thy great big one on me."[16]

Lorenzo's message to Pedringano is particularly suggestive in view of the common Elizabethan characterizations of Christ's sacrifice as a pardon already written that will deliver us from the devil at the uttermost. John Donne concludes a Holy Sonnet with the assurance than an inner faith in the Lord's forgiveness is "as good / As if thou'hadst sealed my pardon, with thy blood"; but in the world of *The Spanish Tragedy* what is written in blood is instead the provocation to revenge, as in Bel-imperia's desperate letter. Pedringano's pardon—and perhaps Christ's—is writ in water. As mortal beings, we all stand on a gallows—"The whole world is but a Cart of condemned persons," as a 1630 tract put it[17]—but (lest we complain) we are told that the magic box to which the hierophant points (with a reassuring smile) holds the imminent pardon promised by our all-powerful intercessor. Like the Lord in the twenty-third Psalm, Lorenzo assures Pedringano that, even in the shadow of death, "He shall not want" (3.4.75).

Kyd seems to highlight the theological parallel by having the hangman warn Pedringano to "hearken to your soul's health," and having Pedringano reply that what "is good for the body is likewise good for the soul: and it may be, in that box is balm for both" (3.6.75-78). Pedringano's jeering from the gallows at his tormentors may be cynical villainy, but it is disquietingly similar to the bravado of the real-life heroes of *The Book of Martyrs,* vaunting their trust in their providential Lord as they faced their own executioners, often clinging to a Bible supposed to hold the ultimate saving Word. At the notorious execution of Bishop Hooper, "When he came to the place appointed where he should die, he smilingly beheld the stake . . . a box was brought and laid before him upon a stool, with his pardon from the queen, if he would turn."[18] In this context, a merely empty box can be more terrifying than Pandora's overflowing one, as annihilation can be more terrifying than damnation.

It is ominous that Lorenzo (and Kyd) can elide the two levels so easily: that a ruthless death-sentence can sound so much like a promise of perfect redemption, and that a bizarre Machiavellian scene at the gallows can sound so much like the standard Christian deathbed scene. This would of course have been an unusual and dangerous perspective for a playwright to express, even in such indirect terms, and even after artificially displacing his story into a pagan society. Remember, however, that "vile hereticall Conceiptes denyinge the deity of Jhesus Christe our Saviour" were "fownd emongst the papers of Thos Kydd prisoner" in 1593;[19] and that doubting the divinity of the Son could easily lead to doubts about the promises of salvation and resurrection that depend so heavily on the New Testament. Though ownership of these papers is commonly attributed to Christopher Marlowe, remember also that it was Kyd himself who, facing torture, initiated that attribution. The passing of the blame onto a recently deceased associate was predictable whether or not it was true. The two men wrote in the same room, and perhaps they wrote in the same skeptical spirit as well.[20]

THE STATE OF NATURE: A TYRANNY IN PALIMPSEST

Lorenzo's ploy can be read as a local political reference rather than as a grand theological allegory: editors commonly cite its resemblance to a trick played by the Earl of Leicester on an underling. Perhaps we can swallow the topical reference and still have our theological cake by recognizing that, in *The Spanish Tragedy* as in several other compelling Renaissance tragedies, the depredations of social hierarchy partly symbolize the equally unjust depredations of an uncaring material universe, where again the promise of a providential lord proves a hollow fiction. Only in the realm of fantasy—Hieronimo's masque, Kyd's play—can personal will reassert any control, and register any meaningful protest against either kind of tyranny.

Current critical orthodoxies make sexual and political subtexts the heart and soul of Renaissance drama; but for all its cynical politics, sexual and otherwise, *The Spanish Tragedy* seems as deeply concerned with the construal of death as with the constructions of social hierarchy. Political control proves hollow: a false witness named Villuppo can easily damage royal honor and royal hopes, and an old madman named Hieronimo can erase two dynasties in a moment. Renaissance societies commonly generated a decorous notion that mortality is at the service of political authority, but the fictionality of that notion is all too clearly on display in *The Spanish Tragedy*—as it is in *The Revenger's Tragedy,* where the corrupt sovereign brushes aside all those who wish him extremely long life, favoring only the ultimate sycophant who wishes he may never die at all. In the opening act of *The Spanish Tragedy,* Hieronimo says of his newly lionized son, "Long may he live to serve my sovereign liege, / And soon decay unless he serve my liege"; the King replies, "Nor thou nor he shall die without reward" (1.2.98-100), as if (by the politically useful formula) divine redemption were virtually indistinguishable from royal approval. Death again appears to be under official command when the Viceroy declares he is "Procrastinating Alexandro's death" by not executing him more promptly (3.1.28). Really, of course, it is only a question of how much he will *accelerate* that death; delaying it even a day was proverbially beyond the power even of kings. Monarchs are finally only human, and in lamenting the "Infortunate condition of kings" that led to his son's death, the Viceroy closely echoes countless commentaries on the mortal human condition in general: "ever subject to the wheel of chance: / And at our highest never joy we so, / As we both doubt and dread our overthrow" (3.1.1-7). Again the play's political commentary lapses into a meditation on mortality.

Perhaps, then, the corrupt power of the state, concerned with its own hierarchies and their maintenance through dynastic marriage, symbolizes the tyranny of natural mutability that imposes death on behalf of the same generational principle. The dynamic equilibrium of the social system, as it coldly overrules personal desire, proves as dismissive of humane concerns as the dynamic equilibrium of generational biology; the same system that forces Bel-imperia to marry according to the patriarchal suffix of her name also necessitates the murder of Horatio. Death is a decree of the seasonal cycle: Hieronimo predicts that his powerful enemies, "as a wintry storm upon a plain, / Will bear me down with their nobility" (3.13.37-38). From this perspective, natural order is a bureaucracy that regularly performs villainies lacking even the perverse appeal of radical selfishness or sadism—as if the princes in *Richard III* had died from a common typhus instead of an extraordinary tyrant.

If the deceits and oppressions of civil government represent metonymically the failures of divine providence, then there is little point waiting around for either kind of authority to provide satisfactory justice. Presumably that is why the protagonists of Renaissance blood-revenge defy the secular government (by appropriating its juridical functions) at the same time that they abrogate (by appropriating) God's *vindicta mihi*. Hieronimo complains that his

> restless passions,
> That winged mount, and, hovering in the air,
> Beat at the windows of the brightest heavens,
> Soliciting for justice and revenge:
> But they are plac'd in those empyreal heights
> Where, countermur'd with walls of diamond,
> I find the place impregnable, and they
> Resist my woes, and give my words no way.
>
> (3.7.11-18)

His restlessness cannot overcome the silence that stands between us and heaven. To get there he must create his Tower of Babel out of the multilingual revenge-masque—and even if he succeeds, heaven seems likely to prove yet another empty box, a mystification of the silent grave.

Hieronimo's play-within-the-play-within-the-play represents both the triumph and the failure of the revenge genre. Its enactment of justice combines and explicates the consolatory and vengeful functions of substitution, but the body-strewn stage starkly refutes any supposition that life has truly been redeemed. Death may still be isolated as the product of aberrant violence, but it has begun escaping from the metadramatic frame into Hieronimo's audience, and therefore warns Kyd's audience that drama is no longer a safe container for their mortal fears or for the aggressions those fears commonly produce:

> Marry, this follows for Hieronimo:
> Here break we off our sundry languages
> And thus conclude I in our vulgar tongue.
> Haply you think, but bootless are your thoughts,
> That this is fabulously counterfeit,
> And that we do as all tragedians do:
> To die today, for fashioning our scene,
> The death of Ajax or some Roman peer,
> And in a minute starting up again,
> Revive to please tomorrow's audience.
> No, princes, know I am Hieronimo,
> The hopeless father of a hapless son,
> Whose tongue is tun'd to tell his latest tale,
> Not to excuse gross errors in the play.
> I see your looks urge instance of these words,
> Behold the reason urging me to this: [*Shows his dead son*]
> See here my show, look on this spectacle:
> Here lay my hope, and here my hope hath end.
>
> (4.4.73-90)

As the elaborate multilingual distancing of the inner-most play falls away into the "bare honesty" of plain English, the mechanisms of cultural denial collapse under the weight of corpses. As Renaissance *memento mori* tracts sometimes warned, death comes speaking in the plainest vernacular, for all the courtier's flourishes of exotic language.

The box holding the secrets of life and death, horribly empty at Pedringano's execution, is now horribly full; and it looks more like a tomb than a stage. Hieronimo explicitly refuses the role of epilogue as dramatic apologist, insisting instead that he is a real man, and a dying one. But he thereby assumes the other standard role of an epilogue, obliterating the boundary between the characters and the audience. His son has been sent, "In black dark night, to pale dim cruel death" (4.4.107), and no one in the audience can hope to escape that sort of erasure. The literary conventions only masked temporarily the actual deaths occurring all around us. Our dismaying position resembles that of Balthazar when Bel-imperia literalizes the Petrarchan metaphor of their courtship in this masque by killing him in earnest. The invasion of reality into Hieronimo's fiction attacks our mythology of denial. Kyd exploits our willing suspension of disbelief in the drama in order to compromise our resolute suspension of belief in mortality. The demystification, the collapse of the metadrama, is itself a danger, because it revives the recognition of our mortal destiny that had been systematically repressed through drama, role-playing, metonymy, substitution. Hieronimo suggests that the royal families should not have mocked his apparent madness before they realized that they, too, would go mad if forced to confront the death of their own kind, of their own immortalizing hopes. Clearly we are next—next for the madhouse, if we fully absorb the implication that we are next for the tomb and oblivion.

Though Revenge does seem to revive the specter of Don Andrea, all it can promise, in the play's final words, is an "endless tragedy." There seems to be no higher level, no divine comedy, to which this resolution releases him;[21] only by a kind of destructive repetition-compulsion can he keep from disappearing. In this Don Andrea suffers the annihilation-anxiety common to many dramatic characters, who must relive their story endlessly in order to exist at all;[22] his position here as a sort of *epi*-epilogue reinforces that impression. The story of Hamlet will suggest that this metatheatrical terror has a parallel in the world outside the theater, a world that composes endless cycles of tragic violence to avoid facing unaccommodated death. By the time Hamlet rests in silence (1601) the ghost has become a skull, and by the beginning of *The Revenger's Tragedy* (1607) the genre has begun to grin jeeringly at its own quest for metonymic consolations, for figurative transformations of the plain facts of death.

The performance of revenge as a play-within-the-play in *The Spanish Tragedy* (as in *Hamlet* and *The*

Revenger's Tragedy) may constitute an acknowledgment that such satisfactions are possible only at the level of fantasy, where actors stand in for real people and geopolitical treachery stands in for the frustrations of ordinary life. At an aesthetic distance, Hieronimo's final massacre becomes an elaborate sacrifice that exorcises demons of helplessness and perceived injustice, demons so common in the human animal, so heightened in the aspiring minds of the Renaissance, and so focused in the fierce economies of Elizabethan England and Elizabeth's court.

Hieronimo finally dispels the aesthetic distance to complain of the forces that have truly killed his son, and justify his revenge. Countless Elizabethans, bereaved by war, poverty, or religious persecution, could have conceived a similar complaint against their monarch; **The Spanish Tragedy** allows them to witness and approve an extreme act of treason that follows naturally, by the logic of revenge, from that complaint. It allows them an extreme blasphemy, too: disguised as a complaint about violence, developing into a complaint about injustice, it is ultimately a complaint about death itself, in all its forms. If the monarch fails to respond, then we may find ourselves dreaming of killing his only begotten son in compensation.[23]

Notes

1. Peter Sacks, "Where Words Prevail Not," *ELH,* 49 (1982), p. 579, offers a brilliant analysis of this transaction. He quotes Durkheim's observation in *The Elementary Forms of Religious Life* that "If every death is attributed to some magic charm, and for this reason it is believed that the dead man ought to be avenged, it is because men must find a victim at any price, upon whom the collective pain and anger may be discharged." Sacks adds that "retribution is sought regardless of whether or not the deceased has been murdered. Thus seen, revenge is a crucial marshalling of anger, but more significantly, an action in which the survivor assumes *for himself* the power that has bereaved him. It is perhaps in this sense that Bacon wrote 'Revenge conquers Death'"; see "Of Unity in Religion," in *The Works of Francis Bacon* (London: C. & J. Rivington, 1826), II, 247. What I would further derive from Durkheim's observation, and add to Sacks's analysis of the drama, is that a valuable supplementary consolation arises from believing that, without murder, there would be no death. This, too, would explain the need for a scapegoat.

2. Cf. Samuel Daniel's 1603 *Panegyrike Congratulatory* on James I's memorial to his executed mother: "he lookes thereon / With th'eye of griefe, not wrath, t'avenge the same, / Since th' Authors are extinct that caus'd that shame" (stanza 31).

3. Helen Gardner, *The Business of Criticism* (Oxford: Clarendon Press, 1959), p. 41.

4. J. R. Mulryne, ed., *The Spanish Tragedy,* New Mermaids ed. (New York: W. W. Norton, 1987), p. xxiv.

5. Compare Browne, p. 141: "*Cain* was not therefore the first murtherer, but *Adam,* who brought in death; whereof hee beheld the practise and example in his owne sonne *Abel,* and saw that verified in the experience of another; which faith could not perswade him in the Theory of himselfe." Browne thus establishes himself as an early critic of the mechanisms of denial, both at the cultural level of mythmaking and at the individual level of narcissistic psychological evasion. Browne's Adam obeys the precept stated by Sigmund Freud in his "Thoughts for the Times on War and Death," *Complete Psychological Works,* Standard ed., trans. James Strachey (London: Hogarth Press), XIV, 289, that we never really believe ourselves to be mortal. Cf. Browne's *Pseudodoxia Epidemica,* p. 172, on Adam and Eve's disbelief in their own mortality.

6. Compare Browne's *Hydriotaphia,* p. 306:

   If they dyed by violent hands, and were thrust into their Urnes, these bones become considerable, and some old Philosophers would honour them, whose souls they conceived most pure, which were thus snatched from their bodies; and to retain a stranger propension unto them: whereas they weariedly left a languishing corps, and with faint desires of reunion. If they fell by long and aged decay, yet wrapt up in the bundle of time, they fall into indistinction, and make but one blot with Infants.

7. Alexander Ross, *Mystagogus Poeticus* (London, 1648), p. 69, speculates that "Christ is truly *Ceres*; which having lost mankinde . . . went down to Hell, and rescued us from thence." He later speculates that Pluto became god of the underworld because he invented the custom of burial (p. 364). On etymological associations between "Proserpine" and "serpent," see Vincenzo Cartari, *The Fountaine of Ancient Fiction* (London, 1599).

8. See Philip Edwards, "Thrusting Elysium into Hell," in *Elizabethan Theatre XI,* ed. A. L. Magnuson and C. E. McGee (Ontario: P. D. Meaney, 1990), which speculates incisively about this play's blasphemous undertones, and finds it "remarkable that Thomas Kyd should provide a pagan context for his story of a modern Christian Spain" (p. 117). As in Shakespeare's *King Lear* (though less subtly), this displacement is intermittently compromised to allow a subversive commentary on the Christian promise of salvation.

9. Freud, XIV, 290-1, notes our tendency "to lay stress on the fortuitous causation of the death," but also that, in war, "the accumulation of death puts an end to the impression of chance."

10. Eamon Duffy, *The Stripping of the Altars* (New Haven: Yale University Press, 1992), p. 350; Theodore Spencer, *Death and Elizabethan Tragedy* (Cambridge: Harvard University Press, 1936), p. 135.

11. When Ben Jonson wrote additions to the play, he characteristically emphasized the failure of art to replace a lost son. As Jonson attempts to identify with his buried son in that poetic epitaph, so Hieronimo attempts to mirror his son's fate of death by hanging—hardly the most efficient choice under the circumstances.

12. The Viceroy will make very much the same offer, claiming that his death in war would somehow have been more "natural" than his son's. When the Viceroy first supposes his son is dead, he also echoes the annihilationist model of death, attributing blindness and deafness to the agency of mortality (here, Fortune), and striving to sustain a connection to his son by plunging himself into essential darkness and silence: "Fortune is blind and sees not my deserts, / So is she deaf and hears not my laments" (1.2.23-24).

13. Michel de Montaigne, "That to philosophize is to learn to die," in *The Complete Essays of Montaigne,* trans. Donald M. Frame (Stanford: Stanford University Press, 1965), p. 65.

14. Balthazar's pride is injured, but so, more importantly, is his narcissism. When he confronts evidence that Bel-imperia is giving her love to Horatio instead, he pleads for all the correlative insensibilities of annihilationist death—sleep, blindness, deafness—to spare himself from recognizing the defeat of his ultimate immortality-strategy:

> O sleep mine eyes, see not my love profan'd;
> Be deaf my ears, hear not my discontent,
> Die heart, another joys what thou deserv'st.

Lorenzo offers the alternative solution to this problem, using revenge to undo all these little deaths, all these foreshocks of oblivion, including dishonor and failed love as well as sensory deprivation:

> Watch still mine eyes, to see this love disjoin'd;
> Hear still mine ears, to hear them both lament,
> Live, heart to joy at fond Horatio's fall.

(2.2.18-23)

15. Later Lorenzo asks, "Thou art assur'd that thou sawest [Pedringano] dead?" and the Page replies, "Or else, my lord, I live not" (3.10.2-3).

16. *The Poetry of Robert Frost,* ed. E. C. Latham (New York: Holt Rinehart, 1969), p. 428.

17. I. C., *A Handkercher for Parents Wet Eyes* (London, 1630), p. 21—a remarkably Existentialist metaphor for a Renaissance writer.

18. John Foxe, *Fox's Book of Martyrs,* ed. William Forbush (Philadelphia: John C. Winston, 1926), pp. 214-15; on the martyrs' trust that their "salvation is already sealed in heaven," see p. 175.

19. Quoted in Arthur Freeman, *Thomas Kyd: Facts and Problems* (London: Oxford University Press, 1967), p. 26.

20. The Introduction to Edwards's edition of the play asserts that "Marlowe never wrote a less Christian play than *The Spanish Tragedy*" (p. lii).

21. Hieronimo does ascend to the lovers' branch of heaven, but that version of redemption only serves to identify his escape as a metaphor for the consolation of progeny he was so desperate to recover.

22. See Stephen Greenblatt's insightful explication of the compulsive repetitions by which Marlowe's characters metadramatically defend their identities; *Renaissance Self-Fashioning* (Chicago: University of Chicago Press, 1980), p. 200. For a comparable infernal metadramatic ending, see *Lust's Dominion* (1600), ed. J. Le Gay Brereton (Louvain: Uystpruyst, 1931), lines 3793-94, where the dying Eleazar promises to "out-act you all in perfect villany" when he arrives in hell.

23. Perhaps the blasphemous implication that Hieronimo is punishing God (in kind) for death helps to explain the fascination his story held for an Elizabethan culture haunted by circumambient death and unstable theology. After identifying with various lesser bereaved fathers, Hieronimo appears to identify with the paternal deity. In accusing the men who hung his son on a tree to die, he sounds strangely like an angry Calvinist God condemning Adam for corrupting the garden, leading to Cain's murder of his brother and humankind's killing of Christ as their ransom:

> They did what heaven unpunish'd would not leave.
> O false Lorenzo, are these thy flattering looks?
> Is this the honour that thou didst my son?
> And Balthazar, bane to thy soul and me,
> Was this the ransom he reserv'd thee for?
> Woe to the cause of these constrained wars,
> Woe to thy baseness and captivity,
> Woe to thy birth, thy body and thy soul,
> Thy cursed father, and thy conquered self!
> And bann'd with bitter execrations be
> The day and place where he did pity thee!
> But wherefore waste I mine unfruitful words,
> When naught but blood will satisfy my woes?

(3.7.56-68)

From the erotic garden to the tree of martyrdom, from procreation to blood-revenge, we cannot seize life without soliciting death. Neither the father's law of talionic punishment nor the son's law of redemptive sacrifice provide reliable answers to the problem of mortality. William Empson may be wrong in defining Christianity as a religion of torture, but it certainly seems like a religion of revenge; see *Milton's God,* revised and expanded ed. (Cambridge: Cambridge University Press, 1981), pp. 229-77. (René Girard would argue that Christianity is instead the sole cure for revenge.) Kyd invests his play with a remarkable level of dramatic tension by simultaneously destabilizing the revenge mytheme and the Christian story, threatening to expose them as merely defensive constructions, and to plunge the culture into the abyss of a renewed mortality-crisis. Partaking of that endless fall, that "endless tragedy," the audience may justly fear sharing Hieronimo's madness and despair, as well as his silent death.

Works Cited

EDITIONS

Kyd, Thomas. *The Spanish Tragedy.* Edited by Philip Edwards. *The Revels Plays.* London: Methuen, 1959.

Shakespeare, William. *The Riverside Shakespeare.* Edited by G. B. Evans et al. Boston: Houghton Mifflin, 1974.

BIBLIOGRAPHY

C., I. *A Handkercher for Parents Wet Eyes.* London, 1630.

Cartari, Vincenzo. *The Fountaine of Ancient Fiction.* London, 1599.

Daniel, Samuel. *A Panegyrike Congratulatory.* 1603.

Duffy, Eamon. *The Stripping of the Altars: Traditional Religion in England, 1400-1580.* New Haven: Yale University Press, 1992.

Edwards, Philip. "Thrusting Elysium into Hell: The Originality of *The Spanish Tragedy.*" In *Elizabethan Theatre XI.* Edited by A. L. Magnuson and C. E. McGee. Ontario: P. D. Meaney, 1990.

Empson, William. *Milton's God.* Revised and Expanded Edition. Cambridge: Cambridge University Press, 1981.

Fox[e], John. *Fox's Book of Martyrs.* Edited by William Forbush. Philadelphia: John C. Winston, 1926.

Freeman, Arthur. *Thomas Kyd: Facts and Problems.* London: Oxford University Press, 1967.

Freud, Sigmund. *Complete Psychological Works.* Standard Edition. Translated by James Strachey. In 24 volumes. London: Hogarth Press, 1953-74.

Greenblatt, Stephen. *Renaissance Self-Fashioning: From More to Shakespeare.* Chicago: University of Chicago Press, 1980.

Kyd, Thomas. *The Spanish Tragedy.* New Mermaids Edition. Edited by J. R. Mulryne. New York: W. W. Norton, 1987.

Lust's Dominion. 1600. Edited by J. Le Gay Brereton. Louvain: Uystpruyst, 1931.

Montaigne, Michel de. *The Complete Essays of Montaigne.* Edited and translated by Donald M. Frame. Stanford: Stanford University Press, 1965.

Ross, Alexander. *Mystagogus Poeticus.* London, 1648.

Sacks, Peter. "Where Words Prevail Not." *ELH* 49 (1982): 576-601.

Spencer, Theodore. *Death and Elizabethan Tragedy: A Study of Convention and Opinion in the Elizabethan Drama.* Cambridge: Harvard University Press, 1936.

Carla Mazzio (essay date spring 1998)

SOURCE: Mazzio, Carla. "Staging the Vernacular: Language and Nation in Thomas Kyd's *The Spanish Tragedy.*" *Studies in English Literature 1500-1900* 38, no. 2 (spring 1998): 207-32.

[*In the following essay, Mazzio argues that the heterogeneous language used in Kyd's* The Spanish Tragedy *complicates interpretations of the play as a nationalist work.*]

> The familiar physiognomy of a word, the feeling that it has taken up its meaning into itself, that it is an actual likeness of its meaning—there could be human beings to whom all this was alien.
>
> —Ludwig Wittgenstein, *Philosophical Investigations*

> Now to express the rupture of my part
> First take my tongue, and afterward my heart.
>
> —Thomas Kyd, ***The Spanish Tragedy***

In his preface to *A Table Alphabeticall* (1604), Robert Cawdrey imagines the discomfort engendered by the English language in strangely familial terms: "Some men seek so far for outlandish English, that they forget altogether their mothers' language, so that if some of their mothers were alive, they were not able to tell, or understand what they say."[1] Cawdrey's vision of the alienation of a native speaker from his own "mother" underlines a common nervousness about the seemingly unnatural and elusive status of the vernacular.[2] The influx of thousands of new words from Latin, Greek, French, Spanish, and Italian in the sixteenth century led to extensive debates about the presence of foreign and "barbaric" elements within the national vocabulary. While some early modern writers argued that enrichment was civilizing and others that it was vulgarizing, all recognized the essential "otherness" of the new terms that seemed to be invading the English language. "Farre feete words," writes Sir Philip Sidney, "[that] may seem Monsters . . . must seeme straungers to any poore English man."[3] And some people, writes Edward Phillips, "if they spy but a hard word, are as much amazed as if they had met with a Hobgoblin."[4] Whether representations of the expanding vernacular are fused with images of monsters, hobgoblins, or uncomprehending mothers, the range of responses to new words in early modern England dramatizes fears about linguistic, cultural, and national stability.[5]

The increasingly heterogeneous linguistic textures and forms of early modern English became a site for the articulation of anxieties about local and national forms of self-representation. Defenders of enrichment repeatedly depicted the expanding lexicon through images of family, nation, and state, arguing that alien terms, with habitual use, would soon seem to be related, "familiar," part of a naturalized racial and linguistic community. Richard Sherry, for example, notes how many strange and foreign words have been "made by continual vse, very familier to most men . . . *as if they had bene of oure owne natiue bloode*."[6] Similarly, in *The Elementarie* (1582), Richard Mulcaster encourages Englishmen to imagine foreign words "as the stranger denisons be to the lawes of our cuntrie."[7] He urges students to take pains to learn new words, linking linguistic borrowing to a kind of cultural imperialism: "[A foreign word] is a metaphor, a learned translation, remoued from where it is proper, into som such place where it is more properlie vsed . . . *And when the foren word hath yeilded it self, & is receiued into fauor, it is no more foren, tho of foren race, the propertie being altered*."[8] While strange words are just "metaphors," they are still imagined as words "of foren race" which need to be fundamentally "altered."[9]

The range of metaphors invoked in early modern discussions about the English language constantly registers a sense of anxiety about a national identity that is at once constituted and threatened by difference, a difference that in the minds of many signaled internal alienation and political chaos. The unprecedented number of foreign words entering English in the sixteenth century inspired Samuel Daniel to imagine foreign signifiers floating "without a Parliament, without any consent or allowance, establish[ing] themselves as Free-denizens in our language."[10] And in *Logonomia Anglica* (1619), Alexander Gill links lexical borrowing with cultural contamination, noting that the "purity of our tongue continues because . . . no dregs of foreign people have infected us."[11] In contrast, Mulcaster, a supporter of enrichment, imagines tongue-taming in terms of political conquest; considering the status of an alien word, he asks, "Is it a stranger? but no Turk. & tho it were an enemies word, yet good is worth the getting, . . . as well by speche of writers, as by spoill of soldiers."[12]

Whether alien linguistic signs were imagined to be invasive enemies or conquered outsiders, the discourse of inclusion and exclusion so common in the period emphasizes the paradox of a mother tongue that, in the words of Mulcaster, "semeth to haue two heds, the one homeborn, the other a stranger."[13] As Steven Mullaney has noted, in early modern England, the "voice of the Other, of the *barbaros*, sounded in the throat whenever the mother tongue was spoken; one's own tongue was strange yet familiar, a foreigner within, a quite literal internal *emigré*."[14] While the practice of borrowing was gradually (if reluctantly) accepted by most, the marked resistance to the linguistic "foreigner within" in a range of late-sixteenth- and early-seventeenth-century texts reflects a general nervousness about the implications of a nation inhabited by unfamiliar signs.[15] Thomas Dekker, for example, goes so far as to imagine the very voice of the Englishman as stolen property, for "all the parts hee playes are but con'd speeches stolne from others, whose voices and actions he counterfeites."[16] The concept of the emergent national tongue as "stolne" property surfaces again and again in early language debates, with George Puttenham, for example, accusing one writer of "pety *larceny* for pilfering other [French] mens devises from them and converting them to his own use."[17]

Indeed, the constellation of terms so often invoked in recent criticism to describe the symbolic economies of early modern England ("exchange," "circulation," "borrowing," "negotiation") tends to imply a condition of neutrality and reciprocity that, in most situations, was not possible. Although acts of cross-cultural "borrowing" were clearly integral to the production of early modern literature, language, and culture, they were less often imagined in terms of reciprocal relations or circulatory energies than in terms of either heroic conquests or criminal transgressions.[18] While the typology of Babel often figured into critiques of English, emphasizing the "curse" of confusion implicit in the heteroglossic national tongue,[19] tensions about the crimes of enrichment were particularly marked by the economic vocabulary of linguistic expansion. Associations between language and economics were commonplace in the period, and a discourse of theft and usury emerges in contemporary discussions of the English language.[20] While Thomas Carew terms linguistic borrowing a sheer "theft of . . . woordes,"[21] George Chapman suggests that "our countrey language were an usurer," associating enrichment and language *itself* with a famously unnatural and illicit form of breeding.[22]

Given the tensions about unnatural and uncontrolled forms of linguistic productivity, it is no surprise that the reproductive capacities of language become literalized and personified, and the "mother tongue" alternately associated with conditions of chastity and wantonness. While Sir John Cheke imagines the ideal mother to be virginal ("[O]ur own tung shold be written cleane and pure, unmixt and unmangeled with borowing of other tunges . . . For then doth our tongue naturallie and praisablie utter her meaning, when she bouroweth no counterfeitness of other tunges to attire her self withall"),[23] Thomas Tomkis stages the mother tongue as "a common whore [who] lets everyone lie with her."[24] The problematic ideal of the virginal mother who is always already contaminated emphasizes the paradox inherent in efforts to establish and stabilize a national tongue.

Nowhere are the associations between discursive and sexual promiscuity more explicitly dramatized than in Tomkis's 1607 *Lingua, or the Combat of the Tongue and the five Senses for Superiority*. In this play, the wanton and endlessly procreative Lingua (a personification of speech and the mother tongue herself) becomes the embodiment of the literal and metaphorical "internal *emigré*." As the one organ that can move in and out of the body, Lingua threatens conventional boundaries of inside and outside; she is unruly, transgressive, expansive, and alienating. Lingua, whose theatrical "part" positions her as the single most disruptive element within *Microcosmus*, goes to trial with a case for expanding the pentarchy of senses and becoming a *bona fide* "sense" herself.[25] At her trial, she begins flexing her muscle, peppering her prose with a range of foreign words:

> My Lord, though the *Imbecillitas* of my feeble sexe, might drawe me backe, from this Tribunall, with the *habenis* to wit *Timoris* and the *Catenis Pudoris*, notwithstanding beeing so fairely led on with the gratis [*epieikeia*] of your [*dikaiosones*]: Especially so aspremente spurd con gli sproni di necessita mia pungente, I will without the helpe of Orators, commit the *totam salutem* of my action to the *Volutabilitati* [*ton gynaikion logov*] which (avec votre bonne playseur) I will finish with more then *Laconica brevitate*.[26]

A far cry from Cheke's image of a mother tongue that could only "borrow with bashfulness,"[27] here Lingua is boldly and shamelessly appropriative, guilty of what Puttenham would call that "intollerable vice" of the English rhetorician (what "the Greekes call *Soraismus* . . . we may call the [*mingle mangle*] as when we make our speach or writinges of sundry languages using some Italian word, or French, or Spanish, or Dutch, or Scottish, not for the nonce or for any purpose . . . but ignorantly and affectedly").[28] Tomkis explicitly associates Lingua's dramatic self-display with enrichment itself as the character "Common Sense" responds, "What's this? Here's a Gallemaufry of speech indeed . . . I am perswaded to think these same language makers have the very quality of colde in their wit, that freezeth all

Heterogeneall languages together, congealing English Tynne, Graecian Gold, Romaine Latine all in a lumpe."[29] Similarly, the character "Memory" "remember[s] about the year 1602 many used this skew kind of language . . . Which in my opinion is not much unlike the man, *Platony* the Sonne of *Lagus*, King of *Agypt*, brought for a spectacle, halfe white half black."[30] Memory's likening of linguistic heteroglossia to a spectacle of racial indeterminacy dramatizes a nervousness about the symbolics of heterogeneity in this little world of man.[31]

Indeed, while linguistic forms are clearly imagined as sites of cultural and representational crises in early modern England, the problematics of hybridization emerge in discussions of topics ranging from race to fashion to translation. Lingua's garbled linguistic "lumpe," for example, is imaginatively translated by "Phantastes" into lumpish garb: "In my imagination [the lump is] like your Fantasticall Gulls Apparell, wearing a Spanish Felt, a French Doblet, a Granado Stocking, a Dutch Slop, an Italian Cloake, with a Welch . . . Jerkin."[32] The link between discourse and fashion as examples of unwanted spectacles of cultural fusion was commonplace in satires of self-representation in late-sixteenth- and early-seventeenth-century England. Just as the vernacular was often imagined to be a grotesque conglomeration of alien elements, so too was the Englishman envisioned as a veritable patchwork of garments and words filched from other countries: "[We] mocke everie Nation for keeping one fashion," writes Dekker in *The Seven Deadly Sins of London*, "yet steale patches from everie one of them, to peece out our pride, as now lauching stockes to them, because their cut so scurvily becomes us."[33]

If, as Richard Helgerson suggests, the successful formation of a nation-state depends upon the ability of "a political or cultural community [to] distinguish itself from its neighbors [and] also from its former self or selves," then the process of nation-formation would be especially vexed in Elizabethan England, where "neighbors" were often imagined to be a little too close to home.[34] While Mulcaster writes, "[W]e have our tung commonlie both stored and enlarged with our neighbours speches," John Lyly imagines the intermingling of lexical parts to be a condition for both national and theatrical representation: In the prologue to the play *Midas* (1592), he writes:

> *Trafficke and trauell hath wouen the nature of all Nations into ours and made this land like a Arras, full of deuise, which was Broadecloth . . . Time hath confounded our mindes, our mindes the matter; but all commeth to this passe, that what heretofore hath beene serued in seuerall dishes for a feast, is now minced in a charger for a Gallimaufrey. If wee present a minglemangle, our fault is to be excused, because the whole worlde is become an Hodge-podge.*[35]

Lyly imagines a nation which (like the theater itself) is caught in the paradox of defining itself in terms of, and as distinct from, its constituent parts. While "trafficke and trauell" has generated a "hodge-podge" of formal and cultural "matter," it has also "wouen the nature of all Nations into ours." The "mingle-mangle" of representational forms (a phrase which itself implies competing forces of integration and fragmentation) at once disrupts epistemological boundaries and constitutes the singular tapestry of the English nation.

These cultural fantasies of the dramatic interplay of lexical parts were particularly potent when dramatized on the early modern stage, not only because the theater—as a medium which demands the successful integration of parts—was structurally and conceptually analogous to the project of national language formation, but because the theater itself was often thought to be a space for the development of the English language. While Lyly's dramatic text claims to mirror the crises of cultural and national self-representation, many early modern writers imagined that plays had the power to alter the conditions of everyday speech. In his *Apology for Actors* (1612), Thomas Heywood writes that English,

> which hath ben the most harsh, uneven, and broken language of the world . . . a gallimaffry of many, but perfect in none, *is now by this secondary meanes of playing, continually refined*, every writer striving in himselfe to adde a new flourish unto it; so that in the processe, from the most rude and unpolisht tongue, it is growne to a most perfect and composed language, and many excellent workes, and elaborate Poems writ in the same, that many Nations grow inamored of our tongue.[36]

The composition of poetry and drama is here inextricably linked with the composition of self, society, and nation. The copiousness and variety of language that marked the early modern stage, however, held of course for many the potential for the disintegration of both theatrical enterprises and national identities. The teleology of representational progress associated with "playing" in Heywood is, in John Green's *Refutation of the Apology for Actors* (1615), re-imagined as a narrative of social and representational decay. The "Play-poets" that Heywood champions for refining the language and strengthening the nation, Green suggests, actually exacerbate confusion and attenuate social bonds:

> [Heywood] sheweth (and to the disgrace of his mother-tongue) that our English was the rudest language in the world, a Gallymafry of Dutch, French, Irish, Saxon, Scotch, and Welsh, but by Play-Poets it hath beene refined. But doth he not forget, that whiles they adde Greeke, Lattine, and Italian, they make a great mingle-mangle . . . ["our English tongue"] is become more obscure, and used amongst few; for the simple vulgar people cannot understand it: And a plaine man can scarce utter his mind, for want of Phrases (as I may say) according to the fashion.[37]

If the theater was imagined as a site for the articulation and transformation of linguistic "fashion," and hence

for the re-negotiation of social and national modes of communication, then the vexed condition of representation in Thomas Kyd's *The Spanish Tragedy,* I want to argue, can be seen as seriously complicating the nationalistic sentiment that the play seems to celebrate.[38] This essay will read *The Spanish Tragedy* in light of contemporary debates about the heterogenous and intertwined fabrics of language, culture, and nation. It will examine the symbolism of discursive rupture and alienation in the play, and will argue that the thematics of linguistic strangeness and national fragmentation signal an ambivalence about forms of cultural fusion inherent in the establishment of a national tongue and the sculpting of a national self. Through Hieronimo's bloody theater of revenge (the polyglot "Soliman and Perseda"), Kyd stages a discursive war zone which conflates murder, contamination, and corruption with the uneasy juxtaposition of alien forms. In many important ways, Hieronimo's ultimate revenge is a revenge on language, on representation, on what he returns to in the end, "our vulgar tongue."[39]

While critics have examined *The Spanish Tragedy* in terms of its representation of violence and revenge,[40] its advances in dramatic form,[41] and its use of classical and Christian sources,[42] the interlocking thematics of linguistic difference, unnatural breeding, and national identity in the play have been relatively neglected.[43] Contemporary debates about the vernacular central to discussions of authorship and translation could hardly have escaped Kyd, who was himself a dramatist, translator, and poet.[44] As a student at the Merchant Taylors' School, he would have had significant exposure to Mulcaster, who headed the school and who was perhaps the most prolific and outspoken champion of the enriched and enriching mother tongue. The structure of *The Spanish Tragedy* itself suggests the extent to which Kyd was concerned with the relationship between language, society, and nation. The first of Hieronimo's theatrical productions, the historical masque in act I which stages England's triple conquest of Spain and Portugal, signals the play's engagement with popular forms of nation-making and historical representation.[45] Hieronimo himself, the central and vengeful figure of the play, is repeatedly associated with questions of translation, linguistic diversity, and the "vulgar tongue." He not only plots his polyglotinous revenge with materials he "wrote as a student at Toledo," but also quotes Seneca, Alan of Lille, and Claudian; speaks English, Latin, Spanish, and Greek throughout the course of the play; and—in his famous staging of "Soliman and Perseda"—kills the court in a spectacular theater of heteroglossic confusion. Indeed, Hieronimo, positioned in the play as a reader, scholar, translator, and inspired artist of sorts (who "translates" the word of God), occupies an identity that is oddly similar to that of his namesake,

Hieronimus, or St. Jerome.[46] The name, while associating Hieronimo with that which is sacred (from the Greek *hieros*), ironizes his ultimate departure from all things holy.[47]

The polyglot structure of Hieronimo's "Soliman and Perseda" is anticipated by the linguistic texture of **The Spanish Tragedy,** which combines the "vulgar tongue" with fragments of Latin (I.ii.12-4, and 55-6; I.iii.15-7; II.i.65-80; III.xi.102-3; and III.xiii.1, 6, 12-3, and 35), Spanish (III.xiv.118, and III.v.87-8), and Italian (III.v.87-8, and III.xv.168). Hieronimo's playlet is positioned as a kind of grotesque culmination of the alienating fusion and confusion of cultural differences that pervade the play. While the geographical location of the play is Spain, for example, "the characters in **The Spanish Tragedy** bear predominantly Italian names, save Don Cyprian, the duke of Castile."[48] And while the play begins with a conventional structure of antitheses (soul/flesh, past/present, freedom/confinement, summer/winter, life/death, love/war, true/false), a series of rhetorical and thematic moves soon calls into question the very logic of difference; we even hear the king of Spain say, "Spain is Portugal / And Portugal is Spain" (I.iv.132-3).[49] While this statement is easily uttered by one who has just conquered Portugal, its uncomfortable implications are theatricalized by Hieronimo's masque in act I, which stages the vulnerability of *both* Spain and Portugal in the face of English power.[50] Further, this seemingly mild form of theatrical subversion (later paralleled by Hieronimo's destruction of the court) establishes the Spanish Hieronimo as being—if not a "confirmed Anglophile"[51]—at least oddly complicit with the conquering powers of "little England" (I.v.160).

The theater's privileged relationship to expressions of internal fragmentation in **The Spanish Tragedy** is suggested by Hieronimo's first masque, which subtly challenges the sovereignty of state and nation. It is no coincidence in this respect that Hieronimo's own condition of psychic fragmentation is fully realized in the final act of the play, where he uses the theater to stage the death of his enemies. He there produces a second masque in which his enemies unwittingly reenact the sins of their past and are literally killed. As many critics have noted, the plot and brutal murders in "Soliman and Perseda" mirror the crimes of Lorenzo and Balthazar, who, in act II, had conspired to kill Hieronimo's son. The self-reflexivity of "Soliman and Perseda," suggested by the sheer multiplicity of representational frames within which it is acted,[52] calls attention to the way in which the highly theatrical and deliberative helps to facilitate the savage and uncivilized in the play (revenge itself).

The anxieties about war as a threat to national integrity (the very sound of which "gapes to swallow neighbor bounding lands"[I.ii.51] and results in corporeal "scattering" [I.ii.62]) are relocated, over the course of the play, in language itself, which becomes a spectacular war zone for the interplay of difference. Hieronimo's decision to stage the murderous "Soliman and Perseda" as a theater of linguistic difference conflates issues of representational excess with savage behavior:

> Each one of us must act his part
> In unknown languages,
> That it may breed the more variety.
> As you, my lord, in Latin, I in Greek,
> You in Italian; and for because I know
> That Bel-Imperia hath practised the French,
> In courtly French shall all her phrases be.
>
> (IV.i.172-9)

The playlet's implicit engagement with contemporary debates about language is signaled by Hieronimo himself, who stages the play in "unknown languages" so that it will "breed the more variety." In Hieronimo's play, the "variety" is cacophonous and the "breeding" profoundly unnatural; barbarism and barbarism converge in the copious spillage of blood and words.[53] While critics have called Hieronimo's motive to "breed the more variety" a "lame and queer explanation,"[54] or seemingly insignificant,[55] its importance in terms of the play as a whole cannot be underestimated. His logic for staging the play in sundry languages is articulated in terms commonly deployed in arguments about the status of English; as we have seen, "breeding" and "variety" are terms invoked time and again in discussions about the vernacular.[56] Eloquence necessitated a fusion of *copia* and *varietas,* and it was in the effort to "breed the more variety" that much linguistic borrowing took place.[57]

Hieronimo manipulates the stage so as to breed representational variety that is at once verbal and visual. By combining poly-glot with poly-garb, he generates a visual spectacle of international cliches:

> You must prouide a Turkish cappe,
> A black mustacio, and a Fauchion.
> You, with a Crosse, like to a Knight of Rhodes.
> And, Madame, you must attire yourself
> Like *Phoebe, Flora,* or the huntresse . . .
>
> (IV.i.144-8)

The disjunction between the verbal and the visual breeds further confusion. The *English* actor who plays *Spanish* Bel-Imperia plays *Italian* Perseda who speaks "courtly *French.*" The *English* actor who plays *Portuguese* Balthazar plays *Turkish* Soliman who speaks *Latin.* The *English* actor who plays the *Castilian* Lorenzo plays a knight of *Rhodes* who speaks *Italian.* And finally, the *English* actor who plays the *Spanish* Hieronimo plays the *Bashaw* who speaks *Greek.*

The mixing of linguistic, cultural, and national identities is meant, at the very least, to signify confusion. In response to Balthazar's "But this will be a meere confusion / And hardly shall we all be vnderstood" (IV.ii.179-80), Hieronimo says, "It must be so; for the conclusion / shall proue the invention . . ." (IV.ii.181-2). Indeed, the polyglossic discord infuses the bloody masque with meta-linguistic significance, emphasizing the fallen state of discourse that has ruptured community throughout the play. While many critics have linked Hieromino's spectacular revenge with a theological model of crime and punishment (Babel),[58] the socio-linguistic confusion enacted in the Spanish court conflates multiple conceptions of "barbarism" and addresses language concerns relevant to the English nation. Indeed, the spectacle of clashing words and garments in Hieronimo's playlet conjures up the image of gross heterogeneity that was central to critiques of "Englishness" in the late sixteenth and early seventeenth-century. Just as linguistic "mingle-mangling" destabilized the logic of national and class difference, so too did the "confuse[d] mingle mangle of apparell," which, as Philip Stubbes wrote in *The Anatomy of Abuses* (1583), "[made it] verie hard to knowe, who is noble, who is worshipfull, who is a gentleman, who is not."[59] A nice gloss on Hieronimo's playlet might be William Harrison's comment about the unsettling morphologies of specifically *English* sartorial splendors, "that to daie there is none to the Spanish guise, to morrow the French toies are most fine and delectable, yer long no such apparell as that which is after the high Alman fashion, by and by the Turkish maner is generallie best liked of."[60] For Stubbes and others, the unstable boundaries of nation are intimately bound up with the unstable boundaries of class.

Similarly, the breeding of languages in "Soliman and Perseda" (and the monstrous spectacle thereof) is explicitly related to the dissolution of class boundaries. Not only was the play

> determined to have been acted
> By scholars and gentlemen
> Such as could tell what to speak
>
>   (IV.i.101-3)

but it is also "played by princes and courtiers, / Such as can tell how to speak" (IV.i.104-5).[61] The discursive elitism of the play itself is emphasized by Hieronimo, when he defends his choice of topic and genre. When Balthazar suggests that "a comedy were better," Hieronimo argues

> Fie, comedies are fit for common wits:
> But to present a kingly troop withal,
> Give me a stately-written tragedy,
> *Tragedia cothurnata,* fitting kings,
> Containing matter, and not common things.
>
>   (IV.i.157-61)

Hieronimo's invocation of the standard "comedies are fit for common wits" echoes the earlier contrast he makes between his own murderous cunning and "the

vulgar wits of men, / With open, but inevitable ills" (III.xiii.21-2). Hieronimo repeatedly emphasizes the boundary between the stately spectacle and the common world, between the aristocratic and the vulgar. This distinction would have been exaggerated to the range of spectators in an Elizabethan/Jacobean audience who literally could not understand the "unknown languages" invoked in the playlet. In many ways, the strange linguistic spectacle becomes an exaggerated metaphor for the enriched vernacular itself, a language that was becoming less and less recognizable, or familiar, to the common man. One seventeenth-century critic pointed out that "Most part of our English termes, are very farre different from our vulgare and maternall speache, in such sort, that those who so fully vnderstandeth not the Latin tongue, yea and also the Greek, can scarse vnderstand them."[62]

While the alienating effect of language in "Soliman and Perseda" accentuates social distinctions in the play and in early modern drama, it also signifies their dissolution. It is through the play, after all, that Hieronimo (the Knight Marshall) asserts his power over the court and (as he deprives both rulers of successors) the destiny of the Spanish and Portuguese nations. Class, cultural, and epistemological differences are collapsed as life bursts through the art of Hieronimo's masque and leaves three fathers standing to behold their dead children: "Speak, Portuguese," says Hieronimo to the stunned viceroy, "whose *loss resembles mine*" (IV.iv.114, my emphasis). The king's earlier rhetorical move, "Spain is Portugal, And Portugal is Spain," has become devastatingly *realized* by Hieronimo (I.iv.132-3).

Yet it is the loss of resemblances, in a very literal and a very metaphorical way, that Hieronimo revenges and ultimately mourns.[63] His transformation of art into "life" in the final act of the play can be seen as his ultimate resistance to the referent-less signs (lies) that constitute most of the discourse and drive much of the action in *The Spanish Tragedy.* While Lorenzo and Balthazar are made to speak in signs without apparent referents, Hieronimo transforms what seem to be theatrical signs into horrifyingly literal referents (dead bodies):

> See here my show, look on this spectacle:
> Here lay my hope, and here my hope has end:
> Here lay my heart, and here my heart was slain:
> Here lay my treasure, here my treasure lost:
> Here lay my bliss, and here my bliss bereft:
> But hope, heart, treasure, joy and bliss,
> All fled, fail'd, died, yea, all decay'd with this.
>
>   (IV. iv)

Hieronimo's first and last words ("See . . . this") and his hammering of the word "here" signify his desperate urge to linguistically signify the presence of his dead son. His plain speech and simple anaphoristic repetitions, while contrasting dramatically with the sundry-tongued polylogy of his enemies, parallels the description of the battle in act I: "Here falls a body scinder'd from his head, / There legs and arms lie bleeding on the grass" (I.ii.57-8). "Here" and "there," simple words signifying direct material presences, are only emphasized in the play in moments of representational or emotional crisis.[64]

From the first, the mimetic impulse that inspires and facilitates Hieronimo's revenge is enacted on the level of representation. In the 1602 additions to the play,[65] before he plots an actual revenge, he asks a painter to reproduce the spectacle of his murdered son:

> paint me this tree, this very tree. Canst paint a doleful cry? . . . paint me a youth run through and through with swords, hanging upon this tree. Canst thou draw a murderer? . . . let them be worse, *stretch thine art*, and let their eye-brows jutty over . . . Then, *after some violent noise*, bring me forth in my shirt and my gown under my arm, with my sword rear'd up thus . . . *Make me curse, make me rave, make me cry, make me mad, make me well again* . . . At last, sir, *bring me to one of the murderers*, were he as strong as Hector, *thus would I tear and drag him up and down*.
>
> (III.xii.235-74, my emphases)

Hieronimo's desire to "stretch" the form of visual art to encompass acoustics, physical movement, and temporal sequence, prefigures his own use of theatrical forms to do the work of bloody revenge. Indeed, his desire to reproduce (and in a way revenge) the murder in the bloodless and contained spheres of painting and narration only leads him to a feverishly confused and actively destructive state. When asked how the painting should "end," Hieronimo responds, "there is no end: the end is death and madness" and he proceeds—in a perfect anticipation of his revenge on the world of representation—to beat the painter, ultimately declaiming, *"Vindicta mihi."*

Hieronimo's reference to the importance of a stately-written tragedy, "containing *matter,*" eerily anticipates the bloody literalization of metaphor in "Soliman and Perseda." His madness itself is an extreme reaction to the disjunction between sign and referent that constitutes the fabric of the play. In his imagination ontological boundaries collapse, word and thing congeal, the discursive becomes physical and the physical, discursive. When the three citizens approach him in search of justice in act III, for example, they come bearing legal documents (a declaration, a bond, and a lease). Hieronimo imagines the social contracts to be the bodies of his enemies and tries to "rent and tear them thus and thus / Shivering their limbs in pieces with my teeth" (III.xiii.122-3). When blamed for tearing the documents, he replies, "That cannot be, I gave it never a wound; / Show me one drop of blood fall from the same: / How

is it possible that I should slay it then" (III.xiii.129-31). Hieronimo's confusion here between the corporeal and the textual, between the scattering of representation and the scattering of bodies, prefigures the allegorical significance of his grotesque self-mutilation.

It is significant in this respect that Hieronimo is associated with Orpheus, a figure whose myth embodies the competing forces of integration and fragmentation. Orpheus, the Renaissance model for eloquence and civility, is torn limb from limb at the very moment he loses linguistic power in Ovid's *Metamorphoses*:

> Orpheus, who stretched out
> His hands in supplication, and whose voice,
> For the first time, moved no one.
> They struck him down . . .
> . . . . .
> The poet's limbs lay scattered
> Where they were flung in cruelty or madness
>
> (9. 36-49)

Appropriately, Hieronimo's *response* to the futility of language[66] is staged—in "Soliman and Perseda"—as a "scattering" of language and body. This scattering, or externalization of psychic fragmentation, is prefigured by Hieronimo's imaginative dismemberment of his enemies in act III, a symbolic tearing of bodies that associates him with the frenzied Bacchae in Ovid's *Metamorphoses*. The fact that Hieronimo articulates a yearning for Orpheus ("Be my Orpheus," he says to the Senex, his allegorical mirror, III.xiii.117) moments before he tears pieces of paper "limb from limb," highlights the tragic extent to which he is complicit in the fractured world of representation that he loathes and upon which he ultimately takes revenge.[67]

Moments before his death, in one of the most unforgettable acts of violence on the early modern stage, Hieronimo "bites out his tongue" (IV.iv.191). Although he has confessed everything,[68] he defies the authority of his questioners by literally dislodging the instrument of speech from his body. In a play where individual speech acts have the power to shape destinies and nations, and where discourse itself is often imagined in the material form of tongues and bodies, it is hard to imagine that Kyd's representation of Hieronimo's madness at this point lacks method. Indeed, it is not long after Hieronimo says, "Here break we off in our sundry languages / And thus conclude I in our vulgar tongue" (IV.iv.75-6) that he, quite literally, concludes his discourse with the vulgar spectacle of a mutilated tongue.

While critics have often noted the sheer sensationalism of the act, the additions to the 1602 edition of the play accentuate its thematic significance by inserting, "Now to express the rupture of my part," before "First take my tongue, and afterward my heart" (IV.iv.215-6).

Hieronimo's metonymic self-representation here dramatizes his sense of partiality, fragmentation, and impotence within established discursive systems. "The rupture of part[s]," a metaphor for Hieronimo's fragmented state, also becomes a metaphor for the relation of words and things in the play as a whole. As language fragments, so do bodies, psyches, and nations. A contemporary of Kyd's seems to have recognized the symbolics of Hieronimo's self-mutilation by equating him with "Ruffinus," whose grotesquely dismembered body is described at length in Claudian's *In Ruffinam.*[69] John Weever writes a comic and punning response to the staged dismemberment in *Epigrammes in the Oldest Cut, and Newest Fashion* (1599):

> *Ruffinus* lost his tongue on stage,
> And wot ye how he made it knowne?
> He spittes it out in bloudy rage,
> And told the people he had none:
> The fond spectators said, he acted wrong,
> The dumbest man may say, he hath no tongue.[70]

While the foolish spectators thought "he acted wrong," Hieronimo's "bloudy rage" is seen here as a way of "making known" the fact that he has *already* "lost his tongue."

The implicit association of Hieronimo with Zeno of Elea further dramatizes issues of discursive and psychic fragmentation in **The Spanish Tragedy.** Zeno, a stoic philosopher, bit out his tongue in an act of resistance that was universally interpreted as heroic.[71] In Plutarch's *De garrulitate,* Zeno becomes an emblem of lingual continence: "Zeno, the philosopher, in order that even against his will no secret should be betrayed by his body when under torture, bit his tongue through and spat it at the despot."[72] In most recapitulations of this story, Zeno's self-mutilation functions to dramatize a unitarity of spirit in contrast to the fragmenting and fragmentable material world.[73] While for Zeno, self-mutilation constitutes an act of stoic heroism, a literalized spit in the face of tyranny, for Kyd it signals a profoundly anti-heroic surrender to (and complicity with) a world of fragments and self-alienation.[74]

Zeno bites out his tongue to express his sense of internal wholeness; Hieronimo does so "to express the rupture [of] his part." The powerful contrast between the two figures thematizes anxieties about the relations between part and whole in **The Spanish Tragedy.** Zeno of Elea was as famous for his unsettling philosophical paradoxes about the relations between part and whole as for his autoglossotomy. He posited, in an argument against plurality, that if parts exist, they must be "so small as to have no size" and "so large as to be infinite."[75] In many ways, Kyd's spectacle of heterogeneous horrors can be seen as a kind of "Zenophobia," a deadly anxiety about the possibility that there is no end to the parts that make us who we are. For if, in Willy Maley's

words, "the nation . . . is always a metonymy of one sort or another, a privileged part made to stand in for an imaginary whole," the metonymy at work in Kyd's *play* speaks only to the representational power of a nation unable to negotiate its own parts, or perhaps more aptly, unable to find, to locate, or ultimately to excise, its own voice.[76]

Notes

1. Ludwig Wittgenstein, *Philosophical Investigations,* trans. G. E. M. Anscombe (Oxford: Blackwell Publishers, 1958), p. 218[e]. Thomas Kyd, *The Spanish Tragedy* (IV.iv.215-6). All citations are from the New Mermaids edition of *The Spanish Tragedy,* ed. J. R. Mulryne (London: A. and C. Black, 1989). Subsequent references will appear parenthetically within the text by act, scene, and line number. Robert Cawdrey, *A Table Alphabeticall,* ed. Robert A. Peters (London, 1604; rprt. Gainesville FL: Scholars' Facsimiles and Reprints, 1966). Cawdrey's unacknowledged source here is Thomas Wilson's *Art of Rhetoric* (London, 1553). Throughout this essay, when I quote from original or reprinted sixteenth- and seventeenth-century texts, I retain the old spelling, but modernize the i, j, and long s. My work in this essay is indebted to seminal work of Richard Jones on the history of English, *The Triumph of the English Language* (Stanford: Stanford Univ. Press, 1953).

2. Needless to say, it is as an effort to bring the vernacular home to mother that Cawdrey writes the first English dictionary (Starnes DeWitt and Gertrude E. Noyes, *The English Dictionary from Cawdrey to Johnson* [Chapel Hill: Univ. of North Carolina, 1946], pp. 13-8).

3. Sir Philip Sidney, *An Apologie for Poetry* (London, 1595; ed. Geoffrey Shepherd, Manchester: Manchester Univ. Press, 1973), p. 138.

4. Edward Phillips, *New World of English Words* (London, 1658), p. 44. I juxtapose Sidney and Phillips to emphasize the ongoing uneasiness about the condition of English.

5. See also Alexander Gill's *Logonomia Anglica,* ed. Bror Danielson and Arvid Garielson, trans. Robin C. Alston (London, 1619; rprt. Stockholm: Almquist and Wiksell, Stockholm Studies in English, 1972), where alien terms are imagined as "monstrous," "illegitimate progeny" (p. 84).

6. Richard Sherry, *A Treatise of Schemes and Tropes,* ed. Herbert W. Hildebrandt (London, 1550; rprt. Gainesville FL: Scholars' Facsimiles and Reprints, 1961), p. 3, my emphasis. As Richard Mulcaster similarly points out, "He must take acquaintace & make the thing familiar if it seme to be strange. For all strange things seme great novelties . . .

till theie be acquainted . . . And words likewise, which either conveie strange matters, or be strangers themselves, either in name or in use, be no wilde beasts, tho theie be unwont, neither is a term a *Tiger* to prove untractable" (*The First Part of the Elementarie,* ed. R. C. Alston [London, 1582; rprt. Menston, England: Scolar Press, Scholar Press Facsimile, 1970], p. 281); and George Pettie emphasizes how quickly the foreign becomes the familiar:

> *for it is not unknowen to all men how many woordes we haue fetcht from thence ["Latin as well as other tongues"] within these few yeeres, which if they should be all counted inkepot terms, I know not how we should speake any thing without blacking our mouthes with inke: for what woord can be more plaine then this word* plaine *and yet what can come more neere to the Latin? What more manifest then* manifest? *. . . What more commune then* rare *or less rare then* commune?

(preface to *The Civile Conuersation of M. Steeuen Guazzo* [London, 1581; rprt. London: Constable, 1925], p. 11).

7. Mulcaster, pp. 173-4.

8. Mulcaster, p. 287, my emphasis.

9. The word "translation" meant of course "altering, changing," as defined in Cawdrey's *Table Alphabeticall.*

10. Samuel Daniel, "A Defence of Rime," in *The Renaissance in England* (Massachusetts: D. C. Heath, 1954), p. 662.

11. Gill, p. 81.

12. Mulcaster, p. 287.

13. Mulcaster, p. 172.

14. Stephen Mullaney, "Strange Things, Gross Terms, Curious Customs: The Rehearsal of Cultures in the Late Renaissance," in *Representing the English Renaissance,* ed. Stephen Greenblatt (Berkeley: Univ. of California Press, 1988), pp. 65-92, 80.

15. For example, in the preface to *A Table Alphabeticall,* Cawdrey critiques "farjornied gentlemen, [who] at their return home, like as they love to go in forraine apparrel, so they will pouder their talke with over-sea language. He that commeth lately out of France, will talk French English, and neuer blush at the matter. Another chops in with English Italianated, and applyeth the Italian phrase to our English speaking." In a similar passage, George Puttenham writes that "we make our speach or writings of sundry languages vsing some Italian word, or French, or Spanish, or Dutch, or Scottish, not for the nonce or for any purpose (which were in part excusable) but ignorantly and affectedly" (*The Art of English Poesy,* ed. Edward Arber [London, 1589; rprt. London: A. Constable, 1906], p. 259). And in the dedicatory epistle to *The Shepheardes Calender* (1579), E. K. critiques those who have imagined the mother tongue to be "barren," and have "patched up the holes with peces and rags of other languages, borrowing here of the French, there of the Italian, every where of the Latine, not weighing how il, those tongues accord with themselves, but much worse with ours: So now they have made our English tongue, a gallimaufray or hodgepodge of al other speches" ("Dedicatory Epistle to *The Shepheardes Calender,*" in *Edmund Spenser's Poetry,* ed. Hugh Maclean and Anne Lake Prescott [New York: Norton, 1993], pp. 501-5, 503).

16. Thomas Dekker, *The Seven Deadly Sins of London,* ed. H. F. B. Brett-Smith (London, 1606; rprt. New York: Houghton Mifflin, 1992), p. 42.

17. Puttenham, p. 260. As Paula Blank writes in the recent *Broken English: Dialects and the Politics of Language in Renaissance Writings* (New York: Routledge, 1997), "The rhetoric of crime, of illegality, of 'peril,' speaks, throughout the period, to the ongoing concern that the new trade in words ultimately endangered both the language and the speakers who exploited them" (p. 46).

18. Theft, for example, an act of taking something that belongs to another, was commonly associated with forms of poetic and cultural "exchange": "The world's a Theatre of theft," writes Thomas Tomkis in the opening lines of *Albumazar: A Comedy,* ed. Hugh G. Dick (Berkeley: Univ. of California Press, 1944), I.i.59. Not only are lawyers, merchants, and poets positioned in the play as pilferers, robbers, and plagiarists, but the whole world is imagined in terms of an implicitly shifty cosmography:

> Great rivers
> Rob smaller brookes; and them the Ocean.
> And in this world of ours, this Micrososm,
> Guts from the stomack steale, and what they spare,
> The meseraicks filch, and lay't i'th liver:
> Where, (least it should be found) turn'd to red Nectar,
> Tis by a thousand theevish veines convey'd
> And hid in flesh, nerves, bones, muscles and sinewes,
> In tendons, skin and haire, so that *the property
> Thus altered, the theft can never be discovered.*
> Now all these pilfries couch'd and composed in order,
> Frame thee and me. *Man's a quick masse of theevery.*
>
> (I.i.59-70, my emphasis)

Whereas borrowing implies a condition of temporary possession, thievery signifies an act of intentional and unapologetic appropriation. Disregarding Harpax's comment that "I thought these parts had lent and borrowed mutuall," Albumazar asserts, "'tis done with full intention / Nere to restore, and that's flat robbery" (I.i.72-4). Tomkis's image of a physiological microcosm energized by "a thousand theevish veines" articulates an increasingly common anxiety in early modern England about a nation which is at once constituted by, and in possession of, stolen goods.

19. "Confusion of language, a curse," writes Ben Jonson, for example, in *The English Grammar* (London, 1640; rprt., ed. Alice Vinton Waite, New York: Sturgis and Walton, 1909), p. 1.

20. Interestingly, Blank draws together the criminalized discursive sphere of cant with the "legitimate" sphere of linguistic enrichment and orthographic reform in the Renaissance, demonstrating that both forms of linguistic innovation functioned as variations of "'secret' systems, codes that could only be cracked by their creators" (p. 28). The early reformers, she suggests, worked to develop and estrange the very language they seemed to explicate, and to establish, paradoxically enough, a highly exclusive common language: "Like the gypsies of the Renaissance underworld, the first English language reformers practiced a kind of sleight of hand," using their own forms of linguistic innovation and enrichment to alienate and privilege the language they claimed to make plain (p. 29).

21. Thomas Carew, "The Excellence of the English Tongue," in *Elizabethan Critical Essays,* 2 vols., ed. G. Gregory Smith (Oxford: Oxford Univ. Press, 1909), 2:285-94, 290.

22. Indeed, the imaginative conflation of borrowing with bankruptcy and usury emerged out of a specific set of anxieties about what it might mean for alien signs to be "circulating" and procreating in the linguistic domain of early modern England. Similarly, Sir John Cheke warns against the dangers of the English language "ever borowing and never payeng, [lest] she shall be fain to keep her house as bankrupt" (Cheke, letter to Sir Thomas Hoby, printed in Hoby's translation of Baldassare Castiglione, *The Courtier* [London, 1561; rprt. in *The Renaissance in England: Non-dramatic Prose and Verse of the Sixteenth Century,* ed. Hyder E. Rollins and Herschel Baker (Lexington MA: D. C. Heath, 1954), pp. 538-9, 538]). Some further examples would be Mulcaster's comment in *The First Part of the Elementarie,* "I think it best for the strange words to yeild to our lawes, bycause we are both their vsuaries and fructuaries, both to enjoy their frutes" (p. 174) and Richard Carew's "For our owne partes, we imploye the borrowed ware soe far to our advantag that we raise a profitt

of new woordes from the same stock which yeat in their owne countrey are not merchantable" (p. 291).

23. Cheke, p. 538.

24. Tomkis, *Lingua, or the Combat of the Tongue and the Five Senses for Superiority,* ed. John Farmer (London, 1607; rprt. Amersham: Tudor Facsimile Reprints, 1913, sig. F3). This academic play seems to have been popular, notes Farmer, as other editions surfaced in 1610, 1617, 1622, 1632, and 1657.

25. Importantly, it is the presence of Ladie Lingua, an "idle pratting dame," that differentiates *Lingua* from other microcosmic allegories of the senses based on Aristotle's model in *De anima.* As Jean Starobinski writes: "For a long while, pain and pleasure were not attributed to a specific sensory system; they were called 'bodily passions,' whereas the traditional term, *internal sense (sensus internus),* referred to the conscious activities that the mind developed in and of itself (reason, memory and imagination) on the basis of information provided by the *external senses* (sight, hearing, taste, touch and smell)." Starobinski draws from *De anima,* in which Aristotle posits that "the information provided by the external senses reached the internal sense only after having been unified by the common sense (*sensorium commune, Koinon aistheterion*)." It is to this figure, Common Sense, that Lingua pleads her case. See Starobinski, "The Natural and Literary History of Bodily Sensation," in *Fragments for a History of the Human Body: Part II,* ed. Michel Feher (New York: Zone, 1989), pp. 351-405, 351, 354. Also, for an excellent discussion of the microcosmic allegories from Plato's *Timaeus* to Spenser's *Faerie Queene,* see Leonard Barkan, *Nature's Work of Art: The Human Body as Image of the World* (New Haven: Yale Univ. Press, 1985).

26. Tomkis, *Lingua,* sig. F2.

27. Cheke, p. 538.

28. Puttenham, p. 259.

29. Tomkis, *Lingua,* sig. F2.

30. Ibid.

31. Tomkis further dramatizes the estrangement of this "little world" from itself by having Lingua not only embody the excesses of an uncontrolled "mother tongue" but also linguistically enact the disease of the mother (indeed, even while asleep, she cannot keep mum: "Mum mum mum mum," mumbles the walking talking mother tongue). "[W]omenn are troubled," notes Phantastes, "especially with this talking disease" (sig. M3). Al-

though the specter of an alien and alienated language becomes successfully displaced, through the medium of theater, onto an alien and alienated mother tongue, the disease and the logic of alienation *is* both the drama and the very crisis of representation in the play. Indeed, it is the impossibility of "keeping mum," in every sense of the phrase, that seems to generate the energy of Tomkis's play. For the characters within the play *depend* on the very "mother tongue" that is so alienated from them. Despite their Latin nominations (Auditus, Gustus, etc.), they all, of course, speak English. And, unlike so many earlier university plays which were written and performed in Latin, this play was first performed by Cambridge undergraduates in the mother tongue. Interestingly, while gendering the instability of representation, the play positions Ladie Lingua as a personification of the condition of speech in this predominantly all-male world: in a description of Memory's endless reminiscences, Anamnestes notes, "Nature thou know'st, knowing what an unruly Engine the tongue is, hat set teeth round about for watchmen; Now Sir, my Master's old age hat cought out all his teeth & that's the cause it runs so much at liberty" (sig. E3). For a discussion of the fetishization of the organ of speech in both *Lingua* and in early modern English culture, see Carla Mazzio, "Sins of the Tongue," in *The Body in Parts: Fantasies of Corporeality in Early Modern Europe,* ed. David Hillman and Carla Mazzio (New York: Routledge, 1997), pp. 53-80. Also, for the gendering of rhetoric and rhetorical tropes in Tomkis's *Lingua,* see Patricia Parker, "On the Tongue: Cross Gendering, Effeminacy, and the Art of Words," *Style* 23, 4 (Winter 1989): 445-63.

32. Tomkis, sig. F2.

33. Dekker, p. 44. Also see Shakespeare's Falconbridge in *The Merchant of Venice.* Despite the humanist emphasis on language and translations, importations of foreign literary matter were often linked to conditions of national fragmentation. Stephen Gosson, for instance, in *Plays Confuted in Five Actions* (London, 1582), criticizes dramatists for "thoroughly ransack[ing]" "Latin, French, Italian, and Spanish" texts, and in his *School of Abuse* equates foreign influence with national self-dispersion: "We have robbed *Greece* of Gluttonie, *Italy* of wantonness, *Spaine* of pride, *Fraunce* of deceite, and *Dutchland* of quaffing. Compare *London* to *Rome* and *England* to *Italy,* you shall find the Theaters of the one, the abuses of the other, to be rife among us" ([London, 1579; rprt. London: Alex Murray and Son, English Reprints, 1868], p. 34). As Gosson's words suggest, the presence of foreign literary and linguistic forms in early modern England simultaneously enhanced and threatened emergent modes of national self-articulation.

The Englishmen who travel and "*return home with such quaesie stomackes, that nothyng wyll downe with them but French, Italian, or Spanish,*" writes Pettie, are responsible for the perceived "barbarism" of English culture by their "*apish imitation of every outlandish Asse in their gestures, behaviour, and apparell*" (pp. 9, 10). Similarly, of "*An affected Traueller,*" Sir Thomas Overbury writes, "His attire speakes *French* or *Italian,* his gate cries, *Behold me*" (*A Wife . . . A most exquisite and singular Poem of the choice of a Wife. Whereunto are added many witty Characters, and conceited Newes,* 3d impression [London, 1614]). On the rise of forms of nationhood in late-sixteenth-century England, see Liah Greenfeld, *Nationalism: Five Roads to Modernity* (Cambridge MA: Harvard Univ. Press, 1992), pp. 31-78; and Richard Helgerson, *Forms of Nationhood: The Elizabethan Writing of England* (Chicago: Univ. of Chicago Press, 1992). My discussion about English self-representation is in many ways indebted to Helgerson's discussion about versification (pp. 21-62).

Also, the nationalized taxonomies of character traits so commonplace in sixteenth-century English satire became increasingly re-imagined in the late sixteenth and early seventeenth centuries as shorthand for local and national forms of *self-description.* That is, what emerged as an articulation of nascent nationalism, as a rhetorical device meant to secure a geographically and nationally demarcated characterology, came—with both the rise of the international marketplace and the dramatic expansion of the national language—to be seen as an act of self-description. This is particularly marked in discussions about the English vernacular where tropes of linguistic otherness are—by necessity—fused with forms of self-representation. Indeed, it can be said that the very trope of cataloguing of foreign "parts" as a mode of self-description had a counterpart in the development of English dictionaries and lists of hard words: "Our *Babels Ruins* this in part repairs," reads the prefatory poem to Thomas Blount's *Glossographia,* by "re-acquainting our self-stranger *Nation* / With its disguised self." See the preface to Blount's *Glossographia: Or, A Dictionarie Interpreting Hard Words,* 4th edn. (London, 1674). For a comprehensive examination of foreignness as a mode of English self-representation, see A. J. Hoenselaars, *Images of Englishness and Foreigners in the Drama of Shakespeare and His Contemporaries* (Rutherford NJ: Fairleigh Dickinson Univ. Press, 1992).

34. Helgerson, p. 22.

35. Mulcaster, p. 173; John Lyly, *Midas,* in *The Complete Works of John Lyly,* 3 vols. (Oxford: Clarendon Press, 1902), 3:106-62, 115. Earlier in the prologue, Lyly writes, "*Enquire at Ordinaries, there must be sallets for the Italian; picktooths for the Spaniard; pots for the German; porridge for the Englishman. At our exercises, Souldiers call for Tragedies, their object is bloud: Courtiers for Commedies, their subject is loue; Countriemen for Pastoralles, Shepheards are their Saintes.*"

36. Thomas Heywood, *An Apology for Actors,* ed. Richard H. Perkinson (London, 1612; rprt. New York: Scholars' Facsimiles and Reprints, 1941), sig. F3.

37. John Green, *A Refutation of the Apologie For Actors* (London, 1615; rprt. New York: Scholars' Facsimiles and Reprints, 1941), pp. 41-2.

38. *The Spanish Tragedy* (with the vilification of Spain and confusion of tongues) seems to lend itself to interpretations which focus on the informing (anti-Spanish, anti-Catholic) Protestant polemic of the 1580s and 1590s. Time and again in the play, however, Kyd calls into question the very logic of cultural difference which makes this reading possible.

39. Kyd, IV.iv.75.

40. See, for example, James Shapiro, "'Tragedies naturally performed': Kyd's Representation of Violence in *The Spanish Tragedy,*" in *Staging the Renaissance: Reinterpretations of Elizabethan and Jacobean Drama,* ed. David Scott Kastan and Peter Stallybrass (New York: Routledge, 1991), pp. 99-113. Also see Jonathan Bate, "The Performance of Revenge: *Titus Andronicus* and *The Spanish Tragedy,*" in *The Show Within: Dramatic and Other Insets: English Renaissance Drama, 1550-1642* (Montpellier: Paul-Valery Univ. Press, 1990), pp. 267-83; Molly Smith, "The Theater and the Scaffold: Death as Spectacle in *The Spanish Tragedy,*" in *SEL* 32, 2 (Spring 1992): 217-32; and Frank Ardolino, "'In Paris? Mass, and Well Remembered': Kyd's *The Spanish Tragedy* and the English Reaction to the St. Bartholomew's Day Massacre," in *SCJ* 21, 3 (Fall 1990): 401-9, 401-2.

41. See, for example, Jonas Barish, "*The Spanish Tragedy,* or The Pleasures and Perils of Rhetoric," in *Elizabethan Theatre,* Stratford-upon-Avon Studies 9, ed. J. R. Brown and B. R. Harris (London: E. Arnold, 1966), pp. 59-85.

42. See Eugene Hill, "Senecan and Vergilian Perspectives in *The Spanish Tragedy,*" in *ELR* 15, 2 (Spring 1985): 143-65; Frederick S. Boas's introduction to *The Works of Thomas Kyd* (Oxford: Clarendon Press, 1901); and Frank Ardolino, *Thomas Kyd's Mystery Play: Myth and Ritual in "The Spanish Tragedy"* (New York: Peter Lang, 1985). Also see Mulryne's introduction to *The Spanish Tragedy.*

43. While critics have not examined the play's engagement with specifically *English* forms of national self-representation, they have often noted the way in which the play is *about* Spain and Portugal, or about anti-Catholic, anti-Spanish sentiment in the late sixteenth century. See Mulryne, "Nationality and Language in Thomas Kyd's *The Spanish Tragedy,*" in *Langues et Nations au Temps de la Renaissance,* ed. M. T. Jones-Davies (Paris: Klincksieck, 1991), pp. 67-91. While Mulryne discusses "nationality and language" in terms of English images of the Spanish and the Portuguese, he does not read the play in terms of debates about language or the status of the English or Spanish vernacular.

44. For the full range of works that Thomas Kyd may have produced, see Frederick S. Boas, *The Works of Thomas Kyd* (Oxford: Clarendon Press, 1901).

45. For a discussion of Kyd's reproduction of popular myths of Anglo-Spanish relations, see Arthur Freeman, *Thomas Kyd: Facts and Problems* (Oxford: Clarendon Press, 1967). For an example of myths in circulation, see Christopher Ockland, *The Valiant Actes and Victorious Battailes of the English Nation* (London, 1585).

46. The onomastic self-reflexiveness of Kyd's play is suggested by the correlations between the names and identities of individual characters. The most notable examples are the villain Villupo and the beautiful heroine Bel-Imperia.

47. Although a full discussion of the significance of Jerome is beyond the scope of this essay, the parallels are extensive and deserve further consideration. Hieronimo is variously spelled Jeronymo and Ieronimo and St. Jerome is variously spelled Hieronymus, Hierome, Jerom, and Jerome. As Ardolino has noted, Shakespeare picked up on the association in *The Taming of the Shrew,* with the allusion to "St. Hieronimo!" (see Ardolino, "Hieronimo as St. Jerome in *The Spanish Tragedy,*" *EA* 36, 4 [1983]: 435-7).

48. Freeman, p. 54.

49. In terms of Spanish/Portuguese relations, the either/or structure which functions to differentiate Spain and Portugal from the first soon begins to collapse in the general's account of the battle

> Both furnish'd well, both full of hope and fear
> Both manacing alike with daring shows,

> Both vaunting sundry colours of device
> Both cheerly sounding trumpets, drums and fifes
> Both raising dreadful clamours to the sky
>
> (I.ii.25-9)

and his description of the leveling spectacle of mutilated bodies that follows. Further, as Spain has just conquered Portugal, Hieronimo's historical masque implicitly equates Spanish with English military power, so that Kyd in effect says—if only for a moment—England is Spain and Spain is England.

50. Hieronimo, "sounding the mystery" of his dumb show, explains that "Earl of Gloucester . . . enforced the king [of Portugal] / To bear the yoke of English monarchy," and "Earl of Kent . . . took the King of Portingale in fight," and "Brave John of Gaunt [who was 'as the rest a valiant Englishman'] . . . took our King of Castile prisoner" (I.v.140-67).

51. S. F. Johnson, "*The Spanish Tragedy*: Or Babylon Revisited," in *Essays on Shakespeare and Elizabethan Drama,* ed. Richard Hosley (Columbia: Univ. of Missouri Press, 1962), pp. 23-36.

52. For a full discussion of the multiple plays within plays in the play, see Ardolino, *Thomas Kyd's Mystery Play: Myth and Ritual in "The Spanish Tragedy."*

53. Hieronimo's theater is literally and figuratively barbaric. As Puttenham writes in *The Arte of English Poesie* (1589), "when any straunge word not of the naturall Greeke or Latin was spoken, in the old time they called it *barbarisme*" (p. 257). While "barbarous" was often invoked to describe discomfort with linguistic or dialectical otherness, it surfaces time and again in early modern texts to signify acts of savage, brutish, uncivilized violence. In Lyly's *Midas,* for example, Sophronia wishes the gods would thrust "Martius, that soundest but bloud and terror, into those barbarous Nations, where nothing is to be found but bloud and terror" (II.i.102-3). Similarly, when Hieronimo confronts the spectacle of his son's dead body, he cries,

> If this inhuman and barbarous attempt
>   . . . . .
> Shall unrevealed and unrevenged pass,
> How should we term your dealings to be just.
>
> (III.ii.6-10)

Indeed, it is no coincidence that as part of his revenge, the learned knight makes the murderers inhabit theatrical identities that are—in every sense of the word—barbaric.

54. Michael Hattaway, "The Spanish Tragedy: Architectonic Design," in *Elizabethan Popular Theater* (London: Routledge, 1982), p. 110. Hattaway goes on to suggest that Kyd was "trying to see whether he could employ a theater language that would, to the unlettered at least, communicate by mere sound" (p. 110). I would argue to the contrary that Hieronimo's displacement of psychic alienation onto language functions as a kind of revenge on representation, a revenge that thwarts—rather than transcends—communication.

55. See Gordon Braden's discussion of Kyd in *Renaissance Tragedy and the Senecan Tradition* (New Haven: Yale Univ. Press, 1985).

56. In his 1577 *Chronicles,* Raphael Holinshed writes "no one speache vnder the sonne spoken in our time . . . hath or can haue more varietie of words and copie of phrases [than English]." Also see Jones, who writes about the idealization of *copia* by Thomas Nashe, Puttenham, Robert Parry, and John Florio. He quotes Holinshed from *The First volume of the Chronicles* (London: imprinted for John Hunne, 1577), 5:197.

57. For a full discussion of *copia* in the Renaissance, see Terence Cave, *The Cornucopian Text: Problems of Writing in the French Renaissance* (Oxford: Clarendon Press, 1979). Also see Patricia Parker, *Literary Fat Ladies: Rhetoric, Gender, Property* (London: Methuen, 1987).

58. For discussions about the significance of Babel and Babylon in *The Spanish Tragedy,* see Ardolino, "'Now Shall I see the Fall of Babylon': *The Spanish Tragedy* as a Reformation Play of Daniel," in *Ren & R* 14, 1 (Winter 1990): 49-55; and Mulryne, "Nationality and Language."

59. Philip Stubbes, *The Anatomy of Abuses* (London, 1583; rprt. New York: Garland, 1973), sig. Ciiv. Quoted in Richard Halpern, *The Poetics of Primitive Accumulation: English Renaissance Culture and the Genealogy of Capital* (Ithaca: Cornell Univ. Press, 1991), p. 39.

60. William Harrison, "The Description of Britaine," in *Holinshed's Chronicles,* 6 vols. (1586; rprt. England, 1807-8) 1:289. Quoted in Halpern, p. 39.

61. For a brilliant reading of this passage and of discursive markers of social distinction in the play as a whole, see James R. Siemon, "Sporting Kyd," in *ELR* 24, 3 (Autumn 1994): 553-82.

62. William Fullwood, *The Enimie of Idlenesse* (London, 1582).

63. Paradoxically, he collapses difference in a violent enforcement of it, enacting a literal and symbolic clash of cultures and identities. Just as meaning is obfuscated by alien linguistic forms in "Soliman & Perseda," so are characters in the play alienated from each other by discursive forms (be they multiple languages, false truths, class, or cultural and national differences).

64. See, for example, I.iii.14, where the Portuguese viceroy falls to the ground, saying "Here let me lye, now am I at the lowest" in a comic prefiguration of Hieronimo's tragic loss.

65. These additions dramatize an element already explicit in the 1592 text. "Revenge on them that murdered my son," he says, while tearing up pieces of paper (III.xiii.121).

66. Literally, Hieronimo cannot get anyone at court to hear his plea for justice.

67. While the allusion to the Thracian god recalls at once Hieronimo's dismembered tongue and anguished loss of a loved one, it also signifies his release from savage forces. Like Orpheus, however, it is only in the *after*-world that he is released from a condition of fragmentation. Earlier in the play, he looks to the enigmatic figure of the Senex to "be my Orpheus" (III.xiii.117). As the Senex functions as a kind of allegorical mirror, coming to the knight marshall to seek justice for the murder of his own son, Hieronimo's plea becomes all the more poignant. What Hieronimo craves is the power (embodied in the myth of Orpheus) to cohere nature and art, savagery and civility, things and words. And yet, like the dismembered Orpheus, he is "scattered," torn apart, unable to escape a condition of utter fragmentation.

68. That is, he has revealed everything but the complicity of Bel-Imperia, who by this time is dead. The exact question that he refuses to answer is, "Who were thy confederates in this?" (IV.iv.176). The answer, however, is self-evident, as is demonstrated by the viceroy's comment:

> That was thy daughter Bel-Imperia;
> For by her hand my Balthazar was slain:
> I saw her stab him.

(IV.iv.177-9)

69. A negative counterpart to Orpheus, Ruffinus (who is like Hieronimo, an official marshall of justice) is punished for his savage sins. The injustice of Claudian's Rufinus is ultimately revenged (Claudian, *The Second Book against Rufinus*, trans. Maurice Platnauer [Cambridge MA: Harvard Univ. Press, 1922], pp. 56-97):

> all pierce him with their spears and tear quivering limb from limb . . . They stamp on that face of greed and while yet he lives pluck out his eyes; others seize and carry off his severed arms. One cuts off his foot, another wrenches a shoulder from the torn sinews; one lays bare the ribs of the cleft spine, another his liver, his heart, his still panting lungs . . . Come portion out Ruffinus' corpse among the lands he has wronged. Give the

Thracians his head; let Greece have her due his body. What shall be given the rest? Give but a limb apiece, there are not enough for the peoples he has ruined.

(pp. 88-9)

70. John Weever, *Epigrammes in the oldest cut, and newest fashion* (London, 1599), sig. C1.

71. For late-sixteenth-century recapitulations of the myth, see John Lyly, *Euphues*, in *The Complete Works of John Lyly*, vol. 1, ed. R. Warwick Bond (Oxford: Clarendon Press, 1967). See also William Baldwin, *Treatise of Moral Philosophy* (1579); Plutarch, *Moralia*; and Boethius, *The Consolation of Philosophy*.

72. Plutarch, *De garrulitate*, trans. W. C. Hembold, in *Plutarch's Moralia*, vol. 6 (Cambridge MA: Harvard Univ. Press), p. 415. Elsewhere Plutarch invokes the topos of heart and tongue to emphasize the relation between bodily fragmentation and spiritual cohesion: "Thus Zeno, the disciple of Parmenides . . . revealed when tried in the fire that the teaching of Parmenides *in his heart was like the purest gold and equal to the proof, and demonstrated by the evidence of deeds* that what a great man fears is shame, whereas pain is feared by children and weak women and men with such women's souls, for he bit off his tongue and spat it in the tyrant's face" (p. 415).

73. Similarly, for Diogenes, Anaxarchus's self-mutilation in the literal face of an irrational tyrant functions to signify his detachment from the very tortures and threats of dismemberment that he (paradoxically) resists: Nicocreon "ordered him to be pounded to death with iron pestles. But he, making light of the punishment, made that well known speech, 'Pound, pound the pouch containing Anaxarchus; ye pound not Anaxarchus.' and when Nicocreon commanded his tongue to be cut out, they say he bit it off and spat it at him" (Diogenes Laertius, *Lives of the Eminent Philosophers*, 2 vols., trans. R. D. Hicks (Cambridge MA: Harvard Univ. Press, 1925), 2:473.

74. Unlike his classical predecessor, Hieronimo has no secrets or "confederates" to betray. Although Johnson argues that the parallel with Zeno "serves to identify Hieronimo as admirably stoic" (p. 24), because Hieronimo lacks a logical motive, his self-mutilation actually inverts the neoclassical symbolics of autoglossotomy. Also see Siemon, who writes, "Like his plays, [Hieronimo's] autoglossotomy is a work of conceptual performance, which forms the matter of his subjection into an assertion of transcendent distinction" (p. 528).

75. Simplicius, *On Aristotle's Physics 6*, trans. David Konstan (London: Gerald Duckworth, 1989).

76. Willy Maley, "'This sceptred isle': Shakespeare and the British Problem," in *Shakespeare and National Culture,* ed. John J. Joughin (Manchester, England: Manchester Univ. Press, 1997), p. 85. The staged excision of the tongue, such a vital and symbolically charged corporeal part, would have had powerful analogies in the emergent national culture of early modern England. The specter of a vulnerable or excised national tongue that haunts *The Spanish Tragedy* also haunts Mulcaster's *Elementarie.* Time and again, Mulcaster invokes analogies of the national body to emphasize the crucial "part" played by the tongue, which, if not tended to, would, according to the anatomical metaphorics at work throughout the text, either weaken the body of the nation or lead to its loss of voice (see especially the peroration, pp. 250-91).

Emma Smith (essay date 1999)

SOURCE: Smith, Emma. "Author v. Character in Early Modern Dramatic Authorship: The Example of Thomas Kyd and *The Spanish Tragedy.*" *Medieval and Renaissance Drama in England* 11 (1999): 129-42.

[*In the following essay, Smith considers the attribution of* The Spanish Tragedy *to Kyd, not to argue against his authorship but to examine the how an influential and extremely popular drama could be presented without specifying an author.*]

Kyd's play *The Spanish Tragedy* was the most influential play of the early modern English theater. It was published in ten separate editions between 1594 and 1613 and prompted a kind of prequel play entitled *The First Part of Jeronimo* with which it may have been played in tandem. To revive it for a new audience, Henslowe commissioned additional passages from Ben Jonson at the end of the century. It is known to have been performed at different theaters by different theater companies, and from an analysis of Henslowe's accounts at the Rose theater, it can be shown to have been performed almost thirty times between 1592 and 1597, placing it among the three frequently performed plays of the period.[1] Doubts over its exact date mean that it can be claimed as the first revenge tragedy, the first play to introduce the Machiavellian villain to the English stage, even the first modern tragedy.[2] References to the play are dotted through other plays and poems over the century after its first performance.[3]

Given the evidence for the play's popularity, it might be expected that Kyd—or some other playwright—would want to claim authorship or that an author would be subsequently added to playtexts published after his

death. There was, for example, no comparable hush around Marlowe's authorship of *Dr. Faustus,* a similarly popular play of the same period which bore its author's name in the (posthumous) quartos of 1604 and 1616, and both Shakespeare and Jonson used, or allowed the usage of, their names to authorize their work in early publication. However, none of the early editions or references to performances of *The Spanish Tragedy* associates the play with Kyd's name. There is no mention of Kyd on the title pages of the numerous editions of the play. He does not feature among the actors, playwrights, debtors, and other associates listed in Henslowe's papers, despite having apparently provided the theatrical entrepreneur with one of his most assured commercial successes. While Dekker includes "industrious Kyd" in his vision of a poetic Elysium in *A Knight's Conjuring* (1607) and Francis Meres states he is "among our best for tragedy" in Palladis Tamia (1598),[4] nowhere before 1612 are Kyd's gifts evidenced by the statement of his authorship of the play *The Spanish Tragedy.* In fact, there is little contemporary evidence for any of his literary activity. A quarto edition of his translation of Robert Garnier's *Cornelia* appeared in 1594 with Kyd's name at the end and with a dedicatory epistle to the Countess of Suffolk signed "T. K." but with no attribution on the title page. A second edition the following year, significantly after Kyd's death, is the only publication attributed to Kyd to carry its author's name on its title page. A sixteenth-century reference to this work corroborates Kyd's authorship, while at the same time suggesting that the tragedy was insufficiently valued. In *Polimenteia,* in a complaint at English philistinism, the author William Covell imagines a better time: "then should not tragicke *Garnier* have his poor *Cornelia* stand naked upon every poste." A marginal note adds, "A work howsoever not respected yet excellently done by Th. Kid."[5] Kyd is listed among those "moderne and extant Poets, that have liv'd togither"[6] in the 1600 anthology *Bel-védere or The Garden of the Muses,* alongside Spenser, Drayton, Shakespeare, Marlowe, and Jonson. The snippets recorded are not identified by author, however, so it is impossible to trace Kyd's contribution, although twenty of the excerpts are from *The Spanish Tragedy* and a similar number from *Soliman and Perseda,* often attributed to Kyd.[7] Another anthology in the same year, Robert Allott's *Englands Parnassus,* does attribute extracts to authors, including Kyd, but none of the quoted passages is from *The Spanish Tragedy.* Frederick Boas has noted Kyd's "seemingly lifelong practice of anonymity"[8]—a practice which extended posthumously—to which Arthur Freeman adds that "one may well wonder if Kyd sought obscurity."[9] Even by the standards of what is known about his fellow playwrights, Kyd's traces are hard to recover from the records of the early modern theater.

Even in places where one might expect Kyd's authorship of the popular play *The Spanish Tragedy,* or its authorship by another named individual, to be asserted, no such identification is made. The satirical play *The Return from Parnassus* of 1606, for example, contains many references to specific dramatic and poetic writers, naming, among others, Lodge, Marston, Marlowe, Spenser, Watson, Daniel, and Nashe. After an extensive discussion of the relative merits of Jonson and Shakespeare in which both playwrights are referred to by name, the characters Burbage and Studioso begin to discuss *The Spanish Tragedy,* quoting from act 2, scene 5:

BURBAGE:

> I think your voice would serve for Hieronimo, observe me how I act it and then imitate mee.

STUDIOSO:

> Who calls *Hieronimo* from his naked bed? And &c.

BURBAGE:

> You will do well after a while.[10]

There is no allusion in the play to the authorship of these lines, apparently so familiar as to render full transcription unnecessary, nor any mention of Kyd. Not until Thomas Heywood's *An Apology for Actors,* published in 1612, is Kyd's authorship of the play asserted. Heywood's text does not allude to many contemporary plays or playwrights by name, but he does give a casual reference to Kyd in order to support his evocation of the culture of ancient Rome in defense of the theater:

> Therefore M. *Kid* in the *Spanish Tragedy,* upon occasion presenting it selfe, thus writes
>
> *Why* Nero *thought it no disparagement*
> *And Kings and Emperours have tane delight*
> *To make experience of their wits in playes.*[11]

As Freeman writes, "[b]eyond this offhand attribution by a member of a later generation, we have no external evidence whatever of Kyd's authorship; by so slender a thread hangs his chief claim to memory."[12]

Kyd's claim to memory does not have an unbroken history, however, as Heywood's slender thread linking Kyd with his most famous work was not always visible. William Winstanley, in his *The Lives of the Most Famous English Poets* (1687), cataloged Kyd as "a writer that seems to have been of pretty good esteem for versifying in former times" and states, "[t]here is particularly remembered his Tragedy, **Cornelia.**"[13] Following the lead of Edward Phillips in *Theatrum Poetarum* (1675), Winstanley does not mention *The Spanish Tragedy* in relation to Kyd, but he does ascribe "a Tragedy entituled *Hieronymo*" to one William Smith, also cred-

ited with the play *The Hector of Germany.*[14] No other evidence seems to point to Smith's authorship of *The Spanish Tragedy,* nor of the play published in 1605 as *The First Part of Jeronimo.* Writing in 1691, Gerard Langbaine takes a self-consciously revisionist attitude to his biographical predecessors and this extends to his treatment of Kyd and the Hieronimo play. In Langbaine's entry under Thomas Kyd, he mentions only **Cornelia** by name among the author's tragedies "which are Nine in Number."[15] Under "William Smith," however, Langbaine takes issue with received wisdom: "*Hieronymo* is ascribed by Mr *Philips* and *Winstanley,* thro' their old Mistake, to our Author; it being an Anonymous play."[16] Langbaine's replacement of a proper name, William Smith, with the decisive and curiously final "Anonymous" seems to deny that there is, or could ever have been, a named and recoverable author of the play. Kyd's occlusion from history of the reception of *The Spanish Tragedy,* which began with his absence from the title pages of the play in print, has reached its apogee.[17]

In outlining the paucity of contemporary material identifying Kyd as the author of *The Spanish Tragedy,* this article does not propose that we should question Heywood's attribution. There is, however, no reason why we shouldn't, but deciding, in the absence of any more compelling evidence, against Kyd and in favor of William Smith, or Anonymous, or someone else, as author of *The Spanish Tragedy* would be to substitute one arbitrary authorial signifier for another. Whether or not Kyd wrote *The Spanish Tragedy* is of lesser interest (as well as being ultimately unverifiable in the absence of additional external evidence) than the effects of the absence of a named author-figure in the play's reception. The immense popularity of the play, its familiarity, and its availability as a cultural reference point are entirely independent of any attribution of authorship. As such, it offers an example of a dramatic text which is, in real terms, unauthored. Instead of attempting to provide evidence which would confirm or reject Kyd as the author of the play, the demonstrable reticence about the authorship of *The Spanish Tragedy* can be used to sketch out some of the manifestations of what Michel Foucault has famously called "the author-function"[18] in early modern theatrical culture.

Much recent work on early modern textual culture has been concerned with its construction of authorship and authority, but little of this investigation has addressed itself to dramatic texts and authors. Jeff Masten's important reminder that early modern theater practice was "predominantly collaborative," both in its textual and its performative aspects, marks a move to destabilize the idea of the unified and self-identical dramatic author at the same time as the ascendance of his poetic counterpart is being reified.[19] Early modern theatrical texts do defy a postromantic scripting of the author-figure: as works frequently attributable to more than one hand, or with later revisions by the author or another writer, with cuts and alternations made by the actors and with changes, rereadings, and omissions introduced into printed texts through the so-called "memorial reconstruction" or the activity of the print house compositors. Even the later term to suggest indistinct authorship, "anonymous," perpetuates the idea of a single, albeit unknowable, point of authorial origin. As the *OED* attests, anonymity was a feature of persons not texts during this period, and it is not until the late seventeenth century that the namelessness the word denotes comes to be attached to literary works. The first *OED* citation of this usage ("anonymous," 2) is dated to 1676. Masten describes the dramatic texts on which he focuses as "texts [which] began as productions in the theater, where their writers were not known, and many of them first appeared in print without ascription of authorship (or anonymity); they are thus 'pre-anonymous'—that is 'anonymous' only in a sense that existed before the word itself emerged with the author to describe their condition."[20] Langbaine's insistence on the anonymity of the Hieronimo play marks this shift in the perception of authorship and texts, in which the anonymity that attached itself by omission to printed editions of *The Spanish Tragedy* becomes semantically solidified as a positive textual attribute. Masten's historical teleology of the interpretation of authorship argues that "the author's emergence is marked by the notice of its absence,"[21] thus claiming for anonymity a decisive interest in the "who is speaking"[22] of the text. For Langbaine, however, the label of anonymity registers not as the shadowy obverse of authorization, Masten's "space for identity," nor as a temporary mystery tolerated "in the guise of an enigma,"[23] but as an alternative, final, and decisive attribution.

In examining the historical construction of the authorship of *The Spanish Tragedy,* I want to discuss the implications of the insistent derogation, or abdication, of the author-function in favor of what might be called a "character-function." Throughout the early modern reception of the play, this discourse of the character-function persistently drowns out that of the author. For when Heywood alludes to "M. Kid," he is, of course, quoting a character from the play rather than its author. Thus, an immediate answer to Foucault's obligatory question "who is speaking" is, in this instance, Hieronimo. Foucault's specific stress on orality as an index of authorship makes it an appropriate attribute not of the writing subject—the author—but the speaking subject—the actor-character. It is Hieronimo who uses the dark example of Nero's dramatic patronage to encourage the uncertain Spanish court to agree to stage the play through which he will take his revenge, and in Heywood's example, it is Hieronimo who stands as a metonym for *The Spanish Tragedy* and its implied author. By extension, Heywood's use of Hieronimo's

speech in his polemic defence of the stage registers the self-authorizing, self-justifying, and habitually self-reflexive mode of early modern dramatic discourse. Similarly, when the character of Burbage in *The Return from Parnassus* refers to *The Spanish Tragedy,* he too cites Hieronimo rather than Kyd, following the authorial names "Jonson" and "Shakespeare" used to denote those playwrights' works with the significantly contrasted character name "Hieronimo" to denote the play *The Spanish Tragedy.*

In numerous other references to the play, attesting to its impact on the theatrical culture of the pre-Civil War period, it is Hieronimo who continues to dominate the history of the reception of Kyd's work. A reference in Ben Jonson's *Every Man in his Humour* (printed 1601), for example, makes a particular joke out of the literary merits of the play, which might be expected to include a sideswipe at its author. It is, after all, hard to believe that Jonson, paid for writing additions to *The Spanish Tragedy,* did not know of its author:

BOBADILLA:

> What new book have you there? what? *Go by, Hieronimo.*

MATHEW:

> I, did you ever see it acted? is't not well pend?

BOBADILLA:

> Well pend! I would fain see all the Poets of our times pen such another play as that was: they'll prate and swagger and keepe a stirre of arte and devises, when, (by Gods so), they are the most shallow, pittifull, fellowes, that live upon the face of the earth againe.

MATHEW:

> Indeede here are a number of fine speeches in this booke. *O eyes, no eyes but fountaines fraught with teares!* there's a conceit! *fountaines fraught with teares! O life, no life, but lively forme of death!* is't not excellent? *O world, no world, but masse of publique wrongs! O Gods mee: Confusde and filde with murther and misdeeds!* Is't not excellent? Is't not simply the best that ever you heard? Ha! how do you like it?

BOBADILLA:

> Tis good.[24]

Elsewhere, Jonson, whose interest in the play was abiding however derisive he tried to be about it, makes more than a dozen identifiable references to *The Spanish Tragedy* but never mentions its author. He alludes directly to Kyd only in the enigmatic phrase "sporting Kid" in "To the Memory of my beloved, the Author. Mr. William Shakespeare: And what he hath left us," his dedicatory poem included in the 1623 Folio of Shakespeare's works. Dekker, Webster, Middleton,

Fletcher, and numerous other writers in drama, poetry, and prose all demonstrate their familiarity with, and assume their readers' familiarity with, the play either by quoting or parodying its famous lines or through the mention of its leading protagonist. Occasionally, other characters in the play are used to signal an allusion, particularly Don Andrea as in this reference from Chapman, Jonson, and Marston's 1605 play *Eastward Hoe*:

QUICKSILVER:

When this eternall substance of my soule.

TOUCHSTONE:

Well said, change your gold ends for your play ends.

QUICKSILVER:

Did live imprison'd in my wanton flesh.

TOUCHSTONE:

What then sir?

QUICKSILVER:

I was a Courtier in the Spanish Court, & Don Andrea was my name.

TOUCHSTONE:

Good maister *Don Andrea* will you marche?

QUICKSILVER:

Sweete *Touchstone,* will you lend me two shillings?[25]

Less frequently, Horatio, as in the reference from the anonymous *The Wasp, or the Subjects Precedent* dating from the 1630s which quotes, "Thanks good Horatio (but take thy glove Againe, she answers no challenges, I am her champeon,"[26] or Bel-Imperia, as in Thomas Dekker's "How dost thou my smug Belimperia?"[27] are cited. In some references, the distinctive rhetorical patterning of *The Spanish Tragedy*'s verse stands as a synecdoche for the whole play, particularly in the numerous parodies of Hieronimo's "O eyes, no eyes" lament. John Cooke's *Greenes Tu Quoque* (1614) is one example:

GERALDINE:

[Love] shall make you fetch your breath short againe.

RASH:

And make mee cry, O eyes, no eyes, but two celestiall starres! A Pox ont, Ide as leive hear a fellow sing through the nose.[28]

While these allusions draw on the recognizability of the play's characters and language, it is clear that it is Hieronimo who dominates this recognition. Most references to the play substitute the name of the play's central protagonist in place of its implied literary patronym. Apart from Heywood's reference in 1612, no writer links the play with its author.[29]

In his essay "From Work to Text," Roland Barthes distinguishes between the two concepts of his title:

> the work can be seen in bookstores, in card catalogues, and on course lists, while the text reveals itself, articulates itself according to, or against certain rules. While the work is held in the hand, the text is held in language; it exists only as discourse.[30]

Barthes discusses the issue of authorship in terms of the myths of paternity and filiation. "The author is regarded as the father and owner of his work," whereas "the Text . . . is read without the father's signature . . . without its father's guarantee." Thus, the author's self-inscription in the text is always as "one of his characters, as another figure sewn into the rug; his signature is no longer privileged and paternal, the locus of genuine truth, but, rather, ludic."[31] If the reception of *The Spanish Tragedy* denies the filiation myth of authorship through the absence of any reference to Kyd, it reinscribes paternity as a crucial governor of dramatic action through its replacement of the author-patriarch with the character-patriarch. Hieronimo's character in the play rests on his paternal relationship to Horatio. It is because of the murder of Horatio that Hieronimo seeks a revenge which is fueled by and ultimately consumes other sons of other fathers. His blunted purpose is whetted by the grief of Don Bazulto, the old man who comes to him in his legal capacity as Knight Marshall but who touches him in his familial, paternal capacity as a matching bereft father. The Viceroy of Portugal sees his son Balthazar killed in the deadly playlet which also takes the life of Lorenzo, son of the Duke of Castile. The carnage of the final scene is strongly focused on the grief of fathers, from the body of Horatio, which acts as a visual explanation of Hieronimo's action, to the anguish of the Viceroy and Castile. The play may surrender the ultimate paternity of fixed, named authorship, in Barthes's terms, but its thematic inscription of paternity is curiously overdetermined. It is strangely appropriate that this emphasis should be further highlighted in a passage added to the original play by someone other than Kyd, perhaps Jonson, and printed for the first time in the 1602 quarto. The existence of these interpolated passages establish the play's fundamental independence from its author, denying the singularity of a paternal model of authorship. At the same time, they stress the particular importance of the father-son relationship as a motif and dynamic of the play. In the additional passages, Hieronimo reiterates the paternal bond in his obsessively circular and recurring musing on "what's a sonne"[32] and his request that the relationship be resurrected through the art of the painter Bazardo—another bereaved father—whom he commissions to paint a family portrait of his "speaking looke to my sonne *Horatio* . . . God blesse thee, my sweete sonne: and my hand leaning on his head" (sig. H3v°). The final addition underlines the play's stress on the father-son relationship and, indeed, proposes it as an explanatory principle for the whole bloody action, in Hieronimo's penultimate speech:

> You had a sonne (as I take it) and your sonne,
> Should ha'e beene married to your daughter: ha wast
>   not so?
> You had a sonne too, he was my Lieges Nephew. . . .
> Looke you this same hand, twas it that stab'd
> His heart, Doe you see this hand?
> For one *Horatio,* if you ever knew him
> A youth, one that they hanged up in his fathers gar-
>   den:
> One that did force your valiant sonne to yeelde,
> While your more valiant sonne did take him prisoner.
>
>   (sig. M)

These additional passages that explicitly challenge the metaphor of paternity as a logic of authorship reinstate it as a logic of dramatic action. Again, the function of external authorship is relegated to a self-authoring dramatic paternity, as Hieronimo occupies center stage as the play's patriarch appropriating textual authority from the absent author-father.

References to **The Spanish Tragedy** establish Hieronimo, not Kyd, as its authorizing patronymic and metonym. Interestingly, the play also establishes Hieronimo as an author, whose only known *oeuvre* bears the same title as a play associated with Kyd. Setting the scene for the playlet designed ostensibly to celebrate the marriage of Bel-Imperia and Balthazar, but really guaranteed to turn nuptials into slaughter, Hieronimo remembers his own efforts as a playwright:

> When in *Tolledo,* there I studied,
> It was my chance to write a Tragedie:
> See heere my Lords,
> Which long forgot, I found this other day.
>
>   (sig. K3-v°)

Hieronimo proceeds to outline the plot of his play, the story of Soliman the Turkish emperor who kills a Knight of Rhodes, Erasto, in order to win his beautiful wife, Perseda. This story, apparently derived from Henry Wotton's *A Courtlie Controversie of Cupids Cautels* (1578), is also retold in a play called **Soliman and Perseda,** entered on the Stationers' Register in 1592 and frequently attributed to Kyd.

The evidence for Kyd's authorship of this play is, as Freeman admits, "entirely internal,"[33] and is based heavily on the plot parallel with Hieronimo's play. Both Freeman and Boas are convinced by perceived similarities of style and expression, and Freeman, arguing that

"one cannot but sense behind [**Soliman and Perseda**] an author of approximately Kyd's level of intelligence and artistry" and that the play is "tinged with the stoical melancholy characteristic of Kyd," concludes that "the weight of the evidence is definitely for Kyd's authorship." Describing this attribution as "a maximal probability," Freeman distinguishes between the uses of the author-function in different contexts. He admits that "by the most conservative standards of cataloguing, of course, the play must remain 'anonymous,' but for the special purposes of scholars and readers in the period I think it safe to assign **Soliman and Perseda** to Kyd."[34] While stylometric and other types of linguistic analysis indeed may discern similarities between **The Spanish Tragedy** and **Soliman and Perseda** from which their shared author might be deduced, the main burden of the claims for Kyd's authorship of **Soliman and Perseda** rests on its similarity with Hieronimo's play. In a curious twist of artistic precedence, Kyd's authorship is constructed by Hieronimo's; ultimately, Hieronimo is seen to write Kyd as author, rather than the other way round, as Kyd becomes an authorial effect rather than effective author. Hieronimo as an actual dramatic author within the play further displaces the idea of an extratextual writing authority. John Kerrigan has observed in his account of the particular kinship of revenge and drama with reference to **The Spanish Tragedy**:

> If revenge attracts the dramatist because, by submitting characters to a scenario, it does as a matter of course what his own writing does perforce, it also attracts him because the revenger is a surrogate artist. (Kyd himself wrote a play called **Soliman and Perseda** published at about the same time as **The Spanish Tragedy**).[35]

Hieronimo is not, however, merely the surrogate artist in general terms but a surrogate and specific author whose function at once underwrites and overshadows that of Kyd himself.

Hieronimo's usurpation of the cultural fiction of the author-function in and through **The Spanish Tragedy** can, therefore, point to some interesting questions about the construction of early modern dramatic authorship and authority. Kyd's role in the textual production and reception of the play is absolutely overtaken and overlaid with that of its main protagonist. This is more than a testimony to the effectiveness of dramatic characterization, although it, indeed, may register the impact of Hieronimo's role on contemporary audiences and readers. Rather the absence of Kyd from the narrative of the play's popularity and influence represents a distinct and significant figuring of dramatic authorship within a discourse of cultural familiarity. Hieronimo authors his play, both intratextually in the masque in the final act of **The Spanish Tragedy** and extratextually as the authority behind the play itself. His name stands as the authority behind and reference for the play, in place of the authorial patronymic. The contrast between Kyd's non-appearance in discourse about *The Spanish Tragedy* and the frequency of references to Hieronimo offers an extreme example of a tendency to divorce dramatic authors from their theatrical creations in the period more generally. There is, in broad terms, a division between a rhetoric of admiration or recognition of named authors—the beginnings of a literary and dramatic canon based on authorship—and an engagement with particular texts, represented not by their playwright but by a fictional character within them. Thus, Meres, Jonson, and Dekker all allude to Kyd but with no reference to his works, whereas in other contexts, Jonson, Dekker, and scores of other writers mention Hieronimo independent of an author.

A couple of other examples bear out this suggestion of a bifurcation between dramatic authors and their works. Christopher Marlowe's notoriety ensured that many of the references to him after his death in 1593 were pseudobiographical in that they were more concerned with the supposed details of his ungodly life than with the literary works produced during it. Thomas Beard's *The Theatre of Gods Judgments* (1597) sets the tone of late-sixteenth-century commentary on Marlowe as one whose impiety and wickedness was punished in the moral justice of his death, believed to be with his own dagger. Parallel with this demonizing discourse on Marlowe, but separate from it, are references to Tamburlaine and Faustus which are not tagged by an author, even when they are similarly used as moral illustrations. Thus, one of Joseph Hall's satires in *Virgidemiaram* (1597-98) refers to "the Turkish Tamburlaine," and Thomas Dekker imagines the plague as a "stalking Tamburlaine" but neither names Marlowe.[36] Shakespeare allusions offer further illustration of the point. Of over thirty allusions to Falstaff, probably Shakespeare's most popular character, up to 1649, only three associate him with his author, and two of these are in unpublished manuscripts. It is not until 1646 that Robert Wild's comedy *The Benefice* mentions Shakespeare and Falstaff in the same breath. Interestingly, two references included in *The Shakespeare Allusion-Book* refer to Falstaff as author. The first, a letter known as "one friend to another, who shewes much trouble for the miscarriage of a letter" (c. 1610) collected by "Sr Tobie Matthews, Knt" quotes "that excellent author, Sr *John Falstaff*."[37] The second, a dedicatory poem to the collection of plays by Francis Beaumont and John Fletcher in 1647, inserts Falstaff as a metonym for the author between two named playwrights:

> I could prayse *Heywood* now: or tell how long,
> *Falstaffe* from cracking Nuts kept the throng:
> But for a *Fletcher*, I must take an Age
> And scarce invent the Title for one page.[38]

Such references are quite independent of any attribution: Shakespeare and Falstaff, like Kyd and Hieronimo, seem mutually exclusive rather than inseparably associated.

There is a strong possibility, then, that the relegation of Kyd and the corresponding authority invested in Hieronimo, marks a pattern inscribed elsewhere in the narrative of the consciousness of early modern dramatic authorship. This raises interesting questions about textual authority in dramatic texts of the period. At what point does Kyd, or Marlowe or Shakespeare—the author-function—gain the upper hand over Hieronimo, or Tamburlaine or Falstaff? How can we historicize the decline in the cultural autonomy of dramatic characters and the authorization of authorship in a metonymic relation to specific texts? When does "Kyd," rather than Hieronimo, come to stand for *The Spanish Tragedy,* and what is the effect of this substitution? Can we account for early modern dramatic authorship in the same terms as other kinds of authorship, or does, as I have been suggesting, the contest between writing author and speaking character make the "who is speaking" altogether more unstable?

Notes

1. See D. F. Rowan, "The Staging of *The Spanish Tragedy,*" in *The Elizabethan Theater V,* ed. G. R. Hibbard (Connecticut: 1975), 112-23.

2. Arthur Freeman, *Thomas Kyd: Facts and Problems* (Oxford: 1967) 70-71.

3. On the references to the play, see "Hieronimo's Afterlives" in *Thomas Kyd, The Spanish Tragedie* ed. Emma Smith (Harmondsworth: 1998).

4. Thomas Dekker, *A Knights Conjuring* (London: 1607), sig. K4v°, Francis Meres quoted in Freeman, *Thomas Kyd,* 19.

5. William Covell, *Polimenteia or, The Meanes lawfull and unlawfull, to judge of the fall of a common-wealth* (Cambridge: 1595), sig. Q3v°.

6. John Bodenham, ed., *Bel-vedére or The Garden of the Muses* (London: 1600), sig. A5v°.

7. On the identification of passages in *Bel-vedére,* see C. Crawford, "Bel-vedere, or the Garden of the Muses." *Englische Studien* 43 (1910-11), 198-228.

8. Frederick S. Boas, ed., *The Works of Thomas Kyd,* rev. ed. (Oxford: 1955), lxxvi.

9. Freeman, *Thomas Kyd,* 49.

10. *The Returne from Parnassus* (Tudor Facsimile Texts, n.p.: 1912), sig. G3.

11. Thomas Heywood, *An Apology for Actors* (New York: 1941), sig. E3v°-E4.

12. Freeman, *Thomas Kyd,* 49.

13. William Winstanley, *The Lives of the Most Famous English Poets,* ed. William Riley Parker (Florida: 1963), 100.

14. Ibid., 218.

15. Gerard Langbaine, *An Account of the English Dramatic Poets* (Menston: 1971), 316.

16. Ibid., 489.

17. It is not until 1773 that Thomas Hawkins excavates Heywood's *An Apology for Actors* as evidence for Kyd's authorship of *The Spanish Tragedy* in 1773, accusing Phillips and Winstanley of error in attributing the play to (Hawkins's own mistake) "Thomas Smith" (*The Origins of the English Drama,* vol. 2, sig. A2).

18. Michel Foucault, "What Is an Author?" in *Textual Strategies: Perspectives in Post-Structuralist Criticism,* trans. and ed. Josué Harari (London: 1980), 141-60, 148.

19. In, for example, Kevin Pask, *The Emergence of the English Author: Scripting the Life of the Poet in Early Modern England* (Cambridge: 1996) and Richard Helgerson, *Self-Crowned Laureates: Spenser, Jonson, Milton, and the Literary System* (Berkeley and London: 1983).

20. Jeffrey A. Masten, "Beaumont and/or Fletcher: Collaboration and the Interpretation of Renaissance Drama" in *The Construction of Authorship: Textual Appropriation in Law and Literature* ed. Martha Woodmansee and Peter Jaszi (Durham and London: 1994), 361-99, 363.

21. Ibid., 361.

22. Foucault, "What Is an Author," 160.

23. Ibid., 150.

24. Ben Jonson, *Every Man in his Humour,* vol. 3 of *Ben Jonson,* ed. C. H. Herford and Percy and Evelyn Simpson (Oxford: 1927), 210.

25. George Chapman, Ben Jonson, and John Marston, *Eastward Hoe* (London: 1605), sig. B3v°.

26. *The Wasp or Subject's Precedent* (Malone Society Reprints, Oxford: 1976), 51.

27. Thomas Dekker, *Satiromastix, or, The Untrussing of the Humorous Poet* in *The Dramatic Works of Thomas Dekker,* vol. 1 ed. Fredson Bowers (Cambridge: 1953), 341.

28. John Cooke, *Greenes Tu Quoque, or the Cittie Gallant* (London: 1614), sig. H2.

29. Over one hundred allusions to *The Spanish Tragedy,* some of them tenuous, are listed but not quoted in Claude Dundrap, "La Tragédie *Espagnole* face à la Critique Elizabéthaine et Jacobéene," in *Dramaturgie et Société,* ed. Jean Jacquot (Paris: 1968), 607-31. Full references to the play from 1598 to 1675 are collected in "Hieronimo's Afterlives" in *Thomas Kyd, The Spanish Tragedie,* ed. Emma Smith, (Harmondsworth: 1998).

30. Roland Barthes, "From Work to Text" in *Textual Strategies: Perspectives in Post-Structuralist Criticism,* trans. and ed. Josué Harari (London: 1980), 73-81, 75.

31. Ibid., 78.

32. Thomas Kyd, *The Spanish Tragedy With Additions* (Malone Society Reprint, Oxford: 1925), sig. G3v°. All subsequent references to the play are to this edition.

33. Freeman, *Thomas Kyd,* 140.

34. See Ibid., 140-46; Boas, *The Works of Thomas Kyd,* lvi-lix.

35. John Kerrigan, *Revenge Tragedy: Aeschylus to Armageddon* (Oxford: 1996), 17.

36. On these and other early modern allusions to Marlowe, see Millar MacLure, ed., *Christopher Marlowe: The Critical Heritage* (London and New York: 1979), 29-50.

37. *The Shakespeare Allusion-Book: A Collection of Allusions to Shakespeare from 1591-1700,* vol. 1 (Oxford: 1932), 88.

38. T. Palmer, quoted in *The Shakespeare Allusion-Book,* 502.

Andrew Sofer (essay date summer 2000)

SOURCE: Sofer, Andrew. "Absorbing Interests: Kyd's Bloody Handkerchief as Palimpsest." *Comparative Drama* 34, no. 2 (summer 2000): 127-53.

[*In the following essay, Sofer proposes that Kyd's bloody handkerchief in* The Spanish Tragedy *is a purposeful reference to previous appearances of holy cloth in English drama, suggesting an analogy between Kyd's appropriation of a Catholic "stage property" and the Elizabethan theater's absorption of religious rituals abandoned in Protestant England.*]

Old stancher! [*Pause.*] You . . . remain.

—Hamm in *Endgame*[1]

After the Protestant Reformation took hold in England, many stage properties familiar from the drama of worship performed by urban trade guilds became politically and religiously suspect. While Elizabethan society debated whether theatrical representation was acceptable on the one hand or idolatrous on the other, Elizabethan authorities sought to curb the theatrical use of Catholic symbolism through legislation. Thus a letter dated 27 May 1576 from the Ecclesiastical Commissioners of York to the bailiff and burgesses of Wakefield decreed that "no Pageant be used or set furth wherin the Ma[jes]tye of God the Father, God the Sonne, or God the Holie Ghoste or the administration of either the Sacramentes of baptisme or of the Lordes Supper be counterfeyted or represented, or anythinge plaied which tende to the maintenaunce of superstition and idolatrie or which be contrarie to the lawes of god [and] or of the realme."[2] By 1580, the Corpus Christi play cycles had either withered away or been suppressed by the Elizabethan authorities, and with them vanished such formerly central properties as the eucharistic Host itself.[3]

Yet the Mass and its symbols did not fade from the awareness of early modern audiences once their overt representation was banned on the stage. The Elizabethan playwrights who wrote for a nascent commercial theater were eager to exploit the rituals of the old religion, although their aim was not necessarily the Reformist propaganda exemplified by Cromwell's aggressively polemical playwright, John Bale. While the political space for expressions of dissent was restricted, in the new economy of the sign developed by commercially-minded playwrights, radically different imaginative contracts with spectators drawn from all levels of society became necessary in order to build an audience largely made up of individual, urban ticket-buyers rather than regional communities united by civic and devotional concerns. And if the new commercial drama risked provoking the authorities by presenting religious material in verbal form, it could smuggle religious imagery and content onto the stage by appealing to the spectators' imagination and memory through gestures and physical objects.

Marvin Carlson's concept of "ghosting" offers a useful way of understanding the mechanism whereby the commercial Elizabethan drama invoked religious symbols and ideas that could no longer be directly represented on stage with impunity. Carlson reminds us that spectators bring associations from previous productions with them to the theater, and that these "ghosts" color their experience of the current performance.[4] When Elizabethan audiences saw Edward Alleyn play Christopher Marlowe's Faustus, for example, Alleyn's performance would have been "ghosted" by his previous appearances as Marlovian overreachers such as Tamburlaine and the Jew of Malta. According to Carlson:

> In semiotic terms, we might say that a signifier, already bonded to a signified in the creation of a stage sign, is moved in a different context to be attached to a differ-

ent signified, but when that new bonding takes place, the receiver's memory of the previous bonding remains, contaminating, or "ghosting" the new sign.[5]

One concrete example of such "ghosting" was the Elizabethan players' use of actual church vestments and properties for satiric ends. In one familiar example, Marlowe's Mephistopheles wears the robes of a Franciscan friar (and thus confirms the audience's presumed suspicion that all friars are devilish).

Another striking example, and the focus of this essay, is the device of the bloody handkerchief popularized by Thomas Kyd's spectacularly successful *The Spanish Tragedy* (1582-92). As it moves through the play, Kyd's bloody handkerchief invokes previous performances by bloody cloths, even as it weaves them into an original narrative. Indeed, at the play's climax the ghost in the bloody handkerchief's folds is the Host itself, the "Real Presence" of Christ's body as it was embodied in the sacrament of the eucharist and metonymically invoked by various sacred cloths on the late medieval stage. By the time of *The Spanish Tragedy*—set in a Catholic country loathed and feared by a great many in Kyd's audience—the Protestant Lord's Supper had replaced the Catholic Mass in the Anglican Church. The Host itself was officially understood to be a commemorative symbol and sign of Christ's spiritual presence in the sacrament rather than the transubstantiated body of Christ.[6] Meanwhile, the commercial Elizabethan playhouses filled a theatrical and spiritual void left by the suppression of the devotional Corpus Christi drama on the one hand and the rituals of the Catholic church on the other.[7]

By analyzing Kyd's subversion of a long tradition linking holy cloths and sacred blood in medieval drama, I wish to demonstrate that the bloody napkin is a ghostly palimpsest that absorbs meaning through intertextual borrowing as well as through fresh symbolic resonance. Further, I wish to argue that Kyd's appropriation of the handkerchief was not didactic, as has been argued by recent scholars of Reformation drama, but an opportunistic bid to recast the late medieval "contract of transformation" embodied by bloody cloth as an addictive "contract of sensation." But to understand Kyd's revision, we must first trace the property-cloth's origins back to the very beginning of liturgical drama.

HOLY CLOTHS AND SACRED BLOOD: THE MEDIEVAL HERITAGE

> He is not here, the sothe to say.
>
> —*The Wakefield Play of the Resurrection*

The first dramatic cloth on the English stage was the symbolic grave-cloth (*linteum*) that provided ocular proof of Christ's resurrection at the climax of the *Visitatio Sepulchri,* the tenth-century Easter liturgical drama that reenacted the visit of the three Marys to Christ's tomb. In the case of the *Regularis Concordia,* a liturgical script prepared at Winchester by Saint Ethelwold, Bishop of Winchester, some time between 965 and 975 for Benedictine use in England, this property-cloth tangibly linked the *Visitatio* to three preceding ceremonies: the *Adoratio, Depositio,* and *Elevatio.* On Good Friday, a veiled cross or crucifix was gradually uncovered by two deacons before being laid on the altar and venerated by each member of the congregation in turn (*Adoratio*). The deacons then wrapped the cross in the linen cloth and "buried" it in an improvised "sepulchre," a part of the altar with a curtain stretched around it (*Depositio*). A "watch" was then posted to "guard" the tomb until the night of the Lord's resurrection; the cross was then "raised" on Easter Sunday before the congregation was admitted to Mass (*Elevatio*). After the *Elevatio,* the linen cloth was left behind on the altar for use in the drama that followed—possibly the earliest liturgical drama to be sung in English churches.[8]

According to the text of the *Visitatio* in the *Regularis Concordia,* as set down by Saint Ethelwold, the monk who represents the angel summons the three Marys to the altar by singing, "Come and see the place [where the Lord had been laid, alleluia.]" The written instructions then read:

> *Saying this, let him rise, and lift the veil and show them the place bare of the cross, with nothing other than the shroud in which the cross had been wrapped. Seeing which, let them set down in that same sepulchre the thuribles which they had carried, and let them take up the shroud and spread it out before the clergy; and, as if demonstrating that the Lord has risen and is not now wrapped in it, let them sing this antiphon: The Lord has risen from the sepulchre . . . And let them lay the cloth upon the altar.[9]*

In this liturgical drama, sung by the clergy in Latin at the end of matins on Easter morning, the linen cloth represents Christ's cerements. David Bevington notes that the ceremony is simple, "dramatic" only in the sense that it reenacts a biblical event: "the costumes are clerical, the simple hand props are ecclesiastical artifacts, and the 'stage' is the choir and altar of the church."[10] Nevertheless, J. L. Styan highlights the dramatic importance of the shroud: "More than just to direct movement and gesture, Ethelwold's business with the property cloth causes it to acquire a symbolic quality and intensity. The magic cloth makes its point first when it is seen to be cast away and then when it is flourished."[11] Christ's "presence" is paradoxically demonstrated by his absence, which is symbolized by the metonymic piece of cloth.

The first substance absorbed by sacred cloth on the English stage is thus the "felt absence" of Christ's resurrected body.[12] The cloth is shown to the congregation as the culminating moment of a divine narrative known intimately by all present. It is a mnemonic device that reenforces a preexisting "contract of revelation": a belief in Christ's resurrection that is based on faith in the unseen. In a sense, the shroud is not "proof" at all. Rather, the shroud is the buffer between audience and player that signals the end of the story and the beginning of faith.

By the time of the vernacular Corpus Christi cycles in the fourteenth and early fifteenth century, which current scholarship suggests developed alongside the liturgical drama rather than evolving out of it, another, more explicitly magical cloth had appeared. Freed from the verbal constraints of the liturgy, which may have limited the expansion of the sung Latin drama, the urban play cycles enthusiastically elaborated on scripture by introducing apocryphal characters, properties, and dialogue. The Corpus Christi pageant of the *Road to Calvary* thus introduced the legendary figure of Veronica, who placed a cloth against Christ's face only to find it magically imprinted with Christ's features.[13] The "image" was of course prestained on the cloth, and in the Lucerne Passion play the Veronica actor repeats the action of visual display familiar from the liturgical drama by lifting the painted cloth toward the people.[14]

The Veronica cloth features in only two surviving English mystery cycle texts, York and N-Town, and Veronica herself appears only in the N-Town *Passion Play II.* On the way to Calvary, Jesus is met by Veronica, who admonishes the crowd:

> Ah! you sinful people, why fare thus?
> For sweat and blood he may not see.
> Alas! holy prophet, Christ Jesus,
> Careful is my heart for thee.
> *And she wipes his face with her kerchief.*

Jesus responds:

> Veronica, thy wiping does me ease.
> My face is clean that was black to see.
> I shall them keep from all mis-ease
> That looken on thy kerchief and remember me.[15]

Here the sacred cloth is not ocular proof of the Resurrection, as in the *Visitatio.* Veronica's napkin is a sacred relic, the very sight of which is said to ward off evil. Christ's sweat, blood, and dirt magically transform the handkerchief into an apotropaic talisman. The symbolic cloth that proposed a contract of revelation, based on the end of narrative and the beginning of faith, now proposes what may be called a "contract of transformation." When Jesus claims, "I shall them keep from all mis-ease / That looken on thy kerchief and remember me," he transforms the napkin from a representational prop to a supernatural relic worthy of veneration.

In the York Shearmen's *Road to Calvary* play, it is the third Mary who bears the relic that becomes imprinted with Christ's features:

> Ah lord, give leave to clean thy face. . . .
> Behold! How he has shewed his grace,
> He that is most of main.
> This sign shall bear witness
> Unto all people plain,
> How God's Son here guiltless
> Is put to peerless pain.[16]

While the third Mary repeats the familiar gesture of visual display to the audience, the dramatic emphasis here (as elsewhere in the York cycle) is on Christ's human suffering as well as on the cosmic implications of his sacrifice. The precise substance the cloth "cleanses" is ambiguous (sweat? blood? dirt?) but clearly the result of acute physical suffering. To the medieval spectator, of course, the distinction between Christ's humanity and his divinity may not have registered, and the napkin would still have been understood as a comforting symbol of divine grace. Yet in the York Shearmen's play the handkerchief's significance cannot be separated from the corporeal extrusions of a body in pain, the very sight of which may have been interpreted as salvific.

Whether or not Kyd was aware of the Veronica cloth, which may have appeared in the York Cycle as late as 1569, he was also able to draw on the powerful religious overtones of stage blood. Clifford Davidson has argued that in the late medieval vernacular plays, stage blood was not sensationalized, as it was on the Elizabethan stage. Rather, the spectacle of stage blood offered the spectator an opportunity for devotional "ocular experience" whose effects were understood to be spiritually transformative.[17] "Such bloody and violent effects," argues Davidson, "were . . . seen as indicative of the gift of grace to all humankind and as reflective of the saving power of the beloved Christ; hence that which for men and women of a later time would be unendurable would potentially have precipitated a deeply spiritual experience."[18] Even the fourteenth-century author of the antitheatrical *Tretise of Miraclis Pleyinge* admitted, "ofte sithis by siche miraclis pleyinge men and wymmen, seinge the passioun of Christ and of his seintis, ben movyd to compassion and devocion, wepinge bitere teris."[19]

As a potentially transformative sight, blood was continually displayed in the Corpus Christi plays. In York and N-Town, for example, Christ visibly sweats both water and blood in the Garden of Gethsemane, and the N-Town *Passion Play II* specifies that Christ should be stripped and beaten with whips *"til he is all blody."*[20] At one point in the Wakefield Scourging a torturer remarks, "Lett me rub on the rust, that the bloode down glide / As swythe."[21] By the time of his crucifixion, Christ's body was covered not only with blood and sweat but often with spittle and mucus as well; "I shall spitt in his face, though it be fare shining," remarks the same Wakefield torturer.[22] According to Davidson, "to devout viewers of the plays, or even to those less devout, the late medieval civic religious drama represented blood in these circumstances as sacred, not as the impure or polluted result of violence."[23] Christ's white leather garment (or "wounded" shirt at York) was visibly imbued with the miraculous traces of His sacred blood and thus worthy of veneration.[24] While many scholars have drawn attention to the ambiguity of blood symbolism in the later Middle Ages, the historical evidence on the whole substantiates Davidson's thesis that the mere sight of stage blood in late medieval Europe was understood by many to have curative and/or salvific powers.[25]

The bloody corpse of Christ and the linen burial shroud literally come together in the Corpus Christi Play of the Death and Burial. In the York Butchers' version, for example, Joseph of Arimathea and Nicodemus remove Christ's body "Nowe blemisght and bolned with bloode" from the Cross, wrap it in the "sudarye" and entomb it in a sepulchre.[26] (Whereas the liturgical *Depositio* ceremony had taken place in a church, Bevington speculates that the Butchers' play may been staged "in a fixed location, with a number of simultaneously-visible scaffolds," since the action would have proved awkward if not impossible on a moveable pageant wagon.)[27] The wrapped body is anointed with ointments, and the kneeling men stress the salvific power of God's blood once more: "This Lorde so goode, / That schedde his bloode, / He mende youre moode, / And buske on this blis for to bide!" (ll. 413-16).

The Corpus Christi Play of the Resurrection, which follows the Harrowing of Hell, then incorporates the Visitatio playlet virtually unaltered from its tenth-century form (apart from its translation into English). Thus in the Wakefield version the three Marys approach the sepulchre and encounter two white-robed angels, one of whom informs the women:

> He is not here, the sothe to say.
> The place is voide therin he lay;
> The sudary here se ye may
> Was on him laide.[28]

As in the *Visitatio,* the cloth is displayed to the audience as ocular proof of Christ's Resurrection. This time, however, its folds have visibly contained not the metonymic substitutions of the Latin liturgical drama (the Cross, the Host) but the actual blood-soaked body of the player-Christ, who rose from the sepulchre just before the arrival of the Marys and proclaimed:

> Behold my body, how Jues it dang
> With knottys of whippys and scorges strang!

As stremes of well, the bloode out-sprang
On every side . . .
The leste drope I for the[e] bled
Might clens the[e] soyn—
All the sin the warld within
If thou had done.[29]

No longer a blank cloth displayed to and by monastic clergy as a symbol of Christ's bodily absence, the Corpus Christi "sudarye" was a theatrical talisman elevated in the public gaze as a metonymic substitute for the Host. Like the sight of the elevated Host itself, the sight of the bloody cloth was now believed to "cleanse sin."[30] Unlike the *Visitatio* shroud, the miraculous Corpus Christi shroud heralded not only revelation but transformation, and this shift was reflected in its changed appearance. The unstained cloth offered to monastic brethren as symbolic "proof" of the Resurrection had now visibly absorbed the magical substance of Christ's blood. For many spectators, denied communion with their savior except for once a year and starved for tactile evidence of salvation, the bloodstained cloth might well have seemed to possess redemptive powers. And once the Corpus Christi plays dwindled—only a decade or so before Kyd's play packed the Rose playhouse—the comforting sight of "God's blood" must indeed have been a painfully felt absence.

DEMYSTIFYING THE HANDKERCHIEF: FROM DRAMA OF DEVOTION TO DRAMA OF ICONOCLASM?

Wee bee blynd [unless God] open our eyes, and take away the kercheefe or veyle that is before them, yea and give us a newe sight.

—John Calvin[31]

What happened to the long theatrical tradition linking holy cloth to sacred blood once the Reformation reached England? Scholars have recently argued that in mid-sixteenth century England, a newly commercial "Protestant" drama severed the link between the stage and devotional "ocular experience." Drama dealing explicitly with religious and political matters was banned by the Proclamation of May 16, 1559, and the Corpus Christi plays were defunct by 1580. Stage blood continued to flow liberally in the Elizabethan playhouses as tragedians drew increasingly on Seneca (whose plays became newly available in complete English translation from 1581), but by the time of *The Spanish Tragedy,* stage blood had apparently lost its theological underpinning as an "ocular experience," the very sight of which had been considered salvific by late medieval spectators.

Protestantism's shift of emphasis from the priestly observance of the sacrament toward the spiritual state of the communicant led to a suspicion of the outer, material means of Christian ritual. In extreme cases, this meant the suspicion that *all* images—whether mental or physical—were idols.[32] For the reformers, the "idolatry" of theatrical representation (worship of the image) was eclipsed by the new "logolatry" (worship of the Word). Michael O'Connell summarizes this "sudden psychic revolution" against a complex of medieval religious practices (such as the cult of images, the sacraments, vestments, relics, and pilgrimage) as a shift from the "incarnationalism" of late medieval culture to "the *textualization of God's body,* the turning of the incarnation (and the devotions and ritual practices associated with it) from expression in physical and material ways to predominantly textual and verbal modes."[33] The theater came under attack because, from a phenomenological perspective, "[t]heatrical presence is not mere sign but a use of corporeality to 'body forth' the fiction it portrays."[34] In other words, the very phenomenology of theater seemed to turn objects into idols, and a steady stream of antitheatricalist tracts accused the theater of doing just that.[35]

Paul Whitfield White concurs that debunking idolatry was a high priority for Puritan activists but conclusively demonstrates that, far from rejecting the drama outright (as O'Connell suggests), beginning with John Bale's virulently anti-Catholic plays in the 1530s, Protestant zealots embraced the drama as a potent didactic weapon in the fight against Papistry: "Well into the 1570s, we find Protestant religious drama calling for further religious reform within the Church of England, and as recent theatrical criticism has demonstrated, the more activist Protestants of later years employed the London playhouses to advance their own ideological interests."[36] At least until around 1580, many reformers believed that the theater—the very temple of idolatry—could be harnessed as a weapon to expose idolatry itself.

In *Staging Reform, Reforming the Stage,* Huston Diehl picks up the historical thread of White's argument and claims that London's public playhouses continued to be just such a tool of reform after 1580. She argues that Elizabethan playwrights such as Kyd and Shakespeare fomented a "drama of iconoclasm" which modeled new, "Protestant" ways of seeing for spectators still emotionally attached to the old religion. Like O'Connell, Diehl discerns a shift from the "purely bodily seeing" of the late Middle Ages to a "transcendent [or intellectual] kind of seeing" encouraged by the reformed church.[37] Diehl highlights this shift by contrasting the veneration of the *Schöne Maria* of Regensburg, an image believed to possess curative and salvific powers, with the stripping of the altars under the Protestant King Edward VI, illustrated in the 1570 edition of John Foxe's *Actes and Monuments.* For Diehl, Foxe's hugely influential work "defines an emerging Protestant aesthetics, one that restrains the power of the image to elicit awe and wonder by forcing the spectator to become conscious about how it signifies."[38] According to Diehl, Elizabethan plays worked in very much the same way, demystifying the power of idolatrous images by exposing their potential to deceive the credulous onlooker.

Among the formerly totemic objects to come under reformist scrutiny was the handkerchief itself.[39] Reformation theologians debated whether such objects as Veronica's napkin and the handkerchiefs sent forth by Saint Paul to cure the sick (Acts 19:11-12) were magical totems or sacramental signs, and Calvin himself warned against fetishizing such handkerchiefs: "For which cause the Papists are more absurd, who wrest this place unto their relics; as if Paul sent his handkerchiefs that men might worship and kiss them in their honor; as in Papistry they worship Francis' shoes and mantle, Rose's girdle, Saint Margaret's comb and such like trifles."[40] According to Diehl, Calvin's project of demystifying sacred handkerchiefs found a theatrical parallel in plays such as **The Spanish Tragedy** and *Othello,* which dramatize the deceptiveness of supposedly "magical" handkerchiefs. For Diehl, the mutation of the handkerchief from magical totem to demystified sign recapitulates the story of holy objects in the first half of the sixteenth century. The "real presences" of the divine-made-visible in sacred images (the drama of devotion) are replaced by the "felt absences" of Protestant signs, which deliberately rupture the medieval bond between the visible and the invisible (the drama of iconoclasm). In Diehl's summary, "The handkerchief is thus a contested site in Reformation disputes about the nature, power, and validity of ocular proof. What is centrally at issue in the commentaries on Paul's handkerchiefs, as well as in popular devotion to relics like Veronica's and Abagarus's napkins, is the role of sight in the practice of faith."[41]

Without wishing to devalue Diehl's and O'Connell's provocative argument that a skeptical, "Protestant" mode of seeing purged an idolatrous "Catholic" one within a quarter of a century, I believe it more useful to see the two attitudes to sacred objects—as totemic "images" on the one hand and representational "signs" on the other—as extreme points on a continuum of audience reception at the most turbulent stage in English religious history. Within a single lifetime, England had gone from Catholicism within the Roman Church, to Catholicism without the Pope, to systematic reform under Edward VI, to Catholicism once more under Mary I, and finally to a moderate Protestantism under the Anglican compromise reached by Elizabeth. Indeed, the Lollard heresy demonstrated that conflicting understandings of the relationship between sign and signified were available to spectators at Mass, or at a miracle play, *prior* to the Reformation. This dissonance erupted into full-fledged semiotic crisis once Protestantism took hold in England.[42] It therefore seems to me implausible to argue that an audience attending *Othello* or **The Spanish Tragedy** would have emerged pondering the theological

distinction between a divinely efficacious sign and an idolatrous fetish. Nor would instilling doctrinal correctness have been the primary intention of the playwright, whose continued employment by the company would largely depend on box-office receipts.

Instead, it is my argument here that Kyd exploited spectators' residual faith in magical handkerchiefs and longing for "ocular experience" by transforming the handkerchief from a token of all believers' salvation into a personalized fetish that embodies the principle of private vengeance ("Remember you must kill"). If by the late sixteenth century the holy *sudarium* of the *Visitatio Sepulchri* and the miracle-working Host of the Croxton *Play of the Sacrament* were long in the past, historical evidence suggests that many ordinary folk clung to their "magical" bits of cloth despite the inroads made by the reformed religion.[43] By introducing a bloody handkerchief into his revenge drama, Kyd deliberately exploited the medieval association between holy cloth and sacred blood—not in order to foment a "Protestant aesthetics," but to appropriate the object's power on behalf of a newly invigorated professional theater freed from the orderly bureaucratic surveillance of a clerical hierarchy.

KYD'S SPANISH PLAYS: THE BLOODY NAPKIN AS TRANSGRESSIVE SPECTACLE

See here my show; look on this spectacle!
—Hieronimo in **The Spanish Tragedy**

By comparison to its more famous cousin in *Othello,* the bloody handkerchief in **The Spanish Tragedy** has received very little critical attention, especially considering its originality. Perhaps the first bloody napkin on the commercial Elizabethan stage, the handkerchief occupies both parts of Kyd's story. When the two parts were performed in repertory, presumably the same property appeared in both plays.[44] In *The First Part of Hieronimo,* the handkerchief appears as the "scarf" which passes from Bel-imperia to Andrea to Horatio, and in **The Spanish Tragedy,** the scarf, now referred to as a "bloody napkin," passes from Bel-imperia to Horatio to Hieronimo. By turns failed love-charm, martial memento, and bloody revenge token, the property continually acquires new connotations for the spectator as it passes from hand to hand in performance. This cumulative absorption of meaning is augmented by moments at which the handkerchief metonymically invokes its medieval predecessors: the Corpus Christi Veronica cloth, the liturgical *sudarium,* and the Host itself. To understand how Kyd uses the handkerchief as a mobile "object lesson" intended to reshape the spectator's emotional response to a disturbingly familiar prop, we must trace the handkerchief's movement both in concrete stage space and through processual stage time.

Kyd's handkerchief first appears in *The First Part of Hieronimo* (c. 1582-92) as a scarf, which Bel-imperia gives to her beloved Don Andrea just before he joins battle with Portugal over its neglected tribute to Spain.[45] As she ties the scarf around his arm, Bel-imperia's stately couplets establish the silken scarf as a courtly love token and at the same time endow the favor with apotropaic powers:

> Lend me thy loving and thy warlike arm,
> On which I knit this soft and silken charm
> Tied with an amorous knot: oh, may it prove
> Enchanted armor being charmed by love;
> That when it mounts up to thy warlike crest,
> It may put by the sword, and so be blest.
>
> (9.15-20)

Ironically, Bel-imperia's "enchanted" talisman fails in its mission. Although the Portuguese are defeated in battle, Andrea himself is slain, and his final words are a confident statement of immortality that can also be interpreted as an ironic comment on the charm's failed magic: "I keep her favor longer than my breath" (11.111). Andrea's pun foreshadows the literal and figural transferral of Bel-imperia's "favor" to his friend, Horatio.

Each time the property changes hands, its meaning for the spectator shifts. When Horatio discovers Andrea's body on the battlefield, he ties the now-bloody scarf about his own arm:

> This scarf I'll wear in memory of our souls,
> And of our mutual loves; here, here, I'll wind it,
> And full as often as I think on thee,
> I'll kiss this little ensign, this soft banner,
> Smear'd with foes' blood, all for the master's honor.
>
> (11.164-68)

Horatio unwittingly appropriates Bel-imperia's pledge of love as a memento of male comradeship, and his erotic affection for "this soft banner" revises its formerly heterosexual valence.[46] (Interestingly, Horatio refuses to acknowledge that the scarf may contain Andrea's blood.) With the scarf attached to his own arm, Horatio visually becomes Andrea's surrogate in the eyes of the audience. Presumably he wears the token in the play's final scene when he is embraced by Andrea's ghost at the latter's funeral procession.

The two exchanges in *1 Hieronimo* establish the scarf as an ambiguous prop whose meaning shifts according to the needs of the scene. In the first exchange, the unspotted scarf is an enchanted love token; in the second, the bloodied scarf is a homoerotic (or at least homosocial) memento. For the spectator the second meaning does not erase the first; rather, the repeated action of tying the scarf increases the property's dramatic interest. Further, the scarf perversely ironizes the meanings ascribed to it by the characters. Instead of "[e]nchanted armor," it becomes a bloody token of ignoble

slaughter (Andrea is outnumbered and overrun). The scarf ominously absorbs blood *instead of* magic, and the repeated stage business of tying the scarf suggests that a similar fate awaits Horatio.

Thus far, it would appear that the handkerchief is being stripped of its prior thaumaturgic powers and hence (in Diehl's terms) demystified. Certainly, the contract of enchantment proposed by Bel-imperia's spell is strikingly negated by Andrea's death. Instead of the eternal contract of grace offered to the community of the faithful by such cloths as Veronica's napkin, we find ourselves caught up in a narrative contract whose outcome is uncertain. The result is both pleasurable dramatic irony (we know more than the characters about the fatal piece of cloth) and eager anticipation (we remain unsure how *this* napkin's story will end).

In *The Spanish Tragedy* the bloody sign on Horatio's arm serves as a constant visual reminder of Andrea, whose vengeful ghost (together with Revenge) acts as chorus throughout.[47] The play repeats *1 Hieronimo*'s courtly love exchange but with a significant difference: the prop is now stained with blood. Horatio explains to the bereaved Bel-imperia how Andrea's scarf came into his possession: "This scarf I pluck'd from off his lifeless arm, / And wear it in remembrance of my friend" (1.4.42-43).[48] As if aware of the erotic implications behind Horatio's action, Bel-imperia denies the possibility that Andrea would have given up the love token voluntarily:

> I know the scarf, would he had kept it still!
> For had he lived, he would have kept it still,
> And worn it for his Bel-imperia's sake;
> For'twas my favor at his last depart.
>
> (1.4.44-47)

Bel-imperia then reappropriates the scarf as hers to give, offering the scarf a second time:

> But now wear thou it both for him and me,
> For after him thou hast deserved it best.
>
> (1.4.48-49)

Despite her awkward disclaimer ("wear thou it both for him and me"), Bel-imperia elides the scarf's function as martial memento by inserting Horatio into the position of recipient formerly occupied by Andrea. Indeed, Bel-imperia has fallen recklessly in love with Horatio.

The staging of this scene, which closely parallels the exchange between Bel-imperia and Andrea in the earlier play, is ambiguous. Does Horatio merely point to the scarf on his arm, or does he try to hand it back to Bel-imperia, only to have her insist that he keep it? In either case, the token now becomes an unintentional emblem of Bel-imperia's faithlessness to Andrea. The contrast between the scarf's spotlessness in *1 Hieronimo* and its soiled appearance in ***The Spanish*** **Tragedy** may carry sexual connotations.[49] Andrea's ghost confirms that his relationship with Bel-imperia was sexual ("In secret I possess'd a worthy dame," [1.1.10]), thereby ironizing the King's later reference to "Young virgins" (2.3.43) and Horatio's comparison of Bel-imperia to the unfaithful goddess Venus (2.4.33). In this scene, the bloodied, recycled scarf suggests that Bel-imperia herself is second-hand goods.

Yet the bloody token symbolizes not only furtive sexuality but impending disaster. During his tryst with Bel-imperia, Horatio is strung up in his father Hieronimo's arbor and stabbed by the jealous Balthazar, Bel-imperia's brother Lorenzo, and two confederates. The scene is iconic in at least two ways. The lovers' bower of bliss becomes a gibbet: J. L. Styan notes that "the rope and the knife used in that order [provide] a version of common hanging and drawing that anyone who paid a gruesome visit to Tyburn would recognize for its popular theatrical value."[50] Moreover, to a contemporary audience the hanging and stabbing of Horatio by four men, on an arbor-property designed to resemble a tree, may well have suggested the Crucifixion on the "tree" dramatized by the Corpus Christi Passion Plays. Thus in the York Crucifixion play, Christ is stretched with ropes to fit the incorrectly bored holes and crucified by four soldiers "symmetrically arranged at the four points of the Cross"; later, in the York play of Christ's Death and Burial, *The blind Longeus goes to Jesus and pierces his side with the spear, and suddenly gains his sight.*[51] But whereas Christ's blood in the Corpus Christi play is both curative and salvific—the Centurion who witnesses the miracle instantly converts—Horatio's slaughter is merely a bloodbath. "These are the fruits of love," quips Lorenzo as the four confederates stab Horatio again and again while the horrified Bel-imperia, like the spectators, is forced to look on (2.4.55). In the starkest terms possible, the spectacle of stage blood is revised from a vehicle of spiritual renewal (modeled by the Centurion's reaction) to a vehicle of theatrical voyeurism (modeled by Bel-imperia's reaction).

As we have seen, the Corpus Christi "sudarye" in which Christ's body is wrapped becomes ocular proof of the Resurrection when it is discovered in the tomb. **The Spanish Tragedy** provides a parallel discovery scene when Hieronimo and his wife Isabella discover the "murd'rous spectacle" of their son's corpse hanging in the arbor (2.5.9). After cutting down his son's body and weeping over it, Hieronimo seizes on the object still attached to Horatio's lifeless arm:

> See'st thou this handkercher besmeared with blood?
> It shall not from me till I take revenge.

> (2.5.51-52)

It is just possible that Hieronimo refers not to Bel-imperia's scarf but to some new property. Nevertheless, the description of the "handkercher" matches the silken scarf "Smeard with foes' blood" in *1 Hieronimo* (11.168), and it seems unlikely that a dramatist as savvy as Kyd would ignore the opportunity to ring the changes on a property already so resonant for the audience and visibly there for the taking. All Hieronimo must do is untie the freshly bloodied scarf from his son's arm, just as Horatio untied it from Andrea's in *1 Hieronimo*—yet another opportunity for ironic visual parallelism. Once again, the love-charm presages doom for the character who picks it up.

If the Corpus Christi cloth suggests the "felt absence" of Christ's body in the tomb, Kyd's handkerchief is now literally imbued with the substance of Hieronimo's dead son:

> Seest thou this handkercher besmeard with blood?
> It shall not from me till I take revenge.
> Seest thou those wounds that yet are bleeding fresh?
> I'll not entomb them till I have reveng'd.
> Then will I joy amidst my discontent;
> Till then my sorrow never shall be spent.

> (2.5.51-56)

Here the scene hinges on yet another visual allusion. As at a public execution, the actor playing Hieronimo dips the handkerchief in Horatio's wounds as he intones these lines, while Hieronimo's reference to the handkerchief together with a *refusal* to entomb his son's body suggests a new twist to the ancient cloth. On the one hand, Hieronimo's virtual canonization of his son invites us to see Horatio as a Christ-figure: Hieronimo describes the "harmless blood" dishonored within "this sacred bower" (2.3.29-27), and in the first addition of 1602 Hieronimo calls Horatio "pure and spotless" (2.5.[80]). On the other hand, we witness the Knight Marshal of Spain preparing to embark on a very un-Christian vendetta against those whom God should punish. Kyd deliberately invokes the *sudarium* motif in order to subvert it; instead of a sacred relic promising divine salvation, in Horatio's hands the prop becomes a bloodthirsty revenge token that gives an unholy charge to the revenger's intent.[52]

Once Hieronimo dips the handkerchief in his son's blood and conceals it on his person in 2.5, the handkerchief makes no explicit appearance until 3.13. Pressed into hearing petitioners' suits, including that of an old man whose son has been murdered, Hieronimo identifies with the senex Bazulto and sees in the latter's grief a mirror for magistrates:

> Oh my son, my son, O my son Horatio!
> But mine, or thine, Bazulto, be content.
> Here, take my handkercher and wipe thine eyes,
> Whiles wretched I in thy mishaps may see

The lively portrait of my dying self.
               He draweth out a bloody napkin.
Oh no, not this; Horatio, this was thine;
And when I dy'd it in thy dearest blood,
This was a token 'twixt thy soul and me
That of thy death revenged I should be.

                                    (3.13.81-89)

Hieronimo seems surprised to discover the handkerchief in his own hand and takes the bloody token as a reproach: "See, see, oh see thy shame, Hieronimo! / See here a loving father to his son!" (3.13.95-96). The handkerchief reminds the audience, as well as Hieronimo, that the motor of the play is Hieronimo's thirst for vengeance; it is as if Hieronimo has forgotten the contract symbolized by the cloth. We cannot tell if the forgotten token is revitalized by Hieronimo's passion or vice versa.

In this scene, the handkerchief triggers a reversion from the Christian frame of the play thus far to the pagan cosmology of the play's Induction. Hieronimo envisages himself "[K]nock[ing] at the dismal gates of Pluto's court" to enlist Proserpine in his revenge cause (3.13.110), a cause Andrea's ghost has already informed us she supports (1.1.78 ff.). Hieronimo betrays his role as impersonal arbiter of justice and hallucinates that Bazulto is Horatio returned from the underworld. He descends into an animal fury and tears the petitioners' bonds with his teeth, seeming almost disappointed when they refuse to bleed. As a hinge between Christian and pagan frames of reference, Hieronimo's napkin anticipates Desdemona's exotic handkerchief in *Othello,* which introduces an eerie pagan coloring into the familiar Christian landscapes of that play.

Neither the magical totem conjured by Bel-imperia nor the ocular proof of divine grace embodied by the sudarium, Kyd's handkerchief thus far is a failed love-charm and a stalled revenge token. But it is in the bloody finale to **The Spanish Tragedy** that Kyd's subversion of medieval tradition becomes most truly apparent. Hieronimo's masque of "Soliman and Perseda" ends with a deliberate parody of the traditional climax of the Mass: the Elevation of the Host. Having staged a murderous entertainment for the Kings of Spain and Portugal which dispatches their heirs, Hieronimo unveils "a strange and wondrous show besides" (4.1.181). Drawing a stage curtain, Hieronimo reveals Horatio's corpse hanging once again from the arbor-property: "See here my show; look on this spectacle!" (4.4.89).[53] Hieronimo's "show" is a theatrical coup that forces his shocked audience to recognize that the murders in the masque of "Soliman and Perseda" were in earnest.

Turning his son's corpse into an explicitly theatrical emblem, Hieronimo enacts a bloody parody of the Corpus Christi Passion Play. Before his captive audience, he demonstrates how "hanging on a tree I found my son, / Through-girt with wounds, and slaughter'd as you see" (4.4.111-12). Not content with displaying the body of the "Son," Hieronimo also elevates his blood. Brandishing the bloody handkerchief, Hieronimo travesties the ritual gesture of visual display common to the Mass and the religious drama of the *sudarium*:

And here behold this bloody handkercher,
Which at Horatio's death I weeping dipp'd
Within the river of his bleeding wounds:
It, as propitious, see, I have reserved,
And never hath it left my bloody heart,
Soliciting remembrance of my vow
With these, oh, these accursed murderers!
Which now perform'd, my heart is satisfied.

                                    (4.4.122-29)

In Hieronimo's grasp the property becomes a fetish: the meaning of Horatio's corpse is reduced to and in some way *replaced by* a bloody piece of cloth. If Hieronimo's onstage audience watched the masque from the gallery situated above the doors in the tiring house wall (as Martin White suggests), Hieronimo must elevate the napkin toward the gallery with his back to the playhouse audience—just like a Catholic priest officiating at Mass.[54]

Through Hieronimo, Kyd transfers our attention from the body itself to the absorbing property in the actor's hand. Hieronimo thus arrogates to the theater the priest's power to orchestrate a spectacle in which the body is conjured by a metonymic object. In a theatrical sleight-of-hand, the prop replaces the corpse as our locus of visual and dramatic interest. Kyd implies that the power of the theater is the power of surrogation: the ability to spin out a potentially infinite chain of metonymic displacements that echo each other (Hieronimo's/Horatio's/Andrea's/Bel-imperia's handkerchief, Veronica cloth, *sudarium, linteum,* Host, Christ).[55] In the case of the handkerchief, the connecting thread is blood.

Hieronimo's sacrilegious perversion of the Mass no doubt played into Kyd's spectators' fear and loathing of Catholic Spain. Like Vindice's use of Gloriana's skull in *The Revenger's Tragedy,* Hieronimo's appropriation of his son's corpse as a theatrical device is shocking, even repulsive.[56] Kyd's transgressive emblem betokens neither salvation nor resurrection. Instead, the "buried" *sudarium* and Host of the liturgical ceremony are transmuted into a bloody prop and a rotting corpse, whose embarrassing material residue evokes what Stephen Greenblatt has called "*the problem of the leftover,* that is, the status of the material remainder" of bread and wine once the formula for consecration has been uttered.[57]

Huston Diehl also detects eucharistic satire in **The Spanish Tragedy** but locates it in the masque. For an Elizabethan audience, she argues, "Soliman and

Perseda" would have been an object lesson on the theatrical meretriciousness of Catholic ritual: "By mystifying and privileging spectacle, literalizing mimetic action, and displaying 'real' bodies and blood, the play-within-the-play manifests the very qualities of the Roman Mass that the Calvinist reformers condemn when they complain that 'of the sacrament' the papists 'make an idol; of commemoration make adoration; instead of receiving, make a deceiving; in place of showing forth Christ's death, make new oblations of his death' (Foxe 5:303)."[58] Yet aside from the fact that Hieronimo's deployment of his "props" provides a more blatant parody of Catholic ritual than his murderous playlet, Diehl's belief that the masque models "true" Protestant seeing by dramatizing its opposite underestimates the shocking immediacy of Kyd's bloody spectacle. The spectator is far more likely to be swept up in the deadly action of the masque than to be busy deconstructing its theatricality. Moreover, instead of confronting the artificiality of the masque, through dramatic irony the offstage audience is made aware that the stage action is *real*. Lorenzo, Balthazar and the rest are murdered, even as the courtly audience applauds the actors' masterly execution. Whereas Diehl claims that "Soliman and Perseda" mimics the very qualities of the Mass condemned by the reformers, it actually reverses them. For the reformers, the Mass passes off the sign (Host) as the thing itself (the Body of Christ), whereas Hieronimo disguises the thing itself (murder) as a sign (masque).

One likely index of Kyd's intended effect on the spectator is the reaction of Andrea's ghost. Rather than being purged by this tragedy of blood, he becomes addicted to its sensationalism. "Ay, these were spectacles to please my soul," Andrea comments, after summarizing each murder with relish (4.5.12). Like any other spectator, the ghost has become swept up in the action; indeed, Andrea has discovered a taste for blood and forgotten that all he desired at first was revenge against Balthazar alone (just as the spectator may have forgotten this original impulse for revenge). Reveling in the deaths of the good as well as the bad, Andrea appoints himself judge of the underworld and sadistically rehearses the various tortures drawn from pagan mythology that lie in store for Lorenzo, Balthazar, and the rest. No Christian redemption awaits these fallen creatures, only the "endless tragedy" promised by Revenge in the play's last line (4.5.48). Andrea's response to tragedy is not catharsis, but a thirst for more bloodshed. Kyd sardonically anticipates the reaction of his own spectators, who (judging by the genre's ensuing popularity) left *The Spanish Tragedy* with an unrestrained appetite for revenge tragedy.[59]

The Spanish Tragedy's handkerchief is no demystified idol, but a fetish endowed by Hieronimo with new and appalling life. Despite the inroads against idolatry made by Protestant reformers, Kyd's handkerchief—stripped of its prior thaumaturgic power, perhaps, but magic *in a new way*—celebrates the enduring capacity of theatrical objects to seduce audiences through an apparently limitless series of metonymic substitutions. Kyd exploits a received visual language (the Elevation of the Host, the ocular proof of the *sudarium*) for his own sensational ends. The old symbols are stripped of their former theological efficacy, but—much like a painted-over rood screen—the old Catholic imagery bleeds through. For Kyd, it was necessary to travesty sacred objects in order to reclaim them for his sensational theater. Through the figure of Hieronimo, Kyd thrusts his bloody "spectacle" in the face of those Puritans who would condemn theater as a temple of idolatry.

Of course, we will never know exactly how Elizabethan spectators reacted to Kyd's tragedy. A given playwright can only propose a particular theatrical contract—in this case, what I have called a contract of sensation, as opposed to the contracts of revelation and transformation proposed by the sight of sacred cloth on the medieval stage—and it is for the individual spectator to accept or reject that contract. What we do know is that *The Spanish Tragedy* and its successors (including *Hamlet*) were immensely popular, suggesting that Andrea's addictive response proved contagious. While it is possible that some of *The Spanish Tragedy*'s spectators left the playhouse with their suspicion of "Papist" idolatry confirmed, it is far more likely that Kyd's theatrically absorbing handkerchief thrilled its audience and left it thirsting for fresh blood.

Such a hypothesis seems confirmed by the slew of bloody handkerchiefs on the Elizabethan and Jacobean stage that followed in Kyd's wake.[60] Indeed, the holy figure embedded in the cloth still occasionally rises to the surface, and as ocular proof I close with an image from our own day. In John Pielmeier's *Agnes of God* (1982), a commercially successful attempt to revive the medieval genre of the saint's play, the pregnant nun Agnes "*presents a hand wrapped in a bloody handkerchief*" as evidence of her stigmata.[61] One last time, rising like a phoenix, the bloody piece of linen is displayed to an astonished audience as a spectacular sign of the phantom beneath the cloth.

Notes

1. Samuel Beckett, *Endgame,* in *The Complete Dramatic Works* (London and Boston: Faber and Faber, 1986), 134.

2. Cited in Louis Montrose, *The Purpose of Playing: Shakespeare and the Cultural Politics of the Elizabethan Theatre* (Chicago: University of Chicago Press, 1996), 25.

3. Among the last recorded dramatic appearances of the Host was during a scurrilous "mock mass" performed for Queen Elizabeth at Hinchenbrook

in 1564, in which a Cambridge student portrayed a Marian bishop as a dog with the Host in his mouth. On this occasion, the anti-Catholic satire backfired: despite her Reformist sympathies, the Queen was so angry at the students' temerity in presuming to instruct her that she stormed out. See Paul Whitfield White, *Theatre and Reformation: Protestantism, Patronage, and Playing in Tudor England* (Cambridge: Cambridge University Press, 1993), 107.

4. Marvin Carlson, "Invisible Presences-Performance Intertextuality," *Theatre Research International* 19 (1994): 111-17. While Carlson is mostly concerned with the intertextual ghosting which haunts the work of famous actors and directors, he notes: "Since every physical element of a production can in fact be recycled in other productions, however, one could extend the workings of 'ghosting' upon audience reception throughout the production apparatus" (114).

5. Marvin Carlson, "The Haunted Stage: Recycling and Reception in the Theatre," *Theatre Survey* 35, no. 1 (May 1994): 12.

6. According to John Stow's *Abridgement of the English Chronicle* (1618), "The 24 of June [1559] the Book of Common Prayer was established, and the Mass clean suppressed in all Churches." Cited in *The Norton Shakespeare*, ed. Stephen Greenblatt (New York and London: W. W. Norton and Company, 1997), 3365.

7. This argument is persuasively put forward by Louis Adrian Montrose, "The Purpose of Playing: Reflections on a Shakespearean Anthropology," *Helios* 7, no. 2 (1980): 51-74. See also Stephen Greenblatt, "Shakespeare and the Exorcists," in *Shakespeare and the Question of Theory*, ed. Patricia Parker and Geoffrey Hartmann (New York and London: Methuen, 1985), 163-187, esp. 181-82.

8. According to Rosemary Woolf, *The English Mystery Plays* (Berkeley: University of California Press, 1972), 7, these ceremonies originally involved burying and raising a consecrated Host instead of a cross and may have evolved out of the custom of "reserving" the Host from Maundy Thursday for use in communion on Good Friday.

9. "The Visit to the Sepulchre (*Visitatio Sepulchri*)," in *Medieval Drama,* ed. David Bevington (Boston: Houghton Mifflin, 1975), 28.

10. Ibid., 24.

11. J. L. Styan, *The English Stage: A History of Drama and Performance* (Cambridge: Cambridge University Press, 1996), 12.

12. I borrow this useful phrase from Bianca in *Othello,* who on seeing the exotic handkerchief in Cassio's possession remarks, "To the felt absence now I feel a cause" (3.4.176). *Othello,* ed. Norman Sanders (Cambridge: Cambridge University Press, 1984).

13. Woolf, *The English Mystery Plays,* 403, note 60: "The incident is included in the three great French *Passions* and [Emile] Mâle argues that these dramatic representations account for the sudden appearance of St. Veronica in late medieval iconographic representations of the road to Calvary (*L'art religieux de la fin du moyen âge,* 64). The handkerchief bearing the face of Christ appeared amongst the instruments of the Passion; cf. *Early English Text Society* 46, 170-3."

14. "Then he [the actor playing Jesus] takes from her hand the cloth, on which a 'veronica' is to be painted, presses it to his face, and gives it back to her. Then Veronica lifts up the outspread cloth towards the people." These stage directions are cited in *The Staging of Religious Drama in Europe in the Later Middle Ages: Texts and Documents in English Translation,* ed. Peter Meredith and John E. Tailby (Kalamazoo, Michigan: Medieval Institute Publications, 1983), 124.

15. *The Corpus Christi Play of the English Middle Ages,* ed. Reginald Thorne Davies (Totowa, New Jersey: Rowman & Littlefield, 1972), 306.

16. *The York Cycle of Mystery Plays: A Complete Version,* ed. J. S. Purvis (New York: Macmillan, 1957), 277-78. Clifford Davidson, *Technology, Guilds, and Early English Drama* (Kalamazoo: Medieval Institute Publications, 1996), 73, offers a fascinating description of the "shearing" process perfected by the York guild, in which the trampled, stretched, and teaseled cloth was clipped with cropping shears to produce a soft, even fabric. In their play, the Shearmen were not only dramatizing a historic miracle but advertising their latest technology. Davidson also notes that although Veronica does not appear in the play, the role is listed in the York *Ordo Paginarum* of 1415, which predates the extant text by about thirty years.

17. Clifford Davidson, "Sacred Blood and the Late Medieval Stage," *Comparative Drama* 31 (1997): 436-58. Davidson borrows the phrase "ocular experience" from Peter Travis, *Dramatic Design in the Chester Cycle* (Chicago: University of Chicago Press, 1982), 15-19.

18. Ibid., 448.

19. *A Tretise of Miraclis Pleyinge,* ed. Clifford Davidson (Kalamazoo, Michigan: Medieval Institute Publications, 1993), 98.

20. "The Passion Play II (N Town)," in *Medieval Drama*, 534.

21. "The Scourging (Wakefield)," in *Medieval Drama*, ll. 137-38.

22. Ibid., l. 72.

23. Davidson, "Sacred Blood," 451.

24. Martin Stevens, "Illusion and Reality in the Medieval Drama," *College English* 32 (1971): 456, notes: "Jesus wears the conventional white robe until the Passion, when he is clad in purple. The stage direction in the *Ludus Coventriae* tells us specifically that the torturers pull off '[t]he purpyl cloth and don on A-geyn his owyn clothis' (31/677f.), which, in a previous stage direction, were identified as white (30/465f)." Stevens quotes from *Ludus Coventriae*, ed. K. S. Block, E.E.T.S. (E.S.) 120 (London: Oxford University Press, 1922).

25. See especially Caroline Walker Bynum, *Holy Feast and Holy Fast: The Religious Significance of Food to Medieval Women* (Berkeley: University of California Press, 1987), 64-65; Jody Enders, "Emotion Memory and the Medieval Performance of Violence," *Theatre Survey* 38, no. 1 (1997): 139-60; John Spalding Gatton, "'There must be blood': mutilation and martyrdom on the medieval stage," in *Violence in Drama*, ed. James Redmond, Themes in Drama Ser. (Cambridge: Cambridge University Press, 1991), 79-91; Victor I. Scherb, "Violence and the social body in the Croxton *Play of the Sacrament*," in *Violence in Drama*, 69-78; Claire Sponsler, *Drama and Resistance: Bodies, Goods, and Theatricality in Late Medieval England*, Medieval Cultures Ser. (Minneapolis: University of Minnesota Press, 1997), 136-60; and Peter W. Travis, "The Social Body of the Dramatic Christ in Medieval England," *Early Drama to 1600* (Acta 13), ed. Albert H. Tricomi (State University of New York at Binghampton: The Center for Medieval and Early Renaissance Studies, 1987), 17-36.

26. "Christ's Death and Burial (York)," in *Medieval Drama*, ll. 370, 387-390.

27. Bevington, *Medieval Drama*, 580.

28. "The Resurrection of the Lord (Wakefield)," in *Medieval Drama*, ll. 388-391.

29. Ibid., ll. 274-277, 300-303.

30. On the belief—widespread from the thirteenth century—that seeing the elevated Host was a "second sacrament," alongside receiving, see Bynum, *Holy Feast and Holy Fast*, 54-55.

31. John Calvin, *The sermons of M. John Calvin upon the Epistle of S. Paul to the Ephesians* (1577). Cited by Huston Diehl, *Staging Reform, Reform-*ing the Stage: Protestantism and Popular Theater in Early Modern England (Ithaca: Cornell University Press, 1997), 142.

32. Thus the iconoclast William Perkins warns, "A thing fained in the mind by imagination is an idoll." William Perkins, "A Warning Against the Idolatrie of the Last Times," in *The Works of the Famous and Worthie Minister of Christ in the Universitie of Cambridge, M. William Perkins* (Cambridge, 1612-13), 1:676. Cited by James R. Siemon, *Shakespearean Iconoclasm* (Berkeley: University of California Press, 1985), 45.

33. Michael O'Connell, "God's Body: Incarnation, Physical Embodiment, and the Fate of Biblical Theater in the Sixteenth Century," in *Subjects on the World's Stage: Essays on British Literature of the Middle Ages and the Renaissance*, ed. David G. Allen and Robert A. White (Newark: University of Delaware Press, 1995), 62-87; 63.

34. Ibid., 64.

35. "The consciousness of the Elizabethan Reformers had been formed by a deep anxiety about the possibility of seeing a god within the physical presence of a statute or painting; such a mode of seeing was for them the very essence of idolatry. The suggestion that the creation of presence is precisely the work of theater thus raises the analogous possibility of idolatry, especially in the context of theater representing sacred narrative." Ibid., 65.

36. White, *Theatre and Reformation*, 4.

37. Diehl, *Staging Reform, Reforming the Stage*, 9-39.

38. Ibid., 38.

39. "It is in the discourse of the reformers that the magical becomes inextricably linked to the strange and the feminine, identified with error and superstition, and repudiated as witchcraft. And it is in the discourse of the reformers that holy images and sacred relics beloved and worshiped by the populace, including numerous well-known handkerchiefs, are systematically and relentlessly demystified." Ibid., 130.

40. John Calvin, *Commentary on* Acts, quoted by Diehl, 132-33.

41. Ibid., 133.

42. See Claire Sponsler, "The Culture of the Spectator: Conformity and Resistance to Medieval Performances," *Theatre Journal* 44 (1992): 15-29.

43. See Gail McMurray Gibson, *The Theater of Devotion: East Anglian Drama and Society in the Late Middle Ages* (Chicago: University of Chicago Press, 1989), 51-65.

44. Henslowe's *Diary* indicates that a performance of *The Spanish Tragedy* was immediately or very closely preceded by a performance of "spanes comodye donne oracoe" on five occasions in 1592 (March 13, 14, 30, 31; April 10, 14, 22, 24; May 21, 22). See Andrew S. Cairncross, Introduction, *The Spanish Comedy,* or] *The First Part of Hieronimo* and [*The Spanish Tragedy* [or *Hieronimo is Mad Again*] (Lincoln: University of Nebraska Press, 1967), xiv-xv. I accept Cairncross' contention, xix, that "*1 Hieronimo* is a memorial version [of] a longer good text by Kyd, *The Spanish Comedy,* which preceded *The Spanish Tragedy* and combined with it to form a two-part play." All citations to Kyd's Spanish plays are to Cairncross' edition and are cited by scene (or act) and line parenthetically in my text.

45. I accept J. R. Mulryne's tentative identification of Bel-imperia's "scarf" with Horatio's bloody napkin in Thomas Kyd, *The Spanish Tragedy,* ed. J. R. Mulryne (New York: Hill & Wang, 1970), 24. Mulryne glosses Hieronimo's word "handkercher" as "handkerchief, small scarf."

46. In *The Spanish Tragedy,* Horatio will describe the comrades' friendship in terms that suggest an Achilles-Patroclus relationship:

> I took him up and wound him in my arms,
> And welding him unto my private tent,
> There laid him down and dew'd him with my tears,
> And sighed and sorrowed as became a friend.
>
> (1.4.34-37)

47. Since the handkerchief and Andrea himself are both present on stage for much of the time, Andrea's blood and body are weirdly bifurcated yet simultaneously staged. Compare the play's final, uneasy double focus on Horatio's hanging corpse and the bloody handkerchief in his father's hand.

48. Horatio's explanation to Bel-imperia has the added explicatory function of filling in those spectators at *The Spanish Tragedy* who may be unfamiliar with *1 Hieronimo.* The scene thus implies two different yet simultaneous narrative contracts: one for those who know that the scarf was given to Andrea by Bel-imperia, and one for those (like Horatio himself) who do not. Presumably the pleasure of being "in the know" may have stimulated repeat attendance at the play.

49. Compare the sleeve offered by Troilus to Cressida and later given by Cressida to Diomedes in Shakespeare's *Troilus and Cressida.* (Although Troilus determines to bloody the favor worn in Diomedes' helmet, as with so much else in the play this threat is never realized.) The soiled handkerchief as an emblem of sexual consummation runs from *The Spanish Tragedy* through *Othello* all the way to August Strindberg's *Miss Julie* (1888).

50. Styan, *The English Stage,* 113-15. Styan adds: "The property 'arbour' was probably an arch of lattice (decorated with leaves and looking a bit like the 'tree' referred to later in the play), sturdy yet portable for convenient hangings; it possibly did double duty when Pedringano was hanged in 3.6. Such a prop is sketched on the title-page of the edition of 1615, where Hieronimo from his bed finds Horatio hanging, while Bel-imperia is pulled away by Lorenzo in a mask," 115.

51. In *Medieval Drama,* 572; 589.

52. On the complex Elizabethan attitude toward the code of blood-revenge, as against the Christian injunction against vengeance ("Vengeance is mine, saith the Lord"), see Fredson Thayer Bowers, *Elizabethan Revenge Tragedy 1587-1642* (1940; reprint, Gloucester, MA: Peter Smith, 1959), 1-40.

53. The arbor-property may double as a gallows to hang Pedringano in 3.6, cementing its association with death. It appears yet again as the "bower" in Hieronimo's garden in 4.2, when Isabella strips its branches and leaves before she stabs herself; it is then moved into place behind the curtain Hieronimo knocks up at the top of the next scene, ready for the discovery of Horatio's body at 4.4.88 where the stage direction reads, *"Shows his dead son."*

54. Martin White, *Renaissance Drama in Action: An Introduction to Aspects of Theatre Practice and Performance* (London: Routledge, 1998), 120.

55. In my thinking about surrogation, I am especially indebted to Joseph Roach, *Cities of the Dead: Circum-Atlantic Performance* (New York: Columbia University Press, 1996). Roach's notion of the *effigy,* an object (or actor) that "fills by means of surrogation a vacancy created by the absence of an original" and "hold[s] open a place in memory into which many different people may step according to circumstances and occasions," applies beautifully to the bloody handkerchief, 36.

56. There is even a touch of Tourneuresque black humor: the fact that Hieronimo has "reserved" the "propitious" handkerchief recalls the liturgical practice of "reserving" the consecrated Host for Easter communion.

57. Stephen Greenblatt, "Remnants of the sacred in Early Modern England," in *Subject and Object in Renaissance Culture,* ed. Margreta de Grazia, Maureen Quilligan, and Peter Stallybrass, Cambridge Studies in Renaissance Literature and Culture Ser. (Cambridge: Cambridge University Press, 1996), 337-45.

58. Huston Diehl, "Observing the Lord's Supper and the Lord Chamberlain's Men: The Visual Rhetoric of Ritual and Play in Early Modern England," *Re-*

naissance Drama n.s. 22 (1991): 162. Diehl quotes from *The Acts and Monuments of John Foxe,* ed. Stephen Reed Cattley (London: 1837-41).

59. In direct contrast, Diehl, "Observing the Lord's Supper," 164, argues that "Kyd's audiences have learned to distrust spectacles of blood."

60. Bloody handkerchiefs subsequently appear in John Lyly's *The Woman in the Moon* (1594-97), the anonymous *A Warning for Fair Women* (1596-1600), Shakespeare's *3 Henry VI* (1590-91), *As You Like It* (1599-1600), *Othello* (c. 1603), and *Cymbeline* (1609-10), Francis Beaumont and John Fletcher's *Cupid's Revenge* (1608), John Webster's *The Duchess of Malfi* (1612), and Sir John Denham's *The Sophy* (1641). On the Restoration stage, the bloody handkerchief featured in three gory tragedies, Nathaniel Lee's *Caesar Borgia* (1679), John Banks' *Vertue Betray'd* (1682), and Colley Cibber's *Xerxes* (1699), before being mocked as a stage cliché in Sir John Vanbrugh's *The Mistake* (1705). In the Georgian era, the handkerchief's contract of sensation was eclipsed by a contract of sentiment: Georgian audiences evidently preferred their "tragedy handkerchiefs" drowned in tears rather than in blood.

61. John Pielmeier, *Agnes of God* (Garden City, New York: Nelson Doubleday, 1982), cited by Gatton, "'There must be Blood,'" 89. I am grateful to Gatton's article for bringing the play to my attention.

Eric Griffin (essay date spring 2001)

SOURCE: Griffin, Eric. "Ethos, Empire, and the Valiant Acts of Thomas Kyd's Tragedy of 'the Spains.'" *English Literary Renaissance* 31, no. 2 (spring 2001): 192-229.

[*In the following essay, Griffin attempts to broaden the historical context in which* The Spanish Tragedy *can be interpreted, connecting the threads of Spanish and English imperial history, Protestant reform, and Catholic expansionism to articulate a "web of significance" in which all aspects of the play resonate in multiple dimensions.*]

For an Historiographer discourseth of affayres orderly as they were done, accounting as well the times and the actions, but a Poet thrusteth into the middest, even where it most concerneth him, and there recoursing to thinges forepaste, and divining of thinges to come, maketh a pleasing Analysis of all.[1]

—Edmund Spenser to Walter Ralegh, January 23, 1589

For heresie and Schisme, were the *Greeke Emperours* discharged, and *the Empire thereby trãslated* to the Germans . . . now our holy father *Sixtus the fifte* . . .

therefore hathe specially intreated Philip the highe and mightie Kinge Catholike of Spaine . . . for his singular love towardes that nation whereof by marriage of Holie Queene Marie of blessed memorie he was once king, for the olde love and league betwixt said cuntrie and the house of Burgogne, for the infinite injuries and dishonours done to his maiestie and people by Elizabethe, and to conclude for his speciall pietie and zeale towards Gods house and the see Apostolicke . . . wold take upon him in the name of God almighty, this sacred and glorious enterprise.[2]

—William Allen, "Englishman"

Declare among the nations, and publish it, and set up a standart, proclaim it *and* conceale it not: say, Babel is taken, Bel is confounded, Merodach is broken down: her idoles are confounded and their images are burnt in pieces.

—Jeremiah 50.2, Geneva translation

As the highly symbolic and multi-vocal name worn by its central character proclaims, *The Spanish Tragedy* comes to us cast in terms of "Empire." To invoke this religio-political problem—which Henry VIII had forced upon England during the 1530s, and which his doctrinally orthodox daughter Mary, along with her Spanish husband Philip and their English Catholic counselors, had tried in the 1550s to reverse—is to recognize that the argument of Kyd's play turns upon a principal crux of Reformation culture, the "implicit trend towards the sovereignty of State over the Church."[3] To strike at the heart of this matter, *The Spanish Tragedy* displaces the *literal* events of the 1580s in order to project them *literarily* into a mythic space at once past and future: in Edmund Spenser's contemporary prescript, by "recoursing to thinges forepaste, and divining of thinges to come," Kyd stands at a critical remove from the structural upheaval that was shaking European culture at the moment of his writing, thrusting "into the middest" in order to make "a pleasing Analysis of all."

In the 1950s William Empson alerted us that "the question" *The Spanish Tragedy* explores is "a major one of current politics."[4] Yet the text has remained strangely resistant to critical efforts that import history, whether by anecdote or allusion.[5] This may be the case because although we have tended to think about Kyd's play in light of the historical dynamics of the short run by fixing it to particular events—that is, either Spain's 1580 resolution to the Portuguese succession crisis, or England's victory over the Armada of 1588—we have failed to consider how the problems he stages are, like these events themselves, the product of a much more global cultural watershed.[6] So while acknowledging at the outset that no appeal to "culture" can ever hope to bridge all of *The Spanish Tragedy*'s formal discontinuities (or its ideological faultlines), any more than historical contextualization can recover some singular originary meaning, I want to offer a much more expansive sense of situation for the drama than commonly has been suggested by re-animating a web of significance that extends well beyond the boundaries of both the text itself and the individual "nations" the play labors to represent.[7]

In what follows I seek to develop *The Spanish Tragedy*'s relation to a number of early modern cultural traditions and formations that previous commentators have touched upon, but failed—probably as a result of the narrow disciplinary temper that occasioned their work—to synthesize narrow disciplinary temper that occasioned their work—to synthesize and draw into formal relation with the play.[8] My second section begins the work of situating Kyd's play against the backdrop of the Iberian consolidation of the 1580s and the discourses of Empire and Idolatry that attend the event. Part III develops the drama's orientation to the imperial religio-political system in opposition to which the nascent English nation is attempting to construct itself at the time of Kyd's writing. Part IV examines how Kyd's representations of English agency in the two plays-with-the-play implicate his audience in the action by performing a critique of transnational dynasticism even as they look forward to the imperial translation in England's future; while Part V considers the multiple function of the sign "Hieronimo," both in the onstage world of the play and within the global "Spanish" Empire that it implicitly critiques. But in order to render these things visible, we must first "open" the name "Bel-imperia" (much in the way a contemporary hermeneut might have opened this sign): to trace the relation of this explicitly allegorical figure to the two highly public traditions of Empire that prevail during the early modern period—one a Latin inheritance, the other Hebrew—is to revivify a neglected interpretive matrix that may have given birth to much of *The Spanish Tragedy*'s meaning.[9]

II

The structures of meaning that Kyd mobilizes are at the time of his writing quite well established[10]: they are at once the common inheritance of all of the "nations" of early modern Europe *and* the discursive raw materials to which each of these emerging national cultures resort in their attempts to construct difference. When we read *The Spanish Tragedy* inter-nationally—that is, in a manner less dependent upon our often anachronistic sense of how fully the national cultures of early modernity had constituted themselves[11]—what seems most significant about the play's relation to the lived history of the late sixteenth century is neither that it alludes specifically to the events of 1580s, nor that it parrots the received apocalyptics of Elizabethan Protestantism.[12] More telling is the way Kyd's apocalyptic rhetoric both plays upon the discursive resources England, Spain, Portugal and Europe's other peoples hold in common,

and how, by way of a number of manifestly English rhetorical practices, his play transforms these traditional cultural codes, co-opting them in service of the newly nationalistic imperial vision of the Tudor regime.[13]

Although generated by the larger cultural tensions that wedge themselves between England and Spain during the early modern period, I do not believe that the meaning of the play depends upon an appeal to some essential Spanish *ethnos* of the kind constructed in the many propagandistic tracts that circulate Northern Europe during the era of Hapsburg dominance (as do many of the "Spanish plays" written by Kyd's contemporaries): instead, *The Spanish Tragedy* explores allegorically the corrupting influence of the imperialist Roman Catholic *ethos* on Iberian society.[14] And unlike the many treatises, polemics and correspondences of the era that betray the uncertainties and anxieties generated by the Portuguese succession, Kyd's play mediates these occurrences by endowing them with positive historical meaning. His largely fictive argument, though vaguely allusive, does not draw attention to "the facts" of history so much as it tries *post facto* to make sense of the cultural recording that is at the time of the play's production still very much in process. It is quite clearly a post-unification Iberia into which we are thrust in *The Spanish Tragedy*; Kyd's tragedy is a tragedy of "the Spains"—as the Iberian kingdoms collectively construct themselves after 1580—in which the new imperial arrangement is already in place.[15] Portugal is not ruled by a Portuguese king in the play, and contrary to what an audience of the 1580s or 1590s might have had reason to expect—for during this period Dom Antonio of Portugal becomes a fixture on the world political stage, pleading before all the courts of Europe the legitimacy of his own succession over Philip II's[16]—a native pretender does not wait in the wings. What must be stressed at the outset, then, is that the difficulties we see staged in Kyd's opening scenes are not so much international as they are *internal*. And within the Spains of the play conflict centers around one character—that figure of Empire, Bel-imperia herself.

A number of *The Spanish Tragedy*'s commentators have recognized that the play stages an act of Providence—a *translatio imperii*—pointing toward "the emergence of England as the new Empire."[17] As Eugene Hill has shown us, Kyd could not have appropriated more fitting models through which to stage this providential translation than the prophetic Vergilian mode, which his play inverts as a kind of "counter-Aeneid," and the tragic Senecan style which he uses to evoke a "nightmarish" political realm reminiscent of Nero's Rome.[18] But precisely how Bel-imperia figures in this Senecan and Vergilian scheme remains a problem. Hill writes that

> what that somewhat tarnished Spanish virgin . . . represents—the glory of Empire—will be transmitted to

another and truer imperial virgin. I mean to Elizabeth, who from captive Princess (the parallel with Bel-imperia's plight is, I think, intended) had become an adept juggler of suitors, a skillful wielder of Empire. Elizabeth will rule on an island at the end of the world, an island which her countrymen—following an ancient tradition—identified with the Elysian fields. And that, of course, was the destination of Aeneas, which he reaches at the center of Virgil's poem. The depths of Kydian implication are Spenserian indeed.[19]

I believe that Hill is right to invoke Spenser. But while it seems evident that Elizabethan theater-goers would feel urged to compare their own Princess with Bel-imperia, we should not rush too quickly toward this positive identification. As Empson stresses (and Hill may sense this too, because he reads Bel-imperia as "somewhat tarnished"), it is also quite probable that they would "be rather shocked by her because it is clear that she goes to bed with her lovers (among the first words of the play are 'In secret I possessed a worthy dame')."[20] Unlike Elizabeth Tudor—or more to the point, unlike the official image so artfully disseminated by the Elizabethan regime—Bel-imperia seems too fraught with imperfections to make this identification so easy.[21]

For although the role she assumes in the play's final masque does help Hieronimo stage his valiant act of revenge, the "facts" of Bel-imperia's previous life—as Empson also underscores, she "hath practised the French" (4.2.177) with Dons Andrea and Horatio—appear far from chaste. But however interesting these details of her private life may be, we should refrain from speaking of this character as though required to regard her solely according to the demands of verisimilitude (that is, as a Princess in a literal or historical sense). Instead, let us begin to unwind the fabric of quite public meaning that her name surely invites us to trace. When we put slightly more pressure on Bel-imperia—casting her both more allegorically and in concert with the typologizing habits of Reformation (and Counter-reformation) culture—Kyd's imperial princess begins to assume a much more multidimensional and culturally relevant shape.

By mobilizing the name "Bel-imperia," Kyd "shadows"—with a multivocality much in line with that we have more commonly associated with his fellow Merchant Taylors' alumnus—a "dark conceit" that "beareth two persons."[22] Indeed *The Spanish Tragedy*'s imperial princess has much in common with a character like Spenser's Duessa, whose "seeming glorious show" could bewitch "all men's sight."[23] For though we may presume her beautiful, alluring and perhaps victimized, and though she does represent, in a strong sense, the beauty or "glory of Empire"[24] (traits that could equally describe Duessa), we should also recognize that there is something terrible about her beauty. This is, of course,

the point, and any attempt to make Bel-imperia stand for simply "beauty," "glory," or "Elizabeth" reduces her interpretive richness. For while we can read Bel-imperia's name after *bella*, so can we read it as though derived from *bellum*, suggesting her relation to "war." We are, after all, from the play's prologue forward, in *Bell*ona's domain "where lovers live, [with] bloody martialists" (1.1.61).[25] And contrary to what Andrea, "who for his love tried fortune of the wars, / And by war's fortune sought both love and life" (1.1.39-40), boasts in the Prologue, the real issue in the play may not be so much the fact that he once possessed Bel-imperia, but that he is—as are each of Kyd's other Dons in their turn: Horatio, Balthazar, and even Hieronimo—possessed by her. But while a foreshadowing such as "Then thus begin our wars" (2.4.35)—coming as it does from a character about to be brutally slain—the more Protestant among his audience would have known far in advance of this allusion that there is something perilous, duplicitous, seductive, and false about Bel-imperia's charms.

In the years since S. F. Johnson showed *The Spanish Tragedy*'s relation to the apocalyptic poetics of Bale and Foxe and other mid-16th century Protestant ideologues, it has been amply demonstrated that Kyd employs a symbolic vocabulary derived from Daniel and Revelation which posits Spain as the "new Babylon" within the received apocalyptic typology of the Calvinist tradition.[26] This exegetical approach furnishes a provocative counterpoint to Hill's resuscitation of the play's Senecan and Vergilian interpolations, which do indeed, as Nashe recognized, ride uneasily with their biblical counterparts because they effectively "thrust Elysium into Hell."[27] However, the implications of how this collision of Latin types with Hebrew works in relation to "Bel-imperia," the figure upon whom *both* of these typological traditions converge, remain undeveloped. It is in relation to the coming together of these Latin and Hebrew codes that we should think of Spenser, and the Protestant allegorical tradition that his poetical "histories" attempt to realize.[28] If we subordinate the Latinate resonances of the sign "Bel-imperia" to the equally resonant tones of English Protestant reformism, we can begin to grasp the name's profound allegorical fullness.[29] For even as "Bel" resounds with "beauty" and "war," it also strikes a far more apocalyptic note, ringing in a more culturally relevant Biblical seductress (and surely Bel-imperia—again like Spenser's Duessa—is as much seductress as seduced).[30] As we are instructed in "Against idolaters" in the Geneva Bible (or in any number of like-minded Elizabethan sermons and commentaries), "Bel" is one of "the chiefe idoles of Babylon."[31]

Thus "Bel-imperia" is a double: the roots of her name are both Latinate and Hebrew.[32] And as Kyd dramatizes a string of incidents (the outcome of which is anything but *bella*), the play unfolds, in Maureen Quilligan's formulation, "a series of running commentaries, related to one another on the most literal of verbal levels,"[33] each implied by the various significations of "Bel" as they converge within the intersections of the play's various interpretive "pretexts": Vergilian epic, Senecan tragedy, and, quite as important, the Protestantized Biblical master-narrative to which the play subordinates these Vergilian and Senecan elements.[34] In other words, if we attend to the allegorical "thickness" of "Bel," we soon hear that this sign is not merely a univocal signifier of "beauty" but a highly multi-vocal sign that comes to us "saturated with meaning."[35] For when Kyd puns the Latinate "Bel" against its Biblical homonyms, the effect is to extend a "verbal echo" that plays against the various senses of their common sound. This allegorizing strategy does indeed thrust Elysium into Hell by collating it within the already-written of the Almighty's (that is, English Protestantism's) apocalyptic plan.[36] As it brings together these Latin and Hebrew codes, *The Spanish Tragedy* dramatizes how an exterior "that conquers kings" (3.10.88) may harbor an unchaste, seductive and insatiable essence, an essence which all of the play's Dons—Balthazar, the succeeding hope of Portugal, like Andrea and Horatio of Castile before him—must, because it has been providentially fore-ordained, find irresistible.[37]

If Kyd seems to go against his age by forgoing stereotypical Spanish Cruelty and granting most of his Dons a nobility they seldom attain in the religio-political discourse of the Protestant North, he goes yet more against the representational status quo in his portrayal of "the Portingale."[38] We encounter in the play no "daring race" of Lusitanians, "bolder in enterprise than any the world has yet seen,"[39] as one of early modernity's most successful Vergilian imitators, Luis Vaz De Camões, constructs Portugal's place in the pantheon of nations in *The Lusiads* (1572), nor do we find, as in Richard Hakluyt's correspondence with Walsingham, a "poor King" like Don Antonio, accompanied by a dwindling retinue that "still hang[s] upon" him.[40] And while the play does mark the loss of both Portugal's national sovereignty and its colonial possessions—"For as we now are," observes the Castilian King, "so sometimes were these, / Kings and commanders of the western Indies" (3.14.6-7)—it does not lament its crushing failure to regain them. Like Cervantes' roughly contemporary play, *The Siege of Numancia* (1580)—which prophesies allegorically the greatness of an Hispanic Empire restored to its ancient unity by "el segundo Felipo sin segundo" (the unrivaled Philip II)[41]—*The Spanish Tragedy* accepts the Portuguese incorporation as an act of historical completion. In what is perhaps a tacit recognition of Philip's dynastic claim, and of the illegitimacy of Antonio's, Portugal's aspirations to legitimacy in the play lie in marriage with Bel-imperia and in submission to the crown of Castile.

The importance of this point cannot be over-emphasized: although it is composed at the very historical moment during which Dom Antonio is soliciting the French and English to mount an enterprise that might help him regain his kingdom's sovereignty, *The Spanish Tragedy* orients us quite differently toward Portugal. None of Kyd's major Portuguese characters—neither the groveling, tribute-hoarding Viceroy nor the doubledealing Villuppo—inspires either admiration or sympathy. And when we meet Prince Balthazar—the heir apparent who will conspire with Bel-Imperia's Machiavellian brother Lorenzo in the murder of Horatio—we find him first "insulting over" the fallen Andrea, and "Breath[ing] out proud vaunts" (1.2.73-74), in recompense for which he is by Horatio "straight . . . beaten from his horse" (1.2.79).[42] Politically admitting the thoroughness of defeat, and his father's "late offense," Balthazar quickly learns to relish his Spanish captivity, as "guest" to Lorenzo, with whom he shares a like "estate" (1.2.186) (that is, rank and social class), and brother in arms to Horatio, "whom he admire[s] and love[s] for chivalry" (1.2.194).[43] Soon we find him "plead[ing] for favour at [Bel-imperia's] hands" (1.4.70) and praising the "pleasing servitude" of the captivity in which his "freedom is enthralled" (1.4.81-83). The Prince's imperial "seduction," mediated of course by the Janus-faced go-between, brother Lorenzo, is signaled by the Petrarchan cliché of his lover's complaint:

> Yes, to your gracious self must I complain,
> In whose fair answer lies my remedy,
> On whose perfection all my thoughts attend,
> On whose aspect mine eyes find beauty's bower,
> In whose translucent breast my heart is lodged.
>
> (1.4.93-97)

In stark contrast with the beaten but un-bowed nationalists of the era's anti-Spanish political propaganda, so driven by imperial ambition—and so seduced by imperial charms—are Kyd's "Portingales" that they are yet more corruptible than his "Spaniards." Indeed, virtually no ideological difference separates the Castilian and Portuguese "nationalities" represented within the play. What draws these erstwhile opponents to both the battlefield and the bed is their mutual admiration for Bel-imperia, the beautiful, war-inspiring Idol of Empire.[44] As Bel-imperia coyly "lets fall her glove," which "Horatio coming out, takes up" (stage direction at 1.4.100), both Horatio's fate and Balthazar's meaning in the play are sealed. For the typological continuum which yokes Babylon with Philip II, and the Spains, and Bel-imperia the figure of Empire, also implicates the Prince of Portugal in *The Spanish Tragedy*'s allegorical exploration of the imperial *ethos*.

We often tend, in English Renaissance studies, to emphasize the "England is Israel" topos of Tudor and Stuart historical thought without recalling that in Christian exegesis "Israel" more traditionally represents an example to "the nations," a type of "every-nation" gone astray.[45] Our error of enthusiasm may help to account for the many interpretations that recognize mainly the English nation in *The Spanish Tragedy*'s apocalyptic stew, or read Bel-imperia and Hieronimo as representatives of English justice.[46] But in Kyd's play it is Portugal that functions as an Israel by providing the negative example of a nation given over to the worship of the golden calf of Empire. This typology provides a key to the actions of our duplicitous Portuguese prince, for Balthazar—a variant of *Bel*teshazzar—derives from the same Biblical root as the name of Kyd's Spanish princess. It is, we should recall, the appellation given to Daniel in his Babylonian captivity by both Nebuchadnezzar, King of Babel, and Ashpenaz, his master of Eunuchs. The Calvinist exegetes of early modern England teach that the names given to the Israelites by their Babylonian masters represent "a great tentation and a signe of servitude, which they were not able to resist."[47] The reformers also believe that it "was a great griefe to Daniel not only to have his name changed, but to be called by the name of [Bel] a vile idole."[48] In addition, and according to a related tradition, they suggest that Daniel's Babylonian name also signifies "he that storeth riches," or "keeper of the treasure"[49] (it is, we should recall, the withholding of riches that occasions the battle with which the play begins and in which Balthazar kills Don Andrea of Spain). Read in concert with "Bel-imperia," then, the name of Kyd's Portuguese prince extends multivocally from an inclination toward servitude to these double "tentations": covetousness, and an attraction or devotion to Idols.

If there is a master sin in early modernity, a catch-all which seems to define irrevocably the "otherness" of religious practices different from those of one's own culture, it is surely Idolatry.[50] No accusation gets bandied about so often by polemicists on either side of the Reformation divide. In England and the Protestant North the militant Catholicism of the Spains, once a devotion so exemplary as to be emulated and partaken of throughout Christendom, is judged to be riddled with idolatrous practices and therefore to be resisted at all cost—even as a native Roman Catholic like William Allen admonishes his English compatriots to oppose the idolatrous royal cult that fashions Elizabeth "a verie nationall idol."[51] By taking up this primal error, the problem of Idolatry, Kyd explores its relation to the *ethos* of the most successful imperial project of his time, the global Empire of the Spains—in the typology current in the Protestant discourse of the day, "Baal"[52]—against which hopeful English Protestants believe themselves to be pitted in a struggle the result of which has been providentially foreordained.

Just when the consolidation of the crowns of Portugal and Castile is being read apocalyptically in Hispano-Catholic prophetic thought, then, so too does Kyd render the event as apocalyptic. But while Hapsburg enthusiasts read the event as a confirmation of Philip II's election as the "Last World Emperor," who will, after he has "defeated the heretic and unified the hemispheres in the Christian faith under his rule,"[53] bring in an era of millennial peace culminating with the return of Christ, *The Spanish Tragedy* interprets the Iberian unification as the ideological reverse of their hubristic prophecy. Read via the apocalyptic logic of the Protestantized Book of Daniel, the Portuguese falling off—which sets the play on the path toward its climactic Babelian bloodbath—is necessary to the fulfillment of an historical plan that will bring in, *not* the peace of Christ under a Hapsburg heir to imperial Rome, but a quite different historical epoch, that of independent national churches and sovereign nations (with England, if its people prove worthy, reserving a chosen place among them) not answerable to universal Roman aspirations.[54]

So when the Castilian King proclaims the dawn of a new era, "Now, lordings, fall to. Spain is Portugal, / And Portugal is Spain" (1.4.132-33), his chiastic recognition chimes the Protestant apocalyptic clock by effectively asserting the historical necessity of the Iberian unification for the realization of Europe's further reformation. And by representing a Spanish society that disavows a marital union between Bel-imperia and at least two native sons (while sanctioning an ill-gotten international proposal), Kyd's godly drama delights in discovering the method behind the madness of imperial dynasty building.[55] In the process, his "doctrine by ensample," to borrow another of Spenser's suggestive formulations, instructs that only a system of governance which guards national sovereignty may hope to preclude the inevitable internal ruptures born of idolatrous devotion to the illusory attractions of transnational imperial dynasticism. This is the lesson that *The Spanish Tragedy*'s Portuguese must, through the experience of their imperial seduction, learn for themselves. The fictional Viceroy's recognition in the last line of the play proper, that "Spain hath no refuge for a Portingale" (4.4.217)—a moralizing aphorism that valorizes national difference in a manner found nowhere else in the play—affirms that he has learned what the nobility of the historical Portugal fail to see: that a nation's affairs are best conducted in the interest of sovereignty rather than in pursuit of the seductive glory of Empire.

Thus we should not read the cycle of attraction and desire that draws *The Spanish Tragedy*'s male characters—Castilians and Portuguese alike—to the allegorical figure of Bel-imperia in terms of the merely sexual, any more than we should read Elizabeth's "virginity" as emblematic of mere physical chastity. Their desires are the symptoms of a deeper, more serious kind of wantonness. For what represents *pietas* in the Spains—where the Hapsburgs adopt an iconography of Aeneas-like piety in order to advertise their strict adherence to the orthodox religious practices demanded by the Counter-Reformation Church—may be figured in the Protestant North as a visible sign of the irremediable "promiscuity" of the "Romish Whore." As militant proponents of Catholic orthodoxy, it is the Spanish who become in Protestant discourse the Babylonian exemplars of those idolatrous practices, or "papisticall supersticions and abuses," which, as they become subsumed within a general argument against "Workes," are seen to encompass everything from bell-ringing, to the ceremony of the Latin Mass, to alms-giving, to the veneration of saints and relics, to the singing of dirges—each of which, while resonating within the world of Kyd's play, remains a vital, authorized ritual of *La Santa Fé*.[56] In order to reprobate the promiscuous excesses of this "irreligion," England's practical preachers commonly mobilize the sexual metaphorics of the Biblical text itself: "Idolatrie is most fitly compared in the scripture unto adulterie," writes the Cambridge-trained John Knewstub, "and the Idolaters called whoores, because as whoores admitte unto their love others than their own husbandes, so Idolaters, and the false worshippers of God, reserve not their faith and confidence unto the Lord alone."[57] So does *The Spanish Tragedy*.

We can now begin to audit the truly Spenserian richness of the play—whose characters are historical only insofar as they live in mythic, apocalyptic or typological time. By reading *The Spanish Tragedy* in such a way as to discover its relation to the Biblicism to which Kyd—in the manner of so many of Protestant England's nation writers—subordinates his classical borrowings, we can hear how the play's orchestration of Latin and Judeo-Christian codes represents an Iberia hubristically torn by its attraction to the beautiful "Idol of Empire," and which is bound, as a result of its promiscuous ambitions toward her, to go down—as had its "type," the Old Testament Babel—to the confusion that inevitably will come to reign within.

III

"Religion is sociologically interesting," writes Clifford Geertz, "not because, as vulgar positivism would have it, it describes the social order (which, insofar as it does, it does not only very obliquely but very incompletely), but because, like environment, political power, wealth, jural obligation, personal affection, and a sense of beauty, it shapes it."[58] Nowhere, perhaps, can the shaping potency of early modern Hispano-Catholicism—and its difference via-à-vis the *soli Deo gloria* pretensions of English Protestantism—be seen more clearly than in the exhortation drafted by the Duke of Medina Sidonia, Commander of the Armada, as the Enterprise of England prepares to sail. The Duke's speech is worth quoting at length, not because it alludes to any event mysteriously represented in *The Spanish Trag-*

edy,[59] but because of the *ethos*—the "set of moods and motivations"[60]—its theological orientation reveals:

> The saints of heaven will go in company with us, and especially the holy patrons of Spain and, indeed, those of England, who are persecuted by the heretics and cry aloud to God for vengeance, will come out to join and help us, and those who gave their lives to establish the holy faith in that land and washed it with their blood. We shall find waiting for us there the help of the Blessed John Fisher, Cardinal-bishop of Rochester, of Thomas More, John Forrest and innumerable saintly Carthusians, Franciscans and other religious, whose blood was cruelly spilt by King Henry and who call on god to avenge them in the land which they died. There shall we be helped by Edmund Campion, Ralph Sherwin, Alexander Briant, Thomas Cotton and many other reverend priests, servants of Our Lord, whom Elizabeth has torn to pieces with ferocious cruelty and nicely calculated tortures. With us will be the blessed and guiltless Mary, Queen of Scotland . . . coming fresh from her sacrifice.[61]

Comforting his troops in the company of the saints, whom the Enterprise aspires both to represent and to appease, Medina Sedonia puts supreme among their collective motivation a desire to become agents of God's "vengeance." Urging his inter-national company "to avenge" the guiltless victims of the English Schism, he affirms their service not to the Spanish nation, but to a much larger community of believers, the *immensum imperii corpus*.[62] The cooperative acts of this body—which inclusively admits a number of beatified Englishmen and women (those so demonized in the histories of the Protestant reformers) whose devotion to the Faith they place above loyalty to the nation—represent for him a kind of Old Testament "sacrifice" of "blood." Further, the Duke characterizes the Enterprise as both a continuation of the work these saintly individuals have begun (the establishment of "the holy faith" in England), and an offering from "us" (the living) to "them" (the dead), "whose blood was cruelly spilt." In this logic of propitiation—the effective opposite of Protestant solfidianism—valiant acts of sacrifice enable the saints' continuing communion with, and intervention on behalf of, the body of earthly believers who hope one day, should their works prove sufficient in His sight, to join their "company." In other words, through human efficacy—which provides visible evidence of the faith upon which God's grace depends—the equilibrium of the heavenly scales remains assured.

It is at the moment during which England is attempting to write a different *ethos* for itself that this theology of propitiation—the active seeking of heavenly favor or appeasement—comes to play an increasingly vital role in shaping the social order of Catholic Iberia. For "the sixteenth century," as Carlos Eire has reminded us, "marked the beginning of a 'golden age of purgatory' in Spain."[63] The same had been true, of course, in the re-

Catholicized England of the Marian years: as the villain of the *Actes and Monuments,* arch-papist Bishop Stephen Gardiner writes (apparently bringing the Latin term into the vulgar), "Withe . . . sacrifices God is made favorable, or God is propitiate, if we shall make new Englishe."[64] As *The Spanish Tragedy* builds to its Act 4 climax—with Bel-imperia brow-beating the "unkind father" (4.1.7) Hieronimo into the recognition "that heaven applies our drift, / And all the saints do sit soliciting / For vengeance on those cursèd murders" (4.1.32-34)—this theological orientation moves to center stage. For when Hieronimo ceremoniously presents the bloody handkerchief—which he preserved in Act 2, scene 5, even as he honored his son by "say[ing] his dirge" (2.5.66) in solemn Latin—he reveals a memorial that has become charged with the kind of agency attributable to a sacred relic.[65] "And here behold this bloody handkerchief," he says,

> Which at Horatio's death I weeping dipped
> Within the river of his bleeding wounds;
> It as *propitious,* see, I have reserved,
> And never hath it left my bloody heart,
> Soliciting remembrance of my vow
> With these, O these accursèd murderers,
> Which, now performed, my heart is satisfied.
>
> (4.4.122-29, my italics)

By embracing the strategy Bel-imperia advocates, becoming at once ambitious to appease the saints through sacrifice and to avenge his personal loss—rather than following his initial (and, from a Protestant nationalist perspective, appropriate) impulse to "plain me to my lord the king . . . for justice" (3.7.69-70)—Hieronimo guarantees the blood-bath that closes the tragedy. But, since it is the Empire he serves that (in the play) "reck[s] no laws that meditate revenge" (1.3.48), we must reemphasize that it is not Hieronimo's action itself that is to blame for the holocaust. Rather, it is the prevailing *ethos* of the society in which his valiant act is carried out—the theological *system* that shapes, supports and sustains the Roman Catholic social order from which Protestant England has so recently withdrawn—that determines its meaning:[66] the *ethos* that demands that God's vengeance be carried out by his servants on earth in behalf of those who have gone before.

The Spanish Tragedy's explicit invocation of the doctrine of propitiation returns us to one of the interpretive problems that has most bothered us about the play, just as it seems to have bothered Nashe. This is the difficulty of Hieronimo's "justice"—in Frank Ardolino's phrase, "the paradox of his being rewarded and his enemies punished in the classical underworld" (p. ix). While it is true that the underworld of the play's prologue and epilogue is "classical," it is the *pagan* quality of Kyd's hellish Elysium that should draw our attention. It is for souls in the "underworld" of purgatory that propitiation is most concerned, a recognition that

does much to answer several of the apparent paradoxes that unsettle the play's opening and closing scenes. For what Kyd must be straining here to represent are "the paradoxes" that Protestants, John Foxe among them, identify as the "fantasies of the later church of Rome concerning purgatory" (I, 84). To recognize this feature of early modern religious culture is to go a long way toward solving both this long-standing hermeneutic enigma and the play's advertised "mystery."

As the "hispanated" William Allen teaches in his first widely circulated apology, *A Defense and Declaration of the Catholicke Churches Doctrine, touching Purgatory, and prayers for the soules departed* (1565), "There be some, which after their death may have absolution of their lighter offenses, in debt whereof they passed out of this life . . . through the prayers and almes of their friends."[67] In *The Spanish Tragedy*'s opening scene we learn that just such an act has been performed "By Don Horatio, our Knight Marshall's son," in the play's prehistory. It is Horatio's administration of these "funerals and obsequies" (1.1.25-26) that enables his fallen compatriot Don Andrea to pass over Avernus and enter the Vergilian underworld in which the play begins and ends. Once there, Andrea is allowed to wind his way "to Pluto's court" so that Proserpine might intercede by awakening sleeping Revenge to the play's action. But what inspires Proserpine "to smile," and so pleases Pluto that he seals (in the manner of a Pope) Don Andrea's doom "with a kiss," is that which has already inspired Minos to issue Don Andrea's passport:

> 'This Knight,' quoth he, 'both lived and died in love,
> And for his love tried fortune of the wars,
> And by war's fortune lost both love and life.'
>
> (1.1.38-40)

As Minos recognizes, Don Andrea has risked everything for love. The object of this love, of course, has been Bel-imperia, the embodiment of Empire. The valiant acts of war Andrea has carried out in her service earn him, in turn, the right to perform his own acts of intercession: as we see in the play's epilogue, Don Andrea is given permission to "consort" his "friends in pleasing sort," taking pleasure in the knowledge that Revenge will hale his enemies "down to deepest hell" (4.5.15, 27).

Whatever relative peace Hieronimo, Horatio and the others seem to attain in the play's Vergilian denouement, we should note that the afterlife we see represented there hardly resembles, even from a Catholic perspective, a place of everlasting bliss. Rather, it has much in common with the "prison house" of the elder Hamlet in a play that more famously takes up the Revenge problem: in Roman Catholic theology (as in Shakespeare's later tragedy) even when one attains its upper, "Elysian" levels, purgatory remains a place where the soul remains aware of its distance from God.[68] That a contemporary like Nashe would object to such a representation of the afterlife as Kyd stages may be a sign of the shaping power of the religio-political ideology of the English state religion. For the official doctrinal position on propitiation and mediation is from the time of the Elizabethan settlement manifestly Protestant, asserting that "the end of [Christ's] coming"—which had "quenched and appeased the wrath of his father"—was "to fulfill the Law . . . to reconcile us in the body of his flesh, to dissolve the workes of the devill, last of all, to become a propitiation for our sinnes."[69] If we look closely at the pagan rewards of *The Spanish Tragedy*'s more "virtuous" characters—which include an eternity for Horatio of "never-dying wars" and Isabella's "train / Where pity weeps but never feeleth pain" (4.5.19-21)—we can see that not even Bel-imperia's "joys" and Hieronimo's orphic "pleasure" (21-24) measure up to the heavenly bliss that English Protestantism assures its elect, who through their Faith are to receive for "eternal days" the "glory" of "his heavenly kingdome," there "to raigne with him," in the refrain of the Elizabethan church's official Christmas sermon, "not for a time, but for ever."[70]

The Spanish Tragedy's relation to the raw material of this propitiation controversy is also borne out by the fact that we do not have to delve very deeply into the larger context out of which this discourse emerges to find that Catholic arguments from tradition are grounded in the teachings of Hieronimo's namesake, "Saincte Hierome," who grants that certain "privileges do serve for few" to lessen purgatory's pains.[71] According to Protestant polemicists like Foxe, these privileges, which reduce the purgatorial period before "the mercy of God doth translate [the deceased] to heavenly bliss," are the basis of the *system* of "Helps and releases . . . pope's pardons and indulgences, sacrifice of the altar, dirges and trentals, prayer, fasting . . . alms and charitable deeds of the living, in satisfying God's justice for them, etc." (pp. 84-85) upon which the temporal authority of the Roman Church rests. Further, it is indeed the Catholic proclivity to thrust Elysium into Hell that provides early modern Protestantism with some of the more forceful rhetoric it employs in order to unmask the pagan inheritance of the Romish theological system. As John Vernon argues, "I thynke [that] this is the privilege, that is described in the Aneides of Virgile, which the Sibylle speaking to Aeneas doeth reherce." As Vernon discovers, this system rewards Catholics "For their valiãt actes and lyfe most commendable . . . [according to] Thys . . . privilege of [the] good doctour [Hierome]," adding "it was easy for Jupiter too obteyne that thinge of his brother Pluto, unto whome, certayne aunciente writers have attributed the keyes of all the infernall regions, and so paynted with keyes in his hãdes as a Pope" (ff. 100-03). It is, then, as a Vergilian underworld ruled by Pluto as by a Pope that Protestants con-

struct purgatory, a place of "Heathenishe superstition and Idolatrie."[72] *The Spanish Tragedy*'s "originality," then, lies not in Kyd's "thrusting Elysium into Hell"; rather, his innovation is to translate the topos for the stage by bodying it forth dramatically.[73] For though he may render it idiosyncratically, Kyd thrusts us into precisely the kind of Vergilian afterlife that the reformers of his day characterize as "pagan." In its discovery of propitiation, *The Spanish Tragedy* reproduces the doctrinal orientation that is at the moment of its production shaping the new social order of the sovereign English empire—with its sole Head, Propitiator and Mediator—a theology advanced not merely in the polemics of hot-gospellers like Vernon and Foxe, but in the approved homilies of the Elizabethan church as well.

IV

If Kyd's translation of empire stages a counter-*Aeneid,* and our discovery of *The Spanish Tragedy*'s logic of propitiation would seem to affirm that it does, it is "counter" in relation to the Hapsburg ideology that provides the sixteenth century's most successful appropriation of that Vergilian iconographic tradition. For it is indeed the exemplary piety of Aeneas that the iconography of Philip II—an image that attracts Catholic apologists like William Allen, who proclaims the Castilian King's "speciall pietie and zeale towards Gods house and the See Apostolike"[74] even as he explains the imperial translation to his English audience—is designed to promulgate. But the *Aeneid* is not the only originary myth mobilized by the Spanish Hapsburgs. Their imperium (like England's) must also be legitimated by the authority of a scriptural genealogy which "christens" its Roman roots. Along with Philip's Solomon-like prudence, it is the Book of Daniel that provides the Hapsburgs with their link to the timeless authority of the Hebrews. In the culminating vision of Daniel 2, "the Dream of the Four Kingdomes," it is written: "And in the days of these kings, shall the God of heaven set up a kingdom, which shall never be destroyed: and this kingdome shall not be given to another people, but it shall break and destroy all these kingdomes, and it shall stand forever" (2.44). While Christian exegetes since Augustine identify this final world kingdom with Rome, imperial panegyrists, Thomas Campanella among them, begin to claim that it is the Spanish Hapsburgs, as the heirs of Augustus, who have been chosen "to be the agents of the final unification of the world."[75] This is the exemplary *translatio imperii* of the early modern period: from Troy to Rome by way of the line of Aeneas, from Rome to the Spanish Hapsburgs by way of the line of Augustus—with the mediation and authorization of the Hebrew prophet himself.[76]

What Kyd's Biblical and classical medley also allegorizes, then, is a collision of two of the dominant imperial ideologies of the day: "empire" understood in its relation to sovereignty (hereafter given a lower case orthography), the rights which accrue to the leader of a particular nation, or people, and synonymous with the term *status,* or state (the sense in which the term is used in the oft-celebrated phrase of Henry VIII's 1533 Act in Restraint of Appeals: "This Realm of England is an Empire"); and, "Empire" as transnational imperium (which I preserve in the upper case)[77] which seeks, in Cardinal Allen's phrase, "the unit[i]e of Gods universall Churche.'"[78] The *translatio imperii* implied in *The Spanish Tragedy* suggests a shift from the transnational or universal imperial model advocated by the Hapsburgs and the Roman Church, which the play represents as covetous, amoral and unworkable, to the less internationally ambitious and (presumably) less corruptible sovereign state that England, along with the United Provinces and several other nations held "captive" within the transnational "Babylonian" system, are in the late-sixteenth century struggling to realize.

But if the Spains of *The Spanish Tragedy* represent an imperial Babylon, what can we say of England's role in the drama? The simple answer is that England exists as the implied theatrical audience, the one that will behold the play's "mystery." But England also exists on stage, in Hieronimo's Act 1 and Act 4 entertainments. While the question of audience is perhaps the most important single consideration for any reading that attempts to recover something of the play's contemporary rhetorical force (a number of its more perceptive readers also try to imagine its early modern setting), I want to set this issue aside for a moment in order to take up the question of England's role in the play itself.

In the comic history of Hieronimo's Act 1 dumb show, Kyd introduces three English knights and three Iberian kings: two Portuguese and a Spaniard.[79] The scene's first action, as Hieronimo glosses it, represents "Robert, Earl of Gloucester,"

> Who, when King Stephen bore sway in Albion,
> Arrived with five and twenty thousand men
> In Portingale, and by success of war
> Enforced the King, then but a Saracen,
> To bear the yoke of the English monarchy.

(1.4.142-46)

It is not clear how Kyd comes by the cultural knowledge his interlude puts to use. Whatever its source, this allusion to the siege of Lisbon embroiders the 1147 event considerably; *contra* the play's imaginative anecdote, the siege did *not* end in the vassalage of Portugal to King Stephen (c.e. 1135-1154) and the English monarchy.[80] Historically inaccurate though it may be, however, the brief scene is quite suggestive in terms of what it reveals about the past, present and *future* of Anglo-Spanish cultural relations.[81]

The particulars of the battle, during which the combined forces of Christendom wrest Lisbon from the "Saracen," are not so important as what the play's representation does with them, and what is most significant about Kyd's improvisation is that it elevates England's role in the ongoing transnational project—realized only in 1492, less than a hundred years prior to his tragedy's composition—that was the Iberian *reconquista.*[82] In the play's providential calculus, Gloucester's "English" victory provides a foundational cornerstone of the towering Spanish Empire. According to this logic, England's agency in the recovery of the Spains for Christendom is a matter of historical necessity: in order that its Babel-like destruction may be enacted when the propitious moment arrives, the Empire's ancient Roman wholeness must first be restored. Though it might seem a trifling consolation from a nationalistic perspective, there *is* something in the anecdote to make the Portingale's "late discomfort seem the less" (1.4.149): to owe tribute to a Christian king in a unified Iberia—surrendering national sovereignty to the greater glory of the Empire—is a far more desirable end than to be ruled by "a Saracen" (a fate even so Protestant a writer as John Foxe cannot wish upon the Spains).[83] It is when we factor in the tales of Hieronimo's second and third knights, however, that the logic of Kyd's somewhat strained history lesson becomes yet more clear. For alongside Robert of Gloucester, Kyd places Edmund of Langley, Duke of York, and John of Gaunt, Duke of Lancaster, patriarchs of the two houses from which the English monarchy descends.[84] Surely, it is here that Kyd's play, however dumbly, portends the "future": for the *translatio imperii* we see in the making is prefigured by the appearance of these highly significant Tudor forebears.

It is the "third and last" of the interlude's episodes— that in which "a valiant Englishman, / Brave John of Gaunt, the Duke of Lancaster . . . with a puissant army came to Spain, / and took our King of Castile prisoner" (1.4.161-67)—that deserves special notice: "not least" because Hieronimo himself gives it emphasis, but also because John of Gaunt's Iberian adventuring was much celebrated in Kyd's day.[85] So highly regarded is the event that it is even represented in one of the standard Latin grammar-school histories of the Elizabethan era, Christopher Ocland's *The Valiant Actes And victorious Battailes of the English Nation.*[86] In the version Englished by John Sharrock in 1585, Gaunt "himself" explains the significance of his Spanish mission to the young Richard II:

> Whilst uncle to your maiestie, and princes offspring, I,
> Beholde my spouse in wedlocke bandes conioyned, of
>   Hispanig land,
> Her fathers onely heir, by force the Spaniard to withstand,
> And barre from Kingdomes rich, which publike lawes
>   her gives as due.

To which Richard responds:

Goe with good luck unto the land which floud Iberus
    streames
Doe famous make, and what as dower unto thy wife
    pertaines,
By custome due, which Nations all have eerst allowed
    for right,
If that the Spaniard wil not yeeld, that stoutly win in
    fight.[87]

The exchange between King Richard and his uncle testifies to the intense cultural anxiety that Europe's received system of dynastic inheritance could often generate, especially when a claim is made by right of matrilineal descent—a matter of tremendous import in the play. *The Spanish Tragedy*'s action, after all, turns upon the expressed desire "To knit a sure, inexplicable bond / Of kingly love and everlasting league / Betwixt the crowns of Spain and Portingale" (3.12.46-48) by the marriage of the niece of the apparently childless King of Castile with Balthazar, "the only hope of [the Portuguese] successive line" (3.1.14). At precisely the historical conjuncture in question, similar succession problems had already engendered tremendous difficulties within the royal houses of the nations Kyd's play represents. Indeed, in the absence of a legitimate "native son," dynastic chaos had ensued: in the British Isles, England and Spain together had experienced the brief Lady Jane Grey debacle and the somewhat more lengthy reign of Mary Tudor and Philip of Hapsburg, while in Iberia, Philip's claim to Portugal had come as a result of that throne's lack of a direct heir.[88]

As significantly, what *The Spanish Tragedy*'s historical dumb show and Ocland's *Valiant Actes* both seem to recognize is that Gaunt's intervention in Spain—like Philip's Portuguese intervention and his attempted Enterprise of England—represents not merely an act justifiable according to historical precedent, but also an acceptable use of military force. The thematic and formal relevance of Kyd's Gaunt anecdote to the argument of the play as a whole deserves emphasis.[89] For when the Portuguese Ambassador observes,

> This is an argument for our viceroy,
> That Spain may not insult for her success,
> Since English warriors likewise conquered Spain,
> And made them bow their knees to Albion,
>
> (1.4.168-71)

the play registers a recognition that the Duke of Lancaster's Iberian adventuring was, as *The Valiant Actes* affirms, as much about *marital* maneuvering of the kind that the Hapsburgs had so perfected—John of Gaunt had succeeded in wedding daughters to the heirs of both Portugal and Spain, even as he claimed the Spanish crown for himself through his own marriage to Constance of Castile—as it was *martial* conquest.[90] In the terms through which Ocland's contemporary history frames the problem, what the Ambassador's observation

implies is that Kyd's fictional Castilian king—having enforced "custome" with arms ("in fight"), and having had his claim affirmed by the victory God grants him—has conducted himself quite properly and in accord with the "publike lawes" of the received dynastic system. In other words, Castile has waged the "Just War." For as in Ocland's imagined exchange between Gaunt and Richard II, each of *The Spanish Tragedy*'s armed encounters—England's with Portugal and Spain, Portugal's with the Saracen, and Castile's with the Portuguese—constitute in early modern political theory an instance of the *Jus Belli,* which, like Philip's Enterprise of England, may be lawfully carried out in defense of the faith, to redress national injuries, or to enforce rightful claims of inheritance.[91] What seems to me most significant about Kyd's incorporation of the play's three English conquests, however, is that these events function not as a criticism of the Spanish themselves, but as yet another way to expose the flaws of the traditional imperial *system* in which all of these polities are embroiled. It is the combination of religion, custom and law that can justify the intervention of foreign princes in the affairs of individual *nations* in order to maintain transnational Empire that comes under scrutiny in *The Spanish Tragedy,* just as in the providential reasoning of English Protestantism it is the idolatrous Roman Catholic *system* that generates the spiritual error of the "pagans" who live according to its propitiatory logic.

The object, then, of Kyd's allegory of imperial idolatry, and of the play's *translatio imperii,* is to valorize and advocate the more local ideology of empire to which Tudor monarchs from Henry VIII, to Edward VI, to Elizabeth I (the notable exception being, of course, the "Spanish Tudor," Mary) cling precariously in the face of the continuing expansion of the dynastic system that opposes them—a system which realizes new, global proportions with the unification of the Spains in 1580. It is between the national/sovereign and Imperial/universal poles of this global structure that the allegorical oscillation of the sign "Bel" freezes long enough for an audience to fix Elizabeth Tudor's place in relation to *The Spanish Tragedy.* For when, in order to carry out her role in Hieronimo's act of revenge, the fictional Bel-imperia is urged to assume a virtue she does not have, attiring herself as "Phoebe, Flora, or the Huntress" (4.1.148), we can momentarily behold the difference between the Spanish princess on stage and the royal actress in whose image she is (for the moment) dramaturgically clothed. These three epithets, three of Elizabeth's most widely circulated ceremonial personae—Phoebe-like beauty and light, Flora-like fertility and renewal, Diana-like resolution and chastity[92]—set off a chain of pretextual resonances that discovers the font from which the "true" (from an English Protestant perspective) glory of empire springs.[93] The valiant act of Elizabeth's militant chastity (a chastity the play's princess has clearly foregone)—which enables the life-giving, realm-enriching fertility celebrated in so many of her own policy statements and the countless encomia of her subjects—opposes the barrenness and death which are the fruits of Bel-imperia's vulnerable promiscuity.[94] For by staging a Spanish Princess who is at once Elizabeth's mirror-image and her ineffectual opposite, Kyd, no less than his more famous contemporary, Edmund Spenser, writes not only his own (and his audience's) subjection to the empire of England, but also that empire's difference (whether real or imagined) in relation to the universalist *ethos* of the Empire of the Spains. And as it rehearses both the mystery and the difference of Elizabeth's power, *The Spanish Tragedy* also allows us to observe the formation of discursive modes and rhetorical strategies through which that power is, by Elizabethan Protestants, written into English culture.[95]

V

If the outcome of *The Spanish Tragedy* ultimately rests upon English Protestantism's orientation toward those doctrinal impurities which support early modern Europe's imperial religio-political system, and I think that the startling number of resonances that pervade these contemporary discourses suggest that it must, we cannot but find it disconcerting that Kyd's protagonist, "Hieronimo," bears a name so sacred—literally *hieros nym,* the sacred name. This fact alone demands exegetical attention.[96] And if such traditional habits of devotion as the idolatrous invocation and propitiation of "dead saints"—"causes" that criticism has largely neglected in its focus on the symptom of revenge—are characterized in Protestant discourse as among those pagan impurities which come into the faith as a result of the Latin corruption of the Primitive Church, it is surely significant that the name of *The Spanish Tragedy*'s "hero" also resounds with that of one of the Church's principal Latinizers, "Saincte Hierome,"[97] whose theology plays so crucial a role in these disputes. Indeed, "Hieronimo" comes to Kyd's play freighted with a thousand years of Christian cultural significance. Although recent scholarship has recognized this, bringing much of the following "data" to bear on Kyd's protagonist, it has been less successful in suggesting how *The Spanish Tragedy* transforms the meaning of his highly significant name. In order to weigh the function of "Hieronimo" within the world of the play, let us explore the fullness of this sign in an openly allegorical and polysemous spirit, tracing not merely its signifying role within the world of sixteenth-century England, but also its relation to the larger, pan-national culture in which it plays a vital, public role.[98]

If Hieronimo, who embraces a propitiatory solution to his ethical dilemma after he is seduced into Bel-imperia's way of thinking, represents traditional Catholic religion in any way, it is a strange Christianity he practices—for the dark ritual he composes in order to exact his revenge runs afoul of both the Levitical letter of the Old Law and the charitable spirit of the New. Indeed, just as *The Spanish Tragedy*'s representation of a pagan afterlife communes with contemporary Protestant refutations of the doctrine of propitiation, so does its representation of Hieronimo's chief work, his final courtly entertainment—which "incorporates many of the elements of the [actual] Roman Mass as constructed by its Protestant detractors"[99]—play into this Protestant discourse of discovery.

Huston Diehl has provided a window into the cultural field of which Kyd's final blood-letting partakes, observing that "by mystifying and privileging spectacle and displaying 'real' bodies and blood, "Soliman and Perseda" manifests the very qualities of the Roman Mass that the Calvinist reformers condemn when they complain that 'of the sacrament' the Papists 'make an idol; of commemoration make adoration; instead of receiving make a deceiving; in place of showing forth Christ's death, make new oblations of his death.'"[100] This is to say that the Roman Catholic sacrament of the Eucharist is *not,* as the reformers argue it ought to be, a ceremony commemorative of Christ's sacrifice; rather, it is an idolatrous Work, a ritual sacrifice, an act of propitiation of the kind authorized by St. Jerome.[101]

What is more, Hieronimo's pattern of behavior in *The Spanish Tragedy* seems the very mirror of the bereaved father in another text often mobilized by England's Protestant reformers in their condemnations of the idolatrous nature of Roman Catholic tradition. While casting Hieronimo's tragedy-within-the-tragedy in terms of the archetypal Old Testament idolaters of Babylon, Kyd also amplifies this typology by answering it with its Apocryphal correlative from the Book of Wisdom, which contains a discussion of the origins of Idolatry that complements the iconophobic arguments drawn from the canonical Books of Law and Prophecy and remains a key text for early modern purifiers of doctrine. Even in William Allen's Douai translation, with its more sympathetic leanings toward *simulacra,* a believer could be instructed that "the beginning of fornication is the devising of idols: and the invention of them is the corruption of life." He or she would read that "a father being afflicted with bitter grief, made to himself the image of his son who was quickly taken away: and him who had then died as a man, he began now to worship as a god, and appointed him rites and sacrifices."[102] And certainly the more scripturally-oriented among Kyd's audience would know—as they watched Hieronimo honor Horatio "as a god" and hear him pronounce over his son's body a solemn Latin incantation—that such "diriges" are yet another pagan sacrifice discovered by English gospellers, who find no precedent for their practice in the Book. Perhaps not surprisingly it is, as Cardinal Allen confirms, upon the authority of "S.

Hyerom" that "diriges" remain justified by canon law and thus propitatorily acceptable to God.[103]

But *The Spanish Tragedy*'s exploration of the societal effects of false doctrine would not be complete if its apocalyptic scriptural journey did not incorporate the appropriate New Testament anti-types as well. In order to see what use Kyd's play makes of the originary moment of the New Dispensation, when the Word becomes revealed to "the nations," let us turn to the second chapter of "The Actes" (the title of which becomes a kind of Protestant code-word for historiographers as various as Foxe and Ocland). As recorded by St. Luke, "when the Day of Pentecost was come," and the Apostles "were all with one accord in one place":

> 2 suddenly there came a sound from heaven, as of a rushing and mightie wind, and it filled all the house where they sate.
>
> 3 And there appeared unto them cloven tongues, like fire, and it sate upon each of them.
>
> 4 And they were all filled with the holy Ghost, & began to speake with other tongues as the Spirit gave them utterance.

The Geneva translation recommends that this "extraordinarie and necessarie gift of tongues" reverses by spiritual means the confusion of Babel in order that the Word may be disseminated to "every nation under heaven."[104] But it can be readily seen, I think, that Hieronimo's valiant acts parody those of St. Luke's spiritually motivated evangelists by effectively inverting their outcome.

Whereas in the historical Pentecost "the holy Ghoste governed [the believer's] tongues" in order "to bring men to salvation by faith,"[105] when Hieronimo demands that each of his actors "must act his part / In unknown languages" (4.1.172-73), he plays at the role assumed by the "holy Ghost" in the Book of Acts, inverting a work of the spirit by transforming the gift of tongues into an idolatrous human invention. Further, the action of Hieronimo's drama does not reverse the effects of Babel: rather, it reproduces them. Filled with the vengeful spirit of the Old Law, his actors receive not the good news of salvation but, as the epilogue bears out, they are condemned instead to an eternity characterized by purgatorial absence from the Father. As the sacred name is profaned, with its bearer literally (and literarily) taking on the Antichristian mantle of "the Turk," as well as the "Scourge-of-God" role Christendom has long accorded the agents of Islam,[106] the representatives of each nation who are audience to Hieronimo's play (Castile, Portugal, and by implication, England) are not granted a moment of inter-national harmony in the holy city: rather, they are thrown into a "divinely" orchestrated discord in its figural opposite, the imperial Spanish Babylon. With each link of the play's apocalyptic

chain in place, we can now grasp the providentially "comic" element of Kyd's tragedy of the Spains. Though the play's Spanish Empire burns itself out, from its ashes rise sovereign nations. For the onstage deaths generate the rebirth of backsliding Portugal, and, for the benefit of those off-stage, agency (as it was in the historical dumb show of Act 1) is once again accorded to England: not this time by way of the English *sword,* but by way of its Christologically metaphoric equivalent, the English *word,* the tongue of the New Jerusalem into which the play's confusion of languages is translated "for the eaiser understanding to every public reader" (stage direction, 4.4.10) during *The Spanish Tragedy*'s climactic blood-letting.

So while we may for analytical purposes privilege the play's Vergilian and Senecan modes, or foreground its Danielic and Apocryphal strains, we must also factor the Acts of the Apostles into Kyd's apocalyptic formula as its prophetic capstone.[107] For when in Act 4 Hieronimo's players talk in tongues, Kyd's culminating invocation of the English vulgar foregrounds yet again the way *The Spanish Tragedy* functions, and a number of its commentators have recognized this, as a *translatio imperii studii*—an "historical rearticulation of privileged cultural models."[108] How utterly appropriate it is that the namesake of the original cultural translator of the Roman Church should orchestrate the play's continuously replicating pattern of *inversio*—for like the Hieronimo of *The Spanish Tragedy,* St. Jerome had been given the gift of tongues.[109] And since, in the logic of national election, the historical Hieronimo's accomplishment, the *Biblia Vulgata,* had been usurped in the service of an idolatrous transnational Empire, how fitting it is that, his role as translator complete and the Word transmitted to the English vulgar, the fictional Hieronimo's tongue should be literally cloven as his diabolized gift for language is revoked in a final, willful (albeit valiant) act.[110] For in his ambition to appease the saints and revenge his son, Hieronimo usurps the power of the Almighty in more ways than one. As "actor" and "author" of the vengeful "Soliman and Perseda" he confuses his civil office, as earthly magistrate or "Knight Marshal of Spain," with his aspirations to heavenly judgment: demanding "blood for blood" in the propitious spirit of the Old Law, he effectively negates the New Dispensation that would have him temper the Law with Charity.[111]

There remains at least one more web of significance which strangely entangles Kyd's Hieronimo. *Los Jerónimos,* who in early modernity become famous for their generous acts of almsgiving, are the religious order most favored by the Spanish Hapsburgs. When Charles V abdicated in 1555, he entrusted himself to the care of the Hieronymites at Yuste, with whom he ended his days. When Charles's son, Philip II, builds his magnificently austere palace/mausoleum at *El*

Escorial—dedicating the edifice to *San Lorenzo,* or St. Lawrence, upon whose day in 1557 he had won, as Philip, King of *England,* his most impressive military victory—he too endows the Hieronymites, into whose care he commends not only the tombs of the past and future Kings of Spain, but also the immense reliquary of some 6000 items he has collected to be housed there. Among the most cherished, and certainly the most famous of the relics Philip obtains, is the preserved head of *San Jerónimo,* St. Jerome.[112] The Hieronymites, however, may have owed the enthusiastic support of the "Spanish" Hapsburgs to that dynasty's Portuguese line. For since 1497, the order had tended—at the behest of the family of Isabel of Portugal, Charles's wife and Philip's mother—the mausoleum of the Portuguese Kings at Belem.[113] One hesitates to make too much of this, but San *Lorenzo* and *Belem* also sound the names of Bel-imperia and her Janus-faced brother.

In any case, the fact that "Hieronimo" presides over the dead bodies of the royal lines of both Spain and Portugal—in the play and in actuality—is surely no coincidence. While certainly Kyd could not have had such a catalogue as we have been constructing at hand when he sat down to write his play, as an inhabitant of a culture that, whether locally Protestant or universally Catholic, valued its imperial Roman cultural and linguistic roots even as it subordinated them to its Judeo-Christian religious inheritance, that ordered Time according to saints-days and martyrdoms, he would not have needed one. For if "societies, like lives, contain their own interpretations,"[114] *The Spanish Tragedy* can engender this astonishingly multi-vocal string of ironies because, like the sign "Hieronimo," it is deeply embedded in a society whose traditions both link and oppose Protestant England and Roman Catholic Spain—both of which read the present in terms of a mythic past and an apocalyptic future that have long since determined its meaning—two "empires" strung together by a web of significance that entangles all European culture during the Reformation.

VI

As we sit down, then, to consider the "mystery" of Thomas Kyd's play, we can now recognize that this "tragedy" of the newly recovered Empire of the Spains discovers the promiscuous *ethos* of the idolatrous system that challenges the legitimacy of his own nation's developing religio-political culture. As it does so, *The Spanish Tragedy* announces biblically authorized national sovereignty as the less adulterous form of empire. By plugging into a received apocalyptic continuum that incorporates figural elements from the Old Testament books of History and Prophecy, the Apocrypha and the New Testament, Kyd effectively stages both imperial translation and national election through his inclusion of Iberian events within the backward reach and

forward trajectory of English history. As his highly multi-vocal allegory probes the theological orientation that maintains the universal monarchy against which the sovereign "nations" of early modern culture both model and measure themselves, the position he dramatizes, like that of the Protestant reformers who seek to redirect contemporary religious practices, is unequivocal in its condemnation of the spiritual whoredom of Romish Works. While revealing the temptations of traditional Catholic internationalism and reaffirming the Protestant national sovereignty into which English culture had been plunged during Henry VIII's reign, Edward VI's minority, and Elizabeth's Settlement, Kyd draws from, participates in, and improvises upon an historiographic formation best exemplified in the writings of Foxe, Hakluyt, Spenser and the nation-writers who are their contemporaries.

But the real richness of *The Spanish Tragedy,* in contrast with the many propagandistic productions of the day that simply recycle the range of available anti-Spanish stereotypes, stems from its manifest reluctance to sink to an easy rhetoric that would cast the play's argument in terms of an essentially corrupt *ethnos.* And perhaps more astonishingly, *The Spanish Tragedy* seems to recognize that any argument that does sink to the level of ethnic demonization is not an argument at all, but an irreversible endgame.[115] For Kyd's quarrel is not so much with the Spains themselves as with an *ethos* that would seek by force to halt the self-determining course his own nation is attempting to set for itself and thereby bring it back within the universalist fold. In this, at least, Kyd's tragedy remains Catholic. The same cannot be said of the texts of his play that will be amended by subsequent "co-writers," who find the demonizing rhetoric of *ethnos* irresistible. For into the later versions of *The Spanish Tragedy* the dark, essentializing "humors" of the Black Legend will steadily creep.

Notes

This essay is for Huston Diehl. I am indebted to Eugene D. Hill's "Senecan and Virgilian Perspectives in *The Spanish Tragedy,*" *English Literary Renaissance* 15 (1985), 143-65, and to J. R. Mulryne's "Nationality and Language in Thomas Kyd's *The Spanish Tragedy,*" *Langues et Nations au Temps de la Renaissance* (Paris, 1991). Mulryne draws upon Hill's important essay in order to "sketch in the framework of political (and religious) associations that would attach to Spain or Spaniards in English minds of the 1580s, or a prominent faction among them, at least, and to identify . . . how such associations might properly influence our understanding of the play . . . , bring the play even more sharply into focus, and . . . more fully in touch with its original structure of feeling," (p. 67). I too attempt to do this by putting Kyd in "conversation" with Edmund

Spenser, William Allen, John Foxe, the Duke of Medina Sidonia, and other contemporaries who undoubtedly "felt" similarly—even when they violently disagreed.

All Biblical quotations are from the Geneva Bible (London, 1599), except where noted.

1. See "A letter of the Authors expounding his whole intention in the course of this worke." Quoted from *The Faerie Queene*, ed. A. C. Hamilton (London and New York, 1977), pp. 737-38.

2. William Allen, *An Admonition to the Nobility and People of England and Ireland* (Antwerp, 1588), XLV-XLIX. STC 368.

3. The phrase is J. E. Neale's; see *Elizabeth I and Her Parliaments, 1584-1603* (New York, 1957), p. 272.

4. William Empson, "The Spanish Tragedy," *Nimbus* 3 (Summer 1956), 16-29, reprinted in *Elizabethan Drama: Modern Essays in Criticism*, ed. Ralph J. Kaufman (New York, 1961), p. 67.

5. Two recent efforts are James R. Siemon, "Sporting Kyd," *English Literary Renaissance* 24.3 (Autumn 1994), 553-82, a Bakhtinian/Voloshinovian analysis of the "specifically social valuations registered in the play" which slips at several points into a mist of biographical speculation; and Frank R. Ardolino, *Apocalypse & Armada in Kyd's Spanish Tragedy* (Kirksville, 1995), which finds an Armada allusion under virtually every noun in the play. José Ramón Díaz-Fernández, "Thomas Kyd: A Bibliography, 1966-1992," *Bulletin of Bibliography,* 52: 1, (1993) indicates the steady interest in *The Spanish Tragedy.*

6. I take up here the methodological injunction offered by John and Jean Comaroff: "The historicity of all social fields, political communities and cultural milieus . . . resides in a complex equation, the elements of which are (1) the internal dynamics of local worlds, their dialectics of the short run and (2) the articulation, over the long term, between those local worlds and the structures and agencies—at once regional and global—that come to make up their total environments." See *Ethnography and the Historical Imagination* (Boulder and Oxford, 1992), p. 98.

7. I receive Max Weber's phrase "web of significance" by way of Clifford Geertz, whose semiotic view of culture inspires this essay. See *The Interpretation of Cultures* (New York, 1973), p. 5.

8. Following Raymond Williams, I intend the "deeper" sense of "tradition": "a deliberately selective and connecting process which offers a historical and cultural ratification of a contemporary order . . . tied to many practical continuities—families, places, institutions, a language—which are indeed directly experienced . . . [the] struggle for and against [which] . . . is understandably a major part of all contemporary cultural activity"; I understand "formations" as "those effective movements and tendencies, in intellectual and artistic life, which have significant and sometimes decisive influence on the active development of a culture, and which have a variable and often oblique relation to formal institutions." See *Marxism and Literature* (Oxford, 1977), pp. 116-17.

9. I feel it important to emphasize that I am not talking about the play's "hidden meaning." Geertz's aphorism is here apropos: "Culture is public because meaning is" (p. 12).

10. Geertz, p. 312.

11. As Eric Wolf writes, "We need to remember that the culture concept came to the fore in a specific historical context, during a period when some European nations were contending for dominance while others were striving for separate identities and independence. The demonstration that each struggling nation possessed a distinctive society, animated by its special spirit or culture, served to legitimate its aspirations to form a separate state of its own. The notion of separate and integral cultures responded to this political project." See *Europe and the People Without History* (Berkeley and Los Angeles, 1982), p. 387.

12. After Patrick Collinson in *The Elizabethan Puritan Movement* (Oxford, 1967), I mean by "Protestantism" a "hot-gospelling" orientation toward what Tyndale described as "the whole course of scripture" (p. 27); I also emphasize the "Chillingworth dictum": "The Bible, the Bible only I say, is the religion of Protestants," which Collinson finds "profoundly true of the Elizabethan and Jacobean Church." See *The Religion of Protestants: The Church in English Society 1559-1625* (Oxford, 1982), pp. viii-ix.

13. "Human agency . . . has the capacity to reproduce and/or transform the substance of social life, its manifest modes of representation and relationship; human agency is at once culturally constituted yet, very often, unpredictable." See Comaroff and Comaroff (p. 98).

14. Raymond Williams notes that in the sixteenth century "ethnic"—from the Greek, *ethnikos,* heathen—"was widely used in the senses of heathen, pagan or Gentile," and that in the nineteenth century this sense was generally superseded by the sense of a racial characteristic. See Williams, *Keywords* (London, 1976), p. 119. The sense of *ethnos*

which incorporates the "racial" element, however, clearly *is* present in the discourse of the Black Legend. Diverging from other recent readers, however, I do not find this spirit in the earliest *Spanish Tragedy*. It is through its relation to the earlier sense of the word—"heathen" or "pagan"— that the play might indeed be said to essentialize *ethnos* (that is, paganism) as the defining characteristic, not of "Hispanicity" per se, but of Roman Catholicism. See also Ivan Hannaford, *Race: The History of an Idea in the West* (Baltimore and London, 1996), pp. 21-28 and 52.

15. The kingdom represented in the play is governed, as were the viceroyalties of Sicily, Sardinia and Naples, New Spain and Peru, by a viceregal subordinate chosen by the crown of Castile.

16. See, for example, *The Explanation of the True and Lawfull Right and Tytle, of the Moste Excellent Prince Anthonie the first of that name, King of Portugal, concerning his warres, againste Phillip King of Castile . . .* (Leyden, 1585), STC 689.

17. Hill, pp. 158-59.

18. Hill notes that "the tragedy is providential in that it is a *Spanish* tragedy that implies an English comedy" (p. 151). But unlike the many contemporary productions that play the era's Hispanophobic tendencies to the hilt by evoking cultural stereotypes which run the gamut from affected buffoonery to essential villainy, *The Spanish Tragedy* resists these low humors in favor of a much more elevated Senecan rhetoric. Thus we might shift the emphasis of Hill's formula slightly, by saying that "the tragedy is *providential*" in its dramatization of the coming *translatio imperii*. Stephen Justice and J. R. Mulryne have also appealed to the currency of the Black Legend in order to suggest that the play's early audiences would have been predisposed toward Spanish villainy, and that it was this predisposition which accounted for *The Spanish Tragedy*'s enduring popularity. As vital as these sentiments seem to have been in late sixteenth-century England, the least convincing moments of several otherwise fine studies are those that try to identify the presence of an Hispanophobic discursive strain within *this particular play,* at least in its earliest version.

19. Hill, p. 161. While I differ with Hill on several key details, I have found his conclusion, that *The Spanish Tragedy* "reveals a poet closer in his meaningful playfulness to Spenser than to the crowd-pleasing hack critics have so often mistaken him" (p. 165), both inspiring and fundamentally sound.

20. The line occurs at 1.1.10. See Empson, p. 68.

21. The sexual readiness Empson recognizes may partially account for the unconvincing air of the many attempts to link the fictional Bel-imperia with the historical Elizabeth. Yet though Kyd's character hardly resembles the Virgin Queen, these attempts persist. It has been argued, for example, that because "Bel-imperia turns against Balthazar by helping Hieronimo to cause the fall of Babylon/ Spain-Portugal . . . she becomes the analogue of Queen Elizabeth, the image of 'beautiful power.'" See Ardolino, (p. 113).

22. See Spenser, p. 113. For Kyd's and Spenser's tenure at Merchant Taylors' School, see Freeman, [*Thomas Kyd: Facts and Problems* (Oxford, 1967)] pp. 6-10.

23. See *The Faerie Queene* Book I, canto 2, stanzas 13-45. Along with Duessa, Bel-imperia also seems related to characters like Marlowe's Bellamira (in *The Jew of Malta*) and Dekker's Madona-Imperia (in *Blurt, Master Constable*), figures who possess outer beauty that, like the Whore of Babylon's, also belies an unchaste spirit. The doubleness of each of these seems to suggest that Kyd is not alone among his contemporaries in employing this "type."

24. See Hill, p. 161; and Ardolino, p. 151-52.

25. If we have missed the implied allusion, the text is explicit at 1.2.52—"Now while Bellona rageth here and there . . ." The play explicitly suggests the dangerous lure of Bel-imperia's charms in her dialogues with Horatio; their love-scenes (2.2.28-40 and 2.4.28-49) are also charged with the language of battle. Citations throughout are to *The Spanish Tragedy,* ed. David Bevington (Manchester, 1996) based on Philip Edwards' edition (Manchester, 1988).

26. See S. F. Johnson, "*The Spanish Tragedy,* or Babylon Revisited" in *Essays on Shakespeare and Elizabethan Drama,* ed. Richard Hosley (Columbia, 1962), pp. 23-36; Ronald Broude, "Time, Truth, and Right in *The Spanish Tragedy,*" *Studies in Philology* 68 (1971), 130-145; and Ardolino, pp. 1-80.

27. Nashe's famous objection, from the Preface to Greene's *Menaphon,* is quoted from Arthur Freeman, *Thomas Kyd: Facts and Problems* (Oxford, 1967), p. 39. I have capitalized "Biblical" throughout in order to emphasize the dominance of this discourse.

28. Louis Montrose's seminal work on Spenser informs my thinking here. See, for example, "'Eliza, Queene of Shepheardes,' and the Pastoral of Power," reprinted in *Renaissance Historicism* (Amherst, 1987), pp. 34-63; "The Elizabethan

Subject and the Spenserian Text," in *Literary Theory/Renaissance Texts* (Baltimore, 1986), pp. 303-40; or "Of Gentlemen and Shepherds: The Politics of Elizabethan Pastoral Form," *ELH* 50 (1983), 415-59. Montrose's continuing project has been to "understand some of the reasons for its [the form's] place within the 'lived system' of Elizabethan 'meanings and values'" (1983, p. 420) by examining the ways in which Elizabethan pastoral allegories like Spenser's "could perform a wide range of symbolic operations upon the network of social relationships at whose center was the sovereign" (1987, p. 35) by means of processes which are "intrinsically social and historical" (1986, p. 307). Thomas Hylland Eriksen, *Ethnicity and Nationalism: Anthropological Perspectives* (London, 1993) has, after Victor Turner, stressed that it is the "ambiguity or 'multivocality' of symbols" that "makes it possible to manipulate them politically" (pp. 73, 101).

29. A growing number of scholars have seen the need to re-sound the depths of Biblicism in early modern English society. See, for example, A. C. Hamilton, "The Renaissance of the Study of the English Literary Renaissance," *English Literary Renaissance* 25, 3 (Autumn 1995), esp. 383-85; Debora Shuger, *Habits of Thought in the English Renaissance: Religion, Politics and the Dominant Culture* (Berkeley, 1990) and *The Renaissance Bible: Scholarship, Sacrifice and Subjectivity* (Berkeley, 1994); and Christopher Hill, *The English Bible and the Seventeenth-Century Revolution* (London, 1993), esp. pp. 3-78.

30. Without pushing the limits of plausibility too far, we can add that even a *sound* can be construed as dangerously seductive in the iconoclastic discourse of the Protestant reformers—as Spenser's commentator, E. K., instructs, glossing *The Shepeardes Calender*: "by such trifles are noted, the reliques and ragges of popish superstition, which put no small religion in Belles . . . Idoles . . . and such lyke trumperies." See *Spenser's Minor Poems,* ed. Ernest de Sélincourt (Oxford, 1910 [1966]), p. 59.

John Foxe also ridicules the Catholic's desire "to be rung for" in "A Christian Man After the Pope's Making, Defined," see *The Actes and Monuments* ed. S. R. Cattley (London, 1841), I, 86. And as M. M. Knappen in *Tudor Puritanism* (Chicago, 1939) notes, "Church bells were rung to call people to services but not at other times—a Protestant rule of the sort frequently found in Episcopal injunctions of the period. The use of the hand bell, formerly carried before corpses, and bidding prayers for the dead were also banned" (p. 254).

31. Isaiah, Chapters 45 and 46. Or as Thomas Wilson, *A Christian Dictionary* (London, 1622), instructs:

"[Bel a contract of Behel, which commeth of Bahall] A Lord, it was not onely the particular Idoll of the Babylonians, but a generall name to the Idols in the East, agreeing to all the Idols of the Gentiles, as some write, Jer. 19.5, I Kin. 18.25." Along with Jeremiah Chapter 50, Bel-imperia's name also evokes the Apocryphal Bel and the Dragon, and by extension virtually the whole typological chain of Babel/Babylon from Genesis through Revelation. More recently, the *Oxford Dictionary of the Christian Church* (2nd edition, 1974), defines "Bel" as "another form of 'Baal' . . . the tutelary god of Babylon, the empire which held the Jews captive" (p. 151).

32. The fact that we have neglected this Biblical presence in "Bel-imperia" may be one measure of the effectiveness of Kyd's allegorizing strategy. For as Angus Fletcher writes, "the whole point of allegory is that it does not need to be read exegetically; it often has a literal level that makes good enough sense by itself. But *somehow,*" Fletcher instructs, "this literal surface suggests a peculiar doubleness of intention, and while it can, as it were, get along without interpretation, it becomes much richer and more interesting if given interpretation." In *The Spanish Tragedy* this *somehow* is that the play immediately announces its allegorical mode by staging the appearance of Don Andrea's Ghost, who, in the presence of the allegorical figure of Revenge, suggests the play's "doubleness" by invoking the character that is at once his lover and the figure around which the drama turns, "hight sweet Bel-imperia by name" (1.1.10-11). See *Allegory: The Theory of a Symbolic Mode* (Ithaca, 1964), p. 7 (my emphasis). The allegorical implications of "Bel-imperia" are determined most broadly by the culture of Reformation Europe, and more specifically, by the culture of English Protestantism. Ardolino, pp. 13-15, raises the issue of allegory in relation to the play, but he has a much different sense of how its allegorical mode operates than I do.

33. Maureen Quilligan, *The Language of Allegory* (Ithaca, 1979), p. 22.

34. Quilligan theorizes that the "pretext" is the source that always stands outside any allegorical narrative and becomes the key to its interpretability (though not necessarily to its interpretation) (p. 23).

35. The phrase I borrow from Antoine de Baeque, "The Allegorical Image of France, 1750-1800: A Political Crisis of Representation," *Representations* 47 (Summer 1994), 114. We might even go so far as to suggest that in Bel-imperia, the Idol of Empire, *The Spanish Tragedy* quite literally embodies *allegoria,* which Puttenham calls variously

the "false" and the "faire semblant" (both of which seem apt to describe Bel-imperia). "Of this figure," he writes, "therefore which for his duplicitie we . . . will speake first as of the chief ringleader and captaine of all other figures, either in the Poeticall or oratorie science." Puttenham then adds, "And ye shall know that we may dissemble, I meane speake otherwise then we thinke, in earnest as well as in *sport,* under covert and darke termes, and in learned and apparent speaches." See *The Arte of English Poesie* (1589) ([facsimile] Kent, 1988), pp. 197, 305 (my emphasis).

36. See Angus Fletcher, *The Prophetic Moment: An Essay on Spenser* (Chicago, 1971), p. 106. Quilligan argues that allegory begins at the level of *sound.* She writes, "we may easily sense the essential affinity of allegory to the pivotal phenomenon of the pun, which provides the basis for the narrative structure characteristic of the genre." Although Quilligan's study is concerned with allegory as a genre of narrative, *The Spanish Tragedy* exemplifies how "a sensitivity to the polysemy in words" may be "the basic component" of dramatic allegory as well. It is through the play of words that the disjunction between word and image is dramatically brought to light—the thing done does not square with the thing said. If allegory were not somehow signaled, we would be in the presence of the merely ironic. It seems clear that this play attempts to stage a much deeper kind of truth. We might go so far as to say, after Quilligan, that the play unfolds as an investigation "into the literal truth inherent in individual words [Bel, bella, bellum], considered in the context of their whole histories as words" (p. 33).

37. Both Bel-imperia's father and brother recognize her lack of chastity. See 3.10.54-55 and 3.14.111-12. Here too we might recall Redcrosse's attraction to Duessa.

38. For a discussion of how thoroughly saturated with the Black Legend of Spanish Cruelty late-Elizabethan culture becomes, see E. Griffin, "Unsainting James: *Othello* and the 'Spanish Spirits' of Shakespeare's Globe," *Representations* 62 (Spring 1998), 58-99.

39. Luis Vaz de Camões, *The Lusiads,* trans. William C. Atkinson (London, 1952), p. 129. First published in 1572, Camões' ten cantos are replete with such appeals to "national pride," and with allusions to the looming Hapsburg Empire that is about to absorb it. To commemorate simultaneously the poet's death and the inevitable union, two editions of Camões' epic were published in Spain in 1580—the earliest date that has been suggested for Kyd's play.

40. "Jan. 7, 1584 Richard Hakluyt, preacher, to same [Fr. Walsingham]." *State Papers, Domestic Series* (London, 1865) CLXVII: 28.

41. See Miguel de Cervantes, *El cerco de Numancia,* ed. Robert Maranst (Salamanca, 1970), I, 55-56; lines 505-28.

42. Although the Machiavellian Lorenzo, who seemingly will do anything to distinguish himself at court (whether by weaseling a share of Horatio's spoils or betraying his own sister) claims half the victory.

43. See Siemon for a discussion of "the mysteries of hierarchy and class solidarity" implied by the Lorenzo/Balthazar subplot, pp. 556-58.

44. The play would thus seem to support John Lynch's thesis that, their long history of dynastic infighting notwithstanding, the former competitors had in the years since Pope Alexander VI engineered the Treaty of Tordesillas come to see that more was to be gained by combining resources than by continuing to play against each other the interests of their various clients. See *Spain 1516-1598: From Nation-State to World Empire* (Oxford, 1991) p. 432.

45. Indeed, an errant Israel seems to provide the era's preachers with a far more common typology. See Patrick Collinson, *The Birthpangs of Protestant England* (New York, 1988), especially pp. 17-27.

46. See, for example, Johnson, p. 36, and Ardolino, p. 113.

47. Daniel 1.7, gloss.

48. Daniel 4.6, gloss e. See also the "briefe Table of the interpretation of the proper names which are chiefly found in the Old Testament" which appends the Geneva translation. "Beel [sic], Baal, Bealim," signifying "lord, lords," is given as "the name of the idol of the Sidonians, or a generall name to all idoles, because they were as the lords and owners of all that worshipped them"; "Belshatsar," "Baltasar," "Belteshazar," "Beleshatsar," or "Beleshazzar" signify "without treasure, or searcher of treasure." "Babel," "confusion" and "Babylon" are given as synonyms.

49. See Ardolino, p. 4.

50. "Idolatry is a fighting word," writes Carlos Eire, suggesting that the term can be understood to refer not simply to "the worship of a physical object, but rather [to] any form of devotion that is judged to be incorrect." See *War Against the Idols* (Cambridge, Eng., 1986), p. 5. See also Margaret Aston, *England's Iconoclasts* (Oxford, 1988), and Patrick Collinson, *From Iconoclasm to Iconophobia* (Reading, 1985), pp. 22-25.

51. Allen, p. vi.

52. As John Hawkins wrote to Walsingham in February 1587, "God will defend us, for we defend the chief cause, our religion, God's own cause; for if we would leave our profession and turn to serve *Baal* (as God forbid, and rather to die a thousand deaths), we might have peace, but not with God." Quoted in Felipe Fernández-Armesto, "Armada Myths: the Formative Phase," in *God's Obvious Design* (London, 1990), p. 23 (my italics).

53. Marie Tanner writes, "In *The Monarchy of Spain,* which he had dedicated to Philip at the end of the 16th century, Tomasso Campanella proclaimed that Philip had realized that plan that God had prognosticated through his prophets: Spain had become the Last World Monarchy. These words expressed a long-held conviction at the Hapsburg court, one that was visually expressed in a treatise dedicated to Philip, where the prophet Daniel reveals his dream of the Four Monarchies directly to Philip," p. 145. See also J. H. Elliott, "Spain and Its Empire in the Sixteenth and Seventeenth Centuries," *Spain and Its World: 1500-1700* (New Haven, 1989), pp. 8-10.

54. As Foxe writes, "we affirm and say, that our church was, when this church of theirs was not yet hatched out of the shell . . . that is, in the time of the apostles, in the primitive age . . . when as yet no universal pope was received publically . . . nor this doctrine of abuse and sacraments yet heard of. In witness whereof we have the old acts and histories of ancient time to give testimony with us, wherein we have sufficient matter to shew that . . . this our present reformed church, are not the beginning of our own but the renewing of the old ancient church of Christ" (I, 8).

55. By way of a time-tested Protestant rhetoric of inversion (we should recall that *inversio* and *allegoria* are virtual synonyms)—quite in the tradition of that which energizes anti-Catholic polemic from Luther to the Enlightenment—the play "corrects" the Roman Catholic mobilization of Daniel's imperial prophecies by subjecting their thematics to a thoroughly Protestant figuration. See Bernard McGinn, "Anti-Christ Divided, Reformers, Catholics and Puritans Debate Antichrist (1500-1660)," in *Anti-Christ: Two Thousand Years of the Human Fascination with Evil* (San Francisco, 1994), pp. 200-30.

56. See "An Homelie, or Sermon, of Good Woorkes Annexed unto Faithe," in *Certaine Sermons and Homilies* (1547), ed. Ronald B. Bond (Toronto, 1987), pp. 103-13, esp. pp. 112-13.

57. See John Knewstub, *Lectures Upon the Twentieth Chapter of Exodus, and certaine other places of Scripture* (London, 1577), p. 34. STC 15042. For Knewstub's prominence in Elizabethan religious affairs, see Collinson, *Elizabethan Puritan Movement,* esp. pp. 455-59, and *The Religion of Protestants,* pp. 155-57. For another deployment of the commonplace see John "Decalogue" Dod's and Robert Cleaver's oft-reissued *A Plaine and familiar exposition of the Ten commandements with a methodical short catechisme* (London, 1606 [3rd ed.]), pp. 55ff. STC 6969. Margaret Aston, *England's Iconoclasts* (Oxford, 1988), I, provides an excellent review of this Protestant theological orientation—see esp. "The Sin of Idolatry: The Teaching of the Decalogue," pp. 342-79. From 1560, the Geneva Bible glosses the condemnation of Idolatry in Hosea, Chapters 1-3, under the headings "Spiritual Whoredome" and "Spiritual Marriage."

58. See "Religion As a Cultural System," p. 119.

59. The second half of Frank Ardolino's otherwise useful study, *Apocalypse and Armada* (1995), strains to find allusions in the play to the Armada. For example, he posits a connection between the Lorenzo of the play, Philip's devotion to St. Lawrence, the site of the Escorial at San Lorenzo, and a ship of the Armada named for the saint.

60. The phrase is Geertz's, p. 118.

61. Quoted in Felipe Fernández-Armesto, *The Spanish Armada* (Oxford, 1988), who also discusses this general tendency of Hispano-Catholicism, and its Protestant opposition, pp. 39-40.

62. The phrase, often used by Cardinal William Allen and the Catholic theorists of universal monarchy, is from Tacitus. See Anthony Pagden, *Lords of All the World: Ideologies of Empire in Spain Britain and France, c. 1500-c. 1800* (New Haven, 1995), p. 13.

63. See Carlos M. N. Eire, *From Madrid to Purgatory: The Art and Craft of Dying in Sixteenth-Century Spain* (Cambridge, Eng., 1995), p. 172.

64. See *Explications* (1551), p. 150. Quoted in the *OED.* Taking the counter-position, Protestant divines rail against propitiatory practices. John Bradford, for example, preaches (hand-in-hand with his anti-Hispanism) that the Catholic view is "perverted and used to a contrary ende, as of sacrifycing propitiatorely for the syns of the quicke and of the dead." See *Two notable Sermons . . . the one of repentance, the other of the Lord's Supper* (1579 [1561]), i. iv. b. STC 3499.5; also printed with *The copye of a letter* (1556). John Knox exhorts "Look Thou to Thy dear Son . . . Our Head . . . Mediator, and onely Propitiator," and is among the many who identify the

tendency as one of the Holy Faith's principal paganisms; see *The Book of Common Order* (1571), p. 151, quoted in the *OED*.

65. See Huston Diehl, *Staging Reform, Reforming the Stage: Protestantism and Popular Theater in Early Modern England* (Ithaca, 1997), p. 113.

66. Stephen Justice, "Spain, Tragedy, and the Spanish Tragedy," *Studies in English Literature* 25 (1985), repeatedly draws our attention to the fact that it is "the *world* of The Spanish Tragedy" (my emphasis) that Kyd wants to examine in the play, and he observes that "The political and polemical context of [its] religious vocabulary suggests . . . that *The Spanish Tragedy* is not 'about' the Old and New Laws; these are the elements with which Kyd portrays a society in which forgiveness and common understanding are impossible" (p. 276). Without denying that Hieronimo elicits our sympathies, Justice recognizes that "As Hieronimo takes upon himself the divine prerogatives of vengeance, he makes his divinity in Spain's image, the image of the society which 'colde not atteine unto the Law of righteousness . . . Because they soght it not by faith, but as it were by workes of the law' (Rom. 9:31-32)," p. 285.

67. See William Allen, *A Defense and Declaration of the Catholicke Churches Doctrine, touching Purgatory, and prayers for the soules departed* (Antwerp, 1565), Chapter 14, fol. 242, STC 371. The Protestant preacher Samuel Cottesford in *A treatise against traitors. Meete for all faithfull subiects in these dayes. Taken out of the 40. chapter of Ieremye* (London, 1591), STC 5840, identifies as "hispanated" those English Catholic priests, like Allen, who have chosen to study at Catholic universities abroad and thereby commit a treasonous, un-English act. See Cottesford's Preface.

68. See *Hamlet* (1.5. 1-90). For this reason, some argue that the doctrine of purgatory is harder on the saint than on the sinner, for the virtuous soul is more conscious of this distance than the reprobate.

69. It is widely thought that Nashe played a role in the production of the anti-Martinist tracts.

70. See "An Homile or Sermon concerning the Nativity and birth of our Saviour Jesus Christ," in the *Seconde Tome of Homilies* (1563) STC 13673.

71. Jean [John] Veron Senonoys [Vernon], *The Huntynge of Purgatorie to death* (1561), STC 24683, ff. 101-03.

72. Ff. 106-07. For a discussion of the presence of "both a 'Virgilian' and a Christian eschatology" in the writings of St. Jerome, see J. H. D. Scourfield, *Consoling Heliodorus: A Commentary on Jerome, Letter 60* (Oxford, 1993), Section 3.2, pp. 98-100.

73. See Philip Edwards, "Thrusting Elysium into Hell: The Originality of *The Spanish Tragedy*," *Elizabethan Theatre XI*, ed. A. L. Magnusson and C. E. McGee (Ontario, 1990), pp. 117-32.

74. Allen, *Admonition*, XLIX.

75. Pp. 42-43. For a discussion of Protestantism's fascination with the Augustinian historical model, which included the *translatio imperii*, see *The Cambridge History of Renaissance Philosophy*, ed. Charles B. Schmidt et al. (Cambridge, Eng., 1988), pp. 750-52.

76. In the Hapsburg view, a long line of events—the completion of Iberian *reconquista*, the discovery of America, the fall of the Empires of the Aztec and the Inca, the victories over the Turk at Tunis or Lepanto, the pacification of the Philippines and the unification of the Spains—provided the unambiguous, visible signs of this translation. This interpretation becomes sufficiently well known in England so that as late as the mid-seventeenth century it is revived in order to foment anti-Spanish feelings in service of Cromwell's Western Design: "The Spaniards," wrote one Protestant polemicist, "hold this as a Delphic oracle and most infallible prophesy that the last Monarchy shall be fixed in Spain." Quoted in Pagden, p. 43.

77. Pagden defines this extended sense of Empire as "the pattern of political relationships which held together groups of peoples in 'an extended system the terms of whose association were not permanently established'" (p. 13).

78. Allen, *Admonition*, XII.

79. Hill notes that "Hieronimo identifies the three Knights as three Englishmen, and the three Kings as two Portuguese and a Spaniard." He observes that "The King and the Ambassador interpret the 'pompous jest' as a reminder of the need for humility, since both states have been 'Enforced . . . / To bear the yoke of the English monarchy' (1.4.145-46)"—from which he concludes:

> the illogic of the Spanish King's explanation is patent, although it goes unremarked amid the carousing. England has compelled one Portuguese King "To bear the yoke of the English monarchy" and captured, on another occasion, a second "King of Portingale"; the English have also taken a King of Spain prisoner; *therefore* (!) the Portuguese should be less discomforted by their loss to the Spaniards, while the Spaniards should not boast too much.
>
> (p. 160)

But is the Castilian King's explanation as marked by "illogic" as an initial reading might tempt us to think? Or can we discover within the dumb show's odd sequence of events in fact some discernible historical plot? Hill continues, "The King's fatuous misreading of the dumb show serves as a warning to Kyd's audience. For the Spanish King, 'little England' (as he calls it; 1.4.160) is peripheral to the meaning of the dumb show; but for the English audience it is the central agent of the dumb show—and of *The Spanish Tragedy* as a whole" (pp. 160-61).

80. An English contingent is known to have participated, but apparently without the aid of Robert of Gloucester, King Stephen's antagonistic bastard brother, who does not seem to have been present. See Bevington's gloss of the scene, and H. V. Livermore, *A New History of Portugal* (Cambridge, 1976), pp. 54-61.

81. The siege was not in and of itself a "conquest," but one event among the many that contributed to the ongoing transnational Empire-building project of the Iberian *reconquista*.

82. The inter-national nature of this effort is not often emphasized. But even so Protestant a chronicle as Edward Hall's—a text that earns a place on the index of prohibited books during the reign of Philip and Mary—goes to great lengths to record England's participation in the event. See *Hall's Chronicle*, ed. J. Johnson et al. (London, 1809 [reprint]), pp. 519-20.

83. John Foxe includes a lengthy examination of the spread of the Islamic Antichrist in the *Acts and Monuments*. See "The History of the Turks," ed. S. R. Cattley (London, 1841), IV, VI, 88-122.

84. Edmund of Langley *did,* "When Richard wore the diadem" (1.4.151-53), come to Lisbon. He *did not,* however, fight against the Portuguese, but with them. In other words, he never "razèd Lisbon walls," nor did he take "the King of Portingale in fight" (ll. 154-55). Edmund Langley was, however, "For . . . other suchlike service," against the troublesome Scots, "after created Duke of York" (ll. 156-57). See *DNB* entry.

85. Well-known accounts include such histories as Sir John Bourchier's translation of Froissart, and the chronicles of Edward Hall and Raphael Holinshed. Gaunt's expedition and subsequent marriage were also celebrated in Spain: the "English" monarchs Katherine of Aragon and Philip of Hapsburg traced their lineage through the Duke of Lancaster.

86. In what remains the most important extended study we have of *The Spanish Tragedy,* Arthur Freeman also notes the similarity between this episode from Hieronimo's Act 1 masque and the Ocland text, although he leaves his discovery undeveloped (pp. 55-56). Sharrock's verse transla-

tion of Christopher Ocland's Latin "epic," *Anglorum Proelia* (1558), was published as *The Valiant Actes and victorious Battailes of the English Nation: from the yeare of our Lord, one thousand three hundred twentie and seven . . . to the yeere 1558* (London, 1585), STC 18777, by Robert Waldegrave, a printer with an undeniably Protestant pedigree. Waldegrave was John Knox's English printer, and subsequently became involved with the Puritan faction, an association which culminated in his participation in the Martin Marprelate controversy. He escaped to Scotland where he became printer to James VI, the future King of Great Britain. See *A Dictionary of Printers and Booksellers in England Scotland and Ireland, and of Foreign Printers of English Books, 1557-1640,* ed. R. B. McKerrow ([reprint] Oxford, 1968), pp. 277-79. While among the glorious English victories of *The Valiant Actes* is counted the famous battle of San Quentin, for which "King Philips laude hye heavens resound," Mary Tudor is represented as a type of Dido, "Whome . . . a treacherous prelate made by perverse councell stray, / Her noble spouse in forraigne coastes dessevered far away . . . the Spanyardes wife, gan to consume away, / whom eating cares, with parching griefe, brought her fatall day." (sig. L3).

87. See Ocland, sig. D3.

88. The ascension of Elizabeth did not do much to relieve these difficulties, for as Cardinal Allen was quick to point out, she could be demonstrated equally a product of "bastardie" according to the prevailing logic of succession—which had allowed Philip, through an appeal to his mother's ancestry, to displace the "illegitimate" Don Antonio's claim to Portugal. Through an only slightly more difficult genealogical manipulation, Philip, by virtue of "his singular love towards that nation whereof by marriage of Holie Queene Marie of blessed memorie he was once kinge," could, after failing to bring England back to the fold by force, advance the suit of his own daughter to displace Elizabeth (which would in turn provide a whiff of legality to any rebellious attempt to install the *infanta* in place of the "Richard-like" queen). See Allen, *Admonition,* pp. XI, XLIX.

89. In lines which some commentators have suggested allude to *The Spanish Tragedy,* Shakespeare too refers to the expedition in *3 Henry VI* ("great John of Gaunt, / Which did subdue the greater part of Spain" [3.3.81-82]), which also seems to have been the subject of a lost play commissioned by Henslowe, *The Conquest of Spayne by John a Gant* [sic]. See *Henslowe's Diary,* ed. R. A. Foakes and R. T. Rickert (Cambridge, 1961), pp. 167-68, 294.

90. The same can be said for the expedition of Edmund Langley, Duke of York, for both he and his brother, John of Gaunt, as Froissart records at length, returned from the Spains linked by marriage to the House of Castile, just as Gaunt had on an earlier expedition wedded his daughter Catherine to the King of Portugal. See *The Chronicle of Froissart Translated out of French by Sir John Bourchier Lord Berners, annis 1523-25,* Tudor Translations edition (London, 1902), II, 372 ff., and IV, 332, 404. The Portuguese Ambassador is therefore right to counsel his viceroy that "English warriors likewise conquered Spain" because they did enforce a suit, that of Gaunt's wife Constance, to the throne of Castile (against the usurpation of the bastard Henry of Trastamara) much like Philip's claim to Portugal. For a summary of Anglo-Portuguese relations during this period, see Livermore, pp. 100-10.

91. See Pagden, pp. 37-52. In the Ciceronian tradition, Cardinal Allen draws this distinction with regard to English activities in the Low Countries in *The Copie of a Letter written by M. Doctor Allen: Concerning the yeelding up; of the citie of Daventrie, unto his Catholike Majestie* (Antwerp, 1587), pp. 8-9.

92. Louis Montrose's "The Elizabethan Subject and the Spenserian Text" informs my reading here. See *Literary Theory/Renaissance Texts,* ed. Patricia Parker and David Quint (Baltimore, 1986), pp. 303-40. "Bellibone," of course, appears in the "Aprill" eclogue earlier in *The Shepheardes Calender* (1579) and Belphoebe in the presumably later *Faerie Queene.* These names may also play against "Bel-imperia." The collective writing of Elizabeth has long been underway by the time Kyd contributes *The Spanish Tragedy,* which clearly participates in this developing tradition.

93. For a discussion of these Elizabethan personae, and of Elizabethan imperial pretensions more generally, see Francis A. Yates, *Astrea: The Imperial Theme in the Sixteenth Century* (London, 1975), pp. 29-87.

94. Montrose discovers the mystery of Elizabeth's imperial ideology in her refusal "to enact the female paradigm . . . to become the medium through which power, authority, and legitimacy are passed between generations of men. . . . Elizabeth perpetuates her maidenhood in a cult of virginity; transfers her wifely duties from the household to the state; and invests her maternity in her political rather than her wifely body" (p. 310). This is precisely the political strategy (or subject position) that *The Spanish Tragedy*'s Bel-imperia is denied.

95. Like the eclogues of *The Shepheards Calender,* the epic romance of *The Faerie Queene,* and any number of reinscriptions by Ralegh, Sidney, Lyly, Drayton and others, *The Spanish Tragedy* works, in Louis Montrose's phrase, "to suggest that the ruler and the ruled are mutually defining, reciprocally constituted" (p. 320).

96. Frank Ardolino has synthesized a view that might be characterized as the Protestant, or literalist extreme. "*The Spanish Tragedy,*" he writes, "is a mystery of divine vengeance exacted against Spain in which Hieronimo, the Danielic figure, the judge, bearer of the sacred name (*hieros nym*), anglophile representative of God's will at the court of Babylon/Spain, author, actor, and revenger, causes the 'fall of Babylon' in his revenge playlet, ostensibly intended to celebrate the marital and dynastic union of Spain and Portugal" (p. 12). Each of Ardolino's propositions do resound with the various roles given Hieronimo in the play.

97. This Latin corruption is clearly implied in John Bradford's condemnation of Propitiation (see note 64 above). It also inspires many a lengthy treatise, the most widely known being the long prefatory matter of the *Actes and Monuments.*

98. "Not only is the semantic structure of the figure a good deal more complex than it appears on the surface, but an analysis of that structure forces one into tracing a multiplicity of referential connections between it and social reality, so that the final picture is one of a configuration of dissimilar meanings out of whose interworking both the expressive power and the rhetorical force of the final symbol derive. This interworking is itself a social process, an occurrence not 'in the head' but in that public world where 'people talk together, name things, make assertions, and to a degree understand each other'" (Geertz, p. 213).

99. See Diehl, p. 112.

100. Diehl quotes Foxe, *Actes and Monuments,* V, 303.

101. Significantly, the ritual of the Eucharist had been, since the reign of Hapsburg patriarch Rudolf I, an important imperial icon. Marie Tanner has recently recalled that the Spanish Hapsburgs, by "vowing on the Eucharist in battles against the Turks and the Protestants," and by establishing by imperial edict "that in processions celebrating . . . military triumphs, the Eucharist would be displayed in a monstrance carried by the archbishop," made the public ritual of Eucharist devotion a powerful ideological tool. Tanner notes that "in celebrations of the Feast of Corpus Christi, the Forty-hours Veneration of the Eucharist, and the Auto[s] Sacramentales, the Eucharist was associated with the royal house," an "awareness [which] reached global proportions when the royal pretensions

were yoked to the good news of the Redemption that reached the New World, for under Philip's sovereignty the mass was said in all four parts of the world for the first time" (p. 215).

102. Wisdom 14.13 and 15, quoted from *The Parallel Apocrypha,* ed. John R. Kohlenberger III (Oxford, 1997), pp. 306-08. My discussion of the Wisdom of Solomon's relation to the play is indebted to Diehl, pp. 113-20.

103. See Allen, *A Defense and Declaration,* whose appeal to "St. Hieronyme" is ridiculed by William Fulke, in *A Confutation of the popish Churches doctrine touching Purgatory & prayer for the dead* (1577), pp. 318-21. STC 11458. Fulke's *Confutation* reprints the whole of Allen's *Defense* and answers the Catholic position point by point over some 460 pages.

104. Acts 2.1 (gloss 1) and 5.

105. Acts 2.1 (gloss 4).

106. It has not often been remarked how appropriately ironic it is that the fall of Babylon/Spain should come at the hands of a character posing as "the Turk." For it was in the holy war against the Islamic Antichrist—a business which the Empire took every bit as seriously as its policing of Northern heresy—that Catholic Spain derived its sense of itself, and it was, in the "authorized view," through her sacrifice that the onslaught of the Turk had been halted at Tunis, Malta and Cyprus. It is one of the enduring ironies of the Black Legend that Philip's greatness was often compared to the Grand Turk's and that the "cruelty" of Catholic Spain was characterized as "more than Turkish." Along with Simon Shepherd, *Marlowe and the Politics of Elizabethan Theater* (London, 1986), p. 144, Mulryne is among those who have appropriately noted this Turkish connection (pp. 75-81).

107. Johnson, p. 27; Justice, pp. 285-86; Mulryne, pp. 85-86; and Ardolino, p. 39, are among those who have drawn our attention to these resonances with the Pentecost of Acts 2.

108. After Hill, Mulryne has emphasized this element of the play (p. 70), while Justice arrives at a similar conclusion independently (pp. 285-86).

109. Frank Ardolino has considered the question of St. Jerome's relation to the play, but has failed to link the two persuasively. See "Hieronimo as St. Jerome in *The Spanish Tragedy,*" *Études Anglaises* 36 (1983), 435-37.

110. As Justice notes, "the persistence of Babel manifests the persistent corruption of self-will that eventually corrupts communication itself . . . in

his search for justice he [Hieronimo] more nearly recapitulates the sin of Nimrod than any of them [the play's other characters]" (pp. 285-86).

111. Though his civil jurisdiction as Knight-Marshall may have extended throughout "the verge," as S. F. Johnson argued, in neither England nor Spain would it have extended to those above him in rank (p. 30). In such cases it would have been his duty, as a servant of the realm, to render unto Caesar the concerns of Empire (in both its sovereign and universal senses). Of course, in this caricatured imperial realm, "Empire" (that is, Bel-imperia) has her own desires which her "masters" cannot contain.

112. See Andrew Wheatcroft, *The Hapsburgs: Embodying Empire* (London, 1995), pp. 145-46.

113. See *The Catholic Encyclopedia* (New York, 1910) VII, 345; and *The New Catholic Encyclopedia* (New York, 1967) VI, 1099-100. Ardolino (pp. 156-58) notes several of the resonances between the Hieronymites, El Escorial, San Lorenzo, and *The Spanish Tragedy.*

114. Geertz, pp. 453, and 5 ff.

115. See note 10 above.

Lukas Erne (essay date 2001)

SOURCE: Erne, Lukas. "*Cornelia.*" In *Beyond* The Spanish Tragedy: *A Study of the Works of Thomas Kyd,* pp. 203-16. New York: Manchester University Press, 2001.

[*In the following essay, Erne discusses the relationship between* Cornelia *and the rest of Kyd's corpus, and between* Cornelia *and the short-lived neoclassical movement in Elizabethan drama.*]

The four plays that have been considered so far, **The Spanish Tragedy,** its forepiece, the lost **Hamlet,** and **Soliman and Perseda,** all share certain characteristics. They were written for and performed on the public stage. As the early references to the Ghost in Hamlet, to Basilisco's clowning and to Hieronimo's revenge suggest, they were notable for their stage action. They are intrigue plays, typically based on novelistic material. Their language stretches from the colloquial to the stately, from prose to verse. **Cornelia** is different in every respect: it is not an original work, but a translation of Robert Garnier's French tragedy *Cornélie* (first published 1574). It is aimed at an educated readership rather than a popular audience and, for all we know, was never performed.[1] Like all plays of the academic, neo-Senecan genre, it is characterised by an almost complete substitution of narrative for stage action and is declaimed rather than performed.

Entered on 26 January 1594 by Nicholas Ling and John Busby ('a booke called *CORNELIA, THOMAS KYDD beinge the Authour*', Arber, II, p. 644), Kyd's translation was printed later the same year with the following title page: 'CORNELIA. / AT LONDON, / Printed by *Iames Roberts,* for *N. L.* / and *John Busbie.* / 1594.' Kyd's name is thus absent from the title page, but his initials stand at the end of the dedication to the Countess of Sussex, and the full name appears at the end of the text. The play seems to have sold badly. According to William Covell's *Polimanteia* (1595), 'tragicke *Garnier* ha[d] his poore *Cornelia* stand naked vpon euery poste' (Q3ᵛ). This refers to the practice of posting extra title pages as advertisements and suggests that *Cornelia* failed to find buyers despite commercial efforts. The play was reissued the same year. Several scholars have taken the reissue for a new edition, thus mistaking a sign of the play's commercial failure for a sign of its popularity.[2] The new title page was the first to bear Kyd's name: 'Pompey the Great, / his faire / *Corneliaes Tragedie*: / Effected by her Father and Hus- / bandes downe-cast, death, / and fortune. / *Written in French, by that excellent / Poet Ro: Garnier; and trans- / lated into English by Thomas / Kid.* / AT LONDON / Printed for Nicholas Ling. / 1595.' The fact that a new and greatly changed title page was printed is unusual. By Elizabethan standards, the original title page is exceptionally plain and uninformative, and it is possible that it was held partly responsible for the poor sales figures. The publisher who reissued the play may also have hoped to profit from the popularity of a play on the public stage. In his diary, Henslowe lists on 8 November 1594 a new play entitled 'sesar & pompie' which received eight performances by the Admiral's Men until 25 June 1595. Significantly, *Cornelia*'s new title page of 1595 prints 'Pompey the Great' in letters double the size of those used for the following 'his faire Corneliaes Tragedie' even though her husband does not appear on stage.

Cornelia, the protagonist of Garnier's play and Kyd's translation, is not to be confused with the famous Cornelia who lived in the second century BC, the daughter of Publius Cornelius Scipio, hero of the Second Punic War and wife of Tiberius Semprionius Gracchus, to whom she bore twelve children. Nor is she identical with Cinna's daughter who married Julius Caesar in 83 BC, but died before his rise to power. The historic figure Kyd's translation deals with is the daughter of Scipio Metellus, who was married first to Publius Licinus Crassus, then to the famous Pompey the Great. Following Garnier, Corneille put the same character at the centre of his play *La Mort de Pompée*.

Robert Garnier (1544-90), the greatest French dramatist before Corneille, wrote eight plays between 1567 and 1583, seven tragedies and one tragicomedy, *Bradamante* (1582), perhaps his best-known play today. *Cornélie* is the third of Garnier's eight plays. For his translation, Kyd did not use the first edition, nor the text printed in the two earliest collected editions of Garnier's works published in 1580 and 1582, but the 1585 (or a later) edition, which show certain cuts also present in Kyd.[3]

Long before the sixteenth century, the topic had been treated by various writers. In a section of the 'argument' Kyd chose not to translate, Garnier conveniently gives his literary references: 'Vous verrez ce Discours amplement traitté en Plutarque ès vies de Pompée, de César, et de Caton d'Utique, en Hirtius vᵉ livre des Commentaires de César: Au vᵉ livre des Guerres civiles d'Appian, et XLIIIᵉ de Dion.' Strangely, Garnier fails to mention Lucan, his most important source. Books VIII and IX of the *Pharsalia* probably did more than any other ancient text to immortalise Cornelia.[4]

The 'plot' of *Cornelia* can be summed up in a few words, for its lack of complexity is in stark contrast with *The Spanish Tragedy*. The drama begins after the disastrous defeat of Pompey's troops on the plain of Pharsalus, Pompey's escape to Egypt, and his treacherous assassination. In Act I, Cicero comments on Rome's fate as she threatens to bring herself down in the ravages of civil war. The theme is taken up by the Chorus who interprets Rome's plight as the gods' vengeance for the crimes of her ancestors. In Act II, Cornelia laments her plight and considers suicide—to which Cicero replies that death is to be appointed by the gods. In III.i, Cornelia relates that the Ghost of Pompey has appeared to her, but she is contradicted by the Chorus who answers that she must have seen some false demon. In the following scene, Cicero foresees that Caesar's tyranny will eventually lead to his overthrow. In the concluding scene of the third act, Philip, who fought with Pompey against Caesar, brings to Rome the ashes of Cornelia's slain husband. She mourns his death and hopes for Caesar's fall. Scene IV.i opposes a fiery Cassius, eager to free Rome from her oppressor, Caesar, to Decimus Brutus who prefers to wait before taking action. The Chorus praises those who free the people from tyrants. In the following scene, Caesar rejoices after defeating his enemies, but is warned by Mark Anthony against a conspirator who will try to kill him. Most of the only scene of the concluding act (V.i) is taken up by the Messenger's speech, which reports Caesar's victory and Scipio's suicide. Cornelia, in her lament, concludes that she must live to bury and mourn the dead.

Approaching *Cornelia* from the angle of contemporary stage plays, what is not dramatised seems more remarkable than what is. Pompey has already been killed and Caesar's assassination, dimly foreshadowed, happens after the end of the play. The chief opponents, Cassius and Brutus on the one hand, and Caesar and Mark Anthony on the other, never meet. Cornelia laments for most of the play, with the sole alteration that whereas she laments her husband's death in Acts II and III, she also mourns for her slain father in the last act. The urn containing Pompey's ashes is the only potential stage prop. Within the five acts and eight scenes into which the play is divided, the action advances preciously little.

Rather than dramatising action, *Cornelia* deals with contemporary political ideas. Garnier described his play as a 'poème à mon regret trop propre aux malheurs de nostre siècle', and the play paints the dangers of civil war with no less clarity than *Gorboduc*.[5] To an age obsessed with the threat (England) or consequences (France) of civil unrest and concerned with the notions of ambition, good and bad rule, and the Monarchy and the Republic, Ancient Rome—and in particular the period of the great civil war—offered one of the chief 'Mirrors for Magistrates'. Towards the end of the sixteenth century, as English power was expanding, many would have seen Julius Caesar as an heroic figure, effecting a providential shift from the Republic to the Empire, and would have gone along with Dante in placing Cassius and Brutus in the ninth circle of hell. Following Lucan, Garnier and Kyd are less inclined to side with Caesar and paint a very different picture of his aspirations. In *Cornelia,* Rome is represented as in decline. Cicero's opening soliloquy addresses Rome as follows:

> See how the Rocks do heaue their heads at thee,
> Which if thou sholdst but touch, thou straight becomst
> A spoyle to *Neptune,* and a sportfull praie
> To th' Glauc's and Trytons, pleasd with thy decay.

> (I. 88-91)

Two acts later, he anticipates with joy the time when Caesar will be overthrown:

> *Caesar,* thou shalt not vaunt thy conquest long,
> Nor longer hold vs in this seruitude,
> Nor shalt thou bathe thee longer in our blood.

> (III.ii.66-8)

Similarly, the Chorus calls for 'another *Brutus* [. . .] / Brauely to fight in *Romes* defence' (II.ii.406-7). Significantly, the only Chorus that does not disparage the future Emperor is 'A Chorus of Caesars friends' (IV.ii.167.1). Kyd, then, introduced to England an unusually skeptical view of Caesar and the beginnings of the Roman Empire.

Interestingly, Kyd and Marlowe, one-time companions and co-founders of modern English tragedy, both translated a work dealing with the Roman Civil War: *Cornelia* and the first book of Lucan's *Pharsalia.* Marlowe's translation, though probably not printed before 1600, was entered on 28 September 1593, only four months before Kyd's, but it is generally supposed that Marlowe had completed his translation much earlier, probably when still in Cambridge. While Lucan and Marlowe focus on the political horror of civil war, Garnier and Kyd look at the events from the personal perspective of Cornelia.

Shakespeare's vivid interest in the decline of the Republic bore fruit a few years later. It cannot be doubted that Shakespeare knew *Cornelia,* since his wide reading on the subject as well as his interest in Kyd's works are well attested. Especially IV.i and IV.ii, the first opposing Cassius and Decimus Brutus, the second Marc Anthony and Caesar, have obvious affinities with Shakespeare's *Julius Caesar.* The dialogue in *Cornelia* IV.i between Cassius and Decimus Brutus shares certain characteristics with that between Cassius and Marcus Brutus in *Julius Caesar* I.ii. Furthermore, Boas pointed out that 'the character of Cassius [. . .]—a character of which only the barest hints are suggested by Plutarch—has its exact prototype in the Cassius of Garnier-Kyd, fiery yet shrewd, envious of Caesar, yet full of a genuinely patriotic passion for liberty' (p. lxxxiii). It is tempting to try to locate more specifically Kyd's influence, but the attempts that have been undertaken seem unconvincing.[6]

Little critical work has been done on Kyd's translation. To my knowledge, only Boas, Carrère, A. M. Witherspoon, and J. A. Roberts and J. F. Gaines have devoted more than cursory remarks to it.[7] With the exception of Roberts and Gaines, even these hardly ever go beyond listing Kyd's alleged mistranslations. Two fundamental misunderstandings underlie Carrère's analysis of *Cornelia* which may help explain more generally why critics have failed to do the work justice. In his dedication to the Countess of Sussex, Kyd qualifies his work as 'small endeuours' which Carrère (p. 315) mistakes as an acknowledgement of the weaknesses of his translation. In fact, Kyd's words display the common understatement of dedicatory rhetoric, comparable to Shakespeare's 'untutored lines' or 'unpolisht lines' in his dedications to the Earl of Southampton.[8] Carrère also misunderstands the last paragraph of Kyd's dedication: 'And so vouchsafing but the passing of a Winters weeke with desolate *Cornelia,* I will assure your Ladiship my next Sommers better trauell with the Tragedy of *Portia.*' A week of *reading* is vouchsafed to the Countess, not a week of *writing,* as Carrère (p. 315) has it. The following sentence makes Kyd's meaning plain: 'And euer spend one howre of the day in some kind seruice to your Honour'. Carrère's misreadings of Kyd's dedication are symptomatic of the spirit in which Kyd's *Cornelia* has been approached: if Kyd admits both his mistakes and his hurry, why should critics take the work seriously?

On close examination, Kyd's *Cornelia* is really more than a translation. Kyd often paraphrases rather than translates Garnier, unlike the Countess of Pembroke who, in her *Antonie,* translates virtually word by word. Not only is the handling of the original relatively free, but what are arguably the best eighteen lines are entirely Kyd's (see below). He omits a good many lines and adds others. As Roberts and Gaines have shown, *Cornelia* is in some ways an original play: 'His amendments constitute a second text, which can be considered independently of Garnier's version, and where the work of the writer can be examined on many planes.'[9] Notably, a good number of changes are concerned with the realm of the supernatural. References to ghosts loom large in Garnier's play, but Kyd misses no opportunity to add more. He adds several images of hell. As in *The Spanish Tragedy,* he seems happy to add Christian to pagan references, as when he invokes the Virgin Mary as 'heauens Queene' (II.401). He replaces general mentions of fate with direct invocations of heaven. In general, his aim seems to have been to impregnate his text with a stronger sense of the supernatural than he found in the original.

From the point of view of the language, *Cornelia* is Kyd's maturest work. Dodsley, who read widely in editing his twelve-volume *Select Collection of Old Plays* (1744), pointed out that its 'stile and versification seem better than ordinary'.[10] The blank verse scans well and flows naturally. Contrary to his earlier plays, *Cornelia* contains a good many *enjambments* displaying the ease with which Kyd had come to write blank verse:

> What end (O race of *Scipio*) will the Fates
> Afford your teares? Will that day neuer come
> That your desastrous griefes shall turne to ioy,

(II.116-18)

> Now *Scipio,* that long'd to shew himselfe
> Discent of Affrican (so fam'd for Armes),
> He durst affront me and my warlike bands,
> Vpon the Coastes of Lybia, till he lost
> His scattred Armie: and to shun the scorne
> Of being taken captiue, kild himselfe.

(IV.ii.67-72)

The verse in *The Spanish Tragedy* and *Soliman and Perseda* was, with very few exceptions, heavily end-stopped. The technical mastery Kyd had acquired also shows in his skilful translation of the various rhymed stanzas. At the end of the third act, for example, the Chorus muses on the workings of Fortune:

Garnier

» Ore elle nous monstre le front

» De mille liesses fecond,
»   Ore elle se retourne,
» Et de son œil au change prompt
»   La faveur ne sejourne.

» Instable en nos prosperitez,
» Instable en nos adversitez,

» De nous elle se joüe,
» Qui tournons sans cesse agitez

»   Au branle de sa roüe.[11]

Kyd

'One while shee bends her angry browe,
'And of no labour will allow;
    Another while
'She fleres againe, I know not how,
    Still to beguile.

'Fickle in our aduersities,
'And fickle when our fortunes rise,
    She scoffs at vs:
'That (blynd herselfe) can bleare our eyes,
    To trust her thus.

With no mean dexterity, Kyd respects simultaneously the rhyme scheme, the varying length of the verses and the sense of the original. Meres, in *Palladis Tamia,* lists Kyd among a group of English poets. Even though Kyd's supposed poetic *oeuvre* is lost, his translation of Garnier's stanzas may allow us a glimpse of it.

It is one of the oddities of the history of Elizabethan drama that Kyd, best remembered today for the popular *Spanish Tragedy,* finished his dramatic career with the closet drama *Cornelia.* This strange fact becomes more easily understandable if we recall the biographical data to which his decision to undertake the translation seem intimately related. By May 1593, Kyd had gotten into trouble with the Privy Council who had found 'certain atheistical tracts' among his papers.[12] Even though Kyd claimed that he had the papers from Marlowe and that they had been 'shufled wth some of myne (vnknown to me) by some occasion of o[r] wryting in one chamber twoe yeares synce', he was imprisoned and tortured.[13] As a consequence, he seems to have lost 'the favo[rs] of my Lord, whom I haue servd almost theis vj yeres nowe', that is from 1587 until his imprisonment in May 1593.[14] It has been argued that *Cornelia,* entered on 26 January 1594 and probably written in the second half of 1593, should be seen in the context of Kyd's attempt to win back the protection of his former patron. Lady Bridget Fitzwalter, the Countess of Sussex, to whom Kyd dedicated his translation, thanking her for her 'fauours past', was the wife of Robert Radcliffe, the fifth Earl of Sussex.[15] Freeman (pp. 32-7) has suggested Radcliffe's father, Henry Radcliffe, the fourth Earl of Sussex until his death in December 1593, as possibly having been Kyd's patron. If, as I argue in the appendix, Kyd was not in the employment of the Earl of Sussex (but of the Earl of Pembroke), it is equally possible that the playwright, after his fall from grace, was looking for patronage elsewhere and therefore dedicated *Cornelia* to the Countess of Sussex.

Cornelia lies on the road English drama did not take. Obvious though this may be from the vantage point of modern literary history, it was perhaps less so in Kyd's own times. In Italy and France, the countries from which England inherited a share of its dramatic tradition, the courtly Senecan tradition bore rich fruit to which Cinthio's and Garnier's plays, among others, bear testimony. In England, 'Seneca's style' was advocated by Sir Philip Sidney, considered by many the paragon of his age.[16] What Willard Farnham calls 'a reactionary Senecan movement' probably looked more like the product of a literary *avant-garde* in its own time.[17]

Several other neoclassical plays were written around the turn of the century. Kyd's *Cornelia* had been preceded by *Antonie,* a translation of Garnier's *Marc Antoine,* undertaken by Mary Herbert, the Countess of Pembroke (the sister of Philip Sidney) in 1590, and was published in 1592. In 1594 appeared Samuel Daniel's *Cleopatra,* the first original play in the manner of Garnier, followed by a number of others, notably Fulke Greville's *Alaham* and *Mustapha.*[18] Earlier critics believed that this group of works grew out of a 'circle' or 'literary coterie' headed by Mary Herbert who took it upon herself, after her brother's untimely death in 1586, to attempt to reform the English tragedy in the way Sidney had called for when lamenting the 'gross absurdities' in contemporary drama and praising *Gorboduc* for its 'stately speeches and well-sounding phrases'.[19] This view is now rightly challenged.[20] Rather than fighting the public stage, Mary Herbert and her husband, the Earl of Pembroke, supported companies of players in the early 1590s just as her uncles Leicester and Warwick had done for a considerable time.

Similarly, it would be an oversimplification to consider *The Spanish Tragedy* and *Cornelia* as examples of two developments within the drama of the early 1590s and to claim that the one grew into Shakespeare, Jonson, and Webster—into plays widely admired and performed today—while the other was aborted after a few attempts and did not leave any traces. Public stage plays such as *The Spanish Tragedy* and closet dramas such as *Cornelia* may be seen more accurately as complementary rather than antagonistic in the influence they exerted. While the former could teach Shakespeare some of his stage craft, the latter may have shown him how to use plays as an eloquent medium to formulate and discuss some of the complex political ideas of his age.

Comparing the early reputations of *The Spanish Tragedy* and *Cornelia* yields telling insights into the relationship between literary recognition and popularity. Denigrated if not forgotten today, Kyd's translation found its admirers after its first publication. A funeral elegy for Lady Helen Branch, wife of the Lord Mayor, who died on 10 April 1594, pays a compliment to the authors of 'chaste *Lucretia*' and of 'sad *Cornelia*', inviting the authors to use their 'siluer pen' not to write about women in foreign countries, but about the life of the deceased, '[m]atter that well deserues your golden stile'.[21] The year after, William Covell, of Christ's College and Queens' College, Cambridge, wrote that *Cornelia* was 'excellently done by Th. Kid'.[22] Furthermore, the literary anthologies *England's Parnassus* (1600) and *Belvedere* (1600) pay *Cornelia* the tribute of citing twenty-one passages each from Kyd's translation.[23] Of the early reception of *The Spanish Tragedy,* in contrast, we best remember the scorn and ridicule Jonson and Marston heaped upon it. Yet, whereas *The Spanish Tragedy* went through eleven editions before 1642, *Cornelia* was not reprinted until the eighteenth century.

It is notable that *Cornelia* and *The Spanish Tragedy,* despite the gulf that separates them on a dramaturgical level, have more in common than their author. Cassius, in a moment of profound doubt about the benevolence, if not the existence, of the gods, suggests the radical scepticism expressed by Hieronimo as his failure to obtain justice drives him mad:

> Yet are there Gods, yet is there heauen and earth,
> That seeme to feare a certaine Thunderer.
> No, no, there are no Gods; or, if there be,
> They leaue to see into the worlds affaires:
> They care not for vs, nor account of men,
> For what we see is done, is done by chaunce.
>
> (IV.i.15-20)

Hieronimo's gods, in comparison, are

> plac'd in those empyreal heights
> Where, countermur'd with walls of diamond,
> I find the place impregnable, and they
> Resist my woes, and give my words no way.
>
> (III.vii.15-18)

The chief correspondences between the two plays, however, are to be found elsewhere: *Cornelia,* to some extent like *The Spanish Tragedy,* is basically a tragedy of grief. While Cornelia laments the loss of her husband and her father, Hieronimo grieves for the death of his son. Cornelia plays no role in the central political events but is told of actions to which she can only react. She is basically a spectator and her strong emotional involvement works as a catalyst for the reader's sympathy. Her passivity is mirrored by Hieronimo's inaction between the discovery of his murdered son and the last act when he takes revenge into his own hands. Their final courses of action are of course diametrically opposed: while Hieronimo destroys himself in the bloody revenge he takes, Cornelia mourns on and endures. Yet despite the plays' disparate conclusions, both characters are essentially rememberers or, in Kyd's word, 'remembrancers' (*Cornelia,* III.i.13).

Interestingly, Kyd's alterations of Garnier's original reveal affinities with *The Spanish Tragedy.* At one point in the last act, Kyd adds five lines, stressing Cornelia's bereavement in terms which are reminiscent of *The Spanish Tragedy*:

> Thy death, deere *Scipio,* Romes eternall losse,
> Whose hopefull life preseru'd our happines,
> Whose siluer haires encouraged the weake,
> Whose resolutions did confirme the rest,
> Whose ende, with it hath ended all my ioyes,
>
> (V.361-5)

Compare this passage with the way Hieronimo mourns for his son:

> Here lay my hope, and here my hope hath end:
> Here lay my heart, and here my heart was slain:
> Here lay my treasure, here my treasure lost:
> Here lay my bliss, and here my bliss bereft:
>
> (IV.iv.90-3)

The one major addition to Garnier's text, the first eighteen verses of the third act, is no less characteristic of Kyd:

> The cheerefull Cock (the sad nights comforter),
> Wayting vpon the rysing of the Sunne,
> Doth sing to see how *Cynthia* shrinks her horne,
> While *Clitie* takes her progresse to the East;
> Where, wringing wet with drops of siluer dew,
> Her wonted teares of loue she doth renew.
> The wandring Swallow with her broken song
> The Country-wench vnto her worke awakes;
> While *Citherea* sighing walkes to seeke
> Her murdred loue trans-form'd into a Rose:
> Whom (though she see) to crop she kindly feares;
> But (kissing) sighes, and dewes hym with her teares:—
> Sweet teares of loue, remembrancers to tyme,
> Tyme past with me that am to teares conuerted;
> Whose mournfull passions dull the mornings ioyes,
> Whose sweeter sleepes are turnd to fearefull dreames,
> And whose first fortunes (fild with all distresse)
> Afford no hope of future happinesse.
>
> (III.1-18)

The image in lines ten to thirteen recalls Hieronimo grieving over the dead body of Horatio: 'Sweet lovely rose, ill-pluck'd before thy time, / [. . .] I'll kiss thee now, for words with tears are stay'd' (II.v.46-8). Even the rhetorical figure anadiplosis in III.i.12-14 is typical of Kyd (cf. *The Spanish Tragedy* II.i.118-29). The lines are among the finest in the play, probably more successful in their lyricism than any passage by Garnier, and the editor of *England's Parnassus,* whose other inclusions from *Cornelia* are all short, never exceeding six lines, paid Kyd the tribute of including the passage almost in its entirety.

Cornelia, a neoclassical play written by the author of the then-most famous play on the public stage, may well seem like the odd man out among Kyd's plays. It is quite possible that Kyd's translation of *Cornelia*

would never have been written if he had not been in pecuniary need after getting into trouble with the authorities. It does not follow, however, that *Cornelia* can be considered as a play outside Kyd's genuine *oeuvre.* Kyd had been interested in Garnier's play long before he came to translate it. As we have seen in chapter 2, it is, in fact, the only contemporary play of which definite traces can be found in *The Spanish Tragedy,* and its influence on Kyd may have been of greater importance than that of any other play of his century. For language and certain passages and ideas, Kyd appears to have looked to *Cornélie* when writing *The Spanish Tragedy* and to *The Spanish Tragedy* when writing *Cornelia.* This relationship of mutual stimulation suggests, as I have pointed out in preceding chapters, that Kyd—rarely disinclined to take clues from his earlier plays—was an author who worked with a limited body of material which he then used and reused, transformed and adapted.

Notes

1. Contrary to the English translations, Garnier's original plays appear to have been acted. See Marie-Madeleine Mouflard, *Robert Garnier, 1545-1590: L'Oeuvre* (La Roche-sur-Yon, 1963), pp. 260-70.

2. See, for instance, Gordon Braden, 'Thomas Kyd', in Fredson Bowers, (ed.), *Elizabethan Dramatists,* Dictionary of Literary Biography, 62 (Detroit, 1987), p. 188. The same mistake is made by Bullough (V, p. 30) and others.

3. This was first pointed out by Markscheffel, 'Thomas Kyd's Tragödien' (1886), 4.

4. See, in particular, Cornelia's two great laments after Pompey's assassination, VIII, ll. 639-61 and IX, ll. 55-108.

5. In the dedication of *Cornélie,* ed. Lebègue, pp. 145-6.

6. Joan Rees ('*Julius Caesar*—An Earlier Play, and an Interpretation', *MLR,* 50 (1955), 135-41) analysed Shakespeare's possible debts to *Cornelia* IV.i and IV.ii; Carrère (pp. 443-4) gives a list of 'parallels' between *Cornelia* and *Julius Caesar*; and Kenneth Muir (*The Sources of Shakespeare's Plays* (London, 1977), pp. 119-20) compares passages in *Cornelia* about indiscriminate slaughter (I.198-200, II.142-3, IV.i.8-10 and IV.i.109) with Antony's vision of murderous chaos (III.i.262-78). In all cases, the 'parallels' are general rather than specific and probably unintentional. Note that it has also been argued that *Cornelia*—along with the Countess of Pembroke's *Antonie* and Samuel Daniel's *Cleopatra*—influenced Shakespeare's *The Rape of Lucrece* (Rolf Soellner, 'Shakespeare's *Lucrece* and the Garnier-Pembroke Connection', *Shakespeare Studies,* 15 (1982), 1-20).

7. Boas, pp. 414-36; Carrère, pp. 315-24; Witherspoon, *The Influence of Robert Garnier on Elizabethan Drama,* pp. 91-9; Roberts and Gaines, 'Kyd and Garnier: The Art of Amendment', *Comparative Literature,* 31 (1979), 124-33. Freeman, for instance, simply states that 'the translation is not altogether accurate' (p. 169) and, for the rest, quotes Witherspoon.

8. Dedications to the narrative poems *Venus and Adonis* (1593) and *The Rape of Lucrece* (1594).

9. 'Kyd and Garnier', 133.

10. *A Select Collection of Plays,* XI, p. 64.

11. Robert Garnier, *Porcie, Cornélie,* ed. Lebègue, p. 197 (ll. 995-1004).

12. For a full account of this portion of Kyd's life, see Freeman, pp. 25-32.

13. Quoted from one of Kyd's two letters to Sir John Puckering, the effectual head of the Privy Council, MS. *Harl.* 6849, fols. 218-19, printed in Freeman, pp. 181-2. As Kyd's authorship of the unsigned letter, which provides details about Marlowe's alleged 'monstruous opinions', has been doubted on paleographical grounds (Robert D. Parsons, 'Thomas Kyd's Letters', *NQ,* 225 [n.s. 27] (1980), 140-1), it may be worthwhile referring to the judgment of Malcolm Parkes, former professor of paleography at the University of Oxford, who has pointed out (by private communication) that the consistency of a series of scribal habits and practices in the two letters strongly suggests that they were written by the same hand.

14. Quoted from Freeman, p. 182.

15. The subtitle 'The Lady Fitzwa[l]ter's Nightingale' of Robert Greene's *Philomela* (1592) was in her honour.

16. 'A Defence of Poetry', in *Miscellaneous Prose of Sir Philip Sidney,* ed. Duncan-Jones and van Dorsten, p. 113.

17. *The Medieval Heritage of Elizabethan Tragedy,* p. 396.

18. The other neoclassical plays were Samuel Brandon's *Virtuous Octavia* (1598), Daniel's *Philotas* (1605), William Alexander's *Darius* (1603), *Cræsus* (1604), *The Alexandræan Tragedy* (1605), and *Julius Cæsar* (1607), and Elizabeth Cary's *Tragedy of Mariam* (1613).

19. 'A Defence of Poetry', ed. Duncan-Jones and van Dorsten, pp. 113-14. T. S. Eliot was among those who held that 'the Countesse of Pembroke tried to assemble a body of wits to compose drama in the proper Senecan style, to make head against the popular melodrama of that time' ('Seneca in Elizabethan Translation', *Selected Essays,* pp. 92-4). For a full account of this view, see A. M. Witherspoon, *The Influence of Robert Garnier on Elizabethan Drama* (New Haven, 1924).

20. See M. E. Lamb, 'The Myth of the Countess of Pembroke: The Dramatic Circle', *The Yearbook of English Studies,* 11 (1981), 195-202, and Margaret P. Hannay, *Philip's Phoenix: Mary Sidney, Countess of Pembroke* (Oxford, 1990), pp. 119-26.

21. *STC* 12751: 'W. Har., Epicedium. A funerall Song, vpon lady Helen Branch. London, printed by Thomas Creede, 1594' (A2^r). W. Har. cannot have been, as has been suggested, the poet Sir William Harbert (or Herbert), who was only eleven years old in 1594 (*DNB,* XXVI, pp. 225-6).

22. *Polimanteia* (*STC* 5883), Q3.

23. Charles Crawford (ed.), *England's Parnassus,* p. 377, and Crawford, '*Belvedere,* or *The Garden of the Muses*', 198-228, esp. 204-7.

Select Bibliography

CONCORDANCE

Crawford, Charles, *A Concordance to the Works of Thomas Kyd,* Materialien zur Kunde des älteren englischen Dramas, 15 (Louvain: David Nutt, 1906-10)

MODERN EDITIONS OF KYD'S WORKS

A Select Collection of Old Plays, ed. by Robert Dodsley, 12 vols. (London, 1744) (*The Spanish Tragedy,* vol. 2; *Cornelia,* vol. 11)

Kyd, Thomas, *The Works of Thomas Kyd,* ed. by Frederick Samuel Boas (Oxford: Clarendon Press, 1901, rpt. with a supplement 1955)

MODERN EDITIONS OF OTHER EARLY WORKS

Garnier, Robert, *Porcie, Cornélie,* ed. by Raymond Lebègue (Paris: Belles Lettres, 1973)

Greene, Robert, *The Plays and Poems of Robert Greene,* 2 vols., ed. by J. Churton Collins (Oxford: Clarendon Press, 1905)

GENERAL CRITICISM AND SCHOLARSHIP ON KYD

Braden, Gordon, 'Thomas Kyd', in Fredson Bowers (ed.), *Elizabethan Dramatists,* Dictionary of Literary Biography, 62 (Detroit: Gale, 1987), 183-95

Carrère, Félix, *Le Théâtre de Thomas Kyd* (Toulouse: Edouard Privat, 1951)

Freeman, Arthur, 'The Printing of *The Spanish Tragedy*', *The Library,* 5th Series, 24 (1969), 187-99

CRITICISM AND SCHOLARSHIP ON KYD'S OTHER PLAYS AND THE KYD APOCRYPHA

Rees, Joan, 'Julius Caesar—An Earlier Play, and an Interpretation', *MLR*, 50 (1955), 135-41

Roberts, Josephine A. and James F. Gaines, 'Kyd and Garnier: The Art of Amendment', *Comparative Literature*, 31 (1979), 124-33

OTHER CRITICISM AND SCHOLARSHIP

Braden, Gordon, *Renaissance Tragedy and the Senecan Tradition: Anger's Privilege* (New Haven: Yale University Press, 1985)

Bullough, Geoffrey (ed.), *Narrative and Dramatic Sources of Shakespeare,* 8 vols. (London: Routledge, 1957-75)

Farnham, Willard, *The Medieval Heritage of Elizabethan Tragedy* (Berkeley: University of California Press, 1936)

Mouflard, Marie-Madeleine, *Robert Garnier, 1545-1590: L'Oeuvre* (La Roche-sur-Yon: Imprimerie Centrale de L'Ouest, 1963)

Muir, Kenneth, *The Sources of Shakespeare's Plays* (London: Methuen, 1977)

Soellner, Rolf, 'Shakespeare's *Lucrece* and the Garnier-Pembroke Connection', *Shakespeare Studies*, 15 (1982), 1-20

Witherspoon, Alexander Maclaren, *The Influence of Robert Garnier on Elizabethan Drama* (New Haven: Yale University Press, 1924)

Marguerite A. Tassi (essay date 2005)

SOURCE: Tassi, Marguerite A. "'Stretch thine art': Painting Passions, Revenge, and the Painter Addition to *The Spanish Tragedy*." In *The Scandal of Images: Iconoclasm, Eroticism, and Painting in Early Modern English Drama*, pp. 152-77. Selinsgrove, Pa.: Susquehanna University Press, 2005.

[*In the following essay, Tassi examines a later addition to* The Spanish Tragedy, *probably written by Ben Jonson. Tassi considers the addition an extension of Kyd's highly visual dramatic style and a possible response to the play's theme of revenge.*]

> Behold a man hanging: and tottering, and tottering as you know the wind will weave a man, and I with a trice to cut him down. And looking upon him by the advantage of my torch, find it to be my son Horatio. There you may show a passion, there you may show a passion. Draw me like old Priam of Troy, crying 'The house is a-fire, the house is a-fire as the torch over my head!' Make me curse, make me rave, make me cry, make me mad. . . .
>
> —Addition to *The Spanish Tragedy*

> Poesie therefore is an arte of imitation, for so *Aristotle* termeth it in his word *Mimesis,* that is to say a representing, counterfetting, or figuring foorth: to speake metaphorically, a speaking picture: with this end, to teach and delight.
>
> —Sir Philip Sidney, *The Defence of Poesie*

The author of the famous Painter Addition to *The Spanish Tragedy* was undoubtedly an appreciative, albeit critical, spectator at one of the early productions of Thomas Kyd's popular revenge tragedy. A number of years after the play's first recorded performance at the Rose Theater in 1592, the anonymous author cast the tragic avenger Hieronimo, by then emblazoned as a stock image of paternal grief and madness in every Elizabethan theatergoer's memory, in a compelling new scene. This addition differed in crucial ways from the dramatic style of the popular play. Retrospective in nature, the scene echoes memorable images and motifs from *The Spanish Tragedy* in a style that heightens the relationship between dramatic language and painting, yet refuses to bear fruit in spectacle. Although its language depends on the potency of images, the scene in performance places greater emphasis on the verbal element of drama—the scene is essentially a conversation, and the imagined pictures find their articulation in language through the elaboration of a painting trope. However, a most remarkable effect of this painting trope can be witnessed in performance: because the painting never materializes on the stage, the actor is motivated to enact the images with his face and body. The player *becomes* the painting; his performance unifies word and image. Thus, the visual element of theater asserts itself through the player in an extraordinary act of compensation for a suppressed visual image.

In no early modern play examined thus far in this study have we witnessed such a fusion of the arts of painting and dramatic impersonation. The energies that resulted in this fusion are arguably competitive, or paragonal, in nature. The dramatist suppressed the material body of the painting in order to draw forth a more striking, moving dramatic painting in which speech, gesture, and passionate expression create living art. The complex nature of the Painter Addition's "speaking picture" and its effects on the audience at an Elizabethan performance of *The Spanish Tragedy* will be the concerns of this chapter. We shall observe, as well, how the scene indulges the audience's iconophilia, while at the same time fostering ambivalence and moral anxiety about the dangers of image-making.

In writing an addition for a play known for its spectacular effects and excessive passions, the Addition's author chose, oddly enough, to present a quiet, moving encounter between two grieving fathers in which the action is conveyed primarily through the motives of rhetoric. A visually charged language compensates for lack of spectacle. A painter, whose son has been murdered, arrives mysteriously at midnight to appeal for justice from Hieronimo. The old Knight Marshal, magistrate of justice in Spain, has himself suffered the brutal murder of a son; "extreme grief and cutting sorrow" (3.12A.14) have driven him into a state of lucid madness in which he contemplates "wild justice."[1] The painter's profession inspires Hieronimo to turn his attention to painting as a medium for consolation and revenge. He gives the artisan a set of instructions for a vivid narrative painting that would feature himself, his wife Isabella, son Horatio, and the murderers as portrait images; the final scene is to depict his revenge. This powerful and moving example of an Elizabethan painting trope reflects the influence both of painting—Tudor portraits, memorial paintings, and the rare, scandalous revenge painting—and poetry—pictorial poetry and the "picture in the gallery" motif.[2]

In synthesizing various influences from poetry and painting, the Painter Addition's author attempts to get at the origin and purpose of the artistic impulse. Because he does this in a theatrical setting with characters who reflect back on prior action in the play, the dramatist's invention of the painting trope proves to be based not only on pictorial genres, but also on an imitation of dramatic performance. The scene offers an allegory of imitation in which Hieronimo momentarily "plays the painter," taking his material from "nature" and painterly models. The work of art he creates is a verbal painting that memorializes scenes from his life and projects new images that help create a meaningful narrative structure. This verbal painting is a fascinating hybrid of representational forms (drama, language, painting) that can be called ekphrastic, yet the extraordinary aspect of this ekphrasis is that it is not conveyed solely in verbal form, nor is it based solely on a visual form. The visual images in Hieronimo's "painting" are realized through dramatic impersonation. As he speaks, Hieronimo suits the word to the action and dramatizes the word painting in an effort to make the images live through performance. The performer's vitality and the vividness of his language (known as *enargeia*) infuse the "painted" images with the liveliness of drama itself. This scene intimately connects drama with painting and demonstrates through the player's performance and a sophisticated use of the painting trope a vivid example of the Elizabethan notion of "painting" passions.

First printed for Thomas Pavier in 1602 along with four other Additions to Kyd's play, the Painter scene has been the subject of controversy for readers of later eras who have debated its authorship, date of composition, and early performance status. While some critics have speculated that Shakespeare, Webster, or Dekker wrote them, the most probable author seems to be Ben Jonson. This view is based on the record in Henslowe's *Diary* of two payments made to Jonson for "new adicyons for

Jeronymo."[3] Given the scene's lack of spectacle and appeal to the ear, Jonson would seem to be an appropriate candidate for authorship. In *Timber: or Discoveries* (printed 1640), he praised painting's ability to "penetrate the inmost affection," while at the same time insisting that poetry is nobler and that "*Picture* tooke her faining from *Poetry*."[4] His well-known quarrel with Inigo Jones appears to have been the culmination of years of repulsion for theatrical spectacle. Furthermore, his known competitiveness with other dramatists could have motivated this critical addition to Kyd's play. In writing the Painter's scene, Jonson was not only competing with Kyd, but with his rival Marston as well, for he was arguably recasting the painter scene from *Antonio and Mellida*. Some critics have argued that Marston parodied the Painter Addition, but the most probable dates for these two works (1599 for Marston, 1601 for the Addition) render the argument untenable. It is not beyond the realm of possibility that a playwright might take a satirical scene as inspiration for serious drama. I propose that this is what occurred.

The 1602 title page features the Painter scene as one of the play's new attractions: "Newly corrected, amended, and enlarged with new additions of the Painters part, and others, as it hath of late beene diuers times acted." This advertisement offers conclusive evidence that "the Painters part" was performed and written before the 1602 publication date, but the question of whether the scene replaced another one or was simply added to Kyd's play remains yet another matter for speculation. In the half dozen quartos printed between 1602 and 1633, the Additions appear as interpolations in Kyd's play. But as Levin L. Schücking has argued, if all the scenes were played, it would make for an atypically long Elizabethan play; the Additions must have been substitutions that catered to changing tastes. He suggests that the Painter scene replaced the outmoded petitioners' episode in which the *senex* Bazulto appeals to Hieronimo for justice for his murdered son.[5] One can certainly detect verbal and thematic echoes of the petitioners' scene in the Painter Addition. The author must have taken his cue from the portrait trope used by Hieronimo to express his identification with a grieving father, Bazulto—"the lively portrait of my dying self" (3.13.85). Hieronimo's passions ride high in that scene, for he tears up the citizens' legal petitions with his teeth in a ludicrous demonstration of lost faith in justice. He also momentarily believes Bazulto to be his son Horatio come back from the dead to haunt him and to urge revenge. By 1601, Henslowe may have felt that these devices seemed laughable and therefore in need of revision if the play was to continue drawing audiences.

Suffice it to say, editors have been baffled by the problem of what to do with the Additions and how to make sense of them as an integral part of Kyd's play. In his

1901 edition of Kyd's works, Frederick S. Boas praised the Painter scene as an "unparalleled 'night piece,'" and a triumph of "Elizabethan romantic art"; he placed the scene between 3.12 and 3.13, exactly where it can be found in the play's seventeenth-century editions, but he agreed with a contemporary reviewer of another edition of Kyd's play who commented that the five Additions turned the play into an "unintelligent mingle-mangle."[6] As a way to eliminate confusion, a number of modern editors have taken the liberty of placing the additional scenes in the appendices of their editions. Philip Edwards states their case succinctly: "Unfortunately, those Additions (which are really substitutions for certain sections of the old play) only hinder one's grasp of Kyd's purposes if one tries to read them with the original text."[7] Most scholars, it would seem, have concurred with this view, for few studies of *The Spanish Tragedy* attempt to make sense of the Additions, and many fail to mention them at all. Yet the five Additions *can* be understood as meaningful extensions of Kyd's play. If read *thematically,* Charles K. Cannon argues, the first four Additions make sense and seem "well integrated with the contexts into which they were placed in the 1602 edition of *The Spanish Tragedy.*"[8] The Painter Addition in particular resonates with Kyd's play because of its concern with art's purpose and potency and its elaboration of the play's central themes—the search for justice, the mystery of evil, and the pursuit of vengeance through art.

The Painter Addition has not been entirely ignored, for it is undeniably good writing and makes for surprisingly good theater. The scene, in fact, demonstrates the power of theater as a mixed art form that need not rely on spectacle for its visual effects. Again, this point argues strongly for Jonson's authorship. Early in the nineteenth century, Charles Lamb reflected his appreciation of the Painter Addition by including it as *the* representative scene from Kyd's play in his *Specimens of English Dramatic Poets* (1808); he called the Addition "the very salt of the old play."[9] More recently, Francis Berry has referred to the "superbly fine additions,"[10] and Peter B. Murray has called the Painter scene "the greatest piece of writing in the play."[11] Murray argues perceptively that "the author's real purpose is to draw our attention to his own great art. In the concentrated power of its rendering of the scene that so well epitomizes the spirit of *The Spanish Tragedy,* the passage is a final microcosm in a play full of microcosms."[12] Michael Hattaway offers a view of the Painter Addition that makes it artistically consistent with Kyd's play. He rightly observes that Kyd "created the 'scene' as the elemental dramatic unit."[13] Each scene in the play is replete with "speaking pictures" such as emblems, tableaux, and pageants. The Painter scene, then, extends Kyd's pictorial method by having Hieronimo ask for paintings of scenes representative of high emotion; the Painter episode, in Hattaway's view, "is a digression apologetical for the nature of the play."[14] It would seem logical, then, that this addition is in fact an *addition* to the drama, rather than a replacement for old material.

Critics typically have focused on the artistic purpose of the Painter Addition, particularly as it functions to clarify Kyd's view of art. Donna B. Hamilton argues that the Painter Addition should be regarded as an important part of the intellectual design of the play, which presents a "progression from painting to poetry and song and finally to drama."[15] She concludes with the astute observation that for Kyd and other Elizabethan dramatists, "drama is the form most capable of expressing the human experience because it is both *poesis* and *pictura,* and has, as well, real sound and action."[16] As a mute picture of *literal* images, Hieronimo's painting fails where only drama can succeed, since drama offers pictures that truly speak both to the understanding and the senses. Like Hamilton, Peter M. Sacks notes Hieronimo's move toward literalism in art, but he finds the collapse of difference between viewer and painted image to occur in the Knight Marshal's use of dramatic art as well. It is literalism, not representation, that Hieronimo wants, and that is what he finally gets when he takes the theater trope seriously and produces *real* rather than *represented* deaths through dramatic performance. The Painter scene, Sacks argues, demonstrates Hieronimo's loss of faith in artistic responses to suffering and death; art fails to compensate for real loss.[17] In contrast, G. Wilson Knight regards the Painter scene as a moving attempt to find comfort and permanence through pictorial art. He remarks on the profundity of the scene in its attempt to imagine the painting as "a *living* transcending of actuality."[18]

These critics have begun to lay the groundwork for an understanding of the Painter scene's significance. However, they do not fully account for the mysterious power of the Painter scene in performance, or for its sophisticated use of the painting trope. Let me start with the painting trope and its manifestation as ekphrasis. First, we should note the author's ingenuity in bringing a literal source for the trope, the professional painter, to the stage: the painter is present to serve as a catalyst for Hieronimo's verbal painting. The imaginative work of ekphrasis and the actor's/character's directing of passion into dramatizing this work brings the audience close to the creative process. One might call the painting produced a "notional ekphrasis," or a verbal representation of an *imagined* work of art, as opposed to an "actual ekphrasis," a verbal representation of an *existing* work of art, to use John Hollander's terms.[19] Indeed, Hieronimo projects the narrative painting in his mind and creates a unique imaginary work of art. Yet some of the imagined scenes belong to Kyd's play, which means that the audience has recently witnessed some of the "painted" events as dramatic action. What we are to perceive, given the suspension of disbelief, is that

Hieronimo as artist imitates life; the Addition's author, however, imitates art.

Both understandings of *imitatio,* imitation of nature and imitation of artistic models, were current during the early modern period. The author, practicing the latter kind of imitation, has based part of the ekphrasis on another work of art that exists in two forms, as text and performance. This is an unusual kind of ekphrasis that functions on two levels: within the illusion of the drama, the artist Hieronimo creates a verbal painting that is an imaginary vision of life as a work of art; from outside the illusion, the author of the scene has created an ekphrasis that is based partly in the actual realm of dramatic performance/text, and partly in the notional realm of imaginary art (i.e., the unique images that are not in Kyd's play). The Painter scene translates drama into painting and painting into drama; these two art forms do not have solid boundaries, nor for that matter do illusion and reality in *The Spanish Tragedy.* The verbal painting as performed has the effect of both distancing the spectators from violent action and bringing it vividly to mind again through an imaginative reenactment.

The Painter scene is Hieronimo's first of three artistic reenactments of the violent scenes of Horatio's murder and his own passionate lament. In 2.4 of Kyd's play, we witness the actual hanging and stabbing of Horatio. The scene begins ominously with Horatio invoking night and darkness as he leads his beloved Bel-Imperia into the bower. Their amorous discourse is interrupted by the villains Lorenzo, Balthazar, and servants, who quickly hang and stab Horatio, and kidnap Bel-Imperia. The scene that follows presents Hieronimo's discovery of the "murderous spectacle" (2.5.9) of his son hanging from a tree in his own garden. His wife, Isabella, joins him, and together they lament the death of their son. Hieronimo vows revenge as he takes up his son's bloodstained handkerchief, a visual memento of vengeance.

The Painter Addition of act three offers a reenactment of these scenes. Set at midnight, the scene opens with Hieronimo's servants burning torches upon their master's order and speaking of his madness. Hieronimo enters the stage in a frantic state; he appears to be searching for Horatio. He cries out against night, the "murderous slut" (3.12A.31), and the moon that lay hidden on the night his son was murdered. He then berates the tree, "wicked wicked" tree (71), upon which his son was killed. Isabella calls out to Hieronimo, "come in a-doors. / O, seek not means so to increase thy sorrow" (54-55). At this moment, a painter arrives, and Hieronimo feels inspired to "paint some comfort" (73) for his sorrow by imagining a painting of the horror he has experienced; at the same time, he appears to have found a means to increase his sorrow through obsessive replaying of his terrible memories. The vivid

description of a painting reenacts the two earlier scenes and projects the moment of revenge, which is yet to come.

The second reenactment centers on vengeance; it occurs as an episode of metadrama in which Hieronimo casts the real "actors in th' accursed tragedy" (3.7.41) of his son's murder as characters in his drama, **"The Tragedy of Soliman and Perseda."** The play-within-a-play recasts and mirrors Horatio's tragedy and allows Hieronimo to take revenge in the guise of playacting a murder. He takes the role of the villain Bashaw, a role that corresponds to that of his son's murderer, Lorenzo, who in turn plays the role of Erasto (the Horatio character), husband of Perseda, played by Bel-Imperia. Hieronimo has created an opportunity for vengeance, as his script calls for the Bashaw to stab Erasto. Ironically, the reenactment of his son's murder becomes the enactment of revenge for his death. The third reenactment occurs when Hieronimo reveals the corpse of his son as a "strange and wondrous show" (4.1.185) and emblem of justification for revenge. He delivers a public "oration" (4.1.184) that recalls again the murder and his discovery of the body. Thus, with the addition of the Painter's scene, the drama reveals Hieronimo to be an artist who transforms personal tragedy and "unfruitful words" (3.7.67) into visual and verbal art forms.

As the first aesthetic reenactment, the Painter scene adds an important stage in Hieronimo's experimentation with artistic forms, for in it we witness the origin of a work of art and the passions that motivate it. Removed from the action, this scene offers a portrait of the artist engaged in the process of invention—imitating nature and arranging images into an agreeable form. We have a brief moment in which dramatic action is suspended; indeed, dramatic action becomes the subject of the imagined painting. The artistic functions of painter and player merge in the character of Hieronimo in this moment of heightened creativity. In his passionate desire to have the Painter *see* his painting, Hieronimo usurps the artist's role and doubles as figurative painter. The Painter says little in the scene; his silence renders him a symbolic representative of his mute art and a compassionate spectator to Hieronimo's verbal and performative art. Not only does Hieronimo describe what he wants to see painted, but also he physically enacts each pictorial scene with gestures and facial expressions so that the Painter may see the action and emotion he should represent. Hieronimo "paints" love, grief, rage, vengeance, and madness in a series of dramatic tableaux. While Kyd's play depended on emblems and other pictorial sources for its dramatic presentation, in this scene the Addition's author ingeniously makes use of stage pictures and dramatic actions from the play itself as inspiration for Hieronimo's painting. This is an ambitious move on the dramatist's part, for it suggests the mysterious power of theater lies in its absorption of the visual arts (pictures, sculpture, funeral effigies, painted cloths, tapestry, emblems, etc.). The theater, he implies, is a kind of superior painting that transcends the limitations of the painter's medium. Hieronimo, in effect, desires to give the moving pictures of drama the constancy and iconic power of static images that one might gaze upon in awe in order to learn the truth.

The connection between the painter's and player's arts can be seen in the way the term *painting* was used in Elizabethan discourses. As we have seen in previous chapters, *painting* referred to a variety of visual arts and to coloring the face with cosmetics; the term could also be used figuratively as a trope to indicate various ways of heightening or falsifying rhetoric and action. Thus, we find countless references to painting that signify verbal style (vivid pictorial description, deceitful speech, artificial or ornate uses of rhetorical "colors") and behavior (pretense, playacting, displaying emotion). We can immediately see the linguistic affiliation between the painter's and player's arts: they both involve colors of a sort that intensify the effect of the work of art on the beholder; they both involve a kind of deception created through their medium; and they both deal in "re-presenting" life, or "counterfeiting" nature. The artistic process for both painters and dramatists/players fell under the general principle of imitation. "The whole doctrine of Comedies and Tragedies," wrote Roger Ascham, "is a perfite *imitation,* or faire liuelie painted picture of the life of euerie degree of man."[20] Players were said to be "painting" passions, dramatists to be "painting" the very life of man. Thus, imitation and painting seem to have been interchangeable concepts in Elizabethan discourses. To phrase it another way, by the late sixteenth century *painting* had become a normative and evaluative term for imitation itself. Both positive and negative connotations could be emphasized in a writer's use of these terms.

A number of early seventeenth-century writers refer explicitly to painting in their descriptions of players' impersonations. In *Microcosmos* (1603), John Davies of Hereford praises the players' "Qualitie" (profession, skill), despite the common prejudice that "the *stage* doth staine pure gentle *bloud*":

> *Players,* I loue yee, and your *Qualitie,*
> As ye are Men, *that* pass time not abus'd:
> And some I loue for *painting, poesie,*
> And say fell *Fortune* cannot be excus'd,
> That hath for better *uses* you refus'd.[21]

The "some" he loves "for painting, poesie" are W. S. (William Shakespeare) and R. B. (Richard Burbage). By way of explanation for the "painting, poesie" reference, Davies invokes the familiar sister arts analogy in the margin: "Simonides saith, that painting is a dumb

Poesy, & Poesy a speaking painting."[22] He loosely applies this popular view of the arts to players who, at their best, become figurative painters. John Webster suggested a similar conceit in a character sketch of the "excellent actor" from 1615: the actor, he exclaims, is "much affected to painting, and 'tis a question whether that make him an excellent Plaier, or his playing an exquisite painter."[23] Webster creates a witty conflation of two meanings of painting: the player literally paints his face with cosmetics and figuratively paints his passions or affections with the colors of rhetoric. In this second meaning of painting, we find the actor presented not only as a word-painter and orator, dependent on the dramatist's poetry, but as an expressive performer who gives language vitality and conviction through performance. In Webster's locution, playing has a kind of agency of its own; playing creates the visual arena of the theater.

Webster, like Davies, may be alluding to Richard Burbage in this passage, for the well-known actor was also an amateur painter.[24] A connection to the Painter Addition may be inferred here, for Burbage was certainly known to have played Hieronimo. "A Funerall Elegye on ye Death of the famous Actor Richard Burbedg . . ." lists "ould Heironymoe" as one of the parts that "liued in him."[25] We might speculate that our clever dramatist wrote the Painter scene for Burbage, the player made famous for his passionate, lifelike performances. Another possible reference to Burbage playing Hieronimo occurs in Thomas May's *The Heir* (1622). The opening passage from this play indicates that the conceit of painting grief was popularly associated with Hieronimo and that he was taken as the pattern for paternal grief (and subject for parody) for dramatists and players of the late sixteenth and early seventeenth centuries. In *The Heir,* a reference to Hieronimo depends on this widely recognized view of Kyd's character. When the old Lord Polimetes plans a jest in which he will counterfeit a father's grief for his dead son, he believes that it will be difficult to feign such profound emotion. His servant Roscius, named for the much admired ancient Roman actor, quickly responds, "Oh no my Lord, / Not for your skill, has not your Lordship seene / A player personate *Jeronimo?*" Polimetes immediately sees the wisdom in modelling his "performance" after the player's (Burbage's) impersonation of Hieronimo:

> By th' masse tis true, I have seen the knave paint
>   griefe
> In such a lively colour, that for false
> And acted passion he has drawne true teares
> From the spectators eyes, Ladyes in the boxes
> Kept time with sighes, and teares to his sad accents
> As had he truely bin the new man he seemd.[26]

"Painting grief" in the "lively colour" of rhetoric and with heightened naturalistic emotion was the recognized mode for personating Hieronimo, and it seems to have been Burbage's trademark as an actor, as well.

Elizabethan dramatists commonly employed the painting trope as a graphic mode of description that enabled their actors to externalize passions, intentions, and moral character. In Shakespeare's *Hamlet*, for example, the painting trope forges a link between acting and painting. When the Players arrive at Elsinore, and Hamlet requests to hear Aeneas's speech, the First Player comes to the famous passage where Pyrrhus is about to take his revenge on Priam. The Player vividly describes a moment of hesitation, the very moment that speaks to Hamlet's own situation: "for lo his sword, / Which was declining on the milky head / Of reverent Priam, seem'd i' th' air to stick. / So as a painted tyrant Pyrrhus stood / [And,] like a neutral to his will and matter, / Did nothing" (2.2.477-82). Pyrrhus appears as an image in a painting, frozen in time with his sword stuck in the air above Priam's head. The Player captures this tense moment of inaction in language, but he also has an opportunity for passionate playing here. *Painted* must have been read as a verbal cue for the actor. He should, in following Hamlet's famous advice to the players, suit the action to the word and take on the physical attitude of the painted Pyrrhus in order to enhance the dramatic intensity of the moment for his spectators. The still moment of hesitation before action captured by the painting analogy indicates precisely *how* the actor should direct his energy and passion.

Through the painting trope, the actor playing Hieronimo in the Painter scene receives a similar cue for playing. He is to evoke the visual power of images, both static and moving, not only through ekphrasis, but also through his expressive voice and physical movements. In Hieronimo's painting, the author has achieved a compelling synthesis of verbal style and performance, word and image that extends Kyd's own use of figures and visual images in a powerful way. The author of the Painter scene successfully produced a passionate language that dramatized the relationship between painting and playing. What emerges from this dramatization is not simply a "critique of rhetoric, an assessment of the limits of impassioned speech," to invoke Jonas Barish's frequently cited argument;[27] rather, the scene offers a compelling example of how the passions give shape and purpose to art. With the painting trope, Hieronimo's speech becomes performative; not only do his words evoke scenes for the audience to imagine, but the player himself brings the verbal painting to life. Through passionate playing, the actor conveys a lively image of grief that demonstrates the very expressiveness he desires to see in the painted figures.

In Pavier's 1602 text and the subsequent quartos that appeared in the early seventeenth century, the Painter scene was placed between Hieronimo's fruitless, lunatic appeal to the Spanish king for justice (3.12) and the momentous "Vindicta mihi" scene in which he resolves to take private revenge (3.13). This positioning is meaningful in that Hieronimo has just turned to the highest earthly authority for justice and has been unsuccessful in communicating anything but his own madness. The well-meaning King does not know that Horatio has been murdered; therefore he cannot understand the cause of his Knight Marshal's unsettled mental state. In the scene following the Painter Addition, Hieronimo commits himself to meting out punishment to the murderers. Poised between the King's rejection and his resolute adoption of the role of avenger, the Painter scene proves to be an imaginative rehearsal of motivation for and vicarious experience of revenge.

Let us examine the Painter's scene in detail. The scene is set forebodingly at midnight in the "hideous orchard" (3.12A.103) with the blood-splattered tree signifying the violence that has erupted in the garden. Hieronimo laments that the tree he planted himself "grew a gallows, and did bear our son. / It bore thy fruit and mine: O wicked, wicked plant" (70-71). A knock at the door interrupts this gruesome reflection on the tree's death-serving fertility. Hieronimo's servant Pedro announces, "It is a painter, sir" (72). A most unexpected arrival at midnight, the Painter's appearance on the stage might suggest the realm of the absurd to a modern audience, but, for Elizabethan spectators, the situation would signal an allegory or symbolic scene in the making. Hieronimo accepts the Painter's arrival without surprise and puns cynically on the word *paint*: "Bid him come in, and paint some comfort, / For surely there's none lives but painted comfort" (73-74). "Painted" in this context refers to the falseness of appearances and inauthentic shows of feeling. Similarly in *Hamlet*, Claudius recognizes his own falseness in terms of painting, or cosmetics: "The harlot's cheek, beautied with plast'ring art, / Is not more ugly to the thing that helps it / Than is my deed to my most painted word" (3.1.50-52). The falsifying or masking of language suggests to Claudius, as it did to many Elizabethan moralists, a resemblance to the literal falsification and masking involved in women's and players' face-painting. For Hieronimo, all shows of comfort seem to be false representations of comfort itself. Yet the element of chance offers hope and despair alike: he calls the Painter in for, as he philosophizes, "One knows not what may chance" (75). Spoken as an antithesis, "Paint some comfort" and "painted comfort" may reflect Hieronimo's sudden insight that art may actually offer comfort. The Painter offers Hieronimo the opportunity to try out this possibility. The meeting with the Painter occurs when Hieronimo is at his most vulnerable—emotionally spent, lonely in his grief, and given to spells of madness. Revenge has entered his consciousness and can no longer be suppressed. Hieronimo begins to perceive, inchoately at first, that some form of art might provide consolation and, later, perhaps a means to avenge Horatio's death. The question of art's consolatory power, of the ability of figurative art to compensate for loss, is most urgent at this moment in the play.

Like Lear and Gloucester in Shakespeare's tragedy, the Painter and Hieronimo sit together and speak feelingly of their madness and suffering: "Come," Hieronimo says, "let's talk wisely now. Was thy son murdered?" "Ay sir," the Painter sadly replies. "So was mine. How dost thou take it?" Hieronimo asks, "Art thou not sometimes mad? Is there no tricks that comes before thine eyes?" "O Lord," the Painter cries, "yes, sir" (106-10). The language is very simple; they speak frankly of their experiences. The "tricks" before their eyes is the crucial image here. In their grief, these men hallucinate or see illusory shapes. The painting that Hieronimo imagines is also a kind of "trick" or visual illusion that comes before his eyes, yet, at the same time, it is a sort of remedy or corrective to the "tricks" of madness. His shaping fantasies are those of lunatic, poet, loving father, and avenger. His imagination bodies forth a painting whose images are truthful; they have a purpose and reality that hallucinations cannot claim to have. "Art a painter?" Hieronimo suddenly asks. "Canst paint me a tear, or a wound, a groan, or a sigh? Canst paint me such a tree as this?" (111-12) he queries, as they look upon the tree that has served as his son's gallows. The Painter, perhaps bristling at the suggestion that he might not know his craft well and, at the same time, evading the impossibility of the request to paint groans and sighs, proudly indicates that he has a name, that is to say, a reputation: "Sir, I am sure you have heard of my painting, my name's Bazardo" (113-14). Hieronimo instantly recognizes the man's name: "Bazardo! afore God, an excellent fellow!" (115) he exclaims, and, with that assurance, he proceeds to describe with many precise details the painting he desires. This "trick" before his eyes begins to gain solidity as he imagines a narrative cycle with at least seven discrete images. Hieronimo seems to have in mind a large narrative painting that contains a series of individual scenes. This design reflects the author's perception of Kyd's method of pictorial scene composition. Scenes from Kyd's play appear complete as stage pictures yet, like Hieronimo's continuous narrative painting, woven within a significant design based on symbolic images and meaningful actions.

Hieronimo first asks for a family portrait that reflects private, emotional ties. This would require an imaginative reconstruction of an affectionate patriarch and his family as they were five years in the past. "I'd have you paint me . . . my gallery," he says to the Painter, "in your oil colours matted, and draw me five years younger than I am . . ." (116-17).[28] He insists that he wants historical accuracy in the depiction of his family: "Do you see sir, let five years go, let them go" (118).

The paradox, of course, lies in the fact that the Painter must use artifice and imaginative license to create this sense of authenticity and truth. It is clear that Hieronimo is aware of the Painter's materials—the "oil colours matted" (116-17), or colors dull in texture—and of the artist's ability to refine and embellish images in order to make the sitter appear younger. Hieronimo's description of poses, gestures, and facial expressions depends upon the conventional iconography of Tudor portraits: "My wife Isabella standing by me, with a speaking look to my son Horatio, which should intend to this or some like purpose: 'God bless thee, my sweet son': and my hand leaning upon his head, thus, sir, do you see?" (119-23). Isabella's look to their son should be a "speaking look" (120)—her eyes, the expression of her face, and her posture should all suggest the expressive quality of speech. Hieronimo speaks the actual words the painted Isabella should seem to be saying: "'God bless thee, my sweet son'" (121-22). He demonstrates his own pose with a gesture—"thus, sir, do you see?" (122-23)—which expresses his affection for and pride in his son.

The portrait exists as a complex example and reversal of Sidney's "speaking picture" trope: Hieronimo is picturing speech; the portrait is to be literal, the speech metaphoric. Yet it is through his speech and action that the painting gains *presence*. Here we seem to have a notional ekphrasis, an image that exists only through language. Yet he himself (the actor/character) transforms into the speaking picture. "May it be done" (123), he anxiously queries the Painter, who responds confidently, "Very well sir" (124). Hieronimo insists, "Nay, I pray mark me sir" (125), compelling the Painter to "mark" how he momentarily embodies the figures. He wants the Painter, like the spectators at the play, to envision the painting by watching his own demonstrations and listening to him "speak" the pictures.

Why, we might ask, does Hieronimo ask for this imaginary family portrait? What will its purpose be in the narrative cycle? As Hieronimo begins to paint his history, he looks back to the past, when he and his family were untouched by violence and cruelty, when their lives seemed coherent, ordered, and meaningful. The family portrait establishes the past good fortune, happiness, and love that governed Hieronimo's life; it is meant to be a truthful image that "speaks" in significant contrast to the other images of chaos, disorder, and wild passion in the painting. His narrative painting has a "beginning" in the image and an implied ideal of familial love.

Hieronimo then moves to the "middle" of his narrative, to continue with the Aristotelian model, in which he projects the horrific events of the recent past. He turns to the fateful tree upon which his son was murdered, and asks if the Painter can "paint me this tree, this very tree" (125-26). With the emphasis on "very," Hieronimo's desire for authenticity, for the representation of this particular tree, is made urgently clear. In the same breath, he asks, "Canst paint a doleful cry?" (126). The Painter responds, "Seemingly, sir" (127), which indicates that he could create an illusion of a person uttering a cry. Painting, he is reminding Hieronimo, is an art of suggestion and appearance; it depends wholly on what can be represented in visual terms. Hieronimo is calling for images that defy painterly representation—the *very* tree, the sound of a cry. "Nay, it should cry" (128), he exclaims passionately, revealing that he wants the painting—or is it the tree?—itself to be animated and crying in pain. The ambiguity in referent suggests that he might want the crying tree to reflect nature weeping at the brutal murder; he also might have in mind the tree as a metonym of both Horatio's and his own pain. The painter's single-word response—"Seemingly" (127)—sums up the paradox of art and, in this case, of painting as an expressive form. Images can appear to weep or express affection, can appear to conjure the thing itself, but in the end they are mute images that rely on the beholder to imagine the implied sounds and narrative. *Seeming* implies a mode of substitution for the thing itself in a painting, which is created by means of style, technique, and conventional iconography.

Hieronimo's painting, like Tudor portraits, is based on patterns, symbolic images, and ideas. He pictures his son as the figure of a youth "run through and through with villains' swords, hanging upon this tree" (129-30). This image is followed by a request for another pattern or figure: "Canst thou draw a murderer?" (130). He is asking the Painter for archetypal or significant iconographic images of youth and villainy rather than naturalistic portraits of the individuals themselves. As Sidney claimed in his *Defence,* "the meaner sort of Painters (who counterfet onely such faces as are sette before them) and the more excellent, who, having no law but wit, bestow that in cullours upon you which is fittest for the eye to see."[29] Hieronimo wants to see virtue and vice reflected in their extremity in the images. The Painter assures Hieronimo that he has "the pattern of the most notorious villains that ever lived in all Spain" (131-32). Hieronimo urges the Painter to "let them be worse, worse: stretch thine art" (133); in other words, he wants the painted images to be the outward show and unmistakable example of villainy. He wants to see the villains painted with thick, threatening eyebrows and red beards to suggest Judas Iscariot, the archetypal betrayer and villain.

He then pictures himself brought forth, much as had happened a few scenes earlier in the play: "Then sir, after some violent noise, bring me forth in my shirt, and my gown under mine arm, with my torch in my hand, and my sword reared up thus: and with these words: *What noise is this? who calls Hieronimo?*" (135-39).

The "thus" in "my sword reared up thus" (138) indicates an accompanying gesture to be performed by the actor, which would serve as the Painter's model. In the text, the words he speaks are italicized and separated from the rest of his speech, which indicates that they are intended as written text in the painting. Hieronimo most likely wants them to appear upon a scroll unfurling above his head, much as they were in the illustrated frontispiece to the 1615 and 1623 editions of *The Spanish Tragedy.* To see words in a visual field such as a painting or woodcut was not unusual in the pictorial arts of Protestant England. The frontispiece is itself a typical example. It presents Hieronimo with torch and sword discovering the body of Horatio hanging by a rope tied to the arch of a trellis. This is most likely a representation of the stage prop used in productions to create the arbor or bower. Hieronimo's words issue directly from his mouth on an unrolled scroll, "Alas it is my son Horatio," which echoes the play's text (2.5.14). The illustration also portrays, in simultaneity with the discovery, the previous scene with Bel-Imperia calling for Hieronimo's help (her text reads, "Murder, helpe Hieronimo," an echo of 2.4.62), and Lorenzo conveying her away with the words, "Stop her mouth" (2.4.63).

Some modern directors of *The Spanish Tragedy* have taken their visual cue from this famous illustration. In one notable example from 1986, the actors in a production of the play at The Shakespeare Center in New York, "startlingly brought to life" the picture of Horatio hanging in the arbour.[30] Like the author of the Painter Addition, the illustrator created a visual representation of the most impressive scandalous scenes from Kyd's play. He appears to have followed Kyd's original text in reproducing three moments from act two. He may very well have been inspired by the Addition in presenting simultaneous actions in visual form.

Unlike the still images depicted on the frontispiece, Hieronimo's pictorial description begins to defy the static quality of painting as he summons up the memory of the horrifying nocturnal scene of murder in which "clouds scowl" (144), the moon is dark, and "the stars extinct" (145). His language animates the scene and conveys a sense of dynamic action and sound: "the winds blowing, the bells tolling, the owl shrieking, the toads croaking, the minutes jarring, and the clock striking twelve" (145-47). He wants to create a ceaseless present that resembles both the phenomenal quality of experience and the vivid tableau of painting. When Hieronimo describes his discovery of Horatio's body hanging from the tree, he remembers first and foremost its movement as he sees it in his mind's eye "tottering, and tottering as you know the wind will weave a man" (148-49). He relives his profound emotion, and cries to the Painter, "There you may show a passion, there you may show a passion" (151-52). The actor's/character's passion is clearly the model for painted passion here.

Hieronimo accompanies his cry with a significant embodiment of emotion. The actor might point "there" to the very place in the bower where Horatio was hanged. He might also enact the gesture of cutting the rope and holding the torch above his son's face.

The passion to be communicated is to be as intense as Priam's passion was at the burning of Troy: "Draw me like old Priam of Troy, crying 'The house is a-fire, the house is a-fire as the torch over my head!'" (153-54). As a classical figure of bereaved fatherhood, Priam is a recognizable model for representations of extreme grief. In Virgil's *Aeneid,* amidst the flames of Troy, Priam witnesses Pyrrhus slaughter his son Polites; in his anguish he calls out for divine retribution. He takes up his sword and attempts to avenge his son's death, but Pyrrhus swiftly kills him. Like Priam, Hieronimo calls to the heavens to take notice of injustice; he, too, will pursue his son's murderer in a final effort to right the wrong that has been done. His world is disintegrating (represented by the burning house) and his inner world is a chaos of passions. "Make me curse," he exhorts the Painter, "make me rave, make me cry, make me mad, make me well again, make me curse hell, invocate heaven, and in the end leave me in a trance; and so forth" (154-57). He has slipped into giving an impossible set of instructions to the Painter—not only are sounds impossible to reproduce, but too many states of mind cannot be represented coherently, even if rendered by more than one or two images. Indeed, Hieronimo cannot finish the painting or see it as a contained object; his passion exceeds the bounds of controlled artistic creation. The Painter quietly asks, "And is this the end?" (158). Hieronimo laments, "O no, there is no end: the end is death and madness!" (159). In his anguish, Hieronimo is driven to distraction; he abandons the painting in a fit of passion as visions of death and madness occupy his raging mind.

In attempting to give significant shape to his life through pictorial narrative, Hieronimo produces a painting that has its visual analogue in actual painting genres of Tudor England. The iconographic "program" he seems to be commissioning resembles an Elizabethan memorial painting. Quite popular in sixteenth-century England, memorial portraits of individuals or families typically functioned as memento mori, a remembrance of death. In the more unusual larger panels and monuments that fused portraiture with narrative, death is solemnly celebrated as man's earthly end. One example that bears some resemblance to Hieronimo's painting is the well-known, flamboyant panel depicting the life and death of the diplomat and soldier Sir Henry Unton (artist unknown, c. 1596). As with Hieronimo's verbal painting, this work of art offers a "selective visual biography," to use Roy Strong's terms.[31] Unton appears as a large figure seated off-center to the left with a blank paper and pen, as if he were about to write his life; he is the bio-

graphical figure, yet one might argue that he is portrayed as an autobiographer, flanked by the miniature figures of Fame at his left and Death at his right, his twin muses. As in an episodic and emblematic medieval painting that depicts the significant events in the life of a saint, Christ, or Mary, Unton's portrait depicts a series of meaningful events in his life that can be read counterclockwise on the right side—infancy, studies at Oriel College, Oxford, travels, diplomatic service, and deathbed. At the center of this half-circle lie images of banqueting and masquing at Wadley House. His funeral and death monument in Faringdon Church dominate the left ("sinister") side of the panel, and the two sides are unified by the funeral procession.

In what ways would this busy narrative painting of an Elizabethan man's life have functioned in English culture? In essence, this narrative portrait is an exemplary public record of an Elizabethan gentleman's life, both in terms of his public and private achievements.[32] Yet, with the predominance of death images, the picture clearly must be a memento mori, which asks us to read Sir Henry Unton's life in the shadow of death. Similarly, Hieronimo's painting offers a portrait of a fortunate and loving family surrounded by images of death. Hieronimo falls short of imagining his own death; he still lives, but clearly he knows that death is near. Unton's portrait emblematizes those moments surrounding his death—the deathbed scene, the preparation and movement of the corpse, and the burial ceremony. Hieronimo's picture illuminates his son's murder, the corpse hanging on the tree, and his discovery of the body.

A crucial point to consider is how the commissioner of the work of art influences the choice of images and the function of the portrait. In the case of Sir Henry Unton, his wife, Lady Unton, requested the painting after her husband's death, as part of the death ritual. Its purpose must have been not only to display her husband's life as exemplary, but also to find consolation in the painted images. Hieronimo's motive for wanting the visual record of the past, the murder, and his suffering may be partly ascribed to these same motives—to memorialize his once-happy family and to find consolation. Clearly, though, he wants more than a family memorial. His line has ended with the death of his son. And he most certainly is not seeking the *aesthetic* adornment of his gallery. These images are motivated by passionate grief and a father's desire to see injustice rendered visible and his son's murderers brought to justice.

A similar dramatic example of a patron requesting a particular image for emotional satisfaction is worth examining at this point. *The Trial of Chivalry,* probably written and performed in the provinces and London public theaters by the Earl of Derby's company around 1600 (printed in 1605),[33] presents another demanding patron and a virtually mute painter who attempts to please, but is held to an unreasonable subjective standard of verisimilitude. The French Princess Katherina calls for a painter to use his "cunningst Arte" (sig. B2ʳ) to draw the image of her beloved, the Earl of Pembrooke.[34] After asking whether his colours are fresh, "pencill" smooth, hand unwavering, and head clear, she commands him, "to the life set downe his counterfet" (sig. B2ʳ). Saying little but that he is well prepared, the Paynter agrees to observe the Earl discretely in order to draw his likeness. Very quickly, he produces a portrait, apparently sketched onstage, which Katherina dotes upon as if it were the man himself. The portrait serves as a material and figurative surrogate for an unattainable beloved. When the Earl rejects her advances, she turns to the "Image far more kind,"

> Then is the substance, whence thou art deriu'd!
> Which way soeuer I diuert my selfe,
> Thou seemst to follow with a louing eye.
> Thee will I therefore hold within mine armes,
> As some small comfort to increasing harmes.

> (sigs. B4ʳ⁻ᵛ)

The portrait seems to be animated: its eyes follow her lovingly with their gaze, and the image even has a material "body" to be embraced. Within moments, however, she grows dissatisfied with this painted substitute for her love, not because it is a mere painting, but because it fails to represent the Earl faithfully. She turns upon the Paynter and chastizes him for grossly neglecting to represent the Earl's stubborn heart: "Where is his stubborne vnrelenting heart, / That lurkes in secret as his master doth, / Disdayning to regard or pity me?" (sig. B4ᵛ). He takes the Princess's rebuke on a literal level and exclaims, "Madam, his heart must be imagined / By the description of the outward parts" (sig. B4ᵛ). The Princess argues that the portrait, although realistic and skillfully made, deceives the eyes, for it fails to reflect an essential element of the Earl's character. To paint "to the life" means, in this case, to paint the subject exactly as the patron perceives him in a given moment of intense feeling. The dramatist has presented the impossible demands of a patron and, at the same time, rejected painting as an inauthentic and inadequate mimetic art. The danger of idolatry, as well, finds expression here. The Princess's rejection of the image reflects the dramatist's critique of painting, and his defense of dramatic characterization and action as the more authentic, "lively" art.

To return to Hieronimo's painting, the last image he evokes in his torment belongs to the future; it is purely fictitious at this point, but indicates much about his purpose: "At the last, sir, bring me to one of the murderers, were he as strong as Hector, thus would I tear and drag him up and down" (162-64). He invokes Achilles' wrath and his vengeance against the Trojan Hector, who had killed Achilles' friend Patroclus. Achilles killed Hector, and then had his body attached to a chariot and dragged three times around the city of Troy; when Priam came to plead for his son's body, Achilles returned the corpse to the father in an act of nobility. Hieronimo imagines his own anger as an Achillean fury that knows no bounds in the encounter with Horatio's murderer; yet his essential decency and sense of justice, we might argue, are implied in the subtext of the justly returned body. While a moment ago, Hieronimo had invoked Priam as the archetypal grieving father, here he envisions Hector, Priam's eldest son, as the pattern of ferocious warrior and killer of a loved one. His disordered mind is reflected in his mixed identification with representative figures in the Trojan war. In his thirst for vengeance, he momentarily sees Hector as an enemy and not a murdered son.

In light of the revenge motif, Hieronimo's painting can be read in a more provocative, scandalous light as a specific kind of memorial, a *memento vindictae,* whose purpose is to incite the viewer and the patron-commissioner to action. Might the author of the Painter Addition have conceived Hieronimo's painting as a vengeance picture? While we cannot know if the author is alluding specifically to this unusual genre of painting, it does offer a useful analogy for interpreting the images in Hieronimo's portrait and their effects on audiences of the time.[35] There are a small number of extant revenge paintings, which are mainly Scottish in origin. One such painting is the life-size portrait of Henry Stewart, the "bonnie earl" of Moray. His corpse looms large in the picture, with death wounds visible on his chest; a scroll issues from his mouth demanding: "God Revenge My Cavs." A panel in the upper right depicts the burning house from which Moray was forced and then murdered by the Earl of Huntley. The revenge painting was commissioned by Henry's mother to present to the King in Edinburgh in an appeal for retributive justice. The artist was most likely John Workman, a decorative painter employed at the Scottish court.[36]

Perhaps the most famous example of a Scottish revenge painting commissioned as part of a campaign for vengeance is *The Memorial of Lord Darnley,* painted by the Antwerp artist Livinus de Vogelaare in England (1568). Vogelaare was instructed by his commissioners, the Earl and Countess of Lennox, to depict in specific iconographical and textual detail the scandalous history of their son's, Lord Henry Darnley's, murder at the hands of the Earl of Bothwell and Mary, Queen of Scots. Formally, the painting resembles a traditional Flemish religious donor picture. Darnley's family kneels in prayer, the effigy of a praying Darnley in arms lies in the center background, and the luminous figure of Christ beside the cross commands the viewer's attention on the left side of the panel. The scrolls of text, however, belie the calm piousness of the picture. From the crowned infant James VI of Scotland's mouth issues the cry: "Arise, O Lord, and avenge the innocent blood of the king my father and, I beseech you, defend me with your right hand."[37] Upon close inspection of the painting's inscriptions, the viewer discovers that the images' express purpose is to inspire revenge.

On a tablet that appears in the upper right corner of the painting, an inscription declares "the reason for this work": that "if they, who are already old, should be deprived of this life before the majority of their descendant, the King of Scots, he may have a memorial from them, in order that he shut not out of his memory the recent atrocious murder of the king his father, until God should avenge it through him."[38] A small rectangular inset to the bottom left depicts the surrender of Mary, Queen of Scots to the Confederate Scottish Lords and the escape of her new husband, Bothwell, whom the painting's texts indict as the murderer. Mary is also clearly implicated. The Lords are carrying a banner depicting Darnley's corpse with the inscription, "Ivdge and Revenge My Cavse O Lord." As Margaret Aston argues, "This inset is critical to the reading of the picture, and the painting as a whole may be seen as a monumentalized version of the famous banner. . . . This picture within the picture . . . forms something like a source from which the whole has developed."[39]

English viewers of the painting must have been moved by Darnley's cause and felt the appropriateness of the family's effort to keep the memory of the murder alive. Roland Mushat Frye has pointed out the tacit acceptance of Darnley's family's call to vengeance from at least one Anglican bishop. In a letter recounting the scandals in Scotland, John Parkhurst, Bishop of Norwich, described (a bit inaccurately) Vogelaare's painting and "conveys not the slightest hint of criticism for that appeal to vengeance."[40] Certainly members of the landed aristocracy (including churchmen) in England would have felt sympathetic with the rebellious Scottish nobility who arrested Mary and named Bothwell as the guilty party. In a similar vein, Hieronimo's painting depicts an injustice done to the family of the Knight Marshal, representative of justice in Spain. For those audience members concerned about, even critical of, the efficacy of law and the state to carry out justice, Hieronimo's predicament may have struck a chord of profound sympathy. Eric Mercer has suggested that we might go so far as to read an English portrait of the Earl of Surrey (executed in 1547 for treason) as a kind of vengeance painting, for revenge may have been implied subtly by the Latin motto "Satis super est" inscribed on a monument in the painting if read as "There is enough left over."[41] His descendents, still alive, were left to take revenge. Neither the English monarchy nor the Church sanctioned private revenge, yet individuals may have refrained from morally condemning revenge causes, such as those of the Earl of Lennox and Surrey's family.

Hieronimo's painting depicts images that specifically justify and motivate revenge. The author has used painting as an imaginative tool in the revenge plot in order to mirror Hieronimo's tormented mind, but the images he sees in the mirror are not mere "tricks" of madness. They possess a degree of realism, as they capture the truth of experience and passion. Donna B. Hamilton argues that the painting fails to give Hieronimo emotional relief and must be rejected because it lacks the universal quality of good art: "he is asking not for interpretive painting, but history in painted form; he wants the painter to paint the events precisely as they happened, and consequently, the painting suggests little relief to him."[42] While Hamilton's focus on art's universal quality as an Elizabethan value is clarifying, her point could lead us to a different conclusion from the one she reaches. Hieronimo desires to see a paradoxical entity—an illusion that is real, a "seeming" that is true, an absence made present. When Hieronimo asks the Painter to "stretch thine art" (133), we should understand that he sees the painter's art as a vehicle for interpreting experience, that is, making sense of a morally chaotic world without justice. He depends upon symbolic gestures and color (red for a Judas beard, signifying villainy and betrayal), as well as antecedent models that have universal significance—Priam as the figure of a grieving father and Hector as a representative of a fierce warrior and murderer. The verbal painting plays an important role in Hieronimo's search for justice and comfort through art, for it embodies the paradoxical drives of art toward both realism and illusion.

The final moment in this scene is ambiguous: Hieronimo "beats the Painter in" (stage direction) just after he describes how he will take revenge. After transforming the energies of violence into the energies of art, Hieronimo is now motivated by his own artistic work to pursue revenge. In fixating momentarily on the painted image of vengeance, however, Hieronimo comes perilously close to madness, for he seems to have truly mistaken the Painter for the murderer. He now literally dramatizes the imagined painted action by treating the Painter as if he were the murderer in his painting. He suffers from confusion between imaginary art and the "tricks" of lunacy. This hallucination resembles the error he will make shortly thereafter when he believes the old man Bazulto to be his son Horatio returning from the dead as a specter to chastise him. Addressing Bazulto, he laments, "And art thou come, Horatio, from the depth, / To ask for justice in this upper earth? / To tell thy father thou art unrevenged . . ." (3.13.133-35). Hieronimo's mistaking his aged double for his son can be explained as an effect of madness once he has recognized that "justice is exiled from the earth" (140). His mistaking the Painter, who is both compassionate audience and Hieronimo's double, for his son's murderer signals a deeper, more troubling truth, which the play's spectators recognize again when they watch him assign himself the role of murderer in **"The Tragedy of Soliman and Perseda."** In beating the Painter, he betrays the dangerous blinding quality of revenge as it consumes the imagination. This moment anticipates Hieronimo's use of drama to enact his revenge. Hieronimo's excessive desire for justice is channeled once more into art as he turns to drama itself to "paint" passions and take revenge.

In the conjuring of this painting, early modern spectators witnessed the dangerous power that resides in the artist and in his images, a power that can prompt men to bloody, scandalous actions. They beheld, as well, the actor animating these images with presence. It was a logical step, then, to move from a dramatized painting to the moving, speaking pictures of drama—or that is, to drama as an extraordinary living form of painting. The player's passion, anticipated in the dramatic enactment of the painting, becomes fully realized in a dramatic performance of a script. Hieronimo turns to the theater because only there can he get results; unlike pure painting or poetry, drama is a mixed medium that depends upon live human impersonations and actions. Hieronimo takes theater one enormous step further than Hamlet does by using actors in a drama to perform *real* actions. Hieronimo has already determined the guilt of his son's murderers and uses a drama of his own to murder the unsuspecting actors/villains. The "fruitless poetry" (4.1.72) of his tragedy will bear bloody fruit when performed. Maurice Hunt has claimed, "In essence, Hieronimo's play-within-the play provides the pattern for vengeance upon actual deeds."[43] But hasn't the Painter Addition already anticipated this dramatic pattern for revenge? Hieronimo's revenge painting serves as the model for a drama of "speaking pictures" that are not only visually compelling, but also capable of literal speech and, even more importantly, real action. He himself had instinctually supplied the speech and actions that made the painting live; the move to drama to take his revenge would seem inevitable.

Hieronimo's use of revenge drama "stretches" his art beyond typical royal entertainments, like the political masque he successfully presented earlier in the play. The illusory images of art serve reality, as real blood is shed during **"The Tragedy of Soliman and Perseda,"** and the spectacle of corpses fills the court's theater. Before his royal audience perceives what has happened, Hieronimo reveals the dead body of his son and begins to tell a tale of woe: "See here my show, look on this spectacle" (4.4.89). The show is an emblem of justified revenge: Horatio's mangled corpse is the image, Hieronimo's tale, the motto. Thus, the drama gives way to another painting of sorts, the emblem, which was the most popular kind of Renaissance "speaking picture."

Dramatic art, punctuated with an emblem, gives compelling aesthetic shape and potency to revenge. Hieronimo, however, loses control of his art, first when he witnesses Bel-Imperia's unscripted suicide and then when he inexplicably murders the Duke of Castile, one of the newly bereaved fathers, before killing himself. As Hunt points out, "the senseless killing of the duke of Castile suggests that the tragic protagonist who uses art as his model for experience can become so carried away by the spirit of his re-enactment that unjust outrages occur, bringing further damnation upon the artisan's head."[44] As Hieronimo's words to the Painter predicted, "there is no end: the end is death and madness! As I am never better than when I am mad, then methinks I am a brave fellow, then I do wonders" (3.12A.159-61).

In his madness, he has performed "wonders" indeed and been avenged, but the revenge, while it may have brought death to the villains, bears no resemblance to the justice that he once safeguarded as Knight Marshal of Spain. Kyd's frame for the play makes this end in lawless revenge inevitable, for Revenge, not Justice, has presided over the human drama like an indifferent theatrical impresario. After the deaths of most of the characters, Revenge proclaims, as if to say that the real show is about the start, "I'll there begin their endless tragedy" (4.5.48). Subject to a destiny watched over by Revenge, Hieronimo cannot quell his raging mind before the images he conjured for the Painter. In a cruel world with Revenge as the reigning deity, art can only momentarily serve the purposes of moral reflection and private consolation. The ingenious artist in Revenge's play has no choice but to follow the imperatives of revenge art and employ its motifs and design.

Like an actor whose passions overflow the measure, Hieronimo pursues his own "wild justice," first through vengeance painting and then through revenge drama, which proves to be a thrilling and appalling spectacle to both onstage and offstage audiences. His use of art for private revenge follows the basic principles of Elizabethan art, originally defined by Horace and articulated by Sidney—to teach and to delight. The instruction, however, is far from morally edifying; it is dark, destructive, and bloody, and the delight, sublimely terrible in its irony. The King of Spain and the Viceroy of Portugal are left to mourn their dead and the loss of heirs (Lorenzo and Balthazar) to their thrones. For Elizabethan spectators, Hieronimo's use of art (and Kyd's metatheatrical device) must have carried a powerful emotional charge and have been perceived as a brilliant technical and aesthetic move, when performed well. The device vividly demonstrates the wondrous lifelike quality of theater and the paradoxes of artistic representation. In the tragic playlet, *real* action makes for compelling illusion, but, for the audience watching Kyd's play, the performance of this real action is itself illusory. Its status as a "representation," however, would not have mitigated against the spectators' experience of visual pleasure and horror at seeing such sights.

Ben Jonson, if he was indeed the author of the Painter Addition, must have found himself caught between fascination and horror as he watched Kyd's brilliant and bloody celebration of the theater's power. In writing his own scene for the play, he chose a quieter tone, deliberately rejecting spectacle as a mode of visual presentation. The heartfelt, vivid images he has Hieronimo call up verbally inspire a nuanced and moving dramatic performance: the pictures speak through the actor, and the implied actions are given movement in time through his embodiment of the images. In this sense, the scene serves as a critical re-visioning of the play. Jonson offers an extraordinary allegorical scene of artistic imitation in which we, as spectators, enter into the creative process of image-making. Insofar as the illusory images of painting represent and provoke the real emotions of wonder, horror and sympathy, they are powerful, dramatically purposeful, and, as the iconoclasts would have it, potentially dangerous in the theater. The dual function of Hieronimo's painting as memento mori and *memento vindictae* reflects Hieronimo's moral dilemma and his conflicting obsessions—to sustain emotional pain, and perhaps find consolation through artistic imitation and vicarious revenge, or to use the compelling images of art to rouse himself to take action against injustice. As a dramatist, the Addition's author recognized the superiority of drama over painting, yet, in this scene, it is an imagined painting that inspires him to tap into the primal destructive and creative forces that drive image-making in all the arts. He brings painting and playing into such intimate contact that we see the brilliant, imaginative melding together of artistic forms. To rephrase Horace's well-known comparison, ut pictura poesis, drama is like painting, or *ut pictura theatrum*. To see the implications of such an analogy played out extensively in the theater and in the dramaturgy of a single artist, we need to turn to the greatest of Elizabethan and early Jacobean dramatists, Shakespeare, who not only created a painter character of his own, but also made extensive use of the visual arts to elicit powerful and sometimes conflicting responses to images from his characters and the plays' spectators.

Notes

References to *The Spanish Tragedy* are from J. R. Mulryne's Norton edition, 2nd ed. (London: A and C Black; New York: W. W. Norton, 1989).

1. "Revenge is a kind of wild justice," Francis Bacon wrote in his essay "On revenge," "which the more man's nature runs to, the more ought law to weed it out." See *Essays, Advancement of Learning, New Atlantis, and Other Pieces,* ed. Richard Foster Jones (New York: The Odyssey Press, Inc., 1937), 13.

2. In *Themes and Conventions of Elizabethan Tragedy* (1935; Cambridge: Cambridge University Press, 1980), Muriel Bradbrook briefly mentions the Painter Addition as a dramatic example of this motif (124-28). She also locates its use in Shakespeare's *The Merchant of Venice* and *Hamlet,* Webster's *The Duchess of Malfi,* and Beaumont's *The Maid's Tragedy.* Bradbrook's best illustratration of self-dramatization through the picture motif is Webster's *The Duchess of Malfi* where the Duchess laments, "Who do I look like now? / Like to your picture in the gallery, / A deal of life in show but none in practice." Hieronimo's verbal painting, however, is unlike the other examples Bradbrook cites as it reflects a long sequence of images analogous to a Tudor "program" that might have been commissioned by a patron.

3. [Philip Henslowe, *Henslowe's Diary,* ed. R. A. Foakes and R. T. Rickert (Cambridge: Cambridge University Press, 1961)] 203. Editors C. H. Herford, Percy Simpson, and Evelyn M. Simpson point out that we have no guarantee that Jonson actually produced these Additions. They assume that Henslowe made Jonson loans rather than payment for completed work. The second date (June 1602) is notably too late for publication in the 1602 edition of the play. See Jonson, *Works* (1925), [vol. 8 (Oxford: Clarendon Press, 1954)] 237-45. The payment, however, could have been made for completed additions.

4. Jonson, *Works,* 610, 611.

5. Levin L. Schücking, "The *Spanish Tragedy* Additions: Acting and Reading Versions," *Times Literary Supplement* (12 June 1937): 442.

6. *The Works of Thomas Kyd,* ed. Frederick S. Boas (Oxford: Clarendon Press, 1901), lxxxix n 1. Boas is quoting from a review of J. Schick's edition of *The Spanish Tragedy* in *The Athenaeum* (Oct. 5, 1899). He continues, "Of the 'mingle-mangle' there is no doubt, but as the Additions were intended chiefly to satisfy the popular craving to see more of Hieronimo in his lunacy, I have little doubt that both Scenes were acted" (lxxxix).

7. Philip Edwards, *Shakespeare and the Confines of Art* (London: Methuen and Company, 1968), 42. Philip Edwards, J. R. Mulryne, and David Bevington are examples of recent editors of *The Spanish Tragedy* who have placed the Additions at the back of their texts.

8. Charles K. Cannon, "The Relation of the Additions of *The Spanish Tragedy* to the Original Play," *Studies in English Literature* 2 (spring 1962): 231.

9. Charles Lamb, *Specimens of English Dramatic Poets* (London: G. Bell and Sons, Ltd., 1911), 11.

10. Francis Berry, *The Shakespeare Inset: Word and Picture* (New York: Theatre Arts Books, 1965), 132.

11. Peter B. Murray, *Thomas Kyd* (New York: Twayne Publishers, Inc., 1969), 158.

12. Ibid.

13. Michael Hattaway, *Elizabethan Popular Theatre: Plays in Performance* (London: Routledge and Kegan Paul, 1982), 104.

14. Ibid., 105.

15. Donna B. Hamilton, "*The Spanish Tragedy*: A Speaking Picture," *English Literary Review* 4 (spring 1974): 215.

16. Ibid., 204-5.

17. Peter M. Sacks, *The English Elegy: Studies in the Genre from Spenser to Yeats* (Baltimore: Johns Hopkins University Press, 1985), 72-73. For another interpretation of the scene as a representation of the failure of painting, see Anat Feinberg-Jütte, "Painters and Counterfeiters," who views this scene as a harsh condemnation of the painter's art. This interpretation seems harsh itself, as the painter is undoubtedly aware of the extreme nature of Hieronimo's passion; Hieronimo's impossible "program" of painted images reflects his state of heightened emotion. In performance, it is quite possible that the actor playing the painter can compensate for the implicit negative view of painting that Feinberg-Jütte detects. For example, when Peter Reeves played the Painter in The Royal Shakespeare Company's production at The Swan Theatre in Stratford that opened April 30, 1997, he patiently, even stoically, listened to Hieronimo. This performance seemed to lend a quiet power to the character of the Painter. See Peter Happé's review in *Research Opportunities in Renaissance Drama* 37 (1998): 70.

18. G. Wilson Knight, "Visual Art in Kyd and Shakespeare," in *Shakespearian Dimensions* (Sussex: Harvester Press; New Jersey: Barnes and Noble Books, 1984), 95.

19. See John Hollander's *The Gazer's Spirit: Poems Speaking to Silent Works of Art* (Chicago: University of Chicago Press, 1995) for a discussion of different kinds of ekphrases, 3-91. The central distinction Hollander makes is between notional and actual ekphrases, the former based on imagined or lost works of art, the latter on real and existing works that may even have been present before the poet as he or she wrote. In a fundamental way, however, all ekphrasis seems to be notional, in that the linguistic construction of visual experience will always be different in kind and phenomenal experience from its visual source. W. J. T. Mitchell makes this point when he argues that ekphrasis "create[s] a specific image that is to be found only in the text as its 'resident alien,' and is to be found nowhere else" (*Picture Theory*, 157, n 19).

20. Ascham, *Scholemaster*, 119.

21. John Davies of Hereford, *Microcosmos* (London, 1603), sig. Ff4^r.

22. Ibid.

23. Overbury, *Overburian Characters*, 76.

24. E. K. Chambers, *Elizabethan Stage* 2:308. Chambers argues that Burbage "was apparently the model for the *Character of an Actor* in the *Characters* of 1615" (2:308).

25. Ibid., 2:309.

26. Thomas May, *The Heire, An Excellent Comedie* (London, 1622), 1.1.

27. Jonas Barish, "*The Spanish Tragedy,* or The Pleasures and Perils of Rhetoric," in *Elizabethan Theatre,* ed. John Russell Brown and Bernard Harris, Stratford-upon-Avon Studies 9 (London: Edward Arnold Ltd., 1966; New York: St. Martin's, 1967), 82.

28. I have followed the 1602 edition for these lines; Mulryne and Bevington edit the line to read, "I'd have you paint me in my gallery." I believe that Hieronimo imagines the portrait being painted for his gallery, rather than the gallery serving as the background motif for the painting. The *OED* indicates that by 1600 "gallery" signified an apartment or building devoted to exhibiting art. Boas took this meaning of the term, as he added "for" in the line: "I'de haue you paint me 'for' my Gallirie. . . ." In altering the line, he follows Schick's edition of *The Spanish Tragedy*.

29. Sidney, *Defence of Poesie*, 90.

30. Harry Keyishian, Review of *The Spanish Tragedy,* by Thomas Kyd, *Shakespeare Bulletin* 4 (May-June 1986): 10.

31. Sir Roy Strong, "Sir Henry Unton and his Portrait: An Elizabethan Memorial Picture and its History," *Archaeologia* 49 (1965): 53.

32. In *The Art of Death: Visual Culture in the English Death Ritual, c. 1500-c. 1800* (London: Reaktion Books, 1991), Nigel Llewellyn emphasizes the public nature of the picture in its depiction of Unton's various public personae, 13-16. He discusses the painting as an example of the extended death ritual in Elizabethan England. See also Strong, "Sir Henry Unton."

33. On the dating of *The Trial of Chivalry,* I have followed E. K. Chambers.

34. References to *The Trial of Chivalry* are from the text edited by John S. Farmer (Amersham, England: Tudor Facsimile Texts, 1912).

35. Roland Mushat Frye makes similar use of revenge paintings in *The Renaissance Hamlet: Issues and Responses in 1600* (Princeton: Princeton University Press, 1984) to establish a context for understanding how an Elizabethan audience would have perceived Prince Hamlet's imperative to avenge his father's death, 29-37. In *The Memorial of Lord Darnley,* King James VI, son of the murdered King of Scots, is represented as the likely candidate for the act of revenge. In the painting's text, his grandparents explicitly call for revenge.

36. This is Duncan Thomson's reasonable speculation. For a reproduction and history of the Earl of Moray's portrait, see *Painting in Scotland, 1570-1650* (Edinburgh: The Trustees of the National Gallery of Scotland, 1975), 34.

37. Qtd. in Duncan Thomson, *Painting in Scotland,* 19. Two contemporary versions of this painting exist: the royal copy descended through the Stewart family of England is at Holyroodhouse, and the other is at Goodwood. The Goodwood version contains the original sixteenth-century inscriptions, while those on the royal painting have been altered, probably by James I and VI in an effort to present his mother, Mary, Queen of Scots, in a more favorable light.

38. Ibid., 18.

39. Margaret Aston, *The King's Bedpost: Reformation and Iconography in a Tudor Group Portrait* (Cambridge: Cambridge University Press, 1993), 24, 25.

40. Frye, *The Renaissance Hamlet,* 37.

41. Eric Mercer, *English Art, 1553-1625* (Oxford: Clarendon Press, 1962), 163-64. Mercer speculates about the "riddling Latin motto": "If questions were asked, and they were, it could be explained away as meaning nothing more than 'There is enough above', his heavenly reward is enough; the other meaning, however, was probably the intended one, 'There are enough left over', his descendants are still alive, with its many and far-reaching implications" (163).

42. Hamilton, "*The Spanish Tragedy*: A Speaking Picture," 214.

43. Maurice Hunt, "Compelling Art in *Titus Andronicus,*" *Studies in English Literature* 28 (spring 1988): 212.

44. Ibid.

FURTHER READING

Criticism

Aggeler, Geoffrey. "The Eschatological Crux in *The Spanish Tragedy*." *Journal of English and Germanic Philology* 86, no. 3 (July 1987): 319-31.

Explores perceived conflicts between the eschatology of Kyd's play and the beliefs of its characters.

Ardolino, Frank. *Apocalypse and Armada in Kyd's* Spanish Tragedy. Kirksville, Mo.: Sixteenth Century Essays and Studies, 1995, 181 p.

Interprets the play in light of biblical traditions and European history.

Byron, Mark. "Logic's Doubt: *The Spanish Tragedy* and *Tamburlaine*." *Comitatus* 30 (1999): 81-94.

Reads *The Spanish Tragedy* and Christopher Marlowe's *Tamburlaine* as complementary reflections on tyranny, each addressing the slippery nature of political language.

Daalder, Joost. "The Role of 'Senex' in Kyd's *The Spanish Tragedy*." *Comparative Drama* 20, no. 3 (fall 1986): 247-60.

Suggests connections between the Senex, or old man, character and the Senecan thought in the play.

Dunn, Kevin. "'Action, Passion, Motion': The Gestural Politics of Counsel in *The Spanish Tragedy*." *Renaissance Drama* 31 (2002): 27-60.

Examines the resonance of gesture, especially as it defines the link between self-definition and legitimate political agency.

Edwards, Philip. "Thrusting Elysium into Hell: The Originality of *The Spanish Tragedy*." In *The Elizabethan Theatre XI,* edited by A. L. Magnusson and C. E. McGee, pp. 117-32. Port Credit, Ontario, Canada: P. D. Meany, 1990.

Considers the theology of the play and the seriousness of its apparent repudiation of Christian justice.

Hopkins, Lisa. "What's Hercules to Hamlet? The Emblematic Garden in *The Spanish Tragedy* and *Hamlet*." *Hamlet Studies* 21, nos. 1-2 (summer-winter 1999): 114-43.

Looks at the use of garden imagery in the plays, particularly as a visual representation of movement toward action or destiny.

Maus, Katherine Eisaman. "*The Spanish Tragedy,* or, The Machiavel's Revenge." In *Revenge Tragedy,* edited by Stevie Simkin, pp. 88-106. Houndmills, Basingstoke, England: Palgrave, 2001.

Analyzes the relationship between inwardness and rebellion in *The Spanish Tragedy,* and suggests that the play ultimately questions the ability of theatrical means to realize the self.

Seimon, James R. "Dialogical Formalism: Word, Object, and Action in *The Spanish Tragedy*." *Medieval and Renaissance Drama in England* 5 (1991): 87-115.

Emphasizes the fluid signifying power of the components of theatrical performance in the play, and proposes a Bakhtinian approach to interpretation.

Additional coverage of Kyd's life and career is contained in the following sources published by Thomson Gale: *British Writers*, **Vol. 1;** *Dictionary of Literary Biography*, **Vol. 62;** *DISCovering Authors Modules: Dramatists*; *Drama Criticism*, **Vol. 3;** *Drama for Students*, **Vol. 21;** *International Dictionary of Theatre: Playwrights*; *Literary Movements for Students*, **Vol. 1;** *Literature Criticism from 1400 to 1800*, **Vol. 22;** *Reference Guide to English Literature*, **Ed. 2;** *Twayne's English Authors*; **and** *World Literature and Its Times*, **Vol. 3.**

The Imaginary Invalid

Molière

The following entry presents criticism on Molière's play *Le Malade imaginaire* (1673; *The Imaginary Invalid*). For discussion of Molière's complete career, see *LC,* Volumes 10, 28, and 64.

INTRODUCTION

When *The Imaginary Invalid* was first performed in 1673, Molière himself performed the role of Argan, the titular "imaginary invalid." A *comédie-ballet* written as a court entertainment for Louis XIV, Molière's last play intersperses comic drama with music and dance loosely related to the plot. The play draws heavily on characters and themes from Molière's earlier plays, especially the character of the unreasonable father figure and the theme of medical satire. In the figure of Argan Molière evokes audience sympathy for the obsessed hypochondriac by revealing a universal fear of death as the root of his mania.

PLOT AND MAJOR CHARACTERS

The plot of *The Imaginary Invalid* centers on the common comic theme of young love frustrated by an unreasonable parent. Angélique is in love with Cléante, whom she hopes to marry. We learn in the first act that her father, the hypochondriac Argan, has arranged for her to marry Thomas Diafoirus, a medical student. Argan threatens to put Angélique in a convent if she does not comply with his wishes. Angélique asks for the help of the family's maid, Toinette, who passes information to Cléante. Meanwhile, in the subplot, Angélique's stepmother, Béline, schemes to inherit all of Argan's estate by encouraging him to change his will.

In the second act Cléante comes to Argan's home disguised as a friend of the music master, soon followed by Thomas and his father. Cléante reveals his wit as he and Angélique sing for Argan a pastoral love song, obliquely describing their frustrated love for each other. In contrast, the absurd medical rhetoric of Thomas and his father make plain their foolishness. Argan continues to insist that Angélique marry Thomas, and Béline brings the conflict to a crisis by informing Argan that she saw

Cléante in Angélique's room. Béline's daughter, Louison, reports that Cléante was kissing Angélique's hands. Argan's brother, Béralde, arrives at the close of the second act, and he is the engine for the play's denouement.

Béralde and Toinette plan, through a series of comic tricks, to frustrate Argan's marriage plans for Angélique, while at the same time convincing Argan to give up his obsession with illness. First, Toinette visits Argan disguised as a doctor, reassuring him that his previous doctors were ignorant. Then Béralde and Toinette convince Argan to feign his own death in order to learn the true feelings that Béline and Angélique hold for him. When Béline believes that Argan is dead, she rejoices; but Angélique is despondent and plans to reject marriage completely. Argan is moved by Angélique's sorrow and allows her to marry Cléante, with the caveat that Cléante become a doctor. Instead, at Béralde's urging, Argan becomes a doctor, and the play concludes with a mock graduation ceremony that demonstrates the absurdity of the profession of medicine.

The primary character in *The Imaginary Invalid* is Argan, who is defined in terms of a single, absurd characteristic—as are Harpagon in *L'Avare* (1668; *The Miser*) and Alceste in *Le Misanthrope* (1666; *The Misanthrope*). Like Harpagon in *The Miser* and also like Orgon in *Tartuffe,* Argan is a volatile, gullible father figure whose efforts to assert his dominance in his family hint at his true lack of control. Having written the role of Argan for himself, Molière depicted the character as sympathetic despite his follies, revealing Argan's genuine affection for his wife and his daughter, and treating his susceptibility to medical malpractice as a forgivable weakness.

Among the secondary characters, the lovers Angélique and Cléante are clever but only mildly rebellious, taking little direct action to move their own love story forward—an action primarily left to the familiar comic character of the clever servant who serves her master best through well-meaning trickery. Toinette's chief motivation is to protect Angélique by preventing Béline from stealing Angélique's inheritance and by stopping Argan from forcing her to marry a ridiculous husband. Part of the play's satire rests on Toinette's ability to outsmart her social superiors, but she nonetheless appears to care genuinely for Angélique and, perhaps to a lesser extent, for Argan himself. Argan also has an advocate in his brother, Béralde, who provides the strongest direct critique of the medical profession in the play. Béralde enters late in the play as the voice of reason, though his efforts to change Argan's behavior could not have been successful without the machinations of Toinette. Though Thomas Diafoirus is nominally the rival of Cléante, he is not a strong enough character to appear as a genuine obstacle to Angélique's desires. Moreover, though Thomas is a medical student, no doctor is a major character in the play; rather, the collection of contradictory medical practitioners functions as a whole as the target of satire. If the play has a villain, it is Béline, whose lavish affection and attention to Argan indicate the depth of her hypocrisy, a cardinal sin in Molière's moral universe.

MAJOR THEMES

The dominant themes of *The Imaginary Invalid* are medicine and the theater itself. Satire at the expense of the medical profession was a significant part of Molière's oeuvre, perhaps driven in part by his own ill health. (The playwright himself was labeled a hypochondriac.) The humor of this theme comes from several sources: Argan's credulity; endless opportunities for scatological jokes; the toppling of authority figures; and the simple absurdity of the doctors themselves. It is easy for modern readers to overestimate, however, just how absurd the doctors are. The "cures" prescribed by Diafoirus and the other doctors of the play would probably have been familiar to many audience members at the time, though they may seem highly unscientific in the twenty-first century. The doctors of *The Imaginary Invalid* are foolish because they blindly follow past precedent, in spite of empirical evidence to the contrary. Thomas Diafoirus is thus a promising doctor, according to his father, because he refuses to accept the circulation of the blood as proven fact.

The Imaginary Invalid is often considered among the most self-reflexive of Molière's works, dramatizing the workings of the theater and the function of comedy. Several of the characters employ play-acting in service of their interests, including Angélique and Cléante as they sing a song together, Toinette as she impersonates a doctor, and Argan as he feigns death. Particularly in the cases of Angélique, Cléante, and Toinette, the ability to stage an illusion indicates each character's cleverness and power in a given situation. For Argan, his willingness to participate in theater becomes his vehicle for reclaiming some power in the family and, arguably, power over his fear of death. If some of the humor of the finale's mock graduation is at Argan's expense, he is nonetheless a willing and joyful participant, visibly altered from his former self.

CRITICAL RECEPTION

The Imaginary Invalid long confused critics, who were inclined to admire Molière's brilliance as a playwright but nonetheless did not understand his purpose or method in this multimedia performance. Not simply a comedy but an "entertainment" for the court of Louis XIV, *The Imaginary Invalid* has often appeared to modern readers to be a hodgepodge of mismatched genres, or a traditional three-act play interrupted by unrelated musical interludes. As a result, the play aroused minimal academic interest for some time, until scholars began to examine the comic styles employed by Molière.

Scholars who have addressed the generic difficulty presented by the play often point out that Molière was not merely a man of words and ideas, but also an actor aware of the multiple senses through which theater reaches its audience. The initial audience for *The Imaginary Invalid* was Louis XIV and his court, who enjoyed music and dance. Molière had created the *comédie-ballet* form in 1661 expressly for Louis's benefit, with *Les Fâcheux* (*The Bores*). H. T. Barnwell has argued that this context for the play should remind us that it is not merely the dramatized story of an angry hypochondriac but part of a larger celebration. Nicholas Cronk's interpretation of the play suggests that this apparent conflict between the joyful *intermèdes* and the gloomy world of Argan not only highlights Argan's isolation from his family and the rational world, but also allows the spectator to experience Molière's process of constructing a work of musical drama, as once-disjointed pieces gradually come together in a grand carnivalesque finale.

Critics have also been interested in what Molière's last play has to say about his worldview. A keen social observer throughout his works, Molière was a moralist and a thinker as well as an entertainer. In that light, D. J. Adams has described *The Imaginary Invalid* as the bleakest of Molière's works, one that demonstrates human ignorance at its utmost. However, other critics have seen in the play a call to live life to its fullest. Scholars have observed that for Molière the family can be a symbol of social order, an order that is often threatened and that must be restored by play's end. Carol Mossman has noted that while many of Molière's plays achieve this order by diminishing the exaggerated role of the father, in *The Imaginary Invalid* balance comes about when the father reclaims his paternal role. As Michael S. Koppisch has also suggested, order for Molière is thus not expressed in hierarchical authority, but in the workings of nature. Béralde, the play's primary voice of reason, also validates this idea of order, which emphasizes that order is not fixed or static but rather depends on allowing nature to follow its course.

PRINCIPAL WORKS

La Jalousie de Barbouillé [*The Jealousy of Barbouillé*] (play) c. 1645

Le Médecin volant [*The Flying Doctor*] (play) c. 1648

L'Éstourdy; ou, Le Contretemps [*The Blunderer*] (play) 1653; also published as *L'Étourdi*, 1888

Le Dépit amoureux [*The Amorous Quarrel*] (play) 1656

Les Précieuses ridicules [*The Affected Young Ladies*] (play) 1659

Sganarelle; ou, Le Cocu imaginaire [*The Imaginary Cuckold*] (play) 1660

Dom Garcie de Navarre; ou, Le Prince jaloux [*Don Garcia of Navarre; or, The Jealous Prince*] (play) 1661

L'École des maris [*The School for Husbands*] (play) 1661

Les Fâcheux [*The Bores*; also translated as *The Impertinents*] (play) 1661

L'École des femmes [*A School for Women*; also translated as *The School for Wives*] (play) 1662

La Critique de "L'École des femmes" [*"The School for Wives" Criticized*] (play) 1663

L'Impromptu de Versailles [*The Versailles Impromptu*] (play) 1663

Le Mariage forcé [*The Forced Marriage*] (play) 1664

La Princesse d'Élide [*The Princess of Elis*] (play) 1664

Le Tartuffe; ou, L'Imposteur [*Tartuffe; or, The Hypocrite*; also translated as *Tartuffe; or, The Imposter*] (play) 1664; revised versions in five acts, 1667, 1669

L'Amour médecin [*The Quacks*; also translated as *Love Is the Best Remedy*] (play) 1665

Dom Juan; ou, Le Festin de Pierre [*Don John; or, The Libertine*; also translated as *Don Juan; or, The Feast with the Statue*] (play) 1665

Le Médecin malgré lui [*The Forced Physician*; also translated as *The Doctor in Spite of Himself*] (play) 1666

Le Misanthrope [*The Man-Hater*; also translated as *The Misanthrope*] (play) 1666

Le Sicilien; ou, L'amour peintre (play) 1667

Amphitryon [*Amphitryon; or, The Two Sosias*] (play) 1668

L'Avare [*The Miser*] (play) 1668

George Dandin; ou, Le Mari confondu [*George Dandin; or, The Wanton Wife*] (play) 1668

Monsieur de Pourceaugnac [*Monsieur de Pourceaugnac; or, Squire Trelooby*; also translated as *The Cornish Squire*] (play) 1669

Les Amants magnifiques [*The Courtly Lovers*] (play) 1670

Le Bourgeois Gentilhomme [*The Bourgeois Gentleman*] (play) 1670

Les Fourberies de Scapin [*The Cheats of Scapin*; also translated as *The Rogueries of Scapin*] (play) 1671

Psiché [*Psyché*] [with Pierre Corneille and Philippe Quinault] (play) 1671

Les Femmes savantes [*The Learned Ladies*] (play) 1672

Le Malade imaginaire [*The Imaginary Invalid*; also translated as *The Hypochondriac*] (play) 1673

The Works of Monsieur de Molière. 6 vols. (plays) 1714

The Dramatic Works of Molière. 6 vols. (plays) 1875-76

Molière: The Plays in French with an English Translation and Notes by A. R. Waller. 8 vols. (plays) 1902-07

CRITICISM

Nicholas Grene (essay date 1980)

SOURCE: Grene, Nicholas. "Quacks and Conmen." In *Shakespeare, Jonson, Molière: The Comic Contract*, pp. 69-92. Totowa, N.J.: Barnes & Noble Books, 1980.

[*In the following essay, Grene considers the treatment of doctors in several plays, including Molière's* Imaginary Invalid *and Jonson's* Alchemist, *emphasizing contemporary beliefs about medicine and the human body.*]

'*The Tempest* is concerned with illusion . . . Jonsonian comedy is concerned with the theory and practice of delusion', as Harry Levin points out in his essay on *The Tempest* and *The Alchemist*.[1] The distinction is a useful one. Though Prospero finally steps back from the images of his conjuring and acknowledges them to be illusion, yet throughout the play the audience is prepared to believe in his magic as magic. We share with him the knowledge of how and why the visitors to the island are hallucinated, but we accept that his powers to enchant are real. To Prospero's art itself we lend willing suspension of disbelief, and we may remind ourselves that disbelief would have been less hard to suspend in 1611, when benevolent white magic was considered to be distinctly possible. Subtle, the alchemist, a year before Prospero, also claimed power over winds and waves:

> No, you scarab,
> I'll thunder you in pieces. I will teach you
> How to beware to tempt a Fury again
> That carries tempest in his hand and voice.
>
> I, i, 59-62

But even though Subtle has the excellent alchemical authority of Paracelsus for such a claim,[2] no audience would ever have dreamed of taking it literally. It is no more than a grotesque comic metaphor in his slanging-match with Face, appropriate to his thundering aggression but a ludicrous boast coming from the conman we see before us. For Jonson deliberately starts his play with his tricksters *en deshabillé,* exposed for what they are, so that we are never likely to grant the least shred of credit to their subsequent pretensions. The scurillous word pictures which each of the two paints of the other provide a deft exposition in which the reality of their characters as frauds is definitely established. From then on the business of the play will be, indeed, deception not illusion. Instead of focusing, as *The Tempest* does, on the strange bewildering effects of magic on the enchanted, we will watch a series of dupes being hoodwinked, cheated, deceived, and we will remain conscious throughout of the fraudulent intentions of the deceivers.

The basic confidence-trick of the play centres around Subtle's profession as alchemist; he blinds with 'science' the gulls who are already blinded with greed. But it is not only pseudo-sciences like alchemy which are regarded in this light in comedy. Very often the more respectable learned professions are seen as an equally dishonest means of exploiting human weaknesses. M. Filerin, the leading spokesman of Molière's doctors in *L'Amour Médecin* puts his own calling on a par with those of alchemists and astrologers:

> Nous ne sommes pas les seuls, comme vous savez, qui tâchons à nous prévaloir de la foiblesse humaine. C'est là qui va l'étude de la plupart du monde, et chacun

s'efforce de prendre les hommes par leur foible, pour en tirer quelque profit . . . Les alchimistes tâchent à profiter de la passion qu'on a pour les richesses, en promettant des montagnes d'or a ceux qui les écoutent; et les diseurs d'horoscope, par leurs prédictions trompeuses, profitent de la vanité et de l'ambition des crédules esprits. Mais le plus grand foible des hommes, c'est l'amour qu'ils ont pour la vie; et nous en profitons, nous autres, par notre pompeux galimatias et savons prendre nos avantages de cette vénération que la peur de mourir leur donne pour notre métier.

> III, i

Molière's medical satires, like *The Alchemist,* are directed towards audiences who are not 'crédules esprits', 'credulous minds'. We are expected to watch the comedies in a spirit of knowing specticism, laughing alike at the credulity of those who believe in the hocus-pocus of medicine or alchemy and at the pretensions of the practitioners. The universal comic impulse to mock the language of learning is sharpened by the knowledge that it is being manipulated for profit. The comedy of the quack and the charlatan is built upon the comedy of the pedant.

Reading or seeing such plays as *The Alchemist* or **Le Malade Imaginaire** in the twentieth century, we may well assume that the attitude Jonson and Molière invite us to adopt is no more than that of commonsense. The alchemical jargon of Subtle is to us pure abracadabra nonsense and the ministrations of Messieurs Purgon and Diafoirus we may regard from the security of modern medicine as equally absurd. It is perhaps necessary to remind ourselves that the seventeenth century audience would not have had the same presuppositions. Alchemy was not by any means universally discredited in Jonson's time: Bacon, for example, though sceptical of the general theory, thought the actual process of making gold possible.[3] Still later, and even more spectacularly, Newton was so absorbed in alchemical experiments that he apparently spent a greater proportion of his time on them than on physics.[4] As for Molière and medicine, however grotesque the double-barrel torture of bleeding and purging may seem to us, it continued to flourish throughout the reign of Louis XIV, whose medical treatment is detailed meticulously in the *Journal de la Santé du Roi*. One of the most apparently fantastic scenes in Molière, the induction of the newly qualified doctor at the end of **Le Malade Imaginaire,** in fact quite closely approximated to the real ceremonial at Montpellier.[5]

We have limited evidence of Molière's personal views on medicine or Jonson's on alchemy outside the context of the plays, though the question with regard to Molière has often been discussed. We are not in a position to take a public opinion poll of an average seventeenth century audience (whatever that may have been) in order to establish what their normal ideas on such professions were. No doubt there were many people who were at times sceptical of the doctors' healing powers: Mme. de Sévigné, although she was not generally a disbeliever in medicine, could applaud heartily the view expressed in *Le Malade Imaginaire.* 'Ah! que j'en veux aux médecins! quelle forfanterie que leur art!'[6]—'Oh! how I hate doctors! what quackery their art is!' Swindling alchemists were notorious in England from the time of Chaucer's Canon down to that Simon Forman. What the comedians appeal to, however, is not the particular opinions of the 'man in the street' of their time, but a strain of comic scepticism which is universal and traditional. After all, medical satires are quite as common in the twentieth century, when we have some grounds for supposing that doctors can cure diseases, as they were in any earlier age when medical success rates must have been far lower. What we have in *The Alchemist* or in Molière's doctor plays is one more type of comic contract in which, instead of disbelief, it is belief which is willingly suspended. To analyse the nature of this response and to illustrate the way in which it is built up we must look to the plays themselves rather than attempting to identify their viewpoint primarily in terms of the background of contemporary ideas.

MOLIÈRE AND MEDICINE

Molière's attacks on doctors, ranging from one end of his writing career to the other through five pieces in which medicine is a central subject beside numerous side-swipes in other plays, may well look like a personal vendetta. Various critics have supplied conjectural biographical motives for this animus against the medical profession. John Palmer, noticing that the first all-out denunciation of doctors comes in 1665 in *Dom Juan,* followed closely by *L'Amour Médecin,* reminds us that it was at this period that Molière's serious illness first began.[7] John Cairncross argues that the hostility to doctors may have originated a year earlier with the deaths of Molière's close friend La Mothe Le Vayer and his own first son.[8] A row with D'Aquin, the Court doctor who was Moliere's landlord in 1665, has been suggested as another personal grievance against the profession at this period.[9] On the other hand, the little we know of Molière's relations with his own doctor, M. de Mauvillain, suggests that they were cordial. In the third 'placet' to the king on behalf of *Tartuffe* we find Molière soliciting a royal favour for him, although he couches the petition in the form of a typically Molièrean anti-doctor joke. What is more important, from our point of view, than Molière's possible motivation for writing medical satires is that the plays accord an opportunity for studying the way in which the subject was adapted for different audiences. The jokes remain much the same from *Le Médecin Volant* down to *Le Malade Imaginaire,* but the character of the comic contract varies depending to some extent on whom Molière was writing for, the provincial audience of his early farces, the Parisians who regularly attended his theatre at the Palais-Royal, or the King and Court at Versailles or elsewhere.

Le Médecin Volant is no more than a brief sketch written for performance in the provinces, and not everyone is agreed that it is Molière's.[10] But whether the actual text is authentic or not, there can be little doubt that Molière did write such farces and that it was from farces like this, close to the Italian tradition, that his doctor satires evolved. Considering how often Molière cannibalised his own earlier work, the fact that the plot of *Le Médecin Volant* reappears in later plays might well be used to strengthen the attribution. What is most striking about the play, in the context of the pieces that were to succeed it, is that it is scarcely an attack on doctors or medicine at all. Sganarelle, who pretends to be a doctor to further his master's love-intrigue, is too gross an imposter to be taken as a parody of the real thing. The humour of the piece derives from the confidence with which he covers up his ignorance:

SGANARELLE:

. . . Il faut que je vous fasse une ordonnance.

GORGIBUS:

Vite une table, du papier, de l'encre.

SGANARELLE:

Y a-t-il quelqu'un qui sache écrire?

GORGIBUS:

Est-ce que vous ne le savez point?

SGANARELLE:

Ah! je ne m'en souvenois point; j'ai tant d'affaires dans la tête, que j'oublie la moitié.

Le Médecin Volant, v

The audience laughs at the simple absurdity of the familiar Sganarelle, the ignorant/cunning valet, in a doctor's gown. In fact, *Le Médecin Volant* contains what may be the only serious appreciation of medical skill in Molière's work. An 'avocat', quite unnecessary to the plot, is brought in to give a eulogy of doctors, addressed to the uncomprehending Sganarelle:

Il faut avouer que tous ceux qui excellent en quelque science sont dignes de grande louange, et particulièrement ceux qui font profession de la médecine, tant à cause du son utilité, que parce qu'elle contient en elle plusieurs autres sciences, ce qui rend sa parfaite connoissance fort difficile . . . Vous n'êtes pas de ces médecins qui ne vous appliquez qu'à là médecine qu'on appelle rationale ou dogmatique, et je crois que vous l'exercez tous les jours avec beaucoup de succès: *experientia magistra rerum.*

Le Médecin Volant, viii

It is of course impossible to say that this represents Molière's own point of view, particularly as there are doubts over the authorship of the farce. But it is consistent with his later attacks on doctors in which it is their tendency to divorce theory from practice, their neglect of empirical observations which is ridiculed. There was certainly little to upset any self-respecting doctor in *Le Médecin Volant.*

Nor yet is there much in *Le Médecin Malgré Lui,* a later more elaborate farce, hastily written, it is often supposed, as a booster to support the dubious success of *Le Misanthrope* in 1666. Again Sganarelle, this time a woodcutter, is a pretend doctor though the pretence is forced upon him. He is given some colour for the success of his disguise in the opening scene in which he is shown as 'un faiseur des fagots qui sache . . . raisonner des choses, qui ait servi six ans un fameux médecin, et qui ait su, dans son jeune âge, son rudiment par coeur', 'a woodcutter who knows how to argue about things, who worked for a famous doctor for six years, and who learned his grammar by heart at an early age'. (*Le Médecin Malgré Lui,* I, i). He has one or two anti-doctor jokes of the traditional variety—no-one ever blames the doctor, he claims, as one of the principal advantages of the profession is that the deceased is always at fault—'c'est toujours la faute de celui qui meurt'. But once again it is the imposture which is funny rather the doctor's role itself, as in his famous line defending his misplacing of the heart and liver:

> Oui, cela étoit autrefois ainsi; mais nous avons changé tout cela, et nous faisons maintenant la médecine d'une méthode toute nouvelle.

> II, iv

This does perhaps catch the absurd complacency of the doctor's belief in progress, but we laugh at it mainly for its delightful implausibility. We take pleasure in the audacity and outrageousness with which Sganarelle carries off his part, and if some of this pleasure derives from the debunking of the learned rigmarole which he mimics, *Le Médecin Malgré Lui* yet remains farcical comedy, not satire.

Turning from the popular farces to the court *comédie-ballets,* we might well expect to find a greater degree of refinement or sophistication, but, if so, we would be disappointed. Molière, like Jonson, catered for the personal tastes of the monarch and both Louis XIV and James I enjoyed simple, not to say crude, forms of humour. The *comédie-ballet* and the Jonsonian masque with anti-masque were both developed to meet royal preferences for a roughly similar combination of dancing, display and dirty jokes. This accounts for why pieces such as *The Gypsies Metamorphosed* or *M. de Pourceaugnac,* neither of which are their authors' most artistic creations, nevertheless met with great success.

Molière in putting together *L'Amour Médecin,* for instance, ('putting together' seems the right phrase, as he assures us in the preface that he composed, rehearsed and produced it in five days) did little more than take one of his stock farce situations and contrive more or less plausible occasions for *entrées de ballet* in between the acts. The plot is virtually the same as that of *Le Médecin Volant* and *Le Médecin Malgré Lui.*

There is, however, an important difference in that *L'Amour Médecin* does attack real doctors rather than making comedy out of pretend doctors, and in fact it caricatures the most eminent practitioners of the time. There is no question here of satire of the species rather than the individual—to the court the identifications would have been unmistakable either by the resemblance of names or physical mannerisms: Tomès is D'Aquin, one of the King's own doctors, Filerin is Yvelin, Des Fonandrès, (the name is taken from Greek roots meaning 'man-killer') is Des Fougerais, Bahis is marked as Esprit by his stammer, Macroton as Guenault by his slow speech. All of these were either attached to the royal household or well-known in Paris. The farcical scenes in which the doctors dispute might have been founded on the real arguments which took place around the death-bed of Cardinal Mazarin as to what he was dying of, or on the controversial crisis over the King's fever in 1658 when D'Aquin, Esprit, Guenault and Yvelin were all involved. The play, in which the doctors are ridiculed as total incompetents, if not frankly conscious hypocrites, does seem remarkable evidence of Molière's hostility towards the medical profession. It may be, however, that the apparent directness of the attack is due to the circumstances of the production. Whether or not Louis actually suggested the subject, Molière would certainly not have ventured on a public mockery of the royal physicians without knowing that the king would approve. It may be, in fact, that he returned to the subject of medicine so often after 1665, not because of any personal animus, but simply because he discovered that it was a favourite comic butt of the king's. 'Les médecins font assez souvent pleurer pour faire rire quelquefois', was Louis' attitude, 'Doctors make us weep often enough for us to laugh at them sometimes.'

If we look at it in the light of a court entertainment, what does the medical satire of *L'Amour Médecin* amount to? Many of the ideas are derived from Montaigne, as so often with Molière, and parts of the speech of M. Filerin, already quoted, are borrowed almost word for word from the long essay which Montaigne devotes to the demolition of the doctor's art.[11] But there can be little of Montaigne's serious purpose in as slight a piece as *L'Amour Médecin* and the whole play gives an impression of spoof rather than satire in earnest. Within the court context, in fact, the personal caricatures of the royal doctors should not necessarily be taken as the measure of Molière's 'impiety in medicine'; they may instead have had something of the character of an enjoyable if slightly malicious in-joke. Personalities in comedy are only funny within a restricted circle—one thinks of undergraduate revues—and it is unlikely that Molière would ever have written *L'Amour Médecin* in the first instance for a public performance. It was no doubt a pleasure for the courtiers who normally had to submit to the authority of Messieurs D'Aquin, Yvelin etc., to see them guyed by the King's actors. It is in this spirit that Mme. de Sévigné much later relished the jealous rage of D'Aquin at the success of an English rival and wished Molière were alive to write a comedy about it.[12] Yet the authority of the doctors need not have been seriously undermined. *L'Amour Médecin* belongs to that very simplest form of comedy which is pure escapism. The audience can laugh with impunity at the antics of the doctors because no real illness is in question. The play ends with the neatly turned claims of La Comédie, Le Ballet, and La Musique to be the only true doctors:

> Sans nous tous les hommes
> Deviendroient mal sains,
> Et c'est nous qui sommes
> Leurs grands médecins.

It is the appropriate finale for this divertissement, light-heartedly setting aside the reality of doctors or disease in its celebration of its own gaiety.

Monsieur de Pourceaugnac seems very much the mixture as before, a cruder, more heavy-handed *comédie-ballet* than *L'Amour Médecin,* in which Molière added to the jargon of the doctors a whole range of different provincial dialects and patois to make up a complete patchwork of barbaric sounding language. *Le Malade Imaginaire,* although it too was planned as a court *comédie-ballet,* is obviously a major work of a quite different kind from the earlier medical satires. It took a long time to produce: projected as an offering for the King's return from the wars in the winter of 1672, it was denied presentation at court, probably by the influence of Molière's rival Lulli, and Molière had to write a new Prologue adapting it for the public theatre where it finally appeared in February 1673. It is the nearest Molière came to a *grande comédie* on the subject of medicine. It has many of the features of his other major comedies, a fully drawn central comic character, a *raisonneur* presenting the logical alternative point of view. If for no other reason, the dreadful ironies of the circumstances of its performance would demand for it a more serious consideration than the other medical satires.

LE MALADE IMAGINAIRE

Argan stands as the last in line of Molière's comic monomaniacs; he is infatuated with medicine, as Harpagon was with money, or Orgon with religion. This infatuation, however, although it dominates his life, does not deprive him of what might pass for practical common sense. When we meet him first he is reading aloud and reckoning up his apothecary's bills for the month, scrutinising each item and making the traditional deductions—seventeenth century apothecaries apparently always charged twice what they expected to be paid. Argan is, in his own eyes, nobody's fool, and is determined to get value for money:

> 'Plus, du vingt-quatrième, un petit clystère insinuatif, préparatif, et rémollient, pour amollir, humecter, et rafraîchir les entrailles de Monsieur'. Ce qui me plaît de Monsieur Fleurant, mon apothicaire, c'est que ses parties sont toujours fort civiles: 'les entrailles de Monsier, trente sols.' Oui, mais, Monsier Fleurant, ce n'est pas tout que d'être civil, il faut être aussi raisonnable, et ne pas écorcher les malades. Trente sols un lavement; Je suis votre serviteur, je vous l'ai déjà dit. Vous ne me les avez mis dans les autres parties qu'à vingt sols, et vingt sols en langage d'apothicaire, c'est-à-dire dix sols; les voilà, dix sols.

> I, i

Argan is not so deranged by his hypochondria that he will let his apothecary cheat him, and in everything that relates to money he can be shrewd enough. Later, when he plans to marry his daughter to the imbecile Thomas Diafoirus, he has calculated on the property Thomas will inherit as well as the advantage of having a qualified doctor as a son-in-law. In one sense this solid pragmatism is the measure of Argan's robust good health, for a man who was really as ill as he imagines himself to be would be too weak or too desperate to haggle over medical expenses. His illness and his doctors are Argan's luxuries, for which he does not grudge payment when he has had satisfaction. This leads to the final lunatic logic of the conclusion of his monologue:

> Si bien donc que ce mois j'ai pris . . . huit médecines, et . . . douze lavements; et l'autre mois il y avoit douze médecines, et vingt lavements. Je ne m'étonne pas si je ne me porte pas si bien ce mois-ci que l'autre.

> I, i

The whole speech has something of the comic impact of the story of the emperor's new clothes; the more literally Argan asses the benefits of medicine, the more clearly the audience realises that its effects are purely imaginary.

Argan's matter-of-fact calculations serve also to highlight the preposterous number of laxatives and enemas he has taken in the past month. The lavatorial humour of purgation is a basic part of most of Molière's medical satires, and is used as a continuing piece of comic business throughout *Le Malade Imaginaire.* For Anglo-

Saxons, with less strong stomachs in such matters than the French, the spectacle of a man who can talk lovingly of a 'bon petit clystère', may be almost too disgusting to be funny. But it is not just for the sake of the scatological jokes that Molière harps upon the mechanics of purgation. It was, after, an essential part of the medicine of his time. For seventeenth-century doctors, committed to the concept of the humours, the primary purpose of any medical treatment was likely to be the evacuation of the malignant substances from the body, and this could only be done by emetics, laxatives or bleeding. In the burlesque dog-Latin catechism of the postulant doctor at the end of the play the automatic treatment for every disease is 'clysterium donare, postea seignare, ensuitta purgare'. This may have been no more than a slight exaggeration of the truth for Molière's contemporaries.

It is likely to be a matter of wonder to many of us in the twentieth century how indeed anyone ever survived this system of medicine. When we consider that the orthodox view of the medical Faculty in Molière's time was that a patient could lose 20 out of his estimated 24 litres of blood without doing him permanent harm, and that babies and pregnant women were not exempt from this calculation, the jokes about doctors as killers seem to have considerable point.[13] With bleeding also used as a regular prophylactic measure on perfectly healthy patients, the result must have been chronic anaemia for those who had nothing worse. Would averagely intelligent laymen in the seventeenth century have been in a position to know that such treatment was anything but helpful? How far could Molière expect to carry his audience with him in mocking these standard practices of evacuation? As we have said, it is impossible to know definitely. But we might apply the analogy of the attitude of many modern people towards the use of antibiotics. Although there can be no doubt that the discovery of antibiotics in this century was a step forward in medicine unlike anything before it, many ordinary patients, besides several medical authorities, have remarked on the tendency of general practitioners to prescribe them promiscuously. Even though the lay patient does not understand the nature of the treatment, he can observe from the mechanical way in which his G. P. reaches for the prescription pad that the antibiotics are being used as placebos of panaceas rather than considered remedies. Surely we can infer from the character of Molière's satire that the situation was similar with the doctors of his time and that, even though his audience believed in the efficacy of laxatives and bleeding, they would have seen enough of normal practice to recognise that they were often used unnecessarily, as in the case of Argan.[14]

In *Le Malade Imaginaire,* however, as in no other medical satire of Molière, there is some evidence that he expected on the part of his audience, not just the attitude of thoughtful common sense, but a fairly informed position on medicine. Monsieur Diafoirus' eulogy of his son Thomas has the following significant conclusion:

> Mais sur toute chose ce qui me plaît en lui, et en quoi il suit mon exemple, c'est qu'il s'attache aveuglement aux opinions de nos anciens, et que jamais il n'a voulu comprendre ni écouter les raisons et les expériences des prétendues découvertes de notre siècle, touchant la circulation du sang, et autres opinions de même farine.
>
> II, v

The speech is heavily ironic throughout, and the Diafoirus, *père et fils,* are intended quite clearly as satiric models of what doctors ought not to be. In the ancients versus moderns controversy there is no doubt where Molière's audience are asked to stand. As Angélique puts it to Thomas—'Les anciens, Monsieur, sont les anciens, et nous sommes les gens de maintenant'—'the ancients, Monsieur, are the ancients, and we are the people of today.' M. Diafoirus' praise for blind devotion to ancient theory as against modern empiricism compares interestingly with the speech of the Avocat in *Le Médecin Volant,* quoted earlier. Molière's irony here suggests that his audience will take for granted the discoveries of their age, including the circulation of the blood. Although Harvey's work on the circulation had been published as long before as 1628, it was still fiercely controversial in France and especially in Paris at the time of *Le Malade Imaginaire.* For in 1671 Louis XIV had decided to institute a chair attached to the Jardin du Roi to teach the new anatomy of the circulation and in 1672 personally intervened in Parliament against the reactionary Faculty of Medicine who were opposing the new chair as an infringement of their privilege. In 1673 the surgeon Pierre Dionys was installed as professor and ordered by the King to give public lectures on anatomy.[15] With this background of public controversy, Molière could no doubt rely on a majority of his audience to follow the King's lead and laugh at the old-fashioned conservatism of the medical establishment.

It may seem, therefore, that Molière in *Le Malade Imaginaire* harnessed the traditional comic scepticism of all medicine to the more specific and topical discredit of one school of medicine. In so far as he seems to be asserting the truth and importance of the anatomical discoveries and empirical methods which form the basis of modern medicine, we may well be tempted to consider Molière as a mind before his time, an avant-garde believer in scientific rationalism. If so, we will be disappointed by the doctrine put forward by Béralde, the play's *raisonneur,* apparently for our approval. Béralde's reasons for disbelieving in the medicine of his time are closer to those of a Christian Scientist than to a twentieth century doctor's. He argues that a disease should be allowed to take its course without interference:

> La nature, d'elle-même, quand nous la laissons faire, se tire doucement du désordre òu elle est tombée. C'est notre inquiétude, c'est notre impatience qui gâte tout, et presque tous les hommes meurent de leurs remèdes, et non pas de leurs maladies.
>
> III, iii

Such passive trust in nature is made necessary by our inability to understand her mysteries:

> Les ressorts de notre machine sont des mystères, jusques ici, où les hommes ne voient goutte, et . . . la nature nous a mis au-devant des yeux des voiles trop épais pour y connoître quelque chose.
>
> III, iii

Although the qualifying 'jusques ici' might be taken to imply the possibility of future understanding, the attitude of Béralde seems to have the quietism of the traditional 'if God had intended us to fly he would have given us wings'.

Béralde's attitude has been related to the philosophy of Gassendi, popularised by Bernier, who is known to have worked with Molière, or to the 'naturism' which originated with Hippocrates but was generally out of fashion in the seventeenth century.[16] But it is surely unnecessary to make *Le Malade Imaginaire* one more debating-ground for the controversy over Molière's philosophical allegiances. The primitivist idealisation of things natural, and its corresponding rejection of everything artificial, is a recurrent phenomenon through the ages, a popular attitude which need not be ascribed to the influence of one current ideology or another. The antipathy for what is felt to be 'meddling with nature' is as strong in the modern environmental and ecological movement as it is in Montaigne—who is as likely a source for Molière as Gassendi. Once again, it is not particularly helpful to place precisely the ideological affiliations of the comic attitudes, or to nail them down as the personal views of Molière. Béralde's position on medicine is available for approval by the comic audience by reason of its strong but vague emotional attractiveness rather than its congruence with the ideas of the seventeenth century. The wishful optimism of assuming that men are naturally inclined to recover from illness is combined with the underlying atavism of accepting nature's decree without question. The result is an attitude which is felt to be humanly valid, however little it may correspond to the religious and scientific beliefs of a given age.

To think of Molière performing *Le Malade Imaginaire* on the point of death, however, is to stop this argument or any other in its tracks. How could Molière, who must have known that he was critically ill if not dying, have jested about illness? Surely here if nowhere else we are entitled to believe that he was speaking from the heart, on an analogous principle to that which gives death-bed confession an especial authority in a court of law? The play can be read as a final laughing defiance of the doctors and their art, attacking their pretensions even while apparently in greatest need of their services. Béralde's explanation to Argan of why Molière will have nothing to do with doctor's remedies has, certainly, the air of a bitter personal joke:

> Il a ses raisons pour n'en point vouloir, et il soutient que cela n'est permis qu'aux gens vigoureux et robustes, et qui ont des forces de reste pour porter les remèdes avec la maladie; mais que, pour lui, il n'a justement de la force que pour porter son mal.
>
> III, iii

But Molière's explanation of the ironies of his own situation is more outrageous and less straightforwardly polemic than this. To begin with, there is the sheer audaciousness of impersonating Argan, the man who pretends to be ill, but whose robust good health is apparent in the raging energy he shows whenever he is thwarted. Argan asks nervously when it is suggested he should sham dead—'N'y a-til point quelque danger à contrefaire le mort?' But even an unsuperstitious person might feel that for an actor who was desperately sick to play a hypochondriac was tempting fate: The joke of Toinette in her disguise as doctor, mechanically ascribing all Argan's symptoms to a single ailment is no doubt a standard one—we meet another version of it in Shaw's *Doctor's Dilemma*. But is there not a frightening audacity in Molière, in the last stages of tuberculosis, having his pretend doctor diagnose his imaginary illness as originating in the lungs?

It is Molière, rather than Sartre's Saint Genet, who deserves the title 'comédien et martyr'. For in *Le Malade Imaginaire* he did martyr himself to his profession of actor. All through his career, Molière had been prepared to exploit caricatures of himself for their comic potential. In *L'Impromptu de Versailles* he painted a delightful, but hardly flattering portrait of M. Molière, the bossy, irritable, harassed theatre director desperately trying to discipline his troupe through a rush rehearsal. From the point when his tubercular cough became so habitual that it could not be suppressed, he wrote it into his parts and turned it to comic advantage, above all in *L'Avare*. Presumably, as with all repertory companies, the pleasure of the audience derived in part from the very familiarity of the actor and the skill with which he could manipulate those familiar features in the interests of a given role. Many critics have suggested that Molière actually took his cue for *Le Malade Imaginaire* from Boulanger du Chalussay's *Elomire Hypocondre*, the malicious portrait in which Elomire/Molière is represented as a querulous hypochondriac. Molière, in taking up the challenge, one might say, was arguing that no-one could satirise him better than he could satirise himself. It was he, playing Argan, who spat with fury when Béralde suggested that a comedy of Molière might do him good:

> Par la mort non de diable! si j'étois que des médecins, je me vengerois de son impertinence; et quand il sera malade, je le laisserois mourir sans secours. Il auroit beau faire et beau dire, je ne lui ordonnerois pas la moindre petite saignée, le moindre petit lavement, et je lui dirois: 'Crève, crève! cela t'apprendra une autre fois à te jouer à la Faculté'.
>
> III, iii

This is so vivid that it even seems to have originated a tradition with apparently little other foundation that Molière did actually die with the doctors refusing him aid. But we should not let the aftermath mislead us as to what Molière was doing with such a speech. It was a means of transferring his private illness into the public arena of comedy, making even of this extremity a subject at which his audience could comfortably laugh.

The speculative autobiographical interpretation of Molière which imagined a disturbed personal life feeding the life of the plays is no longer in fashion, if only because the increased caution of twentieth-century scholarship has driven us back to a realisation of how little we know of the facts. What we are left with is the sense of his role as a clown whose art so often includes an element of self-caricature. Molière may really have shared the scepticism about doctors which had been expressed by Montaigne and others before him. He may well have had the impatience of so many chronic invalids with the absurdities of their examinations and prescriptions. What he put upon the stage, however, was not these opinions as opinions, but a version of such views corresponding to a pre-established comic paradigm. In the early farces this amounted to the simple reductivism of the ignorant impersonating the learned. In the *comédie-ballets*, prepared for the King, the farcical jokes of popular tradition were spiked with a personal satire which the exclusive audience of the court could be expected to relish. For the Palais-Royal, where *La Malade Imaginaire* was finally played, the comedy of the doctors was once again generalised beyond personalities—and could incorporate a more serious and informed attitude to the subject. But even here, the realities of pain and death, which must have been so very real to Molière by then, are tacitly ignored, while the audience can observe with uninfatuated amusement the infatuation of Argan and the 'gallimatias' of his doctors.

THE ALCHEMIST

To turn back from Molière's medical satires to Jonson's *Alchemist* is to turn from respectable to disreputable imposture. Although the early links forged between

medicine and alchemy—Paracelsus styled himself 'Prince of Philosophy and medicine'—had not been broken by the seventeenth century, there was already an orthodox medical establishment, whereas alchemy, however it may have fascinated individual scientists, belonged in the public mind in the half-light at the edge of the underworld. To anyone less dazzled by the chimeras of their own greed than Dapper, Drugger, or Mammon, the very fact of Subtle's obscure residence in the Blackfriars and his lack of antecedents would have seemed fishy. Messieurs Filerin, Des Fonandrès, Diafoirus etc. were, by contrast, the counterparts of real life doctors of eminent reputation in court and city. Yet for the purposes of comedy the process remains that of imposture, however different the normal credibility of doctors and alchemists. *The Alchemist*, like Molière's medical plays, is a study of deceivers and deceived.

In *The Alchemist*, also, as in *Le Malade Imaginaire*, we laugh as much at the deceived as at the deceivers. One of the play's great pieces of character-drawing is Sir Epicure Mammon, as obsessed with alchemy as Argan is with medicine. By contrast with Argan, however, Mammon is an extravagant and fantastic personality who impresses us not by his simple foolishness but by the extraordinary and abnormal scale of his delusions, his 'elephantiasis of the imagination', as Harry Levin calls it.[17] When we meet him first the disease is already far advanced and the imagination is swollen to monstrous proportions:

> My meat shall all come in in Indian shells,
> Dishes of agate, set in gold, and studded,
> With emeralds, sapphires, hyacinths, and rubies.
> The tongues of carps, dormice, and camels' heels,
> Boil'd i' the spirit of Sol, and dissolved pearl,
> (Apicius' diet, 'gainst the epilepsy)
> And I will eat these broths with spoons of amber,
> Headed with diamond and carbuncle.
> My foot-boy shall eat pheasants, calvered salmons,
> Knots, godwits, lampreys. I myself will have
> The beards of barbels, serv'd instead of salads;
> Oil'd mushrooms; and the swelling unctuous paps
> Of a fat pregnant sow, newly cut off,
> Dress'd with an exquisite and poignant sauce.
>
> II, ii, 72-85

But though the monomanias of Mammon and Argan take such different forms and are so differently expressed, they have a similar underlying tendency. Mammon and Argan are both taken in by a vision of bettering nature. Béralde argues, 'lorsqu' un médecin vous parle d'aider, de secourir, de soulager la nature, de lui ôter ce qui lui nuit et lui donner ce qui lui manque . . . il vous dit justement le roman de la médecine'. 'When a doctor talks to you about aiding, assisting, relieving nature, taking away from it what is harmful or giving it what it needs . . . he is giving you the old fairy-tale of medicine'. The 'roman' of alchemy is closely related—to 'teach dull nature what her own forces are', as Mammon puts it to Doll Common. Both have their origins in a theological concept of fallen nature which might conceivably be restored to its prelapsarian capacities. Medicine and alchemy, therefore, offer hope to those who are too impatient, too restless, or too greedy to put up with the natural limitations of the real world.

Molière gives us Béralde to point the moral of Argan's failure to accept nature's way. In *The Alchemist* there is no such clear-cut spokesman for the audience. Surly, Mammon's friend, reasons with him but is not the *raisonneur* of the play in the technical sense. Surly can see through Subtle and Face, as can the audience, and yet the audience is not encouraged to identify with Surly. It is interesting to try to analyse why this should be so. Mammon brings Surly along as a 'heretic' to be converted to the true faith of alchemy. As Mammon's rhetoric soars at the prospect of the new world of riches in view, Surly sticks fast to his attitude of incredulity—'Faith, I have a humour, I would not willingly be gull'd'. The very word 'humour', and the way in which this fear of gulling quickly becomes established as Surly's mechanical catch-word—'Sir Epicure, your friend to use: yet, still, loth to be gull'd'—might be enough to place him for us as one of Jonson's 'humourists', with a single comic over-developed character-trait. But the tone of Surly's deflations of Mammon, also, is important in removing him from the possibility of audience identification. Virtually Surly's first lines in the play are his response to Mammon's assurance that proofs of the alchemical process will convince him:

MAMMON:

. . . You will believe me.

SURLY:

Yes, when I see't, I will.
But if my eyes do cozen me so and I
Giving 'em no occasion, sure I'll have
A whore, shall piss 'em out next day.

II, i, 42-5

There is a gratuitous violence and crudity, here, which marks this as an over-reaction, Surly's aggressiveness turned against himself for want of any other object. We hardly need the courteous and good-humoured tones of Béralde arguing with his brother for contrast to convince us that Surly is not a character to be trusted.

Surly's ancestor in Jonsonian comedy is Downright of *Every Man in His Humour* who also makes a profession out of being gruff and grum. With Surly as with Downright, Jonson can undercut and expose the pretensions of the affected and fantastic characters, without implying any approval of offensive frankness in itself. Surly, listed in the *dramatis personae* as a 'gamester', is partly

discredited as one who can see through the alchemist's cheating only because he is so familiar with cheating at cards himself. He constantly equates the two:

alchemy is a pretty kind of game,
Somewhat like tricks o' the cards, to cheat a man
With charming.

II, iii, 180-2

His scoffing asides or interruptions are mostly knowing allusions to London underworld life—thieving, swindling, the bawdy-houses of Pict-hatch—and in placing alchemy in this context we feel he is bringing it down to his own level. While Face and Subtle are putting on their display for the benefit of Mammon, Surly's reductive gibes point the irony, and no doubt even the crudest of his puns and *double-entendres* raised a laugh among some of the Jacobean audience. But it is striking that he does not win the argument with Subtle when it comes to a formal debate, and the virtuoso rhetoric of Subtle's exposition of alchemy, though it cannot convince him (or us), leaves Surly looking rather stupid. His disbelief seems the result of temperamental cussedness and Philistine ignorance, rather than an intelligent and reasonable scepticism.

Surly's attitude is that of the proudly uneducated mocking the alchemist's 'worlds of strange ingredients would burst a man to name'. But *The Alchemist* was not written for the Surlys of Jonson's audience. To us the language of alchemy is nothing more than a nonsensical hocus-pocus intended to deceive, and so it probably was for many Jacobeans. But there would have been those, also, who, like Jonson, knew the literature of alchemy and could appreciate the accuracy with which he reproduced the alchemical arguments. We may well laugh at the absurd if unanswerable logic of Subtle's defence of his profession against Surly:

SUBTLE:

Why, what have you observed, sir, in our art,
Seems so impossible?

SURLY:

But your whole work, no more.
That you should hatch gold in a furnace, sir,
As they do eggs in Egypt!

SUBTLE:

Sir, do you
Believe that eggs are hatched so?

SURLY:

If I should?

SUBTLE:

Why, I think that the greater miracle.
No egg but differs from a chicken more
Than metals in themselves.

SURLY:

                              That cannot be.
         The egg's ordained by nature to that end,
         And is a chicken *in potentia.*

SUBTLE:

         The same we say of lead and other metals,
         Which would be gold if they had time.

                                        II, iii, 125-36

But once Surly mentioned the Egyptian practice of artificial incubation of chickens, the more alert members of Jonson's audience might have realised that he had played into Subtle's hands, for this was one of the analogies used to support alchemical theory, and Subtle's argument is taken virtually word for word from the Latin of Martin Delrio's *Disquisitiones Magicae.*[18] Sir Epicure's authorities for the truth of alchemy—'a book where Moses and his sister, and Solomon have written of the art . . . a treatise penn'd by Adam . . . in high Dutch'—may seem too much even for such a glutton for belief as Mammon to swallow. But again such supposed authentic manuscripts were taken seriously by alchemists and Jonson even owned one such work himself.[19] When Mammon goes on to make of the golden fleece an alchemist's book, to see in 'Pythagoras' thigh', 'Pandora's tub', and many more, metaphors for the alchemist's art, he is following a well-established tradition of reinterpreting the classical myths as alchemical allegory.[20]

Those who had used alchemy as the subject of comedy before Jonson had been content to mock its grotesque and fantastic jargon. Lyly, for example, in *Gallathea,* does little more than copy out the barbaric technical terms from Chaucer's *Canon's Yeoman's Tale,* and gives us the simple humour of the prentice sending up his master's learning. But Jonson, in *The Alchemist* as in his court masques, was meticulous in his research, and it is a work of bizarre scholarship as well as a theatrical *tour de force.* Why should Jonson have taken the trouble to read Paracelsus, Arnold de Villa Nova, Geber, or Martin Delrio, in order to get right what he was convinced was nonsense anyhow? If there were people in the audience who were also familiar with these authors, what sort of pleasure did they get from recognising the learned reasoning of such authorities reproduced in the mouth of a conman? It almost seems a breach of decorum to accord so much knowledge to the down-at-heel Subtle.

Jonson allows to Subtle the best answer an alchemist could supply, 'less out of generosity than out of the thorough-going candour of the scholar', as Herford and Simpson put it.[21] It is indeed Jonson's scholarly temperament which enables him to display in *The Alchemist* alchemical learning far beyond anything on medicine we find in Molière. We are sometimes inclined to think of his scholarship as a handicap rather than an asset to Jonson, sitting rather heavily upon his writing, but here it is the very source of comic achievement. The play yields a special delight for those capable of recognising that these fantastic arabesques of argument are not the products of imagination but of genuine authorities, that truth, if one could call alchemical theory truth, is indeed wilder than fiction. Most comic writers who mock learning are not sufficiently interested in learning to go beyond superficial caricature. But there is a tradition of perverse scholarship turned to the benefit of a sort of fantastic dead-pan comedy which runs (at least) from Rabelais to Joyce, and it is in this tradition that Jonson belongs. A part of Joyce or of Jonson enjoys the mock scientific language of 'Ithaca' or Subtle's alchemy for its own sake. It is a parody which is half in love with what it parodies, to the point where the reader or audience may feel puzzled as to whether it is parody at all.

If we return them to Surly and consider why we are not asked to identify with his scepticism, it may be that his attitude of coarse disbelief is felt to be inappropriate to the sheer intricacy of Subtle's deceptions. He sees through alchemy as a swindle, but he fails to see what an accomplished swindle it is. In a similar way, when Stephen Dedalus propounds theories of aesthetics or literary criticism founded upon the scholastic principles of Aquinas, although Joyce invites an ironic reaction, he disassociates us from the trivial sneers of Lynch or Mulligan. Those who have no real respect for the creations of the mind cannot truly appreciate the grotesqueness of its abortions. Jonson wants us to feel the sheer beauty of the alchemical system, meaningless as it is. As Subtle expounds the nature of 'remote matter' (II, iii, 143-76), each step in his exposition follows on logically from the previous one and the whole argument is a model of clarity which might have an audience nodding understanding assent. The language of alchemy is a hypnotic Sirens' song, whose enchanting attraction we can feel, while ourselves ensured against its spell.

Whatever its attractions, there is certainly no possibility of anyone in the audience actually believing in alchemy, any more than anyone in the audience of *Le Malade Imaginaire* could believe in medicine. We start, in both cases, with a basic assumption of scepticism. What is more in *The Alchemist,* we laugh at people in direct proportion to the degree they become involved in belief. The simpletons, Dapper or Drugger, are mocked mercilessly, though their pretensions are harmless, relatively speaking, because of the ridiculousness of the charades they are willing to credit. Sir Epicure's imagination has become so saturated in alchemy that he speaks almost entirely in alchemical metaphors, whether appropriate or not. In a different context, Ananias is the more absurd of the two Puritans because he believes literally in the hypocritical attitudes his sect adopts. A flexible capacity for disengaging from any role is the greatest possible asset in *The Alchemist*. This is where Surly finally falls down. He is cynical about everything except his own role as cynic, and while he is self-righteously glorying in his exposure of the tricksters, Face can set going a whole batch of further deceptions which defeat him. It is this same flexibility which may explain why it is ultimately Face rather than Subtle who wins out. Subtle can play his alchemist part in all sorts of different moods and styles—as a religious anchorite for Mammon, as a temperamental artist for Ananias, as a man of the world, expert in rules of honour to Kastril; he can adjust his act to suit the special weaknesses of the individual gulls. Yet it is always basically the same role and from the fact that he, like Mammon, uses his alchemical jargon out of context we sense that he has half begun to believe in his own powers, or at least to take for granted the awing effects of his persona. He is like an actor who has played star parts too long. Face, the perfect character actor by contrast, can double and treble, now as the blustering Captain, now as the technician Lungs, and finally as 'smooth Jeremy' the butler. Face is ironically faceless because each successive mask is equally plausible. If we feel that there is comic justice in his triumph it is because he matches virtuosity in deception, which all the rogues share, with the mental agility to see when each deception must be replaced by a new one. In a comedy where we are asked to see through and admire every form of cheating trick, the man who can participate in all of them, yet believe in none, may end up as something like the hero.

Disbelief in medicine or alchemy in *The Alchemist* or *Le Malade Imaginaire* has been related by several critics to religious belief or disbelief. Molière's 'impiety in medicine' has been linked with the naturalism of Gassendi, as we have seen, and more generally to Molière's alleged 'libertinage'.[22] It has been claimed that *Le Malade Imaginaire* is a disguised attack upon religion and that 'the play actually gains in coherence whenever a metaphor, an attitude, a gesture suggests an analogy between medical doctors and theologians.'[23] To challenge the authority of the Faculty of Medicine could be construed as a step towards challenging the authority of Theology, and of course the two were closely linked. Under cover of mocking the credulity of Argan, who imagines himself in need of doctoring, Molière is perhaps satirising the orthodox Christian who allowed his priests to convince him that he was in constant need of spiritual attention.

For those who interpret *The Alchemist* as a play with religious significance, Jonson's position is the very opposite of Molière's. Through the religious echoes of the alchemist's patter can be detected not a satire on Christianity, but on the age which has debased Christian language into a swindler's stock-in-trade. Edward B. Par-

tridge, who is the outstanding spokesman of this view in Jonson criticism, sums up:

> the alchemist (Subtle or gold) becomes a parody of the Creator. To sincere alchemists who were mystical idealists, alchemy was a religion or quasi-religion. To Jonson, a moral idealist and a dogmatic Christian who approached alchemy with no sympathy for the religious impulse at its heart, it seemed only an obscure fraud, and alchemic terms only a parody of the Word.[24]

As his attacks on medicine are used to support the image of Molière the progressive freethinker, so *The Alchemist* provides further evidence for Jonson the conservative moralist. Subtle and Face are not only confidence tricksters, they are in some sort blasphemers, and it is this undercurrent of blasphemy which, for such critics as Partridge, deepens and darkens the meaning of the play.

At issue here is the relation of the life of the comedy to the life of ideas of the playwright's time. How far did the audience of *Le Malade Imaginaire* or of *The Alchemist* bring to the theatre with them all their normal ethical, social and spiritual commitments within the real world? How open were they to ideological suggestions in comedy? As a first example let us look at the scene in which Monsieur Purgon anathematises Argan for having refused to take his 'clystère' on time. An effect of ritual is built up with the interjections of Argan and Toinette serving to heighten the rhythm of the denunciation:

M. Purgon:

> Mais puisque vous n'avez pas voulu guérir par mes mains

Argan:

> Ce n'est pas ma faute

M. Purgon:

> Puisque vous vous êtes soustrait de l'obéissance que l'on doit à son médecin,

Toinette:

> Cela crie vengeance.

M. Purgon:

> Puisque vous vous êtes déclaré rebelle aux remèdes que je vous ordonnois . . .

Argan:

> Hé! point du tout.

M. Purgon:

> J'ai à vous dire que je vous abandonne â votre mauvaise constitution, à l'intempérie de vos entrailles, à la corruption de votre sang, à l'âcreté de votre bile et à la féculence de vos humeurs.

III, v

M. Purgon then proceeds to project the course of Argan's degeneration—'De la bradypepsie dans la dyspepsie', 'De la dyspepsie dans l'apepsie'—so convincingly that Argan cries out at last 'Ah, mon Dieu! je suis mort'.

This might quite plausibly be compared to an excommunication ceremony, the procedure by which a disobedient heretic is solemnly cut off as a diseased limb of the Church. But the laugh here is against the doctors who take upon themselves an authority as absolute as that of the Church, rather than a disguised satire on the Church itself. It is the disproportion of the sentence to the offence, the absurdity of the doctor's tyrannical pretensions, which is the basis of the parody. Its effect upon the unfortunate Argan, ironically the last person who could justly be accused of medical heresy, is that of an annihilating barrage because it comes from the authority he holds in awe. The sceptical audience, however, can relish the attack as a purely nonsensical rite. The tactics are the same in *The Alchemist,* when Subtle routs Ananias. Ananias has objected to Subtle's 'heathen Greek' alchemical terms, and in indignant demonstration Subtle puts Face through a mock catechism:

Subtle:

> Sirrah, my varlet, stand you forth, and speak to him
> Like a philosopher. Answer i' the language,
> Name the vexations, and the martyrizations
> Of metals in the work.

Face:

>   Sir, putrefaction,
> Solution, ablution, sublimation,
> Cohobation, calcination, ceration, and
> Fixation.

Subtle:

> This is heathen Greek to you now?
> And when comes vivification?

Face:

>   After mortification.

Subtle:

> What's cohobation?

Face:

>   'Tis the pouring on
> Your aqua regis, and then drawing him off,
> To the trine circle of the seven spheres.

Subtle:

> What's the proper passion of metals?

Face:

>   Malleation.

Subtle:

> What's your *ultimum supplicium auri*?

Face:

>   Antimonium.

Subtle:

> This's heathen Greek to you?

>   II, v, 18-31

Of course, the comedy here is that the terms become more and more 'Greek' to Ananias who is nevertheless driven back on his heels by this onslaught of quick-fire learning. Once again, as with Purgon, the combination of wrathful authority and a command of mysterious language gives the imposter success, and Subtle ends by denouncing 'wicked Ananias', 'the varlet that cozen'd the Apostles', in the style of one of Ananias's own Puritan preachers.

The language of alchemy is closely related to the language of mystical religion as Partridge points out, and as we can see from the excerpt from Subtle's catechism. 'Martyrization', 'sublimation', 'mortification', 'passion'—all of these terms have spiritual significance, and the association is not accidental. The alchemist was part scientist, part philosopher, but also part mystic, as Surly reminds Mammon:

>   he must be *homo frugi,*
> A pious, holy, and religious man,
> One free from mortal sin, a very virgin.

But just because there is a normal and accepted relation between alchemical concepts and those of theology, the parody detected by Jonson's critics may not have been so striking as they would have us think. Jonson here is unlike Joyce, who does deliberately use liturgical or sacred images in a profane context with a fully self-conscious sense of parody. The inverted use of Christian symbols does not force itself upon the reader or audience of *The Alchemist* with the shock of Buck Mulligan's shaving Mass. Instead it is part of a much more general inflation and abuse of language. To see Subtle and Face as blasphemers would be to take the claims of alchemy far more seriously than Jonson ever encourages his audience to do. The comic catechism works less by its undercurrent of religious parody, than by the sheer grotesqueness of its literal concepts, the anthropomorphic character of the metaphors applied to the alchemical process. It is the pure absurdity of imagining inanimate metals being 'mortified', 'tortured', 'sublimed', which Jonson mocks here, and which he dramatises so amusingly in his masque *Mercury Vindicated from the Alchemists at Court.*

What Molière and Jonson invite is a general rather than a specific scepticism. Molière's medical satires are not slyly directed against the orthodoxies of the Church, nor is *The Alchemist* intended to satirise those who debased such orthodoxies. In both cases the language of religion is included as it is cognate to all professional language, which, for the purposes of this sort of comedy, can be defined as language which works by means of its obscurity rather than its clarity, its systematic dogmatism rather than its real significance, its emotional charge rather than its logical force. At its simplest we see this in Molière's early medical farces, where the imposter crudely apes the airs of the learned doctor. It is rather different in plays such as *Le Malade Imaginaire* or *The Alchemist,* when the audience is presumed to have a fairly detailed knowledge of what is being parodied. There the pleasure is rather that of seeing the familiar and real, by a process of perhaps only slight exaggeration, turned into the fantastically monstrous. (To read or to watch *Le Malade Imaginaire* is to realise that the techniques of absurdist farce are not innovations of the twentieth century.) While the seamy richness of detail in Jonson makes for a very different texture from the tight mad logic of Molière, in both cases it is the mechanics of deception which we are observing, the psychology both of the gulls or fools and of the professionals who cheat them.

Jonson and Molière are not here finally dependent on the private opinions of their audience on medicine or alchemy. As always the comedian will make capital out of the local or the topical, and so Molière caricatured the court doctors, D'Aquin and the rest, and Jonson no doubt relied on the notoriety of men like Kelly, Forman, and Dee to give immediacy to his play. But if we try to characterise the audience attitudes that Molière or Jonson seem to expect towards *Le Malade Imaginaire* or *The Alchemist,* they are not those of any definite sect or faction of the time. They are assumed to be people of common sense, as always, but common sense, in this instance, takes the form of a sceptical disbelief in what as individuals they might have credited or half credited. They are encouraged to watch with no trace of illusion the comedy of human weakness and credulity which plays in tandem with the comedy of mystification; with no trace of illusion, but without indignation either, for indignation is itself a form of self-righteous pretension which may be left to the Surlys. They are above all understood to be pragmatic plain-speakers, those for whom the only true function of language is communication, and who suspect the alchemists or the doctors most of all for their opacity. In the next chapter we shall turn to a different sort of language, but this underlying norm of a plain-speaking audience will remain the same.

Notes

1. Harry Levin, 'Two Magian comedies: *The Tempest* and *The Alchemist*', *Shakespeare Survey* 22 (1969), 51.

2. See Edgar Hill Duncan 'Jonson's *Alchemist* and the literature of Alchemy', *PMLA* 61 (1946), 669-710.

3. Bacon, *Sylva Sylvarum* (1626), p. 86. Quoted in Herford & Simpson X, p. 48.

4. Frances Yates, 'Did Newton connect his maths and alchemy?' *Times Higher Educational Supplement,* 18 March 1977.

5. Critics have conjectured that Molière may have had help with the details of this scene from his own doctor M. de Mauvillain, a graduate of Montpellier. Certainly the evidence of the induction of a doctor in Montpellier witnessed by Locke in 1676, with its musical accompaniments, and the professor's long speech against innovation, suggests that Molière was not altogether exaggerating. See *Locke's Travels in France 1675-79* ed. John Lough (Cambridge U.P. 1953), p. 57.

6. *Letters de Mme. de Sévigné* 3 vols. (Paris 1953-6), Vol. 2, p. 203.

7. John Palmer, *Molière: his life and works* (London 1930), p. 348.

8. Cairncross, *Molière: bourgeois et libertin,* p. 24.

9. See Joseph Girard, *A propos de L'Amour Médecin, Molière et Louis-Henry Daquin* (Paris 1948).

10. A. Gill tried to restore the play definitely to the Molière canon in '"The Doctor in the Farce" and Molière', *French Studies* 2 (1948), 101-28.

11. 'De la ressemblance des Enfans aux Peres', *Essais,* livre 2 (Paris 1969), pp. 421-48.

12. *Lettres,* 2, pp. 890-1.

13. The principle behind the frequent use of bleeding was the idea that the body created fresh new blood to replace the old stagnant blood removed, as a well produces all the more clean water the more dirty water is taken from it. See François Millepierres, *La Vie Quotidienne des Médecins au temps de Molière* (Paris 1964).

14. In his apology for medicine, G. de Bezançon was prepared to admit that there were any number of bad doctors for whom a crude routine of the Diafoirus variety did instead of the arduous and continuous study of different cases and different remedies which the good doctor undertook. *Les Médecins à la censure ou entretiens sur la médecine* (Paris 1677).

15. See L. Chauvois 'Molière, Boileau, La Fontaine et la circulation du sang', *La Presse Medicale* 62 (1954), 1219-20.

16. See René Jasinski 'Sur Molière et la médecine', *Mélanges de philologie, d'histoire et de littérature offerts à Joseph Vianey* (Paris 1934), pp. 249-54,

and Guy Godlewski 'Les Médecins de Molière et leurs modèles', *La Semaine des Hôpitaux* 46 (1970), 3490-500.

17. Levin, 'Two Magian Comedies', 55.

18. See Herford & Simpson X, p. 81.

19. Salomon, King of Israel *Opus de arte magica, ab Honorio ordinatum,* a fourteenth century manuscript now in the British Museum which Herford and Simpson cite among the books in Jonson's library—Herford and Simpson I, Appendix IV.

20. See Duncan, 'Jonson's Alchemist and the Literature of Alchemy'.

21. Herford and Simpson II, p. 101.

22. See John Cairncross 'Impie en Médecine', *Cahiers de L'Association Internationales des Etudes Françaises* 16 (1965), 269-84.

23. J. D. Hubert, *Molière and the comedy of intellect* (Berkeley & Los Angeles 1962), p. 255. The same idea is pursued to absurd lengths by Carlo François who detects a parody of the nativity in the pastoral prologue to *Le Malade Imaginaire*—'Médecine et religion chez Molière: deux facettes d'un même absurdité', *French Review* 42 (1969), 665-72.

24. Partridge, *The Broken Compass,* p. 127.

Bibliography

A. TEXTS

SHAKESPEARE

The Tempest, ed. Frank Kermode (New Arden, London 1954).

JONSON

The Alchemist, ed. Alvin B. Kernan (Yale Ben Jonson, New Haven 1974).

MOLIÈRE

Oeuvres Complètes de Molière, ed. Robert Jouanny (Paris 1962) 2 vols.

OTHER TEXTS REFERRED TO INCLUDE:

Ben Jonson, ed. C. H. Herford and Percy and Evelyn Simpson (Oxford 1925-52) 11 vols (Brief reference—Herford & Simpson).

B. SECONDARY SOURCES

COMEDY: GENERAL AND COMPARATIVE

Levin, Harry 'Two Magian Comedies: *The Tempest* and *The Alchemist*', *Shakespeare Survey* 22 (1969), 47-58.

JONSON CRITICISM

Duncan, Edgar Hill 'Jonson's *Alchemist* and the literature of Alchemy', PMLA 61 (1946), 699-710.

Partridge, Edward B. *The Broken Compass: a study of the major comedies of Ben Jonson* (London 1958).

MOLIÈRE CRITICISM

Cairncross, John *Molière Bourgeois et Libertin* (Paris 1963).

Cairncross, John 'Impie en médecine', *Cahiers de l'association internationales des études françaises* 16 (1965), 269-84.

Chauvois, L. 'Molière, Boileau, La Fontaine et la circulation du sang', *La Presse Medicale* 62 (1954), 1219-20.

Gill, A. '"The Doctor in the Farce" and Molière', *French Studies* 2 (1948), 101-28.

Girard, Joseph *A propos de L'Amour Médecin, Molière et Louis-Henry Daquin* (Paris 1948).

Godlewski, Guy 'Les médecins de Molière et leurs modèles', *La Semaine des Hôpitaux* 46 (1970), 3490-500.

Hubert, J. D. *Molière and the Comedy of Intellect* (Berkeley & Los Angeles 1962).

Jasinski, René 'Sur Molière et la médecine', in *Mélanges de philologie, d'histoire et de littérature offerts à Joseph Vianey* (Paris 1934), pp. 249-54.

Millepierres, François *La Vie Quotidienne des Médecins au temps de Molière* (Paris 1964).

Palmer, John *Molière: his life and work* (London 1930).

OTHER WORKS CITED

Bezançon, G. de *Les médecins à la censure ou entretiens sur la médecine* (Paris 1677).

Lough, John (ed.) *Locke's Travels in France 1675-1679* (Cambridge 1953).

H. T. Barnwell (essay date 1982)

SOURCE: Barnwell, H. T. "Traditions and Conventions" and "Comic Devices and Comic Language." In *Molière: Le Malade imaginaire,* pp. 9-17; 58-68. London: Grant & Cutler, 1982.

[*In the following essays, Barnwell discusses the modern critical challenge of understanding the generic conventions within which* The Imaginary Invalid *operates. Barnwell examines Molière's use of varied comic and linguistic styles, suggesting that much of the comedy of the play arises from the awkward fit between a character's rhetoric and the context in which it is employed.*]

TRADITIONS AND CONVENTIONS

Molière's last play has been the subject of bewilderingly diverse interpretations. Until recently, *Le Malade imaginaire* was not deemed worthy of serious academic study, but was dismissed as a badly-constructed and sometimes gross farce, grouped with a number of others as being fit only for popular entertainment and not to be thought of as a suitable partner for such acknowledged masterpieces as *Tartuffe, Dom Juan* or *Le Misanthrope.* At the other extreme stands André Gide's estimate of the play as achieving 'une grandeur que le théâtre n'a jamais dépassée'. It is perhaps thanks to Jacques Arnavon's edition of *Le Malade imaginaire* that the comedy has now achieved a certain respectability, but he could treat it seriously only if it were mutilated in such a way as to become an altogether 'serious' play, without farcical elements and without the ballet sequences. The tradition of ignoring the latter has persisted, both in editions and even in sensitive and generous studies of Molière's work, like W. G. Moore's, presumably because they are thought of as extraneous to the comedy proper or as having outlived their ephemeral importance as part of a seventeenth-century Court entertainment.

While it is true that the first Prologue, in particular, may be difficult to stage convincingly within modern theatrical conventions, the spirit of the play as Molière presented it can be grasped only through some understanding of it. By 1672, when the comedy was being written, Molière had acted for a number of years as a provider for the Court of Louis XIV of entertainments which took the form of *comédies-ballets,* and he had collaborated with the Florentine musician, Lulli, who composed the music. *Le Malade imaginaire,* the Prologue tells us, was conceived as a *comédie-ballet* to celebrate the King's victories in the Low Countries in the summer of 1672, and to be performed in his presence as a *divertissement* and a *délassement* during the season of Carnival (the weeks immediately preceding Lent) in the following year. It so happened, however, that Molière's association with Lulli came to an abrupt end and, since the composer had secured for himself a monopoly of musical entertainments for the Court, the dramatist had to seek the collaboration of Marc-Antoine Charpentier and to resign himself to putting on the first performance, on 10th February 1673, at the public theatre of the Palais Royal. (The first Court performance did not take place, at Versailles, until eighteen months later.)

The facts that Molière's partnership with Lulli had ceased and that the dramatist, after playing the part of Argan, was taken home to die from the fourth performance have tended to obscure its nature and conception as a *divertissement* and to encourage the most sombre and bitter interpretations, as though the playwright foresaw exactly what his fate would be and as though its hero were, like himself, really a sick and perhaps a dying man. Elaborate and learned hypotheses have been erected, on evidence—biographical and historical—external to the play, in order to demonstrate that Molière's purpose was to make a satirical attack on medicine and doctors. Much patient research has been devoted to the discovery of his sources and of the genesis of the comedy. Ingenious attempts have been made to put it into one of the artificial, academically constructed categories: *comédie d'intrigue, de mœurs, de caractère.* When it has refused to fit, it has been condemned as a loosely constructed hybrid, unworthy of the great artist who created it.

Thanks to the pioneering work of W. G. Moore and René Bray, however, we have begun in the last thirty years or so to see Molière in a different light, not as a didactic social commentator or moral satirist or profound psychologist, nor even as the exponent of 'classical' comedy (however that may be understood), but as an infinitely various and flexible actor-manager, producer and writer of comic plays at which we need not feel ashamed to laugh. Laughter need not imply frivolity: on the contrary, it may be the means by which a serious moral vision is conveyed to us, but that is not the same thing as an alleged moral lesson vouchsafed to us by a spokesman for the author in the play or by some edifying dénouement. Yet ever since the eighteenth century commentators have assumed that if Molière (or for that matter Corneille or Racine or La Fontaine) was a 'grand classique', he must be serious in the sense of providing that kind of lesson and edification, and that a work of art conveys its significance by the same means as does a moral tract.

If indeed Molière's aim in *Le Malade imaginaire* is to teach that kind of lesson in that way, then presumably the medium he adopts is satire, and he seeks 'to persuade and convince' and to make his spectators 'agree with him in identifying and condemning behaviour and men he regards as vicious'.[1] As Dryden—a contemporary of Molière—put it, 'the true end of satire is the amendment of vices'. On these assumptions who, in the play, is the author's target? And whom does he hope to correct? If we are to be persuaded, three hundred years later, we need to share his moral and social viewpoint; and if we do not, how is it that the play can still be successfully performed, even—and most clearly—when not adapted to some current psychological or sociological fashion?

These questions are not rhetorical. The following pages represent an attempt to answer them by asking a different set of questions based on quite other assumptions

The production of The Imaginary Invalid *in the gardens of the Chateau de Versailles, 1674.*

and, in particular, the assumption that Molière was essentially an artist and a man of the theatre, and that going to the theatre implies on the part of the spectator a willingness and a desire to catch a vision of life which depends not on direct observation and mimicry of life as it is, in the street outside, but on imagination and fantasy in the strict sense which does not suggest mere waywardness or formlessness.

Reading and studying the play are not of course the same thing as going to see it performed, but we must not lose sight of the fact that it was written for the stage and that any satisfactory reading must be directed towards an imaginary performance of which exits and entrances, groupings of actors, gestures and movements, tones of voice and emphases are all parts, like the setting. Molière himself, in the short preface to *L'Amour médecin,* first performed in 1665, makes it clear:

> On sait bien que les comédies ne sont faites que pour être jouées, et je ne conseille de lire celle-ci qu'aux personnes qui ont des yeux pour découvrir, dans la lecture, tout le jeu du théâtre.

Such advice is particularly important for plays like *Le Malade imaginaire* which include a strong visual element, especially in the dance sequences. In *Les Amants magnifiques* (1670), Cléonice introduces the dancers in the following terms (I, 5):

> Ce sont des personnes qui par leurs pas, leurs gestes et leurs mouvements, expriment aux yeux toutes choses; et on appelle cela pantomimes

—that is to say mimes. But the gestures and movements of the actors in a play speak as eloquently as their words to the spectator, real or imaginary.

Le Malade imaginaire: Comédie mêlée de musique et de danse. So runs the full title of the play: in other terms a *comédie-ballet*, a play in a genre virtually invented by Molière in 1661 for the festivities offered by Foucquet to the King at Vaux-le-Vicomte. In the *Avertissement* to ***Les Fâcheux,*** the play in question, Molière tells us that, although he had little time to compose it, he did his best to incorporate the dances into the comedy proper. (Louis XIV was a great lover of dancing and himself an accomplished performer.) Molière's aim was expressed as 'ne faire qu'une seule chose du ballet et de la comédie', but he admits that the attempt was not entirely successful. On more than a dozen subsequent occasions, culminating in his last play, he was to make the same endeavour, and it is on the basis of the remarks of 1661 that we should try to see *Le Malade imaginaire.* We should look for connexions between the dances and the comedy, but not expect to find them uniformly close.

I should interpolate that the modern tradition of ballet is misleading for our purposes. The *ballet de cour,* which came into vogue in the sixteenth century, was a sequence of song, dance and recitation rather tenuously held together by some usually allegorical thread. The spectators were provided with a *livre* or *livret* in which the sung and spoken words were printed, together with an explanation of the dance movements and, sometimes, of their interpretation. It is from the *livret* given to the spectators of 1673 that the first Prologue of our play comes: the second, composed after Molière's death for the Court performance of the following year after the celebratory occasion had passed, need not concern us. The *ballet de cour* was essentially, as its name implies, an aristocratic entertainment and pastime. The Prologue is conceived in the rather formal style appropriate to it, with many repetitions and instrumental interludes (featuring also in the *intermèdes*), which go to give to the three-act comedy a length proportionate to a straight five-act play. Parts of the *intermèdes* may be a kind of parody of the formal style and, therefore, particularly fitting in a comedy. Apart from the special suitability of the ballet to a celebration in honour of Louis XIV, dance, in the form of the masked ball, was of course a feature of the festivities of Carnival. As we shall see, mask and disguise and pretence, in various forms, are also a vital element in the comedy proper as well as in the *intermèdes*. Even if the Prologue, having lost its topicality, can no longer be staged (at least without modification), we ought still to read it in order clearly to understand that the play was conceived as a joyous entertainment and as a fantasy, and not as a dark comedy about hypochondria or real illness or as a satirical attack on the shortcomings of the medical profession.

Although it is tempting to think that comedy necessarily provokes laughter, it has to be remembered that, certainly for Molière and his contemporaries, this was not so. The word *comédie* was generally applied, in the first half of the seventeenth century, to plays, usually in five acts and in verse, involving a complex love-intrigue, featuring mistaken motives and identities, deliberate or unconscious deceptions and conceit-laden language which was frequently, and naturally enough, full of ambiguities and double meanings. In many instances little, other than the absence of public or dynastic issues, distinguished such plays from tragi-comedy. For convenience, this type of play, derived in part from the Spanish *comedia* and the Italian *commedia erudita,* can be called 'literary comedy'. As such, it was of course the

entertainment principally of the educated, those who, provided that they possessed the social graces, polite manners and a lack of pretentiousness, were called 'les honnêtes gens'. Laughter was the prerogative of farce, a form of entertainment beneath the dignity of such people.

But in 1662, Molière produced *L'Ecole des Femmes,* a *comedy* in which he dared to provoke laughter. When the play was attacked by the staider critics, he wrote a defence in two one-act pieces, *La Critique de l'Ecole des Femmes* and *L'Impromptu de Versailles,* in the first of which he admitted that 'c'est une étrange entreprise que celle de faire rire les honnêtes gens', but claimed that, since most spectators had enjoyed the comedy, it must have achieved its purpose: 'Je voudrais bien savoir si la grande règle de toutes les règles n'est pas de plaire'. He had succeeded in his enterprise 'de faire rire des personnes qui nous inspirent du respect, et ne rient que quand ils veulent' (*Critique,* sc. 6; *Impromptu,* sc. 1).

Evidence of this kind points in the direction, not so much of the specific sources on which Molière may have drawn for *Le Malade imaginaire* or any other play, as of the theatrical traditions which he inherited and combined, just as he fused comedy and ballet. In 1660, Somaize called him 'le premier farceur de France'. This was two years after his return from his tours in the provinces and a few months after the success of *Les Précieuses ridicules,* termed a farce by a contemporary, Mlle Desjardins. By then, Molière had written several farces, including what is probably his first surviving play, *La Jalousie du Barbouillé.* These were one-act plays in prose, often gross in their humour, and based on conjugal disputes and quarrels, husbands almost always being threatened with cuckoldry and seeking in vain expert advice from doctors. It has been shown[2] that, even in his most sophisticated comedies—*Le Misanthrope,* for example—Molière made use of aspects of the farce and of his experience as an actor and producer of farces. The actor Montfleury's remark about Molière being the successor of Scaramouche (Scaramuccia) and Molière's presence along with actors of farce and *commedia dell'arte* portrayed in the painting of 1670 in the Comédie Française, reveal another strand which is inextricably bound up with that of farce, the improvised Italian comedy popular in France since the sixteenth century. Inextricably bound up, not only because of close similarities of subject-matter and character (the old setting up obstacles to the marriage of the young, servants—stupid or more usually resourceful (*zanni*)—seeking to outwit their masters with trickery (*lazzi*), doctors volubly pouring out irrelevant advice), but also because, after his return to Paris, Molière shared a theatre with the Italian actors and learnt much from their wonderfully expressive style of acting. The fusion of farce and *commedia dell'arte* can perhaps be seen to be symbolised in the presence, in *Les Précieuses ridicules,* of Jodelet, the *enfariné* of farce, side by side with Mascarille, the mask of the *commedia*. The simplicity of plot in both genres, the recurrence of certain roles and characters, as well as of situations and episodes, all with infinite variations, the liveliness of action and dialogue, the verbal inventiveness and the humour are to be found in all Molière's plays from 1662 onwards, even if the formal basis of the 'great' comedies appears to lie in literary comedy at which he had also by then tried his hand.[3] The paradox is that in the 'great' plays the farcical foundation is made to serve a seriousness far deeper than that of earlier literary comedy, even when in some form the outward characteristics of farce (caricature, beatings-up, slapstick and the like) survive. One of the most persistent of those characteristics is the doctor-figure—he need not always be a doctor: see Alceste in *Le Misanthrope* or Philaminte in *Les Femmes savantes*—for which Molière had, in Métaphraste in *Le Dépit amoureux* as early as 1656, fused the loquacious doctor of the *commedia dell'arte* with the professional, wordy, sentfrom the tradition of the pedant of the *commedia erudita*.[4]

If, as many do, applying to comedy the Aristotelian criteria of strict logic and verisimilitude appropriate to tragedy, we find the plot of *Le Malade imaginaire* slender and episodic (though I shall suggest that its structure is solid if approached from another viewpoint), then that aspect of the play owes nothing to literary comedy in which contrivance of a dénouement to solve the intricate problems of the plot was a *sine qua non*. It clearly stems from the farcical tradition (French and Italian), as do Molière's manner of creating a character dominated by a single obsessive characteristic, fixed and unchanging like the mask, the dupe being gulled and fleeced by the tricksters who assail him in a succession of varying situations, usually contrived by themselves, the verbal play (repetitions, variations, mimicry, etc.), and the comic portrayal of domestic dissension. Although the problem of the plot which the play must solve concerns the marriage of Angélique, this is only the occasion for the family dissension and its causes in which our interest, and Molière's, really lies. In the *Argument* at the head of the *Ballet du Roi* in *Le Mariage forcé* (1664), Molière writes:

> Comme il n'y a rien au monde qui soit si commun que le mariage, et que c'est une chose sur laquelle les hommes ordinairement se tournent le plus en ridicule, il n'est pas merveilleux que ce soit toujours la matière de la plupart des comédies, aussi bien que des ballets, qui sont des comédies muettes; et c'est par là qu'on a pris l'idée de cette comédie-mascarade.

It is not in the fortunes of young love, in which perhaps the only comic possibility is the lovers' tiff ('le dépit amoureux') that Molière finds his subject-matter (though it does feature, for example, in *Tartuffe* and *Le Bourgeois gentilhomme*), but in family life after marriage (in *Le Malade imaginaire* after a second marriage). This theme is infinitely rich, as Molière says, in comic possibilities (which can be exploited also in ballet), even if one of its perpetual manifestations is the conflict between strong and sometimes wayward wife and weak husband (as in *George Dandin, Le Bourgeois gentilhomme, Les Femmes savantes* . . . , as well as in *Le Malade imaginaire*). Such conflict, based on living reality and rooted in a particular form of society in which the man was supposed to be the respected head of the family to whom wife and children ought to give loyalty and obedience, is full of dramatic as well as comic potentialities, and it was from the tradition of farce that Molière took and developed it.

A conflict of this kind lies at the heart of *Le Malade imaginaire,* as we shall see. Make the husband weak-willed and wilful, the prey to an obsession, put him in comfortable financial circumstances, surround him with members of his family some of whom wish to save him from himself or at least his children from unhappiness, and others—in particular his wife, partly abetted by intruding charlatans—who seek to exploit him for material gain even at the expense of the children, and you have the essentially farcical basis[5] on which in this play Molière has elaborated, thanks partly to his borrowings from other comic genres and partly to his own inventiveness and his insights into human nature. If we begin from this point, which is the theatrical reality of Molière's professional life (the only part of his life of which we really know anything for certain), and not from some arbitrarily imposed idea about satire or autobiography, moral didacticism or psychological drama, we shall perhaps see that Molière has created a perfectly coherent *comédie-ballet* which, far from being a crude farce provoking laughter and nothing more, is a highly sophisticated play imaginatively suggesting a profound moral vision. The opening of the play, including the Prologue, shall be our starting point.

. . . . .

COMIC DEVICES AND COMIC LANGUAGE

In analysing aspects of plot, structure and characterisation, I have touched upon a number of points connected with the kind of theatrically comic devices and language which feature in *Le Malade imaginaire*—inevitably, because they are integral to the play and not gratuitous or decorative. 'Le style est l'homme même', wrote Buffon, and certainly their style characterises the stage-figures in Molière's plays. The language of the theatre is not, however, the language of everyday life, for three reasons: first, from a purely practical standpoint, the language of ordinary conversation would simply make no more impression on the audience than would the tones of voice of such conversation; second, that language would be inappropriate to something which is itself not a representation of day-to-day reality but an artistic and imaginative transmutation of that reality; and third, if language is to contribute to the total comic effect, one must expect to find in the author, as has been said of Molière, 'la volonté d'outrer les défauts et d'accentuer les ridicules',[6] linguistically as in other respects. Exaggeration of linguistic characteristics may seem to the reader, as opposed to the spectator, to produce crude effects, such as feature in those passages in which Argan's medical treatment is discussed. Yet even those must be seen in their context: the world of his imagination, which he treats so respectfully and, at times, so lyrically, is concerned in fact with the grossest physical realities (see Béline's account in III, 12). The language he uses, derived from the technical jargon of the doctors, is a source of comedy, not simply because it is extravagant, but because the form of the extravagance is so inappropriate to the expression of those realities and masks them in supposedly scientific verbiage. That verbiage, when used by lawyers and doctors, typifies them as members of their professions and indicates their place in society—and that applies even to the final *intermède*—but it is handled in such a way as to make us aware of its deceit: it is empty of real substance. Again we see the incongruity between their extravagant claims and what passes for their expert knowledge. Argan is ridiculous because we are made aware, through the comic action, of his failure to see it and of his entry into the world of extravagance. And language is inseparable from the form of the episodes and of the dramatic situations. In analysing aspects of it, I shall make no attempt to isolate it from them.

Some of the most obvious sources of comic effect are certain kinds of repetition, duplication or deliberate mimicry, all of which suggest an automatism and rigidity alien to the suppleness and adaptability of the life of normal people. The cyclic sequence of some of the episodes in *Le Malade imaginaire* is an important aspect of comic repetition, because it enables Molière to represent the mechanical, fixed, predictable nature of the responses of the characters, and particularly of Argan; but the fact that the repetition is never exact in form draws attention all the more clearly to that fixity.

Examples occur quite early in the play. Part of Act I, scene 5 is a second version of Toinette's provocation of Argan's anger in scene 2. Anger is established as his automatic response to contradiction. It is characteristic of the self-centred 'imaginaire', but it is comic precisely by virtue of being mechanical, and Toinette knows it. The terms of abuse addressed to her are one important factor in the automatism. In the same Act, one of the farcical episodes derived from the *lazzi* of *commedia dell'arte*—Argan, the invalid, being physically provoked (358-79)—is repeated, with variations, in the presence of Béline (432-46): on both occasions

his anger enables him to exert himself in spite of his alleged weakness, just as his departure in the usual direction is so precipitate on one occasion (III, 1) that Toinette has to remind him to pick up his walking-stick, itself a reminder of his asking for it earlier (I, 3), the stick having been picked up in the meantime as a weapon with which to strike her (363-64). All these things and others like them are on one level farcical and purely laughter-provoking, but they also contribute to our comic perception of Argan's behaviour and are not, as are their equivalents in the *lazzi*,[7] gratuitous improvisations contrived simply to enliven a flagging action: they are integrated into the comic action because they express the character himself and arise from the attempts to dupe or to save him.

The most elaborate example occurs in the mock-doctor scenes of Act III, which are also a parody—and therefore a partial repetition—of the real-doctor episode of Act II. In spite of the sheer fun, these scenes, too, are integral to the action, moving it on from the desertion of Fleurant and Purgon towards the solution of the dramatic problem in Argan's acceptance of and involvement in the final ceremony; and they demonstrate, in the most theatrical manner, the grip on him of his imagination.

The solution of the dramatic problem, that of the marriage of Angélique, is twofold. First, Argan the 'imaginaire' being incurable, a way has to be found of using his imagination so as to make Cléante acceptable as a son-in-law and to provide a substitute for the departed doctors: the substitute is partly in Toinette's impersonation, partly in the final ceremony which will also turn Cléante, so Argan believes, as well as himself, into the much-desired doctor. Second, it is equally important both to reconcile Argan to Angélique and to make him well disposed to her marriage: her true feelings for him must be revealed, as must those of Béline, so that the work of disinheritance can be prevented or undone. Argan must be deceived with regard to the new doctors and undeceived with regard to his family. The means adopted for both processes is the same: pretence.

The undeceiving (III, 11-14), its counterpart, follows immediately upon the deceiving (III, 8-10), a parallel without direct repetition, and one in which the part played by Argan is reversed. In the deceiving, he is the victim of the trick played; in the undeceiving, he is its agent. In different ways, his imagination is being played upon in both episodes—the old farcical idea of 'le trompeur trompé' being turned round into 'le trompé trompeur'. The parallel is, however, more complex than that suggests, because in 'le trompé trompeur' is expressed the change from Argan's being taken in by Louison's shamming to Béline's and Angélique's (and not Louison's) being fooled by his.

Such parallels and symmetries, both aesthetically satisfying and consistent with the dramatic and comic function of the play, are also instanced in Argan's repeated outbursts of anger whenever the course of his delusion is disturbed: the intrusion of domestic reality into the world of the doctors (I, 1-2); the discovery of Angélique's love for Cléante when acquiescence in the projected marriage to Thomas Diafoirus is expected (I, 5), etc. The sudden changes from affability to anger are in their turn paralleled by that in the doctors, all sweetness and light when Argan is the compliant dupe (II, 5-6) but quite the reverse when he is not (III, 4-5).

His predictability is exploited by the other characters and our expectation of it raised when, on three successive occasions, Toinette and Béralde play the impresario: their common capacity for so doing is an important factor in their mutual understanding and their alliance. When Toinette announces the arrival of the doctors (II, 4), she enters into the spirit of Argan's exaggerated respect for them (comically contrasted—see the stage direction, 'par dérision'—with her real feelings: 868-73) and arranges a ceremonial entry, which duly takes place. Parallel to this are her announcement of her own entry as doctor (III, 7-8) and Béralde's ushering in of the dancers before the second and third *intermèdes*. On each occasion, but in different ways, Argan's imagination is being played upon, always with predictable—and therefore laughable—success.

Indeed, so eager is he to put himself at its service that, when Diafoirus comes on the scene, he becomes involved in a 'dialogue de sourds' in which the two men talk simultaneously. On the one hand, this is comic because they behave like mechanical toys which have been wound up and put down together and go on working each in its own independent way. On the other, each pursues relentlessly, because self-centredly, his own greeting, but at the same time, if all the little pieces of the speeches are put together in the order in which they are printed, they make a different kind of sense, though not always perfectly coherent:[8] three lines develop simultaneously, Argan's, Diafoirus's and the combined one, of which neither is aware. A comic perception is conveyed through the laughter, of the perversion of language: it is free to go its own way in spite of the single-mindedness of the speakers, and they are not in control of it.

Immediately afterwards, Thomas delivers himself of the first of his prepared speeches: this is a different kind of automatism, the mechanical repetition of verbiage learnt by heart: Toinette's ironical comment (939; cf. 965-66, 970-71, 1181-83) draws the comic contrast between appearance and reality. The divorce between the realms of appearance (to which the doctors belong) and of reality is evident in the way in which Thomas addresses Angélique as his future mother-in-law (945-46). The actual words have no meaning for him—they are made up of distorted and disparate bits and pieces from Cicero and commonplaces of literary rhetoric—and he fails to perceive either the reality of the girl the fathers propose he should marry—although she is there, in front of him—or the incongruity of the language he has learnt by heart. The rote learning is itself rendered comic by the way in which, having delayed the entry of Béline, Molière arranges for the mechanism to start again in the following scene—when it breaks down. The mechanical nature of the greetings, emphasised by the false starts and the breakdown, is made comic by our attention being drawn to what Bergson calls the form of the social ceremonial and away from its substance. The ceremonial becomes meaningless, 'une mascarade sociale', inert, contrived, ready-made.[9]

These episodes follow hard on the heels of Cléante's arrival at the house and his greeting of Argan. This, too, is comic not simply because, as has been said, 'you cannot tell a hypochondriac that he is looking well',[10] but because Cléante, too, is merely repeating conventional social formulas without being aware or without taking account of the reality of the person in front of him. Thomas Diafoirus's error may be more gross—and is the more laughable for following Cléante's—but it is of the same kind and springs also from mechanical behaviour. Cléante, however, quickly recovers (though he will appear to make another mistake later (2167-68), when he inverts the medical hierarchy) and demonstrates his adaptability and quickwittedness in the remainder of the conversation with Argan and in the singing-lesson. Unaware of it though he is, Argan is greeted by the bogus doctor in a deliberately inverted way: instead of the doctor being famous (what, in real life, one would expect), the patient is 'un illustre malade' who has a great reputation (1910-13) and is evidently worth a doctor's visit. The relationship between these parallel episodes is complex: each throws light on the other in such a way as to draw attention to empty automatism and to present, in the last case, a parody which escapes Argan's notice—except that he is flattered by it.

That automatism is comic not simply because it is mechanical and made to seem inconsistent with the flexibility of real life but because, very often, it is meaningless. When talking about his 'illness' and its treatment, Argan merely repeats the forms of words he has memorised. We actually see Thomas Diafoirus going through the process of automatically producing the theoretical answers to questions put to him in a diagnosis. He is learning his trade. In all such cases the expression bears a false relation or no relation to the reality.[11] It is mere words.

Another type of repetition occurs, as we saw earlier, in modes of address and terms of endearment. The dialogues between Argan and Béline (I, 6-7) are the most important instance. On the one hand, Argan repeatedly utters 'mamie', 'mon coeur', 'mamour', and means what he says. On the other, Béline uses similar expressions to encourage him in the mistaken belief that she loves him. Both the deception and the error are finally dissipated when it is Argan who adopts the pretence (III, 12) and addresses his wife simply as 'Madame ma femme' (2104) while she makes no reply at all. Further aspects of the comedy of the earlier dialogues are seen in Béline's use of the expressions, 'mon fils', 'pauvre petit fils' (the maternal pose adopted by a wife much younger than her husband) and in the contrast between Argan's language of endearment addressed to the wife who is a fraud and that of abuse to the servant who is honest.

Then the scenes between husband and wife are echoed in Argan's conversation with Louison (II, 8—immediately afterwards), first in the girl's repetition of 'mon papa' with all the variations of feeling from security and affection to dismay and contrition, and then in Argan's insistent 'Hé bien?' and 'Et puis après?', the latter being repeated by his daughter. These elements, together with the similarities of rhythm and length of phrase and sentence, constitute part of what has been called the 'ballet des mots'[12]—another connexion between the ballet sequences and the comedy proper—which puts the emphasis on theatricality rather than realism and suggests mimicry, whether conscious or not, and lessons in good manners being as carefully observed as the medical formulations. Like other aspects of the play we have studied, the repetitions and variations form a pattern. They are akin to musical counterpoint and fugue.

The most remarkable example is in Argan's altercation with Purgon (III, 5). This scene falls into two main parts, the first for three voices (Argan, Purgon, Toinette: 1762-1817), the second for two (Argan, Purgon: (1818-35). In the first, Purgon utters complete phrases and sentences, relentlessly pursued despite Argan's short attempted (and always incomplete) interruptions, while Toinette interpolates laconic comments[13] putting the blame for the situation on Argan. The pattern is perfectly regular (as it is throughout the scene), Purgon having twice as many (and twice as long) speeches as the other speakers (voluble self-importance of the traditional doctor—and his refusal to listen), while the counterpoint, as it were, is provided alternately and in different directions by Argan and Toinette. Purgon's theme reaches its climax and Toinette withdraws (1817). Then follow the curses and Argan's repeated cries of despair and supplication: the pattern is exactly that of a litany, with variations in the petitions (here the curses) though not in their form, uniformity in the responses. This is of course entirely appropriate because Argan really does hold the doctors and their powers in religious awe, as we have already seen ('les ordonnances de la médecine',

etc.) and his cries of 'Monsieur Purgon!' are the exact equivalent of the 'miserere mei'.

Purgon's curses take the form of a sequence of names of illnesses, all Greek in origin and all ending in -ie, but the climax falls into bathos (1834-35) when the last words are no longer learned compounds but simple words of everyday speech with the same ending, vie and folie, which return Argan from fantasy to reality—and terrify him. Still, however, 'la privation de la vie' is a circumlocution for 'la mort' (the verbosity persists), and the irony is that if Argan were to die it would certainly be thanks to his 'folie' (madness of the 'imaginaire' as well as simple foolishness)—but not, as Purgon thinks, the folly of refusing medical treatment, rather that of accepting its surfeit. Highly farcical though the episode is in concept, it is also a most complex and sophisticated piece of writing, marking an important development in the action and putting the behaviour of both doctor and patient in a comic perspective.

Pascal's remark—'Deux visages semblables, dont aucun ne fait rire en particulier, font rire ensemble par leur ressemblance'[14]—applies not only to faces but to acts and words and suggests the mechanism that is at work in such examples as this. But resemblances run in families, and Thomas Diafoirus is very much a younger version of his father, showing what the father was like in his own student days, and the father showing what the son will eventually become. Angélique is also a younger version of her father in her persistence and outspokenness, but he does not show us what she will become because she is without his mania. Resemblances run in professions, too, and Purgon's jargon (III, 5) echoes that of Fleurant (his bill in I, 1), but with violence, and that of Diafoirus (II, 6). Such resemblances are comic (and in the case of the doctors are accentuated by their garb) because they reveal habit which has become unthinking and mechanical.

The middle scenes of Act II are important in this respect. The two fathers resemble each other in their unheeding pursuit of their own greetings, as we have seen, as well as in their determination to marry their children off and their anxiety to put them on show. But the children's behaviour is strongly contrasted. Thomas can only mouth what he has learnt by heart and, in direct dialogue with Angélique, import into his would-be wooing the syllogistic and formulaic rhetoric of his studies. She, on the other hand, is straightforward and direct, and speaks her own mind in her own language. This immediately follows the scene in which she and Cléante have improvised their musical duet: that it expresses something spontaneous and natural beneath the appearance of artificiality is evident even to Argan (1124-25—he speaks truer than he knows—and 1160-62). We are allowed to perceive the comedy of the contrast between the mechanical, empty use of convention and its adaptable, significant use. Closely allied to it is of course the use of jargon: the love-duet is couched in conventional, stylised language (the jargon of *préciosité*, with its 'appas', 'transports', 'supplices', etc.) but is made to express an authentic emotion, whereas the ready-made formulas of the doctors—another convention—, whether those of their profession or, in the case of Thomas, those of courtship, are mere words acquired at second hand and signifying nothing; but they are sufficiently impressive to dupe Argan, as Béralde clearly sees (1614-45). The difference is that between the mask deliberately donned to communicate something real in secret and the mask unconsciously worn to say openly something without substance.

We are made aware, through this kind of contrast, of the gap between artificial verbiage and real experience which was particularly perceptible and comic to the 'honnêtes gens' whose rejection of jargon of any kind had been expressed in the doctrines of Malherbe and Vaugelas. But so much an 'imaginaire' is Argan that he accepts literally what Béralde, having drawn the distinction between 'les discours' and 'les choses' (1675-79), finally says: 'L'on n'a qu'à parler; avec une robe et un bonnet, tout galimatias devient savant, et toute sottise devient raison' (2188-89). It is no wonder that Argan is taken in by the verbal fantasies of Fleurant (I, 1) or by their parody by Toinette (III, 8, 10). In the same way, the comic view is suggested by contradictions between general principles (mental constructs) and particular instances (living realities)[15], especially when Angélique and Argan or Toinette and Argan (I, 5), for instance, or Argan and Béralde (III, 3), agree on the first and differ on the second. In such cases, the argument develops to establish agreement on the general principle and, when it stumbles against a particular reality which does not fit, goes into reverse in the direction of dissension.

Connected with this is the importance of set rules. Thomas Diafoirus observes them in his encomia—and they fail; and in his diagnosis—and it is at variance with that of an experienced doctor. Béralde argues that rules have no bearing on real life (1634-36, 1676-79), while Toinette-as-doctor produces a parody (III, 10) of a diagnosis carried out according to the rules (II, 6) in a parody of Argan's ill-fated dialogue with Purgon: here it is the doctor's repeated phrases which reply to the patient's remarks, and the exclamations ('Ignorant!') are anything but helpless appeals. The pattern of the dialogue closely follows that between Argan and Purgon, but the roles and meaning are turned upside down. At the end, Toinette follows logic to its ridiculous conclusion in her prescription for amputation: at that point Argan does in fact awake to reality—'Oui, mais j'ai besoin de mon bras' (2001)—though only

fleetingly. In *L'Amour médecin* (1665), Bahis had said: 'Il vaut mieux mourir selon les règles que de réchapper contre les règles' (II, 5).

The contradiction between truth and illusion is evident even in the names given to some of the characters. While Fleurant and Purgon are aptly named for what seem to be their principal functions, Bonnefoy's character is suggested by ironical antiphrasis. Béline's activities and Argan's blindness to their real nature are also indicated by her name: 'béline', meaning in Old French 'sheep', came to be used as a term of endearment, the equivalent of Argan's 'mamour', etc. But it surely also gives a clue to her real character and behaviour: the wolf in sheep's clothing. Diafoirus is usually held to suggest 'diarrhoea'. But why not 'diagnosis', since the play features two? Molière may however have derived the name from the Greek 'diaphoros', meaning both 'different' (at variance) and 'excellent', and particularly appropriate to the controversies between the doctors in the play and to their (and Argan's) estimate of their worth. Alternatively, the name could be of mixed and more fanciful derivation: Greek 'dia' ('throughout') and French 'foi' ('faith'—on the part of Argan) and Latin suffix (appropriate to the Latinised jargon of the pedant). All these possibilities suggest contradictions between appearance and reality.

The episodes, the language adopted by the characters, their behaviour, all are in themselves theatrical and have to do with disguise, pretence, illusion, deception. Dressing-up (shepherds, actors of the *commedia dell'arte,* doctors real and unreal), deliberate play-acting within the play (Béline and Bonnefoy, Cléante and Angélique, Louison, Toinette, Argan himself), advancement of false arguments (Béralde), use of empty jargon (the doctors, imitated by Argan) combine to make *Le Malade imaginaire* not only a highly theatrical play but to suggest its theme: the 'imaginaire' duped by deceitful appearance. And it is that theme to which every episode, every dialogue, every word makes an indispensable contribution.

Notes

1. A. Pollard, *Satire* (London, Methuen, 1970), p. 1.

2. See, for example, the articles by Lanson, Lebègue, and Gill.

3. *L'Etourdi* (1655), *Le Dépit amoureux* (1656).

4. See Gill, p. 124.

5. To which Boileau was one of the first to take exception: see *L'Art poétique,* ch. III, 11. 391-400.

6. Larthomas, P. *Le Langage dramatique,* [Paris, Colin, 1972] p. 191.

7. Both Riccoboni (*Histoire du théâtre italien*, Paris, 1728) and Bertoli (*Notizie istoriche dei comici*

italiani, Padua, 1781) emphasise the impromptu nature of the *lazzi,* many of which were stereotypes.

8. Cf. R. McBride, p. 16.

9. [Bergson, Henri] *Le Rire* [*Essai sur la signification du comique* (Paris, Paris, Presses Universitaires de France, 1978; first published, 1900)] pp. 34-35.

10. Q. M. Hope, 'The Scene of Greeting in Molière', *Romanic Review,* L (1950), p. 246.

11. Cf. Bergson, *Le Rire,* p. 30: '. . . l'incompatibilité naturelle entre l'enveloppant et l'enveloppé'.

12. See Garapon, p. 242; Larthomas, *Le Langage dramatatique,* p. 274.

13. Cf. Toinette and Angélique (I, 4). See J. Cameron Wilson, 'Expansion and Brevity in Molière's Style' in *Molière, Stage and Study: Essays in honour of W. G. Moore,* ed. W. D. Howarth and M. Thomas (Oxford University Press, 1973), pp. 93-113.

14. *Pensées,* 13 [in *Œuvres complètes,* ed. L. Lafuma (Paris), Seuil, 1963].

15. See W. G. Moore, 'Molière's Last Word' in *Studies in Romance Philology and French Literature presented to John Orr,* Manchester University Press, 1953, pp. 191-92.

Select Bibliography

Garapon, R. *La Fantaisie verbale et le comique dans le théâtre français.* Paris, Colin, 1957.

Gill, A. 'The Doctor in the Farce'. *French Studies,* II (1948), 101-28.

Lanson, G. 'Molière et la farce'. *Revue de Paris,* 1 May 1901, 129-53.

Lebègue. 'Molière et la farce'. *Etudes sur le théâtre français.* 2 vols. Paris, Nizet, 1978. Vol. II, 50-68.

McBride, R. 'The sceptical view of medicine and the comic vision in Molière'. *Studi Francesi,* 67 (1979), 27-42.

D. J. Adams (essay date March 1983)

SOURCE: Adams, D. J. "A Reading of *Le Malade imaginaire.*" *Modern Languages* 64, no. 1 (March 1983): 42-7.

[*In the following essay, Adams interprets* The Imaginary Invalid *as Molière's bleakest play, a grim response to the human inability to grasp truth.*]

Some years ago, W. G. Moore wrote of Molière that 'he made in fourteen years what it may take over four hundred to make out.'[1] This frank acknowledgement of the difficulties facing anyone who attempts to interpret Molière's plays is merely a modern restatement of a conclusion to which many previous commentators, in their several ways, had already come. Some, like Boileau, were confounded by the scandalous proximity of grotesque buffoonery and comic genius: 'Dans ce sac ridicule où Scapin s'enveloppe / Je ne reconnais plus l'auteur du **Misanthrope.**'[2] Others, like the querulous Sabatier de Castres, were driven to enquire in exasperation:

> Comment avec une Prose si négligée, des vers peu exacts, des caractères outrés, est—il parvenu à se faire regarder, à juste titre, comme le premier Poëte comique de tous les Théâtres connus?[3]

Even when they were more indulgent, critics found Molière hard to fathom. La Harpe declared:

> [. . .] mon voisin et moi nous rions du meilleur coeur du monde de nous voir ou sots, ou faibles, ou impertinens, et nous serions furieux, si on nous disait d'une autre façon la moitié de ce que nous dit Molière. Eh! qui t'avait appris cet art, divin Molière?[4]

When they turned their attention to *Le Malade imaginaire,* commentators showed themselves no less acutely aware of the central paradoxes of form and content. The play offered few footholds to those who, like Voltaire, felt most secure when basing their judgements on traditional literary categories. The considerable limitations dictated by such an approach are evident in his remark that *Le Malade imaginaire* is 'une des farces de Molière dans laquelle on trouve beaucoup de scènes dignes de la haut comédie',[5] which merely reveals the inadequacies of the categories by which such judgements are formulated.

A century or more later, Jules Lemaitre, who was no less conscious than Voltaire of the merits of the play, was troubled not by the challenge which it offered to literary convention, but by the dangerous example which it set before children:

> Je me demande quelle impression bienfaisante et quelle leçon de morale les enfants peuvent bien rapporter du *Malade imaginaire* [. . .] Je doute que cette admirable farce leur ait été une leçon de respect.[6]

Even in more recent times, when commentators such as Jacques Arnavon ceased to concern themselves with affixing labels to the play,[7] problems of another kind readily materialised as critics debated the extent to which the work could be considered autobiographical. Pierre Brisson believed that, in its boundless verve and gaiety, the play betrayed none of the despondency which must have weighed on Molière as his own health inexorably worsened; it was, he concluded, 'le contraire d'une oeuvre—testament sans aucun doute'.[8] Others did not hesitate to draw a somewhat different conclusion. René Benjamin was persuaded that

> Argan, c'est Molière quand il souffre, faible, égoïste, colérique . . . ridicule; Béralde, c'est son portrait, chaque fois qu'il redevient sage, qu'il se sent sauvé, qu'il juge les médecins.[9]

This interpretation does not, however, commend itself to Robert Garapon, who writes: 'Molière s'est bien mis dans sa pièce, mais sous les traits de Béralde, et non d'Argan.'[10]

It would be quite easy, though largely superfluous, to extend this litany of critical responses to *Le Malade imaginaire*; there is already evidence enough that, for two centuries or more, the play has faced commentators with a variety of problems literary, philosophical and autobiographical. What is more, their collective responses do not seem to have produced any interpretation of the play which commands widespread assent. My own view will, I hope, provoke questions in its turn!

I believe that *Le Malade imaginaire* is less a play about hypochondria, or the foibles of 17th century French doctors, than a study of intellectual conflicts and human attitudes to truth. No doubt, one can say as much of many plays by Molière, but these preoccupations are central to *Le Malade,* and the elaboration of them as it progresses provides us with what is perhaps the bleakest of his writings.

The legitimacy of this claim can, I think, be substantiated by an examination of the contribution made to the moral climate of the play even by the minor characters. As W. G. Moore noted, the theme of deception runs throughout it like a seam.[11]

Broadly speaking, the instances in which it is practised can be divided into the benevolent, which result in no real harm to anyone, and the malevolent; examples of each are to be found in the behaviour of the secondary figures. Into the benevolent class fall the musical interlude provided by Angélique and her 'teacher' Cléante (II, 6), and Louison's attempt in II, 11 to ward off her father's anger by pretending to be dead. The significance of this episode is not merely to illustrate that Argan can at times prove more amenable to normal emotions than he generally appears, but also to indicate, as young Louison has appreciated, that, even when played as a game, deception has its uses. In the category of benevolent deceptions one may also include Toinette's attempt to wean Argan away from his mania by disguising herself as a doctor (III, 14).

Malevolent deception reveals itself in Béline's calculated endeavour to milk Argan of his money, in the execution of which she obtains the willing cooperation not only of the victim himself, but of the lawyer Bonnefoi too, who complacently outlines no fewer than three ways in which the law forbidding husbands to leave money to their widows can be circumvented (I, 9), and who admits to having 'des expédients pour passer doucement par—dessus la loi et rendre juste ce qui n'est pas permis.'

The cumulative effect of these varied examples of trickery practised for a variety of ends is to create the impression that it is the normal means of obtaining whatever one seeks, and to undermine to a considerable extent any attempt to derive from the behaviour of the secondary characters the kind of positive moral precepts which it was once customary to regard as the *raison d'être* of any play by Molière. It may be true that the conduct of Angélique and Louison towards Argan is of no great moral importance in itself; it is nevertheless true that their behaviour exemplifies attitudes which are worked out more clearly in the conduct of a far more important character, namely Béralde.

If it is true that no positive moral precepts can be deduced from the actions of the secondary characters, the same can be said more emphatically still for what Béralde has to offer. It is conventional to regard Béralde as a *raisonneur*,[12] whose function is to offer counsels of wisdom to palliate the unbridled eccentricities of Argan. Although, in recent years, the role of the *raisonneur* in Molière has become a matter of some controversy,[13] it is not difficult to understand why commentators should have applied the term to a man who can say 'Je ne vois rien de plus ridicule qu'un homme qui se veut mêler d'en guérir un autre' (III, 3),[14] or 'La nature d'elle—même, quand nous la laissons faire, se tire doucement du désordre où elle est tombée [. . .] presque tous les hommes meurent de leurs remèdes, et non de leurs maladies' (*ibid.*), for such robustly sane ideas can be paralleled in *Le Médecin malgré lui, L'Amour médecin* and *M. de Pourceaugnac,* to say nothing of *Dom Juan,*[15] the protagonist of which tells his scandalised servant that doctors

> ne font rien que de recevoir la gloire des heureux succès, et tu peux profiter comme eux du bonheur du malade, et voir attribuer à tes remèdes tout ce qui peut venir des faveurs du hasard et des forces de la nature.
>
> (II, 1)

Yet there are reasons for rejecting the view that Béralde is a conventional *raisonneur.* In the first place, the very fact that Béralde shares his opinions on doctors with Dom Juan and with the Sganarelle of *Le Médecin malgré lui* ought to give pause to anyone who insists that such views alone are enough to qualify him as a *raisonneur*: a category which is elastic enough to include without difficulty three diverse characters such as these is clearly not of great use in establishing the principal characteristics of the *raisonneur.*

In the second, Béralde's comments do not, on the whole, fit the pattern established by the 'reasonable' characters in other plays, for their advice is generally more positive in tone than his. In *Le Tartuffe,* Cléante defines precisely the 'dévots de coeur':

> Ils attachent leur haine au péché seulement,
> Et ne veulent point prendre avec un zele extreme
> Les intérêts du ciel plus qu'il ne veut lui—meme.
> Voilà mes gens, voilà comment il en faut user,
> Voilà l'exemple enfin qu'il faut se proposer.

(I, 5)

In *L'Ecole des Femmes,* Chrysalde bluntly admonishes Arnolphe:

> . . . qui rit d'autrui
> Doit craindre qu'en revanche on rie aussi de lui . . .
> Et l'on ne doit jamais jurer, sur de tels cas,
> De ce qu'on pourra faire ou bien ne faire pas.

(I, 1)

Philinte cautions Alceste in *Le Misanthrope*: '. . . parfois, n'en déplaise à votre austère honneur, Il est bon de cacher ce qu'on a dans le coeur'. (I, 1)

In contrast, Béralde's advice to Argan is characterised not by positive injunctions and precise guidance on the best conduct to be adopted if one is to succeed in the world, but rather by a refusal to dogmatise on any subject:

> [. . .] les ressorts de notre machine sont des mystères, jusques ici, où les hommes ne voient goutte, et [. . .] la nature nous a mis au—devant des yeux des voiles trop épais pour y reconnaître quelque chose [. . .] Moi, mon frère, je ne prends point à tâche de combattre la médecine, et chacun, à ses périls et fortune, peut croire tout ce qu'il lui plaît.

(III, 3)

The *raisonneur* whose reasoning is largely negative is not a typical Molière character; Béralde's pyrrhonism, with its echoes of Montaigne[16], seems to me to contribute, albeit in a different fashion, to the undermining of any positive moral doctrines the play might offer which is one of the principal contributions of the minor characters to whom attention has been drawn. One might add that Béralde's willingness to practise on Argan a deception which leads him to suppose that he is being inducted into the Faculty of Medicine (III, 23) forges, in the final moments of the play, a strong link between the pyrrhonist who carefully refrains from enunciating any moral values, and the characters of Angélique and Cléante who, having once pulled the wool over Argan's eyes, are induced, after only a brief moment of hesitation, to lend themselves to this second piece of dupery.

Béralde's categorical refusal to acquiesce in the superiority which doctors claim to enjoy over ordinary morals leads him not only into this last-minute alliance with Angélique and Cléante, but also, and more significantly for the action of the play into a sympathetic understanding with Toinette, who, like Béralde, makes no secret of her distrust of doctors when speaking to Argan:

> Ce monsieur Fleurant—là et ce monsieur Purgon s'égayent bien sur votre corps; ils ont en vous une bonne vache à lait, et je voudrais bien leur demander quel mal vous avez pour vous faire tant de remèdes.

(I, 2)

Yet I believe that Molière's purpose in allowing Béralde and Toinette to share a hostility towards the doctors who surround Argan is not merely to enable them to unite their forces in a common attack, but to demonstrate the relationship between Argan and his doctors which has its culmination in the climactic ceremony arranged by Béralde himself.

Both Béralde and Toinette exhibit attitudes which bring them into conflict with authority either in the person of the doctors or in that of Argan himself. M. Fleurant cannot permit Béralde to advise Argan against taking the clyster he has prescribed:

> De quoi vous mêlez—vous de vous opposer aux ordonnances de la médecine et d'empêcher monsieur de prendre mon clystère? Vous êtes bien plaisant d'avoir cette hardiesse—là.

(III, 4)

The same irritated resentment at the interference of a third party who will not defer to superior authority is evident in Toinette's debate with Argan on Angélique's marriage:

A:

> Je lui commande absolument de se préparer à prendre le mari que je dis.

T:

> Et moi je lui défends absolument d'en faire rien.

A:

> Où est—ce donc que nous sommes? Et quelle audace est—ce là à une coquine de servante de parler de la sorte devant son maître?

T:

> Quand un maître ne songe pas à ce qu'il fait, une servante bien sensée est en droit de le redresser.

(I, 5)[17]

A dislike of having their authority questioned is not the only characteristic which the doctors share with Argan: neither they nor he can readily accept evidence which conflicts with cherished beliefs. As M. Diafoirus tells Argan à propos of Thomas:

> Mais, sur toute chose, ce qui me plaît en lui, et en quoi il suit mon exemple, c'est qu'il s'attache aveuglément aux opinions de nos anciens, et que jamais il n'a voulu comprendre ni écouter les raisons et les expériences des prétendues découvertes de notre siècle touchant la circulation du sang et autres opinions de la même farine.
>
> (II, 5)

In spite of the plethora of learned articles which this speech has provoke,[18] it is not necessary to be equipped with a knowledge of 17th century French medical controversies in order to evaluate M. Diafoirus' words. What matters far more for an understanding of the play is the attitude which underlies them. I believe it is this blind adherence to theory, irrespective of facts, which Béralde has in mind when he claims that Molière is attacking not 'les médecins' but 'le ridicule de la médecine' (III, 3), a comment which in itself ought to have turned many commentators away from the temptation to dismiss the doctors merely as charlatans. So far as one can tell, the Diafoirus and their associates hold their beliefs in all sincerity, and their conduct is no more to be explained away as a sustained confidence-trick than Argan's certainty that he is ill can be ascribed to a persistent wish to deceive his doctors. On the contrary, they and he organise the greater part of their lives around the conviction that they know the truth, and that it cannot be impugned by the facts of experimental science or of everyday experience. Hence Argan's infuriated rejection of Toinette's sceptical question:

T:

> Mais, monsieur, mettez la main à la conscience. Est—ce que vous êtes malade?

A:

> Comment, coquine, si je suis malade? si je suis malade, impudente!
>
> (I, 5; cf. III, 4)

Although Argan does retain sufficient lucidity to decline to pay his doctors' bills (I, 1), or to reject the advice proffered in III, 10 by Toinette disguised as a doctor, such reactions do not change in any essential respect his quite manifest *need* to go on believing that he is ill.

Like the Diafoirus *père et fils,* Argan cannot face the idea that the world could be other than as he chooses to see it; none of them can face the idea of change, none of them is willing to examine alternative views of the subjects closest to their hearts, and all reject out of hand whatever does not correspond to the reassuringly familiar view of life to which they cling. With such a disposition, Argan is obviously an excellent candidate for induction into a Faculty of Medicine which numbers among its ornaments M. Diafoirus and his son.

What conclusions, then, are to be drawn from these considerations? It is clearly not sufficient to regard *Le Malade imaginaire* as merely an attack on pretention, self-importance and duplicity, though undeniably such human shortcomings are not to Molière's taste. Nor is it enough to see the play as yet another study of eccentricity in the person of Argan, for he has too much in common with his doctors for us to dismiss out of hand the parallels between them. The play is, rather, a blend of these things: Molière gives us on the one hand the scepticism of Béralde and Toinette, the one founded on a deeper pyrrhonism, the other on native good sense, though neither has any very positive ideas to offer; on the other hand, he gives us the crass authoritarianism and resistance to change of any kind exhibited by the doctors and by Argan. That is to say, *Le Malade imaginaire* offers a choice between refusal to believe in anything, and a dogmatism whose drawbacks are all to apparent.

It is this stark alternative which, I believe, lies at the core of *Le Malade imaginaire,* and which explains why the play is so disturbing and yet so tantalisingly unclear behind its substantial veneer of comedy. To interpret it as I have tried to do requires us to make some unsuspected connections between characters and to dismiss some traditional assumptions not the least unsatisfactory aspect of which is they have not led to a wholly convincing understanding of the work.

I want, finally, to suggest one further parallel. I believe that Molière is addressing himself, in his fashion, to a problem which, only a few years previously, Pascal had made one of the central preoccupations of the *Pensées,* where it is written:

> Je m'arrête à l'unique fort des dogmatistes, qui est qu'en parlant de bonne foi et sincèrement, on ne peut douter des principes naturels. Contre quoi les pyrrhoniens opposent en un mot l'incertitude de notre origine, qui enferme celle de notre nature; à quoi les dogmatistes sont encore à répondre depuis que le monde dure.
>
> Voilà la guerre ouverte entre les hommes, où il faut que chacun prenne parti, et se range necessairement ou au dogmatisme, ou au pyrrhonisme [. . .] Que fera donc l'homme en cet état?[19]

Pascal's answer to this dilemma was that men should turn to the truths of the Christian religion. In *Malade imaginaire,* Molière omits to indicate any middle way between dogmatism and disbelief. It is for this reason that his last play, its uproarious comedy notwithstanding, is also his most despondent.

Notes

1. *French Classical Literature* (Oxford, 1961), p. 82.

2. *L'Art poétique* (1674), Chant troisième, 11. 399-400, *Oeuvres* (Paris, 1740), II, 305.

3. *Les trois siècles de la littérature francaise,* quatrième édition, 4 vols (Paris, 1779), III, 128.

4. *Idées sur Molière, Oeuvres,* 6 vols (Paris, 1778), IV, 60-61.

5. *Vie de Molière* (1739), *Oeuvres,* ed. Beaumarchais *et al.,* 70 vols (Kehl, 1784-87), XLVII, 177.

6. Quoted by Yves Hucher in his edition of *Le Malade imaginaire* (Paris, 1970), p. 167.

7. See his *'Le Malade imaginaire' de Molière* (Paris, 1947), *passim.*

8. Quoted by Hucher, p. 167.

9. Ibid.

10. *Le dernier Molière. Des 'Fourberies de Scapin' au 'Malade imginaire'* (Paris, 1977), p. 155.

11. See his *Molière: a new criticism* (Oxford, 1949), pp. 75-76; Moore is concerned, however, to show that the deception practised by the minor characters centres upon Argan, and he does not explore their contribution to the moral problems of the play.

12. See Robert McBride, *Aspects of seventeenth-century French Drama and Thought* (London, 1979), p. 74.

13. Cf. ibid, and Moore, *French Classical Literature,* pp. 82, 87.

14. *Oeuvres de Molière,* ed. Georges Couton, 2 vols (Paris, 1971) II, 1152. All references are to this edition.

15. Respectively in III, I; II, 2, 3, 4; I, II, etc.

16. '[. . .] condamner [. . .] une chose pour fauce et impossible, c'est se donner l'avantage d'avoir dans la teste les bornes et limites de la volonté de Dieu et de la puissance de nostre mere nature; et [. . .] il n'y a point de plus notable folie au monde que de les ramener à la mesure de nostre capacité et suffisance' (I, XXVII, *C'est folie de rapporter le vray et le faux à nostre suffisance, Montaigne: Selected Essays,* ed. Tilley & Boase (Manchester, 1962), p. 9).

17. 'Toinette [est] la plus téméraire des servantes de la grande comédie' (Marcel Gutwirth, *Molière ou l'invention comique* (Paris, 1966), p. 54).

18. Cf. Couton, II, pp. 1078-80, and the *Oeuvres de Molière,* ed. Maurice Rat, 2 vols (Paris, 1956), II, 1022.

19. *Pensées,* ed. Léon Brunschvicg (Paris, 1964), No. 434. The comparison of Pascal and Molière is not as far-fetched as might be thought: Sainte-Beuve writes: 'Pascal et *Les précieuses ridicules,* ce sont les deux grands précédents modernes et les modèles de Despréaux. Pascal avait flétri le mauvais goût dans le sacré, Molière le frappait dans le profane' (*Port-Royal,* troisième édition, 7 vols (Paris, 1867), V, 486-87). Cf. Alfred Simon, *Molière par lui-même* (Paris, 1865), p. 79.

Carol A. Mossman (essay date spring 1986)

SOURCE: Mossman, Carol A. "The Restitution of Paternity in Molière's *Le Malade imaginaire.*" *South Central Review* 3, no. 1 (spring 1986): 50-6.

[*In the following essay, Mossman reads the action of the play as an unraveling and eventual restoration of the traditional family structure. Mossman contends that in following this pattern,* The Imaginary Invalid *is unique among Molière's plays.*]

It is remarkable indeed that in his final play, **Le Malade imaginaire,** Molière should have introduced three elements hitherto unexploited by him in his theater. To an already well-established cast of characters, the playwright chose to add two new roles: that of the child, Louison, and her "evil" stepmother, Béline. It will be seen that the dramatic functions of these two new roles are interrelated and, to a great extent, the play's main character, Argan the invalid, is only defined in juxtaposition to them. These women and a third new ingredient—the Oedipal nature of the discourse linking husband to wife—conspire to dismantle that family structure which forms the pillars upon which Molière had erected his theatrical edifice.

Argan may well be listed as the *pater familias* in the cast of characters, but he functions in the play as a child. At last, the monomania and egocentrism typical of all Molière's tyrant-fathers has been taken to such an extreme as to become subversive: if dramatic resolution in **L'Avare** or **Tartuffe** depends on mitigating a paternal authority which has become exaggerated to monstrous proportions, *dénouement* in **Le Malade imaginaire** will depend on restoring Argan to his fatherly status in order that the "healthy" marriage of his daughter, Angélique, to her suitor, Cléante, may go forward according to the natural scheme of things.

The Arganian illusion of regression into childhood, though internally created, as we shall see, is reinforced from the exterior. From the first, the spectator is plunged into a fantasy as the play opens on a pastoral scene in which shepherdesses, fauns, and Pan are all beckoned to attend this play which, as a *comédie-ballet,* is punctuated with musical interludes. The instructional virtues which form the *sine qua non* of morally-acceptable fiction of seventeenth-century France thus blend periodically with the *divertissement* to suggest a certain diversion from and distortion of reality.

The possibility of illusion is subsequently perpetuated by two dreams which are invoked during the course of the play, first by the eligible daughter, Angélique, and later by Béralde, Argan's brother and the inevitable proponent of moderation and rational behavior who declares that "it is like those lovely dreams which, on waking, leave us only with the displeasure of having believed them" (III.iii).[1] And yet this is the very sort of illusion which Béralde himself will orchestrate in the burlesque finale during which the imaginary invalid is inducted into the august medical corps, exchanging one illusion for another.

Thus, notwithstanding the scatological nature of Argan's malady, which admittedly betokens a certain realism, *Le Malade imaginaire* shares borders with fantasy. In fact, one might even maintain that the world of fairy tale stands behind the play as an intertext. The anomalous presence of a child, Louison, coupled with that of a scheming and usurpatory stepmother (whose interests are pitted against those of the legitimate heiress), sets the stage for a narrative with a child-hero,[2] and Argan's hypochondriacal behavior is indeed very close to the narcissism of a child: it is by virtue of his illness that Argan becomes the "helpless" center of attention, making demands on all around him.[3] His wishes he utters with all the undisguised egotism of an *enfant terrible,* and these take the form of primitive proclamations which invariably begin with "I want." If, on the one hand, Argan has wished himself into a position of total dependence on his family, the family is in turn forced to focus its attention on this counterfeit child when instead it should be concentrating its energies on how best to marry its true progeny.

Argan consolidates his status of child through a behavioral identification with his youngest daughter. (Herein lies the dramatic utility of this new role.) As he engages in a puerile game of "my little finger tells me . . ." with Louison, the latter shames her father with the withering reply that "your little finger is telling you lies." On her exit from the stage, Argan sighs the nostalgic revelation: "Ah! There are no children anymore!" (II.viii). Argan's identification is then cemented through the repetition of a highly significant action in the play: Louison pretends to be dead after Argan has struck her, just as in act V it is he who will feign death in order to uncover the projects of his wife. Argan's childlike narcissism attains its most brutal expression in act I, scene v, in which he explains to his eldest daughter, Angélique, why she must marry Thomas Diafoirus: "My reason is that, seeing myself sickly and ill as I am, I want to find myself a step-son and allies who are doctors so that I can have in my family the medical resources necessary to me. . . ."

It is because she has designs on the family fortune that Béline aids and abets in the infantilization of Argan. As he trembles with impotent rage at the effrontery of the servant, Toinette, who has intimated that he may be less sick than he seems, Argan cries out to his *mamie* (mon amour→mamour→mon amie→mamie) who hurries to rescue her *petit fils* in distress. Béline calms him with words of maternal commiseration, and he sulks: "I've just been put into a fit of anger. . . . She made me mad, mamie. . . . For one whole hour, she opposed the things I want to do" (I.vi). Later, when Béralde questions the extent of his brother's illness, the scene is repeated. Argan flies into a rage which culminates in a fit of exasperation. This time, however, more is at stake, for Doctor Purgon has overheard Béralde's irreverent speech on the medical profession made to Argan (who has listened with some interest), and although Argan tattles on his brother, heaping all the blame on him, Purgon threatens to sever relations with his patient. Argan's excursion into filial insurrection, however fleeting, lays the groundwork for the final ceremony in which Argan will assume the authority of the doctor.

In the meantime, however, he is completely paralyzed by the medical malediction which the doctor has pronounced over him. In Argan's eyes, the doctor represents the adult *par excellence,* not only because of the aggressive manner in which he performs feats of ratiocination, but, more interestingly, by virtue of his possession of the secrets of procreation.

Argan, it seems, has lost this secret, and this particular memory "loss," I maintain, is the key to the production of his grand illusion. "The only regret I'll have if I die, mamie," he confides to his spouse, "is not having a child by you. Mr. Purgon told me that he would make me one" (I.viii). This is a most economically-expressed wish. In the first place, Argan's implication that he has forgotten how children are begotten reveals the Oedipal nature of his desire for his *mamie:* here, as earlier, his infantilization is being spotlighted. What is more to the point, however, is that by wishing himself backwards to a time when a son could love a mother with impunity, Argan is also attempting to erase his own status of *pater familias.*

Still, the project of paternity's disavowal is not so easily accomplished. For impeding the Arganian plot to rewrite his own genealogy are his two daughters, Angélique and Louison: they stand as flesh-and-blood accusations of their father's paternity. And it is his eldest daughter's coming-of-age which forces Argan to envisage radical measures in order to ensure that the unraveling of his personal narrative may proceed uninterrupted.

Critics have commented on Argan's infantilism, which has traditionally been seen as his comic flaw—and an end in itself. This conception, however, bespeaks a particularly static view of the play and its main character. In fact, infantilization of the father is far more than a simple inflection of that egotism typifying Molière's "heavy fathers," to borrow Harold Knutson's expression.[4] I maintain that it is organically linked to the play's dramatic economy . . . and, moreover, that it is only part of the fantasy which Argan is bent on staging. Dramatic resolution of *Le Malade imaginaire* in favor of Béline actually requires Argan's infantilization: until the latter's death, his wife would function as a ward supervising a child, a vantage point from which she could slowly discredit his true children and eventually cause them to be disinherited. Comic resolution of the play (in favor of Angélique, Nature, and propagation of the species) demands that Argan's daughter marry the suitor of her choice and that Argan recognize that one of his own offspring stands on the threshold of adulthood.

Now as far as Argan is concerned, there are only two possible solutions for his painfully eligible elder daughter: either she can marry the uninspired son of a doctor, Thomas Diafoirus, himself a doctor-to-be, or she can take herself to a nunnery. In the first case, Argan would actually inherit—in filial manner—a doctor for a son-in-law, which would enable him to perpetuate his role of child/invalid indefinitely. Should Angélique not wish to marry the repugnant Diafoirus, the expedient Ancien Régime convent solution affords Argan the double advantage of banishing this reminder of paternity from his sight while simultaneously blocking any ramifications of the genealogical tree. Once Angélique is removed from the world, it would be as if she had never existed.[5] Once the vows are taken, no new generation could issue forth to remind Argan that his time is nearly up.

It is the *extremism* of the solutions envisaged by Argan which betrays what is at stake: indeed, for him it is quite literally a matter of life and death. I suggest that by erasing the barriers between reality and illusion, between adult and child, begetter and begotten, Argan is attempting to deny the fact of his mortality. And we cannot forget that the true "danger" of the play revolves around how Argan is going to dispose of his money, that is, whether his wife will manage to wheedle away the family fortune or whether it will fall to its legitimate heirs.

The drama being played out around Argan is thus one which presupposes his own decease. Apart from *Dom Juan* (whose storyline, it should be remembered, was borrowed), *Le Malade imaginaire* is the sole play in Molière's otherwise rather joyful theater in which morbidity and decay are central to the plot, as Knutson has shown.[6] This is apparent from the opening scene in which Argan, after having with glee tallied up the total cost of his various enemas and purgatives, realizes that he is alone: "Is it possible that they would leave a poor sick man all alone like this? . . . Ah! My God! They're going to leave me here to die!" Later, while arguing with Toinette, Argan collapses: "Ah! Ah! I can't take any more. This is going to kill me."

Clearly the conclusions of Argan's tendentious logic equate descendance and death: beyond the notion of posterity, he glimpses the idea of *posthumous*. Thus not only must Angélique be prevented from reproducing (unless she marries a doctor, which would merely prolong the status quo), but she herself must be veiled from view, inasmuch as visible she constitutes a *memento mori*. It is Argan's unnatural design to foil time by rolling back its registers fully three generations: initially, he will "sacrifice" his own daughter by removing her from view and with the same gesture prevent her from reproducing. This accomplished, he will install himself in a permanent state of childhood.

What is at issue for Argan, when all is said and done, is how to convert Historical Time into Mythical Time, how one mere mortal might immortalize himself. And as I have indicated, the possibility of the existence of such mediation (which is being debated on the thematic level) actually suggests itself *formally*, that is, in the way that the rigorous narrative of the comedy periodically fades into the fantasy of the ballet and also through the notion that this dramatic plot possesses clear structural affinities with fairy tale. Furthermore, slippage from the chronological into the eternal occurs from time to time within the individual acts of the play itself. In one of his hyperbolic descriptions (II.v), Thomas Diafoirus refers to the statue of Memnon whom, as legend has it, Zeus immortalized after he had fallen in battle, the victim of Achilles. Later, when the two lovers Angélique and Cléante must communicate their secret desires to each other in the presence of the family, they slip into the pastoral mode in a striking example of the incorporation of the immutable into a narrative in which time and timing are of the essence.

Thus, the atemporal figures in several registers of the text, and it scarcely comes as a surprise to note that at the thematic level, too, the flight from time is being plotted out by Argan. To this end, he has chosen the role of invalid, a casting paradoxical enough until one realizes that this is the persona which best allows him to enter into the sort of dependency which approximates that of the child. It is through the role of the hypochondriac that Argan plans to turn the tables on time.

If at first play-acting serves Argan's interests alone, his theatrical penchant will later be exploited in favor of Angélique's marriage to Cléante. For the play is most certainly the thing here, and in this regard it would not be inaccurate to rank *Le Malade imaginaire* among Molière's most "meta-dramatic" plays because its *dénouement* devolves directly from the characters' staging of their own plays within the play and from the exchanging of dramatic masks. This internally-motivated play-acting is both more frequent and more fundamental than the "mamamouchification" of Jourdain in *Le Bourgeois gentilhomme*.

In fact, twice during the play Argan is called upon to assume a role other than that of the hypochondriac which he had permanently adopted. And interestingly enough, in both cases the role chosen closely corresponds to Argan's own source of anxiety. Now such correspondences, I maintain, can scarcely be fortuitous. It is as if all these histrionics were spotlighting an Argan in the process of staging his anxieties, of repeating these, of working them through (to use the Freudian terminology), in order to arrive at some resolution. To say this, of course, is to suggest that there is a therapeutic function in his role-playing, or, in other words, that in the course of the drama, this character undergoes significant change, something most unusual in the Molièresque theater. Furthermore, on close scrutiny, a *progression* can be observed in these roles: Argan's assuming of the final mask of Doctor presupposes the *mise en scène* of a particular cameo-drama.

Let us return to the scene in question. In act III, scene xii, Argan plays the dead man in order to trick his wife into betraying her nefarious schemes. Bearing in mind that death lies at the very heart of Argan's personal drama, one recognizes in this role-playing, besides its purely dramatic function of unmasking the villainess, the working-through of an anxiety by means of identification with the actual source of fear. Argan "dies," surrendering to that fate which he most dreads, only to be resurrected, and gloriously so, for his descent into hell has led to a revelation—of his wife's perfidy, of his children's devotion—and to a softening of his own fear of death.

However, it seems that Argan will only shed one mask if he can next cast himself in a different role, his "comic flaw" lying less in his hypochondria than in his being condemned to perpetual "actorhood," not unlike Molière's own theatrical destiny. The death mask finds its dramatic justification in the way that it leads Argan to assume his final role, that of Doctor of Medicine. To recapitulate the sequence of symbolic events, the would-be child has practiced the dance of death, thereby exorcizing his fear, and there is no longer any reason for him to refuse identification with that other object of dread, the Adult. And as an adult, he is at last brought to acknowledge his paternity, to recognize his daughter as his own, and to bestow the paternal blessing upon her marriage, one which cannot fail to set the cycle of re-generation into motion.

Structurally, then, *Le Malade imaginaire* enjoys a certain kinship with classical comedy in which *dénouement* often depends on the recognition and reunion of family members, who, after trials and peregrinations, find their way home. Certainly, one must qualify the Arganian *nostos* as a psychological one, but it functions nonetheless to restore the Family to its original configuration.

Whereas in other Molière dramas centering around a tyrant-father the comic solution is to eject the domineering paternal figure outside the family group, in *Le Malade imaginaire,* where the family structure actually threatens to *implode*, it is a matter of restoring the father to his proper place. Up to this point a moralist for whom dramatic evolution consisted in eliminating undesirable elements from society, Molière has ventured beyond the static theater of types by staging a change within the individual himself.

In the entire span of Molière's work, only his last play, *Le Malade imaginaire,* features an evolution of the main character in conjunction with the *dénouement*. A Tartuffe purged of his hypocrisy is unthinkable: Tartuffe must remain faithful to his vice. And by the same token, in *L'Avare,* Cléante and Mariane become husband and wife without Harpagon ever relinquishing his coveted money-box. Indeed, Argan is as unique in the Molièresque theater as Béline and Louison are. The concatenation of these three roles gives rise to a different sort of dramatic disequilibrium, one which threatens to subvert the integrity of the family unless Argan acknowledges, to himself and to others, the fact of his paternity and, beyond that, his mortality. And, on reflection, it may well be that in this, his final play, Molière himself plumbed the depths of death the better to accept it.

Notes

1. Translation from the French is my own.

2. It is curious that the unique presence of the child in this play has gone unnoticed. My contention that the creation of the role of Louison and Argan's infantilization are intimately linked is borne out inversely, as it were, by Karolyn Waterson in *Molière et l'autorité: structures sociales, structures comiques,* French Forum Monographs, No. 1 (Lexington: French Forum, 1976), p. 18. Here she remarks (erroneously) that there are no children in Molière's theater, and asserts that *likewise* no father-children exist: "D'habitude peu soucieux des règles classiques, Molière accepte la convention qui bannit de la scène les enfants en bas âge et . . . ne crée pas de personnage qui se définisse simultanément en tant que père ou mère et enfant."

3. Argan's infantilism (but not the darker reasons behind it) has been pointed out by Charles Mauron in *Des Métaphores obsédantes au mythe personnel: introduction à la psychocritique,* 3rd ed. (Paris: José Corti, 1962), p. 297, and by Harold Knutson in *Molière: An Archetypal Approach* (Toronto: Univ. of Toronto Press, 1976), p. 103.

4. Among the "heavy fathers" Knutson includes Sgnarelle (*L'Ecole des maris*), Arnolphe (*L'Ecole des femmes*), Orgon (*Tartuffe*), Harpagon (*L'Avare*), Argan, and Jourdain (*Le Bourgeois gentilhomme*).

5. Although Knutson does not address the issue of the convent in *Le Malade imaginaire,* he refers to it elsewhere in Molière's theater as a "form of suicide" if the heroine has voluntarily chosen the convent (p. 77) or as "living death" if the father has imposed claustration upon her (p. 95).

6. On moral decay and its relation to Argan's fecal preoccupation, see Knutson (p. 107).

Nicholas Cronk (essay date January 1993)

SOURCE: Cronk, Nicholas. "The Play of Words and Music in Molière-Charpentier's *Le Malade Imaginaire.*" *French Studies* 47, no. 1 (January 1993): 6-19.

[*In the following essay, Cronk investigates the apparent disjunction between the spoken sections of* The Imaginary Invalid *and its musical interludes, suggesting that the tension between sung and spoken sections of the play reflects Molière's exploration of their combined artistic potential.*]

> C'est une grande question de savoir si la Musique ajoûte à la passion, ou si elle la diminue.
>
> (Grimarest)[1]

WORDS AND MUSIC: THE THEATRE OF SPECTACLE

'Est-ce que c'est la mode de parler en musique?' exclaims Polichinelle, as he is suddenly confronted by singing guards of the watch in the first *intermède* of *Le Malade imaginaire*.[2] The question was a pertinent one in early 1673, at a time when opera was enjoying enormous success with Parisian audiences. The work usually described as the first French opera, *Pomone,* had run for eight months in 1671, and this had been followed by a second pastoral opera the following year, *Les Peines et les plaisirs de l'amour.* Molière could hardly ignore this revolution in public taste, and *Le Malade imaginaire* can be seen as both a product of, and a response to, the popular success of *Pomone.* Then, only two months after the first performance of *Le Malade imaginaire,* came the première of *Cadmus et Hermione,* the first of a succession of *tragédies en musique* by Lully and Quinault which would establish definitively the form of French opera for the rest of the century and beyond.

Le Malade imaginaire, the only full-length collaboration between Molière and Charpentier, is more spectacular by far than any of the *comédiés-ballets* which

Molière had written with Lully. The elaborate combination of music, dance and speech is unprecedented in its ambition and takes the work to the threshold of operatic form (more precisely, to the threshold of *opéra-comique*).[3] However, an important consequence of this innovative complexity is the problematic nature of the work's structure: how do the various constituent parts relate to each other? This structural problem is not posed so acutely by Molière's other musical works, despite the inherent instability of the *comédie-ballet*: in *Le Bourgeois Gentilhomme,* for example, the *intermèdes* extend and develop the action of the preceding spoken scenes, so that comedy and ballet seem, at the end of the play, to fuse naturally. *Le Malade imaginaire* presents a quite different prospect. The brilliant finale, clearly indebted to that of *Le Bourgeois Gentilhomme,* is similarly successful in integrating the twin threads of *comédie* and *ballet.* The prologue and *intermèdes* are much more puzzling, however, since these episodes of pastoral, *commedia dell'arte,* and exotic dance appear perversely dislocated from the spoken scenes which precede and follow them. The 1673 'Églogue en musique et en danse', for example, a lavish pastoral in hyperbolic praise of the King, requires six singers and takes some thirty minutes to perform; it has no point of contact at all with the scene which follows, the monologue in which Argan enumerates his medical bills.

Critics view this apparent looseness of structure in different ways. A few admit bluntly to finding the work incoherent, but the majority are keen to demonstrate that, despite appearances, the work does cohere at some level.[4] Certainly it seems reasonable to identify elements which link the spoken scenes and the musical *intermèdes.* Many of the comic routines in the spoken scenes, for example, have (or should have) a balletic quality in performance; more generally, there is the influence of the Italian theatre, equally strong in both spoken and sung sections of the work; most significant of all (we shall return to this point) is the thematization of theatricality, evident in almost every scene, whether spoken or sung.

The identification of such recurrent themes does not however amount to evidence of coherence. A theatrical work must be judged by its theatrical impact, and it has required considerable ingenuity on the part of critics to smooth over the provocative disjunction of a sung pastoral prologue and a spoken comic monologue. This essay will seek to show that the clash between words and music in *Le Malade imaginaire* is pivotal, and that Molière exploits it both to construct his work, and to comment on the genre which he is constructing: the word-music tension has a function which is at once theatrical and theoretical.

WORDS VERSUS MUSIC: A THEATRICAL STRUCTURE

The first observation to be made about the musical sections of the work is that their length and complexity make them far more than merely incidental or decorative interludes. In reading the text it is easy to underestimate their full extent; in performance they constitute half the total work, and possibly, for Molière's early audiences, the more important half.

Secondly, the *intermèdes* are sharply differentiated from each other. We are presented with four types of musical entertainment: pastoral, *commedia,* court dance, and burlesque; and these alternate, in order of performance, between high and low: pastoral (noble), *commedia* (low), court dance (noble), and burlesque (low). This lends the work an extraordinary dynamic, for the musical scenes contrast with each other as much as, collectively, they contrast with the spoken scenes. It is as if Molière and Charpentier were celebrating the idea of theatre (and showing off their own skills?) by constructing a sample-book containing a set-piece of each type of theatrical spectacle. The very fact of bringing these different forms together is both a provocation and a celebration.

The structural function of the final *intermède* is clear: it combines words and music in what is perhaps Molière's most skilful *dénouement,* and brings the work happily to its carnivalesque conclusion. Obviously it is with the earlier *intermèdes* that difficulties of interpretation arise. One strategy is to focus on the protagonist and to identify his relationship with the various musical happenings. The contrast between the prologue and the first scene could hardly be more violent: from the pastoral world of nobility and grace, of refined and delicate emotion, we are brutally translated into a bourgeois interior and confronted with a comic figure crudely obsessed with his bowel movements. While the participants in the prologue turn outward to others, singing in praise of the King and in declarations of love, Argan, alone on the steps, is turned inward on himself, his obsession with his bodily functions cutting him off irrevocably from the imaginative world of music which preceded.

Love is again a central theme of the music and of the *commedia* routines of the first *intermède*; the noble love of the shepherds and shepherdesses in the prologue is relativized by the parodic love of Polichinelle, but Argan is excluded even from this. The first occasion on which Argan comes unavoidably face to face with music is in II, 5, and this scene, in which music is the medium of love, is situated, hardly by chance, exactly in the middle of the work. The young lovers Cléante and Angélique, embarrassed in the presence of Argan and of the ridiculous fiancé whom he is wishing on Angélique, need urgently to communicate. The couple, who first met at the theatre, put their knowledge of theatre to good use, by improvising 'un petit opéra impromptu', so contriving to converse spontaneously through the stilted conventions of pastoral opera (which we, the audience, have already experienced in the prologue). Argan, who at first is only mildly interested in what is going on, begins gradually to become sensitive to the truth underlying this music, and abruptly brings the performance to a halt: 'Cette comédie-là est de fort mauvais exemple'. Thomas Diafoirus, needless to say, is impervious to the world of music, and therefore blissfully unaware of what is happening.

The second *intermède* at the end of this act reverts to the courtly atmosphere of the prologue, as four Moorish women dancers sing conventionally of young love (the fourth woman being sung in early performances by a male alto). The form is conventional enough: Molière and Lully had already written 'morescas', as such entertainments were called, in *Le Sicilien* and *Les Amants magnifiques.* What is most remarkable about the scene is the fact that Argan remains present on stage throughout. Béralde brings on the dancers at the end of Act II, saying to Argan 'this is just what the doctor ordered':

> Je vous amène ici un divertissement, que j'ai rencontré, qui dissipera votre chagrin, et vous rendra l'âme mieux disposée aux choses que nous avons à dire [. . .]. Cela vaudra bien une ordonnance de Monsieur Purgon.
>
> (II, 9)

The therapy of art and music is thus proposed as an alternative to the therapy of medicine.[5] The stage directions tell us that Argan is seated at this point, so he must presumably remain sitting, a passive spectator, centre-stage, as the singers and dancers swirl around him.

Here, for the first time, Argan finds himself at the centre of the musical action, though as yet he is no more than a passive participant. The music must seduce Argan as much as the audience, and Charpentier's dramatic sense prompts him to write music of remarkable beauty. This performance, staged-managed by Béralde, is Argan's true initiation into the world of music, art, and imagination, and it paves the way for the final scene. As the work reaches its climax in the concluding *intermède*, Argan makes the decisive shift from passive to active participant, emerging finally as the pivotal point of the musical as well as of the theatrical action. Argan, for the first time, is integrated fully into the harmony of his surroundings.

Molière's stage directions concerning set changes underline this essential structure: the instruction 'le théâtre change' occurs between the Prologue and Act I (outside to inside, from 'un lieu champêtre' to 'une chambre'), between Act I and the first *intermède* (inside to outside, from a room into an urban street) and again between the first *intermède* and Act II (from outside back into the room). The installation of theatre machinery at the Palais-Royal in 1671 had made available to Molière a radically different form of décor: the two fixed angle wings which until then had been standard could now be replaced by pairs of flat wings painted in perspective, and these, being machine-operated and therefore movable at will, permitted multiple set-changes.[6] *Le Malade imaginaire* is the first comedy in which Molière chose to exploit the potential of this new ('operatic') technology, and he deploys the changes of set to establish a series of fundamental dichotomies: town/country, indoors/outdoors, reality/fantasy, and, most importantly, speech/music.

Since, in the first half of the work, music is confined to the *intermèdes* and Argan to the spoken scenes, the set changes which keep the two worlds of speech and music firmly apart also preserve Argan from all possible contact with the world of music. But half-way through Act II, at the mid-point of the work, music invades the world of speech, and his home, in the form of the 'petit opéra impromptu'; thereafter there are no further set changes. The various oppositions cited above are conflated as Act II leads seamlessly, thanks to Béralde, into the second *intermède,* which itself flows into the third Act, and on into the concluding *intermède.* The 'realism' of the room which isolates Argan from the outside world dissolves as Argan is encircled fantastically by singers and dancers. The stage directions could not be more eloquent: in the first half of the work, the separateness of the different worlds of speech and music is underpinned by the separateness of different sets; at the work's half-way point, these barriers are broken down, and thereafter the action plays continuously on one set, permitting the spheres of music and speech to converge and ultimately coalesce.

When we have once identified this underlying theatrical structure, Argan's illness becomes much easier to diagnose. His malady is essentially a spiritual one, his dilemma, in common with other of Molière's monomaniac protagonists, that he is 'out of tune' with his surroundings. The very structure of the work excludes him initially from 'the music of the spheres',[7] and the dramatic momentum of the work is created by the need to reclaim Argan, to save him from himself, by integrating him in the world of fantasy and imagination as embodied in music. The work thus describes the progress of a 'musicien malgré lui' who moves in stages from being first outside music (prologue, first *intermède*), to being an unwilling spectator of music (the 'petit opéra impromptu'), then a willing, though passive, spectator (second *intermède*), and becoming, finally, an active and central participant in carnival (third *intermède*).

Such a juxtaposition of Comedy and Music is not unique to *Le Malade imaginaire.* There is an anticipation of Molière-Charpentier's last work in the final scene of *L'Amour médecin* (1665), in which 'La Comédie', 'Le Ballet' and 'La Musique' sing in unison about their therapeutic powers:

> Sans nous tous les hommes
> Deviendraient mal sains,
> Et c'est nous qui sommes
> Leurs grands médecins;

and the 'Prologue' to Thomas Corneille's *Circé* (1675) concludes with a 'Dialogue de la Musique et de la Comédie' in which the two join forces to enhance their celebration of the King. More broadly, tensions between the component elements of the *comédie-ballet* may be said to be intrinsic to the genre.[8] The particularity of *Le Malade imaginaire* derives from the way in which it generates theatre out of this rivalry.

At the start of the work, the two worlds of music and speech stand apart from and opposed to each other. The same stark contrast is found, for example, in *George Dandin* (or rather, in *Le Grand Divertissement royal de Versailles*), in the contrast between peasant and pastoral; but whereas in that work the two worlds of speech and music remain distinct, in *Le Malade imaginaire,* they tend increasingly to converge as the work proceeds. The calculated disjunction between different linguistic registers is a recurrent and crucial characteristic of Molière's theatrical language. *Le Malade imaginaire* extends this process by juxtaposing different musical registers and by further juxtaposing spoken and musical registers, and in a manner more sophisticated than in any of the earlier musical works. The pastoral prologue which opens the work, in itself purely conventional, is not merely different from Argan's following monologue; it is intended to shock us by its difference into a realization of Argan's spiritual isolation. Thus the tension between words and music, so far from being a problem, constitutes the mainspring of the work's structure, for it is in the resolution of the apparent conflict between words and music that Argan's theatrical salvation lies.

WORDS VERSUS MUSIC: A THEATRICAL MANIFESTO

If the tension between words and music is central to *Le Malade imaginaire,* it is no less central to contemporary theoretical discussion about vocal music in the theatre. The biggest single stumbling-block in the creation of opera, in France as elsewhere, lay in establishing a reciting style or form of declamation which achieved the appropriate balance between poetry and music. The French, more even than the Italians, were especially anxious that music should not detract from the power of the spoken word (which is why spectators of the *comédies-ballets* held *livrets* containing the texts of the

songs and choruses, though not the spoken dialogue).[9]
The potency of the tragic declamation was widely appreciated in this period—witness Mme de Sévigné on
La Champmeslé's performances of Racine—and there
was an understandable suspicion that music could only
diminish the impact of the spoken word. In his preface
to *Andromède* (1651), Corneille insists rather engag-
ingly that he has made his work comprehensible by ensuring that only unimportant parts of the text are set to
music:

> Je me suis bien gardé de faire rien chanter qui fût
> nécessaire à l'intelligence de la Pièce, parce que
> communément les paroles qui se chantent étant mal
> entendues des auditeurs, pour la confusion qu'y apporte
> la diversité des voix qui les prononcent ensemble, elles
> auraient fait une grande obscurité dans le corps de
> l'ouvrage, si elles avaient eu à instruire l'Auditeur de
> quelque chose d'important.

('Argument')

Pierre Perrin's 'Lettre écrite à Monseigneur
l'archevêque de Turin' of 1659, the first *art poétique* of
French opera, is almost uniquely preoccupied with the
relationship of words to music, and its author launches
a comprehensive attack on Italian opera before defending his own *Pastorale*:

> Ce qui m'est pareillement singulier en cette Comedie,
> c'est une maniere particuliere de traitter les paroles de
> Musique Françoises, dans laquelle il y a des observa-
> tions et des delicatesses jusqu'icy peu connuës et qui
> demandent un art et un genie tout particulier.[10]

The received opinion of Molière's generation about the
primacy of language in vocal music is best summed up
in Bacilly's influential *Remarques curieuses sur l'art de
chanter*:

> Je sçay qu'autrefois on avoit peu d'égard aux Paroles
> que l'on chantoit, et que la Prononciation estoit presque
> comptée pour rien: ainsi il semble que l'on a beaucoup
> fait, lors qu'on l'a introduite dans le Chant, quand ce
> ne seroit que pour faire entendre distinctement les Pa-
> roles. Mais à present qu'il semble que le Chant est
> venu au plus haut degré de perfection qu'il puisse
> jamais estre, il ne suffit pas de prononcer simplement,
> mais il le faut faire avec la force necessaire; et c'est un
> abus de dire qu'il faut Chanter comme l'on parle, à
> moins que d'ajouter comme on parle *en Public*, et non
> pas comme l'on parle dans le Langage familier.[11]

In other words, Bacilly wants to have the best of both
worlds: the beauty of music, but without in any way
sacrificing the power of declaimed speech. The break-up
of the Lully-Molière partnership in 1672 seems to have
been, at least in part, on account of an underlying difference of operatic aesthetic: Lully aspired towards
works of continuous music with recitative, while
Molière wished to retain the spoken word to a significant extent even in 'musical' works. There was, in ef-

fect, a trial of strength between composer and poet.[12]
Lully's great success, beginning with *Cadmus* in the
months after Molière's death, was that he did precisely
what Bacilly wanted: he brought to perfection a style of
recitative which was much less florid than that of Italian opera and was even moulded, so he boasted, on
contemporary spoken theatre.[13]

Not everyone however was convinced by Lully's answer to the problem of combining poetry and music,
and in the late 1670s both La Fontaine and Boileau
were still exercised by this tension. In his 'Épître à M.
de Niert, sur l'opéra', written in 1677 (and first published in the following century), La Fontaine insists that
poetry, dance and music are best appreciated as separate
arts:

> Ces beautés, néanmoins, toutes trois séparées,
> Si tu veux l'avouer, seraient mieux savourées.
> De genres si divers le magnifique appas
> Aux règles de chaque art ne s'accommode pas [. . .].
> Mais ne vaut-il pas mieux, dis-moi ce qu'il t'en
>   semble,
> Qu'on ne puisse sentir tous les plaisirs ensemble,
> Et que, pour en goûter les douceurs purement,
> Il faille les avoir chacun séparément?[14]

During these same years, Boileau was invited to compose a prologue for an opera which Racine was supposed to be writing for Lully. The project came to nothing, but Boileau did complete the prologue, and his
choice of subject is revealing: a dramatization of the
conflict between 'la Poésie' and 'la Musique'. Poetry
declares that she can express more than Music, and in
vain Music argues back that she can embellish Poetry:

LA POÉSIE:

> Quoy, par de vains accords et des sons impuissans
> Vous croiés exprimer tout ce que je sçay dire?

LA MUSIQUE:

> Aux doux transports, qu'Apollon vous inspire
> Je croy pouvoir mesler la douceur de mes chants.

LA POÉSIE:

> Oui, vous pouvés au bord d'une fontaine
> Avec moi soupirer une amoureuse peine,
> Faire gemir Tyrsis, faire plaindre Climene.
> Mais, quand je fais parler les Heros et les Dieux,
>   Vos chants audacieux
> Ne me sçauroient prester qu'une cadence vaine.
>   Quittés ce soin ambitieux.[15]

There is a happy ending to this argument, but only just.
As they are about to separate, Poetry and Music are
reconciled by the last-minute arrival of 'la divine
Harmonie, / Qui descend des Cieux!'. It is clear, despite
the final reconciliation, that Boileau's own sympathies

lie with those who believe in the supremacy of Poetry. And it is hard to think that Lully would have much relished having to set to music Boileau's text.

A more extended discussion of this question, and one exactly contemporary with *Le Malade imaginaire,* is Saint-Évremond's essay 'Sur les opéra', which was mostly written (though not published) in 1669-70, just prior to Lully's first operas and to *Le Malade imaginaire.*[16] Saint-Évremond proclaims his dislike of 'les Comédies en Musique' (p. 149) as they are currently performed, and declares that he finds them boring, a charge which La Bruyère was to echo. Saint-Évremond's objections to opera are twofold. Firstly, the subject-matter is thin, and the poetry bad: 'Une sottise chargée de Musique, de Danses, de Machines, de Décorations, est une sottise magnifique, mais toûjours sottise' (p. 151). Secondly, and more interestingly, he is nervous that the mixing of poetry and music ends up being to the detriment of both: 'Si vous voulez savoir ce que c'est qu'un Opera, je vous dirai que c'est un travail bizarre de Poësie et de Musique, où le Poëte et le Musicien également gênés l'un par l'autre, se donnent bien de la peine à faire un méchant ouvrage' (p. 154).

So far, this sounds very much like Boileau and La Fontaine, and critics from Voltaire onwards have caricatured Saint-Évremond as an opponent of opera. In fact, he was a passionate lover of music, and a particular enthusiast for opera.[17] What is habitually overlooked in Saint-Évremond's essay is the fact that he is attempting to outline a different operatic aesthetic from the one then taking shape in France. Saint-Évremond insists that the poet rather than the composer should be in overall control of the work: 'Il faut que la Musique soit faite pour les Vers, bien plus que les Vers pour la Musique' (p. 155). Saint-Évremond finds it absurd to use music to express banal and simple phrases, and in his comedy *Les Opéra* (written 1676-78), about a young girl who has been driven mad by her infatuation for opera and who communicates only in song, he particularly pokes fun at the notion of setting to music such trivial utterances as 'Comment, Monsieur, vous portez-vous?' and 'Je me porte à vôtre service' (I, 4).[18]

But this does not mean that he is mocking opera in general; his target is the type of opera which sets to music every single word of the text. Such works, in Saint-Évremond's view, lack verisimilitude: 'Car l'harmonie ne doit être qu'un simple accompagnement, et les grands maîtres du Théatre l'ont ajoûtée comme agréable, non pas comme nécessaire, après avoir réglé tout ce qui regarde le sujet et le discours' (pp. 151-52). On the other hand, it is quite possible to sing a part of the text without offending 'la bien-séance' and 'la raison'— Saint-Évremond cites the example of the chorus in Greek tragedy (p. 153)—and he goes on to outline his preferred form of 'music drama', in which a spoken

text is broken up by interludes of music and dance, exactly in the manner of the English semi-opera which was first seen in London in the 1670s, and which Saint-Évremond must have known. Molière could not have read Saint-Évremond's essay, any more than Saint-Évremond could have seen *Le Malade imaginaire*: yet there is a quite remarkable sympathy of spirit between his ideas and those of Molière and Charpentier:

> Si je me sentois capable de donner conseil aux Honnêtes-gens qui se plaisent au Théatre, je leur conseillerois de reprendre le goût de nos belles Comédies, où l'on pourroit introduire des Danses et de la Musique, qui ne nuiroient en rien à la représentation. On y chanteroit un Prologue avec des accompagnemens agréables; dans les Intermèdes le Chant animeroit des paroles qui seroient comme l'esprit de ce qu'on auroit représenté; la représentation finie, on viendroit à chanter une [sic] Epilogue, ou quelque réflexion sur les plus grandes beautés de l'ouvrage en fortifieroit l'idée, et feroit conserver plus cherement l'impression qu'elles auroient fait [sic] sur les Spectateurs.

(p. 154)

The reference to 'nos belles Comédies, où l'on pourroit introduire des Danses et de la Musique' recalls Molière-Charpentier's coinage for their first joint work, 'comédie mêlée de musique et de danses': *Le Malade imaginaire,* at least by Saint-Évremond's criteria, is an opera.

Words and Music: The Theatricality of Spectacle

Just as Saint-Évremond expressed some of his views about opera through the medium of a comedy, so Molière, not for the first time, conceived of a play which embodied a theoretical statement about theatre. *Le Malade imaginaire* should be read, among other things, as an artistic manifesto. The work is a deliberate demonstration of the viability of a certain form of music theatre in which music is an essential element, yet does not swamp the spoken word.

The concept of the 'semi-opera' was not universally admired. Gabriel Gilbert, the librettist to Cambert's next work after *Pomone, Les Peines et les plaisirs de l'amour* (1672), clearly believed that a work of continuous music was superior to a work which alternated between music and spoken dialogue:

> Je ne puis m'empescher de dire que la Musique est une beauté essencielle qui manque [aux Comedies], et qui est le plus grand ornement de la Scene. Les Grecs qui sont les Inventeurs du Poëme Dramatique, ont finy tous les Actes de leurs Tragedies par des Chœurs de Musique, où ils ont mis ce qu'ils ont imaginé de plus beau sur les mœurs. Les Inventeurs de l'Opera ont enrichy sur les Grecs, ils ont meslé la Musique dans toutes les parties du Poëme pour le rendre plus accomply, et donner une nouvelle ame aux Vers.[19]

This was Lully's view too, but it was not the only possible operatic aesthetic, and Molière and Charpentier propose an alternative which accords separate status to words and music, while none the less making each fully dependent on the other.

Le Malade imaginaire propounds therefore a particular theatrical aesthetic and, moreover, one constructed in deliberate opposition to Lully. this debate with his erstwhile collaborator bubbles to the surface in two scenes in particular. The first is II, 5, when Cléante and Angélique adopt pastoral roles to sing their 'petit opéra impromptu'. At one level, Molière parodies the contemporary vogue for concert performances in private houses, all the more ironical here as Argan is as yet immune to music.[20] At another level, the scene allows Molière and Charpentier to show their skill in using music as a dramatic device. As this improvised performance proceeds, it becomes abundantly clear that the pastoral convention, far from inhibiting spontaneous expression, is actually the only way in which the lovers can express themselves 'naturally'.[21] This is an object lesson, not least for Lully and Quinault, in the proper and effective use of sung text, and Charpentier rises to the challenge with music which is subtly sensitive to the dramatic situation.[22]

To Argan's question 'Les vers en sont-ils beaux?', Cléante replies:

> C'est proprement ici un petit opéra impromptu, et vous n'allez entendre chanter que de la prose cadencée, ou des manières de vers libres, tels que la passion et la nécessité peuvent faire trouver à deux personnes qui disent les choses d'eux-mêmes, et parlent sur-le-champ.

It is an odd response in as much as it is not really an answer to Argan's question. Remembering that Lully and Quinault were at that moment at work on their first major joint project, Cléante's answer sounds more like Molière's own view on the proper relationship of words to music. The clarity of the sung text must not be obscured by the music, it should remain 'de la prose cadencée'; and it must involve the expression of immediate emotion, not the exchange of trivial thoughts. These are all principles, of course, which are observed in Molière-Charpentier's own work.

Having halted the performance, Argan observes that Angélique and Cléante have been singing from music with no words, and the situation is saved only by Cléante's quick-wittedness: 'Est-ce que vous ne savez pas, Monsieur, qu'on a trouvé depuis peu l'invention d'écrire les paroles avec les notes mêmes?'. The joke is not only or even principally on Argan, however; Perrin, in the 'Avant-Propos' to his 'Recueil de paroles de musique' (1667), had boasted of 'plusieures [sic] choses curieuses et par moy inventées, entre autres la maniere de composer des paroles sur un chant noté sur la note mesme'.[23] Molière must have been galled that Perrin, a thoroughly mediocre poet, had been given the first

privilège to perform opera and had scored such a convincing success with *Pomone*; this jibe at the man who had written tirelessly on the problems of setting the French language to music, and had announced his intention of writing an 'Art Lyrique' on the same subject, is further evidence of Molière's engagement in this work with contemporary debate about the nature of opera.

The second scene which reflects directly upon contemporary theoretical issues is the opening section of the first *intermède,* which amusingly highlights and dramatizes the clash between words and music which we have seen to be central to the work as a whole. The struggle between Polichinelle and the violins which repeatedly interrupt him is a known *lazzo,*[24] and Molière cleverly employs the routine here as a device to dramatize the theoretical crux of the work. In a monologue, Polichinelle describes his unrequited love, and decides to serenade his beloved, when he is cut short by the intrusion of the violins:

VIOLONS

POLICHINELLE:

   Quelle impertinente harmonie vient interrompre ici ma voix?

VIOLONS

POLICHINELLE:

   Paix là, taisez-vous, violons. Laissez-moi me plaindre à mon aise des cruautés de mon inexorable.

VIOLONS

POLICHINELLE:

   Taisez-vous, vous dis-je. C'est moi qui veux chanter.

VIOLONS

POLICHINELLE:

   Paix donc!

The struggle of wills continues, Polichinelle mimics the sound of the violins, the violins play out of tune in mimicry of him, leading Polichinelle finally to explain in exasperation: 'La musique est accoutumée à ne point faire ce qu'on veut' (again, a remark which Molière may well have intended for Lully). Polichinelle then embarks on an elaborate routine which involves tuning his lute, when some *archers* arrive, singing 'Qui va là, qui va là?'. Polichinelle mocks the notion of singing such a banal phrase, in just the same way that Saint-Évremond in *Les Opéra* mocks the attempt to sing 'Comment, Monsieur, vous portez-vous?'. Polichinelle replies deliberately in prose, and throughout the ensuing exchange—'Qui va là, qui va là?' (sung) / 'Moi, moi, moi' (spoken)—the spoken word repeatedly answers the sung question. This staged battle between words and music stands as a microcosm of a battle which underlies the work as a whole. Hence the particular resonance of Polichinelle's response to the *archers* (which is also the response of Molière and Charpentier to Lully and Quinault): 'Qui diable est cela? Est-ce que c'est la mode de parler en musique?'.

Le Malade imaginaire is quintessentially a product of the moment when opera was establishing itself on the Paris stage. Molière-Charpentier's work may be seen at one level as a comic opera about the problem of opera, and as such it is a forebear of Salieri's *Prima la musica, poi le parole* and of Richard Strauss's *Capriccio*. The pivotal tension between music and speech which determines the internal dynamic of the work also reflects (and contributes to) external theorizing about the place of the spoken word in music theatre: the drama is constructed out of its own theoretical preoccupations.

Molière's most spectacular work is also therefore his most self-consciously spectacular, and this quality of self-reflecting theatricality gives *Le Malade imaginaire* its particular dramatic charge.[25] Many previous plays had experimented with the theme: *La Critique de l'École des Femmes* and *L'Impromptu de Versailles* are only the best-known cases of a theatrical self-awareness which is manifest to some degree in all the musical works, from the opening of *Les Fâcheux,* and Éraste's apology for his lateness on account of being detained—where else?—at the theatre. The skill and complexity with which the theme of theatricality is exploited in *Le Malade imaginaire* is however unprecedented in Molière's œuvre. The conflict between words and music, a recurrent feature of contemporary theoretical discourse, becomes here the driving force of the plot (how to integrate Argan?) while also being central to the aesthetic manifesto which is being advocated (how may the spoken and sung word be made to coexist fruitfully?). Through the world of music and the theatre, Argan learns to make contact with those around him; and the word-music tension is resolved when he is finally absorbed into the world of carnival. Meanwhile, we, as audience, are being taught how to construct a music drama, as well as how to profit from it. By a neat *mise en abyme,* as Argan learns about the theatre, so do we.

Notes

1. J.-L. Le Gallois de Grimarest, *Traité du récitatif* (Paris, Le Fèvre, 1707), p. 196.

2. Quotations from Molière use the text of the *Œuvres complètes,* ed. by Georges Couton, 2 vols, Pléiade (Paris, Gallimard, 1971).

3. See my article 'Molière-Charpentier's *Le Malade imaginaire*: The First *Opéra-comique*?', *Forum for Modern Language Studies,* forthcoming.

4. For example, 'Sauf la fameuse "Cérémonie", les intermèdes sont moins des agréments qu'une surcharge. *Le Malade imaginaire* n'est plus une comédie-ballet; c'est une comédie, et ce sont des ballets' (Pierre Mélèse, 'Molière à la cour', *XVIIᵉ Siècle,* 98-99 (1973), 57-65 (p. 64)). On the other hand, Claude Abraham finds in the work 'a profound structural unity' (*On the Structure of Molière's Comédies-Ballets* (Paris, PFSCL, 1984), p. 86). The most suggestive discussion of this problem is that of Louis E. Auld, 'The Unity of Molière's Comedy-Ballets: A Study of their Structure, Meanings, and Values' (Ph.D. thesis, Bryn Mawr, 1968), p. 75.

5. See Philip R. Berk, 'The Therapy of Art in *Le Malade imaginaire*', *French Review,* 40 (1972), special issue No. 4, 39-48.

6. See Roger W. Herzel, 'The Decor of Molière's Stage: The Testimony of Brissart and Chauveau', *PMLA,* 93 (1978), 925-54 (pp. 950-51). On the expense of set-changes, see Édouard Thierry, *Documents sur le Malade imaginaire* (Paris, Berger-Levrault, 1880), pp. 121-35.

7. See Louis E. Auld, 'The Music of the Spheres in the Comedy-Ballets', *L'Esprit créateur,* 6 (1966), 176-87.

8. See Louis E. Auld: 'The comedy-ballet dealt with the still-unresolved challenge of musical theatre by attaching elements from the French ballet tradition to the dramatic frame of comedy in a flexible association. Its specific *trouvaille* was the incorporation within its structure of a calculated play of juxtapositions or contrasts between the musical and non-musical sections' (*The Lyric Art of Pierre Perrin, Founder of French Opera,* 3 vols (Henryville, Pennsylvania, Institute of Mediaeval Music, 1986), I, 82).

9. See Claude-François Menestrier: 'Il faut [. . .] assujettir le chant et la Symphonie aux paroles, et aux vers dont les recits et les sentimens doivent être entendus dans ces actions de Theatre' (*Des représentations en musique anciennes et modernes* (Paris, Guignard, 1681), p. 135); *Quellentexte,* p. 147. The subservience of music to language in French opera remained unchallenged until the second half of the eighteenth century; see Catherine Kintzler, *Poétique de l'opéra français de Corneille à Rousseau* (Paris, Minerve, 1991), pp. 355-430.

10. Perrin, 'Lettre écrite à Monseigneur l'archevêque de Turin le 30 avril 1659', in *Les Œuvres de poésie* (Paris, Loyson, 1661), pp. 273-90 (p. 288). The 'Lettre' is reprinted in *Quellentexte zur Konzeption der europäischen Oper im 17. Jahrhundert* (Kassel, Bärenreiter, 1981), ed. by Heinz Becker, 105-111 (p. 110).

11. Bénigne de Bacilly, *Remarques curieuses sur l'art de bien chanter* (Paris, Ballard, 1668), pp. 249-50.

12. See Philippe Beaussant, 'Molière et l'opéra', *Europe,* 50, Nos 523-24 (November-December 1972), 155-68.

13. See Jean-Laurent Le Cerf de la Viéville de Freneuse: '*Mon Récitatif n'est fait que pour parler, je veux qu'il soit tout uni* [. . .]. [Lully] le vouloit si uni [. . .], qu'on prétend qu'il alloit le former à la Comedie sur les tons de la *Chanmêlé.* Il écoutoit déclamer la Chanmêlé, retenoit ses tons, puis leur donnoit la grace, l'harmonie et le degré de force qu'ils devoient avoir dans la bouche d'un Chanteur, pour convenir à la Musique à laquelle il les aproprioit de cette maniere' (*Comparaison de la musique italienne et de la musique française,* 2nd ed., 3 pts (Brussels, Foppens, 1705-06), II, 204). See also: 'Je regarde déja la declamation, comme une autre espece de musique; et dans mon sens un musicien, qui saura bien reciter ses vers, aura de grands avantages pour y mettre une note savante et naturelle. Le recit des Comediens est une maniere de chant, et vous m'avoüerez bien, que la Champmeslé ne nous plairoît pas tant, si elle avoit une voix moins agreable. Mais elle là sçait conduire avec beaucoup d'art, et elle y donne à propos des inflexions si naturelles, qu'il semble, qu'elle ait veritablement dans le cœur une passion, qui n'est que dans sa bouche' (*Entretiens galans,* 2 vols (Paris, Ribou, 1681), II, pp. 89-90).

14. *Œuvres diverses,* ed. by Pierre Clarac, Pléiade (Paris, Gallimard, 1958), pp. 617, 619.

15. 'Prologue d'opéra' (written 1678-79), *Œuvres complètes,* ed. by Françoise Escal, Pléiade (Paris, Gallimard, 1966), p. 279.

16. The praise of Lully in this essay is a later (1675-76) addition. References to the work are to Saint-Évremond, *Œuvres en prose,* ed. by René Ternois, 4 vols (1962-69), vol. III (Paris, Didier, 1966).

17. See the introduction to Saint-Évremond, *Les Opéra,* ed. by Robert Finch and Eugène Joliat (Geneva, Droz, 1979).

18. See also: 'Vous ne voudriez pas qu'on vint dire en chantant, le Roy vient, la Reine s'avance, et vous établiriez sans doute pour premiere regle, qu'on n'y chantât, que les endroits qui sont susceptibles de quelque passion. Le chant n'est pas fait pour des recits. Il les rend toûjours trop longs, et ils ne sauroient estre assez courts' (*Entretiens galans,* II, pp. 79-80); on the subject of people driven mad by opera who sing rather than speak, see *Entretiens galans,* II, pp. 100-02.

19. Gabriel Gilbert, 'Épitre à Monseigneur Colbert', *Opera pastorale heroique, Des Peines et des plaisirs de l'amour* (Paris, Varennes, 1672); *Quellentexte,* p. 121.

20. See also *Le Bourgeois Gentilhomme*: 'Il faut qu'une personne comme vous, qui êtes magnifique, et qui avez de l'inclination pour les belles choses, ait un concert de musique chez soi tous les mercredis ou tous les jeudis' (II, 1); within a few years, it becomes the fashion to have opera scenes performed at home: 'Il n'y a presque pas une maison où l'on n'en chante des Scenes entieres' (Saint-Évremond, *Les Opéra,* II, 3). Something akin to the device of the 'petit opéra impromptu' had already been used in *Le Sicilien* (sc. 8); it is imitated in Poisson's *Les Fous divertissants* (1680), in a scene (II, 9) in which young lovers perform duets from Lully's recent operas in the presence of an unwelcome and uncomprehending suitor (see John S. Powell, 'Charpentier's Music for Molière's *Le Malade imaginaire* and its Revisions', *Journal of the American Musicological Society,* 39 (1986), 87-142 (p. 114)).

21. Already in *Le Bourgeois Gentilhomme,* Molière had explained through the mouth of the *Maître à danser* the nature of the pastoral convention: 'Lorsqu'on a des personnes à faire parler en musique, il faut bien que, pour la vraisemblance, on donne dans la bergerie. Le chant a été de tout temps affecté aux bergers; et il n'est guère naturel en dialogue que des princes ou des bourgeois chantent leurs passions' (I, 2).

22. See John S. Powell: 'Here the music is not merely ornament or entertainment. It is the instrument which allows Angélique and Cléante to declare their passion directly to one another for the first time, and thereby to develop in music a courtship that is hindered by spoken dialogue earlier in the play. Especially striking is Charpentier's sensitivity to the dramatic nuances and humour in this scene, and his musical depiction of the quicksilver changes of emotion that typify young people in love' ('Music, Fantasy and Illusion in Molière's *Le Malade imaginaire*', *Music and Letters,* 73 (1992), 222-43 (pp. 230-31)).

23. See Auld, *The Lyric Art of Pierre Perrin,* II, p. 146, and III, p. xii. Molière may not have read the 'Recueil de paroles de musique' (1667), which was in manuscript, but he would have heard of its ideas: Perrin was tireless in publicizing his projects. Molière had already poked fun at him in *Le Bourgeois Gentilhomme*: Perrin is the author of the words of the song 'Je croyais Janneton' which Jourdain sings with ridiculous effect (I, 2); see Louis E. Auld, 'Une rivalité sournoise: Molière

contre Pierre Perrin', in *Le 'Bourgeois Gentilhomme': Problèmes de la comédie-ballet*, ed. by Volker Kapp (Paris, PFSCL, 1991), pp. 123-37.

24. See Cordelia Gundolf, 'Molière and the Commedia dell'arte', *AUMLA*, 39 (1973), 22-34 (p. 33).

25. See also Gay McAuley, 'Language and theatre in *Le Malade imaginaire*', *Australian Journal of French Studies*, 11 (1974), 4-18.

Andrew Calder (essay date 1993)

SOURCE: Calder, Andrew. "Medicine." In *Molière: The Theory and Practice of Comedy*, pp. 123-37. London: Athlone Press, 1993.

[*In the following essay, Calder examines Molière's treatment of medicine in several plays. He suggests that in* The Imaginary Invalid *Molière's satire extends to medical authority itself.*]

1. MEDICAL PEDANTS

Molière's doctors share most of the characteristics of his Aristotelian pedants. The younger Diafoirus, in *Le Malade imaginaire* (1673), a recent graduate from medical school, has precisely the qualities which, in Molière's view, would equip him for a career in either scholastic philosophy or medicine. His father, Monsieur Diafoirus, also a doctor, is proud of his son's education:

> He never showed signs of a lively imagination, nor of the quick intelligence you find in some; but it was these qualities which led me to foresee that his judgement would be strong, a quality essential to the exercise of our art. When he was little, he was never what you might call high-spirited or alert. You would find him always mild, peaceful and taciturn, never saying a word or playing any of those little games peculiar to children. It was a long, hard struggle teaching him to read and, at nine, he still didn't know his alphabet. 'Good,' I said to myself, 'it's the late-blossoming trees that bear the best fruit; it's harder to engrave on marble than on sandstone, but the inscriptions last longer, and this slowness of understanding, this sluggishness of the imagination, are marks of a sound judgement to come.' When I sent him to school, he found it hard; but he stiffened himself against difficulties and his masters always spoke highly of his assiduity and perseverance. Eventually, after much hard slog, he succeeded in graduating with glory; and I can say without vanity that, in his two years on the benches, no candidate has made more noise than he in the disputes of our School. He has made himself formidable, and no thesis can be advanced without his arguing the opposite case to its ultimate extreme. He is unbudgeable in dispute, strong as a Turk on principles, never modifies his opinions and pursues his reasonings into every last retreat of logic.
>
> (II, 5)

However, if doctors and pedants shared the same inflexibility, the same vanity and vindictiveness in dispute, they differed in other respects. Pedants were harmless figures of fun; grown men could look back with serenity upon their school and university days; the posturing of their verbose teachers and professors could be recalled with amusement—even, for some at least, with nostalgia. Women of all stations and men from the lower orders could live out their whole lives without ever having to suffer at the hands of pedants. Doctors were more substantial objects of satire. More people felt need of them (though the majority were too poor to afford them); they commanded much better incomes, and were more widely feared and revered. The discrepancy between theory and practice in medicine, between the confidently prescribed cures and the sudden deaths which often followed treatment, offered the satirist a rich source of humour. Above all, medicine deals with the functioning of the body and provided an inexhaustible fund of jokes, comic gestures and farcical routines.

2. FARCE WITHOUT SATIRE

Molière's earliest medical play, *Le Médecin volant*—a traditional one-act farce, probably part of the repertoire of Molière's troupe when he returned to Paris in 1658—presents many of the features which will recur in his later medical satires: a patient who is suffering from nothing more serious than lovesickness, a doctor who is a *valet* in disguise, some scatological humour, an allusion to the alleged venality of doctors, and mockery both of doctors' reliance on ancient authority and of their professional jargon (Scs 2-5). In this play, however, the laughter is benign. The scatological jokes revolve around Lucile's urine: Sganarelle drinks it, likes the taste, asks for more, then, hearing that she cannot produce more, prescribes a 'pissing potion'. The allusion to doctors who can say nothing without reference to ancient authority occurs in Sganarelle's citing of Galen and Hippocrates to prove that a person is not well when he is ill. Molière will use a similar joke in *Le Médecin malgré lui* (1666), where another Sganarelle invokes the authority of Hippocrates for the wearing of hats indoors at the beginning of a consultation (II, 2). The mockery of medical jargon is equally good-humoured. The ignorant Sganarelle quotes all the magic-sounding formulae he can dredge up: an Arab greeting, half a line from Corneille's *Le Cid*, a couple of fragments of Italian and Spanish and a Latin liturgical phrase picked up in church: 'Salamalec, salamalec. "Rodrigue, as-tu du cœur?" Signor, si; segnor, non. Per omnia saecula saeculorum.'

Molière goes out of his way to emphasize that the satire is friendly. He introduces an honest lawyer whose only function is to deliver an elegant encomium of doctors. 'One must confess', he says, 'that all who excel in any science are worthy of great praise, and particularly those in the medical profession' (Sc. 8). He underlines the special difficulties of medicine with an apposite quotation from the *Aphorisms* of Hippocrates, and quotes a line from Ovid to support the view that a doctor, however skilled, can never guarantee success. He recalls that doctors were once held in such esteem that people numbered them among the gods.

A modest polemical note is introduced with no hint of mockery when the lawyer expresses his hope that Sganarelle does not practise 'rational or dogmatic' medicine. Quoting Erasmus's adage 'experientia magistra rerum', the lawyer indicates his preference for empirical medicine. Molière appears to be supporting the campaign of doctors such as Joseph Duchesne, Jean Fabre, Estienne de Clave and David de Planis, who opposed the dogmatically based humoral medicine of such conservative bodies as the Paris Faculty and called for the use of empirically based chemical remedies.[1]

This urbane, well-informed and articulate lawyer is not a stock comic character. He shows a seriousness of tone and a familiarity with wider cultural and scientific questions quite foreign to Sganarelle, Gorgibus and the world of low farce.

This brief moment of warmth and approval for doctors was never to be repeated in the later medical plays.

3. BITING SATIRE

Molière did not return to medical themes until 1665, in **Dom Juan,** just eight years before his death. The tone of his satire had changed: 'their whole art is pure hypocrisy', says Dom Juan, and 'it is one of the great errors among men' (III, 1). From 1665 until his last play, **Le Malade imaginaire** (1673), Molière's satire of all doctors, whether advocates of modern chemical medicine or of the conservative Aristotelian dogmatic approach taught in the Paris Faculty, was consistently biting.

We cannot be sure why Molière began to ridicule the medical profession in 1665. It has been suggested that it might have been a consequence of contacts with doctors resulting from his own ill health. Perhaps the deaths of his ten-month-old son in November 1664, and—just a few weeks earlier—of his friend the abbé Le Vayer, son of La Mothe Le Vayer, at the age of thirty-five, left him with bitter memories of doctors. These deaths occurred around the time Molière was writing **Dom Juan,** a few months before the first performance in February 1665. Gui Patin, doctor and prolific letter-writer, asserts that Le Vayer's doctors poisoned him with antimony.[2] Antimony, commonly prepared and administered as *vin émétique,* is the remedy which Molière singles out in **Dom Juan** as the most lethal of all the cures popular in his day. Sganarelle cites its use on a patient who, at

death's door for six days, failed to respond to all remedies until the doctors administered 'de l'émétique'; its effect was immediate, Sganarelle boasts: he died instantly.

Molière's mockery of doctors, however, may have had nothing to do with his own personal experience. He used the *raisonneur* Béralde, in *Le Malade imaginaire,* to point out that 'it is not doctors he is mocking, but the folly of medicine' (III, 3). He belonged to the sceptical humanist tradition of Montaigne, who had written that many doctors were 'honest men, worthy of affection. It is not against them that I harbour ill feeling but against their art' (*Essais,* II, 37, p. 780). It is an anachronism to view Molière's distrust of medicine as excessive. The views he expresses through Béralde are no more extreme than Montaigne's. Like Montaigne, he believed that the mechanisms of the body were mysteries hidden from man's understanding, that man's best hope of recovering from illness was to trust patiently to the healing powers of nature, that sick men especially should avoid doctors as they needed all their strength to withstand their illnesses and had none to spare for fighting off the ill effects of medication. Both observe that doctors speak with great confidence about the theoretical functioning and malfunctioning of the body, but are powerless when faced with the problem of curing real illnesses.[3] Another sceptic, Pascal, who was also a scientist, shared the view that medicine was not a science. In a passage on the imagination in the *Pensées,* he points out in a matter-of-fact way, without polemical venom, that doctors and pedants were obliged to wear academic dress in order to capture the imagination of their public, because the sciences on which their expertise was based were wholly illusory (82).

It was doubly appropriate for Molière to parade doctors on stage: they were part of the heritage of farce and, in their stock roles as pedant-clowns, a rich source of visual and linguistic comedy; equally, their claims appeared genuinely absurd to a sceptical humanist; like Aristotelian pedants, they offered comic examples of would-be experts, looking back to a worn-out corpus of theory while remaining blind to the real complexities of the world about them.

4. COURT DOCTORS

L'Amour médecin, a *comédie-ballet* written at the King's request, composed and rehearsed—according to Molière—in five days was Molière's first full-blooded medical satire. It was performed at Versailles in 1665, seven months after **Dom Juan.** The play is a three-act entertainment, with a conventional plot, a slight central action and a musical tableau, with singing and ballet, at the beginning and end of each act. Molière used this light structure, with music composed by Lulli, to present a delightfully comic and bitingly satirical portrait of the doctors at court.

As the play was written at the King's request, it is not unlikely that he suggested the subject, too. At the very least, Molière must have sought prior approval for his play; the court doctors were important figures, close to the persons of the King and his immediate family, and neither Molière nor the courtiers would have laughed at them in the King's presence if he had not led the laughter. Allusions to particular doctors were quite clear to contemporaries. Bahys's stammer allegedly imitated a speech impediment of Jean Esprit, doctor to Monsieur, the King's brother; Des Fonandrès's horse, in place of the traditional doctor's mule, is an allusion to Guénaut, doctor to the Queen, and to his unconventional habit of visiting his patients on horseback; Macroton's slow speech was said also to be modelled on Guénaut's intonation; other court doctors and Des Fougerais, a successful Paris doctor, were also cited as possible models. Contemporary sources indicate that Molière made the allusions even clearer by having masks made for his actors which resembled leading doctors of the day.[4]

It is nevertheless fruitless to attempt to tie each of the doctors to a particular model. As we have seen, Molière gave Guénaut's horse to Des Fonandrès and his intonation to Macroton; he no doubt collected and rearranged characteristics from many models to construct five distinctive caricatural doctors. All five bear the stamp of the traditional stage doctor: they are wealthy; they agree that their patients, however healthy, always need expensive treatment; they diagnose illness with reference to the conventions of medicine, paying scant attention to the patient and none at all to her or his case history; they care more for the reputation of medicine than for the health of the patient—as Tomès says, 'A dead man is merely a dead man and of no consequence, but a neglected formality inflicts damage upon the whole body of doctors' (II, 3); finally, all have left behind them, in their rise to the top of their profession, countless dead and dying patients; as Filerin says, 'I've made my little pile, thank God. Let the winds blow, let it rain and hail, the dead are dead and I have enough put by to do without the living' (III, 1).

Superimposed on this general medical character, each of the five doctors represents something a little more precise. Tomès, as his Greek name indicates, was an advocate of bleeding; in this he represents the typical graduate of the Paris Faculty, practising humoral medicine (**G.E.** [Molière's **Œuvres,** ed. Despois et Mesnard, in *Grands Écrivains de la France*], V, p. 269). If Lucinde, the lovesick patient, is not bled instantly, Tomès asserts, 'she is a dead woman' (II, 4). He displays another distinguishing feature of the Paris doctor: he will have nothing to do with doctors from other faculties, as only Paris graduates can practise in the region of Paris; he boasts that on one occasion he allowed a patient to die rather than share a consultation with a doctor from outside (II, 3).

In opposition to Tomès, the arch-conservative from Paris, Molière portrays the ultra-modern horse-riding doctor, Des Fonandrès, who swears by chemical medicine, symbolized by his keenness to prescribe antimony. The contrast is crude, as befits the medium of farce, but it is clear that Des Fonandrès represents the empirical chemists from Montpellier who flourished at court, which was exempt from the jurisdiction of the Paris Faculty. Molière does not enter into the details of the rival claims of Paris and Montpellier. He now shows no more faith in the modern supposedly empirical medicine of the chemists than in traditional humoral medicine.[5] Both Tomès and Des Fonandrès are presented as dangerous fanatics, each believing absolutely in the efficacy of his chosen treatment. Each is quite sure that while his own method is infallible, that of his rival will prove fatal. Molière reflected and shared Montaigne's view that the irreconcilable differences of opinion between doctors interpreting the same symptoms were evidence enough that the claims of medicine had no basis in science (II, 37, pp. 770-76).

The next pair of doctors to take over the consultation, Bahys and Macroton, are quite different. Their priority is to sustain the reputation of medicine with a display of solidarity. Bahys with his stutter and Macroton with his slow speech are a delightfully absurd double act, but they do not fall out; they harmonize their diagnosis of Lucinde's condition with a consummate display of mutual deference and flattery. They begin cautiously, recalling the Hippocratic aphorism which emphasizes the difficulties and dangers of diagnosis and treatment. They give the patient value for money by dwelling lovingly and at length on the complexities of her very interesting condition: her humours are 'over-cooked and have acquired that malign condition in which their smoke spreads through the region of the brain' (II, 5). Most important of all, Bahys and Macroton are wily old doctors who will prescribe radical treatments only as a last resort. Before turning to 'vigorous purgation' and bleeding, they recommend that Lucinde try 'little, harmless remedies, that is, little softening and cleansing enemas, juleps and refreshing syrups to be mixed in her *tisane*'. She is to be given a chance to recover on her own before being exposed to the more lethal remedies. Finally, the two doctors prudently offer no guarantee of success, consoling Sganarelle with the assurance that if his daughter must die, they will see to it at least that she dies 'according to the rules' (II, 6).

The fifth doctor, Filerin, is introduced to restore peace between Tomès and Des Fonandrès. Molière uses the artifice of putting him on stage with his fellow doctors and no non-medical witnesses, so that he can speak his mind, confess openly the failures of medicine, and outline the policies and procedures doctors should follow to hide them (III, 1). His speech is redolent of Montaigne's influence. He shares Montaigne's view that the scientific claims of medicine are fraudulent and that the success of the medical profession is built upon the gullibility of people unmanned by the fear of death. To conceal the lack of scientific certainties in medicine, Filerin calls upon doctors to keep their quarrels secret. Montaigne had said of doctors:

> They should have contented themselves with the perpetual discrepancies in the opinions of the principal masters and ancient authors of this science which are known only to those who are well-read, without showing the common people as well the controversies and inconsistent judgements which they nurture and keep going between them.
>
> (II, 37, p. 771)

Filerin says:

> Do you not see the harm these sorts of quarrels do us in the opinion of people? And isn't it enough that learned men see the contradictions and disagreements between our authors and our ancient masters, without revealing to the common people as well, by our debates and quarrels, the charlatanism of our art.
>
> (III, 1)

Molière shows Filerin enthusiastically developing Montaigne's argument that doctors are no worse than most people who try to profit from the silliness of others; flatterers, alchemists and astrologers all work on the same principle.[6] In short, Filerin argues, as medicine is built upon the gullibility of the patient, the doctors' highest priority should be to conceal their differences and present a public façade of perfect harmony and unity.

5. THE FACULTY OF PARIS

Molière's remaining doctors—two in *Monsieur de Pourceaugnac,* and Monsieur Purgon, Monsieur Diafoirus and his son Thomas in *Le Malade imaginaire*—are all fiercely loyal graduates of the Paris Faculty and staunch defenders of the principles and practices of humoral medicine. Molière portrays the Faculty and its graduates through the reductive perspective of comic hyperbole. Any redeeming features in the behaviour of individual doctors or of the Faculty as a body, however interesting to historians of medicine, were of no concern to Molière as satirist and comic artist. The picture he paints is delightfully clear, rigorously stripped of complications which might weaken the impact of the comedy, perceptive in its analysis of the general defects in the Paris Faculty's practices, and quite unfair on questions of detail.

Antimony, or *vin émétique,* the remedy associated with innovating doctors from Montpellier, is mentioned no more after *L'Amour médecin.* Paris doctors confined themselves to the three techniques for purifying the humours: enemas, bleeding and purging. In the mock graduation ceremony at the end of *Le Malade imaginaire,* the candidate answers all questions on the treatments appropriate to different illnesses with the same refrain:

> Clysterium donare
> Postea seignare,
> Ensuitta purgare.

On each occasion, the examining Faculty doctors congratulate him on his excellent reply. Bleeding is the favourite remedy of the two doctors in *Monsieur de Pourceaugnac.* They diagnose their healthy patient as a severe melancholic, and the first doctor opines with evident relish that it may prove necessary 'to open a vein in his brow'; 'let the opening be wide,' he adds, 'to let out the thicker blood' (I, 8). Monsieur Purgon, on the other hand, as his name suggests, is an out-and-out purger.

For Molière, Paris doctors, though conservative and backward-looking in their treatment, kill just as many patients as the antimony poisoners. The apothecary in *Monsieur de Pourceaugnac,* who has complete faith in his doctor, praises him for his decisiveness: 'he's not one of those doctors who make concessions to illnesses: he's a quick worker who loves to deal with his patients at speed; and when you have to die, it's over as quickly as possible' (I, 5). This doctor has already despatched three of the apothecary's children into the next world in less than four days. The remaining two are under his care, and the apothecary adds with satisfaction: 'he treats and governs them as he pleases, with no interference from me; and, as often as not, when I get home from town, I'm amazed to find that he's had them bled or purged' (I, 5). It is these out-and-out doctors who believe in the efficacy of their art who are the most dangerous. Monsieur Purgon (*Le Malade imaginaire*) is another of the same kind. According to Béralde, Monsieur Purgon

> is nothing but doctor from head to toe; a man who has more faith in his rules than in any mathematical demonstration, and who would think it criminal to wish to examine them; a man who sees nothing obscure in medicine, nothing doubtful, nothing difficult, and who, with the impetuosity of conviction, an inflexibility born of confidence, with the brutality of common sense and reason, indiscriminately hands out purgations and bleedings, never hesitating over anything. You mustn't bear him ill will for any harm he does you: it's with unquestionable good faith that he'll polish you off and, in killing you, he's doing no more than he has already done for his wife and children and, if the need arises, will do for himself, too.
>
> (III, 3)

Molière did not embrace all doctors in this condemnation. Béralde encourages Argan, if he cannot do without doctors, to find another with whom he would be less at risk. A healthy man like Argan would have no difficulty surviving the anodyne treatments of a Bahys or a Macroton.

6. MEDICINE AND AUTHORITY

Molière presents a picture of the Paris Faculty obsessed with its exclusive rights and privileges. In the Paris region, they alone could practise; we saw how Tomès, in *L'Amour médecin,* let a patient die rather than share him with an intruder from another faculty. Their patients were their property and their income; in *Monsieur de Pourceaugnac,* the doctor, trying to recapture his escaped patient, describes him as 'a piece of property which belongs to me, and which I count among my effects' (II, 2).

Even more jealously guarded than the right to the exclusive exploitation of their patients was the right to determine the rules and laws of medicine. The Faculty of Paris, as seen by Molière, was a world-in-itself, isolated from medical scholarship and practice elsewhere in France and Europe; the candidate in the graduation ceremony in *Le Malade imaginaire* must swear to use no remedies except those approved by the Faculty of Paris. For Monsieur Diafoirus, the particular strength of his son is his refusal even to listen to new theories and discoveries:

> What pleases me most about him—and in this he is following my example—is that he holds on blindly to the opinions of our ancients, and has never wished to understand or listen to the so-called discoveries of our century on the circulation of the blood and other opinions of the same kind.
>
> (II, 5)

Diafoirus has no hesitation treating the fact of circulation as an opinion.

Molière's Paris doctors were isolated not only from other doctors but from the whole realm of empirical observation. As guardians of the hallowed principles passed down through generations of doctors, they could not risk opening their eyes, ears and minds to the evidence of the day-to-day illnesses under their care, for fear that what they observed might not tally with the theories of their masters. To highlight this blindness to evidence, Molière used the technique of presenting his doctors only with patients enjoying excellent health; first of all, they fail to notice that their patients have nothing wrong with them; then, with barely a glance at them, they launch into a mass of pre-learned theory which has no connection with the patients whose condition they are supposed to be discussing.

The strategy of Molière's Paris doctors is to keep their body of theories and codes of practice intact. To do this, they reduce the whole field of medicine to a verbally self-contained system; they banish the world of phenomena and experience from their discipline and replace it with a self-referential linguistic code. When asked to explain why opium induces sleep, the graduand answers:

> Quia est in eo
> Virtus dormitiva
> Cujus est natura
> Sensus assoupire.

The answer tells us nothing of the chemical composition of opium or of the body's responses to it. Instead, it is a perfect circle of words: opium brings sleep 'because it contains sleep-making properties whose nature is to induce drowsiness in the senses'.

The method harnesses the same scholastic techniques as those used by the Jesuit father Noël 'proving' that a vacuum in nature is impossible; it is a method designed to produce accounts of phenomena which will ensure that they fit into a preconceived cosmology and physiology.

In the cut-off world of Paris medicine, the candidate for examination need have no worries about the truth or falsehood of what he has learned. His knowledge will not be tested empirically. He is answerable only to the doctors of Paris who, so long as he parrots the orthodox views, will greet his every reply with the acclamation:

> Bene, bene, bene, bene respondere:
> Dignus, dignus est entrare
> In nostro docto corpore.

> [He replies well and is worthy to be admitted into our learning body.]

Where all the experts agree, who can question their authority?

The need for unanimity in such a system is paramount. If agreement between the experts is to be the cornerstone of medical authority, then the experts must be seen to agree. It was easy enough for doctors to speak with one voice on the general principles of humoral medicine, but according to Molière, when it came to individual cases their diagnoses were so arbitrary that doctors regularly ran into the problem of incompatible opinions. When two Paris doctors are on stage together, the problem is easily solved; in *Monsieur de Pourceaugnac,* the second doctor listens while the first doctor speaks and then has only to deliver an encomium of his colleague's wisdom. Such is the beauty of the first doctor's diagnosis of melancholic hypochondria, according to the second doctor, that a mere layman would be proud to develop the symptoms described as a sort of homage to the doctor's wisdom and eloquence (I, 8).

However, when a doctor is invited to offer a second opinion in a case where he has not heard the opinion of the first doctor, problems arise. In *Le Malade imaginaire,* Molière presents the opinions of three doctors at once: the young Thomas Diafoirus, on no more evidence than one measurement of the patient's pulse, offers his diagnosis of Argan's condition; the earlier opinion of the absent Purgon is reported by Argan himself; the third doctor, Thomas's father, who is taking the pulse of Argan's other wrist, has the difficult role of agreeing with everything his son says and then of harmonizing his son's opinion with the quite different analysis of Purgon. For Thomas the illness originates in the spleen, while for Purgon it begins in the liver. Monsieur Diafoirus quickly intervenes with some obfuscating medical jargon designed to prove that their differences are only on the surface and that, medically speaking, spleen and liver are virtually the same thing. However, he then falls into the trap of offering an opinion himself, surmising that Purgon has prescribed a diet of roast meat for his patient; in fact, he had prescribed only stewed meat. Monsieur Diafoirus quickly brings the consultation to a close and leaves, having re-established his authority by declaring firmly that the grains of salt Argan takes with his eggs should always be counted in even numbers (II, 6).

Molière pushes his satire of Paris doctors to its logical extreme by suggesting that, in their own eyes, they have achieved the power and stature of kings and even gods. Pascal had accused Noël of arrogating a godlike position in relation to nature, inventing and ignoring phenomena to prove whatever he wished. Molière's Paris doctors behave in a similar manner. In the insular world of the Paris region, where every patient is in their power and only the medical opinions of the teachers and graduates of the Faculty of Paris are accepted, Paris doctors are omnipotent; they are free to create and remove illnesses entirely as they please. When the patient of a doctor in *Monsieur de Pourceaugnac* escapes before his treatment is completed, the doctor tells Oronte that if he finds him and fails to restore him to the doctor's custody, he will be 'struck down by whatever diseases the Faculty chooses' (II, 2). When Argan fails to observe the precise instructions of his doctor—he wishes to delay an enema—Purgon, in a blind rage, condemns his patient to a whole sequence of illnesses of increasing gravity which, he promises, will leave him incurable within four days and, soon after that, will lead to certain death (III, 5).

The quasi-divine powers which Paris doctors claim for themselves are compared mockingly to the divinely instituted powers of kingship. Argan's postponement of his enema is anathematized by Monsieur Purgon as an act of *lèse-Faculté.* The new graduate in the mock ceremony praises his elders in terms more suited to an encomium of *le Roi soleil:*

> Ce serait sans douta à moi chosa folla,
> 　Inepta et ridicula,
> 　Si j'alloibam m'engageare
> 　Vobis louangeas donare,
> Et entreprenoibam adjoutare
> 　Des lumieras au soleillo,
> 　Et des étoilas au cielo,
> 　Des ondas à l'Oceano,
> 　Et des rosas au printanno.

[It would no doubt be a mad, inept and ridiculous thing if I were to engage in praising you, and undertake to add light to the sun, stars to the sky, waves to the ocean, and roses to the spring.]

The student's gratitude to his Faculty teachers is expressed in even more excessive terms. He speaks as if he were offering thanks to his Creator:

> Vobis, vobis debeo
> Bien plus qu'à naturae et qu' à patri meo:
> 　Natura et pater meus
> 　Hominem me habent factum;
> 　Mais vos me, ce qui est bien plus,
> 　Avetis factum medicum.

[To you, to you I owe much more than to nature and to my father: nature and my father made me a man, but you, much more importantly, have made me a doctor.][7]

Molière was never to turn his doctors into the subject of high comedy; they were never to achieve the status of such figures as Arnolphe, Alceste, Dom Juan, or even Philaminte. They belonged to the world of farce, and on stage they performed as clowns, in clownish medical costumes, with funny voices and mechanical gestures. This is not to say that his medical plays were innocent farces with no satirical edge to them. On the contrary, Molière's choice of a farcical medium was a reflection of his low opinion of the medical profession. Doctors, like Aristotelian pedants, did not deserve more serious attention: their absurd scientific pretensions, their vanity and their cupidity made them natural figures of fun.

But Molière's blame did not fall too heavily on the doctors themselves; it was not entirely their fault that the whole discipline of medicine was built on uncertain foundations. To underline his view that it was the discipline itself that was absurd, Molière had his stage doctors use real diagnoses, with the correct technical terms; the first doctor's analysis of hypochondriacal melancholy in *Monsieur de Pourceaugnac* has been hailed as a masterly summary of seventeenth-century medical opinion on this condition (*O.C.* [*Œvres complètes*], II, 1402, n. 3). Molière felt that medical eloquence was funny enough to stand on its own, without any need of comic exaggeration. He blamed the public, too, for the state of medicine: the fear of death made people gullible and much too keen to spend money on their health; as Montaigne and Molière pointed out, doctors flourished and multiplied in response to public demand.

However, Molière's satire of doctors, for all the laughter they inspire, is much harsher than his satire of pedants; the audience is not allowed to forget that the models for these strutting clowns, in the real world, never tired of sending men, women and children to an early grave. Both the delightful humour and lightness of his portrait of doctors and the chilling realities of medical practice are captured in Molière's last words on the subject, and the last words he wrote for the stage:

> Vivat, vivat, vivat, vivat, cent fois vivat
> Novus doctor, qui tam bene parlat!
> Mille, mille annis et manget et bibat,
> Et seignet et tuat!

[Long live, long live, long live, long live, a hundred times long live the new Doctor, who speaks so well! For a thousand and a thousand years may he eat, drink, bleed and kill!]

Notes

1. See Andrew Wear, 'Aspects of seventeenth-century French medicine', in *Newsletter of the Society for Seventeenth-Century French Studies,* 4, 1982, pp. 118-32, especially pp. 120-24.

2. See *G.E.,* IX, pp. 577-8. Molière wrote a sonnet and a letter to La Mothe Le Vayer, consoling him for the death of his son, published in *O.C.,* II, p. 1184, and *G.E.,* IX, pp. 577-80.

3. Montaigne's views on medicine are contained in *Essais,* II, 37, 'De la ressemblance des enfans aux pères', especially pp. 765-82, and III, 13, 'De l'expérience', pp. 1079, 1087-92.

4. For a discussion of the possible models for Molière's doctors in *L'Amour médecin,* see Despois and Mesnard's introduction and notes in *G.E.,* V, pp. 268-76. The evidence for the use of masks appeared in contemporary letters, quoted by Couton, in *O.C.,* II, pp. 1320-21, note 2.

5. See Wear, p. 118, who, writing as an impartial historian, shares Molière's view, pointing out that 'antimony (the chemical remedy of the 'moderns') could kill just as much as bleeding (the treatment of the 'ancients')'.

6. See Montaigne, p. 780. In another chapter, I, 32, 'Qu'il faut sobrement se mesler de juger des ordonnances divines', Montaigne groups 'alchemists, soothsayers, astrologers, palmists and doctors' together as charlatans whose claims have no foundation in reality (p. 215).

7. There is a double irony in this stanza. As well as mocking doctors for their vanity, Molière is reminding us that once a man becomes a doctor, he loses his status as a man—a process illustrated earlier in *Le Malade imaginaire* through the portrait of the halfwitted, dehumanized and mechanical figure of Thomas Diafoirus, reciting his memorized compliments and proposing to celebrate his engagement by taking his young mistress out to a dissection.

Bibliography

The best edition of Molière's complete works remains the *Œuvres,* ed. Despois et Mesnard, *Grands Écrivains de la France* (13 vols) (Paris, 1873-1900) [abbreviated *G.E.*].

The best recent edition is the *Œvres complètes,* ed. G. Couton, *Bibliothèque de la Pléiade* (2 vols) (Paris, 1971) [abbreviated *O.C.*]

Montaigne, M. de, *Essais* (1588), ed. P. Villey and V.-L. Saulnier (2 vols) (Paris, 1965)

Pascal, B., *Pensées,* ed. L. Brunschvicg (3 vols) (Paris, 1904)

Wear, A., 'Aspects of seventeenth-century French medicine', *Newsletter of the Society for Seventeenth-Century French Studies,* 4 (1982), pp. 118-32

Roxanne Decker Lalande (essay date 1996)

SOURCE: Lalande, Roxanne Decker. "*Le Malade imaginaire*: The Symbolic and the Mimetic." In *Intruders in the Play World: The Dynamics of Gender in Molière's Comedies,* pp. 168-85. Madison, N.J.: Fairleigh Dickinson University Press, 1996.

[*In the following essay, Lalande discusses the structural coherence of* The Imaginary Invalid, *suggesting that careful construction underlies the apparently disjointed arrangement of the plot and musical interludes.*]

> L'on n'a qu'à parler avec une robe et un bonnet, tout galimatias devient savant, et toute sottise devient raison.
>
> —*Le Malade imaginaire,* III, 14

Many critics indulgently dismiss Molière's apparent lack of attention to structural unity as unimportant in view of his comic genius, which liberates him from the constraints facing ordinary playwrights. Without arguing against the poetic license of genius, I should like to point out that this view of Molière's plays as a series of sketches favoring the display of comic character does very little justice to his talent for plot construction. I hope to have justified this point of view already in my analysis of *Le Bourgeois gentilhomme,* which, along with *Le Malade imaginaire,* has been cited as one of Molière's most dismembered plots. Naturally, the negative perception has a great deal to do with the fact that both plays are *comédies-ballets.* The incorporation of music and dance into a broadly farcical main plot may appear somewhat arbitrary, and Molière's attempts at careful integration of the interludes seem, at least initially, very casual. Paradoxically, this flagrant lack of integration is, as I shall try to prove, a very important feature of the structural unity of *Le Malade imaginaire.* The key to the play's fundamental symmetry lies in uncovering the dialectics of opposition between two radically different ludic spheres that are largely determined by gender.

The first scene of act 1 is of critical importance to our understanding of Argan, for the spectator is made aware of the semi-conscious nature of his game. The fact that the protagonist is engrossed in monologue indicates his self-absorption within an illusory circle of his own creation. On the other hand, his need to be surrounded by others manifests his desire for an audience: "Il n'y a personne. J'ai beau dire, on me laisse toujours seul; il n'y a pas moyen de les arrêter ici"[1] (I,1). [There's nobody here. No matter what I say, they always leave me alone; there's no way to keep them here.] He is therefore presented as a comedian, but as one who is only semiconscious of his playacting. His infantilism and helplessness are merely attention-getting artifices that allow him to manipulate his audience. This child-subject cannot be satisfied with self-appraisal. He needs the gaze of others to substantiate his being. Argan therefore simultaneously depends upon and controls this gaze. Carol Mossman points out the paradoxical nature of Argan's manoeuvre: "If, on the one hand, Argan has wished himself into a position of total dependence on his family, the family is in turn forced to focus its attention on this counterfeit child."[2]

Argan is an invalid who measures the state of his health by the number of medications he has ingested. "Si bien donc que, de ce mois, j'ai pris une, deux, trois, quatre, cinq, six, sept et huit médecines et un, deux, trois, quatre, cinq, six, sept, huit, neuf, dix, onze et douze lavements; et l'autre mois, il y avait douze médecines et vingt lavements. Je ne m'étonne pas si je ne me porte pas si bien ce mois-ci que l'autre" (I,1). [So this month I've taken one, two, three, four, five, six, seven, eight doses of medicine and one, two, three, four, five, six, seven, eight, nine, ten, eleven, twelve enemas; and last month there were twelve doses of medicine and twenty enemas. I don't wonder that I'm not as well as this month as last.] This comical use of inverted logic points to the equivalence of pleasure and pain. This masochistic propensity of Argan, for whom illness is a veritable source of pleasure, is a means whereby to become the center of attention in a circle of ludic activity of his own creation. According to Philip Berk, "He has the pleasure of knowing . . . that his helplessness is willed and therefore a function of his strength."[3] One should never underestimate Argan's puerile behavior and seeming dependency, which serve as a pernicious smoke screen for authoritarianism. His patriarchal powers remain intact, perhaps all the more so because of the false security his childish disposition inspires in his entourage.

Although Argan's play world may seem utterly foolish to those who do not share in his obsessions, absorption is intense for those who take any game and its rules seriously. Ralph Albanese describes the carefully constructed demarcation line between reality and play in the following terms: "L'univers chimérique dans lequel il s'enferme doit être perçu, on le verra, comme une stratégie de défense contre les impératifs de l'univers réel."[4] [The chimerical universe in which he encloses himself must be perceived, we shall see, as a defensive strategy against the demands of the real world.] (Translation by author) It is participation or nonparticipation in Argan's play world that marks the delineation between the two groups of opponents within the play. The attributes and activities of the two circles of adversaries, though diametrically opposed, will eventually overlap and fuse. It is in this respect that Molière reveals his true talent for plot construction.

A primarily male society has formed around the patriarch Argan, consisting of members of the medical profession: Diafoirus Père and Fils, M. Fleurant, and Docteur Purgon. Béline's rather marginal presence within this society will be examined at some length later on. One thing that these male characters share is their serious regard for their profession. Indeed, even the skeptical Béralde must concede that Purgon's intentions are sincere, in spite of their disastrous consequences. "Votre Monsieur Purgon, par exemple, n'y sait point de finesse; c'est un homme tout médecin de la tête jusqu'aux pieds; un homme qui croit à ses règles plus qu'à toutes les démonstrations des mathématiques, et qui croirait du crime à les vouloir examiner . . . Il ne faut point vouloir mal de tout ce qu'il pourra vous faire; c'est de la meilleure foi du monde qu'il vous expédiera, et il ne fera, en vous tuant, que ce qu'il fait à sa femme et à ses enfants, et ce qu'en un besoin il ferait à lui-même" (III,3). [Your Monsieur Purgon, for example, doesn't try to fool anybody: he's a man who's all doctor, from head to foot, a man who believes in his rules more than in all the demonstrations of mathematics, and who would think it a crime to want to examine them; . . . You mustn't bear him ill will for anything he may do to you; it's in the best faith in the world that he'll expedite you; and in killing you he will do only what he's done to his wife and children, and what, if the need arose, he would do to himself.]

This impression of Purgon is confirmed in scene 5 of act 3, when Béralde, Argan's more sensible brother, attempts to dismiss the overeager M. Fleurant, who has prepared yet another of Purgon's prescribed enemas. Purgon's outrage is vented in a litany of imprecations and threats of impending doom. By association, Argan is characterized as rebellious, insubordinate, even sacrilegious. His subsequent excommunication from the sacred realm of medicine leaves him feeling the anguish of an outcast from that very group of which he was initially the center. The equivalence between the science of medicine and religious doctrine established by the text, demonstrates once again the utter seriousness of the endeavor and the ethical overtones that the participants confer upon their activity, but most importantly it indicates the exclusive nature of enclosure within the ludic circle.

Diafoirus Père is portrayed as obsequious, conservative, and unjustifiably proud of his foolish son Thomas. Unwittingly, he reveals the faults of the very person he desires to praise: "Il n'a jamais eu l'imagination bien vive, ni ce feu d'esprit qu'on remarque dans quelques-uns; mais c'est par là que j'ai toujours bien auguré de sa judiciaire, qualité requise pour l'exercice de notre art. Lorsqu'il était petit, il n'a jamais été ce qu'on appelle mièvre et éveillé. On le voyait toujours doux, paisible et taciturne, ne disant jamais mot, et ne jouant jamais à tous ces petits jeux que l'on nomme enfantins" (II,5). [He has never had a very lively imagination, nor that sparkling wit that you notice in some; but it's by this that I have always augured well of his judgment, a quality required for the exercise of our art. When he was small, he was never what you'd call mischievous or lively. He was always mild, peaceful and taciturn, never saying a word, and never playing all those little games that we call childish.] Thomas' predicament is that he is intrinsically colorless, having no imagination, no gift for spontaneity, and no desire to play. His inability to reason for himself is demonstrated by his rote memorization of medical theory and his constant need for parental guidance. One of the main attributes of all those within Argan's sphere is a humorless disposition. Because the boundaries of ludic activity are largely undiscernible to them, their playacting is executed in dead earnest. This confusion between reality and play, medicine and comedy, is further illustrated by Thomas' proposal to take Angélique to a dissection for an evening's entertainment. Toinette rebukes him in the following manner: "Le divertissement sera agréable. Il y en a qui donnent la comédie à leurs maîtresses; mais donner une dissection est quelque chose de plus galant" (II,5). [That will be a delightful entertainment. There are some who put on a play for their sweethearts, but to put on a dissection is a much more gallant thing.]

With the exception of Béline, Argan's cohorts all abide by the laws of medicine in utter devotion. As his name indicates, Purgon's practice is almost exclusively based on purgative remedies. When he threatens Argan, it is with severe digestive disorders. Based on medical theories of the time, one can assume that Argan suffers primarily from melancholia, attributed to a malfunction of the spleen, which produces inordinate amounts of black

bile and black vapors. Hellebore, a medicinal laxative plant, was the habitual cure for this ailment, although it is interesting to note that the other commonly prescribed cure was laughter. Thus, melancholy patients were often enjoined to attend comic plays. The evacuation of anguish could hence be a physical or a psychic phenomenon. Purgon's heavy reliance on enemas can be attributed to his insensitivity to the comic spirit.

The constant cleansing of Argan's digestive track has a theatrical effect. It allows the protagonist to interrupt the action at frequent intervals, riveting the audience's attention on his physical presence. According to Albanese, "L'hypocondrie permet à Argan de faire de son corps un pur objet d'exhibition, de l'ériger en spectacle . . . La passivité de son corps est telle que l'on assiste à un processus permanent de prise et d'évacuation de médicaments sous forme de substances malignes."[5] [Hypochondria allows Argan to turn his body into an object of pure exhibition, to erect it as a showpiece . . . The passiveness of his body is such that one witnesses a permanent process of ingestion and evacuation of medications in the form of malignant substances.] (Translation by author) Small wonder that Béline heaves a sigh of relief at the simulated death of her loathsome husband: "Un homme incommode à tout le monde, malpropre, dégoûtant, sans cesse un lavement ou une médecine dans le ventre, mouchant, toussant, crachant toujours, sans esprit, ennuyeux, de mauvaise humeur, fatiguant sans cesse les gens, et grondant jour et nuit servantes et valets" (III, 12). [A man who was a nuisance to everyone, dirty, disgusting, always with an enema or a dose of medicine in his stomach; always blowing his nose, coughing, and spitting; devoid of wit, boring, bad-humored, constantly wearying people, and scolding all the servants day and night.] The audience is left with an impression of uncleanliness, humorlessness and irritability. The constant process of ingestion and excretion is in essence destructive, draining Argan physically, emotionally, and financially, and proving the ineffectiveness of the cure.

Béline forms a striking contrast to the other members of Argan's clan. Argan's wife accurately perceives the delineation between reality and play, and her astuteness is a measure of her effectiveness as a player. Unlike the other characters surrounding Argan, Béline's game is consciously hypocritical and motivated by self-interest. Angélique's youthful stepmother is a cheat, a female incarnation of the trickster. The false player pretends to be playing the game and, on the face of it, still acknowledges the rules of the game. This is why Argan is so much more lenient toward Béline than toward the other members of his family who refuse to condone his fantasies and who reveal the relative fragility of the play world in which he has shut himself up with others. In contrast to Mme Jourdain, Béline is an example of a wife whose speech is listened to and whose opinion is respected, but this is only because she has made herself the receptacle of her husband's projections and an echo of her husband's voice. Béline says what Argan wants to hear and it is only at this cost, the cost of losing her identity in speech, that she retains his interest. However, Béline's loss is a short-term sacrifice for a long-term gain. Like Tartuffe, her ultimate goal is to gain control of the family fortune by disinheriting the rightful heirs. Her strategy is to help Argan reinforce and define the boundaries of his play world by casting out the dissenting others. By reflecting her husband's gaze, allowing it thereby to turn back on itself, and by offering herself as the mirror in which the narcissistic gaze can consume itself, Béline becomes an object of fascination for Argan.[6]

Béline's role as wife-mother to Argan, in spite of her youth, casts a murky shadow over the nature of their matrimony. Béline refers to her husband as "mon pauvre mari" [my poor little hubby] and "mon petit fils" [my sweet boy (son)] in almost the same breath, whereas her husband refers to her as "mamie" [my dear], which is homonymous with "mamy" [granny]. The ambiguity of Argan's own assertion that he would require the assistance of Purgon in order to conceive a child with Béline has been interpreted by some as an abdication of paternal power and a desire to return to the irresponsibility of childhood: "Tout le regret que j'aurai, si je meurs, mamie, c'est de n'avoir point un enfant de vous. Monsieur Purgon m'avait dit qu'il m'en ferait faire un" (I,7). [The only regret I'll have if I die, my darling, is not to have a child by you. Monsieur Purgon told me he'd have me have one.] However, this allusion to Argan's sexual impotence allows one to draw the conclusion that the protagonist's enthrallment with his wife is purely narcissistic and that this willed impotence represents not an abdication, but a reaffirmation of paternal authority through the vehicle of the false child, namely Argan, who is controlled by and controls his mother; who desires his mother, but only as an extension of himself.

There is an interesting correlation between Béline's specular role and Argan's desire to sire her child: "The point being that man is *the* procreator, that sexual *production-reproduction* is referable to his 'activity' alone, to his pro-ject alone. Woman is nothing but the receptacle that passively *receives* his *product . . .*"[7] The reabsorption of femininity into maternity is a stultifying reduction process allowing man to assimilate the otherness of woman into Mother, the complement of man's primary narcissism.

The opposing cast of characters includes Cléante, Angélique, Louison, and Toinette: all those whose actions are directed against Argan's egocentric fantasies. Although Béralde takes the side of the younger generation, he will be only marginally involved in their plotting. Béralde's function is primarily dramatic. Though he may sympathize with the young, he belongs to Argan's generation and he will attempt to exploit the advantages of age by acting as go-between for the two groups of opponents. His moralizing tone indicates his adherence to the serious values of an older generation, yet his long-windedness has very little real effect on his brother. Unlike the comic spirit, didactic reason has not the ability to divert (entertain), and it is precisely a diversion from his obsession that Argan so vitally needs. The thematic value of Béralde's position as intermediary is thus established by the seriousness of his logical argumentation, while he remains nonetheless a proponent of the healing power of comedy.

It is therefore significant that it is Béralde who initially suggests the equivalence of comedy and medicine. In his view, medical practice is a superfluous art, for the body has the inherent power of healing itself. The primary function of doctors is not to heal, but to name, to enumerate, and to classify diseases: "Ils savent la plupart de fort belles humanités, savent parler en beau latin, savent nommer en grec toutes les maladies, les définir et les diviser; mais, pour ce qui est de les guérir, c'est ce qu'ils ne savent point du tout . . . Toute l'excellence de leur art consiste en un pompeux galimatias, en un spécieux babil, qui vous donne des mots pour des raisons et des promesses pour des effets" (III,3). [Most of them know a lot in the humanities, know how to talk in fine Latin, know how to name all the diseases in Greek, define them, and classify them; but as for curing them, that's what they don't know how to do at all . . . and the whole excellence of their art consists of a pompous mumbo-jumbo, a specious chatter, which gives you words for reasons and promises for results.] Medicine is thus closely connected to the nominative function of linguistic discourse, as well as to the art of deception and disguise. It is in this respect that medical practice is truly an art similar to that of comedy, based on illusion rather than substantive acts. Doctors can be seen as comedians whose sense of self-importance leaves them prey to self-deception. As Albanese points out, the doctors "font de leur art l'objet d'une érudition puérile and sclérosée, une expérience essentiellement discursive et formaliste."[8] [turn their art into the object of sterile and ossified erudition, into an essentially discursive and formalistic experience.] (Translation by author)

In his endeavor to free his brother from the tenacious ascendancy of medical practitioners, Béralde addresses him with the following exhortation: "Songez que les principes de votre vie sont en vous-même, et que le courroux de Monsieur Purgon est aussi peu capable de vous faire mourir que ses remèdes de vous faire vivre" (III,6). [Remember that the principles of your life are in yourself, and that the wrath of Monsieur Purgon is as little capable of making you die as are his remedies of making you live.] Béralde's alternative to physical purgation is, of course, the intake of comedy, the true means for the elimination of psychic anguish. The medicinal value of pleasure and laughter operates by means of diversion, allowing for a psychic discharge of anxiety. Not content to prove his point in the abstract, Béralde has brought with him a band of Egyptians for Argan's entertainment: "Ce sont des Egyptiens, vêtus en Mores, qui font des danses mêlées de chansons où je suis sûr que vous prendrez du plaisir; et cela vaudra bien une ordonnance de Monsieur Purgon" (II,9). [They are Gypsies dressed as Moors, who put on dances mingled with songs. I'm sure you'll enjoy them, and they'll do you as much good as one of Monsieur Purgon's prescriptions.] Béralde also highly recommends that his brother attend a comedy by none other than Molière. This metaliterary allusion allows the spectator to consider for a moment the benefits of his own activity. The correlation between mental and physical well-being is further emphasized by Argan's distraction after viewing the spectacle: he momentarily forgets that he is unable to walk without his cane.

At this point in the play the theme of medicine as comedy and comedy as medicine has been firmly established by Béralde, who thus provides an important link between the two circles of ludic activity present within the play. It is this link that accounts for the very central importance of this character and his somewhat lengthy discourse. It will now be up to the others to put his suggestions to work.

If the art of medicine is the bond between the members of Argan's group, the art of comedy is certainly the common link between their adversaries. Indeed, Angélique and Cléante's first encounter takes place at the theater. As Toinette reminds Cléante, "l'on vous a dit l'étroite garde où elle est retenue, qu'on ne la laisse ni sortir, ni parler à personne, et que ce ne fut que la curiosité d'une vieille tante qui nous fit accorder la liberté d'aller à cette comédie qui donna lieu à la naissance de votre passion" (II,1). [you've been told of the tight guard she's kept under, how they don't let her go out, and that it was only the curiosity of an elderly aunt of hers that got us permission to go to that play that was the scene of the birth of your passion . . .] According to Berk: "the gesture of liberation transports Angélique to the comédie, quintessentially a place of art and illusion, but where too nature can run its course, a locus of freedom and love not unlike the pastoral *locus amoenus* of medieval and Renaissance romance. It is then at the theater that are born the forces that will oppose Argan's hypochondria."[9] Comedy is thus associated with liberation from the constraints of Argan's hegemony.

With the exception of the suitor Cléante, the circle of comedians is primarily composed of women: Angélique, Louison, and Toinette, who plays the leading role. Nor should we forget Béline's role as comedienne and tactician within the opposing group. The exclusion of women from the medical circle is partially attributable to what is perceived as their inability to grasp the symbolic. Hélène Cixous contends that "woman is said to be 'outside the Symbolic': outside the Symbolic, that is outside language, the place of the Law, excluded from any possible relationship with culture and cultural order."[10] Though outside the symbolic, women are not outside the mimetic. Deprived of language, they employ their bodies as signs. Jane Gallop comments upon the relation between the Kristevan semiotic and the Lacanian imaginary in the following terms: "Both are defined in contradistinction to 'the symbolic'; the semiotic is revolutionary, breaks closure, and disrupts the symbolic . . . It is noteworthy that the male theorist sees the paternal as disruptive, the maternal as stagnant, whereas the female theorist reverses the positions."[11] Although Molière's female characters seem to share a common aversion to participating in a man's game that has lost sight of its playful origins, they are not at all adverse to forming a play world of their own. From Argan's point of view, these characters are spoil-sports, refusing as they do to participate in his circle of fantasy. By withdrawing from his game, they reveal the falsehood of his hypochondria and shatter the illusion of his play world. This is all the more distressing to Argan, as he has lost sight of the temporal and spacial limitations of his game.

The women, however, do gradually form a locus of play of their own. It is not surprising that Cléante, the lone male participant in this circle, is initially met with distrust. It is interesting to note that his presence in the female locus is structurally analogous to Béline's presence within the masculine circle of medical practitioners. It is the more worldly Toinette who cautions Angélique against the perils of love and the deceit of men: "Hé! hé! ces choses-là, parfois, sont un peu sujettes à caution. Les grimaces d'amour ressemblent fort à la vérité, et j'ai vu de grands comédiens là-dessus" (I,4). The doubt thus cast upon the authenticity of Cléante's intentions is further heightened by his first appearance on stage under the assumed identity of Angélique's music instructor. Cléante is in fact a consummate actor, the "grand comédien" of Toinette's warning. However, any initial ambivalence toward Cléante is immediately tempered by admiration for his skill, especially in view of the contrast established between himself and Thomas Diafoirus. Unlike his rival, Cléante is creative, playful, spontaneous, boldly imaginative, and he is, besides, a skillful improvisor. Whatever the initial distrust, one cannot help but be drawn to such a beguiling entertainer.

Despite Cléante's charismatic presence, it is the servant girl Toinette who is the most protean character of all: changing roles to suit the moment. Toinette's inferior social status affords her freedom from behavioral norms in spite of her economic dependency. Béline's reluctance to fire her spirited maid in spite of Argan's insistence demonstrates the soubrette's indispensable position in the household. Furthermore, Toinette's freedom is attributable to her status as unattached female. She is the only woman in the play unfettered by a male consort or a father and thus the only woman who is able to speak for herself. This allows her to assume the leadership of the group opposing Argan's wishes. The brief appearance of her suitor Polichinelle in the first interlude only serves to emphasize her complete detachment. She has no interest in her aging admirer and merely summons him to use him as an emissary. Furthermore, no actual encounter will take place at any time between Toinette and Polichinelle. Such freedom will allow her to assume a number of different identities in the course of the play.

When she first appears on stage, summoned by her master, she pretends to have knocked her head against a shutter. This tactic allows her to continuously interrupt Argan's discourse with her cries of pain, frustrating thereby his desire to quarrel with her: "Tais-toi donc, conquine, que je te querelle" (I,2). [Will you shut up, you hussy, and let me scold you?] Like Jourdain's servant Nicole, Toinette makes a mockery of her master's attempts to impose his authoritative voice while stiffling hers. However, unlike Nicole's involuntary convulsions, Toinette's behavior is willfully disruptive. By her own admission, she can turn the tears on and off: "Si vous querellez, je pleurerai" (I,2). [If you scold me, I'll cry.] She opposes her own form of body language to paternal authority, forcing the father into silence by blocking the reception of the message and forcing him to shout to the point of hoarseness. The effectiveness of a command is shown to be inversely proportional to the loudness of its transmission.

Toinette's second role as Angélique's confidante is equally one at which she excels. Understanding the ingenue's need to talk about her love, to recreate emotions through speech, and to gain self-confidence through approval, Toinette keeps her replies to a monosyllabic minimum, laced with gentle irony. Her only statement of any length cautions Angélique to distinguish the mask from the person, reality from illusion. The accomplished actor must never confuse the two. It is therefore appropriate that it be Toinette who issues such a statement.

In the next scene, Toinette will step in for Angélique, whose reticence leaves her prey to her father's commands. The servant will speak for her mistress, giving voice to the latter's objections to a marriage with Thomas Diafoirus. She will play her role for her while Angélique remains silently present. Finding, however, that paternal authority prevails and that Argan discredits

her ability to reason, Toinette will usurp the voice of the father, taking over the prerogative to issue commands, the masculine voice:

ARGAN:

Je lui commande absolument de se préparer à prendre le mari que je dis.

TOINETTE:

Et moi, je lui défends absolument d'en faire rien . . . Quand un maître ne songe pas à ce qu'il fait, une servante bien sensée est en droit de le redresser.

(I,5)

[ARGAN:

I absolutely command her to prepare to take the husband I say.

TOINETTE:

And *I* absolutely forbid her to do anything of the sort. . . . When a master doesn't think what he's doing, a sensible servant has the right to correct him.]

Argan immediately detects the subversiveness of this intrusive move into absolutist political discourse and counters with: "Viens, viens, que je t'apprenne à parler!" (I,5) [Come here, come here, I'll teach you how to talk.] What Argan really wants is to teach Toinette to speak like a woman who allows a man to in-form her speech. The servant has overstepped the boundaries of propriety by using the traditionally masculine imperative voice.

Although Toinette uses very little circumspection to reply to her master, her behavior changes radically in the presence of Béline. Both women are playacting, but Toinette is the more skillful of the two, as she is able to deceive the deceitful wife. Toinette has vowed to employ her talents in the service of young love. Her machinations will lead to the gradual integration of spectacle within the structural framework of the play. This integration parallels the disintegration of Argan's illusory circle of play and the gradual shifting of his loyalties from the medical clan to that of the comedians, the final substitution being that of comedy for medicine.

The intention of the prologue, for example, is obvious. Molière makes no attempt to disguise the obsequious flattery directed at his benefactor, the king, for whose entertainment this comedy has been devised. In a pastoral setting, shepherds and shepherdesses sing of the ailment and fatal suffering of love, as well as of its pleasures, laughter, and games. Despite the fact that for most spectators the transition between the artificial convention of the bucolic scene and Argan's first appearance on stage seems tenuous, the juxtaposition of pleasure and pain, vaguely sketched out in the prologue, will form one of the major thematic building blocks of the play.

Another point of interest that is frequently overlooked is that it is presumably the shepherds and shepherdesses of the prologue who perform *Le Malade imaginaire,* which can therefore be perceived from its inception as a play within a play, a royal *divertissement.* The main plot is thus on a plane of illusion once removed from that of the eclogue, and yet, strangely enough, the vivid realism of Argan's first monologue makes the audience perceive the preceding ballet as the less "real" of the two. Nonetheless, a framework is established from the outset, whereby *Le Malade imaginaire* is presented first and foremost as a theatrical diversion. It is interesting to note that this framework will remain open, for the play will never return to the initial pastoral illusion and thus one loses sight of the pretext for the play.

The pretext for the first interlude can be located within the first act. Toinette needs to advise Cléante of the impending marriage between Angélique and his rival. To this effect, she summons her admirer Polichinelle. Although the first interlude appears somewhat better integrated than the prologue, its introduction of music, mime, and rhythmic movement gives it a more stylized atmosphere than that of the rest of the play. Once again, the martyrdom of love is evoked; however, this time Polichinelle's laments are interrupted by a beating in the vein of farce. More importantly, Toinette's message to Cléante will never be transmitted and Argan will remain unaware of the events. Cléante will have to appear of his own volition in the next scene to hear of his misfortunes. Thus, the pretext for the first interlude seems to be rather transparent: the simple desire to add a gratuitous comic spectacle to the play, the justification being solely the pleasure it affords.

Aside from Toinette, with her frequent role playing, Cléante is the first character to offer a formal comic presentation. His impromptu opera is the first true spectacle to occur within an act of the play and to be carefully integrated, as it contributes directly to plot development. Argan insists upon witnessing his daughter's music lesson, adding a comment on his appreciation of the fine arts. This claim will soon reveal itself false, as the protagonist has little patience for the impertinent love duet. The previously silent Angélique now comes alive under the tutelage of her lover, as he coaxes her to break her silence and teaches her what to say/sing. Cléante's thinly disguised commentary on paternal tyranny irritates Argan who puts a halt to the spectacle. Once again, comedy is a vehicle for the freedom to communicate and the liberation from external constraints. Even more pertinent is the fact that the operatic subject matter is that of the play itself. Cléante thus affords us a glimpse at a miniature version of his own reality-as-comedy.

Argan's growing irritation at his daughter Angélique's insubordination is further compounded by his discovery that the music master has visited her within the confines of her private chambers. His attempt to force his younger daughter Louison into a sisterly betrayal is countered by her pretending to be dead. For one so young, she is an accomplished actress in her own right and shows an awareness of female solidarity. This time, Argan is taken in by a deception that has aroused his greatest fear, that of death. He is so jarred by his daughter's comedy that he momentarily forgets his own ailment: "Ah! que d'affaires! je n'ai pas seulement le loisir de songer à ma maladie" (II,8). [Oh, what a lot of troubles! I don't even have time to think about my illness.]

Argan's state of confusion is so great by this time, that he barely has the energy to counter the next offensive by Béralde, who has brought a band of gypsies to distract and amuse his brother. The song and dance constitute the second interlude, which again removes Argan for a moment from his troubled illusions. Integration is more complete than for the first interlude. Not only does the spectator understand the motives for the introduction of the diversion, but s/he also witnesses its effects on Argan.

The healing effect of comic diversion may have been proven to the audience, but Argan's conversion will be obtained with greater difficulty. The first step in extricating him from the doctors' grip will be taken by Béralde. By dismissing M. Fleurant, Argan's brother causes the ire of Docteur Purgon, who will subsequently expel Argan from his circle of support. As Gérard Defaux points out, "Ce n'est pas lui qui quitte la médecine mais, avec un Purgon offensé, la médecine qui le quitte."[12] [It isn't he who abandons medicine but, with an offended Purgon, it is medicine that abandons him.] (Translation by author) At this crucial moment, Toinette's intervention becomes imperative, for fear that the patient find some way to regain his medical sanctuary by placating the offended physician. Toinette understands that the only means of shattering Argan's play world is from within, by invading his ludic space and gaining his confidence within his own frame of reference. She is also perceptive enough to understand that the only way to gain stature and credibility in Argan's mind is to assume a masculine identity. By donning the disguise of a physician—that is, through the mimetic—Toinette gains access to the symbolic and consequently to authoritative discourse. Understandably, this is a concession on her part, as her ability to reason was established from the start. In his study of *Le Malade imaginaire,* Marc Fumaroli corroborates this assertion by stating that Béralde and Toinette change their tactics in the following manner: "Dès lors les deux complices, 'le génie du foyer' Toinette et le 'bon enchanteur' Béralde, doivent se rabattre sur une autre voie. De la *démonstration* au sens logique et rationnel, ils vont passer à la *démonstration* au sens esthétique."[13] [From this point on, the two accomplices, the "household genie" Toinette and the "kindly enchanter" Béralde, must resort to other means. From the logical and rational *demonstration,* they must pass on to an aesthetic *demonstration.*] (Translation by author)

Toinette's strategy is simple. Initially she discredits Purgon and his consorts by proposing remedies contrary to those that have been prescribed. Having accomplished this, she proceeds to discredit her own remedies by prescribing such a drastic cure that even Argan must flinch at its execution: "Voilà un bras que je me ferais couper tout à l'heure si j'étais de vous" (III,10). [That's an arm that I'd have cut off right away, if I were you.] It should not escape notice that Toinette's proposed remedy is a thinly disguised form of castration. The maid servant thereby calls upon the father to do in actuality what he has already done symbolically: relinquish the phallus and the accompanying paternal power by assuming the role of the unsexed child. Argan is thus forced to finally distinguish between reality and his fantasy world, when all of his concerted efforts have so far been focused on erasing the boundaries between the two. Mossman concludes: "I suggest that by erasing the barriers between reality and illusion, between adult and child, begetter and begotten, Argan is attempting to deny the fact of his mortality."[14] Argan is also jarred into recognizing that his infantilism was never in fact an abdication of power, but a pernicious means of consolidating it. Toinette's suggested castration is a means to feminine empowerment since the phallus is said to constitute the *a priori* condition of all symbolic functioning. Naturally, Argan will refuse this final solution. Although by now the disintegration of Argan's play world is nearly complete, one further step will prove necessary.

Béline's importance within the circle of Argan's illusions has been discussed at some length. As long as her presence reflects the image of himself that he wants to see, Argan can retreat to her mirror gaze as he projects himself into the space she provides for him. This mother figure is the last remaining shelter from the harshness of reality. In order to pry Argan loose from his narcissistic contemplation, it becomes necessary to afford him a view of Béline as Other. This can only be done by enlisting his participation in a subterfuge. Argan must become Other himself—a comedian—but in order to do so he must first subdue his overriding fear of death: "N'y a-t-il point quelque danger à contrefaire le mort?" (III,11) [Isn't there some danger in pretending to be dead?] The effort involved in acting out his own death is cathartic and relieves some of his morbid anguish. It allows him to merge with the image of death rather than be riveted by it. Argan's abandonment by the doctors and his subsequent disengagement from Béline leaves him nowhere to turn for refuge but to the opposing clan.

The final shift in loyalties is momentarily delayed by the protagonist's obstinacy, as he consents to his daughter's betrothal to Cléante but only on condition that Cléante become a doctor himself: "Qu'il se fasse médecin, je consens au mariage. Oui, faites-vous médecin, je vous donne ma fille" (III,14). [Let him become a doctor and I'll consent to the marriage. Yes, become a doctor and I'll give you my daughter.] Thus, Argan's permutation takes place within the structural permanence of illusion. Although his obsession with medicine does not seem to have diminished and in this respect no change is apparent, he does seem to have grasped the playful nature of the transformation and the inherent kinship between comedy and medicine. If the authority of medicine rests upon the art of deception, disguise and language, then it is essentially a theatrical art: "En recevant la robe et le bonnet de médecin, vous apprendrez tout cela . . . L'on n'a qu'à parler, avec une robe et un bonnet, tout galimatias devient savant, et toute sottise devient raison" (III, 14). [As you receive the doctor's cap and gown, you'll learn all that . . . One has only to talk with a cap and gown on. Any gibberish becomes learned, and any nonsense becomes reason.] To which Toinette slyly adds: "Tenez, monsieur, quand il n'y aurait que votre barbe, c'est déjà beaucoup; et la barbe fait plus de la moitié d'un médecin" (III, 14) [Look here, sir, if all you had was your beard, that's already a lot and a beard makes more than half a doctor], thereby obliquely acknowledging the inherent kinship between the masculine identity and the realm of the symbolic. However, if comedy proves more effective than medicine, it is ultimately because it makes use of magical, poetic, and evocative language rather than nominative discourse; of creation and mimesis rather than symbolic representation. When considered from such a vantage point, it is obviously Cléante the inveterate actor, not the unimaginative Thomas, who will afford the better cure.

It is not enough, however, for Argan to surround himself with comedians: he needs to exchange one fantasy for another, becoming a comedian himself. His stubborn clinging to his former illusion, his insistence on surrounding himself with doctors, forces a bilateral compromise. Though he may have to make do with make-believe doctors, the comedians must comply with his obsessions. Béralde exhorts his brother to become a doctor himself, thus reiterating his previous plea that he cure himself from within. As a doctor-comedian, Argan will internalize and assimilate comedy, the ultimate remedy. Thus, the ingestion and incorporation of comedy-as-medicine is symbolically represented onstage by the donning of a doctor's gown, and the fusion of the initially separate play worlds of the symbolic and the mimetic is complete. Although the solution is fantastic, it is eminently logical within the context of the play. Healing will take place in an atmosphere of complete comic liberation and rebirth authorized by carnival. Beralde explains that "Ce n'est pas tant le jouer que s'accommoder à ses fantaisies. Tout ceci n'est qu'entre nous. Nous y pouvons aussi prendre chacun un personnage, et nous donner ainsi la comédie les uns aux autres. Le carnaval autorise cela" (III, 14). [But niece, it's not so much our making fun of him, than accommodating ourselves to his fancies. All this is just between us. We can also each of us take a part, and thus put on a comedy for one another. Carnival time authorizes that.] The term "entre nous" stresses the exclusivity of the play world's membership and the awareness of its temporal and spatial limitations.

In spite of the liberating experience of comedy, the structural paradigm of patriarchy remains intact. For the women in particular, the experience of freedom has definite temporal limitations. Having managed to extricate Argan from the shelter of his hypochondria, Toinette will now, at Béralde's behest, relinquish her leadership position within this group, deferring to the Father. The power switch is marked by the third interlude, which can be seen as an initiation ritual confirming Argan's adherence to this new group in which a fusion of comedy and medicine has taken place. It is interesting to note that it is Béralde, Argan's male sibling and member of the older generation, who seeks to firmly establish the patriarch's centrality to this new group: "Les comédiens ont fait un petit intermède de la réception d'un médecin, avec des danses et de la musique; je veux que nous en prenions ensemble le divertissement, et que mon frère y fasse le premier personnage" (III, 14). [I have some actors who have composed a little act about accepting a man as a doctor, with music and dances. I want us to enjoy the entertainment together, and I want my brother to play the leading part.] It must be remembered that Argan has never entirely lost his grip on power and that his shift to Toinette's group was contingent upon his retention of the male hegemony. Hence his stubborn insistence on retaining the right to give his daughter away. In fact, his switch becomes an imperative move in his struggle to retain paternal power. Although the author seems to recognize woman's ability to perform and improvise in the realm of the mimetic, the inaccessibility of the symbolic leaves her outside of authoritative discourse, outside of any possible relationship to the cultural order. This engenders a void that will ultimately be filled by Argan's appropriation of comedy.

Paralleling this development—that is, the progressive fusion of the initially separate worlds of comedy and medicine—the spectacular elements and most notably the play's interludes, which are initially almost separate entities, become increasingly incorporated into the fabric of the plot, as the play ends on a note of delirium. Thus, *Le Malade imaginaire,* the last opus of a brilliant comic playwright, with its complete integration of metadramatic reflections on the nature and value of comedy, can been regarded as one of the most autoreferential of Molière's works: comedy ingesting it-

self. In the words of Defaux; "Molière, en rejoignant dans sa dernière comédie la grande et ancienne tradition du rire médical, nous apprend, après Hippocrate, L. Joubert et Rabelais, que le rire est non seulement le propre de l'homme, mais encore son salut, sa plus belle sagesse et sa dignité."[15] [By joining in his last comedy the great and ancient tradition of medical laughter, Molière teaches us, after Hippocrates, L. Joubert and Rabelais, that laughter is not only characteristic of mankind, but his salvation, his greatest wisdom and his dignity as well.] (Translation by author) I will simply add that the word "homme" in this citation could be viewed as gender specific.

Notes

1. Translation of *Le Malade imaginaire* from: Molière, *Comedies,* trans. Donald M. Frame (Oxford: Oxford University Press, 1985, 1986).

2. Carol A. Mossman, "The Restitution of Paternity in Molière's *Le Malade imaginaire," The South Central Review* 3, no. 1 (spring 1986): 51.

3. Philip R. Berk, "The Therapy of Art in *Le Malade imaginaire," The French Review* 45, Special Issue, no. 4, (spring 1972): 41.

4. Ralph Albanese Jr., "*Le Malade imaginaire,* ou le jeu de la mort et du hasard," *Dix-septième siècle* 154 (1987): 4.

5. Ibid., 6-7.

6. Irigaray suggests that "the desire for the same, for the self-identical, the self (as) same, and again of the similar, the alter ego and, to put it in a nutshell, the desire for the auto . . . the homo . . . the male, dominates the representational economy. 'Sexual difference' is a derivation of the problematics of sameness, it is, now and forever, determined within the project, the projection, the sphere of representation, of the same" (*Speculum,* 26-27).

7. Ibid., 18.

8. Albanese, "Jeu de la mort," 9.

9. Berk, "Therapy of Art," 39.

10. Hélène Cixous, "Castration," 46.

11. Jane Gallop, *The Daughter's Seduction. Feminism and Psychoanalysis* (Ithaca: Cornell University Press, 1982): 124.

12. Gérard Defaux, *Métamorphoses,* 298.

13. Marc Fumaroli, "Aveuglement et déabusement dans *Le Malade imaginaire,"* in *Vérité et illusion dans le théâtre au temps de la Renaissance* (Paris: Touzot, 1983): 110.

14. Mossman, "Restitution of Paternity," 54.

15. Defaux, *Métamorphoses,* 301.

Bibliography

Albanese, Ralph Jr. "*Le Malade imaginaire,* ou le jeu de la mort et du hasard." *Dix-septième siècle* 154 (1987): 3-15.

Berk, Philip R. "The Therapy of Art in *Le Malade imaginaire.*" *The French Review* 45, Special Issue no. 4 (spring 1972): 39-48.

Cixous, Hélène. "Castration or Decapitation?" Translated by Annette Kuhn. *Signs: Journal of Women in Culture and Society* 7, no. 1 (Autumn 1982): 36-55.

Defaux, Gérard. *Molière ou les métamorphoses du comique: de la comédie morale au triomphe de la folie.* Lexington, Ky.: French Forum Publishers, 1980.

Fumaroli, Marc. "Aveuglement et désabusement dans *Le Malade imaginaire.*" In *Vérité et illusion dans le théâtre au temps de la Renaissance.* Edited by M. T. Jones-Davies. Paris: Touzot, 1983: 105-14.

Gallop, Jane. *The Daughter's Seduction: Feminism and Psychoanalysis.* Ithaca: Cornell University Press, 1982.

Irigaray, Luce. *Speculum of the Other Woman.* Translated by Gillian Gill. Ithaca: Cornell University Press, 1985.

Molière. *Comedies.* Translated by Donald M. Frame. Oxford: Oxford University Press, 1968, 1985.

Mossman, Carol A. "The Restitution of Paternity in Molière's *Le Malade imaginaire.*" *The South Central Review* 3, no. 1 (spring 1986): 50-56.

Mitchell Greenberg (essay date 2001)

SOURCE: Greenberg, Mitchell. "Molière's Body Politic." In *Baroque Bodies: Psychoanalysis and the Culture of French Absolutism,* pp. 22-61. Ithaca, N.Y.: Cornell University Press, 2001.

[*In the following essay, Greenberg interprets* The Imaginary Invalid *within a psychoanalytic and historicist framework, linking the physical obsessions of Argan to the economic obsessions of* The Miser'*s Harpagon. Greenberg also considers the potential for political critique in the play, in light of Louis XIV's patronage.*]

> To be truthful, the monarch seems to spend a large part of his time on the *chaise percée.* We constantly hear of purges and enemas, of intestinal irritations that sometimes go on for an entire day; of bowel movements repeated up to a dozen times.
>
> François Millepierres, *La vie quotidienne des médecins au temps de Molière*

> The body is also directly involved in a political field; power relations have an immediate hold upon it; they invest it, mark it, train it, torture it, force it to carry out tasks, to perform ceremonies, to emit signs. This political investment of the body is bound up in accordance with complex reciprocal relations with its economic use.
>
> Michel Foucault, *Discipline and Punish*

The comfortingly monochromatic and slightly marmoreal image of the "Grand Siècle" has been a notable victim of the renewed attention literary critics and theoreticians have brought to the study of the Classical age. Gone from recent discussions of seventeenth-century France is that hieratically fixed notion of a structured world in which things and people were believed to be neatly arranged in an ordered and "organic" whole (a vision resonant with the ideological yearnings of certain twentieth-century bourgeois critics). French society of the period is no longer envisioned as a pyramid the apex of which would be fixed at Versailles, seen as the shiny apogee of a Classical moment more ideal than real. In its place, we have been offered a vision of a society in radical transformation. France, like other countries of seventeenth-century Europe situated at the crossroads of epochal changes—changes in epistemology, in economies, in theology and philosophy, in the arts—appears to us now as a rich, often extremely violent nation where political, sexual, and economic differences commingle, divide, are reconfigured.[1]

In his many provocative and innovative readings of the origins and ramifications of the "modern" subject, Michel Foucault returns time and again to the seventeenth century. He goes so far as to define this period that retained its fascination for him, whether in his early history of madness, or in his later works on epistemological and sexual revolutions, as one of the two decisive moments of radical change that mark the "modern" period, a moment in which the parameters defining human subjectivity are decisively realigned.[2] At the same time that Foucault marks off the seventeenth century as a period of fundamental realignment of epistemology, he also (and this, of course, is intimately related to epistemology) situates the coming into being, through his mapping of a new confessional policy of morality, of sexuality.[3] This change in sexuality/epistemologies corresponds to the transformation of the concept of "family" that is impelled by the reconfigurations of the socioeconomic sphere that recent demographic historians have also situated during the course of the century. "It seems clear," Jean-Louis Flandrin writes, "that between the sixteenth century and the end of the eighteenth the family radically changed and that a new familial morality had been outlined."[4] For such diverse historians as Flandrin, Lawrence Stone, Peter Laslett, Philippe Ariès, the seventeenth century in

Europe marks a moment of essential realignment in the conception of the family which gradually shifts (under the impetus of an emerging precapitalist economy?) from that rather large, inchoate definition of those people who all live and work under the same (extended) roof, be they servants, kinsfolk or other dependents, to the more restricted sense of family as that limited group of blood-relations (parents and children) that the eighteenth century will come to cherish.[5] When we understand the seventeenth century as a period of radical change in both the epistemological and sexual configurations, configurations that are inextricably interwoven with the emerging changes in polity (the imposition of an absolutist conception of the monarchy) and economics (the beginnings of the first precapitalist ventures), we see that the family is situated as the focal point of these various intermeshings (insofar as the family's main function is to produce new subjects for this network, and thus to reproduce the network).[6] These configurations are not separate but intimately interwoven as the family becomes the center of a seamless roundelay where the economic, social, and political laws governing subjectivity are, by that very subjectivity they subtend, intermeshed with sexuality, in its pleasures and limits. The family thus becomes, in the words of Foucault, "the interchange of sexuality and alliance: it conveys the law and the juridical dimension in the deployment of sexuality; and it conveys the economy of pleasure and the intensity of sensations in the regime of alliance."[7]

In another context I have argued that we must view the theater of the seventeenth century as being essentially the arena in which an inchoate and as yet unbounded ideology of the family is essayed. It strikes me that here the theater's role is proleptically to represent changes in social formations that are still only immanent in society at large.[8] It seems like more than a fortuitous coincidence that the theater should be the privileged form of representation in a society undergoing such fundamental realignment of its most basic structures. Since Aristotle, critics have pointed to the mediating function of theater. The stage mediates between the individual and the collective in an extraordinarily charged moment of dramatic exchange. Anne Ubersfeld, in a Marxist-semiotic perspective, tells us that the theater "appears to be a privileged form of art of capital importance since it demonstrates better than other forms of art how the individual psyche is invested in a collective relation." Furthermore she goes on to say that "every theatrical text is the response to a desire on the part of the audience, and it is in this relation that the articulation of theatrical discourse with history and ideology is most easily made."[9] In a similar vein the French psychoanalyst André Green writes:

> Between the two, at the meeting-point of the individual and society, between the personal resonance of the work's content and its social function, art occupies a transitional position, which qualifies the domain of illusion, which permits an inhibited and displaced *jouissance* obtained by means of objects that both are and are not what they represent.[10]

In his book *The Place of the Stage,* Steven Mullaney, as the title suggests, seductively analyzes the mediating social function of the theater in Elizabethan England. Although he is obviously indebted to Foucault for much of his theoretical vision, Mullaney turns to Raymond Williams's work to argue persuasively for viewing cultural sites (such as the theater) as inclusive (of differences) rather than exclusive.[11] Although Mullaney makes much of the geographical ambivalence of the "place of the stage" in late sixteenth- and early seventeenth-century London, situated in a juridical no-mans-land between the city of London on the one hand and the feudal jurisdictions that prevailed beyond the city's limits on the other, he argues that the theater because of this "neither/nor" relation to law inscribed within itself these diverse and contradictory "jurisdictions."[12] While the French stage of the seventeenth century, unlike the English, was not ex-centric to the sites of power but, on the contrary, situated directly at the seats of power (at Versailles or in the bustle of Paris, at the Hôtel de Bourgogne or the Théâtre du Marais), surely the metaphysical role of the theater as a mediating locus of conflicting and contradictory discourses that Mullaney analyzes is equally valid for France. Although we have too easily a tendency to view the productions of France's great playwrights—Corneille, Racine, Molière—as representing, not unproblematically, but rather monolithically the hegemonic discourse of French Classicism as a reflection of the Absolutism of Richelieu and Louis XIV, we would do well to bear in mind Mullaney's rich redefinition of the role of dominant ideology in dramatic productions:

> Hegemonic culture is (moreover) a historical dynamic, an ongoing, diachronic negotiation between the old and the new. The dominant culture in any given period cannot hope to include or even account for all human aspirations and energies; present culture is continually limited, challenged or modified by culture past and culture yet to come.[13]

How are we to understand this meeting of pleasure and law/economics (*alliance*) in the conflicting representations of seventeenth-century theater? How are we to locate it, how did the seventeenth century locate it, if not by representing this strange configuration—this new configuration, emerging out of and still intimately inextricable from other, older subjective patterns—if not by incorporating this intermeshing network in/on/as the body? I am speaking of those bodies of the passionate, comic personages that the seventeenth century figures for us (and this is not the least of its radical representations of the human subject) within the dramatic scenarios (the first in European literature) of the family—

the family that is born on the stage with all the passion and rage of a deeply conflicted sexuality, and all its comic hilarity too.

But what are we to make of these bodies given to us in representation? Is there a reality there that points to anything other than precisely the configuration and reconfiguration of discursive practices? For, and this is my point here, the body does not exist, is not available to us in some empirical "thereness" but always as a complex nexus of ideological investments. Just as we have seen that for critics, despite their different theoretical perspectives, the theater was perceived as a mediating locus so too, the body is another construct that different critics, especially recent critics of early modern culture, refuse to see as simply a biological given. Although it is the body as cadaver that in an objectifying gaze receives the attention of the seventeenth century anatomist, it is precisely not this "object" that contemporary theoreticians analyze in their discussions. Much recent work, from scholars in varying disciplines, has been brought to bear on the "body" in these cultures, so near, and yet so removed from us. In *The Tremulous Private Body,* for instance, one of the most provocative recent attempts to circumscribe the site and function of the body in early modern culture, Francis Barker argues for seeing the body as "not a hypostasized object, still less a simple biological mechanism of given desires and needs acted on externally by controls and enticements, but a relation in a system of liaisons which are material, discursive, psychic, sexual, but without stop or centre."[14] In their book *The Politics and Poetics of Transgression,* Peter Stallybrass and Allon White, who share many of the same materialist premises of Barker, insist that the "body cannot be thought separately from the social formation, symbolic topography and the constitution of the subject. The body is neither a purely natural given nor is it merely a textual metaphor, it is a privileged operator for the transcoding of these other areas. Thinking the body is thinking social topography and vice versa."[15] In a more new historicist perspective Gail Kern Paster has written persuasively about seventeenth-century English society's relation to the body. In her *The Body Embarrassed: Drama and the Discipline of Shame in Early Modern England,* she too returns to this complex nexus of intermeshing imperatives that we call the "body": "In the continuous series of negotiations by which the body is inscribed as a social text it also becomes a social 'sub' or 'infra' text, the outward manifestation of an container for desire's inner workings, less visible than the external habitus but no less subject to social formation and judgments."[16]

In a sense all of these works owe a great debt, on the one hand, to Mikhail Bakhtin's study of Rabelais (to which I shall return in a moment) and, on the other, to the work of anthropologist Mary Douglas. Douglas's influential *Purity and Danger: An Analysis of the Concepts of Pollution and Taboo* provides a structural account of the social symbolization of the body which is congenial to critics who wish precisely to deal with the body as a symbolic system without appealing to the symbolizing processes of psychoanalysis. Douglas's study of the interpretive strategies at work in archaic and primitive societies, where the body is seen as a reflection of the larger world and vice versa, has proved particularly useful as a critical tool, as it seems in a strangely sympathetic fashion to mirror early modern Europe's own interpretive, that is, "analogic" (in Foucault's terms) perception of the world (man being a microcosm that reflects the macrocosm):

> The body is a model which can stand for any bounded system. Its boundaries can represent any boundaries which are threatened or precarious. The body is a complex structure. The functions of its different parts and their relations afford a source of symbols for other complex structures. We cannot possibly interpret rituals concerning excreta, breast milk, saliva and the rest unless we are prepared to see in the body a symbol of society, and to see the powers and dangers credited to social structures reproduced in small on the human body.[17]

From Freud's early studies on hysteria, psychoanalysis has also taught us that the body is a symbolic production. By this is meant of course that there is a complex interweave of the physical and psychic functions in which is produced a "phantasmatic" image in each of us of our own corporeality. Our bodily image reflects as much of how we are inserted in the symbolic, signifying systems of our culture as how that culture is manifested in and as that image.[18] As the French psychoanalyst and critic Guy Rosolato writes, "we cannot approach the subject of the formation of the body image without bearing in mind the complex interaction of libidinal investments, the imaginary narcissistic apprehension of images, and the substitutive and symbolic potential of language which directs identification in general."[19] The body is inscribed at the interstice of "reality" (social, economic, physiological) and "fantasy" (desire). Furthermore this split between reality and desire is never unilateral, there is no perception of the body—one's own, or others'—that can be separated out from the desiring, phantasmatic structures into which it is inserted, and which it reproduces as its symptoms at the same time, of course, that these "phantasmatic" structures bear the impress of exterior social imperatives.[20]

These different attempts to circumscribe the body in either social-anthropological or psychoanalytical grids, although in many important aspects antithetical in the basic assumptions, can be bridged, it seems to me, by an appeal to the very process of "symbolization" which underpins them all. In a sense Stallybrass and White are provocatively suggestive when they offer the hypothesis: "It might . . . seem plausible to view the discourses of neurosis as the psychic eruption of social practices which have been suppressed."[21] Stallybrass and White of course are referring in their analysis to the evolution of "bourgeois culture" during the nineteenth century. Nevertheless, it seems to me that their remark may be generalized to speak about the symptomatic resistances that the appeal to the body represents in all cultures in crisis, in those fraught historical moments, to return to the conundrum of seventeenth-century France, of history's "becoming."

In the seventeenth century, and particularly on the seventeenth-century stage, questions of the body are inextricably tied to the way(s) the different comic or tragic scenarios insert the body, the body of their contentious protagonist, into the social, sexual, and economic parameters that are waiting to accommodate them. Marriage is the most overdetermined social/sexual apparatus in which and through which the sexed bodies of the seventeenth century are inserted into the familial narratives that Janus-like point both toward the past from whence the subject comes and forward into the future of renewed familial generations. Marriage, by serving as the crossroads in which and by which the past and the future generations meet in the newly consecrated heterosexual couple, serves the oedipal scenario where the difference of generations and of sexes becomes the crucial dilemma that the fractious Classical protagonist must successfully navigate in order to assume his/her proper place in absolutist society.

Where are we to situate Molière, and his cast of characters in the oedipal scheme of things? On the one hand we might say that his comedy, which plays out the same scenario over and over again, a scenario in which curmudgeonly *barbons* are continually outwitted and ridiculed by cunning servants and innocent young lovers, besides repeating a culturally inherited scenario, also affirms by this very repetition a social and sexual narrative in which normal love ("nature") successfully parries the invasive threats of perversion. In this overly simplified account of Molière's sexual plots he would clearly seem to proclaim his alignment with and affirmation of a normative oedipal scenario: the triumph of the young (male) over the old (father) for the possession of the coveted sexual (female) prize. On the other hand, a much more ambivalent response might just as well be in order. To begin with, it might be responded that the initial question is flawed, presenting as a universalizing account of sexuality (the oedipal scheme) what for many is a historically circumscribed production of a particular period and culture (late-nineteenth-century Vienna). What can an "oedipal scenario," the product of a developed bourgeois society, its prejudices and peculiarities, have to do with a seventeenth-century playwright and his cast of characters—living and play

acting in a world whose subjective parameters are clearly different from, not to say entirely alien to, those of Freud and his patients?

For the time being, rather then situate myself on one side or the other of this dilemma, I shall fence-sit by saying that the question is not as simple as it might first appear and that it admits of no easy answer, neither the apparent transparency of plot, nor the equally simplistic dismissal by those who refuse to look at any early modern social production through the twentieth-century's (supposedly distorting) lenses. When we examine the Molieresque corpus within the complex social networking of seventeenth-century France, we see that what a certain critical shorthand describes as the oedipal problematic does not admit of unidimensional answers. Rather, at the same time that any consideration of the oedipal scenario is necessarily an examination of the sexual (defined in its broadest sense), it is also inseparably linked to the social, political, economic, and religious coordinates that in any culture attend the arrival of the newly born human subject and attend this subject's inscription in his or her culture. These coordinates lay out for the infant an intricately elaborated labyrinth that s/he must negotiate in order to be eventually recognized by that culture as a viable "man" or "woman." That this path is convoluted, full of obstacles, ruts, and dead ends, is readily apparent. One only has to look at those members whom society has branded as its pariahs, those internal outsiders who for reasons that are never quite comprehensible appear (as often as not to themselves and to the others in whose gaze they stand) and are defined as having definitely and inexplicably at one moment or another of their past taken a wrong turn. They remain forever fixed in a position from which there is no return. This point of no return, this position of failed social negotiations, can be ritualistically encoded by the community only with rites of exclusion, either a sacred exclusion (shamanistic), or a ridiculous one (from laughter). In either case the community defends itself from the difference in its midst by taking its revenge on the person who has let it down, who is viewed, if we wish to use a cruel economic metaphor, as having squandered its psychic (mythic, ideological) capital, and who remains, within the psychic (but also very much within the real) economy of that community in the position of dilapidation, representing a waste of economic potential.

For Oedipus in his myth is not only about sexuality. He is, the myth is, also about "sexuality" as community, sexuality connected to yet inextricable from politics, from the economic, social, and mythic interweave that is necessary to constitute any human grouping as a society.[22] Sexuality, therefore, especially reduced to its narrow confines of genitality is not what is at issue here, but rather sexuality in the much larger sense—the scenario of an economy of desire—in which capitalization, exchange, propagation and generation are all inseparable from the particular structures of political power that are at work, in different ways at different times, to produce what any given society names as its own or rejects as its other.

Let us then return to the seventeenth century, using in this case two plays of Molière, to trace the ways a certain dramaturgy figures the transformations of the human subject in the period between the end of the Renaissance and the apogee of the Classical moment. In so doing I hope to be able to circumscribe the emergence of the subject of modernity in its varied convolutions, with the acuity of vision that is permitted, paradoxically, only as this subject, objectified in our attentive gaze, is, so we are told, disappearing forever from our field of vision.

Molière's last play, *Le malade imaginaire,* during the fourth performance of which he suffered his fatal (tubercular?) attack, was written to be staged in celebration of Louis XIV's triumphal return from his Dutch campaign (1672). It was first given on February 10, 1673, that is, if we consult the ecclesiastical calendar, during carnival. At the very end of the comedy, in the concluding lines of Béralde, Argan's brother, there is a direct reference to carnival, and to those liberties that traditionally are permitted during the pre-Lenten festivities. In response to Angélique's timid protest that perhaps the masquerade proposed by Béralde is too cruel a joke to play on Argan, Béralde responds:

> Mais, ma nièce, ce n'est pas tant le jouer que s'accommoder à ses fantaisies. Tout ceci n'est qu'entre nous. Nous y pouvons aussi prendre chacun un personnage, et nous donner ainsi la comédie les uns aux autres. Le carnaval autorise cela.[23]

> (III. xiv; 4:454)

Carnival forms the overarching structure inside of which *Le malade imaginaire* plays out its farcical attack on seventeenth-century medicine in and across the body of the hypochondriac, Argan. These obvious references to carnival and the carnivalesque allow me to fix our attention on two highly invested moments in the history of modern literary/social criticism which will form the outside parameters of my own discussion of Molière, and the subject of political modernity—at the one end of my spectrum I situate Bakhtin, and more precisely, his much commented, highly debated idea of the "carnivalesque," and at the other Freud, or rather a certain twentieth-century "psychoanalytical" vision of the human subject. In between, torn between the one and the other, objects of mediation and change, I shall place Molière, or rather those two characters of Moliere's theater, Harpagon and Argan, the protagonists of *L'avare* and *Le malade imaginaire.*

Bakhtin's rich use of the term "carnivalesque," and the carnivalesque ("grotesque") body to describe what he believed to be a different, premodern subjectivity, exemplified most notably by Rabelais, has proven to be an extremely fertile concept for contemporary criticism. Although the concept is so widely used as to be familiar to most students of the sixteenth and seventeenth centuries I shall highlight just a few aspects of the notion that I find particularly useful for my own discussion. First of all, Bakhtin's description of the carnivalesque body is authorized in his book by its dialectical relation to its supposedly historically later, other—the closed Classical body. In other words the distinction between a carnivalesque and the Classical is one other way of delimiting the difference, the perceived difference in the periods of the Middle Ages and Renaissance from the Classical and modern age. This distinction is, thus, superimposable, it seems to me, on the Foucauldian separation of these two periods—on the one hand the analogic universe of the Renaissance, on the other, and this after the moment of "the great enclosure," the period of Classical representation. I want to stress once again how periods of transition lend themselves to binary powered oppositions, how difficult it is to conceive of the imbrication, the moment of mediation in which the oppositions, not yet separated out, form an inchoate whole.

For Bakhtin, then, here is the grotesque body:

> The grotesque body . . . is a body in the act of becoming. It is never finished, never completed; it is continually built, created, and builds and creates another body. Moreover, the body swallows the world and is itself swallowed by the world . . . This is why the essential role belongs to those parts of the grotesque body in which it outgrows its own self, transgressing its own body, in which it conceives a new second body: the bowels and the phallus. These two areas play the leading role in the grotesque image, and it is precisely for this reason that they are predominantly subject to positive exaggeration, to hyperbolization; they can even detach themselves from the body and lead an independent life, for they hide the rest of the body, as something secondary. . . . Next to the bowels and the genital organs is the mouth, through which enters the world to be swallowed up. And next is the anus. All these convexities and orifices have a common characteristic; it is within them that the confines between bodies and between the body and the world are overcome: there is an interchange and an interorientation. This is why the main events in the life of the grotesque body, the acts of the bodily drama, take place in this sphere. Eating, drinking, defecation and other elimination (sweating, blowing of the nose, sneezing), as well as copulation, pregnancy, dismemberment, swallowing up by another body—all these acts are performed on the confines of the body and the outer world, or on the confines of the old and new body. In all these events the beginning and end of life are closely linked and interwoven.[24]

I have quoted this passage extensively because it is important for its description of the grotesque body as a body of organic excess, of openness, of incompletion, in a constantly renewable cycle of life and death. The grotesque is a body that knows no limits, to which limits are death. The social activity that corresponds to the grotesque body is, of course, the carnival which Bakhtin tells us cannot be thought of as a function that "distinguishes," or separates out. Once again it is not a (social) organism that creates an exterior and an interior, an in and out: "Carnival is not a spectacle seen by the people: they live in it, and every one participates because it very idea embraces all the people."[25] The utopian, perhaps naively utopian aspect of Bakhtin's description of carnival has been severely criticized by almost all contemporary scholars who have adopted, nevertheless, his delineations of both the grotesque body and the carnival as heuristic devises in their own work.[26]

Although the concept of the grotesque body may be but one way among many to describe a different subjective imbrication of the human being in an epistemic formation that has become for us but a nostalgic memory, it does seem to correspond, as an image, to the medical science of the late Middle Ages and the early modern period. Such historians as Thomas Laquer or Caroline Walker-Bynum and literary scholars such as Marie-Hélène Huet and Gail Kern Paster have reminded us not only of the principles of Galenic medicine but of the enormous patriarchal investments such a humoral conception of the human body both obfuscates and reveals.[27] The early modern English and, we can assume, French subject, according to Paster, "grew up with an understanding of his or her body as a semipermeable, irrigated container in which humors moved sluggishly. People imagined that health consisted of a state of internal solubility to be perilously maintained often through a variety of evacuations either self-administered or in consultation with a healer."[28] Obviously, in the masculinized ideology that informed such a conception of the body, the male body was the ideal object of creation, being both more "hot" than the female, and particularly more "closed."[29] The female body because of its effluents was famously described as a "leaky vessel," tautologically dangerous for a society that in the seventeenth century was growing increasingly wary of any "unbounded system."[30]

On the one hand, therefore, we have the open, unfinished, female grotesque body, on the other the Classical closed, male body. And who best represented the shining ideal of bodily and political perfection but the king, the extolled, idolized, and triumphant Louis XIV? *Le malade imaginaire,* let us remember, was written as part of the ceremonies celebrating Louis's triumphal return from the Dutch campaign of 1672. The French had gone off to punish the too-wealthy, too-commercially successful, too-Protestant Dutch Republic. Although the purpose of this particular military action undertaken by the French with Louis at their head was not ostensibly to enlarge their territory, the campaign must obviously be seen as forming an integral part of the policy of ter-

ritorial aggrandizement of the French state under both Louis XIII and Louis XIV. Rather then simply a disguised form of landgrabbing such as those pre-Classical dynastic marriages, with the ensuing back-and-forth bickering over what territories did and did not become a permanent part of the crown (although, this activity too continues throughout the century, witness the Clèves-Juliers affair), the territorial policy of the French crown in the seventeenth century becomes essentially a consistent and organized attempt to secure natural boundaries (natural in the sense of geography or cultural spheres) for the state. These borders, once secured, were thought to protect the state from the vulnerability of openness. By closing off the frontiers—at the Pyrenees, the Rhine, the Atlantic coast—France became a secured, bounded entity. Once of course this entity was separated out from and defended against external threats, attention could then be directed at securing the internal vulnerabilities of the state. When the outside was kept at bay, the inside could be cleansed of those troublesome others who undermined the state from within: the Huguenots are expulsed (1685), pushed beyond the borders of the realm.

I am suggesting simply that a homology is working throughout the seventeenth century between the geographic integrity of the realm and the ideal of a classical body which Bakhtin defines in the following way: "The new bodily canon . . . presents an entirely finished, completed, strictly limited body, which is shown from the outside as something individual. That which protrudes, bulges, sprouts, or branches off . . . is eliminated, hidden or moderated. All orifices of the body are closed."[31] Mary Douglas, as I mentioned above, has spoken about this analogy between the social body and the physical body in an attempt to equate how the fear of permeable social/political boundaries is reflected by the anxiety associated with bodily orifices, margins: "Any structure of ideas is vulnerable at its margins. We should expect the orifices of the body to symbolize its specially vulnerable points."[32] In a world where precisely not only the political boundaries were in flux but the prevalent (although changing) medical notion of the body was one of contained but infinitely variable fluidity, anxiety about borders, openings, bodily orifices would seem, on still another level, to symbolize a ceaseless back-and-forth dialectic, a struggle between chaos and order, between bodily and social disintegration and societal stability and governance. To instill the conception of an integral body politic in the individual subject, an image must be substantiated which is at once familiar and august, both near and distant. The idea of the state must be made to correspond to the image of the individual body just as the image of the body (of the subject) is made to mediate the distance separating metaphysical ideology from an anchoring in the physical. The conception of the body fixes the ideological aporia of the state by first identifying with what is recognizably similar in the body of the God/prince and then by denying this equivalence in a metaphysical leap beyond the physical body of the king to his other body—the body royal wherein the state in its transcendental essence resides. The body that mediates between the transcendental concept of the perfect state, and the physical reality of the body in its evanescence becomes fixed upon the shining body Royal, the "corps glorieux" of the king: Louis XIV as he was produced in and as a spectacular embodiment of the ideals toward which the French state moved.[33]

The constant pressure throughout the century to eliminate the extravagant, the obtrusive, the vulgar—the movement that we have come to define as the refining so essential to our contemporary views of French culture this finesse that is the quintessence of abstract sophistication, that marks French Classicism off from the excesses of seventeenth-century English or Spanish culture, so shot through with plebeian elements rather than some simple given of cultural superiority—is the product of a long politicoesthetic struggle to impose order on a threatening chaos.[34] This imposition however was contested and hotly resisted—the Frondes, the peasant rebellions, the Protestant revolts—to name just the most obvious political manifestations. It was a long ongoing struggle, often bloody, in which the first modern totalitarian state attempted with more or less success to impose a homogenous image by subsuming the state in and under the image of the king—finally the image of the Classical male body—on the heterogeneous mixture of French life.

The important point to bear in mind, however, the point Stallybrass and White stress, is the dialectical nature of this change, the way, even as we see in Bakhtin, one form ("the grotesque") exists in an inextricable relation to its other ("the Classical"):

> The classical body splits precisely along the rigid edge which is its defense against heterogeneity: Its closure and purity are quite illusory and it will perpetually rediscover in itself, often with a sense of shock or inner revulsion, the grotesque, the protean and the motley, the neither/nor, the double negation of high and low which was the very precondition for its social identity.[35]

So, although the glorious body royal becomes an icon too sacred to be touched and remaining incorruptible even into advanced old age,[36] the king's surrogate, the father, the king of his family, lends himself to more ambivalence, to the ambivalence of the clash of cultural codes and values, in a way that is more tragic and more comic than the "real" hieratic image of the *père du peuple* ever could.[37]

Borrowing the term "oikodespotès" from Jürgen Habermas who uses it to describe familial-economic organization in Greek society, I suggest that the word fits admirably into our own purposes as a way of introducing the sociosexual dimension of the role of the father in Molière's comedy.[38] It combines the etymological connotations of house and home (and by extension husbandry, household-economy) with the term for controller, ruler. This latter term echoes with the proleptic resonance of despot, tyrant, dictator and in this sense sends us back to the metaphorical conundrum uniting father/king in seventeenth-century culture. The father remains, for seventeenth-century patriarchy, the central figure in familial economy. I think it best to map the economic change, the change that is written on the bodies of these men, and this is, I suggest, interestingly perverse—because, in the Classical period we are discussing, "men" and "bodies" have almost become exclusionary terms. In the emerging redistribution of patriarchal monarchies that mark the introduction of the modern, men who are the arbiters of value and meaning, who are at work in the chancelleries, in the learned societies, in the amphitheaters where more and more readily anatomical dissections and lessons are carried out accentuate the split between the body and the soul, the body and the mind. This metaphysical difference becomes, true to its roots in Aristotelian logic, even more the split between male and female, between masculine and feminine. In this split, women are essentialized as "le sexe" for the men who, although they may "have a sex," certainly refuse any notion that they are "le sexe."[39]

"Le sexe" of course, is always the "other," the female other, who in the emergent order of corporate statism, proves all the more necessary for the economic distribution of wealth accumulated and passed down in patrilineal descent. Thus, on the most simple level, the confusion, the heated confusion of "le sexe," sex and money, comes to rest on that roc incontournable of (emergent) bourgeois economies—marriage. It is in terms of marriage that sex and money are inextricably linked to desire and the body politic in Molière's comedy, be it the serious comedy of *L'avare* or the more carnivalesque farce of *Le malade imaginaire,* and they are linked most forcefully through paternal mediation, a mediation that in Molière is always comic because of a flaw in the father that puts him at odds with the system, its values, ideals, and simulacra that he is supposed to embody.

Let us turn our attention to the two father/protagonists of *Le malade imaginaire* and *L'avare* and, rather than view them as separate, exclusive entities (which on the textual level they obviously are), look at them as two sides of the same conflicted coin—the site of political, economic, and sexual agencies that traverse their representation, their beings, their "bodies." On the one side we have a pull toward the carnivalesque, toward the grotesque body, the lower bodily stratum, the body of birthing, of excretion, the open, organic, constantly evolving body, even (if we wish to follow the logic of Bakhtin) the maternal body. On the other there is a pull toward the classical, the closed precapitalist body of state corporatism as it reaches its apogee in Louis XIV's France, the body of the father, of the law, the oedipal body of emerging modernity. In other words, it is in and across the body of Harpagon/Argan that Molière traces the emergence—with all its conflicts and tensions, all its halts, insecurities, and regressions—of the *mise-en-place* of the modern. He does this by the ways he incorporates the bodies of the father(s) within the intermeshing flow, through and across these bodies of different but interrelated economies—the economy of excreta (the anal economy), the economy of material exchange (the precapitalist economy of conflict between systems of inheritance and systems of venture capitalism), and the mixed economy of oedipal sexuality (genital and material, i.e., the marriage economy). That these different economies exist together, that one really is not easily isolated from the others, is what makes Molière's plays so perversely comic; for in another sense these different economies of plot and character are all subsumed in the economy of laughter which they generate and which, in turn, effects our own system, the audience's system, of bodily economies.

I have already mentioned the carnivalesque framing inside of which *Le malade imaginaire* is inscribed. If we look at *L'avare,* written and performed five years earlier (1668), we find repeatedly stamped in its very center that other, diluted, Bakhtinian category, the "fair." In his attempts at courting Mariane, Harpagon has enlisted the services of Frosine, a go-between. On Harpagon's behalf Frosine has arranged for Mariane pay a visit to Elise, Harpagon's own daughter, and while waiting to dine with the Harpagon family, to accompany her to the fair:[40]

HARPAGON:

> C'est que je suis obligé, Frosine, de donner à souper au seigneur Anselme; et je serai bien aise qu'elle soit du régal.

FROSINE:

> Vous avez raison. Elle doit, après dîner, rendre visite à votre fille, d'où elle fait son compte d'aller faire un tour à la foire, pour venir ensuite au souper.

HARPAGON:

> Hé bien! elles iront ensemble dans mon carrosse, que je leur prêterai.

> (II,v; 3:346-47)

I point to this apparently inconsequential plot devise because for, as marginal as it seems, it indicates for us another inscription of a public economic locus that in its contrast to the invocation of carnival in the *Malade*

imaginaire is revelatory of at least a competing economic sphere coexisting simultaneously in Molière's theatrical universe. While the carnival is used as a metaphor for unlimited spending, for a world that knows no bounds, that knows no hoarding, and while it thus corresponds economically to a (utopian) world of indifference (i.e., wealth in the capitalist sense, of individual, separate possession, is negated in the vast, unregulated carnivalesque disbursing), the fair, as Stallybrass and White tell us, is a much more ambivalent economic locus:

> In so far as it was purely a commercial event it could be envisaged as a practical agency in the progress of capital, an instrument of modernization and a means of connecting up local and communal "markets" to the world market. . . . From the perspective of cultural studies, folklore and social history, the fair has been predominantly thought of in terms of popular revelry and political subversion. From the perspective of economic history . . . fairs have been seen above all as the sites of commercial distribution whose rise and fall depended upon national and international market forces.[41]

So, in the one case, at least at the very outset, we have a comedy, *Le malade imaginaire,* that with its reference to carnival would seem to be backward looking, economically speaking, while the other *L'avare,* with its reference to the fair, would appear to be pointing toward the (capitalist) future, at least insofar as the realities of seventeenth-century economic life seem to intrude within the confines of the play. This division is, of course, only a heuristic devise: quite clearly what we have is the coexistence in Molière's theater of the transitional moment, the moment that contains both systems, without choosing between them.[42] But let us for the time being continue to view these two plays as representing clearly opposed worldviews, two radically separated views of economics realities. How then are these exterior differences embodied in the comedies?

Argan, the hypochondriacal father of *Le malade imaginaire* is evidently a wealthy bourgeois who, as the introductory scene shows us, is, even in throes of his mania, very close to his *sous.* The play begins with Argan counting his different medications and calculating their cost.

> Trois et deux font cinq, et cinq font dix et dix font vingt. Trois et deux font cinq. "Plus, du vingt-quatrième, un petit clystère insinuatif, préparatif, et rémollient, pour amollir, humecter, et rafraîchir les entrailles de Monsieur." Ce qui me plaît de Monsieur Fleurant, mon apothicaire, c'est que ses parties sont toujours fort civiles: "les entrailles de Monsieur, trente sols." Oui, mais, Monsieur Fleurant, ce n'est pas tout que d'être civil, il faut être aussi raisonnable, et ne pas écorcher les malades. Trente sols un lavement: Je suis votre serviteur, je vous l'ai déjà dit. Vous ne me les avez mis dans les autres parties qu'à vingt sols, et vingt

sols en langage d'apothicaire, c'est-à-dire dix sols; les voilà, dix sols.

(I.i; 4:388)

Argan is ill, so he believes, and because he is ill with a sickness unto death ("Ah mon Dieu! Ils me laisseront ici mourir"), he desperately tries to restore his health, or at least maintain it in its precarious equilibrium, by fetishistic ministrations to his bowels, ministrations for which he pays dearly. But although from the very beginning the comedy establishes a running equation between the economy of the body and the economy of the marketplace, the laughter of this play is generated by the former rather than the latter. The entire play's comedy turns around the obsessive references Argan makes to his excretory functions. He is continually administering to himself or having others administer to him purges, enemas, and the like. Of all the works in the French canon, including Rabelais's oeuvre, no other is so persistently scatological, no other as André Glucksmann informs us, so insistently rubs our noses in shit.[43]

For a twentieth-century audience Argan's obsession with his bowels appears much more "symptomatic" than what a contemporary seventeenth-century public would at first notice. In the seventeenth century, during which prevailed, as I mentioned above, a humoral concept of the body, purges, that is the artificially induced elimination of "nefarious" internal "humors," were, as Paster reminds us, a quotidinally familiar treatment. Most of the audience would often have had purges administered to them.[44] The desired effect of these purges was to reestablish a harmonious equilibrium in the body that illness had disturbed. Clearly, however, Argan's attention to his bowel functions, his obsessive interest in maintaining a constant "ebb and flow" of intake and output, goes beyond the socially accepted limits of his time (that is why there is laughter, but not why there is riotous laughter) and places him in the realm of the scatologically outrageous.

If Argan focuses obsessively on his bowels, it is properly because in any society that puts a high price on order, on closure, on a complete, integral structure (any society, in other words, which views the father as embodying a totalizing fantasy of corporate integrity—patriarchy, in sum), the anus is that bodily orifice that first comes up against the social imperatives of renunciation.[45] The control of bodily excretions becomes the locus of a continuing battle between the internal economy of the infant and the external law of his world. It is a battle whose consequences, so Freud tells us, has repercussions on the entire future sociosexual life of the individual. In the *Three Essays on the Theory of Sexuality*, Freud first describes the importance of the "anal zone": "It is to be presumed that the erotogenic significance of this part of the body is very great from the

first. We learn with some astonishment from psychoanalysis of the transmutations normally undergone by the sexual excitations arising from this zone and of the frequency with which it retains a considerable amount of susceptibility to genital stimulation throughout life."[46] It is this genital excitability that is, once again according to analytic theory, like all forms of infantile pleasure, so difficult to renounce. Under the pressure of society the anal zone becomes the object of the child's first struggle with the law, the law that says "no": no to his/her pleasure, no to what is quickly defined as dirt, "bad," unacceptable. For Melanie Klein, continuing the theoretical speculations of Karl Abraham, the fixation of the anal stage is marked as "sadistic" in that there seems to predominate an aggressively hostile attitude toward the world—the desire to dominate and destroy the ambient social locus through the manipulation (in the attempts of control) of the anal muscles and the control of the contents of the intestines.[47] The struggle between the child's pleasure and social injunction is an early and deciding factor in the child's relation to his own body, to the psychic image he or she has of his or her own body, and consequently to other peoples' bodies, and to the law:

> Defecation affords the first occasion on which the child must decide between narcissistic and an object-loving attitude. He either parts obediently with his faeces, "sacrifices them" to his love, or else retains them for purposes of autoerotic gratification and later as a means of asserting his own will.[48]

But Argan's fixation on his bowels is only a symptom of his larger problem, hypochondria. What, and this will come as no surprise, underlies Argan's obsessive anal fixation is the fear of/and desire for control. Argan wants order in his world ("Je le dirai à Monsieur Purgon, afin qu'il mette ordre à cela"). From the very beginning, the play underlines the points of intersection between chaos/order, passivity/activity, loss of control/mastery and the mounting anxiety that is produced when one side of the dichotomy (chaos, passivity, loss of control) seems to Argan to be gaining the upper hand. In the first speech is a growing crescendo of anxiety, marked by the comic buildup of the maniacal economies of Argan, which lead to his anxious outburst—"Il n'y a personne: j'ai beau dire, on me laisse toujours seul. . . . Ils n'entendent point, et ma sonnette ne fait pas assez de bruit. . . . Ils me laisseront ici mourir"—which we can assume is the eruption of the heart of his anxiety and which can be translated as the underlying cry, "I am defenseless, I am vulnerable, I am a helpless (infant) in distress." The anxiety forms the underside, the nonarticulable underside to the public persona Argan, as pater familias, one who is expected to project to the world—"I am strong, I am the father (king), I am one and invincible." Here Argan's angst, which he focalizes on his bowels, represents his desire to create a perfect economy of control, to render his body, in its

Kreaturlichkeit, unthreatening to his fragile sense of security and integrity. We could see this personal angst (but also this so spectacularly public angst) as expressing—unbeknownst to him, and to Molière—the larger ambient insecurity of boundaries of the emerging nation-states which on the another level the play is purportedly celebrating. It would seem that neither the nation nor the ego is as yet securely buttressed by firm definition. Argan's angst is the anxiety of conflict, the conflict between a pull toward a system into which he (and we may assume the father in general) does not perfectly dovetail but whose lure nevertheless entices him.[49]

In other words, in whatever code we desire to place his symptoms—the humoral code of the seventeenth century, or the analytical code of ours—Argan's initial presentation at the beginning of the play, with the heavily underlined emphasis on the body—the leaky, grotesque body of Galenic theory, or the hypochondriacal anal-sadistic (psychic) body of analysis—places him, as father (that is, as a male subject in a patriarchal culture) at odds with the ambient ideology of masculinity. In both instances Argan is not integral. For the humoral theory, he is split by the constant "quiddity" of his lower bodily stratum which represents a female intrusion into what should be a male subject. His integrity is constantly sundered by the apertures, the flux of excreta, in which he delights, and which constantly call attention to him as an open, effluent body. In Freudian terms Argan would be split between a narcissistic attention to his own body, a sign which Freud considers as a particularly feminine attitude, and a normatively masculine "object-love."[50] At the same time Argan's delectation in his anality would also in a more complex fashion indicate that he is—that the carnivalesque body is—in a schema of Oedipal sexuality in a pregenital stage, a stage that refuses castration and therefore the law of difference, refuses the construction of a "self" that would be defined off from its/an other.[51] So in the first instance what marks Argan as comic, beyond the scatology, beyond the tirades for or against the medical profession, is the copresence in the father, of what seventeenth-century psychology, medicine, theology, and esthetics would suppress—the body, and most particularly, the body coded as feminine and thus passive.

Argan's attention to his excretory functions—although it is, like all psychic phenomena, anchored in the physicality of the body and in ambient bodily practices obviously exceeds these social realities. His own internal economy has only a tenuous relation to external reality.[52] It does, on the other hand, have quite a rich and forceful influence on the members of his household. Marriage forms the central conundrum of Molièresque comedy because it is a heavily overinvested locus where social and political economy meets with and is inseparable from personal sexual economy. This extremely enchafed locus produces equally the tragic and comic scenarios of familial/social conflict in seventeenth-century drama. In *Le malade imaginaire* we have two negative types of marriage, the proposed marriage of Angélique to Thomas Diafoirus, and the actual marriage of Argan and Béline. Both, I suggest, correspond to Argan's anal economy in which the passive and aggressive sides of his anality take precedence over any "genital" economy that would supersede it.

Although we might suggest that Argan's hypochondria fixes him in a pregenital relation to sexuality, a relation marked by a desire to control, it interferes with the sexual fulfillment of the other members of his household—particularly his daughter, Angélique. While Argan's anality attempts to control his household economy by an obsessive attention to the free flowing of his intestinal tract, this enforced fluidity leaves his daughter "dammed up" (bouchée):

> il n'est rien de plus fâcheux que la contrainte où l'on me tient, qui bouche tout commerce aux doux empressements de cette mutuelle ardeur que le Ciel nous inspire.
>
> (I.iv; 4:393)

Both father and daughter envisage the same type of therapy for this problem (being "blocked" or "backed" up)—marriage. But here, once again, despite his invocation of "nature" ("Cela est plaisant, oui, ce mot de mariage; il n'y a rien de plus drôle pour les jeunes filles: ah! nature, nature!"), the difference between Argan's anal economy and the more "natural" economy of Angélique come into conflict. Angélique desires to marry the young, bright, good-looking fellow who has been courting her (Cléante), while Argan, of course, entirely possessed by his hypochondriacal mania, wishes to use his daughter as part of his economy, wishes to secure through her (through a bartering of her sexuality) a closed circuit where symptoms and on-site medical aid exist in a copresent cycle of need and fulfillment. Argan wants a live-in physician, present *à demeure* to minister to his every demand:

> Ma raison est que, me voyant infirme et malade comme je suis, je veux me faire un gendre et des alliés médecins, afin de m'appuyer de bons secours contre ma maladie, d'avoir dans ma famille les sources des remèdes qui me sont nécessaires, et d'être à même des consultations et des ordonnances.
>
> (I.v; 4:395)

Argan's desire to possess Angélique, to use her as but an extension of his body, represents the sadistic totalizing side of his anality. In a sense we can interpret Argan's tyrannical abuse of his daughter as but one more metaphor for the control of his feces which is so vitally important to him—staving off as it does the undoing of his being, its total collapse into death. On another level, a level that Freud also analyzed and that we have already seen operative in Argan, his interest in feces is displaced (but only partially) onto that other currency, money.[53] Argan, although wealthy in his own right, has not forgotten what this exchange of his daughter for a doctor son-in-law will also bring him financially:

> le parti est plus avantageux qu'on ne pense. Monsieur Diafoirus n'a que ce fils-là pour tout héritier; et, de plus, Monsieur Purgon, qui n'a ni femme, ni enfants, lui donne tout son bien, en faveur de ce mariage; et Monsieur Purgon est un homme qui a huit mille bonnes livres de rente. . . . Huit mille livres de rente sont quelque chose, sans compter le bien du père.
>
> (I.v; 4:396)

This obsessive intrusion of Argan's anality into the general economy of marriage as it was practiced in the seventeenth century (an "unnatural" institution in Molière's terms, repeated in comedy after comedy) is precisely society's desire to confuse the libidinal (i.e. natural) economy with the economy of the marketplace. In his defense of young lovers against aged, maniacal fathers, Molière at first appears to be defending a liberatory position, which is radically disruptive of the patriarchal economy of his day. Argan's case, however, is complex: in either its passive or active forms, his anality clearly situates Argan on the near side of phallic sexuality, the sexuality of the emergent bourgeois family.[54] For, although by his insistence on the continued heartless exploitation of his daughter he participates in an economy of patriarchal aggrandizement, this very economy is corrupted by the intrusion of his lower bodily stratum into the integrity of his position as father. It undoes the orthopedic rigidity necessary to support the economic law of marriage he would, as *oikodespotès,* impose. We might say that his own fascination with his bowels, with his anal economy, precludes his phallic valorization as father—that is the *Aufhebung* by which biology (Argan as *genitor*) becomes one with ideology (Argan as *pater*).[55]

His own marriage is striking precisely because it is peculiarly unphallic. His relation to his wife, who we know from the very outset of the play is interested only in inheriting his wealth, corresponds to the passive infantile side of his anality. She caters to his mania, to his hypochondria, in a blatantly hypocritical way that fools no one but Argan. Argan adores his wife because in his relation to her he can safely regress to the position of the infant. (We might remark that this marriage is childless, the sign, perhaps, of a lack of genital sexuality?) Their sexual relation consists of his moaning to her about his maladies, about the indignities of his body (i.e., offering up to her his body in its "femaleness" rather than, following "humoral" theory, its "maleness") and her responses, couched significantly in infantilizing

terms of endearment: "mon fils," "mon petit fils." We can assume that in his relation to his wife, Argan must find a pleasure similar to the one he achieves through his constant purges, a pleasure in which he regresses to an infantile state of indifference, a pregenital state of the child for whom the distinction between outer and inner worlds and thus between a sense of self and a sense of other is only barely beginning to be formed.[56] He regresses (or exists) precisely in a body without limits, a body of constant flux, a body that for him must be highly eroticized and thus both extremely pleasurable and extremely dangerous—the grotesque body of the carnival.

Yet, for the economy of the play, it is this body that threatens, as it has threatened the happiness of his daughter, the economic well-being of the family unit. Lost as he is in the pleasurable illusion of his marriage, lost in the anal pleasure of Béline, he is ready to sacrifice his family's financial security. We might even suggest that unaware of phallic jouissance he has no qualms about handing over to his wife the "family jewels," which in this case are much less valuable to him than his wife's tender (verbal) ministrations to his erotically more invested intestinal tract. It is only because of the cunning of his servant, his brother, and his daughter, of his "household," that is, that Argan is saved from this act of financial auto-castration. It is their economic interests that seem to be rational and not libidinalized ("mature," according to Freud), that reassert themselves at the hour of their destitution and rally the cunning necessary to unmask Béline as the ruthless fortune hunter she is. Argan's family is saved in extremis and saved in spite of the master of the household, who is unable to see reality until he feigns, acts out what he most fears—his own demise. Like a comic Lear, Argan passes through death to find his right, that is paternal, place in the reactions of his anal-sadistic wife ("Le ciel en soit loué! Me voilà délivrée d'un grand fardeau. . . . Un homme incommode à tout le monde, malpropre, dégôutant, sans cesse un lavement ou une médecine dans le ventre, mouchant, toussant, crachant toujours, sans esprit, ennuyeux," III.xiii) and his dutiful daughter, ready to renounce her own hopes of erotic fulfillment to please her dead father ("O ciel! quelle infortune! quelle atteinte cruelle! Hélas! faut-il que je perde mon père, la seule chose qui me restait au monde?" . . . Ah! Cléante ne parlons plus de rien. Laissons-là toutes les pensées du mariage. Après la perte de mon père je ne veux plus être du monde," III.xiii, xiv).

The play ends, appropriately enough, by dissolving into a carnivalesque charivari, where Argan is duped by his entire entourage into submitting to a mock-heroic induction into the ranks of the physicians. Through the comic use of "un latin de basoche," through infantile chanting and rhymes (can we see this as a parody of the infants' induction into language, and therefore, according to Kristeva, the superseding of the anal stage for an entrance into the "symbolic" of language, into castration, and thus "phallic desire")?[57] Argan "becomes" a doctor, achieves narcissistic self-sufficiency and self-enclosure—he is at once patient and healer, a closed economy of supply and demand, an auto-erotic circle of a suffering body/soul and its healer/lover.[58] But, and this is equally important, there does not seem, despite the (mock) initiation into the symbolics of medicine a going beyond the body, but rather a total, "grotesque" acquiescence to the body, its quiddity, its ever-present and never ending demands. The *Malade imaginaire* offers no sublimated economy that would place the body in another (repressed) locale. Rather the body seems to end the play as triumphantly present as ever, only more ominously so, for the body's triumph in the *Malade* signals, as we know from Molière's biography, quite literally the death of its author.

When we step back in time to *L'avare,* written and performed five years prior to the *Malade,* we appear to have advanced in the development of the bourgeois family and its precapitalist milieu. This step back from the carnival to the fair indicates, it seems to me, a certain cultural indeterminacy that lends itself equally to different comic treatments. For although it has been claimed that *L'avare* is a very physical comedy, for our purposes this earlier play seems to be already situated on the far side of the divide where the body in its quiddity is no longer present.[59] What we have in its stead is precisely "Classical representation," in which and for which the body exists, if at all, as an object of discourse, as a discursive, that is, absent reality.[60] In its place we find, however, an entire play structured around the symbolic systems of exchange—sex and money—which although they never make any direct mention of the physicality of the body, all in one way or another bear its traces.

I would like to propose simply that when the grotesque body of free-flowing excreta is suppressed—a suppression that both Foucault and Elias, each in his own terms, map out for us—what is repressed returns in the sublimated, symbolized form of another currency. When we pass from Argan's *chaise percée* to Harpagon's *cassette,* the feces that was so amply apparent in the carnivalesque world of *Le malade imaginaire* continues to exist in the libidinalized fetishization of money (*trésor*) of *L'avare.* Despite the long tradition that traces the play's plot to Plautus and the *Aulularia,* I think that the *Avare* can be properly understood—not only as a reflection of the seventeenth century's economic and cultural turmoil but in our own terms as well as a harbinger of modern subjectivity, by which I mean, modern sexual, "oedipal" economy—only if we see it in relation to the *Malade.* The anal economy of Molière's last play resurfaces in/as the Classical economy of representation of *L'avare,* where the symbol stands in for

(thus kills) its missing (repressed) referent. As I have already mentioned, one of Freud's most shocking but by now sufficiently banalized insights suggests that in the unconscious there exists a contiguous relation between feces and money ("in unconscious thoughts and dreams, and in neuroses—money comes into the closest relation with excrement").[61] When we move in Molière's universe, a convoluted, conflicted, and often contradictory universe, from the farces to the "high" (i.e. "Classical") comedies, we move, in a sense, from a subaltern to a hegemonic discourse. Ideologically speaking "the Classical" (despite the resistances to it) was becoming the master narrative of the emerging absolutist/mercantilist state. But, as Stallybrass and White point out, the grotesque remains the hidden, underside, informing Classicism's self-definition.[62] In a sense then, the body so flagrantly present in the *Malade,* disappears here, and in its stead we have a new "grotesque," the mental grotesquery of Harpagon's fetishization of money which threatens, for very different reasons, the household of which he is the head.[63]

What I am suggesting is that we are dealing with a chiasmatic reversal in our comparison of the two comedies which is perfectly consonant with the idea I put forward at the beginning of this chapter—the theater is a mediating locus that contains in itself the conflicting forces of competing ideologies that are particularly active in seventeenth century France. While in the *Malade* we had the predominance of anality that is allied to the carnivalesque, over "genitality," in the *Avare* we have a reverse situation the dominance of the "phallic" (i.e. the "genital") over the anal. In each case, however, one does not exist without the other: they exist in a dialectical codependency with different, but weighted, valencies defining the comic of each play.

In a series of essays Freud returns to the problem of anality, to the importance of the anal zone in the development of our sexual (in the widest sense) subjectivities.[64] Now, before going further, I must stress that the body that Freud presupposes in his discussion is the "classical" "closed" (socially, ideologically, sexually) body. But rather than see that as being only the fully formed body of nineteenth-century bourgeois Vienna, we can see it already as the emerging hegemonic bodily structure toward which, as Foucault and Elias have shown, the society of late seventeenth-century France was moving—the body of Harpagon, for instance, especially as he/it exists in a tendentious relation to Argan and the grotesque. In both "Character and Anal Eroticism" and "On the Transformation of Instincts with Special Reference to Anal Erotism" Freud comes back to the anal stage to suggest how certain character traits met with in adults—traits of "orderliness, parsimony, and obstinacy"—can be seen as the result of a particularly ill-navigated passage from (in his own normative description of sexual chronology) the predominance of the anal to the genital zone. This "ill-navigation" (another term would be "neurosis") can take several different forms in the constitution of the mature character: "the permanent character-traits are either unchanged prolongations of the original impulses, or sublimations of them, or reaction-formations against them."[65] In the case of our protagonist we have no trouble recognizing both parsimony and obstinacy which seem to predominate while orderliness can be seen clearly peering through his tyrannical desire for control of his children and household. They are all intertwined with his retentive delight in acquiring and holding onto his money (but not only money: according to the list of usury conditions La Flèche reads Cléante in the contract Harpagon has drawn up (II.i), we see that he hoards, pack-rat style, objects of all and sundry provenance). The people in whom these traits predominate, according to Freud's speculations, are those who as children experienced a particularly intense erotogenic pleasure in the act of withholding or releasing the contents of their bowels.[66]

Freud goes on to speculate that in those people who retain, consciously, the erotic pleasure of their anal zone, these traits do not develop. Rather, it is only by the ego's giving in to ambient social pressure and renouncing the infantile pleasure associated with defecation that pleasure remains in the unconscious, transformed into these character traits.[67] At the same time that the pleasure becomes attached to the character trait, the object of that pleasure, the feces, is itself transformed.

The relation that Freud draws between feces and money, as shocking and seductive as it may seem, is only one small part of a complicated chain of symbolic displacements that can, he hypothesizes, exist in the unconscious of the infant and that can later continue to exist in sublimated form in the adult. In the essay "On the Transformation of Instincts with Special Reference to Anal Erotism" Freud continues to refine, this time with relation to the object (feces) of anal erotism, the symbolic displacement from infancy to adulthood. Here Freud suggests that for the infant, at a very early stage of his development, a chain of symbolic displacements is elaborated, infused already with erotic pleasure, wherein the equation "feces (money, gift), child and penis are seldom distinguished and are easily interchangeable."[68] Freud goes on to offer a distinct evolution of this signifying chain for the normal development of women and men. Here I focus only on what he has to say about male evolution:

> A different series of relation can be observed much more distinctly in the male. It is formed when the boy's sexual curiosity leads him to discover the absence of a penis in women. He concludes that the penis must be a detachable part of the body, something analogous to faeces, the first bodily substance the child had to part with. Thus the original anal defiance enters into the composition of the castration complex.[69]

Ilana Reiss-Schimmel glosses Freud's dense essay to point out the following predominant traits: feces as it is transformed into "gift" already bears the impress of desire—the child's desire to please its mother and receive her love in return—as such the object (feces/gift) is already an ambivalent object.[70] Freud's symbolic chain of displacements is established, she says, on an analogy of separation that is understandable only in relation to an originary fantasy of castration, which alone allows for the substitution of one element for another. Underlying, therefore, this substitutive chain (for the male subject) is, as we have seen in Freud, the castration complex which, will retroactively determine the libidinal intensity of the invested object ("money," "penis").[71]

In his study of the "Wolfman" (*From the History of an Infantile Neurosis*) Freud returns to his speculations on anal sexuality and its effects on psychic life and offers the following summary:

> Since the column of faeces stimulates the erotogenic mucous membrane of the bowel, it plays the part of an active organ in regard to it; it behaves just as the penis does to the vaginal mucous membrane, and acts as it were as its forerunner during the cloacal epoch. The handing over of faeces for the sake of (out of love for) some one else becomes a prototype of castration; it is the first occasion upon which an individual parts with a piece of his own body in order to gain the favor of some other person whom he loves. So that a person's love of his own penis, which is in other respects narcissistic, is not without an element of anal erotism. 'Faeces,' 'baby,' and 'penis' thus form a unity, an unconscious concept (sit venia verbo)—the concept, namely, of 'a little one' that can become separated from one body.[72]

A relation is thus clearly established by Freud which intermeshes anality, the castration complex (itself directly related to the outcome of the oedipal development of the child), and the establishment of adult character traits that bear the mark of these differently connected unconscious processes. For our present purposes what is particularly important to "retain" is first the idea of psychic transmutability (i.e. feces = money) and then the inherent fear of losing a part of one's self, a part that is highly invested with narcissistic libido.

While it was Argan's anality that presided over his familial economy, the Harpagon household seems, at first, to be firmly situated in an mercantilist economy with a correlative dominance of oedipal (that is genital) sexuality. *L'avare* appears as probably the most glaringly oedipal of Molière's many conflicted familial comedies. The rivalry between the father and son for the sexual prize (Mariane), as comically ludicrous as it might appear to the audience, provokes at the same time as laughter a sense of unease. Sexuality reveals its hostilely aggressive side in the rivalry of Harpagon and Cléante, a rivalry intensely marked by death wishes on both sides ("Cléante—Voilà où les jeunes gens sont réduits . . . et on s'étonne après cela que les fils souhaitent qu'ils meurent" II.i; 3:342 "Frosine—Il faudra vous assommer, . . . et vous mettrez en terre et vos enfants, et les enfants de vos enfants. Harpagon—Tant mieux" II.v; 3:345).[73] It is in fact this mortiferous rivalry ("mon père est mon rival") between father and son that forms the central plot device of the play. Only when we comprehend that this desire, the disruptive intrusion of the body into the world of mercantilism, is inseparable from the economy of the marketplace, can we understand that *L'avare,* even at this early date, presents us with a world where people are already in Marx's terms "fetishized commodities" and thus can we understand the seamless interweave between sexuality and avarice as structurally necessary in this comedy of the oedipal family.[74] This family from its very inception—here on the seventeenth-century stage—is shown to be dysfunctional: although the two economies, libidinal and financial, may overlap they cannot be made to coincide.

The comedy configures a clear sexual symmetry between the young members of the household—both of Harpagon's children are in love and wish to marry, and then immediately triangularizes that symmetry through the rivalrous relation between Harpagon and his son Cléante, and by the censorious pressure Harpagon brings to bear on Élise. The mediation for this triangularization of desire is financial. From the very outset the desire of the children is frustrated by the avarice of the father:

> Figurez-vous, ma soeur, quelle joie ce peut être que de relever la fortune d'une personne que l'on aime; que de donner adroitement quelques petits secours aux modestes nécessités d'une vertueuse famille; et concevez quel déplaisir ce m'est de voir que, par l'avarice d'un père, je sois dans l'impuissance de goûter cette joie, et de faire éclater à cette belle aucun témoignage de mon amour.
>
> (I.ii; 3:327)

Cléante's opening declarations to his sister while couched in terms of desire ("goûter cette joie" and further on "nous ne serons plus dans le bel âge d'en jouir") and frustration ("impuissance") are also and as fully imbricated in an economy of mercantile exchange—in which his desire for Mariane can, he knows, be mediated by his family's wealth. His desire comes up against what he calls the "rigoureuse épargne" of his father and is frustrated. In a simple sense, therefore, the oedipal rivalry between father and child is mediated in and through money—the new law of emerging capitalist France. It is the "no" of the father but, here, transcoded as a question of financial tyranny. In this play Harpagon's controlling the family purse strings effectively controls the son's *bourses* as well. Élise fares no better with her father than her brother. She becomes a

bartered bride. In the financial machinations of her father, where what counts is not to have one's estate diminished, not to lose what one has accumulated, she is given to the *moins coûtant,* to Anselme, whose chief claim to her in her father's eyes is that he is willing to take her as a wife without a dowry (*sans dot*) without, that is, there being any loss of property on the part of Harpagon.

This fear of loss is at the very heart of Harpagon's mania. From his first entrance on stage, Harpagon appears obsessed with the thought that everyone is trying to get the better of him, which becomes in his fantasy the idea that everyone is trying to rob him. His interchange with La Flèche sets the comic tone for the rest of the play:

> Va-t'en l'attendre dans la rue, et ne sois point dans ma maison planté tout droit comme un piquet, à observer ce qui se passe, et faire ton profit de tout. Je ne veux point avoir sans cesse devant moi un espion de mes affaires, un traître, dont les yeux maudits assiègent toutes mes actions, dévorent ce que je possède, et furètent de tous côtés voir s'il n'y rien à voler.
>
> (I.iii; 3:328)

The anxiety of being robbed is exacerbated for comic effect by the presence in the home of a large sum of money that Harpagon received the day before. He is frantically trying to hide it from all those prying eyes he imagines around him:

> Certes ce n'est pas une petite peine que de garder chez soi une grande somme d'argent; et bienheureux qui a tout son fait bien placé, et ne conserve seulement que ce qu'il faut pour sa dépense. On n'est pas peu embarrassé à inventer dans toute une maison une cache fidèle; car pour moi, les coffres-forts me sont suspects, et je ne veux jamais m'y fier: je les tiens justement une franche amorce à voleurs, et c'est toujours la première chose que l'on va attaquer. Cependant je ne sais si j'aurai bien fait d'avoir enterré dans mon jardin dix mille écus qu'on me rendit hier. Dix mille écus en or chez soi est une somme assez . . .
>
> (I.iv; 3:331)

Harpagon has buried the money, locked in the famous *cassette* in his garden. For the time being I want to point out only the obvious: if we can, for the moment, accept Freud's chain of equivalencies feces = money, Harpagon's choice of a "cache" is particularly rich in analogies. He buries his money, out of sight, in the ground. The only safe place he can find for his treasure is in the "bowels" of the earth. But even here, of course, the hiding place is not entirely secure; other eyes can peer into ground, discover and carry off the precious *cassette.* What is intriguing in Harpagon's mania is its monolithic intensity. In a sense Harpagon's avarice insofar as it reduces the entire world to a series of things that can be possessed (and therefore at the same time to a series of things of which one can be dispossessed) reflects a totalitarian psychic system that would constantly attempt to enclose the world in the same way the body is phantasmatically shut. If we remember that the original choice of the infant in relation to his bowel is presented as a dichotomy, either to retain his feces in the auto-erotic enclosure of narcissism, or to surrender it as a love offering to an object (person) in the world, we see that we are presented with a choice, *grosso modo*, between closing in on the self, or opening up the self to the world. We can understand the enormous tension that exists in Harpagon—the comic tension of a character who is situated on the horns of this one very crucial dilemma. He is presented as a totally self-enclosed (but paranoid) narcissist, a position that would seem to parody in a negative reversal the ideal of corporate/bodily integrity that underpins the evolution of absolutist patriarchy. And yet at the same time he is tempted by the opening up of this enclosed, defended structure as it reaches out for object-love. There is a conflict, I am suggesting, between these two very basic tendencies—the desire to retain, to remain in a self-enclosed tyrannical psychic structure that is in conflict with his genital desire for Mariane. It is this conflict that points to an impossible tension in the "father," his presentation as split being, and that, I believe, accounts in great part for the hilarity of Harpagon's character.

What could be more comic than a desirous "barbon?" What more perverse than the spectacle of a wizened, maniacal old miser (let us not forget the traditional iconographic representation of Avarice is a withered hag) who nevertheless is presented as concupiscent? The body returns, elliptically, in this comedy as that which resists the retentive psychic economy of sublimation. It is the conflict between the desire of the body and the resistance of sublimated retention that forms the comic nexus of the play.

We witness the reappearance of the body most pointedly in the interchanges between Harpagon and his procuress, Frosine. Although La Flèche warns her that she is dealing with a particularly obstinate case, that Harpagon is, as he strategically says, "le plus dur et le plus serré" of men (and I suggest that in the French "serré" there is the same sense we have in the English "tight-assed"), she maintains that she, desire's spokeswoman, knows how to loosen up the most obdurate cases. In a sense, Frosine (although she will meet defeat) is presented as a combination of all those cunning female servants who populate Molière's theatrical universe, but to her is added here the aura of a ministering mother. Like all those stereotypical figures of the go-between, these women, in relation to the "man/child" they are called upon to service ("il y a certains services qui touchent merveilleusement"), promise to supply those bodily comforts (sexual pleasure), and attend to their charges in a way that reproduces the mother's initial bodily ministration to the baby.[75] Frosine's description of herself as an expert in catering to men's innermost secrets is couched in terms of opening up the enclosed body of adult males. In a sense, therefore, she (Molière) creates the analogy that equates the "jouissance" of the body to "openness." Pleasure, the body's desire to be opened, to be available, to be made, so to speak, like a woman, is positioned as a feminization and thus, as the inverse of what the dominant ideology says a man must be—closed, "serré," bounded:

> Mon Dieu! je sais l'art de traire les hommes, j'ai le secret de m'ouvrir leur tendresse, de chatouiller leurs coeurs, de trouver les endroits par où ils sont sensibles.
>
> (II.iv; 3:345)

Desire, when it announces itself in this play in the body of Harpagon, declares itself as precisely what patriarchal Absolutism as it evolves toward ideological hegemony, had to suppress. It signals quite unconsciously that it desires the presence, as pleasure, as, once again in Bakhtin's terms, the "grotesque" (as female) of precisely what it has had to repress. It is this persistence, in the dominant discourse, of the fantasy of its own obverse which is being played out in the tension between Harpagon's retentiveness and the desire that is bred in that retention for release—the Classical body's yearning for its own grotesque.[76]

Frosine begins her attack on Harpagon where she thinks he is most vulnerable—his (bodily) vanity:

FROSINE:

> Ah! mon Dieu! que vous vous portez bien! et que vous avez là un vrai visage de santé!

HARPAGON:

> Qui, moi?

FROSINE:

> Jamais je ne vous vis un teint si frais et si gaillard.

HARPAGON:

> Tout de bon?

FROSINE:

> Comment! vous n'avez de votre vie été si jeune que vous êtes; et je vois des gens de vingt-cinq ans qui sont plus vieux que vous.

HARPAGON:

> Cependant, Frosine, j'en ai soixante bien comptés.

FROSINE:

> Hé bien! qu'est-ce que cela, soixante ans? Voilà bien de quoi! C'est la fleur de l'âge, cela, et vous entrez maintenant dans la belle saison de l'homme.
>
> (II.v; 3:345)

But his vanity is no match for his avarice. Although Frosine presents herself on one level as a ministering mother, catering to the bodily needs of her charges, on another level, these ministrations are themselves part of a financial system of exchange—sex for money—and it is here that her own vulnerability comes too directly into conflict with Harpagon's mania and is undone ("Que la fièvre te serre, chien de vilain à tous les diables! Le ladre a été ferme à toutes mes attaques" II.v; 3:350). Harpagon remains impenetrable to pleasure. His desire, after its destructive meandering through and across the desires of his children, gives way to the force of his own mania.

Of course, any attempt to divorce sexuality ("love") from economy is already precluded from the ideological universe of the play. Although there is a yearning for their separation especially in the gesture that would place passion on the side of the natural (i.e. youth, heterosexuality, and the like) and economy on the side of "perversion" (i.e. avarice), in truth, as we have seen, this is an untenable dichotomy in a world totally immersed in the bourgeois culture of the seventeenth century. For that (still primitive) bourgeoisie, marriage remains the most overinvested institution for the exchange of financial and sexual economies. For this reason the plot of *L'avare* can crescendo to a dizzying height of comic misprisions in the dialogue between Harpagon and Valère, the former panic-stricken over the loss of his "cassette," the latter pleading his "love." It is precisely because there is a *chassé-croisé* between Harpagon's relation to his hoarded treasure and Valère's desire for Élise, a chiasmus that comes to rest on the linguistic indeterminacy where passion and avarice overlap (such words as "treasure," "love," "engagement") that lends itself, indiscriminately, to entirely opposed economic interpretations depending on the code into which they are placed, the code of financial avarice, or the code of traditional passion. Despite or rather because of the blurring of (linguistic) codes, the risible of the play underlines and therefore puts into comic relief what otherwise would be obfuscated in the simply quotidian acceptation of either one of the codes in its home idiolect—that the woman as object of desire (in a bourgeois) economy is also a "treasure" (an economic investment) in the same (but parodically exaggerated) way the hoarded stash of money for Harpagon is an object of libidinal lust.

How can we understand the immensely comic (for us) displacement of lust onto his *cassette* if not precisely by seeing it as the highly overdetermined instance where libidinal energy is captured and fixed on a symbolic object of psychic exchange? The scene of Harpagon's distress upon discovering the theft of his cassette is among the most hilarious in Molière's repertoire. It is a bravura piece of writing (and of acting) that focuses in so concentrated a fashion all of the lines of contradictory

tensions between market and libidinal economies in the play, into this one paroxystic moment where the symbolic systems of finance and the body come to rest in and on the miser's anguish over his loss—a distress that is figured most poignantly and most comically as a loss of one's self—Harpagon cries that his body has been attacked, that he has been murdered:

> Au voleur! au voleur! à l'assassin! au meutrier! Justice, juste Ciel! je suis perdu, je suis assassiné, on m'a coupé la gorge, on m'a dérobé mon argent. . . . Mon esprit est troublé, et j'ignore où je suis, qui je suis, et ce que je fais. Hélas! mon pauvre argent, mon pauvre argent, mon cher ami! on m'a privé de toi, et puisque tu m'es enlevé, j'ai perdu mon support, ma consolation, ma joie; tout est fini pour moi, et je n'ai plus que faire au monde: sans toi il m'est impossible de vivre. C'en est fait, je n'en puis plus; je me meurs, je suis mort, je suis enterré . . .

> (IV.vii; 3:374)

In the high comedy of this scene Harpagon describes the disintegration of his self. But, curiously this disintegration is metaphorized in a highly symbolic fashion, a fashion that, I suggest, allows us (some) entry into the phantasmatic system that underpins Harpagon's anxiety. He tells us that he has been "murdered," but this murder is significantly couched in particularly symbolic terms, "on m'a coupé la gorge" ("they've slit my throat"), a cry that is immediately coupled with "on m'a dérobé mon argent" ("they've stolen my money"). I would propose that the equation of having one's throat cut and having one's money stolen allows us some insight into why Harpagon's psychic trauma is so comically intense and why, finally, it leads us back into the conflict between anal and genital sexuality we have been tracing through the two comedies.

In a simple way, if we take into account the "economic" phenomenon of psychic displacement discussed by Freud in relation to dream interpretation, we will be able to unravel what is at work in Harpagon's mania. Laplanche and Pontalis offer a succinct summary of displacement: "The psycho-analytic theory of displacement depends upon the economic hypothesis of a cathectic energy able to detach itself from ideas and to run along associative pathways."[7] In other words, an affect can be detached from its source and displaced onto another psychic or physical structure. In Harpagon's case I think we can assume that we have a "vertical displacement" from the lower bodily stratum to the higher, from the genitals to the throat (neck, head). In another searingly funny cry Harpagon reveals the profound investment at work in this psychic configuration, when after referring to the theft in abstract, that is legal-social terms, calling it a "un guet-apens," "un assassinat," where "les choses les plus sacrées ne sont plus en sûreté," he returns to the physicality of his attachment referring to his treasure as "mon sang," "mes entrailles" (V.iii; 3:379). He constantly oscillates from the abstract to the body, from the higher to the lower. In his impassioned cry at having his throat slashed I think we can hear a more primitive castration anxiety, an anxiety that returns us once again to the confusion we have already alluded to in Freud's discussion of the symbolic displacements of anality. But in this case, both the displacements and the affect are stronger and more complicated than we might first imagine.

On one level it is reasonably clear that in the passage from anality to genitality, from Argan to Harpagon, from "grotesque" to "Classical," Harpagon represents a snag in any clearly defined, unproblematic navigation from the one to the other. Let us recall (one of) the associative chains Freud proposed in his discussion of the persistence of the anal stage in the character traits of a mature individual "feces = penis = money", and then let us also remember that the passage from the anal to the genital stage is intimately connected to the "castration complex" and to the different traumatic avatars of this complex for the psycho-sexual development of the male child. Although it would be unproductive to offer an analysis of Harpagon, who is, after all, not a real psychic entity (not a person) but merely a character in a play, by considering him as a nexus of conflicting and conflicted social, sexual, and economic vectors, we can see how, through a "personal" analysis, we can arrive at a sociohistoric description.

Harpagon, in his obsessive miserliness, would represent a "misplaced" investment of libidinal energy onto his bowels—onto, that is, the pleasure of the retention of his bowels, onto money—or we could turn this around and say that there is the invasion of genital sexuality by the misplaced intensity of anality. In either case the vehemence of this displacement is explicable only if we concede that the intermediary term in the associative chain—penis—has dropped out, been displaced. It has been consigned to the invisibility of the unconscious, resurfacing as concentrated affect, the fear of loss, the fear of self-destruction, the fear of death. This fear of loss—the representative of the castration complex—has been, I believe, sutured into the psychic construction of Harpagon by and through the insistence on still another displacement, the metonymic displacement from money (viz. penis) to *cassette* (from a part to a whole, from contained to container). The cassette functions, on one level, as a fetish object, which allows Harpagon to have his money (feces/penis) and to relinquish it too (transform it into, in a sense, object love). The vehemence of his attachment to his cassette ("O ma chère cassette"), takes on the lure of another man's (Valère's, for example) attachment to a woman. In his essay "The Theme of the Three Caskets" Freud talks about how the casket (box, i.e. "cassette") is a symbol of "the essential thing in woman, and therefore of a woman herself" He goes on, however, to show how in folklore and fairytales, this "woman herself" is an ambiguous construction where the "casket" does not represent just woman in general, but a particular ambivalent projection of woman, both the figure of "Atropos," a symbol of death and (as a reaction formation) the image of woman as the youthful, life-giving goddess of Love.[78] This ambivalence functioning bivalently, I believe, acts as the hinge between the sexual and financial economies in the play, allowing their mutual displacement. As we have seen, especially in the stychomachia that opposes Harpagon and Valère, this ambivalence (essentially on the level of linguistic economies, between metaphor and metonymy) relays the sexual into the linguistic creating the comic quid pro quo of the double misprision in the dialogue, the sexual/economic chiasmus of woman and money.

But, as this dialogue also makes clear, while Valère talks about his love in more traditionally "metaphorical" terms, Harpagon understands these metaphors only metonymically, because for him, first and foremost, the cassette represents a displaced part of himself. So on one level we can see that the cassette might represent a woman but for Harpagon this is a special phantasm of a woman, the fetishistic "woman-with-a-penis." And, I would suggest, it is to this final displacement that Harpagon is most attached; one he cannot give up and that finally presides over his divesting himself of his genital/oedipal desire for Mariane—a desire in which, as in all desire, he risks (or so it appears to him) his annihilation in the woman-as-other, the woman as object and proof of castration (for the male psyche)—and remains in the protected, self-enclosed narcissistic position where as long as he has his beloved cassette (his feces/penis) he is protected from loss, protected from castration, protected from death.

With the restitution of his cassette, the play can end, as all comedies do with the promise of marriage—the marriage of the children. On an important level, therefore, the comedy ends by reaffirming a familial model of oedipal/genitality. The lost, good father has been found. The family is reconstituted: brother and sister are introduced to each other and all go off to gather around the silently, suffering absence of this play, the mother. While the stage is cleared by the exit of all the characters gone off to share the news of their impending wedding with this never-realized maternal presence, Harpagon, alone, returns to his obsession, returns to the position from which he was almost budged but which proved too obdurate. He returns to the contemplation of what completes and assures him of his integrity; he reverts to the closed circle where, with his cassette, he retains an entire libidinal economy, protected from the anxiety of risk and loss.

L'avare and *Le malade imaginaire* form a chiasmatic economy of their own, emblematic of the conflicted and contradictory economies, libidinal and financial, that

Molière's theater mediates. On the one hand we have the predominance of the farce, of the carnivalesque grotesque body, the open, effluent body of Argan; on the other, "high comedy" of Classicism with its sublimation of the body, its disappearance in an economy of retention and symbolization. This dichotomy, of course, is too rigidly opposed here to account fully for the overlaps, exchanges, and interconnections that unite rather than oppose the multiple economies that coexist within Molière's theater and which finally come to rest in that ultimate economy, the economy of laughter, the laughter of the spectators of these, and other Molièresque comedies. How are we to understand this laughter, this "sideration of the body" in its voluptuous abandonment to its own pleasure? The history of laughter, of the comic, is long and complex. I do not wish to enter here into a long debate that begins with ancient Greece and continues down through the ages with important modern contributions by Bergson, Freud, and others. Here, as a coda, I add only a small note on what I believe is the role of the laughter spawned by Molière's comedy, spawned by Harpagon and Argan.

If we return to Bakhtin, who comments extensively on "carnivalesque laughter," he tells us that the laughter of the marketplace, the laughter of the premodern, nonindividuated ego is

> first of all, a festive laughter. Therefore, it is not an individual reaction to some "comic" event. Carnival laughter is the laughter of all the people. Second, it is universal in scope; it is directed at all and everyone, including the carnival's participants. The entire world is seen in its droll aspect, in its gay relativity. Third, this laughter is ambivalent: it is gay, triumphant at the same time mocking deriding. It asserts and denies, it buries and revives.[79]

Bakhtin's description of laughter, although nuanced at the end, remains nevertheless, like most of his description of the "carnivalesque," a paean to some utopian notion of the "people." What is repressed from his enormously rich contribution to the study of laughter, of the carnival, is precisely, as Stallybrass and White point out, the negative, destructive side of the grotesque, which rather than empowering as often as not authorizes itself by degrading, demeaning society's outcasts while maintaining its own complicitious relation with the dominant social structures.[80] Although Freud in his essay "Humour" claims that "Humour is not resigned; it is rebellious. It signifies not only the triumph of the ego but of the pleasure principle,"[81] the question for Molière remains, it seems to me, undecidable, situated somewhere between the unavowed repression inherent in Bakhtin's carnival and the structuring of the modern ego—as much product of what has been unconsciously repressed as what is consciously expressed.

What generates the laughter, the mirth of the spectators in the comedies we have been discussing? On the one hand we might say that it is the mania—the hypochon-

dria, the fixation of Argan on his bowels, or the avarice of Harpagon fixated on his cassette (his money, therefore, also his bowels). In both cases we are made to laugh, our laughter is spawned by an *écart*, a split in the image we have of the main character, the father, head of the household (*oikodespotès*).[82] In the patriarchal world of seventeenth century France, in this world which ideologically tends ideally toward the order of the absolute, the order of the "one" which is "embodied" most tellingly in the persona of the king and of all his paternal declensions, declensions that span the celestial and terrestrial realms from "God the Father," to the king "father of his people," to finally the father, head of each individual household, the unacceptable, the monstrous is precisely a "split" in this unitary phantasy. For, as we have seen, in either the Galenic or Freudian schema the split in the subject, the subject that is not integral, is the sign of the intrusion into the world of masculine perfection of the "other"—the other coded as feminine.

We laugh at Harpagon/Argan, precisely because in the context of their world, they are excessive, split by their monomania which, rather than confirming them as absolute, has the contrary effect of revealing their flaw, and thus the flaw of their world. They reveal what all seventeenth-century culture in its hegemonic drive would keep hidden—that the king, the father, is not one, but two, that in other words under the austere reverence of the one, is the many, the multifarious, and this many is the other—the children, the wily servants, the submissive (and the plotting) women. Harpagon/Argan in their mania reveal what the culture of patriarchy would keep hidden, that the father's "split is showing." It is this split that causes our laughter, I believe, on one level the release of our pent-up economies of repression and control. We laugh at the ridicule that is not so much in the characters as in the system, in the system that controls us all.

So, on one hand, this laughter can be seen, as it often has been, as "liberatory," "rebellious," Molière as the underside of Classicism's repression. But on the other hand, bearing in mind the critique of the "carnivalesque," the thought that the carnival, that Molière, are inextricably involved in the dominant political narratives of their time, narratives in which his (their) social, economic, and sexual interests are invested, we might then think that rather then being disruptive of social order, the laughter spawned by his plays is simply recuperative rather than rebellious. For, when we look at the target of our laughter—Argan/Harpagon—we realize that we are laughing at the bad father, the father as *pharamakos*, the ritual victim led out onto the stage of our own repressive fantasies and sacrificed to them. But this sacrifice, like all sacrifice, tends to finally maintain in place an entire worldview: when we laugh at the bad father, when we see Argan/

Harpagon as risible, "feminized," maniacal, we do so only because we can compare them, as failed fathers, to that image of the ideal father, the absolute father, who continues, in this comparison, to reign in our thoughts, in our repressions, in our fantasies. How else can we explain both the benign patronage of Louis XIV laughing at the antics of Molière's preposterous bourgeois, or the more enchafed reactions of the archbishop of Paris for whom Molière and his cast of characters represented a threat to the well-run order of seventeenth-century France? Both were surely right, but to his credit Louis XIV was probably more sanguine about the effects of Molieresque laughter: being directed as it was at those imperfect bodies of the father, knowing, in his own splendid isolation, in the impervious isolation of his body royal, that the real father, the state, Louis, were only enhanced by the raucous laughter spawned by the debasement of his imperfect earthly simulacra.

Notes

1. I am referring in this brief opening paragraph to the idea of a crisis of the seventeenth century, the century seen as period of radical, even revolutionary change that we see expressed in works by historians, philosophers, literary critics. See for the broad general ideas *Crisis in Europe, 1560-1660,* ed. by Trevor Aston (New York Doubleday, 1967); Michel Foucault's *Les mots et les choses: Une archéologie des sciences humaines* (Paris: Gallimard, 1966, trans. *The Order of Things: An Archeology of the Human Sciences* (New York: Pantheon 1971); and *Folie et déraison: Histoire de la folie à l'âge classique* (Paris: Gallimard, 1961, trans. Richard Howard, *Madness and Civilization; A History of Insanity in the Age of Reason,* New York: Pantheon, 1965).

2. "Now, this archaeological inquiry has revealed two great discontinuities in the *episteme* of Western culture: the first inaugurates the Classical age (roughly half-way through the seventeenth century) and the second, at the beginning of the nineteenth century, marks the beginning of the modern age" (*The Order of Things,* xxii).

3. Cf. *La volonté de savoir: Histoire de la sexualité,* vol. 1 (Paris: Gallimard, 1976), trans. Robert Hurley, *The History of Sexuality,* vol. 1 (New York: Vintage, 1978).

4. Jean-Louis Flandrin, *Familles, parenté, maison, sexualité dans l'ancienne société* (Paris: Seuil, 1976), 208.

5. For a more detailed discussion, see Mitchell Greenberg, *Subjectivity and Subjugation in Seventeenth-Century Drama and Prose: The Family Romance of French Classicism,* (Cambridge: Cambridge University Press, 1992), introduction.

6. This "productive" definition of the family is taken from Louis Althusser's well-known essay "L'idéologie et appareils idéologiques de l'état," in *Positions* (Paris: Éditions Sociales, 1970).

7. Foucault, *The History of Sexuality,* 108.

8. I have been arguing for this view of the theater/family in my *Corneille, Classicism and the Ruses of Symmetry* (Cambridge, Cambridge University Press, 1986); *Subjectivity and Subjugation,* (Cambridge: Cambridge Un. Press, 1992) and most recently in *Canonical States, Canonical Stages: Oedipus, Othering and Seventeenth Century Drama* (Minneapolis: University of Minnesota Press, 1994).

9. Anne Ubersfeld, *Lire le théâtre* (Paris: Éditions Sociales, 1978), 15 and 265.

10. André Green, *Un oeil en trop, le complexe d'Oedipe dans la tragédie* (Paris: Minuit, 1969), trans. Alan Sheridan, *The Tragic Effect: The Oedipus Complex in Tragedy* (Cambridge: Cambridge University Press, 1979), 23.

11. By this I mean that Mullaney and Williams seem to react to the early Foucault where Foucault is more interested in pointing to cultural "ruptures," to (too) clearly defined and separated phenomena, rather than to a later Foucault who, having modified his views, did come to see, especially in transitional periods such as the "baroque," the coexistence of varying and vying discursive possibilities. See Mullaney, *The Place of the Stage: License, Play and Power in Renaissance England* (Chicago: University of Chicago Press, 1988), and cf. for instance Williams *Problems in Materialism and Culture: Selected Essays* (London: Verso, 1980).

12. Mullaney, *The Place of the Stage,* cf. esp. the chap. 1, "Toward a Rhetoric of Space in Elizabethan London," 1-25.

13. *The Place of the Stage,* 130. Here Mullaney is amplifying Williams's distinction between "residual" and "emergent" cultures.

14. Francis Barker, *The Tremulous Private Body: Essays in Subjection* (London: Methuen, 1984), 12.)

15. Peter Stallybrass and Allon White, *The Politics and Poetics of Transgression* (Ithaca: Cornell University Press, 1986), 192.

16. Gail Kern Paster, *The Body Embarrassed: Drama and the Discipline of Shame in Early Modern England* (Ithaca: Cornell University Press, 1993), 4.

17. Mary Douglas, *Purity and Danger: An Analysis of the Concepts of Pollution and Taboo* (London: Routledge and Kegan Paul, 1966), 115.

18. For a feminist psychoanalytic reading of hysteria, see Monique David-Ménard, *L'hystérique entre Freud et Lacan: Corps et langage en psychanalyse* (Paris: Éditions Universitaires, 1983), trans. Catherine Porter, *Hysteria from Freud to Lacan: Body and Language in Psychoanalysis,* (Ithaca: Cornell University Press, 1989).

19. Cf. for example these preliminary remarks of Guy Rosolato, in his introductory essay, "Recension du corps," in *Lieux du corps* issue of *Nouvelle Revue de Psychanalyse,* no. 3 (spring 1971): 17. Elaborating even more explicitly on this same idea, François Gantheret, in the same issue, writes, "The body becomes symbolic only when it enters into a relation of meaning with other elements by substituting itself as a symbol for the repressed. There is symbolization only at the intersection of a series of associations and through an anchoring in a signifying system, only when an imaginary series, attaching itself to a biological reality acquires the value of a sign, that is, becomes a part of a system" ("Remarque sur la place et le statut du corps en psychanalyse," 142).

20. For the important impossible distinction in psychic life between reality and fantasy, cf. Jean Laplanche, *Problématiques,* esp. vol. 2, *Castration, Symbolisations,* and vol. 3 *La Sublimation* (Paris: P.U.F, 1980).

21. Stallybrass and White, *The Politics and Poetics of Transgression,* 176.

22. Cf. Marie Delcourt, *Oedipe ou la légende du conquérant* (Paris: Faculté de philosophie et lettres, 1944), xxxi: "The story of Oedipus is certainly the most complete of all political myths."

23. All references to Molière are to Molière, *Oeuvres complètes,* 4 vols. (Paris: Flammarion, 1979), *L'avare* (vol. 3), *Le malade imaginaire* (vol. 4). Act and scene numbers are given first in references, followed by volume and page numbers.

24. Mikhail Bakhtin, *Rabelais and His World,* trans. Helen Iswolsky, (Cambridge Mass.: M.I.T. Press, 1968), 317.

25. Ibid., 7.

26. Perhaps the richest use of Bakhtin is by Stallybrass and White. They are careful, however, to distinguish between this optimistic, utopic, and perhaps a-political invocation of carnival and a more nuanced perception. See *The Politics and Poetics of Transgression,* "the politics of carnival cannot be resolved outside of a close historical examination of particular conjunctures: there is not a-priori revolutionary vector to carnival and transgression" (16), and also "the problems raised so far concerning the politics of carnival: its nostalgia; its uncritical populism (carnival often violently abuses and demonizes weaker, not stronger, social groups—women, ethnic and religious minorities, those who 'don't belong'—in a process of displaced abjection); its failure to do away with the official dominant culture, its licensed complicity" (19).

27. Caroline Walker-Bynum, *Fragmentation and Redemption: Essays on Gender and the Human Body in Medieval Religion* (New York: Zone Books, 1992) particularly chaps. 3, 4, 6; Marie-Hélène Huet, *Monstrous Imagination* (Cambridge Mass.: Harvard University Press, 1994); Thomas Laqueur, *Making Sex: Body and Gender from the Greeks to Freud,* (Cambridge Mass.: Harvard University Press, 1990); Paster, *The Body Embarrassed.*

28. Paster, *The Body Embarrassed,* 8.

29. Walker-Bynum succinctly sums up the patriarchal ideology of Galenic medical theory: "Ancient biology, especially in its Aristotelian form, made the male body paradigmatic. The male was the form or quiddity of what we are as humans; what was particularly womanly was the unformed-ness, the stuff-ness or physicality, of our humanness. Such a notion identified woman with breaches in boundaries, with lack of shape or definition, with opening and exudings and spillings forth. But this conception also, we should note, put men and women on a continuum. All human beings were form and matter. Women were merely less of what men were more" (*Fragmentation and Redemption,* 109).

30. Cf. Paster, *The Body Embarrassed,* 25: "Representations of the female body as a leaking vessel display that body as beyond the control of the female subject, and thus as threatening the acquisitive goal of the family and its maintenance of status and power."

31. Bakhtin, *Rabelais and His World,* 320.

32. Douglas, *Purity and Danger,* 121.

33. For a lengthy discussion of the idea of the king, as a representation, as "spectacle," see: Jean-Marie Apostolidès, *Le roi machine,* and the works of Louis Marin, *Portrait of the King* and *Food for Thought.* The by-now classic study of medieval theologico-politics that underlies the above mentioned works is Ernst Kantorowicz, *The King's Two Bodies: A Study in Medieval Political Theology.* (Full references to these works are in introduction, n.7.)

34. Throughout *The Tremulous Private Body* Barker speaks of the seventeenth century as the period that eliminated the body from discourse. Cf. his

comments, for instance, on the "Cartesian body," 99: "The Cartesian body is 'outside' language; it is given to discourse as an object (when it is not in its absent moment exiled altogether) but it is never of language in its essence." In a sense, Barker's argument could be extended to the entire movement of seventeenth-century bienséances as it was imposed upon the rhetorical, theatrical, and artistic practice throughout the century. As many have noted, the French stage becomes disembodied, the characters appearing finally as "talking heads."

35. Stallybrass and White, *The Politics and Poetics of Transgression,* 113.

36. See, for instance, Marin's discussion of the "body" of Louis XIV in Rigaud's regal portrait, "The Portrait of the King's Glorious Body" (189-217), in *Food for Thought.*

37. For an analysis of the declension, so important for Absolutism, of the slippage the word "father" precipitates from God the father, to the king as "father of his people," to, finally, the father as head of the individual household, see the introduction to Greenberg, *Subjectivity and Subjugation.*

38. Jürgen Habermas, *L'espace public,* French translation, Marc de Launay (Paris: Payot, 1985), 13-17.

39. Barker, talking of this same split, writes: "It is with an identical gesture that the modern structure . . . excludes the body from the proper realm of discourse and simultaneously genders that very structuration. . . . For if the new regime in inaugurating itself deploys a pattern of speech and silence, a semiosis in which the discoursing 'I' is held to be constitutive then it is clear that the designated woman is positioned extraneously to the constitutive centre where the male voice speaks: The woman is allotted to the place of the body outside discourse and therefore also outside the pertinent domain of legitimate subjecthood" (*The Tremulous Private Body,* 100). Eugène Enriquez, (*De la horde à l'état: Essai de psychanalyse du lien social* [Paris: Gallimard, 1986], 274) writes: "It is only later when incest has been prohibited that the vision will be born and developed of woman as the archaic devouring mother, or of the woman empowered by a precocious sexuality and thus able to exclude men from her intense pleasure, or having such an overabundant sexuality that men can only be overcome by it. It is the triumph of men that engenders the fear of women. The body of man is thus as much in question as the body of the woman. But man has successfully engineered this forceful 'coup' of having eliminated his body from the comparison."

40. Paris had several major fairs, of course. The most important were the Foire St. Germain and the Foire St. Laurent. It is not clear to which of these fairs Molière is referring.

41. Stallybrass and White, *The Politics and Poetics of Transgression,* 30.

42. But is this really so? Why then the qualitative difference of esthetic judgment? Why is *L'avare* a *grande comédie,* while the *Malade* is but a farce. Doesn't this hierarchy already speak, or does it only come later, for the (capitalist) future rather than for the (carnivalesque) past?

43. André Glucksmann, *La bêtise* (Paris: Grasset, 1985), 233: "There is no more daring play in the western repertory. *Le Malade Imaginaire* pushes the spectator's nose in shit. Never before, never after, has the theater presented such purtrefaction, floating in an almost nauseating sweatiness."

44. Paster, *The Body Embarrassed,* 113, refers to "the centrality to early modern medical practice of the alimentary purge, administered in the form of emetics, laxatives, and enemas, which was experienced from time to time by nearly everyone from infancy on."

45. Norbert Elias, *The Civilizing Process,* trans. Edmund Jephcott (New York: Urizen Books, 1978), is the classic "sociological" study of the history of the laws of propriety, of manners. Starting with Erasmus, Elias traces the history of bodily policing in Western Europe.

46. Freud, *Three Essays on the Theory of Sexuality,* Standard Edition (above, introduction, n.2), 7:185.

47. Melanie Klein, "Some Theoretical Conclusions regarding the emotional life of the infant," in *Developments in Psychoanalysis,* ed. Joan Riviere (London: Hogarth Press, 1952) 198-273.

48. Freud, "On the Transformation of Instincts with Special Reference to Anal Erotism," Standard Edition, 7:130.

49. See Douglas, *Purity and Danger,* 124: "Here I am suggesting that when rituals express anxiety about the body's orifices the sociological counterpart of this anxiety is a care to protect the political and cultural unity."

50. Freud, "On Narcissism: An Introduction," Standard Edition, 14:88: "A comparison of the male and female sexes then show that there are fundamental differences between them in respect of their type of object-choice. . . . Complete object-love of the attachment type is, properly speaking, characteristic of the male. . . . Women, especially if they grow up with good looks, develop a certain self-contentment which compensates them for the social restrictions that are imposed upon them in

their choice of object. Strictly speaking, it is only themselves that such women love with an intensity comparable to that of the man's love for them."

51. For a detailed analysis of this problematic see Julia Kristeva's *Pouvoirs de l'horreur* (Paris: Seuil, 1980), trans. Leon Roudiez, *Powers of Horror: An Essay on Abjection* (New York: Columbia University Press, 1982) esp. the chapters "Something to Be Scared Of" and "From Filth to Defilement."

52. Didier Anzieu states in *The Skin Ego,* trans. Chris Turner (New Haven: Yale University Press, 1989), 96, that "every psychical function develops by supporting itself upon a bodily function whose workings it transposes on to the mental plane."

53. As Freud writes, "In reality, wherever archaic modes of thought predominate or have persisted—in ancient civilizations, in myth, fairy-tale and superstition, in unconscious thoughts and dreams, and in neuroses—money comes into the closest relation with excrement" ("Character and Anal Erotism," Standard Edition, 9:174).

54. Kaja Silverman has recently written on the different possibilities of "male subjectivity" that would not be based on a phallic (i.e, oedipal) model all while defining phallic model as the dominant cultural mode of sexuality in (patriarchal) modern culture: "our present dominant fiction is above all the representational system through which the subject is accommodated to the Name-of-the-Father. Its most central signifier of unity is the (paternal) family and its primary signifier of privilege the phallus." See her *Male Subjectivity at the Margins* (New York: Routledge, 1992), 34.

55. For this interesting distinction within the economy of patriarchy of "genitor/genitrix" and "pater/mater," see Jean Joseph Goux, *Freud, Marx, économie et symbolique* (Paris: Seuil, 1973), esp. "La génération matérielle," 239-56.

56. Paster's comment on the double valency of purging is relevant for Argan: "Purging recalls the deeply pleasurable ministrations of passive early experience, but it also threatens the bodily boundaries of self-mastery of the subject" (*The Body Embarrassed,* 21).

57. See Kristeva, *Powers of Horror,* 56-89.

58. François Dagognet in his *Le corps multiple et un* (Paris: Les empêcheurs de penser en rond, 1992) reminds us that for the Greeks "Medicine, according to Erixymacus, is entirely governed by Eros" (18).

59. Will Moore in his *Molière, a New Criticism* (Oxford: Oxford University Press, 1949) underlines what is for him the physicality of the play (30)

"*L'avare* is full of concrete illustrations of moral qualities; nothing is described, everything is shown in many physical acts: Harpagon searches his man's clothes, runs after his money, wears glasses and a ring on his finger, crawls under the table."

60. Barker writes in *The Tremulous Private Body* (62), "the carnality of the body has been dissolved and dissipated until it can be reconstituted in writing at a distance from itself."

61. Freud, "Character and Anal Erotism." See also Ilana Reiss-Schimmel *La psychanalyse et l'argent* (Paris: Odile Jacob, 1993), 51-52: "Thus from the perspective of the theory of symbolism money is considered a sexual symbol, the equivalent, both univocal and universal of excrement," and Jean Laplanche *Problématiques, vol. 5, Le baquet: Transcendence du transfert* (Paris: P.U.F., 1987), 174: "Money has a libidinal value. Here we are obliged to push our thought to the extreme and to remind ourselves that the libidinal value of money is above all anal: excrement, penis, anus, or asswipes."

62. Stallybrass and White, *The Politics and Poetics of Transgression,* 113:"The Classical body . . . rediscover[s] in itself, often with a sense of shock or inner revulsion, the grotesque, the protean, and the motley, the neither/nor, the double negation of high and low which was the very precondition for its social identity."

63. Goux, *Freud, Marx, économie et symbolique,* 35, insists on the importance of symbolic exchanges in defining the human subject: "What Marx teaches us, just as what Freud teaches us, is that the subject is made up of only an ensemble of social relations. Either as the subject of ideology or the subject of neurosis (a private ideology), the subject is constituted as one pole in a relation of complex exchanges, exchanges of vital activity. The subject is always a subject of exchange."

64. "The multifarious instinctual impulses which are comprised under the name of anal erotism play an extraordinarily important part, which it would be quite impossible to over-estimate, in building up sexual life and mental activity in general" (*From the History of an Infantile Neurosis,* Standard Edition, vol. 17:72).

65. See "Character and Anal Erotism," Standard Edition, 9:175.

66. "Character and Anal Erotism," 9:170. "As infants they seem to have been among those who refuse to empty the bowel when placed on the chamber, because they derive an incidental pleasure from the act of defecation; for they assert that even in

somewhat later years they have found a pleasure in holding back their stools. . . . From these indications we infer that the erotogenic significance of the anal zone is intensified in the innate sexual constitution of these persons."

67. "On the Transformation of Instincts," Standard Edition, 17:128: "the organic sources of anal erotism cannot be buried as a result of the emergence of the genital organization."

68. Ibid., 204.

69. Ibid., 208.

70. Reiss-Schimmel, *La psychanalyse et l'argent,* 57: "The gift is not just the vehicle of amorous feelings, but may also be invested with hostile wishes."

71. Ibid., 76-77 "For Freud it is the different ways of integrating anal eroticism that determine the symbolic value of money," and "the symbolic value that an individual attributes to money is a function of his level of libidinal organisation."

72. Freud, *From the History of an Infantile Neurosis,* Standard Edition, 17:84.

73. Georges Mongrédien, the editor of the Molière edition I am using, articulates this "discomfit" (we might call it a rather overdetermined and thus particularly interesting discomfit, coming as it does from one of the representatives of high French bourgeois culture) in the following way: "Without a doubt, the spectator feels a discomfiture, a feeling of being ill at ease spending two hours in the midst of the poisonous atmosphere of this family" (*Oeuvres complètes* 3:318). For a history of the critical reception of *L'avare* in general and of the relation of Harpagon and Cléante in particular, see Barbara W. Alsip, "*L'Avare*: History of Scholarship," in *Oeuvres et critiques,* 6/1 (summer 1981): 99-110.

74. For Marx's classic definition of "fetishism," see "The Fetishism of Commodities and the Secret Thereof" (sect. 4 of chap. 1 "Commodities" in *Capital,* in *The Portable Karl Marx,* ed. E. Kamenka (London: Penguin Books, 1983) 437-61.

75. In his article "Notre corps ou le présent d'une illusion" (*Nouvelle Revue de Psychanalyse,* 3[1971], 34), talking about the primordial importance of the infant/mother bond in forming the "phantasmatic" image of the subject's body, Jean-Claude Lavie says: "In relation to our body, it is less our body that counts than the relation it allows us to have with our mother."

76. Talking about the imposition of Classicism in England in the eighteenth century, Stallybrass and White write (*The Politics and Poetics of Transgression,* 105): "The production and reproduction of a body of classical writing required a labour of suppression, a perpetual work of exclusion upon the grotesque body and it was that supplementary yet unavoidable labour which troubled the identity of the classical. It brought the grotesque back into the classical . . . as a vast labour of exclusion requiring and generating its own equivocal energies. Quae negata, grata—what is denied is desired."

77. Jean Laplanche and Jean-Bertrand Pontalis, *The Language of Psychoanalysis,* trans, Donald Nicholson-Smith (New York: Norton, 1973), 121.

78. Standard Edition, 12:72: "The goddess of Death was replaced by the goddess of Love." Freud goes on to generalize from these speculations (73): "The great Mother-goddesses of the oriental peoples, . . . all seem to have been both founts of being and destroyers: goddesses of life and of fertility, and death goddesses."

79. Bakhtin, *Rabelais and His World,* 11-12.

80. Stallybrass and White, *The Politics and Poetics of Transgression,* 19: "the politics of carnival: its nostalgia; its uncritical populism (carnival often violently abuses and demonizes *weaker,* not stronger, social groups—women, ethnic and religious minorities, those who 'don't belong'—in a process of *displaced abjection*); its failure to do away with the official dominant culture, its licensed complicity."

81. "Humour" Standard Edition, 21:160.

82. Here I would seem to reach a similar but diametrically opposed view of mania in Molière from Glucksmann who in his *La bêtise* (228), when talking about this desire for the absolute writes: "The comedies of Molière take as their theme the thousand and one ways a hero, one and indivisible, begins to gravitate around his own person. Without ever allowing himself to be distracted or troubled he pursues, in a vertiginous spiral, his fetish object, a man, a woman, some strongboxes, or an enema—wherein the absolute and exclusive relation that makes him eternal plays itself out."

Michael S. Koppisch (essay date 2004)

SOURCE: Koppisch, Michael S. "Doctors and Actors: The Victory of Comedy in *Le Malade imaginaire*." In *Rivalry and the Disruption of Order in Molière's Theater,* pp. 173-86. Madison, N.J.: Fairleigh Dickinson University Press, 2004.

[*In the following essay, Koppisch describes* The Imaginary Invalid'*s movement toward order and a concurrent awareness that order cannot be fixed or permanent.*]

Of all Molière's plays, the one most favored by André Gide was *Le Malade imaginaire*: "c'est elle qui me paraît la plus neuve, la plus hardie, la plus belle—et de beaucoup"[1] [it is the one that seems to me the newest, the boldest, the finest—and by far]. What moved Gide in this chef d'oeuvre is the prose of an author who has arrived at the summit of his art. And yet, Molière uses this magnificent prose in the service of a plot that at times surprises an audience familiar with his theater by its lack of originality. Numerous critics have pointed out the similarities between *Le Malade imaginaire* and other Molière plays. As Antoine Adam says, *Tartuffe, L'Avare, Le Bourgeois gentilhomme,* and *Les Femmes savantes* all put on stage a parent, usually a father, who selects for his daughter a husband who fulfills parental needs rather than those of his future wife.[2] For Gérard Defaux, "*Le Malade imaginaire* ressemble étrangement, et d'une façon presque gênante" [*Le Malade imaginaire* resembles strangely and in an almost embarrassing way] these same plays.[3] Robert Garapon and John Cairncross emphasize the links between *Le Malade imaginaire* and *Tartuffe*.[4] Patrick Dandrey calls Argan "ce nouvel Orgon"[5] [this new Orgon]. Financial considerations having made it advantageous for the actors in Molière's troupe to put off its publication in France (they had the sole right to perform the work until it appeared in print), his last play was first published in 1674 by Daniel Elzevir in Amsterdam.[6] In this edition, whose lack of fidelity to Molière's text is noteworthy, there is an extremely interesting mistake: Argan's name appears as Orgon. The Elzevir edition seems to be a transcription of the text done by someone who had attended a performance of *Le Malade imaginaire* and had tried to reconstitute the play from memory. It is not difficult to understand why a spectator who had seen *Tartuffe* might make such an error.

In both plays, Molière presents a myopic, obsessive character taken in, one by false piety and the other by medicine. Haunted by the desire to be seen by others as "divinely absolute,"[7] Orgon does his best to integrate Tartuffe into his family. No less tormented by his health than Orgon by his soul, Argan responds in similar fashion, surrounding himself with doctors. The two servants, Dorine and Toinette, make fun of their masters. Each of them takes charge of the life of a daughter ill treated by a father whose egotism could thwart her love. Neither Cléante nor Béralde can overcome the madness of these monomaniacs with solid good sense, because in the final analysis, Orgon and Argan are not just a pair of simpletons tricked by a couple of rogues more clever than they, but rather willing victims, characters whose passivity in the face of fraud obscures their real aggressiveness. What Lionel Gossman says of Alceste—"'Je veux' is never far from his lips"[8]—is equally true for these two patresfamilias. The scene in which Orgon tries to convince his daughter to accept Tartuffe as her husband is structurally identical to that

in which Argan announces that he has chosen Thomas Diafoirus for Angélique. As long as they think that their fathers' ideas coincide with their own, the daughters swear obedience. Their submissiveness vanishes once they discover their fathers' true intentions. When Mariane explains to her father that she would be lying to say that she loves Tartuffe, Orgon replies stridently: "Mais je veux que cela soit une vérité" (2.1.451) [I want it to be true]. Argan responds similarly to Toinette's protestation that Angélique "n'est point faite pour être Madame Diafoirus": "Et je veux, moi, que cela soit" (1.5)[9] [she's not cut out to be Madame Diafoirus / And *I* want that to be]. Although the father has, by virtue of his paternity, a certain power over his daughter, that does not suffice. His often repeated "Je veux" is a measure of the intensity of his desire for power. He insists "je veux qu'elle exécute la parole que j'ai donnée" (1.5) [I want her to carry out the promise I've given]. If the servant thinks him incapable of anything so cruel as locking his daughter up in a convent for the rest of her life, she is mistaken: "Ouais! voici qui est plaisant: je ne mettrai pas ma fille dans un couvent, si je veux?" (1.5) [Well now! That's a good one! I won't put my daughter in a convent if I want to?]. Flying into a rage at the intervention of Toinette, who speaks of her master's natural goodness, Argan is reminiscent of the Orgon who does not want to be loved (2.2.545): "Je ne suis pas bon, et je suis méchant quand je veux" (1.5) [I am not good, I'm bad when I want to be]. By emphasizing their desire for a power that, as heads of households they already possess, the two men make plain their profound lack of confidence in themselves.[10]

Argan's project to assume an identity that distinguishes him from others and makes of him a superior being originates in his inferiority complex, as his affectation itself, sickness, suggests. Although his illnesses are imaginary, he does suffer from them, and they debilitate him psychologically. He is totally lacking in self-assurance. His certainty that he is sick lifts the veil on his secret vision of himself as inferior. Convinced, albeit wrongly, that his wife, Béline, loves him, he still finds it hard to believe that she could love a man like him: "Voilà une femme qui m'aime . . . cela n'est pas croyable" (2.6) [There's a woman who loves me so . . . It's incredible]. His insecurity is magnified by Béline and Angélique, who resist him, which they would not dare to do were he firmly in command of his household. With so little self-esteem, he hopes to win for himself a place of dominance and superiority in the small world of his family by manipulating the external manifestation of his inner weakness, his imagined ill health.

To consolidate his own superiority, Argan sets out to prove his difference from others. The familial order he has in mind would be based on a hierarchical system of differences with Argan on the highest rung of the ladder. However, his dependence on others constitutes a major impediment to the realization of his vision. No sooner does Argan appear on stage than his desire to be seen by others becomes clear. He is infuriated that his family has abandoned him: "Il n'y a personne: j'ai beau dire, on me laisse toujours seul; il n'y a pas moyen de les arrêter ici" (1.1) [There's nobody here. No matter what I say, they always leave me alone; there's no way to keep them here]. He demands the undivided attention of those around him, and when his servants do not immediately respond to his ring, begins to scream abusively, enraged that they would leave "un pauvre malade tout seul" (1.1) [a poor invalid all alone like this]. Like Pascal's miserable human being, Argan cannot endure solitude, which leaves him bereft of an identity that only others can grant. Contemplating his illness in solitude reduces it to a mere affliction, but in the presence of others, his bad health gives meaning and value to an otherwise purposeless existence. In short, his ill health is his path to distinction.

As so often in Molière's theater, wealth too plays a significant role in the attempts of this rich bourgeois to rise above others. *Le Malade imaginaire* opens with a comic monologue in which Argan divides his vigilance between money and the medications his pharmacist, Monsieur Fleurant, inflicts upon him.[11] Noticing the high price of one of his treatments, he exclaims: "Ah! Monsieur Fleurant, tout doux, s'il vous plaît; si vous en usez comme cela, on ne voudra plus être malade" (1.1) [Ah! Monsieur Fleurant, gently, if you please; if you treat people like that, they won't want to be sick any more]. Good health cannot be bought, nor does Argan really want to buy it, but surrounding himself with doctors and all their medical paraphernalia has little to do with being cured of illness. For their part, the doctors themselves do not deny their preoccupation with money. Toinette ironically supports Monsieur Diafoirus's complaint that people of high social rank expect their doctors to cure them. "Cela est plaisant," she remarks, "et ils sont bien impertinents de vouloir que vous autres messieurs les guérissiez: vous n'êtes point auprès d'eux pour cela; vous n'y êtes que pour recevoir vos pensions, et leur ordonner des remèdes; c'est à eux à guérir s'ils peuvent" (2.5) [That's a funny one, and they are mighty presumptuous to insist that you gentlemen cure them; you're not there for that; you're there only to receive your fees and prescribe remedies for them; it's up to them to be cured if they can]. Diafoirus responds with a simple "cela est vrai" [That's true]. Obviously, as long as his money holds out, Argan can count on the doctors. Money, moreover, unlike health, is a material, substantial commodity. Argan wants to accumulate it in order to give his life a solidity it lacks. The fortune that Thomas Diafoirus will inherit impresses him as much as the medical skill of his future son-in-law: "Monsieur Diafoirus n'a que ce fils-là pour tout héritier; et, de

plus, Monsieur Purgon . . . lui donne tout son bien, en faveur de ce mariage; et Monsieur Purgon est un homme qui a huit mille bonnes livres de rente" (1.5) [Monsieur Diafoirus has only that son for his sole heir, and what's more, Monsieur Purgon . . . will leave him his entire estate in view of this marriage; and Monsieur Purgon is a man who has a good eight thousand francs a year of income]. In the third act, Purgon will break with his patient, and Argan's punishment begins with the loss of what Purgon had promised Diafoirus: "pour finir toute liaison avec vous, voilà la donation que je faisais à mon neveu, en faveur du mariage" (3.5) [to end all dealings with you, here is the donation I was making to my nephew in favor of the marriage]. Money, like the presence of the doctors who take care of him, is a tangible sign of Argan's superiority. Purgon understands instinctively how tightly bound in his patient's mind are money and medicine. To have value, distinctiveness, whether financial or medical, requires recognition by others. Insofar as they serve the same end, Argan confuses in his mind a band of doctors and the great sums of money that permit him to buy their services.

To center his family's attention on himself is for Argan a way to establish his mastery, which, as will become apparent, is his greatest desire. His tone when speaking to his daughter parallels Orgon's rough treatment of Mariane. Both fathers have the same objective, domination. They want to bring into their families a son-in-law they choose, and they see their demands for their daughters' acquiescence as proof of their own power. Obedience, which ought to be inspired by filial affection, is instead a mark of submission to the tyrannical desire of the father. These overbearing parents care little about being loved; they want to rule, absolutely and unchallenged. Like a typical Molière character, Argan reveals his desire without taking full cognizance of the truth he utters. To call himself "maître" when speaking to Toinette in the first act of the play may be little more than a convention of language indicative of their roles.[12] The response that Argan gives later to a question posed by his brother is not:

BÉRALDE:

> D'où vient, mon frère, qu'ayant le bien que vous avez, et n'ayant d'enfants qu'une fille . . . que vous parlez de la mettre dans un couvent?

ARGAN:

> D'où vient, mon frère, que je suis maître dans ma famille pour faire ce que bon me semble?

(3.3)

[BÉRALDE:

> How does it happen, brother, that with the money you have, and no children but one daughter . . . that you're talking about putting her into a convent?

ARGAN:

> How does it happen, brother, that I am master in my family to do what seems good to me?]

Argan could not express his will to power more explicitly.

Medicine and its practitioners open for him the road to supremacy. By playing them against the healthy—that is to say, against others in general—Argan means to establish the difference between himself and them so as to institute within the family an order in which he can reign as absolute master. Sickness is a disorder, but, paradoxically, Argan uses it to create order. The role of invalid seems perfectly adaptable to his quest for an identity that will signify his mastery over his household. Without behaving inhumanely, after all, the others cannot ignore the plaints of a sick man, especially a sick man who might at any moment die. He must be listened to, cared for, cosseted, and, finally, obeyed. Such is his thinking, in any case. Illness permits Argan to impose his will on his family and to feel assured of his own existence. By distinguishing him from others, it furnishes him with a clearly defined identity.

Argan does not stray far from the path already beaten by many characters in Molière's earlier plays.[13] His poor health has the same usefulness that contempt for society's codes of behavior had for Dom Juan, virtue for Alceste, social pretensions for Monsieur Jourdain, or pedantry for Philaminte. All of these characters enlist their obsessions in the struggle to gain superiority over others. The greatest obstacle to their desire for power comes from the hollowness of the human heart, as Pascal has it. They feel the emptiness keenly. Argan can no more find happiness within himself than can other Molière characters. He must search it out elsewhere, as they do, in others' eyes and words. Argan's mania, however, is distinct from theirs in its total inability to bring happiness of any kind. Harpagon can tell himself he will perhaps be happy when he has more money. Nor is it beyond the realm of possibility to think that Monsieur Jourdain might find a degree of contentment were he to attain a higher social rank, and the virtue that Alceste claims to crave has value in itself. Being sick, on the other hand, is unlikely to result in anything positive. Thus, in this, his last play, Molière shows more explicitly and definitively than in his earlier works that his characters' obsessions are but pretexts to hide a profound desire for self-affirmation through the domination of others.

In the final analysis, personal superiority in Molière's plays is almost always built upon nothing more substantial than the recognition others grant. If characters are to experience the feeling of superiority so necessary to their sense of self, others must affirm it by their recognition. The natural resistance of those others both fascinates and intrigues. It also creates rivalry between characters that is the source of a disorder threatening their world.[14] Orgon competes for control with the members of his family and even, toward the end of the play, with Tartuffe himself. Dom Juan, though superior to the likes of Pierrot, becomes the peasant's rival. In *Le Misanthrope*, Alceste vies with others in the domains of love, virtue, literature, and the law. To avoid the disorder that stems from rivalry, the character guilty of introducing it must be neutralized. Someone must be sacrificed; someone must serve as the scapegoat.[15]

In *Le Malade imaginaire*, the illness on which Argan counts to distinguish himself compels him to live a life of contradiction, as Toinette's description of her master suggests: "Il marche, dort, mange, et boit tout comme les autres; mais cela n'empêche pas qu'il ne soit fort malade" (2.2) [He walks, sleeps, eats, and drinks just like anyone else; but that doesn't keep him from being very sick]. He is sick, but he is not sick. Although his sickness makes him different from everyone else, he behaves "tout comme les autres." Not surprisingly, therefore, Toinette must remind Argan, as he leaves the stage, that he is sick and cannot "marcher sans bâton" (3.1) [walk without a stick]. Béralde, in the same act, turns his brother's supposed illness against him. The proof that Argan is, in fact, a quite healthy specimen "c'est qu'avec tous les soins que vous avez pris, vous n'avez pas pu parvenir encore à gâter la bonté de votre tempérament, et que vous n'êtes point crevé de toutes les médecines qu'on vous a fait prendre" (3.3) [is that with all the cares you have taken you haven't yet succeeded in ruining the soundness of your system, and that you haven't burst with all the medicines they've had you take]. Argan can do whatever he wants to distinguish himself from others, he always ends by resembling them. His treatments have an effect antithetical to that intended: they demonstrate the good health that he shares with those to whom he would be superior through bad health. The difference between Argan and the other members of his family is not accentuated. It is erased.

Medicine and doctors actually prevent the imaginary invalid from accomplishing what he sets out to do. If medicine can give Argan a kind of prestige, it also has the contrary quality of blurring distinctions. Before the Diafoiruses, father and son, leave his house, Argan asks them to tell him "un peu comment je suis" (2.6) [how I am]. Thomas's diagnosis is peremptory: his future father-in-law has "le pouls d'un homme qui ne se porte point bien" [the pulse of a man who is not well], a sign of an "intempérie dans le *parenchyme splénique,* c'est-à-dire la rate" (2.6) [an intemperance in the splenic parenchyma, that is to say the spleen]. The dialogue that follows shows how medicine, which in Argan's eyes should make him different, acts instead to level difference:

ARGAN:

Non: Monsieur Purgon dit que c'est mon foie qui est malade.

MONSIEUR DIAFOIRUS:

Eh! oui: qui dit *parenchyme,* dit l'un et l'autre, à cause de l'étroite sympathie qu'ils ont ensemble. . . . Il vous ordonne sans doute de manger force rôti?

ARGAN:

Non, rien que du bouilli.

MONSIEUR DIAFOIRUS:

Eh! oui: rôti, bouilli, même chose.

(2.6)

[ARGAN:

No. Monsieur Purgon says it's my liver that's sick.

MONSIEUR DIAFOIRUS:

Oh, yes! If anyone says *parenchyma,* he says both, because of the close sympathy they have with each other . . . No doubt he orders you to eat a lot of roast meat?

ARGAN:

No, nothing but boiled.

MONSIEUR DIAFOIRUS:

Oh, yes! Roast, boiled, all the same thing.]

By repeating the words "Eh! Oui" before each negation of a self-evident distinction, Molière comically underscores medicine's refusal to distinguish even between completely different things. Argan says "non" and the doctor says "oui," but medicine's "oui" only confirms the doctors' tendency to obscure differences. When Toinette disguises herself as a doctor, she picks up on this characteristic of medicine by attributing all of Argan's symptoms—whether those associated with his liver or his spleen, his eyes or his stomach—to his lung (3.10). The laughter in this scene is the laughter of a writer who fully understands his protagonist's turn of mind, who wants comic doctors to cure rather than encourage their patient and to cure not with medicine but with ridicule.

The rivalry so typical of Argan's way of relating to others extends to his relations with his doctors. From his first monologue, Argan, although intimidated by the doctors and their allies, the apothecaries, nevertheless threatens Fleurant with the loss of a profitable patient. Argan wants the doctors to recognize his individual worth, but the individuality he hopes to acquire by the agency of medicine is denied from the moment he finds himself in their company. When Monsieur Diafoirus comes to introduce his son to Argan, a dialogue of the deaf ensues between the imaginary invalid and Thomas's father:

ARGAN:

Je reçois, Monsieur . . .

MONSIEUR DIAFOIRUS:

Nous venons ici, Monsieur . . .

ARGAN:

Avec beaucoup de joie . . .

MONSIEUR DIAFOIRUS:

Mon fils Thomas, et moi. . . .

(2.5)

[ARGAN:

Sir, I receive . . .

MONSIEUR DIAFOIRUS:

We come here, sir . . .

ARGAN:

With great joy . . .

MONSIEUR DIAFOIRUS:

My son Thomas and I . . .]

Stage directions for the scene suggest that Argan loses his individuality as his voice and that of Monsieur Diafoirus blend together in cacophony: "Ils parlent tous deux en même temps, s'interrompent et confondent" (2.5)[16] [They both speak at the same time, interrupting each other]. Their entangled speeches make it difficult, if not impossible, to sort out what they are trying to say. Each hopes to impress the other by his politeness, but they end up merging in a single gush of babble into one ridiculous entity.

In his attitude toward his family, Argan sounds very much like Purgon. Before understanding that he intends to marry her off to Thomas Diafoirus, Angélique tries to please her father, and Argan allows that "Je suis bien aise d'avoir une fille si obéissante" (1.5) [I'm very glad to have such an obedient daughter]. In point of fact, he exacts this obedience from her. Purgon is no different. He expects his patients to submit to the will of their doctor and refuses to continue to care for Argan, "[p]uisque vous vous êtes soustrait de l'obéissance que l'on doit à son médecin" (3.5) [(s)ince you absconded from the obedience that a man owes to his doctor]. Purgon and his patient, identical in their desire for control, often speak the same language. When Béralde proposes that his brother stop dwelling on his own condition and distract himself with Molière's comedy, Argan damns the author as "un bon impertinent" [a really impertinent fellow] and imagines himself in the role of an avenging doctor who would extract the appropriate punishment for Molière's insolence: "si j'étais que des médecins, je me vengerais de son impertinence; et quand il sera malade, je le laisserait mourir sans secours . . . et je lui dirais: 'Crève, crève! cela t'apprendra une autre fois à te jouer à la Faculté'" (3.3) [If I were a doctor, I'd take revenge on his impertinence; and when he's sick, I'd let him die without any help . . . and I'd say to him: "Croak! Croak! That'll teach you another time to make fun of the Faculty of Medicine!"]. Not long after, Purgon, in his turn, denounces Argan with a condemnation identical to the attack of the imaginary invalid against Molière. Argan identifies with his doctor in order to be different from those who challenge medicine, but contrary to his expectations—though clearly not to the expectations of those who, unlike him, appreciate Molière—his individuality evaporates in that identification.[17]

Without knowing it, Argan undergoes an identity crisis, causing the good order of his family to unravel. His madness prevents the natural course of events. Nothing could be more in conformity with nature than Angélique's love for Cléante, which cannot progress normally toward marriage, as it ought. Argan's passion for medicine and for doctors places an immovable obstacle in love's path. According to Béralde, confidence in medicine is misplaced, even in the face of illness: "Il ne faut que demeurer en repos. La nature, d'elle-même, quand nous la laissons faire, se tire doucement du désordre où elle est tombée" (3.3) [All you have to do is rest. Nature, by herself, when we let her be, gently makes her way out of the disorder into which she has fallen]. Order is a beneficent law of nature applicable to life in general as to matters of health. Yet all of Argan's actions run counter to it. He sows turmoil in his family, which falls into a dysfunctional state. One of his daughters is obliged to feign death to protect herself against her father, and venality weighs on the whole household. Béline, the doctors, and even, from time to time, Argan himself show as much or more interest in money as in the well-being of the family. Disorder smolders just below the surface and moral deterioration testifies to it.

In play after play, Molière demonstrates that despite the flaws of characters who almost never cast off their imperfections, order can be restored, if only temporarily and within the strict confines of the play's conclusion. The vital principle of comedy followed here is, as Jacques Guicharnaud puts it, "le triomphe nécessaire de l'ordre sur la corruption assuré par des moyens non héroïques"[18] [the necessary triumph of order over corruption ensured by non-heroic means]. In short, order triumphs in the very midst of corruption, but for that to happen, the perpetrator of disorder must be rendered ineffective. Thus, George Dandin is sacrificed in an atmosphere of cruelty and violence; an unrepentant Dom Juan descends into hell; and Tartuffe is escorted to prison. Violence counters violence to reestablish order without the characters' having to change in a funda-

mental way. For Monsieur Jourdain, Molière chooses an equally efficacious though less harsh and more comic method of expulsion,[19] but the result is the same, the chosen victim is ousted, if only in the imagination, from the community he has disrupted. In *Le Malade imaginaire,* with an eye no doubt on the scapegoat mechanism that had served so well against disorder in his earlier plays, Molière has Argan's family call upon comedy itself to cure the invalid of his imagined illness by administering to him an inoculation, a weakened, less active dose of the very illness from which he suffers.

In Harold Knutson's view, Béline is "the true scapegoat of *Le Malade imaginaire.*"[20] By her expression of joy and avarice at the sight of her supposedly dead husband, she lowers herself to the level of a frightful shrew. She leaves the stage debased, her power in the house nullified. Argan realizes at last that his wife's corrupt character justifies Béralde's negative opinion of her. Her defeat changes nothing essential, even temporarily, in the circumstances of the family. Argan remains as attached as ever to his obsession, and his daughter still refuses to obey him. If the goal of the scapegoat's expulsion is to restore order to the family, Béline as sacrificial victim fails. Eliminating her might rid the family of avarice, but that is not the major illness from which it suffers.

The character who ought logically be the object of an exorcism is Argan. Indeed, Purgon does condemn him to death for not having followed the prescribed regimen of enemas. The mere pronouncement has its effect on a terrified Argan who cries out, "Ah, mon Dieu! je suis mort" (3.6) [Oh, good Lord! I'm a dead man]. When Toinette assumes the role of a "médecin passager" [traveling doctor], who seeks out only "des maladies d'importance" (3.10) [important illnesses], she ends her visit to the imaginary invalid by suggesting that her new patient have one of his arms cut off and one eye put out so as not to limit nourishment to the other one, its rival for food. This satirical prescription for improving Argan's health resonates with the ritual mutilation of a scapegoat or *sparagmos* and also reminds the audience, however comically, that rivalry leads inevitably to violence.[21] Medicine, with which Argan has always collaborated, becomes a ferocious adversary. Molière has already shown the close resemblance between Argan and Purgon; he now puts on display the violence that typically follows upon rivalry in so much of his work. In these scenes, he places in full view the violence inherent in the scapegoat mechanism. Ridicule is his instrument, but the laughter he provokes has meaningful implications for his audience. If, in some of his earlier works, the violence of an exorcism put an end to the violence between rivals, in his last play, Molière looks to another way—comedy—to exorcise the demon and reestablish order.

The malady from which Argan suffers is, according to Béralde, "la maladie des médecins" (3.4) [the malady of doctors], and its cure is a vaccination composed of the same virus. Argan will be immunized against doctors by becoming a doctor himself: "Voilà le vrai moyen de vous guérir bientôt; il n'y a point de maladie si osée, que de se jouer à la personne d'un médecin" (3.14) [That's the real way to get well soon; and there is no illness so daring as to trifle with the person of a doctor]. This treatment is less painful but structurally similar to the banishment of a scapegoat. René Girard compares vaccination and Purgon's enemas with certain rites of purification, including that of the *pharmakos* punished:

> L'opération bénéfique est toujours conçue sur le mode de l'invasion repoussée, de l'intrus maléfique chassé hors de la place. . . . L'intervention médicale consiste à inoculer "un peu" de la maladie, exactement comme les rites qui injectent "un peu" de violence dans le corps social pour le rendre capable de résister à la violence.[22]

> [The benefic operation is always conceived of as a kind of invasion repelled, an evil intruder chased away. . . . Medical intervention consists of inoculating with "a little" of the illness to be cured, just like those rites that inject "a little" violence into the social body in order to make it capable of resisting violence.]

Laughter replaces violence as the constitutive element in the vaccine that restores Argan's health and acts to reestablish order in the family. Although Argan "fasse le premier personnage" [play(s) the leading part] in the curative *divertissement* (3.14), everybody is inoculated in the little comedy in which all play a role: "Nous y pouvons aussi prendre chacun un personnage, et nous donner ainsi la comédie les uns aux autres" (3.14) [We can also each of us take a part, and thus put on a comedy for one another]. Without everyone's participation, there can be no recovery of order. Disorder is a social illness; its cure must be social as well. Comedy, "une cérémonie burlesque d'un homme qu'on fait médecin en récit, chant, et danse" (3.14) [a burlesque, with recitative, song, and dance, of the conferral of the degree of Doctor of Medicine on a candidate (a Bachelor) by the Faculty], is a regulated disorder that drives out real disorder. Disguised as a doctor, Argan becomes, for just a moment and under tightly controlled circumstances, the doctor who had previously been his master and rival, and this without wreaking the chaos that such a loss of identity usually holds in store.

Comedy's role in the resolution of Argan's identity crisis cannot be exaggerated. The love of Angélique and Cléante wins out in the end, but comedy as much as love, Philip R. Berk remarks, is "responsible for defeating the professional schemes of the doctors to subjugate Argan and Argan's own tyrannical fiction of ill health."[23] Molière sees in his comic art the capacity that sacrifi-

cial rites once had. When Argan refuses to go to a Molière play, Béralde arranges to make his brother an actor in another comedy. Béralde must be taken seriously when he says that in his play, everyone, rather than duping Argan, will "s'accommoder à ses fantaisies" (3.14) [(be) accommodating ourselves to his fancies]. To cure his brother, Béralde seizes upon those "fantaisies" and manipulates them skillfully. He understands that Argan's imaginary illness has a quite real dimension. Argan may not be physically ill, but his desire to be different and superior to others and his identification with doctors are not for that any the less destructive. Society must protect itself against Argan's sickness despite its imaginary character, and comedy is the vaccine of choice.

The imagination, which Pascal calls "cette maîtresse d'erreur et de fausseté" (fragment 82) [this mistress of error and falsehood], is at the root of much of the action in Molière's last play.[24] Critics have often commented that Argan does not change, even after having discovered his wife's perversity and the essential goodness of the daughter who disobeys him. He retains his belief in medicine and orders Cléante to become a doctor before marrying Angélique. Nor does his attachment to money lessen. Béralde understands this as he reassures his brother that becoming a doctor "ne vous coûtera rien" (3.14) [It won't cost you a thing]. The power of Argan's imaginary illness calls to mind Pascal's texts on the imagination, "[c]ette superbe puissance, ennemie de la raison qui se plaît à la contrôler et à la dominer" (fragment 82)[25] [this haughty power, the enemy of reason, that takes pleasure in controlling and dominating reason]. Doctors, who have grasped this truth, derive their power from a costume that speaks to the imagination of their patients. Pascal calls the mask that doctors wear "cette montre si authentique" (fragment 82).[26] His tone in this passage is at once ironic and serious, for even though the doctors' power is based only on appearances, people need doctors. Pascal condemns the contrivances of the imagination while recognizing that human beings cannot live without the imaginary. They must somehow escape the feeling of their own emptiness, whose most striking and disturbing image is death. Argan's illness is a diversion that permits him to close his eyes to his greatest fear, death.[27]

Le Malade imaginaire begins and ends with death. At the conclusion of his long opening monologue, Argan exposes his real fear in a desperate, comic cry: "ah, mon Dieu! ils me laisseront ici mourir" (1.1)[28] [oh, good Lord! They're going to leave me here to die]. Death is mentioned in the play more than sixty times,[29] and the final word uttered on stage is a salutation in macaronic Latin to the newly initiated doctor: "Et seignet et tuat!" (Troisième Intermède) [Et bleedet et killat!]. The use of words like "tuat" and "occidendi" in the play's conclusion and the hasty departure of Toinette in her doctor's outfit to attend "une grande consultation qui se doit faire pour un homme qui mourut hier" (3.10) [a big consultation to be held for a man who died yesterday] tie the practice of medicine to death. To consult a doctor is to play with death. Béralde does not question Purgon's good faith. On the contrary, he explains to his brother, "c'est un homme tout médecin, depuis la tête jusqu'aux pieds; un homme qui croit à ses règles plus qu'à toutes les démonstrations des mathématiques, et qui croirait du crime à les vouloir examiner . . . c'est de la meilleure foi du monde qu'il vous expédiera" (3.3) [he's a man who's all doctor, from head to foot, a man who believes in his rules more than all the demonstrations of mathematics, and who would think it a crime to want to examine them . . . it's in the best faith in the world that he'll expedite you]. The doctor's role is to help his patient die more easily, more surely, in a better state of health. Argan is no less terrified by death than Pascal's human beings, but his fear comes out in an obsessive, comic way. Death hangs over and haunts him. Louison, his younger daughter, pretends to be dead to escape her father's whipping, and Purgon pronounces a death sentence upon him.[30] Twice in succession, Argan encounters death by imitating it. In these two scenes, death is, for a very short time, brought to heel. To fake death is a way of reassuring oneself against its power. It goes without saying, though, that the Argan who rises from his "death bed" remains fearful of death. He redirects his thoughts away from it by his continued insistence on bringing a doctor into his family. Death, of course, stays on the prowl no matter what Argan does.[31]

By playing with death, Argan tries to neutralize it, which explains his lack of fear when he plays dead. Comedy domesticates noxious forces by integrating them into quotidian life, rendering them commonplace. A small dose of medicine cures the sickness of medicine for a short time and "a little bit" of death has the same passing effect upon the fear of dying. What Molière portrays in *Le Malade imaginaire* is the necessarily temporary character of such a cure. Argan's secret desire not to die is utterly fanciful. By forgetting that Orgon does not really change, it might be possible to imagine that the order restored by Tartuffe's expulsion could endure, but Argan's "cure," given the nature of his illness, must be ephemeral. It is impossible to escape death. At the end of *Le Malade imaginaire*, as in most comedy, order is restored, but this time it is necessarily and explicitly short-lived. The fixity represented by a permanent order that Argan seeks cannot be realized. Pascal experiences the impossibility of finding "une assiette ferme, et une dernière base constante" (fragment 72) [a firm, stable position and an ultimate, unchanging foundation] as a source of anguish.[32] Molière, who contemplates the same truth at the moment of his death, makes of it a subject of comedy. The search for some stable, fixed order animates much of

the theater of Molière, who shares with Pascal a sense of the impossibility of permanence. The great genius of *Le Malade imaginaire* is to strip away all illusions and speak this sad truth with a laughter devoid of bitterness.

Notes

1. *Journal 1939-49. Souvenirs*, 82.

2. *Histoire*, 3:396-97.

3. *Molière ou les métamorphoses du comique*, 295. Defaux does not include *L'Avare* in this comparison.

4. Robert Garapon, *Le Dernier Molière* (Paris: Société d'Edition d'Enseignement Supérieur, 1977), 158; John Cairncross, "Impie en médecine," *Cahiers de l'Association Internationale des Etudes Françaises* 16 (1964): 279-81.

5. Patrrick Dandrey, *La Médecine et la maladie dans le théâtre de Molière*, 2 vols. (Paris: Klincksieck, 1998), 2:284.

6. Despois and Mesnard describe this edition in some detail (*Oeuvres*, 9:252-53).

7. *Men and Masks*, 102.

8. Ibid., 67.

9. The source of translations of passages from *Le Malade imaginaire* is Molière, *Comedies*, trans. Donald M. Frame (Franklin Center, Pa.: Franklin Library, 1985). This edition was published by arrangement with Penguin Group (USA) Inc., which has kindly granted permission to use Donald Frame's translation.

10. Ralph Albanese addresses Argan's "insécurité fondamentale" [fundamental insecurity], which he has in common not only with Orgon but with other Molière characters as well ("*Le Malade imaginaiare* ou le jeu de la mort et du hasard," *XVIIe Siècle* 154 [1987]: 4).

11. As James F. Gaines points out, "Argan has hopelessly confused the medical and economic codes, and keeps parallel records of expenses and enemas." Gaines also observes that Argan "is sure that he can buy health just as Orgon attempted to buy salvation by extending charity to Tartuffe" (*Social Structures in Molière's Theater*, 220).

12. "Où est-ce donc que nous sommes? et quelle audace est-ce là à une coquine de servante de parler de la sorte devant son maître?" (1.5) [What are we coming to? And what kind of effrontery is that, for a slut of a maidservant to talk that way in front of her master?].

13. Patrick Dandrey makes the interesting point that Argan's madness "se complique en effet d'un paramètre absent chez tous les autres imaginaires

de Molière: c'est que la lubie porte ici sur un objet très particulier . . . *le corps* du sujet désirant et délirant" (*La Médecine et la maladie dans le théâtre de Molière,* 2:286) [is indeed complicated by a parameter absent in all of Molière's other fanciful characters: the whim bears here on a quite particular object . . . *the body* of the desiring and raving subject].

14. Paisley Livingston does not ignore this point in his study of Molière's farcical depiction of medicine ("Comic Treatment: Molière and the Farce of Medicine," *MLN* 94 [1979]: 678).

15. Harold Knutson places emphasis on the presence of the scapegoat in Molière's theater (*Molière: An Archetypal Approach,* 15-16).

16. According to Despois and Mesnard, this stage direction does not appear in all editions of the play (*Oeuvres,* 9:347).

17. Ralph Albanese speaks in psychological terms of Argan's encounter with the doctors, whom he sees as mirror images of Argan (*"Le Malade imaginaire* ou le jeu de la mort et du hasard," 8).

18. *Molière: une aventure théâtrale,* 143.

19. Gérard Defaux's distinction between "la comédie morale" [moral comedy] and a later comedy of a new kind in Molière's theater seems especially pertinent to this question (*Molière ou les métamorphoses du comique,* 300).

20. *Molière: An Archetypal Approach,* 169.

21. Harold Knutson remarks upon the resemblance between Toinette's proposal and a *sparagmos* (ibid., 107).

22. *La Violence et le sacré,* 401-2.

23. Philip R. Berk, "The Therapy of Art in *Le Malade imaginaire,*" *French Review* 45, special issue no. 4 (1972): 39.

24. *Pensées et opuscules,* 363.

25. Ibid.

26. Ibid., 366.

27. For Ralph Albanese, Argan's hypochondria "est une conséquence extrême de sa peur de la maladie et de la mort" (*"Le Malade imaginaire* ou le jeu de la mort et du hasard," 3-4) [is an extreme consequence of his fear of illness and death].

28. Jean Serroy sees Purgon's fear of death as "fondamentale" ("Argan et la mort. Autopsie du malade imaginaire," in *L'Art du théâtre. Mélanges en hommage à Robert Garapon* [Paris: Presses Universitaires de France, 1992], 244) but argues that Molière, to celebrate life in his last play, makes death ridiculous.

29. See Jacques Arnavon, Le Malade imaginaire *de Molière: essai d'interprétation dramatique* (1938; reprint, Geneva: Slatkine Reprints, 1970), 26.

30. Louison plays a minor role in the play, appearing only once. Her greatest importance is to place Argan face to face with death. According to Robert Garapon, among others, Argan is not really taken in by his daughter's feigned death. Nor, however, can he stand the image of death confronting him as his daughter's body goes limp before his eyes (*Le Dernier Molière,* 183).

31. The prominence of death in *Le Malade imaginaire* prompted Gide to see a tragic element in this comedy, which he refers to as "cette farce tragique" (*Journal 1939-49. Souvenirs,* 83) [this tragic farce].

32. *Pensées et opuscules,* 354.

Works Cited

Adam, Antoine. *Histoire de la littérature française au XVIIe siècle.* 5 vols. Paris: del Duca, 1948-56.

Albanese, Ralph. "*Le Malade imaginaire* ou le jeu de la mort et du hasard." *XVIIe Siècle* 154 (1987): 3-15.

Arnavon, Jacques. Le Malade imaginaire *de Molière: essai d'interprétation dramatique.* 1938. Reprint, Geneva: Slatkine Reprints, 1970.

Berk, Philip R. "The Therapy of Art in *Le Malade imaginaire.*" *French Review* 45, special issue no. 4 (1972): 39-48.

Cairncross, John. "Impie en médecine." *Cahiers de l'Association Internationale des Etudes Françaises* 16 (1964): 269-84.

Dandrey, Patrick. *La Médecine et la maladie dans le théâtre de Molière.* 2 vols. Paris: Klincksieck, 1998.

Defaux, Gérard. *Molière ou les métamorphoses du comique: de la comédie morale au triomphe de la folie.* Lexington: French Forum Publishers, 1980.

Gaines, James F. *Social Structures in Molière's Theater.* Columbus: Ohio State University Press, 1984.

Garapon, Robert. *Le Dernier Molière.* Paris: Société d'Édition d'Enseignement Supérieur, 1977.

Gide, André. *Journal 1939-49. Souvenirs.* Paris: Gallimard, 1954.

Girard, René. *La Violence et le sacré.* Paris: Grasset, 1972.

Gossman, Lionel. *Men and Masks.* Baltimore: Johns Hopkins University Press, 1963.

Knutson, Harold. *Molière: An Archetypal Approach.* Toronto: University of Toronto Press, 1976.

Livingston, Paisley. "Comic Treatment: Molière and the Farce of Medicine." *MLN* 94 (1979): 676-87.

Molière. *Comedies*. Translated by Donald M. Frame. Franklin Center, Pa.: Franklin Library, 1985.

———. *Oeuvres*. Edited by Eugène Despois and Paul Mesnard. 13 vols. Grands Ecrivains de la France. Paris: Hachette, 1873-1900.

Pascal, Blaise. *Pensées et opuscules*. Edited by Léon Brunschvicg. Paris: Hachette, n.d.

Serroy, Jean. "Argan et la mort. Autopsie du malade imaginaire." In *L'Art du théâtre. Mélanges en hommage à Robert Garapon*, 239-46. Paris: Presses Universitaires de France, 1992.

FURTHER READING

Criticism

Abraham, Claude. "Teaching *Fête: Le Malade imaginaire*." In *Approaches to Teaching Molière's Tartuffe and Other Plays*, edited by James F. Gaines and Michael S. Koppisch, pp. 110-16. New York: Modern Language Association of America, 1995.

Argues for the importance of the music in understanding *The Imaginary Invalid*; counters interpretations that focus on Molière's awareness of impending death.

Bermel, Albert. "*The Imaginary Invalid*." In *Molière's Theatrical Bounty: A New View of the Plays*, pp. 182-92. Carbondale: Southern Illinois University Press, 1990.

Interprets the play as a call to live life fully in the face of the reality of death and emphasizes the joyfulness of the play.

Crawshaw, Robert. "An Original Canvas? *Le Malade Imaginaire* Restored." In *Exploring French Text Analysis: Interpretations of National Identity*, edited by Robert Crawshaw and Karin Tusting, pp. 88-95. London: Routledge, 2000.

Discusses French critics' reviews of a 1990 production of *The Imaginary Invalid*, to which the missing score had been "restored."

Howarth, W. D. "Molière: A Playwright and His Audience." In *Comedy and Ballet*, pp. 213-26. Cambridge: Cambridge University Press, 1982.

Describes *The Imaginary Invalid* as a successful marriage of Molière's character comedy with the *comédie-ballet* form.

Powell, John S. "Music, Fantasy and Illusion in Molière's *Le Malade Imaginaire*." *Music and Letters* 73 (1992): 222-43.

Argues that the interrelationship between play and music is crucial to understanding *The Imaginary Invalid*'s artistic significance.

Shaw, David. "Molière and the Doctors." *Nottingham French Studies* 33, no. 1 (spring 1994): 133-42.

Argues that Molière's depiction of doctors was intended as comic but not satirical.

Gian Francesco Poggio Bracciolini
1380-1459

Italian dialogist, essayist, and humorist.

INTRODUCTION

Poggio Bracciolini's contributions to the rise of humanism range from dirty jokes to moral dialogues. His most enduring achievement is his extensive and successful effort to recover lost classical manuscripts and to restore them for a Renaissance audience seeking more information on ancient Roman culture. As a secretary to several popes and as a friend to influential Italian political leaders, Poggio engaged in numerous debates, often with abusive polemics aimed at the enemies of his patrons. As his dialogues demonstrate, however, Poggio was also an adept author who embodied the humanist belief in the power of eloquence.

BIOGRAPHICAL INFORMATION

Poggio Bracciolini was born in Tuscany, in the village of Terranuova, the son of an impoverished notary. He briefly studied law at Bologna, but soon adopted the shorter, less expensive course of notary studies in Florence. There he also studied classical languages with a large cohort of young men who would, like Poggio himself, contribute to the rise of Italian humanism. During this period he likely began working as a scribe, and he developed a reputation for having a good hand for copying antique manuscripts. In 1402 he took a position at the Vatican, serving as a secretary under Pope Boniface IX. Poggio's position within the church was that of a layman, and accounts of his personal life suggest that his affiliation with the Holy See did little to dampen his taste for worldly pleasures, especially in his early years. His first experiments with writing can be found in his *Facetiæ* (published 1438-52), a collection of clever quips, jokes, and ribald anecdotes that often reveal an impertinent attitude toward religion.

Poggio worked for the church during the Western Schism, when a split among the cardinals and the royal families of Europe produced two popes, each with his own supporters. In 1409 the situation grew even more complicated and acute when a group of cardinals convened to produce a third pope. In 1414 the three concurrent popes, John XXIII, Gregory XII, and Benedict XIII, were all pressed to abdicate, and in 1417 the

church was united once more under one pontiff, Martin V. It was during the intervening years that Poggio, with no pope to serve, traveled around Europe—to Cluni, St. Gallen, Langres, and other sites in Italy, Germany, and France—and located several speeches by Cicero, a rare complete copy of Quintilian's *Institutio Oratoria,* and countless other manuscripts in untended monastic libraries. From 1418 to 1422 he traveled through England, where he wrote of his disappointment in the pre-Renaissance culture.

In 1423 Poggio resumed his role as papal secretary, under Martin V; however, his ability to travel was severely limited. At this same time, a widespread movement for reform sought to remove worldly influence from the inner chambers of the papacy, thus jeopardizing Poggio's position in the church. This tension may have been among the influences for Poggio's first dialogue, *De avaritia* (1428-29; *On Avarice*). The dialogue became one of Poggio's primary genres: later examples include *De varietate fortunae* (1431-48; *On the Vicissitudes of Fortune*), *An seni sit uxor ducenda* (1436), *De nobilitate* (1440; *Dialogue on Nobility*), and *De miseria humanae conditionis* (1455; *A Treatise upon the Woes of Human Fate*).

The papacy fell back into turmoil under Eugenius IV, with whom Poggio was forced to flee when the pope was expelled from the city of Rome. Profits from Poggio's scribal work allowed him to build a villa in Valdarno, part of the seigniory of Florence, to house the collection of antique relics he had acquired during his searches for ancient manuscripts. He was not yet prepared to settle there, however, and he continued to travel with Eugenius IV in his attempts to quell the reform efforts of the Council of Basel. Eugenius was successful, and by the time of Eugenius's death in 1447, the church was largely united again. The subsequent peace and the generous patronage of Eugenius's successor, Nicholas V, enabled Poggio to pursue his studies in earnest again.

Though he maintained a certain distance from much of the ecclesiastic strife of his time, Poggio engaged in many scholarly and social controversies during his career. He wrote a letter in defense of the heretic Jerome of Prague, and he took up the banner of his patron Cosimo de' Medici in the Scipio-Caesar controversy of the 1430s, suggesting that the Florentine leader's quiet virtue resembled that of the classical hero Scipio. Poggio later spoke on behalf of the Medici when they were removed from power in Florence, attacking Francesco Filelfo in particular. Poggio also published an extensive critique of rival humanist Lorenzo Valla and his scholarly method.

In 1452 Poggio retired permanently to the Republic of Florence, and in 1453 he was appointed chancellor and historiographer there. While serving in that office he wrote his *Historiae Florentinae* (published 1715; *History of Florence*). Poggio died in 1459 and was buried in the church of Santa Croce in Florence. The Renaissance sculptor Donatello was commissioned to create a statue of Poggio for the façade of the cathedral, or Duomo, of Florence, but the statue was relocated in 1569 to stand near a grouping of the Twelve Apostles.

MAJOR WORKS

Of all Poggio's writings, the most significant are his dialogues. These works revive the Ciceronian style of debate, but are tempered by the influence of Augustine. The structure of *On Avarice* represents the pattern of most of the dialogues: friends gather for dinner and discussion, and a debate takes place. Two speakers present opposing points of view on a chosen topic, but the framework shifts when a third speaker introduces a religious perspective to the issue, citing scripture and the church fathers for support. The dialogues also take their characters from among the *literati* of Poggio's day, including Antonio Loschi, Niccolo Niccoli, and Cosimo de' Medici. The structure of the discussion is at least as important as the arguments presented; the dialogue works on the humanist assumption that the free exchange of ideas among unbiased, learned men will produce the truth. Whether with genuine or false humility, Poggio offered his written dialogues with the hope that the circulation of thought would continue, with wiser men making further progress in the search for truth. The notion of philosophical progress is also central to Renaissance humanism and the humanist belief that individuals possess the capacity to come ever closer to perfection through the skillful exercise of reason.

CRITICAL RECEPTION

Poggio did not become one of the major figures of the Renaissance simply because of his writings. His gift to Renaissance humanism and thus to Western culture in general was his enthusiastic recovery and recopying of classical texts, which has been a major focus of critical attention. While Petrarch is better known to modern students of the Italian Renaissance, critics point out that, in practical terms, Poggio did far more than Petrarch to make the classical revival possible. Scholars have also observed that Poggio originated a movement toward a new type of handwriting—the humanistic script—which was better suited to copying ancient Roman texts.

With regard to Poggio's own writing, critical opinions have often been deeply colored by early assessments of Poggio's personal life and his personality—whether he is considered charmingly scandalous and eccentric or merely obscene and repugnant. Later readers of his invectives against Lorenzo Valla and Francesco Filelfo suggest that the violence of Poggio's attacks reveals more about Poggio's intemperance than about the flaws of his enemies. In the case of the *Facetiæ*, however, Poggio's penchant for irreverence and indecency has earned him admiration as the author of the first modern joke-book. Scholars have generally chosen to pass over these minor works and to focus on Poggio's dialogues—especially *On Avarice*—for their vivid portraits of humanist culture as it evolved in the fifteenth century. Assessing their value for students of the Italian Renaissance, scholar David Marsh concluded, "Poggio's dialogues are unequaled."

PRINCIPAL WORKS

De avaritia [*On Avarice*] (dialogue) 1428-29
*India Recognita [*The Indies Rediscovered*] (dialogue) 1429

De varietate fortunae [*On the Vicissitudes of Fortune*] (dialogue) 1431-48

An seni sit uxor ducenda (dialogue) 1436

Facetiæ (humor) 1438-52

De infelicitate principum [*A Treatise upon the Unhappiness of Princes*] (dialogue) 1440

De nobilitate [*Dialogue on Nobility*] (dialogue) 1440

Contra hypocritas [*On Hypocrisy*] (dialogue) 1447-48

Historia tripartita disceptativa convivalis (dialogues) 1450

De miseria humanae conditionis [*A Treatise upon the Woes of Human Fate*] (dialogue) 1455

Opera omnia. 4 vols. (dialogues, letters, nonfiction, humor) 1538

†*Historiae Florentinae* [*History of Florence*] (history) 1715

Opera omnia. 4 vols. [edited by Riccardo Fubini] (dialogues, letters, nonfiction, humor) 1964-69

*This text is the fourth book of *On the Vicissitudes of Fortune* and circulated independently as a manuscript prior to its official publication in 1429.

†This text was written sometime between 1453 and Poggio's death in 1459.

CRITICISM

Sidney Hellman Ehrman (essay date 1928)

SOURCE: Ehrman, Sidney Hellman. "Poggio Guccio Bracciolini, 1380-1459 A.D." In *Three Renaissance Silhouettes*, pp. 27-48. New York: G. P. Putnam's Sons, 1928.

[*In the following essay, Ehrman surveys the life and work of Poggio, asserting his centrality to the Italian Renaissance and to the development of humanism.*]

> Virtue Alone Constitutes the Character of a Truly Great Man.[1]

The sun was slowly sinking over the hills of Rome. Its rays, softened and golden, sped across the gardens of the Vatican. Their gleam rested upon the windows of the pontifical palace, peering through the narrow latticed panes of the loggia.

Within, all appeared tranquil and serene. The long galleries connecting the wings with the main building were deserted and noiseless. Everything breathed a spirit of contentment and peace, of work well done.

At one extremity of a cozy room in the west wing a small fire place held fast dying embers. Before these, in a sort of semicircle, were to be found a half score of men seated in comfortable chairs, laughing and joking. Now and again one of their number recounted some coarse or witty anecdote concerning a well known citizen, perhaps his Holiness himself. As the speaker finished, his sally was greeted by a burst of laughter. Jeers and questions hurled at him by the incredulous, generally provoked but another tale.[2]

Upon such a scene the chimes of St. Peter's resounded, marking the close of day. One by one the assemblage sauntered from the *Bugiale*.[3] Priests, arm in arm with gaily clad courtiers, laughing or arguing as the case might be, leisurely quitted the chamber. Finally but one man remained, who seemingly lost in revery, stared steadily at the now darkening embers. Occasionally a satiric smile crept over his countenance, only to be erased by a more thoughtful air.

The person so musing, was a young man in his early thirties, of medium stature, rather slightly built. His olive complexioned face, long and lean, was framed by a crop of dark curly hair, which, already beginning to recede, displayed a high broad forehead. Two large piercing eyes looked out from beneath finely penciled eyebrows. A long aquiline nose with broad nostrils gave further proof to a full sensuous underlip which protruded and curled sardonically. A square chin completes the portrait of the gentleman about whom there was an unmistakable air of passionate resoluteness combined with delicate sensuality.[4] This man was Poggio Bracciolini who, for forty-seven years, was an apostolic secretary, who aided greatly in the discovery of classic manuscripts, who was to prove himself a writer of no mean ability, and with whose name the Renaissance is indubitably linked.

Poggio[5] Bracciolini was born in Terranuova, a village near Arezzo, in Tuscany, in the year 1380. His father was a notary who had completely ruined himself. At an early age, he was sent to study at Florence where he acquired Latin under the guidance of the noted scholar, John of Ravenna, and Greek under the tutelage of the brilliant and gifted Chrysoloras. The school of Florence already possessed a great reputation, and Poggio had for classmates such boys as Lionardo Aretino, Pallas Strozza, Paulo Vergerio and Guarino Veronese, all of whom as men were to leave behind them long records of humanist achievements.

Due to the fame of his teachers and in part to the brilliancy of his own work, Poggio found scant difficulty in securing an appointment to the papal court. At twenty, he was created apostolic secretary by Boniface IX, a position which he was destined to fill for nearly half a century. Thus, at an early age he embarked upon a career which, notwithstanding its apparent simplicity, became a remarkably troubled one, owing to the schismatic disturbance of the times.

During the first ten years of his service, Poggio conducted himself in much the same fashion as any young Roman of limited means and good education. He spent his leisure hours in reading and studying and from the company of his fellow scribes gathered a great deal of the material later employed in his *Facetiæ.* He also took the opportunity to improve his friendship with Lionardo Aretino,[6] a friendship which was to produce much in later years. These occupations, together with his work as secretary and social duties of a lighter and often less circumspect nature, filled his days and nights.

In 1414 the Pontiff, John XXIII, together with his court repaired to the Council of Constance. Here, for the first time, Poggio's writings and interest in antiquity take on a more formal and methodical character, presaging what was to follow. With the flight of the pope, Poggio was left, for the time being, more or less his own master. For the next two years he devoted himself to the study of Hebrew, which he disliked,[7] and to an enthusiastic as well as highly successful pursuit of lost manuscripts.[8] During this time he traveled extensively, making a trip to Baden in order to enjoy the waters, and in a letter addressed to his friend Niccolo Niccoli, the mode of living which he discovered there is charmingly described.[9]

At the elevation of Otto Colonna, Martin V, to the papal throne, the Western Schism drew to a close. With its ending, Poggio's freedom precipitately vanished. Not reappointed to his former office and thus lacking means of sustenance, he took refuge with Beaufort, Bishop of Winchester, from whom he had received a flattering invitation, couched in the most promising terms. However, his English visit was doomed to disappointment. The promised rewards proved to be nothing more than a scant benefice; books were scarce, and antiquity practically unknown. It is not strange that under such circumstances he soon returned to Italy, where, having secured his reappointment, he resumed his former life.

From 1420, the main work of Poggio is directed into different channels. The author replaces the antiquarian. Shortly after his return, he wrote his first dialogue *On Avarice,* which was well received. A second was in preparation when, due to the flight from Rome of the new Pontiff, Eugenius IV, Poggio was forced to leave the capital in company with his master. After many vicissitudes of fortune, including being stopped on the way and held for ransom, the papal secretary reached Florence, worn and exasperated by his experience.

Upon his arrival at the Tuscan capital, Poggio learned of the eviction from power of the Medici. Fervently espousing the cause of his banished patron, Cosimo, he threw himself into the fray, penning a series of invectives against Francesco Filelfo[10] who had enlisted on the opposite side.[11] These writings, scurrilous and unworthy as they were, nevertheless won for him the lasting friendship of the Medici, and upon Cosimo's return to power, he and his children were, by decree, declared forever exempt from the payment of all taxes.

In those days the copying of manuscripts was evidently a gainful occupation, for Poggio now proceeded to purchase a villa at Valdarno from the profits of a Livy which he had copied. Here he set about storing a collection of statues and coins, hunting these with as much enthusiasm as he had before shown in his search for old manuscripts. During this time, at the age of fifty-five, he married. He discarded his mistress by whom he had twelve children,[12] marrying Vaggia de Buondelmonte, an eighteen year old girl of noble family who "combined beauty and discretion,"[13] virtues which were apparently lacking in the happy bridegroom.

Occupations of such a nature did not, however, prevent Poggio from following Eugenius to Bologna. Here he effected a reconciliation between the Pope and Cardinal Julian thus frustrating the efforts of the Council at Basle. The turbulent period of the papacy having now ended, one finds Poggio devoting himself more and more to his writing. In the next decade he published a collection of his letters, wrote his *Dialogue on Nobility,* The Eulogies upon Niccolo Niccoli, Lorenzo de Medici,[14] Cardinal Santa-Croce and Lionardo Aretino, as well as *A Treatise upon the Unhappiness of Princes,* dedicated to Tomasso de Sarzana who was soon to assume the purple as Nicholas V. The result of these labors firmly established Poggio as one of the leading literary figures in Italy, a position which he succeeded in maintaining up to the time of his death.

In 1447 Eugenius IV died, and was succeeded by Nicholas V. To this pontiff, regarded as a man of letters and a patron of the arts, Poggio wrote and solicited an annuity, pleading old age and a desire to pursue more closely his literary endeavors.[15] His request was most generously complied with and Poggio now found himself definitely shielded from want. Never was he more prolific. In quick succession were produced the dialogues, *On the Vicissitudes of Fortune, On Hypocrisy,* his *Historia Disceptativa Convivialis* and an invective against the weak anti-pope, Felix V. He also kept his friends in constant laughter with invectives directed against Lorenzo Valla which proved, that despite age's usually heavy toll, the irascibility of the author's temper remained quite unimpaired.

But this was his last quarrel. In 1453, due to the protection and patronage granted him by the Medici, Poggio was tendered the office of Chancellor of the Florentine Republic, whither he repaired together with his wife, five sons and a daughter. Soon after his arrival, he was made Prior of the Arts of Florence, a position which greatly pleased his dignity. In this capacity, and in comparative tranquillity, he spent the remaining days of his life writing his *Facetiæ, A Treatise upon the Woes of Human Fate* and an excellent *History of Florence*. He died, greatly mourned, on the thirtieth of October, 1459, at the age of seventy-nine. His remains were paid signal honor and interred in the church of Santa Croce while his portrait was hung in the Proconsolo, and a statue erected to his memory on the façade of Santa Maria del Fiore.

Such in brief was the life of Poggio Bracciolini, pontifical secretary and critic of the church, writer of invectives and lover of the beautiful, an immoral moralist. Surely no greater paradox has visited this paradoxical world, no more obstruce and yet illuminating a figure has ever provided a keynote to the times. To invoke an *apologia* for Poggio, to attempt to vindicate his contradictions of thought and action by reconciling them to the period in which he lived, would merely result in casting the man himself into obscurity. The sesame to the character of Bracciolini lies in the fact that he belongs to an age so distinctly individualistic in action, that generalities can play no part in its description.

Intense egotism was a characteristic of Renaissance Italy, and represented an attitude generally shared in by all. Humility and humbleness were never so frankly cast aside. In riotous colors, the realization of Being swept the Italian peninsula, enveloping all in its voluminous mantle of conceit and curiosity. Its effect upon people was startling; rulers wrote verse, while poets ruled countries; priests enacted plays in the Vatican while actors played the roles of priests. All sense of order was swept away in one mad dash for the delirious goal—recognition and homage in every field of human endeavor.

Now there lies in the individual a lack of direct interrelation between self-conscious romance and its crystallization, as well as between self-conscious thought and action. It is difficult at such times to arrive at the whys and wherefores of an act, for, while thinking man is a distinctly rational being, he is scarcely a consistent one.[16] Therefore, if thinking man is inconsistent in his thought, how much more inconsistent must he be when his thoughts are translated into actions. He himself must realize this incongruity. To excuse himself in his own eyes, he believes himself to be outside the rules of action which he has set down. If this condition be borne in mind, Poggio may be understood. Otherwise, the contradictions and equivocations which beset his thoughts and actions will remain an unordered mass, perplexing and bewildering the reader.

Poggio can be best explained as a frank realist. A superficial study of the man serves to show that he was a po-

seur, frankly out for glory and above all, for material gain. In a letter to Guarino Veronese, written at the time he found the lost Quintillian, he said: "It is my glory to restore to the present age, by my labor and diligence, the writings of excellent authors. . . . Oh, what a valuable acquisition! What an unexpected pleasure."[17] Yet a few years later, after haggling for his price, he sold his only copy of St. Jerome to Leonardo d'Este, without a qualm.[18] It is in the light of such contradictory evidence that a fairly balanced insight to the mind of this Renaissance Humanist must be sought.

Above all, Poggio was self conscious. Even in his most sublime moments of passion or anger, he never forgot the importance of his own position. Feeling in himself the reincarnation of the glories of ancient literature, he rushed into quarrels, treated his contemporaries and rivals with barely concealed contempt, and refused to obey in any way those rules of conduct which he had laid down for others.[19]

In a study of the character of Poggio, due attention must be payed to his invectives. Student though he was, and possessing a facile and well managed pen, he never succeeded in becoming a great writer, though surely he never allowed one to imagine that he was aware of his shortcomings in any field. His frank criticism of the works of others, leads one to believe that the man thought that only Cicero and he were writers of true Latin.[20] And yet his friend Lionardo tells us: "Poggio's is a sensative soul easily wounded . . . of wondrous beauty . . . and most shy."[21] Perhaps with age, a realization of his shortcomings came to Poggio, and, unhappy in the knowledge of his impotence, he sought to disguise his weakness under a mask of bitter raillery and bluster. One likes to believe this as the reason for his famous invectives against Valla, which otherwise appear a needless work "tarnishing the lustre attached to his name,"[22] and presenting him to posterity in the guise of a ridiculous old man, cruel tongued and venomous. However, much as one might wish to credit this conjecture, it stands so opposed to his makeup that it can be given little weight.

His ambition to become one of the Great was boundless. There can be no quarrel with Poggio on this score. It is the smallness of his nature, his love of tinselled notoriety as a means to obtain his objective, that sickens. Manifestations of character, thought by him to be instruments on the path to success, were but productive of contempt. To vilify a Filelfo, to scurriously attack a Guarino, did not alone draw attention to himself and to his writings and so prove his superior knowledge in the eyes of the world. These phillipics cannot, like the ones against Valla, be condoned with on the grounds of age and a realization of failure. Poggio at the time of their production was a man in his thirties, young, tempestuous, and self confident. They must stand as the work of a small soul steeped in vulgarity, of one who deliberately defied the canons of good taste in order to grasp publicity and glory. No plea of whimsicality can be attached to, or pardon such statements as, "Filelfo is a defamer of women vomiting obscenity from the succulent stores of his putrid mouth."[23] Such words hold neither beauty or truth. Stripped of their pretense and *raison d'être*,[24] these invectives bare a small soul, a nature cancered and petty, frivolous and vindictive. They are unworthy of a "seeker of the highest in art," of a Humanist and lover of the truth.

Though quick to take offense, this bloody dualist was, on the one hand, as good a friend as he was fierce an enemy on the other. Often he hurried to the aid of a comrade, proffering all that he had whether in money or in love. His friendship for Niccoli and Aretino are, like precious jewels, deep colored, tranquil, emitting warmth and brilliancy. Between these men is found a community of feeling that is profound and gentle. It is a rich, sonorous harmony held together and dominated by the powerful melody of the era, a reverent love for the beautiful. His panegyric upon Lionardo, after the latter's death, is a truly noble expression of friendship. Dignified and pathetic, simple in its structure, showing true love and grief, it remains a monument not alone to Aretino, but to the author as well.[25] Contrast this work with his invectives. What explanation can be tendered for these two so different works emanating from the pen of one man? A logical interpretation would be futile. The answer must be sensed. It is but one more proof of the duality of this man, his complexity of character and his strange contradictions.

Perhaps the most illuminating sidelight on the character of Poggio is exhibited in his curiosity. Whatever else this man may have possessed, he certainly had curiosity. His search for the works of antiquity did not confine itself to the collection and investigation of old manuscripts. As a young man in Rome, he daily made excursions to the imperial ruins, spending much time in exploring, with minute accuracy describing the deserted and fast crumbling buildings, and in nothing all that he observed.[26] His collection of old coins was a very noted one. He filled his villa with statuary which he had collected and acquired on his excursions as an antiquarian. In addition, "struck with awe by the genius of the artist who represents the power of nature herself, put in marble, and carrying an infirmity, an admiration for the works of excellent sculpters,"[27] he wrote to a celebrated collector, Suffretus of Rhodes, whom he knew only by reputation, informing him that he could not bestow upon Poggio a greater pleasure than by transmitting to him one or more pieces of sculpture which he, Suffretus, might be able to spare from his well furnished gallery.[28]

Poggio exhibited this extraordinary curiosity not only towards antiquity and art, but towards the lives of his fellow men as well. His letters from Constance, from Baden, and from England show him to have been deeply concerned with an investigation of his new surroundings and the character of the people he encountered. From Baden he wrote: "every day, I visit the baths so that I may study the people,"[29] and with cleverness and minuteness born from acute observation, he paints a vivid picture of the lives of the frequenters of this watering place. From Constance, he sent an excellent description of the trial of Jerome of Prague[30] in which he not only exposed the corruption and discomfiture of the judges, but, as a certain writer says, gives us a touching and thoroughly understanding portrait of the man.[31]

Egoism is manifested in his curiosity as well as in the writings of Poggio. One can easily imagine this intense Humanist walking at night through the narrow streets of Rome, watching the windows, observing the passers by, analyzing, philosophizing. Or, on a sunny day, one can see him sauntering by the gaily painted stalls of Florentine merchants, sniffing at a flower, testing the hardness of a piece of fruit, playing the great lord incognito, curious, patronizing, stopping here and there to chat, exchanging the time of day with his acquaintances. For him the world was a stage, and its inhabitants all enacting roles for his special benefit. To Niccoli he writes: "It gives me pleasure to stand aloof and watch the wandering throngs, to join in their activities now and again but merely for a closer observance of their actions."[32] He imagined himself, like Petrarch, seated upon the summit of a lofty mountain, looking about him, philosophizing upon the fragility of the world at his feet—of *genus homo*, but not *homo sapiens*.

In only one respect were Poggio's actions consistent with his thoughts. This consistency, which is, however, irreconcilable with his professed loftiness and "supremacy of mind" ideal,[33] is found in his moral life. That was habitually loose. Often chided for this laxity, he never took the trouble to conceal or deny it but contented himself with politely sneering at the morality of his advisors.

Yet moral laxity is more easily understood and forgivable than were other traits in the character of Poggio. The times in which he lived are noted for just this sort of looseness. It was an age in which a pope not only openly recognized his children but caused them to be installed in apartments in the Vatican, creating them princes of the Holy See.[34] It was, therefore, perfectly natural that Poggio failed to observe certain moral precepts. In addition to this excuse of environment, he consistently expressed himself on the subject of celibacy. It was on this account that he refused to take religious orders although they would have bestowed upon him further material advancement. He frankly says: "I am not like Menendemus, a moral rejector of pleasure."[35] Never bawdy, Poggio ever continued to enjoy to their utmost the pleasures of the body and of the senses. He was indeed in all things a sensualist, gratifying his tastes whenever possible, whether it was in realizing beauty in works of art, in literature, or in love.

The paradox of Life is revealed by Poggio in the many sidedness of his character. Covetous, he was, yet liberal to a fault where his friends were concerned; the materialist and realist battled with the romantic in his character; a literary light, he often wielded his pen with such injustice that it became the tool of a professional dualist and scandal monger rather than the weapon of truth and beauty; possessing a remarkable aptitude towards learning, some of his knowledge was of a curiously distorted nature; at times endowed with a frankness that was alarming, he could, when occasion arose, dissimulate and fawn like the best of them; courageous in his attacks upon his enemies and quick to laugh and mock, he cried and writhed before derision; admiring and extolling bravery, he yet feared poverty or any sort of hardship. One can not seek to understand him, to explain his actions by his thoughts. He is a man apart, an arresting figure, because of his deeds, and because of his attempts.

In the evening, as the moonlight steals through the stained glass windows of Santa Maria del Fiore, the traveler can see the statue of Poggio standing in the shadows of the nave, watching with symbolic calm the passing of the world, waiting for what is to come. Slowly it appears to stir. The diaphanous folds of velvet marble, draped toga-like about the body of the man, rustle in the pregnant quiet of the cathedral air. Originally forming a part of the façade, it was taken down a century later when the church was redecorated and replaced in the nave where it now stands in the midst of a group representing the twelve apostles.[36] Thus the narrator of the *Facetiæ* today keeps on good terms with the narrators of the Gospel. As the pale silver light falls upon the lips they tremble slightly. Perhaps they are parted in silent laughter. One wonders. . . .

Notes

1. "Poggii Opera," Basle, 1513, 358.

2. The probability of this purely imaginative scene finds support in Liseux's explanation of the *Facetiæ,* Paris, 1887, II, 230-232.

3. Name given to this room wherein originated the anecdotes later recounted in the *Facetiæ*. The term *Bugiale* means a falsehood.

4. This description has been taken from a portrait of Poggio by Pollainolo hung in the Proconsolo, as well as from a statue of him in the church of Santa Maria del Fiore, Florence.

5. The following outline has been taken and reduced from lives of Poggio as recorded by Recanati, Shepherd and L'Enfant.

6. More familiarly known as Lionardo Bruni, 1369-1444 A.D. As his writings, however, are listed under the name of Aretino, it has been considered expedient to employ in this work the latter designation.

7. "Poggii Opera," op. cit., 29.

8. For a complete list of the manuscripts found during this time see Liseux, op. cit., I, XI.

9. Merau "Les Bains de Bade au xv° Siècle," Paris, 1876.

10. An Italian who became one of the most noted Greek scholars of the day, 1398-1481.

11. These invectives, to be again referred to, may be found in "Poggii Opera," op. cit., 198-257.

12. Lorenzo Valla: "Antidota," in "Mancini vita di Lorenzo Valla," Florence, 1891, 287.

13. "Poggii Epistolæ," lvii., Epist. xxxvii.

14. Brother of Cosimo de Medici and not to be confounded with Lorenzo il Magnifico.

15. "Poggii Opera," op. cit., 287-292.

16. Glaring contradictions appear even in the works of such men as Berkeley, Hegel, etc.

17. L'Enfant: "Poggiana." Tom.II, 509-513.

18. Walser: "Poggius Florentinus," Leipzig, 1914, 501.

19. The presumption in sending an open letter to Beccatelli, "Poggii Opera," op. cit., 349-350, criticizing the obscenity of the latter's work "Hermaphrodite," and then writing his *Facetiæ* is illustrative of the strange mixture of audacity and contradiction which besets his actions.

20. Invectives against Valla, "Poggio Opera," op. cit., 141-176.

21. Lionardo Aretino, "Opera," 324.

22. Recanati: op. cit., 57.

23. "Poggii Opera", op. cit., 339.

24. The first invective, culled into being under the cloak of a defense of the character of Niccolo Niccoli, was, in reality, a threat aimed at the vilifier of the Medici.

25. To be found in the preface of the Mehus edition of the letters of Lionardo Aretino.

26. The results of this labor are contained in "Ruinarum Urbis Romæ Descripto," Poggii Opera, op. cit.

27. "Poggio, Epist.," op. cit., lvii, 118.

28. "Mehi Vita Ambrosii Traversarii," lii.

29. Merau: op. cit.

30. "Poggii Opera," op. cit., 301-305.

31. Shepherd: "Life of Poggio Braccilolini," Liverpool, 1802, 89.

32. "Poggii Epistolæ," op. cit., lxvi, 204.

33. "Dialogue on the Respective Merits of Cæsar and Scipio."

34. Alexander VI.

35. "Poggii Epistolæ": op. cit., xii, 45.

36. Shepherd: op. cit. (a) 484.

Bibliography

PRIMARY SOURCE

Poggio Bracciolini: "Opera," Basle, 1513.

SECONDARY SOURCES

Aretino, Lionardo: "Opera" from Photastadts.

L'Enfant, Jacobo: "Poggiana," Amsterdam, 1720.

Recanati, Giovanbatista: "Osservazioni Critiche e Apologetiche Sopra il Libro de Signor Jacopo L'Enfant Intotilate Poggiana," Venice, 1721.

Shepard, William: "The Life of Poggio Bracciolini," Liverpool, 1902.

Walser, Ernst, "Poggius Florentinus," Leipzig, 1914.

Renee Neu Watkins (essay date January 1967)

SOURCE: Watkins, Renee Neu. "The Death of Jerome of Prague: Divergent Views." *Speculum* 42, no. 1 (January 1967): 104-29.

[*In the following excerpt, Watkins observes the influence of Poggio's humanism in his defense of the scholar Jerome of Prague, who was executed as a heretic. Watkins finds in Poggio's assessment of Jerome a belief in the moral character of both education and eloquence in language.*]

"And when they sentenced [John Hus, in 1415], the King Sigismund sat on the judgment seat, and it was he that had given safe conduct to Master Hus. And they ordered him to be burned at the stake, and also Master Jerome, but him only in the year after. . . . And when such things came to pass, the Czechs and Moravians were filled with wrath. . . ."[1] Thus a Hussite chronicler sums up the executions at Constance which inspired in Bohemia both sermons and military deeds.[2] He stresses

the perfidy of the emperor, some others, the piety of the martyrs. German and Italian clerics at the Council naturally did not share the Bohemian view. To them what mattered was the turbulence of the reform movement and the heretical character which they attributed to the leaders. Perhaps most interesting is the view of those "learned men" who, according to one observer, "were grieved that Jerome had to die, for he was a far greater scholar than Hus."[3] These persons, whose main concern was apparently neither political nor theological, are represented for posterity by Poggio Bracciolini, the Florentine humanist.

When we compare Poggio's well-known letter on the death of Jerome of Prague with the reports of other churchmen who were not humanists, we find a difference of assumptions, a conflict of perceptions, a divergence of conclusions. Scholars have, on the whole, been satisfied to overlook this divergence and to view Poggio's account merely as a corroboration of other, more detailed, reports. Thus R. R. Betts, presenting Jerome's biography, smoothly weaves together the account of Poggio—"one of the ablest journalists of the time"—with other accounts of Jerome's last days. He constructs a good composite picture without analyzing the contrasting attitudes expressed by his sources.[4] Milada Nedvědová, editing a Czech anthology of documents concerning the Hussite trials at Constance, especially admired Poggio's description as "not only a splendid example of humanist writing," but also as a "text of permanent truth."[5] A recent French biographer of John Hus assesses the letter less favorably:

> C'est un reportage étonnant, écrit malheureusement dans ce latin cicéronien qui allait remplacer le latin scolastique si ferme et si précis, par des "équivalences" tirées de l'antique, que l'on trouvait d'une élégance suprême et qui, en réalité, ne sont que des clichés mis bout à bout.

Boulier also observes something of the effect of Poggio's humanism on the substance of his account:

> Jerome de Prague rencontrera [les humanistes] à Constance et forcera leur admiration. Il est de leur caste naissante. Ils salueront en lui, jusque dans son malheur, la constance d'un philosophe de cette antiquité dont ils sont idolâtres et dont, sans toujours en être conscients, ils mettent la virtu plus haut que la sagesse chrétienne.[6]

What Boulier views as the unconscious expression of a professional humanist's aesthetic and moral values, I believe was a consciously chosen point of view, and one of some political significance.

As the basis of discussion, some documents are necessary. I have made a fresh translation of Poggio's letter, based for the first time on the critical edition.[7] I have also translated part of what seems to have been a quasi-official transcription of Jerome's speeches before the Council of Constance on 23, 26, and 30 May 1416.[8] This record is followed by an account of Jerome's death attributed by the scribe to certain anonymous "old historians." It is, in fact, part of the work of Peter of Mladoňovice, an ardent friend of Jerome. Peter witnessed some of the earlier events leading to Jerome's death, and obtained his account of the execution from a sworn eyewitness.[9] In addition to this favorable account, the fullest we have, I have also translated a vivid and outspokenly hostile description by Theodore of Vrie, a German monk.[10] The translations are presented below in an appendix.

The semi-official record, only a small part of which is translated here, devotes far more space to the articles of accusation and to the speeches of the prosecutors than to the defense. Distortions of Jerome's speeches are discernible here and there within it, when Jerome improbably incriminates himself or Hus.[11] I would describe the tone of the document, however, as largely objective. Karl August Fink, a scholar currently engaged in extended research on the Council, also views this work as a semi-official record based on some sort of official notes. Concerning the text, he remarks that "die Nachprüfungen der Texte Van der Hardt's für die allgemeinen Sitzungen [haben] ergeben dass seine Edition zuverlässig ist und mit gutem gewissen benutzt werden kann."[12]

There are a good many unofficial accounts from persons who were at the Council and who perhaps attended the execution. Altogether they corroborate the picture as given below by the anonymous clerk, by Mladoňovic, and by Vrie. They agree so closely on the facts that they serve as a standard by which to measure the story, unique on several counts, as told by Poggio. In Hardt, one may find: Gobelinus Persona (I, 772); Theodorus Niemus (I, 307, and II, 454); Erdwinus Erdmannus (IV, 772); Magdeburg Chronicle (IV, 772). In L. R. Loomis' translations, one may read Guillaume Filastre (283-284) and Ulrich Richental (129-135). In Novotný's edition, along with Peter of Mladoňovice's *Narration,* there are two anonymous less full accounts: *Notae de Concilio Constantiensis* and *De Vita Magistri Ieronimi.* Another important Hussite source is Laurentius of Březová.[13]

The French cardinal, Guillaume Filastre, comprehensively sums up the case. Concerning his point of view, J. H. Mundy remarks: "His background, interests and intellectual bent were Gallican. By the end of the Council of Constance, however, he was first, last, and always the man who best expressed the point of view of the Sacred College."[14] He is cited here to demonstrate the point of view which in fact decreed the death of Jerome.

Filastre's summation:

> On Wednesday, 27 May 1416, the second year of the Council, the vigil of the Lord's Ascension, the Council held a session, without solemnities, and gave public audience to Jerome of Prague, at his own request. For the new commissioners had begun new proceedings against him, an examination on the charge of heresy. He made a great speech to prove that hatred, false witnesses, and lies were being employed to convict him. In the course of it, he cited many examples from the Old and New Testaments of holy men who had suffered for the truth from false testimony and hate, and showed that noone had ever been overcome by so many false means as he. At the end he revoked forever, as he said, the abjuration, confession, and declaration which he had made in the session of the Council on Monday, 23 September 1415, in which he had approved and assented to the sentence of condemnation passed on Wyclif and John Hus, condemned for heresy of teaching and writing. This John Hus had been condemned for heresy in July and burned by the secular court, and the memory of Wyclif, long dead, had been condemned.

> Jerome now said that he had made that confession and abjuration and had assented to and approved those verdicts wickedly and falsely, in foolish terror of an imaginary fire. He was not afraid to confess his falsehood and spoke of Hus always as a good man. But with regard to the article on the sacrament of the altar and the transubstantiation of the bread into the body of Christ, he said he held and believed what the Church believed and on this point he prefered to believe Augustine and the other doctors rather than Wyclif or Hus.

> On the Saturday after the Lord's Ascension, 30 May, the Council held a session with solemnities, in miters and copes, and Mass was performed. The lord Cardinal Bishop of Ostia presided at the condemnation of Jerome. After Mass and the customary prayers, the oft-mentioned Bishop of Lodi preached a fine sermon, taking his text from the Gospel for the Lord's Ascension: "He upbraided them for their unbelief and hardness of heart." He spoke with great eloquence, urging Jerome, who was present, to repent and save his soul. After the sermon, the Patriarch of Constantinople read the declaration which Jerome had made on the 23rd of the previous September, before the Council, as stated above, and said that Jerome had revoked it some days since and therefore had relapsed into heresy. In a loud voice Jerome confessed that he had revoked it, as he did on the Wednesday preceding, and went on to make many allegations, asserting, as he did before, that he was overcome by false witnesses, hatred, and lies and citing the examples of Paul and Christ, who were overcome by the Jews.

> Finally, he professed the Catholic faith in general and refused to recant in any particular. He said also that Hus had been called a heretic because he preached against the arrogance of the clergy. To which the Cardinal of St Mark replied that he ought not to invent such grounds for Hus's condemnation. The sacred Council knew and deplored the fact that many ecclesiastics did assume excessive arrogance and pomp, and had assembled in order to reform that and other bad customs, and expected to do so. But it was characteristic of heretics to mix some truth in with their false doctrines, so that simple people who heard the truth would believe the false remainder was true also.

The Patriarch of Constantinople then read the sentence against Jerome. . . . After the reading of the sentence, a paper cap, painted over with devils, was given to Jerome, who took it boldly and set it on his head, saying: "Christ wore a crown of thorns." And he was received by the secular court, led to the fire, and burned.

This is the core of the story. The anonymous record provides a far fuller description of Jerome's speech, explaining how he came to ask for a "public audience," as Filastre tells us, and showing how he justified his charge that the opposing witnesses were committing perjury. Peter of Mladoňovice's and Vrie's accounts of the last hours of Jerome's life supplement Filastre's laconic statement; from them we learn of the dramatic manner in which Jerome bore witness both to his convictions and to his loyalty to Hus.

The altercation with the Cardinal of St Mark concerning the reasons for Hus's condemnation is uniquely preserved in Filastre. We know from others that Jerome thought Hus had truly aroused the conciliar ire only by attacking clerical corruption, but here we learn that there was an official answer to this charge. The answer expresses an important and pervasive attitude: when a heretic speaks some truth it is merely to further his heresy—even a truthful statement merely cloaks the Devil. Precisely this thought becomes a question rather than a certainty for Poggio. Poggio tells us, first, that Jerome uttered "not one idea unworthy of a good man." Second, Poggio describes how, after he had practically cleared himself of heresy, Jerome insisted on courting death by defending Hus. In defense of Hus, Jerome had said "that he never held any belief opposed to the Church of God, but had opposed clerical abuses, the pride, luxury, and pomp of the prelates." In the end, Poggio vaguely rejects Jerome's erroneous opinions. The "errors" are rejected, but not all the rest of what Jerome has to say. The closest Poggio comes to the position of the Cardinal, that virtue or truth in heretics can only be a device to mislead us, is the much less severe notion that the heretic's splendid gifts all turn in the end to his *own* destruction. "I do not praise him for holding some opinions contrary to those the church has established," says Poggio, "but I admire his learning, his wide knowledge, his eloquence, the elegance of his speech, and his wit in reply; yet I fear that he was given all these gifts by nature for his own destruction." This does not mean that Jerome's very gifts only make him more dangerous to the orthodox. Ignoring the problem of "simple people," Poggio implies that at least some hearers could profit from the words of the heretic, to which they could listen selectively. All this amounts to an implicit argument against burning heretics.

Poggio attributes to Jerome a remark about the early church fathers which argues explicitly for tolerance in matters of religious belief. It goes beyond merely sort-ing out the good from the dangerous. "He had also asserted that, in matters of faith, the learned and most holy men of ancient times were accustomed to disagree sometimes, not in order to harm the faith, but in order to find out the truth." St Jerome and St Augustine are given as examples. The anonymous account not only does not indicate that Jerome made this statement, but mentions the same two church fathers only as authorities who agree in giving the basis for the orthodox view of the Eucharist. Who made the statement about diversity of opinion leading to truth—was this Jerome or Poggio? After considering the rest of what we know of Jerome's views, I think we shall find it hardly fits as it stands, and that we must attribute this radically untraditional view of the problem of heresy to Poggio.

To understand the confrontation of Poggio and Jerome better, one certainly needs some idea of the events which had brought each of them to the situation of the trial of May 1416. With the help of scholars writing in Western European languages and of the documentation in Hardt, I should like to review here briefly some of the salient facts and problems of Jerome's life.[15] I shall turn thereafter to the easier task of summarizing Poggio's situation at Constance, which is richly documented by his own writings and has been interpreted by biographers.

Jerome of Prague became a bachelor of arts at Prague in 1398, at perhaps about the age of twenty-five. He studied for three years at Oxford (1399-1402), then taught at Paris, Cologne, and Heidelberg before returning home. Persons from these three universities accused him of having taught heresies when they confronted him at Constance. He had certainly taught extreme Realism and used unconventional arguments to clarify the mystery of the trinity. After persistently teaching in a manner which led to trouble with university authorities, he brought back to Prague certain of the books of Wycliffe: the *Trialogus,* the *De Eucharistia,* the *Dialogus,* and the *De Simonia.*[16] These writings apparently supplemented the philosophical works of Wycliffe already known there.

John Hus, a student of theology at the University of Prague, based his own writing on the problem of the nature of the church largely on Wycliffe, and he defended the English heretic's books from those who wished to have them all publicly burnt. Some years older than Jerome, Hus became dean of the faculty of philosophy at the University of Prague in 1401, and served for a short term as rector, in 1402-03. From 1402 on he was the regular preacher at the Bethlehem Chapel in Prague, which had, even in earlier decades, been the main pulpit of popular preachers of church reform. Hus urged the public to demonstrations and refusals to pay the tithe to notoriously negligent or loose-living clergy. He thus acted as the leader of a practical movement as well as of a scholastic one: the practical movement was conducted in Czech and concerned the daily life of the church; the scholastic one, conducted in Latin, was mainly concerned with the theoretical character of the church as the Body of Christ and with the Realist doctrine concerning the objective existence of universals. While Wycliffe's writings inspired the scholasticism of Hus, it is clear that he read Wycliffe selectively. That he did not follow him in rejecting transubstantiation is quite certain. Both Hus and Jerome were, nonetheless, accused of this heresy at Constance.

In January 1409, Jerome played a leading role in a great debate at the University of Prague on the problem of universals. The debate, as Betts says, "resolved itself into a defense of and an attack on Wyclif, the modern champion of Realism; it was Czech against German, reformer against conservative."[17] Jerome's final speech, as partly preserved and as translated by Betts, shows what he then thought of the problem of heresy. Jerome concluded his first section by saying "they are not logicians, but diabolical heretics, who say that universals are mere names." These persons are heretics "in life and morals." Their behavior is inconsistent with Czech feelings, for "no true Czech can be a heretic." Jerome calls on all his hearers to protect "the good name of this most holy city of Prague." As to Wycliffe, Jerome has learnt much that is good from him. He does not believe everything Wycliffe says, nor "any other doctor." Only holy scripture is infallible. Readers of Wycliffe should sort out the many truths from the occasional errors, remembering that "gold and silver and precious stones are often buried in foul earth." What is contrary to faith in Wycliffe, they should not conceal, nor accept. In conclusion, however, Jerome clearly defended Wycliffe as a "grave doctor" in spite of his errors, and said he wished "that God would grant that my soul were where Wycliffe's is." Jerome can see that there are teachings to reject as well as teachings to accept in his favorite master; but one can hardly construe his remarks as a defense of doubt, debate, and rational tolerance.

Later in 1409, in the course of a political struggle between the university and Wenceslas, the King of Bohemia, the Bohemian professors gained an unprecedented control of the university administration. Hus, himself, was appointed rector. The German faculty did not accept this loss of power, and a large number withdrew from Prague. In Jerome's speech of defense as preserved by the anonymous clerk, he refers at length to these events, for, as a member of the Bohemian faculty and a chief supporter of Hus, he had made many enemies in the struggle.

The following year Jerome travelled to Vienna, boldly to face the university authorities there who accused him of heresy. He was put on trial for heresy but managed to flee for his life. The result was excommunication by the archbishop, but, as Betts says, "this does not seem to have worried him or prevented his participation in the services and sacraments of the church."[18] Back in Prague, he led the protests against a new papal indulgence of 1412 being sold to support John XXIII's "crusade" against Ladislas of Naples. Jerome seems to have been not only an ardent travelling missionary of his scholastic and reforming views, but a fiery leader of the city populace. In a document of protest against the indulgences which de Vooght associates with Jerome's authorship or influence, those who promulgate the indulgence are described as "disciples of Asmodeus, Belial, and Mammon."[19] On 17 June 1412, Jerome even publicly defied Hus, who wished to pacify a crowd of students, in order to lead a public demonstration against the indulgence.[20]

On 10 July, a public protest was followed by the arrest and execution of three young men. A crowd got hold of their bodies and walked in a funeral procession led by Master John of Jicin, Hus's friend, chanting for the dead, not the usual funeral hymns, but the hymn "Isti sunt sancti . . ." from the liturgy for the ancient Christian martyrs.[21] Another demonstration took place, probably in August, organized by Vok of Valdstein, at which a student dressed as a prostitute handed out mock-indulgences.[22] While the role of Jerome in these demonstrations is not clear, the funeral procession seems to reflect his cast of mind or to have influenced it. In his own last hours he likewise used the liturgy to express very precisely his protest and his faith. His connection with popular gatherings and with the translation of religious texts into Bohemian, moreover, reached such a level in 1412 that Betts feels he can say, "Jerome was well on the way to the establishment of an autonomous Protestant community."[23] Fears of this sort, in any case, led to a clerical appeal from Prague to Rome and to the papal excommunication of Hus and Jerome. They then attempted to appeal the excommunication, first at Rome, then at Constance.

The Council of Constance undertook from the first to deal with the problem of heresy in Bohemia, a problem both of church authority and of the political power of Sigismund over Wenceslas. Hus wished to present his own case at Constance, and was offered a safe conduct by the emperor. He arrived in the city on 3 November 1414, but was charged with continuing to celebrate the mass and preaching, and arrested on 28 November. As a prisoner arraigned for heresy, moreover, he was given a very limited opportunity to state his views before the Council.

Jerome, in spite of Hus's warnings, followed him to Constance and arrived on 4 April, hoping to set his friend and spiritual leader free. He stayed in hiding, apparently in a castle at Überlingen, very near Constance. He caused notices to be put up at night on the doors of the main churches and of the cardinals' residences, protesting against the breach of Hus's safe conduct. He asked for a safe conduct for himself, so that he might appear publicly and defend the teachings common to Hus and himself. The only force, however, with which he could back his plea to be heard and not to be treated as a known heretic before he could defend himself, was the rather vague threat of public disapproval.

> . . . paratus sum venire Constanciam et innocenciam meam fidem quoque orthodoxam non latenter in angulis aut coram privatis personis sed aperte et publice coram toto concilio ostendere. . . . Quod si michi venienti et me tante equitati offerenti ante probacionem in me cuiusquam culpe quequam arrestacio, captivacio vel violencia fieret, extunc toti mundo patesceret, quod hoc generale concilium non secundum iusticiam atque equitatem procederet. . . .[24]

On 9 April, Jerome departed secretly from Constance. We have, curiously enough, the record of a cautiously worded safe conduct for him issued by the Council on 11 or 12 April.[25] He probably never received it. On 17 April, the Council cited Jerome to appear before it to answer charges of heresy. On his journey through Bavaria, he stopped and had dinner with some parish clergy and apparently spoke very vehemently against the Council; his indiscreet words led to his arrest. He was returned to Constance on 23 May in chains and paraded thus around the city, a large man with a bushy black beard. Then he was imprisoned in the tower of St Paul's cemetery under the care of Walrode, bishop of Riga. At first he was kept chained up with his arms above his head, unable to sit down even to sleep; this torture lasted two days.[26]

The commission set up to examine Jerome's case included Henry of Piro and John Scribanis, men who were simultaneously the chief prosecutors in the case against John XXIII. As early as 18 April, they heard a large group of witnesses, headed by one Michael of Brod, an official of the church of St Albert of Prague; they all testified that Jerome had been known to disturb church services and incite the public to violence.[27] On 23 May, when Jerome himself was in their hands, the commission heard no less a personage than Jean Gerson, chancellor of the University of Paris, register complaints against Jerome. "While you were in Paris, Jerome," said Gerson, "you thought you were an Angel with all your eloquence, and you disturbed the university by stating many erroneous conclusions in the schools, along with their correlates, especially on the subject of universals, on Ideas, and on other matters still more controversial." Jerome replied by saying that all he had taught in Paris had been spoken as a philosopher and teacher speaking philosophically. If he had stated something wrong and were now shown his error, he would willingly and humbly retract what he had taught.[28]

On 6 July Hus was burned. Jerome remained in prison. Mladoňovic mentions, not only his physical sufferings, but also the threats of execution with which he was taunted. By all this, he explains the prisoner's capitulation early in September. On 11 September, Jerome signed a full confession and revocation. On the 12th, he sent a letter to Lacek of Kravař in Bohemia saying he had come to see his errors and that he now fully accepted the Council's execution of Hus.[29] On 23 September, he read his submission before a full session of the Council. He repudiated all the teachings of Wycliffe and Hus condemned by the Council and joined in their condemnation.[30] After that his chains were at last taken off, but he was still not released from prison.

At a meeting on 19 December of all the nations at the Council, John Naso (Náz), speaking for the German nation, insisted on a decision concerning the "suspected heretic," Jerome. In February, therefore, we again find Jerome publicly charged with heresy. Henry of Piro read some accusations before the Council, and a new commission headed by John of Rochetaillée, Patriarch of Constantinople, and Nicolas Dinckelspuel, was set up to look into the matter further.[31] That the commission was, as Jerome later claimed, predisposed to condemn him, is confirmed by the fact that Dinckelspuel, who was a canon of All Saints and of St Stephen in Vienna, appears as a witness on the archiepiscopal excommunication of Jerome issued at Vienna, 30 September 1410.[32] Jerome continued to languish in prison while these men inquisitioned him. There were public examinations, beginning 27 April, and ending in Jerome's appearance before the fully assembled Council on 23 and 26 May. On 26 and 30 May he spoke in his own defense, asserting that John Hus himself was never a heretic, that he had repudiated Hus only from fear of the fire, that both Hus and he were good Christians. He was condemned by vote of the Council on 26 May, the sentence carried out 30 May 1416.

During the year or so which Jerome spent in the hands of the Council, Poggio was in the city as a papal secretary, a *scriptor* in the *Poenitentieria,* an official, in other words, of the department of the Curia which issued indulgences.[33] He had been appointed by John XXIII, whom the Council deposed in May 1415, and his position and future were necessarily somewhat insecure. His friend, Leonardo Bruni, for whom Poggio had obtained a similar position with the Curia, departed early in 1415 to accept the post of chancellor of the Florentine republic. He left, in fact, only a week before the flight of the pope himself.[34] He had had the opportunity, therefore, to see Hus and to observe his imprisonment, but he did not witness the arrival of Jerome.

Poggio remained at Constance but took frequent trips, mainly to search in nearby monasteries for classical manuscripts, but also to enjoy the baths at Baden. He was looking for a personal protector to replace the pope, and he found Henry of Beaufort, bishop of Winchester, who eventually took Poggio to England.[35] Poggio, according to Voight, "looked upon this stormy time as a literary vacation, encouraged as he was by Florentine and Venetian friends who thought of him as a missionary on German soil for the cult of letters."[36] It may also be true, as Voight suggests, that "he laughed silently as the prelates and doctors got involved in long expositions and discussions concerning the schism and the Hussite heretics."[37]

Yet Poggio found the last days of the trial of Jerome remarkably interesting, and he described the events in his letter to Leonardo Bruni. He disclaimed any authority to judge the guilt or innocence of Jerome, but he clearly said that Jerome's speech of defense was unstained by any heresy and that, if Jerome defended the heretic, Hus, it was for the sake of the reforming, not the heretical, qualities of the heretic. Poggio declares, moreover, that he found convincing Jerome's claim that all of the testimony against him was biased, false, and fabricated. These thoughts seem to challenge the infallibility of the Council, to say the least. We have already noted that Poggio seems to disagree with prevailing ideas, represented by Filastre, in that he permits himself to admire much of what this man, officially condemned for heresy, thinks and feels. Subtly but effectively, Poggio suggests that divergent opinions on matters of faith may lead to truth. He thus comes close to doing for Jerome of Prague what the latter had just done for Hus. No wonder Leonardo Bruni's reply called for more caution:

> The day before yesterday we received a copy of your letter sent by Barbaro concerning the execution of Jerome, the elegance of which I do most heartily commend. You seem, however, to give him more credit than I would wish, and though you correct your own judgment several times, you somehow show too much favor to him. I think one should write more cautiously about these things.[38]

For all its elegance, Poggio's letter was not merely a literary exercise. It was the defense, barely within the bounds of the permitted, of a heretic, Why? Richental's remark gives us a first answer: "Many learned men were grieved that he had to die, for he was a far greater scholar than Hus." Ernst Walser suggests that Poggio's words "represent neither a pagan nor a disinterested aesthete, but a warm hearted Christian layman, who had the courage to say openly what many were thinking, and who set upon the death of Jerome an immortal aura of beauty."[39] This judgment seems to me sound as far as it goes. That Poggio's feeling was moral, rather than disinterestedly "pagan" or aesthetic, is clear both from the letter itself and from his whole attitude to scholarship, the purpose of which, for him, is emphatically moral.[40] Why does he put so much faith in education as the means to morality, and in classical education particularly—how, in the case of Jerome, does he move from the admirable learning and eloquence of the man

to his admirable character? This question may be partially answered by closer examination of the letter.

Walser also does not take up the quite basic question of Poggio's historical veracity. Comparison with other witnesses indicates that Poggio sharply modified the actual story and, probably consciously, altered the character of his central figures in some important ways. While Poggio explicitly disclaims any intention of fully narrating the case, his selective description betrays a definite intention to use the episode as an illustration of a certain kind of greatness. What moral purpose did he think to serve by his artful modifications? Though Poggio was, doubtless, from a modern point of view like Walser's, as Christian as any man who recorded his impressions of the trial of Jerome, yet the contrasts between his view and that of others indicate that his Christianity, like his style, moved away from the established norm. A substantive comparison with Hardt's anonymous chronicle will make the point clearer.

Poggio and the semi-official account agree on at least certain major parts of the story. They tell us that Jerome faced a series of charges read before the whole Council by a commission of investigators who declared that he had long been and still, despite his denials, was a heretic. They agree that he wished to make a speech in his own defense and was granted the opportunity to do so on 26 May. They agree that he said: that his judges were unfair; many excellent persons in both pagan and biblical antiquity had been unjustly condemned and might serve as models for Jerome's own case; the witnesses for the prosecution were lying, and there were historical reasons for their vindictiveness; he was not a heretic; John Hus had been a good man and a good Christian, not a heretic, and mainly concerned with reforming abuses in the church. They agree also that the speech was one which, by insisting on Hus's having been wrongfully condemned, was not calculated to incline the Council to mercy. They tell us that Jerome was condemned and that he was led out to the stake on 30 May. The anonymous chronicler and Theodore of Vrie assure us that he sang parts of the litany, the *credo,* in fact, and certain significant hymns. Poggio confirms that he did sing. All agree that he was pertinacious to the end in his defense of Hus and, whatever the spirit in which they report it, brave.

Differences of style and intention are apparent. Poggio's letter has form: an introduction, a report of Jerome's speech interrupted by comments on his gestures and manner, and a conclusion. The others, by contrast, merely put down a series of observations in chronological order. While all three report particularly the words of Jerome, Theodore of Vrie and the anonymous clerk do so according to what struck them as interesting, sometimes shocking, or important; Poggio, as he clearly tells us, reports what struck him as eloquent. We find

Poggio more concerned than the others to assess, to evaluate, both the argument and the manner of the speaker. Theodore, though he vituperates against Jerome, does not really discuss him, nor does the anonymous clerk or Mladoňovic in his narration of the final drama. Poggio, however, not only seeks to explain exactly how Jerome achieved an effect of eloquence, but also, to some degree, what was the strength of his claim not to be a heretic, what kind of man he was if he *was* a heretic, and why he was defying the Council.

The main part of Jerome's defense, as all agree, took part on 26 May. Poggio also reports the protest of 23 May which preceded Jerome's being granted the right to make a continuous speech. It is only from Poggio that we understand that Jerome claimed the Council had been prejudiced by listening only to his enemies up to this time. Poggio alone reports Jerome's complaints about the filth in his prison and the terrible darkness. The anonymous clerk, on the other hand, and not Poggio, tells that Jerome made another brief speech in the assembly on the very day of his execution. This speech as he and others give it, summed up Jerome's belief in himself, in Hus, and in Bohemia. Poggio may omit it partly for the sake of artistic economy, since he thus makes a stark and almost silent drama of the last hours of Jerome's life. He makes little of Jerome's chanting and singing which most witnesses report in detail, perhaps partly for the same aesthetic reason. The singing of the *credo,* etc., was obviously intended by Jerome as an eloquent statement of his own innocence; the orthodox observers whose impressions we have found it shocking, disturbing, and bold: Poggio may have felt that it added nothing to the logic of the defense, and as to the figure of heroism in the face of death which such singing might be thought to enhance, Poggio had another, more silent and aloof, ideal.

Poggio enjoyed and understood the rational coherence of Jerome's list of earlier martyrs to the miscarriage of justice, while the anonymous source somewhat garbled the list. The chronicler gives "Socrates, Boethius, Maro (mistake for Soranus?), Seneca, and Plato." Poggio says Jerome named "Socrates, Anaxagoras, Zeno, Rutilius, and Boethius." As Poggio shows us, Jerome derived his pagan examples mainly from Boethius, who speaks of Socrates, Anaxagoras, Zeno, Canius, Seneca, and Soranus[41]—Jerome, according to Poggio, put in Plato (Boethius had said certain philosophers had been unjustly condemned "even before the age of Plato") and Rutilius, and of course Boethius himself. Rutilius, an almost proverbial ancient martyr to unjust class-biased judgment, may have been familiar to Jerome from Cicero, Quintilian, or Seneca, to name only the most widely read authorities.[42] Poggio apparently edited out Seneca as poorly suited to illustrate the point. As Poggio well understood, Jerome had chosen examples which would build up an argument for the fallibility of high,

and even of ecclesiastical, courts. To this end, a second list of examples from the Bible was essential; one wonders, nevertheless, about the taste and tact of Jerome when he flew from such figures as Zeno and Rutilius to Moses, Joseph, Isaiah, Daniel, and Susanah. One is reminded of Paul Arendt's general comment on the sermons given at the Council by both Northerners and Italians, "a youthful enthusiasm, one might say an ebullient infatuation, for classical antiquity . . . resurrects all Olympus and lets the ancient gods and heroes appear amidst scholastic holiday sermons and even in the midst of dark sermons of penance."[43]

Still more are we taken aback to find Jerome ending his list of martyrs with John the Baptist and "Christ himself" whom "all are agreed . . . were condemned by false witnesses and by the false decisions of their judges . . ." Or was it Poggio who made the comparison in this way? The anonymous account omits it. Guillaume Filastre says that, on the day of the execution, when Jerome again spoke before the Council, he made "many allegations," and cited "the examples of Paul and Christ, who were overcome by the Jews." Jerome compared himself to Christ, as we read in Theodore of Vrie and in Filastre, when he put on his heretic's cap. Yet the bald listing of Christ himself to conclude a series of martyrs can be credited rather to Poggio's relentless schematization than to Jerome's passionate self-identification with the Saviour, for it seems to be Poggio, not Jerome, who has absorbed from classical literature concepts of justice and heroism by which he might measure even Christ. As for Jerome's own erudition and classical interests, in truth, we see but darkly through our witnesses' eyes.

The anonymous account indicates that perhaps half of Jerome's main speech in his own defense was devoted to the story of a political struggle between Bohemians and Germans. On the day of the execution, Jerome again asserts that "what he had argued and said . . . he had always done for the good and welfare of Bohemia, as a faithful subject." By political intrigues, Jerome explains the alleged prejudice of the court against Hus and himself. The description of these intrigues in the anonymous chronicle is pithy, persuasive, and a gem for the historian of heresy. Poggio's account passes over it with the remark, "the causes of their hatred he set forth so clearly that there was no need for further explanation." The Italian humanist leaves in the shadow a whole story of German and Bohemian rancour, and casts a strong light on those of Jerome's complaints against his judges which dealt with elements also dangerous to Poggio and his Italian friends—the elements of clerical panic in the face of anti-clerical criticism.

> When they said, among other things, that he spoke evil
> of the Apostolic See, opposed the Roman pope, stood
> against the cardinals, persecuted the prelates and hated

the clergy of the Christian religion, he arose and said in a voice of prayer with his arms outstretched: 'Where, then, shall I turn, fathers of the Council? Whose help shall I implore? . . . these, my persecutors, have already alienated your minds from any concern for my welfare, for they have made me out to be the enemy of all who are judges here.'

Poggio deals subtly with the question of Jerome's stand on specific theological issues where he was accused of heresy. On one of the most important, the matter of transubstantiation, Poggio recounts Jerome's answer, "the bread does remain—at the baker's" as a monument of wit. The reply is, of course, also a sufficient indication, which Poggio need not interpret to friends as wise as Leonardo Bruni, that Jerome repudiated the remanentist heresy of which he was accused. His orthodox views on this point are confirmed by the anonymous clerk, who says,

> Finally, however, where these same men, John Wycliffe and John Hus, speak their opinion concerning the sacrament of the altar, insofar as they contradict the doctors of the church, he did not follow them in that part of their teaching nor hold their view. There he believed, on the contrary, with the four doctors of the church, namely Gregory, Ambrose, Augustine, and Jerome, and others who today are leaders in the church.

Filastre, too, tells us Jerome rejected both Wycliffe and Hus on this point. It seems that this is probably a distortion, which may well have come into Filastre's account from the official record of the session. That it is a distortion is likely because Hus repeatedly denied this heresy both in Prague and when arraigned before the Council;[44] and it is almost incredible that Jerome should thus turn and accuse him. The heresy was Wycliffe's, of course, and Jerome may well have wished to make clear the limits of his defense of Wycliffe, whom he did consider, nonetheless, unfairly condemned. It is clear that neither of our sources finds it wise to give a full and explicit account of what we can surmise was Jerome's assertion of his own innocence and that of Hus in the matter of Eucharistic doctrine.

Poggio most strikingly omits all reference to the revocation made by Jerome the previous September, as if this had never happened. It is hard to believe that he thought that his Florentine friends would not learn of this prominent aspect of the case, and one wonders whether he left it out simply to enhance the purity of the *exemplum,* so that he could more fittingly remark "the death of the man you might have described from a text in philosophy." But, as with the whole letter, an alteration which seems primarily aesthetic also changes the moral and practical picture.

The revocation, of course, made a difference to Jerome's final situation and to the character of his defense. Poggio was greatly underrating the legal difficulties if, as he listened to Jerome's speech, he really hoped that the accused man "would now proceed to clear himself by retracting the objectionable points in his teaching or to ask pardon for his errors," and so save his life. Instead Jerome burst into a defense of Hus and so "courted death." After Jerome's revocation of September, 1415, a fresh admission of errors or plea for forgiveness—such as the bishops of Florence and Lodi and the patriarch of Constantinople until the very hour of execution urged upon him—would indeed have restored the condemned man to "the bosom of the church" and perhaps caused that church to breathe easier, but would only have altered his sentence to a more merciful form of death.

To escape execution altogether, Jerome would have had to convince the Council that he had not relapsed from a revocation which had been sincere; and while thus defying the commission which accused him, he would also have had to persuade the Council of his continuing wholly submissive spirit. This difficult defense he seemed in fact to be attempting in the first part of his speech of 26 May. He certainly tried to cast doubt on the commission's findings, to discredit all the witnesses who had accused him. It is questionable, however, that, for all his spirited attack on his accusers, Jerome ever thought that he could persuade the Council to move against the recommendation of its own eminent commission and declare him innocent. But he indeed arrived at a turning point when, though repudiating all heresies of doctrine, he openly defended Hus. To do so was to flout the authority of the Council, and the problem of authority was actually the most fundamental one preventing the reconciliation of Hus and the Council. Jerome apparently did not, as Poggio claims, court death by associating himself with his friend; rather he was inviting the most drastic form of a fate he could hardly have avoided.

Why did Jerome give up the slim chance of a successful defense and insist by his pertinacity on a painful end by burning? He had been tortured and had yielded, torturing his conscience. Perhaps he hoped then for a fate like that which later befell one Henry Lacembok of Chlum, a Bohemian nobleman, who was accused of the Hussite heresy and obtained his freedom by swearing that he had never been a Hussite and condemning both Hus and Jerome posthumously, only to return to Bohemia and die "in the Hussite faith."[45] Lacembok, however, was not, like Jerome, a notorious leader, and his German name may also have helped confuse the authorities as to his real loyalties. Any hope of this kind of outcome must have died during Jerome's months of imprisonment after he had abjured and written his letter of abjuration to Bohemia. He then at last returned to his open faith in Hus as a Christian and a leader, and by implication reasserted the right of the laity and lower clergy to reform the church. He was a man of tortured conscience, as Poggio entirely fails to tell us, who burst free at last from the fear of the fire, as he says, to express his real hopes and loyalties.

Poggio tells us Jerome argued for the idea of tolerance—diversity of belief "not in order to harm the faith, but in order to find out the truth." Did he express this notion, perhaps to defend Wycliffe? The notion itself is far more radical than what the anonymous clerk records Jerome answering Gerson: "that he spoke as a philosopher and teacher of philosophy," or than his analogous defense at Vienna in 1410, that he spoke only "scholastically." The implied idea of the two truths (of faith and of reason) carries with it less support for tolerance than does Poggio's idea of diversity helping truth. Jerome, in his proclamations on the church doors of Constance, believed that he could openly present his own and Hus's opinions to the Council and prove that they were not heretical. He expected disputation to end in unanimity. What he found instead, he regarded as the blind persecution of enemies—enemies to himself, to the Bohemians, and to God.

Even in Poggio's account, Jerome prays that he "might be given such thoughts and such powers of speech as would conduce to his welfare and the safety of his soul." In the anonymous account, more anguished in spirit, Jerome prays that he may not imperil his soul. In Poggio he declared himself ready to suffer burning

> . . . with a strong and constant spirit, to yield to his enemies and to the witnesses who had lied shamelessly, who, however, would have to render an account of the things they had said when they came before God and would not be able to deceive him.

In the anonymous account the threat to his tormentors is more desperate, the issue is justice in a broader sense:

> . . . for an occasion would come after this life when they would see him again, and they would find him, the very same man, standing before them and calling them all to judgment. What would they think of then to say to God and to himself if they had acted unjustly towards him?

Logically, though not historically, Jerome could be depicted as Poggio depicted him, not as a man entangled in national fights or a religious soul anxious concerning his salvation, not as a man of fiery temper and an anguished conscience, but as a calm and fearless philosopher who faces death for justice's sake—a Mutius Scaevola, a Cato, a Socrates. The actual Jerome is replaced by an ideal of calm and constancy.

The discrepancy between Poggio's account of Jerome's last hours and that of Theodore of Vrie only confirms this interpretation of Poggio's letter. Theodore and other accounts tell us that there was widespread feeling against Jerome; whatever the learned might think, the crowd was hostile. The reference to the crown of thorns, the pointed choice of hymns and the persistence in singing, the lack of any sign of penitence confirm the assurance of Jerome: "Verus Christianus sum." After he recited the *credo* in Latin he turned to the spectators and confirmed in German that what he had just said was what he believed.[46] Richental, too, reports the efforts of Jerome thus to state his faith in a way that would reach the crowd. He did not die singing, according to Richental, but suffered a long drawn-out torture in the fire and died screaming horribly. Mladoňovic, or his eyewitness source, tells us that Jerome's body showed blisters the size of eggs during his prolonged agony.

By Poggio's account, Jerome asks for the fire to be lit before his very eyes, an episode which seems to crown Poggio's heroic image of the man. If we consider Jerome's repeated admissions, according to the anonymous record, of his fearing the fire, this episode—if we may believe it—takes on a different, but no less heroic, meaning. Poggio omits the cap painted with devils, nor does he dwell on prayers and hymns which might affect the simpler spectators. Poggio's Jerome, almost silent, contemplates his own courage; the Jerome of other, more ingenuous, observers, constantly, pointedly, and loudly reasserts his faith. Though a speaker to the last, Jerome seeks to remind us, and did remind his sympathisers, of the Passion. Only to and through Poggio could his death call up the memory of the tranquil Socrates, the imperturbable Cato.

CONCLUDING COMMENTS

Poggio was concerned with Jerome's eloquence. This eloquence posed a problem, to which the humanist saw two solutions. He did not definitely decide to choose one or the other. The first, and less acceptable, solution was expressed in the thought, "Yet I fear that he was given all these gifts by nature for his own destruction." This idea underlies the limitations put on Jerome by the remark, "whether he acted as he did for treason or from stubbornness, the death of the man you might have described from a text in philosophy." Here Poggio assumes that eloquence and even philosophy may be morally neutral, tools for good or for evil, but not a way to become good.

The more acceptable solution for the humanist, though never formulated so directly, is the one which dominates the letter and explains much of its character. Eloquence, specifically classical eloquence, produces virtue. This virtue is in Jerome. Jerome, like the heroes of classical philosophy, dies for justice. The Council was misguided in condemning him. The virtue which Poggio attributes to Jerome, the view he takes of Jerome, deviates from historical reality. It serves, on the other hand, not only to justify classical learning by showing what Jerome, a learned man, should have been like; it also serves to show an alternative to the kind of thinking and the kind of virtue actually present in the historical moment of Jerome's death. Poggio transforms the events to create, beyond what happened, a more rational, less tragic, alternative. Politics does not appear, personal loyalty and the desire to survive play no part; true Christians can recognize each other in spite of diversities of doctrine and theory; the cause of reform, officially the purpose of both sides, can unite its adherents; in short, a fight seen by the participants as a struggle between God and Satan, a fight to eternal extinction, becomes theoretically negotiable from Poggio's point of view. The Northern accounts of the case were, I think, more direct as observation, and they ring historically truer than Poggio's, but they accept the assumptions of the trial as well as the facts: criticism of the Council's decision, support of a condemned heretic, is outright rebellion. Jerome, himself, like his opponents, seems to have believed that Satanic forces were arraigned against him, and that he and Hus alone stood for the one just cause, the cause of the Church. Poggio suggests that *eloquentia*—that is, the classical moral tradition—offers another standard of justice—constancy, honesty, observation of the rules of evidence—on which men might meet.

Aeneas Silvius Piccolomini, who labored as a diplomat, and later as Pope Pius II, to save the church by some kind of alliance between the papacy and the critical, self-willed princes, praised this letter of Poggio's. Though a little hard on clerical practises, it was, in his view, "elegant."[47] Bruni likewise called it elegant, and elegant, of course, is one of Poggio's terms for Jerome's admirable erudition, rhetoric, and style. This quality is far from being merely formal or decorative in the eyes of these humanists. To Theodore of Vrie it is a two-edged sword: "He revoked his heresy as elegantly as he had propounded it." To Poggio and to Piccolomini, however, it has the great attraction of a style that enables writers to resolve in their own minds, and among themselves, the deadlocked conflicts of their time.

Notes

1. Kronika velmi pěkná o Janovi Žižkovi . . . cited by Frederick G. Heymann, *John Žizka and the Hussite Revolution* (Princeton, 1955), pp. 3-4.

2. Sermons may be sampled in K. Höfler, *Geschichtschreiber der hussitischen Bewegung in Böhmen, Fontes Rerum Austriacarum,* Abt. 1, v. 2, 6, 7. Also in Václav Novotný, *Fontes Rerum Bohemicarum,* VIIII (Prague, 1932).

3. Ulrich Richental, *Chronicle,* tr. L. R. Loomis, in J. H. Mundy and K. M. Woody, *The Council of Constance* (New York, 1961), p. 135.

4. R. R. Betts, "Jerome of Prague," *University of Birmingham Historical Journal,* I (1947-48), 51-91.

5. Milada Nedvědová, *Hus a Jeronym v Kostnici* (Prague, 1953), p. 269.

6. Jean Boulier, *Jean Hus* (Paris, 1958), p. 68.

7. Poggii *Epistolae,* Tomaso de Tonellis ed. v. I (Florence, 1832), pp. 11-20. The letter was more freely translated and partially paraphrased by William Shepherd, in his *The Life of Poggio Bracciolini* (Liverpool, 1802), pp. 78-88. This translation was republished in J. Ross and M. M. McLaughlin, *The Portable Renaissance Reader* (New York, 1953), pp. 615-624.

8. Hermann Van der Hardt, *Corpus Actorum et Decretorum Magni Constantiensis Concilii* (Frankfurt and Leipzig, 1692-1700), IV, 755-791.

9. Peter of Mladoňovice is edited by Václav Novotný, *Fontes Rerum Bohemicarum,* VIII, 339-350. On his reliability, see Matthew Spinka, *John Hus and the Council of Constance* (New York, 1965) pp. 82 ff.

10. Hardt, II, 202.

11. R. R. Betts, *op. cit.,* 86, note 119; see below, p. 117.

12. A. Franzen and W. Müller, ed., *Das Konzil von Konstanz; Festschrift . . . Schaufele* (Basel and Vienna, 1964), p. 472.

13. Laurentii de Březová, *Historia Hussitica,* ed. Joseph Emler, *Fontes Rerum Rohemicarum,* v. (Prague, 1893).

14. J. H. Mundy, *op. cit.,* p. 201. Extract given here, 282-284.

15. As complete a biography of Jerome as the documents seem to permit is given by R. R. Betts, "Jerome of Prague," *op. cit.* In addition Jerome must be seen in his association with Hus and the Hussites. On Hus, and his character as a leader, see H. B. Workman and R. M. Pope, edd., *The Letters of John Hus* (London, 1904); likewise Matthew Spinka, ed., *Advocates of Reform* (Philadelphia, 1953). Jean Boulier, *Jean Hus, op. cit.,* narrates the biography. Spinka has provided two monographs on the teaching of Hus: *John Hus and the Czech Reform* (Chicago, 1941), and *John Hus's Concept of the Church* (Princeton, 1966). In *John Hus and the Council of Constance* (New York, 1965), Spinka makes a general assessment of Hus's position and gives a full translation of Mladoňovic's account of Huss' experience at Constance. Johann Loserth, *Hus und Wiclif* (Munich, 1925), is still helpful on the preaching and teaching of Hus. For a correction of Loserth on Hus's relation to Wycliffe, it is essential to see R. R. Betts, "English and Czech Influences on the

Hussite Movement," *Transactions of the Royal Historical Society,* XXXI, (1939). The theological issues are most fully discussed by Paul de Vooght, *L'Heresie de Jean Hus,* and *Hussiana,* both Louvain, 1960. He modifies certain of his ideas in "Jean Hus et ses juges," in *Das Konzil von Konstanz, Festschrift . . . Schaufele, op. cit.,* pp. 152-173.

16. R. R. Betts, "English and Czech Influences . . ." *op. cit.,* 82.

17. R. R. Betts, "Jerome of Prague," *op. cit.,* 58. The speech of Jerome, 59-60.

18. Ibid., 69.

19. Paul de Vooght, *L'Heresie . . . , op. cit.* 198-199.

20. R. R. Betts, "Jerome of Prague," *op. cit.,* 71.

21. *Ibid.,* 73, cf. Boulier, pp. 97 ff. Spinka, *John Hus and the Czech Reform, op. cit.,* 46.

22. R. R. Betts, "Jerome of Prague," *op. cit.,* 72.

23. *loc. cit.*

24. Mladoňovic, ed. Novotný, *op. cit.,* gives full text of notices which Peter of Mladoňovice himself posted for Jerome, he says.

25. Hardt, IV, 107. Betts notes the weak wording, "Jerome . . ." op. cit., 77.

26. Mladoňovic, ed. Novotný, *op. cit.,* 343, Cf. Betts, *loc. cit.,* 79.

27. Hardt, IV. 146 ff.

28. Hardt, IV, 217. He had given essentially the same defense of his teachings concerning universals in Vienna in 1410. Betts, "Jerome . . ." *op. cit.,* 66.

29. František Palacký, ed., *Documenta Mag. Joannis Hus Vitam . . . illustrantia* (Prague, 1869), doc. 89.

30. Hardt, IV, 497-600, gives abbreviated text of revocation.

31. Hardt, IV, 557 and 615. On the various commissions to deal with the Hussite problem, cf. K. Woody, "The Organization of the Council," in Mundy and Woody, *op. cit.,* 59-60.

32. Palacký, *op. cit.,* doc. 32.

33. Chiefly helpful on Poggio's life are Ernst Walser's *Poggius Florentinus Leben und Werke* (Leipzig, 1914), and Georg Voigt, *Wiederbelebung des Klassischen Altertums* (1893), I, 235-260 and II, 251-254. A recent view is Lauro Martines, *The Social World of the Florentine Humanists* (Princeton, 1963), p. 285 and *passim.*

34. Lorenzo Mehus, in the introduction to Leonardo Bruni Aretini *Epistolarum Libri VIII* (Florence, 1741), xlii, says that Bruni was in Constance from 31 December 1414 until 14 March 1415.

35. Voigt, *op. cit.,* II, 251.

36. Voigt, I, 235.

37. *Loc. cit.*

38. L. Bruni *Epistolarum libri VIII,* ep. IV. 9, v. I, 120.

39. Ernst Walser, op. cit., p. 69.

40. His attitude is most fully attested, perhaps, in his funeral oration for Leonardo Bruni (1444), which looks back over the many years of their literary friendship. Bruni, *Epistolarum Libri VIII,* I, CXV-CXXVI. On the moral purposes of humanism, see the diverse studies of Eugenio Garin.

41. Boethius, *Consolation of Philosophy* I.3 (Loeb edition, Cambridge [1918], 139-40).

42. Pauly-Wissowa, *Real-Encyclopädie,* 2 Reihe, v. I, 1274.

43. Paul Arendt, *Die Predigten des Konstanzer Konzils* (Freiburg, 1933), pp. 56-57.

44. Cf. R. R. Betts, *op. cit.,* 101 and Loserth, *op. cit.,* 189 ff. But Hus is most fully cleared by de Vooght, "Jean Hus et ses juges," *op. cit.* 160.

45. Richental, *op. cit.,* 144. Richental's spelling: Latzenborck. Another variant: Lucernbok.

46. Mladoňovic, *op. cit.,* 349. Laurentius of Březová, *op. cit.,* 343. Anon. *Vita Magistri Ieronimi,* ed. Novotný, *op. cit.,* 337, gives: "Lyben kyden, alzo geleb ych, unde nicht anders, alzo eczunt hob ich gesungen; sundir ich mus dorume sterben, daz ich nicht mit concilium volde seyen unde helden, daz Iohannes Hus wier helig unde rechtig verortelt, wem ich yn hob wol begent, daz her gut und worheftig prediger des ewangelium Christi ist gewest."

47. A. S. Piccolomini, *Historia Bohemorum,* ch. 36, quoted Hardt, III, 773. "Poggius Florentinus aetatis nostrae nobilis scriptor, de morte Hieronymi ad Nicolaum Nicoli concivem suum, elegantem scripsit epistolam, quamvis paululum sua consuetudine in mores cleri invectus videatur."

John W. Oppel (essay date winter 1977)

SOURCE: Oppel, John W. "Poggio, San Bernardino of Siena, and the Dialogue *On Avarice.*" *Renaissance Quarterly* 30, no. 4 (winter 1977): 564-87.

[*In the following essay, Oppel reads Poggio's dialogue* On Avarice *in the context of a power struggle within the Catholic church—which Poggio witnessed firsthand in his role as a papal secretary.*]

The early fifteenth century was the age of conciliarism, of a crisis in the church; it was a time of fragmentation. In such an age it may be difficult to tell the separate parties apart, to distinguish the defenders of the old order from its critics. Whatever the nature of the parties, each may claim to stand for its own particular version of reform. This paper deals with such a rivalry as it surfaces in **On Avarice,** one of the dialogues of a prominent curial humanist, Poggio Bracciolini (1380-1459). Though the point has never been noted, it will be seen that the essence of this work is to be found in the conflict between curial humanists or secretaries and mendicant friars, two groups whose fortunes had traditionally been closely identified with those of the papacy. **On Avarice,** I think, reveals a jockeying for position between these two traditional rivals in an age of reform, a competition in which neither group is content to be identified with the forces of tradition, the *status quo,* but in which each tries to recast its image as that of an agent of change.

I

Poggio Bracciolini was a Florentine humanist whose professional ties to the papal curia began in 1402 and were to continue over half a century.[1] Poggio, as a papal secretary, was identified with the more worldly side of the church, the institutional church whose structure had been so elaborated by the Avignon Popes but whose activities, after centuries of growth, came in for a new barrage of criticism in the conciliar epoch.[2] As a layman and, by reputation, something of a hedonist, Poggio seemed to certain contemporaries to typify the worst abuses of the 'worldly' church, a judgment which has been echoed by later critics as well.[3] Whatever the traditional rationale for the presence of educated laymen at the curia, the role of the humanist secretary, always something of an outsider, seemed more and more of an anomaly.

One of the salient features of the crisis of the medieval church in the early 1400's was the rise to new influence of classically educated laymen, the humanist secretaries. In the confusion and chaos of the Great Schism the popes of the Roman obedience had come more and more to depend on the support of secular states and their curia had come more and more to resemble the secular courts of Italy. A certain *rapprochement* had thus taken place between the traditionally secular culture of the communal chanceries and that of the papal curia. A symptom of this change was the rise, within the papal administration, of humanist secretaries, laymen whose very presence was something of a novelty (the office of papal secretary had been created in the 1300's by the Avignon Popes) and whose steadily growing influence on the highest levels of the church seemed to many critics one of the principal signs of its decay. Poggio himself was one of these parvenus, having made

his fortune at the curia in 1402-03. A more egregious example, however, was offered by one of the main speakers in **On Avarice,** Antonio Loschi, who, after a long and very secular career in the chancery of the Milanese Visconti, shook off the dust of the world to become a kind of elder statesman among the papal secretaries. Loschi's tainted background and his unabashedly secular way of life seem to have made him a center of controversy and, even, scandal. By the decade of the 1420's, when the church's 'decline' seemed to have been halted and when the momentum now lay with the forces seeking its 'reform' (forces of which the conciliar movement was just one manifestation), the position of the humanist secretaries shifted more and more to the defensive. The need to justify what seemed to many a kind of usurpation, the power and prestige of the humanist secretaries, is the essential background for an understanding of **On Avarice.**[4]

Ever since the thirteenth century, no group was more inclined to criticism of the this-worldly or organizational side of the church than the Franciscans. Indeed, a major source of difficulties for Poggio in his dual role as a Florentine citizen and a servant of the papal curia was the activities of the mendicant orders or preaching friars. In particular, Poggio's difficulties concerned the order of the *Osservanti,* or Observants, Franciscans who preached a (moderately) strict observance of the original rule of Saint Francis and who were sharply critical of the more orthodox branch of Franciscan monasticism, the Conventuals, though without lapsing into either the heresy or the social radicalism of the earlier 'Spirituals.'[5]

Poggio's sharpest clash with the Observants occurred in 1429, when he was accused by Florentine critics of personally interfering to prevent the building, by the Observants, of a new monastery near his home in Terranuova.[6] Poggio replied to these accusations that, as a papal secretary, he had been personally involved in the drafting of a new rule for the Observants, one of whose chief features was the provision that no new monasteries should be built. As such, he could not be expected to ignore an infraction of this rule, particularly in his own backyard.[7]

Poggio's position on this question seems to have been justified. He *was* a servant of the papacy, and there were too many monasteries in Tuscany.[8] However, the impression Poggio gives in this letter, that he is a man on the defensive, falsely accused by his enemies, is misleading; Poggio, throughout his life, was an enemy of the Observants, and of the mendicants in general. In this same letter, moreover, Poggio characterizes the preaching of San Bernardino of Siena, the most famous of the mendicants, in terms which will be pertinent to our understanding of **On Avarice**:

> Brother Bernardino, a learned and prudent man, brings
> to his sermons the greatest moderation, the greatest

diligence in speaking: the one thing for which he has been a little criticized he passed over with the greatest equanimity, and he is so adroit in a variety of circumstances that he has given rise to no error or commotion among the people.[9]

The same comment always seems to recur when Poggio deals with San Bernardino. In another letter to Niccoli, in which he discusses the genesis and purpose of *On Avarice,* Poggio makes the following, similar comment on San Bernardino and the mendicants in general: "On account of their ineptitudes it seemed fitting to add in what ways they go wrong, when they do not assail those vices which are most harmful to the multitude."[10] In particular, as we shall see from the opening passages of *On Avarice,* the vices which the mendicants fail to denounce are avarice and its counterpart, usury. This must be the 'one thing' Poggio has in mind here, in his letter on the construction of the Observantine monastery.

The fact that the composition of *On Avarice* is almost exactly contemporaneous with Poggio's involvement in this rather intense dispute with the mendicants has not attracted sufficient attention. We first hear, with assurance, about the completion of *On Avarice* in June of 1428. Poggio's letter to Niccoli criticizing the mendicants is from December of the following year, but his involvement with them clearly goes back a good deal earlier. Let us see what can be made of this coincidence.

San Bernardino of Siena (1380-1444) is a difficult figure to approach. A symbol of piety and activism, it is difficult to visualize him in the *Quattrocento,* an age supposedly lacking in both these qualities. To an austere rationalist, San Bernardino might appear a know-nothing and a rabble-rouser, but Iris Origo considers him a latter-day Saint Francis.[11] Eugenio Garin finds in him a combination of humane learning and practical piety characteristic of the Renaissance at its best.[12] The best account of San Bernardino's career, a collection of essays by Italian Catholic scholars, stresses his ability to combine a unique—almost a primitive—emotional vigor with practical concessions to the spirit of his times. In the case of San Bernardino's own preaching this fusion of apparently conflicting elements is expressed in his combination of an earthy, almost a vulgar style of delivery with a real sense of literary form, such as to make of him, in the words of one scholar, 'the perfect popular preacher.'[13] In the case of his movement, the Franciscan Observants, this fusion of contrasting values expressed itself in, on the one hand, a personal life-style that was austere and self-denying, and, on the other, the sponsorship of a building program, throughout Northern Italy, characterized by architectural elegance.[14] It is interesting that Poggio's clash with the Observants should have focused on just this point: the construction of one of their monasteries.

San Bernardino was a Franciscan, in an age when heretical Franciscans (*fraticelli*) had been burned by the Inquisition in Avignon, Florence, and elsewhere, but he was not a heretic. In fact, the keynote of his writings seems to be peaceful change, persuasion, love, humility. The theme which predominates in all of San Bernardino's life and work as a writer and popular preacher is that of a general pacification, an attack on discord in the name of the public good. San Bernardino, who had many ties to the humanists, was denoted by one of them, Maffeo Veggio, as a 'Christian Cicero.' In his life of Bernardino, Veggio points out the many ways in which he conforms to the classical ideal of the orator, both in his moving vehemence and in his conscious use of literary techniques.[15] Many of the humanists were influenced by San Bernardino, and much can be made of the parallels between these two groups, humanists and mendicant friars, both Christian orators, both committed to a vision of the reform of the church as proceeding through a grass-roots, moral revival.[16] For all of this, however, the similarity of his teaching to that of many so-called 'civic' humanists and the closeness of his personal ties to such figures as Leonardo Bruni and Guarino of Verona, San Bernardino's intimacy with the humanists should not be exaggerated. Beside the parallels must also be set the antagonisms, and one of these, in the economic sphere, is the subject of this study. The fundamental reason for hostility between San Bernardino and the humanists, where it existed, was not that he was a Franciscan, nor, surely, that he was a Christian reformer, but that he was a scholastic philosopher. All of the somewhat condescending praise by men of letters for San Bernardino's 'eloquence' cannot conceal the fact that he was a representative of a fundamentally separate intellectual tradition—that of speculative philosophy with its emphasis on truth as opposed to that of Ciceronian eloquence with its emphasis on persuasion. One wonders what San Bernardino would have made of the humanist descriptions of him as a 'Christian Cicero'—whether, in the final analysis, he would really have been flattered. One writer who was never close to San Bernardino personally at all or—even more emphatically—to the Observants as a group was Poggio. An analysis of his writings will enable us more clearly to bring out these differences.

San Bernardino is famous as a preacher, a statesman of the church, and a doer of miracles. It has recently been pointed out that he was remarkable in another way too, as an economic theorist.[17] This is an assertion which calls for more careful examination.

We have a good, easily accessible source for San Bernardino's economic views in a sermon which he delivered in September 1427, in Siena, on the subject of the ethics of trade and of the merchant.[18] This series of sermons delivered in the *campo* of Siena in 1427 was San Bernardino's most famous achievement as a preacher, and it might not be going too far to see in this sermon the immediate stimulus to Poggio's *On Avarice,* which dates from around this time.[19] The thrust of San Bernardino's sermon, as we might expect, is an attack on the malpractices and deceits practiced by merchants. Proceeding in scholastic fashion, Bernardino breaks these down into eighteen different categories, analyzing each separately, and maintaining the interest of his audience by the use of rather homely, but effective examples. The malpractices Bernardino criticizes are the expected ones: misrepresentation, monopolistic buying and selling, usury, the practice of trade by clerics, and other commonplaces of medieval sermon literature. It is noteworthy that the examples Bernardino chooses are small businessmen of rather low standing—butchers, wine sellers, and the like—rather than the Francesco Datinis or the Giovanni Bicci de' Medicis.

The interest of Bernardino's sermon, however, lies not in his criticisms of merchants, or their malpractice, but in his description of their positive role in society. Thus, after he has dealt with the eighteen varieties of malpractice, San Bernardino turns to what he considers the *legitimate* role of the merchant in society. This consists essentially of three activities, bringing goods from, or to, faraway places, storing and reselling these goods, and processing them, that is, turning them into new, finished products.[20] This procedure in itself is not original, though the emphasis on the positive role of the merchant is interesting, as is the emphasis placed by San Bernardino, throughout his sermon, on the contributions of the merchant to the public good,[21] an emphasis which will receive an echo in the 'defense' of avarice by Antonio Loschi in Poggio's dialogue.

This general bias in favor of the positive role of the merchant in society constitutes the real significance of San Bernardino's sermon. He sums it up in a single sentence:

> You have seen eighteen ways of sinning in the activities of the merchant, from which you may also be able to deduce the way to carry on these activities in the world *without* sin, in the manner prescribed by the sacred authorities.[22]

'Al modo che ci amaestrano e sacri dottori': the sacred authorities, scholastic and others, seem called upon here to give not so much a *critique* of the activities of the merchant as a justification for them.

This sermon is a good example of San Bernardino's popular preaching style in the 1420's—a style which some of the humanists applauded but which others, at the time, deplored. Particularly vocal in their disapproval of San Bernardino were the curial humanists, secretaries at the curia of Martin V—Poggio, Antonio Loschi, Bartolomeo da Montepulciano, and others—the speakers in the dialogue *On Avarice.* To see the reasons

for their disapproval it is necessary to go beyond the text of this single sermon—in itself rather innocuous—and to explore Bernardino's teaching more carefully.

A good starting point is offered by the authoritative source on which San Bernardino's Sienese sermon was based, the writings of the Franciscan thinker John Duns Scotus. Bernardino often refers to Scotus as an authority in economic matters, and this particular sermon is a commentary on his teaching. In particular, Bernardino cites Scotus for his principal thesis, the basis, really, for his apology for the merchant: 'El settimo ci agognamo, che è di Scoto, che per lo ben comune si dìe esercitare la mercantia.'[23] The activities of the merchant must be subordinated to the public good. This thesis is central to the discussion in *On Avarice,* and it is interesting to explore, though very briefly, Scotus' original ideas.

The Franciscan tradition is almost always—in nearly all historical writing—associated with the defense of poverty.[24] There are legitimate reasons for this, and yet it should be noted that one of the most positive portrayals of the activities of the merchant, his role in society, is offered by a Franciscan, Duns Scotus.[25] Scotus is, of course, a critic of usury and of malpractices in the medieval Christian tradition—he is a very practical thinker. He does not, however, condemn mercantile activity or commerce *per se.* On the contrary, he praises them for their positive contribution to what he calls the *servitium communitatis,* the common good. According to Scotus, the activities of the merchant may be censured insofar as they proceed from zeal for a private, personal end. Insofar as they contribute to the well being of all, however, he will gladly allow them. Indeed, he will go so far as to admonish the lawgiver, the head of the state, that if the invaluable contributions of the merchants to the community are lacking, he should see that they are provided for. Those who perform these necessary functions—bringing in goods from afar, providing for their storage, etc.—should receive their appropriate return.[26] The merchant should receive his just due from the commonwealth. This, as will be seen, is the heart of the discussion in *On Avarice.*

The Sienese sermon illustrates one side of San Bernardino, the popular preacher, a facet of his activities which the humanists were, as a rule, willing to praise and emulate. Another side, however, is offered by his Latin writings. In these, his more systematic treatises, San Bernardino often took a more permissive, less censorious view of social questions than he did in his more popular, moralistic sermons. This is a contradiction which has struck latter-day commentators and which may have appeared remarkable to contemporaries as well. Raymond De Roover, in his examination of San Bernardino's economic attitudes (and of those of his contemporary San Antonino, as well), has concluded that San Bernardino places the minimal ethical restraints on the merchant—that he not do business on Sunday, or in church, for example.[27] Bernardino develops in his Latin works something which sounds, to the modern economist, like a 'utility' theory of value;[28] in general he seems progressive enough to this modern business historian to merit the title of the greatest medieval economist.[29] John F. McGovern has culled the following, somewhat fatuous remark to show just how far San Bernardino could go in justifying the activities of the wealthy man in society:

> When God sees that a soul can be better saved through riches than through poverty, God bestows riches. . . . God calls each one of us to the state that befits him best. The rich are necessary to the State, and the poor to the rich.[30]

De Roover has remarked on the paradox of finding anticipations of modern economic theory in the writings of 'toothless, emaciated, and ascetic saints.'[31]

Paradoxical indeed; in fact, we might go so far as to call it, with the humanist, 'hypocritical,' or at least to see what the humanists might have meant in referring to the mendicants as 'hypocrites.'[32] The contradiction between the fiery preacher in the marketplace denouncing avarice and its ill effects and then, in the musty recesses of a scholastic treatise, justifying the activities of the merchant and praising his contribution to the common good was a sharp one. The public image of San Bernardino, as a stern critic of avarice, seems to contrast with the impression to be gained from reading his Latin works. This is a point which his curial critics, in **On Avarice,** will be careful to make.

Finally, it is necessary to look very briefly at one of Bernardino's Latin works, the sermon on merchants and their vices delivered in Siena in 1425. This work is the specific source for Poggio's **On Avarice.** In general, San Bernardino's Latin works were intended to provide the theoretical basis for his preaching as well as to offer a model for other speakers. Here, in the greater privacy of a Latin text, San Bernardino seems considerably less censorious, more the prototype of a modern 'scientific' economist and less of a moralist. The activities of the merchant, he writes, are not among those which can be classed as either good or bad in themselves but must be judged by a relative standard. Bernardino comments on the famous passage in Matthew: that Christ went into the Temple and threw out all the money lenders:

> And Jesus went into the temple of God, and cast out all them that sold and bought in the temple, and overthrew the tables of the money changers and the seats of them that sold doves. And said unto them, It is written, my house shall be called the house of prayer, but ye have made of it a den of thieves.

> (Matthew 21.12-13)

What is meant by this phrase in the Vulgate, to 'cast out,' *eicere*? Not, really, that merchants should be banned from the community altogether, but, rather, that they should be banished under certain conditions. When, in their hearts, they serve their own private good, the idol avarice, rather than the common welfare, then indeed—but only, according to San Bernardino, in this limited sense—should they be 'cast out.'[33] The way the merchant himself 'casts out' avarice, however, is by exercising his proper and legitimate functions, not by withdrawing from trade altogether.

Bernardino continues to assert that there is much in trade which contributes to the 'service and well being of the *res publica.*'[34] He says that he will prove this claim by what he calls the *via naturae,* natural reasoning. Commerce, then, is a natural activity.[35] This is a point which the last speaker in Poggio's dialogue, Andrea of Constantinople, will vehemently rebut. Bernardino goes on to describe in glowing terms the activity of the merchant, remarking that his social standing all too often does not measure up to his real contribution to the *res publica,* nor, indeed, to what it costs him in terms of anxiety and exertion.[36] Perhaps it should be noted that San Bernardino—Bernardo degli Albizzeschi—was the scion of a Sienese patrician family, whereas his antagonist, Poggio, was the offspring of a humble and unsuccessful farmer.

Bernardino continues here, but we need not follow him in detail.[37] Sacred scripture, he claims, in no place condemns mercantile practice.[38] Still, there are many dangers, and San Bernardino now, in the bulk of his presentation, proceeds to list these. He returns, at the end, to the basic question: Should the merchant, for all this, be 'cast out'? The authorities brought to bear here are weighty indeed. Not only a single passage in Matthew but an authoritative interpretation of that passage, embodied in canon law, in the decree *Eiciens Dominus.* In this text, attributed at that time to John Chrysostom, the activities of the merchant are condemned in no uncertain terms. San Bernardino does not, here, question the authenticity of this passage.[39] He interprets it, however, in a peculiar way. Not all merchants should be cast out, he observes, but only those who, guilty of malpractice, sin against the common good. The number of these, according to the saint, will not be very large—perhaps two or three—but their sinfulness is apparent and cannot be excused. It consists, at least in part, in giving the others a bad name.[40]

This passage gets to the heart of **On Avarice,** and the speaker chosen to refute San Bernardino, Andrea of Constantinople, will be an embodiment of Chrysostom himself. Poggio's dialogue is directed, however, not only against Bernardino the theologian but against the preacher as well. He mocks the one, the orator, and refutes the other, the philosopher. Let us now turn to the work itself.

II

It should be apparent, by now, why Poggio began his dialogue *On Avarice* with a condemnation of the methods of the mendicant preachers and with an explicit mention of San Bernardino (against the advice of his friend Niccoli). We are also in a good position to understand the force of the following passage, from the opening pages of the dialogue:

> Your friend Bernardino, Antonio, whom you praise so highly, has never covered this subject [avarice], though he may have touched on usurers, moving the people more to laugh at than to detest such a great crime. Avarice, however, which is the source of usury, he left intact.[41]

It is, perhaps, a detail worth mentioning that Antonio, who is here described as a 'friend' of Bernardino (*Bernardinus tuus, Antoni*), will later be the 'defender' of avarice in the dialogue.

The aggressive tone of the dialogue is apparent from the start. Poggio thus, in his preface (directed to Francesco Barbaro, the Venetian nobleman), states that he has abandoned here the studied classicism and elegance of his letters in order to achieve a wider audience and a more direct approach:

> So that, if my style appears here excessively plain or unadorned to anyone, or my level of argument on too low a plane, let him consider that I prefer that kind of eloquence in which the labor of understanding is no greater than that of reading.[42]

Thus, already, or so it would seem, the humanist is prepared to compete on the same grounds as the mendicants, and for the same wide audience. The curial party, here represented by the papal secretaries, is prepared to take the offensive.

The opening passages of the dialogue proper make clear that the target of the work is the mendicants and, in particular, San Bernardino. The talk of the town is a series of sermons given by San Bernardino in Rome, of which the papal secretaries engage in a discussion. In the course of the discussion, some *pro forma* praise is offered of Bernardino's piety and eloquence, but the general tone of the discussion is critical. Significantly, Antonio Loschi is twice singled out as the admirer and friend of San Bernardino, not, perhaps, without irony, but then the whole role of Antonio in this dialogue will be ironic, as we shall see.[43] The secretaries criticize Bernardino, as we have seen, for pandering to the frivolous tastes of his audience—for moving them to ridicule rather than to condemn vices—and, in particular, for his softness on the questions of usury and avarice and their counterpart, luxury. The stage is thus set for a discussion of these vices, one which, presumably, will serve as a contrast to the mendicants' treatment of the problem, and in which the papal secretaries may show their own social usefulness:

> They are not alone of value to the state who are placed over others, who tend the guilty, who treat of peace and war, but also those who imbue the soul with virtue, who, finding others in pursuit of luxury and wealth, admonish and restrain. Therefore let us try ourselves if we may not be good for something in this our discourse—if not to others, at least to ourselves.[44]

At this point, when the discussion is about to begin, a needed note of gravity is added by the entrance of a Greek theologian, Andrea of Constantinople. After the exchange of pleasantries, the discussion begins.[45]

The first speaker, Bartolomeo da Montepulciano, characterizes his own discussion of the problem as lightweight, designed only to stimulate the others.[46] This is a fair characterization: Bartolomeo's contribution is of the most shopworn, schematic variety, complete with an allegorical explanation of the meaning of Vergil. The only real interest of Bartolomeo's presentation lies in his explicit, moralistic condemnation of avarice, and in his bald statement that the avaricious should be driven from the state:

> For which reason I think him [the avaricious man] worthy of the common hatred of all mortals, as the public enemy of all, and fit to be removed from the company of men as the sower of evils. For in what way can he be loved who, that I may omit his other crimes, destroys these two—love and benevolence, the bonds of human society, without which no association, neither private nor public, can stand? What is this but to destroy utterly the human race? . . . He should be denied fire and water, useless to the city, harmful to the republic. That he lives in a city is an outrage: if all were to imitate him, we should have no cities.[47]

This vice is not to be moderated, but to be driven out; here, already, we are brought back to the passage in Matthew and to the decretal *Eiciens Dominus*. Perhaps Bartolomeo, we are led to reflect, has been too modest about his own contribution, which foreshadows, as will be seen, the main argument of the dialogue. Bartolomeo's modesty may, however, have a point. The main speaker, Andrea of Constantinople, has not been heard from, has yet to dominate the discussion, and the much longer presentation of Antonio Loschi will be a lively *jeu d'esprit,* to be disowned, ultimately, by the speaker himself.[48] Bartolomeo is hesitant but sincere. Perhaps he is so modest because he is the presence of a much more weighty authority, Andrea of Constantinople, a cleric and a theologian. It is the nervousness of the secretary that is indicated here, an upstart and a parvenu, a layman in a clerical milieu. Bartolomeo's audacity in speaking out on this question, however, will be rewarded, when his argument is 'confirmed' by the weightier authority of Andrea. This in itself is a central point of the dialogue.

The way is now open for Antonio Loschi's much more interesting presentation, a 'defense' of avarice. Antonio begins by pursuing an interesting sideline, a secondary theme whose presence in the dialogue has never been adequately explained. Which is the worse of the two vices, he asks, avarice or luxury? Luxury, he answers, differing with Bartolomeo and, thereby, immediately aligning himself with the mendicants who, it may be argued, treated the *symptoms* but not the roots of evil, by criticizing the elegance of dress and the flashiness of manners of the towns, but not the greed of the merchants on which they rested. Antonio proceeds to argue that by the sumptuary laws of the Italian towns luxury was banned but not avarice, hardly a very forceful moral position but one which reminds us of the scholastic approach to economic questions, which was, as John T. Noonan has remarked, intimately linked to that of the Roman lawyers.[49] It is apparent that Antonio's presentation is to be a kind of parody—or, rather, a mockery—of the preachings of the friars.[50]

In the course of this presentation, a number of sacred cows are satirized. Among them is the philosophical authority of Aristotle. Antonio cites Aristotle as an authority who, by precept and example, was in favor of avarice. It would be possible, here, to see a reference to the works of Poggio's humanist friend and colleague Leonardo Bruni, whose translations of the Greek philosopher into the language of Cicero were changing Aristotle's image from that of an abstract, speculative thinker into that of a practical moralist suffused with moral concern. The 'Aristotle' in question here is, however, much more probably, the 'barbarized' authority of the scholastics, not the reformed philosopher discovered by Bruni.[51]

Antonio's presentation, without much formal structure, gives a lively picture of avarice run rampant, of avarice as a universal malady of the day and, therefore, as somehow justified. All classes of people, we learn, are motivated by avarice: doctors, lawyers, and, by no means last or least, priests and monks.

> For not by these inert and semiawake creatures, who enjoy the greatest peace, but by our labors are cities to be constructed, by those whose skills are accommodated to the preservation of the human species, so that, if no one cared to earn more than his own living, we should all be returned to the fields.[52]

One theme which seems, though in a strange and ironic way, to echo San Bernardino is Antonio's emphasis on the social usefulness of the rich man, as expressed in his philanthropic giving:

> Avarice is not harmful in any way. Consider that the rich men often confer much ornament and splendor on their city. How many (if I may omit the ancient times) magnificent homes, splendid villas, temples, porticos,

and hospitals have been constructed in our age by the wealth of the avaricious, so that, if these were driven out, our cities would lack their most beautiful ornaments?[53]

Here we have a direct reflection, in the most telling way, of San Bernardino's emphasis on the public usefulness of the man of wealth.

But the most telling passage, and the one which strongly echoes San Bernardino and the mendicants, is Antonio's argument that avarice, far from destroying the other virtues, can easily coexist with them:

> You have ascribed many evils to the life of avarice. But the case of some of the avaricious is not necessarily that of all, as I have shown. You will find many among them beneficent, humble, benign, civil, upright, anything but obnoxious.[54]

Or again:

> There are, indeed, many whom I myself would spurn, not so much for their avarice as because they are hard, insensitive, ignorant, truculent, miserable and greedy, the basest and most vile kind of men who have derived their harsh and brutal habits not from avarice but from the malignity of nature. I have known many of the 'avaricious' who were generous, splendid, distinguished, humane, good-tempered, and whose homes were filled with guests and friends.[55]

This point, apparently the most plausible defense of avarice, is the one which the last speaker, Andrea of Constantinople, will particularly try to counteract, with the Pauline dictum that avarice is the root of all evils. What is it, after all, that Antonio is here expounding except the 'hypocrisy' of which Poggio had shown himself such a consistent critic? To what, after all, does the passionate eloquence of San Bernardino amount but a 'defense' of avarice, since he attacks the other vices but leaves this one, the source of them all, unscathed? The more measured, restrained eloquence of the curial humanist is, it will be shown, more nearly on target. Again, the humanists' point, in their criticism of the mendicants, is not that they fail to criticize the vices but that they criticize the wrong ones, leaving the way open for a covering over of the worst defects in a semblance of virtue.

The speech of Antonio Loschi is, therefore, a spoof, directed at the 'hypocrisy' of the mendicants and based on the incongruity of the fact that one who is their avowed enemy could adopt so many of their arguments. It is, however, an artful piece, and it raises the level of discussion far higher than it was left by Bartolomeo da Montepulciano. The stage is now set for a resolution, which the dialogue finds in the discourse of Andrea of Constantinople, its principal speaker.

Andrea is clearly, and by his own frequent admission,[56] modeled on St. John Chrysostom. Chrysostom was a fourth-century Byzantine saint whose works Poggio had come to know during a sojourn in England in 1418-22. Chrysostom was, at the same time, a great orator, the citizen of a great *polis,* and a loyal adherent of the Roman Church, friendly but not submissive to the papacy.[57] Particularly important, of course, is Chrysostom's reputation as a violent enemy of avarice, both among clerics and among laymen. He seems to fit Poggio's purpose in **On Avarice** perfectly, and we can hardly doubt that he stands behind Andrea of Constantinople or that Andrea is meant to be the main speaker in the work.

Andrea's significance, however, goes beyond this. He is labeled, from the moment of his appearance, a *theologus.* Whereas Bartolomeo da Montepulciano, a Ciceronian, used the tools of the orator, eloquence and persuasion, to combat the sin of avarice, Andrea will add to these the 'wisdom' of the philosopher. Not just Andrea, however, but Poggio too, since in this work Andrea of Constantinople is his spokesman. In **On Avarice,** therefore, the humanist speaks as philosopher, and it is just this combination of wisdom and eloquence which distinguishes the presentation of the last from that of the first speaker and which is the ideal aspired to at this time not just by Poggio but by many other humanists as well.[58]

Andrea's presentation deserves careful consideration. It is a humanist's response not just to San Bernardino—or not just to San Bernardino as a preacher—but to the whole scholastic tradition of economic thought, summed up in the work of one of its greatest masters. Poggio will not here make much of an original contribution to economics. He will, however, show himself an effective—if destructive—critic of the scholastics on their own ground. This is, of course, a primary importance of humanism, as destructive criticism.

Andrea's argument closely parallels San Bernardino's in the treatise referred to above. Antonio Loschi, with evident flippancy and nonchalance, had argued that avarice, far from being, as so commonly supposed, an evil, is both natural and useful. He ends his presentation with precisely these assertions.[59] These claims seem to be the logical outcome of all that has gone before—or, more accurately, Antonio's perverse extolling of what seem so many variations of antisocial behavior follows, really, from his adherence to these principles. Andrea does not take Antonio seriously, and he will not take up his humorous defense of greedy priests, greedy citizens, and the like. He does, however, go straight to the matter of principle. San Bernardino had not defended avarice, but he did claim that the activity of its practitioners, merchants, was 'useful' and that commerce was a natural activity. This is the first point of his sermon, and Andrea denies it. There is nothing 'natural' about avarice. On the contrary, nature abhors it. What is 'natural' is not avarice but its opposite, liberality, of which Anto-

nio Loschi, known for his generosity, is himself a pertinent example. 'To call this "natural," if you will excuse me, is the act of one who takes little account of nature and its wonders.'[60] Andrea is not addressing Antonio here, known for his generosity, but Bernardino, who begins with the statement, noted above, that trade is natural.[61] In fact, he follows very closely Bernardino's—not Antonio's—presentation, and he refutes it point by point.

Avarice is not natural. On the contrary, nature is everywhere the opposite of avarice. She is generous, she is open, she is free. Everything else is natural, especially liberality, but not avarice. Those who believe that men are, by nature, avaricious, or that there is some form of greed inherent in human nature commit a serious error, nor can their opinions be supported by philosophical authority. There are those who cite the authority of philosophers in praise of avarice, but they cite them wrongly, out of context. A case in point is Aristotle, who never praised avarice but always—in his writings at least, if not in his life—condemned it.[62] Philosophy, rightly defined, is free of vice, and if all too many of its practitioners are moved by desire for gain that does not change the nature of the thing itself. 'I will boldly assert that no philosopher was ever greedy—no philosopher, that is, who was worthy of the name.'[63] Humanists were fond of claiming that the enthusiasts of other disciplines than their own *studia humanitatis* were moved by ulterior, inferior motives. This passage is a reflection of that position.

Andrea now continues: Antonio has cited many examples of avarice in practice. He has cited the avarice of kings. The humanists, dependent on secular patronage, could hardly allow this, and Andrea rebuts him accordingly. He has cited the avarice of priests and, in the course of his speech, he has given a vivid picture of the corruption of the church. Andrea himself will not refute this—it would not be fitting to his status, as a cleric, to do so. He yields the floor to one of the secretaries, Cincio de' Rustici, who begins a vehement attack. We shall return to this issue in a moment, but let us consider first the remainder of Andrea's points.

Antonio has claimed that avarice is natural, and he has been refuted—not on the basis of false or perverted, but of true, philosophy. He has also claimed that avarice is useful, and it is to this point that Andrea now turns. 'You claimed, which seemed to me, at the time, most ridiculous, that the avaricious were useful to the state because many are enriched by their wealth and because they are a public benefit.'[64] Here was a basic staple of Bernardino's preaching and of that of the Franciscans in general, beginning with Scotus—that avarice was justified, in some sense, by its utility. Antonio reflects and perverts it in his speech. Andrea finds the claim ridiculous. To be sure, it is an ill wind which has no good effects, but if 'avarice' is a blessing can't you say the same for any other evil? If the activities of the avaricious have beneficent side effects they are entirely unintended and, thus, to be discounted. The evil effects of avarice far outweigh the good. Andrea now presents his own sermon, showing the hardness of heart, the rascality, of the man of wealth. He is the last to whom we should turn, whom we may expect to succor our cities in time of need. Avarice is the very antithesis of a public spirit. Antonio claims that the avaricious are universally liked, that they are surrounded by friends. Liberality, however, is the source of friendship, and the avaricious man, however frequently he may be solicited, is always alone. The traits of the avaricious man are the very reverse of those of the good citizen. Antonio has insisted so on this point—the utility of the avaricious—that Andrea feels he must refute him point for point: 'Let us examine a little this utility of the avaricious.'[65] All virtue proceeds from a love of the common good, but the avaricious man perceives only his own good, not that of others. 'It follows, therefore, that he will hate the common good and do harm to all.'[66] To justify avarice in terms of its utility is the equivalent, in moral philosophy, of squaring the circle.

Andrea now draws toward a conclusion. The avaricious man, far from being a common benefactor, will be a kind of moral outcast. Far from seeking his service, the proper role of the legislator, at least according to Andrea, should be to drive him out. Just as Plato was selective concerning his *res publica,* let us follow his example:

> So that I, if these others will agree, declare that by my decree all the avaricious are to be cast out of the state, by whom—not by words but by deeds, not by teaching but by example—the spirit of the citizens is corrupted.[67]

The language here is worthy of note: 'avaros omnes decreto meo eiiciendos.' Here is Chrysostom, here is his decree, and here is a humanist citing against a future saint the authority of canon law.

III

It is difficult to know how Poggio's *On Avarice* should be taken. For some time, by many critics, Poggio has been identified with the views of Antonio Loschi, the 'defender' of avarice in the dialogue. This view is superficial and cannot be maintained.[68] Quite to the contrary, Poggio's work is a conscious attack on a long scholastic tradition which, starting from the Christian church's original prohibition of 'usury,' had so defined it, analyzed it, and striven to reconcile it with the demands of reason as to amount almost to an *apologia.* From this point of view, Poggio's stance seems very conservative indeed.

It would be a mistake to go to the other extreme, however. It is difficult to believe that Poggio, a layman and a Florentine citizen, really took a dimmer view of commercial activity than San Bernardino, a Christian preacher. Similarly, it is very questionable whether Poggio's position in *On Avarice* can be fully identified with that of his principal spokesman, Andrea of Constantinople. The line drawn in this dialogue between the humanist secretaries and Andrea, a foreigner, is very sharp, and this is entirely appropriate. He is from another world and, even more to the point, of another era. As 'Chrysostom' he embodies a remote but still a very powerful reform tradition, one with which the secretaries wish to be identified but which they see, nevertheless, at some remove.

Finally, it is important to note that Poggio was by no means a thoroughgoing and stringent critic of avarice, a despiser of this-worldly values. On the contrary, he was identified with the school of 'civic' humanism embodied by Leonardo Bruni. At just this time, in the 1420's, Bruni was translating classical works on the subject of household management or economics. Similarly, in 1427, Xenophon's treatise, the *Oeconomicus,* was published for the first time. Certain passages in this work celebrate good management and wealth in much the same way as San Bernardino did in his treatises or as Antonio Loschi in *On Avarice.* Consider, for example, the following interchange:

> 'do you really want to be rich and to have much, along with much trouble to take care of it?'
>
> 'The answer to your questions,' said he 'is, Yes, I do indeed. For I would fain honor the gods without counting the cost, Socrates, help friends in need, and look to it that the city lacks no adornment that my means can supply.'[69]

Of course, neither Bruni nor Xenophon—nor, for that matter, anyone else—praises avarice *per se* or, even, the pursuit of wealth in anything but carefully qualified terms.[70] In fact, Bruni's praise of wealth and that of San Bernardino closely parallel each other in the Florentine, civic sphere, and it would be difficult on this point to draw a sharp line between humanist and Franciscan teachings.[71] It seems, then, quite inconsistent that Poggio, who is identified with a rather lenient, permissive attitude toward the pursuit of wealth—or, indeed, toward this-worldly values in general—should, on this occasion, be their violent critic. It seems a complete reversal.

The contradiction, however, is only apparent. In fact, there is no contradiction but, rather, a consistency. It is consistent that Poggio, a layman and a citizen, should apologize for and even endorse this-worldly values in the civic sphere and condemn them in the church. *On Avarice* is set in the Roman curia, not in Florence. Its subject, really, is the church's penetration by worldly values, even in the person of its most zealous reformers. Most important for an understanding of this work is the special position of the humanist secretaries. Many of them, such as Antonio Loschi, came to the curia after long experience in Italy's lay chanceries. They could hardly shed their this-worldly identities—nor, indeed, did they show much inclination to do so. **On Avarice** dramatizes the situation of laymen in a clerical milieu at the height of a reform era. The laymen here, however, humanist secretaries, become spokesmen for reform by identifying themselves not with the ecclesiastical milieu of their day but with an earlier, revered tradition—that of the Greek fathers.

Notes

1. See Ernst Walser, *Poggius Florentinus, Leben and Werke* (Leipzig and Berlin, 1913), the best biography.

2. For the revolutionary character of this criticism, the way in which structures whose elaboration had, for so long, been uncritically accepted came, suddenly, to seem unnatural and undesirable, see the classic discussion of J. Haller, *Papstum und Kirchenreform* (Berlin, 1903).

3. For evidence of Poggio's vulnerability to contemporary criticisms on account of his uninhibited way of life, see his *Epistolario*, ed. Tomasso di Tonelli, I (Florence, 1832), 107, where an English emissary characterizes the secretary as a 'vile, ribald ass.' For a modern Catholic historian whose sternness in these matters surpasses even that of the fifteenth century, see L. Von Pastor, *The History of the Popes, from the End of the Middle Ages,* I (London, 1923). Pastor considers Poggio 'as a man, one of the most repulsive figures of the period' (p. 29).

4. On the humanist secretaries and their functions in the late medieval church see W. Hoffman, *Forschungen zur Geschichte der kurialen Behörden* (Rome, 1914). Poggio's short, angry *Invectiva in delatores,* written in 1426, shows the tensions to which, increasingly, the humanist secretary was subjected in a reforming age (Poggio Bracciolini, *Opera Omnia,* ed. R. Fubini, 4 vols. [Turin, 1964-69], II, 709-717). For the career and writings of Antonio Loschi, who deserves more careful study, see Giovanni da Schio, *Sulla vita e sugli scritti di Antonio Loschi vicentino* (Padua, 1858). On Loschi's role in the curia see G. Voigt, *Il risorgimento dell'antichità classica,* 2 vols. (Florence, 1890), II, 19-22.

5. There is no good study of the *Osservanti.* See Iris Origo, *The World of San Bernardino* (London, 1963), pp. 205-228.

6. See *Epistolario,* I, 296. Also, Origo, *World of San Bernardino,* p. 220.

7. 'Haec igitur cum ita decreta essent, mihique nota, qui illa edideram, essem autem in patria, audiremque silvas cedi, locum designari, aedificia tolli; dixi statim id fieri non posse propter novas leges.' *Epistolario,* I, 299.

8. See Gene Brucker, *Renaissance Florence* (New York, 1969), pp. 190-194.

9. 'Frater Bernardinus homo doctus, et prudens affert ad suos sermones summam moderationem, summamque in dicendo diligentiam: unum, quod videbatur in eo paulo reprehendendum, magna cum aequitate animi omisit, atque ita versutus est plurimis in locis, ut nullius erroris, aut commotionis in populo causam praebuerit.' *Epistolario,* I, 297.

10. 'Nam quod mentio fratris Bernardini displicit, eaque in Dialogum introductio; id ego non feci ad eum laudandum, sed ad exagitandum paulisper hos molestos latratores, ac rabulas francos. Simul per eorum ineptias visum est apte subjici posse quibus in rebus delinquant, cum non reprehendant ea vitia, quae magis vulgo nocent.' *Ibid.,* p. 279. A critical text of this letter has been published by Helene Harth in her article 'Niccolò Niccoli als Literarischer Zensor: Untersuchungen zur Textgeschichte von Poggio's *De Avaritia,*' *Rinascimento,* 2nd ser., 7 (1967), 35.

11. See Origo, *World of San Bernardino,* p. 228: 'It was Saint Francis' own spirit that he renewed.'

12. See E. Garin, *L'umanesimo italiano,* 2nd ed. (Bari, 1965), pp. 47-48, on the relationship between Bruni and the mendicants.

13. Gustavo Canfini, 'San Bernardino da Siena, perfetto predicatore popolare,' in *San Bernardino da Siena: saggi e ricerche pubblicati nel quinto centenario della morte* (Milan: Università Cattolica del S. Cuore, 1945), pp. 203-245.

14. Ilarino da Milano, 'San Bernardino da Siena e l'Osservanza Minoritica,' *ibid.,* p. 387: 'Il balzo dalle *humiles aediculae* della prima età agli *elegantia coenobia,* dai tuguri e dalle cappelle all'arte sobria e decorosa delle chiese stilizzate ed ornate come templi e dei conventi spaziati e luminosi, segna esteriormente l'ingresso dell'Osservanza nel mondo della Rinascita.'

15. See Veggio's life of Bernardino in Luke Wadding, *Annales Minorum,* 25 vols. (Rome, 1731-1886), X, 8: 'tantum apud animas hominum valet ut nihil plus eo valere maximi oratores attestantur.'

16. See Joseph Bernard, 'San Bernardino of Siena: His Relation to the Humanist World of the Early Italian Renaissance' (Ph.D. diss., Yale University, 1972).

17. By Raymond De Roover, in his *San Bernardino of Siena and Sant' Antonino of Florence: The Two Great Economic Thinkers of the Middle Ages* (Cambridge, Mass., 1967).

18. Published in San Bernardino da Siena, *La fonte della vita,* ed. G. V. Sabatelli (Florence, 1964).

19. It is first mentioned in November 1428 in a letter to Francesco Barbaro: 'Ego enim nonnihil tibi excudi, sed edere non audeo propter tempora: est enim contra avaritiam.' *Epistolario,* I, 260. Helene Harth has traced the inspiration of Poggio's *On Avarice* to a series of Roman sermons of 1429 in her 'Niccolò Niccoli,' p. 260. Whether the content of the Roman sermons differed significantly from that of the Sienese one is another, open question, but it seems unlikely.

20. San Bernardino da Siena, *La fonte della vita,* pp. 412ff.

21. This was to be San Bernardino's last major point, as he outlined the contents of his sermon: 'El settimo ci agognamo, che è di Scoto, che per lo ben comune si dìe esercitare la mercantia.' *Ibid.,* p. 371.

22. 'Tu hai veduto diciotto modi di peccato sopra de le mercantie, dove puoi avere compresi i modi di poterli esercitare senza peccato al mondo e al modo che ci amaestrano e sacri dottori.' *Ibid.,* p. 406.

23. *Ibid.,* p. 371.

24. See the article by Hans Baron, 'Franciscan Poverty and Civic Wealth as Factors in the Rise of Humanistic Thought,' *Speculum,* 13 (1938), 1-37.

25. See Edmund Schreiber, *Die Volkswirtschaftlichen Anschauungen der Scholastik seit Thomas von Aquin* (Jena, 1913), p. 154: 'Fast mit einer gewissen Wärme wird die industria, diligentia und sollicitudo des Kaufmanns hervorgehoben. . . . So bezeichnet Duns Scotus den Handel als ein ehrenhaftes und nützbringendes "servitium communitatis".'

26. 'legislator autem justus deberet conducere operas transferentium res, quibus indiget Respublica, ergo et ipsi possunt suos labores, industriam, pericula, et reliqua pretio aestimabilia vendere.' *Quaestiones in Quartum Librum Sententiarum,* dist. 15, question 2, in Joannes Duns Scotus, *Opera Omnia,* XII (Paris, 1904), 318.

27. Raymond De Roover, *San Bernardino of Siena and Sant' Antonino of Florence,* pp. 9-16.

28. *Ibid.,* pp. 16-23.

29. *Ibid.,* p. 7.

30. John F. McGovern, 'The Rise of New Economic Attitudes—Economic Humanism, Economic Nationalism—during the Later Middle Ages and the Renaissance, A.D. 1200-1500,' *Traditio,* 26 (1970),

232. McGovern, in his useful survey, argues that humanist attitudes parallel those of the mendicants on economic questions. I am going to argue the reverse: that humanists began to write on economic matters in reaction against this sort of preaching. My argument, however, only applies to a particular work, *On Avarice,* in a particular setting, that of curial humanism.

31. *San Bernardino and Sant' Antonino,* p. 41.

32. See Poggio's dialogue *Contra hypocritas,* in his *Opera Omnia,* II, 45-80. Leonardo Bruni composed another attack on the mendicants, with the same title.

33. 'Eice ergo tu, mercator et artifex, hanc ancillam et filium eius [i.e., avarice and her 'son,' usury] de corde tuo. Quos tunc illos vere eicies, cum secundum rectitudinem et iustitiam illa perficies. . . .' San Bernardino da Siena, 'De mercationibus et artificibus,' *Quadragesimale de Evangelio Aeterno,* Sermon 33 (San Bernardino of Siena, *Opera Omnia,* IV [Florence, 1956], 141).

34. 'in mercatione concurrunt multa pro reipublicae servitio et utilitate.' *Ibid.,* p. 142.

35. 'Primo quidem probatur via *naturae* licitam esse mercationem.' *Ibid.,* p. 142.

36. 'insuper addi potest quod cum antedictis industriis, sollicitudinibus, laboribus et periculis non semper lucrosis haec exercent; et quia ex his omnibus reipublicae sunt utiles et opportuni . . . inde possunt et debent rationaliter reportare.' *Ibid.,* p. 143.

37. See De Roover's more extended discussion in his *San Bernardino and Sant' Antonino.*

38. 'De mercationibus et artificibus,' p. 143.

39. Though, according to Raymond De Roover, he did elsewhere. See *San Bernardino and Sant' Antonino,* p. 10.

40. 'contra tales loquitur Chrysostomus, 88 dist., in can. *Eiciens.* . . . Tales quidem, secundum Chrysostomum et Scotum, de patria deberent esterminari atque expelli et in exilium dari, quia duo vel tres in una civitate magna corrumpant totam multitudinem mercatorum.' 'De mercationibus et artificibus,' p. 150.

41. 'Hanc Bernardinus tuus, Antoni, quem adeo laudas, nunquam tetigit, semel dixit in usurarios, magis movens populum ad risum, quam ad horrorem tanti criminis. Avaritiam vero quae foenus persuadet, intactam reliquit.' *Opera Omnia,* I, 4.

42. 'Quod si cui forte aut planum nimis atque humile videbitur dicendi genus, aut non satis explicata ra-

tio muneris suscepti, is intelligat primum me delectari ea eloquentia, in quo non maior existat intelligendi, quam legendi labor.' *Ibid.,* p. 1.

43. Once on page 2: Bernardinus was in Rome: 'Quem cum Antonius, qui eum frequens audierat, maiorum in modum commendaret,' etc. Again, on page 3 (see above, n. 41).

44. 'Non solum eos prodesse reipublicae qui assunt aliis, qui tuentur reos, qui de pace belloque censent, sed illos quoque qui virtute instituunt animum, qui in luxuriam pecuniamque currentes prestant ac retrahunt. Quare tentemus et ipsi, si quid possumus prodesse hoc sermone nostro, et si non caeteris, at saltem nobis.' *Ibid.,* p. 5.

45. Of the speakers in *On Avarice* only Poggio himself has been the subject of a full-scale, modern study, by Ernst Walser. He came to the curia in 1402, became a secretary in 1413, under John XXIII, and only definitively broke with the clerical milieu in 1453, though retaining until his death in 1459 the title and privileges of a *secretarius.* On Antonio Loschi, see above, n. 4. He came to the curia in 1406, at the age of about thirty-eight, and died in 1441 after some thirty-five years of service. Voigt credits him with attempting, like Salutati in Florence, a reform of the curial style of letter writing (*Il risorgimento,* II, 21). Bartolomeo da Montepulciano seems to have been associated with the very vice of avarice which we find him criticizing in Poggio's dialogue. A close associate of Poggio, Bartolomeo was the epitome of a professional curialist, coming from a family of papal functionaries. His death in 1429 was itself an occasion for controversy and criticism directed at his supposedly ill-gotten wealth and the ostentatious tomb constructed in his honor—a symbol of the pride of a papal secretary. (See Leonardo Bruni, *Epistolarum Libri VIII,* ed. L. Mehus, 2 vols. [Florence, 1741], II, 45-48). Cincio de' Rustici, a pupil of Francesco da Fiano, was a classical scholar, an occasional anti-cleric, and a Roman patriot, all roles which he seems to embody in Poggio's dialogue. For all these personalities and for the little that can be known about Andrea of Constantinople as well see the notes to Phyllis Goodhart Gordan's *Two Renaissance Book Hunters: The Letters of Poggius Bracciolini to Nicolaus de Niccolis* (New York and London, 1974).

46. 'Faciam quod iubes ille inquit, non tam disserendi causa, quam aut te, aut hunc provocandi . . . dummodo ego te audiam.' *Ibid.,* p. 6.

47. 'Quam ob rem est hic dignus communi odio mortalium, veluti publicus omnium hostis, amovendusque ab hominum consortio tanquam seminarium malorum. Nam quomodo amari eum

decet, qui ut caetera omittam, haec duo, scilicet amorem et benivolentiam, humanae societatis vincula, sine quibus nulla, neque privata, neque publica res consistit, aufert a nobis? Quod quid est aliud quam delere funditus humanum genus? At ipse potius delendus esset. Ipse aqua et igni interdicendus, inutilis civitati, reipublicae pernitiosus. Iniquum est enim ei locum esse in civitate, quem si omnes imitaremur, nullas omnino civitates haberemus.' *Ibid.,* p. 8.

48. Andrea himself accuses Antonio of levity: 'non ex animi sententia, sed gratia aliorum reor Antonium disseruisse' (*ibid.,* p. 17). His position, not Antonio's, will be supported by all the other secretaries (*ibid.,* p. 27), and in the closing passages of the dialogue Antonio as much as admits to Andrea his intention to provoke: 'Laetor inquit Antonius me pro avaris sensisse, quo ista a te audiremus' (*ibid.,* p. 31).

49. 'Ego sane multos audivi, neque contemnendos homines, qui nulla ratione unquam cum Bartolomaeo sentirent, qui et rem mea sententia gravissimam reddidit leviusculam verbis suis: et item rem non admodum magni ponderis, nimium depressit mole sermonis, ut si iretur in suffragium populi, non dubitarem quin ferme omnes aliter ac nos essent iudicaturi, cum in luxuriam multa sint illius arbitrio, ac legibus constituta iudicia, in avaritiam nulla.' *Ibid.,* p. 10. See John T. Noonan, Jr., *The Scholastic Analysis of Usury* (Cambridge, Mass., 1957), p. 2: 'The scholastics are disciples of Roman law, and from the earliest revival of medieval culture canon law and moral theology are impregnated with the concepts of Roman jurisprudence.'

50. For a different opinion, which sees in Antonio's presentation the true message of the dialogue, see E. Garin, *L'umanesimo italiano,* pp. 54-55. Garin has been followed by many others.

51. 'Est enim peroportuna ad usum communem, et civilem vitam pecunia, quam necessario Aristoteles inventam tradit ad commercia hominum, resque mutuo contrahendas.' *Opera Omnia,* I, 12. Poggio, in fact, sent Bruni a copy of his dialogue, but he was a little nervous about his reaction: 'Quamquam vereor, ne se offensum putet hoc sermone propter avaritiae suspicionem.' *Epistolario,* I, 274.

52. 'Non enim ex istis inertibus et larvatis hominibus, qui summa cum quiete feruntur, nostris laboribus sunt nobis civitates constituendae, sed ex his qui sint accommodati ad conservationem generis humani, quorum si untisquisque neglexerit operari quicquid excedat usum suum, necesse erit ut omittam reliqua, nos omnes agrum colere.' *Ibid.,* p. 13.

53. 'Nulla in re nocuit avaritia. Adde quod afferunt persaepe magnum ornamentum et decorem suis civitatibus. Quot enim (ut vetera omittam) nostris diebus fuerunt magnificae domus, egregiae villae, templa, porticus, hospitalia avarorum pecuniis constructa, ut nisi hi fuissent carerent omnino urbes maximis ac pulcherrimis ornamentis.' *Ibid.,* p. 15.

54. 'Multa insuper vitia in avari vitam contulisti. Non eadem est ut dixi causa avarorum omnium sicuti caeterorum. Reperies ex eis multos beneficos, humiles, mansuetos, benignos, probos, minime molestos.' *Ibid.,* p. 16.

55. 'Sunt quidem quamplures, quos ego etiam reprehendo, non avari illi quidem, sed stipites, stupidi, plumbei, miseri, truculenti, tenaces, ex infima hominum sorde ac fece, qui mores duros atque asperos sortiuntur, non ab avaritia, sed ex naturae malignitate. Avaros vero cognovi multos lautos, splendidos, ornatos, sumptuosos, humanos, perfacetos, quorum domus plena esset hospitibus et amicis.' *Ibid.*

56. *Ibid.,* p. 28, where Andrea admits his debt to Chrysostom and regrets that the available translations of his works should be so poor.

57. See the article on Chrysostom by P. W. Harkins in the *New Catholic Encyclopedia* (Washington, D.C., 1967), VII, 1041-44.

58. See J. E. Seigel, *Rhetoric and Philosophy in Renaissance Humanism* (Princeton, 1968).

59. 'Quo sit ut non tantum naturalem, sed utilem et necessariam rem quandam constet esse in homine avaritiam.' *Opera Omnia,* I, 17.

60. 'Hanc secundum naturam dicere hominis est (pace tua dixerim) parum naturae munera atque opera inspicientis.' *Ibid.,* p. 18.

61. See above, n. 35.

62. In fact, none of the ancient philosophers had much to say about economics or considered it worthy of note. The scholastics—perhaps because of their link to the law—were more tolerant. See the article by T. F. Divine on 'Usury' in the *New Catholic Encyclopedia* (Washington, D.C., 1967), XIV, 498-500 at 499.

63. 'aperte affirmaverim, neminem philosophum fuisse unquam avarum, qui quidem esset dignus philosophi nomine.' *Opera Omnia,* I, 20.

64. 'Dixisti, quod mihi quidem inter loquendum ridiculum visum est, avaros prodesse civitatibus, quod et multis opitulentur suis pecuniis, et reipublicae sint adiumento.' *Ibid.,* p. 22.

65. 'Verum excutiamus paulum hanc avarorum utilitatem.' *Ibid.,* p. 25.

66. 'avari est et nocere omnibus, et communem utilitatem odisse.' *Ibid.*

67. 'Ita ego si tamen hi mecum sentiunt, avaros omnes decreto meo eiiciendos sentio e civitatibus, quorum non verbis, sed factis, non doctrina, sed exemplo civium animi corrumpuntur.' *Ibid.,* p. 27.

68. For another critic, in addition to Garin, who takes this position, see George Holmes, *The Florentine Enlightenment, 1400-50* (London, 1969), pp. 147-148. Holmes does not think that any of the speakers, however, can really be taken seriously. For a more extreme position, see G. Saitta, *Il pensiero italiano nell'umanesimo e nel Rinascimento,* I (Bologna, 1949), 317: 'Poggio per bocca di Lusco accarezza con visibile compiacenza . . . il principale motore delle operazioni umane . . . ; l'utilitarismo inglese dell'epoca moderna è tutto preannunciato.'

69. Xenophon, *Memorabilia et Oeconomicus,* tr. E. C. Marchant (London and Cambridge, Mass., 1938), p. 455 (*Oeconomicus,* XI, ix).

70. Thus, even for Bruni, riches are not good in themselves: 'Sunt enim utiles divitiae, cum et ornamenta sint possidentibus et ad virtutem exercendam suppeditent facultatem.' *Epistolarum Leonardi Aretini Libri Octo* (Basel, 1535), p. 209.

71. This, however, is what Hans Baron tries to do in the article cited above on 'Franciscan Poverty.' He argues that humanism emerges, in the *Trecento,* in an atmosphere dominated by Franciscan social ideals, notably the exaltation of poverty, but that, in the course of time, it outgrows these, to take a new and 'more mature' attitude toward thisworldly goods. Whereas Baron considers the humanist tradition to be dynamic and changing, his view of that of the Franciscans seems to be that it is fixed and static. His view thus takes little account of such a figure as San Bernardino or of the general complexity of the Franciscan tradition. In fact, the parallelism for which Baron argues in the *Trecento*—when both humanists and mendicants idealized poverty—can be extended into the following century when both groups praised wealth, though with careful qualifications. There is, I think, a more general issue involved here: that of humanism and its environment. The humanist movement grew up in the same environment as that of many other traditions: Franciscanism, Roman law, scholasticism. On many points—simply because it is a product of the same milieu—it parallels these traditions. On the other hand, it never merges with any of them—that is, it never loses its own identity. Scholarship is, it seems to me, often confused on this point.

David Marsh (essay date 1980)

SOURCE: Marsh, David. "Poggio Bracciolini and the Moral Debate." In *The Quattrocento Dialogue: Classical Tradition and Humanist Innovation*, pp. 38-54. Cambridge, Mass.: Harvard University Press, 1980.

[*In the following essay, Marsh examines Poggio's use of the dialogue form, exploring the possible influence of Augustine, Cicero, and Poggio's contemporary Leonardo Bruni.*]

> I know you are afraid that someone whom you correctly judge may think himself offended, but all are allowed to speak the truth.

The dialogues of Poggio Bracciolini (1380-1459) constitute the first modern example of the form used generically in an extended literary program.[1] Whereas humanist epistolary collections are common after the example of Petrarch, Poggio is the first to base his literary reputation on a series of dialogues rather than on his collected letters. To be sure, Poggio had already begun to collect his own letters when he wrote his first dialogue, *De avaritia,* in 1428, and the moralistic criticism of his dialogues merely elaborates the lively reportage of his epistles. Yet Poggio reserved the honor of first publication to his dialogue *De avaritia,* which he intended for a wider readership than his more outspoken epistles, and the work proved an immediate literary success.[2] Poggio's *De avaritia* provides a significant link between Bruni's *Dialogi ad Petrum Histrum* and Valla's *De vero falsoque bono,* and it also serves as a useful introduction to the themes and methods developed in Poggio's later dialogues.

The dialogue portrays the conversation of a gathering of secretaries from the Roman Curia, who have dined at the house of Bartolomeo da Montepulciano near St. John Lateran in Rome. The principal interlocutors are Bartolomeo, Antonio Loschi, Cincio Romano, and the theologian Andreas of Constantinople. The conversation begins after dinner with a discussion of the recent sermons of Fra Bernardino in Rome. Antonio praises the friar's eloquence and his power to move the people, but Cincio objects that, like other preachers of the day, Bernardino fails to cure the spiritual ills of his hearers. Bartolomeo concurs, noting that the greatest of these ills are lust and avarice, of which the latter is more pernicious and more widespread, being rarely condemned by the clergy. Antonio asks Bartolomeo to discourse on this important topic, and Bartolomeo accepts, on condition that Antonio shall succeed him in speaking (I, 2-5).

At this point, Andreas of Constantinople arrives and inquires about the nature of the discussion. The group is at first reduced to silence by his dignity and authority, but he begs that the discussion continue. In a three-part speech Bartolomeo undertakes the condemnation of avarice that he promised, first defining avarice, then demonstrating its destructive effects on human society, and finally denouncing its prevalence among old men. Antonio replies to Bartolomeo's discourse by returning to his initial comparison of lust and avarice, which extenuates the effects of avarice by contrast with those of lust, and then answers the several arguments of Bartolomeo's speech in order. He is succeeded by Andreas, who excuses Antonio's speech in defense of avarice as insincere and then responds to his arguments in order, occasionally interrupted by the polemical asides of Cincio. Andreas concludes with a lengthy peroration condemning avarice on the basis of scriptural and patristic texts, and all, including Antonio, welcome his beneficial homily. Night having fallen, the group breaks up (I, 6-31).

This simple, three-part debate on the moral topic of avarice follows in part the model of Ciceronian discussions *in utramque partem,* while the final role of Andreas reflects the influence of Augustine's Cassiciacum dialogues. As a neo-Ciceronian dialogue, *De avaritia* resembles Bruni's *Dialogi ad Petrum Histrum.* In both works an initial discussion concerning the benefits of discourse—Salutati's praise of disputation and the praise of Bernardino's sermons—leads to a denunciation of contemporary standards of eloquence: Bruni's Niccoli laments the decline of classical wisdom in Scholastic quibbles, and Poggio's interlocutors question the moral efficacy of the preachers of the day. These initial exchanges introduce the central debate in both works, involving opposing discourses based on the rhetorical antithesis of praise and blame.

In Bruni's *Dialogi,* the Niccoli of Book I attacks the reputation of Dante, Petrarch, and Boccaccio, while his recantation in Book II provides a defense and laudation of them. This antithesis is clearly formulated by Poggio when he summarizes the *Dialogi* in his funeral oration of 1444 for Bruni: "He published a very eloquent dialogue, in the first book of which he attacked the excellent and learned men Dante, Petrarch, and Boccaccio and their learning, eloquence and works; in the second book, their virtue is praised in defense of the first" (II, 668-669).

The same antithesis of attack and defense found in Bruni's *Dialogi* appears in the first two lengthy discourses on avarice in Poggio's dialogue. Discussing a first draft of the work in a letter of June 10, 1429, to Niccoli, Poggio describes his original choice of interlocutors: "I had assigned the first role of attacking avarice to Cincio, who is considered greedy, and the role of defending it to Antonio, who is rather prodigal. I had done that intentionally, so that a greedy man would attack avarice and a spendthrift defend it" (Ton., I, 278).[3] On Antonio Loschi's advice, Poggio had later substituted Bartolomeo for Cincio (Ton., I, 273), but he had clearly planned the antithetical debate as an argument between unlikely proponents and opponents of avarice. In part, this ethical irony was necessary to protect the integrity of the speaker defending avarice: thus Antonio, "who is something of a spendthrift, defends avarice, for the vice is more safely defended by someone far removed from it" (Ton., I, 273). But Poggio's use of this ethical irony also serves to reinforce the "rhetorical" aspect of the debate, for even in his revised version Poggio's first two interlocutors begin their discourses by admitting that they speak primarily to promote the discussion. Introducing his attack on avarice in words more suited to Cincio, Bartolomeo says that he will address the group not so much to speak his mind as to provoke Antonio or Andreas (I, 6). Similarly, Antonio prefaces his defense of avarice by invoking the Academic custom, condemned a thousand years before by Augustine, of arguing on both sides of a question, *in utramque partem*: "Following the custom of the Academics, who used to debate against what others said, I shall relate a view different from Bartolomeo's; you shall judge whether it is acceptable" (I, 6).

The conclusion of *De avaritia,* where Andreas denounces the vice, arrives at a general agreement such as that reached by Niccoli's recantation in Bruni's *Dialogus II.* In the latter work, Bruni himself imposes the sentence on Niccoli "to defend the same men whom he had attacked the previous day," to which Niccoli agrees, prefacing his defense of the Florentine poets with a personal excuse: "Above all be assured that I attacked them yesterday only to arouse Coluccio to praise them. But it proved difficult to make this most prudent of men think I had spoken sincerely and had not invented my view" (p. 82). In Poggio's *De avaritia,* Andreas likewise begins his attack on avarice by excusing the insincerity of Antonio's defense of the vice:

> Besides, I think Antonio spoke not sincerely, but for some other reason . . . As we hear of someone who praised the immoral tyrant Dionysius of Sicily and blamed the pious Plato in order to exercise his eloquence, so I perceive that you, a very liberal man, undertook the defense of this vice which you knew should be condemned before all others. I'm sure that you have spoken not to excuse the vice, but to attack it, so that from your arguments I might have greater ability to refute what can be said in its favor and to expose the ugliness and baseness of this great evil. We know that you, Antonio, as a liberal man are far from any taint of avarice and even from any suspicion of it.
>
> (I, 17-18)[4]

Although this passage recalls Poggio's fear of slandering his contemporaries (Ton., I, 274), it also suggests the influence of Bruni's *Dialogi.* After Niccoli's condemnation of the *iniquitas temporum* in *Dialogus I,* Salutati responds that Niccoli has in fact confuted his own arguments: "I think that his elaborate speech served not so much to excuse him as to condemn him, for what he argued with words his speech disproved in fact and in truth" (p. 64).

More significant, however, is the affinity of this passage with Niccoli's recantation in *Dialogus II,* where Niccoli himself indicates the discrepancy between the insincerity of his attack upon the Florentine poets and the reality of his devotion to them. By absolving Antonio from possible charges of avarice, Andreas prepares the way for the unanimity expressed at the conclusion of *De avaritia* where, as in Bruni, the formerly dissident speaker is restored to the consensus of the group, which may then adjourn without fear of public reproach:

ANT.:

> I am glad that I argued in favor of the greedy, so that we could hear your remarks.

AND.:

> I only hope they were worthy of your hearing. And if you approve them, I have no reason to fear the judgment of others. But since we have conversed enough and night has fallen, I think we should go.
>
> (I, 31)

The design of Poggio's *De avaritia* nevertheless cannot be said to be directly modeled on the structure of Bruni's *Dialogi,* which had been written some twenty years earlier. Yet it is probable that Poggio was familiar with Bruni's work and found in it confirmation of his own concept of the dialogue according to the notion of arguing *in utramque partem* for the sake of discussion rather than from personal conviction. As a close friend of Niccoli, Poggio would have sensed the irony of Bruni's *Dialogi,* in which the true-to-life portrayal of Niccoli in Book I as a "sharp man quick in provoking," is discredited by the recantation of Book II.[5] The Niccoli of Poggio's later dialogues never changes his true-to-life position. Thus in *De avaritia* the initial debate between Bartolomeo, originally Cincio, and Antonio serves as a rhetorical exposition of the problems that are to be resolved by the third speaker, Andreas. Just as Niccoli's recantation leads from the debate of *Dialogus I* to the acceptable laudation of *Dialogus II,* so Andreas' exoneration of Antonio turns the dispute concerning avarice, which was originally to be argued by the unlikely opponents Cincio *contra* and Antonio *pro,* into an elevated homily denouncing avarice and praising virtue.

From the beginning Poggio had reserved to Andreas the task of condemning avarice definitively. Writing to Niccoli about his first draft of *De avaritia,* Poggio calls the work "a dialogue against the avaricious," and he discusses in the same letter the suitability of Andreas as an exponent of the Christian condemnation of avarice:

"In the second place, avarice is attacked by Andreas of Constantinople, who as a religious man seemed a suitable person to answer Antonio and to use the authority of Holy Scripture in censuring the vice of avarice" (Ton., I, 272-273). The authority of Andreas is emphasized by his late entrance, when his friends allude, with a suggestion of antiecclesiastical irony, to his dignity as censor and theologian.[6] His discourse, which is as long as the whole debate between Bartolomeo and Antonio, supplies the verisimilitude missing in the preceding arguments by rejecting them as insincere (*non ex animi sententia*) and by responding with a Christian discourse appropriate to his character and office. Andreas' condemnation of avarice as the root of all evils constitutes the central moral lesson of the dialogue as Poggio describes it in the preface to his **Contra Hypocritas** of 1447 (II, 45); and the ample citations from St. John Chrysostom reflect Poggio's enthusiasm for patristic homilies, dating from his years in England (cf. Ton., I, 30-31). Having responded to the arguments of Bartolomeo and Antonio, Andreas delivers an exhortation against avarice not found in the sermons of contemporary preachers, thereby both resolving the debate and providing the moral benefits that were the purpose of the discussion.

This "Christian" resolution of the dialogue, in which a pious and authoritative figure dismisses the previous debate between two disputants of a classicizing bent, recalls the Cassiciacum dialogues of Augustine in general and the first book of his dialogue *Contra Academicos* in particular. In the latter work, which marks the end of the classical dialogue in antiquity, the youthful Licentius and Trygetius argue whether philosophers may ultimately know the truth. Their debate is interrupted by their teacher Augustine, who praises their skill in discussion but insists that he now act as arbiter between them (*PL*, 32, 918).[7] Christian authority thus pronounces sentence on a two-part classical debate. Augustine likewise intervenes in Books II and III to resolve the discussion for the moral and spiritual betterment of all (929, 941). Poggio's **De avaritia** follows this Augustinian pattern while asserting Ciceronian freedom in debate, but Poggio's use of Augustine in structure and theme constitutes a singularly unAugustinian argument.

The three-part debate of the **De avaritia** examines various arguments concerning avarice in the speeches of Bartolomeo, Antonio, and Andreas. Bartolomeo and Antonio begin by comparing avarice and lust. Bartolomeo compares the moral effects of avarice and lust, applying the social standard that characterizes his discourse, and extenuates the effects of lust as being limited to the individual, while condemning avarice as injurious to all mankind (I, 4). Responding to Bartolomeo, Antonio reverses the criterion from social to individual—a reversal fundamental to his defense of

avarice—and after adducing the deleterious effects of lust, he expounds the compatibility of avarice with qualities of excellence (I, 10-11).

Upon the arrival of Andreas, Bartolomeo begins his discussion in the traditional manner by defining the term *avaritia* according to the classical etymology *avidus aeris* ("greedy for bronze") found in Gellius and Isidorus (I, 6).[8] Antonio immediately takes exception to this archaic derivation, noting that "contemporaries are moved by a desire for gold and silver, not bronze" (I, 6: *Auri enim argentique nostri homines cupiditate ducuntur, non aeris*), and this insistence on contemporary realities sets the tone for his subsequent discourse (I, 14). Despite the humor of his objection, Antonio later takes full advantage of this neutral definition. Stripping the concept of avarice of all but an economic sense, he rapidly identifies avarice with the universal human motivations of gain and self-preservation:

> In the first place you said that the avaricious are so called because they are too desirous of bronze, gold, and silver, but if all those desirous of money are called avaricious, nearly everyone will be thought guilty in these terms. For we all undertake all our actions for the sake of money; we are all moved by a desire for profit—and great profit at that—and if you remove this desire, all business and work will cease entirely. Who would do anything with no hope for his own benefit? The larger the profit, the more readily we undertake an affair; all pursue and desire this profit.
>
> (I, 11)[9]

Having exploited this economic sense of avarice in order to prove its universality, Antonio boldly seizes on a definition given by none other than Augustine and argues that avarice is the basis of altruism:

> In his book *On Free Will,* the most learned of the Latin fathers, St. Augustine, wrote that avarice is wanting more than what is enough, a definition less weighty than yours. If he is right, we must admit that we are all avaricious by nature, for that which everyone desires must be regarded as derived from nature and arising by her influence. Indeed, you will find no one who does not desire more than what is enough, no one who does not want a large surplus for himself . . . One sows only to provide enough both for himself and for his family. Think what general confusion would result if we only wanted what was enough for ourselves. The practice of the most welcome public virtues, mercy and charity, would be eliminated, and no one could be either beneficent or generous. For who will give to another if he has no surplus to give?
>
> (I, 12-13)[10]

Responding to Antonio, Andreas corrects both his definition of avarice and his conclusion that avarice is a natural impulse. First, Andreas distinguishes between desire (*cupiditas*) and avarice (*avaritia*), which is merely a special type of desire. Since the desire to accumulate wealth is necessary to the preservation of life and to the performance of generous actions, it may be considered natural, provided it is only a moderate desire. Avarice, on the contrary, is immoderate. It also replaces man's natural independence—a notion derived from Cicero's *De officiis*, I, 4, 13—with an unnatural slavery to gain. Andreas restores to the discussion the moral implications of the notion of avarice, which had been eliminated by Antonio's economic use of Augustine's simple definition of avarice as wanting more than enough. Conceding the natural existence of moderate desire, Andreas observes that an excessive desire of gain conflicts with another natural impulse in man, his desire to remain free and even to dominate and excel others. But whoever is possessed by overwhelming greed subjects his will to the slavery of desire. Andreas thus accepts part of Antonio's argument—the existence of natural impulses in man—but indicates the ethical ideal of moderation as reconciling man's diverse natural impulses. As proof of the servitude of the greedy to their passion, Andreas cites a passage from Chrysostom, whom he subsequently quotes repeatedly, not for his theological position but for his persuasive formulations of the psychology of the avaricious. According to Chrysostom, the desire for money is more savage than a tyrant and subjects its victim to a slavery of the passions more bitter than servitude to a human master (I, 19).

Bartolomeo had proceeded from his definition to a twofold condemnation of avarice from a social perspective (I, 7-8): the greedy are both harmful to the general welfare (*communis utilitas*) and lacking in the virtues essential to social bonds (*amicitia et benivolentia*). Antonio at first responds to this general charge by identifying avarice with the simple accumulation of wealth. He says that money is necessary for the common needs of civil life and that Aristotle in his *Politics* regards money as a means of doing business and drawing up contracts. Thus, if one condemns this appetite, one must condemn the other appetites that nature has given mankind. By nature, Antonio continues, all people seek to preserve themselves, and money is the means of doing so (I, 12).[11]

Antonio identifies the avaricious with the rich and, with the contemporary evidence characteristic of Poggio's writings, praises the civic magnificence that rich men contribute to modern civilization. Money is necessary as a sort of lifeblood of the commonwealth; and since the avaricious abound in money, they must be deemed the basis and foundation of society: "For if the commonwealth should need help, would we turn to the poor merchants and those who profess to despise wealth, or to the rich, that is, to the avaricious (for without avarice money is seldom amassed)? Is it better for the city to be full of wealthy citizens, who can protect themselves and others with their wealth, or of the needy, who can

aid neither themselves nor others?" Many who are considered avaricious nonetheless aid the commonwealth and exercise great civic authority, avarice being no hindrance to participation in public affairs: "In fact, the avaricious often contribute great ornaments and beauty to their cities. To omit ancient examples, how many magnificent houses, outstanding villas, churches, colonnades, and hospitals have been built in our day by the money of the avaricious: if it had not been for them, our cities would entirely lack their greatest and most beautiful ornaments!" (I, 15).[12]

Responding to Bartolomeo's charge that the avaricious are incapable of friendship and generosity, Antonio reverses his position: denying the importance of money in benevolence, he separates the notion of wealth from the alleged virtues of the avaricious. The central duty of friendship is concerned not with money but with obligations and benevolence, which Antonio thinks the greedy may practice since wealth plays only a small role in maintaining friendships (I, 16). Antonio continues this reversal when he returns to the problem of the general welfare; reversing the ideal standard of the common good (*communis utilitas*) to the practical reality of general usage (*communis usus*), Antonio states the economic principle that one man's profit is another man's loss. As for Bartolomeo's objection that the greedy forget the general good in an eagerness for their own, Antonio maintains that such is the custom of almost everyone, not just the greedy. Who really seeks the public good without regard to private gain? Speaking from experience, Antonio says that he has to the present day never known anyone who could safely neglect his own interest:

> The philosophers say a good deal about placing the common good (*communis utilitas*) first, assertions more specious than true. But we must not regulate our lives by the standards of philosophy. It is usual and accepted by general usage (*communis usus*), and indeed has been the practice since the world began, that our own affairs affect us more than public affairs. We must admit this fact unless we prefer to speak in lofty phrases rather than according to usage. Yet if you think avarice harmful because making money entails many people's losses, you must also detest commerce and any other activity which seeks to make a profit. For no profit can be made without someone's loss, since whatever one person gains is taken from another.
>
> (I, 16-17)[13]

In his response to Antonio, Andreas shifts the discussion back to the moral level of Bartolomeo's discourse. He deals first with the problem of friendship, a classical concept which he identifies with Christian love. As in his proof that avarice is unnatural, he corroborates his opinion by citing Chrysostom's analysis of the psychology of the avaricious; the value of the citation, he adds, consists in an authority confirmed by reason itself (I,

24). Replying to Antonio's praise of the avaricious as contributors to the general welfare, Andreas denies *a priori* the compatibility of avarice with social virtues, again citing Chrysostom:

> Avarice is destructive of all good qualities: hear how it is described by Chrysostom, whose opinions I cull as from a fertile field. "Avarice," he says, "is a destructive thing which deadens both sight and hearing, making men more savage than beasts. It permits no thought of friendship, of society, or even of the soul's salvation, but like a fierce tyrant makes slaves of its captives and, what is worse, forces them to love the author of their slavery, causing incurable sickness at heart. Avarice has declared a thousand wars, filling the streets with blood and the cities with mourning."
>
> (I, 26)[14]

Bartolomeo's discourse ended with a condemnation of avarice in old men, his interpretation of Virgil's description of the Harpies providing a lengthy peroration probably intended to compete with the allegorical preaching of St. Bernardine himself (I, 8).[15] At the end of Bartolomeo's discourse, Antonio asserts that the avarice of old men is a result of their experience, not a contradiction of it. Realizing the value of money in combatting life's hardships, avaricious old men provide for themselves and their families by acquiring and accumulating wealth. Again assuming a pragmatic and pessimistic stance, Antonio blames the realities of "nature" for the necessity of heaping up riches:

> If you think the greed of old men a base thing, the fault lies not in the prudence of a man who prepares himself against unexpected and unforeseen events, but in the frailty of nature, which subjects us to so many tests, abandons us in so many exigencies, and surrounds us with so many difficulties, against which we must seek the support of wealth, unless we wish to philosophize idly about words rather than about realities. Consequently, it is certain that greed is not only natural to man but useful and necessary, since it teaches him to provide himself with the securest means known of enduring the frailty of human nature and of avoiding misfortune.
>
> (I, 17)[16]

The topic of avarice in old men invites Andreas' apparent conclusion. With an allusion to Plato's *Republic,* Andreas expresses the opinion that the avaricious should be banished from the ideal state. Bartolomeo assents, and Cincio formulates a law which Cicero himself had surprisingly omitted from his ideal republic: "Let there be no greedy men in the cities; let any such be expelled by public decree" (I, 27). With this consent established, Andreas proceeds to his final point, which he makes succinctly by citing Cicero's remark that he cannot understand the point of old men's greed, since nothing could be less prudent than to seek more provisions when the journey remaining is shorter.[17] This Ciceronian dic-

tum merely restates the observation of Bartolomeo that old men have even less cause to be anxious about wealth since they have fewer years ahead (I, 8).

Andreas has now addressed the principal arguments of the discussion begun by Bartolomeo and Antonio. Yet instead of ending with the allusion to *De senectute,* Andreas pronounces moral judgment on avaricious old men. As a peroration, he delivers a Christian homily on avarice as the root of all evils, taking Paul as his text (I Tim. 6:10). Poggio later wrote to Niccoli that he was not entirely satisfied with the conclusion of his dialogue (Ton., I, 273); he may have been displeased by either the homiletic style or the mixture of classical and Christian elements. Yet Poggio drew upon an eminent humanist source for the peroration of Andreas, Petrarch's letter against the avarice of bishops (*Fam.,* VI, 1), which foreshadows Poggio's antiecclesiastical diatribe, interspersing classical maxims with Biblical citations.

The peroration of Andreas identifies the Pauline *cupiditas* of the Vulgate with the *avaritia* he denounces, in order to preserve his previous distinction between cupidity and avarice while citing the Latin Bible. Antonio's statement that avarice is necessary is obviously not true, Andreas argues, for avarice is in fact useless and destructive; nothing could be more destructive than the source of all ills. Paul attests that all ills arise from avarice: his golden saying is that the root of all ills is cupidity, by which he means that from which avarice proceeds. In his peroration, Andreas treats the topic of avarice for the first time from a Christian viewpoint. The classical notion of friendship (*amicitia*) here becomes Pauline love (*charitas*), and the vice of avarice is now identified with idolatry and heresy according to passages from Paul and Augustine. To be sure, even here the import of Andreas' citations from the Church Fathers is not theological, for he wishes to encourage the humanists to translate Chrysostom into eloquent Latin, and in the conclusion he quotes both Plautus and Horace (I, 27-30). But after his classical reply to Antonio, Andreas' hortatory invocations of sin and damnation, addressed not to the *tu* of Stoic diatribe but to the *vos* of Paul's Epistles and Christian sermons, marks a shift to the eternal verities of religion.

The shift is not absolute, for classical expressions and concepts pervade the lessons drawn, and Christ and salvation are not mentioned in Andreas' stoicizing final words: "When you depart this life, riches will desert you, and you will go forth naked, poor, and abandoned, descending to the underworld to plead your cause without an advocate before that terrible judge who cannot be corrupted by gold. You will have no help, no protector, no defense, but that provided by virtue and good deeds." This classicizing tendency is affirmed in Bartolomeo's approbation of Andreas' discourse, where

Lucian and Silius Italicus are cited to corroborate the classical notion of an underworld judgment in which worldly goods play no part. Andreas welcomes these citations, not as ancient authorities but as testimonies of the truth: "So they have written, and others have written much as well; yet these are not the voices of one man or another, but of nature and truth itself" (I, 30). Antonio adds his voice to the consensus of the group, who then adjourn.

The discussion thus arrives at a consensus confirmed by the opinions of great men who agree concerning the truth. In Poggio's dialogues, the truth emerges from rational examination of opinions and arguments, and transcends traditional values of authority and position. In *De avaritia,* for example, classical and Christian authorities are evaluated in the same manner. Antonio cites the testimony of Lucian that Aristotle and many other philosophers were avaricious; yet although their example would suffice to defend avarice by their authority alone, he proposes to set aside any question of authority and to examine the question rationally (I, 11). Andreas replies to the example of Aristotle's alleged avarice by discounting his possible moral failing and by insisting instead on his recognition of the truth: "nowhere in his works does he praise avarice, but places it rather among the vices, far removed from virtue; so that even if he were himself avaricious, he would still be compelled by the force of truth to declare avarice an evil" (I, 19).

The independence of truth from individual ethical limitations is reflected as well in Poggio's constitution of the initial debate *in utramque partem* between Bartolomeo (originally Cincio) and Antonio. While the defense of avarice requires an unlikely advocate in order to avoid recriminations, Poggio also chooses an unlikely interlocutor to denounce the vice, thereby implying that the validity of the arguments is independent of their exponents' characters. Similarly, the maxims (*sententiae*) of authorities both classical and ecclesiastical are cited for their suitability in the argument and for their consonance with reason; as Andreas says when the group reaches their rational agreement, "these are not the voices of one man or another, but of nature and of truth itself" (I, 30). Whereas Bruni's *Dialogi* created a sort of debate *in utramque partem* through the device of Niccoli's "recantation" and thereby removed the dialogue from the realm of historical fidelity, Poggio boldly announces his constitution of the dialogue as a revival of the Academic custom condemned by Augustine. In a novel and un-Ciceronian manner, he consciously exploits the discrepancy between speaker and viewpoint, both as a means of dealing with a controversial topic and as a mode of examining arguments without reference to the authority of individuals.

The revival of the Academic method of argument in *De avaritia,* which characterizes Poggio's later dialogues as well, clearly reflects the direct encounter between the humanist's ideal of discussion and the historical obstacle posed by Augustine. In striving to re-establish the Ciceronian model of structure and method for the dialogue, Poggio had to confront the Augustinian objections voiced in *Contra Academicos.* In so doing, Poggio has in part adopted the structure of *Contra Academicos,* in which an initial two-part debate is subsequently resolved by a religious figure with Christian authority. At the same time, Poggio has reduced the authority of Scripture to a secular level of judgment subject to rational examination, as one of the "voices of truth itself," and Augustine himself is cited by three of the interlocutors of *De avaritia* for various purposes. Antonio quotes Augustine's definition of avarice in order to defend the deadly sin which Augustine would have condemned (I, 12). Cincio cites Augustine's complaint against the avaricious clergy for his own polemical purposes (I, 22). Andreas quotes Augustine, who likens the avaricious to heretics (I, 29), but he characterizes this Augustinian comparison in classicizing terms, calling it a "divine saying issued from God's oracle" (*sententiam divinam tam ex oraculo Dei emissam*).

Like Petrarch before him, Poggio does not argue merely from authority and reason but appeals to experience as well, especially in Antonio's defense of avarice. This experience is not the personal experience of an individual, as in Petrarch, but the collective experience of contemporary practice. Poggio is the first to advance the criterion of usage later expounded by Valla and Pontano, for whom usage generally assumes a linguistic connotation. Valla and Pontano both assert that all philosophy must derive from correct linguistic usage, since language properly employed corresponds to the immediate reality of human experience. This linguistic approach to philosophy is already implicit in Poggio's *De avaritia.* In a significant passage, Antonio says that we must not regulate our lives by the standards of philosophy (I, 16: *vita mortalium non est exigenda nobis ad stateram philosophiae*). This assertion echoes Cicero's description of the orator's language in *De oratore* II, where Antonius observes that the orator deals with questions that are weighed "not in the goldsmith's balance, but in a sort of popular scale" (II, 38, 159: *non aurificis statera, sed populari quadam trutina*). Poggio thus anticipates the "rhetorical" philosophy of Valla, who quotes the Ciceronian passage in his *Dialecticae disputationes.*[18]

Following the methodological hints of Petrarch's *Secretum,* the prerequisite to the search for truth in Poggio's dialogues is the freedom, repeatedly asserted, of each person to form and maintain his own opinion. This freedom, which is essential to the spirit of dialogue, is a dominant theme in the dialogues of Cicero, and is revived by Petrarch in his *Secretum.*[19] In *De avaritia,* Antonio introduces the defense of avarice by professing to follow the custom of the ancient Academics, arguing the opposite position to that already heard and allowing the hearers to judge for themselves (I, 6). Introducing the discussion of fortune in his *De varietate fortunae,* Poggio says that he does not wish to oppose Aristotle and Aquinas; still, "since everyone is free to believe what he will," a discussion is possible (II, 529). At the conclusion of the dialogue *De nobilitate,* Niccoli leaves the final decision of the question of nobility to those with "a keener talent for debate; all are free to feel as they will" (I, 83). In his *Contra hypocritas* Poggio asserts the right of others to their own opinion before he expresses his own (II, 78); and in his *Historia convivialis* he begins the debate concerning medicine and law by expressing his own doubts on the subject, leaving the solution of the problem to his more perceptive companions (I, 37). Introducing the discussion in *De miseria humanae conditionis,* Cosimo de' Medici says that the validity of the arguments presented may be judged by those with greater learning; he himself will speak whatever comes to mind, while others may maintain their own opinions (I, 94).

The freedom of opinion established in the dialogues applies to Poggio's readers as well as to his interlocutors. Thus, in the preface to his *An seni sit uxor ducenda,* Poggio writes to Cosimo de' Medici that he is sending him the dialogue in order to elicit his opinion (II, 684). Similarly, in *De varietate fortunae,* Antonio Loschi exhorts anyone who is qualified for the task to narrate contemporary history, and he later asserts the right of readers to judge for themselves concerning historical writings (II, 537, 580)—such as, by implication, the dialogue itself.

The interaction of dialogue and reader is essential to Poggio's notion of progress in literary and philosophical endeavors. In the preface to *De avaritia* Poggio writes that he has published his dialogue as a small beginning from which others may produce a more perfect or elegant treatment of the subject: "It seemed to me enough to publish my little efforts (for what they are worth), from which those wishing to undertake the task of revision and fuller exposition might derive and perfect something more complete" (I,1).[20] His reasons for publishing *De nobilitate* are the same; and in his preface to that dialogue, Poggio expounds his conception of progress in philosophy, a notion derived from Cicero's *Brutus:*

> It seemed reasonable to me to publish a sort of beginning for the treatment of this topic, which more learned men, aroused by me, might afterwards render more polished and elegant with their wisdom. For in every endeavor, the first to write about a subject have generally been considered less brilliant and refined. Nothing has ever arisen at the outset both invented and established without later generations adding to it and improving it. Even in philosophy, the mother of wisdom, and in the liberal arts, we see that this has been the

case: since all of them arrived at the peak of perfection by degrees, it was enough for the originators to provide some incitements and give the spur, as it were, to others for seeking greater perfection. In the same way, I expect that this essay of mine will arouse someone with talent to apply himself to improving whatever he sees I have omitted or mistaken.

(I, 64)[21]

The related notion of challenge (*provocatio*), in the sense of both promoting debate within the dialogue and eliciting response from readers, is found in Poggio's preface to his *De infelicitate principum*: "When I found the time, I wrote down this discussion once held between learned men, so that whoever might wish to write more copiously on the subject may have greater ability as a result of my challenge" (I, 394).[22] In his preface to the second book of *De miseria humanae conditionis,* Poggio repeats the notion of progress in the arts and the hope that others may be aroused to improve upon his work:

> I ask my readers to consider this treatment written not as a display of my talent but as an exercise of my wits. I deemed it better to spend what little time might be free from my affairs in praiseworthy endeavors, rather than to waste it in lazy and sluggish idleness. Others perhaps will be aroused to treat this material more copiously and learnedly, thereby contributing much, in my opinion, to learned studies and to the sciences. For such great progress (*progressio*) would not have been made in philosophy or in any other excellent art if the earlier writers had not by their contributions offered matter for correction and profounder understanding.

(I, 112)

Contrasted to the freedom of opinion among the learned friends in Poggio's dialogues is an awareness of the need for restraint in alluding specifically to contemporaries. In publishing his *De avaritia,* Poggio was afraid of offending contemporaries, notably Bruni.[23] Within the dialogue itself Bartolomeo expresses a reluctance to use examples which might offend (I, 4: *Nolo exemplis uti, ne quem mea verba offendant*). In the third book of his *De varietate fortunae* Poggio fears to offend contemporaries if he narrates recent history, citing the Terentian dictum that the truth breeds enmity (II, 591).[24] In his *De infelicitate principum* Poggio similarly chooses to abstain from discussing the happiness of popes (I, 397). Although in the same dialogue Poggio attributes freedom of expression to the Florentine Niccoli, even the latter soon explains that he is speaking not about specific individuals but about the subject in general (I, 397). Likewise, in *Contra hypocritas* Carlo Marsuppini cautions Poggio against discussing the pope in order to avoid giving offense; and after a pointed remark concerning the late Eugenius IV, Poggio consents to pass over pontifical examples (II, 75). A similar fear of recriminations from the clergy is expressed by Cosimo de' Medici in *De miseria humanae conditionis* (I, 100).

After a general denunciation of mendicants in the same work, Matteo Palmieri proposes to leave them in their erroneous felicity lest he provoke them (I, 102). When Cosimo later asks about the happiness of popes, Poggio confesses his inability to speak freely on the subject (I, 115).

The fear of offending others thus constitutes the negative complement to Poggio's goal of arousing learned readers, by the positive *provocatio* of the dialogues, to participate in a continuing pursuit of truth and eloquence, as described in his theory of progress. On the one hand, Poggio strives to represent the freedom of opinion that promotes inquiry; on the other, he fears offending contemporaries who may resent his moral pronouncements. Yet Poggio's dialogues also contain a great deal of open polemic, generally aimed at the group which humanists condemned most and feared least, the friars of the mendicant orders.

In **De avaritia,** Cincio is the most outspoken critic of the clergy. During the initial discussion of Bernardino, Cincio attacks the vainglory of contemporary preachers, who seek the applause rather than the spiritual improvement of their hearers (I, 2-3). Later in the discussion, after Andreas has argued that not all men are moved by avarice, Cincio sarcastically comments that Antonio's general attribution of avarice is intended to refer only to priests, and he traces the avarice of priests to the greed of Judas, adding the testimonies of Augustine and Petrarch on clerical corruption. Yet even Cincio recognizes the need for silence in this matter, observing acidly that it is better to be silent about avaricious priests than to say too little (I, 22). Andreas resumes his discourse, noting that the purpose of their discussion does not properly admit this question.

In general, the anger of powerful individuals is what Poggio seeks to avoid, but his interlocutors also manifest caution in alluding to the masses. In **De miseria humanae conditionis,** Cosimo de' Medici deprecates allusions to his own family lest they arouse envy, adding that in order to avoid the unstable opinion of the mob, he will restrict his discussion to ancient examples: "Let us cease . . . to speak of ourselves, lest we seem to indulge in self-praise, which would cause envy. Yet I can truly observe that many of our citizens died happily, whose names I omit in order to avoid the unstable judgment of the masses; I may more properly confine my remarks to citing ancient examples" (I, 94). This dismissal of fluctuating popular opinion (*vulgi varia sentientis opinio*) is an important feature of Poggio's dialogues. Surprisingly, it is Antonio in **De avaritia** who insists "that we argue not according to popular judgment, but by reason" (I, 10), for much of his defense of avarice relies on the citing of example and usage. Otherwise, it is the Stoic idealist Niccoli who rejects unstable popular opinion in order to affirm the

eternal truths discovered by reason. This antithesis is central to the argument of **De nobilitate,** as in Niccoli's reply to the concept of nobility derived by Lorenzo de' Medici from common usage:

> "Do you think," said Niccolò, "that we should argue by the judgment of learned men or by that of the masses and populace? For if you are swayed by the opinions and customs of men, you will see that there is no foundation for the concept of nobility: these are so various and contradictory that I fail to see what standard of nobility they offer. The word exists everywhere, but the thing differs . . . Now if there is such a thing as nobility and if it has a source (as we must admit) in a certain reality and reason, then it must be one and the same everywhere. Yet since the opinion of the masses values nothing less than virtue or reason . . . I often am forced to think that "nobility" is merely an empty name."

> (I, 66)

Similarly, in **De infelicitate principum** Niccoli asserts that the truth, not popular opinion, is the object of the inquiry (I, 395: *non existimationem vulgi, sed veritatem quaerimus*).

The humanist circle depicted in Poggio's dialogues thus places itself in the position of an educated minority, elevated above the masses and above the clergy who exploit the masses. Like Cicero's dialogues, Poggio's dialogues depict a select gathering of learned company. Yet Ciceronian leisure (*otium*) suggests the occupations (*negotium*) of the interlocutors' daily affairs, whereas the settings of Poggio's dialogues both imply a respite from the turmoil of the Curia (which was subject to frequent disturbances in the first half of the Quattrocento) and create a sort of literary immunity for the discussion of controversial topics. Poggio's dialogues are characterized by an innovative and polemical treatment of contemporary questions of morality, and thus their setting reflects the caution necessary in expounding controversial views.[25] The provocative intent of the dialogues extends especially to Poggio's readership, and by the composition of his last dialogue, **De miseria humanae conditionis** (1455), Poggio's faith lies rather in the formative value of writing than in an enthusiasm for personal debate.[26] Yet as a vivid record of the humanists' discussions during the early Quattrocento and of their novel concerns and attitudes, Poggio's dialogues are unequaled.

Notes

Epigraph: Poggio Bracciolini, *Opera omnia,* ed. Riccardo Fubini (Turin: Bottega d'Erasmo, 1964-1969), I, 100: "scio te vereri, ut quis eorum de quibus recte sentis se existimet a te offensum, sed vera loqui unicuique licet." All citations for Poggio's work refer to this edition. The letters, from the edition of Tommaso Tonelli (Florence, 1832-1861) which appears in vol. III of the Fubini edition, are cited as "Ton."

1. See esp. Ernst Walser, *Poggius Florentinus, Leben und Werke* (Leipzig: Teubner, 1914); Francesco Tateo, "Poggio Bracciolini e la dialogistica del Quattrocento," *Pubblicazioni dell'Università di Bari, Annali della Facoltà di Lettere e Filologia,* 7 (1961), 167-204; Tateo, *Tradizione* (Bari: Dedalo, 1967), pp. 223-277; Helene Harth, "Niccolò Niccoli als literarischer Zensor: Untersuchungen zur Textgeschichte von Poggios 'De avaritia,'" *Rinascimento,* II, 7 (1967), 29-53; Riccardo Fubini, "Intendimenti umanistici e riferimenti patristici dal Petrarca al Valla," *Giornale storico della letteratura italiana,* 151 (1974), 520-578.

2. Cf. Ton. I, 273, 280; *De avaritia,* I, 1: "Quod si cui forte aut planum nimis atque humile videbitur dicendi genus, aut non satis explicata ratio muneris suscepti, is intelligat primum me delectari ea eloquentia, in qua non maior existat intelligendi quam legendi labor."

3. Cf. Harth, "Niccolò Niccoli," p. 35.

4. Cf. Tateo, *Tradizione,* p. 257. Poggio originally left a blank for the name of the classical orator (here "someone": *quendam*) who praised Dionysius and blamed Plato, and he asked Niccoli to supply the name, which he had forgotten (Ton. I, 275). Poggio may have had in mind a passage from Quintilian, *Inst. orat.,* II, 17, 4, in which a certain Polycrates is said to have praised the tyrant Busiris and blamed Socrates. At the same time as *De avaritia* was being composed, Leon Battista Alberti misquoted the Quintilian passage. See Alberti, *De commodis litterarum atque incommodis,* ed. Laura Goggi Carotti, Nuova collezione di testi umanistici inediti o rari, 17 (Florence: Olschki, 1976), pp. 40-41.

5. Cf. *Dialogus I,* p. 44: "Nicolaus . . . et in dicendo est promptus, et in lacessendo acerrimus," and Poggio's description of Niccoli in a letter of 1447 to Pietro Tommasi, Ton., II, 334: "vir acer, ac promptus . . . ad lacessendum." See also Poggio, *De infelicitate principum,* I, 394.

6. Antonio says to the newly arrived Andreas, "Te vero praesente tacemus pudore commoti, ne fias nostrarum censor ineptiarum," and Bartolomeo, "Ea est . . . ratio ut taceamus, cum te videamus et virum doctrissimum et theologum" (I, 6). See also Fubini, "Intendimenti," p. 563; Harth, "Niccolò Niccoli," p. 45.

7. Patristic texts are hereafter cited from Migne, *Patrologia latina* (*PL*) and *Patrologia graeca* (*PG*).

8. Cf. Gellius, *Noctes Atticae,* X, 5; Isidorus, *Origines,* X, 9.

9. The argument is imitated by Valla, *De vero falsoque bono,* ed. M. De Panizza Lorch (Bari: Adriatica, 1971), p. 87.

10. Cf. Augustine, *De libero arbitrio,* III, 17, 48 (*PL,* 32, 1294).

11. Cf. Aristotle, *Politics,* I, 7; VII, 8. The argument of animal instinct for self-preservation is used by Valla to defend pleasure in *De vero falsoque bono,* p. 35: "nihil est generi animantium tam a natura tributum quam ut se, vitam corpusque tueatur declinetque ea que nocitura videantur. Nunc autem quid magis vitam conservat quam voluptas?"

12. Cf. Hans Baron, "Franciscan Poverty and Civic Wealth," *Speculum,* 13 (1938), 31-33.

13. Cf. Petrarch, *Fam.,* XXIII, 12, 6: "omittamus ista magnifica et loquamur ut ceteri."

14. Cf. Chrysostom, *Sermon on John,* 65, 3 (*PG,* 59, 363).

15. Cf. the allegory of the spider as *avaro* in a sermon preached by St. Bernardine in Florence during Lent, 1425, in *Le prediche volgari inedite,* ed. D. Pacetti (Siena: Cantagalli, 1935), I, 293-315. In the revised version of the dialogue, Poggio includes a passage against this allegorical interpretation of poets (Garin, ed., *Prosatori,* p. 1129). Cf. Harth, "Niccolò Niccoli," p. 30n3.

16. The topic of old men's avarice had been discussed in Petrarch's *Secretum,* where Franciscus defended his concern over money with an argument similar to Antonio's here. See Petrarca, *Prose,* p. 88: "Senectutis pauperiem ante prospiciens si fatigate etati adiumenta conquiro, quid hic tam reprehensible est?" In *Fam.,* XX, 14, 19, Petrarch observes that old men are generally avaricious, according to Aristotle (*Rhet.* 1389a 14-16). A similar defense of money from a pessimistic viewpoint is that of Adovardo in Book III of Alberti's *Famiglia: Opere volgari,* ed. C. Grayson, I (Bari, 1960), 246-247.

17. Cicero, *De senectute,* 18, 66, a text quoted by Petrarch (*Fam.,* XIV, 4, 17; XVII, 8, 8) and paraphrased by him in his *Secretum,* pp. 86-88: "Nunc mutatis moribus, infelix, quo magis ad terminum appropinquas, eo viatici reliquum conquiris attentius."

18. Valla quotes the passage to contrast the Stoic abstractions, implicit in Cicero's context, to common usage. See his *Opera omnia,* I, 688.

19. Cf. Cicero, *De or.,* II, 28, 121; *De leg.,* I, 13, 36; *Tusc. disp.,* II, 2, 5; IV, 4, 7; *De nat. deor.,* III, 1, 1; *Lucullus,* 3, 7-8; *De div.,* II, 72, 150.

20. See Harth, "Niccolò Niccoli," pp. 51-53.

21. The notion of progress from the inception of a discipline derives from Cicero, *Brutus,* 18, 71: "nescio an reliquis in rebus omnibus idem eveniat: nihil est enim simul et inventum et perfectum." The same passage is cited in Leon Battista Alberti's *Della pittura* of 1436, *Opere volgari,* III (Bari, 1973), 106-107.

22. Cf. *De avaritia,* I, 6: "non tam disserendi causa, quam aut te aut hunc provocandi," and Cicero, *De fin.,* I, 8, 26: "Quae cum dixissem, magis ut illum provocarem quam ut ipse loquerer." In Cicero, however, the sense of the *provocatio* does not extend to his readership.

23. See Ton. I, 273; Walser, *Poggius,* p. 429.

24. Terence, *Andria,* 68: "veritas solet odium parere," also quoted by Poggio in *Contra hypocritas* (II, 51) and *De miseria humanae conditionis* (I, 100) in religious contexts.

25. On the "reversal" of traditional treatments inherent in Poggio's choice of titles, see Fubini, "Intendimenti", p. 553n52.

26. In a letter of 1455 to Andrea Alamanni, Poggio declares that reading and meditation are superior to teaching and discussion in the pursuit of eloquence, citing the examples of learned men from Petrarch to his own generation (Ton. III, 184-186).

A. Bartlett Giamatti (essay date 1982)

SOURCE: Giamatti, A. Bartlett. "Hippolytus among the Exiles: The Romance of Early Humanism." In *Poetic Traditions of the English Renaissance,* edited by Maynard Mack and George deForest Lord, pp. 1-23. New Haven, Conn.: Yale University Press, 1982.

[*In the following essay, Giamatti describes Poggio as the leader of the second wave of humanism, a successor to Petrarch in Renaissance efforts to rescue the writings of classical authors from neglect and fragmentation.*]

Exile was a central and abiding preoccupation of Petrarch's life, as it would be for that cultural epoch, the Renaissance, that he seems to initiate. In his fragmentary autobiographical piece, the *Letter to Posterity,* written near the end of his life, Petrarch says:

> My parents were worthy people, of Florentine origin, middling well-off, indeed, to confess the truth, on the edge of poverty. As they were expelled from their home city, I was born in exile in Arezzo, in the 1304th year of Christ's era, at dawn on a Monday, the 20th of July.[1]

Or again, in the prefatory epistle to his *Familiares,* or *Letters on Familiar Affairs* (that massive epic of the self in twenty-four books, comprising 350 letters writ-ten between 1325 and 1366), Petrarch tells his closest friend, the Belgian musician Lodewyck Heyliger, whom he called "Socrates," "Compare my wanderings with those of Ulysses; if we were equal in name and fame, it would be known that he traveled no longer or farther than I. He was a mature man when he left his hometown; though nothing lasts long at any age, everything runs very fast in old age. But I was conceived in exile and born in exile."[2] "Ego in exilio genitus, in exilio natus sum." "Ego . . . sum"—his deepest concern: "genitus," "natus"—the life of man: and through it, balancing and ordering the terse, pregnant span of the sentence, and the life, the dominant chord—"in exilio," "in exilio." This is January 1350.

Petrarch's whole existence, his sense of himself, would be determined by his obsession with origin and exile; by his conviction that he was displaced and marginal. Unlike Ulysses, who wandered but came home, he, Petrarch, was never at home save in books. Only in books, and in words, did he feel at peace and at rest, only then not moving, as he says in the broken last sentence of his *Letter to Posterity,* "like a sick man, to be rid of distress by shifting position."[3] Petrarch's odyssey, his endless exile, depended—as his courtship of Laura depended—on not achieving what he said he desired. His sense of identity depended on being displaced, for only in perpetual exile could Petrarch gain the necessary perspective on himself truly to determine, or create, who he was. Only by being eccentric, could he center, or gather in and collect, his self.[4] Exile was essential to his view of himself, and it was, as we will see, essential in varying ways to his culture's view of itself. Both Petrarch, the individual, and humanism, the dominant elite culture of Europe for the next three centuries, had to assert exile, whether from secular antiquity and its ethics or Scriptural Paradise and its bliss, in order to refashion, or revive, or give rebirth to, or regain, what had once been purer, holier, or simply more whole.

For the Renaissance, integration of self and culture meant seeing Origin or the Original as distant and lost, so that one could imitate and emulate and thus make oneself a new copy or assert a genuine revision. A seminal tension in Renaissance culture, as in individuals like Petrarch, stems from the conviction that, on the one hand, origins so distant were also for the first time clearly perceived after the darkness, but that, on the other hand, what was recreated on that clear model would never be truly authentic. The Renaissance, for all its assertive, expansive, cultural imperialism—its revival of the past, its new texts, institutions and perceptions—would never completely shake the sense that what it made was removed, not quite worthy of the original; if not secondrate, at least secondhand, just as beneath the oft-repeated boast of each people that their land had been colonized by a hero from Troy—Italy by Aeneas, France by Francus, Portugal by the sons of

Lusus, Britain by Brutus—there would be the constant awareness that Europe was founded by the losers, that the European people were colonists who, for all their glory, were exiled from the Homeland, that in the Westering of culture, much had been gained but something had also been lost.

But this is to anticipate the sixteenth century, the end of the Renaissance, and we are at the beginning, in the fourteenth, and my point is simple: exile is the precondition to identity.[5] So Petrarch, never truly at home, always refuses to return. In March 1315, Giovanni Boccaccio carries to Padua a letter to Petrarch from the governors of Florence promising restitution of his patrimony and a chair at their new university. Petrarch writes two letters of refusal—one, to Zanobi da Strada (*Ep. Met.* 3.8) in early 1351, saying he must bear his exile with equanimity; the other, to the Priors and People of Florence (*Fam.*, 11.5) of April 1351, thanking them but saying the Pope had called him to Avignon. He needed his exile. And we get even better insight into why he needed it in two letters (*Fam.* 2.3-4) to an otherwise unknown correspondent, Severo Appenninicola, letters of consolation for the other's fate. Since the letters are long, I shall summarize.

The letter to Appenninicola begins with an etymology of "exilium," a derivation not remarkable in itself but interesting because the etymologizing habit, the philological cast of mind, is, of course, typical of the whole humanist effort to uncover and reconstitute meaning by returning to origins. Whether through single words or whole bodies of texts, philology reaffirms the humanist's exile from true meaning as he struggles to overcome it. We shall return to this philological impulse. Then Petrarch goes on to say that exile resides in one's attitude when one is outside one's homeland; if one feels beaten, one is an exile; if one goes with dignity, one is a traveler. Exile consists of an attitude; the attitude is the fear of loss—loss of riches, fame, life. Exile is therefore an error in judgement, and anyone can make this error. But, and Petrarch adopts the perspective of his correspondent,

> if you firmly believe that whoever is absent from his native land is without question an exile, where are those who are not exiles? For what man, unless he were lazy and soft, has not departed from his home and his native land several times either because he was desirous of seeing new things, or of learning, or of enlightening his mind, or was concerned about his health, or was desirous of increasing his wealth, or because of the demands or wars, or at the command of his state, of his master, of his parents?[6]

But Petrarch explains—and this is the heart of the matter—one can be forced into exile, but not forced to despair of returning:

> We have seen men sent into exile who, before they had arrived at their destination, were called back to the homeland because of the unbearable grief of the citi-

zens. Others, after a long time, returned with so much honor. . . . No one was committed to such a horrible place that he was not allowed to raise his eyes; no one viewed the loss of his belongings as so deplorable that he was unable to hope for better things.[7]

Let us pause here, for it strikes me that there is more at issue than simply a moralizing injunction to be optimistic. Petrarch, in his meditation on exile, is saying not that one will, or even should, come home, but that the hope of returning is ever alive—indeed, that the hope of returning home is as strong as the force that sends one away in the first place. The man who would not go home always had to believe he could. Indeed, much as life—for Petrarch—was an endless marginality, so also was it sustained, precisely because of that marginality, by the belief that one might become central. Petrarch's need to believe he was displaced was the only way he could believe in genuine return, revival, recall.

This perspective is what we may call the Romance of Early Humanism—the secondary culture's deep belief that, despite distance and loss, it might become primary; the conviction that, through effort and emulation, the copy might become an original, the removed might restore the beginning, the exile might—through purposeful wandering—become a point, or recapture the point, of origin. Petrarch tells his friend to imitate the virtue of those ancients in exile, so that he may not despair that what has been done so often cannot be done again. And as he goes on, he seems to be saying: as we imitate the virtue of the ancients, we become virtuous; as we become virtuous, we are at home; we are at home because we are at one with the ancients, and they are our home. So he writes in 1359 to his beloved Socrates: "Homeland is for a man in any niche in the universe; only by impatience can he make himself believe [he is] in exile."[8]

He is groping for a definition; to call this a "theory" of exile is to make it sound too systematic, too abstract. He is working out, constantly, his attitudes toward exile, always fixing his intuitions in the balanced periods of his prose, his style both affirming his distance from the ancients and seeking, by imitation, to bridge that gulf. For it was finally the ancients, not Florence, or friends, or Tuscany, that Petrarch felt most exiled from, and because he expressed this perspective so powerfully, Renaissance culture, after him, would imitate him—both in his sense of exile and his efforts to return.

Petrarch's radical solitude stemmed from what we would call his sense of history. "He would have liked," says Peter Burke, "to have lived in Augustan Rome. For him, the period before the conversion of Constantine (the *aetas antiqua*) was an age of light; the *aetas nova*, the modern age which succeeded it, was an age of darkness. This was the reversal of the traditional Christian distinction."⁹ Others, like Flavio Biondo, after him would speak of a "media aetas" between antiquity and the present; and still later others, like Vasari, would speak of the present as a "rebirth."¹⁰ But the essential perspective on the ancients as distinct, distant, and the home we had left was established by Petrarch and his language of exile.

His efforts to find his true self in their selves is expressed in everything he wrote but never more clearly, or poignantly, than in the last ten letters of the last book, the twenty-fourth, of his *Familiares*—written between 1345 and 1360 to the great figures of Antiquity. These letters, two to Cicero, one each to Seneca, Varro, Quintilian, Livy, Pollio, and then, building to the summit of poets and receding in time, to Horace, Virgil and Homer, are meditations on his distance from them, his desire to be with them. They are exercises in exile: fruitless efforts to go home that at the same time allow Petrarch to create himself. We need only look at one of these letters, keeping in mind what exile means for Petrarch, to see where the course of Renaissance humanism would run for some time to come. This is the fifth letter in the series, to Quintilian.

Petrarch wrote to Quintilian on December 7, 1350, the very day when, passing through Florence on his way to Rome, he was given an incomplete manuscript of Quintilian's *Institutes* by a young scholar named Lapo di Castiglionchio. Deeply moved, Petrarch wrote a lovely letter, finally praising Quintilian himself for being a great man, but saying, "greater than you, your highest merit lay in your ability to ground and to mold great men."¹¹ Shape others as he may, however, it is Quintilian's own shape that concerns Petrarch most and that draws his attention in the opening lines: "Your book, called *Institutes of Oratory*, has come to my hands, but alas how mangled and mutilated. I recognize therein the hand of time—the destroyer of all things."¹² Then, after saying how he admires Quintilian, Petrarch returns to his figure again: "I saw the dismembered limbs of a beautiful body and admiration mingled with grief seized me."¹³

This language for the incomplete book is crucial for what humanism would come to mean: the text is a beautiful body, a "corpus" whose limbs are scattered, a body mutilated and mangled. Petrarch uses the words *discerptus*, from *discerpere*, ("to mutilate") and *lacer*, meaning mangled, lacerated. The words have their own enormous resonances. *Discerptus* for instance, is the word Virgil uses in the *Fourth Georgic* (l. 522) to describe the mutilated Orpheus; *lacer* occurs in *Aeneid* 6.495 to describe how Deiphobus appeared to Aeneas in the underworld; and it is used again in *Aeneid* 9.491 to describe Euryalus, he who fell as a purple flower cut by the plow. Potent words, and images, for anyone steeped—as Petrarch was—in Virgil. But I would suggest that beneath the image of the book as mutilated body, beneath Deiphobus and Euryalus and even Orpheus, another Virgilian passage is buried so deep that Petrarch does not seem to know it, though others, imitating him, would almost instinctively bring it to the surface. This is *Aeneid* 7.765-73, describing the death of Hippolytus and his resurrection at the hands of Aesculapius:

> For they tell how that Hippolytus, when he fell by a
> 　Stepmother's craft,
> and slaked his father's vengeance in blood,
> ripped apart by terrified horses, came again to the
> 　starry firmament,
> and heaven's upper air, recalled by the Healer's
> herbs and the love of Diana. Then the Father
> omnipotent, angry that any mortal should rise
> from the nether shades to the light of life,
> hurled with his thunder beneath the Stygian waves
> the finder of such healing-craft, him Apollo-born.¹⁴

Virgil goes on to say that Hippolytus, now named Virbius, was taken to live out his life in Italy, and that his son, also Virbius, now rode another chariot to join the army of Turnus.¹⁵ I suggest this passage, in conjunction with Petrarch's images of Quintilian mutilated, for two reasons. Here again, as with Deiphobus, Euryalus, and Orpheus, we are dealing with the story of a lacerated body, and this time with the story of one who came back, one who was "revocatus," says Virgil, as Petrarch's exiled ancients were sometimes recalled, "to the starry firmament and heaven's upper air." Jove was angry that one should go from "the nether shades to the light of life," but Hippolytus did it—then to find a home in Italy. His healer was punished with exile to Hell, but the shredded Hippolytus came home again, whole.

I suggest that in the story of Hippolytus and Aesculapius we have a version of what I have been calling the Romance of Early Humanism—the sense that return or rebirth or restoration of origin and original form is possible, a hope that not only sustained but necessitated Petrarch's sense of exile. I suggest that in the mutilated body of Hippolytus, mangled like those other Virgilian heroes but older than all save Orpheus, Petrarch might see a figure for the shapes of all those ancients, now known only in fragmentary texts, in mangled corpora, whom he desired to see whole, and be with—if not one of. And I suggest, lest you think I lack the courage of my aberrations, that in Aesculapius, the healer who could not be cured, the victim of his own powers, the scion of Apollo to whom the light was denied, Petrarch might see figured the humanist's power to restore—texts, bodies, traditions—and also his inability to experience the integrity, the wholeness, thus wrought.¹⁶ A humanist might see the endless dialectic of his own dilemma—always being exiled so that he might find himself, always bringing the curative balm of ancient ethics to his culture, yet himself shifting like a sick man in distress.

II

I cannot prove that the Virgilian story of Hippolytus and Aesculapius is the link that binds Petrarch's sense of his and his culture's exile to his desire to integrate himself by restoring the fragments of the past; but I do know that Humanists would use a language alluding to exile, fragmented bodies, and Aesculapius shortly after Petrarch, in ways that would have been impossible, I think, without him. And I know it is possible once again to affirm that if Petrarch did not create all the formulations humanism would use for itself, he did at least define the fundamental issues to which those formulations would respond—and those were the issues of how one saw oneself, particularly in relation to the ethical wisdom of the ancient world, and what that relationship meant for the modern individual and his society—indeed, what it meant to be modern at all.

At the end of his letter to Quintilian, Petrarch says: "I ardently desire to find you entire; and if you are anywhere in such condition, pray do not hide from me any longer. Vale."[17] This humanist-physician was forever barred from reassembling that Hippolytus, and thus barred from restoring his own wounds, from ending his exile from his homeland in ancient culture, because Lapo di Castiglionchio had given him only a partial manuscript. But Quintilian was "totus," "entire"; was—as Petrarch had prophetically hoped earlier in the letter—"resting intact in someone's library."[18] He was resting, to be precise, in his entire twelve-book body in the tower of the monastery at St. Gall, outside Constance. And there he was found, and revived, in June or July of 1416, one afternoon, by Poggio Bracciolini and two friends.

With Poggio, the second phase of our inquiry, and the second generation of Italian humanism, can be said to begin. Poggio (1380-1459), native of Arezzo, student of Salutati, who had studied with Petrarch, served the papacy as apostolic secretary for fifty years, would be chancellor of Florence at the end of his life, learned, acerb, shrewd, was one of the great discoverers of lost manuscripts in the Renaissance. Some of his greatest finds came when he was attending the Council of Constance in 1416.[19] There he and his friends made four sallies to search for pagan texts while the Church was convulsed in disputes. On the second trip, in the tower of St. Gall, Poggio found books 1-4 of the *Argonautica* of Valerius Flaccus, commentary on five orations of Cicero, and all of Quintilian. Like America, Quintilian whole had been known to others since Petrarch; but like Columbus, Poggio gets credit for the find because he knew how to publicize the discovery. Poggio immediately wrote his learned friend and fellow bibliophile, Niccolò de Niccolis in Florence, and the letter circu-

lated. On September 15, 1416, a former and future chancellor of Florence, Leonardo Bruni, having read of Poggio's finds, wrote him from Florence in ecstatic terms:

> Just as Camillus was called a second founder of Rome after Romulus, who established the city, while Camillus restored it after it was lost, so you will deservedly be called the second author of all the works which were once lost and now returned to us by your integrity and diligence.[20]

Here the references to being the "second founder," "second author," carry the pride and pleasure of rediscovery, and not—as they would have earlier, and might later—a note of melancholy at being derivative of that which remained just beyond reach. Here, the pride and confidence of early humanism asserts itself; and why not? The promise of a return to former glory, and indeed a surpassing new glory, seemed at hand. Bruni then turns to specific concerns:

> For Quintilian, who used to be mangled and in pieces, will recover all his parts through you. I have seen the headings of the chapters; he is whole, while we used to have only the middle section and that incomplete.[21]

And then he addresses Quintilian directly:

> Oh wondrous treasure! Oh unexpected joy! Shall I see you, Marcus Fabius, whole and undamaged, and how much will you mean to me now? For I loved you even when you were cruelly deprived of your mouth, of your mouth and both your hands, when you were "spoiled of your nose and shorten'd of your ears;" still I loved you for your grace.[22]

The language of mutilation and wholeness is reminiscent of the figures of Petrarch. Yet it derives more immediately from Poggio. For Poggio doubtless used to Niccolò de Niccolis the same language he uses on December 15, 1416 when he writes from Constance to Guarino da Verona. First he extols language to Guarino in classic humanist fashion as that which alone

> we use to express the power of our mind and which separates us from the other beings. And so we must be deeply grateful to the pioneers in the other liberal arts and especially those who by their concern and efforts have given us rules for speaking and a pattern of perfection. They have made it possible for us to excel other men in the ability in which all men excel beasts.[23]

This celebration of rhetoric and the power of speech as the formative energy in human affairs—what Petrarch had praised in his letter—leads naturally to the greatest rhetorician and trainer of Orators, Quintilian. He alone—even without Cicero—could have taught us all we needed to know of oratory. But among us Italians, says Poggio, "Quintilian was to be had only in such a mangled and mutilated state (the fault of the times, I think), that neither the figure nor the face of the man was to be distinguished in him."[24] So far, in the adjectives and the allusion to time, Poggio says immediately, "So far you have seen the man only thus,"[25] and cites *Aeneid* 6.495-97:

> his whole frame mangled
> His face cruelly torn, his face and either hand,
> His ears wrenched from despoiled brows, and
> His nostrils lopped by a shameful wound.[26]

This is the Virgilian passage about Deiphobus, one of those passages latent in Petrarch's use of the word "lacer." Thus, beneath the imagery of fragments—applied to Quintilian—we get an actual instance—in the Virgilian reminiscences—of the way humanists would handle and reintegrate fragments for their own purposes. We have humanist texts talking about reassembling Quintilian on one level, and the same texts fragmenting and reintegrating Virgil on another level—enacting what they talk about. Again, we see the process of aggression and accommodation towards antiquity that we saw in the notion of exile—a constant longing for origins that serves to allow the humanist the distance to make himself over into something like an original.

Poggio is the master of this method. After the illusion to Deiphobus mangled, he tells how he found the actual Quintilian text, now figured as a man in prison: he speaks of the squalor of his jail, the cruelty of his jailers, and describes Quintilian "with ragged beard, with hair matted with blood,"[27] this time alluding to *Aeneid* 2.277, where the figure of Hector appears to Aeneas in a dream before the sack of Troy.

All of these mangled Virgilian heroes, Hector, Deiphobus, Euryalus, tend to link the massive weight and authority of the *Aeneid* to the humanist enterprise, and tend to imply that the humanist enterprise, like the *Aeneid* itself, is a celebration of the way limbs, or a people dispersed, like the Trojans, may be brought home—home to Italy where, like Hippolytus, they live out their lives whole, healthy, and secure. The progress in the *Aeneid* of Aeneas himself, from exiled individual to restored institution, becomes another analogue to the Romance of Early Humanism, the hope for restoration: restoration of humanists to the ancients, of ancient texts to Italy.

Indeed, this much Poggio implies in a passage separating the two Virgilian allusions: we should congratulate ourselves, he says, that "he [Quintilian] has now been restored to us in his original appearance and grandeur, whole and in perfect condition."[28] The thrust is still to find origins, but where Petrarch wanted to go back across distance to Rome, Poggio will bring Romans across the distance to home:

> For if Marcus Tullius rejoiced so fervently when Marcus Marcellus was returned from exile, and that at a time when Rome had a great many able and out-standing men like Marcellus both at home and abroad, what should men do now in learned circles, and especially men who devote themselves to oratory, when the one and only light of the Roman name, except for whom there was no one but Cicero and he likewise cut to pieces and scattered, has through our efforts been called back not only from exile but from almost complete destruction?[29]

For the exiled Petrarch, return was only a hope; for Poggio, the return of the exiled ancients is a fact. In this reversal of the basic image, we sense the massive confidence acquired by humanism in two generations: they now know the tide flows toward them; they know they are Aesculapiuses who can restore lacerated heroes, and bring them to Italian woods, and incorporate the potent ethical virtues of those heroes into their civic institutions. Poggio has no doubt the fragments are whole, their exile is over.

Nor does another of his correspondents—the last we will consider—have any doubts. Indeed, that writer—Francesco Barbaro, a distinguished Venetian humanist—congratulates Poggio on his discoveries in terms that bring to the full light of consciousness the images I have mentioned. Barbaro writes to Poggio on July 6, 1417—about a year after the whole series of discoveries. He praises the apostolic secretary for "releasing the monuments of literature from darkness into light"[30]—the imagery for history is beginning to acquire the Dark Ages/New Dawn antithesis so familiar, alas, to us. Then:

> You and your helpful companion Bartholomeus have endowed Tertullian with life, and M. Fabius Quintilian, Q. Asconius Pedianus, Lucretius, Silius Italicus, Marcellinus, Manilius the astronomer, Lucius Septimus, Valerius Flaccus; you have revived the grammarians Caprus, Eutychius, and Probus, and many others who had suffered a like fate, or you have brought them back to Latium from a long absence.[31]

The metaphors are of resuscitation and return from exile, and the result is that all the Gods are home.

Then Barbaro praises Poggio by reminding him of Lycurgus, who "was the first to bring back whole to Greece from Asia the work of Homer scattered in bits in various places"[32] and this, by now, traditional language of fragments—following on the image of exile—leads Barbaro to the figure that I believe has been present by implication ever since Petrarch first looked upon the mutilated corpus of Quintilian:

> We accept Aesculapius as belonging among the gods because he called back Hippolytus, as well as others from the underworld, when he had reached the day fixed as the last of his life, and thus allowed him [Hippolytus] to die only some years later. If peoples, nations, and provinces have dedicated shrines to him, what might I think ought to be done for you, if that custom had not already been forgotten? You have re-

vived so many illustrious men and such wise men, who were dead for eternity, through whose minds and teachings not only we but our descendants will be able to live well and honorably.[33]

Now not a single text but a series of texts, not one mangled Hippolytus but a Pantheon of Hippolyti, have been revived and brought home. (Barbaro adds to the myth the idea that Aesculapius refashioned not only Hippolytus but "others" as well, to accommodate his paradigm to the actual series of books discovered by Poggio.) And from this act of restoration, this successful ending to the Romance of Early Humanism, Barbaro draws the proper humanistic conclusion: this act is not only glorious in itself, but, and this has been implicit in the figure of Aesculapius all along, the curative and healing powers of the restored bodies of work will pass into the new culture, to subsequent generations. This view of ancient virtue, once whole, now infused, is the essence of the humanist vision. It was adumbrated in Petrarch's exile who imitated the virtue of the ancient heroes, and thus found a home; it rings out in a glorious period as Barbaro, finishing another figure of praise for Poggio—the commander who has liberated those besieged—says that "there must be no doubt that culture and mental training which are adapted to a good and blessed life and fair speech, can bring no trifling advantages not only to private concerns but to cities, nations, and finally to all mankind."[34] The relation of private impulse and public good, the ethically educated regard of the one for the many, is the goal of the whole humanist movement, particularly as interpreted by those whose native city was, as for Barbaro, the Venetian or, as for Poggio, the Florentine Republic.

We have seen what in Petrarch was a sense of exile and a perception of fragmentation become in Poggio and his friends a triumphant image of return and conviction of integrity. There remains one last text for us to examine in the light of our Aesculapian concerns, one last document where we can see early Renaissance humanism asserting its self-consciousness. It falls, in time, between Petrarch and Poggio. I refer to Giovanni Boccaccio's preface to his massive *Genealogia Deorum Gentilium,* the *Genealogy of the Gods,* which occupied the last thirty years of his life, from the 1340s almost until his death, a year after his beloved Petrarch, in 1375. The *Genealogia* is an encyclopedic work on myth—on the nature, relationship and meaning of the Gods of the Gentiles—and it stands like Janus at the threshold of the new era, looking back at ancient treatises on the Gods, like Cicero's *De Natura Deorum,* and Hyginus' *Fables,* and Fulgentius' sixth century *Mythologiae.* Boccaccio's huge work gathers in all that flows from ancient treatises and writers, from Church Father and Christian poet, and then circulates its lore through later writers, providing in its medieval format an overwhelming image of Renaissance eclecticism.

The book is, like its author, learned, human, genial, devout; though also like its author it is not a little redundant, too pleased with its own efforts at times, too deferential before authorities like Petrarch and others. This splendid monster, like something from the past, could never have been produced in the past; not only is it written by a man who has tried to learn Greek, who is aware of the latest discoveries of the day, but it exudes, in its very syncretism, the spirit of revival and restoration we have spoken of—although in its own particular way as a massive prose epic, a work in many ways comparable to the great epics and romances in verse produced by poets from Pulci to Milton, save that the subject now is not the death lament of some chivalric past or the loss of some paradisiacal beginning, but a song of revival, a huge hymn to ancient culture, now restored.

We catch these notes in his preface, which Boccaccio writes in the form of a dialogue between himself and one Donino, emissary of Hugo IV, King of Cyprus and Jerusalem, who had commissioned the work but died in 1359, well before it was completed—though that seemed to bother neither Boccaccio nor his book, both author and subject swelling to fullness, rushing on, one king more or less a mere speck on the landscape. Can it be done? asks Boccaccio.

> Doubtless—if mountains offer easy passage and trackless deserts an open and travelled road; if rivers are fordable and seas tranquil; if Aeolus from his cave sends me in my course strong and favorable winds; or, better still, if a man might have on his feet the golden sandals of Argeiphontes, to fly whithersoever he pleased for the asking. Hardly then could he cover such extent of land and sea, though his life were never so long, and he did nothing else.[35]

Certainly it can be done, says Boccaccio—by an epic hero. But beneath the epic impulse, here presented obliquely, of the author-hero, is the view of Antiquity, its myths and writers, as a landscape, a vast, difficult terrain to be sure, but a landscape that is, with good fortune and great heart, chartable, knowable. For Boccaccio, Antiquity is not a distant shore—as it was for lonely, riven Petrarch; to the more robust, less tentative Boccaccio, it is new world, fabulous but now available. Boccaccio is coy; to handle those languages and people, it will take someone, he says, "strong enough, keen enough, and with good enough memory, first to observe what is relevant, then to understand it, retain it, note it down, and finally reduce it to order."[36] He suggests Petrarch. Donino sidesteps gracefully. When Boccaccio is at last persuaded, he addresses his patron, King Hugo. He will take his frail bark to sea: "I may trace every shore and traverse every mountain grove; I may, if need be, explore dyke and den afoot, descend even to hell, or, like another Daedalus, go winging to the ether."[37] The epic hero, and his labor, are launched:

Aeneas, St. Paul, Dante—all are caught up in this epic opening. And what will our hero find? In his words immediately following, we hear the familiar humanist accent:

> Everywhere . . . I will find and gather, like fragments of a mighty wreck strewn on some vast shore, the relics of the Gentile gods. These relics, scattered through almost infinite volumes, shrunk with age, half consumed, well-nigh a blank, I will bring into such single genealogical order as I can.[38]

There is the deep preoccupation with assembling the fragments of antiquity and recreating an original shape, the shape of "genealogical order," or "in unum genealogie corpus." Genealogy is humanist philology writ large, the probing for the past, the translation of significance to the present, on an epic scale. That will be Boccaccio's great voyage, a journey of discovery which is a labor of recovery.

Because now not a single lacerated text, nor a series of texts, but rather "almost infinite volumes" confront the humanist, his new book, made up of all these old books, will not "have a body [*corpus*] of perfect proportion. It will, alas, be maimed—not, I hope, in too many members—and for reasons aforesaid distorted, shrunken, and warped."[39] His book, finished, will look like all the fragments it has absorbed and reassembled, and so be a true copy of the originals. Boccaccio's implication is that his book will be an original of its own kind, in which the king will see "not only the art of the ancient poets, and the consanguinity and relations of the false gods, but certain natural truths, hidden with an art that will surprise you, together with deeds and moral civilization of the Ancients that are not a matter of every-day information."[40] As the plan of the book is new, so is the content. This is as close as early humanists ever come or could come to saying they were original.

Boccaccio concludes: do not be surprised at discrepancies, falsehoods, contradictions. They belong to the ancients, not to me. "Satis enim mihi erit comperta rescribere"—"I will be satisfied only to write down [write again] what is found." The humanist epic consists in "rescribere," in rewriting or reassembling in language, what the mind of man has found. Like Apollo's son, who would heal, but not judge, the scattered limbs, the early humanist revives the past; only later generations would criticize. Not now. So, before his final prayer to God for aid, Boccaccio summons in full the image for his effort, for the effort of all of them, that he has twice touched on:

> I can quite realize this labor to which I am committed—this vast system of gentile gods and their progeny, torn limb from limb [*membratim discerptum*: Petrarch's word, Virgil's word] and scattered among the rough and desert places of antiquity and the thorns of hate,

wasted away, sunk almost to ashes; and here am I setting forth to collect these fragments, hither and yon, and fit them together, like another Aesculapius restoring Hippolytus.[41]

From Petrarch gazing at the mutilated body of one old book, through the whole—entire—bodies of Poggio's books by way of the mighty corpus of Boccaccio's new book, made of the limbs of the old, the humanist has implicitly or overtly seen himself as physician-restorer. But the early humanist is also Hippolytus, for as he reassembles the past, he assembles himself. The humanist's supreme reaction is finally his own sense of himself; his crucial composition is the reconstitution of self out of what the past has given him—a sense of self that is defined by the activity of making up the self. The humanist is Aesculapius to his own Hippolytus, restorer of himself out of the fragments old and new of his own humanity.

We remember that in the seminal account of Hippolytus in book 7 of the *Aeneid,* Virgil tells us that when Hippolytus was made whole, he went to live "in silvis italis," and was called "Virbius," as his son was called after him. Virbius, of course, means "twice man"—man a second time, man as he is reborn.[42] Let that finally be our emblem for the early humanist—the man made again, whole, assembled out of the fragments of his own past; the humanist, one who, by a sense of loss that is also an effort of historical imagination, has made himself up, his essential self both derivative and integrated; his consciousness old but very new; a scholar confident that, in his Italian woods, his exile is finally over and the Rome he so longed for is again alive.

Notes

1. Honestibus parentibus, Florentinis origine, fortuna mediocri et (ut verum fatear) ad inopiam vergente, sed patria pulsis, Aretti in exilio natus sum, anno huius aetatis ultimae, quae a Christo incipit, M. CCC. IIII. die Lunae, ad auroram XIII. Cal. Augusti (*Francisci Petrarcae Epistolae De Rebus Familiaribus Et Variae,* ed. Giuseppe Fracassetti [Florence: Typis Felicis Le Monnier, 1859], 1:2; Morris Bishop, trans., *Letters From Petrarch* [Bloomington: Indiana University Press, 1966], p. 7).

2. Ulysseos errores erroribus meis confer: profecto si nominis et returm claritas una foret, nec diutius erravit ille, nec latius. Ille patrios fines iam senior excessit: cum nihil in ulla aetate longum sit, omnia sunt in senectute brevissima. Ego in exilio genitus, in exilio natus sum (Fracassetti, *Epistolae,* 1:18; Bishop, *Letters,* pp. 18-19).

3. Et licet filius sibi successerit prudentissimus et clarissimus vir, et qui per paterna vestigia me carum semper atque honoratum habuit, ego tamen

illo amisso cum quo magis mihi praesertim de aetate convenerat, redii rursus in Gallias, stare nescius, non tam desiderio visa millies revisendi, quam studio, more aegrorum, loci mutatione taediis consulendi. (Fracassetti, *Epistolae,* 1:11; Bishop, *Letters,* p. 12).

4. See on this theme in later Renaissance epics, A. Bartlett Giamatti, "Headlong Horses, Headless Horsemen: An Essay on the Chivalric Epics of Pulci, Boiardo, and Ariosto," in *Italian Literature: Roots and Branches: Essays in Honor of Thomas Goddard Bergin,* ed. Giose Rimanelli and Kenneth John Atchity (New Haven: Yale University Press, 1976), pp. 265-307.

5. For a later version of this idea as located in lost children and foundlings, see A. Bartlett Giamatti, "Primitivism and the Process of Civility in Spenser's *Faerie Queene,*" in *First Images of America: The Impact of the New World on the Old,* ed. Fredi Chiappelli, Michael J. B. Allen, and Robert L. Benson (Berkeley: University of California Press, 1976), pp. 71-82.

6. Quod si tu mihi, quicumque a patria absunt exulare sine ulla distinctione firmaveris, rari ergo non exules. Quis enim hominum, nisi desidiosus ac mollis, non aliquotiens aut visendi avidus, aut discendi studio, aut illustrandi animi, aut curandi corporis, aut amplificandae rei familiaris proposito, aut necessitate bellorum, aut suae reipublicae seu domini seu parentis imperio, domum linquit et patriam? (Fracassetti, *Epistolae,* 1:90; Francesco Petrarca, *Rerum familiarium libri I-VIII,* trans. Aldo S. Bernardo [Albany: State University of New York Press, 1975], p. 71.)

7. Vidimus in exilium missos, priusquam ad destinatum pervenissent, immenso patriae desiderio revocatus: alios vero, post tempus, tanto cum honore . . . reversos. . . . Nemo unquam tam iniquo loco iacuit, ut non ei liceret oculos attollere: nemo tam deploratum rerum suarum vidit exitum, ut prohibetur sperare meliora (Fracassetti, *Epistolae,* 1:90-91; Bernardo, *Rerum familiarium,* pp. 71-72).

8. Patriam viro omnem mundi angulum, exilium nusquam esse, nisi quod impatientia fecerit (Fracassetti, *Epistolae* (1863), 3:80; my translation).

9. *The Renaissance Sense of the Past* (London: Edward Arnold, 1969), p. 21.

10. For these matters the basic text is Wallace Ferguson, *The Renaissance in Historical Thought: Five Centuries of Interpretation* (Cambridge: Harvard University Press, 1948).

11. Magnus fateor vir fuisti, sed instituendis formandisque magnis viris maximus. (Fracassetti,

Epistolae, 3:279; Mario Cosenza, trans. *Petrarch's Letters to Classical Authors* [Chicago: University of Chicago Press, 1910], p. 88. Where I have used Cosenza's translation, I have somewhat modernized his diction.)

12. Oratoriarum institutionum liber heu! discerptus et lacer venit ad manus meas. Agnovi aetatem vastatricem omnium (Fracassetti, *Epistolae,* 3:278; Cosenza, *Petrarch's Letters,* p. 84).

13. Vidi formosi corporis artus effusos: admiratio animum dolorque concussit (Fracassetti, *Epistolae,* 3:278; Cosenza, *Petrarch's Letters,* pp. 84-85).

14.

> namque ferunt fama Hyppolytum, postquam arte novercae
> occiderit patriasque explerit sanguine poenas
> turbatis distractus equis, ad sidera rursus
> aetheria et superas caeli venisse sub auras,
> Paeoniis revocatum herbis et amore Dianae.
> tum pater omnipotens, aliquem indignatus ab umbris
> mortalem infernis ad lumina surgere vitae,
> ipse repertorem medicinae talis et artis
> fulmine Phoebigenam Stygias detrusit ad undas.

(Text and translation from *Virgil,* Loeb Classical Library, ed. H. R. Fairclough, 2 vols., rev. ed. [Cambridge: Harvard University Press, 1969, 1974]. Although I have used Fairclough's translation, I have modernized his diction and arranged the prose in verse form.)

15. On Virbius, particularly in Dante, see Marguerite Mills Chiarenza, "Hippolytus' Exile: *Paradiso* XVII, vv. 46-48," *Dante Studies* 84 (1966), 65-68.

16. On the tradition of the healer in the Christian middle ages, see Rudolph Arbesmann, "The Concept of 'Christus Medicus' in St. Augustine," *Traditio* 10 (1954), 1-28.

17. Opto te incolumem videre, et sicubi totus es, oro ne diutius me lateas. Vale (Fracassetti, *Epistolae,* 3:280; Cosenza, *Petrarch's Letters,* p. 89).

18. Et fortasse nunc apud aliquem totus es (Fracassetti, *Epistolae,* 3:278; Cosenza, *Petrarch's Letters,* p. 85).

19. Remigio Sabbadini, *Le Scoperte dei codici latini e greci ne' secoli, XIV e XV,* rev. and ed. Eugenio Garin (Florence: Sansoni, 1967), 1:78. For an older account, see J. E. Sandys, *A History of Classical Scholarship* (Cambridge: Cambridge University Press, 1908), 2:27. For further bibliography on Poggio's four expeditions, see the excellent account of Rudolf Pfeiffer, *History of Classical Scholarship from 1300 to 1850* (Oxford: Oxford University Press, Clarendon Press, 1976), pp. 31-34.

20. Vtque Camillus secundus a romulo conditor dictus est: qui ille statuit urbem. hic amissam restituit. Sic tu omnium quae iam amissa: tua virtute ac diligentia nobis restituta fuerint secundus auctor: merito nuncupabere. (*Epistolarum familiarium libri VIII,* ed. Antonio Moreto and Girolamo Squarciafico [Venice: Damianus de Gorgonzola and Petrus de Quarengis, 1495], bk. 4, ltr. 5, n. p.; Phyllis Gordan, trans., *Two Renaissance Book Hunters* [New York: Columbia University Press, 1974], p. 191. I cite the Latin text of 1495 with all abbreviations expanded).

21. Quintilianus enim prius lacer: atque discerptus concta membra sua per te recuperabit. Vidi enim capita librorum Totus est: cum uix nobis media pars & ea ipsa lacera superesset (Moreto and Squarciafico, *Epistolarum,* n. p.; Gordan, *Book Hunters,* p. 192).

22. O lucrum ingens. O insperatum gaudium. Ego te o Marce Fabi totum integrumque aspiciam. Et quanti tu mihi nunc eris: quem ego quamuis lacerum crudeliter ora: Ora manusque ambas: populataque tempora raptis Auribus: & truncas inhonesto uulnere nares. Tamen propter decorem tuum in deliciis habebam (Moreto and Squarciafico, *Epistolarum,* n. p.; Gordan, *Book Hunters,* p. 192).

23. Nos utentes ad exprimendam animi virtutem, ab reliquis animantibus segregamur. Permagna igitur habenda est gratia tum reliquarum liberalium artium inventoribus, tum vel praecipue iis, qui dicendi praecepta, et normam quandam perfecte loquendi suo studio, et diligentia nobis tradiderunt. Effecerunt enim, ut qua in re homines caeteris animantibus maxime praestant, nos ipsos etiam homines antecelleremus (*Poggii Epistolae,* ed. Thomas de Tonellis [Florence: Typis L. Marchini, 1832], bk. I, ltr. 5, vol. I, p. 26; reprinted in *Poggii Opera Omnia,* ed. Riccardo Fubini [Turin: Bottega d'Erasmo, 1964], vol. 3; Gordan, *Book Hunters,* p. 193).

24. Is vero apud nos antea, Italos dico, ita laceratus erat, ita circumcisus, culpa, ut opinor, temporum, ut nulla forma, nullus habitus hominis in eo recognosceretur (de Tonellis, *Epistolae,* 1:27; Consenza, *Petrarch's Letters,* p. 92).

25. Tute hominem vidisti hactenus (de Tonellis, *Epistolae,* 1:27; Gordan, *Book Hunters,* p. 194).

26.   Atque hic Priamiden laniatum corpore toto
       Deiphobum vidit, lacerum crudeliter ora,
       ora manusque ambas, populataque tempora raptis
       auribus et truncas inhonesto volnere naris.

                    Fairclough, *Virgil*

27.   squalentem barbam et concretos sanguine crinis

                    Fairclough, *Virgil*

28. Cum sit in pristinum habitum et dignitatem, in antiquam formam, atque integram valetudinem . . . restitutus (de Tonellis, *Epistolae,* 1:27; Gordan, *Book Hunters,* p. 194).

29. Nam si Marcus Tullius magnum praesefert gaudium pro Marco Marcello restituto ab exilio, et eo quidem tempore, quo Romae plures erant Marcelli similes, domi, forisque egregii, ac praestantes viri, quid nunc agere docti homines debent, et praesertim studiosi eloquentiae, cum singulare, et unicum lumen Romani nominis, quo extincto nihil praeter Ciceronem supererat, et eum modo simili lacerum, ac dispersum, non tantum ab exilio, sed ab ipso paene interitu revocaverimus? (de Tonellis, *Epistolae,* 1:27-28; Gordan, *Book Hunters,* p. 194.)

30. Ut monumenta litterarum e tenebris in lucem erueres (*Francisci Barbari et aliorum ad ipsum Epistolae,* ed. A. M. Quirini [Brescia: Joannes-Maria Rizzardi, 1743], p. 2; Gordan, *Book Hunters,* p. 196).

31. Tu Tertullianum, tu M. Fabium Quintilianum, tu Q. Asconium Pedianum, tu Lucretium, Silium Italicum, Marcellinum, tu Manilium Astronomum, Lucium Septimium, Valerium Flaccum, tu Caprum, Eutychium, Probum Grammaticos, tu complures alios, Bartholomaeo collega tuo adjutore, vel fato functos vita donastis, vel longo, ut ajunt, postliminio in Latium reduxistis (Quirini, *Epistolae,* p. 2; Gordan, *Book Hunters,* pp. 196-97).

32. Cum primus Homerum variis in locis per frustra dispersum . . . ex Asia totum Graeciam reportasset (Quirini, *Epistolae,* p. 2; Gordan, *Book Hunters,* p. 197).

33. Aesculapium inter Deos relatum accepimus, propterea quod cum alios nonnullos, tum Hippolytum supremum vitae diem functum, aliquot tamen post annos moriturum, ab inferis revocavit. Cui si populi, nationes, provinciae sacras aedes dicaverunt, quid vobis, nisi haec consuetudo jampridem obsolevisset, faciendum putarem? qui tot illustres, ac sapientissimos viros mortuos in perpetuum resuscitastis, quorum ingeniis, ac institutis non solum nos, sed etiam posteri bene dicere & honeste vivere poterunt (Quirini, *Epistolae,* pp. 2-3; Gordan, *Book Hunters,* p. 197).

34. Sic humanitatem, & disciplinam, quae ad bene beateque vivendum, & ornate dicendum accommodatae sunt, non modo privatis rationibus, sed urbibus, nationibus, universis denique

hominibus non mediocres utilitates afferre posse dubitandum non est (Quirini, *Epistolae*, p. 3; Gordan, *Book Hunters*, p. 198).

35. Equidem si present montes faciles transitus: & solitudines inuie apertum notumque iter. Si flumina uada: & maria tranquillas undas: ac transfretanti emittat ab antro Aeolus uentos tam ualidos quam secundos: & quod maius est: sint Argiphontis talaria aurea uolucri cuicumque homini alligata pedibus: & pro uotis quocumque libuerit euolet: uix tam longos terrarum marisque tractus. etiam si illi presteret permaxima seculorum annositas ne dum aliud agat: solum poterit peragrasse (*Genealogia Deorum Gentilium* [Venice: Wendelin von Speyer, 1472], n. p.; Charles Osgood, trans., *Boccaccio on Poetry*, 2nd ed. [New York: Bobbs-Merrill, 1956], pp. 5-6. I cite the Latin text of 1472 with abbreviations expanded).

36. Tam solide: tam perspicax ingenium: tamque tenax memoria: ut omnia queat uidere apposita: & intelligere uisa: & intellecta seruare: & demum calamo etiam exarare: & in opus collecta deducere. (*Genealogia*, n. p.; Osgood, *Boccaccio*, p. 6).

37. Si omnia legero littora & montuosa etiam nemora: scrobes & antra: si opus sit peragrauero pedibus: ad inferos usque descendere & Dedalus alter factus: ad aethera transuolauero undique (*Genealogia*, n. p.; Osgood, *Boccaccio*, p. 10).

38. Non aliter quam si per uastum litus ingentis naufragii fragmenta colligerem: sparsas per infinita poene uolumina deorum gentilium reliquas colligam: quas comperiam: & collectas euo diminutas atque semessas & fere attritas in unum genealogie corpus: quo potero ordine . . . redigam (*Genealogia*, n. p.; Osgood, *Boccaccio*, pp. 10-11).

39. Corpus huiusmodi habere perfectum. multum quippe: & utinam non membrorum plurium & fortasse distortum seu contractum gibbosumque habendum est. Iam rationibus premonstratis (*Genealogia*, n. p.; Osgood, *Boccaccio*, p. 11).

40. Preter artificium fingentium poetarum & futilium deorum consanguinitates & affinitates explicitas: naturalia quedam uidebis tanto occultata misterio ut mireris: sic & procerum gesta moresque non per omne trivium euagantia (*Genealogia*, n. p.; Osgood, *Boccaccio*, p. 12).

41. Satis aduertere possum quid mihi faciendum sit: qui inter fragosa uetustatis aspreta & aculeos odiorum membratim discerptum attritum & in cineres fere redactum ingens olim corpus deorum procerumque gentilium nunc huc illuc collecturus: & quasi esculapius alter ad instar hippolyti

consolidaturus sum (*Genealogia*, n. p.; Osgood, *Boccaccio*, p. 13).

42. See Chiarenza, "Hippolytus' Exile," pp. 65-66.

Salvatore I. Camporeale (essay date 2001)

SOURCE: Camporeale, Salvatore I. "Poggio Bracciolini versus Lorenzo Valla: The *Orationes in Laurentium Vallam*." In *Perspectives on Early Modern and Modern Intellectual History: Essays in Honor of Nancy S. Struever,* edited by Joseph Marino and Melinda W. Schlitt, pp. 27-48. Rochester, N.Y.: University of Rochester Press, 2001.

[*In the following essay, Camporeale considers the dispute between Poggio and Valla as reflecting opposing views of humanism. He also examines Erasmus's unflattering evaluation of the dispute, casting Poggio as an uneducated, indecent "petty clerk."*]

Humanist culture spread throughout Europe and reached its highest flourishing on the last decades of the fifteenth and the first half of the sixteenth century. The epistolary of Erasmus is rightly considered as a primary source for the unravelling of the densely woven fabric of Renaissance humanism at the turn of the sixteenth century. It provides a retrospective insight into the birth and early development of Renaissance humanism, a rich mine of information about its origins and the ways the *humanae litterae* were studied in the early fifteenth century. At the same time, Erasmus' historical and theoretical comments and judgments are constantly focused on the many facets of his own contemporary humanism, which by the first decades of the sixteenth century are hardly to be described as unified.[1]

ERASMUS' DEFENSE OF LORENZO VALLA

Concerning the question of the origins and first developments of humanism in Italy in the early decades of the fifteenth century, the exchange of letters in the summer of 1489 between Erasmus and Cornelius Gherard, embodies in almost emblematic fashion contrasting points of view.[2]

Erasmus writing from Steyn, and his friend Gherard replying from Lopsen (near Gouda), discuss the controversy between Poggio Bracciolini and Lorenzo Valla that had taken place in 1452-53. Erasmus and Gherard are familiar with Bracciolini's text (the ***Orationes in L. Vallam*** or ***Invectivae***) and with that of Valla (the *Antidota in Pogium*). And they know both the immediate circumstances and later developments which surrounded the controversy between the two Italian humanists.

In his letter to Gherard of June 1489, Erasmus notes that the study of Latin and Greek literature has become widely diffused in Northern Europe. He points to Agricola (who had just died a few years earlier, in 1485) and to his disciples and followers as the most important promoters of the new culture in the Netherlands, Rheinlands and Westphalia—in "our Germany," as he puts it. But this new culture has its roots in Italy, and the first humanists were Italians. Erasmus mentions some of these: Aeneas Silvius Piccolomini, Agostino Dati, Guarino Veronese, Poggio Bracciolini, Gasparino Barzizza. But for him the most important are Lorenzo Valla and Francesco Filelfo, and the former, author of the *Elegantiae,* laid the foundations for the new classical studies.[3]

Gherard is basically in agreement with Erasmus. Nonetheless in his reply of July 1489, he reminds Erasmus of Poggio's criticisms of Valla's works in general, and the *Elegantiae* in particular. Gherard's intended reference to Poggio's *Orationes* is clear, and it provoked a detailed response from Erasmus. This response, the first complete statement of Erasmus' position in regard to Valla's works and to the Poggio-Valla controversy, is nothing less than a *defensio* of Valla and his humanism.[4]

Let us consider the salient features of this defense. Above all, Erasmus rejects the commonly held image of Valla. This, he says, is derived solely from Bracciolini's criticisms of him. The idea that Valla was conceited, sarcastic, and hyper critical, and that his work was concerned with linguistic trivia, has its source in Poggio's anti-Valla writings. From the same source comes the idea that Poggio himself was the scourge of intellectual dishonesty and champion of genuine culture. Instead, Erasmus continues, an attentive reading of the evidence regarding the Poggio-Valla controversy leads to almost opposite conclusions. While Bracciolini was distinguished for his talents as a stylist and for his recovery of ancient *loquentia* (in the Ciceronian sense), he was not the equal of Valla. Going beyond the *loquentia* of Poggio, Valla vanquished his Florentine rival through his mastery of *eloquentia* and *eruditio.*[5]

By alluding to *eloquentia* and *eruditio,* Erasmus couches his argument in the terminology of classical rhetoric. *Eloquentia* concerns grammar and syntax. *Eruditio,* instead, refers to the historical formation of a language, and its literary documents. It is precisely in terms of *eloquentia* and *eruditio* that Valla is superior to Bracciolini. The work of J. W. Aldridge on the hermeneutics of Erasmus has demonstrated the richness and importance of this word—*eruditio*—in Erasmus' writings. For Erasmus, *eruditio* meant the analysis of texts by means of philological, historical, and theological criticism.[6]

Taking Erasmus' retrospective evaluation of the Poggio-Valla controversy as my point of departure, I shall now examine the *Orationes in L. Vallam* in greater detail. At the end, having explored the complex interrelationship between the two Italian humanists' theoretical stand through a closer reading of their own texts, I will return to Erasmus.[7]

The Literary Debate between Poggio and Valla

In February of 1452, Bracciolini composed an *Oratio in L. Vallam.* For the first time, Bracciolini was publicly criticizing the *Elegantiae* and Valla's method in academic and private teaching. Valla replied with the three "books" of the *Antidotum in Pogium,* written between May and June of 1452. Within six months, came Bracciolini's response, this time in a trilogy of *Orationes,* in which he dealt with Valla's writings in a thoroughgoing fashion. He considered them, along with Valla's lifestyle and ideological pursuit, within the context of contemporary Roman humanistic ambience. At the same time, Valla expanded his own earlier *Antidotum* with an *Apologus* (in two "acts"). But, learning of the *First Oratio* in Poggio's trilogy, Valla put aside the unfinished *Apologus* in order to write a second *Antidotum in Pogium.* This text, which I have described elsewhere as an "apologia pro vita sua," was written in a short span of weeks, March through April of 1453. Yet, before Valla could publish it, Bracciolini had written a *Fifth Oratio,* this time confronting Valla's *Apologus.*

In brief, the controversy began early 1452 and ended in the first half of 1453. It produced, on Bracciolini's part, five *Orationes in L. Vallam,* written in three distinct moments, though close together in time. Their sequence was, first, *Oratio I,* then the trilogy of *Orationes II, III,* and *IV,* and finally the last *Oratio V.* Valla's contribution was the *Antidotum I,* the *Apologus,* and the *Antidotum II.* I have used the designation *Orationes* for Bracciolini's writings and not *Invectivae,* because the former is the title given by their author whereas the latter, "invectivae," was the term by which Valla referred to them in the debate. Interestingly, they were and are more widely known, both in manuscripts and printed publications, by Valla's title for them.[8]

The controversy took place within the cultural circle of the Roman curia where both humanists were employed by Nicholas V. Valla also taught grammar privately and held the chair of rhetoric at the *Studium Urbis,* beginning in the academic year of 1450-51. While Valla thus remained in Rome working for Popes Nicholas V and Callixtus III and teaching, Poggio left Rome for Florence in the summer of 1453. The Florentine Signoria had appointed him as chancellor on April 27, three days after the death of Carlo Marsuppini, the preceding chancellor in office.

Poggio's move to Florence ended his direct confrontation with Valla. Yet, it also spread the controversy to other humanist centers, and scholars from Naples to Venice joined the ranks of either "poggiani" or "laurenziani." Positions hardened, and despite the efforts of Francesco Barbaro, Filelfo, Tommasi, and others to reconcile the protagonists of the controversy, they remained bitterly opposed. These later developments, in which they continued to elaborate new points of disagreement, are not of central interest here.[9]

Bracciolini's *Orationes* are at once a critique of the theoretical stand and related fundamental assumptions of Valla's humanism and a moral denunciation of Valla's personality as lacking any intellectual integrity and ethical norms. Thus, the discussion of theory is liberally peppered with stinging sarcasm. Valla's position is made to seem comic and almost grotesque, even while the most serious points of debate are under discussion. No occasion for ridiculing his adversary is missed: Valla's education, his lifestyle, and even his appearance are scourged with sarcastic irony, edging to insult. The figure of Valla as invented by Bracciolini is an extraordinary one: an eccentric, almost monstrous character, embodying the radical intellectual of the new humanist culture. For Erasmus, Bracciolini's skill in painting this portrait demonstrates a virtuosic application of his Latin *loquentia*. By a high literary standard, the *Orationes* of Braccioli are to be considered an exemplary work of epideictic oration, the third function of rhetoric, which consists in the oratory skill of praise and blame (*ars laudandi et vituperandi*) but here reduced in reality totally to the order of blame (*ad vituperandum*). All of the criticisms leveled against Valla by Bracciolini arise from Valla's constant and overall radicalism. Valla sets himself up as supreme judge and master of the classical and postclassical tradition, as well as of the Christian patristic and medieval tradition, but in reality a "new Maxentius, desecrator of temples and humanity." He thinks himself to be better than his contemporaries and is ever engaged in contradicting them. He goes even further, claiming that future generations will applaud his work, considering it the indispensable basis for further research. His own conceit is the sole criterion by which Valla judges past, present, and future. He sees himself as the "universal man," possessing definitive understanding of all texts, and he believes in the absolute certainty of his method of investigation. So inflated is his idea of himself that he seems superhuman, "as having in his hands the power of turning at will the wheel of fortune."

Valla's cultural radicalism is, in Bracciolini's view, expressed, or better, enacted, in his provocative nonconformity. So extreme is this nonconformity of Valla's that it seems to be his only rule of behavior. His is a life outside of every moral code: he rejects sexual restraints, disdains the basic rules of social comportment,

directs sarcasm at both people and institutions whether political or academic, is unhealthy in his eating habits, careless in dress, and crude in his manner. His whole person is repugnant, and his dead-white, emaciated face arouses hatred in all who see him.

This is Bracciolini's image of Valla. He undoubtedly uses antivallan precedents (such as the "Invectivae" of Bartolomeo Fazio) and other literary sources (such as the personage Demea in the *Adelphi* of Terence). But Bracciolini gives great concreteness and veracity to his discourse, collecting actual references and facts, circumstances situated in time and place: all a series of documented events and occasions conveyed by contemporary testimony. The reader of the *Orationes* finds himself persuaded of the truth of the account. Moreover, the portrait is drawn in such a way as to seem, in every respect, the opposite of Poggio himself. At the same time that he mocked Valla, Poggio boasted of his own career in the papal curia, and of the dignity and prestige to which he had been rising at most in that circle. A reading of his *Orationes* in the light of the Freudian theory of reaction-formation might suggest that Poggio was simultaneously obsessed and fascinated by Valla's personality, his originality, and his importance for the new culture. Support for such an interpretation, I think, is provided by the fact that Poggio had his children educated by none other than the hated Valla!

Even from an objective standpoint, however, Poggio was undoubtedly correct in pointing to Valla's nonconformity and radicalism as essential components of his writings and cultural activity. This led him to call for Valla's condemnation as a "heretic" who should be burnt at the stake. He repeats this accusation several times, not only in the *Orationes* but also in his private correspondence. And as late as 1454, in a letter to Tommasi, Poggio desires for Valla the same punishment which he saw meted out to Jerome of Prague at the time of the Council of Constance.[10]

The controversy between Bracciolini and Valla was thus not merely a formal literary duel as conventional historiography may have been claiming. Instead, far more profoundly, it raises questions about the origins and nature of the early humanism, and about its later development in the fifteenth to the first decades of the sixteenth century. It is therefore of importance to investigate the main issues taken up and questioned by the *Orationes* of Poggio.

POGGIO'S *ORATIONES* AND VALLA'S *ANTIDOTA*

The **First Oratio** is dedicated to the discussion of Valla's *Elegantiae*. Bracciolini singles out and evaluates Valla's original contribution both in terms of content and method. His critique is brought to a total rejection of the *Elegantiae,* with the motivation that Valla by his work is undermining the whole of Latin culture with unhesitating criticism of classical and Christian literature. Valla "with a certain savage enmity condemns and spurns all of those most learned men of antiquity, whose *memoria* had been celebrated with the highest praise and veneration for so many a century." Classical and Christian literary testimonies of the past—argues Bracciolini in dissension with Valla—possess knowledge and wisdom so authoritative (*auctoritas*) that they are not to be questioned according to criterion of "truth" and "falsity"; such a criterion cannot be properly applied to them. Naturally, it is allowed after adequate investigation to come to prefer or privilege some authors instead of others, or choose poetry and/or prose models as more suitable for emulation, always of course drawing from the most correct Latin texts. These philological analyses contribute to the renewal of the *humanae litterae.* But it is "madness" on the part of Valla to imagine that he has the right to discover "errors and deceits" within the classical and Christian tradition. This tradition, as expounded and substantiated by the great authors of the past, expresses inalienable values; it is valid in the absolute insofar as it constitutes the "memory" of the West, the origin and foundation of our culture as a universal norm of thinking and living. For this reason, to that *traditio* has been accorded the highest value for more than a thousand years—in Bracciolini's words, "most highly venerated by all peoples." Arguing forcefully on these premises, Bracciolini could not but utterly reject the *Elegantiae* of Valla.

At this point before going further, we have to examine in more general and comprehensive terms the different conceptions held by Bracciolini and Valla concerning the revival of classical and Christian literature. In reality it was that theoretical diversity about the meaning of cultural rebirth that came to be both the immediate context and the ultimate motivation of the controversy. Both Bracciolini and Valla felt that humanistic rebirth had to be authentic renewal of classical and Christian tradition. But they differed on *how* this had to be done and on *what* had to be assumed as being its very content. For Bracciolini, the recovery of the ancient cultural tradition had to be guided by *imitatio.* Understood as a method and also as a process, *imitatio* implied studied recovery of the past and creative assimilation. But going beyond the limits of Poggio's approach, Valla applied a historical-philological analysis to classical and Christian literature. No longer relying only on *imitatio,* Valla intended first, and then implemented, a new dimension into that method, that of "critical" investigation. Thus "imitatio" came to imply at its very foundation the *eruditio,* the analysis of texts by means of philological, historical, and theological criticism. And consequently "eruditio," a specifically philological heuristic technique, led inevitably to a new historicism and

to a recognition of relativity in regard to both textual form and content. And, moreover, this new approach was applied to all literary production from antiquity to the present day, not exempting even the most authoritative authors. It is in this sense that the *Elegantiae* may be considered as the first attempt at synchronic and diachronic analysis of Latin language and Latin literature.[11]

Valla had clear consciousness that with his *Elegantiae* he had introduced a new tool of research ("eruditio") to humanistic endeavors, and that with this he had gone far beyond the earlier approach ("imitatio") to classical and Christian literature. The prefaces to the individual books which comprise the *Elegantiae* testify to this awareness. And it is no accident that Bracciolini refers often in his **First Oratio** precisely to these *proemii* in which the new method was systematically expounded. Bracciolini and Valla both saw that humanistic studies were opening out into new directions, although their feelings about the wisdom of this were diametrically opposed. The split between the formal "imitatio" and the critical "eruditio" introduced by Valla's *Elegantiae* led Bracciolini to write that one had now to speak of two schools ("scholae") of humanist studies: these were the former one ("illa prior," "illa nostra antiqua") of which Guarino Veronese was the last representative, and the new school, that of Valla and his followers. The latter, for Poggio, were like conspirators plotting the "great transgression" of that humanist culture whose first promoter had been Petrarch.[12]

Next in importance to the **First Oratio** is the **Second Oratio** in which Bracciolini delineates the areas of his disagreement with Valla in greater detail. While the **First Oratio** is restricted to a critique of the *Elegantiae,* the second takes up Valla's entire literary production. The analysis pin-points the basic position of Valla and retraces the implications of his position. Valla, after all, had proclaimed himself to be the all-knowledgeable intellectual ("grammaticus," "rhetor," "philosophus," "mathematicus," "theologus") whose work was acclaimed by specialists in every branch of doctrine.[13] It was therefore up to Bracciolini to pass in review these various aspects of Valla's activity, pointing out errors and lies. Although the *Elegantiae* entertain the focal point of controversy, in the **Second Oratio** Poggio's real target is Valla's criticism of philosophical and theological language and speculation.

In Poggio's view, Valla's *Dialecticae disputationes* undermines the linguistic and conceptual foundations of Aristotelianism and of the philosophical and theological works inspired by the Stagirite—from Boethius to Albertus Magnus, Thomas Aquinas, and the major part of the Schoolmen. The three books of the *Disputationes* had applied a philological method of analysis to the key words of the metaphysical system of Scholasticism and to the structure of the Aristotelian syllogistic argumentation, only to conclude that the whole of Scholastic philosophical language is nothing but an agglomeration of senseless verbal expressions. But Valla goes even further, writes Poggio. Having attacked the ontological foundation of Aristotelian metaphysics, logic, physics, and ethics, he passes to theology. In his *De libero arbitrio,* Valla opposes Augustine's and Boethius' position on freedom and predestination. And not only this: according to Poggio, Valla's rejection of Boethius' definition of "persona" makes his position on the dogma of the Trinity heterodoxical with respect to patristic and postpatristic theology.[14] Finally, Valla with his *Adnotationes* to the New Testament is edging at the extreme of intellectual and ethical perversion. Here, even the Latin version of the New Testament, the Vulgate, is subject to a radical philological analysis by which Valla is brought to the unprecedented assertion that the Greek New Testament should take its place as the primary text in the absolute of Christian revelation. Valla calls for the dethroning of "Jerome's" Vulgate in favor of the *veritas graeca* of the original New Testament text.[15] In so doing, Valla imperils the traditional authority of the Latin text in the Western Church, insofar as for him the Vulgate, being a "translation," may have only minimal relative value, and not the primary absolute validity of the original Greek of the sacred text. Yet, argues the Florentine humanist, it is precisely that Latin version, the Vulgate, which has served as the primary source for theological discourse in the West from the beginnings of Latin Christianity and, even earlier, as ground and source of dogmatic and liturgical language in the Western Church. This, in brief, is the content of Poggio's *Second Oratio.* It must be emphasized that Poggio attains here full comprehension of Valla's cultural position and defines it with perfect clarity. Because of this, the *Second Oratio* has always been a crucial tool for subsequent historiography and investigations on the life and thought of Valla and his writings.[16]

Earlier, I noted that the split between *imitatio* and *eruditio* was the key area of disagreement between Bracciolini and Valla. Now, using the *Second Oratio,* we can pursue this point further. A precise understanding of this issue is necessary in order to grasp the essential differences between the two humanists—differences which by now should be apparent as clearly underlying the entire controversy.

With the first and especially the *Second Oratio,* Poggio had shown that he had fully understood meaning and import of Valla's critical approach. It did not escape him that for Valla, language, when considered morphologically and semantically, became the paradigm of cultural enquiry. And he realized also that implementing such a tool of investigation had far-reaching implications. Since all modes of knowledge are expressed in words and proceed by argumentation, the analysis of

the linguistic structure of a specific doctrine meant analyzing the knowledgeable content of that doctrine at its very foundations. The standard approach to such analysis is the discipline of rhetoric. Thus rhetoric, the art of persuasion and technique of formal discourse, became with Valla the science of language in general and the primary tool for analyzing the process and specific content of argumentation in any branch of knowledge. Thus rhetoric was assumed by Valla as an alternate *science-of-method,* a new *Wissenschaftslehre.*[17]

Once Valla had assumed the philological criticism as his new method of analytical and historical investigation of the *humanae litterae* (classical Greek and Latin literature), he expanded the same methodology to the *divinae litterae* (the biblical Judeo-Christian literature, the "sacred scriptures"). Valla considered such a transfer of methodology not only legitimate but also necessary, in order to provide research alternative tools to Scholasticism and thus overcome the crisis in which contemporary theology had floundered.[18] Although profane (*humanae*) and sacred (*divinae*) literature (*litterae*) may profoundly differ in content, form, and contextual formation, the fact that both consist of historical languages and written texts means that they fall under the same linguistic and scriptural laws; and as such, they are to be subject to a single methodology: the critical and historical analysis of philology. On this overarching premise (which will be heavily disputed by his own contemporary humanists and schoolmen alike, and will be increasingly questioned through the century, reaching its climax with Erasmus) Valla was to reopen the argument and make the movement from classical to biblical philology in Western culture for the first time since Jerome.[19] By contrast, Bracciolini denied the possibility of such an approach to the biblical literature. For him, the Judeo-Christian texts of revelation could not be subject, by merit of its specific content and formation, to historical and philological analysis as such. Thus, while Valla believed and promoted the idea that humanist research and theological speculation could, indeed should, interpenetrate, insofar as the latter could profit from the former, for Poggio, on the contrary, humanism and theology were entirely different areas of inquiry whose separateness had to be maintained. Humanism and theology were, for him, autonomous subject matters of investigation, and with this he came to negate and directly undermine the assumption on which Valla had transferred philological criticism from classical to biblical literature, Jewish and Christian. Valla's and Bracciolini's overt and continuing disagreement on the possibility of a marriage between "humanism," as philological investigation of classical literature, and "theology," as biblical exegesis, has to be considered as emblematic of a conflict already running deep through the literary renaissance of the early fifteenth century, and having its climax in depth and expansion during the next century with Erasmus and the coming of the Reformation and the Counter-Reformation.

Poggio's correspondence with friendly humanists and other political figures sheds further light on the issues argued in the *Orationes.* The embattled tone of some of these letters, written during the controversy and in the years following it, betrays his sense of being at a loss to cope with Valla's ideas. One detects his sense of having been cast up on unknown shores, or of having discovered the limitless spaces of a new continent. His feeling that Valla had gone beyond all intellectual limits and broken the boundaries of reason, is a recurrent theme of the *Orationes.* Precisely because Valla's work seems outside of, or in opposition to, any known philosophical and/or theological tradition, it is almost impossible for Bracciolini to test its validity through references and comparisons. And since Valla's position is no longer within the realm of reason, it must surely lie within the realm of madness. The theme of Valla's *dementia* is reiterated at length in the five *Orationes.* Bracciolini's need to dramatize this triumph of lunacy leads him to parody, to depict Valla as a full comical personage, bordering on the grotesque.

Poggio concentrates all his literary skill on the task of leading Valla through a carnivalesque triumph whose itinerary goes from earth (the streets of imperial Rome), to the inferno (of Satan and his demons), to the Elysian fields of immortal heroes, and finally back on earth into Valla's miserable hut. In the last pages of the *First Oratio*—but it will be a recurring topic in the other four—Poggio writes: "Let us decree for and dedicate to Valla, prince of all things that creep and swarm over the surface of the earth, a majestic triumph, similar to those which my fellow citizens dedicate to lunatics during carnival time in Florence."[20]

Poggio paints a detailed scene of this witless triumph, intended as a parody of the writings and personality of Valla. When in the *Third Oratio* Valla is conducted to Hell, he is invited by Satan and his demons to proclaim himself the grand heresiarch of Christianity, receiving from them lordship over all earthly knowledge and sciences.[21] Finally, in the *Fourth Oratio,* we find Valla in the Elysian fields, when he aspires to be counted among the immortals, to share in the glory of the blessed. The merit of his request is debated by Homer and Aristotle, Cicero and Theophrastus, together with other great grammarians, lawyers, and writers of antiquity. In his defense, Valla expounds his work to them. But his explanations evoke profound disdain; the humanist is expelled from the Elysian fields. The masses welcome him at the exit of the Elysian fields and escort him at home, riding backwards on an ass, crowned with animal intestines and accompanied by a din of deafening music.[22] Thus, with the carnivalesque mockery of the

charivari and *Katzenmusik,* Poggio brings his philippic against Valla to a close.

These passages of the *Orationes* employ modes of expression drawn from popular humor and carnival. The wild gaiety of popular festivals informs the hyperbolic language, grotesque images, and references to current events in Poggio's parody. So, too, the mocking triumph of lunatics recalls carnival themes. Michail Bakhtin's work, *Rabelais,* comes to mind in this context, for it seems to me that Poggio's *Orationes* provide strong support for the central thesis of his book. In Bakhtin's words: "In Renaissance literature . . . the very concept that the Renaissance held of the world, was deeply permeated by a carnivalesque perception of reality, and often took on its forms and symbols."[23]

THE FRUITION OF VALLA'S BIBLICAL EXEGESIS BY ERASMUS

My comments on the *Orationes in L. Vallam* have begun with a consideration of the letters exchanged between Erasmus and Gherard in 1489. I shall now return to Erasmus' correspondence with Gherard to reconsider a further aspect of those letters before concluding the present contribution. What follows is intended as an outline for a reassessment of the after effects of the Valla-Bracciolini controversy—its impact on the theological and exegetical disputes about Scriptures, which reoccurred among the Northern humanists in the first decades of the sixteenth century.[24]

In 1505 Erasmus discovered a manuscript of Valla's *Adnotationes in Novum Testamentum* in the library of Parc monastery, near Louvain. Before having this previously unpublished work printed, Erasmus thought it prudent to obtain the protection of a member of the Roman curia: Christopher Fisher. A long dedicatory letter to Fisher serves as introduction to the publication of the Valla's *Adnotationes.* In it, Erasmus develops the *defensio* of Valla we have already encountered in his letter to Gherard of August 1489. Once again, he declares his desire to write an apologia in favor of the Roman humanist, defending Valla from the *invidia,* past and present, of ancient and contemporary scholars in biblical disciplines.[25]

The contrast that Erasmus draws between Bracciolini and Valla is extremely sharp. Indeed, his negative assessment of the former hardly does justice to Poggio's complexity. "Poggio," he says, "is a petty clerk so uneducated that even if he were not indecent he would still not be worth reading, and so indecent that he would deserve to be rejected by good men however learned he was."[26] Valla, on the other hand, is praised for his research in classical and Christian literature, and in general for his literary production. Valla's endeavor and production were both informed by the pursuit of truth, underlines Erasmus. And the assumption of a new methodology, philological analysis, and consequent implementation of such a method, which aroused the opposition of many among his contemporaries, was deemed by the Roman humanist not only desirable and appropriate but also a scholarly obligation. Thus, following on the path of Quintilian, Valla sought to demonstrate (especially in the *Elegantiae*) that, while not every classical writer was worth imitating, all classical literature was indeed to be searched for and analytically studied. In sum: for Erasmus, Valla's *mordacitas*—his radical criticism of contemporary humanism for a comprehensive philological and historical enquiry of the ancient literary legacy—was more decisive and useful for the renaissance of the humanities than the formal aesthetic appreciation with which many of his fellow humanists handled classical and Christian literature.[27]

The main focus of Erasmus' apology is, however, Valla's biblical exegesis and his transaction of philological criticism from classical to biblical literature. In so doing, Erasmus was resuming the argumentation of Valla's self-defense in the *Antidotum I* against Bracciolini, and of his *Adnotationes in Novum Testamentum,* and expanding the context of that self-defense.[28] Erasmus' own contribution here is his insistence on the continuity between the patristic tradition, particularly Jerome, and Valla's work, which is dependent on that tradition. Far from being heterodox, the *Adnotationes* are obedient to the decrees of the Church councils and norms of canon law. All language, even the language of theology—writes Erasmus—is subject to the laws of grammar. Following on this premise, Erasmus continues:

> Theology herself, the queen of all sciences, will not be offended if some share is claimed in her and due deference shown to her by her humble attendant Grammar. For, though Grammar is of less consequence in some men's eyes, no help is more indispensable than hers. She is concerned with small details, but details such as have always been indispensable for the attainment of greatness. Perhaps she discusses trivial questions, but these have important corollaries. If they protest that a theologian is too grand to be bound by rules of grammar, and that the whole business of interpretation depends on the inspiration of the Holy Spirit, what a novel distinction is offered to theologians, who are to have the exclusive privilege of expressing themselves ungrammatically! But I should like them to explain the meaning of Jerome's remark to his friend Desiderius that "it is one thing to be a prophet, another to be an interpreter! In the one case the Holy Ghost prophesies the future; in the other scholarship, together with the resources of language, conveys the meaning it apprehends." Again, what point would there be in the advice from Jerome himself on the proper method of translating the Scriptures if the power to do so is bestowed by divine inspiration? Lastly, why has Paul been called more eloquent in the Hebrew tongue than in the Greek? But if it were possible for the translators of the Old Testament to make mistakes occasionally, especially where the faith is not impugned, could not the translators have done likewise in the New Testament? For Jerome indeed did not translate the latter so much as emend it, though moderately, leaving (as he himself testifies), the words of the text; and it is the words that Valla discusses with particular care.[29]

Erasmus has recourse to Jerome's *auctoritas* again in rebutting Poggio's other accusation of Valla—that by emending the Vulgate, Valla desecrated the most venerated text of Western Christianity. On this point, too, Erasmus is clear and firm. In reality, Valla had completed the task begun by Jerome and promoted by Pope Damasus. Valla's contribution, like Jerome's, was intended to combat the errors and superficiality of biblical exegesis flawed by insufficient command of Latin and Greek. While Valla brought to bear on the New Testament his linguistic skills and literary erudition, he did not forget that these texts were fundamental for Christianity. Moreover, asserts Erasmus, Valla's research was in conformity with the norms established by the Council of Vienne (1311-12), and later included in the *Constitutiones Clementinae*. These norms imposed the study of biblical language on students of theology, in order to secure a correct understanding of the Holy Scriptures.

HUMANIST THEOLOGY ON THE EVE OF REFORMATION

These, in brief, are the points which Erasmus makes in his 1505 introduction to the *Adnotationes* of Valla. He could not have foreseen that, despite the caution evidenced by his dedication of the printed text to Christopher Fisher, he himself would be criticized ten years later on the same grounds, and with arguments similar to those by which Valla had been attacked by Poggio. In 1514-15, Erasmus was completing the *Novum Instrumentum,* the first bilingual version of the New Testament. Before it left the press of Froben (Basel, March 1516), Martin van Dorp, spokesman for the Louvain theologians, denounced Erasmus on account of its audacious novelties. To Erasmus' reply, and van Dorp's counter-reply, was added Thomas More's *Epistola apologetica* on behalf of Erasmus. In the writings of these three, we recognize the Valla-Bracciolini controversy or, more precisely, its fundamental issues. The arguments of Erasmus and More were formulated first in Valla's *Antidota*; van Dorp reiterates the criticisms of Poggio's *Orationes*. Like Poggio, van Dorp believes that classical philology has no role in biblical exegesis and, therefore, that theological discussion can never be based on it. Retracing Poggio's steps, van Dorp writes: "Now the grammarians sit enthroned and act as censors of all other disciplines. They bring forth our new theology (*novam theologiam*) which will be born some day with the proverbial mouse." The Erasmus-More position is in perfect antithesis to that of van Dorp: philology is the best analytic tool for the epistemological re-foundation of all branches of knowledge, and therefore also for theology; that is, for the foundation of a new theology: *humanist theology.*[30]

Of course, the contexts of these two controversies—occurring respectively in 1452-53 and 1514-15—are different in important ways. The cultural dimensions and geographic extension of the later dispute (that of van Dorp, Erasmus, and More), on the eve of the Reformation, have resonances far beyond those of the Bracciolini-Valla controversy. Yet, in their essential outlines, these two events are closely related. The controversy between these two Quattrocento humanists was important for Italian humanists, dividing them into opposed camps on the question of the meaning and application of rhetoric. But its impact on Europeans humanists of the early sixteenth century was perhaps even more influential, serving to polarize those biblical and theological disputes which gave birth to the Reformation, the Council of Trent, and the Counter-Reformation.

Notes

1. See the recent study of Erasmus as a sixteenth century European humanist: Lisa Jardine, *Erasmus. Man of Letters: the Construction of Charisma in Print* (Princeton, 1993). For the Letters, *Opus epistolarum Des. Erasmi Roterodami,* 12 vols. (Oxford, 1906-58), eds., P. S. Allen et al.; English translation, *The Correspondence of Erasmus,* trans. R. A. B. Mynors and D. F. S. Thomson, annotated by Wallace K. Ferguson (Toronto, 1974-92), vols. 1-7, 10.

2. Erasmus, *Opus epistolarum,* cit. I, pp. 92-122, nn. 17-30; but also see, pp. 586ff. The letters of Erasmus and Gherard that are most relevant are nos. 22, 24, 26 and 29. Noting the same epistolary exchange between Erasmus and Gherard is Jacques Chomarat, *Erasme lecteur des "Elegantiae" de Valla,* in *Acta Conventus Neo-latini Amstelodamensis,* ed. P. Tuynman, G. C. Kuiper and E. Kessler (Monaco, 1979), pp. 206-43.

3. For the diffusion of humanism in the North and for consideration of the Italian humanists, Allen, *Erasmus,* I, n. 23, pp. 103ff. For the *Elegantiae,* I refer to the introduction to the works of Valla, M. Regoliosi, *Nel Cantiere del Valla. Elaborazione e montaggio delle "Elegantie"* (Roma: Bulzoni Editore, Humanistica 13, 1993), p. 137.

4. The reply of Gherard is in Allen, *Erasmus,* I, n. 24, pp. 109ff; the anti-Vallian critique seems to refer, particularly, *Oratio I* of Bracciolini. The epistolary defense of Erasmus, ibid., n. 26, pp. 112-15. Erasmus writes, ". . . quemadmodum apud Platonem Glauco vituperata iusticia Socratem ad iusticiae defensionem provocat, ita tu me ad Vallae

defensionem proliceres, recensens quam indignis conviciis stolidissimi barbariei mystae in virum literatissimum debacchentur." (113.14-17; ". . . just as Glaucon in Plato by reviling justice incites Socrates to undertake its defence, so you would draw me on to defend Valla by rehearsing the disgraceful slanders, the drunken ravings against a first-rate scholar, of perfect fools who have graduated in barbarism." Allen, *Erasmus,* I, n. 26, p. 45).

5. The discourse of Erasmus is important for several reasons beyond the Bracciolini-Valla controversy. To be noted are the considerations on the divergent opinions, rather frequent, about the culture of classical letters. It is also necessary to underline the reference to the debate between Girolamo and Rufino, concerning issues similar to those in the discussion between the two early Quattrocento Italians (Allen, *Erasmus,* p. 114.52). One also notes the three references from Terence, *Andria* 68, *Adelphi* 855, *Eunuchus* 251-53 (Allen, 54, 55, 60): "inevitably when one compares two individuals that behave in diametrically opposed ways, one finds among the multitude some parasite that lives in more servile conformity." Here, Erasmus follows a recurring topos in the *Antidota* of Valla. Noteworthy are two other passages of Erasmus' letter. The first: "Pogius hoc erat animo ut doctissimus haberi mallet quam reddi doctior. Quem ego sic inter eruditos poni feram ut non sit omnino a consortio barbarorum alienus; siquidem magis ille natura facundus quam eruditione, et plus habet loquentiae quam eloquentiae" (113.46-50; ". . . it was Poggio's nature to prefer to be regarded as most learned rather than to acquire more learning. I should myself accept his inclusion among scholars, with the reservation that he is not entirely remote from association with barbarous men, being naturally fluent rather than erudite and possessing a greater capacity for loquacity than eloquence," ibid., p. 46). With all probability—not noted in Allen, i.l.—Erasmus refers to Pliny, *Epist.* 5, 20.5: "Iulius Candidus non invenuste solet dicere aliud esse 'eloquentiam,' aliud 'loquentiam.' Nam eloquentia vix uni alteri, immo, si Marco Antonio credimus, nemini; haec vero, quam Candidus loquentiam appellat; multis atque etiam impudentissimo cuique maxime contigit."

The other Erasmian passage: "Quis tam exigui animi est, cuius pectus tantis invidiae angustiis concluditur, ut Vallam non et magnifice laudet et amet quam maxime; qui tanta industria, tanto studio, tantis sudoribus barbarorum ineptias refellit, literas pene sepultas ab interitu vindicavit, prisco eloquentiae splendori reddidit Italiam, doctis etiam id praestitit, ut posthac circunspectius loqui cogantur?" (115.103-8; ". . . is anyone so small-minded, so pinched at heart by the narrowest sort of ill-will, as not to accord generous praise and the warmest possible affection to Valla, who bestowed such intense industry, application, and exertion in combating the follies of the barbarians and rescuing literature from extinction when it was all but buried, in restoring Italy to her ancient literary glory, and even in conferring a benefit on scholars by obliging them to express themselves more carefully in future?," ibid., p. 48). As in this, so in the entire epistolary defense, Erasmus takes up themes, commonplaces and literary expressions that make up the Vallian Prefaces to the six books of the *Elegantiae*. The text of the Prefaces (Latin and Italian translation) is in *Prosatori latini del Quattrocento*, ed. E. Garin (Milano, 1952) pp. 594-631.

6. J. W. Aldridge, *The Hermeneutic of Erasmus*, (Zürich & Richmond, Virginia, 1966) pp. 57-97; J. J. Murphy, *Rhetoric in the Middle Ages: A History of Rhetorical Theory from St. Augustine to the Renaissance* (Berkeley, Los Angeles, London, 1974), pp. 23-26 and *passim; Renaissance Eloquence: Studies in the Theory and Practice of Renaissance Rhetoric*, ed. J. J. Murphy (Berkeley, Los Angeles, London, 1983); F. E. Cranz, "Quintilian as Ancient Thinker," *Rhetorica: A Journal of the History of Rhetoric* 13 (1995): 219-30; J. O. Ward, "Quintilian and the Rhetorical Revolution of the Middle Ages," ibid., pp. 231-84.

7. The Poggio/Valla controversy was the primary theme of my study, *Lorenzo Valla: Umanesimo e Teologia* (Firenze, 1972). The controversy and the writings which took place by the two humanists, its origin, context, and themes, serve as the basis of my analysis of Valla's entire work as well as my interpretive perspective. I have treated the controversy again in a contribution for *Poggio Bracciolini: 1380-1980. Nel VI centenario della nascita* (Firenze, 1982), entitled, "Poggio Bracciolini contro Lorenzo Valla. Le *Orationes in L. Vallam*," pp. 137-61. In this essay, focused on the "orationes" of Bracciolini and on the judgment given by Erasmus and other humanists in the early Cinquecento concerning this controversy, I sought to highlight the Poggian perspective on the debate in comparison to Valla, and the impact of that debate in the first half of the sixteenth century. Further developed in seminars and public lectures, that which is presented here is an up to date reworking of that 1982 study.

It is important to note, *Lorenzo Valla, Antidotum Primum: La prima apologia contro Poggio Bracciolini*, a critical edition with introduction and notes, edited by Ari Wesseling (Assen-Amsterdam, 1978). As the editor himself admits, he has amply used my 1972 study, in the introduction more than in the commentary, contributing to the critical edition of the text, and not helping better to contextualize the controversy between the two humanists. Also see, A. Wesseling, "Per l'edizione del secondo *Antidotum* contro Poggio Bracciolini," in *Lorenzo Valla e l'Umanesimo Italiano,* edited by O. Besomi and M. Regoliosi (Padova, 1986), pp. 133-39. The Bracciolini-Valla controversy was variously taken up again after my 1972 study in articles and essays. I limit myself here to two fundamental studies on the question of the "lingua latina," one of the themes of the debate between the two—studies also critical for comparison with my interpretation (1972) of the Vallian texts. These are, M. Tavoni, *Latino, grammatica, volgare: Storia di una questione umanistica* (Padova, 1984); A. Mazzocco, *Linguistic Theories in Dante and the Humanists: Studies of Language and Intellectual History in Late Medieval and Early Renaissance Italy* (Leiden and New York, 1993).

8. The texts of the controversy are found in the following editions: (1) Poggio, *Opera omnia*, 4 vols., edited by R. Fubini (Torino, 1964-69). The first volume reproduces, in anastatic edition, the 1538 Basel edition; the *Invectivae in L. Vallam* (taken from the fourth) comprises pp. 188-251. The second volume contains various writings of Bracciolini, edited and unedited, among which is the *Invectiva IV in L. Vallam,* pp. 865-85 (from cod. ms. of the Laurenziana of Firenze *90 sup. 7,* sec. XV). For the epistolary of Bracciolini, we now have the critical edition, Poggio Bracciolini, *Lettere,* 3 vols., ed. H. Harth (Firenze, 1984-87). (2) Laurentius Valla, *Opera,* 2 vols., ed. E. Garin (Torino, 1962). The first volume reproduces, in anastatic edition, the 1540 Basel folio edition. The *Antidota in Pogium* and the l'*Apologus* comprise pp. 253-389; for the text, often incorrect and *in lacunae,* it is necessary to use the autographed copy in Valla's *Lat. 8691* in the Bibliothèque Nationale, Paris. The second volume contains the unedited nonpublished writings, and the most up to date collection (since 1969) of Valla's letters. (3) To these publications of the Bottega d'Erasmo, one adds Lorenzo Valla, *Antidotum Primum,* ed. crit. of Wesseling (op. cit. n. 7). For the *Apologus,* there is the annotated edition of the Vallian autograph, referred to in Camporeale, *L. Valla,* pp. 469-534; in Tavoni, *Grammatica,* (op. cit. n. 7), pp. 260-73, partial critical edition of the *Apologus* ("secundus").

9. The incidents from the Bracciolini and Valla controversies in the Italian humanist circles and in the culture in general between the Quattro and

Cinquecento are treated amply in my *L. Valla,* pp. 374ff, with the relevant documentation. Essential with regard to these are, now, *Laurentii Valle Epistole,* edited by O. Besomi and M. Regoliosi (Padova, 1981), pp. 357-89; for the text of the correspondence and historical commentary of the editors, see *Lorenzo Valla e l'Umanesimo italiano,* (op. cit. n. 7), O. Besomi and M. Regoliosi, "Laurentii Valle Epistole: Addendum," pp. 77-110, and M. Davis, "Lettere inedite tra Valla e Perotti," pp. 94-106.

10. For the sections in which Bracciolini characterizes the physical and moral figure of Valla, see in particular, Poggio, *Opera* I, pp. 189-90, 197, 201-2, 209-10, 213, 215-18, 220-34, 243-48. For the "invectivae" of Bartolomeo Fazio, following the vulgate title and the letter of di Poggio to Tommasi, see *L. Valla,* pp. 28, 311-15, 399-402. Cf. the best critical edition with introduction and notes, *Laurentii Valle Antidotum in Facium,* ed. Mariangela Regoliosi (Padova, 1981).

11. "Il problema della *imitatio* nel primo Quattrocento. Differenze e controversia tra Bracciolini e Valla," *Annali d'Architettura* 9 (1997):149-54.

12. For *Oratio I,* see Poggio, *Opera* I, pp. 189, 190, 194-95, 200, 202-3, for the referred-to passages and, *passim* for the most complete of the Poggian discourse. Further, Camporeale, *L. Valla,* pp. 106ff; Camporeale, "Lorenzo Valla tra Medioevo e Rinascimento. 'L'Encomion s. Thomae'—1457," *Memorie Domenicane,* n.s. 7 (1976), pp. 110-43. Bracciolini speaks on various occasions of the "due scuole": *Lettere* III, pp. 240, 347, 408; and again, *Opera* II, p. 815 and *passim* in the Poggian invective, *In Nicolaum Perottum infamem pusionem,* an extremely significant text for the controversy in question. Here, one again refers to "tamquam novus Maxentius, deorum hominumque contemptor" e della "laurentiana coniuratio," pp. 801 and 802.

13. On the Roman humanist as the "uomo universale" of several branches of learning, see *Valle Antidotum in Facium,* ed. cit., pp. 370-400, pages that constitute a first "apologia pro vita sua" at the conclusion of his response to Fazio, taken up again in *Antidotum II in Pogium* (cf. Camporeale, *L. Valla,* p. 402). Again, the introduction of Lorch to the English translation, *Lorenzo Valla, On Pleasure—De Voluptate,* eds. A. Kent Hieatt and M. Panizza Lorch (New York, 1977); for "mathematicus," Poggio, *Opera* I, p. 240 (*Oratio III*), and Besomi and Regoliosi, "Laurentii Valle Epistole: Addendum II," op. cit. pp. 99-100.

14. Camporeale, *L. Valla. Umanesimo e teologia,* pp. 235-76 ("La questione trinitaria"), and now most

recently, C. Trinkaus, "Lorenzo Valla on the Problem of Speaking about the Trinity," *Journal of the History of Ideas* 57 (1996): 27-53.

15. Camporeale, *L. Valla,* pp. 277-403 ("Le *Adnotationes*: prima e seconda stesura"); Camporeale, "Lorenzo Valla tra Medioevo e Rinascimento," pp. 102-40, 141-86 (appendix with unedited text of the "Adnotationes"); J. H. Bentley, *Humanists and Holy Writ* (Princeton, 1983); Ch. S. Celenza, "Renaissance Humanism and the New Testament: Lorenzo Valla's Annotations to the Vulgate," *Journal of Medieval and Renaissance Studies* 24 (1994), pp. 33-52; P. Lombardi, *La Bibbia contes: Tra umanesimo e razionalismo* (Firenze, 1992), pp. 19-38.

16. I have written (of Poggio's part) of the *Adnotationes in Novum Testamentum.* In reality, in the *Orationes* of Bracciolini the reference to the New Testament exegetical work of Valla is to the *prima* draft of the same, the *Collatio Novi Testamenti* (after 1450). The *Adnotationes* constitute a later draft (dated from the last years of the life of the Roman humanist, between 1550 and 1557, the year of his death). Meanwhile, the first redaction (*Collatio*) remains unedited since the recent edition; Lorenzo Valla, *Collatio Novi Testamenti,* redazione inedita, edited by A. Perosa, (Firenze, 1970); the second (*Adnotationes*) was published by Erasmus in 1505, by Froben in Basel. See, Camporeale, *L. Valla. Umanesimo e teologia,* pp. 23-24, and 277-403. For the Vulgata, see the important observations in W. Ullmann, *Medieval Foundations of Renaissance Humanism* (London, 1977), pp. 35, 41, 111-12.

17. D. R. Kelley, *Foundations of Modern Historical Scholarship. Language, Law, and History in the French Renaissance* (New York & London, 1970), pp. 20-50; Camporeale, *L. Valla. Umanesimo e teologia,* cit. pp. 31-108; Camporeale, "Lorenzo Valla: la retorica come critica filologica e superamento della filosofia," AA.VV., *Ulisse. Enciclopedia della ricerca e della scoperta,* dir. L. Lombardo Radice (Roma, 1977) vol. 3, pp. 70-76, 78-80, 194-96.

18. Camporeale, *L. Valla,* pp. 209-33 ("La crisi della teologia contemporanea e il rinnovamento della teologia"); Camporeale, "Renaissance Humanism and the Origins of Humanist Theology," in *Humanity and Divinity in Renaissance and Reformation: Essays in Honor of Charles Trinkaus,* eds. J. W. O'Malley, T. M. Izbicki, and G. Christianson (New York, Köln, 1993), pp. 101-24.

19. The terms, *humanae litterae* and *studia humanitatis,* acquire greater specificity; see Ullmann, *Medieval Foundations,* passim, but es-

pecially, pp. 151ff and 20ff. From the Vallian perspective of the *studia humanitatis,* they necessarily must modify the *studia divinitatis.* See Camporeale, "Renaissance Humanism and the Origins of Humanist Theology," in *Humanity and Divinity in Renaissance and Reformation,* pp. 101-24.

20. ". . . decernemus ei triumphum et lauream coronam, ne amplius addubitari possit Vallam notrum stultorum atque insanorum principatum possidere. Itaque ut florentini solent in festis suis aliquando curru triumphali insanos vehere—quod est iucundissimum spectaculum—ita nos isti triumphum decernamus tanquam doctorum omnium victori, ob omnes gentes ingenii acumine superatas . . . ," Poggio, *Opera* I, p. 203.

21. Ibid., *Oratio III,* pp. 234-38.

22. "Hunc ergo poëtam laetamur—ends the *Oratio IV*—temporibus nostris datum, qui sit omnes priscos insania et dementia superaturus. Celebremus diem illius natalem et calicibus vino plenis agamus choreas, ut saltem inter ebrios aliquam laudem mereatur," *Opera* II, p. 885.

23. Michail Bakhtin, *L'opera di Rabelais e la cultura popolare. Riso, carnevale e festa nella tradizione medievale e rinascimentale* (Torino, 1979) p. 301, but for context, pp. 299-302. For the charivari see also N. Zemon Davis, *Le culture del popolo. Sapere, rituali e resistenze nella Francia del Cinquecento* (Torino, 1980), pp. 130-74, 189-91.

24. In addition, *L. Valla. Umanesimo e teologia,* pp. 277-403 cited in note 15. See also, S. Camporeale, "Da Lorenzo Valla a Tommaso Moro. Lo statuto umanistico della teologia," *Memorie Domenicane,* n.s. 4 (1973), pp. 9-102; the essay is dedicated to the dispute between Erasmus, van Dorp, and Thomas More—a dispute with which I will conclude the present contribution. Further, H. Holeczek, *Humanistische Bibelphilologie als Reformproblem bei Erasmus, Thomas More und William Tyndale* (Leiden, 1975), pp. 138-65; H. Holeczek, historical-critical introduction and bibliography to "Faksimile-Neudruck": *Erasmus, Novum Instrumentum, Basel 1516* (Stuttgart-Bad Cannstatt, 1986), pp. v-xli. Due to their lack of precise knowledge of New Testament biblical exegesis, both of Valla and of Erasmus' intense study of Valla's work, and notwithstanding the historiography on Valla that appeared in the 1970s in Italy and in the U. S., J. H. Bentley, *Humanists and Holy Writ: New Testament Scholarship in the Renaissance* (Princeton, 1983) and Holeczek, in the introduction cited above, have repeated the past historiographical errors; namely, that Erasmus had discovered the Vallian manuscript of the

Adnotationes in the monastery at Parc near Lovanio "by serendipity" or even "stumbled across" it (Bentley, pp. 116 and 35—cf. my review of the work in *Journal of Modern History,* 57 [1985]: 574s) and "zufällig" (Holeczek, p. xx). Quite the contrary: after his stay in England and the shift toward biblical studies that followed his sojourn (cf. G. Faludy, *Erasmus,* "The English Influence," pp. 73-111, New York, 1971), Erasmus consciously searched for Valla's work. The *Adnotationes* of Valla were already noted by Erasmus; he, in fact, had complete knowledge of the *Antidota* of Valla against Poggio, and Valla speaks of the *Adnotationes* in self-defense against Poggio—as also occurs in the correspondence between Erasmus and Gherard with which I began this present essay. Bentley and Holeczek were incorrect about the relation between Valla's biblical exegesis and that of Erasmus. To the preceding bibliography, one now adds, Cecilia Asso, *La teologia e la grammatica. La controversia tra Erasmo ed Edward Lee* (Firenze, 1993).

25. The text of the dedicatory letter to Fisher, in Allen (op. cit. n. 1) I, n. 182, pp. 406-12, with the annotations of the editor. Again, Erasmus refers to Terence, *Andria* 68: "obsequium amicos, veritas odium parit," already cited in the Vallian *defensio* of 1489 directed at Cornelius Gherard. I refer to one of the central passages of the Erasmian text, of which I will provide more than the English version: "Ac ne ipsa quidem, opinor, disciplinarum omnium regina theologia ducet indignum admoveri sibi manus, ac debitum exhiberi obsequium a pedissequa grammatica; quae tametsi nonnullis est dignitate posterior, nullius certe opera magis necessaria. In minimis versatur, sed sine quibus nemo evasit maximus; nugas agitat, sed quae seria ducant. Quod si reclament maiorem esse theologiam quam ut grammaticae legibus teneatur, totum interpretandi negocium de sacri Spiritus afflatu pendere, nova vero theologorum dignitas, si solis illis licet barbare loqui. Sed expediant interim quid sibi velit, quod Desyderio suo scribit Hieronymus, Aliud est, inquiens, esse vatem et aliud interpretem. Ibi Spiritus ventura praedicit; hic eruditio et verborum copia quae intelligit transfert. Tum quorsum attinuerit eundem de ratione vertendi divinas litteras praecipere, si facultas ista divino contingit afflatu? Postremo quur Paulus in Hebraica lingua quam Graeca dictus est dissertior? Quod si fieri potuit ut Veteris interpretes Testamenti erraverint alicubi, in his praesertim in quibus fides non violatur, quidni potuerint labi et Novi? quod quidem Hieronymus non tam vertit quam emendavit, idque modice, relictis ut ipse ut ipse testatur verbis, quae potissimum excutit Laurentius. Verum num etiam

nostros errores ad Spiritum authorem referamus? Esto bene verterint interpretes; sed bene versa pervertuntur. Emendavit Hieronymus; at rursum depravantur emendata. Nisi forte nunc aut minor audacia semidoctorum, aut peritia linguarum maior, aut non facillima depravatio propter artem calchographicam, quae unicum mendum repente in mille propagat exemplaria. At fas non est, inquiunt, in sacris scripturis quicquam immutare, propterea quod illic ne apiculi quidem mysterio vacant. Imo tanto magis nefas est depravare, tantoque attentius corrigendum a doctis quod per inscitiam est adulteratum; ea tamen cautione temperantiaque, quae quum omnibus libris tam sacris in primis debetur. Verum non recte, aiunt, sibi sumit Laurentius quod Hieronymus mandante Damaso suscepit. Ne propositum quidem simile. Hieronymus veterem ediotionem nova sustulit; Laurentius quod annotavit, in privatos commentarios refert, neque postulat ut hinc quicquam in tuo codice demutes, quanquam ipsa nostrorum exemplarium variestas satis arguit ea non carere mendis. Porro ut veterum librorum fides de Hebraeis voluminibus examinanda est, ita novorum veritas Graeci sermonis normam desyderat, Authore Augustino cuius verba referuntur in Decretis distin. IX" (Allen, *Erasmus,* pp. 410-11). For the Vallian text (in polemic with Poggio) here addressed to Erasmus, cf. *L. Valla,* pp. 145ff, and especially, 277ff. In note 29 below, the English translation of the first part ("Ac ne ipsa quidem . . . Laurentius") of the pages of Erasmus here cited.

26. Allen, *Erasmus,* I, p. 409: "Pogius, rabula adeo indoctus ut etiam si vacaret obscoenitate, tamen indignus esset qui legeretur, adeo autem obscoenus ut etiam si doctissimus fuisset, tamen esset a bonis viris reiiciendus."

27. Ibid., pp. 407-9.

28. L. Valla, *Antidotum Primum,* pp. 112, 188.

29. Allen, *Erasmus,* II, p. 182.

30. The controversy among Erasmus, van Dorp, and More, together with the relevant texts, is treated amply in S. I. Camporeale, "Da Lorenzo Valla a Tommaso Moro. Lo statuto umanistico della teologia," (op. cit. n. 24). See also H. Holeczek, *Humanistische Bibelphilologie als Reformproblem bei Erasmus von Rotterdam, Thomas More und William Tyndale,* (Leiden, 1975), pp. 138-65; but above all, St. Thomas More, *In Defense of Humanism,* vol. 15 (The Yale Edition of The Complete Works), edited by D. Kinney, (New Haven & London, 1986), pp. xix-cxxx, 1-127. The cited passage of van Dorp, in Allen, *Erasmus,* II, n. 347, pp. 130-31.

FURTHER READING

Biography

Shepherd, William. *The Life of Poggio Bracciolini.* London: Longman, Rees, Orme, Brown, Green & Longman, 1837, 462 p.
> First and still the primary biography of Poggio in English; includes extensive translations of correspondence.

Criticism

Baron, Hans. "*Dialogus II* and the Florentine Environment." In *The Crisis of the Early Italian Renaissance: Civic Humanism and Republican Liberty in an Age of Classicism and Tyranny,* rev. ed., pp. 245-69. Princeton, N.J.: Princeton University Press, 1966.
> Discusses Poggio's debate with Coluccio Salutati in the Petrarch controversy of 1405-06, in the context of the life of Leonardo Bruni.

Bradley, Dennis R. "Poggio's Noble Dialogue: Textual Variations in Three Early Printed Editions." *Renaissance Studies* 8, no. 1 (March 1994): 1-12.
> Discusses variations in editions of Poggio's *Dialogue on Nobility* as they reflect on the authority of the first published edition.

Dunstan, A. J. "The Hand of Poggio." *Scriptorum* 19 (1965): 53-70.
> Discusses identifying elements of Poggio's handwriting to further illuminate his contribution to the development of a humanistic script.

Hammond, Lincoln Davis. Introduction to *Travelers in Disguise: Narratives of Eastern Travel by Poggio Bracciolini and Ludovico de Varthema,* pp. vii-xxxii. Cambridge, Mass.: Harvard University Press, 1963.
> Explains the context and content of Poggio's *The Indies Rediscovered,* the final section of his dialogue *On the Vicissitudes of Fortune*; connects the work to the development of humanism and travel writing.

Hellinga, Lotte. "The Link between Two Early Printed Books: Two Editions of Poggio Bracciolini, *Facetiæ,* c. 1470-1471." In *Book Production and Letters in the Western European Renaissance: Essays in Honour of Conor Fahy,* ed. Anna Laura Lepschy, John Took, and Dennis E. Rhodes, pp. 166-83. London: Modern Humanities Research Association, 1986.
> Examines two editions of Poggio's book of jests in an attempt to illuminate early publication and printing practices.

Kajanto, Iiro. *Poggio Bracciolini and Classicism: A Study in Early Italian Humanism.* Helsinki: Suomalainen Tiedeakatemia, 1987, 43 p.

Discusses Poggio's contributions and limitations as a classicist and suggests a greater affinity for modernism than Poggio himself might have acknowledged.

Marsh, David. "Poggio and Alberti: Three Notes." *Rinascimento* 23 (1983): 189-215.
Compares Poggio's translation of Lucian's *Iuppiter confutatus* with a similar work by Leon Battista Alberti, highlighting Poggio's failings.

Martines, Lauro. "The Relation between Humanism and Florentine Society: An Essay." In *The Social World of the Florentine Humanists, 1390-1460,* pp. 263-310. London: Routledge & Kegan Paul, 1963.
Includes Poggio in a study of civic roles and social class as they related to the development of humanism.

Mazzocco, Angelo. "Petrarca, Poggio, and Biondo: Humanism's Foremost Interpreters of Roman Ruins." In *Francis Petrarch, Six Centuries Later: A Symposium,* edited by Aldo Scaglione, pp. 353-63. Chapel Hill: Department of Romance Languages, University of North Carolina, 1975.
Compares Poggio's accounts of seeking ancient relics to those of other Italian humanists.

Newhauser, Richard. "Patristic Poggio? The Evidence of Györ, Egyházmegyei Könyvtár Ms. 1.4." *Rinascimento* 26 (1986): 231-39.
Uses manuscript evidence suggesting readers' reception of the text to support interpreting Poggio's *On Avarice* within a patristic tradition.

Oppel, John W. "Peace vs. Liberty in the Quattrocento: Poggio, Guarino, and the Scipio-Caesar Controversy." *Journal of Medieval and Renaissance Studies* 4 (1974): 221-65.
Argues that Poggio acted as a partisan propagandist for the house of Medici in the Scipio-Caesar controversy.

Robin, Diana. "A Reassessment of the Character of Francesco Filelfo (1398-1481)." *Renaissance Quarterly* 36, no. 2 (summer 1983): 202-24.

Questions the veracity of Poggio's representation of Francesco Filelfo in his *Invectivae*; concludes that much of Poggio's account is fabricated or exaggerated as part of his defense of his friend Niccolo Niccoli.

Sandys, John Edwin. "The Recovery of the Classics: Poggio, Aurispa, Filelfo, Janus Lascaris." In *A History of Classical Scholarship,* Vol. II, pp. 25-39. Cambridge: Cambridge University Press, 1908.
Discusses Poggio's role in finding and acquiring classical texts.

Spencer, Walter E., and Kirk M. Summers. "An Unpublished Fragment of *An seni sit uxor ducenda* of Poggio Bracciolini." *Manuscripta* 38, no. 2 (July 1994): 156-70.
Reports the physical features, including humanistic script and grammar, of a variant copy of Poggio's manuscript.

Ullman, B. L. "The Inventor—Poggio Bracciolini." In *The Origin and Development of Humanistic Script,* pp. 21-57. Rome: Edizioni de Storia e Letteratura, 1960.
Considers Poggio's reputation as the inventor of the humanistic script; includes detailed descriptions of his manuscripts.

———. "Poggio's Manuscripts of Livy." *Scriptorum* 19 (1965): 71-5.
Debates A. J. Dunstan's claim that one of Poggio's scribes, rather than Poggio himself, was responsible for a manuscript copy of Livy; discusses the details of the script and the practices of manuscript production.

Wilcox, Donald J. "Poggio Bracciolini and the *Historica fiorentina.*" In *The Development of Florentine Humanist Historiography in the Fifteenth Century,* pp. 130-53. Cambridge, Mass.: Harvard University Press, 1969.
Highlights the moral and psychological dimensions of Poggio's historiography; contends that Poggio failed to connect those dimensions effectively with political issues.

CDALBS = *Concise Dictionary of American Literary Biography Supplement*
CDBLB = *Concise Dictionary of British Literary Biography*
CMW = *St. James Guide to Crime & Mystery Writers*
CN = *Contemporary Novelists*
CP = *Contemporary Poets*
CPW = *Contemporary Popular Writers*
CSW = *Contemporary Southern Writers*
CWD = *Contemporary Women Dramatists*
CWP = *Contemporary Women Poets*
CWRI = *St. James Guide to Children's Writers*
CWW = *Contemporary World Writers*
DA = *DISCovering Authors*
DA3 = *DISCovering Authors 3.0*
DAB = *DISCovering Authors: British Edition*
DAC = *DISCovering Authors: Canadian Edition*
DAM = *DISCovering Authors: Modules*
   DRAM: *Dramatists Module;* **MST:** *Most-studied Authors Module;*
   MULT: *Multicultural Authors Module;* **NOV:** *Novelists Module;*
   POET: *Poets Module;* **POP:** *Popular Fiction and Genre Authors Module*
DFS = *Drama for Students*
DLB = *Dictionary of Literary Biography*
DLBD = *Dictionary of Literary Biography Documentary Series*
DLBY = *Dictionary of Literary Biography Yearbook*
DNFS = *Literature of Developing Nations for Students*
EFS = *Epics for Students*
EXPN = *Exploring Novels*
EXPP = *Exploring Poetry*
EXPS = *Exploring Short Stories*
EW = *European Writers*
FANT = *St. James Guide to Fantasy Writers*
FW = *Feminist Writers*
GFL = *Guide to French Literature,* Beginnings to 1789, 1798 to the Present
GLL = *Gay and Lesbian Literature*
HGG = *St. James Guide to Horror, Ghost & Gothic Writers*
HW = *Hispanic Writers*
IDFW = *International Dictionary of Films and Filmmakers: Writers and Production Artists*
IDTP = *International Dictionary of Theatre: Playwrights*
LAIT = *Literature and Its Times*
LAW = *Latin American Writers*
JRDA = *Junior DISCovering Authors*
MAICYA = *Major Authors and Illustrators for Children and Young Adults*
MAICYAS = *Major Authors and Illustrators for Children and Young Adults Supplement*
MAWW = *Modern American Women Writers*
MJW = *Modern Japanese Writers*
MTCW = *Major 20th-Century Writers*
NCFS = *Nonfiction Classics for Students*
NFS = *Novels for Students*
PAB = *Poets: American and British*
PFS = *Poetry for Students*
RGAL = *Reference Guide to American Literature*
RGEL = *Reference Guide to English Literature*
RGSF = *Reference Guide to Short Fiction*
RGWL = *Reference Guide to World Literature*
RHW = *Twentieth-Century Romance and Historical Writers*
SAAS = *Something about the Author Autobiography Series*
SATA = *Something about the Author*
SFW = *St. James Guide to Science Fiction Writers*
SSFS = *Short Stories for Students*
TCWW = *Twentieth-Century Western Writers*
WLIT = *World Literature and Its Times*
WP = *World Poets*
YABC = *Yesterday's Authors of Books for Children*
YAW = *St. James Guide to Young Adult Writers*

How to Use This Index

The main references

> **Calvino, Italo**
> 1923-1985 .... CLC 5, 8, 11, 22, 33, 39,
> 73; SSC 3, 48

list all author entries in the following Thomson Gale Literary Criticism series:

AAL = *Asian American Literature*
BG = *The Beat Generation: A Gale Critical Companion*
BLC = *Black Literature Criticism*
BLCS = *Black Literature Criticism Supplement*
CLC = *Contemporary Literary Criticism*
CLR = *Children's Literature Review*
CMLC = *Classical and Medieval Literature Criticism*
DC = *Drama Criticism*
FL = *Feminism in Literature: A Gale Critical Companion*
GL = *Gothic Literature: A Gale Critical Companion*
HLC = *Hispanic Literature Criticism*
HLCS = *Hispanic Literature Criticism Supplement*
HR = *Harlem Renaissance: A Gale Critical Companion*
LC = *Literature Criticism from 1400 to 1800*
NCLC = *Nineteenth-Century Literature Criticism*
NNAL = *Native North American Literature*
PC = *Poetry Criticism*
SSC = *Short Story Criticism*
TCLC = *Twentieth-Century Literary Criticism*
WLC = *World Literature Criticism, 1500 to the Present*
WLCS = *World Literature Criticism Supplement*

The cross-references

> See also CA 85-88, 116; CANR 23, 61;
> DAM NOV; DLB 196; EW 13; MTCW 1, 2;
> RGSF 2; RGWL 2; SFW 4; SSFS 12

list all author entries in the following Thomson Gale biographical and literary sources:

AAYA = *Authors & Artists for Young Adults*
AFAW = *African American Writers*
AFW = *African Writers*
AITN = *Authors in the News*
AMW = *American Writers*
AMWR = *American Writers Retrospective Supplement*
AMWS = *American Writers Supplement*
ANW = *American Nature Writers*
AW = *Ancient Writers*
BEST = *Bestsellers*
BPFB = *Beacham's Encyclopedia of Popular Fiction: Biography and Resources*
BRW = *British Writers*
BRWS = *British Writers Supplement*
BW = *Black Writers*
BYA = *Beacham's Guide to Literature for Young Adults*
CA = *Contemporary Authors*
CAAS = *Contemporary Authors Autobiography Series*
CABS = *Contemporary Authors Bibliographical Series*
CAD = *Contemporary American Dramatists*
CANR = *Contemporary Authors New Revision Series*
CAP = *Contemporary Authors Permanent Series*
CBD = *Contemporary British Dramatists*
CCA = *Contemporary Canadian Authors*
CD = *Contemporary Dramatists*
CDALB = *Concise Dictionary of American Literary Biography*

Literary Criticism Series
Cumulative Author Index

Anderson, C. Farley
See Mencken, H(enry) L(ouis); Nathan, George Jean

Anderson, Jessica (Margaret) Queale
1916- .... **CLC 37**
See also CA 9-12R; CANR 4, 62; CN 4, 5, 6, 7

Anderson, Jon (Victor) 1940- .... **CLC 9**
See also CA 25-28R; CANR 20; CP 1, 3, 4; DAM POET

Anderson, Lindsay (Gordon)
1923-1994 .... **CLC 20**
See also CA 125; 128; 146; CANR 77

Anderson, Maxwell 1888-1959 .... **TCLC 2, 144**
See also CA 105; 152; DAM DRAM; DFS 16, 20; DLB 7, 228; MAL 5; MTCW 2; MTFW 2005; RGAL 4

Anderson, Poul (William)
1926-2001 .... **CLC 15**
See also AAYA 5, 34; BPFB 1; BYA 6, 8, 9; CA 1-4R, 181; 199; CAAE 181; CAAS 2; CANR 2, 15, 34, 64, 110; CLR 58; DLB 8; FANT; INT CANR-15; MTCW 1, 2; MTFW 2005; SATA 90; SATA-Brief 39; SATA-Essay 106; SCFW 1, 2; SFW 4; SUFW 1, 2

Anderson, Robert (Woodruff)
1917- .... **CLC 23**
See also AITN 1; CA 21-24R; CANR 32; CD 6; DAM DRAM; DLB 7; LAIT 5

Anderson, Roberta Joan
See Mitchell, Joni

Anderson, Sherwood 1876-1941 .. **SSC 1, 46; TCLC 1, 10, 24, 123; WLC**
See also AAYA 30; AMW; AMWC 2; BPFB 1; CA 104; 121; CANR 61; CDALB 1917-1929; DA; DA3; DAB; DAC; DAM MST, NOV; DLB 4, 9, 86; DLBD 1; EWL 3; EXPS; GLL 2; MAL 5; MTCW 1, 2; MTFW 2005; NFS 4; RGAL 4; RGSF 2; SSFS 4, 10, 11; TUS

Andier, Pierre
See Desnos, Robert

Andouard
See Giraudoux, Jean(-Hippolyte)

Andrade, Carlos Drummond de ..... **CLC 18**
See Drummond de Andrade, Carlos
See also EWL 3; RGWL 2, 3

Andrade, Mario de .... **TCLC 43**
See de Andrade, Mario
See also DLB 307; EWL 3; LAW; RGWL 2, 3; WLIT 1

Andreae, Johann V(alentin)
1586-1654 .... **LC 32**
See also DLB 164

Andreas Capellanus fl. c. 1185- .... **CMLC 45**
See also DLB 208

Andreas-Salome, Lou 1861-1937 ... **TCLC 56**
See also CA 178; DLB 66

Andreev, Leonid
See Andreyev, Leonid (Nikolaevich)
See also DLB 295; EWL 3

Andress, Lesley
See Sanders, Lawrence

Andrewes, Lancelot 1555-1626 .... **LC 5**
See also DLB 151, 172

Andrews, Cicily Fairfield
See West, Rebecca

Andrews, Elton V.
See Pohl, Frederik

Andreyev, Leonid (Nikolaevich)
1871-1919 .... **TCLC 3**
See Andreev, Leonid
See also CA 104; 185

Andric, Ivo 1892-1975 .... **CLC 8; SSC 36; TCLC 135**
See also CA 81-84; 57-60; CANR 43, 60; CDWLB 4; DLB 147; EW 11; EWL 3; MTCW 1; RGSF 2; RGWL 2, 3

Androvar
See Prado (Calvo), Pedro

Angela of Foligno 1248(?)-1309 .... **CMLC 76**

Angelique, Pierre
See Bataille, Georges

Angell, Roger 1920- .... **CLC 26**
See also CA 57-60; CANR 13, 44, 70, 144; DLB 171, 185

Angelou, Maya 1928- ... **BLC 1; CLC 12, 35, 64, 77, 155; PC 32; WLCS**
See also AAYA 7, 20; AMWS 4; BPFB 1; BW 2, 3; BYA 2; CA 65-68; CANR 19, 42, 65, 111, 133; CDALBS; CLR 53; CP 4, 5, 6, 7; CPW; CSW; CWP; DA; DA3; DAB; DAC; DAM MST, MULT, POET, POP; DLB 38; EWL 3; EXPN; EXPP; FL 1:5; LAIT 4; MAICYA 1; MAICYAS 1; MAL 5; MAWW; MTCW 1, 2; MTFW 2005; NCFS 2; NFS 2; PFS 2, 3; RGAL 4; SATA 49, 136; TCLE 1:1; WYA; YAW

Angouleme, Marguerite d'
See de Navarre, Marguerite

Anna Comnena 1083-1153 .... **CMLC 25**

Annensky, Innokentii Fedorovich
See Annensky, Innokenty (Fyodorovich)
See also DLB 295

Annensky, Innokenty (Fyodorovich)
1856-1909 .... **TCLC 14**
See also CA 110; 155; EWL 3

Annunzio, Gabriele d'
See D'Annunzio, Gabriele

Anodos
See Coleridge, Mary E(lizabeth)

Anon, Charles Robert
See Pessoa, Fernando (Antonio Nogueira)

Anouilh, Jean (Marie Lucien Pierre)
1910-1987 . **CLC 1, 3, 8, 13, 40, 50; DC 8, 21**
See also AAYA 67; CA 17-20R; 123; CANR 32; DAM DRAM; DFS 9, 10, 19; DLB 321; EW 13; EWL 3; GFL 1789 to the Present; MTCW 1, 2; MTFW 2005; RGWL 2, 3; TWA

Anselm of Canterbury
1033(?)-1109 .... **CMLC 67**
See also DLB 115

Anthony, Florence
See Ai

Anthony, John
See Ciardi, John (Anthony)

Anthony, Peter
See Shaffer, Anthony (Joshua); Shaffer, Peter (Levin)

Anthony, Piers 1934- .... **CLC 35**
See also AAYA 11, 48; BYA 7; CA 200; CAAE 200; CANR 28, 56, 73, 102, 133; CPW; DAM POP; DLB 8; FANT; MAI-CYA 2; MAICYAS 1; MTCW 1, 2; MTFW 2005; SAAS 22; SATA 84, 129; SATA-Essay 129; SFW 4; SUFW 1, 2; YAW

Anthony, Susan B(rownell)
1820-1906 .... **TCLC 84**
See also CA 211; FW

Antiphon c. 480B.C.-c. 411B.C. .... **CMLC 55**

Antoine, Marc
See Proust, (Valentin-Louis-George-Eugene) Marcel

Antoninus, Brother
See Everson, William (Oliver)
See also CP 1

Antonioni, Michelangelo 1912- .... **CLC 20, 144**
See also CA 73-76; CANR 45, 77

Antschel, Paul 1920-1970
See Celan, Paul
See also CA 85-88; CANR 33, 61; MTCW 1; PFS 21

Anwar, Chairil 1922-1949 .... **TCLC 22**
See Chairil Anwar
See also CA 121; 219; RGWL 3

Anzaldua, Gloria (Evanjelina)
1942-2004 .... **CLC 200; HLCS 1**
See also CA 175; 227; CSW; CWP; DLB 122; FW; LLW; RGAL 4; SATA-Obit 154

Apess, William 1798-1839(?) .... **NCLC 73; NNAL**
See also DAM MULT; DLB 175, 243

Apollinaire, Guillaume 1880-1918 .... **PC 7; TCLC 3, 8, 51**
See Kostrowitzki, Wilhelm Apollinaris de
See also CA 152; DAM POET; DLB 258, 321; EW 9; EWL 3; GFL 1789 to the Present; MTCW 2; RGWL 2, 3; TWA; WP

Apollonius of Rhodes
See Apollonius Rhodius
See also AW 1; RGWL 2, 3

Apollonius Rhodius c. 300B.C.-c. 220B.C. .... **CMLC 28**
See Apollonius of Rhodes
See also DLB 176

Appelfeld, Aharon 1932- ... **CLC 23, 47; SSC 42**
See also CA 112; 133; CANR 86; CWW 2; DLB 299; EWL 3; RGSF 2; WLIT 6

Apple, Max (Isaac) 1941- .... **CLC 9, 33; SSC 50**
See also CA 81-84; CANR 19, 54; DLB 130

Appleman, Philip (Dean) 1926- .... **CLC 51**
See also CA 13-16R; CAAS 18; CANR 6, 29, 56

Appleton, Lawrence
See Lovecraft, H(oward) P(hillips)

Apteryx
See Eliot, T(homas) S(tearns)

Apuleius, (Lucius Madaurensis)
125(?)-175(?) .... **CMLC 1**
See also AW 2; CDWLB 1; DLB 211; RGWL 2, 3; SUFW

Aquin, Hubert 1929-1977 .... **CLC 15**
See also CA 105; DLB 53; EWL 3

Aquinas, Thomas 1224(?)-1274 ..... **CMLC 33**
See also DLB 115; EW 1; TWA

Aragon, Louis 1897-1982 .... **CLC 3, 22; TCLC 123**
See also CA 69-72; 108; CANR 28, 71; DAM NOV, POET; DLB 72, 258; EW 11; EWL 3; GFL 1789 to the Present; GLL 2; LMFS 2; MTCW 1, 2; RGWL 2, 3

Arany, Janos 1817-1882 .... **NCLC 34**

Aranyos, Kakay 1847-1910
See Mikszath, Kalman

Aratus of Soli c. 315B.C.-c. 240B.C. .... **CMLC 64**
See also DLB 176

Arbuthnot, John 1667-1735 .... **LC 1**
See also DLB 101

Archer, Herbert Winslow
See Mencken, H(enry) L(ouis)

Archer, Jeffrey (Howard) 1940- .... **CLC 28**
See also AAYA 16; BEST 89:3; BPFB 1; CA 77-80; CANR 22, 52, 95, 136; CPW; DA3; DAM POP; INT CANR-22; MTFW 2005

Archer, Jules 1915- .... **CLC 12**
See also CA 9-12R; CANR 6, 69; SAAS 5; SATA 4, 85

Archer, Lee
See Ellison, Harlan (Jay)

Archilochus c. 7th cent. B.C.- .... **CMLC 44**
See also DLB 176

Arden, John 1930- .... CLC 6, 13, 15
See also BRWS 2; CA 13-16R; CAAS 4;
CANR 31, 65, 67, 124; CBD; CD 5, 6;
DAM DRAM; DFS 9; DLB 13, 245;
EWL 3; MTCW 1

Arenas, Reinaldo 1943-1990 .. CLC 41; HLC
1
See also CA 124; 128; 133; CANR 73, 106;
DAM MULT; DLB 145; EWL 3; GLL 2;
HW 1; LAW; LAWS 1; MTCW 2; MTFW
2005; RGSF 2; RGWL 3; WLIT 1

Arendt, Hannah 1906-1975 .... CLC 66, 98
See also CA 17-20R; 61-64; CANR 26, 60;
DLB 242; MTCW 1, 2

Aretino, Pietro 1492-1556 .... LC 12
See also RGWL 2, 3

Arghezi, Tudor .... CLC 80
See Theodorescu, Ion N.
See also CA 167; CDWLB 4; DLB 220;
EWL 3

Arguedas, Jose Maria 1911-1969 .... CLC 10,
18; HLCS 1; TCLC 147
See also CA 89-92; CANR 73; DLB 113;
EWL 3; HW 1; LAW; RGWL 2, 3; WLIT
1

Argueta, Manlio 1936- .... CLC 31
See also CA 131; CANR 73; CWW 2; DLB
145; EWL 3; HW 1; RGWL 3

Arias, Ron(ald Francis) 1941- .... HLC 1
See also CA 131; CANR 81, 136; DAM
MULT; DLB 82; HW 1, 2; MTCW 2;
MTFW 2005

Ariosto, Lodovico
See Ariosto, Ludovico
See also WLIT 7

Ariosto, Ludovico 1474-1533 ... LC 6, 87; PC
42
See Ariosto, Lodovico
See also EW 2; RGWL 2, 3

Aristides
See Epstein, Joseph

Aristophanes 450B.C.-385B.C. .... CMLC 4,
51; DC 2; WLCS
See also AW 1; CDWLB 1; DA; DA3;
DAB; DAC; DAM DRAM, MST; DFS
10; DLB 176; LMFS 1; RGWL 2, 3; TWA

Aristotle 384B.C.-322B.C. .... CMLC 31;
WLCS
See also AW 1; CDWLB 1; DA; DA3;
DAB; DAC; DAM MST; DLB 176;
RGWL 2, 3; TWA

Arlt, Roberto (Godofredo Christophersen)
1900-1942 .... HLC 1; TCLC 29
See also CA 123; 131; CANR 67; DAM
MULT; DLB 305; EWL 3; HW 1, 2;
IDTP; LAW

Armah, Ayi Kwei 1939- . BLC 1; CLC 5, 33,
136
See also AFW; BRWS 10; BW 1; CA 61-
64; CANR 21, 64; CDWLB 3; CN 1, 2,
3, 4, 5, 6, 7; DAM MULT, POET; DLB
117; EWL 3; MTCW 1; WLIT 2

Armatrading, Joan 1950- .... CLC 17
See also CA 114; 186

Armitage, Frank
See Carpenter, John (Howard)

Armstrong, Jeannette (C.) 1948- .... NNAL
See also CA 149; CCA 1; CN 6, 7; DAC;
SATA 102

Arnette, Robert
See Silverberg, Robert

Arnim, Achim von (Ludwig Joachim von
Arnim) 1781-1831 .. NCLC 5, 159; SSC
29
See also DLB 90

Arnim, Bettina von 1785-1859 ...... NCLC 38,
123
See also DLB 90; RGWL 2, 3

Arnold, Matthew 1822-1888 ..... NCLC 6, 29,
89, 126; PC 5; WLC
See also BRW 5; CDBLB 1832-1890; DA;
DAB; DAC; DAM MST, POET; DLB 32,
57; EXPP; PAB; PFS 2; TEA; WP

Arnold, Thomas 1795-1842 .... NCLC 18
See also DLB 55

Arnow, Harriette (Louisa) Simpson
1908-1986 .... CLC 2, 7, 18
See also BPFB 1; CA 9-12R; 118; CANR
14; CN 2, 3, 4; DLB 6; FW; MTCW 1, 2;
RHW; SATA 42; SATA-Obit 47

Arouet, Francois-Marie
See Voltaire

Arp, Hans
See Arp, Jean

Arp, Jean 1887-1966 .... CLC 5; TCLC 115
See also CA 81-84; 25-28R; CANR 42, 77;
EW 10

Arrabal
See Arrabal, Fernando

Arrabal (Teran), Fernando
See Arrabal, Fernando
See also CWW 2

Arrabal, Fernando 1932- ... CLC 2, 9, 18, 58
See Arrabal (Teran), Fernando
See also CA 9-12R; CANR 15; DLB 321;
EWL 3; LMFS 2

Arreola, Juan Jose 1918-2001 .... CLC 147;
HLC 1; SSC 38
See also CA 113; 131; 200; CANR 81;
CWW 2; DAM MULT; DLB 113; DNFS
2; EWL 3; HW 1, 2; LAW; RGSF 2

Arrian c. 89(?)-c. 155(?) .... CMLC 43
See also DLB 176

Arrick, Fran .... CLC 30
See Gaberman, Judie Angell
See also BYA 6

Arrley, Richmond
See Delany, Samuel R(ay), Jr.

Artaud, Antonin (Marie Joseph)
1896-1948 .... DC 14; TCLC 3, 36
See also CA 104; 149; DA3; DAM DRAM;
DFS 22; DLB 258, 321; EW 11; EWL 3;
GFL 1789 to the Present; MTCW 2;
MTFW 2005; RGWL 2, 3

Arthur, Ruth M(abel) 1905-1979 ..... CLC 12
See also CA 9-12R; 85-88; CANR 4; CWRI
5; SATA 7, 26

Artsybashev, Mikhail (Petrovich)
1878-1927 .... TCLC 31
See also CA 170; DLB 295

Arundel, Honor (Morfydd)
1919-1973 .... CLC 17
See also CA 21-22; 41-44R; CAP 2; CLR
35; CWRI 5; SATA 4; SATA-Obit 24

Arzner, Dorothy 1900-1979 .... CLC 98

Asch, Sholem 1880-1957 .... TCLC 3
See also CA 105; EWL 3; GLL 2

Ascham, Roger 1516(?)-1568 .... LC 101
See also DLB 236

Ash, Shalom
See Asch, Sholem

Ashbery, John (Lawrence) 1927- .. CLC 2, 3,
4, 6, 9, 13, 15, 25, 41, 77, 125; PC 26
See Berry, Jonas
See also AMWS 3; CA 5-8R; CANR 9, 37,
66, 102, 132; CP 1, 2, 3, 4, 5, 6, 7; DA3;
DAM POET; DLB 5, 165; DLBY 1981;
EWL 3; INT CANR-9; MAL 5; MTCW
1, 2; MTFW 2005; PAB; PFS 11; RGAL
4; TCLE 1:1; WP

Ashdown, Clifford
See Freeman, R(ichard) Austin

Ashe, Gordon
See Creasey, John

Ashton-Warner, Sylvia (Constance)
1908-1984 .... CLC 19
See also CA 69-72; 112; CANR 29; CN 1,
2, 3; MTCW 1, 2

Asimov, Isaac 1920-1992 ..... CLC 1, 3, 9, 19,
26, 76, 92
See also AAYA 13; BEST 90:2; BPFB 1;
BYA 4, 6, 7, 9; CA 1-4R; 137; CANR 2,
19, 36, 60, 125; CLR 12, 79; CMW 4;
CN 1, 2, 3, 4, 5; CPW; DA3; DAM POP;
DLB 8; DLBY 1992; INT CANR-19;
JRDA; LAIT 5; LMFS 2; MAICYA 1, 2;
MAL 5; MTCW 1, 2; MTFW 2005;
RGAL 4; SATA 1, 26, 74; SCFW 1, 2;
SFW 4; SSFS 17; TUS; YAW

Askew, Anne 1521(?)-1546 .... LC 81
See also DLB 136

Assis, Joaquim Maria Machado de
See Machado de Assis, Joaquim Maria

Astell, Mary 1666-1731 .... LC 68
See also DLB 252; FW

Astley, Thea (Beatrice May)
1925-2004 .... CLC 41
See also CA 65-68; 229; CANR 11, 43, 78;
CN 1, 2, 3, 4, 5, 6, 7; DLB 289; EWL 3

Astley, William 1855-1911
See Warung, Price

Aston, James
See White, T(erence) H(anbury)

Asturias, Miguel Angel 1899-1974 .... CLC 3,
8, 13; HLC 1
See also CA 25-28; 49-52; CANR 32; CAP
2; CDWLB 3; DA3; DAM MULT, NOV;
DLB 113, 290; EWL 3; HW 1; LAW;
LMFS 2; MTCW 1, 2; RGWL 2, 3; WLIT
1

Atares, Carlos Saura
See Saura (Atares), Carlos

Athanasius c. 295-c. 373 .... CMLC 48

Atheling, William
See Pound, Ezra (Weston Loomis)

Atheling, William, Jr.
See Blish, James (Benjamin)

Atherton, Gertrude (Franklin Horn)
1857-1948 .... TCLC 2
See also CA 104; 155; DLB 9, 78, 186;
HGG; RGAL 4; SUFW 1; TCWW 1, 2

Atherton, Lucius
See Masters, Edgar Lee

Atkins, Jack
See Harris, Mark

Atkinson, Kate 1951- .... CLC 99
See also CA 166; CANR 101; DLB 267

Attaway, William (Alexander)
1911-1986 .... BLC 1; CLC 92
See also BW 2, 3; CA 143; CANR 82;
DAM MULT; DLB 76; MAL 5

Atticus
See Fleming, Ian (Lancaster); Wilson,
(Thomas) Woodrow

Atwood, Margaret (Eleanor) 1939- ... CLC 2,
3, 4, 8, 13, 15, 25, 44, 84, 135; PC 8;
SSC 2, 46; WLC
See also AAYA 12, 47; AMWS 13; BEST
89:2; BPFB 1; CA 49-52; CANR 3, 24,
33, 59, 95, 133; CN 2, 3, 4, 5, 6, 7; CP 1,
2, 3, 4, 5, 6, 7; CPW; CWP; DA; DA3;
DAB; DAC; DAM MST, NOV, POET;
DLB 53, 251; EWL 3; EXPN; FL 1:5;
FW; GL 2; INT CANR-24; LAIT 5;
MTCW 1, 2; MTFW 2005; NFS 4, 12,
13, 14, 19; PFS 7; RGSF 2; SATA 50;
SSFS 3, 13; TCLE 1:1; TWA; WWE 1;
YAW

Aubigny, Pierre d'
See Mencken, H(enry) L(ouis)

Aubin, Penelope 1685-1731(?) .... LC 9
See also DLB 39

Auchincloss, Louis (Stanton) 1917- .. CLC 4, 6, 9, 18, 45; SSC 22
See also AMWS 4; CA 1-4R; CANR 6, 29, 55, 87, 130; CN 1, 2, 3, 4, 5, 6, 7; DAM NOV; DLB 2, 244; DLBY 1980; EWL 3; INT CANR-29; MAL 5; MTCW 1; RGAL 4

Auden, W(ystan) H(ugh) 1907-1973 . CLC 1, 2, 3, 4, 6, 9, 11, 14, 43, 123; PC 1; WLC
See also AAYA 18; AMWS 2; BRW 7; BRWR 1; CA 9-12R; 45-48; CANR 5, 61, 105; CDBLB 1914-1945; CP 1, 2; DA; DA3; DAB; DAC; DAM DRAM, MST, POET; DLB 10, 20; EWL 3; EXPP; MAL 5; MTCW 1, 2; MTFW 2005; PAB; PFS 1, 3, 4, 10; TUS; WP

Audiberti, Jacques 1899-1965 .... CLC 38
See also CA 25-28R; DAM DRAM; DLB 321; EWL 3

Audubon, John James 1785-1851 . NCLC 47
See also ANW; DLB 248

Auel, Jean M(arie) 1936- .... CLC 31, 107
See also AAYA 7, 51; BEST 90:4; BPFB 1; CA 103; CANR 21, 64, 115; CPW; DA3; DAM POP; INT CANR-21; NFS 11; RHW; SATA 91

Auerbach, Erich 1892-1957 .... TCLC 43
See also CA 118; 155; EWL 3

Augier, Emile 1820-1889 .... NCLC 31
See also DLB 192; GFL 1789 to the Present

August, John
See De Voto, Bernard (Augustine)

Augustine, St. 354-430 .... CMLC 6; WLCS
See also DA; DA3; DAB; DAC; DAM MST; DLB 115; EW 1; RGWL 2, 3

Aunt Belinda
See Braddon, Mary Elizabeth

Aunt Weedy
See Alcott, Louisa May

Aurelius
See Bourne, Randolph S(illiman)

Aurelius, Marcus 121-180 .... CMLC 45
See Marcus Aurelius
See also RGWL 2, 3

Aurobindo, Sri
See Ghose, Aurabinda

Aurobindo Ghose
See Ghose, Aurabinda

Austen, Jane 1775-1817 ...... NCLC 1, 13, 19, 33, 51, 81, 95, 119, 150; WLC
See also AAYA 19; BRW 4; BRWC 1; BRWR 2; BYA 3; CDBLB 1789-1832; DA; DA3; DAB; DAC; DAM MST, NOV; DLB 116; EXPN; FL 1:2; GL 2; LAIT 2; LATS 1:1; LMFS 1; NFS 1, 14, 18, 20, 21; TEA; WLIT 3; WYAS 1

Auster, Paul 1947- .... CLC 47, 131
See also AMWS 12; CA 69-72; CANR 23, 52, 75, 129; CMW 4; CN 5, 6, 7; DA3; DLB 227; MAL 5; MTCW 2; MTFW 2005; SUFW 2; TCLE 1:1

Austin, Frank
See Faust, Frederick (Schiller)

Austin, Mary (Hunter) 1868-1934 . TCLC 25
See also ANW; CA 109; 178; DLB 9, 78, 206, 221, 275; FW; TCWW 1, 2

Averroes 1126-1198 .... CMLC 7
See also DLB 115

Avicenna 980-1037 .... CMLC 16
See also DLB 115

Avison, Margaret (Kirkland) 1918- .. CLC 2, 4, 97
See also CA 17-20R; CANR 134; CP 1, 2, 3, 4, 5, 6, 7; DAC; DAM POET; DLB 53; MTCW 1

Axton, David
See Koontz, Dean R.

Ayckbourn, Alan 1939- ...... CLC 5, 8, 18, 33, 74; DC 13
See also BRWS 5; CA 21-24R; CANR 31, 59, 118; CBD; CD 5, 6; DAB; DAM DRAM; DFS 7; DLB 13, 245; EWL 3; MTCW 1, 2; MTFW 2005

Aydy, Catherine
See Tennant, Emma (Christina)

Ayme, Marcel (Andre) 1902-1967 ... CLC 11; SSC 41
See also CA 89-92; CANR 67, 137; CLR 25; DLB 72; EW 12; EWL 3; GFL 1789 to the Present; RGSF 2; RGWL 2, 3; SATA 91

Ayrton, Michael 1921-1975 .... CLC 7
See also CA 5-8R; 61-64; CANR 9, 21

Aytmatov, Chingiz
See Aitmatov, Chingiz (Torekulovich)
See also EWL 3

Azorin .... CLC 11
See Martinez Ruiz, Jose
See also DLB 322; EW 9; EWL 3

Azuela, Mariano 1873-1952 .. HLC 1; TCLC 3, 145
See also CA 104; 131; CANR 81; DAM MULT; EWL 3; HW 1, 2; LAW; MTCW 1, 2; MTFW 2005

Ba, Mariama 1929-1981 .... BLCS
See also AFW; BW 2; CA 141; CANR 87; DNFS 2; WLIT 2

Baastad, Babbis Friis
See Friis-Baastad, Babbis Ellinor

Bab
See Gilbert, W(illiam) S(chwenck)

Babbis, Eleanor
See Friis-Baastad, Babbis Ellinor

Babel, Isaac
See Babel, Isaak (Emmanuilovich)
See also EW 11; SSFS 10

Babel, Isaak (Emmanuilovich) 1894-1941(?) . SSC 16, 78; TCLC 2, 13, 171
See Babel, Isaac
See also CA 104; 155; CANR 113; DLB 272; EWL 3; MTCW 2; MTFW 2005; RGSF 2; RGWL 2, 3; TWA

Babits, Mihaly 1883-1941 .... TCLC 14
See also CA 114; CDWLB 4; DLB 215; EWL 3

Babur 1483-1530 .... LC 18

Babylas 1898-1962
See Ghelderode, Michel de

Baca, Jimmy Santiago 1952- . HLC 1; PC 41
See also CA 131; CANR 81, 90, 146; CP 7; DAM MULT; DLB 122; HW 1, 2; LLW; MAL 5

Baca, Jose Santiago
See Baca, Jimmy Santiago

Bacchelli, Riccardo 1891-1985 .... CLC 19
See also CA 29-32R; 117; DLB 264; EWL 3

Bach, Richard (David) 1936- .... CLC 14
See also AITN 1; BEST 89:2; BPFB 1; BYA 5; CA 9-12R; CANR 18, 93; CPW; DAM NOV, POP; FANT; MTCW 1; SATA 13

Bache, Benjamin Franklin 1769-1798 .... LC 74
See also DLB 43

Bachelard, Gaston 1884-1962 ...... TCLC 128
See also CA 97-100; 89-92; DLB 296; GFL 1789 to the Present

Bachman, Richard
See King, Stephen

Bachmann, Ingeborg 1926-1973 .... CLC 69
See also CA 93-96; 45-48; CANR 69; DLB 85; EWL 3; RGWL 2, 3

Bacon, Francis 1561-1626 .... LC 18, 32
See also BRW 1; CDBLB Before 1660; DLB 151, 236, 252; RGEL 2; TEA

Bacon, Roger 1214(?)-1294 .... CMLC 14
See also DLB 115

Bacovia, George 1881-1957 .... TCLC 24
See Vasiliu, Gheorghe
See also CDWLB 4; DLB 220; EWL 3

Badanes, Jerome 1937-1995 .... CLC 59
See also CA 234

Bagehot, Walter 1826-1877 .... NCLC 10
See also DLB 55

Bagnold, Enid 1889-1981 .... CLC 25
See also BYA 2; CA 5-8R; 103; CANR 5, 40; CBD; CN 2; CWD; CWRI 5; DAM DRAM; DLB 13, 160, 191, 245; FW; MAICYA 1, 2; RGEL 2; SATA 1, 25

Bagritsky, Eduard .... TCLC 60
See Dzyubin, Eduard Georgievich

Bagrjana, Elisaveta
See Belcheva, Elisaveta Lyubomirova

Bagryana, Elisaveta .... CLC 10
See Belcheva, Elisaveta Lyubomirova
See also CA 178; CDWLB 4; DLB 147; EWL 3

Bailey, Paul 1937- .... CLC 45
See also CA 21-24R; CANR 16, 62, 124; CN 1, 2, 3, 4, 5, 6, 7; DLB 14, 271; GLL 2

Baillie, Joanna 1762-1851 ...... NCLC 71, 151
See also DLB 93; GL 2; RGEL 2

Bainbridge, Beryl (Margaret) 1934- . CLC 4, 5, 8, 10, 14, 18, 22, 62, 130
See also BRWS 6; CA 21-24R; CANR 24, 55, 75, 88, 128; CN 2, 3, 4, 5, 6, 7; DAM NOV; DLB 14, 231; EWL 3; MTCW 1, 2; MTFW 2005

Baker, Carlos (Heard) 1909-1987 .... TCLC 119
See also CA 5-8R; 122; CANR 3, 63; DLB 103

Baker, Elliott 1922- .... CLC 8
See also CA 45-48; CANR 2, 63; CN 1, 2, 3, 4, 5, 6, 7

Baker, Jean H. .... TCLC 3, 10
See Russell, George William

Baker, Nicholson 1957- .... CLC 61, 165
See also AMWS 13; CA 135; CANR 63, 120, 138; CN 6; CPW; DA3; DAM POP; DLB 227; MTFW 2005

Baker, Ray Stannard 1870-1946 .... TCLC 47
See also CA 118

Baker, Russell (Wayne) 1925- .... CLC 31
See also BEST 89:4; CA 57-60; CANR 11, 41, 59, 137; MTCW 1, 2; MTFW 2005

Bakhtin, M.
See Bakhtin, Mikhail Mikhailovich

Bakhtin, M. M.
See Bakhtin, Mikhail Mikhailovich

Bakhtin, Mikhail
See Bakhtin, Mikhail Mikhailovich

Bakhtin, Mikhail Mikhailovich 1895-1975 .... CLC 83; TCLC 160
See also CA 128; 113; DLB 242; EWL 3

Bakshi, Ralph 1938(?)- .... CLC 26
See also CA 112; 138; IDFW 3

Bakunin, Mikhail (Alexandrovich) 1814-1876 .... NCLC 25, 58
See also DLB 277

Baldwin, James (Arthur) 1924-1987 . BLC 1; CLC 1, 2, 3, 4, 5, 8, 13, 15, 17, 42, 50, 67, 90, 127; DC 1; SSC 10, 33; WLC
See also AAYA 4, 34; AFAW 1, 2; AMWR 2; AMWS 1; BPFB 1; BW 1; CA 1-4R; 124; CABS 1; CAD; CANR 3, 24; CDALB 1941-1968; CN 1, 2, 3, 4; CPW; DA; DA3; DAB; DAC; DAM MST, MULT, NOV, POP; DFS 11, 15; DLB 2, 7, 33, 249, 278; DLBY 1987; EWL 3;

EXPS; LAIT 5; MAL 5; MTCW 1, 2;
MTFW 2005; NCFS 4; NFS 4; RGAL 4;
RGSF 2; SATA 9; SATA-Obit 54; SSFS
2, 18; TUS

Baldwin, William c. 1515-1563 .... **LC 113**
See also DLB 132

Bale, John 1495-1563 .... **LC 62**
See also DLB 132; RGEL 2; TEA

Ball, Hugo 1886-1927 .... **TCLC 104**

Ballard, J(ames) G(raham) 1930- . **CLC 3, 6,
14, 36, 137; SSC 1, 53**
See also AAYA 3, 52; BRWS 5; CA 5-8R;
CANR 15, 39, 65, 107, 133; CN 1, 2, 3,
4, 5, 6, 7; DA3; DAM NOV, POP; DLB
14, 207, 261, 319; EWL 3; HGG; MTCW
1, 2; MTFW 2005; NFS 8; RGEL 2;
RGSF 2; SATA 93; SCFW 1, 2; SFW 4

Balmont, Konstantin (Dmitriyevich)
1867-1943 .... **TCLC 11**
See also CA 109; 155; DLB 295; EWL 3

Baltausis, Vincas 1847-1910
See Mikszath, Kalman

Balzac, Honore de 1799-1850 ... **NCLC 5, 35,
53, 153; SSC 5, 59; WLC**
See also DA; DA3; DAB; DAC; DAM
MST, NOV; DLB 119; EW 5; GFL 1789
to the Present; LMFS 1; RGSF 2; RGWL
2, 3; SSFS 10; SUFW; TWA

Bambara, Toni Cade 1939-1995 .... **BLC 1;
CLC 19, 88; SSC 35; TCLC 116;
WLCS**
See also AAYA 5, 49; AFAW 2; AMWS 11;
BW 2, 3; BYA 12, 14; CA 29-32R; 150;
CANR 24, 49, 81; CDALBS; DA; DA3;
DAC; DAM MST, MULT; DLB 38, 218;
EXPS; MAL 5; MTCW 1, 2; MTFW
2005; RGAL 4; RGSF 2; SATA 112; SSFS
4, 7, 12, 21

Bamdad, A.
See Shamlu, Ahmad

Bamdad, Alef
See Shamlu, Ahmad

Banat, D. R.
See Bradbury, Ray (Douglas)

Bancroft, Laura
See Baum, L(yman) Frank

Banim, John 1798-1842 .... **NCLC 13**
See also DLB 116, 158, 159; RGEL 2

Banim, Michael 1796-1874 .... **NCLC 13**
See also DLB 158, 159

Banjo, The
See Paterson, A(ndrew) B(arton)

Banks, Iain
See Banks, Iain M(enzies)
See also BRWS 11

Banks, Iain M(enzies) 1954- .... **CLC 34**
See Banks, Iain
See also CA 123; 128; CANR 61, 106; DLB
194, 261; EWL 3; HGG; INT CA-128;
MTFW 2005; SFW 4

Banks, Lynne Reid .... **CLC 23**
See Reid Banks, Lynne
See also AAYA 6; BYA 7; CLR 86; CN 4,
5, 6

Banks, Russell (Earl) 1940- .... **CLC 37, 72,
187; SSC 42**
See also AAYA 45; AMWS 5; CA 65-68;
CAAS 15; CANR 19, 52, 73, 118; CN 4,
5, 6, 7; DLB 130, 278; EWL 3; MAL 5;
MTCW 2; MTFW 2005; NFS 13

Banville, John 1945- .... **CLC 46, 118**
See also CA 117; 128; CANR 104; CN 4,
5, 6, 7; DLB 14, 271; INT CA-128

Banville, Theodore (Faullain) de
1832-1891 .... **NCLC 9**
See also DLB 217; GFL 1789 to the Present

Baraka, Amiri 1934- .... **BLC 1; CLC 1, 2, 3,
5, 10, 14, 33, 115, 213; DC 6; PC 4;
WLCS**
See Jones, LeRoi
See also AAYA 63; AFAW 1, 2; AMWS 2;
BW 2, 3; CA 21-24R; CABS 3; CAD;
CANR 27, 38, 61, 133; CD 3, 5, 6;
CDALB 1941-1968; CP 4, 5, 6, 7; CPW;
DA; DA3; DAC; DAM MST, MULT,
POET, POP; DFS 3, 11, 16; DLB 5, 7,
16, 38; DLBD 8; EWL 3; MAL 5; MTCW
1, 2; MTFW 2005; PFS 9; RGAL 4;
TCLE 1:1; TUS; WP

Baratynsky, Evgenii Abramovich
1800-1844 .... **NCLC 103**
See also DLB 205

Barbauld, Anna Laetitia
1743-1825 .... **NCLC 50**
See also DLB 107, 109, 142, 158; RGEL 2

Barbellion, W. N. P. .... **TCLC 24**
See Cummings, Bruce F(rederick)

Barber, Benjamin R. 1939- .... **CLC 141**
See also CA 29-32R; CANR 12, 32, 64, 119

Barbera, Jack (Vincent) 1945- .... **CLC 44**
See also CA 110; CANR 45

Barbey d'Aurevilly, Jules-Amedee
1808-1889 .... **NCLC 1; SSC 17**
See also DLB 119; GFL 1789 to the Present

Barbour, John c. 1316-1395 .... **CMLC 33**
See also DLB 146

Barbusse, Henri 1873-1935 .... **TCLC 5**
See also CA 105; 154; DLB 65; EWL 3;
RGWL 2, 3

Barclay, Alexander c. 1475-1552 .... **LC 109**
See also DLB 132

Barclay, Bill
See Moorcock, Michael (John)

Barclay, William Ewert
See Moorcock, Michael (John)

Barea, Arturo 1897-1957 .... **TCLC 14**
See also CA 111; 201

Barfoot, Joan 1946- .... **CLC 18**
See also CA 105; CANR 141

Barham, Richard Harris
1788-1845 .... **NCLC 77**
See also DLB 159

Baring, Maurice 1874-1945 .... **TCLC 8**
See also CA 105; 168; DLB 34; HGG

Baring-Gould, Sabine 1834-1924 ... **TCLC 88**
See also DLB 156, 190

Barker, Clive 1952- .... **CLC 52, 205; SSC 53**
See also AAYA 10, 54; BEST 90:3; BPFB
1; CA 121; 129; CANR 71, 111, 133;
CPW; DA3; DAM POP; DLB 261; HGG;
INT CA-129; MTCW 1, 2; MTFW 2005;
SUFW 2

Barker, George Granville
1913-1991 .... **CLC 8, 48**
See also CA 9-12R; 135; CANR 7, 38; CP
1, 2, 3, 4; DAM POET; DLB 20; EWL 3;
MTCW 1

Barker, Harley Granville
See Granville-Barker, Harley
See also DLB 10

Barker, Howard 1946- .... **CLC 37**
See also CA 102; CBD; CD 5, 6; DLB 13,
233

Barker, Jane 1652-1732 .... **LC 42, 82**
See also DLB 39, 131

Barker, Pat(ricia) 1943- ...... **CLC 32, 94, 146**
See also BRWS 4; CA 117; 122; CANR 50,
101; CN 6, 7; DLB 271; INT CA-122

Barlach, Ernst (Heinrich)
1870-1938 .... **TCLC 84**
See also CA 178; DLB 56, 118; EWL 3

Barlow, Joel 1754-1812 .... **NCLC 23**
See also AMWS 2; DLB 37; RGAL 4

Barnard, Mary (Ethel) 1909- .... **CLC 48**
See also CA 21-22; CAP 2; CP 1

Barnes, Djuna 1892-1982 .... **CLC 3, 4, 8, 11,
29, 127; SSC 3**
See Steptoe, Lydia
See also AMWS 3; CA 9-12R; 107; CAD;
CANR 16, 55; CN 1, 2, 3; CWD; DLB 4,
9, 45; EWL 3; GLL 1; MAL 5; MTCW 1,
2; MTFW 2005; RGAL 4; TCLE 1:1;
TUS

Barnes, Jim 1933- .... **NNAL**
See also CA 108; 175; CAAE 175; CAAS
28; DLB 175

Barnes, Julian (Patrick) 1946- . **CLC 42, 141**
See also BRWS 4; CA 102; CANR 19, 54,
115, 137; CN 4, 5, 6, 7; DAB; DLB 194;
DLBY 1993; EWL 3; MTCW 2; MTFW
2005

Barnes, Peter 1931-2004 .... **CLC 5, 56**
See also CA 65-68; 230; CAAS 12; CANR
33, 34, 64, 113; CBD; CD 5, 6; DFS 6;
DLB 13, 233; MTCW 1

Barnes, William 1801-1886 .... **NCLC 75**
See also DLB 32

Baroja (y Nessi), Pio 1872-1956 .... **HLC 1;
TCLC 8**
See also CA 104; EW 9

Baron, David
See Pinter, Harold

Baron Corvo
See Rolfe, Frederick (William Serafino
Austin Lewis Mary)

Barondess, Sue K(aufman)
1926-1977 .... **CLC 8**
See Kaufman, Sue
See also CA 1-4R; 69-72; CANR 1

Baron de Teive
See Pessoa, Fernando (Antonio Nogueira)

Baroness Von S.
See Zangwill, Israel

Barres, (Auguste-)Maurice
1862-1923 .... **TCLC 47**
See also CA 164; DLB 123; GFL 1789 to
the Present

Barreto, Afonso Henrique de Lima
See Lima Barreto, Afonso Henrique de

Barrett, Andrea 1954- .... **CLC 150**
See also CA 156; CANR 92; CN 7

Barrett, Michele .... **CLC 65**

Barrett, (Roger) Syd 1946- .... **CLC 35**

Barrett, William (Christopher)
1913-1992 .... **CLC 27**
See also CA 13-16R; 139; CANR 11, 67;
INT CANR-11

Barrett Browning, Elizabeth
1806-1861 ... **NCLC 1, 16, 61, 66; PC 6,
62; WLC**
See also AAYA 63; BRW 4; CDBLB 1832-
1890; DA; DA3; DAB; DAC; DAM MST,
POET; DLB 32, 199; EXPP; FL 1:2; PAB;
PFS 2, 16, 23; TEA; WLIT 4; WP

Barrie, J(ames) M(atthew)
1860-1937 .... **TCLC 2, 164**
See also BRWS 3; BYA 4, 5; CA 104; 136;
CANR 77; CDBLB 1890-1914; CLR 16;
CWRI 5; DA3; DAB; DAM DRAM; DFS
7; DLB 10, 141, 156; EWL 3; FANT;
MAICYA 1, 2; MTCW 2; MTFW 2005;
SATA 100; SUFW; WCH; WLIT 4; YABC
1

Barrington, Michael
See Moorcock, Michael (John)

Barrol, Grady
See Bograd, Larry

Barry, Mike
See Malzberg, Barry N(athaniel)

Barry, Philip 1896-1949 .... **TCLC 11**
See also CA 109; 199; DFS 9; DLB 7, 228;
MAL 5; RGAL 4

Bart, Andre Schwarz
See Schwarz-Bart, Andre

EXPN; EXPS; HGG; LAIT 3, 5; LATS 1:2; LMFS 2; MAL 5; MTCW 1, 2; MTFW 2005; NFS 1, 22; RGAL 4; RGSF 2; SATA 11, 64, 123; SCFW 1, 2; SFW 4; SSFS 1, 20; SUFW 1, 2; TUS; YAW

Braddon, Mary Elizabeth
1837-1915 .... **TCLC 111**
See also BRWS 8; CA 108; 179; CMW 4; DLB 18, 70, 156; HGG

Bradfield, Scott (Michael) 1955- .... **SSC 65**
See also CA 147; CANR 90; HGG; SUFW 2

Bradford, Gamaliel 1863-1932 .... **TCLC 36**
See also CA 160; DLB 17

Bradford, William 1590-1657 .... **LC 64**
See also DLB 24, 30; RGAL 4

Bradley, David (Henry), Jr. 1950- .... **BLC 1; CLC 23, 118**
See also BW 1, 3; CA 104; CANR 26, 81; CN 4, 5, 6, 7; DAM MULT; DLB 33

Bradley, John Ed(mund, Jr.) 1958- . **CLC 55**
See also CA 139; CANR 99; CN 6, 7; CSW

Bradley, Marion Zimmer
1930-1999 .... **CLC 30**
See Chapman, Lee; Dexter, John; Gardner, Miriam; Ives, Morgan; Rivers, Elfrida
See also AAYA 40; BPFB 1; CA 57-60; 185; CAAS 10; CANR 7, 31, 51, 75, 107; CPW; DA3; DAM POP; DLB 8; FANT; FW; MTCW 1, 2; MTFW 2005; SATA 90, 139; SATA-Obit 116; SFW 4; SUFW 2; YAW

Bradshaw, John 1933- .... **CLC 70**
See also CA 138; CANR 61

Bradstreet, Anne 1612(?)-1672 ...... **LC 4, 30; PC 10**
See also AMWS 1; CDALB 1640-1865; DA; DA3; DAC; DAM MST, POET; DLB 24; EXPP; FW; PFS 6; RGAL 4; TUS; WP

Brady, Joan 1939- .... **CLC 86**
See also CA 141

Bragg, Melvyn 1939- .... **CLC 10**
See also BEST 89:3; CA 57-60; CANR 10, 48, 89; CN 1, 2, 3, 4, 5, 6, 7; DLB 14, 271; RHW

Brahe, Tycho 1546-1601 .... **LC 45**
See also DLB 300

Braine, John (Gerard) 1922-1986 . **CLC 1, 3, 41**
See also CA 1-4R; 120; CANR 1, 33; CD-BLB 1945-1960; CN 1, 2, 3, 4; DLB 15; DLBY 1986; EWL 3; MTCW 1

Braithwaite, William Stanley (Beaumont)
1878-1962 .... **BLC 1; HR 1:2; PC 52**
See also BW 1; CA 125; DAM MULT; DLB 50, 54; MAL 5

Bramah, Ernest 1868-1942 .... **TCLC 72**
See also CA 156; CMW 4; DLB 70; FANT

Brammer, Billy Lee
See Brammer, William

Brammer, William 1929-1978 .... **CLC 31**
See also CA 235; 77-80

Brancati, Vitaliano 1907-1954 .... **TCLC 12**
See also CA 109; DLB 264; EWL 3

Brancato, Robin F(idler) 1936- .... **CLC 35**
See also AAYA 9, 68; BYA 6; CA 69-72; CANR 11, 45; CLR 32; JRDA; MAICYA 2; MAICYAS 1; SAAS 9; SATA 97; WYA; YAW

Brand, Dionne 1953- .... **CLC 192**
See also BW 2; CA 143; CANR 143; CWP

Brand, Max
See Faust, Frederick (Schiller)
See also BPFB 1; TCWW 1, 2

Brand, Millen 1906-1980 .... **CLC 7**
See also CA 21-24R; 97-100; CANR 72

Branden, Barbara .... **CLC 44**
See also CA 148

Brandes, Georg (Morris Cohen)
1842-1927 .... **TCLC 10**
See also CA 105; 189; DLB 300

Brandys, Kazimierz 1916-2000 .... **CLC 62**
See also CA 239; EWL 3

Branley, Franklyn M(ansfield)
1915-2002 .... **CLC 21**
See also CA 33-36R; 207; CANR 14, 39; CLR 13; MAICYA 1, 2; SAAS 16; SATA 4, 68, 136

Brant, Beth (E.) 1941- .... **NNAL**
See also CA 144; FW

Brant, Sebastian 1457-1521 .... **LC 112**
See also DLB 179; RGWL 2, 3

Brathwaite, Edward Kamau
1930- .... **BLCS; CLC 11; PC 56**
See also BW 2, 3; CA 25-28R; CANR 11, 26, 47, 107; CDWLB 3; CP 1, 2, 3, 4, 5, 6, 7; DAM POET; DLB 125; EWL 3

Brathwaite, Kamau
See Brathwaite, Edward Kamau

Brautigan, Richard (Gary)
1935-1984 .... **CLC 1, 3, 5, 9, 12, 34, 42; TCLC 133**
See also BPFB 1; CA 53-56; 113; CANR 34; CN 1, 2, 3; CP 1, 2, 3, 4; DA3; DAM NOV; DLB 2, 5, 206; DLBY 1980, 1984; FANT; MAL 5; MTCW 1; RGAL 4; SATA 56

Brave Bird, Mary .... **NNAL**
See Crow Dog, Mary (Ellen)

Braverman, Kate 1950- .... **CLC 67**
See also CA 89-92; CANR 141

Brecht, (Eugen) Bertolt (Friedrich)
1898-1956 ..... **DC 3; TCLC 1, 6, 13, 35, 169; WLC**
See also CA 104; 133; CANR 62; CDWLB 2; DA; DA3; DAB; DAC; DAM DRAM, MST; DFS 4, 5, 9; DLB 56, 124; EW 11; EWL 3; IDTP; MTCW 1, 2; MTFW 2005; RGWL 2, 3; TWA

Brecht, Eugen Berthold Friedrich
See Brecht, (Eugen) Bertolt (Friedrich)

Bremer, Fredrika 1801-1865 .... **NCLC 11**
See also DLB 254

Brennan, Christopher John
1870-1932 .... **TCLC 17**
See also CA 117; 188; DLB 230; EWL 3

Brennan, Maeve 1917-1993 ... **CLC 5; TCLC 124**
See also CA 81-84; CANR 72, 100

Brenner, Jozef 1887-1919
See Csath, Geza
See also CA 240

Brent, Linda
See Jacobs, Harriet A(nn)

Brentano, Clemens (Maria)
1778-1842 .... **NCLC 1**
See also DLB 90; RGWL 2, 3

Brent of Bin Bin
See Franklin, (Stella Maria Sarah) Miles (Lampe)

Brenton, Howard 1942- .... **CLC 31**
See also CA 69-72; CANR 33, 67; CBD; CD 5, 6; DLB 13; MTCW 1

Breslin, James 1930-
See Breslin, Jimmy
See also CA 73-76; CANR 31, 75, 139; DAM NOV; MTCW 1, 2; MTFW 2005

Breslin, Jimmy .... **CLC 4, 43**
See Breslin, James
See also AITN 1; DLB 185; MTCW 2

Bresson, Robert 1901(?)-1999 .... **CLC 16**
See also CA 110; 187; CANR 49

Breton, Andre 1896-1966 .. **CLC 2, 9, 15, 54; PC 15**
See also CA 19-20; 25-28R; CANR 40, 60; CAP 2; DLB 65, 258; EW 11; EWL 3; GFL 1789 to the Present; LMFS 2; MTCW 1, 2; MTFW 2005; RGWL 2, 3; TWA; WP

Breytenbach, Breyten 1939(?)- .. **CLC 23, 37, 126**
See also CA 113; 129; CANR 61, 122; CWW 2; DAM POET; DLB 225; EWL 3

Bridgers, Sue Ellen 1942- .... **CLC 26**
See also AAYA 8, 49; BYA 7, 8; CA 65-68; CANR 11, 36; CLR 18; DLB 52; JRDA; MAICYA 1, 2; SAAS 1; SATA 22, 90; SATA-Essay 109; WYA; YAW

Bridges, Robert (Seymour)
1844-1930 .... **PC 28; TCLC 1**
See also BRW 6; CA 104; 152; CDBLB 1890-1914; DAM POET; DLB 19, 98

Bridie, James .... **TCLC 3**
See Mavor, Osborne Henry
See also DLB 10; EWL 3

Brin, David 1950- .... **CLC 34**
See also AAYA 21; CA 102; CANR 24, 70, 125, 127; INT CANR-24; SATA 65; SCFW 2; SFW 4

Brink, Andre (Philippus) 1935- . **CLC 18, 36, 106**
See also AFW; BRWS 6; CA 104; CANR 39, 62, 109, 133; CN 4, 5, 6, 7; DLB 225; EWL 3; INT CA-103; LATS 1:2; MTCW 1, 2; MTFW 2005; WLIT 2

Brinsmead, H. F(ay)
See Brinsmead, H(esba) F(ay)

Brinsmead, H. F.
See Brinsmead, H(esba) F(ay)

Brinsmead, H(esba) F(ay) 1922- ...... **CLC 21**
See also CA 21-24R; CANR 10; CLR 47; CWRI 5; MAICYA 1, 2; SAAS 5; SATA 18, 78

Brittain, Vera (Mary) 1893(?)-1970 . **CLC 23**
See also BRWS 10; CA 13-16; 25-28R; CANR 58; CAP 1; DLB 191; FW; MTCW 1, 2

Broch, Hermann 1886-1951 .... **TCLC 20**
See also CA 117; 211; CDWLB 2; DLB 85, 124; EW 10; EWL 3; RGWL 2, 3

Brock, Rose
See Hansen, Joseph
See also GLL 1

Brod, Max 1884-1968 .... **TCLC 115**
See also CA 5-8R; 25-28R; CANR 7; DLB 81; EWL 3

Brodkey, Harold (Roy) 1930-1996 .. **CLC 56; TCLC 123**
See also CA 111; 151; CANR 71; CN 4, 5, 6; DLB 130

Brodsky, Iosif Alexandrovich 1940-1996
See Brodsky, Joseph
See also AITN 1; CA 41-44R; 151; CANR 37, 106; DA3; DAM POET; MTCW 1, 2; MTFW 2005; RGWL 2, 3

Brodsky, Joseph . **CLC 4, 6, 13, 36, 100; PC 9**
See Brodsky, Iosif Alexandrovich
See also AMWS 8; CWW 2; DLB 285; EWL 3; MTCW 1

Brodsky, Michael (Mark) 1948- .... **CLC 19**
See also CA 102; CANR 18, 41, 58; DLB 244

Brodzki, Bella ed. .... **CLC 65**

Brome, Richard 1590(?)-1652 .... **LC 61**
See also BRWS 10; DLB 58

Bromell, Henry 1947- .... **CLC 5**
See also CA 53-56; CANR 9, 115, 116

Bromfield, Louis (Brucker)
1896-1956 .... **TCLC 11**
See also CA 107; 155; DLB 4, 9, 86; RGAL
4; RHW

Broner, E(sther) M(asserman)
1930- .... **CLC 19**
See also CA 17-20R; CANR 8, 25, 72; CN
4, 5, 6; DLB 28

Bronk, William (M.) 1918-1999 .... **CLC 10**
See also CA 89-92; 177; CANR 23; CP 3,
4, 5, 6, 7; DLB 165

Bronstein, Lev Davidovich
See Trotsky, Leon

Bronte, Anne 1820-1849 ..... **NCLC 4, 71, 102**
See also BRW 5; BRWR 1; DA3; DLB 21,
199; TEA

Bronte, (Patrick) Branwell
1817-1848 .... **NCLC 109**

Bronte, Charlotte 1816-1855 ...... **NCLC 3, 8,
33, 58, 105, 155; WLC**
See also AAYA 17; BRW 5; BRWC 2;
BRWR 1; BYA 2; CDBLB 1832-1890;
DA; DA3; DAB; DAC; DAM MST, NOV;
DLB 21, 159, 199; EXPN; FL 1:2; GL 2;
LAIT 2; NFS 4; TEA; WLIT 4

Bronte, Emily (Jane) 1818-1848 ... **NCLC 16,
35, 165; PC 8; WLC**
See also AAYA 17; BPFB 1; BRW 5;
BRWC 1; BRWR 1; BYA 3; CDBLB
1832-1890; DA; DA3; DAB; DAC; DAM
MST, NOV, POET; DLB 21, 32, 199;
EXPN; FL 1:2; GL 2; LAIT 1; TEA;
WLIT 3

Brontes
See Bronte, Anne; Bronte, Charlotte; Bronte,
Emily (Jane)

Brooke, Frances 1724-1789 .... **LC 6, 48**
See also DLB 39, 99

Brooke, Henry 1703(?)-1783 .... **LC 1**
See also DLB 39

Brooke, Rupert (Chawner)
1887-1915 ..... **PC 24; TCLC 2, 7; WLC**
See also BRWS 3; CA 104; 132; CANR 61;
CDBLB 1914-1945; DA; DAB; DAC;
DAM MST, POET; DLB 19, 216; EXPP;
GLL 2; MTCW 1, 2; MTFW 2005; PFS
7; TEA

Brooke-Haven, P.
See Wodehouse, P(elham) G(renville)

Brooke-Rose, Christine 1926(?)- ..... **CLC 40,
184**
See also BRWS 4; CA 13-16R; CANR 58,
118; CN 1, 2, 3, 4, 5, 6, 7; DLB 14, 231;
EWL 3; SFW 4

Brookner, Anita 1928- .. **CLC 32, 34, 51, 136**
See also BRWS 4; CA 114; 120; CANR 37,
56, 87, 130; CN 4, 5, 6, 7; CPW; DA3;
DAB; DAM POP; DLB 194; DLBY 1987;
EWL 3; MTCW 1, 2; MTFW 2005; TEA

Brooks, Cleanth 1906-1994 . **CLC 24, 86, 110**
See also AMWS 14; CA 17-20R; 145;
CANR 33, 35; CSW; DLB 63; DLBY
1994; EWL 3; INT CANR-35; MAL 5;
MTCW 1, 2; MTFW 2005

Brooks, George
See Baum, L(yman) Frank

Brooks, Gwendolyn (Elizabeth)
1917-2000 ... **BLC 1; CLC 1, 2, 4, 5, 15,
49, 125; PC 7; WLC**
See also AAYA 20; AFAW 1, 2; AITN 1;
AMWS 3; BW 2, 3; CA 1-4R; 190; CANR
1, 27, 52, 75, 132; CDALB 1941-1968;
CLR 27; CP 1, 2, 3, 4, 5, 6, 7; CWP; DA;
DA3; DAC; DAM MST, MULT, POET;
DLB 5, 76, 165; EWL 3; EXPP; FL 1:5;
MAL 5; MAWW; MTCW 1, 2; MTFW
2005; PFS 1, 2, 4, 6; RGAL 4; SATA 6;
SATA-Obit 123; TUS; WP

Brooks, Mel .... **CLC 12, 217**
See Kaminsky, Melvin
See also AAYA 13, 48; DLB 26

Brooks, Peter (Preston) 1938- .... **CLC 34**
See also CA 45-48; CANR 1, 107

Brooks, Van Wyck 1886-1963 .... **CLC 29**
See also AMW; CA 1-4R; CANR 6; DLB
45, 63, 103; MAL 5; TUS

Brophy, Brigid (Antonia)
1929-1995 .... **CLC 6, 11, 29, 105**
See also CA 5-8R; 149; CAAS 4; CANR
25, 53; CBD; CN 1, 2, 3, 4, 5, 6; CWD;
DA3; DLB 14, 271; EWL 3; MTCW 1, 2

Brosman, Catharine Savage 1934- ..... **CLC 9**
See also CA 61-64; CANR 21, 46

Brossard, Nicole 1943- .... **CLC 115, 169**
See also CA 122; CAAS 16; CANR 140;
CCA 1; CWP; CWW 2; DLB 53; EWL 3;
FW; GLL 2; RGWL 3

Brother Antoninus
See Everson, William (Oliver)

The Brothers Quay
See Quay, Stephen; Quay, Timothy

Broughton, T(homas) Alan 1936- ..... **CLC 19**
See also CA 45-48; CANR 2, 23, 48, 111

Broumas, Olga 1949- .... **CLC 10, 73**
See also CA 85-88; CANR 20, 69, 110; CP
7; CWP; GLL 2

Broun, Heywood 1888-1939 .... **TCLC 104**
See also DLB 29, 171

Brown, Alan 1950- .... **CLC 99**
See also CA 156

Brown, Charles Brockden
1771-1810 .... **NCLC 22, 74, 122**
See also AMWS 1; CDALB 1640-1865;
DLB 37, 59, 73; FW; GL 2; HGG; LMFS
1; RGAL 4; TUS

Brown, Christy 1932-1981 .... **CLC 63**
See also BYA 13; CA 105; 104; CANR 72;
DLB 14

Brown, Claude 1937-2002 ... **BLC 1; CLC 30**
See also AAYA 7; BW 1, 3; CA 73-76; 205;
CANR 81; DAM MULT

Brown, Dan 1964- .... **CLC 209**
See also AAYA 55; CA 217; MTFW 2005

Brown, Dee (Alexander)
1908-2002 .... **CLC 18, 47**
See also AAYA 30; CA 13-16R; 212; CAAS
6; CANR 11, 45, 60; CPW; CSW; DA3;
DAM POP; DLBY 1980; LAIT 2; MTCW
1, 2; MTFW 2005; NCFS 5; SATA 5, 110;
SATA-Obit 141; TCWW 1, 2

Brown, George
See Wertmueller, Lina

Brown, George Douglas
1869-1902 .... **TCLC 28**
See Douglas, George
See also CA 162

Brown, George Mackay 1921-1996 ... **CLC 5,
48, 100**
See also BRWS 6; CA 21-24R; 151; CAAS
6; CANR 12, 37, 67; CN 1, 2, 3, 4, 5, 6;
CP 1, 2, 3, 4; DLB 14, 27, 139, 271;
MTCW 1; RGSF 2; SATA 35

Brown, (William) Larry 1951-2004 . **CLC 73**
See also CA 130; 134; 233; CANR 117,
145; CSW; DLB 234; INT CA-134

Brown, Moses
See Barrett, William (Christopher)

Brown, Rita Mae 1944- .... **CLC 18, 43, 79**
See also BPFB 1; CA 45-48; CANR 2, 11,
35, 62, 95, 138; CN 5, 6, 7; CPW; CSW;
DA3; DAM NOV, POP; FW; INT CANR-
11; MAL 5; MTCW 1, 2; MTFW 2005;
NFS 9; RGAL 4; TUS

Brown, Roderick (Langmere) Haig-
See Haig-Brown, Roderick (Langmere)

Brown, Rosellen 1939- .... **CLC 32, 170**
See also CA 77-80; CAAS 10; CANR 14,
44, 98; CN 6, 7

Brown, Sterling Allen 1901-1989 ...... **BLC 1;
CLC 1, 23, 59; HR 1:2; PC 55**
See also AFAW 1, 2; BW 1, 3; CA 85-88;
127; CANR 26; CP 3, 4; DA3; DAM
MULT, POET; DLB 48, 51, 63; MAL 5;
MTCW 1, 2; MTFW 2005; RGAL 4; WP

Brown, Will
See Ainsworth, William Harrison

Brown, William Hill 1765-1793 .... **LC 93**
See also DLB 37

Brown, William Wells 1815-1884 ...... **BLC 1;
DC 1; NCLC 2, 89**
See also DAM MULT; DLB 3, 50, 183,
248; RGAL 4

Browne, (Clyde) Jackson 1948(?)- ... **CLC 21**
See also CA 120

Browne, Sir Thomas 1605-1682 .... **LC 111**
See also BRW 2; DLB 151

Browning, Robert 1812-1889 . **NCLC 19, 79;
PC 2, 61; WLCS**
See also BRW 4; BRWC 2; BRWR 2; CD-
BLB 1832-1890; CLR 97; DA; DA3;
DAB; DAC; DAM MST, POET; DLB 32,
163; EXPP; LATS 1:1; PAB; PFS 1, 15;
RGEL 2; TEA; WLIT 4; WP; YABC 1

Browning, Tod 1882-1962 .... **CLC 16**
See also CA 141; 117

Brownmiller, Susan 1935- .... **CLC 159**
See also CA 103; CANR 35, 75, 137; DAM
NOV; FW; MTCW 1, 2; MTFW 2005

Brownson, Orestes Augustus
1803-1876 .... **NCLC 50**
See also DLB 1, 59, 73, 243

Bruccoli, Matthew J(oseph) 1931- ... **CLC 34**
See also CA 9-12R; CANR 7, 87; DLB 103

Bruce, Lenny .... **CLC 21**
See Schneider, Leonard Alfred

Bruchac, Joseph III 1942- .... **NNAL**
See also AAYA 19; CA 33-36R; CANR 13,
47, 75, 94, 137; CLR 46; CWRI 5; DAM
MULT; JRDA; MAICYA 2; MAICYAS 1;
MTCW 2; MTFW 2005; SATA 42, 89,
131

Bruin, John
See Brutus, Dennis

Brulard, Henri
See Stendhal

Brulls, Christian
See Simenon, Georges (Jacques Christian)

Brunetto Latini c. 1220-1294 .... **CMLC 73**

Brunner, John (Kilian Houston)
1934-1995 .... **CLC 8, 10**
See also CA 1-4R; 149; CAAS 8; CANR 2,
37; CPW; DAM POP; DLB 261; MTCW
1, 2; SCFW 1, 2; SFW 4

Bruno, Giordano 1548-1600 .... **LC 27**
See also RGWL 2, 3

Brutus, Dennis 1924- ... **BLC 1; CLC 43; PC
24**
See also AFW; BW 2, 3; CA 49-52; CAAS
14; CANR 2, 27, 42, 81; CDWLB 3; CP
1, 2, 3, 4, 5, 6, 7; DAM MULT, POET;
DLB 117, 225; EWL 3

Bryan, C(ourtlandt) D(ixon) B(arnes)
1936- .... **CLC 29**
See also CA 73-76; CANR 13, 68; DLB
185; INT CANR-13

Bryan, Michael
See Moore, Brian
See also CCA 1

Bryan, William Jennings
1860-1925 .... **TCLC 99**
See also DLB 303

Bryant, William Cullen 1794-1878 . NCLC 6, 46; PC 20
See also AMWS 1; CDALB 1640-1865; DA; DAB; DAC; DAM MST, POET; DLB 3, 43, 59, 189, 250; EXPP; PAB; RGAL 4; TUS

Bryusov, Valery Yakovlevich 1873-1924 .... TCLC 10
See also CA 107; 155; EWL 3; SFW 4

Buchan, John 1875-1940 .... TCLC 41
See also CA 108; 145; CMW 4; DAB; DAM POP; DLB 34, 70, 156; HGG; MSW; MTCW 2; RGEL 2; RHW; YABC 2

Buchanan, George 1506-1582 .... LC 4
See also DLB 132

Buchanan, Robert 1841-1901 .... TCLC 107
See also CA 179; DLB 18, 35

Buchheim, Lothar-Guenther 1918- .... CLC 6
See also CA 85-88

Buchner, (Karl) Georg 1813-1837 .... NCLC 26, 146
See also CDWLB 2; DLB 133; EW 6; RGSF 2; RGWL 2, 3; TWA

Buchwald, Art(hur) 1925- .... CLC 33
See also AITN 1; CA 5-8R; CANR 21, 67, 107; MTCW 1, 2; SATA 10

Buck, Pearl S(ydenstricker) 1892-1973 .... CLC 7, 11, 18, 127
See also AAYA 42; AITN 1; AMWS 2; BPFB 1; CA 1-4R; 41-44R; CANR 1, 34; CDALBS; CN 1; DA; DA3; DAB; DAC; DAM MST, NOV; DLB 9, 102; EWL 3; LAIT 3; MAL 5; MTCW 1, 2; MTFW 2005; RGAL 4; RHW; SATA 1, 25; TUS

Buckler, Ernest 1908-1984 .... CLC 13
See also CA 11-12; 114; CAP 1; CCA 1; CN 1, 2, 3; DAC; DAM MST; DLB 68; SATA 47

Buckley, Christopher (Taylor) 1952- .... CLC 165
See also CA 139; CANR 119

Buckley, Vincent (Thomas) 1925-1988 .... CLC 57
See also CA 101; CP 1, 2, 3, 4; DLB 289

Buckley, William F(rank), Jr. 1925- . CLC 7, 18, 37
See also AITN 1; BPFB 1; CA 1-4R; CANR 1, 24, 53, 93, 133; CMW 4; CPW; DA3; DAM POP; DLB 137; DLBY 1980; INT CANR-24; MTCW 1, 2; MTFW 2005; TUS

Buechner, (Carl) Frederick 1926- . CLC 2, 4, 6, 9
See also AMWS 12; BPFB 1; CA 13-16R; CANR 11, 39, 64, 114, 138; CN 1, 2, 3, 4, 5, 6, 7; DAM NOV; DLBY 1980; INT CANR-11; MAL 5; MTCW 1, 2; MTFW 2005; TCLE 1:1

Buell, John (Edward) 1927- .... CLC 10
See also CA 1-4R; CANR 71; DLB 53

Buero Vallejo, Antonio 1916-2000 ... CLC 15, 46, 139; DC 18
See also CA 106; 189; CANR 24, 49, 75; CWW 2; DFS 11; EWL 3; HW 1; MTCW 1, 2

Bufalino, Gesualdo 1920-1996 .... CLC 74
See also CA 209; CWW 2; DLB 196

Bugayev, Boris Nikolayevich 1880-1934 .... PC 11; TCLC 7
See Bely, Andrey; Belyi, Andrei
See also CA 104; 165; MTCW 2; MTFW 2005

Bukowski, Charles 1920-1994 ... CLC 2, 5, 9, 41, 82, 108; PC 18; SSC 45
See also CA 17-20R; 144; CANR 40, 62, 105; CN 4, 5; CP 1, 2, 3, 4; CPW; DA3; DAM NOV, POET; DLB 5, 130, 169; EWL 3; MAL 5; MTCW 1, 2; MTFW 2005

Bulgakov, Mikhail (Afanas'evich) 1891-1940 ..... SSC 18; TCLC 2, 16, 159
See also BPFB 1; CA 105; 152; DAM DRAM, NOV; DLB 272; EWL 3; MTCW 2; MTFW 2005; NFS 8; RGSF 2; RGWL 2, 3; SFW 4; TWA

Bulgya, Alexander Alexandrovich 1901-1956 .... TCLC 53
See Fadeev, Aleksandr Aleksandrovich; Fadeev, Alexandr Alexandrovich; Fadeyev, Alexander
See also CA 117; 181

Bullins, Ed 1935- ... BLC 1; CLC 1, 5, 7; DC 6
See also BW 2, 3; CA 49-52; CAAS 16; CAD; CANR 24, 46, 73, 134; CD 5, 6; DAM DRAM, MULT; DLB 7, 38, 249; EWL 3; MAL 5; MTCW 1, 2; MTFW 2005; RGAL 4

Bulosan, Carlos 1911-1956 .... AAL
See also CA 216; DLB 312; RGAL 4

Bulwer-Lytton, Edward (George Earle Lytton) 1803-1873 .... NCLC 1, 45
See also DLB 21; RGEL 2; SFW 4; SUFW 1; TEA

Bunin, Ivan Alexeyevich 1870-1953 ... SSC 5; TCLC 6
See also CA 104; DLB 317; EWL 3; RGSF 2; RGWL 2, 3; TWA

Bunting, Basil 1900-1985 ...... CLC 10, 39, 47
See also BRWS 7; CA 53-56; 115; CANR 7; CP 1, 2, 3, 4; DAM POET; DLB 20; EWL 3; RGEL 2

Bunuel, Luis 1900-1983 ... CLC 16, 80; HLC 1
See also CA 101; 110; CANR 32, 77; DAM MULT; HW 1

Bunyan, John 1628-1688 ..... LC 4, 69; WLC
See also BRW 2; BYA 5; CDBLB 1660-1789; DA; DAB; DAC; DAM MST; DLB 39; RGEL 2; TEA; WCH; WLIT 3

Buravsky, Alexandr .... CLC 59

Burckhardt, Jacob (Christoph) 1818-1897 .... NCLC 49
See also EW 6

Burford, Eleanor
See Hibbert, Eleanor Alice Burford

Burgess, Anthony . CLC 1, 2, 4, 5, 8, 10, 13, 15, 22, 40, 62, 81, 94
See Wilson, John (Anthony) Burgess
See also AAYA 25; AITN 1; BRWS 1; CD-BLB 1960 to Present; CN 1, 2, 3, 4, 5; DAB; DLB 14, 194, 261; DLBY 1998; EWL 3; RGEL 2; RHW; SFW 4; YAW

Burke, Edmund 1729(?)-1797 .... LC 7, 36; WLC
See also BRW 3; DA; DA3; DAB; DAC; DAM MST; DLB 104, 252; RGEL 2; TEA

Burke, Kenneth (Duva) 1897-1993 ... CLC 2, 24
See also AMW; CA 5-8R; 143; CANR 39, 74, 136; CN 1, 2; CP 1, 2, 3, 4; DLB 45, 63; EWL 3; MAL 5; MTCW 1, 2; MTFW 2005; RGAL 4

Burke, Leda
See Garnett, David

Burke, Ralph
See Silverberg, Robert

Burke, Thomas 1886-1945 .... TCLC 63
See also CA 113; 155; CMW 4; DLB 197

Burney, Fanny 1752-1840 .... NCLC 12, 54, 107
See also BRWS 3; DLB 39; FL 1:2; NFS 16; RGEL 2; TEA

Burney, Frances
See Burney, Fanny

Burns, Robert 1759-1796 ... LC 3, 29, 40; PC 6; WLC
See also AAYA 51; BRW 3; CDBLB 1789-1832; DA; DA3; DAB; DAC; DAM MST, POET; DLB 109; EXPP; PAB; RGEL 2; TEA; WP

Burns, Tex
See L'Amour, Louis (Dearborn)

Burnshaw, Stanley 1906- .... CLC 3, 13, 44
See also CA 9-12R; CP 1, 2, 3, 4, 5, 6, 7; DLB 48; DLBY 1997

Burr, Anne 1937- .... CLC 6
See also CA 25-28R

Burroughs, Edgar Rice 1875-1950 . TCLC 2, 32
See also AAYA 11; BPFB 1; BYA 4, 9; CA 104; 132; CANR 131; DA3; DAM NOV; DLB 8; FANT; MTCW 1, 2; MTFW 2005; RGAL 4; SATA 41; SCFW 1, 2; SFW 4; TCWW 1, 2; TUS; YAW

Burroughs, William S(eward) 1914-1997 .. CLC 1, 2, 5, 15, 22, 42, 75, 109; TCLC 121; WLC
See Lee, William; Lee, Willy
See also AAYA 60; AITN 2; AMWS 3; BG 1:2; BPFB 1; CA 9-12R; 160; CANR 20, 52, 104; CN 1, 2, 3, 4, 5, 6; CPW; DA; DA3; DAB; DAC; DAM MST, NOV, POP; DLB 2, 8, 16, 152, 237; DLBY 1981, 1997; EWL 3; HGG; LMFS 2; MAL 5; MTCW 1, 2; MTFW 2005; RGAL 4; SFW 4

Burton, Sir Richard F(rancis) 1821-1890 .... NCLC 42
See also DLB 55, 166, 184; SSFS 21

Burton, Robert 1577-1640 .... LC 74
See also DLB 151; RGEL 2

Buruma, Ian 1951- .... CLC 163
See also CA 128; CANR 65, 141

Busch, Frederick 1941- ... CLC 7, 10, 18, 47, 166
See also CA 33-36R; CAAS 1; CANR 45, 73, 92; CN 1, 2, 3, 4, 5, 6, 7; DLB 6, 218

Bush, Barney (Furman) 1946- .... NNAL
See also CA 145

Bush, Ronald 1946- .... CLC 34
See also CA 136

Bustos, F(rancisco)
See Borges, Jorge Luis

Bustos Domecq, H(onorio)
See Bioy Casares, Adolfo; Borges, Jorge Luis

Butler, Octavia E(stelle) 1947- .. BLCS; CLC 38, 121
See also AAYA 18, 48; AFAW 2; AMWS 13; BPFB 1; BW 2, 3; CA 73-76; CANR 12, 24, 38, 73, 145; CLR 65; CN 7; CPW; DA3; DAM MULT, POP; DLB 33; LATS 1:2; MTCW 1, 2; MTFW 2005; NFS 8, 21; SATA 84; SCFW 2; SFW 4; SSFS 6; TCLE 1:1; YAW

Butler, Robert Olen, (Jr.) 1945- ...... CLC 81, 162
See also AMWS 12; BPFB 1; CA 112; CANR 66, 138; CN 7; CSW; DAM POP; DLB 173; INT CA-112; MAL 5; MTCW 2; MTFW 2005; SSFS 11

Butler, Samuel 1612-1680 .... LC 16, 43
See also DLB 101, 126; RGEL 2

Butler, Samuel 1835-1902 .... TCLC 1, 33; WLC
See also BRWS 2; CA 143; CDBLB 1890-1914; DA; DA3; DAB; DAC; DAM MST, NOV; DLB 18, 57, 174; RGEL 2; SFW 4; TEA

Butler, Walter C.
See Faust, Frederick (Schiller)

Canfield, Dorothea F.
See Fisher, Dorothy (Frances) Canfield
Canfield, Dorothea Frances
See Fisher, Dorothy (Frances) Canfield
Canfield, Dorothy
See Fisher, Dorothy (Frances) Canfield
Canin, Ethan 1960- .... **CLC 55; SSC 70**
See also CA 131; 135; MAL 5
Cankar, Ivan 1876-1918 .... **TCLC 105**
See also CDWLB 4; DLB 147; EWL 3
Cannon, Curt
See Hunter, Evan
Cao, Lan 1961- .... **CLC 109**
See also CA 165
Cape, Judith
See Page, P(atricia) K(athleen)
See also CCA 1
Capek, Karel 1890-1938 .... **DC 1; SSC 36;**
TCLC 6, 37; WLC
See also CA 104; 140; CDWLB 4; DA;
DA3; DAB; DAC; DAM DRAM, MST,
NOV; DFS 7, 11; DLB 215; EW 10; EWL
3; MTCW 2; MTFW 2005; RGSF 2;
RGWL 2, 3; SCFW 1, 2; SFW 4
Capote, Truman 1924-1984 . **CLC 1, 3, 8, 13,**
19, 34, 38, 58; SSC 2, 47; TCLC 164;
WLC
See also AAYA 61; AMWS 3; BPFB 1; CA
5-8R; 113; CANR 18, 62; CDALB 1941-
1968; CN 1, 2, 3; CPW; DA; DA3; DAB;
DAC; DAM MST, NOV, POP; DLB 2,
185, 227; DLBY 1980, 1984; EWL 3;
EXPS; GLL 1; LAIT 3; MAL 5; MTCW
1, 2; MTFW 2005; NCFS 2; RGAL 4;
RGSF 2; SATA 91; SSFS 2; TUS
Capra, Frank 1897-1991 .... **CLC 16**
See also AAYA 52; CA 61-64; 135
Caputo, Philip 1941- .... **CLC 32**
See also AAYA 60; CA 73-76; CANR 40,
135; YAW
Caragiale, Ion Luca 1852-1912 ...... **TCLC 76**
See also CA 157
Card, Orson Scott 1951- .... **CLC 44, 47, 50**
See also AAYA 11, 42; BPFB 1; BYA 5, 8;
CA 102; CANR 27, 47, 73, 102, 106, 133;
CPW; DA3; DAM POP; FANT; INT
CANR-27; MTCW 1, 2; MTFW 2005;
NFS 5; SATA 83, 127; SCFW 2; SFW 4;
SUFW 2; YAW
Cardenal, Ernesto 1925- .... **CLC 31, 161;**
HLC 1; PC 22
See also CA 49-52; CANR 2, 32, 66, 138;
CWW 2; DAM MULT, POET; DLB 290;
EWL 3; HW 1, 2; LAWS 1; MTCW 1, 2;
MTFW 2005; RGWL 2, 3
Cardinal, Marie 1929-2001 .... **CLC 189**
See also CA 177; CWW 2; DLB 83; FW
Cardozo, Benjamin N(athan)
1870-1938 .... **TCLC 65**
See also CA 117; 164
Carducci, Giosue (Alessandro Giuseppe)
1835-1907 .... **PC 46; TCLC 32**
See also CA 163; EW 7; RGWL 2, 3
Carew, Thomas 1595(?)-1640 . **LC 13; PC 29**
See also BRW 2; DLB 126; PAB; RGEL 2
Carey, Ernestine Gilbreth 1908- ...... **CLC 17**
See also CA 5-8R; CANR 71; SATA 2
Carey, Peter 1943- .... **CLC 40, 55, 96, 183**
See also CA 123; 127; CANR 53, 76, 117;
CN 4, 5, 6, 7; DLB 289; EWL 3; INT CA-
127; MTCW 1, 2; MTFW 2005; RGSF 2;
SATA 94
Carleton, William 1794-1869 .... **NCLC 3**
See also DLB 159; RGEL 2; RGSF 2
Carlisle, Henry (Coffin) 1926- .... **CLC 33**
See also CA 13-16R; CANR 15, 85
Carlsen, Chris
See Holdstock, Robert P.

Carlson, Ron(ald F.) 1947- .... **CLC 54**
See also CA 105, 189; CAAE 189; CANR
27; DLB 244
Carlyle, Thomas 1795-1881 ..... **NCLC 22, 70**
See also BRW 4; CDBLB 1789-1832; DA;
DAB; DAC; DAM MST; DLB 55, 144,
254; RGEL 2; TEA
Carman, (William) Bliss 1861-1929 ... **PC 34;**
TCLC 7
See also CA 104; 152; DAC; DLB 92;
RGEL 2
Carnegie, Dale 1888-1955 .... **TCLC 53**
See also CA 218
Carossa, Hans 1878-1956 .... **TCLC 48**
See also CA 170; DLB 66; EWL 3
Carpenter, Don(ald Richard)
1931-1995 .... **CLC 41**
See also CA 45-48; 149; CANR 1, 71
Carpenter, Edward 1844-1929 .... **TCLC 88**
See also CA 163; GLL 1
Carpenter, John (Howard) 1948- ... **CLC 161**
See also AAYA 2; CA 134; SATA 58
Carpenter, Johnny
See Carpenter, John (Howard)
Carpentier (y Valmont), Alejo
1904-1980 . **CLC 8, 11, 38, 110; HLC 1;**
SSC 35
See also CA 65-68; 97-100; CANR 11, 70;
CDWLB 3; DAM MULT; DLB 113; EWL
3; HW 1, 2; LAW; LMFS 2; RGSF 2;
RGWL 2, 3; WLIT 1
Carr, Caleb 1955- .... **CLC 86**
See also CA 147; CANR 73, 134; DA3
Carr, Emily 1871-1945 .... **TCLC 32**
See also CA 159; DLB 68; FW; GLL 2
Carr, John Dickson 1906-1977 .... **CLC 3**
See Fairbairn, Roger
See also CA 49-52; 69-72; CANR 3, 33,
60; CMW 4; DLB 306; MSW; MTCW 1,
2
Carr, Philippa
See Hibbert, Eleanor Alice Burford
Carr, Virginia Spencer 1929- .... **CLC 34**
See also CA 61-64; DLB 111
Carrere, Emmanuel 1957- .... **CLC 89**
See also CA 200
Carrier, Roch 1937- .... **CLC 13, 78**
See also CA 130; CANR 61; CCA 1; DAC;
DAM MST; DLB 53; SATA 105
Carroll, James Dennis
See Carroll, Jim
Carroll, James P. 1943(?)- .... **CLC 38**
See also CA 81-84; CANR 73, 139; MTCW
2; MTFW 2005
Carroll, Jim 1951- .... **CLC 35, 143**
See also AAYA 17; CA 45-48; CANR 42,
115; NCFS 5
Carroll, Lewis ..... **NCLC 2, 53, 139; PC 18;**
WLC
See Dodgson, Charles L(utwidge)
See also AAYA 39; BRW 5; BYA 5, 13; CD-
BLB 1832-1890; CLR 2, 18; DLB 18,
163, 178; DLBY 1998; EXPN; EXPP;
FANT; JRDA; LAIT 1; NFS 7; PFS 11;
RGEL 2; SUFW 1; TEA; WCH
Carroll, Paul Vincent 1900-1968 ...... **CLC 10**
See also CA 9-12R; 25-28R; DLB 10; EWL
3; RGEL 2
Carruth, Hayden 1921- ..... **CLC 4, 7, 10, 18,**
84; PC 10
See also CA 9-12R; CANR 4, 38, 59, 110;
CP 1, 2, 3, 4, 5, 6, 7; DLB 5, 165; INT
CANR-4; MTCW 1, 2; MTFW 2005;
SATA 47
Carson, Anne 1950- .... **CLC 185; PC 64**
See also AMWS 12; CA 203; DLB 193;
PFS 18; TCLE 1:1
Carson, Ciaran 1948- .... **CLC 201**
See also CA 112; 153; CANR 113; CP 7

Carson, Rachel
See Carson, Rachel Louise
See also AAYA 49; DLB 275
Carson, Rachel Louise 1907-1964 .... **CLC 71**
See Carson, Rachel
See also AMWS 9; ANW; CA 77-80; CANR
35; DA3; DAM POP; FW; LAIT 4; MAL
5; MTCW 1, 2; MTFW 2005; NCFS 1;
SATA 23
Carter, Angela (Olive) 1940-1992 ...... **CLC 5,**
41, 76; SSC 13, 85; TCLC 139
See also BRWS 3; CA 53-56; 136; CANR
12, 36, 61, 106; CN 3, 4, 5; DA3; DLB
14, 207, 261, 319; EXPS; FANT; FW; GL
2; MTCW 1, 2; MTFW 2005; RGSF 2;
SATA 66; SATA-Obit 70; SFW 4; SSFS
4, 12; SUFW 2; WLIT 4
Carter, Nick
See Smith, Martin Cruz
Carver, Raymond 1938-1988 ..... **CLC 22, 36,**
53, 55, 126; PC 54; SSC 8, 51
See also AAYA 44; AMWS 3; BPFB 1; CA
33-36R; 126; CANR 17, 34, 61, 103; CN
4; CPW; DA3; DAM NOV; DLB 130;
DLBY 1984, 1988; EWL 3; MAL 5;
MTCW 1, 2; MTFW 2005; PFS 17;
RGAL 4; RGSF 2; SSFS 3, 6, 12, 13;
TCLE 1:1; TCWW 2; TUS
Cary, Elizabeth, Lady Falkland
1585-1639 .... **LC 30**
Cary, (Arthur) Joyce (Lunel)
1888-1957 .... **TCLC 1, 29**
See also BRW 7; CA 104; 164; CDBLB
1914-1945; DLB 15, 100; EWL 3; MTCW
2; RGEL 2; TEA
Casal, Julian del 1863-1893 .... **NCLC 131**
See also DLB 283; LAW
Casanova, Giacomo
See Casanova de Seingalt, Giovanni Jacopo
See also WLIT 7
Casanova de Seingalt, Giovanni Jacopo
1725-1798 .... **LC 13**
See Casanova, Giacomo
Casares, Adolfo Bioy
See Bioy Casares, Adolfo
See also RGSF 2
Casas, Bartolome de las 1474-1566
See Las Casas, Bartolome de
See also WLIT 1
Casely-Hayford, J(oseph) E(phraim)
1866-1903 .... **BLC 1; TCLC 24**
See also BW 2; CA 123; 152; DAM MULT
Casey, John (Dudley) 1939- .... **CLC 59**
See also BEST 90:2; CA 69-72; CANR 23,
100
Casey, Michael 1947- .... **CLC 2**
See also CA 65-68; CANR 109; CP 2, 3;
DLB 5
Casey, Patrick
See Thurman, Wallace (Henry)
Casey, Warren (Peter) 1935-1988 .... **CLC 12**
See also CA 101; 127; INT CA-101
Casona, Alejandro .... **CLC 49**
See Alvarez, Alejandro Rodriguez
See also EWL 3
Cassavetes, John 1929-1989 .... **CLC 20**
See also CA 85-88; 127; CANR 82
Cassian, Nina 1924- .... **PC 17**
See also CWP; CWW 2
Cassill, R(onald) V(erlin)
1919-2002 .... **CLC 4, 23**
See also CA 9-12R; 208; CAAS 1; CANR
7, 45; CN 1, 2, 3, 4, 5, 6, 7; DLB 6, 218;
DLBY 2002
Cassiodorus, Flavius Magnus c. 490(?)-c.
583(?) .... **CMLC 43**
Cassirer, Ernst 1874-1945 .... **TCLC 61**
See also CA 157

Christie, Agatha (Mary Clarissa)
1890-1976 .. CLC 1, 6, 8, 12, 39, 48, 110
See also AAYA 9; AITN 1, 2; BPFB 1;
BRWS 2; CA 17-20R; 61-64; CANR 10,
37, 108; CBD; CDBLB 1914-1945; CMW
4; CN 1, 2; CPW; CWD; DA3; DAB;
DAC; DAM NOV; DFS 2; DLB 13, 77,
245; MSW; MTCW 1, 2; MTFW 2005;
NFS 8; RGEL 2; RHW; SATA 36; TEA;
YAW
Christie, Philippa .... CLC 21
See Pearce, Philippa
See also BYA 5; CANR 109; CLR 9; DLB
161; MAICYA 1; SATA 1, 67, 129
Christina of Sweden 1626-1689 .... LC 124
Christine de Pizan 1365(?)-1431(?) ...... LC 9;
PC 68
See also DLB 208; RGWL 2, 3
Chuang Tzu c. 369B.C.-c.
286B.C. .... CMLC 57
Chubb, Elmer
See Masters, Edgar Lee
Chulkov, Mikhail Dmitrievich
1743-1792 .... LC 2
See also DLB 150
Churchill, Caryl 1938- .... CLC 31, 55, 157;
DC 5
See Churchill, Chick
See also BRWS 4; CA 102; CANR 22, 46,
108; CBD; CD 6; CWD; DFS 12, 16;
DLB 13, 310; EWL 3; FW; MTCW 1;
RGEL 2
Churchill, Charles 1731-1764 .... LC 3
See also DLB 109; RGEL 2
Churchill, Chick
See Churchill, Caryl
See also CD 5
Churchill, Sir Winston (Leonard Spencer)
1874-1965 .... TCLC 113
See also BRW 6; CA 97-100; CDBLB
1890-1914; DA3; DLB 100; DLBD 16;
LAIT 4; MTCW 1, 2
Chute, Carolyn 1947- .... CLC 39
See also CA 123; CANR 135; CN 7
Ciardi, John (Anthony) 1916-1986 . CLC 10,
40, 44, 129; PC 69
See also CA 5-8R; 118; CAAS 2; CANR 5,
33; CLR 19; CP 1, 2, 3, 4; CWRI 5; DAM
POET; DLB 5; DLBY 1986; INT
CANR-5; MAICYA 1, 2; MAL 5; MTCW
1, 2; MTFW 2005; RGAL 4; SAAS 26;
SATA 1, 65; SATA-Obit 46
Cibber, Colley 1671-1757 .... LC 66
See also DLB 84; RGEL 2
Cicero, Marcus Tullius
106B.C.-43B.C. .... CMLC 3, 81
See also AW 1; CDWLB 1; DLB 211;
RGWL 2, 3
Cimino, Michael 1943- .... CLC 16
See also CA 105
Cioran, E(mil) M. 1911-1995 .... CLC 64
See also CA 25-28R; 149; CANR 91; DLB
220; EWL 3
Cisneros, Sandra 1954- .... CLC 69, 118, 193;
HLC 1; PC 52; SSC 32, 72
See also AAYA 9, 53; AMWS 7; CA 131;
CANR 64, 118; CN 7; CWP; DA3; DAM
MULT; DLB 122, 152; EWL 3; EXPN;
FL 1:5; FW; HW 1, 2; LAIT 5; LATS 1:2;
LLW; MAICYA 2; MAL 5; MTCW 2;
MTFW 2005; NFS 2; PFS 19; RGAL 4;
RGSF 2; SSFS 3, 13; WLIT 1; YAW
Cixous, Helene 1937- .... CLC 92
See also CA 126; CANR 55, 123; CWW 2;
DLB 83, 242; EWL 3; FL 1:5; FW; GLL
2; MTCW 1, 2; MTFW 2005; TWA
Clair, Rene .... CLC 20
See Chomette, Rene Lucien

Clampitt, Amy 1920-1994 .... CLC 32; PC 19
See also AMWS 9; CA 110; 146; CANR
29, 79; CP 4; DLB 105; MAL 5
Clancy, Thomas L., Jr. 1947-
See Clancy, Tom
See also CA 125; 131; CANR 62, 105;
DA3; INT CA-131; MTCW 1, 2; MTFW
2005
Clancy, Tom .... CLC 45, 112
See Clancy, Thomas L., Jr.
See also AAYA 9, 51; BEST 89:1, 90:1;
BPFB 1; BYA 10, 11; CANR 132; CMW
4; CPW; DAM NOV, POP; DLB 227
Clare, John 1793-1864 .. NCLC 9, 86; PC 23
See also BRWS 11; DAB; DAM POET;
DLB 55, 96; RGEL 2
Clarin
See Alas (y Urena), Leopoldo (Enrique
Garcia)
Clark, Al C.
See Goines, Donald
Clark, Brian (Robert)
See Clark, (Robert) Brian
See also CD 6
Clark, (Robert) Brian 1932- .... CLC 29
See Clark, Brian (Robert)
See also CA 41-44R; CANR 67; CBD; CD
5
Clark, Curt
See Westlake, Donald E(dwin)
Clark, Eleanor 1913-1996 .... CLC 5, 19
See also CA 9-12R; 151; CANR 41; CN 1,
2, 3, 4, 5, 6; DLB 6
Clark, J. P.
See Clark Bekederemo, J(ohnson) P(epper)
See also CDWLB 3; DLB 117
Clark, John Pepper
See Clark Bekederemo, J(ohnson) P(epper)
See also AFW; CD 5; CP 1, 2, 3, 4, 5, 6, 7;
RGEL 2
Clark, Kenneth (Mackenzie)
1903-1983 .... TCLC 147
See also CA 93-96; 109; CANR 36; MTCW
1, 2; MTFW 2005
Clark, M. R.
See Clark, Mavis Thorpe
Clark, Mavis Thorpe 1909-1999 ...... CLC 12
See also CA 57-60; CANR 8, 37, 107; CLR
30; CWRI 5; MAICYA 1, 2; SAAS 5;
SATA 8, 74
Clark, Walter Van Tilburg
1909-1971 .... CLC 28
See also CA 9-12R; 33-36R; CANR 63,
113; CN 1; DLB 9, 206; LAIT 2; MAL 5;
RGAL 4; SATA 8; TCWW 1, 2
Clark Bekederemo, J(ohnson) P(epper)
1935- .... BLC 1; CLC 38; DC 5
See Bekederemo, J. P. Clark; Clark, J. P.;
Clark, John Pepper
See also BW 1; CA 65-68; CANR 16, 72;
DAM DRAM, MULT; DFS 13; EWL 3;
MTCW 2; MTFW 2005
Clarke, Arthur C(harles) 1917- .... CLC 1, 4,
13, 18, 35, 136; SSC 3
See also AAYA 4, 33; BPFB 1; BYA 13;
CA 1-4R; CANR 2, 28, 55, 74, 130; CN
1, 2, 3, 4, 5, 6, 7; CPW; DA3; DAM POP;
DLB 261; JRDA; LAIT 5; MAICYA 1, 2;
MTCW 1, 2; MTFW 2005; SATA 13, 70,
115; SCFW 1, 2; SFW 4; SSFS 4, 18;
TCLE 1:1; YAW
Clarke, Austin 1896-1974 .... CLC 6, 9
See also CA 29-32; 49-52; CAP 2; CP 1, 2;
DAM POET; DLB 10, 20; EWL 3; RGEL
2

Clarke, Austin C(hesterfield) 1934- .. BLC 1;
CLC 8, 53; SSC 45
See also BW 1; CA 25-28R; CAAS 16;
CANR 14, 32, 68, 140; CN 1, 2, 3, 4, 5,
6, 7; DAC; DAM MULT; DLB 53, 125;
DNFS 2; MTCW 2; MTFW 2005; RGSF
2
Clarke, Gillian 1937- .... CLC 61
See also CA 106; CP 3, 4, 5, 6, 7; CWP;
DLB 40
Clarke, Marcus (Andrew Hislop)
1846-1881 .... NCLC 19
See also DLB 230; RGEL 2; RGSF 2
Clarke, Shirley 1925-1997 .... CLC 16
See also CA 189
Clash, The
See Headon, (Nicky) Topper; Jones, Mick;
Simonon, Paul; Strummer, Joe
Claudel, Paul (Louis Charles Marie)
1868-1955 .... TCLC 2, 10
See also CA 104; 165; DLB 192, 258, 321;
EW 8; EWL 3; GFL 1789 to the Present;
RGWL 2, 3; TWA
Claudian 370(?)-404(?) .... CMLC 46
See also RGWL 2, 3
Claudius, Matthias 1740-1815 .... NCLC 75
See also DLB 97
Clavell, James (duMaresq)
1925-1994 .... CLC 6, 25, 87
See also BPFB 1; CA 25-28R; 146; CANR
26, 48; CN 5; CPW; DA3; DAM NOV,
POP; MTCW 1, 2; MTFW 2005; NFS 10;
RHW
Clayman, Gregory .... CLC 65
Cleaver, (Leroy) Eldridge
1935-1998 .... BLC 1; CLC 30, 119
See also BW 1, 3; CA 21-24R; 167; CANR
16, 75; DA3; DAM MULT; MTCW 2;
YAW
Cleese, John (Marwood) 1939- .... CLC 21
See Monty Python
See also CA 112; 116; CANR 35; MTCW 1
Cleishbotham, Jebediah
See Scott, Sir Walter
Cleland, John 1710-1789 .... LC 2, 48
See also DLB 39; RGEL 2
Clemens, Samuel Langhorne 1835-1910
See Twain, Mark
See also CA 104; 135; CDALB 1865-1917;
DA; DA3; DAB; DAC; DAM MST, NOV;
DLB 12, 23, 64, 74, 186, 189; JRDA;
LMFS 1; MAICYA 1, 2; NCFS 4; NFS
20; SATA 100; YABC 2
Clement of Alexandria
150(?)-215(?) .... CMLC 41
Cleophil
See Congreve, William
Clerihew, E.
See Bentley, E(dmund) C(lerihew)
Clerk, N. W.
See Lewis, C(live) S(taples)
Cleveland, John 1613-1658 .... LC 106
See also DLB 126; RGEL 2
Cliff, Jimmy .... CLC 21
See Chambers, James
See also CA 193
Cliff, Michelle 1946- .... BLCS; CLC 120
See also BW 2; CA 116; CANR 39, 72; CD-
WLB 3; DLB 157; FW; GLL 2
Clifford, Lady Anne 1590-1676 .... LC 76
See also DLB 151
Clifton, (Thelma) Lucille 1936- .... BLC 1;
CLC 19, 66, 162; PC 17
See also AFAW 2; BW 2, 3; CA 49-52;
CANR 2, 24, 42, 76, 97, 138; CLR 5; CP
2, 3, 4, 5, 6, 7; CSW; CWP; CWRI 5;

DA3; DAM MULT, POET; DLB 5, 41;
EXPP; MAICYA 1, 2; MTCW 1, 2;
MTFW 2005; PFS 1, 14; SATA 20, 69,
128; WP

Clinton, Dirk
See Silverberg, Robert

Clough, Arthur Hugh 1819-1861 .. **NCLC 27,**
163
See also BRW 5; DLB 32; RGEL 2

Clutha, Janet Paterson Frame 1924-2004
See Frame, Janet
See also CA 1-4R; 224; CANR 2, 36, 76,
135; MTCW 1, 2; SATA 119

Clyne, Terence
See Blatty, William Peter

Cobalt, Martin
See Mayne, William (James Carter)

Cobb, Irvin S(hrewsbury)
1876-1944 .... **TCLC 77**
See also CA 175; DLB 11, 25, 86

Cobbett, William 1763-1835 .... **NCLC 49**
See also DLB 43, 107, 158; RGEL 2

Coburn, D(onald) L(ee) 1938- .... **CLC 10**
See also CA 89-92

Cocteau, Jean (Maurice Eugene Clement)
1889-1963 ..... **CLC 1, 8, 15, 16, 43; DC**
17; TCLC 119; WLC
See also CA 25-28; CANR 40; CAP 2; DA;
DA3; DAB; DAC; DAM DRAM, MST,
NOV; DLB 65, 258, 321; EW 10; EWL
3; GFL 1789 to the Present; MTCW 1, 2;
RGWL 2, 3; TWA

Codrescu, Andrei 1946- .... **CLC 46, 121**
See also CA 33-36R; CAAS 19; CANR 13,
34, 53, 76, 125; CN 7; DA3; DAM POET;
MAL 5; MTCW 2; MTFW 2005

Coe, Max
See Bourne, Randolph S(illiman)

Coe, Tucker
See Westlake, Donald E(dwin)

Coen, Ethan 1958- .... **CLC 108**
See also AAYA 54; CA 126; CANR 85

Coen, Joel 1955- .... **CLC 108**
See also AAYA 54; CA 126; CANR 119

The Coen Brothers
See Coen, Ethan; Coen, Joel

Coetzee, J(ohn) M(axwell) 1940- ..... **CLC 23,**
33, 66, 117, 161, 162
See also AAYA 37; AFW; BRWS 6; CA 77-
80; CANR 41, 54, 74, 114, 133; CN 4, 5,
6, 7; DA3; DAM NOV; DLB 225; EWL
3; LMFS 2; MTCW 1, 2; MTFW 2005;
NFS 21; WLIT 2; WWE 1

Coffey, Brian
See Koontz, Dean R.

Coffin, Robert P(eter) Tristram
1892-1955 .... **TCLC 95**
See also CA 123; 169; DLB 45

Cohan, George M(ichael)
1878-1942 .... **TCLC 60**
See also CA 157; DLB 249; RGAL 4

Cohen, Arthur A(llen) 1928-1986 ...... **CLC 7,**
31
See also CA 1-4R; 120; CANR 1, 17, 42;
DLB 28

Cohen, Leonard (Norman) 1934- ...... **CLC 3,**
38
See also CA 21-24R; CANR 14, 69; CN 1,
2, 3, 4, 5, 6; CP 1, 2, 3, 4, 5, 6, 7; DAC;
DAM MST; DLB 53; EWL 3; MTCW 1

Cohen, Matt(hew) 1942-1999 .... **CLC 19**
See also CA 61-64; 187; CAAS 18; CANR
40; CN 1, 2, 3, 4, 5, 6; DAC; DLB 53

Cohen-Solal, Annie 1948- .... **CLC 50**
See also CA 239

Colegate, Isabel 1931- .... **CLC 36**
See also CA 17-20R; CANR 8, 22, 74; CN
4, 5, 6, 7; DLB 14, 231; INT CANR-22;
MTCW 1

Coleman, Emmett
See Reed, Ishmael (Scott)

Coleridge, Hartley 1796-1849 .... **NCLC 90**
See also DLB 96

Coleridge, M. E.
See Coleridge, Mary E(lizabeth)

Coleridge, Mary E(lizabeth)
1861-1907 .... **TCLC 73**
See also CA 116; 166; DLB 19, 98

Coleridge, Samuel Taylor
1772-1834 ...... **NCLC 9, 54, 99, 111; PC**
11, 39, 67; WLC
See also AAYA 66; BRW 4; BRWR 2; BYA
4; CDBLB 1789-1832; DA; DA3; DAB;
DAC; DAM MST, POET; DLB 93, 107;
EXPP; LATS 1:1; LMFS 1; PAB; PFS 4,
5; RGEL 2; TEA; WLIT 3; WP

Coleridge, Sara 1802-1852 .... **NCLC 31**
See also DLB 199

Coles, Don 1928- .... **CLC 46**
See also CA 115; CANR 38; CP 7

Coles, Robert (Martin) 1929- .... **CLC 108**
See also CA 45-48; CANR 3, 32, 66, 70,
135; INT CANR-32; SATA 23

Colette, (Sidonie-Gabrielle)
1873-1954 .... **SSC 10; TCLC 1, 5, 16**
See Willy, Colette
See also CA 104; 131; DA3; DAM NOV;
DLB 65; EW 9; EWL 3; GFL 1789 to the
Present; MTCW 1, 2; MTFW 2005;
RGWL 2, 3; TWA

Collett, (Jacobine) Camilla (Wergeland)
1813-1895 .... **NCLC 22**

Collier, Christopher 1930- .... **CLC 30**
See also AAYA 13; BYA 2; CA 33-36R;
CANR 13, 33, 102; JRDA; MAICYA 1,
2; SATA 16, 70; WYA; YAW 1

Collier, James Lincoln 1928- .... **CLC 30**
See also AAYA 13; BYA 2; CA 9-12R;
CANR 4, 33, 60, 102; CLR 3; DAM POP;
JRDA; MAICYA 1, 2; SAAS 21; SATA 8,
70; WYA; YAW 1

Collier, Jeremy 1650-1726 .... **LC 6**

Collier, John 1901-1980 . **SSC 19; TCLC 127**
See also CA 65-68; 97-100; CANR 10; CN
1, 2; DLB 77, 255; FANT; SUFW 1

Collier, Mary 1690-1762 .... **LC 86**
See also DLB 95

Collingwood, R(obin) G(eorge)
1889(?)-1943 .... **TCLC 67**
See also CA 117; 155; DLB 262

Collins, Billy 1941- .... **PC 68**
See also AAYA 64; CA 151; CANR 92;
MTFW 2005; PFS 18

Collins, Hunt
See Hunter, Evan

Collins, Linda 1931- .... **CLC 44**
See also CA 125

Collins, Tom
See Furphy, Joseph
See also RGEL 2

Collins, (William) Wilkie
1824-1889 .... **NCLC 1, 18, 93**
See also BRWS 6; CDBLB 1832-1890;
CMW 4; DLB 18, 70, 159; GL 2; MSW;
RGEL 2; RGSF 2; SUFW 1; WLIT 4

Collins, William 1721-1759 .... **LC 4, 40**
See also BRW 3; DAM POET; DLB 109;
RGEL 2

Collodi, Carlo .... **NCLC 54**
See Lorenzini, Carlo
See also CLR 5; WCH; WLIT 7

Colman, George
See Glassco, John

Colman, George, the Elder
1732-1794 .... **LC 98**
See also RGEL 2

Colonna, Vittoria 1492-1547 .... **LC 71**
See also RGWL 2, 3

Colt, Winchester Remington
See Hubbard, L(afayette) Ron(ald)

Colter, Cyrus J. 1910-2002 .... **CLC 58**
See also BW 1; CA 65-68; 205; CANR 10,
66; CN 2, 3, 4, 5, 6; DLB 33

Colton, James
See Hansen, Joseph
See also GLL 1

Colum, Padraic 1881-1972 .... **CLC 28**
See also BYA 4; CA 73-76; 33-36R; CANR
35; CLR 36; CP 1; CWRI 5; DLB 19;
MAICYA 1, 2; MTCW 1; RGEL 2; SATA
15; WCH

Colvin, James
See Moorcock, Michael (John)

Colwin, Laurie (E.) 1944-1992 .... **CLC 5, 13,**
23, 84
See also CA 89-92; 139; CANR 20, 46;
DLB 218; DLBY 1980; MTCW 1

Comfort, Alex(ander) 1920-2000 ...... **CLC 7**
See also CA 1-4R; 190; CANR 1, 45; CN
1, 2, 3, 4; CP 1, 2, 3, 4, 5, 6, 7; DAM
POP; MTCW 2

Comfort, Montgomery
See Campbell, (John) Ramsey

Compton-Burnett, I(vy)
1892(?)-1969 .... **CLC 1, 3, 10, 15, 34**
See also BRW 7; CA 1-4R; 25-28R; CANR
4; DAM NOV; DLB 36; EWL 3; MTCW
1, 2; RGEL 2

Comstock, Anthony 1844-1915 ...... **TCLC 13**
See also CA 110; 169

Comte, Auguste 1798-1857 .... **NCLC 54**

Conan Doyle, Arthur
See Doyle, Sir Arthur Conan
See also BPFB 1; BYA 4, 5, 11

Conde (Abellan), Carmen
1901-1996 .... **HLCS 1**
See also CA 177; CWW 2; DLB 108; EWL
3; HW 2

Conde, Maryse 1937- ..... **BLCS; CLC 52, 92**
See also BW 2, 3; CA 110; 190; CAAE 190;
CANR 30, 53, 76; CWW 2; DAM MULT;
EWL 3; MTCW 2; MTFW 2005

Condillac, Etienne Bonnot de
1714-1780 .... **LC 26**
See also DLB 313

Condon, Richard (Thomas)
1915-1996 .... **CLC 4, 6, 8, 10, 45, 100**
See also BEST 90:3; BPFB 1; CA 1-4R;
151; CAAS 1; CANR 2, 23; CMW 4; CN
1, 2, 3, 4, 5, 6; DAM NOV; INT CANR-
23; MAL 5; MTCW 1, 2

Condorcet .... **LC 104**
See Condorcet, marquis de Marie-Jean-
Antoine-Nicolas Caritat
See also GFL Beginnings to 1789

Condorcet, marquis de
Marie-Jean-Antoine-Nicolas Caritat
1743-1794
See Condorcet
See also DLB 313

Confucius 551B.C.-479B.C. .... **CMLC 19, 65;**
WLCS
See also DA; DA3; DAB; DAC; DAM
MST

Congreve, William 1670-1729 ... **DC 2; LC 5,**
21; WLC
See also BRW 2; CDBLB 1660-1789; DA;
DAB; DAC; DAM DRAM, MST, POET;
DFS 15; DLB 39, 84; RGEL 2; WLIT 3

Conley, Robert J(ackson) 1940- .... **NNAL**
See also CA 41-44R; CANR 15, 34, 45, 96;
DAM MULT; TCWW 2

Connell, Evan S(helby), Jr. 1924- . **CLC 4, 6,**
45
See also AAYA 7; AMWS 14; CA 1-4R;
CAAS 2; CANR 2, 39, 76, 97, 140; CN
1, 2, 3, 4, 5, 6; DAM NOV; DLB 2;
DLBY 1981; MAL 5; MTCW 1, 2;
MTFW 2005

Cummins, Maria Susanna
1827-1866 .... NCLC 139
See also DLB 42; YABC 1

Cunha, Euclides (Rodrigues Pimenta) da
1866-1909 .... TCLC 24
See also CA 123; 219; DLB 307; LAW;
WLIT 1

Cunningham, E. V.
See Fast, Howard (Melvin)

Cunningham, J(ames) V(incent)
1911-1985 .... CLC 3, 31
See also CA 1-4R; 115; CANR 1, 72; CP 1,
2, 3, 4; DLB 5

Cunningham, Julia (Woolfolk)
1916- .... CLC 12
See also CA 9-12R; CANR 4, 19, 36; CWRI
5; JRDA; MAICYA 1, 2; SAAS 2; SATA
1, 26, 132

Cunningham, Michael 1952- .... CLC 34
See also AMWS 15; CA 136; CANR 96;
CN 7; DLB 292; GLL 2; MTFW 2005

Cunninghame Graham, R. B.
See Cunninghame Graham, Robert
(Gallnigad) Bontine

Cunninghame Graham, Robert (Gallnigad)
Bontine 1852-1936 .... TCLC 19
See Graham, R(obert) B(ontine) Cunning-
hame
See also CA 119; 184

Curnow, (Thomas) Allen (Monro)
1911-2001 .... PC 48
See also CA 69-72; 202; CANR 48, 99; CP
1, 2, 3, 4, 5, 6, 7; EWL 3; RGEL 2

Currie, Ellen 19(?)- .... CLC 44

Curtin, Philip
See Lowndes, Marie Adelaide (Belloc)

Curtin, Phillip
See Lowndes, Marie Adelaide (Belloc)

Curtis, Price
See Ellison, Harlan (Jay)

Cusanus, Nicolaus 1401-1464 .... LC 80
See Nicholas of Cusa

Cutrate, Joe
See Spiegelman, Art

Cynewulf c. 770- .... CMLC 23
See also DLB 146; RGEL 2

Cyrano de Bergerac, Savinien de
1619-1655 .... LC 65
See also DLB 268; GFL Beginnings to
1789; RGWL 2, 3

Cyril of Alexandria c. 375-c. 430 . CMLC 59

Czaczkes, Shmuel Yosef Halevi
See Agnon, S(hmuel) Y(osef Halevi)

Dabrowska, Maria (Szumska)
1889-1965 .... CLC 15
See also CA 106; CDWLB 4; DLB 215;
EWL 3

Dabydeen, David 1955- .... CLC 34
See also BW 1; CA 125; CANR 56, 92; CN
6, 7; CP 7

Dacey, Philip 1939- .... CLC 51
See also CA 37-40R, 231; CAAE 231;
CAAS 17; CANR 14, 32, 64; CP 4, 5, 6,
7; DLB 105

Dacre, Charlotte c. 1772-1825(?) . NCLC 151

Dafydd ap Gwilym c. 1320-c. 1380 ..... PC 56

Dagerman, Stig (Halvard)
1923-1954 .... TCLC 17
See also CA 117; 155; DLB 259; EWL 3

D'Aguiar, Fred 1960- .... CLC 145
See also CA 148; CANR 83, 101; CN 7;
CP 7; DLB 157; EWL 3

Dahl, Roald 1916-1990 ...... CLC 1, 6, 18, 79;
TCLC 173
See also AAYA 15; BPFB 1; BRWS 4; BYA
5; CA 1-4R; 133; CANR 6, 32, 37, 62;
CLR 1, 7, 41; CN 1, 2, 3, 4; CPW; DA3;
DAB; DAC; DAM MST, NOV, POP;

DLB 139, 255; HGG; JRDA; MAICYA 1,
2; MTCW 1, 2; MTFW 2005; RGSF 2;
SATA 1, 26, 73; SATA-Obit 65; SSFS 4;
TEA; YAW

Dahlberg, Edward 1900-1977 .. CLC 1, 7, 14
See also CA 9-12R; 69-72; CANR 31, 62;
CN 1, 2; DLB 48; MAL 5; MTCW 1;
RGAL 4

Daitch, Susan 1954- .... CLC 103
See also CA 161

Dale, Colin .... TCLC 18
See Lawrence, T(homas) E(dward)

Dale, George E.
See Asimov, Isaac

Dalton, Roque 1935-1975(?) ..... HLCS 1; PC
36
See also CA 176; DLB 283; HW 2

Daly, Elizabeth 1878-1967 .... CLC 52
See also CA 23-24; 25-28R; CANR 60;
CAP 2; CMW 4

Daly, Mary 1928- .... CLC 173
See also CA 25-28R; CANR 30, 62; FW;
GLL 1; MTCW 1

Daly, Maureen 1921- .... CLC 17
See also AAYA 5, 58; BYA 6; CANR 37,
83, 108; CLR 96; JRDA; MAICYA 1, 2;
SAAS 1; SATA 2, 129; WYA; YAW

Damas, Leon-Gontran 1912-1978 .... CLC 84
See also BW 1; CA 125; 73-76; EWL 3

Dana, Richard Henry Sr.
1787-1879 .... NCLC 53

Daniel, Samuel 1562(?)-1619 .... LC 24
See also DLB 62; RGEL 2

Daniels, Brett
See Adler, Renata

Dannay, Frederic 1905-1982 .... CLC 11
See Queen, Ellery
See also CA 1-4R; 107; CANR 1, 39; CMW
4; DAM POP; DLB 137; MTCW 1

D'Annunzio, Gabriele 1863-1938 ... TCLC 6,
40
See also CA 104; 155; EW 8; EWL 3;
RGWL 2, 3; TWA; WLIT 7

Danois, N. le
See Gourmont, Remy(-Marie-Charles) de

Dante 1265-1321 .... CMLC 3, 18, 39, 70; PC
21; WLCS
See Alighieri, Dante
See also DA; DA3; DAB; DAC; DAM
MST, POET; EFS 1; EW 1; LAIT 1;
RGWL 2, 3; TWA; WP

d'Antibes, Germain
See Simenon, Georges (Jacques Christian)

Danticat, Edwidge 1969- .... CLC 94, 139
See also AAYA 29; CA 152, 192; CAAE
192; CANR 73, 129; CN 7; DNFS 1;
EXPS; LATS 1:2; MTCW 2; MTFW
2005; SSFS 1; YAW

Danvers, Dennis 1947- .... CLC 70

Danziger, Paula 1944-2004 .... CLC 21
See also AAYA 4, 36; BYA 6, 7, 14; CA
112; 115; 229; CANR 37, 132; CLR 20;
JRDA; MAICYA 1, 2; MTFW 2005;
SATA 36, 63, 102, 149; SATA-Brief 30;
SATA-Obit 155; WYA; YAW

Da Ponte, Lorenzo 1749-1838 .... NCLC 50

d'Aragona, Tullia 1510(?)-1556 .... LC 121

Dario, Ruben 1867-1916 .... HLC 1; PC 15;
TCLC 4
See also CA 131; CANR 81; DAM MULT;
DLB 290; EWL 3; HW 1, 2; LAW;
MTCW 1, 2; MTFW 2005; RGWL 2, 3

Darley, George 1795-1846 .... NCLC 2
See also DLB 96; RGEL 2

Darrow, Clarence (Seward)
1857-1938 .... TCLC 81
See also CA 164; DLB 303

Darwin, Charles 1809-1882 .... NCLC 57
See also BRWS 7; DLB 57, 166; LATS 1:1;
RGEL 2; TEA; WLIT 4

Darwin, Erasmus 1731-1802 .... NCLC 106
See also DLB 93; RGEL 2

Daryush, Elizabeth 1887-1977 ...... CLC 6, 19
See also CA 49-52; CANR 3, 81; DLB 20

Das, Kamala 1934- .... CLC 191; PC 43
See also CA 101; CANR 27, 59; CP 1, 2, 3,
4, 5, 6, 7; CWP; FW

Dasgupta, Surendranath
1887-1952 .... TCLC 81
See also CA 157

Dashwood, Edmee Elizabeth Monica de la
Pasture 1890-1943
See Delafield, E. M.
See also CA 119; 154

da Silva, Antonio Jose
1705-1739 .... NCLC 114

Daudet, (Louis Marie) Alphonse
1840-1897 .... NCLC 1
See also DLB 123; GFL 1789 to the Present;
RGSF 2

d'Aulnoy, Marie-Catherine c.
1650-1705 .... LC 100

Daumal, Rene 1908-1944 .... TCLC 14
See also CA 114; EWL 3

Davenant, William 1606-1668 .... LC 13
See also DLB 58, 126; RGEL 2

Davenport, Guy (Mattison, Jr.)
1927-2005 .... CLC 6, 14, 38; SSC 16
See also CA 33-36R; 235; CANR 23, 73;
CN 3, 4, 5, 6; CSW; DLB 130

David, Robert
See Nezval, Vitezslav

Davidson, Avram (James) 1923-1993
See Queen, Ellery
See also CA 101; 171; CANR 26; DLB 8;
FANT; SFW 4; SUFW 1, 2

Davidson, Donald (Grady)
1893-1968 .... CLC 2, 13, 19
See also CA 5-8R; 25-28R; CANR 4, 84;
DLB 45

Davidson, Hugh
See Hamilton, Edmond

Davidson, John 1857-1909 .... TCLC 24
See also CA 118; 217; DLB 19; RGEL 2

Davidson, Sara 1943- .... CLC 9
See also CA 81-84; CANR 44, 68; DLB
185

Davie, Donald (Alfred) 1922-1995 .... CLC 5,
8, 10, 31; PC 29
See also BRWS 6; CA 1-4R; 149; CAAS 3;
CANR 1, 44; CP 1, 2, 3, 4; DLB 27;
MTCW 1; RGEL 2

Davie, Elspeth 1918-1995 .... SSC 52
See also CA 120; 126; 150; CANR 141;
DLB 139

Davies, Ray(mond Douglas) 1944- ... CLC 21
See also CA 116; 146; CANR 92

Davies, Rhys 1901-1978 .... CLC 23
See also CA 9-12R; 81-84; CANR 4; CN 1,
2; DLB 139, 191

Davies, (William) Robertson
1913-1995 .... CLC 2, 7, 13, 25, 42, 75,
91; WLC
See Marchbanks, Samuel
See also BEST 89:2; BPFB 1; CA 33-36R;
150; CANR 17, 42, 103; CN 1, 2, 3, 4, 5,
6; CPW; DA; DA3; DAB; DAC; DAM
MST, NOV, POP; DLB 68; EWL 3; HGG;
INT CANR-17; MTCW 1, 2; MTFW
2005; RGEL 2; TWA

Davies, Sir John 1569-1626 .... LC 85
See also DLB 172

Davies, Walter C.
See Kornbluth, C(yril) M.

Davies, William Henry 1871-1940 ... **TCLC 5**
See also BRWS 11; CA 104; 179; DLB 19, 174; EWL 3; RGEL 2

Da Vinci, Leonardo 1452-1519 ..... **LC 12, 57, 60**
See also AAYA 40

Davis, Angela (Yvonne) 1944- .... **CLC 77**
See also BW 2, 3; CA 57-60; CANR 10, 81; CSW; DA3; DAM MULT; FW

Davis, B. Lynch
See Bioy Casares, Adolfo; Borges, Jorge Luis

Davis, Frank Marshall 1905-1987 ...... **BLC 1**
See also BW 2, 3; CA 125; 123; CANR 42, 80; DAM MULT; DLB 51

Davis, Gordon
See Hunt, E(verette) Howard, (Jr.)

Davis, H(arold) L(enoir) 1896-1960 . **CLC 49**
See also ANW; CA 178; 89-92; DLB 9, 206; SATA 114; TCWW 1, 2

Davis, Natalie Zemon 1928- .... **CLC 204**
See also CA 53-56; CANR 58, 100

Davis, Rebecca (Blaine) Harding 1831-1910 .... **SSC 38; TCLC 6**
See also CA 104; 179; DLB 74, 239; FW; NFS 14; RGAL 4; TUS

Davis, Richard Harding 1864-1916 .... **TCLC 24**
See also CA 114; 179; DLB 12, 23, 78, 79, 189; DLBD 13; RGAL 4

Davison, Frank Dalby 1893-1970 ..... **CLC 15**
See also CA 217; 116; DLB 260

Davison, Lawrence H.
See Lawrence, D(avid) H(erbert Richards)

Davison, Peter (Hubert) 1928-2004 .. **CLC 28**
See also CA 9-12R; 234; CAAS 4; CANR 3, 43, 84; CP 1, 2, 3, 4, 5, 6, 7; DLB 5

Davys, Mary 1674-1732 .... **LC 1, 46**
See also DLB 39

Dawson, (Guy) Fielding (Lewis) 1930-2002 .... **CLC 6**
See also CA 85-88; 202; CANR 108; DLB 130; DLBY 2002

Dawson, Peter
See Faust, Frederick (Schiller)
See also TCWW 1, 2

Day, Clarence (Shepard, Jr.) 1874-1935 .... **TCLC 25**
See also CA 108; 199; DLB 11

Day, John 1574(?)-1640(?) .... **LC 70**
See also DLB 62, 170; RGEL 2

Day, Thomas 1748-1789 .... **LC 1**
See also DLB 39; YABC 1

Day Lewis, C(ecil) 1904-1972 . **CLC 1, 6, 10; PC 11**
See Blake, Nicholas; Lewis, C. Day
See also BRWS 3; CA 13-16; 33-36R; CANR 34; CAP 1; CP 1; CWRI 5; DAM POET; DLB 15, 20; EWL 3; MTCW 1, 2; RGEL 2

Dazai Osamu .... **SSC 41; TCLC 11**
See Tsushima, Shuji
See also CA 164; DLB 182; EWL 3; MJW; RGSF 2; RGWL 2, 3; TWA

de Andrade, Carlos Drummond
See Drummond de Andrade, Carlos

de Andrade, Mario 1892(?)-1945
See Andrade, Mario de
See also CA 178; HW 2

Deane, Norman
See Creasey, John

Deane, Seamus (Francis) 1940- ...... **CLC 122**
See also CA 118; CANR 42

de Beauvoir, Simone (Lucie Ernestine Marie Bertrand)
See Beauvoir, Simone (Lucie Ernestine Marie Bertrand) de

de Beer, P.
See Bosman, Herman Charles

De Botton, Alain 1969- .... **CLC 203**
See also CA 159; CANR 96

de Brissac, Malcolm
See Dickinson, Peter (Malcolm de Brissac)

de Campos, Alvaro
See Pessoa, Fernando (Antonio Nogueira)

de Chardin, Pierre Teilhard
See Teilhard de Chardin, (Marie Joseph) Pierre

de Crenne, Helisenne c. 1510-c. 1560 .... **LC 113**

Dee, John 1527-1608 .... **LC 20**
See also DLB 136, 213

Deer, Sandra 1940- .... **CLC 45**
See also CA 186

De Ferrari, Gabriella 1941- .... **CLC 65**
See also CA 146

de Filippo, Eduardo 1900-1984 ... **TCLC 127**
See also CA 132; 114; EWL 3; MTCW 1; RGWL 2, 3

Defoe, Daniel 1660(?)-1731 .... **LC 1, 42, 108; WLC**
See also AAYA 27; BRW 3; BRWR 1; BYA 4; CDBLB 1660-1789; CLR 61; DA; DA3; DAB; DAC; DAM MST, NOV; DLB 39, 95, 101; JRDA; LAIT 1; LMFS 1; MAICYA 1, 2; NFS 9, 13; RGEL 2; SATA 22; TEA; WCH; WLIT 3

de Gourmont, Remy(-Marie-Charles)
See Gourmont, Remy(-Marie-Charles) de

de Gournay, Marie le Jars 1566-1645 .... **LC 98**
See also FW

de Hartog, Jan 1914-2002 .... **CLC 19**
See also CA 1-4R; 210; CANR 1; DFS 12

de Hostos, E. M.
See Hostos (y Bonilla), Eugenio Maria de

de Hostos, Eugenio M.
See Hostos (y Bonilla), Eugenio Maria de

Deighton, Len .... **CLC 4, 7, 22, 46**
See Deighton, Leonard Cyril
See also AAYA 6; BEST 89:2; BPFB 1; CD-BLB 1960 to Present; CMW 4; CN 1, 2, 3, 4, 5, 6, 7; CPW; DLB 87

Deighton, Leonard Cyril 1929-
See Deighton, Len
See also AAYA 57; CA 9-12R; CANR 19, 33, 68; DA3; DAM NOV, POP; MTCW 1, 2; MTFW 2005

Dekker, Thomas 1572(?)-1632 ..... **DC 12; LC 22**
See also CDBLB Before 1660; DAM DRAM; DLB 62, 172; LMFS 1; RGEL 2

de Laclos, Pierre Ambroise Franois
See Laclos, Pierre-Ambroise Francois

Delacroix, (Ferdinand-Victor-)Eugene 1798-1863 .... **NCLC 133**
See also EW 5

Delafield, E. M. .... **TCLC 61**
See Dashwood, Edmee Elizabeth Monica de la Pasture
See also DLB 34; RHW

de la Mare, Walter (John) 1873-1956 . **SSC 14; TCLC 4, 53; WLC**
See also CA 163; CDBLB 1914-1945; CLR 23; CWRI 5; DA3; DAB; DAC; DAM MST, POET; DLB 19, 153, 162, 255, 284; EWL 3; EXPP; HGG; MAICYA 1, 2; MTCW 2; MTFW 2005; RGEL 2; RGSF 2; SATA 16; SUFW 1; TEA; WCH

de Lamartine, Alphonse (Marie Louis Prat)
See Lamartine, Alphonse (Marie Louis Prat) de

Delaney, Franey
See O'Hara, John (Henry)

Delaney, Shelagh 1939- .... **CLC 29**
See also CA 17-20R; CANR 30, 67; CBD; CD 5, 6; CDBLB 1960 to Present; CWD; DAM DRAM; DFS 7; DLB 13; MTCW 1

Delany, Martin Robison 1812-1885 .... **NCLC 93**
See also DLB 50; RGAL 4

Delany, Mary (Granville Pendarves) 1700-1788 .... **LC 12**

Delany, Samuel R(ay), Jr. 1942- .... **BLC 1; CLC 8, 14, 38, 141**
See also AAYA 24; AFAW 2; BPFB 1; BW 2, 3; CA 81-84; CANR 27, 43, 116; CN 2, 3, 4, 5, 6, 7; DAM MULT; DLB 8, 33; FANT; MAL 5; MTCW 1, 2; RGAL 4; SATA 92; SCFW 1, 2; SFW 4; SUFW 2

De la Ramee, Marie Louise (Ouida) 1839-1908
See Ouida
See also CA 204; SATA 20

de la Roche, Mazo 1879-1961 .... **CLC 14**
See also CA 85-88; CANR 30; DLB 68; RGEL 2; RHW; SATA 64

De La Salle, Innocent
See Hartmann, Sadakichi

de Laureamont, Comte
See Lautreamont

Delbanco, Nicholas (Franklin) 1942- .... **CLC 6, 13, 167**
See also CA 17-20R; 189; CAAE 189; CAAS 2; CANR 29, 55, 116; CN 7; DLB 6, 234

del Castillo, Michel 1933- .... **CLC 38**
See also CA 109; CANR 77

Deledda, Grazia (Cosima) 1875(?)-1936 .... **TCLC 23**
See also CA 123; 205; DLB 264; EWL 3; RGWL 2, 3; WLIT 7

Deleuze, Gilles 1925-1995 .... **TCLC 116**
See also DLB 296

Delgado, Abelardo (Lalo) B(arrientos) 1930-2004 .... **HLC 1**
See also CA 131; 230; CAAS 15; CANR 90; DAM MST, MULT; DLB 82; HW 1, 2

Delibes, Miguel .... **CLC 8, 18**
See Delibes Setien, Miguel
See also DLB 322; EWL 3

Delibes Setien, Miguel 1920-
See Delibes, Miguel
See also CA 45-48; CANR 1, 32; CWW 2; HW 1; MTCW 1

DeLillo, Don 1936- ..... **CLC 8, 10, 13, 27, 39, 54, 76, 143, 210, 213**
See also AMWC 2; AMWS 6; BEST 89:1; BPFB 1; CA 81-84; CANR 21, 76, 92, 133; CN 3, 4, 5, 6, 7; CPW; DA3; DAM NOV, POP; DLB 6, 173; EWL 3; MAL 5; MTCW 1, 2; MTFW 2005; RGAL 4; TUS

de Lisser, H. G.
See De Lisser, H(erbert) G(eorge)
See also DLB 117

De Lisser, H(erbert) G(eorge) 1878-1944 .... **TCLC 12**
See de Lisser, H. G.
See also BW 2; CA 109; 152

Deloire, Pierre
See Peguy, Charles (Pierre)

Deloney, Thomas 1543(?)-1600 .... **LC 41**
See also DLB 167; RGEL 2

Deloria, Ella (Cara) 1889-1971(?) ..... **NNAL**
See also CA 152; DAM MULT; DLB 175

Deloria, Vine (Victor), Jr. 1933-2005 .... **CLC 21, 122; NNAL**
See also CA 53-56; CANR 5, 20, 48, 98; DAM MULT; DLB 175; MTCW 1; SATA 21

del Valle-Inclan, Ramon (Maria)
See Valle-Inclan, Ramon (Maria) del
See also DLB 322

Del Vecchio, John M(ichael) 1947- .. **CLC 29**
See also CA 110; DLBD 9

Dillard, R(ichard) H(enry) W(ilde)
1937- .... **CLC 5**
See also CA 21-24R; CAAS 7; CANR 10;
CP 2, 3, 4, 5, 6, 7; CSW; DLB 5, 244

Dillon, Eilis 1920-1994 .... **CLC 17**
See also CA 9-12R, 182; 147; CAAE 182;
CAAS 3; CANR 4, 38, 78; CLR 26; MAI-
CYA 1, 2; MAICYAS 1; SATA 2, 74;
SATA-Essay 105; SATA-Obit 83; YAW

Dimont, Penelope
See Mortimer, Penelope (Ruth)

Dinesen, Isak ..... **CLC 10, 29, 95; SSC 7, 75**
See Blixen, Karen (Christentze Dinesen)
See also EW 10; EWL 3; EXPS; FW; GL
2; HGG; LAIT 3; MTCW 1; NCFS 2;
NFS 9; RGSF 2; RGWL 2, 3; SSFS 3, 6,
13; WLIT 2

Ding Ling .... **CLC 68**
See Chiang, Pin-chin
See also RGWL 3

Diphusa, Patty
See Almodovar, Pedro

Disch, Thomas M(ichael) 1940- ... **CLC 7, 36**
See Disch, Tom
See also AAYA 17; BPFB 1; CA 21-24R;
CAAS 4; CANR 17, 36, 54, 89; CLR 18;
CP 7; DA3; DLB 8; HGG; MAICYA 1, 2;
MTCW 1, 2; MTFW 2005; SAAS 15;
SATA 92; SCFW 1, 2; SFW 4; SUFW 2

Disch, Tom
See Disch, Thomas M(ichael)
See also DLB 282

d'Isly, Georges
See Simenon, Georges (Jacques Christian)

Disraeli, Benjamin 1804-1881 ... **NCLC 2, 39, 79**
See also BRW 4; DLB 21, 55; RGEL 2

Ditcum, Steve
See Crumb, R(obert)

Dixon, Paige
See Corcoran, Barbara (Asenath)

Dixon, Stephen 1936- .... **CLC 52; SSC 16**
See also AMWS 12; CA 89-92; CANR 17,
40, 54, 91; CN 4, 5, 6, 7; DLB 130; MAL
5

Dixon, Thomas, Jr. 1864-1946 ..... **TCLC 163**
See also RHW

Djebar, Assia 1936- .... **CLC 182**
See also CA 188; EWL 3; RGWL 3; WLIT
2

Doak, Annie
See Dillard, Annie

Dobell, Sydney Thompson
1824-1874 .... **NCLC 43**
See also DLB 32; RGEL 2

Doblin, Alfred .... **TCLC 13**
See Doeblin, Alfred
See also CDWLB 2; EWL 3; RGWL 2, 3

Dobroliubov, Nikolai Aleksandrovich
See Dobrolyubov, Nikolai Alexandrovich
See also DLB 277

Dobrolyubov, Nikolai Alexandrovich
1836-1861 .... **NCLC 5**
See Dobroliubov, Nikolai Aleksandrovich

Dobson, Austin 1840-1921 .... **TCLC 79**
See also DLB 35, 144

Dobyns, Stephen 1941- .... **CLC 37**
See also AMWS 13; CA 45-48; CANR 2,
18, 99; CMW 4; CP 4, 5, 6, 7; PFS 23

Doctorow, E(dgar) L(aurence)
1931- .... **CLC 6, 11, 15, 18, 37, 44, 65, 113, 214**
See also AAYA 22; AITN 2; AMWS 4;
BEST 89:3; BPFB 1; CA 45-48; CANR
2, 33, 51, 76, 97, 133; CDALB 1968-
1988; CN 3, 4, 5, 6, 7; CPW; DA3; DAM
NOV, POP; DLB 2, 28, 173; DLBY 1980;

EWL 3; LAIT 3; MAL 5; MTCW 1, 2;
MTFW 2005; NFS 6; RGAL 4; RHW;
TCLE 1:1; TCWW 1, 2; TUS

Dodgson, Charles L(utwidge) 1832-1898
See Carroll, Lewis
See also CLR 2; DA; DA3; DAB; DAC;
DAM MST, NOV, POET; MAICYA 1, 2;
SATA 100; YABC 2

Dodsley, Robert 1703-1764 .... **LC 97**
See also DLB 95; RGEL 2

Dodson, Owen (Vincent) 1914-1983 .. **BLC 1; CLC 79**
See also BW 1; CA 65-68; 110; CANR 24;
DAM MULT; DLB 76

Doeblin, Alfred 1878-1957 .... **TCLC 13**
See Doblin, Alfred
See also CA 110; 141; DLB 66

Doerr, Harriet 1910-2002 .... **CLC 34**
See also CA 117; 122; 213; CANR 47; INT
CA-122; LATS 1:2

Domecq, H(onorio Bustos)
See Bioy Casares, Adolfo

Domecq, H(onorio) Bustos
See Bioy Casares, Adolfo; Borges, Jorge
Luis

Domini, Rey
See Lorde, Audre (Geraldine)
See also GLL 1

Dominique
See Proust, (Valentin-Louis-George-Eugene)
Marcel

Don, A
See Stephen, Sir Leslie

Donaldson, Stephen R(eeder)
1947- .... **CLC 46, 138**
See also AAYA 36; BPFB 1; CA 89-92;
CANR 13, 55, 99; CPW; DAM POP;
FANT; INT CANR-13; SATA 121; SFW
4; SUFW 1, 2

Donleavy, J(ames) P(atrick) 1926- .... **CLC 1, 4, 6, 10, 45**
See also AITN 2; BPFB 1; CA 9-12R;
CANR 24, 49, 62, 80, 124; CBD; CD 5,
6; CN 1, 2, 3, 4, 5, 6, 7; DLB 6, 173; INT
CANR-24; MAL 5; MTCW 1, 2; MTFW
2005; RGAL 4

Donnadieu, Marguerite
See Duras, Marguerite

Donne, John 1572-1631 ... **LC 10, 24, 91; PC 1, 43; WLC**
See also AAYA 67; BRW 1; BRWC 1;
BRWR 2; CDBLB Before 1660; DA;
DAB; DAC; DAM MST, POET; DLB
121, 151; EXPP; PAB; PFS 2, 11; RGEL
3; TEA; WLIT 3; WP

Donnell, David 1939(?)- .... **CLC 34**
See also CA 197

Donoghue, Denis 1928- .... **CLC 209**
See also CA 17-20R; CANR 16, 102

Donoghue, P. S.
See Hunt, E(verette) Howard, (Jr.)

Donoso (Yanez), Jose 1924-1996 ... **CLC 4, 8, 11, 32, 99; HLC 1; SSC 34; TCLC 133**
See also CA 81-84; 155; CANR 32, 73; CD-
WLB 3; CWW 2; DAM MULT; DLB 113;
EWL 3; HW 1, 2; LAW; LAWS 1; MTCW
1, 2; MTFW 2005; RGSF 2; WLIT 1

Donovan, John 1928-1992 .... **CLC 35**
See also AAYA 20; CA 97-100; 137; CLR
3; MAICYA 1, 2; SATA 72; SATA-Brief
29; YAW

Don Roberto
See Cunninghame Graham, Robert
(Gallnigad) Bontine

Doolittle, Hilda 1886-1961 . **CLC 3, 8, 14, 31, 34, 73; PC 5; WLC**
See H. D.
See also AAYA 66; AMWS 1; CA 97-100;
CANR 35, 131; DA; DAC; DAM MST,

POET; DLB 4, 45; EWL 3; FW; GLL 1;
LMFS 2; MAL 5; MAWW; MTCW 1, 2;
MTFW 2005; PFS 6; RGAL 4

Doppo, Kunikida .... **TCLC 99**
See Kunikida Doppo

Dorfman, Ariel 1942- .... **CLC 48, 77, 189; HLC 1**
See also CA 124; 130; CANR 67, 70, 135;
CWW 2; DAM MULT; DFS 4; EWL 3;
HW 1, 2; INT CA-130; WLIT 1

Dorn, Edward (Merton)
1929-1999 .... **CLC 10, 18**
See also CA 93-96; 187; CANR 42, 79; CP
1, 2, 3, 4, 5, 6, 7; DLB 5; INT CA-93-96;
WP

Dor-Ner, Zvi .... **CLC 70**

Dorris, Michael (Anthony)
1945-1997 .... **CLC 109; NNAL**
See also AAYA 20; BEST 90:1; BYA 12;
CA 102; 157; CANR 19, 46, 75; CLR 58;
DA3; DAM MULT, NOV; DLB 175;
LAIT 5; MTCW 2; MTFW 2005; NFS 3;
RGAL 4; SATA 75; SATA-Obit 94;
TCWW 2; YAW

Dorris, Michael A.
See Dorris, Michael (Anthony)

Dorsan, Luc
See Simenon, Georges (Jacques Christian)

Dorsange, Jean
See Simenon, Georges (Jacques Christian)

Dorset
See Sackville, Thomas

Dos Passos, John (Roderigo)
1896-1970 ... **CLC 1, 4, 8, 11, 15, 25, 34, 82; WLC**
See also AMW; BPFB 1; CA 1-4R; 29-32R;
CANR 3; CDALB 1929-1941; DA; DA3;
DAB; DAC; DAM MST, NOV; DLB 4,
9, 274, 316; DLBD 1, 15; DLBY 1996;
EWL 3; MAL 5; MTCW 1, 2; MTFW
2005; NFS 14; RGAL 4; TUS

Dossage, Jean
See Simenon, Georges (Jacques Christian)

Dostoevsky, Fedor Mikhailovich
1821-1881 .. **NCLC 2, 7, 21, 33, 43, 119, 167; SSC 2, 33, 44; WLC**
See Dostoevsky, Fyodor
See also AAYA 40; DA; DA3; DAB; DAC;
DAM MST, NOV; EW 7; EXPN; NFS 3,
8; RGSF 2; RGWL 2, 3; SSFS 8; TWA

Dostoevsky, Fyodor
See Dostoevsky, Fedor Mikhailovich
See also DLB 238; LATS 1:1; LMFS 1, 2

Doty, M. R.
See Doty, Mark (Alan)

Doty, Mark
See Doty, Mark (Alan)

Doty, Mark (Alan) 1953(?)- .... **CLC 176; PC 53**
See also AMWS 11; CA 161, 183; CAAE
183; CANR 110

Doty, Mark A.
See Doty, Mark (Alan)

Doughty, Charles M(ontagu)
1843-1926 .... **TCLC 27**
See also CA 115; 178; DLB 19, 57, 174

Douglas, Ellen .... **CLC 73**
See Haxton, Josephine Ayres; Williamson,
Ellen Douglas
See also CN 5, 6, 7; CSW; DLB 292

Douglas, Gavin 1475(?)-1522 .... **LC 20**
See also DLB 132; RGEL 2

Douglas, George
See Brown, George Douglas
See also RGEL 2

Douglas, Keith (Castellain)
1920-1944 .... **TCLC 40**
See also BRW 7; CA 160; DLB 27; EWL
3; PAB; RGEL 2

Dunbar, William 1460(?)-1520(?) .... **LC 20; PC 67**
See also BRWS 8; DLB 132, 146; RGEL 2

Dunbar-Nelson, Alice .... **HR 1:2**
See Nelson, Alice Ruth Moore Dunbar

Duncan, Dora Angela
See Duncan, Isadora

Duncan, Isadora 1877(?)-1927 .... **TCLC 68**
See also CA 118; 149

Duncan, Lois 1934- .... **CLC 26**
See also AAYA 4, 34; BYA 6, 8; CA 1-4R; CANR 2, 23, 36, 111; CLR 29; JRDA; MAICYA 1, 2; MAICYAS 1; MTFW 2005; SAAS 2; SATA 1, 36, 75, 133, 141; SATA-Essay 141; WYA; YAW

Duncan, Robert (Edward)
1919-1988 .... **CLC 1, 2, 4, 7, 15, 41, 55; PC 2**
See also BG 1:2; CA 9-12R; 124; CANR 28, 62; CP 1, 2, 3, 4; DAM POET; DLB 5, 16, 193; EWL 3; MAL 5; MTCW 1, 2; MTFW 2005; PFS 13; RGAL 4; WP

Duncan, Sara Jeannette
1861-1922 .... **TCLC 60**
See also CA 157; DLB 92

Dunlap, William 1766-1839 .... **NCLC 2**
See also DLB 30, 37, 59; RGAL 4

Dunn, Douglas (Eaglesham) 1942- .... **CLC 6, 40**
See also BRWS 10; CA 45-48; CANR 2, 33, 126; CP 1, 2, 3, 4, 5, 6, 7; DLB 40; MTCW 1

Dunn, Katherine (Karen) 1945- .... **CLC 71**
See also CA 33-36R; CANR 72; HGG; MTCW 2; MTFW 2005

Dunn, Stephen (Elliott) 1939- .. **CLC 36, 206**
See also AMWS 11; CA 33-36R; CANR 12, 48, 53, 105; CP 3, 4, 5, 6, 7; DLB 105; PFS 21

Dunne, Finley Peter 1867-1936 ...... **TCLC 28**
See also CA 108; 178; DLB 11, 23; RGAL 4

Dunne, John Gregory 1932-2003 ..... **CLC 28**
See also CA 25-28R; 222; CANR 14, 50; CN 5, 6, 7; DLBY 1980

Dunsany, Lord .... **TCLC 2, 59**
See Dunsany, Edward John Moreton Drax Plunkett
See also DLB 77, 153, 156, 255; FANT; IDTP; RGEL 2; SFW 4; SUFW 1

Dunsany, Edward John Moreton Drax Plunkett 1878-1957
See Dunsany, Lord
See also CA 104; 148; DLB 10; MTCW 2

Duns Scotus, John 1266(?)-1308 ... **CMLC 59**
See also DLB 115

du Perry, Jean
See Simenon, Georges (Jacques Christian)

Durang, Christopher (Ferdinand)
1949- .... **CLC 27, 38**
See also CA 105; CAD; CANR 50, 76, 130; CD 5, 6; MTCW 2; MTFW 2005

Duras, Claire de 1777-1832 .... **NCLC 154**

Duras, Marguerite 1914-1996 . **CLC 3, 6, 11, 20, 34, 40, 68, 100; SSC 40**
See also BPFB 1; CA 25-28R; 151; CANR 50; CWW 2; DFS 21; DLB 83, 321; EWL 3; FL 1:5; GFL 1789 to the Present; IDFW 4; MTCW 1, 2; RGWL 2, 3; TWA

Durban, (Rosa) Pam 1947- .... **CLC 39**
See also CA 123; CANR 98; CSW

Durcan, Paul 1944- .... **CLC 43, 70**
See also CA 134; CANR 123; CP 1, 7; DAM POET; EWL 3

Durfey, Thomas 1653-1723 .... **LC 94**
See also DLB 80; RGEL 2

Durkheim, Emile 1858-1917 .... **TCLC 55**

Durrell, Lawrence (George)
1912-1990 ..... **CLC 1, 4, 6, 8, 13, 27, 41**
See also BPFB 1; BRWS 1; CA 9-12R; 132; CANR 40, 77; CDBLB 1945-1960; CN 1, 2, 3, 4; CP 1, 2, 3, 4; DAM NOV; DLB 15, 27, 204; DLBY 1990; EWL 3; MTCW 1, 2; RGEL 2; SFW 4; TEA

Durrenmatt, Friedrich
See Duerrenmatt, Friedrich
See also CDWLB 2; EW 13; EWL 3; RGWL 2, 3

Dutt, Michael Madhusudan
1824-1873 .... **NCLC 118**

Dutt, Toru 1856-1877 .... **NCLC 29**
See also DLB 240

Dwight, Timothy 1752-1817 .... **NCLC 13**
See also DLB 37; RGAL 4

Dworkin, Andrea 1946-2005 ..... **CLC 43, 123**
See also CA 77-80; 238; CAAS 21; CANR 16, 39, 76, 96; FL 1:5; FW; GLL 1; INT CANR-16; MTCW 1, 2; MTFW 2005

Dwyer, Deanna
See Koontz, Dean R.

Dwyer, K. R.
See Koontz, Dean R.

Dybek, Stuart 1942- .... **CLC 114; SSC 55**
See also CA 97-100; CANR 39; DLB 130

Dye, Richard
See De Voto, Bernard (Augustine)

Dyer, Geoff 1958- .... **CLC 149**
See also CA 125; CANR 88

Dyer, George 1755-1841 .... **NCLC 129**
See also DLB 93

Dylan, Bob 1941- .... **CLC 3, 4, 6, 12, 77; PC 37**
See also CA 41-44R; CANR 108; CP 1, 2, 3, 4, 5, 6, 7; DLB 16

Dyson, John 1943- .... **CLC 70**
See also CA 144

Dzyubin, Eduard Georgievich 1895-1934
See Bagritsky, Eduard
See also CA 170

E. V. L.
See Lucas, E(dward) V(errall)

Eagleton, Terence (Francis) 1943- .. **CLC 63, 132**
See also CA 57-60; CANR 7, 23, 68, 115; DLB 242; LMFS 2; MTCW 1, 2; MTFW 2005

Eagleton, Terry
See Eagleton, Terence (Francis)

Early, Jack
See Scoppettone, Sandra
See also GLL 1

East, Michael
See West, Morris L(anglo)

Eastaway, Edward
See Thomas, (Philip) Edward

Eastlake, William (Derry)
1917-1997 .... **CLC 8**
See also CA 5-8R; 158; CAAS 1; CANR 5, 63; CN 1, 2, 3, 4, 5, 6; DLB 6, 206; INT CANR-5; MAL 5; TCWW 1, 2

Eastman, Charles A(lexander)
1858-1939 .... **NNAL; TCLC 55**
See also CA 179; CANR 91; DAM MULT; DLB 175; YABC 1

Eaton, Edith Maude 1865-1914 .... **AAL**
See Far, Sui Sin
See also CA 154; DLB 221, 312; FW

Eaton, (Lillie) Winnifred 1875-1954 .... **AAL**
See also CA 217; DLB 221, 312; RGAL 4

Eberhart, Richard 1904-2005 ...... **CLC 3, 11, 19, 56**
See also AMW; CA 1-4R; 240; CANR 2, 125; CDALB 1941-1968; CP 1, 2, 3, 4, 5, 6, 7; DAM POET; DLB 48; MAL 5; MTCW 1; RGAL 4

Eberhart, Richard Ghormley
See Eberhart, Richard

Eberstadt, Fernanda 1960- .... **CLC 39**
See also CA 136; CANR 69, 128

Echegaray (y Eizaguirre), Jose (Maria Waldo) 1832-1916 .... **HLCS 1; TCLC 4**
See also CA 104; CANR 32; EWL 3; HW 1; MTCW 1

Echeverria, (Jose) Esteban (Antonino)
1805-1851 .... **NCLC 18**
See also LAW

Echo
See Proust, (Valentin-Louis-George-Eugene) Marcel

Eckert, Allan W. 1931- .... **CLC 17**
See also AAYA 18; BYA 2; CA 13-16R; CANR 14, 45; INT CANR-14; MAICYA 2; MAICYAS 1; SAAS 21; SATA 29, 91; SATA-Brief 27

Eckhart, Meister 1260(?)-1327(?) .. **CMLC 9, 80**
See also DLB 115; LMFS 1

Eckmar, F. R.
See de Hartog, Jan

Eco, Umberto 1932- .... **CLC 28, 60, 142**
See also BEST 90:1; BPFB 1; CA 77-80; CANR 12, 33, 55, 110, 131; CPW; CWW 2; DA3; DAM NOV, POP; DLB 196, 242; EWL 3; MSW; MTCW 1, 2; MTFW 2005; NFS 22; RGWL 3; WLIT 7

Eddison, E(ric) R(ucker)
1882-1945 .... **TCLC 15**
See also CA 109; 156; DLB 255; FANT; SFW 4; SUFW 1

Eddy, Mary (Ann Morse) Baker
1821-1910 .... **TCLC 71**
See also CA 113; 174

Edel, (Joseph) Leon 1907-1997 .. **CLC 29, 34**
See also CA 1-4R; 161; CANR 1, 22, 112; DLB 103; INT CANR-22

Eden, Emily 1797-1869 .... **NCLC 10**

Edgar, David 1948- .... **CLC 42**
See also CA 57-60; CANR 12, 61, 112; CBD; CD 5, 6; DAM DRAM; DFS 15; DLB 13, 233; MTCW 1

Edgerton, Clyde (Carlyle) 1944- ...... **CLC 39**
See also AAYA 17; CA 118; 134; CANR 64, 125; CN 7; CSW; DLB 278; INT CA-134; TCLE 1:1; YAW

Edgeworth, Maria 1768-1849 ... **NCLC 1, 51, 158; SSC 86**
See also BRWS 3; DLB 116, 159, 163; FL 1:3; FW; RGEL 2; SATA 21; TEA; WLIT 3

Edmonds, Paul
See Kuttner, Henry

Edmonds, Walter D(umaux)
1903-1998 .... **CLC 35**
See also BYA 2; CA 5-8R; CANR 2; CWRI 5; DLB 9; LAIT 1; MAICYA 1, 2; MAL 5; RHW; SAAS 4; SATA 1, 27; SATA-Obit 99

Edmondson, Wallace
See Ellison, Harlan (Jay)

Edson, Margaret 1961- ...... **CLC 199; DC 24**
See also CA 190; DFS 13; DLB 266

Edson, Russell 1935- .... **CLC 13**
See also CA 33-36R; CANR 115; CP 2, 3, 4, 5, 6, 7; DLB 244; WP

Edwards, Bronwen Elizabeth
See Rose, Wendy

Edwards, G(erald) B(asil)
1899-1976 .... **CLC 25**
See also CA 201; 110

Edwards, Gus 1939- .... **CLC 43**
See also CA 108; INT CA-108

Edwards, Jonathan 1703-1758 .... **LC 7, 54**
See also AMW; DA; DAC; DAM MST; DLB 24, 270; RGAL 4; TUS

Fairfield, Flora
See Alcott, Louisa May
Fairman, Paul W. 1916-1977
See Queen, Ellery
See also CA 114; SFW 4
Falco, Gian
See Papini, Giovanni
Falconer, James
See Kirkup, James
Falconer, Kenneth
See Kornbluth, C(yril) M.
Falkland, Samuel
See Heijermans, Herman
Fallaci, Oriana 1930- .... **CLC 11, 110**
See also CA 77-80; CANR 15, 58, 134; FW;
MTCW 1
Faludi, Susan 1959- .... **CLC 140**
See also CA 138; CANR 126; FW; MTCW
2; MTFW 2005; NCFS 3
Faludy, George 1913- .... **CLC 42**
See also CA 21-24R
Faludy, Gyoergy
See Faludy, George
Fanon, Frantz 1925-1961 .... **BLC 2; CLC 74**
See also BW 1; CA 116; 89-92; DAM
MULT; DLB 296; LMFS 2; WLIT 2
Fanshawe, Ann 1625-1680 .... **LC 11**
Fante, John (Thomas) 1911-1983 .... **CLC 60;
SSC 65**
See also AMWS 11; CA 69-72; 109; CANR
23, 104; DLB 130; DLBY 1983
Far, Sui Sin .... **SSC 62**
See Eaton, Edith Maude
See also SSFS 4
Farah, Nuruddin 1945- ...... **BLC 2; CLC 53,
137**
See also AFW; BW 2, 3; CA 106; CANR
81; CDWLB 3; CN 4, 5, 6, 7; DAM
MULT; DLB 125; EWL 3; WLIT 2
Fargue, Leon-Paul 1876(?)-1947 .... **TCLC 11**
See also CA 109; CANR 107; DLB 258;
EWL 3
Farigoule, Louis
See Romains, Jules
Farina, Richard 1936(?)-1966 .... **CLC 9**
See also CA 81-84; 25-28R
Farley, Walter (Lorimer)
1915-1989 .... **CLC 17**
See also AAYA 58; BYA 14; CA 17-20R;
CANR 8, 29, 84; DLB 22; JRDA; MAI-
CYA 1, 2; SATA 2, 43, 132; YAW
Farmer, Philip Jose 1918- .... **CLC 1, 19**
See also AAYA 28; BPFB 1; CA 1-4R;
CANR 4, 35, 111; DLB 8; MTCW 1;
SATA 93; SCFW 1, 2; SFW 4
Farquhar, George 1677-1707 .... **LC 21**
See also BRW 2; DAM DRAM; DLB 84;
RGEL 2
Farrell, J(ames) G(ordon)
1935-1979 .... **CLC 6**
See also CA 73-76; 89-92; CANR 36; CN
1, 2; DLB 14, 271; MTCW 1; RGEL 2;
RHW; WLIT 4
Farrell, James T(homas) 1904-1979 . **CLC 1,
4, 8, 11, 66; SSC 28**
See also AMW; BPFB 1; CA 5-8R; 89-92;
CANR 9, 61; CN 1, 2; DLB 4, 9, 86;
DLBD 2; EWL 3; MAL 5; MTCW 1, 2;
MTFW 2005; RGAL 4
Farrell, Warren (Thomas) 1943- ...... **CLC 70**
See also CA 146; CANR 120
Farren, Richard J.
See Betjeman, John
Farren, Richard M.
See Betjeman, John
Fassbinder, Rainer Werner
1946-1982 .... **CLC 20**
See also CA 93-96; 106; CANR 31

Fast, Howard (Melvin) 1914-2003 .. **CLC 23,
131**
See also AAYA 16; BPFB 1; CA 1-4R, 181;
214; CAAE 181; CAAS 18; CANR 1, 33,
54, 75, 98, 140; CMW 4; CN 1, 2, 3, 4, 5,
6, 7; CPW; DAM NOV; DLB 9; INT
CANR-33; LATS 1:1; MAL 5; MTCW 2;
MTFW 2005; RHW; SATA 7; SATA-
Essay 107; TCWW 1, 2; YAW
Faulcon, Robert
See Holdstock, Robert P.
Faulkner, William (Cuthbert)
1897-1962 .... **CLC 1, 3, 6, 8, 9, 11, 14,
18, 28, 52, 68; SSC 1, 35, 42; TCLC
141; WLC**
See also AAYA 7; AMW; AMWR 1; BPFB
1; BYA 5, 15; CA 81-84; CANR 33;
CDALB 1929-1941; DA; DA3; DAB;
DAC; DAM MST, NOV; DLB 9, 11, 44,
102, 316; DLBD 2; DLBY 1986, 1997;
EWL 3; EXPN; EXPS; GL 2; LAIT 2;
LATS 1:1; LMFS 2; MAL 5; MTCW 1,
2; MTFW 2005; NFS 4, 8, 13; RGAL 4;
RGSF 2; SSFS 2, 5, 6, 12; TUS
Fauset, Jessie Redmon
1882(?)-1961 .. **BLC 2; CLC 19, 54; HR
1:2**
See also AFAW 2; BW 1; CA 109; CANR
83; DAM MULT; DLB 51; FW; LMFS 2;
MAL 5; MAWW
Faust, Frederick (Schiller)
1892-1944 .... **TCLC 49**
See Brand, Max; Dawson, Peter; Frederick,
John
See also CA 108; 152; CANR 143; DAM
POP; DLB 256; TUS
Faust, Irvin 1924- .... **CLC 8**
See also CA 33-36R; CANR 28, 67; CN 1,
2, 3, 4, 5, 6, 7; DLB 2, 28, 218, 278;
DLBY 1980
Faustino, Domingo 1811-1888 ...... **NCLC 123**
Fawkes, Guy
See Benchley, Robert (Charles)
Fearing, Kenneth (Flexner)
1902-1961 .... **CLC 51**
See also CA 93-96; CANR 59; CMW 4;
DLB 9; MAL 5; RGAL 4
Fecamps, Elise
See Creasey, John
Federman, Raymond 1928- .... **CLC 6, 47**
See also CA 17-20R, 208; CAAE 208;
CAAS 8; CANR 10, 43, 83, 108; CN 3,
4, 5, 6; DLBY 1980
Federspiel, J(uerg) F. 1931- .... **CLC 42**
See also CA 146
Feiffer, Jules (Ralph) 1929- ...... **CLC 2, 8, 64**
See also AAYA 3, 62; CA 17-20R; CAD;
CANR 30, 59, 129; CD 5, 6; DAM
DRAM; DLB 7, 44; INT CANR-30;
MTCW 1; SATA 8, 61, 111, 157
Feige, Hermann Albert Otto Maximilian
See Traven, B.
Feinberg, David B. 1956-1994 .... **CLC 59**
See also CA 135; 147
Feinstein, Elaine 1930- .... **CLC 36**
See also CA 69-72; CAAS 1; CANR 31,
68, 121; CN 3, 4, 5, 6, 7; CP 2, 3, 4, 5, 6,
7; CWP; DLB 14, 40; MTCW 1
Feke, Gilbert David .... **CLC 65**
Feldman, Irving (Mordecai) 1928- ..... **CLC 7**
See also CA 1-4R; CANR 1; CP 1, 2, 3, 4,
5, 6, 7; DLB 169; TCLE 1:1
Felix-Tchicaya, Gerald
See Tchicaya, Gerald Felix
Fellini, Federico 1920-1993 .... **CLC 16, 85**
See also CA 65-68; 143; CANR 33
Felltham, Owen 1602(?)-1668 .... **LC 92**
See also DLB 126, 151

Felsen, Henry Gregor 1916-1995 ..... **CLC 17**
See also CA 1-4R; 180; CANR 1; SAAS 2;
SATA 1
Felski, Rita .... **CLC 65**
Fenno, Jack
See Calisher, Hortense
Fenollosa, Ernest (Francisco)
1853-1908 .... **TCLC 91**
Fenton, James Martin 1949- .... **CLC 32, 209**
See also CA 102; CANR 108; CP 2, 3, 4, 5,
6, 7; DLB 40; PFS 11
Ferber, Edna 1887-1968 .... **CLC 18, 93**
See also AITN 1; CA 5-8R; 25-28R; CANR
68, 105; DLB 9, 28, 86, 266; MAL 5;
MTCW 1, 2; MTFW 2005; RGAL 4;
RHW; SATA 7; TCWW 1, 2
Ferdowsi, Abu'l Qasem
940-1020(?) .... **CMLC 43**
See Firdawsi, Abu al-Qasim
See also RGWL 2, 3
Ferguson, Helen
See Kavan, Anna
Ferguson, Niall 1964- .... **CLC 134**
See also CA 190
Ferguson, Samuel 1810-1886 .... **NCLC 33**
See also DLB 32; RGEL 2
Fergusson, Robert 1750-1774 .... **LC 29**
See also DLB 109; RGEL 2
Ferling, Lawrence
See Ferlinghetti, Lawrence (Monsanto)
Ferlinghetti, Lawrence (Monsanto)
1919(?)- .. **CLC 2, 6, 10, 27, 111; PC 1**
See also BG 1:2; CA 5-8R; CAD; CANR 3,
41, 73, 125; CDALB 1941-1968; CP 1, 2,
3, 4, 5, 6, 7; DA3; DAM POET; DLB 5,
16; MAL 5; MTCW 1, 2; MTFW 2005;
RGAL 4; WP
Fern, Fanny
See Parton, Sara Payson Willis
Fernandez, Vicente Garcia Huidobro
See Huidobro Fernandez, Vicente Garcia
Fernandez-Armesto, Felipe .... **CLC 70**
Fernandez de Lizardi, Jose Joaquin
See Lizardi, Jose Joaquin Fernandez de
Ferre, Rosario 1938- ...... **CLC 139; HLCS 1;
SSC 36**
See also CA 131; CANR 55, 81, 134; CWW
2; DLB 145; EWL 3; HW 1, 2; LAWS 1;
MTCW 2; MTFW 2005; WLIT 1
Ferrer, Gabriel (Francisco Victor) Miro
See Miro (Ferrer), Gabriel (Francisco
Victor)
Ferrier, Susan (Edmonstone)
1782-1854 .... **NCLC 8**
See also DLB 116; RGEL 2
Ferrigno, Robert 1948(?)- .... **CLC 65**
See also CA 140; CANR 125
Ferron, Jacques 1921-1985 .... **CLC 94**
See also CA 117; 129; CCA 1; DAC; DLB
60; EWL 3
Feuchtwanger, Lion 1884-1958 .... **TCLC 3**
See also CA 104; 187; DLB 66; EWL 3
Feuerbach, Ludwig 1804-1872 ..... **NCLC 139**
See also DLB 133
Feuillet, Octave 1821-1890 .... **NCLC 45**
See also DLB 192
Feydeau, Georges (Leon Jules Marie)
1862-1921 .... **TCLC 22**
See also CA 113; 152; CANR 84; DAM
DRAM; DLB 192; EWL 3; GFL 1789 to
the Present; RGWL 2, 3
Fichte, Johann Gottlieb
1762-1814 .... **NCLC 62**
See also DLB 90
Ficino, Marsilio 1433-1499 .... **LC 12**
See also LMFS 1
Fiedeler, Hans
See Doeblin, Alfred

Fiedler, Leslie A(aron) 1917-2003 ..... **CLC 4, 13, 24**
See also AMWS 13; CA 9-12R; 212; CANR 7, 63; CN 1, 2, 3, 4, 5, 6; DLB 28, 67; EWL 3; MAL 5; MTCW 1, 2; RGAL 4; TUS

Field, Andrew 1938- .... **CLC 44**
See also CA 97-100; CANR 25

Field, Eugene 1850-1895 .... **NCLC 3**
See also DLB 23, 42, 140; DLBD 13; MAICYA 1, 2; RGAL 4; SATA 16

Field, Gans T.
See Wellman, Manly Wade

Field, Michael 1915-1971 .... **TCLC 43**
See also CA 29-32R

Fielding, Helen 1958- .... **CLC 146, 217**
See also AAYA 65; CA 172; CANR 127; DLB 231; MTFW 2005

Fielding, Henry 1707-1754 .... **LC 1, 46, 85; WLC**
See also BRW 3; BRWR 1; CDBLB 1660-1789; DA; DA3; DAB; DAC; DAM DRAM, MST, NOV; DLB 39, 84, 101; NFS 18; RGEL 2; TEA; WLIT 3

Fielding, Sarah 1710-1768 .... **LC 1, 44**
See also DLB 39; RGEL 2; TEA

Fields, W. C. 1880-1946 .... **TCLC 80**
See also DLB 44

Fierstein, Harvey (Forbes) 1954- ..... **CLC 33**
See also CA 123; 129; CAD; CD 5, 6; CPW; DA3; DAM DRAM, POP; DFS 6; DLB 266; GLL; MAL 5

Figes, Eva 1932- .... **CLC 31**
See also CA 53-56; CANR 4, 44, 83; CN 2, 3, 4, 5, 6, 7; DLB 14, 271; FW

Filippo, Eduardo de
See de Filippo, Eduardo

Finch, Anne 1661-1720 .... **LC 3; PC 21**
See also BRWS 9; DLB 95

Finch, Robert (Duer Claydon)
1900-1995 .... **CLC 18**
See also CA 57-60; CANR 9, 24, 49; CP 1, 2, 3, 4; DLB 88

Findley, Timothy (Irving Frederick)
1930-2002 .... **CLC 27, 102**
See also CA 25-28R; 206; CANR 12, 42, 69, 109; CCA 1; CN 4, 5, 6, 7; DAC; DAM MST; DLB 53; FANT; RHW

Fink, William
See Mencken, H(enry) L(ouis)

Firbank, Louis 1942-
See Reed, Lou
See also CA 117

Firbank, (Arthur Annesley) Ronald
1886-1926 .... **TCLC 1**
See also BRWS 2; CA 104; 177; DLB 36; EWL 3; RGEL 2

Firdawsi, Abu al-Qasim
See Ferdowsi, Abu'l Qasem
See also WLIT 6

Fish, Stanley
See Fish, Stanley Eugene

Fish, Stanley E.
See Fish, Stanley Eugene

Fish, Stanley Eugene 1938- .... **CLC 142**
See also CA 112; 132; CANR 90; DLB 67

Fisher, Dorothy (Frances) Canfield
1879-1958 .... **TCLC 87**
See also CA 114; 136; CANR 80; CLR 71; CWRI 5; DLB 9, 102, 284; MAICYA 1, 2; MAL 5; YABC 1

Fisher, M(ary) F(rances) K(ennedy)
1908-1992 .... **CLC 76, 87**
See also CA 77-80; 138; CANR 44; MTCW 2

Fisher, Roy 1930- .... **CLC 25**
See also CA 81-84; CAAS 10; CANR 16; CP 1, 2, 3, 4, 5, 6, 7; DLB 40

Fisher, Rudolph 1897-1934 . **BLC 2; HR 1:2; SSC 25; TCLC 11**
See also BW 1, 3; CA 107; 124; CANR 80; DAM MULT; DLB 51, 102

Fisher, Vardis (Alvero) 1895-1968 .... **CLC 7; TCLC 140**
See also CA 5-8R; 25-28R; CANR 68; DLB 9, 206; MAL 5; RGAL 4; TCWW 1, 2

Fiske, Tarleton
See Bloch, Robert (Albert)

Fitch, Clarke
See Sinclair, Upton (Beall)

Fitch, John IV
See Cormier, Robert (Edmund)

Fitzgerald, Captain Hugh
See Baum, L(yman) Frank

FitzGerald, Edward 1809-1883 ...... **NCLC 9, 153**
See also BRW 4; DLB 32; RGEL 2

Fitzgerald, F(rancis) Scott (Key)
1896-1940 ... **SSC 6, 31, 75; TCLC 1, 6, 14, 28, 55, 157; WLC**
See also AAYA 24; AITN 1; AMW; AMWC 2; AMWR 1; BPFB 1; CA 110; 123; CDALB 1917-1929; DA; DA3; DAB; DAC; DAM MST, NOV; DLB 4, 9, 86, 219, 273; DLBD 1, 15, 16; DLBY 1981, 1996; EWL 3; EXPN; EXPS; LAIT 3; MAL 5; MTCW 1, 2; MTFW 2005; NFS 2, 19, 20; RGAL 4; RGSF 2; SSFS 4, 15, 21; TUS

Fitzgerald, Penelope 1916-2000 . **CLC 19, 51, 61, 143**
See also BRWS 5; CA 85-88; 190; CAAS 10; CANR 56, 86, 131; CN 3, 4, 5, 6, 7; DLB 14, 194; EWL 3; MTCW 2; MTFW 2005

Fitzgerald, Robert (Stuart)
1910-1985 .... **CLC 39**
See also CA 1-4R; 114; CANR 1; CP 1, 2, 3, 4; DLBY 1980; MAL 5

FitzGerald, Robert D(avid)
1902-1987 .... **CLC 19**
See also CA 17-20R; CP 1, 2, 3, 4; DLB 260; RGEL 2

Fitzgerald, Zelda (Sayre)
1900-1948 .... **TCLC 52**
See also AMWS 9; CA 117; 126; DLBY 1984

Flanagan, Thomas (James Bonner)
1923-2002 .... **CLC 25, 52**
See also CA 108; 206; CANR 55; CN 3, 4, 5, 6, 7; DLBY 1980; INT CA-108; MTCW 1; RHW; TCLE 1:1

Flaubert, Gustave 1821-1880 .... **NCLC 2, 10, 19, 62, 66, 135; SSC 11, 60; WLC**
See also DA; DA3; DAB; DAC; DAM MST, NOV; DLB 119, 301; EW 7; EXPS; GFL 1789 to the Present; LAIT 2; LMFS 1; NFS 14; RGSF 2; RGWL 2, 3; SSFS 6; TWA

Flavius Josephus
See Josephus, Flavius

Flecker, Herman Elroy
See Flecker, (Herman) James Elroy

Flecker, (Herman) James Elroy
1884-1915 .... **TCLC 43**
See also CA 109; 150; DLB 10, 19; RGEL 2

Fleming, Ian (Lancaster) 1908-1964 . **CLC 3, 30**
See also AAYA 26; BPFB 1; CA 5-8R; CANR 59; CDBLB 1945-1960; CMW 4; CPW; DA3; DAM POP; DLB 87, 201; MSW; MTCW 1, 2; MTFW 2005; RGEL 2; SATA 9; TEA; YAW

Fleming, Thomas (James) 1927- ...... **CLC 37**
See also CA 5-8R; CANR 10, 102; INT CANR-10; SATA 8

Fletcher, John 1579-1625 .... **DC 6; LC 33**
See also BRW 2; CDBLB Before 1660; DLB 58; RGEL 2; TEA

Fletcher, John Gould 1886-1950 .... **TCLC 35**
See also CA 107; 167; DLB 4, 45; LMFS 2; MAL 5; RGAL 4

Fleur, Paul
See Pohl, Frederik

Flieg, Helmut
See Heym, Stefan

Flooglebuckle, Al
See Spiegelman, Art

Flora, Fletcher 1914-1969
See Queen, Ellery
See also CA 1-4R; CANR 3, 85

Flying Officer X
See Bates, H(erbert) E(rnest)

Fo, Dario 1926- .... **CLC 32, 109; DC 10**
See also CA 116; 128; CANR 68, 114, 134; CWW 2; DA3; DAM DRAM; DLBY 1997; EWL 3; MTCW 1, 2; MTFW 2005; WLIT 7

Fogarty, Jonathan Titulescu Esq.
See Farrell, James T(homas)

Follett, Ken(neth Martin) 1949- .... **CLC 18**
See also AAYA 6, 50; BEST 89:4; BPFB 1; CA 81-84; CANR 13, 33, 54, 102; CMW 4; CPW; DA3; DAM NOV, POP; DLB 87; DLBY 1981; INT CANR-33; MTCW 1

Fondane, Benjamin 1898-1944 ..... **TCLC 159**

Fontane, Theodor 1819-1898 . **NCLC 26, 163**
See also CDWLB 2; DLB 129; EW 6; RGWL 2, 3; TWA

Fonte, Moderata 1555-1592 .... **LC 118**

Fontenot, Chester .... **CLC 65**

Fonvizin, Denis Ivanovich
1744(?)-1792 .... **LC 81**
See also DLB 150; RGWL 2, 3

Foote, Horton 1916- .... **CLC 51, 91**
See also CA 73-76; CAD; CANR 34, 51, 110; CD 5, 6; CSW; DA3; DAM DRAM; DFS 20; DLB 26, 266; EWL 3; INT CANR-34; MTFW 2005

Foote, Mary Hallock 1847-1938 .. **TCLC 108**
See also DLB 186, 188, 202, 221; TCWW 2

Foote, Samuel 1721-1777 .... **LC 106**
See also DLB 89; RGEL 2

Foote, Shelby 1916-2005 .... **CLC 75**
See also AAYA 40; CA 5-8R; 240; CANR 3, 45, 74, 131; CN 1, 2, 3, 4, 5, 6, 7; CPW; CSW; DA3; DAM NOV, POP; DLB 2, 17; MAL 5; MTCW 2; MTFW 2005; RHW

Forbes, Cosmo
See Lewton, Val

Forbes, Esther 1891-1967 .... **CLC 12**
See also AAYA 17; BYA 2; CA 13-14; 25-28R; CAP 1; CLR 27; DLB 22; JRDA; MAICYA 1, 2; RHW; SATA 2, 100; YAW

Forche, Carolyn (Louise) 1950- .... **CLC 25, 83, 86; PC 10**
See also CA 109; 117; CANR 50, 74, 138; CP 4, 5, 6, 7; CWP; DA3; DAM POET; DLB 5, 193; INT CA-117; MAL 5; MTCW 2; MTFW 2005; PFS 18; RGAL 4

Ford, Elbur
See Hibbert, Eleanor Alice Burford

Ford, Ford Madox 1873-1939 ... **TCLC 1, 15, 39, 57, 172**
See Chaucer, Daniel
See also BRW 6; CA 104; 132; CANR 74; CDBLB 1914-1945; DA3; DAM NOV; DLB 34, 98, 162; EWL 3; MTCW 1, 2; RGEL 2; TEA

Ford, Henry 1863-1947 .... **TCLC 73**
See also CA 115; 148

Ford, Jack
See Ford, John
Ford, John 1586-1639 .... **DC 8; LC 68**
See also BRW 2; CDBLB Before 1660;
DA3; DAM DRAM; DFS 7; DLB 58;
IDTP; RGEL 2
Ford, John 1895-1973 .... **CLC 16**
See also CA 187; 45-48
Ford, Richard 1944- .... **CLC 46, 99, 205**
See also AMWS 5; CA 69-72; CANR 11,
47, 86, 128; CN 5, 6, 7; CSW; DLB 227;
EWL 3; MAL 5; MTCW 2; MTFW 2005;
RGAL 4; RGSF 2
Ford, Webster
See Masters, Edgar Lee
Foreman, Richard 1937- .... **CLC 50**
See also CA 65-68; CAD; CANR 32, 63,
143; CD 5, 6
Forester, C(ecil) S(cott) 1899-1966 . **CLC 35;
TCLC 152**
See also CA 73-76; 25-28R; CANR 83;
DLB 191; RGEL 2; RHW; SATA 13
Forez
See Mauriac, Francois (Charles)
Forman, James
See Forman, James D(ouglas)
Forman, James D(ouglas) 1932- .... **CLC 21**
See also AAYA 17; CA 9-12R; CANR 4,
19, 42; JRDA; MAICYA 1, 2; SATA 8,
70; YAW
Forman, Milos 1932- .... **CLC 164**
See also AAYA 63; CA 109
Fornes, Maria Irene 1930- .... **CLC 39, 61,
187; DC 10; HLCS 1**
See also CA 25-28R; CAD; CANR 28, 81;
CD 5, 6; CWD; DLB 7; HW 1, 2; INT
CANR-28; LLW; MAL 5; MTCW 1;
RGAL 4
Forrest, Leon (Richard)
1937-1997 .... **BLCS; CLC 4**
See also AFAW 2; BW 2; CA 89-92; 162;
CAAS 7; CANR 25, 52, 87; CN 4, 5, 6;
DLB 33
Forster, E(dward) M(organ)
1879-1970 ...... **CLC 1, 2, 3, 4, 9, 10, 13,
15, 22, 45, 77; SSC 27; TCLC 125;
WLC**
See also AAYA 2, 37; BRW 6; BRWR 2;
BYA 12; CA 13-14; 25-28R; CANR 45;
CAP 1; CDBLB 1914-1945; DA; DA3;
DAB; DAC; DAM MST, NOV; DLB 34,
98, 162, 178, 195; DLBD 10; EWL 3;
EXPN; LAIT 3; LMFS 1; MTCW 1, 2;
MTFW 2005; NCFS 1; NFS 3, 10, 11;
RGEL 2; RGSF 2; SATA 57; SUFW 1;
TEA; WLIT 4
Forster, John 1812-1876 .... **NCLC 11**
See also DLB 144, 184
Forster, Margaret 1938- .... **CLC 149**
See also CA 133; CANR 62, 115; CN 4, 5,
6, 7; DLB 155, 271
Forsyth, Frederick 1938- .... **CLC 2, 5, 36**
See also BEST 89:4; CA 85-88; CANR 38,
62, 115, 137; CMW 4; CN 3, 4, 5, 6, 7;
CPW; DAM NOV, POP; DLB 87; MTCW
1, 2; MTFW 2005
Forten, Charlotte L. 1837-1914 .... **BLC 2;
TCLC 16**
See Grimke, Charlotte L(ottie) Forten
See also DLB 50, 239
Fortinbras
See Grieg, (Johan) Nordahl (Brun)
Foscolo, Ugo 1778-1827 .... **NCLC 8, 97**
See also EW 5; WLIT 7
Fosse, Bob .... **CLC 20**
See Fosse, Robert Louis
Fosse, Robert Louis 1927-1987
See Fosse, Bob
See also CA 110; 123

Foster, Hannah Webster
1758-1840 .... **NCLC 99**
See also DLB 37, 200; RGAL 4
Foster, Stephen Collins
1826-1864 .... **NCLC 26**
See also RGAL 4
Foucault, Michel 1926-1984 . **CLC 31, 34, 69**
See also CA 105; 113; CANR 34; DLB 242;
EW 13; EWL 3; GFL 1789 to the Present;
GLL 1; LMFS 2; MTCW 1, 2; TWA
**Fouque, Friedrich (Heinrich Karl) de la
Motte** 1777-1843 .... **NCLC 2**
See also DLB 90; RGWL 2, 3; SUFW 1
Fourier, Charles 1772-1837 .... **NCLC 51**
Fournier, Henri-Alban 1886-1914
See Alain-Fournier
See also CA 104; 179
Fournier, Pierre 1916-1997 .... **CLC 11**
See Gascar, Pierre
See also CA 89-92; CANR 16, 40
Fowles, John (Robert) 1926- . **CLC 1, 2, 3, 4,
6, 9, 10, 15, 33, 87; SSC 33**
See also BPFB 1; BRWS 1; CA 5-8R;
CANR 25, 71, 103; CDBLB 1960 to
Present; CN 1, 2, 3, 4, 5, 6, 7; DA3; DAB;
DAC; DAM MST; DLB 14, 139, 207;
EWL 3; HGG; MTCW 1, 2; MTFW 2005;
NFS 21; RGEL 2; RHW; SATA 22; TEA;
WLIT 4
Fox, Paula 1923- .... **CLC 2, 8, 121**
See also AAYA 3, 37; BYA 3, 8; CA 73-76;
CANR 20, 36, 62, 105; CLR 1, 44, 96;
DLB 52; JRDA; MAICYA 1, 2; MTCW
1; NFS 12; SATA 17, 60, 120; WYA;
YAW
Fox, William Price (Jr.) 1926- .... **CLC 22**
See also CA 17-20R; CAAS 19; CANR 11,
142; CSW; DLB 2; DLBY 1981
Foxe, John 1517(?)-1587 .... **LC 14**
See also DLB 132
Frame, Janet .. **CLC 2, 3, 6, 22, 66, 96; SSC
29**
See Clutha, Janet Paterson Frame
See also CN 1, 2, 3, 4, 5, 6, 7; CP 2, 3, 4;
CWP; EWL 3; RGEL 2; RGSF 2; TWA
France, Anatole .... **TCLC 9**
See Thibault, Jacques Anatole Francois
See also DLB 123; EWL 3; GFL 1789 to
the Present; RGWL 2, 3; SUFW 1
Francis, Claude .... **CLC 50**
See also CA 192
Francis, Dick
See Francis, Richard Stanley
See also CN 2, 3, 4, 5, 6
Francis, Richard Stanley 1920- ... **CLC 2, 22,
42, 102**
See Francis, Dick
See also AAYA 5, 21; BEST 89:3; BPFB 1;
CA 5-8R; CANR 9, 42, 68, 100, 141; CD-
BLB 1960 to Present; CMW 4; CN 7;
DA3; DAM POP; DLB 87; INT CANR-9;
MSW; MTCW 1, 2; MTFW 2005
Francis, Robert (Churchill)
1901-1987 .... **CLC 15; PC 34**
See also AMWS 9; CA 1-4R; 123; CANR
1; CP 1, 2, 3, 4; EXPP; PFS 12; TCLE
1:1
Francis, Lord Jeffrey
See Jeffrey, Francis
See also DLB 107
Frank, Anne(lies Marie)
1929-1945 .... **TCLC 17; WLC**
See also AAYA 12; BYA 1; CA 113; 133;
CANR 68; CLR 101; DA; DA3; DAB;
DAC; DAM MST; LAIT 4; MAICYA 2;
MAICYAS 1; MTCW 1, 2; MTFW 2005;
NCFS 2; SATA 87; SATA-Brief 42; WYA;
YAW
Frank, Bruno 1887-1945 .... **TCLC 81**
See also CA 189; DLB 118; EWL 3

Frank, Elizabeth 1945- .... **CLC 39**
See also CA 121; 126; CANR 78; INT CA-
126
Frankl, Viktor E(mil) 1905-1997 ...... **CLC 93**
See also CA 65-68; 161
Franklin, Benjamin
See Hasek, Jaroslav (Matej Frantisek)
Franklin, Benjamin 1706-1790 .... **LC 25;
WLCS**
See also AMW; CDALB 1640-1865; DA;
DA3; DAB; DAC; DAM MST; DLB 24,
43, 73, 183; LAIT 1; RGAL 4; TUS
**Franklin, (Stella Maria Sarah) Miles
(Lampe)** 1879-1954 .... **TCLC 7**
See also CA 104; 164; DLB 230; FW;
MTCW 2; RGEL 2; TWA
Franzen, Jonathan 1959- .... **CLC 202**
See also AAYA 65; CA 129; CANR 105
Fraser, Antonia (Pakenham) 1932- . **CLC 32,
107**
See also AAYA 57; CA 85-88; CANR 44,
65, 119; CMW; DLB 276; MTCW 1, 2;
MTFW 2005; SATA-Brief 32
Fraser, George MacDonald 1925- .... **CLC 7**
See also AAYA 48; CA 45-48, 180; CAAE
180; CANR 2, 48, 74; MTCW 2; RHW
Fraser, Sylvia 1935- .... **CLC 64**
See also CA 45-48; CANR 1, 16, 60; CCA
1
Frayn, Michael 1933- .... **CLC 3, 7, 31, 47,
176; DC 27**
See also BRWC 2; BRWS 7; CA 5-8R;
CANR 30, 69, 114, 133; CBD; CD 5, 6;
CN 1, 2, 3, 4, 5, 6, 7; DAM DRAM,
NOV; DFS 22; DLB 13, 14, 194, 245;
FANT; MTCW 1, 2; MTFW 2005; SFW
4
Fraze, Candida (Merrill) 1945- .... **CLC 50**
See also CA 126
Frazer, Andrew
See Marlowe, Stephen
Frazer, J(ames) G(eorge)
1854-1941 .... **TCLC 32**
See also BRWS 3; CA 118; NCFS 5
Frazer, Robert Caine
See Creasey, John
Frazer, Sir James George
See Frazer, J(ames) G(eorge)
Frazier, Charles 1950- .... **CLC 109**
See also AAYA 34; CA 161; CANR 126;
CSW; DLB 292; MTFW 2005
Frazier, Ian 1951- .... **CLC 46**
See also CA 130; CANR 54, 93
Frederic, Harold 1856-1898 .... **NCLC 10**
See also AMW; DLB 12, 23; DLBD 13;
MAL 5; NFS 22; RGAL 4
Frederick, John
See Faust, Frederick (Schiller)
See also TCWW 2
Frederick the Great 1712-1786 .... **LC 14**
Fredro, Aleksander 1793-1876 .... **NCLC 8**
Freeling, Nicolas 1927-2003 .... **CLC 38**
See also CA 49-52; 218; CAAS 12; CANR
1, 17, 50, 84; CMW 4; CN 1, 2, 3, 4, 5,
6; DLB 87
Freeman, Douglas Southall
1886-1953 .... **TCLC 11**
See also CA 109; 195; DLB 17; DLBD 17
Freeman, Judith 1946- .... **CLC 55**
See also CA 148; CANR 120; DLB 256
Freeman, Mary E(leanor) Wilkins
1852-1930 .... **SSC 1, 47; TCLC 9**
See also CA 106; 177; DLB 12, 78, 221;
EXPS; FW; HGG; MAWW; RGAL 4;
RGSF 2; SSFS 4, 8; SUFW 1; TUS
Freeman, R(ichard) Austin
1862-1943 .... **TCLC 21**
See also CA 113; CANR 84; CMW 4; DLB
70

French, Albert 1943- .... **CLC 86**
See also BW 3; CA 167

French, Antonia
See Kureishi, Hanif

French, Marilyn 1929- .. **CLC 10, 18, 60, 177**
See also BPFB 1; CA 69-72; CANR 3, 31, 134; CN 5, 6, 7; CPW; DAM DRAM, NOV, POP; FL 1:5; FW; INT CANR-31; MTCW 1, 2; MTFW 2005

French, Paul
See Asimov, Isaac

Freneau, Philip Morin 1752-1832 .. **NCLC 1, 111**
See also AMWS 2; DLB 37, 43; RGAL 4

Freud, Sigmund 1856-1939 .... **TCLC 52**
See also CA 115; 133; CANR 69; DLB 296; EW 8; EWL 3; LATS 1:1; MTCW 1, 2; MTFW 2005; NCFS 3; TWA

Freytag, Gustav 1816-1895 .... **NCLC 109**
See also DLB 129

Friedan, Betty (Naomi) 1921- .... **CLC 74**
See also CA 65-68; CANR 18, 45, 74; DLB 246; FW; MTCW 1, 2; MTFW 2005; NCFS 5

Friedlander, Saul 1932- .... **CLC 90**
See also CA 117; 130; CANR 72

Friedman, B(ernard) H(arper) 1926- .... **CLC 7**
See also CA 1-4R; CANR 3, 48

Friedman, Bruce Jay 1930- ...... **CLC 3, 5, 56**
See also CA 9-12R; CAD; CANR 25, 52, 101; CD 5, 6; CN 1, 2, 3, 4, 5, 6, 7; DLB 2, 28, 244; INT CANR-25; MAL 5; SSFS 18

Friel, Brian 1929- .... **CLC 5, 42, 59, 115; DC 8; SSC 76**
See also BRWS 5; CA 21-24R; CANR 33, 69, 131; CBD; CD 5, 6; DFS 11; DLB 13, 319; EWL 3; MTCW 1; RGEL 2; TEA

Friis-Baastad, Babbis Ellinor 1921-1970 .... **CLC 12**
See also CA 17-20R; 134; SATA 7

Frisch, Max (Rudolf) 1911-1991 ... **CLC 3, 9, 14, 18, 32, 44; TCLC 121**
See also CA 85-88; 134; CANR 32, 74; CD-WLB 2; DAM DRAM, NOV; DLB 69, 124; EW 13; EWL 3; MTCW 1, 2; MTFW 2005; RGWL 2, 3

Fromentin, Eugene (Samuel Auguste) 1820-1876 .... **NCLC 10, 125**
See also DLB 123; GFL 1789 to the Present

Frost, Frederick
See Faust, Frederick (Schiller)

Frost, Robert (Lee) 1874-1963 .. **CLC 1, 3, 4, 9, 10, 13, 15, 26, 34, 44; PC 1, 39; WLC**
See also AAYA 21; AMW; AMWR 1; CA 89-92; CANR 33; CDALB 1917-1929; CLR 67; DA; DA3; DAB; DAC; DAM MST, POET; DLB 54, 284; DLBD 7; EWL 3; EXPP; MAL 5; MTCW 1, 2; MTFW 2005; PAB; PFS 1, 2, 3, 4, 5, 6, 7, 10, 13; RGAL 4; SATA 14; TUS; WP; WYA

Froude, James Anthony 1818-1894 .... **NCLC 43**
See also DLB 18, 57, 144

Froy, Herald
See Waterhouse, Keith (Spencer)

Fry, Christopher 1907-2005 ... **CLC 2, 10, 14**
See also BRWS 3; CA 17-20R; 240; CAAS 23; CANR 9, 30, 74, 132; CBD; CD 5, 6; CP 1, 2, 3, 4, 5, 6, 7; DAM DRAM; DLB 13; EWL 3; MTCW 1, 2; MTFW 2005; RGEL 2; SATA 66; TEA

Frye, (Herman) Northrop 1912-1991 .... **CLC 24, 70; TCLC 165**
See also CA 5-8R; 133; CANR 8, 37; DLB 67, 68, 246; EWL 3; MTCW 1, 2; MTFW 2005; RGAL 4; TWA

Fuchs, Daniel 1909-1993 .... **CLC 8, 22**
See also CA 81-84; 142; CAAS 5; CANR 40; CN 1, 2, 3, 4, 5; DLB 9, 26, 28; DLBY 1993; MAL 5

Fuchs, Daniel 1934- .... **CLC 34**
See also CA 37-40R; CANR 14, 48

Fuentes, Carlos 1928- .. **CLC 3, 8, 10, 13, 22, 41, 60, 113; HLC 1; SSC 24; WLC**
See also AAYA 4, 45; AITN 2; BPFB 1; CA 69-72; CANR 10, 32, 68, 104, 138; CDWLB 3; CWW 2; DA; DA3; DAB; DAC; DAM MST, MULT, NOV; DLB 113; DNFS 2; EWL 3; HW 1, 2; LAIT 3; LATS 1:2; LAW; LAWS 1; LMFS 2; MTCW 1, 2; MTFW 2005; NFS 8; RGSF 2; RGWL 2, 3; TWA; WLIT 1

Fuentes, Gregorio Lopez y
See Lopez y Fuentes, Gregorio

Fuertes, Gloria 1918-1998 .... **PC 27**
See also CA 178, 180; DLB 108; HW 2; SATA 115

Fugard, (Harold) Athol 1932- . **CLC 5, 9, 14, 25, 40, 80, 211; DC 3**
See also AAYA 17; AFW; CA 85-88; CANR 32, 54, 118; CD 5, 6; DAM DRAM; DFS 3, 6, 10; DLB 225; DNFS 1, 2; EWL 3; LATS 1:2; MTCW 1; MTFW 2005; RGEL 2; WLIT 2

Fugard, Sheila 1932- .... **CLC 48**
See also CA 125

Fujiwara no Teika 1162-1241 .... **CMLC 73**
See also DLB 203

Fukuyama, Francis 1952- .... **CLC 131**
See also CA 140; CANR 72, 125

Fuller, Charles (H.), (Jr.) 1939- .... **BLC 2; CLC 25; DC 1**
See also BW 2; CA 108; 112; CAD; CANR 87; CD 5, 6; DAM DRAM, MULT; DFS 8; DLB 38, 266; EWL 3; INT CA-112; MAL 5; MTCW 1

Fuller, Henry Blake 1857-1929 .... **TCLC 103**
See also CA 108; 177; DLB 12; RGAL 4

Fuller, John (Leopold) 1937- .... **CLC 62**
See also CA 21-24R; CANR 9, 44; CP 1, 2, 3, 4, 5, 6, 7; DLB 40

Fuller, Margaret
See Ossoli, Sarah Margaret (Fuller)
See also AMWS 2; DLB 183, 223, 239; FL 1:3

Fuller, Roy (Broadbent) 1912-1991 ... **CLC 4, 28**
See also BRWS 7; CA 5-8R; 135; CAAS 10; CANR 53, 83; CN 1, 2, 3, 4, 5; CP 1, 2, 3, 4; CWRI 5; DLB 15, 20; EWL 3; RGEL 2; SATA 87

Fuller, Sarah Margaret
See Ossoli, Sarah Margaret (Fuller)

Fuller, Sarah Margaret
See Ossoli, Sarah Margaret (Fuller)
See also DLB 1, 59, 73

Fuller, Thomas 1608-1661 .... **LC 111**
See also DLB 151

Fulton, Alice 1952- .... **CLC 52**
See also CA 116; CANR 57, 88; CP 7; CWP; DLB 193

Furphy, Joseph 1843-1912 .... **TCLC 25**
See Collins, Tom
See also CA 163; DLB 230; EWL 3; RGEL 2

Fuson, Robert H(enderson) 1927- .... **CLC 70**
See also CA 89-92; CANR 103

Fussell, Paul 1924- .... **CLC 74**
See also BEST 90:1; CA 17-20R; CANR 8, 21, 35, 69, 135; INT CANR-21; MTCW 1, 2; MTFW 2005

Futabatei, Shimei 1864-1909 .... **TCLC 44**
See Futabatei Shimei
See also CA 162; MJW

Futabatei Shimei
See Futabatei, Shimei
See also DLB 180; EWL 3

Futrelle, Jacques 1875-1912 .... **TCLC 19**
See also CA 113; 155; CMW 4

Gaboriau, Emile 1835-1873 .... **NCLC 14**
See also CMW 4; MSW

Gadda, Carlo Emilio 1893-1973 ...... **CLC 11; TCLC 144**
See also CA 89-92; DLB 177; EWL 3; WLIT 7

Gaddis, William 1922-1998 ... **CLC 1, 3, 6, 8, 10, 19, 43, 86**
See also AMWS 4; BPFB 1; CA 17-20R; 172; CANR 21, 48; CN 1, 2, 3, 4, 5, 6; DLB 2, 278; EWL 3; MAL 5; MTCW 1, 2; MTFW 2005; RGAL 4

Gaelique, Moruen le
See Jacob, (Cyprien-)Max

Gage, Walter
See Inge, William (Motter)

Gaiman, Neil (Richard) 1960- .... **CLC 195**
See also AAYA 19, 42; CA 133; CANR 81, 129; DLB 261; HGG; MTFW 2005; SATA 85, 146; SFW 4; SUFW 2

Gaines, Ernest J(ames) 1933- .. **BLC 2; CLC 3, 11, 18, 86, 181; SSC 68**
See also AAYA 18; AFAW 1, 2; AITN 1; BPFB 2; BW 2, 3; BYA 6; CA 9-12R; CANR 6, 24, 42, 75, 126; CDALB 1968-1988; CLR 62; CN 1, 2, 3, 4, 5, 6, 7; CSW; DA3; DAM MULT; DLB 2, 33, 152; DLBY 1980; EWL 3; EXPN; LAIT 5; LATS 1:2; MAL 5; MTCW 1, 2; MTFW 2005; NFS 5, 7, 16; RGAL 4; RGSF 2; RHW; SATA 86; SSFS 5; YAW

Gaitskill, Mary (Lawrence) 1954- .... **CLC 69**
See also CA 128; CANR 61; DLB 244; TCLE 1:1

Gaius Suetonius Tranquillus
See Suetonius

Galdos, Benito Perez
See Perez Galdos, Benito
See also EW 7

Gale, Zona 1874-1938 .... **TCLC 7**
See also CA 105; 153; CANR 84; DAM DRAM; DFS 17; DLB 9, 78, 228; RGAL 4

Galeano, Eduardo (Hughes) 1940- . **CLC 72; HLCS 1**
See also CA 29-32R; CANR 13, 32, 100; HW 1

Galiano, Juan Valera y Alcala
See Valera y Alcala-Galiano, Juan

Galilei, Galileo 1564-1642 .... **LC 45**

Gallagher, Tess 1943- .... **CLC 18, 63; PC 9**
See also CA 106; CP 3, 4, 5, 6, 7; CWP; DAM POET; DLB 120, 212, 244; PFS 16

Gallant, Mavis 1922- ..... **CLC 7, 18, 38, 172; SSC 5, 78**
See also CA 69-72; CANR 29, 69, 117; CCA 1; CN 1, 2, 3, 4, 5, 6, 7; DAC; DAM MST; DLB 53; EWL 3; MTCW 1, 2; MTFW 2005; RGSF 2

Gallant, Roy A(rthur) 1924- .... **CLC 17**
See also CA 5-8R; CANR 4, 29, 54, 117; CLR 30; MAICYA 1, 2; SATA 4, 68, 110

Gallico, Paul (William) 1897-1976 ..... **CLC 2**
See also AITN 1; CA 5-8R; 69-72; CANR 23; CN 1, 2; DLB 9, 171; FANT; MAICYA 1, 2; SATA 13

Gallo, Max Louis 1932- .... **CLC 95**
See also CA 85-88

Gallois, Lucien
See Desnos, Robert

Gallup, Ralph
See Whitemore, Hugh (John)

Gent, Peter 1942- .... CLC 29
See also AITN 1; CA 89-92; DLBY 1982
Gentile, Giovanni 1875-1944 .... TCLC 96
See also CA 119
Gentlewoman in New England, A
See Bradstreet, Anne
Gentlewoman in Those Parts, A
See Bradstreet, Anne
Geoffrey of Monmouth c.
1100-1155 .... CMLC 44
See also DLB 146; TEA
George, Jean
See George, Jean Craighead
George, Jean Craighead 1919- .... CLC 35
See also AAYA 8; BYA 2, 4; CA 5-8R;
CANR 25; CLR 1; 80; DLB 52; JRDA;
MAICYA 1, 2; SATA 2, 68, 124; WYA;
YAW
George, Stefan (Anton) 1868-1933 . TCLC 2,
14
See also CA 104; 193; EW 8; EWL 3
Georges, Georges Martin
See Simenon, Georges (Jacques Christian)
Gerald of Wales c. 1146-c. 1223 ... CMLC 60
Gerhardi, William Alexander
See Gerhardie, William Alexander
Gerhardie, William Alexander
1895-1977 .... CLC 5
See also CA 25-28R; 73-76; CANR 18; CN
1, 2; DLB 36; RGEL 2
Gerson, Jean 1363-1429 .... LC 77
See also DLB 208
Gersonides 1288-1344 .... CMLC 49
See also DLB 115
Gerstler, Amy 1956- .... CLC 70
See also CA 146; CANR 99
Gertler, T. .... CLC 34
See also CA 116; 121
Gertsen, Aleksandr Ivanovich
See Herzen, Aleksandr Ivanovich
Ghalib .... NCLC 39, 78
See Ghalib, Asadullah Khan
Ghalib, Asadullah Khan 1797-1869
See Ghalib
See also DAM POET; RGWL 2, 3
Ghelderode, Michel de 1898-1962 ..... CLC 6,
11; DC 15
See also CA 85-88; CANR 40, 77; DAM
DRAM; DLB 321; EW 11; EWL 3; TWA
Ghiselin, Brewster 1903-2001 .... CLC 23
See also CA 13-16R; CAAS 10; CANR 13;
CP 1, 2, 3, 4, 5, 6, 7
Ghose, Aurabinda 1872-1950 .... TCLC 63
See Ghose, Aurobindo
See also CA 163
Ghose, Aurobindo
See Ghose, Aurabinda
See also EWL 3
Ghose, Zulfikar 1935- .... CLC 42, 200
See also CA 65-68; CANR 67; CN 1, 2, 3,
4, 5, 6, 7; CP 1, 2, 3, 4, 5, 6, 7; EWL 3
Ghosh, Amitav 1956- .... CLC 44, 153
See also CA 147; CANR 80; CN 6, 7;
WWE 1
Giacosa, Giuseppe 1847-1906 .... TCLC 7
See also CA 104
Gibb, Lee
See Waterhouse, Keith (Spencer)
Gibbon, Edward 1737-1794 .... LC 97
See also BRW 3; DLB 104; RGEL 2
Gibbon, Lewis Grassic .... TCLC 4
See Mitchell, James Leslie
See also RGEL 2
Gibbons, Kaye 1960- .... CLC 50, 88, 145
See also AAYA 34; AMWS 10; CA 151;
CANR 75, 127; CN 7; CSW; DA3; DAM
POP; DLB 292; MTCW 2; MTFW 2005;
NFS 3; RGAL 4; SATA 117

Gibran, Kahlil 1883-1931 . PC 9; TCLC 1, 9
See also CA 104; 150; DA3; DAM POET,
POP; EWL 3; MTCW 2; WLIT 6
Gibran, Khalil
See Gibran, Kahlil
Gibson, Mel 1956- .... CLC 215
Gibson, William 1914- .... CLC 23
See also CA 9-12R; CAD; CANR 9, 42, 75,
125; CD 5, 6; DA; DAB; DAC; DAM
DRAM, MST; DFS 2; DLB 7; LAIT 2;
MAL 5; MTCW 2; MTFW 2005; SATA
66; YAW
Gibson, William (Ford) 1948- ... CLC 39, 63,
186, 192; SSC 52
See also AAYA 12, 59; BPFB 2; CA 126;
133; CANR 52, 90, 106; CN 6, 7; CPW;
DA3; DAM POP; DLB 251; MTCW 2;
MTFW 2005; SCFW 2; SFW 4
Gide, Andre (Paul Guillaume)
1869-1951 ..... SSC 13; TCLC 5, 12, 36;
WLC
See also CA 104; 124; DA; DA3; DAB;
DAC; DAM MST, NOV; DLB 65, 321;
EW 8; EWL 3; GFL 1789 to the Present;
MTCW 1, 2; MTFW 2005; NFS 21;
RGSF 2; RGWL 2, 3; TWA
Gifford, Barry (Colby) 1946- .... CLC 34
See also CA 65-68; CANR 9, 30, 40, 90
Gilbert, Frank
See De Voto, Bernard (Augustine)
Gilbert, W(illiam) S(chwenck)
1836-1911 .... TCLC 3
See also CA 104; 173; DAM DRAM, POET;
RGEL 2; SATA 36
Gilbreth, Frank B(unker), Jr.
1911-2001 .... CLC 17
See also CA 9-12R; SATA 2
Gilchrist, Ellen (Louise) 1935- .. CLC 34, 48,
143; SSC 14, 63
See also BPFB 2; CA 113; 116; CANR 41,
61, 104; CN 4, 5, 6, 7; CPW; CSW; DAM
POP; DLB 130; EWL 3; EXPS; MTCW
1, 2; MTFW 2005; RGAL 4; RGSF 2;
SSFS 9
Giles, Molly 1942- .... CLC 39
See also CA 126; CANR 98
Gill, Eric .... TCLC 85
See Gill, (Arthur) Eric (Rowton Peter
Joseph)
Gill, (Arthur) Eric (Rowton Peter Joseph)
1882-1940
See Gill, Eric
See also CA 120; DLB 98
Gill, Patrick
See Creasey, John
Gillette, Douglas .... CLC 70
Gilliam, Terry (Vance) 1940- .... CLC 21, 141
See Monty Python
See also AAYA 19, 59; CA 108; 113; CANR
35; INT CA-113
Gillian, Jerry
See Gilliam, Terry (Vance)
Gilliatt, Penelope (Ann Douglass)
1932-1993 .... CLC 2, 10, 13, 53
See also AITN 2; CA 13-16R; 141; CANR
49; CN 1, 2, 3, 4, 5; DLB 14
Gilligan, Carol 1936- .... CLC 208
See also CA 142; CANR 121; FW
Gilman, Charlotte (Anna) Perkins (Stetson)
1860-1935 ...... SSC 13, 62; TCLC 9, 37,
117
See also AMWS 11; BYA 11; CA 106; 150;
DLB 221; EXPS; FL 1:5; FW; HGG;
LAIT 2; MAWW; MTCW 2; MTFW
2005; RGAL 4; RGSF 2; SFW 4; SSFS 1,
18

Gilmour, David 1946- .... CLC 35
Gilpin, William 1724-1804 .... NCLC 30
Gilray, J. D.
See Mencken, H(enry) L(ouis)
Gilroy, Frank D(aniel) 1925- .... CLC 2
See also CA 81-84; CAD; CANR 32, 64,
86; CD 5, 6; DFS 17; DLB 7
Gilstrap, John 1957(?)- .... CLC 99
See also CA 160; CANR 101
Ginsberg, Allen 1926-1997 .... CLC 1, 2, 3, 4,
6, 13, 36, 69, 109; PC 4, 47; TCLC
120; WLC
See also AAYA 33; AITN 1; AMWC 1;
AMWS 2; BG 1:2; CA 1-4R; 157; CANR
2, 41, 63, 95; CDALB 1941-1968; CP 1,
2, 3, 4, 5, 6; DA; DA3; DAB; DAC; DAM
MST, POET; DLB 5, 16, 169, 237; EWL
3; GLL 1; LMFS 2; MAL 5; MTCW 1, 2;
MTFW 2005; PAB; PFS 5; RGAL 4;
TUS; WP
Ginzburg, Eugenia .... CLC 59
See Ginzburg, Evgeniia
Ginzburg, Evgeniia 1904-1977
See Ginzburg, Eugenia
See also DLB 302
Ginzburg, Natalia 1916-1991 .... CLC 5, 11,
54, 70; SSC 65; TCLC 156
See also CA 85-88; 135; CANR 33; DFS
14; DLB 177; EW 13; EWL 3; MTCW 1,
2; MTFW 2005; RGWL 2, 3
Giono, Jean 1895-1970 .... CLC 4, 11; TCLC
124
See also CA 45-48; 29-32R; CANR 2, 35;
DLB 72, 321; EWL 3; GFL 1789 to the
Present; MTCW 1; RGWL 2, 3
Giovanni, Nikki 1943- .... BLC 2; CLC 2, 4,
19, 64, 117; PC 19; WLCS
See also AAYA 22; AITN 1; BW 2, 3; CA
29-32R; CAAS 6; CANR 18, 41, 60, 91,
130; CDALBS; CLR 6, 73; CP 2, 3, 4, 5,
6, 7; CSW; CWP; CWRI 5; DA; DA3;
DAB; DAC; DAM MST, MULT, POET;
DLB 5, 41; EWL 3; EXPP; INT CANR-
18; MAICYA 1, 2; MAL 5; MTCW 1, 2;
MTFW 2005; PFS 17; RGAL 4; SATA
24, 107; TUS; YAW
Giovene, Andrea 1904-1998 .... CLC 7
See also CA 85-88
Gippius, Zinaida (Nikolaevna) 1869-1945
See Hippius, Zinaida (Nikolaevna)
See also CA 106; 212
Giraudoux, Jean(-Hippolyte)
1882-1944 .... TCLC 2, 7
See also CA 104; 196; DAM DRAM; DLB
65, 321; EW 9; EWL 3; GFL 1789 to the
Present; RGWL 2, 3; TWA
Gironella, Jose Maria (Pous)
1917-2003 .... CLC 11
See also CA 101; 212; EWL 3; RGWL 2, 3
Gissing, George (Robert)
1857-1903 .... SSC 37; TCLC 3, 24, 47
See also BRW 5; CA 105; 167; DLB 18,
135, 184; RGEL 2; TEA
Gitlin, Todd 1943- .... CLC 201
See also CA 29-32R; CANR 25, 50, 88
Giurlani, Aldo
See Palazzeschi, Aldo
Gladkov, Fedor Vasil'evich
See Gladkov, Fyodor (Vasilyevich)
See also DLB 272
Gladkov, Fyodor (Vasilyevich)
1883-1958 .... TCLC 27
See Gladkov, Fedor Vasil'evich
See also CA 170; EWL 3
Glancy, Diane 1941- .... CLC 210; NNAL
See also CA 136, 225; CAAE 225; CAAS
24; CANR 87; DLB 175

Gordone, Charles 1925-1995 .. **CLC 1, 4; DC 8**
  See also BW 1, 3; CA 93-96, 180; 150; CAAE 180; CAD; CANR 55; DAM DRAM; DLB 7; INT CA-93-96; MTCW 1

Gore, Catherine 1800-1861 .... **NCLC 65**
  See also DLB 116; RGEL 2

Gorenko, Anna Andreevna
  See Akhmatova, Anna

Gorky, Maxim .... **SSC 28; TCLC 8; WLC**
  See Peshkov, Alexei Maximovich
  See also DAB; DFS 9; DLB 295; EW 8; EWL 3; TWA

Goryan, Sirak
  See Saroyan, William

Gosse, Edmund (William)
  1849-1928 .... **TCLC 28**
  See also CA 117; DLB 57, 144, 184; RGEL 2

Gotlieb, Phyllis (Fay Bloom) 1926- .. **CLC 18**
  See also CA 13-16R; CANR 7, 135; CN 7; CP 1, 2, 3, 4; DLB 88, 251; SFW 4

Gottesman, S. D.
  See Kornbluth, C(yril) M.; Pohl, Frederik

Gottfried von Strassburg fl. c. 1170-1215 .... **CMLC 10**
  See also CDWLB 2; DLB 138; EW 1; RGWL 2, 3

Gotthelf, Jeremias 1797-1854 .... **NCLC 117**
  See also DLB 133; RGWL 2, 3

Gottschalk, Laura Riding
  See Jackson, Laura (Riding)

Gould, Lois 1932(?)-2002 .... **CLC 4, 10**
  See also CA 77-80; 208; CANR 29; MTCW 1

Gould, Stephen Jay 1941-2002 .... **CLC 163**
  See also AAYA 26; BEST 90:2; CA 77-80; 205; CANR 10, 27, 56, 75, 125; CPW; INT CANR-27; MTCW 1, 2; MTFW 2005

Gourmont, Remy(-Marie-Charles) de 1858-1915 .... **TCLC 17**
  See also CA 109; 150; GFL 1789 to the Present; MTCW 2

Gournay, Marie le Jars de
  See de Gournay, Marie le Jars

Govier, Katherine 1948- .... **CLC 51**
  See also CA 101; CANR 18, 40, 128; CCA 1

Gower, John c. 1330-1408 .... **LC 76; PC 59**
  See also BRW 1; DLB 146; RGEL 2

Goyen, (Charles) William
  1915-1983 .... **CLC 5, 8, 14, 40**
  See also AITN 2; CA 5-8R; 110; CANR 6, 71; CN 1, 2, 3; DLB 2, 218; DLBY 1983; EWL 3; INT CANR-6; MAL 5

Goytisolo, Juan 1931- .... **CLC 5, 10, 23, 133; HLC 1**
  See also CA 85-88; CANR 32, 61, 131; CWW 2; DAM MULT; DLB 322; EWL 3; GLL 2; HW 1, 2; MTCW 1, 2; MTFW 2005

Gozzano, Guido 1883-1916 .... **PC 10**
  See also CA 154; DLB 114; EWL 3

Gozzi, (Conte) Carlo 1720-1806 .... **NCLC 23**

Grabbe, Christian Dietrich
  1801-1836 .... **NCLC 2**
  See also DLB 133; RGWL 2, 3

Grace, Patricia Frances 1937- .... **CLC 56**
  See also CA 176; CANR 118; CN 4, 5, 6, 7; EWL 3; RGSF 2

Gracian y Morales, Baltasar
  1601-1658 .... **LC 15**

Gracq, Julien .... **CLC 11, 48**
  See Poirier, Louis
  See also CWW 2; DLB 83; GFL 1789 to the Present

Grade, Chaim 1910-1982 .... **CLC 10**
  See also CA 93-96; 107; EWL 3

Graduate of Oxford, A
  See Ruskin, John

Grafton, Garth
  See Duncan, Sara Jeannette

Grafton, Sue 1940- .... **CLC 163**
  See also AAYA 11, 49; BEST 90:3; CA 108; CANR 31, 55, 111, 134; CMW 4; CPW; CSW; DA3; DAM POP; DLB 226; FW; MSW; MTFW 2005

Graham, John
  See Phillips, David Graham

Graham, Jorie 1950- .... **CLC 48, 118; PC 59**
  See also AAYA 67; CA 111; CANR 63, 118; CP 4, 5, 6, 7; CWP; DLB 120; EWL 3; MTFW 2005; PFS 10, 17; TCLE 1:1

Graham, R(obert) B(ontine) Cunninghame
  See Cunninghame Graham, Robert (Gallnigad) Bontine
  See also DLB 98, 135, 174; RGEL 2; RGSF 2

Graham, Robert
  See Haldeman, Joe (William)

Graham, Tom
  See Lewis, (Harry) Sinclair

Graham, W(illiam) S(idney)
  1918-1986 .... **CLC 29**
  See also BRWS 7; CA 73-76; 118; CP 1, 2, 3, 4; DLB 20; RGEL 2

Graham, Winston (Mawdsley)
  1910-2003 .... **CLC 23**
  See also CA 49-52; 218; CANR 2, 22, 45, 66; CMW 4; CN 1, 2, 3, 4, 5, 6, 7; DLB 77; RHW

Grahame, Kenneth 1859-1932 ...... **TCLC 64, 136**
  See also BYA 5; CA 108; 136; CANR 80; CLR 5; CWRI 5; DA3; DAB; DLB 34, 141, 178; FANT; MAICYA 1, 2; MTCW 2; NFS 20; RGEL 2; SATA 100; TEA; WCH; YABC 1

Granger, Darius John
  See Marlowe, Stephen

Granin, Daniil 1918- .... **CLC 59**
  See also DLB 302

Granovsky, Timofei Nikolaevich
  1813-1855 .... **NCLC 75**
  See also DLB 198

Grant, Skeeter
  See Spiegelman, Art

Granville-Barker, Harley
  1877-1946 .... **TCLC 2**
  See Barker, Harley Granville
  See also CA 104; 204; DAM DRAM; RGEL 2

Granzotto, Gianni
  See Granzotto, Giovanni Battista

Granzotto, Giovanni Battista
  1914-1985 .... **CLC 70**
  See also CA 166

Grass, Guenter (Wilhelm) 1927- ... **CLC 1, 2, 4, 6, 11, 15, 22, 32, 49, 88, 207; WLC**
  See Grass, Gunter (Wilhelm)
  See also BPFB 2; CA 13-16R; CANR 20, 75, 93, 133; CDWLB 2; DA; DA3; DAB; DAC; DAM MST, NOV; DLB 75, 124; EW 13; EWL 3; MTCW 1, 2; MTFW 2005; RGWL 2, 3; TWA

Grass, Gunter (Wilhelm)
  See Grass, Guenter (Wilhelm)
  See also CWW 2

Gratton, Thomas
  See Hulme, T(homas) E(rnest)

Grau, Shirley Ann 1929- .... **CLC 4, 9, 146; SSC 15**
  See also CA 89-92; CANR 22, 69; CN 1, 2, 3, 4, 5, 6, 7; CSW; DLB 2, 218; INT CA-89-92; CANR-22; MTCW 1

Gravel, Fern
  See Hall, James Norman

Graver, Elizabeth 1964- .... **CLC 70**
  See also CA 135; CANR 71, 129

Graves, Richard Perceval
  1895-1985 .... **CLC 44**
  See also CA 65-68; CANR 9, 26, 51

Graves, Robert (von Ranke)
  1895-1985 .. **CLC 1, 2, 6, 11, 39, 44, 45; PC 6**
  See also BPFB 2; BRW 7; BYA 4; CA 5-8R; 117; CANR 5, 36; CDBLB 1914-1945; CN 1, 2, 3; CP 1, 2, 3, 4; DA3; DAB; DAC; DAM MST, POET; DLB 20, 100, 191; DLBD 18; DLBY 1985; EWL 3; LATS 1:1; MTCW 1, 2; MTFW 2005; NCFS 2; NFS 21; RGEL 2; RHW; SATA 45; TEA

Graves, Valerie
  See Bradley, Marion Zimmer

Gray, Alasdair (James) 1934- .... **CLC 41**
  See also BRWS 9; CA 126; CANR 47, 69, 106, 140; CN 4, 5, 6, 7; DLB 194, 261, 319; HGG; INT CA-126; MTCW 1, 2; MTFW 2005; RGSF 2; SUFW 2

Gray, Amlin 1946- .... **CLC 29**
  See also CA 138

Gray, Francine du Plessix 1930- ..... **CLC 22, 153**
  See also BEST 90:3; CA 61-64; CAAS 2; CANR 11, 33, 75, 81; DAM NOV; INT CANR-11; MTCW 1, 2; MTFW 2005

Gray, John (Henry) 1866-1934 ...... **TCLC 19**
  See also CA 119; 162; RGEL 2

Gray, John Lee
  See Jakes, John (William)

Gray, Simon (James Holliday)
  1936- .... **CLC 9, 14, 36**
  See also AITN 1; CA 21-24R; CAAS 3; CANR 32, 69; CBD; CD 5, 6; CN 1, 2, 3; DLB 13; EWL 3; MTCW 1; RGEL 2

Gray, Spalding 1941-2004 .... **CLC 49, 112; DC 7**
  See also AAYA 62; CA 128; 225; CAD; CANR 74, 138; CD 5, 6; CPW; DAM POP; MTCW 2; MTFW 2005

Gray, Thomas 1716-1771 .... **LC 4, 40; PC 2; WLC**
  See also BRW 3; CDBLB 1660-1789; DA; DA3; DAB; DAC; DAM MST; DLB 109; EXPP; PAB; PFS 9; RGEL 2; TEA; WP

Grayson, David
  See Baker, Ray Stannard

Grayson, Richard (A.) 1951- .... **CLC 38**
  See also CA 85-88; 210; CAAE 210; CANR 14, 31, 57; DLB 234

Greeley, Andrew M(oran) 1928- ...... **CLC 28**
  See also BPFB 2; CA 5-8R; CAAS 7; CANR 7, 43, 69, 104, 136; CMW 4; CPW; DA3; DAM POP; MTCW 1, 2; MTFW 2005

Green, Anna Katharine
  1846-1935 .... **TCLC 63**
  See also CA 112; 159; CMW 4; DLB 202, 221; MSW

Green, Brian
  See Card, Orson Scott

Green, Hannah
  See Greenberg, Joanne (Goldenberg)

Green, Hannah 1927(?)-1996 .... **CLC 3**
  See also CA 73-76; CANR 59, 93; NFS 10

Green, Henry .... **CLC 2, 13, 97**
  See Yorke, Henry Vincent
  See also BRWS 2; CA 175; DLB 15; EWL 3; RGEL 2

Green, Julian .... **CLC 3, 11, 77**
  See Green, Julien (Hartridge)
  See also EWL 3; GFL 1789 to the Present; MTCW 2

Guillen, Nicolas (Cristobal)
    1902-1989 .... **BLC 2; CLC 48, 79; HLC 1; PC 23**
    See also BW 2; CA 116; 125; 129; CANR 84; DAM MST, MULT, POET; DLB 283; EWL 3; HW 1; LAW; RGWL 2, 3; WP

Guillen y Alvarez, Jorge
    See Guillen, Jorge

Guillevic, (Eugene) 1907-1997 .... **CLC 33**
    See also CA 93-96; CWW 2

Guillois
    See Desnos, Robert

Guillois, Valentin
    See Desnos, Robert

Guimaraes Rosa, Joao 1908-1967 .... **HLCS 2**
    See Rosa, Joao Guimaraes
    See also CA 175; LAW; RGSF 2; RGWL 2, 3

Guiney, Louise Imogen
    1861-1920 .... **TCLC 41**
    See also CA 160; DLB 54; RGAL 4

Guinizelli, Guido c. 1230-1276 ...... **CMLC 49**
    See Guinizzelli, Guido

Guinizzelli, Guido
    See Guinizelli, Guido
    See also WLIT 7

Guiraldes, Ricardo (Guillermo)
    1886-1927 .... **TCLC 39**
    See also CA 131; EWL 3; HW 1; LAW; MTCW 1

Gumilev, Nikolai (Stepanovich)
    1886-1921 .... **TCLC 60**
    See Gumilyov, Nikolay Stepanovich
    See also CA 165; DLB 295

Gumilyov, Nikolay Stepanovich
    See Gumilev, Nikolai (Stepanovich)
    See also EWL 3

Gump, P. Q.
    See Card, Orson Scott

Gunesekera, Romesh 1954- .... **CLC 91**
    See also BRWS 10; CA 159; CANR 140; CN 6, 7; DLB 267

Gunn, Bill .... **CLC 5**
    See Gunn, William Harrison
    See also DLB 38

Gunn, Thom(son William)
    1929-2004 . **CLC 3, 6, 18, 32, 81; PC 26**
    See also BRWS 4; CA 17-20R; 227; CANR 9, 33, 116; CDBLB 1960 to Present; CP 1, 2, 3, 4, 5, 6, 7; DAM POET; DLB 27; INT CANR-33; MTCW 1; PFS 9; RGEL 2

Gunn, William Harrison 1934(?)-1989
    See Gunn, Bill
    See also AITN 1; BW 1, 3; CA 13-16R; 128; CANR 12, 25, 76

Gunn Allen, Paula
    See Allen, Paula Gunn

Gunnars, Kristjana 1948- .... **CLC 69**
    See also CA 113; CCA 1; CP 7; CWP; DLB 60

Gunter, Erich
    See Eich, Gunter

Gurdjieff, G(eorgei) I(vanovich)
    1877(?)-1949 .... **TCLC 71**
    See also CA 157

Gurganus, Allan 1947- .... **CLC 70**
    See also BEST 90:1; CA 135; CANR 114; CN 6, 7; CPW; CSW; DAM POP; GLL 1

Gurney, A. R.
    See Gurney, A(lbert) R(amsdell), Jr.
    See also DLB 266

Gurney, A(lbert) R(amsdell), Jr.
    1930- .... **CLC 32, 50, 54**
    See Gurney, A. R.
    See also AMWS 5; CA 77-80; CAD; CANR 32, 64, 121; CD 5, 6; DAM DRAM; EWL 3

Gurney, Ivor (Bertie) 1890-1937 ... **TCLC 33**
    See also BRW 6; CA 167; DLBY 2002; PAB; RGEL 2

Gurney, Peter
    See Gurney, A(lbert) R(amsdell), Jr.

Guro, Elena (Genrikhovna)
    1877-1913 .... **TCLC 56**
    See also DLB 295

Gustafson, James M(oody) 1925- ... **CLC 100**
    See also CA 25-28R; CANR 37

Gustafson, Ralph (Barker)
    1909-1995 .... **CLC 36**
    See also CA 21-24R; CANR 8, 45, 84; CP 1, 2, 3, 4; DLB 88; RGEL 2

Gut, Gom
    See Simenon, Georges (Jacques Christian)

Guterson, David 1956- .... **CLC 91**
    See also CA 132; CANR 73, 126; CN 7; DLB 292; MTCW 2; MTFW 2005; NFS 13

Guthrie, A(lfred) B(ertram), Jr.
    1901-1991 .... **CLC 23**
    See also CA 57-60; 134; CANR 24; CN 1, 2, 3; DLB 6, 212; MAL 5; SATA 62; SATA-Obit 67; TCWW 1, 2

Guthrie, Isobel
    See Grieve, C(hristopher) M(urray)

Guthrie, Woodrow Wilson 1912-1967
    See Guthrie, Woody
    See also CA 113; 93-96

Guthrie, Woody .... **CLC 35**
    See Guthrie, Woodrow Wilson
    See also DLB 303; LAIT 3

Gutierrez Najera, Manuel
    1859-1895 .... **HLCS 2; NCLC 133**
    See also DLB 290; LAW

Guy, Rosa (Cuthbert) 1925- .... **CLC 26**
    See also AAYA 4, 37; BW 2; CA 17-20R; CANR 14, 34, 83; CLR 13; DLB 33; DNFS 1; JRDA; MAICYA 1, 2; SATA 14, 62, 122; YAW

Gwendolyn
    See Bennett, (Enoch) Arnold

H. D. .... **CLC 3, 8, 14, 31, 34, 73; PC 5**
    See Doolittle, Hilda
    See also FL 1:5

H. de V.
    See Buchan, John

Haavikko, Paavo Juhani 1931- .. **CLC 18, 34**
    See also CA 106; CWW 2; EWL 3

Habbema, Koos
    See Heijermans, Herman

Habermas, Juergen 1929- .... **CLC 104**
    See also CA 109; CANR 85; DLB 242

Habermas, Jurgen
    See Habermas, Juergen

Hacker, Marilyn 1942- ...... **CLC 5, 9, 23, 72, 91; PC 47**
    See also CA 77-80; CANR 68, 129; CP 3, 4, 5, 6, 7; CWP; DAM POET; DLB 120, 282; FW; GLL 2; MAL 5; PFS 19

Hadewijch of Antwerp fl. 1250- ... **CMLC 61**
    See also RGWL 3

Hadrian 76-138 .... **CMLC 52**

Haeckel, Ernst Heinrich (Philipp August)
    1834-1919 .... **TCLC 83**
    See also CA 157

Hafiz c. 1326-1389(?) .... **CMLC 34**
    See also RGWL 2, 3; WLIT 6

Hagedorn, Jessica T(arahata)
    1949- .... **CLC 185**
    See also CA 139; CANR 69; CWP; DLB 312; RGAL 4

Haggard, H(enry) Rider
    1856-1925 .... **TCLC 11**
    See also BRWS 3; BYA 4, 5; CA 108; 148; CANR 112; DLB 70, 156, 174, 178; FANT; LMFS 1; MTCW 2; RGEL 2; RHW; SATA 16; SCFW 1, 2; SFW 4; SUFW 1; WLIT 4

Hagiosy, L.
    See Larbaud, Valery (Nicolas)

Hagiwara, Sakutaro 1886-1942 .... **PC 18; TCLC 60**
    See Hagiwara Sakutaro
    See also CA 154; RGWL 3

Hagiwara Sakutaro
    See Hagiwara, Sakutaro
    See also EWL 3

Haig, Fenil
    See Ford, Ford Madox

Haig-Brown, Roderick (Langmere)
    1908-1976 .... **CLC 21**
    See also CA 5-8R; 69-72; CANR 4, 38, 83; CLR 31; CWRI 5; DLB 88; MAICYA 1, 2; SATA 12; TCWW 2

Haight, Rip
    See Carpenter, John (Howard)

Hailey, Arthur 1920-2004 .... **CLC 5**
    See also AITN 2; BEST 90:3; BPFB 2; CA 1-4R; 233; CANR 2, 36, 75; CCA 1; CN 1, 2, 3, 4, 5, 6, 7; CPW; DAM NOV, POP; DLB 88; DLBY 1982; MTCW 1, 2; MTFW 2005

Hailey, Elizabeth Forsythe 1938- ..... **CLC 40**
    See also CA 93-96, 188; CAAE 188; CAAS 1; CANR 15, 48; INT CANR-15

Haines, John (Meade) 1924- .... **CLC 58**
    See also AMWS 12; CA 17-20R; CANR 13, 34; CP 1, 2, 3, 4; CSW; DLB 5, 212; TCLE 1:1

Hakluyt, Richard 1552-1616 .... **LC 31**
    See also DLB 136; RGEL 2

Haldeman, Joe (William) 1943- .... **CLC 61**
    See Graham, Robert
    See also AAYA 38; CA 53-56, 179; CAAE 179; CAAS 25; CANR 6, 70, 72, 130; DLB 8; INT CANR-6; SCFW 2; SFW 4

Hale, Janet Campbell 1947- .... **NNAL**
    See also CA 49-52; CANR 45, 75; DAM MULT; DLB 175; MTCW 2; MTFW 2005

Hale, Sarah Josepha (Buell)
    1788-1879 .... **NCLC 75**
    See also DLB 1, 42, 73, 243

Halevy, Elie 1870-1937 .... **TCLC 104**

Haley, Alex(ander Murray Palmer)
    1921-1992 .... **BLC 2; CLC 8, 12, 76; TCLC 147**
    See also AAYA 26; BPFB 2; BW 2, 3; CA 77-80; 136; CANR 61; CDALBS; CPW; CSW; DA; DA3; DAB; DAC; DAM MST, MULT, POP; DLB 38; LAIT 5; MTCW 1, 2; NFS 9

Haliburton, Thomas Chandler
    1796-1865 .... **NCLC 15, 149**
    See also DLB 11, 99; RGEL 2; RGSF 2

Hall, Donald (Andrew, Jr.) 1928- ...... **CLC 1, 13, 37, 59, 151; PC 70**
    See also AAYA 63; CA 5-8R; CAAS 7; CANR 2, 44, 64, 106, 133; CP 1, 2, 3, 4, 5, 6, 7; DAM POET; DLB 5; MAL 5; MTCW 2; MTFW 2005; RGAL 4; SATA 23, 97

Hall, Frederic Sauser
    See Sauser-Hall, Frederic

Hall, James
    See Kuttner, Henry

Hall, James Norman 1887-1951 ..... **TCLC 23**
    See also CA 123; 173; LAIT 1; RHW 1; SATA 21

Hall, Joseph 1574-1656 .... **LC 91**
    See also DLB 121, 151; RGEL 2

Hewes, Cady
See De Voto, Bernard (Augustine)
Heyen, William 1940- .... **CLC 13, 18**
See also CA 33-36R; 220; CAAE 220;
CAAS 9; CANR 98; CP 3, 4, 5, 6, 7; DLB
5
Heyerdahl, Thor 1914-2002 .... **CLC 26**
See also CA 5-8R; 207; CANR 5, 22, 66,
73; LAIT 4; MTCW 1, 2; MTFW 2005;
SATA 2, 52
Heym, Georg (Theodor Franz Arthur)
1887-1912 .... **TCLC 9**
See also CA 106; 181
Heym, Stefan 1913-2001 .... **CLC 41**
See also CA 9-12R; 203; CANR 4; CWW
2; DLB 69; EWL 3
Heyse, Paul (Johann Ludwig von)
1830-1914 .... **TCLC 8**
See also CA 104; 209; DLB 129
Heyward, (Edwin) DuBose
1885-1940 .... **HR 1:2; TCLC 59**
See also CA 108; 157; DLB 7, 9, 45, 249;
MAL 5; SATA 21
Heywood, John 1497(?)-1580(?) .... **LC 65**
See also DLB 136; RGEL 2
Heywood, Thomas 1573(?)-1641 .... **LC 111**
See also DAM DRAM; DLB 62; LMFS 1;
RGEL 2; TEA
Hibbert, Eleanor Alice Burford
1906-1993 .... **CLC 7**
See Holt, Victoria
See also BEST 90:4; CA 17-20R; 140;
CANR 9, 28, 59; CMW 4; CPW; DAM
POP; MTCW 2; MTFW 2005; RHW;
SATA 2; SATA-Obit 74
Hichens, Robert (Smythe)
1864-1950 .... **TCLC 64**
See also CA 162; DLB 153; HGG; RHW;
SUFW
Higgins, Aidan 1927- .... **SSC 68**
See also CA 9-12R; CANR 70, 115; CN 1,
2, 3, 4, 5, 6, 7; DLB 14
Higgins, George V(incent)
1939-1999 .... **CLC 4, 7, 10, 18**
See also BPFB 2; CA 77-80; 186; CAAS 5;
CANR 17, 51, 89, 96; CMW 4; CN 2, 3,
4, 5, 6; DLB 2; DLBY 1981, 1998; INT
CANR-17; MSW; MTCW 1
Higginson, Thomas Wentworth
1823-1911 .... **TCLC 36**
See also CA 162; DLB 1, 64, 243
Higgonet, Margaret ed. .... **CLC 65**
Highet, Helen
See MacInnes, Helen (Clark)
Highsmith, (Mary) Patricia
1921-1995 .... **CLC 2, 4, 14, 42, 102**
See Morgan, Claire
See also AAYA 48; BRWS 5; CA 1-4R; 147;
CANR 1, 20, 48, 62, 108; CMW 4; CN 1,
2, 3, 4, 5; CPW; DA3; DAM NOV, POP;
DLB 306; MSW; MTCW 1, 2; MTFW
2005
Highwater, Jamake (Mamake)
1942(?)-2001 .... **CLC 12**
See also AAYA 7; BPFB 2; BYA 4; CA 65-
68; 199; CAAS 7; CANR 10, 34, 84; CLR
17; CWRI 5; DLB 52; DLBY 1985;
JRDA; MAICYA 1, 2; SATA 32, 69;
SATA-Brief 30
Highway, Tomson 1951- ...... **CLC 92; NNAL**
See also CA 151; CANR 75; CCA 1; CD 5,
6; CN 7; DAC; DAM MULT; DFS 2;
MTCW 2
Hijuelos, Oscar 1951- .... **CLC 65; HLC 1**
See also AAYA 25; AMWS 8; BEST 90:1;
CA 123; CANR 50, 75, 125; CPW; DA3;
DAM MULT, POP; DLB 145; HW 1, 2;
LLW; MAL 5; MTCW 2; MTFW 2005;
NFS 17; RGAL 4; WLIT 1

Hikmet, Nazim 1902-1963 .... **CLC 40**
See Nizami of Ganja
See also CA 141; 93-96; EWL 3; WLIT 6
Hildegard von Bingen 1098-1179 . **CMLC 20**
See also DLB 148
Hildesheimer, Wolfgang 1916-1991 .. **CLC 49**
See also CA 101; 135; DLB 69, 124; EWL
3
Hill, Geoffrey (William) 1932- ...... **CLC 5, 8,
18, 45**
See also BRWS 5; CA 81-84; CANR 21,
89; CDBLB 1960 to Present; CP 1, 2, 3,
4, 5, 6, 7; DAM POET; DLB 40; EWL 3;
MTCW 1; RGEL 2
Hill, George Roy 1921-2002 .... **CLC 26**
See also CA 110; 122; 213
Hill, John
See Koontz, Dean R.
Hill, Susan (Elizabeth) 1942- ...... **CLC 4, 113**
See also CA 33-36R; CANR 29, 69, 129;
CN 2, 3, 4, 5, 6, 7; DAB; DAM MST,
NOV; DLB 14, 139; HGG; MTCW 1;
RHW
Hillard, Asa G. III .... **CLC 70**
Hillerman, Tony 1925- .... **CLC 62, 170**
See also AAYA 40; BEST 89:1; BPFB 2;
CA 29-32R; CANR 21, 42, 65, 97, 134;
CMW 4; CPW; DA3; DAM POP; DLB
206, 306; MAL 5; MSW; MTCW 1, 2;
MTFW 2005; RGAL 4; SATA 6; TCWW
2; YAW
Hillesum, Etty 1914-1943 .... **TCLC 49**
See also CA 137
Hilliard, Noel (Harvey) 1929-1996 ... **CLC 15**
See also CA 9-12R; CANR 7, 69; CN 1, 2,
3, 4, 5, 6
Hillis, Rick 1956- .... **CLC 66**
See also CA 134
Hilton, James 1900-1954 .... **TCLC 21**
See also CA 108; 169; DLB 34, 77; FANT;
SATA 34
Hilton, Walter (?)-1396 .... **CMLC 58**
See also DLB 146; RGEL 2
Himes, Chester (Bomar) 1909-1984 .. **BLC 2;
CLC 2, 4, 7, 18, 58, 108; TCLC 139**
See also AFAW 2; BPFB 2; BW 2; CA 25-
28R; 114; CANR 22, 89; CMW 4; CN 1,
2, 3; DAM MULT; DLB 2, 76, 143, 226;
EWL 3; MAL 5; MSW; MTCW 1, 2;
MTFW 2005; RGAL 4
Himmelfarb, Gertrude 1922- .... **CLC 202**
See also CA 49-52; CANR 28, 66, 102
Hinde, Thomas .... **CLC 6, 11**
See Chitty, Thomas Willes
See also CN 1, 2, 3, 4, 5, 6; EWL 3
Hine, (William) Daryl 1936- .... **CLC 15**
See also CA 1-4R; CAAS 15; CANR 1, 20;
CP 1, 2, 3, 4, 5, 6, 7; DLB 60
Hinkson, Katharine Tynan
See Tynan, Katharine
Hinojosa(-Smith), Rolando (R.)
1929- .... **HLC 1**
See Hinojosa-Smith, Rolando
See also CA 131; CAAS 16; CANR 62;
DAM MULT; DLB 82; HW 1, 2; LLW;
MTCW 2; MTFW 2005; RGAL 4
Hinton, S(usan) E(loise) 1950- .. **CLC 30, 111**
See also AAYA 2, 33; BPFB 2; BYA 2, 3;
CA 81-84; CANR 32, 62, 92, 133;
CDALBS; CLR 3, 23; CPW; DA; DA3;
DAB; DAC; DAM MST, NOV; JRDA;
LAIT 5; MAICYA 1, 2; MTCW 1, 2;
MTFW 2005 !**; NFS 5, 9, 15, 16; SATA
19, 58, 115, 160; WYA; YAW
Hippius, Zinaida (Nikolaevna) .... **TCLC 9**
See Gippius, Zinaida (Nikolaevna)
See also DLB 295; EWL 3

Hiraoka, Kimitake 1925-1970
See Mishima, Yukio
See also CA 97-100; 29-32R; DA3; DAM
DRAM; GLL 1; MTCW 1, 2
Hirsch, E(ric) D(onald), Jr. 1928- .... **CLC 79**
See also CA 25-28R; CANR 27, 51; DLB
67; INT CANR-27; MTCW 1
Hirsch, Edward 1950- .... **CLC 31, 50**
See also CA 104; CANR 20, 42, 102; CP 7;
DLB 120; PFS 22
Hitchcock, Alfred (Joseph)
1899-1980 .... **CLC 16**
See also AAYA 22; CA 159; 97-100; SATA
27; SATA-Obit 24
Hitchens, Christopher (Eric)
1949- .... **CLC 157**
See also CA 152; CANR 89
Hitler, Adolf 1889-1945 .... **TCLC 53**
See also CA 117; 147
Hoagland, Edward (Morley) 1932- .. **CLC 28**
See also ANW; CA 1-4R; CANR 2, 31, 57,
107; CN 1, 2, 3, 4, 5, 6, 7; DLB 6; SATA
51; TCWW 2
Hoban, Russell (Conwell) 1925- ... **CLC 7, 25**
See also BPFB 2; CA 5-8R; CANR 23, 37,
66, 114, 138; CLR 3, 69; CN 4, 5, 6, 7;
CWRI 5; DAM NOV; DLB 52; FANT;
MAICYA 1, 2; MTCW 1, 2; MTFW 2005;
SATA 1, 40, 78, 136; SFW 4; SUFW 2;
TCLE 1:1
Hobbes, Thomas 1588-1679 .... **LC 36**
See also DLB 151, 252, 281; RGEL 2
Hobbs, Perry
See Blackmur, R(ichard) P(almer)
Hobson, Laura Z(ametkin)
1900-1986 .... **CLC 7, 25**
See also BPFB 2; CA 17-20R; 118; CANR
55; CN 1, 2, 3, 4; DLB 28; SATA 52
Hoccleve, Thomas c. 1368-c. 1437 ...... **LC 75**
See also DLB 146; RGEL 2
Hoch, Edward D(entinger) 1930-
See Queen, Ellery
See also CA 29-32R; CANR 11, 27, 51, 97;
CMW 4; DLB 306; SFW 4
Hochhuth, Rolf 1931- .... **CLC 4, 11, 18**
See also CA 5-8R; CANR 33, 75, 136;
CWW 2; DAM DRAM; DLB 124; EWL
3; MTCW 1, 2; MTFW 2005
Hochman, Sandra 1936- .... **CLC 3, 8**
See also CA 5-8R; CP 1, 2, 3, 4; DLB 5
Hochwaelder, Fritz 1911-1986 .... **CLC 36**
See Hochwalder, Fritz
See also CA 29-32R; 120; CANR 42; DAM
DRAM; MTCW 1; RGWL 3
Hochwalder, Fritz
See Hochwaelder, Fritz
See also EWL 3; RGWL 2
Hocking, Mary (Eunice) 1921- .... **CLC 13**
See also CA 101; CANR 18, 40
Hodgins, Jack 1938- .... **CLC 23**
See also CA 93-96; CN 4, 5, 6, 7; DLB 60
Hodgson, William Hope
1877(?)-1918 .... **TCLC 13**
See also CA 111; 164; CMW 4; DLB 70,
153, 156, 178; HGG; MTCW 2; SFW 4;
SUFW 1
Hoeg, Peter 1957- .... **CLC 95, 156**
See also CA 151; CANR 75; CMW 4; DA3;
DLB 214; EWL 3; MTCW 2; MTFW
2005; NFS 17; RGWL 3; SSFS 18
Hoffman, Alice 1952- .... **CLC 51**
See also AAYA 37; AMWS 10; CA 77-80;
CANR 34, 66, 100, 138; CN 4, 5, 6, 7;
CPW; DAM NOV; DLB 292; MAL 5;
MTCW 1, 2; MTFW 2005; TCLE 1:1
Hoffman, Daniel (Gerard) 1923- . **CLC 6, 13,
23**
See also CA 1-4R; CANR 4, 142; CP 1, 2,
3, 4, 5, 6, 7; DLB 5; TCLE 1:1

Jordan, June (Meyer)
　　1936-2002 .. **BLCS; CLC 5, 11, 23, 114; PC 38**
　　　See also AAYA 2, 66; AFAW 1, 2; BW 2, 3; CA 33-36R; 206; CANR 25, 70, 114; CLR 10; CP 3, 4, 5, 6, 7; CWP; DAM MULT, POET; DLB 38; GLL 2; LAIT 5; MAICYA 1, 2; MTCW 1; SATA 4, 136; YAW

Jordan, Neil (Patrick) 1950- .... **CLC 110**
　　　See also CA 124; 130; CANR 54; CN 4, 5, 6, 7; GLL 2; INT CA-130

Jordan, Pat(rick M.) 1941- .... **CLC 37**
　　　See also CA 33-36R; CANR 121

Jorgensen, Ivar
　　　See Ellison, Harlan (Jay)

Jorgenson, Ivar
　　　See Silverberg, Robert

Joseph, George Ghevarughese .... **CLC 70**

Josephson, Mary
　　　See O'Doherty, Brian

Josephus, Flavius c. 37-100 .... **CMLC 13**
　　　See also AW 2; DLB 176

Josiah Allen's Wife
　　　See Holley, Marietta

Josipovici, Gabriel (David) 1940- ...... **CLC 6, 43, 153**
　　　See also CA 37-40R, 224; CAAE 224; CAAS 8; CANR 47, 84; CN 3, 4, 5, 6, 7; DLB 14, 319

Joubert, Joseph 1754-1824 .... **NCLC 9**

Jouve, Pierre Jean 1887-1976 .... **CLC 47**
　　　See also CA 65-68; DLB 258; EWL 3

Jovine, Francesco 1902-1950 .... **TCLC 79**
　　　See also DLB 264; EWL 3

Joyce, James (Augustine Aloysius)
　　1882-1941 .... **DC 16; PC 22; SSC 3, 26, 44, 64; TCLC 3, 8, 16, 35, 52, 159; WLC**
　　　See also AAYA 42; BRW 7; BRWC 1; BRWR 1; BYA 11, 13; CA 104; 126; CD-BLB 1914-1945; DA; DA3; DAB; DAC; DAM MST, NOV, POET; DLB 10, 19, 36, 162, 247; EWL 3; EXPN; EXPS; LAIT 3; LMFS 1, 2; MTCW 1, 2; MTFW 2005; NFS 7; RGSF 2; SSFS 1, 19; TEA; WLIT 4

Jozsef, Attila 1905-1937 .... **TCLC 22**
　　　See also CA 116; 230; CDWLB 4; DLB 215; EWL 3

Juana Ines de la Cruz, Sor
　　1651(?)-1695 ...... **HLCS 1; LC 5; PC 24**
　　　See also DLB 305; FW; LAW; RGWL 2, 3; WLIT 1

Juana Inez de La Cruz, Sor
　　　See Juana Ines de la Cruz, Sor

Judd, Cyril
　　　See Kornbluth, C(yril) M.; Pohl, Frederik

Juenger, Ernst 1895-1998 .... **CLC 125**
　　　See Junger, Ernst
　　　See also CA 101; 167; CANR 21, 47, 106; DLB 56

Julian of Norwich 1342(?)-1416(?) . **LC 6, 52**
　　　See also DLB 146; LMFS 1

Julius Caesar 100B.C.-44B.C.
　　　See Caesar, Julius
　　　See also CDWLB 1; DLB 211

Junger, Ernst
　　　See Juenger, Ernst
　　　See also CDWLB 2; EWL 3; RGWL 2, 3

Junger, Sebastian 1962- .... **CLC 109**
　　　See also AAYA 28; CA 165; CANR 130; MTFW 2005

Juniper, Alex
　　　See Hospital, Janette Turner

Junius
　　　See Luxemburg, Rosa

Junzaburo, Nishiwaki
　　　See Nishiwaki, Junzaburo
　　　See also EWL 3

Just, Ward (Swift) 1935- .... **CLC 4, 27**
　　　See also CA 25-28R; CANR 32, 87; CN 6, 7; INT CANR-32

Justice, Donald (Rodney)
　　1925-2004 .... **CLC 6, 19, 102; PC 64**
　　　See also AMWS 7; CA 5-8R; 230; CANR 26, 54, 74, 121, 122; CP 1, 2, 3, 4, 5, 6, 7; CSW; DAM POET; DLBY 1983; EWL 3; INT CANR-26; MAL 5; MTCW 2; PFS 14; TCLE 1:1

Juvenal c. 60-c. 130 .... **CMLC 8**
　　　See also AW 2; CDWLB 1; DLB 211; RGWL 2, 3

Juvenis
　　　See Bourne, Randolph S(illiman)

K., Alice
　　　See Knapp, Caroline

Kabakov, Sasha .... **CLC 59**

Kabir 1398(?)-1448(?) .... **LC 109; PC 56**
　　　See also RGWL 2, 3

Kacew, Romain 1914-1980
　　　See Gary, Romain
　　　See also CA 108; 102

Kadare, Ismail 1936- .... **CLC 52, 190**
　　　See also CA 161; EWL 3; RGWL 3

Kadohata, Cynthia (Lynn)
　　1956(?)- .... **CLC 59, 122**
　　　See also CA 140; CANR 124; SATA 155

Kafka, Franz 1883-1924 ... **SSC 5, 29, 35, 60; TCLC 2, 6, 13, 29, 47, 53, 112; WLC**
　　　See also AAYA 31; BPFB 2; CA 105; 126; CDWLB 2; DA; DA3; DAB; DAC; DAM MST, NOV; DLB 81; EW 9; EWL 3; EXPS; LATS 1:1; LMFS 2; MTCW 1, 2; MTFW 2005; NFS 7; RGSF 2; RGWL 2, 3; SFW 4; SSFS 3, 7, 12; TWA

Kahanovitsch, Pinkhes
　　　See Der Nister

Kahn, Roger 1927- .... **CLC 30**
　　　See also CA 25-28R; CANR 44, 69; DLB 171; SATA 37

Kain, Saul
　　　See Sassoon, Siegfried (Lorraine)

Kaiser, Georg 1878-1945 .... **TCLC 9**
　　　See also CA 106; 190; CDWLB 2; DLB 124; EWL 3; LMFS 2; RGWL 2, 3

Kaledin, Sergei .... **CLC 59**

Kaletski, Alexander 1946- .... **CLC 39**
　　　See also CA 118; 143

Kalidasa fl. c. 400-455 .... **CMLC 9; PC 22**
　　　See also RGWL 2, 3

Kallman, Chester (Simon)
　　1921-1975 .... **CLC 2**
　　　See also CA 45-48; 53-56; CANR 3; CP 1, 2

Kaminsky, Melvin 1926-
　　　See Brooks, Mel
　　　See also CA 65-68; CANR 16; DFS 21

Kaminsky, Stuart M(elvin) 1934- ..... **CLC 59**
　　　See also CA 73-76; CANR 29, 53, 89; CMW 4

Kamo no Chomei 1153(?)-1216 .... **CMLC 66**
　　　See also DLB 203

Kamo no Nagaakira
　　　See Kamo no Chomei

Kandinsky, Wassily 1866-1944 .... **TCLC 92**
　　　See also AAYA 64; CA 118; 155

Kane, Francis
　　　See Robbins, Harold

Kane, Henry 1918-
　　　See Queen, Ellery
　　　See also CA 156; CMW 4

Kane, Paul
　　　See Simon, Paul (Frederick)

Kanin, Garson 1912-1999 .... **CLC 22**
　　　See also AITN 1; CA 5-8R; 177; CAD; CANR 7, 78; DLB 7; IDFW 3, 4

Kaniuk, Yoram 1930- .... **CLC 19**
　　　See also CA 134; DLB 299

Kant, Immanuel 1724-1804 ..... **NCLC 27, 67**
　　　See also DLB 94

Kantor, MacKinlay 1904-1977 .... **CLC 7**
　　　See also CA 61-64; 73-76; CANR 60, 63; CN 1, 2; DLB 9, 102; MAL 5; MTCW 2; RHW; TCWW 1, 2

Kanze Motokiyo
　　　See Zeami

Kaplan, David Michael 1946- .... **CLC 50**
　　　See also CA 187

Kaplan, James 1951- .... **CLC 59**
　　　See also CA 135; CANR 121

Karadzic, Vuk Stefanovic
　　1787-1864 .... **NCLC 115**
　　　See also CDWLB 4; DLB 147

Karageorge, Michael
　　　See Anderson, Poul (William)

Karamzin, Nikolai Mikhailovich
　　1766-1826 .... **NCLC 3**
　　　See also DLB 150; RGSF 2

Karapanou, Margarita 1946- .... **CLC 13**
　　　See also CA 101

Karinthy, Frigyes 1887-1938 .... **TCLC 47**
　　　See also CA 170; DLB 215; EWL 3

Karl, Frederick R(obert)
　　1927-2004 .... **CLC 34**
　　　See also CA 5-8R; 226; CANR 3, 44, 143

Karr, Mary 1955- .... **CLC 188**
　　　See also AMWS 11; CA 151; CANR 100; MTFW 2005; NCFS 5

Kastel, Warren
　　　See Silverberg, Robert

Kataev, Evgeny Petrovich 1903-1942
　　　See Petrov, Evgeny
　　　See also CA 120

Kataphusin
　　　See Ruskin, John

Katz, Steve 1935- .... **CLC 47**
　　　See also CA 25-28R; CAAS 14, 64; CANR 12; CN 4, 5, 6, 7; DLBY 1983

Kauffman, Janet 1945- .... **CLC 42**
　　　See also CA 117; CANR 43, 84; DLB 218; DLBY 1986

Kaufman, Bob (Garnell) 1925-1986 . **CLC 49**
　　　See also BG 1:3; BW 1; CA 41-44R; 118; CANR 22; CP 1; DLB 16, 41

Kaufman, George S. 1889-1961 ...... **CLC 38; DC 17**
　　　See also CA 108; 93-96; DAM DRAM; DFS 1, 10; DLB 7; INT CA-108; MTCW 2; MTFW 2005; RGAL 4; TUS

Kaufman, Moises 1964- .... **DC 26**
　　　See also CA 211; DFS 22; MTFW 2005

Kaufman, Sue .... **CLC 3, 8**
　　　See Barondess, Sue K(aufman)

Kavafis, Konstantinos Petrou 1863-1933
　　　See Cavafy, C(onstantine) P(eter)
　　　See also CA 104

Kavan, Anna 1901-1968 .... **CLC 5, 13, 82**
　　　See also BRWS 7; CA 5-8R; CANR 6, 57; DLB 255; MTCW 1; RGEL 2; SFW 4

Kavanagh, Dan
　　　See Barnes, Julian (Patrick)

Kavanagh, Julie 1952- .... **CLC 119**
　　　See also CA 163

Kavanagh, Patrick (Joseph)
　　1904-1967 .... **CLC 22; PC 33**
　　　See also BRWS 7; CA 123; 25-28R; DLB 15, 20; EWL 3; MTCW 1; RGEL 2

Kawabata, Yasunari 1899-1972 ..... **CLC 2, 5, 9, 18, 107; SSC 17**
See Kawabata Yasunari
See also CA 93-96; 33-36R; CANR 88; DAM MULT; MJW; MTCW 2; MTFW 2005; RGSF 2; RGWL 2, 3

Kawabata Yasunari
See Kawabata, Yasunari
See also DLB 180; EWL 3

Kaye, M(ary) M(argaret) 1908-2004 .... **CLC 28**
See also CA 89-92; 223; CANR 24, 60, 102, 142; MTCW 1, 2; MTFW 2005; RHW; SATA 62; SATA-Obit 152

Kaye, Mollie
See Kaye, M(ary) M(argaret)

Kaye-Smith, Sheila 1887-1956 .... **TCLC 20**
See also CA 118; 203; DLB 36

Kaymor, Patrice Maguilene
See Senghor, Leopold Sedar

Kazakov, Iurii Pavlovich
See Kazakov, Yuri Pavlovich
See also DLB 302

Kazakov, Yuri Pavlovich 1927-1982 . **SSC 43**
See Kazakov, Iurii Pavlovich; Kazakov, Yury
See also CA 5-8R; CANR 36; MTCW 1; RGSF 2

Kazakov, Yury
See Kazakov, Yuri Pavlovich
See also EWL 3

Kazan, Elia 1909-2003 .... **CLC 6, 16, 63**
See also CA 21-24R; 220; CANR 32, 78

Kazantzakis, Nikos 1883(?)-1957 .... **TCLC 2, 5, 33**
See also BPFB 2; CA 105; 132; DA3; EW 9; EWL 3; MTCW 1, 2; MTFW 2005; RGWL 2, 3

Kazin, Alfred 1915-1998 ..... **CLC 34, 38, 119**
See also AMWS 8; CA 1-4R; CAAS 7; CANR 1, 45, 79; DLB 67; EWL 3

Keane, Mary Nesta (Skrine) 1904-1996
See Keane, Molly
See also CA 108; 114; 151; RHW

Keane, Molly .... **CLC 31**
See Keane, Mary Nesta (Skrine)
See also CN 5, 6; INT CA-114; TCLE 1:1

Keates, Jonathan 1946(?)- .... **CLC 34**
See also CA 163; CANR 126

Keaton, Buster 1895-1966 .... **CLC 20**
See also CA 194

Keats, John 1795-1821 ...... **NCLC 8, 73, 121; PC 1; WLC**
See also AAYA 58; BRW 4; BRWR 1; CD-BLB 1789-1832; DA; DA3; DAB; DAC; DAM MST, POET; DLB 96, 110; EXPP; LMFS 1; PAB; PFS 1, 2, 3, 9, 17; RGEL 2; TEA; WLIT 3; WP

Keble, John 1792-1866 .... **NCLC 87**
See also DLB 32, 55; RGEL 2

Keene, Donald 1922- .... **CLC 34**
See also CA 1-4R; CANR 5, 119

Keillor, Garrison .... **CLC 40, 115**
See Keillor, Gary (Edward)
See also AAYA 2, 62; BEST 89:3; BPFB 2; DLBY 1987; EWL 3; SATA 58; TUS

Keillor, Gary (Edward) 1942-
See Keillor, Garrison
See also CA 111; 117; CANR 36, 59, 124; CPW; DA3; DAM POP; MTCW 1, 2; MTFW 2005

Keith, Carlos
See Lewton, Val

Keith, Michael
See Hubbard, L(afayette) Ron(ald)

Keller, Gottfried 1819-1890 .... **NCLC 2; SSC 26**
See also CDWLB 2; DLB 129; EW; RGSF 2; RGWL 2, 3

Keller, Nora Okja 1965- .... **CLC 109**
See also CA 187

Kellerman, Jonathan 1949- .... **CLC 44**
See also AAYA 35; BEST 90:1; CA 106; CANR 29, 51; CMW 4; CPW; DA3; DAM POP; INT CANR-29

Kelley, William Melvin 1937- .... **CLC 22**
See also BW 1; CA 77-80; CANR 27, 83; CN 1, 2, 3, 4, 5, 6, 7; DLB 33; EWL 3

Kellogg, Marjorie 1922-2005 .... **CLC 2**
See also CA 81-84

Kellow, Kathleen
See Hibbert, Eleanor Alice Burford

Kelly, Lauren
See Oates, Joyce Carol

Kelly, M(ilton) T(errence) 1947- ...... **CLC 55**
See also CA 97-100; CAAS 22; CANR 19, 43, 84; CN 6

Kelly, Robert 1935- .... **SSC 50**
See also CA 17-20R; CAAS 19; CANR 47; CP 1, 2, 3, 4, 5, 6, 7; DLB 5, 130, 165

Kelman, James 1946- .... **CLC 58, 86**
See also BRWS 5; CA 148; CANR 85, 130; CN 5, 6, 7; DLB 194, 319; RGSF 2; WLIT 4

Kemal, Yasar
See Kemal, Yashar
See also CWW 2; EWL 3; WLIT 6

Kemal, Yashar 1923(?)- .... **CLC 14, 29**
See also CA 89-92; CANR 44

Kemble, Fanny 1809-1893 .... **NCLC 18**
See also DLB 32

Kemelman, Harry 1908-1996 .... **CLC 2**
See also AITN 1; BPFB 2; CA 9-12R; 155; CANR 6, 71; CMW 4; DLB 28

Kempe, Margery 1373(?)-1440(?) ... **LC 6, 56**
See also DLB 146; FL 1:1; RGEL 2

Kempis, Thomas a 1380-1471 .... **LC 11**

Kendall, Henry 1839-1882 .... **NCLC 12**
See also DLB 230

Keneally, Thomas (Michael) 1935- ... **CLC 5, 8, 10, 14, 19, 27, 43, 117**
See also BRWS 4; CA 85-88; CANR 10, 50, 74, 130; CN 1, 2, 3, 4, 5, 6, 7; CPW; DA3; DAM NOV; DLB 289, 299; EWL 3; MTCW 1, 2; MTFW 2005; NFS 17; RGEL 2; RHW

Kennedy, A(lison) L(ouise) 1965- ... **CLC 188**
See also CA 168, 213; CAAE 213; CANR 108; CD 5, 6; CN 6, 7; DLB 271; RGSF 2

Kennedy, Adrienne (Lita) 1931- .... **BLC 2; CLC 66; DC 5**
See also AFAW 2; BW 2, 3; CA 103; CAAS 20; CABS 3; CAD; CANR 26, 53, 82; CD 5, 6; DAM MULT; DFS 9; DLB 38; FW; MAL 5

Kennedy, John Pendleton 1795-1870 .... **NCLC 2**
See also DLB 3, 248, 254; RGAL 4

Kennedy, Joseph Charles 1929-
See Kennedy, X. J.
See also CA 1-4R, 201; CAAE 201; CANR 4, 30, 40; CWRI 5; MAICYA 2; MAIC-YAS 1; SATA 14, 86, 130; SATA-Essay 130

Kennedy, William (Joseph) 1928- ..... **CLC 6, 28, 34, 53**
See also AAYA 1; AMWS 7; BPFB 2; CA 85-88; CANR 14, 31, 76, 134; CN 4, 5, 6, 7; DA3; DAM NOV; DLB 143; DLBY 1985; EWL 3; INT CANR-31; MAL 5; MTCW 1, 2; MTFW 2005; SATA 57

Kennedy, X. J. .... **CLC 8, 42**
See Kennedy, Joseph Charles
See also AMWS 15; CAAS 9; CLR 27; CP 1, 2, 3, 4, 5, 6, 7; DLB 5; SAAS 22

Kenny, Maurice (Francis) 1929- ..... **CLC 87; NNAL**
See also CA 144; CAAS 22; CANR 143; DAM MULT; DLB 175

Kent, Kelvin
See Kuttner, Henry

Kenton, Maxwell
See Southern, Terry

Kenyon, Jane 1947-1995 .... **PC 57**
See also AAYA 63; AMWS 7; CA 118; 148; CANR 44, 69; CP 7; CWP; DLB 120; PFS 9, 17; RGAL 4

Kenyon, Robert O.
See Kuttner, Henry

Kepler, Johannes 1571-1630 .... **LC 45**

Ker, Jill
See Conway, Jill K(er)

Kerkow, H. C.
See Lewton, Val

Kerouac, Jack 1922-1969 ...... **CLC 1, 2, 3, 5, 14, 29, 61; TCLC 117; WLC**
See Kerouac, Jean-Louis Lebris de
See also AAYA 25; AMWC 1; AMWS 3; BG 3; BPFB 2; CDALB 1941-1968; CP 1; CPW; DLB 2, 16, 237; DLBD 3; DLBY 1995; EWL 3; GLL 1; LATS 1:2; LMFS 2; MAL 5; NFS 8; RGAL 4; TUS; WP

Kerouac, Jean-Louis Lebris de 1922-1969
See Kerouac, Jack
See also AITN 1; CA 5-8R; 25-28R; CANR 26, 54, 95; DA; DA3; DAB; DAC; DAM MST, NOV, POET, POP; MTCW 1, 2; MTFW 2005

Kerr, (Bridget) Jean (Collins) 1923(?)-2003 .... **CLC 22**
See also CA 5-8R; 212; CANR 7; INT CANR-7

Kerr, M. E. .... **CLC 12, 35**
See Meaker, Marijane (Agnes)
See also AAYA 2, 23; BYA 1, 7, 8; CLR 29; SAAS 1; WYA

Kerr, Robert .... **CLC 55**

Kerrigan, (Thomas) Anthony 1918- .. **CLC 4, 6**
See also CA 49-52; CAAS 11; CANR 4

Kerry, Lois
See Duncan, Lois

Kesey, Ken (Elton) 1935-2001 ... **CLC 1, 3, 6, 11, 46, 64, 184; WLC**
See also AAYA 25; BG 1:3; BPFB 2; CA 1-4R; 204; CANR 22, 38, 66, 124; CDALB 1968-1988; CN 1, 2, 3, 4, 5, 6, 7; CPW; DA; DA3; DAB; DAC; DAM MST, NOV, POP; DLB 2, 16, 206; EWL 3; EXPN; LAIT 4; MAL 5; MTCW 1, 2; MTFW 2005; NFS 2; RGAL 4; SATA 66; SATA-Obit 131; TUS; YAW

Kesselring, Joseph (Otto) 1902-1967 .... **CLC 45**
See also CA 150; DAM DRAM, MST; DFS 20

Kessler, Jascha (Frederick) 1929- ...... **CLC 4**
See also CA 17-20R; CANR 8, 48, 111; CP 1

Kettelkamp, Larry (Dale) 1933- .... **CLC 12**
See also CA 29-32R; CANR 16; SAAS 3; SATA 2

Key, Ellen (Karolina Sofia) 1849-1926 .... **TCLC 65**
See also DLB 259

Keyber, Conny
See Fielding, Henry

Keyes, Daniel 1927- .... **CLC 80**
See also AAYA 23; BYA 11; CA 17-20R, 181; CAAE 181; CANR 10, 26, 54, 74; DA; DA3; DAC; DAM MST, NOV; EXPN; LAIT 4; MTCW 2; MTFW 2005; NFS 2; SATA 37; SFW 4

Klinger, Friedrich Maximilian von
1752-1831 .... NCLC 1
See also DLB 94

Klingsor the Magician
See Hartmann, Sadakichi

Klopstock, Friedrich Gottlieb
1724-1803 .... NCLC 11
See also DLB 97; EW 4; RGWL 2, 3

Kluge, Alexander 1932- .... SSC 61
See also CA 81-84; DLB 75

Knapp, Caroline 1959-2002 .... CLC 99
See also CA 154; 207

Knebel, Fletcher 1911-1993 .... CLC 14
See also AITN 1; CA 1-4R; 140; CAAS 3;
CANR 1, 36; CN 1, 2, 3, 4, 5; SATA 36;
SATA-Obit 75

Knickerbocker, Diedrich
See Irving, Washington

Knight, Etheridge 1931-1991 ... BLC 2; CLC
40; PC 14
See also BW 1, 3; CA 21-24R; 133; CANR
23, 82; CP 1, 2, 3, 4; DAM POET; DLB
41; MTCW 2; MTFW 2005; RGAL 4;
TCLE 1:1

Knight, Sarah Kemble 1666-1727 .... LC 7
See also DLB 24, 200

Knister, Raymond 1899-1932 .... TCLC 56
See also CA 186; DLB 68; RGEL 2

Knowles, John 1926-2001 ... CLC 1, 4, 10, 26
See also AAYA 10; AMWS 12; BPFB 2;
BYA 3; CA 17-20R; 203; CANR 40, 74,
76, 132; CDALB 1968-1988; CLR 98; CN
1, 2, 3, 4, 5, 6, 7; DA; DAC; DAM MST,
NOV; DLB 6; EXPN; MTCW 1, 2;
MTFW 2005; NFS 2; RGAL 4; SATA 8,
89; SATA-Obit 134; YAW

Knox, Calvin M.
See Silverberg, Robert

Knox, John c. 1505-1572 .... LC 37
See also DLB 132

Knye, Cassandra
See Disch, Thomas M(ichael)

Koch, C(hristopher) J(ohn) 1932- .... CLC 42
See also CA 127; CANR 84; CN 3, 4, 5, 6,
7; DLB 289

Koch, Christopher
See Koch, C(hristopher) J(ohn)

Koch, Kenneth (Jay) 1925-2002 .... CLC 5, 8,
44
See also AMWS 15; CA 1-4R; 207; CAD;
CANR 6, 36, 57, 97, 131; CD 5, 6; CP 1,
2, 3, 4, 5, 6, 7; DAM POET; DLB 5; INT
CANR-36; MAL 5; MTCW 2; MTFW
2005; PFS 20; SATA 65; WP

Kochanowski, Jan 1530-1584 .... LC 10
See also RGWL 2, 3

Kock, Charles Paul de 1794-1871 . NCLC 16

Koda Rohan
See Koda Shigeyuki

Koda Rohan
See Koda Shigeyuki
See also DLB 180

Koda Shigeyuki 1867-1947 .... TCLC 22
See Koda Rohan
See also CA 121; 183

Koestler, Arthur 1905-1983 ... CLC 1, 3, 6, 8,
15, 33
See also BRWS 1; CA 1-4R; 109; CANR 1,
33; CDBLB 1945-1960; CN 1, 2, 3;
DLBY 1983; EWL 3; MTCW 1, 2; MTFW
2005; NFS 19; RGEL 2

Kogawa, Joy Nozomi 1935- ...... CLC 78, 129
See also AAYA 47; CA 101; CANR 19, 62,
126; CN 6, 7; CP 1; CWP; DAC; DAM
MST, MULT; FW; MTCW 2; MTFW
2005; NFS 3; SATA 99

Kohout, Pavel 1928- .... CLC 13
See also CA 45-48; CANR 3

Koizumi, Yakumo
See Hearn, (Patricio) Lafcadio (Tessima
Carlos)

Kolmar, Gertrud 1894-1943 .... TCLC 40
See also CA 167; EWL 3

Komunyakaa, Yusef 1947- .. BLCS; CLC 86,
94, 207; PC 51
See also AFAW 2; AMWS 13; CA 147;
CANR 83; CP 7; CSW; DLB 120; EWL
3; PFS 5, 20; RGAL 4

Konrad, George
See Konrad, Gyorgy

Konrad, Gyorgy 1933- .... CLC 4, 10, 73
See also CA 85-88; CANR 97; CDWLB 4;
CWW 2; DLB 232; EWL 3

Konwicki, Tadeusz 1926- .... CLC 8, 28, 54,
117
See also CA 101; CAAS 9; CANR 39, 59;
CWW 2; DLB 232; EWL 3; IDFW 3;
MTCW 1

Koontz, Dean R. 1945- .... CLC 78, 206
See also AAYA 9, 31; BEST 89:3, 90:2; CA
108; CANR 19, 36, 52, 95, 138; CMW 4;
CPW; DA3; DAM NOV, POP; DLB 292;
HGG; MTCW 1; MTFW 2005; SATA 92,
165; SFW 4; SUFW 2; YAW

Koontz, Dean Ray
See Koontz, Dean R.

Koontz, Dean Ray
See Koontz, Dean R.

Kopernik, Mikolaj
See Copernicus, Nicolaus

Kopit, Arthur (Lee) 1937- ...... CLC 1, 18, 33
See also AITN 1; CA 81-84; CABS 3;
CAD; CD 5, 6; DAM DRAM; DFS 7, 14;
DLB 7; MAL 5; MTCW 1; RGAL 4

Kopitar, Jernej (Bartholomaus)
1780-1844 .... NCLC 117

Kops, Bernard 1926- .... CLC 4
See also CA 5-8R; CANR 84; CBD; CN 1,
2, 3, 4, 5, 6, 7; CP 1, 2, 3, 4, 5, 6, 7; DLB
13

Kornbluth, C(yril) M. 1923-1958 .... TCLC 8
See also CA 105; 160; DLB 8; SCFW 1, 2;
SFW 4

Korolenko, V. G.
See Korolenko, Vladimir Galaktionovich

Korolenko, Vladimir
See Korolenko, Vladimir Galaktionovich

Korolenko, Vladimir G.
See Korolenko, Vladimir Galaktionovich

Korolenko, Vladimir Galaktionovich
1853-1921 .... TCLC 22
See also CA 121; DLB 277

Korzybski, Alfred (Habdank Skarbek)
1879-1950 .... TCLC 61
See also CA 123; 160

Kosinski, Jerzy (Nikodem)
1933-1991 .... CLC 1, 2, 3, 6, 10, 15, 53,
70
See also AMWS 7; BPFB 2; CA 17-20R;
134; CANR 9, 46; CN 1, 2, 3, 4; DA3;
DAM NOV; DLB 2, 299; DLBY 1982;
EWL 3; HGG; MAL 5; MTCW 1, 2;
MTFW 2005; NFS 12; RGAL 4; TUS

Kostelanetz, Richard (Cory) 1940- .. CLC 28
See also CA 13-16R; CAAS 8; CANR 38,
77; CN 4, 5, 6; CP 2, 3, 4, 5, 6, 7

Kostrowitzki, Wilhelm Apollinaris de
1880-1918
See Apollinaire, Guillaume
See also CA 104

Kotlowitz, Robert 1924- .... CLC 4
See also CA 33-36R; CANR 36

Kotzebue, August (Friedrich Ferdinand) von
1761-1819 .... NCLC 25
See also DLB 94

Kotzwinkle, William 1938- ..... CLC 5, 14, 35
See also BPFB 2; CA 45-48; CANR 3, 44,
84, 129; CLR 6; CN 7; DLB 173; FANT;
MAICYA 1, 2; SATA 24, 70, 146; SFW
4; SUFW 2; YAW

Kowna, Stancy
See Szymborska, Wislawa

Kozol, Jonathan 1936- .... CLC 17
See also AAYA 46; CA 61-64; CANR 16,
45, 96; MTFW 2005

Kozoll, Michael 1940(?)- .... CLC 35

Kramer, Kathryn 19(?)- .... CLC 34

Kramer, Larry 1935- .... CLC 42; DC 8
See also CA 124; 126; CANR 60, 132;
DAM POP; DLB 249; GLL 1

Krasicki, Ignacy 1735-1801 .... NCLC 8

Krasinski, Zygmunt 1812-1859 .... NCLC 4
See also RGWL 2, 3

Kraus, Karl 1874-1936 .... TCLC 5
See also CA 104; 216; DLB 118; EWL 3

Kreve (Mickevicius), Vincas
1882-1954 .... TCLC 27
See also CA 170; DLB 220; EWL 3

Kristeva, Julia 1941- .... CLC 77, 140
See also CA 154; CANR 99; DLB 242;
EWL 3; FW; LMFS 2

Kristofferson, Kris 1936- .... CLC 26
See also CA 104

Krizanc, John 1956- .... CLC 57
See also CA 187

Krleza, Miroslav 1893-1981 .... CLC 8, 114
See also CA 97-100; 105; CANR 50; CD-
WLB 4; DLB 147; EW 11; RGWL 2, 3

Kroetsch, Robert (Paul) 1927- .... CLC 5, 23,
57, 132
See also CA 17-20R; CANR 8, 38; CCA 1;
CN 2, 3, 4, 5, 6, 7; CP 7; DAC; DAM
POET; DLB 53; MTCW 1

Kroetz, Franz
See Kroetz, Franz Xaver

Kroetz, Franz Xaver 1946- .... CLC 41
See also CA 130; CANR 142; CWW 2;
EWL 3

Kroker, Arthur (W.) 1945- .... CLC 77
See also CA 161

Kroniuk, Lisa
See Berton, Pierre (Francis de Marigny)

Kropotkin, Peter (Aleksieevich)
1842-1921 .... TCLC 36
See Kropotkin, Petr Alekseevich
See also CA 119; 219

Kropotkin, Petr Alekseevich
See Kropotkin, Peter (Aleksieevich)
See also DLB 277

Krotkov, Yuri 1917-1981 .... CLC 19
See also CA 102

Krumb
See Crumb, R(obert)

Krumgold, Joseph (Quincy)
1908-1980 .... CLC 12
See also BYA 1, 2; CA 9-12R; 101; CANR
7; MAICYA 1, 2; SATA 1, 48; SATA-Obit
23; YAW

Krumwitz
See Crumb, R(obert)

Krutch, Joseph Wood 1893-1970 ..... CLC 24
See also ANW; CA 1-4R; 25-28R; CANR
4; DLB 63, 206, 275

Krutzch, Gus
See Eliot, T(homas) S(tearns)

Krylov, Ivan Andreevich
1768(?)-1844 .... NCLC 1
See also DLB 150

Kubin, Alfred (Leopold Isidor)
1877-1959 .... TCLC 23
See also CA 112; 149; CANR 104; DLB 81

Kubrick, Stanley 1928-1999 .... **CLC 16; TCLC 112**
See also AAYA 30; CA 81-84; 177; CANR 33; DLB 26

Kumin, Maxine (Winokur) 1925- ..... **CLC 5, 13, 28, 164; PC 15**
See also AITN 2; AMWS 4; ANW; CA 1-4R; CAAS 8; CANR 1, 21, 69, 115, 140; CP 2, 3, 4, 5, 6, 7; CWP; DA3; DAM POET; DLB 5; EWL 3; EXPP; MTCW 1, 2; MTFW 2005; PAB; PFS 18; SATA 12

Kundera, Milan 1929- . **CLC 4, 9, 19, 32, 68, 115, 135; SSC 24**
See also AAYA 2, 62; BPFB 2; CA 85-88; CANR 19, 52, 74, 144; CDWLB 4; CWW 2; DA3; DAM NOV; DLB 232; EW 13; EWL 3; MTCW 1, 2; MTFW 2005; NFS 18; RGSF 2; RGWL 3; SSFS 10

Kunene, Mazisi (Raymond) 1930- ... **CLC 85**
See also BW 1, 3; CA 125; CANR 81; CP 1, 7; DLB 117

Kung, Hans .... **CLC 130**
See Kung, Hans

Kung, Hans 1928-
See Kung, Hans
See also CA 53-56; CANR 66, 134; MTCW 1, 2; MTFW 2005

Kunikida Doppo 1869(?)-1908
See Doppo, Kunikida
See also DLB 180; EWL 3

Kunitz, Stanley (Jasspon) 1905- .. **CLC 6, 11, 14, 148; PC 19**
See also AMWS 3; CA 41-44R; CANR 26, 57, 98; CP 1, 2, 3, 4, 5, 6, 7; DA3; DLB 48; INT CANR-26; MAL 5; MTCW 1, 2; MTFW 2005; PFS 11; RGAL 4

Kunze, Reiner 1933- .... **CLC 10**
See also CA 93-96; CWW 2; DLB 75; EWL 3

Kuprin, Aleksander Ivanovich 1870-1938 .... **TCLC 5**
See Kuprin, Aleksandr Ivanovich; Kuprin, Alexandr Ivanovich
See also CA 104; 182

Kuprin, Aleksandr Ivanovich
See Kuprin, Aleksander Ivanovich
See also DLB 295

Kuprin, Alexandr Ivanovich
See Kuprin, Aleksander Ivanovich
See also EWL 3

Kureishi, Hanif 1954- .. **CLC 64, 135; DC 26**
See also BRWS 11; CA 139; CANR 113; CBD; CD 5, 6; CN 6, 7; DLB 194, 245; GLL 2; IDFW 4; WLIT 4; WWE 1

Kurosawa, Akira 1910-1998 ..... **CLC 16, 119**
See also AAYA 11, 64; CA 101; 170; CANR 46; DAM MULT

Kushner, Tony 1956- .... **CLC 81, 203; DC 10**
See also AAYA 61; AMWS 9; CA 144; CAD; CANR 74, 130; CD 5, 6; DA3; DAM DRAM; DFS 5; DLB 228; EWL 3; GLL 1; LAIT 5; MAL 5; MTCW 2; MTFW 2005; RGAL 4; SATA 160

Kuttner, Henry 1915-1958 .... **TCLC 10**
See also CA 107; 157; DLB 8; FANT; SCFW 1, 2; SFW 4

Kutty, Madhavi
See Das, Kamala

Kuzma, Greg 1944- .... **CLC 7**
See also CA 33-36R; CANR 70

Kuzmin, Mikhail (Alekseevich) 1872(?)-1936 .... **TCLC 40**
See also CA 170; DLB 295; EWL 3

Kyd, Thomas 1558-1594 .. **DC 3; LC 22, 125**
See also BRW 1; DAM DRAM; DFS 21; DLB 62; IDTP; LMFS 1; RGEL 2; TEA; WLIT 3

Kyprianos, Iossif
See Samarakis, Antonis

L. S.
See Stephen, Sir Leslie

Laȝamon
See Layamon
See also DLB 146

Labe, Louise 1521-1566 .... **LC 120**

Labrunie, Gerard
See Nerval, Gerard de

La Bruyere, Jean de 1645-1696 .... **LC 17**
See also DLB 268; EW 3; GFL Beginnings to 1789

Lacan, Jacques (Marie Emile) 1901-1981 .... **CLC 75**
See also CA 121; 104; DLB 296; EWL 3; TWA

Laclos, Pierre-Ambroise Francois 1741-1803 .... **NCLC 4, 87**
See also DLB 313; EW 4; GFL Beginnings to 1789; RGWL 2, 3

Lacolere, Francois
See Aragon, Louis

La Colere, Francois
See Aragon, Louis

La Deshabilleuse
See Simenon, Georges (Jacques Christian)

Lady Gregory
See Gregory, Lady Isabella Augusta (Persse)

Lady of Quality, A
See Bagnold, Enid

La Fayette, Marie-(Madelaine Pioche de la Vergne) 1634-1693 .... **LC 2**
See Lafayette, Marie-Madeleine
See also GFL Beginnings to 1789; RGWL 2, 3

Lafayette, Marie-Madeleine
See La Fayette, Marie-(Madelaine Pioche de la Vergne)
See also DLB 268

Lafayette, Rene
See Hubbard, L(afayette) Ron(ald)

La Flesche, Francis 1857(?)-1932 ...... **NNAL**
See also CA 144; CANR 83; DLB 175

La Fontaine, Jean de 1621-1695 .... **LC 50**
See also DLB 268; EW 3; GFL Beginnings to 1789; MAICYA 1, 2; RGWL 2, 3; SATA 18

Laforet, Carmen 1921-2004 .... **CLC 219**
See also CWW 2; DLB 322; EWL 3

Laforgue, Jules 1860-1887 . **NCLC 5, 53; PC 14; SSC 20**
See also DLB 217; EW 7; GFL 1789 to the Present; RGWL 2, 3

Lagerkvist, Paer (Fabian) 1891-1974 ..... **CLC 7, 10, 13, 54; TCLC 144**
See Lagerkvist, Par
See also CA 85-88; 49-52; DA3; DAM DRAM, NOV; MTCW 1, 2; MTFW 2005; TWA

Lagerkvist, Par .... **SSC 12**
See Lagerkvist, Paer (Fabian)
See also DLB 259; EW 10; EWL 3; RGSF 2; RGWL 2, 3

Lagerloef, Selma (Ottiliana Lovisa) .... **TCLC 4, 36**
See Lagerlof, Selma (Ottiliana Lovisa)
See also CA 108; MTCW 2

Lagerlof, Selma (Ottiliana Lovisa) 1858-1940
See Lagerloef, Selma (Ottiliana Lovisa)
See also CA 188; CLR 7; DLB 259; RGWL 2, 3; SATA 15; SSFS 18

La Guma, (Justin) Alex(ander) 1925-1985 . **BLCS; CLC 19; TCLC 140**
See also AFW; BW 1, 3; CA 49-52; 118; CANR 25, 81; CDWLB 3; CN 1, 2, 3; CP 1; DAM NOV; DLB 117, 225; EWL 3; MTCW 1, 2; MTFW 2005; WLIT 2; WWE 1

Laidlaw, A. K.
See Grieve, C(hristopher) M(urray)

Lainez, Manuel Mujica
See Mujica Lainez, Manuel
See also HW 1

Laing, R(onald) D(avid) 1927-1989 . **CLC 95**
See also CA 107; 129; CANR 34; MTCW 1

Laishley, Alex
See Booth, Martin

Lamartine, Alphonse (Marie Louis Prat) de 1790-1869 .... **NCLC 11; PC 16**
See also DAM POET; DLB 217; GFL 1789 to the Present; RGWL 2, 3

Lamb, Charles 1775-1834 ..... **NCLC 10, 113; WLC**
See also BRW 4; CDBLB 1789-1832; DA; DAB; DAC; DAM MST; DLB 93, 107, 163; RGEL 2; SATA 17; TEA

Lamb, Lady Caroline 1785-1828 ... **NCLC 38**
See also DLB 116

Lamb, Mary Ann 1764-1847 .... **NCLC 125**
See also DLB 163; SATA 17

Lame Deer 1903(?)-1976 .... **NNAL**
See also CA 69-72

Lamming, George (William) 1927- ... **BLC 2; CLC 2, 4, 66, 144**
See also BW 2, 3; CA 85-88; CANR 26, 76; CDWLB 3; CN 1, 2, 3, 4, 5, 6, 7; CP 1; DAM MULT; DLB 125; EWL 3; MTCW 1, 2; MTFW 2005; NFS 15; RGEL 2

L'Amour, Louis (Dearborn) 1908-1988 .... **CLC 25, 55**
See also AAYA 16; AITN 2; BEST 89:2; BPFB 2; CA 1-4R; 125; CANR 3, 25, 40; CPW; DA3; DAM NOV, POP; DLB 206; DLBY 1980; MTCW 1, 2; MTFW 2005; RGAL 4; TCWW 1, 2

Lampedusa, Giuseppe (Tomasi) di .... **TCLC 13**
See Tomasi di Lampedusa, Giuseppe
See also CA 164; EW 11; MTCW 2; MTFW 2005; RGWL 2, 3

Lampman, Archibald 1861-1899 ... **NCLC 25**
See also DLB 92; RGEL 2; TWA

Lancaster, Bruce 1896-1963 .... **CLC 36**
See also CA 9-10; CANR 70; CAP 1; SATA 9

Lanchester, John 1962- .... **CLC 99**
See also CA 194; DLB 267

Landau, Mark Alexandrovich
See Aldanov, Mark (Alexandrovich)

Landau-Aldanov, Mark Alexandrovich
See Aldanov, Mark (Alexandrovich)

Landis, Jerry
See Simon, Paul (Frederick)

Landis, John 1950- .... **CLC 26**
See also CA 112; 122; CANR 128

Landolfi, Tommaso 1908-1979 .... **CLC 11, 49**
See also CA 127; 117; DLB 177; EWL 3

Landon, Letitia Elizabeth 1802-1838 .... **NCLC 15**
See also DLB 96

Landor, Walter Savage 1775-1864 .... **NCLC 14**
See also BRW 4; DLB 93, 107; RGEL 2

Landwirth, Heinz 1927-
See Lind, Jakov
See also CA 9-12R; CANR 7

Lane, Patrick 1939- .... **CLC 25**
See also CA 97-100; CANR 54; CP 3, 4, 5, 6, 7; DAM POET; DLB 53; INT CA-97-100

Lang, Andrew 1844-1912 .... **TCLC 16**
See also CA 114; 137; CANR 85; CLR 101; DLB 98, 141, 184; FANT; MAICYA 1, 2; RGEL 2; SATA 16; WCH

Leavitt, David 1961- .... **CLC 34**
See also CA 116; 122; CANR 50, 62, 101, 134; CPW; DA3; DAM POP; DLB 130; GLL 1; INT CA-122; MAL 5; MTCW 2; MTFW 2005

Leblanc, Maurice (Marie Emile) 1864-1941 .... **TCLC 49**
See also CA 110; CMW 4

Lebowitz, Fran(ces Ann) 1951(?)- ... **CLC 11, 36**
See also CA 81-84; CANR 14, 60, 70; INT CANR-14; MTCW 1

Lebrecht, Peter
See Tieck, (Johann) Ludwig

le Carré, John .... **CLC 3, 5, 9, 15, 28, 220**
See Cornwell, David John Moore
See also AAYA 42; BEST 89:4; BPFB 2; BRWS 2; CDBLB 1960 to Present; CMW 4; CN 1, 2, 3, 4, 5, 6, 7; CPW; DLB 87; EWL 3; MSW; MTCW 2; RGEL 2; TEA

Le Clezio, J(ean) M(arie) G(ustave) 1940- .... **CLC 31, 155**
See also CA 116; 128; CWW 2; DLB 83; EWL 3; GFL 1789 to the Present; RGSF 2

Leconte de Lisle, Charles-Marie-Rene 1818-1894 .... **NCLC 29**
See also DLB 217; EW 6; GFL 1789 to the Present

Le Coq, Monsieur
See Simenon, Georges (Jacques Christian)

Leduc, Violette 1907-1972 .... **CLC 22**
See also CA 13-14; 33-36R; CANR 69; CAP 1; EWL 3; GFL 1789 to the Present; GLL 1

Ledwidge, Francis 1887(?)-1917 .... **TCLC 23**
See also CA 123; 203; DLB 20

Lee, Andrea 1953- .... **BLC 2; CLC 36**
See also BW 1, 3; CA 125; CANR 82; DAM MULT

Lee, Andrew
See Auchincloss, Louis (Stanton)

Lee, Chang-rae 1965- .... **CLC 91**
See also CA 148; CANR 89; CN 7; DLB 312; LATS 1:2

Lee, Don L. .... **CLC 2**
See Madhubuti, Haki R.
See also CP 2, 3, 4

Lee, George W(ashington) 1894-1976 .... **BLC 2; CLC 52**
See also BW 1; CA 125; CANR 83; DAM MULT; DLB 51

Lee, (Nelle) Harper 1926- . **CLC 12, 60, 194; WLC**
See also AAYA 13; AMWS 8; BPFB 2; BYA 3; CA 13-16R; CANR 51, 128; CDALB 1941-1968; CSW; DA; DA3; DAB; DAC; DAM MST, NOV; DLB 6; EXPN; LAIT 3; MAL 5; MTCW 1, 2; MTFW 2005; NFS 2; SATA 11; WYA; YAW

Lee, Helen Elaine 1959(?)- .... **CLC 86**
See also CA 148

Lee, John .... **CLC 70**

Lee, Julian
See Latham, Jean Lee

Lee, Larry
See Lee, Lawrence

Lee, Laurie 1914-1997 .... **CLC 90**
See also CA 77-80; 158; CANR 33, 73; CP 1, 2, 3, 4; CPW; DAB; DAM POP; DLB 27; MTCW 1; RGEL 2

Lee, Lawrence 1941-1990 .... **CLC 34**
See also CA 131; CANR 43

Lee, Li-Young 1957- .... **CLC 164; PC 24**
See also AMWS 15; CA 153; CANR 118; CP 7; DLB 165, 312; LMFS 2; PFS 11, 15, 17

Lee, Manfred B(ennington) 1905-1971 .... **CLC 11**
See Queen, Ellery
See also CA 1-4R; 29-32R; CANR 2; CMW 4; DLB 137

Lee, Nathaniel 1645(?)-1692 .... **LC 103**
See also DLB 80; RGEL 2

Lee, Shelton Jackson 1957(?)- .. **BLCS; CLC 105**
See Lee, Spike
See also BW 2, 3; CA 125; CANR 42; DAM MULT

Lee, Spike
See Lee, Shelton Jackson
See also AAYA 4, 29

Lee, Stan 1922- .... **CLC 17**
See also AAYA 5, 49; CA 108; 111; CANR 129; INT CA-111; MTFW 2005

Lee, Tanith 1947- .... **CLC 46**
See also AAYA 15; CA 37-40R; CANR 53, 102, 145; DLB 261; FANT; SATA 8, 88, 134; SFW 4; SUFW 1, 2; YAW

Lee, Vernon .... **SSC 33; TCLC 5**
See Paget, Violet
See also DLB 57, 153, 156, 174, 178; GLL 1; SUFW 1

Lee, William
See Burroughs, William S(eward)
See also GLL 1

Lee, Willy
See Burroughs, William S(eward)
See also GLL 1

Lee-Hamilton, Eugene (Jacob) 1845-1907 .... **TCLC 22**
See also CA 117; 234

Leet, Judith 1935- .... **CLC 11**
See also CA 187

Le Fanu, Joseph Sheridan 1814-1873 .... **NCLC 9, 58; SSC 14, 84**
See also CMW 4; DA3; DAM POP; DLB 21, 70, 159, 178; GL 3; HGG; RGEL 2; RGSF 2; SUFW 1

Leffland, Ella 1931- .... **CLC 19**
See also CA 29-32R; CANR 35, 78, 82; DLBY 1984; INT CANR-35; SATA 65

Leger, Alexis
See Leger, (Marie-Rene Auguste) Alexis Saint-Leger

Leger, (Marie-Rene Auguste) Alexis Saint-Leger 1887-1975 .. **CLC 4, 11, 46; PC 23**
See Perse, Saint-John; Saint-John Perse
See also CA 13-16R; 61-64; CANR 43; DAM POET; MTCW 1

Leger, Saintleger
See Leger, (Marie-Rene Auguste) Alexis Saint-Leger

Le Guin, Ursula K(roeber) 1929- ..... **CLC 8, 13, 22, 45, 71, 136; SSC 12, 69**
See also AAYA 9, 27; AITN 1; BPFB 2; BYA 5, 8, 11, 14; CA 21-24R; CANR 9, 32, 52, 74, 132; CDALB 1968-1988; CLR 3, 28, 91; CN 2, 3, 4, 5, 6, 7; CPW; DA3; DAB; DAC; DAM MST, POP; DLB 8, 52, 256, 275; EXPS; FANT; FW; INT CANR-32; JRDA; LAIT 5; MAICYA 1, 2; MAL 5; MTCW 1, 2; MTFW 2005; NFS 6, 9; SATA 4, 52, 99, 149; SCFW 1, 2; SFW 4; SSFS 2; SUFW 1, 2; WYA; YAW

Lehmann, Rosamond (Nina) 1901-1990 .... **CLC 5**
See also CA 77-80; 131; CANR 8, 73; CN 1, 2, 3, 4; DLB 15; MTCW 2; RGEL 2; RHW

Leiber, Fritz (Reuter, Jr.) 1910-1992 .... **CLC 25**
See also AAYA 65; BPFB 2; CA 45-48; 139; CANR 2, 40, 86; CN 2, 3, 4, 5; DLB 8; FANT; HGG; MTCW 1, 2; MTFW 2005; SATA 45; SATA-Obit 73; SCFW 1, 2; SFW 4; SUFW 1, 2

Leibniz, Gottfried Wilhelm von 1646-1716 .... **LC 35**
See also DLB 168

Leimbach, Martha 1963-
See Leimbach, Marti
See also CA 130

Leimbach, Marti .... **CLC 65**
See Leimbach, Martha

Leino, Eino .... **TCLC 24**
See Lonnbohm, Armas Eino Leopold
See also EWL 3

Leiris, Michel (Julien) 1901-1990 ..... **CLC 61**
See also CA 119; 128; 132; EWL 3; GFL 1789 to the Present

Leithauser, Brad 1953- .... **CLC 27**
See also CA 107; CANR 27, 81; CP 7; DLB 120, 282

le Jars de Gournay, Marie
See de Gournay, Marie le Jars

Lelchuk, Alan 1938- .... **CLC 5**
See also CA 45-48; CAAS 20; CANR 1, 70; CN 3, 4, 5, 6, 7

Lem, Stanislaw 1921- ...... **CLC 8, 15, 40, 149**
See also CA 105; CAAS 1; CANR 32; CWW 2; MTCW 1; SCFW 1, 2; SFW 4

Lemann, Nancy (Elise) 1956- .... **CLC 39**
See also CA 118; 136; CANR 121

Lemonnier, (Antoine Louis) Camille 1844-1913 .... **TCLC 22**
See also CA 121

Lenau, Nikolaus 1802-1850 .... **NCLC 16**

L'Engle, Madeleine (Camp Franklin) 1918- .... **CLC 12**
See also AAYA 28; AITN 2; BPFB 2; BYA 2, 4, 5, 7; CA 1-4R; CANR 3, 21, 39, 66, 107; CLR 1, 14, 57; CPW; CWRI 5; DA3; DAM POP; DLB 52; JRDA; MAICYA 1, 2; MTCW 1, 2; MTFW 2005; SAAS 15; SATA 1, 27, 75, 128; SFW 4; WYA; YAW

Lengyel, Jozsef 1896-1975 .... **CLC 7**
See also CA 85-88; 57-60; CANR 71; RGSF 2

Lenin 1870-1924
See Lenin, V. I.
See also CA 121; 168

Lenin, V. I. .... **TCLC 67**
See Lenin

Lennon, John (Ono) 1940-1980 .. **CLC 12, 35**
See also CA 102; SATA 114

Lennox, Charlotte Ramsay 1729(?)-1804 .... **NCLC 23, 134**
See also DLB 39; RGEL 2

Lentricchia, Frank, (Jr.) 1940- .... **CLC 34**
See also CA 25-28R; CANR 19, 106; DLB 246

Lenz, Gunter .... **CLC 65**

Lenz, Jakob Michael Reinhold 1751-1792 .... **LC 100**
See also DLB 94; RGWL 2, 3

Lenz, Siegfried 1926- .... **CLC 27; SSC 33**
See also CA 89-92; CANR 80; CWW 2; DLB 75; EWL 3; RGSF 2; RGWL 2, 3

Leon, David
See Jacob, (Cyprien-)Max

Leonard, Elmore (John, Jr.) 1925- . **CLC 28, 34, 71, 120**
See also AAYA 22, 59; AITN 1; BEST 89:1, 90:4; BPFB 2; CA 81-84; CANR 12, 28, 53, 76, 96, 133; CMW 4; CN 5, 6, 7; CPW; DA3; DAM POP; DLB 173, 226; INT CANR-28; MSW; MTCW 1, 2; MTFW 2005; RGAL 4; SATA 163; TCWW 1, 2

Leonard, Hugh .... **CLC 19**
See Byrne, John Keyes
See also CBD; CD 5, 6; DFS 13; DLB 13

Limonov, Eduard
  See Limonov, Edward
  See also DLB 317
Limonov, Edward 1944- .... **CLC 67**
  See Limonov, Eduard
  See also CA 137
Lin, Frank
  See Atherton, Gertrude (Franklin Horn)
Lin, Yutang 1895-1976 .... **TCLC 149**
  See also CA 45-48; 65-68; CANR 2; RGAL
  4
Lincoln, Abraham 1809-1865 .... **NCLC 18**
  See also LAIT 2
Lind, Jakov .... **CLC 1, 2, 4, 27, 82**
  See Landwirth, Heinz
  See also CAAS 4; DLB 299; EWL 3
Lindbergh, Anne (Spencer) Morrow
  1906-2001 .... **CLC 82**
  See also BPFB 2; CA 17-20R; 193; CANR
  16, 73; DAM NOV; MTCW 1, 2; MTFW
  2005; SATA 33; SATA-Obit 125; TUS
Lindsay, David 1878(?)-1945 .... **TCLC 15**
  See also CA 113; 187; DLB 255; FANT;
  SFW 4; SUFW 1
Lindsay, (Nicholas) Vachel
  1879-1931 .... **PC 23; TCLC 17; WLC**
  See also AMWS 1; CA 114; 135; CANR
  79; CDALB 1865-1917; DA; DA3; DAC;
  DAM MST, POET; DLB 54; EWL 3;
  EXPP; MAL 5; RGAL 4; SATA 40; WP
Linke-Poot
  See Doeblin, Alfred
Linney, Romulus 1930- .... **CLC 51**
  See also CA 1-4R; CAD; CANR 40, 44,
  79; CD 5, 6; CSW; RGAL 4
Linton, Eliza Lynn 1822-1898 .... **NCLC 41**
  See also DLB 18
Li Po 701-763 .... **CMLC 2; PC 29**
  See also PFS 20; WP
Lipsius, Justus 1547-1606 .... **LC 16**
Lipsyte, Robert (Michael) 1938- ...... **CLC 21**
  See also AAYA 7, 45; CA 17-20R; CANR
  8, 57; CLR 23, 76; DA; DAC; DAM
  MST, NOV; JRDA; LAIT 5; MAICYA 1,
  2; SATA 5, 68, 113, 161; WYA; YAW
Lish, Gordon (Jay) 1934- ... **CLC 45; SSC 18**
  See also CA 113; 117; CANR 79; DLB 130;
  INT CA-117
Lispector, Clarice 1925(?)-1977 .... **CLC 43;**
  HLCS 2; SSC 34
  See also CA 139; 116; CANR 71; CDWLB
  3; DLB 113, 307; DNFS 1; EWL 3; FW;
  HW 2; LAW; RGSF 2; RGWL 2, 3; WLIT
  1
Littell, Robert 1935(?)- .... **CLC 42**
  See also CA 109; 112; CANR 64, 115;
  CMW 4
Little, Malcolm 1925-1965
  See Malcolm X
  See also BW 1, 3; CA 125; 111; CANR 82;
  DA; DA3; DAB; DAC; DAM MST,
  MULT; MTCW 1, 2; MTFW 2005
Littlewit, Humphrey Gent.
  See Lovecraft, H(oward) P(hillips)
Litwos
  See Sienkiewicz, Henryk (Adam Alexander
  Pius)
Liu, E. 1857-1909 .... **TCLC 15**
  See also CA 115; 190
Lively, Penelope 1933- .... **CLC 32, 50**
  See also BPFB 2; CA 41-44R; CANR 29,
  67, 79, 131; CLR 7; CN 5, 6, 7; CWRI 5;
  DAM NOV; DLB 14, 161, 207; FANT;
  JRDA; MAICYA 1, 2; MTCW 1, 2;
  MTFW 2005; SATA 7, 60, 101, 164; TEA
Lively, Penelope Margaret
  See Lively, Penelope

Livesay, Dorothy (Kathleen)
  1909-1996 .... **CLC 4, 15, 79**
  See also AITN 2; CA 25-28R; CAAS 8;
  CANR 36, 67; CP 1, 2, 3, 4; DAC; DAM
  MST, POET; DLB 68; FW; MTCW 1;
  RGEL 2; TWA
Livy c. 59B.C.-c. 12 .... **CMLC 11**
  See also AW 2; CDWLB 1; DLB 211;
  RGWL 2, 3
Lizardi, Jose Joaquin Fernandez de
  1776-1827 .... **NCLC 30**
  See also LAW
Llewellyn, Richard
  See Llewellyn Lloyd, Richard Dafydd Viv-
  ian
  See also DLB 15
Llewellyn Lloyd, Richard Dafydd Vivian
  1906-1983 .... **CLC 7, 80**
  See Llewellyn, Richard
  See also CA 53-56; 111; CANR 7, 71;
  SATA 11; SATA-Obit 37
Llosa, (Jorge) Mario (Pedro) Vargas
  See Vargas Llosa, (Jorge) Mario (Pedro)
  See also RGWL 3
Llosa, Mario Vargas
  See Vargas Llosa, (Jorge) Mario (Pedro)
Lloyd, Manda
  See Mander, (Mary) Jane
Lloyd Webber, Andrew 1948-
  See Webber, Andrew Lloyd
  See also AAYA 1, 38; CA 116; 149; DAM
  DRAM; SATA 56
Llull, Ramon c. 1235-c. 1316 .... **CMLC 12**
Lobb, Ebenezer
  See Upward, Allen
Locke, Alain (Le Roy)
  1886-1954 .... **BLCS; HR 1:3; TCLC 43**
  See also AMWS 14; BW 1, 3; CA 106; 124;
  CANR 79; DLB 51; LMFS 2; MAL 5;
  RGAL 4
Locke, John 1632-1704 .... **LC 7, 35**
  See also DLB 31, 101, 213, 252; RGEL 2;
  WLIT 3
Locke-Elliott, Sumner
  See Elliott, Sumner Locke
Lockhart, John Gibson 1794-1854 .. **NCLC 6**
  See also DLB 110, 116, 144
Lockridge, Ross (Franklin), Jr.
  1914-1948 .... **TCLC 111**
  See also CA 108; 145; CANR 79; DLB 143;
  DLBY 1980; MAL 5; RGAL 4; RHW
Lockwood, Robert
  See Johnson, Robert
Lodge, David (John) 1935- .... **CLC 36, 141**
  See also BEST 90:1; BRWS 4; CA 17-20R;
  CANR 19, 53, 92, 139; CN 1, 2, 3, 4, 5,
  6, 7; CPW; DAM POP; DLB 14, 194;
  EWL 3; INT CANR-19; MTCW 1, 2;
  MTFW 2005
Lodge, Thomas 1558-1625 .... **LC 41**
  See also DLB 172; RGEL 2
Loewinsohn, Ron(ald William)
  1937- .... **CLC 52**
  See also CA 25-28R; CANR 71; CP 1, 2, 3,
  4
Logan, Jake
  See Smith, Martin Cruz
Logan, John (Burton) 1923-1987 .... **CLC 5**
  See also CA 77-80; 124; CANR 45; CP 1,
  2, 3, 4; DLB 5
Lo Kuan-chung 1330(?)-1400(?) .... **LC 12**
Lombard, Nap
  See Johnson, Pamela Hansford
Lombard, Peter 1100(?)-1160(?) ... **CMLC 72**
London, Jack 1876-1916 .. **SSC 4, 49; TCLC**
  9, 15, 39; WLC
  See London, John Griffith
  See also AAYA 13; AITN 2; AMW; BPFB
  2; BYA 4, 13; CDALB 1865-1917; DLB

8, 12, 78, 212; EWL 3; EXPS; LAIT 3;
MAL 5; NFS 8; RGAL 4; RGSF 2; SATA
18; SFW 4; SSFS 7; TCWW 1, 2; TUS;
WYA; YAW
London, John Griffith 1876-1916
  See London, Jack
  See also CA 110; 119; CANR 73; DA; DA3;
  DAB; DAC; DAM MST, NOV; JRDA;
  MAICYA 1, 2; MTCW 1, 2; MTFW 2005;
  NFS 19
Long, Emmett
  See Leonard, Elmore (John, Jr.)
Longbaugh, Harry
  See Goldman, William (W.)
Longfellow, Henry Wadsworth
  1807-1882 .... **NCLC 2, 45, 101, 103; PC**
  30; WLCS
  See also AMW; AMWR 2; CDALB 1640-
  1865; CLR 99; DA; DA3; DAB; DAC;
  DAM MST, POET; DLB 1, 59, 235;
  EXPP; PAB; PFS 2, 7, 17; RGAL 4;
  SATA 19; TUS; WP
Longinus c. 1st cent. - .... **CMLC 27**
  See also AW 2; DLB 176
Longley, Michael 1939- .... **CLC 29**
  See also BRWS 8; CA 102; CP 1, 2, 3, 4, 5,
  6, 7; DLB 40
Longstreet, Augustus Baldwin
  1790-1870 .... **NCLC 159**
  See also DLB 3, 11, 74, 248; RGAL 4
Longus fl. c. 2nd cent. - .... **CMLC 7**
Longway, A. Hugh
  See Lang, Andrew
Lonnbohm, Armas Eino Leopold 1878-1926
  See Leino, Eino
  See also CA 123
Lonnrot, Elias 1802-1884 .... **NCLC 53**
  See also EFS 1
Lonsdale, Roger ed. .... **CLC 65**
Lopate, Phillip 1943- .... **CLC 29**
  See also CA 97-100; CANR 88; DLBY
  1980; INT CA-97-100
Lopez, Barry (Holstun) 1945- .... **CLC 70**
  See also AAYA 9, 63; ANW; CA 65-68;
  CANR 7, 23, 47, 68, 92; DLB 256, 275;
  INT CANR-7, -23; MTCW 1; RGAL 4;
  SATA 67
Lopez de Mendoza, Inigo
  See Santillana, Inigo Lopez de Mendoza,
  Marques de
Lopez Portillo (y Pacheco), Jose
  1920-2004 .... **CLC 46**
  See also CA 129; 224; HW 1
Lopez y Fuentes, Gregorio
  1897(?)-1966 .... **CLC 32**
  See also CA 131; EWL 3; HW 1
Lorca, Federico Garcia
  See Garcia Lorca, Federico
  See also DFS 4; EW 11; PFS 20; RGWL 2,
  3; WP
Lord, Audre
  See Lorde, Audre (Geraldine)
  See also EWL 3
Lord, Bette Bao 1938- .... **AAL; CLC 23**
  See also BEST 90:3; BPFB 2; CA 107;
  CANR 41, 79; INT CA-107; SATA 58
Lord Auch
  See Bataille, Georges
Lord Brooke
  See Greville, Fulke
Lord Byron
  See Byron, George Gordon (Noel)
Lorde, Audre (Geraldine)
  1934-1992 .... **BLC 2; CLC 18, 71; PC**
  12; TCLC 173
  See Domini, Rey; Lord, Audre
  See also AFAW 1, 2; BW 1, 3; CA 25-28R;
  142; CANR 16, 26, 46, 82; CP 2, 3, 4;
  DA3; DAM MULT, POET; DLB 41; FW;
  MAL 5; MTCW 1, 2; MTFW 2005; PFS
  16; RGAL 4

McGinley, Patrick (Anthony) 1937- . **CLC 41**
See also CA 120; 127; CANR 56; INT CA-127

McGinley, Phyllis 1905-1978 .... **CLC 14**
See also CA 9-12R; 77-80; CANR 19; CP 1, 2; CWRI 5; DLB 11, 48; MAL 5; PFS 9, 13; SATA 2, 44; SATA-Obit 24

McGinniss, Joe 1942- .... **CLC 32**
See also AITN 2; BEST 89:2; CA 25-28R; CANR 26, 70; CPW; DLB 185; INT CANR-26

McGivern, Maureen Daly
See Daly, Maureen

McGrath, Patrick 1950- .... **CLC 55**
See also CA 136; CANR 65; CN 5, 6, 7; DLB 231; HGG; SUFW 2

McGrath, Thomas (Matthew)
1916-1990 .... **CLC 28, 59**
See also AMWS 10; CA 9-12R; 132; CANR 6, 33, 95; CP 1, 2, 3, 4; DAM POET; MAL 5; MTCW 1; SATA 41; SATA-Obit 66

McGuane, Thomas (Francis III)
1939- .... **CLC 3, 7, 18, 45, 127**
See also AITN 2; BPFB 2; CA 49-52; CANR 5, 24, 49, 94; CN 2, 3, 4, 5, 6, 7; DLB 2, 212; DLBY 1980; EWL 3; INT CANR-24; MAL 5; MTCW 1; MTFW 2005; TCWW 1, 2

McGuckian, Medbh 1950- .... **CLC 48, 174; PC 27**
See also BRWS 5; CA 143; CP 4, 5, 6, 7; CWP; DAM POET; DLB 40

McHale, Tom 1942(?)-1982 .... **CLC 3, 5**
See also AITN 1; CA 77-80; 106; CN 1, 2, 3

McHugh, Heather 1948- .... **PC 61**
See also CA 69-72; CANR 11, 28, 55, 92; CP 4, 5, 6, 7; CWP

McIlvanney, William 1936- .... **CLC 42**
See also CA 25-28R; CANR 61; CMW 4; DLB 14, 207

McIlwraith, Maureen Mollie Hunter
See Hunter, Mollie
See also SATA 2

McInerney, Jay 1955- .... **CLC 34, 112**
See also AAYA 18; BPFB 2; CA 116; 123; CANR 45, 68, 116; CN 5, 6, 7; CPW; DA3; DAM POP; DLB 292; INT CA-123; MAL 5; MTCW 2; MTFW 2005

McIntyre, Vonda N(eel) 1948- .... **CLC 18**
See also CA 81-84; CANR 17, 34, 69; MTCW 1; SFW 4; YAW

McKay, Claude .... **BLC 3; HR 1:3; PC 2; TCLC 7, 41; WLC**
See McKay, Festus Claudius
See also AFAW 1, 2; AMWS 10; DAB; DLB 4, 45, 51, 117; EWL 3; EXPP; GLL 2; LAIT 3; LMFS 2; MAL 5; PAB; PFS 4; RGAL 4; WP

McKay, Festus Claudius 1889-1948
See McKay, Claude
See also BW 1, 3; CA 104; 124; CANR 73; DA; DAC; DAM MST, MULT, NOV, POET; MTCW 1, 2; MTFW 2005; TUS

McKuen, Rod 1933- .... **CLC 1, 3**
See also AITN 1; CA 41-44R; CANR 40; CP 1

McLoughlin, R. B.
See Mencken, H(enry) L(ouis)

McLuhan, (Herbert) Marshall
1911-1980 .... **CLC 37, 83**
See also CA 9-12R; 102; CANR 12, 34, 61; DLB 88; INT CANR-12; MTCW 1, 2; MTFW 2005

McManus, Declan Patrick Aloysius
See Costello, Elvis

McMillan, Terry (L.) 1951- . **BLCS; CLC 50, 61, 112**
See also AAYA 21; AMWS 13; BPFB 2; BW 2, 3; CA 140; CANR 60, 104, 131; CN 7; CPW; DA3; DAM MULT, NOV, POP; MAL 5; MTCW 2; MTFW 2005; RGAL 4; YAW

McMurtry, Larry 1936- .... **CLC 2, 3, 7, 11, 27, 44, 127**
See also AAYA 15; AITN 2; AMWS 5; BEST 89:2; BPFB 2; CA 5-8R; CANR 19, 43, 64, 103; CDALB 1968-1988; CN 2, 3, 4, 5, 6, 7; CPW; CSW; DA3; DAM NOV, POP; DLB 2, 143, 256; DLBY 1980, 1987; EWL 3; MAL 5; MTCW 1, 2; MTFW 2005; RGAL 4; TCWW 1, 2

McNally, T. M. 1961- .... **CLC 82**

McNally, Terrence 1939- ... **CLC 4, 7, 41, 91; DC 27**
See also AAYA 62; AMWS 13; CA 45-48; CAD; CANR 2, 56, 116; CD 5, 6; DA3; DAM DRAM; DFS 16, 19; DLB 7, 249; EWL 3; GLL 1; MTCW 2; MTFW 2005

McNamer, Deirdre 1950- .... **CLC 70**

McNeal, Tom .... **CLC 119**

McNeile, Herman Cyril 1888-1937
See Sapper
See also CA 184; CMW 4; DLB 77

McNickle, (William) D'Arcy
1904-1977 .... **CLC 89; NNAL**
See also CA 9-12R; 85-88; CANR 5, 45; DAM MULT; DLB 175, 212; RGAL 4; SATA-Obit 22; TCWW 1, 2

McPhee, John (Angus) 1931- .... **CLC 36**
See also AAYA 61; AMWS 3; ANW; BEST 90:1; CA 65-68; CANR 20, 46, 64, 69, 121; CPW; DLB 185, 275; MTCW 1, 2; MTFW 2005; TUS

McPherson, James Alan 1943- . **BLCS; CLC 19, 77**
See also BW 1, 3; CA 25-28R; CAAS 17; CANR 24, 74, 140; CN 3, 4, 5, 6; CSW; DLB 38, 244; EWL 3; MTCW 1, 2; MTFW 2005; RGAL 4; RGSF 2

McPherson, William (Alexander)
1933- .... **CLC 34**
See also CA 69-72; CANR 28; INT CANR-28

McTaggart, J. McT. Ellis
See McTaggart, John McTaggart Ellis

McTaggart, John McTaggart Ellis
1866-1925 .... **TCLC 105**
See also CA 120; DLB 262

Mead, George Herbert 1863-1931 . **TCLC 89**
See also CA 212; DLB 270

Mead, Margaret 1901-1978 .... **CLC 37**
See also AITN 1; CA 1-4R; 81-84; CANR 4; DA3; FW; MTCW 1, 2; SATA-Obit 20

Meaker, Marijane (Agnes) 1927-
See Kerr, M. E.
See also CA 107; CANR 37, 63, 145; INT CA-107; JRDA; MAICYA 1, 2; MAIC-YAS 1; MTCW 1; SATA 20, 61, 99, 160; SATA-Essay 111; YAW

Medoff, Mark (Howard) 1940- .... **CLC 6, 23**
See also AITN 1; CA 53-56; CAD; CANR 5; CD 5, 6; DAM DRAM; DFS 4; DLB 7; INT CANR-5

Medvedev, P. N.
See Bakhtin, Mikhail Mikhailovich

Meged, Aharon
See Megged, Aharon

Meged, Aron
See Megged, Aharon

Megged, Aharon 1920- .... **CLC 9**
See also CA 49-52; CAAS 13; CANR 1, 140; EWL 3

Mehta, Deepa 1950- .... **CLC 208**

Mehta, Gita 1943- .... **CLC 179**
See also CA 225; CN 7; DNFS 2

Mehta, Ved (Parkash) 1934- .... **CLC 37**
See also CA 1-4R; 212; CAAE 212; CANR 2, 23, 69; MTCW 1; MTFW 2005

Melanchthon, Philipp 1497-1560 .... **LC 90**
See also DLB 179

Melanter
See Blackmore, R(ichard) D(oddridge)

Meleager c. 140B.C.-c. 70B.C. ...... **CMLC 53**

Melies, Georges 1861-1938 .... **TCLC 81**

Melikow, Loris
See Hofmannsthal, Hugo von

Melmoth, Sebastian
See Wilde, Oscar (Fingal O'Flahertie Wills)

Melo Neto, Joao Cabral de
See Cabral de Melo Neto, Joao
See also CWW 2; EWL 3

Meltzer, Milton 1915- .... **CLC 26**
See also AAYA 8, 45; BYA 2, 6; CA 13-16R; CANR 38, 92, 107; CLR 13; DLB 61; JRDA; MAICYA 1, 2; SAAS 1; SATA 1, 50, 80, 128; SATA-Essay 124; WYA; YAW

Melville, Herman 1819-1891 ..... **NCLC 3, 12, 29, 45, 49, 91, 93, 123, 157; SSC 1, 17, 46; WLC**
See also AAYA 25; AMW; AMWR 1; CDALB 1640-1865; DA; DA3; DAB; DAC; DAM MST, NOV; DLB 3, 74, 250, 254; EXPN; EXPS; GL 3; LAIT 1, 2; NFS 7, 9; RGAL 4; RGSF 2; SATA 59; SSFS 3; TUS

Members, Mark
See Powell, Anthony (Dymoke)

Membreno, Alejandro .... **CLC 59**

Menand, Louis 1952- .... **CLC 208**
See also CA 200

Menander c. 342B.C.-c. 293B.C. .... **CMLC 9, 51; DC 3**
See also AW 1; CDWLB 1; DAM DRAM; DLB 176; LMFS 1; RGWL 2, 3

Menchu, Rigoberta 1959- .. **CLC 160; HLCS 2**
See also CA 175; CANR 135; DNFS 1; WLIT 1

Mencken, H(enry) L(ouis)
1880-1956 .... **TCLC 13**
See also AMW; CA 105; 125; CDALB 1917-1929; DLB 11, 29, 63, 137, 222; EWL 3; MAL 5; MTCW 1, 2; MTFW 2005; NCFS 4; RGAL 4; TUS

Mendelsohn, Jane 1965- .... **CLC 99**
See also CA 154; CANR 94

Mendoza, Inigo Lopez de
See Santillana, Inigo Lopez de Mendoza, Marques de

Menton, Francisco de
See Chin, Frank (Chew, Jr.)

Mercer, David 1928-1980 .... **CLC 5**
See also CA 9-12R; 102; CANR 23; CBD; DAM DRAM; DLB 13, 310; MTCW 1; RGEL 2

Merchant, Paul
See Ellison, Harlan (Jay)

Meredith, George 1828-1909 .. **PC 60; TCLC 17, 43**
See also CA 117; 153; CANR 80; CDBLB 1832-1890; DAM POET; DLB 18, 35, 57, 159; RGEL 2; TEA

Meredith, William (Morris) 1919- .... **CLC 4, 13, 22, 55; PC 28**
See also CA 9-12R; CAAS 14; CANR 6, 40, 129; CP 1, 2, 3, 4, 5, 6, 7; DAM POET; DLB 5; MAL 5

Merezhkovsky, Dmitrii Sergeevich
See Merezhkovsky, Dmitry Sergeyevich
See also DLB 295

Merezhkovsky, Dmitry Sergeevich
See Merezhkovsky, Dmitry Sergeyevich
See also EWL 3
Merezhkovsky, Dmitry Sergeyevich
1865-1941 .... **TCLC 29**
See Merezhkovsky, Dmitrii Sergeevich;
Merezhkovsky, Dmitry Sergeevich
See also CA 169
Merimee, Prosper 1803-1870 ... **NCLC 6, 65;
SSC 7, 77**
See also DLB 119, 192; EW 6; EXPS; GFL
1789 to the Present; RGSF 2; RGWL 2,
3; SSFS 8; SUFW
Merkin, Daphne 1954- .... **CLC 44**
See also CA 123
Merleau-Ponty, Maurice
1908-1961 .... **TCLC 156**
See also CA 114; 89-92; DLB 296; GFL
1789 to the Present
Merlin, Arthur
See Blish, James (Benjamin)
Mernissi, Fatima 1940- .... **CLC 171**
See also CA 152; FW
Merrill, James (Ingram) 1926-1995 .. **CLC 2,
3, 6, 8, 13, 18, 34, 91; PC 28; TCLC
173**
See also AMWS 3; CA 13-16R; 147; CANR
10, 49, 63, 108; CP 1, 2, 3, 4; DA3; DAM
POET; DLB 5, 165; DLBY 1985; EWL 3;
INT CANR-10; MAL 5; MTCW 1, 2;
MTFW 2005; PAB; PFS 23; RGAL 4
Merriman, Alex
See Silverberg, Robert
Merriman, Brian 1747-1805 .... **NCLC 70**
Merritt, E. B.
See Waddington, Miriam
Merton, Thomas (James)
1915-1968 . **CLC 1, 3, 11, 34, 83; PC 10**
See also AAYA 61; AMWS 8; CA 5-8R;
25-28R; CANR 22, 53, 111, 131; DA3;
DLB 48; DLBY 1981; MAL 5; MTCW 1,
2; MTFW 2005
Merwin, W(illiam) S(tanley) 1927- ... **CLC 1,
2, 3, 5, 8, 13, 18, 45, 88; PC 45**
See also AMWS 3; CA 13-16R; CANR 15,
51, 112, 140; CP 1, 2, 3, 4, 5, 6, 7; DA3;
DAM POET; DLB 5, 169; EWL 3; INT
CANR-15; MAL 5; MTCW 1, 2; MTFW
2005; PAB; PFS 5, 15; RGAL 4
Metastasio, Pietro 1698-1782 .... **LC 115**
See also RGWL 2, 3
Metcalf, John 1938- .... **CLC 37; SSC 43**
See also CA 113; CN 4, 5, 6, 7; DLB 60;
RGSF 2; TWA
Metcalf, Suzanne
See Baum, L(yman) Frank
Mew, Charlotte (Mary) 1870-1928 .. **TCLC 8**
See also CA 105; 189; DLB 19, 135; RGEL
2
Mewshaw, Michael 1943- .... **CLC 9**
See also CA 53-56; CANR 7, 47; DLBY
1980
Meyer, Conrad Ferdinand
1825-1898 .... **NCLC 81; SSC 30**
See also DLB 129; EW; RGWL 2, 3
Meyer, Gustav 1868-1932
See Meyrink, Gustav
See also CA 117; 190
Meyer, June
See Jordan, June (Meyer)
Meyer, Lynn
See Slavitt, David R(ytman)
Meyers, Jeffrey 1939- .... **CLC 39**
See also CA 73-76, 186; CAAE 186; CANR
54, 102; DLB 111
**Meynell, Alice (Christina Gertrude
Thompson)** 1847-1922 .... **TCLC 6**
See also CA 104; 177; DLB 19, 98; RGEL
2

Meyrink, Gustav .... **TCLC 21**
See Meyer, Gustav
See also DLB 81; EWL 3
Michaels, Leonard 1933-2003 ..... **CLC 6, 25;
SSC 16**
See also CA 61-64; 216; CANR 21, 62, 119;
CN 3, 45, 6, 7; DLB 130; MTCW 1;
TCLE 1:2
Michaux, Henri 1899-1984 .... **CLC 8, 19**
See also CA 85-88; 114; DLB 258; EWL 3;
GFL 1789 to the Present; RGWL 2, 3
Micheaux, Oscar (Devereaux)
1884-1951 .... **TCLC 76**
See also BW 3; CA 174; DLB 50; TCWW
2
Michelangelo 1475-1564 .... **LC 12**
See also AAYA 43
Michelet, Jules 1798-1874 .... **NCLC 31**
See also EW 5; GFL 1789 to the Present
Michels, Robert 1876-1936 .... **TCLC 88**
See also CA 212
Michener, James A(lbert)
1907(?)-1997 .. **CLC 1, 5, 11, 29, 60, 109**
See also AAYA 27; AITN 1; BEST 90:1;
BPFB 2; CA 5-8R; 161; CANR 21, 45,
68; CN 1, 2, 3, 4, 5, 6; CPW; DA3; DAM
NOV, POP; DLB 6; MAL 5; MTCW 1, 2;
MTFW 2005; RHW; TCWW 1, 2
Mickiewicz, Adam 1798-1855 . **NCLC 3, 101;
PC 38**
See also EW 5; RGWL 2, 3
Middleton, (John) Christopher
1926- .... **CLC 13**
See also CA 13-16R; CANR 29, 54, 117;
CP 1, 2, 3, 4, 5, 6, 7; DLB 40
Middleton, Richard (Barham)
1882-1911 .... **TCLC 56**
See also CA 187; DLB 156; HGG
Middleton, Stanley 1919- .... **CLC 7, 38**
See also CA 25-28R; CAAS 23; CANR 21,
46, 81; CN 1, 2, 3, 4, 5, 6, 7; DLB 14
Middleton, Thomas 1580-1627 ...... **DC 5; LC
33, 123**
See also BRW 2; DAM DRAM, MST; DFS
18, 22; DLB 58; RGEL 2
Migueis, Jose Rodrigues 1901-1980 . **CLC 10**
See also DLB 287
Mikszath, Kalman 1847-1910 .... **TCLC 31**
See also CA 170
Miles, Jack .... **CLC 100**
See also CA 200
Miles, John Russiano
See Miles, Jack
Miles, Josephine (Louise)
1911-1985 .... **CLC 1, 2, 14, 34, 39**
See also CA 1-4R; 116; CANR 2, 55; CP 1,
2, 3, 4; DAM POET; DLB 48; MAL 5;
TCLE 1:2
Militant
See Sandburg, Carl (August)
Mill, Harriet (Hardy) Taylor
1807-1858 .... **NCLC 102**
See also FW
Mill, John Stuart 1806-1873 .... **NCLC 11, 58**
See also CDBLB 1832-1890; DLB 55, 190,
262; FW 1; RGEL 2; TEA
Millar, Kenneth 1915-1983 .... **CLC 14**
See Macdonald, Ross
See also CA 9-12R; 110; CANR 16, 63,
107; CMW 4; CPW; DA3; DAM POP;
DLB 2, 226; DLBD 6; DLBY 1983;
MTCW 1, 2; MTFW 2005
Millay, E. Vincent
See Millay, Edna St. Vincent

Millay, Edna St. Vincent 1892-1950 ..... **PC 6,
61; TCLC 4, 49, 169; WLCS**
See Boyd, Nancy
See also AMW; CA 104; 130; CDALB
1917-1929; DA; DA3; DAB; DAC; DAM
MST, POET; DLB 45, 249; EWL 3;
EXPP; FL 1:6; MAL 5; MAWW; MTCW
1, 2; MTFW 2005; PAB; PFS 3, 17;
RGAL 4; TUS; WP
Miller, Arthur 1915-2005 ..... **CLC 1, 2, 6, 10,
15, 26, 47, 78, 179; DC 1; WLC**
See also AAYA 15; AITN 1; AMW; AMWC
1; CA 1-4R; 236; CABS 3; CAD; CANR
2, 30, 54, 76, 132; CD 5, 6; CDALB
1941-1968; DA; DA3; DAB; DAC; DAM
DRAM, MST; DFS 1, 3, 8; DLB 7, 266;
EWL 3; LAIT 1, 4; LATS 1:2; MAL 5;
MTCW 1, 2; MTFW 2005; RGAL 4;
TUS; WYAS 1
Miller, Henry (Valentine)
1891-1980 .... **CLC 1, 2, 4, 9, 14, 43, 84;
WLC**
See also AMW; BPFB 2; CA 9-12R; 97-
100; CANR 33, 64; CDALB 1929-1941;
CN 1, 2; DA; DA3; DAB; DAC; DAM
MST, NOV; DLB 4, 9; DLBY 1980; EWL
3; MAL 5; MTCW 1, 2; MTFW 2005;
RGAL 4; TUS
Miller, Hugh 1802-1856 .... **NCLC 143**
See also DLB 190
Miller, Jason 1939(?)-2001 .... **CLC 2**
See also AITN 1; CA 73-76; 197; CAD;
CANR 130; DFS 12; DLB 7
Miller, Sue 1943- .... **CLC 44**
See also AMWS 12; BEST 90:3; CA 139;
CANR 59, 91, 128; DA3; DAM POP;
DLB 143
Miller, Walter M(ichael, Jr.)
1923-1996 .... **CLC 4, 30**
See also BPFB 2; CA 85-88; CANR 108;
DLB 8; SCFW 1, 2; SFW 4
Millett, Kate 1934- .... **CLC 67**
See also AITN 1; CA 73-76; CANR 32, 53,
76, 110; DA3; DLB 246; FW; GLL 1;
MTCW 1, 2; MTFW 2005
Millhauser, Steven (Lewis) 1943- .... **CLC 21,
54, 109; SSC 57**
See also CA 110; 111; CANR 63, 114, 133;
CN 6, 7; DA3; DLB 2; FANT; INT CA-
111; MAL 5; MTCW 2; MTFW 2005
Millin, Sarah Gertrude 1889-1968 ... **CLC 49**
See also CA 102; 93-96; DLB 225; EWL 3
Milne, A(lan) A(lexander)
1882-1956 .... **TCLC 6, 88**
See also BRWS 5; CA 104; 133; CLR 1,
26; CMW 4; CWRI 5; DA3; DAB; DAC;
DAM MST; DLB 10, 77, 100, 160; FANT;
MAICYA 1, 2; MTCW 1, 2; MTFW 2005;
RGEL 2; SATA 100; WCH; YABC 1
Milner, Ron(ald) 1938-2004 ..... **BLC 3; CLC
56**
See also AITN 1; BW 1; CA 73-76; 230;
CAD; CANR 24, 81; CD 5, 6; DAM
MULT; DLB 38; MAL 5; MTCW 1
Milnes, Richard Monckton
1809-1885 .... **NCLC 61**
See also DLB 32, 184
Milosz, Czeslaw 1911-2004 .... **CLC 5, 11, 22,
31, 56, 82; PC 8; WLCS**
See also AAYA 62; CA 81-84; 230; CANR
23, 51, 91, 126; CDWLB 4; CWW 2;
DA3; DAM MST, POET; DLB 215; EW
13; EWL 3; MTCW 1, 2; MTFW 2005;
PFS 16; RGWL 2, 3
Milton, John 1608-1674 ..... **LC 9, 43, 92; PC
19, 29; WLC**
See also AAYA 65; BRW 2; BRWR 2; CD-
BLB 1660-1789; DA; DA3; DAB; DAC;
DAM MST, POET; DLB 131, 151, 281;
EFS 1; EXPP; LAIT 1; PAB; PFS 3, 17;
RGEL 2; TEA; WLIT 3; WP

Oskison, John Milton
1874-1947 .... NNAL; TCLC 35
See also CA 144; CANR 84; DAM MULT;
DLB 175

Ossian c. 3rd cent. - .... CMLC 28
See Macpherson, James

Ossoli, Sarah Margaret (Fuller)
1810-1850 .... NCLC 5, 50
See Fuller, Margaret; Fuller, Sarah Margaret
See also CDALB 1640-1865; FW; LMFS 1;
SATA 25

Ostriker, Alicia (Suskin) 1937- .... CLC 132
See also CA 25-28R; CAAS 24; CANR 10,
30, 62, 99; CWP; DLB 120; EXPP; PFS
19

Ostrovsky, Aleksandr Nikolaevich
See Ostrovsky, Alexander
See also DLB 277

Ostrovsky, Alexander 1823-1886 .. NCLC 30,
57
See Ostrovsky, Aleksandr Nikolaevich

Otero, Blas de 1916-1979 .... CLC 11
See also CA 89-92; DLB 134; EWL 3

O'Trigger, Sir Lucius
See Horne, Richard Henry Hengist

Otto, Rudolf 1869-1937 .... TCLC 85

Otto, Whitney 1955- .... CLC 70
See also CA 140; CANR 120

Otway, Thomas 1652-1685 ... DC 24; LC 106
See also DAM DRAM; DLB 80; RGEL 2

Ouida .... TCLC 43
See De la Ramee, Marie Louise (Ouida)
See also DLB 18, 156; RGEL 2

Ouologuem, Yambo 1940- .... CLC 146
See also CA 111; 176

Ousmane, Sembene 1923- ... BLC 3; CLC 66
See Sembene, Ousmane
See also BW 1, 3; CA 117; 125; CANR 81;
CWW 2; MTCW 1

Ovid 43B.C.-17 .... CMLC 7; PC 2
See also AW 2; CDWLB 1; DA3; DAM
POET; DLB 211; PFS 22; RGWL 2, 3;
WP

Owen, Hugh
See Faust, Frederick (Schiller)

Owen, Wilfred (Edward Salter)
1893-1918 ... PC 19; TCLC 5, 27; WLC
See also BRW 6; CA 104; 141; CDBLB
1914-1945; DA; DAB; DAC; DAM MST;
POET; DLB 20; EWL 3; EXPP; MTCW
2; MTFW 2005; PFS 10; RGEL 2; WLIT
4

Owens, Louis (Dean) 1948-2002 .... NNAL
See also CA 137, 179; 207; CAAE 179;
CAAS 24; CANR 71

Owens, Rochelle 1936- .... CLC 8
See also CA 17-20R; CAAS 2; CAD;
CANR 39; CD 5, 6; CP 1, 2, 3, 4, 5, 6, 7;
CWD; CWP

Oz, Amos 1939- ...... CLC 5, 8, 11, 27, 33, 54;
SSC 66
See also CA 53-56; CANR 27, 47, 65, 113,
138; CWW 2; DAM NOV; EWL 3;
MTCW 1, 2; MTFW 2005; RGSF 2;
RGWL 3; WLIT 6

Ozick, Cynthia 1928- .... CLC 3, 7, 28, 62,
155; SSC 15, 60
See also AMWS 5; BEST 90:1; CA 17-20R;
CANR 23, 58, 116; CN 3, 4, 5, 6, 7;
CPW; DA3; DAM NOV, POP; DLB 28,
152, 299; DLBY 1982; EWL 3; EXPS;
INT CANR-23; MAL 5; MTCW 1, 2;
MTFW 2005; RGAL 4; RGSF 2; SSFS 3,
12

Ozu, Yasujiro 1903-1963 .... CLC 16
See also CA 112

Pabst, G. W. 1885-1967 .... TCLC 127

Pacheco, C.
See Pessoa, Fernando (Antonio Nogueira)

Pacheco, Jose Emilio 1939- .... HLC 2
See also CA 111; 131; CANR 65; CWW 2;
DAM MULT; DLB 290; EWL 3; HW 1,
2; RGSF 2

Pa Chin .... CLC 18
See Li Fei-kan
See also EWL 3

Pack, Robert 1929- .... CLC 13
See also CA 1-4R; CANR 3, 44, 82; CP 1,
2, 3, 4, 5, 6, 7; DLB 5; SATA 118

Padgett, Lewis
See Kuttner, Henry

Padilla (Lorenzo), Heberto
1932-2000 .... CLC 38
See also AITN 1; CA 123; 131; 189; CWW
2; EWL 3; HW 1

Page, James Patrick 1944-
See Page, Jimmy
See also CA 204

Page, Jimmy 1944- .... CLC 12
See Page, James Patrick

Page, Louise 1955- .... CLC 40
See also CA 140; CANR 76; CBD; CD 5,
6; CWD; DLB 233

Page, P(atricia) K(athleen) 1916- ...... CLC 7,
18; PC 12
See Cape, Judith
See also CA 53-56; CANR 4, 22, 65; CP 1,
2, 3, 4, 5, 6, 7; DAC; DAM MST; DLB
68; MTCW 1; RGEL 2

Page, Stanton
See Fuller, Henry Blake

Page, Stanton
See Fuller, Henry Blake

Page, Thomas Nelson 1853-1922 .... SSC 23
See also CA 118; 177; DLB 12, 78; DLBD
13; RGAL 4

Pagels, Elaine Hiesey 1943- .... CLC 104
See also CA 45-48; CANR 2, 24, 51; FW;
NCFS 4

Paget, Violet 1856-1935
See Lee, Vernon
See also CA 104; 166; GLL 1; HGG

Paget-Lowe, Henry
See Lovecraft, H(oward) P(hillips)

Paglia, Camille (Anna) 1947- .... CLC 68
See also CA 140; CANR 72, 139; CPW;
FW; GLL 2; MTCW 2; MTFW 2005

Paige, Richard
See Koontz, Dean R.

Paine, Thomas 1737-1809 .... NCLC 62
See also AMWS 1; CDALB 1640-1865;
DLB 31, 43, 73, 158; LAIT 1; RGAL 4;
RGEL 2; TUS

Pakenham, Antonia
See Fraser, Antonia (Pakenham)

Palamas, Costis
See Palamas, Kostes

Palamas, Kostes 1859-1943 .... TCLC 5
See Palamas, Kostis
See also CA 105; 190; RGWL 2, 3

Palamas, Kostis
See Palamas, Kostes
See also EWL 3

Palazzeschi, Aldo 1885-1974 .... CLC 11
See also CA 89-92; 53-56; DLB 114, 264;
EWL 3

Pales Matos, Luis 1898-1959 .... HLCS 2
See Pales Matos, Luis
See also DLB 290; HW 1; LAW

Paley, Grace 1922- .. CLC 4, 6, 37, 140; SSC
8
See also AMWS 6; CA 25-28R; CANR 13,
46, 74, 118; CN 2, 3, 4, 5, 6, 7; CPW;
DA3; DAM POP; DLB 28, 218; EWL 3;
EXPS; FW; INT CANR-13; MAL 5;
MAWW; MTCW 1, 2; MTFW 2005;
RGAL 4; RGSF 2; SSFS 3, 20

Palin, Michael (Edward) 1943- .... CLC 21
See Monty Python
See also CA 107; CANR 35, 109; SATA 67

Palliser, Charles 1947- .... CLC 65
See also CA 136; CANR 76; CN 5, 6, 7

Palma, Ricardo 1833-1919 .... TCLC 29
See also CA 168; LAW

Pamuk, Orhan 1952- .... CLC 185
See also CA 142; CANR 75, 127; CWW 2;
WLIT 6

Pancake, Breece Dexter 1952-1979
See Pancake, Breece D'J
See also CA 123; 109

Pancake, Breece D'J .... CLC 29; SSC 61
See Pancake, Breece Dexter
See also DLB 130

Panchenko, Nikolai .... CLC 59

Pankhurst, Emmeline (Goulden)
1858-1928 .... TCLC 100
See also CA 116; FW

Panko, Rudy
See Gogol, Nikolai (Vasilyevich)

Papadiamantis, Alexandros
1851-1911 .... TCLC 29
See also CA 168; EWL 3

Papadiamantopoulos, Johannes 1856-1910
See Moreas, Jean
See also CA 117

Papini, Giovanni 1881-1956 .... TCLC 22
See also CA 121; 180; DLB 264

Paracelsus 1493-1541 .... LC 14
See also DLB 179

Parasol, Peter
See Stevens, Wallace

Pardo Bazan, Emilia 1851-1921 .... SSC 30
See also EWL 3; FW; RGSF 2; RGWL 2, 3

Pareto, Vilfredo 1848-1923 .... TCLC 69
See also CA 175

Paretsky, Sara 1947- .... CLC 135
See also AAYA 30; BEST 90:3; CA 125;
129; CANR 59, 95; CMW 4; CPW; DA3;
DAM POP; DLB 306; INT CA-129;
MSW; RGAL 4

Parfenie, Maria
See Codrescu, Andrei

Parini, Jay (Lee) 1948- .... CLC 54, 133
See also CA 97-100, 229; CAAE 229;
CAAS 16; CANR 32, 87

Park, Jordan
See Kornbluth, C(yril) M.; Pohl, Frederik

Park, Robert E(zra) 1864-1944 ..... TCLC 73
See also CA 122; 165

Parker, Bert
See Ellison, Harlan (Jay)

Parker, Dorothy (Rothschild)
1893-1967 . CLC 15, 68; PC 28; SSC 2;
TCLC 143
See also AMWS 9; CA 19-20; 25-28R; CAP
2; DA3; DAM POET; DLB 11, 45, 86;
EXPP; FW; MAL 5; MAWW; MTCW 1,
2; MTFW 2005; PFS 18; RGAL 4; RGSF
2; TUS

Parker, Robert B(rown) 1932- .... CLC 27
See also AAYA 28; BEST 89:4; BPFB 3;
CA 49-52; CANR 1, 26, 52, 89, 128;
CMW 4; CPW; DAM NOV, POP; DLB
306; INT CANR-26; MSW; MTCW 1;
MTFW 2005

Parkin, Frank 1940- .... CLC 43
See also CA 147

Parkman, Francis, Jr. 1823-1893 .. NCLC 12
See also AMWS 2; DLB 1, 30, 183, 186,
235; RGAL 4

Parks, Gordon (Alexander Buchanan)
1912- .... BLC 3; CLC 1, 16
See also AAYA 36; AITN 2; BW 2, 3; CA
41-44R; CANR 26, 66, 145; DA3; DAM
MULT; DLB 33; MTCW 2; MTFW 2005;
SATA 8, 108

Parks, Suzan-Lori 1964(?)- .... **DC 23**
See also AAYA 55; CA 201; CAD; CD 5, 6; CWD; DFS 22; RGAL 4

Parks, Tim(othy Harold) 1954- ...... **CLC 147**
See also CA 126; 131; CANR 77, 144; CN 7; DLB 231; INT CA-131

Parmenides c. 515B.C.-c. 450B.C. .... **CMLC 22**
See also DLB 176

Parnell, Thomas 1679-1718 .... **LC 3**
See also DLB 95; RGEL 2

Parr, Catherine c. 1513(?)-1548 .... **LC 86**
See also DLB 136

Parra, Nicanor 1914- ... **CLC 2, 102; HLC 2; PC 39**
See also CA 85-88; CANR 32; CWW 2; DAM MULT; DLB 283; EWL 3; HW 1; LAW; MTCW 1

Parra Sanojo, Ana Teresa de la 1890-1936 .... **HLCS 2**
See de la Parra, (Ana) Teresa (Sonojo)
See also LAW

Parrish, Mary Frances
See Fisher, M(ary) F(rances) K(ennedy)

Parshchikov, Aleksei 1954- .... **CLC 59**
See Parshchikov, Aleksei Maksimovich

Parshchikov, Aleksei Maksimovich
See Parshchikov, Aleksei
See also DLB 285

Parson, Professor
See Coleridge, Samuel Taylor

Parson Lot
See Kingsley, Charles

Parton, Sara Payson Willis 1811-1872 .... **NCLC 86**
See also DLB 43, 74, 239

Partridge, Anthony
See Oppenheim, E(dward) Phillips

Pascal, Blaise 1623-1662 .... **LC 35**
See also DLB 268; EW 3; GFL Beginnings to 1789; RGWL 2, 3; TWA

Pascoli, Giovanni 1855-1912 .... **TCLC 45**
See also CA 170; EW 7; EWL 3

Pasolini, Pier Paolo 1922-1975 .. **CLC 20, 37, 106; PC 17**
See also CA 93-96; 61-64; CANR 63; DLB 128, 177; EWL 3; MTCW 1; RGWL 2, 3

Pasquini
See Silone, Ignazio

Pastan, Linda (Olenik) 1932- .... **CLC 27**
See also CA 61-64; CANR 18, 40, 61, 113; CP 3, 4, 5, 6, 7; CSW; CWP; DAM POET; DLB 5; PFS 8

Pasternak, Boris (Leonidovich) 1890-1960 ...... **CLC 7, 10, 18, 63; PC 6; SSC 31; WLC**
See also BPFB 3; CA 127; 116; DA; DA3; DAB; DAC; DAM MST, NOV, POET; DLB 302; EW 10; MTCW 1, 2; MTFW 2005; RGSF 2; RGWL 2, 3; TWA; WP

Patchen, Kenneth 1911-1972 .... **CLC 1, 2, 18**
See also BG 1:3; CA 1-4R; 33-36R; CANR 3, 35; CN 1; CP 1; DAM POET; DLB 16, 48; EWL 3; MAL 5; MTCW 1; RGAL 4

Pater, Walter (Horatio) 1839-1894 . **NCLC 7, 90, 159**
See also BRW 5; CDBLB 1832-1890; DLB 57, 156; RGEL 2; TEA

Paterson, A(ndrew) B(arton) 1864-1941 .... **TCLC 32**
See also CA 155; DLB 230; RGEL 2; SATA 97

Paterson, Banjo
See Paterson, A(ndrew) B(arton)

Paterson, Katherine (Womeldorf) 1932- .... **CLC 12, 30**
See also AAYA 1, 31; BYA 1, 2, 7; CA 21-24R; CANR 28, 59, 111; CLR 7, 50; CWRI 5; DLB 52; JRDA; LAIT 4; MAICYA 1, 2; MAICYAS 1; MTCW 1; SATA 13, 53, 92, 133; WYA; YAW

Patmore, Coventry Kersey Dighton 1823-1896 .... **NCLC 9; PC 59**
See also DLB 35, 98; RGEL 2; TEA

Paton, Alan (Stewart) 1903-1988 ...... **CLC 4, 10, 25, 55, 106; TCLC 165; WLC**
See also AAYA 26; AFW; BPFB 3; BRWS 2; BYA 1; CA 13-16; 125; CANR 22; CAP 1; CN 1, 2, 3, 4; DA; DA3; DAB; DAC; DAM MST, NOV; DLB 225; DLBD 17; EWL 3; EXPN; LAIT 4; MTCW 1, 2; MTFW 2005; NFS 3, 12; RGEL 2; SATA 11; SATA-Obit 56; TWA; WLIT 2; WWE 1

Paton Walsh, Gillian 1937- .... **CLC 35**
See Paton Walsh, Jill; Walsh, Jill Paton
See also AAYA 11; CANR 38, 83; CLR 2, 65; DLB 161; JRDA; MAICYA 1, 2; SAAS 3; SATA 4, 72, 109; YAW

Paton Walsh, Jill
See Paton Walsh, Gillian
See also AAYA 47; BYA 1, 8

Patterson, (Horace) Orlando (Lloyd) 1940- .... **BLCS**
See also BW 1; CA 65-68; CANR 27, 84; CN 1, 2, 3, 4, 5, 6

Patton, George S(mith), Jr. 1885-1945 .... **TCLC 79**
See also CA 189

Paulding, James Kirke 1778-1860 ... **NCLC 2**
See also DLB 3, 59, 74, 250; RGAL 4

Paulin, Thomas Neilson 1949-
See Paulin, Tom
See also CA 123; 128; CANR 98

Paulin, Tom .... **CLC 37, 177**
See Paulin, Thomas Neilson
See also CP 3, 4, 5, 6, 7; DLB 40

Pausanias c. 1st cent. - .... **CMLC 36**

Paustovsky, Konstantin (Georgievich) 1892-1968 .... **CLC 40**
See also CA 93-96; 25-28R; DLB 272; EWL 3

Pavese, Cesare 1908-1950 .... **PC 13; SSC 19; TCLC 3**
See also CA 104; 169; DLB 128, 177; EW 12; EWL 3; PFS 20; RGSF 2; RGWL 2, 3; TWA; WLIT 7

Pavic, Milorad 1929- .... **CLC 60**
See also CA 136; CDWLB 4; CWW 2; DLB 181; EWL 3; RGWL 3

Pavlov, Ivan Petrovich 1849-1936 . **TCLC 91**
See also CA 118; 180

Pavlova, Karolina Karlovna 1807-1893 .... **NCLC 138**
See also DLB 205

Payne, Alan
See Jakes, John (William)

Payne, Rachel Ann
See Jakes, John (William)

Paz, Gil
See Lugones, Leopoldo

Paz, Octavio 1914-1998 . **CLC 3, 4, 6, 10, 19, 51, 65, 119; HLC 2; PC 1, 48; WLC**
See also AAYA 50; CA 73-76; 165; CANR 32, 65, 104; CWW 2; DA; DA3; DAB; DAC; DAM MST, MULT, POET; DLB 290; DLBY 1990, 1998; DNFS 1; EWL 3; HW 1, 2; LAW; LAWS 1; MTCW 1, 2; MTFW 2005; PFS 18; RGWL 2, 3; SSFS 13; TWA; WLIT 1

p'Bitek, Okot 1931-1982 .... **BLC 3; CLC 96; TCLC 149**
See also AFW; BW 2, 3; CA 124; 107; CANR 82; CP 1, 2, 3; DAM MULT; DLB 125; EWL 3; MTCW 1, 2; MTFW 2005; RGEL 2; WLIT 2

Peacham, Henry 1578-1644(?) .... **LC 119**
See also DLB 151

Peacock, Molly 1947- .... **CLC 60**
See also CA 103; CAAS 21; CANR 52, 84; CP 7; CWP; DLB 120, 282

Peacock, Thomas Love 1785-1866 .... **NCLC 22**
See also BRW 4; DLB 96, 116; RGEL 2; RGSF 2

Peake, Mervyn 1911-1968 .... **CLC 7, 54**
See also CA 5-8R; 25-28R; CANR 3; DLB 15, 160, 255; FANT; MTCW 1; RGEL 2; SATA 23; SFW 4

Pearce, Philippa
See Christie, Philippa
See also CA 5-8R; CANR 4, 109; CWRI 5; FANT; MAICYA 2

Pearl, Eric
See Elman, Richard (Martin)

Pearson, T(homas) R(eid) 1956- .... **CLC 39**
See also CA 120; 130; CANR 97; CSW; INT CA-130

Peck, Dale 1967- .... **CLC 81**
See also CA 146; CANR 72, 127; GLL 2

Peck, John (Frederick) 1941- .... **CLC 3**
See also CA 49-52; CANR 3, 100; CP 4, 5, 6, 7

Peck, Richard (Wayne) 1934- .... **CLC 21**
See also AAYA 1, 24; BYA 1, 6, 8, 11; CA 85-88; CANR 19, 38, 129; CLR 15; INT CANR-19; JRDA; MAICYA 1, 2; SAAS 2; SATA 18, 55, 97, 110, 158; SATA-Essay 110; WYA; YAW

Peck, Robert Newton 1928- .... **CLC 17**
See also AAYA 3, 43; BYA 1, 6; CA 81-84; 182; CAAE 182; CANR 31, 63, 127; CLR 45; DA; DAC; DAM MST; JRDA; LAIT 3; MAICYA 1, 2; SAAS 1; SATA 21, 62, 111, 156; SATA-Essay 108; WYA; YAW

Peckinpah, (David) Sam(uel) 1925-1984 .... **CLC 20**
See also CA 109; 114; CANR 82

Pedersen, Knut 1859-1952
See Hamsun, Knut
See also CA 104; 119; CANR 63; MTCW 1, 2

Peele, George 1556-1596 .... **DC 27; LC 115**
See also BRW 1; DLB 62, 167; RGEL 2

Peeslake, Gaffer
See Durrell, Lawrence (George)

Peguy, Charles (Pierre) 1873-1914 .... **TCLC 10**
See also CA 107; 193; DLB 258; EWL 3; GFL 1789 to the Present

Peirce, Charles Sanders 1839-1914 .... **TCLC 81**
See also CA 194; DLB 270

Pellicer, Carlos 1897(?)-1977 .... **HLCS 2**
See also CA 153; 69-72; DLB 290; EWL 3; HW 1

Pena, Ramon del Valle y
See Valle-Inclan, Ramon (Maria) del

Pendennis, Arthur Esquir
See Thackeray, William Makepeace

Penn, Arthur
See Matthews, (James) Brander

Penn, William 1644-1718 .... **LC 25**
See also DLB 24

PEPECE
See Prado (Calvo), Pedro

Author Index

Pepys, Samuel 1633-1703 ... **LC 11, 58; WLC**
See also BRW 2; CDBLB 1660-1789; DA;
DA3; DAB; DAC; DAM MST; DLB 101,
213; NCFS 4; RGEL 2; TEA; WLIT 3

Percy, Thomas 1729-1811 .... **NCLC 95**
See also DLB 104

Percy, Walker 1916-1990 .... **CLC 2, 3, 6, 8,
14, 18, 47, 65**
See also AMWS 3; BPFB 3; CA 1-4R; 131;
CANR 1, 23, 64; CN 1, 2, 3, 4; CPW;
CSW; DA3; DAM NOV, POP; DLB 2;
DLBY 1980, 1990; EWL 3; MAL 5;
MTCW 1, 2; MTFW 2005; RGAL 4; TUS

Percy, William Alexander
1885-1942 .... **TCLC 84**
See also CA 163; MTCW 2

Perec, Georges 1936-1982 .... **CLC 56, 116**
See also CA 141; DLB 83, 299; EWL 3;
GFL 1789 to the Present; RGWL 3

**Pereda (y Sanchez de Porrua), Jose Maria
de** 1833-1906 .... **TCLC 16**
See also CA 117

Pereda y Porrua, Jose Maria de
See Pereda (y Sanchez de Porrua), Jose
Maria de

Peregoy, George Weems
See Mencken, H(enry) L(ouis)

Perelman, S(idney) J(oseph)
1904-1979 .. **CLC 3, 5, 9, 15, 23, 44, 49;
SSC 32**
See also AITN 1, 2; BPFB 3; CA 73-76;
89-92; CANR 18; DAM DRAM; DLB 11,
44; MTCW 1, 2; MTFW 2005; RGAL 4

Peret, Benjamin 1899-1959 .... **PC 33; TCLC
20**
See also CA 117; 186; GFL 1789 to the
Present

Peretz, Isaac Leib
See Peretz, Isaac Loeb
See also CA 201

Peretz, Isaac Loeb 1851(?)-1915 ...... **SSC 26;
TCLC 16**
See Peretz, Isaac Leib
See also CA 109

Peretz, Yitzkhok Leibush
See Peretz, Isaac Loeb

Perez Galdos, Benito 1843-1920 ..... **HLCS 2;
TCLC 27**
See Galdos, Benito Perez
See also CA 125; 153; EWL 3; HW 1;
RGWL 2, 3

Peri Rossi, Cristina 1941- .. **CLC 156; HLCS
2**
See also CA 131; CANR 59, 81; CWW 2;
DLB 145, 290; EWL 3; HW 1, 2

Perlata
See Peret, Benjamin

Perloff, Marjorie G(abrielle)
1931- .... **CLC 137**
See also CA 57-60; CANR 7, 22, 49, 104

Perrault, Charles 1628-1703 .... **LC 2, 56**
See also BYA 4; CLR 79; DLB 268; GFL
Beginnings to 1789; MAICYA 1, 2;
RGWL 2, 3; SATA 25; WCH

Perry, Anne 1938- .... **CLC 126**
See also CA 101; CANR 22, 50, 84; CMW
4; CN 6, 7; CPW; DLB 276

Perry, Brighton
See Sherwood, Robert E(mmet)

Perse, St.-John
See Leger, (Marie-Rene Auguste) Alexis
Saint-Leger

Perse, Saint-John
See Leger, (Marie-Rene Auguste) Alexis
Saint-Leger
See also DLB 258; RGWL 3

Persius 34-62 .... **CMLC 74**
See also AW 2; DLB 211; RGWL 2, 3

Perutz, Leo(pold) 1882-1957 .... **TCLC 60**
See also CA 147; DLB 81

Peseenz, Tulio F.
See Lopez y Fuentes, Gregorio

Pesetsky, Bette 1932- .... **CLC 28**
See also CA 133; DLB 130

Peshkov, Alexei Maximovich 1868-1936
See Gorky, Maxim
See also CA 105; 141; CANR 83; DA;
DAC; DAM DRAM, MST, NOV; MTCW
2; MTFW 2005

Pessoa, Fernando (Antonio Nogueira)
1888-1935 ..... **HLC 2; PC 20; TCLC 27**
See also CA 125; 183; DAM MULT; DLB
287; EW 10; EWL 3; RGWL 2, 3; WP

Peterkin, Julia Mood 1880-1961 ...... **CLC 31**
See also CA 102; DLB 9

Peters, Joan K(aren) 1945- .... **CLC 39**
See also CA 158; CANR 109

Peters, Robert L(ouis) 1924- .... **CLC 7**
See also CA 13-16R; CAAS 8; CP 1, 7;
DLB 105

Petofi, Sandor 1823-1849 .... **NCLC 21**
See also RGWL 2, 3

Petrakis, Harry Mark 1923- .... **CLC 3**
See also CA 9-12R; CANR 4, 30, 85; CN
1, 2, 3, 4, 5, 6, 7

Petrarch 1304-1374 .... **CMLC 20; PC 8**
See also DA3; DAM POET; EW 2; LMFS
1; RGWL 2, 3; WLIT 7

Petronius c. 20-66 .... **CMLC 34**
See also AW 2; CDWLB 1; DLB 211;
RGWL 2, 3

Petrov, Evgeny .... **TCLC 21**
See Kataev, Evgeny Petrovich

Petry, Ann (Lane) 1908-1997 .. **CLC 1, 7, 18;
TCLC 112**
See also AFAW 1, 2; BPFB 3; BW 1, 3;
BYA 2; CA 5-8R; 157; CAAS 6; CANR
4, 46; CLR 12; CN 1, 2, 3, 4, 5, 6; DLB
76; EWL 3; JRDA; LAIT 1; MAICYA 1,
2; MAICYAS 1; MTCW 1; RGAL 4;
SATA 5; SATA-Obit 94; TUS

Petursson, Halligrimur 1614-1674 .... **LC 8**

Peychinovich
See Vazov, Ivan (Minchov)

Phaedrus c. 15B.C.-c. 50 .... **CMLC 25**
See also DLB 211

Phelps (Ward), Elizabeth Stuart
See Phelps, Elizabeth Stuart
See also FW

Phelps, Elizabeth Stuart
1844-1911 .... **TCLC 113**
See Phelps (Ward), Elizabeth Stuart
See also DLB 74

Philips, Katherine 1632-1664 . **LC 30; PC 40**
See also DLB 131; RGEL 2

Philipson, Morris H. 1926- .... **CLC 53**
See also CA 1-4R; CANR 4

Phillips, Caryl 1958- .... **BLCS; CLC 96**
See also BRWS 5; BW 2; CA 141; CANR
63, 104, 140; CBD; CD 5, 6; CN 5, 6, 7;
DA3; DAM MULT; DLB 157; EWL 3;
MTCW 2; MTFW 2005; WLIT 4; WWE
1

Phillips, David Graham
1867-1911 .... **TCLC 44**
See also CA 108; 176; DLB 9, 12, 303;
RGAL 4

Phillips, Jack
See Sandburg, Carl (August)

Phillips, Jayne Anne 1952- .... **CLC 15, 33,
139; SSC 16**
See also AAYA 57; BPFB 3; CA 101;
CANR 24, 50, 96; CN 4, 5, 6, 7; CSW;
DLBY 1980; INT CANR-24; MTCW 1,
2; MTFW 2005; RGAL 4; RGSF 2; SSFS
4

Phillips, Richard
See Dick, Philip K(indred)

Phillips, Robert (Schaeffer) 1938- .... **CLC 28**
See also CA 17-20R; CAAS 13; CANR 8;
DLB 105

Phillips, Ward
See Lovecraft, H(oward) P(hillips)

Philostratus, Flavius c. 179-c.
244 .... **CMLC 62**

Piccolo, Lucio 1901-1969 .... **CLC 13**
See also CA 97-100; DLB 114; EWL 3

Pickthall, Marjorie L(owry) C(hristie)
1883-1922 .... **TCLC 21**
See also CA 107; DLB 92

Pico della Mirandola, Giovanni
1463-1494 .... **LC 15**
See also LMFS 1

Piercy, Marge 1936- .... **CLC 3, 6, 14, 18, 27,
62, 128; PC 29**
See also BPFB 3; CA 21-24R, 187; CAAE
187; CAAS 1; CANR 13, 43, 66, 111; CN
3, 4, 5, 6, 7; CP 1, 2, 3, 4, 5, 6, 7; CWP;
DLB 120, 227; EXPP; FW; MAL 5;
MTCW 1, 2; MTFW 2005; PFS 9, 22;
SFW 4

Piers, Robert
See Anthony, Piers

Pieyre de Mandiargues, Andre 1909-1991
See Mandiargues, Andre Pieyre de
See also CA 103; 136; CANR 22, 82; EWL
3; GFL 1789 to the Present

Pilnyak, Boris 1894-1938 . **SSC 48; TCLC 23**
See Vogau, Boris Andreyevich
See also EWL 3

Pinchback, Eugene
See Toomer, Jean

Pincherle, Alberto 1907-1990 ...... **CLC 11, 18**
See Moravia, Alberto
See also CA 25-28R; 132; CANR 33, 63,
142; DAM NOV; MTCW 1; MTFW 2005

Pinckney, Darryl 1953- .... **CLC 76**
See also BW 2, 3; CA 143; CANR 79

Pindar 518(?)B.C.-438(?)B.C. .... **CMLC 12;
PC 19**
See also AW 1; CDWLB 1; DLB 176;
RGWL 2

Pineda, Cecile 1942- .... **CLC 39**
See also CA 118; DLB 209

Pinero, Arthur Wing 1855-1934 .... **TCLC 32**
See also CA 110; 153; DAM DRAM; DLB
10; RGEL 2

Pinero, Miguel (Antonio Gomez)
1946-1988 .... **CLC 4, 55**
See also CA 61-64; 125; CAD; CANR 29,
90; DLB 266; HW 1; LLW

Pinget, Robert 1919-1997 .... **CLC 7, 13, 37**
See also CA 85-88; 160; CWW 2; DLB 83;
EWL 3; GFL 1789 to the Present

Pink Floyd
See Barrett, (Roger) Syd; Gilmour, David;
Mason, Nick; Waters, Roger; Wright, Rick

Pinkney, Edward 1802-1828 .... **NCLC 31**
See also DLB 248

Pinkwater, D. Manus
See Pinkwater, Daniel Manus

Pinkwater, Daniel
See Pinkwater, Daniel Manus

Pinkwater, Daniel M.
See Pinkwater, Daniel Manus

Pinkwater, Daniel Manus 1941- .... **CLC 35**
See also AAYA 1, 46; BYA 9; CA 29-32R;
CANR 12, 38, 89, 143; CLR 4; CSW;
FANT; JRDA; MAICYA 1, 2; SAAS 3;
SATA 8, 46, 76, 114, 158; SFW 4; YAW

Pinkwater, Manus
See Pinkwater, Daniel Manus

DLBY 1980; EWL 3; EXPS; LAIT 3; MAL 5; MAWW; MTCW 1, 2; MTFW 2005; NFS 14; RGAL 4; RGSF 2; SATA 39; SATA-Obit 23; SSFS 1, 8, 11, 16; TCWW 2; TUS

Porter, Peter (Neville Frederick)
1929- .... **CLC 5, 13, 33**
See also CA 85-88; CP 1, 2, 3, 4, 5, 6, 7; DLB 40, 289; WWE 1

Porter, William Sydney 1862-1910
See Henry, O.
See also CA 104; 131; CDALB 1865-1917; DA; DA3; DAB; DAC; DAM MST; DLB 12, 78, 79; MAL 5; MTCW 1, 2; MTFW 2005; TUS; YABC 2

Portillo (y Pacheco), Jose Lopez
See Lopez Portillo (y Pacheco), Jose

Portillo Trambley, Estela 1927-1998 .. **HLC 2**
See Trambley, Estela Portillo
See also CANR 32; DAM MULT; DLB 209; HW 1

Posey, Alexander (Lawrence)
1873-1908 .... **NNAL**
See also CA 144; CANR 80; DAM MULT; DLB 175

Posse, Abel .... **CLC 70**

Post, Melville Davisson
1869-1930 .... **TCLC 39**
See also CA 110; 202; CMW 4

Potok, Chaim 1929-2002 ... **CLC 2, 7, 14, 26, 112**
See also AAYA 15, 50; AITN 1, 2; BPFB 3; BYA 1; CA 17-20R; 208; CANR 19, 35, 64, 98; CLR 92; CN 4, 5, 6; DA3; DAM NOV; DLB 28, 152; EXPN; INT CANR-19; LAIT 4; MTCW 1, 2; MTFW 2005; NFS 4; SATA 33, 106; SATA-Obit 134; TUS; YAW

Potok, Herbert Harold -2002
See Potok, Chaim

Potok, Herman Harold
See Potok, Chaim

Potter, Dennis (Christopher George)
1935-1994 .... **CLC 58, 86, 123**
See also BRWS 10; CA 107; 145; CANR 33, 61; CBD; DLB 233; MTCW 1

Pound, Ezra (Weston Loomis)
1885-1972 .. **CLC 1, 2, 3, 4, 5, 7, 10, 13, 18, 34, 48, 50, 112; PC 4; WLC**
See also AAYA 47; AMW; AMWR 1; CA 5-8R; 37-40R; CANR 40; CDALB 1917-1929; CP 1; DA; DA3; DAB; DAC; DAM MST, POET; DLB 4, 45, 63; DLBD 15; EFS 2; EWL 3; EXPP; LMFS 2; MAL 5; MTCW 1, 2; MTFW 2005; PAB; PFS 2, 8, 16; RGAL 4; TUS; WP

Povod, Reinaldo 1959-1994 .... **CLC 44**
See also CA 136; 146; CANR 83

Powell, Adam Clayton, Jr.
1908-1972 .... **BLC 3; CLC 89**
See also BW 1, 3; CA 102; 33-36R; CANR 86; DAM MULT

Powell, Anthony (Dymoke)
1905-2000 .... **CLC 1, 3, 7, 9, 10, 31**
See also BRW 7; CA 1-4R; 189; CANR 1, 32, 62, 107; CDBLB 1945-1960; CN 1, 2, 3, 4, 5, 6; DLB 15; EWL 3; MTCW 1, 2; MTFW 2005; RGEL 2; TEA

Powell, Dawn 1896(?)-1965 .... **CLC 66**
See also CA 5-8R; CANR 121; DLBY 1997

Powell, Padgett 1952- .... **CLC 34**
See also CA 126; CANR 63, 101; CSW; DLB 234; DLBY 01

Powell, (Oval) Talmage 1920-2000
See Queen, Ellery
See also CA 5-8R; CANR 2, 80

Power, Susan 1961- .... **CLC 91**
See also BYA 14; CA 160; CANR 135; NFS 11

Powers, J(ames) F(arl) 1917-1999 ..... **CLC 1, 4, 8, 57; SSC 4**
See also CA 1-4R; 181; CANR 2, 61; CN 1, 2, 3, 4, 5, 6; DLB 130; MTCW 1; RGAL 4; RGSF 2

Powers, John J(ames) 1945-
See Powers, John R.
See also CA 69-72

Powers, John R. .... **CLC 66**
See Powers, John J(ames)

Powers, Richard (S.) 1957- .... **CLC 93**
See also AMWS 9; BPFB 3; CA 148; CANR 80; CN 6, 7; MTFW 2005; TCLE 1:2

Pownall, David 1938- .... **CLC 10**
See also CA 89-92, 180; CAAS 18; CANR 49, 101; CBD; CD 5, 6; CN 4, 5, 6, 7; DLB 14

Powys, John Cowper 1872-1963 ... **CLC 7, 9, 15, 46, 125**
See also CA 85-88; CANR 106; DLB 15, 255; EWL 3; FANT; MTCW 1, 2; MTFW 2005; RGEL 2; SUFW

Powys, T(heodore) F(rancis)
1875-1953 .... **TCLC 9**
See also BRWS 8; CA 106; 189; DLB 36, 162; EWL 3; FANT; RGEL 2; SUFW

Pozzo, Modesta
See Fonte, Moderata

Prado (Calvo), Pedro 1886-1952 ... **TCLC 75**
See also CA 131; DLB 283; HW 1; LAW

Prager, Emily 1952- .... **CLC 56**
See also CA 204

Pratchett, Terry 1948- .... **CLC 197**
See also AAYA 19, 54; BPFB 3; CA 143; CANR 87, 126; CLR 64; CN 6, 7; CPW; CWRI 5; FANT; MTFW 2005; SATA 82, 139; SFW 4; SUFW 2

Pratolini, Vasco 1913-1991 .... **TCLC 124**
See also CA 211; DLB 177; EWL 3; RGWL 2, 3

Pratt, E(dwin) J(ohn) 1883(?)-1964 . **CLC 19**
See also CA 141; 93-96; CANR 77; DAC; DAM POET; DLB 92; EWL 3; RGEL 2; TWA

Premchand .... **TCLC 21**
See Srivastava, Dhanpat Rai
See also EWL 3

Prescott, William Hickling
1796-1859 .... **NCLC 163**
See also DLB 1, 30, 59, 235

Preseren, France 1800-1849 .... **NCLC 127**
See also CDWLB 4; DLB 147

Preussler, Otfried 1923- .... **CLC 17**
See also CA 77-80; SATA 24

Prevert, Jacques (Henri Marie)
1900-1977 .... **CLC 15**
See also CA 77-80; 69-72; CANR 29, 61; DLB 258; EWL 3; GFL 1789 to the Present; IDFW 3, 4; MTCW 1; RGWL 2, 3; SATA-Obit 30

Prevost, (Antoine Francois)
1697-1763 .... **LC 1**
See also DLB 314; EW 4; GFL Beginnings to 1789; RGWL 2, 3

Price, (Edward) Reynolds 1933- ... **CLC 3, 6, 13, 43, 50, 63, 212; SSC 22**
See also AMWS 6; CA 1-4R; CANR 1, 37, 57, 87, 128; CN 1, 2, 3, 4, 5, 6, 7; CSW; DAM NOV; DLB 2, 218, 278; EWL 3; INT CANR-37; MAL 5; MTCW 2005; NFS 18

Price, Richard 1949- .... **CLC 6, 12**
See also CA 49-52; CANR 3; CN 7; DLBY 1981

Prichard, Katharine Susannah
1883-1969 .... **CLC 46**
See also CA 11-12; CANR 33; CAP 1; DLB 260; MTCW 1; RGEL 2; RGSF 2; SATA 66

Priestley, J(ohn) B(oynton)
1894-1984 .... **CLC 2, 5, 9, 34**
See also BRW 7; CA 9-12R; 113; CANR 33; CDBLB 1914-1945; CN 1, 2, 3; DAM DRAM, NOV; DLB 10, 34, 77, 100, 139; DLBY 1984; EWL 3; MTCW 1, 2; MTFW 2005; RGEL 2; SFW 4

Prince 1958- .... **CLC 35**
See also CA 213

Prince, F(rank) T(empleton)
1912-2003 .... **CLC 22**
See also CA 101; 219; CANR 43, 79; CP 1, 2, 3, 4, 5, 6, 7; DLB 20

Prince Kropotkin
See Kropotkin, Peter (Aleksieevich)

Prior, Matthew 1664-1721 .... **LC 4**
See also DLB 95; RGEL 2

Prishvin, Mikhail 1873-1954 .... **TCLC 75**
See Prishvin, Mikhail Mikhailovich

Prishvin, Mikhail Mikhailovich
See Prishvin, Mikhail
See also DLB 272; EWL 3

Pritchard, William H(arrison)
1932- .... **CLC 34**
See also CA 65-68; CANR 23, 95; DLB 111

Pritchett, V(ictor) S(awdon)
1900-1997 ... **CLC 5, 13, 15, 41; SSC 14**
See also BPFB 3; BRWS 3; CA 61-64; 157; CANR 31, 63; CN 1, 2, 3, 4, 5, 6; DA3; DAM NOV; DLB 15, 139; EWL 3; MTCW 1, 2; MTFW 2005; RGEL 2; RGSF 2; TEA

Private 19022
See Manning, Frederic

Probst, Mark 1925- .... **CLC 59**
See also CA 130

Procaccino, Michael
See Cristofer, Michael

Proclus c. 412-485 .... **CMLC 81**

Prokosch, Frederic 1908-1989 ...... **CLC 4, 48**
See also CA 73-76; 128; CANR 82; CN 1, 2, 3, 4; CP 1, 2, 3, 4; DLB 48; MTCW 2

Propertius, Sextus c. 50B.C.-c. 16B.C. .... **CMLC 32**
See also AW 2; CDWLB 1; DLB 211; RGWL 2, 3

Prophet, The
See Dreiser, Theodore (Herman Albert)

Prose, Francine 1947- .... **CLC 45**
See also CA 109; 112; CANR 46, 95, 132; DLB 234; MTFW 2005; SATA 101, 149

Proudhon
See Cunha, Euclides (Rodrigues Pimenta) da

Proulx, Annie
See Proulx, E. Annie

Proulx, E. Annie 1935- .... **CLC 81, 158**
See also AMWS 7; BPFB 3; CA 145; CANR 65, 110; CN 6, 7; CPW 1; DA3; DAM POP; MAL 5; MTFW 2005; SSFS 18

Proulx, Edna Annie
See Proulx, E. Annie

Proust, (Valentin-Louis-George-Eugene) Marcel 1871-1922 ..... **SSC 75; TCLC 7, 13, 33; WLC**
See also AAYA 58; BPFB 3; CA 104; 120; CANR 110; DA; DA3; DAB; DAC; DAM MST, NOV; DLB 65; EW 8; EWL 3; GFL 1789 to the Present; MTCW 1, 2; MTFW 2005; RGWL 2, 3; TWA

Prowler, Harley
See Masters, Edgar Lee

Prudentius, Aurelius Clemens 348-c.
405 .... **CMLC 78**
See also EW 1; RGWL 2, 3

Prus, Boleslaw 1845-1912 .... **TCLC 48**
See also RGWL 2, 3

Pryor, Richard (Franklin Lenox Thomas)
1940-2005 .... **CLC 26**
See also CA 122; 152

Przybyszewski, Stanislaw
1868-1927 .... **TCLC 36**
See also CA 160; DLB 66; EWL 3

Pteleon
See Grieve, C(hristopher) M(urray)
See also DAM POET

Puckett, Lute
See Masters, Edgar Lee

Puig, Manuel 1932-1990 .... **CLC 3, 5, 10, 28, 65, 133; HLC 2**
See also BPFB 3; CA 45-48; CANR 2, 32, 63; CDWLB 3; DA3; DAM MULT; DLB 113; DNFS 1; EWL 3; GLL 1; HW 1, 2; LAW; MTCW 1, 2; MTFW 2005; RGWL 2, 3; TWA; WLIT 1

Pulitzer, Joseph 1847-1911 .... **TCLC 76**
See also CA 114; DLB 23

Purchas, Samuel 1577(?)-1626 .... **LC 70**
See also DLB 151

Purdy, A(lfred) W(ellington)
1918-2000 .... **CLC 3, 6, 14, 50**
See also CA 81-84; 189; CAAS 17; CANR 42, 66; CP 1, 2, 3, 4, 5, 6, 7; DAC; DAM MST, POET; DLB 88; PFS 5; RGEL 2

Purdy, James (Amos) 1923- .... **CLC 2, 4, 10, 28, 52**
See also AMWS 7; CA 33-36R; CAAS 1; CANR 19, 51, 132; CN 1, 2, 3, 4, 5, 6, 7; DLB 2, 218; EWL 3; INT CANR-19; MAL 5; MTCW 1; RGAL 4

Pure, Simon
See Swinnerton, Frank Arthur

Pushkin, Aleksandr Sergeevich
See Pushkin, Alexander (Sergeyevich)
See also DLB 205

Pushkin, Alexander (Sergeyevich)
1799-1837 .... **NCLC 3, 27, 83; PC 10; SSC 27, 55; WLC**
See Pushkin, Aleksandr Sergeevich
See also DA; DA3; DAB; DAC; DAM DRAM, MST, POET; EW 5; EXPS; RGSF 2; RGWL 2, 3; SATA 61; SSFS 9; TWA

P'u Sung-ling 1640-1715 .... **LC 49; SSC 31**

Putnam, Arthur Lee
See Alger, Horatio, Jr.

Puttenham, George 1529(?)-1590 ...... **LC 116**
See also DLB 281

Puzo, Mario 1920-1999 .... **CLC 1, 2, 6, 36, 107**
See also BPFB 3; CA 65-68; 185; CANR 4, 42, 65, 99, 131; CN 1, 2, 3, 4, 5, 6; CPW; DA3; DAM NOV, POP; DLB 6; MTCW 1, 2; MTFW 2005; NFS 16; RGAL 4

Pygge, Edward
See Barnes, Julian (Patrick)

Pyle, Ernest Taylor 1900-1945
See Pyle, Ernie
See also CA 115; 160

Pyle, Ernie .... **TCLC 75**
See Pyle, Ernest Taylor
See also DLB 29; MTCW 2

Pyle, Howard 1853-1911 .... **TCLC 81**
See also AAYA 57; BYA 2, 4; CA 109; 137; CLR 22; DLB 42, 188; DLBD 13; LAIT 1; MAICYA 1, 2; SATA 16, 100; WCH; YAW

Pym, Barbara (Mary Crampton)
1913-1980 .... **CLC 13, 19, 37, 111**
See also BPFB 3; BRWS 2; CA 13-14; 97-100; CANR 13, 34; CAP 1; DLB 14, 207; DLBY 1987; EWL 3; MTCW 1, 2; MTFW 2005; RGEL 2; TEA

Pynchon, Thomas (Ruggles, Jr.)
1937- ...... **CLC 2, 3, 6, 9, 11, 18, 33, 62, 72, 123, 192, 213; SSC 14, 84; WLC**
See also AMWS 2; BEST 90:2; BPFB 3; CA 17-20R; CANR 22, 46, 73, 142; CN 1, 2, 3, 4, 5, 6, 7; CPW 1; DA; DA3; DAB; DAC; DAM MST, NOV, POP; DLB 2, 173; EWL 3; MAL 5; MTCW 1, 2; MTFW 2005; RGAL 4; SFW 4; TCLE 1:2; TUS

Pythagoras c. 582B.C.-c. 507B.C. . **CMLC 22**
See also DLB 176

Q
See Quiller-Couch, Sir Arthur (Thomas)

Qian, Chongzhu
See Ch'ien, Chung-shu

Qian, Sima 145B.C.-c. 89B.C. .... **CMLC 72**

Qian Zhongshu
See Ch'ien, Chung-shu
See also CWW 2

Qroll
See Dagerman, Stig (Halvard)

Quarles, Francis 1592-1644 .... **LC 117**
See also DLB 126; RGEL 2

Quarrington, Paul (Lewis) 1953- ..... **CLC 65**
See also CA 129; CANR 62, 95

Quasimodo, Salvatore 1901-1968 .... **CLC 10; PC 47**
See also CA 13-16; 25-28R; CAP 1; DLB 114; EW 12; EWL 3; MTCW 1; RGWL 2, 3

Quatermass, Martin
See Carpenter, John (Howard)

Quay, Stephen 1947- .... **CLC 95**
See also CA 189

Quay, Timothy 1947- .... **CLC 95**
See also CA 189

Queen, Ellery .... **CLC 3, 11**
See Dannay, Frederic; Davidson, Avram (James); Deming, Richard; Fairman, Paul W.; Flora, Fletcher; Hoch, Edward D(entinger); Kane, Henry; Lee, Manfred B(ennington); Marlowe, Stephen; Powell, (Oval) Talmage; Sheldon, Walter J(ames); Sturgeon, Theodore (Hamilton); Tracy, Don(ald Fiske); Vance, John Holbrook
See also BPFB 3; CMW 4; MSW; RGAL 4

Queen, Ellery, Jr.
See Dannay, Frederic; Lee, Manfred B(ennington)

Queneau, Raymond 1903-1976 ..... **CLC 2, 5, 10, 42**
See also CA 77-80; 69-72; CANR 32; DLB 72, 258; EW 12; EWL 3; GFL 1789 to the Present; MTCW 1, 2; RGWL 2, 3

Quevedo, Francisco de 1580-1645 .... **LC 23**

Quiller-Couch, Sir Arthur (Thomas)
1863-1944 .... **TCLC 53**
See also CA 118; 166; DLB 135, 153, 190; HGG; RGEL 2; SUFW 1

Quin, Ann (Marie) 1936-1973 .... **CLC 6**
See also CA 9-12R; 45-48; CN 1; DLB 14, 231

Quincey, Thomas de
See De Quincey, Thomas

Quindlen, Anna 1953- .... **CLC 191**
See also AAYA 35; CA 138; CANR 73, 126; DA3; DLB 292; MTCW 2; MTFW 2005

Quinn, Martin
See Smith, Martin Cruz

Quinn, Peter 1947- .... **CLC 91**
See also CA 197

Quinn, Simon
See Smith, Martin Cruz

Quintana, Leroy V. 1944- ...... **HLC 2; PC 36**
See also CA 131; CANR 65, 139; DAM MULT; DLB 82; HW 1, 2

Quintilian c. 40-c. 100 .... **CMLC 77**
See also AW 2; DLB 211; RGWL 2, 3

Quintillian 0035-0100 .... **CMLC 77**

Quiroga, Horacio (Sylvestre)
1878-1937 ... **HLC 2; SSC 89; TCLC 20**
See also CA 117; 131; DAM MULT; EWL 3; HW 1; LAW; MTCW 1; RGSF 2; WLIT 1

Quoirez, Francoise 1935-2004 .... **CLC 9**
See Sagan, Francoise
See also CA 49-52; 231; CANR 6, 39, 73; MTCW 1, 2; MTFW 2005; TWA

Raabe, Wilhelm (Karl) 1831-1910 . **TCLC 45**
See also CA 167; DLB 129

Rabe, David (William) 1940- .. **CLC 4, 8, 33, 200; DC 16**
See also CA 85-88; CABS 3; CAD; CANR 59, 129; CD 5, 6; DAM DRAM; DFS 3, 8, 13; DLB 7, 228; EWL 3; MAL 5

Rabelais, Francois 1494-1553 .... **LC 5, 60; WLC**
See also DA; DAB; DAC; DAM MST; EW 2; GFL Beginnings to 1789; LMFS 1; RGWL 2, 3; TWA

Rabinovitch, Sholem 1859-1916
See Aleichem, Sholom
See also CA 104

Rabinyan, Dorit 1972- .... **CLC 119**
See also CA 170

Rachilde
See Vallette, Marguerite Eymery; Vallette, Marguerite Eymery
See also EWL 3

Racine, Jean 1639-1699 .... **LC 28, 113**
See also DA3; DAB; DAM MST; DLB 268; EW 3; GFL Beginnings to 1789; LMFS 1; RGWL 2, 3; TWA

Radcliffe, Ann (Ward) 1764-1823 ... **NCLC 6, 55, 106**
See also DLB 39, 178; GL 3; HGG; LMFS 1; RGEL 2; SUFW 1; WLIT 3

Radclyffe-Hall, Marguerite
See Hall, (Marguerite) Radclyffe

Radiguet, Raymond 1903-1923 ...... **TCLC 29**
See also CA 162; DLB 65; EWL 3; GFL 1789 to the Present; RGWL 2, 3

Radnoti, Miklos 1909-1944 .... **TCLC 16**
See also CA 118; 212; CDWLB 4; DLB 215; EWL 3; RGWL 2, 3

Rado, James 1939- .... **CLC 17**
See also CA 105

Radvanyi, Netty 1900-1983
See Seghers, Anna
See also CA 85-88; 110; CANR 82

Rae, Ben
See Griffiths, Trevor

Raeburn, John (Hay) 1941- .... **CLC 34**
See also CA 57-60

Ragni, Gerome 1942-1991 .... **CLC 17**
See also CA 105; 134

Rahv, Philip .... **CLC 24**
See Greenberg, Ivan
See also DLB 137; MAL 5

Raimund, Ferdinand Jakob
1790-1836 .... **NCLC 69**
See also DLB 90

Raine, Craig (Anthony) 1944- .. **CLC 32, 103**
See also CA 108; CANR 29, 51, 103; CP 3, 4, 5, 6, 7; DLB 40; PFS 7

Raine, Kathleen (Jessie) 1908-2003 .. **CLC 7, 45**
See also CA 85-88; 218; CANR 46, 109; CP 1, 2, 3, 4, 5, 6, 7; DLB 20; EWL 3; MTCW 1; RGEL 2

Rainis, Janis 1865-1929 .... **TCLC 29**
See also CA 170; CDWLB 4; DLB 220; EWL 3

Rakosi, Carl .... **CLC 47**
See Rawley, Callman
See also CA 228; CAAS 5; CP 1, 2, 3, 4, 5, 6, 7; DLB 193

Ralegh, Sir Walter
See Raleigh, Sir Walter
See also BRW 1; RGEL 2; WP

Raleigh, Richard
See Lovecraft, H(oward) P(hillips)

Raleigh, Sir Walter 1554(?)-1618 .... **LC 31, 39; PC 31**
See Ralegh, Sir Walter
See also CDBLB Before 1660; DLB 172; EXPP; PFS 14; TEA

Rallentando, H. P.
See Sayers, Dorothy L(eigh)

Ramal, Walter
See de la Mare, Walter (John)

Ramana Maharshi 1879-1950 .... **TCLC 84**

Ramoacn y Cajal, Santiago 1852-1934 .... **TCLC 93**

Ramon, Juan
See Jimenez (Mantecon), Juan Ramon

Ramos, Graciliano 1892-1953 .... **TCLC 32**
See also CA 167; DLB 307; EWL 3; HW 2; LAW; WLIT 1

Rampersad, Arnold 1941- .... **CLC 44**
See also BW 2, 3; CA 127; 133; CANR 81; DLB 111; INT CA-133

Rampling, Anne
See Rice, Anne
See also GLL 2

Ramsay, Allan 1686(?)-1758 .... **LC 29**
See also DLB 95; RGEL 2

Ramsay, Jay
See Campbell, (John) Ramsey

Ramuz, Charles-Ferdinand 1878-1947 .... **TCLC 33**
See also CA 165; EWL 3

Rand, Ayn 1905-1982 ...... **CLC 3, 30, 44, 79; WLC**
See also AAYA 10; AMWS 4; BPFB 3; BYA 12; CA 13-16R; 105; CANR 27, 73; CDALBS; CN 1, 2, 3; CPW; DA; DA3; DAC; DAM MST, NOV, POP; DLB 227, 279; MTCW 1, 2; MTFW 2005; NFS 10, 16; RGAL 4; SFW 4; TUS; YAW

Randall, Dudley (Felker) 1914-2000 . **BLC 3; CLC 1, 135**
See also BW 1, 3; CA 25-28R; 189; CANR 23, 82; CP 1, 2, 3, 4; DAM MULT; DLB 41; PFS 5

Randall, Robert
See Silverberg, Robert

Ranger, Ken
See Creasey, John

Rank, Otto 1884-1939 .... **TCLC 115**

Ransom, John Crowe 1888-1974 .. **CLC 2, 4, 5, 11, 24; PC 61**
See also AMW; CA 5-8R; 49-52; CANR 6, 34; CDALBS; CP 1, 2; DA3; DAM POET; DLB 45, 63; EWL 3; EXPP; MAL 5; MTCW 1, 2; MTFW 2005; RGAL 4; TUS

Rao, Raja 1909- .... **CLC 25, 56**
See also CA 73-76; CANR 51; CN 1, 2, 3, 4, 5, 6; DAM NOV; EWL 3; MTCW 1, 2; MTFW 2005; RGEL 2; RGSF 2

Raphael, Frederic (Michael) 1931- ... **CLC 2, 14**
See also CA 1-4R; CANR 1, 86; CN 1, 2, 3, 4, 5, 6, 7; DLB 14, 319; TCLE 1:2

Ratcliffe, James P.
See Mencken, H(enry) L(ouis)

Rathbone, Julian 1935- .... **CLC 41**
See also CA 101; CANR 34, 73

Rattigan, Terence (Mervyn) 1911-1977 .... **CLC 7; DC 18**
See also BRWS 7; CA 85-88; 73-76; CBD; CDBLB 1945-1960; DAM DRAM; DFS 8; DLB 13; IDFW 3, 4; MTCW 1, 2; MTFW 2005; RGEL 2

Ratushinskaya, Irina 1954- .... **CLC 54**
See also CA 129; CANR 68; CWW 2

Raven, Simon (Arthur Noel) 1927-2001 .... **CLC 14**
See also CA 81-84; 197; CANR 86; CN 1, 2, 3, 4, 5, 6; DLB 271

Ravenna, Michael
See Welty, Eudora (Alice)

Rawley, Callman 1903-2004
See Rakosi, Carl
See also CA 21-24R; 228; CANR 12, 32, 91

Rawlings, Marjorie Kinnan 1896-1953 .... **TCLC 4**
See also AAYA 20; AMWS 10; ANW; BPFB 3; BYA 3; CA 104; 137; CANR 74; CLR 63; DLB 9, 22, 102; DLBD 17; JRDA; MAICYA 1, 2; MAL 5; MTCW 2; MTFW 2005; RGAL 4; SATA 100; WCH; YABC 1; YAW

Ray, Satyajit 1921-1992 .... **CLC 16, 76**
See also CA 114; 137; DAM MULT

Read, Herbert Edward 1893-1968 ..... **CLC 4**
See also BRW 6; CA 85-88; 25-28R; DLB 20, 149; EWL 3; PAB; RGEL 2

Read, Piers Paul 1941- .... **CLC 4, 10, 25**
See also CA 21-24R; CANR 38, 86; CN 2, 3, 4, 5, 6, 7; DLB 14; SATA 21

Reade, Charles 1814-1884 .... **NCLC 2, 74**
See also DLB 21; RGEL 2

Reade, Hamish
See Gray, Simon (James Holliday)

Reading, Peter 1946- .... **CLC 47**
See also BRWS 8; CA 103; CANR 46, 96; CP 7; DLB 40

Reaney, James 1926- .... **CLC 13**
See also CA 41-44R; CAAS 15; CANR 42; CD 5, 6; CP 1, 2, 3, 4, 5, 6, 7; DAC; DAM MST; DLB 68; RGEL 2; SATA 43

Rebreanu, Liviu 1885-1944 .... **TCLC 28**
See also CA 165; DLB 220; EWL 3

Rechy, John (Francisco) 1934- ...... **CLC 1, 7, 14, 18, 107; HLC 2**
See also CA 5-8R, 195; CAAE 195; CAAS 4; CANR 6, 32, 64; CN 1, 2, 3, 4, 5, 6, 7; DAM MULT; DLB 122, 278; DLBY 1982; HW 1, 2; INT CANR-6; LLW; MAL 5; RGAL 4

Redcam, Tom 1870-1933 .... **TCLC 25**

Reddin, Keith 1956- .... **CLC 67**
See also CAD; CD 6

Redgrove, Peter (William) 1932-2003 .... **CLC 6, 41**
See also BRWS 6; CA 1-4R; 217; CANR 3, 39, 77; CP 1, 2, 3, 4, 5, 6, 7; DLB 40; TCLE 1:2

Redmon, Anne .... **CLC 22**
See Nightingale, Anne Redmon
See also DLBY 1986

Reed, Eliot
See Ambler, Eric

Reed, Ishmael (Scott) 1938- . **BLC 3; CLC 2, 3, 5, 6, 13, 32, 60, 174; PC 68**
See also AFAW 1, 2; AMWS 10; BPFB 3; BW 2, 3; CA 21-24R; CANR 25, 48, 74, 128; CN 1, 2, 3, 4, 5, 6, 7; CP 1, 2, 3, 4, 5, 6, 7; CSW; DA3; DAM MULT; DLB 2, 5, 33, 169, 227; DLBD 8; EWL 3; LMFS 2; MAL 5; MSW; MTCW 1, 2; MTFW 2005; PFS 6; RGAL 4; TCWW 2

Reed, John (Silas) 1887-1920 .... **TCLC 9**
See also CA 106; 195; MAL 5; TUS

Reed, Lou .... **CLC 21**
See Firbank, Louis

Reese, Lizette Woodworth 1856-1935 . **PC 29**
See also CA 180; DLB 54

Reeve, Clara 1729-1807 .... **NCLC 19**
See also DLB 39; RGEL 2

Reich, Wilhelm 1897-1957 .... **TCLC 57**
See also CA 199

Reid, Christopher (John) 1949- .... **CLC 33**
See also CA 140; CANR 89; CP 4, 5, 6, 7; DLB 40; EWL 3

Reid, Desmond
See Moorcock, Michael (John)

Reid Banks, Lynne 1929-
See Banks, Lynne Reid
See also AAYA 49; CA 1-4R; CANR 6, 22, 38, 87; CLR 24; CN 1, 2, 3, 7; JRDA; MAICYA 1, 2; SATA 22, 75, 111, 165; YAW

Reilly, William K.
See Creasey, John

Reiner, Max
See Caldwell, (Janet Miriam) Taylor (Holland)

Reis, Ricardo
See Pessoa, Fernando (Antonio Nogueira)

Reizenstein, Elmer Leopold
See Rice, Elmer (Leopold)
See also EWL 3

Remarque, Erich Maria 1898-1970 . **CLC 21**
See also AAYA 27; BPFB 3; CA 77-80; 29-32R; CDWLB 2; DA; DA3; DAB; DAC; DAM MST, NOV; DLB 56; EWL 3; EXPN; LAIT 3; MTCW 1, 2; MTFW 2005; NFS 4; RGWL 2, 3

Remington, Frederic S(ackrider) 1861-1909 .... **TCLC 89**
See also CA 108; 169; DLB 12, 186, 188; SATA 41; TCWW 2

Remizov, A.
See Remizov, Aleksei (Mikhailovich)

Remizov, A. M.
See Remizov, Aleksei (Mikhailovich)

Remizov, Aleksei (Mikhailovich) 1877-1957 .... **TCLC 27**
See Remizov, Alexey Mikhaylovich
See also CA 125; 133; DLB 295

Remizov, Alexey Mikhaylovich
See Remizov, Aleksei (Mikhailovich)
See also EWL 3

Renan, Joseph Ernest 1823-1892 . **NCLC 26, 145**
See also GFL 1789 to the Present

Renard, Jules(-Pierre) 1864-1910 .. **TCLC 17**
See also CA 117; 202; GFL 1789 to the Present

Renault, Mary .... **CLC 3, 11, 17**
See Challans, Mary
See also BPFB 3; BYA 2; CN 1, 2, 3; DLBY 1983; EWL 3; GLL 1; LAIT 1; RGEL 2; RHW

Rendell, Ruth (Barbara) 1930- .. **CLC 28, 48**
See Vine, Barbara
See also BPFB 3; BRWS 9; CA 109; CANR 32, 52, 74, 127; CN 5, 6, 7; CPW; DAM POP; DLB 87, 276; INT CANR-32; MSW; MTCW 1, 2; MTFW 2005

Renoir, Jean 1894-1979 .... **CLC 20**
See also CA 129; 85-88

Resnais, Alain 1922- .... **CLC 16**

Revard, Carter (Curtis) 1931- .... **NNAL**
See also CA 144; CANR 81; PFS 5

Reverdy, Pierre 1889-1960 .... **CLC 53**
See also CA 97-100; 89-92; DLB 258; EWL 3; GFL 1789 to the Present

Rexroth, Kenneth 1905-1982 .... **CLC 1, 2, 6, 11, 22, 49, 112; PC 20**
See also BG 1:3; CA 5-8R; 107; CANR 14, 34, 63; CDALB 1941-1968; CP 1, 2, 3; DAM POET; DLB 16, 48, 165, 212; DLBY 1982; EWL 3; INT CANR-14; MAL 5; MTCW 1, 2; MTFW 2005; RGAL 4

Reyes, Alfonso 1889-1959 .... **HLCS 2; TCLC 33**
See also CA 131; EWL 3; HW 1; LAW

Robbins, Tom .... CLC 9, 32, 64
  See Robbins, Thomas Eugene
  See also AAYA 32; AMWS 10; BEST 90:3;
  BPFB 3; CN 3, 4, 5, 6, 7; DLBY 1980
Robbins, Trina 1938- .... CLC 21
  See also AAYA 61; CA 128
Roberts, Charles G(eorge) D(ouglas)
  1860-1943 .... TCLC 8
  See also CA 105; 188; CLR 33; CWRI 5;
  DLB 92; RGEL 2; RGSF 2; SATA 88;
  SATA-Brief 29
Roberts, Elizabeth Madox
  1886-1941 .... TCLC 68
  See also CA 111; 166; CLR 100; CWRI 5;
  DLB 9, 54, 102; RGAL 4; RHW; SATA
  33; SATA-Brief 27; TCWW 2; WCH
Roberts, Kate 1891-1985 .... CLC 15
  See also CA 107; 116; DLB 319
Roberts, Keith (John Kingston)
  1935-2000 .... CLC 14
  See also BRWS 10; CA 25-28R; CANR 46;
  DLB 261; SFW 4
Roberts, Kenneth (Lewis)
  1885-1957 .... TCLC 23
  See also CA 109; 199; DLB 9; MAL 5;
  RGAL 4; RHW
Roberts, Michele (Brigitte) 1949- .... CLC 48,
  178
  See also CA 115; CANR 58, 120; CN 6, 7;
  DLB 231; FW
Robertson, Ellis
  See Ellison, Harlan (Jay); Silverberg, Robert
Robertson, Thomas William
  1829-1871 .... NCLC 35
  See Robertson, Tom
  See also DAM DRAM
Robertson, Tom
  See Robertson, Thomas William
  See also RGEL 2
Robeson, Kenneth
  See Dent, Lester
Robinson, Edwin Arlington
  1869-1935 .... PC 1, 35; TCLC 5, 101
  See also AMW; CA 104; 133; CDALB
  1865-1917; DA; DAC; DAM MST,
  POET; DLB 54; EWL 3; EXPP; MAL 5;
  MTCW 1, 2; MTFW 2005; PAB; PFS 4;
  RGAL 4; WP
Robinson, Henry Crabb
  1775-1867 .... NCLC 15
  See also DLB 107
Robinson, Jill 1936- .... CLC 10
  See also CA 102; CANR 120; INT CA-102
Robinson, Kim Stanley 1952- .... CLC 34
  See also AAYA 26; CA 126; CANR 113,
  139; CN 6, 7; MTFW 2005; SATA 109;
  SCFW 2; SFW 4
Robinson, Lloyd
  See Silverberg, Robert
Robinson, Marilynne 1944- ...... CLC 25, 180
  See also CA 116; CANR 80, 140; CN 4, 5,
  6, 7; DLB 206; MTFW 2005
Robinson, Mary 1758-1800 .... NCLC 142
  See also DLB 158; FW
Robinson, Smokey .... CLC 21
  See Robinson, William, Jr.
Robinson, William, Jr. 1940-
  See Robinson, Smokey
  See also CA 116
Robison, Mary 1949- .... CLC 42, 98
  See also CA 113; 116; CANR 87; CN 4, 5,
  6, 7; DLB 130; INT CA-116; RGSF 2
Roches, Catherine des 1542-1587 ...... LC 117
Rochester
  See Wilmot, John
  See also RGEL 2

Rod, Edouard 1857-1910 .... TCLC 52
Roddenberry, Eugene Wesley 1921-1991
  See Roddenberry, Gene
  See also CA 110; 135; CANR 37; SATA 45;
  SATA-Obit 69
Roddenberry, Gene .... CLC 17
  See Roddenberry, Eugene Wesley
  See also AAYA 5; SATA-Obit 69
Rodgers, Mary 1931- .... CLC 12
  See also BYA 5; CA 49-52; CANR 8, 55,
  90; CLR 20; CWRI 5; INT CANR-8;
  JRDA; MAICYA 1, 2; SATA 8, 130
Rodgers, W(illiam) R(obert)
  1909-1969 .... CLC 7
  See also CA 85-88; DLB 20; RGEL 2
Rodman, Eric
  See Silverberg, Robert
Rodman, Howard 1920(?)-1985 .... CLC 65
  See also CA 118
Rodman, Maia
  See Wojciechowska, Maia (Teresa)
Rodo, Jose Enrique 1871(?)-1917 .... HLCS 2
  See also CA 178; EWL 3; HW 2; LAW
Rodolph, Utto
  See Ouologuem, Yambo
Rodriguez, Claudio 1934-1999 .... CLC 10
  See also CA 188; DLB 134
Rodriguez, Richard 1944- .... CLC 155; HLC
  2
  See also AMWS 14; CA 110; CANR 66,
  116; DAM MULT; DLB 82, 256; HW 1,
  2; LAIT 5; LLW; MTFW 2005; NCFS 3;
  WLIT 1
Roelvaag, O(le) E(dvart) 1876-1931
  See Rolvaag, O(le) E(dvart)
  See also CA 117; 171
Roethke, Theodore (Huebner)
  1908-1963 .... CLC 1, 3, 8, 11, 19, 46,
  101; PC 15
  See also AMW; CA 81-84; CABS 2;
  CDALB 1941-1968; DA3; DAM POET;
  DLB 5, 206; EWL 3; EXPP; MAL 5;
  MTCW 1, 2; PAB; PFS 3; RGAL 4; WP
Rogers, Carl R(ansom)
  1902-1987 .... TCLC 125
  See also CA 1-4R; 121; CANR 1, 18;
  MTCW 1
Rogers, Samuel 1763-1855 .... NCLC 69
  See also DLB 93; RGEL 2
Rogers, Thomas Hunton 1927- .... CLC 57
  See also CA 89-92; INT CA-89-92
Rogers, Will(iam Penn Adair)
  1879-1935 .... NNAL; TCLC 8, 71
  See also CA 105; 144; DA3; DAM MULT;
  DLB 11; MTCW 2
Rogin, Gilbert 1929- .... CLC 18
  See also CA 65-68; CANR 15
Rohan, Koda
  See Koda Shigeyuki
Rohlfs, Anna Katharine Green
  See Green, Anna Katharine
Rohmer, Eric .... CLC 16
  See Scherer, Jean-Marie Maurice
Rohmer, Sax .... TCLC 28
  See Ward, Arthur Henry Sarsfield
  See also DLB 70; MSW; SUFW
Roiphe, Anne (Richardson) 1935- .. CLC 3, 9
  See also CA 89-92; CANR 45, 73, 138;
  DLBY 1980; INT CA-89-92
Rojas, Fernando de 1475-1541 ... HLCS 1, 2;
  LC 23
  See also DLB 286; RGWL 2, 3
Rojas, Gonzalo 1917- .... HLCS 2
  See also CA 178; HW 2; LAWS 1
Roland (de la Platiere), Marie-Jeanne
  1754-1793 .... LC 98
  See also DLB 314

Rolfe, Frederick (William Serafino Austin
  Lewis Mary) 1860-1913 .... TCLC 12
  See Al Siddik
  See also CA 107; 210; DLB 34, 156; RGEL
  2
Rolland, Romain 1866-1944 .... TCLC 23
  See also CA 118; 197; DLB 65, 284; EWL
  3; GFL 1789 to the Present; RGWL 2, 3
Rolle, Richard c. 1300-c. 1349 ...... CMLC 21
  See also DLB 146; LMFS 1; RGEL 2
Rolvaag, O(le) E(dvart) .... TCLC 17
  See Roelvaag, O(le) E(dvart)
  See also DLB 9, 212; MAL 5; NFS 5;
  RGAL 4
Romain Arnaud, Saint
  See Aragon, Louis
Romains, Jules 1885-1972 .... CLC 7
  See also CA 85-88; CANR 34; DLB 65,
  321; EWL 3; GFL 1789 to the Present;
  MTCW 1
Romero, Jose Ruben 1890-1952 .... TCLC 14
  See also CA 114; 131; EWL 3; HW 1; LAW
Ronsard, Pierre de 1524-1585 . LC 6, 54; PC
  11
  See also EW 2; GFL Beginnings to 1789;
  RGWL 2, 3; TWA
Rooke, Leon 1934- .... CLC 25, 34
  See also CA 25-28R; CANR 23, 53; CCA
  1; CPW; DAM POP
Roosevelt, Franklin Delano
  1882-1945 .... TCLC 93
  See also CA 116; 173; LAIT 3
Roosevelt, Theodore 1858-1919 ..... TCLC 69
  See also CA 115; 170; DLB 47, 186, 275
Roper, William 1498-1578 .... LC 10
Roquelaure, A. N.
  See Rice, Anne.
Rosa, Joao Guimaraes 1908-1967 ... CLC 23;
  HLCS 1
  See Guimaraes Rosa, Joao
  See also CA 89-92; DLB 113, 307; EWL 3;
  WLIT 1
Rose, Wendy 1948- . CLC 85; NNAL; PC 13
  See also CA 53-56; CANR 5, 51; CWP;
  DAM MULT; DLB 175; PFS 13; RGAL
  4; SATA 12
Rosen, R. D.
  See Rosen, Richard (Dean)
Rosen, Richard (Dean) 1949- .... CLC 39
  See also CA 77-80; CANR 62, 120; CMW
  4; INT CANR-30
Rosenberg, Isaac 1890-1918 .... TCLC 12
  See also BRW 6; CA 107; 188; DLB 20,
  216; EWL 3; PAB; RGEL 2
Rosenblatt, Joe .... CLC 15
  See Rosenblatt, Joseph
  See also CP 3, 4, 5, 6, 7
Rosenblatt, Joseph 1933-
  See Rosenblatt, Joe
  See also CA 89-92; CP 1, 2; INT CA-89-92
Rosenfeld, Samuel
  See Tzara, Tristan
Rosenstock, Sami
  See Tzara, Tristan
Rosenstock, Samuel
  See Tzara, Tristan
Rosenthal, M(acha) L(ouis)
  1917-1996 .... CLC 28
  See also CA 1-4R; 152; CAAS 6; CANR 4,
  51; CP 1, 2, 3, 4; DLB 5; SATA 59
Ross, Barnaby
  See Dannay, Frederic
Ross, Bernard L.
  See Follett, Ken(neth Martin)
Ross, J. H.
  See Lawrence, T(homas) E(dward)
Ross, John Hume
  See Lawrence, T(homas) E(dward)

Ross, Martin 1862-1915
See Martin, Violet Florence
See also DLB 135; GLL 2; RGEL 2; RGSF 2

Ross, (James) Sinclair 1908-1996 ... **CLC 13; SSC 24**
See also CA 73-76; CANR 81; CN 1, 2, 3, 4, 5, 6; DAC; DAM MST; DLB 88; RGEL 2; RGSF 2; TCWW 1, 2

Rossetti, Christina 1830-1894 ... **NCLC 2, 50, 66; PC 7; WLC**
See also AAYA 51; BRW 5; BYA 4; DA; DA3; DAB; DAC; DAM MST, POET; DLB 35, 163, 240; EXPP; FL 1:3; LATS 1:1; MAICYA 1, 2; PFS 10, 14; RGEL 2; SATA 20; TEA; WCH

Rossetti, Christina Georgina
See Rossetti, Christina

Rossetti, Dante Gabriel 1828-1882 . **NCLC 4, 77; PC 44; WLC**
See also AAYA 51; BRW 5; CDBLB 1832-1890; DA; DAB; DAC; DAM MST, POET; DLB 35; EXPP; RGEL 2; TEA

Rossi, Cristina Peri
See Peri Rossi, Cristina

Rossi, Jean-Baptiste 1931-2003
See Japrisot, Sebastien
See also CA 201; 215

Rossner, Judith (Perelman) 1935- . **CLC 6, 9, 29**
See also AITN 2; BEST 90:3; BPFB 3; CA 17-20R; CANR 18, 51, 73; CN 4, 5, 6, 7; DLB 6; INT CANR-18; MAL 5; MTCW 1, 2; MTFW 2005

Rostand, Edmond (Eugene Alexis)
1868-1918 .... **DC 10; TCLC 6, 37**
See also CA 104; 126; DA; DA3; DAB; DAC; DAM DRAM, MST; DFS 1; DLB 192; LAIT 1; MTCW 1; RGWL 2, 3; TWA

Roth, Henry 1906-1995 ..... **CLC 2, 6, 11, 104**
See also AMWS 9; CA 11-12; 149; CANR 38, 63; CAP 1; CN 1, 2, 3, 4, 5, 6; DA3; DLB 28; EWL 3; MAL 5; MTCW 1, 2; MTFW 2005; RGAL 4

Roth, (Moses) Joseph 1894-1939 ... **TCLC 33**
See also CA 160; DLB 85; EWL 3; RGWL 2, 3

Roth, Philip (Milton) 1933- ... **CLC 1, 2, 3, 4, 6, 9, 15, 22, 31, 47, 66, 86, 119, 201; SSC 26; WLC**
See also AAYA 67; AMWR 2; AMWS 3; BEST 90:3; BPFB 3; CA 1-4R; CANR 1, 22, 36, 55, 89, 132; CDALB 1968-1988; CN 3, 4, 5, 6, 7; CPW 1; DA; DA3; DAB; DAC; DAM MST, NOV, POP; DLB 2, 28, 173; DLBY 1982; EWL 3; MAL 5; MTCW 1, 2; MTFW 2005; RGAL 4; RGSF 2; SSFS 12, 18; TUS

Rothenberg, Jerome 1931- .... **CLC 6, 57**
See also CA 45-48; CANR 1, 106; CP 1, 2, 3, 4, 5, 6, 7; DLB 5, 193

Rotter, Pat ed. .... **CLC 65**

Roumain, Jacques (Jean Baptiste)
1907-1944 .... **BLC 3; TCLC 19**
See also BW 1; CA 117; 125; DAM MULT; EWL 3

Rourke, Constance Mayfield
1885-1941 .... **TCLC 12**
See also CA 107; 200; MAL 5; YABC 1

Rousseau, Jean-Baptiste 1671-1741 ...... **LC 9**

Rousseau, Jean-Jacques 1712-1778 .... **LC 14, 36, 122; WLC**
See also DA; DA3; DAB; DAC; DAM MST; DLB 314; EW 4; GFL Beginnings to 1789; LMFS 1; RGWL 2, 3; TWA

Roussel, Raymond 1877-1933 .... **TCLC 20**
See also CA 117; 201; EWL 3; GFL 1789 to the Present

Rovit, Earl (Herbert) 1927- .... **CLC 7**
See also CA 5-8R; CANR 12

Rowe, Elizabeth Singer 1674-1737 ..... **LC 44**
See also DLB 39, 95

Rowe, Nicholas 1674-1718 .... **LC 8**
See also DLB 84; RGEL 2

Rowlandson, Mary 1637(?)-1678 .... **LC 66**
See also DLB 24, 200; RGAL 4

Rowley, Ames Dorrance
See Lovecraft, H(oward) P(hillips)

Rowley, William 1585(?)-1626 ... **LC 100, 123**
See also DFS 22; DLB 58; RGEL 2

Rowling, J. K. 1966- .... **CLC 137, 217**
See also AAYA 34; BYA 11, 13, 14; CA 173; CANR 128; CLR 66, 80; MAICYA 2; MTFW 2005; SATA 109; SUFW 2

Rowling, Joanne Kathleen
See Rowling, J.K.

Rowson, Susanna Haswell
1762(?)-1824 .... **NCLC 5, 69**
See also AMWS 15; DLB 37, 200; RGAL 4

Roy, Arundhati 1960(?)- .... **CLC 109, 210**
See also CA 163; CANR 90, 126; CN 7; DLBY 1997; EWL 3; LATS 1:2; MTFW 2005; NFS 22; WWE 1

Roy, Gabrielle 1909-1983 .... **CLC 10, 14**
See also CA 53-56; 110; CANR 5, 61; CCA 1; DAB; DAC; DAM MST; DLB 68; EWL 3; MTCW 1; RGWL 2, 3; SATA 104; TCLE 1:2

Royko, Mike 1932-1997 .... **CLC 109**
See also CA 89-92; 157; CANR 26, 111; CPW

Rozanov, Vasilii Vasil'evich
See Rozanov, Vassili
See also DLB 295

Rozanov, Vasily Vasilyevich
See Rozanov, Vassili
See also EWL 3

Rozanov, Vassili 1856-1919 .... **TCLC 104**
See Rozanov, Vasilii Vasil'evich; Rozanov, Vasily Vasilyevich

Rozewicz, Tadeusz 1921- ...... **CLC 9, 23, 139**
See also CA 108; CANR 36, 66; CWW 2; DA3; DAM POET; DLB 232; EWL 3; MTCW 1, 2; MTFW 2005; RGWL 3

Ruark, Gibbons 1941- .... **CLC 3**
See also CA 33-36R; CAAS 23; CANR 14, 31, 57; DLB 120

Rubens, Bernice (Ruth) 1923-2004 . **CLC 19, 31**
See also CA 25-28R; 232; CANR 33, 65, 128; CN 1, 2, 3, 4, 5, 6, 7; DLB 14, 207; MTCW 1

Rubin, Harold
See Robbins, Harold

Rudkin, (James) David 1936- .... **CLC 14**
See also CA 89-92; CBD; CD 5, 6; DLB 13

Rudnik, Raphael 1933- .... **CLC 7**
See also CA 29-32R

Ruffian, M.
See Hasek, Jaroslav (Matej Frantisek)

Ruiz, Jose Martinez .... **CLC 11**
See Martinez Ruiz, Jose

Ruiz, Juan c. 1283-c. 1350 .... **CMLC 66**

Rukeyser, Muriel 1913-1980 . **CLC 6, 10, 15, 27; PC 12**
See also AMWS 6; CA 5-8R; 93-96; CANR 26, 60; CP 1, 2, 3; DA3; DAM POET; DLB 48; EWL 3; FW; GLL 2; MAL 5; MTCW 1, 2; PFS 10; RGAL 4; SATA-Obit 22

Rule, Jane (Vance) 1931- .... **CLC 27**
See also CA 25-28R; CAAS 18; CANR 12, 87; CN 4, 5, 6, 7; DLB 60; FW

Rulfo, Juan 1918-1986 .. **CLC 8, 80; HLC 2; SSC 25**
See also CA 85-88; 118; CANR 26; CD-WLB 3; DAM MULT; DLB 113; EWL 3; HW 1, 2; LAW; MTCW 1, 2; RGSF 2; RGWL 2, 3; WLIT 1

Rumi, Jalal al-Din 1207-1273 ...... **CMLC 20; PC 45**
See also AAYA 64; RGWL 2, 3; WLIT 6; WP

Runeberg, Johan 1804-1877 .... **NCLC 41**

Runyon, (Alfred) Damon
1884(?)-1946 .... **TCLC 10**
See also CA 107; 165; DLB 11, 86, 171; MAL 5; MTCW 2; RGAL 4

Rush, Norman 1933- .... **CLC 44**
See also CA 121; 126; CANR 130; INT CA-126

Rushdie, (Ahmed) Salman 1947- .... **CLC 23, 31, 55, 100, 191; SSC 83; WLCS**
See also AAYA 65; BEST 89:3; BPFB 3; BRWS 4; CA 108; 111; CANR 33, 56, 108, 133; CN 4, 5, 6, 7; CPW 1; DA3; DAB; DAC; DAM MST, NOV, POP; DLB 194; EWL 3; FANT; INT CA-111; LATS 1:2; LMFS 2; MTCW 1, 2; MTFW 2005; NFS 22; RGEL 2; RGSF 2; TEA; WLIT 4

Rushforth, Peter (Scott) 1945- .... **CLC 19**
See also CA 101

Ruskin, John 1819-1900 .... **TCLC 63**
See also BRW 5; BYA 5; CA 114; 129; CD-BLB 1832-1890; DLB 55, 163, 190; RGEL 2; SATA 24; TEA; WCH

Russ, Joanna 1937- .... **CLC 15**
See also BPFB 3; CA 25-28; CANR 11, 31, 65; CN 4, 5, 6, 7; DLB 8; FW; GLL 1; MTCW 1; SCFW 1, 2; SFW 4

Russ, Richard Patrick
See O'Brian, Patrick

Russell, George William 1867-1935
See A.E.; Baker, Jean H.
See also BRWS 8; CA 104; 153; CDBLB 1890-1914; DAM POET; EWL 3; RGEL 2

Russell, Jeffrey Burton 1934- .... **CLC 70**
See also CA 25-28R; CANR 11, 28, 52

Russell, (Henry) Ken(neth Alfred)
1927- .... **CLC 16**
See also CA 105

Russell, William Martin 1947-
See Russell, Willy
See also CA 164; CANR 107

Russell, Willy .... **CLC 60**
See Russell, William Martin
See also CBD; CD 5, 6; DLB 233

Russo, Richard 1949- .... **CLC 181**
See also AMWS 12; CA 127; 133; CANR 87, 114

Rutherford, Mark .... **TCLC 25**
See White, William Hale
See also DLB 18; RGEL 2

Ruyslinck, Ward .... **CLC 14**
See Belser, Reimond Karel Maria de

Ryan, Cornelius (John) 1920-1974 ..... **CLC 7**
See also CA 69-72; 53-56; CANR 38

Ryan, Michael 1946- .... **CLC 65**
See also CA 49-52; CANR 109; DLBY 1982

Ryan, Tim
See Dent, Lester

Rybakov, Anatoli (Naumovich)
1911-1998 .... **CLC 23, 53**
See Rybakov, Anatolii (Naumovich)
See also CA 126; 135; 172; SATA 79; SATA-Obit 108

Rybakov, Anatolii (Naumovich)
See Rybakov, Anatoli (Naumovich)
See also DLB 302

Ryder, Jonathan
  See Ludlum, Robert
Ryga, George 1932-1987 .... **CLC 14**
  See also CA 101; 124; CANR 43, 90; CCA
  1; DAC; DAM MST; DLB 60
S. H.
  See Hartmann, Sadakichi
S. S.
  See Sassoon, Siegfried (Lorraine)
Sa'adawi, al- Nawal
  See El Saadawi, Nawal
  See also AFW; EWL 3
Saadawi, Nawal El
  See El Saadawi, Nawal
  See also WLIT 2
Saba, Umberto 1883-1957 .... **TCLC 33**
  See also CA 144; CANR 79; DLB 114;
  EWL 3; RGWL 2, 3
Sabatini, Rafael 1875-1950 .... **TCLC 47**
  See also BPFB 3; CA 162; RHW
Sabato, Ernesto (R.) 1911- .... **CLC 10, 23;**
  HLC 2
  See also CA 97-100; CANR 32, 65; CD-
  WLB 3; CWW 2; DAM MULT; DLB 145;
  EWL 3; HW 1, 2; LAW; MTCW 1, 2;
  MTFW 2005
Sa-Carneiro, Mario de 1890-1916 . **TCLC 83**
  See also DLB 287; EWL 3
Sacastru, Martin
  See Bioy Casares, Adolfo
  See also CWW 2
Sacher-Masoch, Leopold von
  1836(?)-1895 .... **NCLC 31**
Sachs, Hans 1494-1576 .... **LC 95**
  See also CDWLB 2; DLB 179; RGWL 2, 3
Sachs, Marilyn 1927- .... **CLC 35**
  See also AAYA 2; BYA 6; CA 17-20R;
  CANR 13, 47; CLR 2; JRDA; MAICYA
  1, 2; SAAS 2; SATA 3, 68, 164; SATA-
  Essay 110; WYA; YAW
Sachs, Marilyn Stickle
  See Sachs, Marilyn
Sachs, Nelly 1891-1970 .... **CLC 14, 98**
  See also CA 17-18; 25-28R; CANR 87;
  CAP 2; EWL 3; MTCW 2; MTFW 2005;
  PFS 20; RGWL 2, 3
Sackler, Howard (Oliver)
  1929-1982 .... **CLC 14**
  See also CA 61-64; 108; CAD; CANR 30;
  DFS 15; DLB 7
Sacks, Oliver (Wolf) 1933- .... **CLC 67, 202**
  See also CA 53-56; CANR 28, 50, 76;
  CPW; DA3; INT CANR-28; MTCW 1, 2;
  MTFW 2005
Sackville, Thomas 1536-1608 .... **LC 98**
  See also DAM DRAM; DLB 62, 132;
  RGEL 2
Sadakichi
  See Hartmann, Sadakichi
Sa'dawi, Nawal al-
  See El Saadawi, Nawal
  See also CWW 2
Sade, Donatien Alphonse Francois
  1740-1814 .... **NCLC 3, 47**
  See also DLB 314; EW 4; GFL Beginnings
  to 1789; RGWL 2, 3
Sade, Marquis de
  See Sade, Donatien Alphonse Francois
Sadoff, Ira 1945- .... **CLC 9**
  See also CA 53-56; CANR 5, 21, 109; DLB
  120
Saetone
  See Camus, Albert
Safire, William 1929- .... **CLC 10**
  See also CA 17-20R; CANR 31, 54, 91

Sagan, Carl (Edward) 1934-1996 .... **CLC 30,**
  112
  See also AAYA 2, 62; CA 25-28R; 155;
  CANR 11, 36, 74; CPW; DA3; MTCW 1,
  2; MTFW 2005; SATA 58; SATA-Obit 94
Sagan, Francoise .... **CLC 3, 6, 9, 17, 36**
  See Quoirez, Francoise
  See also CWW 2; DLB 83; EWL 3; GFL
  1789 to the Present; MTCW 2
Sahgal, Nayantara (Pandit) 1927- .... **CLC 41**
  See also CA 9-12R; CANR 11, 88; CN 1,
  2, 3, 4, 5, 6, 7
Said, Edward W. 1935-2003 .... **CLC 123**
  See also CA 21-24R; 220; CANR 45, 74,
  107, 131; DLB 67; MTCW 2; MTFW
  2005
Saint, H(arry) F. 1941- .... **CLC 50**
  See also CA 127
St. Aubin de Teran, Lisa 1953-
  See Teran, Lisa St. Aubin de
  See also CA 118; 126; CN 6, 7; INT CA-
  126
Saint Birgitta of Sweden c.
  1303-1373 .... **CMLC 24**
Saint Gregory of Nazianzus
  329-389 .... **CMLC 82**
Sainte-Beuve, Charles Augustin
  1804-1869 .... **NCLC 5**
  See also DLB 217; EW 6; GFL 1789 to the
  Present
Saint-Exupery, Antoine (Jean Baptiste
  Marie Roger) de 1900-1944 .... **TCLC 2,**
  56, 169; WLC
  See also AAYA 63; BPFB 3; BYA 3; CA
  108; 132; CLR 10; DA3; DAM NOV;
  DLB 72; EW 12; EWL 3; GFL 1789 to
  the Present; LAIT 3; MAICYA 1, 2;
  MTCW 1, 2; MTFW 2005; RGWL 2, 3;
  SATA 20; TWA
St. John, David
  See Hunt, E(verette) Howard, (Jr.)
St. John, J. Hector
  See Crevecoeur, Michel Guillaume Jean de
Saint-John Perse
  See Leger, (Marie-Rene Auguste) Alexis
  Saint-Leger
  See also EW 10; EWL 3; GFL 1789 to the
  Present; RGWL 2
Saintsbury, George (Edward Bateman)
  1845-1933 .... **TCLC 31**
  See also CA 160; DLB 57, 149
Sait Faik .... **TCLC 23**
  See Abasiyanik, Sait Faik
Saki .... **SSC 12; TCLC 3**
  See Munro, H(ector) H(ugh)
  See also BRWS 6; BYA 11; LAIT 2; RGEL
  2; SSFS 1; SUFW
Sala, George Augustus 1828-1895 . **NCLC 46**
Saladin 1138-1193 .... **CMLC 38**
Salama, Hannu 1936- .... **CLC 18**
  See also EWL 3
Salamanca, J(ack) R(ichard) 1922- .. **CLC 4,**
  15
  See also CA 25-28R, 193; CAAE 193
Salas, Floyd Francis 1931- .... **HLC 2**
  See also CA 119; CAAS 27; CANR 44, 75,
  93; DAM MULT; DLB 82; HW 1, 2;
  MTCW 2; MTFW 2005
Sale, J. Kirkpatrick
  See Sale, Kirkpatrick
Sale, Kirkpatrick 1937- .... **CLC 68**
  See also CA 13-16R; CANR 10
Salinas, Luis Omar 1937- .... **CLC 90; HLC 2**
  See also AMWS 13; CA 131; CANR 81;
  DAM MULT; DLB 82; HW 1, 2
Salinas (y Serrano), Pedro
  1891(?)-1951 .... **TCLC 17**
  See also CA 117; DLB 134; EWL 3

Salinger, J(erome) D(avid) 1919- .. **CLC 1, 3,**
  8, 12, 55, 56, 138; SSC 2, 28, 65; WLC
  See also AAYA 2, 36; AMW; AMWC 1;
  BPFB 3; CA 5-8R; CANR 39, 129;
  CDALB 1941-1968; CLR 18; CN 1, 2, 3,
  4, 5, 6, 7; CPW 1; DA; DA3; DAB; DAC;
  DAM MST, NOV, POP; DLB 2, 102, 173;
  EWL 3; EXPN; LAIT 4; MAICYA 1, 2;
  MAL 5; MTCW 1, 2; MTFW 2005; NFS
  1; RGAL 4; RGSF 2; SATA 67; SSFS 17;
  TUS; WYA; YAW
Salisbury, John
  See Caute, (John) David
Sallust c. 86B.C.-35B.C. .... **CMLC 68**
  See also AW 2; CDWLB 1; DLB 211;
  RGWL 2, 3
Salter, James 1925- .. **CLC 7, 52, 59; SSC 58**
  See also AMWS 9; CA 73-76; CANR 107;
  DLB 130
Saltus, Edgar (Everton) 1855-1921 . **TCLC 8**
  See also CA 105; DLB 202; RGAL 4
Saltykov, Mikhail Evgrafovich
  1826-1889 .... **NCLC 16**
  See also DLB 238:
Saltykov-Shchedrin, N.
  See Saltykov, Mikhail Evgrafovich
Samarakis, Andonis
  See Samarakis, Antonis
  See also EWL 3
Samarakis, Antonis 1919-2003 .... **CLC 5**
  See Samarakis, Andonis
  See also CA 25-28R; 224; CAAS 16; CANR
  36
Sanchez, Florencio 1875-1910 .... **TCLC 37**
  See also CA 153; DLB 305; EWL 3; HW 1;
  LAW
Sanchez, Luis Rafael 1936- .... **CLC 23**
  See also CA 128; DLB 305; EWL 3; HW 1;
  WLIT 1
Sanchez, Sonia 1934- .... **BLC 3; CLC 5, 116,**
  215; PC 9
  See also BW 2, 3; CA 33-36R; CANR 24,
  49, 74, 115; CLR 18; CP 2, 3, 4, 5, 6, 7;
  CSW; CWP; DA3; DAM MULT; DLB 41;
  DLBD 8; EWL 3; MAICYA 1, 2; MAL 5;
  MTCW 1, 2; MTFW 2005; SATA 22, 136;
  WP
Sancho, Ignatius 1729-1780 .... **LC 84**
Sand, George 1804-1876 ..... **NCLC 2, 42, 57;**
  WLC
  See also DA; DA3; DAB; DAC; DAM
  MST, NOV; DLB 119, 192; EW 6; FL 1:3;
  FW; GFL 1789 to the Present; RGWL 2,
  3; TWA
Sandburg, Carl (August) 1878-1967 . **CLC 1,**
  4, 10, 15, 35; PC 2, 41; WLC
  See also AAYA 24; AMW; BYA 1, 3; CA
  5-8R; 25-28R; CANR 35; CDALB 1865-
  1917; CLR 67; DA; DA3; DAB; DAC;
  DAM MST, POET; DLB 17, 54, 284;
  EWL 3; EXPP; LAIT 2; MAICYA 1, 2;
  MAL 5; MTCW 1, 2; MTFW 2005; PAB;
  PFS 3, 6, 12; RGAL 4; SATA 8; TUS;
  WCH; WP; WYA
Sandburg, Charles
  See Sandburg, Carl (August)
Sandburg, Charles A.
  See Sandburg, Carl (August)
Sanders, (James) Ed(ward) 1939- .... **CLC 53**
  See Sanders, Edward
  See also BG 1:3; CA 13-16R; CAAS 21;
  CANR 13, 44, 78; CP 1, 2, 3, 4, 5, 6, 7;
  DAM POET; DLB 16, 244
Sanders, Edward
  See Sanders, (James) Ed(ward)
  See also DLB 244
Sanders, Lawrence 1920-1998 .... **CLC 41**
  See also BEST 89:4; BPFB 3; CA 81-84;
  165; CANR 33, 62; CMW 4; CPW; DA3;
  DAM POP; MTCW 1

Sanders, Noah
See Blount, Roy (Alton), Jr.

Sanders, Winston P.
See Anderson, Poul (William)

Sandoz, Mari(e Susette) 1900-1966 .. CLC 28
See also CA 1-4R; 25-28R; CANR 17, 64;
DLB 9, 212; LAIT 2; MTCW 1, 2; SATA
5; TCWW 1, 2

Sandys, George 1578-1644 .... LC 80
See also DLB 24, 121

Saner, Reg(inald Anthony) 1931- .... CLC 9
See also CA 65-68; CP 3, 4, 5, 6, 7

Sankara 788-820 .... CMLC 32

Sannazaro, Jacopo 1456(?)-1530 .... LC 8
See also RGWL 2, 3; WLIT 7

**Sansom, William 1912-1976 . CLC 2, 6; SSC
21**
See also CA 5-8R; 65-68; CANR 42; CN 1,
2; DAM NOV; DLB 139; EWL 3; MTCW
1; RGEL 2; RGSF 2

Santayana, George 1863-1952 .... TCLC 40
See also AMW; CA 115; 194; DLB 54, 71,
246, 270; DLBD 13; EWL 3; MAL 5;
RGAL 4; TUS

Santiago, Danny .... CLC 33
See James, Daniel (Lewis)
See also DLB 122

**Santillana, Inigo Lopez de Mendoza,
Marques de 1398-1458 .... LC 111**
See also DLB 286

**Santmyer, Helen Hooven
1895-1986 .... CLC 33; TCLC 133**
See also CA 1-4R; 118; CANR 15, 33;
DLBY 1984; MTCW 1; RHW

Santoka, Taneda 1882-1940 .... TCLC 72

**Santos, Bienvenido N(uqui)
1911-1996 ... AAL; CLC 22; TCLC 156**
See also CA 101; 151; CANR 19, 46; CP 1;
DAM MULT; DLB 312; EWL; RGAL 4;
SSFS 19

Sapir, Edward 1884-1939 .... TCLC 108
See also CA 211; DLB 92

Sapper .... TCLC 44
See McNeile, Herman Cyril

Sapphire
See Sapphire, Brenda

Sapphire, Brenda 1950- .... CLC 99

**Sappho fl. 6th cent. B.C.- ... CMLC 3, 67; PC
5**
See also CDWLB 1; DA3; DAM POET;
DLB 176; FL 1:1; PFS 20; RGWL 2, 3;
WP

Saramago, Jose 1922- ..... CLC 119; HLCS 1
See also CA 153; CANR 96; CWW 2; DLB
287; EWL 3; LATS 1:2

**Sarduy, Severo 1937-1993 .... CLC 6, 97;
HLCS 2; TCLC 167**
See also CA 89-92; 142; CANR 58, 81;
CWW 2; DLB 113; EWL 3; HW 1, 2;
LAW

Sargeson, Frank 1903-1982 .... CLC 31
See also CA 25-28R; 106; CANR 38, 79;
CN 1, 2, 3; EWL 3; GLL 2; RGEL 2;
RGSF 2; SSFS 20

**Sarmiento, Domingo Faustino
1811-1888 .... HLCS 2**
See also LAW; WLIT 1

Sarmiento, Felix Ruben Garcia
See Dario, Ruben

**Saro-Wiwa, Ken(ule Beeson)
1941-1995 .... CLC 114**
See also BW 2; CA 142; 150; CANR 60;
DLB 157

**Saroyan, William 1908-1981 ... CLC 1, 8, 10,
29, 34, 56; SSC 21; TCLC 137; WLC**
See also AAYA 66; CA 5-8R; 103; CAD;
CANR 30; CDALBS; CN 1, 2; DA; DA3;
DAB; DAC; DAM DRAM, MST, NOV;
DFS 17; DLB 7, 9, 86; DLBY 1981; EWL

3; LAIT 4; MAL 5; MTCW 1, 2; MTFW
2005; RGAL 4; RGSF 2; SATA 23; SATA-
Obit 24; SSFS 14; TUS

**Sarraute, Nathalie 1900-1999 .... CLC 1, 2, 4,
8, 10, 31, 80; TCLC 145**
See also BPFB 3; CA 9-12R; 187; CANR
23, 66, 134; CWW 2; DLB 83, 321; EW
12; EWL 3; GFL 1789 to the Present;
MTCW 1, 2; MTFW 2005; RGWL 2, 3

**Sarton, (Eleanor) May 1912-1995 ..... CLC 4,
14, 49, 91; PC 39; TCLC 120**
See also AMWS 8; CA 1-4R; 149; CANR
1, 34, 55, 116; CN 1, 2, 3, 4, 5, 6; CP 1,
2, 3, 4; DAM POET; DLB 48; DLBY
1981; EWL 3; FW; INT CANR-34; MAL
5; MTCW 1, 2; MTFW 2005; RGAL 4;
SATA 36; SATA-Obit 86; TUS

**Sartre, Jean-Paul 1905-1980 . CLC 1, 4, 7, 9,
13, 18, 24, 44, 50, 52; DC 3; SSC 32;
WLC**
See also AAYA 62; CA 9-12R; 97-100;
CANR 21; DA; DA3; DAB; DAC; DAM
DRAM, MST, NOV; DFS 5; DLB 72,
296, 321; EW 12; EWL 3; GFL 1789 to
the Present; LMFS 2; MTCW 1, 2; MTFW
2005; NFS 21; RGSF 2; RGWL 2, 3;
SSFS 9; TWA

**Sassoon, Siegfried (Lorraine)
1886-1967 .... CLC 36, 130; PC 12**
See also BRW 6; CA 104; 25-28R; CANR
36; DAB; DAM MST, NOV; DLB
20, 191; DLBD 18; EWL 3; MTCW 1, 2;
MTFW 2005; PAB; RGEL 2; TEA

Satterfield, Charles
See Pohl, Frederik

Satyremont
See Peret, Benjamin

Saul, John (W. III) 1942- .... CLC 46
See also AAYA 10, 62; BEST 90:4; CA 81-
84; CANR 16, 40, 81; CPW; DAM NOV,
POP; HGG; SATA 98

Saunders, Caleb
See Heinlein, Robert A(nson)

Saura (Atares), Carlos 1932-1998 .... CLC 20
See also CA 114; 131; CANR 79; HW 1

Sauser, Frederic Louis
See Sauser-Hall, Frederic

Sauser-Hall, Frederic 1887-1961 ...... CLC 18
See Cendrars, Blaise
See also CA 102; 93-96; CANR 36, 62;
MTCW 1

**Saussure, Ferdinand de
1857-1913 .... TCLC 49**
See also DLB 242

Savage, Catharine
See Brosman, Catharine Savage

Savage, Richard 1697(?)-1743 .... LC 96
See also DLB 95; RGEL 2

Savage, Thomas 1915-2003 .... CLC 40
See also CA 126; 132; 218; CAAS 15; CN
6, 7; INT CA-132; SATA-Obit 147;
TCWW 2

Savan, Glenn 1953-2003 .... CLC 50
See also CA 225

Sax, Robert
See Johnson, Robert

**Saxo Grammaticus c. 1150-c.
1222 .... CMLC 58**

Saxton, Robert
See Johnson, Robert

**Sayers, Dorothy L(eigh) 1893-1957 . SSC 71;
TCLC 2, 15**
See also BPFB 3; BRWS 3; CA 104; 119;
CANR 60; CDBLB 1914-1945; CMW 4;
DAM POP; DLB 10, 36, 77, 100; MSW;
MTCW 1, 2; MTFW 2005; RGEL 2;
SSFS 12; TEA

Sayers, Valerie 1952- .... CLC 50, 122
See also CA 134; CANR 61; CSW

**Sayles, John (Thomas) 1950- .... CLC 7, 10,
14, 198**
See also CA 57-60; CANR 41, 84; DLB 44

Scammell, Michael 1935- .... CLC 34
See also CA 156

Scannell, Vernon 1922- .... CLC 49
See also CA 5-8R; CANR 8, 24, 57, 143;
CN 1, 2; CP 1, 2, 3, 4, 5, 6, 7; CWRI 5;
DLB 27; SATA 59

Scarlett, Susan
See Streatfeild, (Mary) Noel

Scarron 1847-1910
See Mikszath, Kalman

Scarron, Paul 1610-1660 .... LC 116
See also GFL Beginnings to 1789; RGWL
2, 3

**Schaeffer, Susan Fromberg 1941- ..... CLC 6,
11, 22**
See also CA 49-52; CANR 18, 65; CN 4, 5,
6, 7; DLB 28, 299; MTCW 1, 2; MTFW
2005; SATA 22

Schama, Simon (Michael) 1945- ..... CLC 150
See also BEST 89:4; CA 105; CANR 39,
91

Schary, Jill
See Robinson, Jill

Schell, Jonathan 1943- .... CLC 35
See also CA 73-76; CANR 12, 117

**Schelling, Friedrich Wilhelm Joseph von
1775-1854 .... NCLC 30**
See also DLB 90

Scherer, Jean-Marie Maurice 1920-
See Rohmer, Eric
See also CA 110

Schevill, James (Erwin) 1920- .... CLC 7
See also CA 5-8R; CAAS 12; CAD; CD 5,
6; CP 1, 2, 3, 4

**Schiller, Friedrich von 1759-1805 ...... DC 12;
NCLC 39, 69**
See also CDWLB 2; DAM DRAM; DLB
94; EW 5; RGWL 2, 3; TWA

Schisgal, Murray (Joseph) 1926- .... CLC 6
See also CA 21-24R; CAD; CANR 48, 86;
CD 5, 6; MAL 5

Schlee, Ann 1934- .... CLC 35
See also CA 101; CANR 29, 88; SATA 44;
SATA-Brief 36

**Schlegel, August Wilhelm von
1767-1845 .... NCLC 15, 142**
See also DLB 94; RGWL 2, 3

Schlegel, Friedrich 1772-1829 .... NCLC 45
See also DLB 90; EW 5; RGWL 2, 3; TWA

**Schlegel, Johann Elias (von)
1719(?)-1749 .... LC 5**

**Schleiermacher, Friedrich
1768-1834 .... NCLC 107**
See also DLB 90

**Schlesinger, Arthur M(eier), Jr.
1917- .... CLC 84**
See also AITN 1; CA 1-4R; CANR 1, 28,
58, 105; DLB 17; INT CANR-28; MTCW
1, 2; SATA 61

Schlink, Bernhard 1944- .... CLC 174
See also CA 163; CANR 116

Schmidt, Arno (Otto) 1914-1979 ...... CLC 56
See also CA 128; 109; DLB 69; EWL 3

Schmitz, Aron Hector 1861-1928
See Svevo, Italo
See also CA 104; 122; MTCW 1

**Schnackenberg, Gjertrud (Cecelia)
1953- .... CLC 40; PC 45**
See also AMWS 15; CA 116; CANR 100;
CP 7; CWP; DLB 120, 282; PFS 13

Schneider, Leonard Alfred 1925-1966
See Bruce, Lenny
See also CA 89-92

Shepherd, Michael
See Ludlum, Robert
Sherburne, Zoa (Lillian Morin)
1912-1995 .... **CLC 30**
See also AAYA 13; CA 1-4R; 176; CANR
3, 37; MAICYA 1, 2; SAAS 18; SATA 3;
YAW
Sheridan, Frances 1724-1766 .... **LC 7**
See also DLB 39, 84
Sheridan, Richard Brinsley
1751-1816 .... **DC 1; NCLC 5, 91; WLC**
See also BRW 3; CDBLB 1660-1789; DA;
DAB; DAC; DAM DRAM, MST; DFS
15; DLB 89; WLIT 3
Sherman, Jonathan Marc 1968- .... **CLC 55**
See also CA 230
Sherman, Martin 1941(?)- .... **CLC 19**
See also CA 116; 123; CAD; CANR 86;
CD 5, 6; DFS 20; DLB 228; GLL 1; IDTP
Sherwin, Judith Johnson
See Johnson, Judith (Emlyn)
See also CANR 85; CP 2, 3, 4; CWP
Sherwood, Frances 1940- .... **CLC 81**
See also CA 146, 220; CAAE 220
Sherwood, Robert E(mmet)
1896-1955 .... **TCLC 3**
See also CA 104; 153; CANR 86; DAM
DRAM; DFS 11, 15, 17; DLB 7, 26, 249;
IDFW 3, 4; MAL 5; RGAL 4
Shestov, Lev 1866-1938 .... **TCLC 56**
Shevchenko, Taras 1814-1861 .... **NCLC 54**
Shiel, M(atthew) P(hipps)
1865-1947 .... **TCLC 8**
See Holmes, Gordon
See also CA 106; 160; DLB 153; HGG;
MTCW 2; MTFW 2005; SCFW 1, 2;
SFW 4; SUFW
Shields, Carol (Ann) 1935-2003 ...... **CLC 91,
113, 193**
See also AMWS 7; CA 81-84; 218; CANR
51, 74, 98, 133; CCA 1; CN 6, 7; CPW;
DA3; DAC; MTCW 2; MTFW 2005
Shields, David (Jonathan) 1956- ...... **CLC 97**
See also CA 124; CANR 48, 99, 112
Shiga, Naoya 1883-1971 .... **CLC 33; SSC 23;
TCLC 172**
See Shiga Naoya
See also CA 101; 33-36R; MJW; RGWL 3
Shiga Naoya
See Shiga, Naoya
See also DLB 180; EWL 3; RGWL 3
Shilts, Randy 1951-1994 .... **CLC 85**
See also AAYA 19; CA 115; 127; 144;
CANR 45; DA3; GLL 1; INT CA-127;
MTCW 2; MTFW 2005
Shimazaki, Haruki 1872-1943
See Shimazaki Toson
See also CA 105; 134; CANR 84; RGWL 3
Shimazaki Toson .... **TCLC 5**
See Shimazaki, Haruki
See also DLB 180; EWL 3
Shirley, James 1596-1666 .... **DC 25; LC 96**
See also DLB 58; RGEL 2
Sholokhov, Mikhail (Aleksandrovich)
1905-1984 .... **CLC 7, 15**
See also CA 101; 112; DLB 272; EWL 3;
MTCW 1, 2; MTFW 2005; RGWL 2, 3;
SATA-Obit 36
Shone, Patric
See Hanley, James
Showalter, Elaine 1941- .... **CLC 169**
See also CA 57-60; CANR 58, 106; DLB
67; FW; GLL 2
Shreve, Susan
See Shreve, Susan Richards
Shreve, Susan Richards 1939- .... **CLC 23**
See also CA 49-52; CAAS 5; CANR 5, 38,
69, 100; MAICYA 1, 2; SATA 46, 95, 152;
SATA-Brief 41

Shue, Larry 1946-1985 .... **CLC 52**
See also CA 145; 117; DAM DRAM; DFS
7
Shu-Jen, Chou 1881-1936
See Lu Hsun
See also CA 104
Shulman, Alix Kates 1932- .... **CLC 2, 10**
See also CA 29-32R; CANR 43; FW; SATA
7
Shuster, Joe 1914-1992 .... **CLC 21**
See also AAYA 50
Shute, Nevil .... **CLC 30**
See Norway, Nevil Shute
See also BPFB 3; DLB 255; NFS 9; RHW;
SFW 4
Shuttle, Penelope (Diane) 1947- .... **CLC 7**
See also CA 93-96; CANR 39, 84, 92, 108;
CP 3, 4, 5, 6, 7; CWP; DLB 14, 40
Shvarts, Elena 1948- .... **PC 50**
See also CA 147
Sidhwa, Bapsi
See Sidhwa, Bapsy (N.)
See also CN 6, 7
Sidhwa, Bapsy (N.) 1938- .... **CLC 168**
See Sidhwa, Bapsi
See also CA 108; CANR 25, 57; FW
Sidney, Mary 1561-1621 .... **LC 19, 39**
See Sidney Herbert, Mary
Sidney, Sir Philip 1554-1586 . **LC 19, 39; PC
32**
See also BRW 1; BRWR 2; CDBLB Before
1660; DA; DA3; DAB; DAC; DAM MST,
POET; DLB 167; EXPP; PAB; RGEL 2;
TEA; WP
Sidney Herbert, Mary
See Sidney, Mary
See also DLB 167
Siegel, Jerome 1914-1996 .... **CLC 21**
See Siegel, Jerry
See also CA 116; 169; 151
Siegel, Jerry
See Siegel, Jerome
See also AAYA 50
Sienkiewicz, Henryk (Adam Alexander Pius)
1846-1916 .... **TCLC 3**
See also CA 104; 134; CANR 84; EWL 3;
RGSF 2; RGWL 2, 3
Sierra, Gregorio Martinez
See Martinez Sierra, Gregorio
Sierra, Maria (de la O'LeJarraga) Martinez
See Martinez Sierra, Maria (de la
O'LeJarraga)
Sigal, Clancy 1926- .... **CLC 7**
See also CA 1-4R; CANR 85; CN 1, 2, 3,
4, 5, 6, 7
Siger of Brabant 1240(?)-1284(?) . **CMLC 69**
See also DLB 115
Sigourney, Lydia H.
See Sigourney, Lydia Howard (Huntley)
See also DLB 73, 183
Sigourney, Lydia Howard (Huntley)
1791-1865 .... **NCLC 21, 87**
See Sigourney, Lydia H.; Sigourney, Lydia
Huntley
See also DLB 1
Sigourney, Lydia Huntley
See Sigourney, Lydia Howard (Huntley)
See also DLB 42, 239, 243
Siguenza y Gongora, Carlos de
1645-1700 .... **HLCS 2; LC 8**
See also LAW
Sigurjonsson, Johann
See Sigurjonsson, Johann
Sigurjonsson, Johann 1880-1919 ... **TCLC 27**
See also CA 170; DLB 293; EWL 3
Sikelianos, Angelos 1884-1951 .... **PC 29;
TCLC 39**
See also EWL 3; RGWL 2, 3

Silkin, Jon 1930-1997 .... **CLC 2, 6, 43**
See also CA 5-8R; CAAS 5; CANR 89; CP
1, 2, 3, 4, 5, 6; DLB 27
Silko, Leslie (Marmon) 1948- .... **CLC 23, 74,
114, 211; NNAL; SSC 37, 66; WLCS**
See also AAYA 14; AMWS 4; ANW; BYA
12; CA 115; 122; CANR 45, 65, 118; CN
4, 5, 6, 7; CP 4, 5, 6, 7; CPW 1; CWP;
DA; DA3; DAC; DAM MST, MULT,
POP; DLB 143, 175, 256, 275; EWL 3;
EXPP; EXPS; LAIT 4; MAL 5; MTCW
2; MTFW 2005; NFS 4; PFS 9, 16; RGAL
4; RGSF 2; SSFS 4, 8, 10, 11; TCWW 1,
2
Sillanpaa, Frans Eemil 1888-1964 ... **CLC 19**
See also CA 129; 93-96; EWL 3; MTCW 1
Sillitoe, Alan 1928- .. **CLC 1, 3, 6, 10, 19, 57,
148**
See also AITN 1; BRWS 5; CA 9-12R, 191;
CAAE 191; CAAS 2; CANR 8, 26, 55,
139; CDBLB 1960 to Present; CN 1, 2, 3,
4, 5, 6; CP 1, 2, 3, 4; DLB 14, 139; EWL
3; MTCW 1, 2; MTFW 2005; RGEL 2;
RGSF 2; SATA 61
Silone, Ignazio 1900-1978 .... **CLC 4**
See also CA 25-28; 81-84; CANR 34; CAP
2; DLB 264; EW 12; EWL 3; MTCW 1;
RGSF 2; RGWL 2, 3
Silone, Ignazione
See Silone, Ignazio
Silver, Joan Micklin 1935- .... **CLC 20**
See also CA 114; 121; INT CA-121
Silver, Nicholas
See Faust, Frederick (Schiller)
Silverberg, Robert 1935- .... **CLC 7, 140**
See also AAYA 24; BPFB 3; BYA 7, 9; CA
1-4R, 186; CAAE 186; CAAS 3; CANR
1, 20, 36, 85, 140; CLR 59; CN 6, 7;
CPW; DAM POP; DLB 8; INT CANR-
20; MAICYA 1, 2; MTCW 1, 2; MTFW
2005; SATA 13, 91; SATA-Essay 104;
SCFW 1, 2; SFW 4; SUFW 2
Silverstein, Alvin 1933- .... **CLC 17**
See also CA 49-52; CANR 2; CLR 25;
JRDA; MAICYA 1, 2; SATA 8, 69, 124
Silverstein, Shel(don Allan)
1932-1999 .... **PC 49**
See also AAYA 40; BW 3; CA 107; 179;
CANR 47, 74, 81; CLR 5, 96; CWRI 5;
JRDA; MAICYA 1, 2; MTCW 2; MTFW
2005; SATA 33, 92; SATA-Brief 27;
SATA-Obit 116
Silverstein, Virginia B(arbara Opshelor)
1937- .... **CLC 17**
See also CA 49-52; CANR 2; CLR 25;
JRDA; MAICYA 1, 2; SATA 8, 69, 124
Sim, Georges
See Simenon, Georges (Jacques Christian)
Simak, Clifford D(onald) 1904-1988 . **CLC 1,
55**
See also CA 1-4R; 125; CANR 1, 35; DLB
8; MTCW 1; SATA-Obit 56; SCFW 1, 2;
SFW 4
Simenon, Georges (Jacques Christian)
1903-1989 .... **CLC 1, 2, 3, 8, 18, 47**
See also BPFB 3; CA 85-88; 129; CANR
35; CMW 4; DA3; DAM POP; DLB 72;
DLBY 1989; EW 12; EWL 3; GFL 1789
to the Present; MSW; MTCW 1, 2; MTFW
2005; RGWL 2, 3
Simic, Charles 1938- .... **CLC 6, 9, 22, 49, 68,
130; PC 69**
See also AMWS 8; CA 29-32R; CAAS 4;
CANR 12, 33, 52, 61, 96, 140; CP 2, 3, 4,
5, 6, 7; DA3; DAM POET; DLB 105;
MAL 5; MTCW 2; MTFW 2005; PFS 7;
RGAL 4; WP
Simmel, Georg 1858-1918 .... **TCLC 64**
See also CA 157; DLB 296

Simmons, Charles (Paul) 1924- .... **CLC 57**
See also CA 89-92; INT CA-89-92

Simmons, Dan 1948- .... **CLC 44**
See also AAYA 16, 54; CA 138; CANR 53, 81, 126; CPW; DAM POP; HGG; SUFW 2

Simmons, James (Stewart Alexander) 1933- .... **CLC 43**
See also CA 105; CAAS 21; CP 1, 2, 3, 4, 5, 6, 7; DLB 40

Simms, William Gilmore 1806-1870 .... **NCLC 3**
See also DLB 3, 30, 59, 73, 248, 254; RGAL 4

Simon, Carly 1945- .... **CLC 26**
See also CA 105

Simon, Claude 1913-2005 ... **CLC 4, 9, 15, 39**
See also CA 89-92; 241; CANR 33, 117; CWW 2; DAM NOV; DLB 83; EW 13; EWL 3; GFL 1789 to the Present; MTCW 1

Simon, Claude Eugene Henri
See Simon, Claude

Simon, Claude Henri Eugene
See Simon, Claude

Simon, Myles
See Follett, Ken(neth Martin)

Simon, (Marvin) Neil 1927- ... **CLC 6, 11, 31, 39, 70; DC 14**
See also AAYA 32; AITN 1; AMWS 4; CA 21-24R; CAD; CANR 26, 54, 87, 126; CD 5, 6; DA3; DAM DRAM; DFS 2, 6, 12, 18; DLB 7, 266; LAIT 4; MAL 5; MTCW 1, 2; MTFW 2005; RGAL 4; TUS

Simon, Paul (Frederick) 1941(?)- ..... **CLC 17**
See also CA 116; 153

Simonon, Paul 1956(?)- .... **CLC 30**

Simonson, Rick ed. .... **CLC 70**

Simpson, Harriette
See Arnow, Harriette (Louisa) Simpson

Simpson, Louis (Aston Marantz) 1923- .... **CLC 4, 7, 9, 32, 149**
See also AMWS 9; CA 1-4R; CAAS 4; CANR 1, 61, 140; CP 1, 2, 3, 4, 5, 6, 7; DAM POET; DLB 5; MAL 5; MTCW 1, 2; MTFW 2005; PFS 7, 11, 14; RGAL 4

Simpson, Mona (Elizabeth) 1957- ... **CLC 44, 146**
See also CA 122; 135; CANR 68, 103; CN 6, 7; EWL 3

Simpson, N(orman) F(rederick) 1919- .... **CLC 29**
See also CA 13-16R; CBD; DLB 13; RGEL 2

Sinclair, Andrew (Annandale) 1935- . **CLC 2, 14**
See also CA 9-12R; CAAS 5; CANR 14, 38, 91; CN 1, 2, 3, 4, 5, 6, 7; DLB 14; FANT; MTCW 1

Sinclair, Emil
See Hesse, Hermann

Sinclair, Iain 1943- .... **CLC 76**
See also CA 132; CANR 81; CP 7; HGG

Sinclair, Iain MacGregor
See Sinclair, Iain

Sinclair, Irene
See Griffith, D(avid Lewelyn) W(ark)

Sinclair, Mary Amelia St. Clair 1865(?)-1946
See Sinclair, May
See also CA 104; HGG; RHW

Sinclair, May .... **TCLC 3, 11**
See Sinclair, Mary Amelia St. Clair
See also CA 166; DLB 36, 135; EWL 3; RGEL 2; SUFW

Sinclair, Roy
See Griffith, D(avid Lewelyn) W(ark)

Sinclair, Upton (Beall) 1878-1968 ..... **CLC 1, 11, 15, 63; TCLC 160; WLC**
See also AAYA 63; AMWS 5; BPFB 3; BYA 2; CA 5-8R; 25-28R; CANR 7; CDALB 1929-1941; DA; DA3; DAB; DAC; DAM MST, NOV; DLB 9; EWL 3; INT CANR-7; LAIT 3; MAL 5; MTCW 1, 2; MTFW 2005; NFS 6; RGAL 4; SATA 9; TUS; YAW

Singe, (Edmund) J(ohn) M(illington) 1871-1909 .... **WLC**

Singer, Isaac
See Singer, Isaac Bashevis

Singer, Isaac Bashevis 1904-1991 .. **CLC 1, 3, 6, 9, 11, 15, 23, 38, 69, 111; SSC 3, 53, 80; WLC**
See also AAYA 32; AITN 1, 2; AMW; AMWR 2; BPFB 3; BYA 1, 4; CA 1-4R; 134; CANR 1, 39, 106; CDALB 1941-1968; CLR 1; CN 1, 2, 3, 4; CWRI 5; DA; DA3; DAB; DAC; DAM MST, NOV; DLB 6, 28, 52, 278; DLBY 1991; EWL 3; EXPS; HGG; JRDA; LAIT 3; MAI-CYA 1, 2; MAL 5; MTCW 1, 2; MTFW 2005; RGAL 4; RGSF 2; SATA 3, 27; SATA-Obit 68; SSFS 2, 12, 16; TUS; TWA

Singer, Israel Joshua 1893-1944 .... **TCLC 33**
See also CA 169; EWL 3

Singh, Khushwant 1915- .... **CLC 11**
See also CA 9-12R; CAAS 9; CANR 6, 84; CN 1, 2, 3, 4, 5, 6, 7; EWL 3; RGEL 2

Singleton, Ann
See Benedict, Ruth (Fulton)

Singleton, John 1968(?)- .... **CLC 156**
See also AAYA 50; BW 2, 3; CA 138; CANR 67, 82; DAM MULT

Siniavskii, Andrei
See Sinyavsky, Andrei (Donatevich)
See also CWW 2

Sinjohn, John
See Galsworthy, John

Sinyavsky, Andrei (Donatevich) 1925-1997 .... **CLC 8**
See Siniavskii, Andrei; Sinyavsky, Andrey Donatovich; Tertz, Abram
See also CA 85-88; 159

Sinyavsky, Andrey Donatovich
See Sinyavsky, Andrei (Donatevich)
See also EWL 3

Sirin, V.
See Nabokov, Vladimir (Vladimirovich)

Sissman, L(ouis) E(dward) 1928-1976 .... **CLC 9, 18**
See also CA 21-24R; 65-68; CANR 13; CP 2; DLB 5

Sisson, C(harles) H(ubert) 1914-2003 .... **CLC 8**
See also BRWS 11; CA 1-4R; 220; CAAS 3; CANR 3, 48, 84; CP 1, 2, 3, 4, 5, 6, 7; DLB 27

Sitting Bull 1831(?)-1890 .... **NNAL**
See also DA3; DAM MULT

Sitwell, Dame Edith 1887-1964 ..... **CLC 2, 9, 67; PC 3**
See also BRW 7; CA 9-12R; CANR 35; CDBLB 1945-1960; DAM POET; DLB 20; EWL 3; MTCW 1, 2; MTFW 2005; RGEL 2; TEA

Siwaarmill, H. P.
See Sharp, William

Sjoewall, Maj 1935- .... **CLC 7**
See Sjowall, Maj
See also CA 65-68; CANR 73

Sjowall, Maj
See Sjoewall, Maj
See also BPFB 3; CMW 4; MSW

Skelton, John 1460(?)-1529 ..... **LC 71; PC 25**
See also BRW 1; DLB 136; RGEL 2

Skelton, Robin 1925-1997 .... **CLC 13**
See Zuk, Georges
See also AITN 2; CA 5-8R; 160; CAAS 5; CANR 28, 89; CCA 1; CP 1, 2, 3, 4; DLB 27, 53

Skolimowski, Jerzy 1938- .... **CLC 20**
See also CA 128

Skram, Amalie (Bertha) 1847-1905 .... **TCLC 25**
See also CA 165

Skvorecky, Josef (Vaclav) 1924- ...... **CLC 15, 39, 69, 152**
See also CA 61-64; CAAS 1; CANR 10, 34, 63, 108; CDWLB 4; CWW 2; DA3; DAC; DAM NOV; DLB 232; EWL 3; MTCW 1, 2; MTFW 2005

Slade, Bernard 1930- .... **CLC 11, 46**
See Newbound, Bernard Slade
See also CAAS 9; CCA 1; CD 6; DLB 53

Slaughter, Carolyn 1946- .... **CLC 56**
See also CA 85-88; CANR 85; CN 5, 6, 7

Slaughter, Frank G(ill) 1908-2001 ... **CLC 29**
See also AITN 2; CA 5-8R; 197; CANR 5, 85; INT CANR-5; RHW

Slavitt, David R(ytman) 1935- ..... **CLC 5, 14**
See also CA 21-24R; CAAS 3; CANR 41, 83; CN 1, 2; CP 1, 2, 3, 4, 5, 6, 7; DLB 5, 6

Slesinger, Tess 1905-1945 .... **TCLC 10**
See also CA 107; 199; DLB 102

Slessor, Kenneth 1901-1971 .... **CLC 14**
See also CA 102; 89-92; DLB 260; RGEL 2

Slowacki, Juliusz 1809-1849 .... **NCLC 15**
See also RGWL 3

Smart, Christopher 1722-1771 . **LC 3; PC 13**
See also DAM POET; DLB 109; RGEL 2

Smart, Elizabeth 1913-1986 .... **CLC 54**
See also CA 81-84; 118; CN 4; DLB 88

Smiley, Jane (Graves) 1949- ...... **CLC 53, 76, 144**
See also AAYA 66; AMWS 6; BPFB 3; CA 104; CANR 30, 50, 74, 96; CN 6, 7; CPW 1; DA3; DAM POP; DLB 227, 234; EWL 3; INT CANR-30; MAL 5; MTFW 2005; SSFS 19

Smith, A(rthur) J(ames) M(arshall) 1902-1980 .... **CLC 15**
See also CA 1-4R; 102; CANR 4; CP 1, 2, 3; DAC; DLB 88; RGEL 2

Smith, Adam 1723(?)-1790 .... **LC 36**
See also DLB 104, 252; RGEL 2

Smith, Alexander 1829-1867 .... **NCLC 59**
See also DLB 32, 55

Smith, Anna Deavere 1950- .... **CLC 86**
See also CA 133; CANR 103; CD 5, 6; DFS 2, 22

Smith, Betty (Wehner) 1904-1972 .... **CLC 19**
See also BPFB 3; BYA 3; CA 5-8R; 33-36R; DLBY 1982; LAIT 3; RGAL 4; SATA 6

Smith, Charlotte (Turner) 1749-1806 .... **NCLC 23, 115**
See also DLB 39, 109; RGEL 2; TEA

Smith, Clark Ashton 1893-1961 .... **CLC 43**
See also CA 143; CANR 81; FANT; HGG; MTCW 2; SCFW 1, 2; SFW 4; SUFW

Smith, Dave .... **CLC 22, 42**
See Smith, David (Jeddie)
See also CAAS 7; CP 3, 4, 5, 6, 7; DLB 5

Smith, David (Jeddie) 1942-
See Smith, Dave
See also CA 49-52; CANR 1, 59, 120; CSW; DAM POET

Smith, Florence Margaret 1902-1971
See Smith, Stevie
See also CA 17-18; 29-32R; CANR 35; CAP 2; DAM POET; MTCW 1, 2; TEA

Smith, Iain Crichton 1928-1998 .... **CLC 64**
See also BRWS 9; CA 21-24R; 171; CN 1,
2, 3, 4, 5, 6; CP 1, 2, 3, 4; DLB 40, 139,
319; RGSF 2
Smith, John 1580(?)-1631 .... **LC 9**
See also DLB 24, 30; TUS
Smith, Johnston
See Crane, Stephen (Townley)
Smith, Joseph, Jr. 1805-1844 .... **NCLC 53**
Smith, Lee 1944- .... **CLC 25, 73**
See also CA 114; 119; CANR 46, 118; CN
7; CSW; DLB 143; DLBY 1983; EWL 3;
INT CA-119; RGAL 4
Smith, Martin
See Smith, Martin Cruz
Smith, Martin Cruz 1942- .. **CLC 25; NNAL**
See also BEST 89:4; BPFB 3; CA 85-88;
CANR 6, 23, 43, 65, 119; CMW 4; CPW;
DAM MULT, POP; HGG; INT CANR-
23; MTCW 2; MTFW 2005; RGAL 4
Smith, Patti 1946- .... **CLC 12**
See also CA 93-96; CANR 63
Smith, Pauline (Urmson)
1882-1959 .... **TCLC 25**
See also DLB 225; EWL 3
Smith, Rosamond
See Oates, Joyce Carol
Smith, Sheila Kaye
See Kaye-Smith, Sheila
Smith, Stevie .... **CLC 3, 8, 25, 44; PC 12**
See Smith, Florence Margaret
See also BRWS 2; CP 1; DLB 20; EWL 3;
PAB; PFS 3; RGEL 2
Smith, Wilbur (Addison) 1933- .... **CLC 33**
See also CA 13-16R; CANR 7, 46, 66, 134;
CPW; MTCW 1, 2; MTFW 2005
Smith, William Jay 1918- .... **CLC 6**
See also AMWS 13; CA 5-8R; CANR 44,
106; CP 1, 2, 3, 4, 5, 6, 7; CSW; CWRI
5; DLB 5; MAICYA 1, 2; SAAS 22;
SATA 2, 68, 154; SATA-Essay 154; TCLE
1:2
Smith, Woodrow Wilson
See Kuttner, Henry
Smith, Zadie 1976- .... **CLC 158**
See also AAYA 50; CA 193; MTFW 2005
Smolenskin, Peretz 1842-1885 .... **NCLC 30**
Smollett, Tobias (George) 1721-1771 ... **LC 2,
46**
See also BRW 3; CDBLB 1660-1789; DLB
39, 104; RGEL 2; TEA
Snodgrass, W(illiam) D(e Witt)
1926- .... **CLC 2, 6, 10, 18, 68**
See also AMWS 6; CA 1-4R; CANR 6, 36,
65, 85; CP 1, 2, 3, 4, 5, 6, 7; DAM POET;
DLB 5; MAL 5; MTCW 1, 2; MTFW
2005; RGAL 4; TCLE 1:2
Snorri Sturluson 1179-1241 .... **CMLC 56**
See also RGWL 2, 3
Snow, C(harles) P(ercy) 1905-1980 ... **CLC 1,
4, 6, 9, 13, 19**
See also BRW 7; CA 5-8R; 101; CANR 28;
CDBLB 1945-1960; CN 1, 2; DAM NOV;
DLB 15, 77; DLBD 17; EWL 3; MTCW
1, 2; MTFW 2005; RGEL 2; TEA
Snow, Frances Compton
See Adams, Henry (Brooks)
Snyder, Gary (Sherman) 1930- . **CLC 1, 2, 5,
9, 32, 120; PC 21**
See also AMWS 8; ANW; BG 1:3; CA 17-
20R; CANR 30, 60, 125; CP 1, 2, 3, 4, 5,
6, 7; DA3; DAM POET; DLB 5, 16, 165,
212, 237, 275; EWL 3; MAL 5; MTCW
2; MTFW 2005; PFS 9, 19; RGAL 4; WP
Snyder, Zilpha Keatley 1927- .... **CLC 17**
See also AAYA 15; BYA 1x; CA 9-12R;
CANR 38; CLR 31; JRDA; MAICYA 1,
2; SAAS 2; SATA 1, 28, 75, 110, 163;
SATA-Essay 112, 163; YAW

Soares, Bernardo
See Pessoa, Fernando (Antonio Nogueira)
Sobh, A.
See Shamlu, Ahmad
Sobh, Alef
See Shamlu, Ahmad
Sobol, Joshua 1939- .... **CLC 60**
See Sobol, Yehoshua
See also CA 200
Sobol, Yehoshua 1939-
See Sobol, Joshua
See also CWW 2
Socrates 470B.C.-399B.C. .... **CMLC 27**
Soderberg, Hjalmar 1869-1941 ...... **TCLC 39**
See also DLB 259; EWL 3; RGSF 2
Soderbergh, Steven 1963- .... **CLC 154**
See also AAYA 43
Sodergran, Edith (Irene) 1892-1923
See Soedergran, Edith (Irene)
See also CA 202; DLB 259; EW 11; EWL
3; RGWL 2, 3
Soedergran, Edith (Irene)
1892-1923 .... **TCLC 31**
See Sodergran, Edith (Irene)
Softly, Edgar
See Lovecraft, H(oward) P(hillips)
Softly, Edward
See Lovecraft, H(oward) P(hillips)
Sokolov, Alexander V(sevolodovich) 1943-
See Sokolov, Sasha
See also CA 73-76
Sokolov, Raymond 1941- .... **CLC 7**
See also CA 85-88
Sokolov, Sasha .... **CLC 59**
See Sokolov, Alexander V(sevolodovich)
See also CWW 2; DLB 285; EWL 3; RGWL
2, 3
Solo, Jay
See Ellison, Harlan (Jay)
Sologub, Fyodor .... **TCLC 9**
See Teternikov, Fyodor Kuzmich
See also EWL 3
Solomons, Ikey Esquir
See Thackeray, William Makepeace
Solomos, Dionysios 1798-1857 .... **NCLC 15**
Solwoska, Mara
See French, Marilyn
Solzhenitsyn, Aleksandr I(sayevich)
1918- .. **CLC 1, 2, 4, 7, 9, 10, 18, 26, 34,
78, 134; SSC 32; WLC**
See Solzhenitsyn, Aleksandr Isaevich
See also AAYA 49; AITN 1; BPFB 3; CA
69-72; CANR 40, 65, 116; DA; DA3;
DAB; DAC; DAM MST, NOV; DLB 302;
EW 13; EXPS; LAIT 4; MTCW 1, 2;
MTFW 2005; NFS 6; RGSF 2; RGWL 2,
3; SSFS 9; TWA
Solzhenitsyn, Aleksandr Isaevich
See Solzhenitsyn, Aleksandr I(sayevich)
See also CWW 2; EWL 3
Somers, Jane
See Lessing, Doris (May)
Somerville, Edith Oenone
1858-1949 .... **SSC 56; TCLC 51**
See also CA 196; DLB 135; RGEL 2; RGSF
2
Somerville & Ross
See Martin, Violet Florence; Somerville,
Edith Oenone
Sommer, Scott 1951- .... **CLC 25**
See also CA 106
Sommers, Christina Hoff 1950- ...... **CLC 197**
See also CA 153; CANR 95
Sondheim, Stephen (Joshua) 1930- . **CLC 30,
39, 147; DC 22**
See also AAYA 11, 66; CA 103; CANR 47,
67, 125; DAM DRAM; LAIT 4
Sone, Monica 1919- .... **AAL**
See also DLB 312

Song, Cathy 1955- .... **AAL; PC 21**
See also CA 154; CANR 118; CWP; DLB
169, 312; EXPP; FW; PFS 5
Sontag, Susan 1933-2004 ... **CLC 1, 2, 10, 13,
31, 105, 195**
See also AMWS 3; CA 17-20R; 234; CANR
25, 51, 74, 97; CN 1, 2, 3, 4, 5, 6, 7;
CPW; DA3; DAM POP; DLB 2, 67; EWL
3; MAL 5; MAWW; MTCW 1, 2; MTFW
2005; RGAL 4; RHW; SSFS 10
Sophocles 496(?)B.C.-406(?)B.C. .... **CMLC 2,
47, 51; DC 1; WLCS**
See also AW 1; CDWLB 1; DA; DA3;
DAB; DAC; DAM DRAM, MST; DFS 1,
4, 8; DLB 176; LAIT 1; LATS 1:1; LMFS
1; RGWL 2, 3; TWA
Sordello 1189-1269 .... **CMLC 15**
Sorel, Georges 1847-1922 .... **TCLC 91**
See also CA 118; 188
Sorel, Julia
See Drexler, Rosalyn
Sorokin, Vladimir .... **CLC 59**
See Sorokin, Vladimir Georgievich
Sorokin, Vladimir Georgievich
See Sorokin, Vladimir
See also DLB 285
Sorrentino, Gilbert 1929- .. **CLC 3, 7, 14, 22,
40**
See also CA 77-80; CANR 14, 33, 115; CN
3, 4, 5, 6, 7; CP 1, 2, 3, 4, 5, 6, 7; DLB 5,
173; DLBY 1980; INT CANR-14
Soseki
See Natsume, Soseki
See also MJW
Soto, Gary 1952- ... **CLC 32, 80; HLC 2; PC
28**
See also AAYA 10, 37; BYA 11; CA 119;
125; CANR 50, 74, 107; CLR 38; CP 4,
5, 6, 7; DAM MULT; DLB 82; EWL 3;
EXPP; HW 1, 2; INT CA-125; JRDA;
LLW; MAICYA 2; MAICYAS 1; MAL 5;
MTCW 2; MTFW 2005; PFS 7; RGAL 4;
SATA 80, 120; WYA; YAW
Soupault, Philippe 1897-1990 .... **CLC 68**
See also CA 116; 147; 131; EWL 3; GFL
1789 to the Present; LMFS 2
Souster, (Holmes) Raymond 1921- .... **CLC 5,
14**
See also CA 13-16R; CAAS 14; CANR 13,
29, 53; CP 1, 2, 3, 4, 5, 6, 7; DA3; DAC;
DAM POET; DLB 88; RGEL 2; SATA 63
Southern, Terry 1924(?)-1995 .... **CLC 7**
See also AMWS 11; BPFB 3; CA 1-4R;
150; CANR 1, 55, 107; CN 1, 2, 3, 4, 5,
6; DLB 2; IDFW 3, 4
Southerne, Thomas 1660-1746 .... **LC 99**
See also DLB 80; RGEL 2
Southey, Robert 1774-1843 .... **NCLC 8, 97**
See also BRW 4; DLB 93, 107, 142; RGEL
2; SATA 54
Southwell, Robert 1561(?)-1595 .... **LC 108**
See also DLB 167; RGEL 2; TEA
Southworth, Emma Dorothy Eliza Nevitte
1819-1899 .... **NCLC 26**
See also DLB 239
Souza, Ernest
See Scott, Evelyn
Soyinka, Wole 1934- .. **BLC 3; CLC 3, 5, 14,
36, 44, 179; DC 2; WLC**
See also AFW; BW 2, 3; CA 13-16R;
CANR 27, 39, 82, 136; CD 5, 6; CDWLB
3; CN 6, 7; CP 1, 2, 3, 4, 5, 6 ,7; DA;
DA3; DAB; DAC; DAM DRAM, MST,
MULT; DFS 10; DLB 125; EWL 3;
MTCW 1, 2; MTFW 2005; RGEL 2;
TWA; WLIT 2; WWE 1
Spackman, W(illiam) M(ode)
1905-1990 .... **CLC 46**
See also CA 81-84; 132

Spacks, Barry (Bernard) 1931- .... **CLC 14**
See also CA 154; CANR 33, 109; CP 3, 4, 5, 6, 7; DLB 105

Spanidou, Irini 1946- .... **CLC 44**
See also CA 185

Spark, Muriel (Sarah) 1918- ..... **CLC 2, 3, 5, 8, 13, 18, 40, 94; SSC 10**
See also BRWS 1; CA 5-8R; CANR 12, 36, 76, 89, 131; CDBLB 1945-1960; CN 1, 2, 3, 4, 5, 6, 7; CP 1, 2, 3, 4, 5, 6, 7; DA3; DAB; DAC; DAM MST, NOV; DLB 15, 139; EWL 3; FW; INT CANR-12; LAIT 4; MTCW 1, 2; MTFW 2005; NFS 22; RGEL 2; TEA; WLIT 4; YAW

Spaulding, Douglas
See Bradbury, Ray (Douglas)

Spaulding, Leonard
See Bradbury, Ray (Douglas)

Speght, Rachel 1597-c. 1630 .... **LC 97**
See also DLB 126

Spence, J. A. D.
See Eliot, T(homas) S(tearns)

Spencer, Anne 1882-1975 .... **HR 1:3**
See also BW 2; CA 161; DLB 51, 54

Spencer, Elizabeth 1921- .... **CLC 22; SSC 57**
See also CA 13-16R; CANR 32, 65, 87; CN 1, 2, 3, 4, 5, 6, 7; CSW; DLB 6, 218; EWL 3; MTCW 1; RGAL 4; SATA 14

Spencer, Leonard G.
See Silverberg, Robert

Spencer, Scott 1945- .... **CLC 30**
See also CA 113; CANR 51; DLBY 1986

Spender, Stephen (Harold) 1909-1995 .... **CLC 1, 2, 5, 10, 41, 91**
See also BRWS 2; CA 9-12R; 149; CANR 31, 54; CDBLB 1945-1960; CP 1, 2, 3, 4; DA3; DAM POET; DLB 20; EWL 3; MTCW 1, 2; MTFW 2005; PAB; PFS 23; RGEL 2; TEA

Spengler, Oswald (Arnold Gottfried) 1880-1936 .... **TCLC 25**
See also CA 118; 189

Spenser, Edmund 1552(?)-1599 ...... **LC 5, 39, 117; PC 8, 42; WLC**
See also AAYA 60; BRW 1; CDBLB Before 1660; DA; DA3; DAB; DAC; DAM MST, POET; DLB 167; EFS 2; EXPP; PAB; RGEL 2; TEA; WLIT 3; WP

Spicer, Jack 1925-1965 .... **CLC 8, 18, 72**
See also BG 1:3; CA 85-88; DAM POET; DLB 5, 16, 193; GLL 1; WP

Spiegelman, Art 1948- .... **CLC 76, 178**
See also AAYA 10, 46; CA 125; CANR 41, 55, 74, 124; DLB 299; MTCW 2; MTFW 2005; SATA 109, 158; YAW

Spielberg, Peter 1929- .... **CLC 6**
See also CA 5-8R; CANR 4, 48; DLBY 1981

Spielberg, Steven 1947- .... **CLC 20, 188**
See also AAYA 8, 24; CA 77-80; CANR 32; SATA 32

Spillane, Frank Morrison 1918-
See Spillane, Mickey
See also CA 25-28R; CANR 28, 63, 125; DA3; MTCW 1, 2; MTFW 2005; SATA 66

Spillane, Mickey .... **CLC 3, 13**
See Spillane, Frank Morrison
See also BPFB 3; CMW 4; DLB 226; MSW

Spinoza, Benedictus de 1632-1677 .. **LC 9, 58**

Spinrad, Norman (Richard) 1940- ... **CLC 46**
See also BPFB 3; CA 37-40R, 233; CAAE 233; CAAS 19; CANR 20, 91; DLB 8; INT CANR-20; SFW 4

Spitteler, Carl (Friedrich Georg) 1845-1924 .... **TCLC 12**
See also CA 109; DLB 129; EWL 3

Spivack, Kathleen (Romola Drucker) 1938- .... **CLC 6**
See also CA 49-52

Spofford, Harriet (Elizabeth) Prescott 1835-1921 .... **SSC 87**
See also CA 201; DLB 74, 221

Spoto, Donald 1941- .... **CLC 39**
See also CA 65-68; CANR 11, 57, 93

Springsteen, Bruce (F.) 1949- .... **CLC 17**
See also CA 111

Spurling, Hilary 1940- .... **CLC 34**
See also CA 104; CANR 25, 52, 94

Spurling, Susan Hilary
See Spurling, Hilary

Spyker, John Howland
See Elman, Richard (Martin)

Squared, A.
See Abbott, Edwin A.

Squires, (James) Radcliffe 1917-1993 .... **CLC 51**
See also CA 1-4R; 140; CANR 6, 21; CP 1, 2, 3, 4

Srivastava, Dhanpat Rai 1880(?)-1936
See Premchand
See also CA 118; 197

Stacy, Donald
See Pohl, Frederik

Stael
See Stael-Holstein, Anne Louise Germaine Necker
See also EW 5; RGWL 2, 3

Stael, Germaine de
See Stael-Holstein, Anne Louise Germaine Necker
See also DLB 119, 192; FL 1:3; FW; GFL 1789 to the Present; TWA

Stael-Holstein, Anne Louise Germaine Necker 1766-1817 .... **NCLC 3, 91**
See Stael; Stael, Germaine de

Stafford, Jean 1915-1979 .. **CLC 4, 7, 19, 68; SSC 26, 86**
See also CA 1-4R; 85-88; CANR 3, 65; CN 1, 2; DLB 2, 173; MAL 5; MTCW 1, 2; MTFW 2005; RGAL 4; RGSF 2; SATA-Obit 22; SSFS 21; TCWW 1, 2; TUS

Stafford, William (Edgar) 1914-1993 .... **CLC 4, 7, 29**
See also AMWS 11; CA 5-8R; 142; CAAS 3; CANR 5, 22; CP 1, 2, 3, 4; DAM POET; DLB 5, 206; EXPP; INT CANR-22; MAL 5; PFS 2, 8, 16; RGAL 4; WP

Stagnelius, Eric Johan 1793-1823 . **NCLC 61**

Staines, Trevor
See Brunner, John (Kilian Houston)

Stairs, Gordon
See Austin, Mary (Hunter)

Stalin, Joseph 1879-1953 .... **TCLC 92**

Stampa, Gaspara c. 1524-1554 .. **LC 114; PC 43**
See also RGWL 2, 3; WLIT 7

Stampflinger, K. A.
See Benjamin, Walter

Stancykowna
See Szymborska, Wislawa

Standing Bear, Luther 1868(?)-1939(?) .... **NNAL**
See also CA 113; 144; DAM MULT

Stanislavsky, Konstantin (Sergeivich) 1863(?)-1938 .... **TCLC 167**
See also CA 118

Stannard, Martin 1947- .... **CLC 44**
See also CA 142; DLB 155

Stanton, Elizabeth Cady 1815-1902 .... **TCLC 73**
See also CA 171; DLB 79; FL 1:3; FW

Stanton, Maura 1946- .... **CLC 9**
See also CA 89-92; CANR 15, 123; DLB 120

Stanton, Schuyler
See Baum, L(yman) Frank

Stapledon, (William) Olaf 1886-1950 .... **TCLC 22**
See also CA 111; 162; DLB 15, 255; SCFW 1, 2; SFW 4

Starbuck, George (Edwin) 1931-1996 .... **CLC 53**
See also CA 21-24R; 153; CANR 23; CP 1, 2, 3, 4; DAM POET

Stark, Richard
See Westlake, Donald E(dwin)

Staunton, Schuyler
See Baum, L(yman) Frank

Stead, Christina (Ellen) 1902-1983 ... **CLC 2, 5, 8, 32, 80**
See also BRWS 4; CA 13-16R; 109; CANR 33, 40; CN 1, 2, 3; DLB 260; EWL 3; FW; MTCW 1, 2; MTFW 2005; RGEL 2; RGSF 2; WWE 1

Stead, William Thomas 1849-1912 .... **TCLC 48**
See also CA 167

Stebnitsky, M.
See Leskov, Nikolai (Semyonovich)

Steele, Richard 1672-1729 .... **LC 18**
See also BRW 3; CDBLB 1660-1789; DLB 84, 101; RGEL 2; WLIT 3

Steele, Timothy (Reid) 1948- .... **CLC 45**
See also CA 93-96; CANR 16, 50, 92; CP 7; DLB 120, 282

Steffens, (Joseph) Lincoln 1866-1936 .... **TCLC 20**
See also CA 117; 198; DLB 303; MAL 5

Stegner, Wallace (Earle) 1909-1993 .. **CLC 9, 49, 81; SSC 27**
See also AITN 1; AMWS 4; ANW; BEST 90:3; BPFB 3; CA 1-4R; 141; CAAS 9; CANR 1, 21, 46; CN 1, 2, 3, 4, 5; DAM NOV; DLB 9, 206, 275; DLBY 1993; EWL 3; MAL 5; MTCW 1, 2; MTFW 2005; RGAL 4; TCWW 1, 2; TUS

Stein, Gertrude 1874-1946 ...... **DC 19; PC 18; SSC 42; TCLC 1, 6, 28, 48; WLC**
See also AAYA 64; AMW; AMWC 2; CA 104; 132; CANR 108; CDALB 1917-1929; DA; DA3; DAB; DAC; DAM MST, NOV; POET; DLB 4, 54, 86, 228; DLBD 15; EWL 3; EXPS; FL 1:6; GLL 1; MAL 5; MAWW; MTCW 1, 2; MTFW 2005; NCFS 4; RGAL 4; RGSF 2; SSFS 5; TUS; WP

Steinbeck, John (Ernst) 1902-1968 ... **CLC 1, 5, 9, 13, 21, 34, 45, 75, 124; SSC 11, 37, 77; TCLC 135; WLC**
See also AAYA 12; AMW; BPFB 3; BYA 2, 3, 13; CA 1-4R; 25-28R; CANR 1, 35; CDALB 1929-1941; DA; DA3; DAB; DAC; DAM DRAM, MST, NOV; DLB 7, 9, 212, 275, 309; DLBD 2; EWL 3; EXPS; LAIT 3; MAL 5; MTCW 1, 2; MTFW 2005; NFS 1, 5, 7, 17, 19; RGAL 4; RGSF 2; RHW; SATA 9; SSFS 3, 6; TCWW 1, 2; TUS; WYA; YAW

Steinem, Gloria 1934- .... **CLC 63**
See also CA 53-56; CANR 28, 51, 139; DLB 246; FW; MTCW 1, 2; MTFW 2005

Steiner, George 1929- .... **CLC 24**
See also CA 73-76; CANR 31, 67, 108; DAM NOV; DLB 67, 299; EWL 3; MTCW 1, 2; MTFW 2005; SATA 62

Steiner, K. Leslie
See Delany, Samuel R(ay), Jr.

Steiner, Rudolf 1861-1925 .... **TCLC 13**
See also CA 107

Stendhal 1783-1842 .. **NCLC 23, 46; SSC 27; WLC**
See also DA; DA3; DAB; DAC; DAM MST, NOV; DLB 119; EW 5; GFL 1789 to the Present; RGWL 2, 3; TWA

Stephen, Adeline Virginia
See Woolf, (Adeline) Virginia
Stephen, Sir Leslie 1832-1904 .... **TCLC 23**
See also BRW 5; CA 123; DLB 57, 144, 190
Stephen, Sir Leslie
See Stephen, Sir Leslie
Stephen, Virginia
See Woolf, (Adeline) Virginia
Stephens, James 1882(?)-1950 .... **SSC 50; TCLC 4**
See also CA 104; 192; DLB 19, 153, 162; EWL 3; FANT; RGEL 2; SUFW
Stephens, Reed
See Donaldson, Stephen R(eeder)
Stephenson, Neal 1959- .... **CLC 220**
See also AAYA 38; CA 122; CANR 88, 138; CN 7; MTCW 2005; SFW 4
Steptoe, Lydia
See Barnes, Djuna
See also GLL 1
Sterchi, Beat 1949- .... **CLC 65**
See also CA 203
Sterling, Brett
See Bradbury, Ray (Douglas); Hamilton, Edmond
Sterling, Bruce 1954- .... **CLC 72**
See also CA 119; CANR 44, 135; CN 7; MTFW 2005; SCFW 2; SFW 4
Sterling, George 1869-1926 .... **TCLC 20**
See also CA 117; 165; DLB 54
Stern, Gerald 1925- .... **CLC 40, 100**
See also AMWS 9; CA 81-84; CANR 28, 94; CP 3, 4, 5, 6, 7; DLB 105; RGAL 4
Stern, Richard (Gustave) 1928- ... **CLC 4, 39**
See also CA 1-4R; CANR 1, 25, 52, 120; CN 1, 2, 3, 4, 5, 6, 7; DLB 218; DLBY 1987; INT CANR-25
Sternberg, Josef von 1894-1969 .... **CLC 20**
See also CA 81-84
Sterne, Laurence 1713-1768 .... **LC 2, 48; WLC**
See also BRW 3; BRWC 1; CDBLB 1660-1789; DA; DAB; DAC; DAM MST, NOV; DLB 39; RGEL 2; TEA
Sternheim, (William Adolf) Carl 1878-1942 .... **TCLC 8**
See also CA 105; 193; DLB 56, 118; EWL 3; IDTP; RGWL 2, 3
Stevens, Margaret Dean
See Aldrich, Bess Streeter
Stevens, Mark 1951- .... **CLC 34**
See also CA 122
Stevens, Wallace 1879-1955 . **PC 6; TCLC 3, 12, 45; WLC**
See also AMW; AMWR 1; CA 104; 124; CDALB 1929-1941; DA; DA3; DAB; DAC; DAM MST, POET; DLB 54; EWL 3; EXPP; MAL 5; MTCW 1, 2; PAB; PFS 13, 16; RGAL 4; TUS; WP
Stevenson, Anne (Katharine) 1933- .. **CLC 7, 33**
See also BRWS 6; CA 17-20R; CAAS 9; CANR 9, 33, 123; CP 3, 4, 5, 6, 7; CWP; DLB 40; MTCW 1; RHW
Stevenson, Robert Louis (Balfour) 1850-1894 ...... **NCLC 5, 14, 63; SSC 11, 51; WLC**
See also AAYA 24; BPFB 3; BRW 5; BRWC 1; BRWR 1; BYA 1, 2, 4, 13; CD-BLB 1890-1914; CLR 10, 11; DA; DA3; DAB; DAC; DAM MST, NOV; DLB 18, 57, 141, 156, 174; DLBD 13; GL 3; HGG; JRDA; LAIT 1, 3; MAICYA 1, 2; NFS 11, 20; RGEL 2; RGSF 2; SATA 100; SUFW; TEA; WCH; WLIT 4; WYA; YABC 2; YAW

Stewart, J(ohn) I(nnes) M(ackintosh) 1906-1994 .... **CLC 7, 14, 32**
See Innes, Michael
See also CA 85-88; 147; CAAS 3; CANR 47; CMW 4; CN 1, 2, 3, 4, 5; MTCW 1, 2
Stewart, Mary (Florence Elinor) 1916- .... **CLC 7, 35, 117**
See also AAYA 29; BPFB 3; CA 1-4R; CANR 1, 59, 130; CMW 4; CPW; DAB; FANT; RHW; SATA 12; YAW
Stewart, Mary Rainbow
See Stewart, Mary (Florence Elinor)
Stifle, June
See Campbell, Maria
Stifter, Adalbert 1805-1868 .. **NCLC 41; SSC 28**
See also CDWLB 2; DLB 133; RGSF 2; RGWL 2, 3
Still, James 1906-2001 .... **CLC 49**
See also CA 65-68; 195; CAAS 17; CANR 10, 26; CSW; DLB 9; DLBY 01; SATA 29; SATA-Obit 127
Sting 1951-
See Sumner, Gordon Matthew
See also CA 167
Stirling, Arthur
See Sinclair, Upton (Beall)
Stitt, Milan 1941- .... **CLC 29**
See also CA 69-72
Stockton, Francis Richard 1834-1902
See Stockton, Frank R.
See also AAYA 68; CA 108; 137; MAICYA 1, 2; SATA 44; SFW 4
Stockton, Frank R. .... **TCLC 47**
See Stockton, Francis Richard
See also BYA 4, 13; DLB 42, 74; DLBD 13; EXPS; SATA-Brief 32; SSFS 3; SUFW; WCH
Stoddard, Charles
See Kuttner, Henry
Stoker, Abraham 1847-1912
See Stoker, Bram
See also CA 105; 150; DA; DA3; DAC; DAM MST, NOV; HGG; MTFW 2005; SATA 29
Stoker, Bram . **SSC 62; TCLC 8, 144; WLC**
See Stoker, Abraham
See also AAYA 23; BPFB 3; BRWS 3; BYA 5; CDBLB 1890-1914; DAB; DLB 304; GL 3; LATS 1:1; NFS 18; RGEL 2; SUFW; TEA; WLIT 4
Stolz, Mary (Slattery) 1920- .... **CLC 12**
See also AAYA 8; AITN 1; CA 5-8R; CANR 13, 41, 112; JRDA; MAICYA 1, 2; SAAS 3; SATA 10, 71, 133; YAW
Stone, Irving 1903-1989 .... **CLC 7**
See also AITN 1; BPFB 3; CA 1-4R; 129; CAAS 3; CANR 1, 23; CN 1, 2, 3, 4; CPW; DA3; DAM POP; INT CANR-23; MTCW 1, 2; MTFW 2005; RHW; SATA 3; SATA-Obit 64
Stone, Oliver (William) 1946- .... **CLC 73**
See also AAYA 15, 64; CA 110; CANR 55, 125
Stone, Robert (Anthony) 1937- ... **CLC 5, 23, 42, 175**
See also AMWS 5; BPFB 3; CA 85-88; CANR 23, 66, 95; CN 4, 5, 6, 7; DLB 152; EWL 3; INT CANR-23; MAL 5; MTCW 1; MTFW 2005
Stone, Ruth 1915- .... **PC 53**
See also CA 45-48; CANR 2, 91; CP 7; CSW; DLB 105; PFS 19
Stone, Zachary
See Follett, Ken(neth Martin)

Stoppard, Tom 1937- ... **CLC 1, 3, 4, 5, 8, 15, 29, 34, 63, 91; DC 6; WLC**
See also AAYA 63; BRWC 1; BRWR 2; BRWS 1; CA 81-84; CANR 39, 67, 125; CBD; CD 5, 6; CDBLB 1960 to Present; DA; DA3; DAB; DAC; DAM DRAM, MST; DFS 2, 5, 8, 11, 13, 16; DLB 13, 233; DLBY 1985; EWL 3; LATS 1:2; MTCW 1, 2; MTFW 2005; RGEL 2; TEA; WLIT 4
Storey, David (Malcolm) 1933- . **CLC 2, 4, 5, 8**
See also BRWS 1; CA 81-84; CANR 36; CBD; CD 5, 6; CN 1, 2, 3, 4, 5, 6; DAM DRAM; DLB 13, 14, 207, 245; EWL 3; MTCW 1; RGEL 2
Storm, Hyemeyohsts 1935- ... **CLC 3; NNAL**
See also CA 81-84; CANR 45; DAM MULT
Storm, (Hans) Theodor (Woldsen) 1817-1888 .... **NCLC 1; SSC 27**
See also CDWLB 2; DLB 129; EW; RGSF 2; RGWL 2, 3
Storni, Alfonsina 1892-1938 . **HLC 2; PC 33; TCLC 5**
See also CA 104; 131; DAM MULT; DLB 283; HW 1; LAW
Stoughton, William 1631-1701 .... **LC 38**
See also DLB 24
Stout, Rex (Todhunter) 1886-1975 ..... **CLC 3**
See also AITN 2; BPFB 3; CA 61-64; CANR 71; CMW 4; CN 2; DLB 306; MSW; RGAL 4
Stow, (Julian) Randolph 1935- ... **CLC 23, 48**
See also CA 13-16R; CANR 33; CN 1, 2, 3, 4, 5, 6, 7; CP 1, 2, 3, 4; DLB 260; MTCW 1; RGEL 2
Stowe, Harriet (Elizabeth) Beecher 1811-1896 .... **NCLC 3, 50, 133; WLC**
See also AAYA 53; AMWS 1; CDALB 1865-1917; DA; DA3; DAB; DAC; DAM MST, NOV; DLB 1, 12, 42, 74, 189, 239, 243; EXPN; FL 1:3; JRDA; LAIT 2; MAICYA 1, 2; NFS 6; RGAL 4; TUS; YABC 1
Strabo c. 64B.C.-c. 25 .... **CMLC 37**
See also DLB 176
Strachey, (Giles) Lytton 1880-1932 .... **TCLC 12**
See also BRWS 2; CA 110; 178; DLB 149; DLBD 10; EWL 3; MTCW 2; NCFS 4
Stramm, August 1874-1915 .... **PC 50**
See also CA 195; EWL 3
Strand, Mark 1934- .. **CLC 6, 18, 41, 71; PC 63**
See also AMWS 4; CA 21-24R; CANR 40, 65, 100; CP 1, 2, 3, 4, 5, 6, 7; DAM POET; DLB 5; EWL 3; MAL 5; PAB; PFS 9, 18; RGAL 4; SATA 41; TCLE 1:2
Stratton-Porter, Gene(va Grace) 1863-1924
See Porter, Gene(va Grace) Stratton
See also ANW; CA 137; CLR 87; DLB 221; DLBD 14; MAICYA 1, 2; SATA 15
Straub, Peter (Francis) 1943- ... **CLC 28, 107**
See also BEST 89:1; BPFB 3; CA 85-88; CANR 28, 65, 109; CPW; DAM POP; DLBY 1984; HGG; MTCW 1, 2; MTFW 2005; SUFW 2
Strauss, Botho 1944- .... **CLC 22**
See also CA 157; CWW 2; DLB 124
Strauss, Leo 1899-1973 .... **TCLC 141**
See also CA 101; 45-48; CANR 122
Streatfeild, (Mary) Noel 1897(?)-1986 .... **CLC 21**
See also CA 81-84; 120; CANR 31; CLR 17, 83; CWRI 5; DLB 160; MAICYA 1, 2; SATA 20; SATA-Obit 48
Stribling, T(homas) S(igismund) 1881-1965 .... **CLC 23**
See also CA 189; 107; CMW 4; DLB 9; RGAL 4

Synge, (Edmund) J(ohn) M(illington)
1871-1909 .... **DC 2; TCLC 6, 37**
See also BRW 6; BRWR 1; CA 104; 141;
CDBLB 1890-1914; DAM DRAM; DFS
18; DLB 10, 19; EWL 3; RGEL 2; TEA;
WLIT 4

Syruc, J.
See Milosz, Czeslaw

Szirtes, George 1948- .... **CLC 46; PC 51**
See also CA 109; CANR 27, 61, 117; CP 4,
5, 6, 7

Szymborska, Wislawa 1923- ... **CLC 99, 190;**
PC 44
See also CA 154; CANR 91, 133; CDWLB
4; CWP; CWW 2; DA3; DLB 232; DLBY
1996; EWL 3; MTCW 2; MTFW 2005;
PFS 15; RGWL 3

T. O., Nik
See Annensky, Innokenty (Fyodorovich)

Tabori, George 1914- .... **CLC 19**
See also CA 49-52; CANR 4, 69; CBD; CD
5, 6; DLB 245

Tacitus c. 55-c. 117 .... **CMLC 56**
See also AW 2; CDWLB 1; DLB 211;
RGWL 2, 3

Tagore, Rabindranath 1861-1941 .... **PC 8;**
SSC 48; TCLC 3, 53
See also CA 104; 120; DA3; DAM DRAM,
POET; EWL 3; MTCW 1, 2; MTFW
2005; PFS 18; RGEL 2; RGSF 2; RGWL
2, 3; TWA

Taine, Hippolyte Adolphe
1828-1893 .... **NCLC 15**
See also EW 7; GFL 1789 to the Present

Talayesva, Don C. 1890-(?) .... **NNAL**

Talese, Gay 1932- .... **CLC 37**
See also AITN 1; CA 1-4R; CANR 9, 58,
137; DLB 185; INT CANR-9; MTCW 1,
2; MTFW 2005

Tallent, Elizabeth (Ann) 1954- .... **CLC 45**
See also CA 117; CANR 72; DLB 130

Tallmountain, Mary 1918-1997 .... **NNAL**
See also CA 146; 161; DLB 193

Tally, Ted 1952- .... **CLC 42**
See also CA 120; 124; CAD; CANR 125;
CD 5, 6; INT CA-124

Talvik, Heiti 1904-1947 .... **TCLC 87**
See also EWL 3

Tamayo y Baus, Manuel
1829-1898 .... **NCLC 1**

Tammsaare, A(nton) H(ansen)
1878-1940 .... **TCLC 27**
See also CA 164; CDWLB 4; DLB 220;
EWL 3

Tam'si, Tchicaya U
See Tchicaya, Gerald Felix

Tan, Amy (Ruth) 1952- . **AAL; CLC 59, 120,**
151
See also AAYA 9, 48; AMWS 10; BEST
89:3; BPFB 3; CA 136; CANR 54, 105,
132; CDALBS; CN 6, 7; CPW 1; DA3;
DAM MULT, NOV, POP; DLB 173, 312;
EXPN; FL 1:6; FW; LAIT 3, 5; MAL 5;
MTCW 2; MTFW 2005; NFS 1, 13, 16;
RGAL 4; SATA 75; SSFS 9; YAW

Tandem, Felix
See Spitteler, Carl (Friedrich Georg)

Tanizaki, Jun'ichiro 1886-1965 ... **CLC 8, 14,**
28; SSC 21
See Tanizaki Jun'ichiro
See also CA 93-96; 25-28R; MJW; MTCW
2; MTFW 2005; RGSF 2; RGWL 2

Tanizaki Jun'ichiro
See Tanizaki, Jun'ichiro
See also DLB 180; EWL 3

Tannen, Deborah F(rances) 1945- .. **CLC 206**
See also CA 118; CANR 95

Tanner, William
See Amis, Kingsley (William)

Tao Lao
See Storni, Alfonsina

Tapahonso, Luci 1953- .... **NNAL; PC 65**
See also CA 145; CANR 72, 127; DLB 175

Tarantino, Quentin (Jerome)
1963- .... **CLC 125**
See also AAYA 58; CA 171; CANR 125

Tarassoff, Lev
See Troyat, Henri

Tarbell, Ida M(inerva) 1857-1944 . **TCLC 40**
See also CA 122; 181; DLB 47

Tarkington, (Newton) Booth
1869-1946 .... **TCLC 9**
See also BPFB 3; BYA 3; CA 110; 143;
CWRI 5; DLB 9, 102; MAL 5; MTCW 2;
RGAL 4; SATA 17

Tarkovskii, Andrei Arsen'evich
See Tarkovsky, Andrei (Arsenyevich)

Tarkovsky, Andrei (Arsenyevich)
1932-1986 .... **CLC 75**
See also CA 127

Tartt, Donna 1964(?)- .... **CLC 76**
See also AAYA 56; CA 142; CANR 135;
MTFW 2005

Tasso, Torquato 1544-1595 .... **LC 5, 94**
See also EFS 2; EW 2; RGWL 2, 3; WLIT
7

Tate, (John Orley) Allen 1899-1979 .. **CLC 2,**
4, 6, 9, 11, 14, 24; PC 50
See also AMW; CA 5-8R; 85-88; CANR
32, 108; CN 1, 2; CP 1, 2; DLB 4, 45, 63;
DLBD 17; EWL 3; MAL 5; MTCW 1, 2;
MTFW 2005; RGAL 4; RHW

Tate, Ellalice
See Hibbert, Eleanor Alice Burford

Tate, James (Vincent) 1943- ..... **CLC 2, 6, 25**
See also CA 21-24R; CANR 29, 57, 114;
CP 1, 2, 3, 4, 5, 6, 7; DLB 5, 169; EWL
3; PFS 10, 15; RGAL 4; WP

Tate, Nahum 1652(?)-1715 .... **LC 109**
See also DLB 80; RGEL 2

Tauler, Johannes c. 1300-1361 ...... **CMLC 37**
See also DLB 179; LMFS 1

Tavel, Ronald 1940- .... **CLC 6**
See also CA 21-24R; CAD; CANR 33; CD
5, 6

Taviani, Paolo 1931- .... **CLC 70**
See also CA 153

Taylor, Bayard 1825-1878 .... **NCLC 89**
See also DLB 3, 189, 250, 254; RGAL 4

Taylor, C(ecil) P(hilip) 1929-1981 .... **CLC 27**
See also CA 25-28R; 105; CANR 47; CBD

Taylor, Edward 1642(?)-1729 . **LC 11; PC 63**
See also AMW; DA; DAB; DAC; DAM
MST, POET; DLB 24; EXPP; RGAL 4;
TUS

Taylor, Eleanor Ross 1920- .... **CLC 5**
See also CA 81-84; CANR 70

Taylor, Elizabeth 1912-1975 ..... **CLC 2, 4, 29**
See also CA 13-16R; CANR 9, 70; CN 1,
2; DLB 139; MTCW 1; RGEL 2; SATA
13

Taylor, Frederick Winslow
1856-1915 .... **TCLC 76**
See also CA 188

Taylor, Henry (Splawn) 1942- .... **CLC 44**
See also CA 33-36R; CAAS 7; CANR 31;
CP 7; DLB 5; PFS 10

Taylor, Kamala (Purnaiya) 1924-2004
See Markandaya, Kamala
See also CA 77-80; 227; MTFW 2005; NFS
13

Taylor, Mildred D(elois) 1943- .... **CLC 21**
See also AAYA 10, 47; BW 1; BYA 3, 8;
CA 85-88; CANR 25, 115, 136; CLR 9,
59, 90; CSW; DLB 52; JRDA; LAIT 3;
MAICYA 1, 2; MTFW 2005; SAAS 5;
SATA 135; WYA; YAW

Taylor, Peter (Hillsman) 1917-1994 .. **CLC 1,**
4, 18, 37, 44, 50, 71; SSC 10, 84
See also AMWS 5; BPFB 3; CA 13-16R;
147; CANR 9, 50; CN 1, 2, 3, 4, 5; CSW;
DLB 218, 278; DLBY 1981, 1994; EWL
3; EXPS; INT CANR-9; MAL 5; MTCW
1, 2; MTFW 2005; RGSF 2; SSFS 9; TUS

Taylor, Robert Lewis 1912-1998 .... **CLC 14**
See also CA 1-4R; 170; CANR 3, 64; CN
1, 2; SATA 10; TCWW 1, 2

Tchekhov, Anton
See Chekhov, Anton (Pavlovich)

Tchicaya, Gerald Felix 1931-1988 .. **CLC 101**
See Tchicaya U Tam'si
See also CA 129; 125; CANR 81

Tchicaya U Tam'si
See Tchicaya, Gerald Felix
See also EWL 3

Teasdale, Sara 1884-1933 .... **PC 31; TCLC 4**
See also CA 104; 163; DLB 45; GLL 1;
PFS 14; RGAL 4; SATA 32; TUS

Tecumseh 1768-1813 .... **NNAL**
See also DAM MULT

Tegner, Esaias 1782-1846 .... **NCLC 2**

Teilhard de Chardin, (Marie Joseph) Pierre
1881-1955 .... **TCLC 9**
See also CA 105; 210; GFL 1789 to the
Present

Temple, Ann
See Mortimer, Penelope (Ruth)

Tennant, Emma (Christina) 1937- .. **CLC 13,**
52
See also BRWS 9; CA 65-68; CAAS 9;
CANR 10, 38, 59, 88; CN 3, 4, 5, 6, 7;
DLB 14; EWL 3; SFW 4

Tenneshaw, S. M.
See Silverberg, Robert

Tenney, Tabitha Gilman
1762-1837 .... **NCLC 122**
See also DLB 37, 200

Tennyson, Alfred 1809-1892 ... **NCLC 30, 65,**
115; PC 6; WLC
See also AAYA 50; BRW 4; CDBLB 1832-
1890; DA; DA3; DAB; DAC; DAM MST,
POET; DLB 32; EXPP; PAB; PFS 1, 2, 4,
11, 15, 19; RGEL 2; TEA; WLIT 4; WP

Teran, Lisa St. Aubin de .... **CLC 36**
See St. Aubin de Teran, Lisa

Terence c. 184B.C.-c. 159B.C. ...... **CMLC 14;**
DC 7
See also AW 1; CDWLB 1; DLB 211;
RGWL 2, 3; TWA

Teresa de Jesus, St. 1515-1582 .... **LC 18**

Teresa of Avila, St.
See Teresa de Jesus, St.

Terkel, Louis 1912-
See Terkel, Studs
See also CA 57-60; CANR 18, 45, 67, 132;
DA3; MTCW 1, 2; MTFW 2005

Terkel, Studs .... **CLC 38**
See Terkel, Louis
See also AAYA 32; AITN 1; MTCW 2; TUS

Terry, C. V.
See Slaughter, Frank G(ill)

Terry, Megan 1932- .... **CLC 19; DC 13**
See also CA 77-80; CABS 3; CAD; CANR
43; CD 5, 6; CWD; DFS 18; DLB 7, 249;
GLL 2

Tertullian c. 155-c. 245 .... **CMLC 29**

Tertz, Abram
See Sinyavsky, Andrei (Donatevich)
See also RGSF 2

Tesich, Steve 1943(?)-1996 .... **CLC 40, 69**
See also CA 105; 152; CAD; DLBY 1983

Tesla, Nikola 1856-1943 .... **TCLC 88**

Teternikov, Fyodor Kuzmich 1863-1927
See Sologub, Fyodor
See also CA 104

Tolkien, J(ohn) R(onald) R(euel)
1892-1973 .... **CLC 1, 2, 3, 8, 12, 38;
TCLC 137; WLC**
See also AAYA 10; AITN 1; BPFB 3;
BRWC 2; BRWS 2; CA 17-18; 45-48;
CANR 36, 134; CAP 2; CDBLB 1914-
1945; CLR 56; CN 1; CPW 1; CWRI 5;
DA; DA3; DAB; DAC; DAM MST, NOV,
POP; DLB 15, 160, 255; EFS 2; EWL 3;
FANT; JRDA; LAIT 1:2; LMFS
2; MAICYA 1, 2; MTCW 1, 2; MTFW
2005; NFS 8; RGEL 2; SATA 2, 32, 100;
SATA-Obit 24; SFW 4; SUFW; TEA;
WCH; WYA; YAW
Toller, Ernst 1893-1939 .... **TCLC 10**
See also CA 107; 186; DLB 124; EWL 3;
RGWL 2, 3
Tolson, M. B.
See Tolson, Melvin B(eaunorus)
Tolson, Melvin B(eaunorus)
1898(?)-1966 .... **BLC 3; CLC 36, 105**
See also AFAW 1, 2; BW 1, 3; CA 124; 89-
92; CANR 80; DAM MULT, POET; DLB
48, 76; MAL 5; RGAL 4
Tolstoi, Aleksei Nikolaevich
See Tolstoy, Alexey Nikolaevich
Tolstoi, Lev
See Tolstoy, Leo (Nikolaevich)
See also RGSF 2; RGWL 2, 3
Tolstoy, Aleksei Nikolaevich
See Tolstoy, Alexey Nikolaevich
See also DLB 272
Tolstoy, Alexey Nikolaevich
1882-1945 .... **TCLC 18**
See Tolstoy, Aleksei Nikolaevich
See also CA 107; 158; EWL 3; SFW 4
Tolstoy, Leo (Nikolaevich)
1828-1910 . **SSC 9, 30, 45, 54; TCLC 4,
11, 17, 28, 44, 79, 173; WLC**
See Tolstoi, Lev
See also AAYA 56; CA 104; 123; DA; DA3;
DAB; DAC; DAM MST, NOV; DLB 238;
EFS 2; EW 7; EXPS; IDTP; LAIT 2;
LATS 1:1; LMFS 1; NFS 10; SATA 26;
SSFS 5; TWA
Tolstoy, Count Leo
See Tolstoy, Leo (Nikolaevich)
Tomalin, Claire 1933- .... **CLC 166**
See also CA 89-92; CANR 52, 88; DLB
155
Tomasi di Lampedusa, Giuseppe 1896-1957
See Lampedusa, Giuseppe (Tomasi) di
See also CA 111; DLB 177; EWL 3; WLIT
7
Tomlin, Lily .... **CLC 17**
See Tomlin, Mary Jean
Tomlin, Mary Jean 1939(?)-
See Tomlin, Lily
See also CA 117
Tomline, F. Latour
See Gilbert, W(illiam) S(chwenck)
Tomlinson, (Alfred) Charles 1927- .... **CLC 2,
4, 6, 13, 45; PC 17**
See also CA 5-8R; CANR 33; CP 1, 2, 3, 4,
5, 6, 7; DAM POET; DLB 40; TCLE 1:2
Tomlinson, H(enry) M(ajor)
1873-1958 .... **TCLC 71**
See also CA 118; 161; DLB 36, 100, 195
Tonna, Charlotte Elizabeth
1790-1846 .... **NCLC 135**
See also DLB 163
Tonson, Jacob fl. 1655(?)-1736 .... **LC 86**
See also DLB 170
Toole, John Kennedy 1937-1969 ..... **CLC 19,
64**
See also BPFB 3; CA 104; DLBY 1981;
MTCW 2; MTFW 2005
Toomer, Eugene
See Toomer, Jean

Toomer, Eugene Pinchback
See Toomer, Jean
Toomer, Jean 1894-1967 .. **BLC 3; CLC 1, 4,
13, 22; HR 1:3; PC 7; SSC 1, 45;
TCLC 172; WLCS**
See also AFAW 1, 2; AMWS 3, 9; BW 1;
CA 85-88; CDALB 1917-1929; DA3;
DAM MULT; DLB 45, 51; EWL 3; EXPP;
EXPS; LMFS 2; MAL 5; MTCW 1, 2;
MTFW 2005; NFS 11; RGAL 4; RGSF 2;
SSFS 5
Toomer, Nathan Jean
See Toomer, Jean
Toomer, Nathan Pinchback
See Toomer, Jean
Torley, Luke
See Blish, James (Benjamin)
Tornimparte, Alessandra
See Ginzburg, Natalia
Torre, Raoul della
See Mencken, H(enry) L(ouis)
Torrence, Ridgely 1874-1950 .... **TCLC 97**
See also DLB 54, 249; MAL 5
Torrey, E(dwin) Fuller 1937- .... **CLC 34**
See also CA 119; CANR 71
Torsvan, Ben Traven
See Traven, B.
Torsvan, Benno Traven
See Traven, B.
Torsvan, Berick Traven
See Traven, B.
Torsvan, Berwick Traven
See Traven, B.
Torsvan, Bruno Traven
See Traven, B.
Torsvan, Traven
See Traven, B.
Tourneur, Cyril 1575(?)-1626 .... **LC 66**
See also BRW 2; DAM DRAM; DLB 58;
RGEL 2
Tournier, Michel (Edouard) 1924- .... **CLC 6,
23, 36, 95; SSC 88**
See also CA 49-52; CANR 3, 36, 74; CWW
2; DLB 83; EWL 3; GFL 1789 to the
Present; MTCW 1, 2; SATA 23
Tournimparte, Alessandra
See Ginzburg, Natalia
Towers, Ivar
See Kornbluth, C(yril) M.
Towne, Robert (Burton) 1936(?)- ..... **CLC 87**
See also CA 108; DLB 44; IDFW 3, 4
Townsend, Sue .... **CLC 61**
See Townsend, Susan Lilian
See also AAYA 28; CA 119; 127; CANR
65, 107; CBD; CD 5, 6; CPW; CWD;
DAB; DAC; DAM MST; DLB 271; INT
CA-127; SATA 55, 93; SATA-Brief 48;
YAW
Townsend, Susan Lilian 1946-
See Townsend, Sue
Townshend, Pete
See Townshend, Peter (Dennis Blandford)
Townshend, Peter (Dennis Blandford)
1945- .... **CLC 17, 42**
See also CA 107
Tozzi, Federigo 1883-1920 .... **TCLC 31**
See also CA 160; CANR 110; DLB 264;
EWL 3; WLIT 7
Tracy, Don(ald Fiske) 1905-1970(?)
See Queen, Ellery
See also CA 1-4R; 176; CANR 2
Trafford, F. G.
See Riddell, Charlotte
Traherne, Thomas 1637(?)-1674 .. **LC 99; PC
70**
See also BRW 2; BRWS 11; DLB 131;
PAB; RGEL 2
Traill, Catharine Parr 1802-1899 .. **NCLC 31**
See also DLB 99

Trakl, Georg 1887-1914 .... **PC 20; TCLC 5**
See also CA 104; 165; EW 10; EWL 3;
LMFS 2; MTCW 2; RGWL 2, 3
Trambley, Estela Portillo .... **TCLC 163**
See Portillo Trambley, Estela
See also CA 77-80; RGAL 4
Tranquilli, Secondino
See Silone, Ignazio
Transtroemer, Tomas Gosta
See Transtromer, Tomas (Goesta)
Transtromer, Tomas (Gosta)
See Transtromer, Tomas (Goesta)
See also CWW 2
Transtromer, Tomas (Goesta)
1931- .... **CLC 52, 65**
See Transtromer, Tomas (Gosta)
See also CA 117; 129; CAAS 17; CANR
115; DAM POET; DLB 257; EWL 3; PFS
21
Transtromer, Tomas Gosta
See Transtromer, Tomas (Goesta)
Traven, B. 1882(?)-1969 .... **CLC 8, 11**
See also CA 19-20; 25-28R; CAP 2; DLB
9, 56; EWL 3; MTCW 1; RGAL 4
Trediakovsky, Vasilii Kirillovich
1703-1769 .... **LC 68**
See also DLB 150
Treitel, Jonathan 1959- .... **CLC 70**
See also CA 210; DLB 267
Trelawny, Edward John
1792-1881 .... **NCLC 85**
See also DLB 110, 116, 144
Tremain, Rose 1943- .... **CLC 42**
See also CA 97-100; CANR 44, 95; CN 4,
5, 6, 7; DLB 14, 271; RGSF 2; RHW
Tremblay, Michel 1942- .... **CLC 29, 102**
See also CA 116; 128; CCA 1; CWW 2;
DAC; DAM MST; DLB 60; EWL 3; GLL
1; MTCW 1, 2; MTFW 2005
Trevanian .... **CLC 29**
See Whitaker, Rod(ney)
Trevor, Glen
See Hilton, James
Trevor, William .. **CLC 7, 9, 14, 25, 71, 116;
SSC 21, 58**
See Cox, William Trevor
See also BRWS 4; CBD; CD 5, 6; CN 1, 2,
3, 4, 5, 6, 7; DLB 14, 139; EWL 3; LATS
1:2; RGEL 2; RGSF 2; SSFS 10; TCLE
1:2
Trifonov, Iurii (Valentinovich)
See Trifonov, Yuri (Valentinovich)
See also DLB 302; RGWL 2, 3
Trifonov, Yuri (Valentinovich)
1925-1981 .... **CLC 45**
See Trifonov, Iurii (Valentinovich); Tri-
fonov, Yury Valentinovich
See also CA 126; 103; MTCW 1
Trifonov, Yury Valentinovich
See Trifonov, Yuri (Valentinovich)
See also EWL 3
Trilling, Diana (Rubin) 1905-1996 . **CLC 129**
See also CA 5-8R; 154; CANR 10, 46; INT
CANR-10; MTCW 1, 2
Trilling, Lionel 1905-1975 ..... **CLC 9, 11, 24;
SSC 75**
See also AMWS 3; CA 9-12R; 61-64;
CANR 10, 105; CN 1, 2; DLB 28, 63;
EWL 3; INT CANR-10; MAL 5; MTCW
1, 2; RGAL 4; TUS
Trimball, W. H.
See Mencken, H(enry) L(ouis)
Tristan
See Gomez de la Serna, Ramon
Tristram
See Housman, A(lfred) E(dward)

Trogdon, William (Lewis) 1939-
See Heat-Moon, William Least
See also AAYA 66; CA 115; 119; CANR 47, 89; CPW; INT CA-119

Trollope, Anthony 1815-1882 .... NCLC 6, 33, 101; SSC 28; WLC
See also BRW 5; CDBLB 1832-1890; DA; DA3; DAB; DAC; DAM MST, NOV; DLB 21, 57, 159; RGEL 2; RGSF 2; SATA 22

Trollope, Frances 1779-1863 .... NCLC 30
See also DLB 21, 166

Trollope, Joanna 1943- .... CLC 186
See also CA 101; CANR 58, 95; CN 7; CPW; DLB 207; RHW

Trotsky, Leon 1879-1940 .... TCLC 22
See also CA 118; 167

Trotter (Cockburn), Catharine 1679-1749 .... LC 8
See also DLB 84, 252

Trotter, Wilfred 1872-1939 .... TCLC 97

Trout, Kilgore
See Farmer, Philip Jose

Trow, George W. S. 1943- .... CLC 52
See also CA 126; CANR 91

Troyat, Henri 1911- .... CLC 23
See also CA 45-48; CANR 2, 33, 67, 117; GFL 1789 to the Present; MTCW 1

Trudeau, G(arretson) B(eekman) 1948-
See Trudeau, Garry B.
See also AAYA 60; CA 81-84; CANR 31; SATA 35

Trudeau, Garry B. .... CLC 12
See Trudeau, G(arretson) B(eekman)
See also AAYA 10; AITN 2

Truffaut, Francois 1932-1984 ... CLC 20, 101
See also CA 81-84; 113; CANR 34

Trumbo, Dalton 1905-1976 .... CLC 19
See also CA 21-24R; 69-72; CANR 10; CN 1, 2; DLB 26; IDFW 3, 4; YAW

Trumbull, John 1750-1831 .... NCLC 30
See also DLB 31; RGAL 4

Trundlett, Helen B.
See Eliot, T(homas) S(tearns)

Truth, Sojourner 1797(?)-1883 ...... NCLC 94
See also DLB 239; FW; LAIT 2

Tryon, Thomas 1926-1991 .... CLC 3, 11
See also AITN 1; BPFB 3; CA 29-32R; 135; CANR 32, 77; CPW; DA3; DAM POP; HGG; MTCW 1

Tryon, Tom
See Tryon, Thomas

Ts'ao Hsueh-ch'in 1715(?)-1763 .... LC 1

Tsushima, Shuji 1909-1948
See Dazai Osamu
See also CA 107

Tsvetaeva (Efron), Marina (Ivanovna) 1892-1941 .... PC 14; TCLC 7, 35
See also CA 104; 128; CANR 73; DLB 295; EW 11; MTCW 1, 2; RGWL 2, 3

Tuck, Lily 1938- .... CLC 70
See also CA 139; CANR 90

Tu Fu 712-770 .... PC 9
See Du Fu
See also DAM MULT; TWA; WP

Tunis, John R(oberts) 1889-1975 ..... CLC 12
See also BYA 1; CA 61-64; CANR 62; DLB 22, 171; JRDA; MAICYA 1, 2; SATA 37; SATA-Brief 30; YAW

Tuohy, Frank .... CLC 37
See Tuohy, John Francis
See also CN 1, 2, 3, 4, 5, 6, 7; DLB 14, 139

Tuohy, John Francis 1925-
See Tuohy, Frank
See also CA 5-8R; 178; CANR 3, 47

Turco, Lewis (Putnam) 1934- ..... CLC 11, 63
See also CA 13-16R; CAAS 22; CANR 24, 51; CP 1, 2, 3, 4, 5, 6, 7; DLBY 1984; TCLE 1:2

Turgenev, Ivan (Sergeevich) 1818-1883 ..... DC 7; NCLC 21, 37, 122; SSC 7, 57; WLC
See also AAYA 58; DA; DAB; DAC; DAM MST, NOV; DFS 6; DLB 238, 284; EW 6; LATS 1:1; NFS 16; RGSF 2; RGWL 2, 3; TWA

Turgot, Anne-Robert-Jacques 1727-1781 .... LC 26
See also DLB 314

Turner, Frederick 1943- .... CLC 48
See also CA 73-76, 227; CAAE 227; CAAS 10; CANR 12, 30, 56; DLB 40, 282

Turton, James
See Crace, Jim

Tutu, Desmond M(pilo) 1931- .. BLC 3; CLC 80
See also BW 1, 3; CA 125; CANR 67, 81; DAM MULT

Tutuola, Amos 1920-1997 ..... BLC 3; CLC 5, 14, 29
See also AFW; BW 2, 3; CA 9-12R; 159; CANR 27, 66; CDWLB 3; CN 1, 2, 3, 4, 5, 6; DA3; DAM MULT; DLB 125; DNFS 2; EWL 3; MTCW 1, 2; MTFW 2005; RGEL 2; WLIT 2

Twain, Mark .... SSC 6, 26, 34, 87; TCLC 6, 12, 19, 36, 48, 59, 161; WLC
See Clemens, Samuel Langhorne
See also AAYA 20; AMW; AMWC 1; BPFB 3; BYA 2, 3, 11, 14; CLR 58, 60, 66; DLB 11; EXPN; EXPS; FANT; LAIT 2; MAL 5; NCFS 4; NFS 1, 6; RGAL 4; RGSF 2; SFW 4; SSFS 1, 7, 16, 21; SUFW; TUS; WCH; WYA; YAW

Tyler, Anne 1941- . CLC 7, 11, 18, 28, 44, 59, 103, 205
See also AAYA 18, 60; AMWS 4; BEST 89:1; BPFB 3; BYA 12; CA 9-12R; CANR 11, 33, 53, 109, 132; CDALBS; CN 1, 2, 3, 4, 5, 6, 7; CPW; CSW; DAM NOV, POP; DLB 6, 143; DLBY 1982; EWL 3; EXPN; LATS 1:2; MAL 5; MAWW; MTCW 1, 2; MTFW 2005; NFS 2, 7, 10; RGAL 4; SATA 7, 90; SSFS 17; TCLE 1:2; TUS; YAW

Tyler, Royall 1757-1826 .... NCLC 3
See also DLB 37; RGAL 4

Tynan, Katharine 1861-1931 .... TCLC 3
See also CA 104; 167; DLB 153, 240; FW

Tyndale, William c. 1484-1536 .... LC 103
See also DLB 132

Tyutchev, Fyodor 1803-1873 .... NCLC 34

Tzara, Tristan 1896-1963 .... CLC 47; PC 27; TCLC 168
See also CA 153; 89-92; DAM POET; EWL 3; MTCW 2

Uchida, Yoshiko 1921-1992 .... AAL
See also AAYA 16; BYA 2, 3; CA 13-16R; 139; CANR 6, 22, 47, 61; CDALBS; CLR 6, 56; CWRI 5; DLB 312; JRDA; MAICYA 1, 2; MTCW 1, 2; MTFW 2005; SAAS 1; SATA 1, 53; SATA-Obit 72

Udall, Nicholas 1504-1556 .... LC 84
See also DLB 62; RGEL 2

Ueda Akinari 1734-1809 .... NCLC 131

Uhry, Alfred 1936- .... CLC 55
See also CA 127; 133; CAD; CANR 112; CD 5, 6; CSW; DA3; DAM DRAM, POP; DFS 11, 15; INT CA-133; MTFW 2005

Ulf, Haerved
See Strindberg, (Johan) August

Ulf, Harved
See Strindberg, (Johan) August

Ulibarri, Sabine R(eyes) 1919-2003 .... CLC 83; HLCS 2
See also CA 131; 214; CANR 81; DAM MULT; DLB 82; HW 1, 2; RGSF 2

Unamuno (y Jugo), Miguel de 1864-1936 .. HLC 2; SSC 11, 69; TCLC 2, 9, 148
See also CA 104; 131; CANR 81; DAM MULT, NOV; DLB 108, 322; EW 8; EWL 3; HW 1, 2; MTCW 1, 2; MTFW 2005; RGSF 2; RGWL 2, 3; SSFS 20; TWA

Uncle Shelby
See Silverstein, Shel(don Allan)

Undercliffe, Errol
See Campbell, (John) Ramsey

Underwood, Miles
See Glassco, John

Undset, Sigrid 1882-1949 ..... TCLC 3; WLC
See also CA 104; 129; DA; DA3; DAB; DAC; DAM MST, NOV; DLB 293; EW 9; EWL 3; FW; MTCW 1, 2; MTFW 2005; RGWL 2, 3

Ungaretti, Giuseppe 1888-1970 ... CLC 7, 11, 15; PC 57
See also CA 19-20; 25-28R; CAP 2; DLB 114; EW 10; EWL 3; PFS 20; RGWL 2, 3; WLIT 7

Unger, Douglas 1952- .... CLC 34
See also CA 130; CANR 94

Unsworth, Barry (Forster) 1930- .... CLC 76, 127
See also BRWS 7; CA 25-28R; CANR 30, 54, 125; CN 6, 7; DLB 194

Updike, John (Hoyer) 1932- . CLC 1, 2, 3, 5, 7, 9, 13, 15, 23, 34, 43, 70, 139, 214; SSC 13, 27; WLC
See also AAYA 36; AMW; AMWC 1; AMWR 1; BPFB 3; BYA 12; CA 1-4R; CABS 1; CANR 4, 33, 51, 94, 133; CDALB 1968-1988; CN 1, 2, 3, 4, 5, 6, 7; CP 1, 2, 3, 4, 5, 6, 7; CPW 1; DA; DA3; DAB; DAC; DAM MST, NOV, POET, POP; DLB 2, 5, 143, 218, 227; DLBD 3; DLBY 1980, 1982, 1997; EWL 3; EXPP; HGG; MAL 5; MTCW 1, 2; MTFW 2005; NFS 12; RGAL 4; RGSF 2; SSFS 3, 19; TUS

Upshaw, Margaret Mitchell
See Mitchell, Margaret (Munnerlyn)

Upton, Mark
See Sanders, Lawrence

Upward, Allen 1863-1926 .... TCLC 85
See also CA 117; 187; DLB 36

Urdang, Constance (Henriette) 1922-1996 .... CLC 47
See also CA 21-24R; CANR 9, 24; CP 1, 2, 3, 4; CWP

Uriel, Henry
See Faust, Frederick (Schiller)

Uris, Leon (Marcus) 1924-2003 ... CLC 7, 32
See also AITN 1, 2; BEST 89:2; BPFB 3; CA 1-4R; 217; CANR 1, 40, 65, 123; CN 1, 2, 3, 4, 5, 6; CPW 1; DA3; DAM NOV, POP; MTCW 1, 2; MTFW 2005; SATA 49; SATA-Obit 146

Urista (Heredia), Alberto (Baltazar) 1947- .... HLCS 1
See Alurista
See also CA 182; CANR 2, 32; HW 1

Urmuz
See Codrescu, Andrei

Urquhart, Guy
See McAlmon, Robert (Menzies)

Urquhart, Jane 1949- .... CLC 90
See also CA 113; CANR 32, 68, 116; CCA 1; DAC

Usigli, Rodolfo 1905-1979 .... HLCS 1
See also CA 131; DLB 305; EWL 3; HW 1; LAW

Usk, Thomas (?)-1388 .... **CMLC 76**
See also DLB 146

Ustinov, Peter (Alexander)
1921-2004 .... **CLC 1**
See also AITN 1; CA 13-16R; 225; CANR
25, 51; CBD; CD 5, 6; DLB 13; MTCW
2

U Tam'si, Gerald Felix Tchicaya
See Tchicaya, Gerald Felix

U Tam'si, Tchicaya
See Tchicaya, Gerald Felix

Vachss, Andrew (Henry) 1942- .... **CLC 106**
See also CA 118, 214; CAAE 214; CANR
44, 95; CMW 4

Vachss, Andrew H.
See Vachss, Andrew (Henry)

Vaculik, Ludvik 1926- .... **CLC 7**
See also CA 53-56; CANR 72; CWW 2;
DLB 232; EWL 3

Vaihinger, Hans 1852-1933 .... **TCLC 71**
See also CA 116; 166

Valdez, Luis (Miguel) 1940- ..... **CLC 84; DC
10; HLC 2**
See also CA 101; CAD; CANR 32, 81; CD
5, 6; DAM MULT; DFS 5; DLB 122;
EWL 3; HW 1; LAIT 4; LLW

Valenzuela, Luisa 1938- .... **CLC 31, 104;
HLCS 2; SSC 14, 82**
See also CA 101; CANR 32, 65, 123; CD-
WLB 3; CWW 2; DAM MULT; DLB 113;
EWL 3; FW; HW 1, 2; LAW; RGSF 2;
RGWL 3

Valera y Alcala-Galiano, Juan
1824-1905 .... **TCLC 10**
See also CA 106

Valerius Maximus fl. 20- .... **CMLC 64**
See also DLB 211

Valery, (Ambroise) Paul (Toussaint Jules)
1871-1945 .... **PC 9; TCLC 4, 15**
See also CA 104; 122; DA3; DAM POET;
DLB 258; EW 8; EWL 3; GFL 1789 to
the Present; MTCW 1, 2; MTFW 2005;
RGWL 2, 3; TWA

Valle-Inclan, Ramon (Maria) del
1866-1936 .... **HLC 2; TCLC 5**
See del Valle-Inclan, Ramon (Maria)
See also CA 106; 153; CANR 80; DAM
MULT; DLB 134; EW 8; EWL 3; HW 2;
RGSF 2; RGWL 2, 3

Vallejo, Antonio Buero
See Buero Vallejo, Antonio

Vallejo, Cesar (Abraham)
1892-1938 .... **HLC 2; TCLC 3, 56**
See also CA 105; 153; DAM MULT; DLB
290; EWL 3; HW 1; LAW; RGWL 2, 3

Valles, Jules 1832-1885 .... **NCLC 71**
See also DLB 123; GFL 1789 to the Present

Vallette, Marguerite Eymery
1860-1953 .... **TCLC 67**
See Rachilde
See also CA 182; DLB 123, 192

Valle Y Pena, Ramon del
See Valle-Inclan, Ramon (Maria) del

Van Ash, Cay 1918-1994 .... **CLC 34**
See also CA 220

Vanbrugh, Sir John 1664-1726 .... **LC 21**
See also BRW 2; DAM DRAM; DLB 80;
IDTP; RGEL 2

Van Campen, Karl
See Campbell, John W(ood, Jr.)

Vance, Gerald
See Silverberg, Robert

Vance, Jack .... **CLC 35**
See Vance, John Holbrook
See also DLB 8; FANT; SCFW 1, 2; SFW
4; SUFW 1, 2

Vance, John Holbrook 1916-
See Queen, Ellery; Vance, Jack
See also CA 29-32R; CANR 17, 65; CMW
4; MTCW 1

**Van Den Bogarde, Derek Jules Gaspard
Ulric Niven** 1921-1999 .... **CLC 14**
See Bogarde, Dirk
See also CA 77-80; 179

Vandenburgh, Jane .... **CLC 59**
See also CA 168

Vanderhaeghe, Guy 1951- .... **CLC 41**
See also BPFB 3; CA 113; CANR 72, 145;
CN 7

van der Post, Laurens (Jan)
1906-1996 .... **CLC 5**
See also AFW; CA 5-8R; 155; CANR 35;
CN 1, 2, 3, 4, 5, 6; DLB 204; RGEL 2

van de Wetering, Janwillem 1931- ... **CLC 47**
See also CA 49-52; CANR 4, 62, 90; CMW
4

Van Dine, S. S. .... **TCLC 23**
See Wright, Willard Huntington
See also DLB 306; MSW

Van Doren, Carl (Clinton)
1885-1950 .... **TCLC 18**
See also CA 111; 168

Van Doren, Mark 1894-1972 .... **CLC 6, 10**
See also CA 1-4R; 37-40R; CANR 3; CN
1; CP 1; DLB 45, 284; MAL 5; MTCW
1, 2; RGAL 4

Van Druten, John (William)
1901-1957 .... **TCLC 2**
See also CA 104; 161; DLB 10; MAL 5;
RGAL 4

Van Duyn, Mona (Jane) 1921-2004 .. **CLC 3,
7, 63, 116**
See also CA 9-12R; 234; CANR 7, 38, 60,
116; CP 1, 2, 3, 4, 5, 6, 7; CWP; DAM
POET; DLB 5; MAL 5; MTFW 2005;
PFS 20

Van Dyne, Edith
See Baum, L(yman) Frank

van Itallie, Jean-Claude 1936- .... **CLC 3**
See also CA 45-48; CAAS 2; CAD; CANR
1, 48; CD 5, 6; DLB 7

Van Loot, Cornelius Obenchain
See Roberts, Kenneth (Lewis)

van Ostaijen, Paul 1896-1928 .... **TCLC 33**
See also CA 163

Van Peebles, Melvin 1932- .... **CLC 2, 20**
See also BW 2, 3; CA 85-88; CANR 27,
67, 82; DAM MULT

van Schendel, Arthur(-Francois-Emile)
1874-1946 .... **TCLC 56**
See also EWL 3

Vansittart, Peter 1920- .... **CLC 42**
See also CA 1-4R; CANR 3, 49, 90; CN 4,
5, 6, 7; RHW

Van Vechten, Carl 1880-1964 ... **CLC 33; HR
1:3**
See also AMWS 2; CA 183; 89-92; DLB 4,
9, 51; RGAL 4

van Vogt, A(lfred) E(lton) 1912-2000 . **CLC 1**
See also BPFB 3; BYA 13, 14; CA 21-24R;
190; CANR 28; DLB 8, 251; SATA 14;
SATA-Obit 124; SCFW 1, 2; SFW 4

Vara, Madeleine
See Jackson, Laura (Riding)

Varda, Agnes 1928- .... **CLC 16**
See also CA 116; 122

Vargas Llosa, (Jorge) Mario (Pedro)
1936- .... **CLC 3, 6, 9, 10, 15, 31, 42, 85,
181; HLC 2**
See Llosa, (Jorge) Mario (Pedro) Vargas
See also BPFB 3; CA 73-76; CANR 18, 32,
42, 67, 116, 140; CDWLB 3; CWW 2;
DA; DA3; DAB; DAC; DAM MST,
MULT, NOV; DLB 145; DNFS 2; EWL

3; HW 1, 2; LAIT 5; LATS 1:2; LAW;
LAWS 1; MTCW 1, 2; MTFW 2005;
RGWL 2; SSFS 14; TWA; WLIT 1

Varnhagen von Ense, Rahel
1771-1833 .... **NCLC 130**
See also DLB 90

Vasari, Giorgio 1511-1574 .... **LC 114**

Vasiliu, George
See Bacovia, George

Vasiliu, Gheorghe
See Bacovia, George
See also CA 123; 189

Vassa, Gustavus
See Equiano, Olaudah

Vassilikos, Vassilis 1933- .... **CLC 4, 8**
See also CA 81-84; CANR 75; EWL 3

Vaughan, Henry 1621-1695 .... **LC 27**
See also BRW 2; DLB 131; PAB; RGEL 2

Vaughn, Stephanie .... **CLC 62**

Vazov, Ivan (Minchov) 1850-1921 . **TCLC 25**
See also CA 121; 167; CDWLB 4; DLB
147

Veblen, Thorstein B(unde)
1857-1929 .... **TCLC 31**
See also AMWS 1; CA 115; 165; DLB 246;
MAL 5

Vega, Lope de 1562-1635 ... **HLCS 2; LC 23,
119**
See also EW 2; RGWL 2, 3

Vendler, Helen (Hennessy) 1933- ... **CLC 138**
See also CA 41-44R; CANR 25, 72, 136;
MTCW 1, 2; MTFW 2005

Venison, Alfred
See Pound, Ezra (Weston Loomis)

Ventsel, Elena Sergeevna 1907-2002
See Grekova, I.
See also CA 154

Verdi, Marie de
See Mencken, H(enry) L(ouis)

Verdu, Matilde
See Cela, Camilo Jose

Verga, Giovanni (Carmelo)
1840-1922 .... **SSC 21, 87; TCLC 3**
See also CA 104; 123; CANR 101; EW 7;
EWL 3; RGSF 2; RGWL 2, 3; WLIT 7

Vergil 70B.C.-19B.C. ... **CMLC 9, 40; PC 12;
WLCS**
See Virgil
See also AW 2; DA; DA3; DAB; DAC;
DAM MST, POET; EFS 1; LMFS 1

Vergil, Polydore c. 1470-1555 .... **LC 108**
See also DLB 132

Verhaeren, Emile (Adolphe Gustave)
1855-1916 .... **TCLC 12**
See also CA 109; EWL 3; GFL 1789 to the
Present

Verlaine, Paul (Marie) 1844-1896 .. **NCLC 2,
51; PC 2, 32**
See also DAM POET; DLB 217; EW 7;
GFL 1789 to the Present; LMFS 2; RGWL
2, 3; TWA

Verne, Jules (Gabriel) 1828-1905 ... **TCLC 6,
52**
See also AAYA 16; BYA 4; CA 110; 131;
CLR 88; DA3; DLB 123; GFL 1789 to
the Present; JRDA; LAIT 2; LMFS 2;
MAICYA 1, 2; MTFW 2005; RGWL 2, 3;
SATA 21; SCFW 1, 2; SFW 4; TWA;
WCH

Verus, Marcus Annius
See Aurelius, Marcus

Very, Jones 1813-1880 .... **NCLC 9**
See also DLB 1, 243; RGAL 4

Vesaas, Tarjei 1897-1970 .... **CLC 48**
See also CA 190; 29-32R; DLB 297; EW
11; EWL 3; RGWL 3

Vialis, Gaston
See Simenon, Georges (Jacques Christian)

Wain, John (Barrington) 1925-1994 . **CLC 2, 11, 15, 46**
See also CA 5-8R; 145; CAAS 4; CANR 23, 54; CDBLB 1960 to Present; CN 1, 2, 3, 4, 5; CP 1, 2, 3, 4; DLB 15, 27, 139, 155; EWL 3; MTCW 1, 2; MTFW 2005

Wajda, Andrzej 1926- .... **CLC 16, 219**
See also CA 102

Wakefield, Dan 1932- .... **CLC 7**
See also CA 21-24R; 211; CAAE 211; CAAS 7; CN 4, 5, 6, 7

Wakefield, Herbert Russell 1888-1965 .... **TCLC 120**
See also CA 5-8R; CANR 77; HGG; SUFW

Wakoski, Diane 1937- ...... **CLC 2, 4, 7, 9, 11, 40; PC 15**
See also CA 13-16R, 216; CAAE 216; CAAS 1; CANR 9, 60, 106; CP 1, 2, 3, 4, 5, 6, 7; CWP; DAM POET; DLB 5; INT CANR-9; MAL 5; MTCW 2; MTFW 2005

Wakoski-Sherbell, Diane
See Wakoski, Diane

Walcott, Derek (Alton) 1930- ... **BLC 3; CLC 2, 4, 9, 14, 25, 42, 67, 76, 160; DC 7; PC 46**
See also BW 2; CA 89-92; CANR 26, 47, 75, 80, 130; CBD; CD 5, 6; CDWLB 3; CP 1, 2, 3, 4, 5, 6, 7; DA3; DAB; DAC; DAM MST, MULT, POET; DLB 117; DLBY 1981; DNFS 1; EFS 1; EWL 3; LMFS 2; MTCW 1, 2; MTFW 2005; PFS 6; RGEL 2; TWA; WWE 1

Waldman, Anne (Lesley) 1945- .... **CLC 7**
See also BG 1:3; CA 37-40R; CAAS 17; CANR 34, 69, 116; CP 1, 2, 3, 4, 5, 6, 7; CWP; DLB 16

Waldo, E. Hunter
See Sturgeon, Theodore (Hamilton)

Waldo, Edward Hamilton
See Sturgeon, Theodore (Hamilton)

Walker, Alice (Malsenior) 1944- .... **BLC 3; CLC 5, 6, 9, 19, 27, 46, 58, 103, 167; PC 30; SSC 5; WLCS**
See also AAYA 3, 33; AFAW 1, 2; AMWS 3; BEST 89:4; BPFB 3; BW 2, 3; CA 37-40R; CANR 9, 27, 49, 66, 82, 131; CDALB 1968-1988; CN 4, 5, 6, 7; CPW; CSW; DA; DA3; DAB; DAC; DAM MST, MULT, NOV, POET, POP; DLB 6, 33, 143; EWL 3; EXPN; EXPS; FL 1:6; FW; INT CANR-27; LAIT 3; MAL 5; MAWW; MTCW 1, 2; MTFW 2005; NFS 5; RGAL 4; RGSF 2; SATA 31; SSFS 2, 11; TUS; YAW

Walker, David Harry 1911-1992 ...... **CLC 14**
See also CA 1-4R; 137; CANR 1; CN 1, 2; CWRI 5; SATA 8; SATA-Obit 71

Walker, Edward Joseph 1934-2004
See Walker, Ted
See also CA 21-24R; 226; CANR 12, 28, 53

Walker, George F(rederick) 1947- .. **CLC 44, 61**
See also CA 103; CANR 21, 43, 59; CD 5, 6; DAB; DAC; DAM MST; DLB 60

Walker, Joseph A. 1935-2003 .... **CLC 19**
See also BW 1, 3; CA 89-92; CAD; CANR 26, 143; CD 5, 6; DAM DRAM, MST; DFS 12; DLB 38

Walker, Margaret (Abigail) 1915-1998 .... **BLC; CLC 1, 6; PC 20; TCLC 129**
See also AFAW 1, 2; BW 2, 3; CA 73-76; 172; CANR 26, 54, 76, 136; CN 1, 2, 3, 4, 5, 6; CP 1, 2, 3, 4; CSW; DAM MULT; DLB 76, 152; EXPP; FW; MAL 5; MTCW 1, 2; MTFW 2005; RGAL 4; RHW

Walker, Ted .... **CLC 13**
See Walker, Edward Joseph
See also CP 1, 2, 3, 4, 5, 6, 7; DLB 40

Wallace, David Foster 1962- ... **CLC 50, 114; SSC 68**
See also AAYA 50; AMWS 10; CA 132; CANR 59, 133; CN 7; DA3; MTCW 2; MTFW 2005

Wallace, Dexter
See Masters, Edgar Lee

Wallace, (Richard Horatio) Edgar 1875-1932 .... **TCLC 57**
See also CA 115; 218; CMW 4; DLB 70; MSW; RGEL 2

Wallace, Irving 1916-1990 .... **CLC 7, 13**
See also AITN 1; BPFB 3; CA 1-4R; 132; CAAS 1; CANR 1, 27; CPW; DAM NOV, POP; INT CANR-27; MTCW 1, 2

Wallant, Edward Lewis 1926-1962 ... **CLC 5, 10**
See also CA 1-4R; CANR 22; DLB 2, 28, 143, 299; EWL 3; MAL 5; MTCW 1, 2; RGAL 4

Wallas, Graham 1858-1932 .... **TCLC 91**

Waller, Edmund 1606-1687 .... **LC 86**
See also BRW 2; DAM POET; DLB 126; PAB; RGEL 2

Walley, Byron
See Card, Orson Scott

Walpole, Horace 1717-1797 .... **LC 2, 49**
See also BRW 3; DLB 39, 104, 213; GL 3; HGG; LMFS 1; RGEL 2; SUFW 1; TEA

Walpole, Hugh (Seymour) 1884-1941 .... **TCLC 5**
See also CA 104; 165; DLB 34; HGG; MTCW 2; RGEL 2; RHW

Walrond, Eric (Derwent) 1898-1966 . **HR 1:3**
See also BW 1; CA 125; DLB 51

Walser, Martin 1927- .... **CLC 27, 183**
See also CA 57-60; CANR 8, 46, 145; CWW 2; DLB 75, 124; EWL 3

Walser, Robert 1878-1956 ..... **SSC 20; TCLC 18**
See also CA 118; 165; CANR 100; DLB 66; EWL 3

Walsh, Gillian Paton
See Paton Walsh, Gillian

Walsh, Jill Paton .... **CLC 35**
See Paton Walsh, Gillian
See also CLR 2, 65; WYA

Walter, Villiam Christian
See Andersen, Hans Christian

Walters, Anna L(ee) 1946- .... **NNAL**
See also CA 73-76

Walther von der Vogelweide c. 1170-1228 .... **CMLC 56**

Walton, Izaak 1593-1683 .... **LC 72**
See also BRW 2; CDBLB Before 1660; DLB 151, 213; RGEL 2

Wambaugh, Joseph (Aloysius), Jr. 1937- .... **CLC 3, 18**
See also AITN 1; BEST 89:3; BPFB 3; CA 33-36R; CANR 42, 65, 115; CMW 4; CPW 1; DA3; DAM NOV, POP; DLB 6; DLBY 1983; MSW; MTCW 1, 2

Wang Wei 699(?)-761(?) .... **PC 18**
See also TWA

Warburton, William 1698-1779 .... **LC 97**
See also DLB 104

Ward, Arthur Henry Sarsfield 1883-1959
See Rohmer, Sax
See also CA 108; 173; CMW 4; HGG

Ward, Douglas Turner 1930- .... **CLC 19**
See also BW 1; CA 81-84; CAD; CANR 27; CD 5, 6; DLB 7, 38

Ward, E. D.
See Lucas, E(dward) V(errall)

Ward, Mrs. Humphry 1851-1920
See Ward, Mary Augusta
See also RGEL 2

Ward, Mary Augusta 1851-1920 ... **TCLC 55**
See Ward, Mrs. Humphry
See also DLB 18

Ward, Nathaniel 1578(?)-1652 .... **LC 114**
See also DLB 24

Ward, Peter
See Faust, Frederick (Schiller)

Warhol, Andy 1928(?)-1987 .... **CLC 20**
See also AAYA 12; BEST 89:4; CA 89-92; 121; CANR 34

Warner, Francis (Robert le Plastrier) 1937- .... **CLC 14**
See also CA 53-56; CANR 11; CP 1, 2, 3, 4

Warner, Marina 1946- .... **CLC 59**
See also CA 65-68; CANR 21, 55, 118; CN 5, 6, 7; DLB 194; MTFW 2005

Warner, Rex (Ernest) 1905-1986 ...... **CLC 45**
See also CA 89-92; 119; CN 1, 2, 3, 4; CP 1, 2, 3, 4; DLB 15; RGEL 2; RHW

Warner, Susan (Bogert) 1819-1885 .... **NCLC 31, 146**
See also DLB 3, 42, 239, 250, 254

Warner, Sylvia (Constance) Ashton
See Ashton-Warner, Sylvia (Constance)

Warner, Sylvia Townsend 1893-1978 .. **CLC 7, 19; SSC 23; TCLC 131**
See also BRWS 7; CA 61-64; 77-80; CANR 16, 60, 104; CN 1, 2; DLB 34, 139; EWL 3; FANT; FW; MTCW 1, 2; RGEL 2; RGSF 2; RHW

Warren, Mercy Otis 1728-1814 ..... **NCLC 13**
See also DLB 31, 200; RGAL 4; TUS

Warren, Robert Penn 1905-1989 .. **CLC 1, 4, 6, 8, 10, 13, 18, 39, 53, 59; PC 37; SSC 4, 58; WLC**
See also AITN 1; AMW; AMWC 2; BPFB 3; BYA 1; CA 13-16R; 129; CANR 10, 47; CDALB 1968-1988; CN 1, 2, 3, 4; CP 1, 2, 3, 4; DA; DA3; DAB; DAC; DAM MST, NOV, POET; DLB 2, 48, 152, 320; DLBY 1980, 1989; EWL 3; INT CANR-10; MAL 5; MTCW 1, 2; MTFW 2005; NFS 13; RGAL 4; RGSF 2; RHW; SATA 46; SATA-Obit 63; SSFS 8; TUS

Warrigal, Jack
See Furphy, Joseph

Warshofsky, Isaac
See Singer, Isaac Bashevis

Warton, Joseph 1722-1800 .... **NCLC 118**
See also DLB 104, 109; RGEL 2

Warton, Thomas 1728-1790 .... **LC 15, 82**
See also DAM POET; DLB 104, 109; RGEL 2

Waruk, Kona
See Harris, (Theodore) Wilson

Warung, Price .... **TCLC 45**
See Astley, William
See also DLB 230; RGEL 2

Warwick, Jarvis
See Garner, Hugh
See also CCA 1

Washington, Alex
See Harris, Mark

Washington, Booker T(aliaferro) 1856-1915 .... **BLC 3; TCLC 10**
See also BW 1; CA 114; 125; DA3; DAM MULT; LAIT 2; RGAL 4; SATA 28

Washington, George 1732-1799 .... **LC 25**
See also DLB 31

Wassermann, (Karl) Jakob 1873-1934 .... **TCLC 6**
See also CA 104; 163; DLB 66; EWL 3

Wiggins, Marianne 1947- .... **CLC 57**
See also BEST 89:3; CA 130; CANR 60, 139; CN 7

Wigglesworth, Michael 1631-1705 .... **LC 106**
See also DLB 24; RGAL 4

Wiggs, Susan .... **CLC 70**
See also CA 201

Wight, James Alfred 1916-1995
See Herriot, James
See also CA 77-80; SATA 55; SATA-Brief 44

Wilbur, Richard (Purdy) 1921- ..... **CLC 3, 6, 9, 14, 53, 110; PC 51**
See also AMWS 3; CA 1-4R; CABS 2; CANR 2, 29, 76, 93, 139; CDALBS; CP 1, 2, 3, 4, 5, 6, 7; DA; DAB; DAC; DAM MST, POET; DLB 5, 169; EWL 3; EXPP; INT CANR-29; MAL 5; MTCW 1, 2; MTFW 2005; PAB; PFS 11, 12, 16; RGAL 4; SATA 9, 108; WP

Wild, Peter 1940- .... **CLC 14**
See also CA 37-40R; CP 1, 2, 3, 4, 5, 6, 7; DLB 5

Wilde, Oscar (Fingal O'Flahertie Wills) 1854(?)-1900 .... **DC 17; SSC 11, 77; TCLC 1, 8, 23, 41, 175; WLC**
See also AAYA 49; BRW 5; BRWC 1, 2; BRWR 2; BYA 15; CA 104; 119; CANR 112; CDBLB 1890-1914; DA; DA3; DAB; DAC; DAM DRAM, MST, NOV; DFS 4, 8, 9, 21; DLB 10, 19, 34, 57, 141, 156, 190; EXPS; FANT; GL 3; LATS 1:1; NFS 20; RGEL 2; RGSF 2; SATA 24; SSFS 7; SUFW; TEA; WCH; WLIT 4

Wilder, Billy .... **CLC 20**
See Wilder, Samuel
See also AAYA 66; DLB 26

Wilder, Samuel 1906-2002
See Wilder, Billy
See also CA 89-92; 205

Wilder, Stephen
See Marlowe, Stephen

Wilder, Thornton (Niven) 1897-1975 .. **CLC 1, 5, 6, 10, 15, 35, 82; DC 1, 24; WLC**
See also AAYA 29; AITN 2; AMW; CA 13-16R; 61-64; CAD; CANR 40, 132; CDALBS; CN 1, 2; DA; DA3; DAB; DAC; DAM DRAM, MST, NOV; DFS 1, 4, 16; DLB 4, 7, 9, 228; DLBY 1997; EWL 3; LAIT 3; MAL 5; MTCW 1, 2; MTFW 2005; RGAL 4; RHW; WYAS 1

Wilding, Michael 1942- ...... **CLC 73; SSC 50**
See also CA 104; CANR 24, 49, 106; CN 4, 5, 6, 7; RGSF 2

Wiley, Richard 1944- .... **CLC 44**
See also CA 121; 129; CANR 71

Wilhelm, Kate .... **CLC 7**
See Wilhelm, Katie (Gertrude)
See also AAYA 20; BYA 16; CAAS 5; DLB 8; INT CANR-17; SCFW 2

Wilhelm, Katie (Gertrude) 1928-
See Wilhelm, Kate
See also CA 37-40R; CANR 17, 36, 60, 94; MTCW 1; SFW 4

Wilkins, Mary
See Freeman, Mary E(leanor) Wilkins

Willard, Nancy 1936- .... **CLC 7, 37**
See also BYA 5; CA 89-92; CANR 10, 39, 68, 107; CLR 5; CP 2, 3, 4; CWP; CWRI 5; DLB 5, 52; FANT; MAICYA 1, 2; MTCW 1; SATA 37, 71, 127; SATA-Brief 30; SUFW 2; TCLE 1:2

William of Malmesbury c. 1090B.C.-c. 1140B.C. .... **CMLC 57**

William of Ockham 1290-1349 ..... **CMLC 32**

Williams, Ben Ames 1889-1953 ..... **TCLC 89**
See also CA 183; DLB 102

Williams, C(harles) K(enneth) 1936- .... **CLC 33, 56, 148**
See also CA 37-40R; CAAS 26; CANR 57, 106; CP 1, 2, 3, 4, 5, 6, 7; DAM POET; DLB 5; MAL 5

Williams, Charles
See Collier, James Lincoln

Williams, Charles (Walter Stansby) 1886-1945 .... **TCLC 1, 11**
See also BRWS 9; CA 104; 163; DLB 100, 153, 255; FANT; RGEL 2; SUFW 1

Williams, Ella Gwendolen Rees
See Rhys, Jean

Williams, (George) Emlyn 1905-1987 .... **CLC 15**
See also CA 104; 123; CANR 36; DAM DRAM; DLB 10, 77; IDTP; MTCW 1

Williams, Hank 1923-1953 .... **TCLC 81**
See Williams, Hiram King

Williams, Helen Maria 1761-1827 .... **NCLC 135**
See also DLB 158

Williams, Hiram Hank
See Williams, Hank

Williams, Hiram King
See Williams, Hank
See also CA 188

Williams, Hugo (Mordaunt) 1942- ... **CLC 42**
See also CA 17-20R; CANR 45, 119; CP 1, 2, 3, 4, 5, 6, 7; DLB 40

Williams, J. Walker
See Wodehouse, P(elham) G(renville)

Williams, John A(lfred) 1925- . **BLC 3; CLC 5, 13**
See also AFAW 2; BW 2, 3; CA 53-56; 195; CAAE 195; CAAS 3; CANR 6, 26, 51, 118; CN 1, 2, 3, 4, 5, 6, 7; CSW; DAM MULT; DLB 2, 33; EWL 3; INT CANR-6; MAL 5; RGAL 4; SFW 4

Williams, Jonathan (Chamberlain) 1929- .... **CLC 13**
See also CA 9-12R; CAAS 12; CANR 8, 108; CP 1, 2, 3, 4, 5, 6, 7; DLB 5

Williams, Joy 1944- .... **CLC 31**
See also CA 41-44R; CANR 22, 48, 97

Williams, Norman 1952- .... **CLC 39**
See also CA 118

Williams, Sherley Anne 1944-1999 ... **BLC 3; CLC 89**
See also AFAW 2; BW 2, 3; CA 73-76; 185; CANR 25, 82; DAM MULT, POET; DLB 41; INT CANR-25; SATA 78; SATA-Obit 116

Williams, Shirley
See Williams, Sherley Anne

Williams, Tennessee 1911-1983 . **CLC 1, 2, 5, 7, 8, 11, 15, 19, 30, 39, 45, 71, 111; DC 4; SSC 81; WLC**
See also AAYA 31; AITN 1, 2; AMW; AMWC 1; CA 5-8R; 108; CABS 3; CAD; CANR 31, 132; CDALB 1941-1968; CN 1, 2, 3; DA; DA3; DAB; DAC; DAM DRAM, MST; DFS 17; DLB 7; DLBD 4; DLBY 1983; EWL 3; GLL 1; LAIT 4; LATS 1:2; MAL 5; MTCW 1, 2; MTFW 2005; RGAL 4; TUS

Williams, Thomas (Alonzo) 1926-1990 .... **CLC 14**
See also CA 1-4R; 132; CANR 2

Williams, William C.
See Williams, William Carlos

Williams, William Carlos 1883-1963 .... **CLC 1, 2, 5, 9, 13, 22, 42, 67; PC 7; SSC 31**
See also AAYA 46; AMW; AMWR 1; CA 89-92; CANR 34; CDALB 1917-1929; DA; DA3; DAB; DAC; DAM MST,

POET; DLB 4, 16, 54, 86; EWL 3; EXPP; MAL 5; MTCW 1, 2; MTFW 2005; NCFS 4; PAB; PFS 1, 6, 11; RGAL 4; RGSF 2; TUS; WP

Williamson, David (Keith) 1942- ..... **CLC 56**
See also CA 103; CANR 41; CD 5, 6; DLB 289

Williamson, Ellen Douglas 1905-1984
See Douglas, Ellen
See also CA 17-20R; 114; CANR 39

Williamson, Jack .... **CLC 29**
See Williamson, John Stewart
See also CAAS 8; DLB 8; SCFW 1, 2

Williamson, John Stewart 1908-
See Williamson, Jack
See also CA 17-20R; CANR 23, 70; SFW 4

Willie, Frederick
See Lovecraft, H(oward) P(hillips)

Willingham, Calder (Baynard, Jr.) 1922-1995 .... **CLC 5, 51**
See also CA 5-8R; 147; CANR 3; CN 1, 2, 3, 4, 5; CSW; DLB 2, 44; IDFW 3, 4; MTCW 1

Willis, Charles
See Clarke, Arthur C(harles)

Willy
See Colette, (Sidonie-Gabrielle)

Willy, Colette
See Colette, (Sidonie-Gabrielle)
See also GLL 1

Wilmot, John 1647-1680 .... **LC 75; PC 66**
See Rochester
See also BRW 2; DLB 131; PAB

Wilson, A(ndrew) N(orman) 1950- .. **CLC 33**
See also BRWS 6; CA 112; 122; CN 4, 5, 6, 7; DLB 14, 155, 194; MTCW 2

Wilson, Angus (Frank Johnstone) 1913-1991 . **CLC 2, 3, 5, 25, 34; SSC 21**
See also BRWS 1; CA 5-8R; 134; CANR 21; CN 1, 2, 3, 4; DLB 15, 139, 155; EWL 3; MTCW 1, 2; MTFW 2005; RGEL 2; RGSF 2

Wilson, August 1945-2005 .. **BLC 3; CLC 39, 50, 63, 118; DC 2; WLCS**
See also AAYA 16; AFAW 2; AMWS 8; BW 2, 3; CA 115; 122; CAD; CANR 42, 54, 76, 128; CD 5, 6; DA; DA3; DAB; DAC; DAM DRAM, MST, MULT; DFS 3, 7, 15, 17; DLB 228; EWL 3; LAIT 4; LATS 1:2; MAL 5; MTCW 1, 2; MTFW 2005; RGAL 4

Wilson, Brian 1942- .... **CLC 12**

Wilson, Colin (Henry) 1931- .... **CLC 3, 14**
See also CA 1-4R; CAAS 5; CANR 1, 22, 33, 77; CMW 4; CN 1, 2, 3, 4, 5, 6; DLB 14, 194; HGG; MTCW 1; SFW 4

Wilson, Dirk
See Pohl, Frederik

Wilson, Edmund 1895-1972 .. **CLC 1, 2, 3, 8, 24**
See also AMW; CA 1-4R; 37-40R; CANR 1, 46, 110; CN 1; DLB 63; EWL 3; MAL 5; MTCW 1, 2; MTFW 2005; RGAL 4; TUS

Wilson, Ethel Davis (Bryant) 1888(?)-1980 .... **CLC 13**
See also CA 102; CN 1, 2; DAC; DAM POET; DLB 68; MTCW 1; RGEL 2

Wilson, Harriet
See Wilson, Harriet E. Adams
See also DLB 239

Wilson, Harriet E.
See Wilson, Harriet E. Adams
See also DLB 243

Wilson, Harriet E. Adams 1827(?)-1863(?) .... **BLC 3; NCLC 78**
See Wilson, Harriet; Wilson, Harriet E.
See also DAM MULT; DLB 50

Wilson, John 1785-1854 .... **NCLC 5**

Wilson, John (Anthony) Burgess 1917-1993
See Burgess, Anthony
See also CA 1-4R; 143; CANR 2, 46; DA3;
DAC; DAM NOV; MTCW 1, 2; MTFW
2005; NFS 15; TEA

Wilson, Lanford 1937- .. **CLC 7, 14, 36, 197;
DC 19**
See also CA 17-20R; CABS 3; CAD; CANR
45, 96; CD 5, 6; DAM DRAM; DFS 4, 9,
12, 16, 20; DLB 7; EWL 3; MAL 5; TUS

Wilson, Robert M. 1941- .... **CLC 7, 9**
See also CA 49-52; CAD; CANR 2, 41; CD
5, 6; MTCW 1

Wilson, Robert McLiam 1964- .... **CLC 59**
See also CA 132; DLB 267

Wilson, Sloan 1920-2003 .... **CLC 32**
See also CA 1-4R; 216; CANR 1, 44; CN
1, 2, 3, 4, 5, 6

Wilson, Snoo 1948- .... **CLC 33**
See also CA 69-72; CBD; CD 5, 6

Wilson, William S(mith) 1932- .... **CLC 49**
See also CA 81-84

Wilson, (Thomas) Woodrow
1856-1924 .... **TCLC 79**
See also CA 166; DLB 47

Wilson and Warnke eds. .... **CLC 65**

Winchilsea, Anne (Kingsmill) Finch
1661-1720
See Finch, Anne
See also RGEL 2

Windham, Basil
See Wodehouse, P(elham) G(renville)

Wingrove, David (John) 1954- .... **CLC 68**
See also CA 133; SFW 4

Winnemucca, Sarah 1844-1891 .... **NCLC 79;
NNAL**
See also DAM MULT; DLB 175; RGAL 4

Winstanley, Gerrard 1609-1676 .... **LC 52**

Wintergreen, Jane
See Duncan, Sara Jeannette

Winters, Arthur Yvor
See Winters, Yvor

Winters, Janet Lewis .... **CLC 41**
See Lewis, Janet
See also DLBY 1987

Winters, Yvor 1900-1968 .... **CLC 4, 8, 32**
See also AMWS 2; CA 11-12; 25-28R; CAP
1; DLB 48; EWL 3; MAL 5; MTCW 1;
RGAL 4

Winterson, Jeanette 1959- .... **CLC 64, 158**
See also BRWS 4; CA 136; CANR 58, 116;
CN 5, 6, 7; CPW; DA3; DAM POP; DLB
207, 261; FANT; FW; GLL 1; MTCW 2;
MTFW 2005; RHW

Winthrop, John 1588-1649 .... **LC 31, 107**
See also DLB 24, 30

Wirth, Louis 1897-1952 .... **TCLC 92**
See also CA 210

Wiseman, Frederick 1930- .... **CLC 20**
See also CA 159

Wister, Owen 1860-1938 .... **TCLC 21**
See also BPFB 3; CA 108; 162; DLB 9, 78,
186; RGAL 4; SATA 62; TCWW 1, 2

Wither, George 1588-1667 .... **LC 96**
See also DLB 121; RGEL 2

Witkacy
See Witkiewicz, Stanislaw Ignacy

Witkiewicz, Stanislaw Ignacy
1885-1939 .... **TCLC 8**
See also CA 105; 162; CDWLB 4; DLB
215; EW 10; EWL 3; RGWL 2, 3; SFW 4

Wittgenstein, Ludwig (Josef Johann)
1889-1951 .... **TCLC 59**
See also CA 113; 164; DLB 262; MTCW 2

Wittig, Monique 1935-2003 .... **CLC 22**
See also CA 116; 135; 212; CANR 143;
CWW 2; DLB 83; EWL 3; FW; GLL 1

Wittlin, Jozef 1896-1976 .... **CLC 25**
See also CA 49-52; 65-68; CANR 3; EWL
3

Wodehouse, P(elham) G(renville)
1881-1975 . **CLC 1, 2, 5, 10, 22; SSC 2;
TCLC 108**
See also AAYA 65; AITN 2; BRWS 3; CA
45-48; 57-60; CANR 3, 33; CDBLB
1914-1945; CN 1, 2; CPW 1; DA3; DAB;
DAC; DAM NOV; DLB 34, 162; EWL 3;
MTCW 1, 2; MTFW 2005; RGEL 2;
RGSF 2; SATA 22; SSFS 10

Woiwode, L.
See Woiwode, Larry (Alfred)

Woiwode, Larry (Alfred) 1941- ... **CLC 6, 10**
See also CA 73-76; CANR 16, 94; CN 3, 4,
5, 6, 7; DLB 6; INT CANR-16

Wojciechowska, Maia (Teresa)
1927-2002 .... **CLC 26**
See also AAYA 8, 46; BYA 3; CA 9-12R;
183; 209; CAAE 183; CANR 4, 41; CLR
1; JRDA; MAICYA 1, 2; SAAS 1; SATA
1, 28, 83; SATA-Essay 104; SATA-Obit
134; YAW

Wojtyla, Karol (Jozef)
See John Paul II, Pope

Wojtyla, Karol (Josef)
See John Paul II, Pope

Wolf, Christa 1929- .... **CLC 14, 29, 58, 150**
See also CA 85-88; CANR 45, 123; CD-
WLB 2; CWW 2; DLB 75; EWL 3; FW;
MTCW 1; RGWL 2, 3; SSFS 14

Wolf, Naomi 1962- .... **CLC 157**
See also CA 141; CANR 110; FW; MTFW
2005

Wolfe, Gene 1931- .... **CLC 25**
See also AAYA 35; CA 57-60; CAAS 9;
CANR 6, 32, 60; CPW; DAM POP; DLB
8; FANT; MTCW 2; MTFW 2005; SATA
118, 165; SCFW 2; SFW 4; SUFW 2

Wolfe, Gene Rodman
See Wolfe, Gene

Wolfe, George C. 1954- .... **BLCS; CLC 49**
See also CA 149; CAD; CD 5, 6

Wolfe, Thomas (Clayton)
1900-1938 ...... **SSC 33; TCLC 4, 13, 29,
61; WLC**
See also AMW; BPFB 3; CA 104; 132;
CANR 102; CDALB 1929-1941; DA;
DA3; DAB; DAC; DAM MST, NOV;
DLB 9, 102, 229; DLBD 2, 16; DLBY
1985, 1997; EWL 3; MAL 5; MTCW 1,
2; NFS 18; RGAL 4; SSFS 18; TUS

Wolfe, Thomas Kennerly, Jr.
1931- .... **CLC 147**
See Wolfe, Tom
See also CA 13-16R; CANR 9, 33, 70, 104;
DA3; DAM POP; DLB 185; EWL 3; INT
CANR-9; MTCW 1, 2; MTFW 2005; TUS

Wolfe, Tom .... **CLC 1, 2, 9, 15, 35, 51**
See Wolfe, Thomas Kennerly, Jr.
See also AAYA 8, 67; AITN 2; AMWS 3;
BEST 89:1; BPFB 3; CN 5, 6, 7; CPW;
CSW; DLB 152; LAIT 5; RGAL 4

Wolff, Geoffrey (Ansell) 1937- .... **CLC 41**
See also CA 29-32R; CANR 29, 43, 78

Wolff, Sonia
See Levitin, Sonia (Wolff)

Wolff, Tobias (Jonathan Ansell)
1945- .... **CLC 39, 64, 172; SSC 63**
See also AAYA 16; AMWS 7; BEST 90:2;
BYA 12; CA 114; 117; CAAS 22; CANR
54, 76, 96; CN 5, 6, 7; CSW; DA3; DLB
130; EWL 3; INT CA-117; MTCW 2;
MTFW 2005; RGAL 4; RGSF 2; SSFS 4,
11

Wolfram von Eschenbach c. 1170-c.
1220 .... **CMLC 5**
See Eschenbach, Wolfram von
See also CDWLB 2; DLB 138; EW 1;
RGWL 2

Wolitzer, Hilma 1930- .... **CLC 17**
See also CA 65-68; CANR 18, 40; INT
CANR-18; SATA 31; YAW

Wollstonecraft, Mary 1759-1797 .... **LC 5, 50,
90**
See also BRWS 3; CDBLB 1789-1832;
DLB 39, 104, 158, 252; FL 1:1; FW;
LAIT 1; RGEL 2; TEA; WLIT 3

Wonder, Stevie .... **CLC 12**
See Morris, Steveland Judkins

Wong, Jade Snow 1922- .... **CLC 17**
See also CA 109; CANR 91; SATA 112

Woodberry, George Edward
1855-1930 .... **TCLC 73**
See also CA 165; DLB 71, 103

Woodcott, Keith
See Brunner, John (Kilian Houston)

Woodruff, Robert W.
See Mencken, H(enry) L(ouis)

Woolf, (Adeline) Virginia 1882-1941 .. **SSC 7,
79; TCLC 1, 5, 20, 43, 56, 101, 123,
128; WLC**
See also AAYA 44; BPFB 3; BRW 7;
BRWC 2; BRWR 1; CA 104; 130; CANR
64, 132; CDBLB 1914-1945; DA; DA3;
DAB; DAC; DAM MST, NOV; DLB 36,
100, 162; DLBD 10; EWL 3; EXPS; FL
1:6; FW; LAIT 3; LATS 1:1; LMFS 2;
MTCW 1, 2; MTFW 2005; NCFS 2; NFS
8, 12; RGEL 2; RGSF 2; SSFS 4, 12;
TEA; WLIT 4

Woollcott, Alexander (Humphreys)
1887-1943 .... **TCLC 5**
See also CA 105; 161; DLB 29

Woolrich, Cornell .... **CLC 77**
See Hopley-Woolrich, Cornell George
See also MSW

Woolson, Constance Fenimore
1840-1894 .... **NCLC 82; SSC 90**
See also DLB 12, 74, 189, 221; RGAL 4

Wordsworth, Dorothy 1771-1855 . **NCLC 25,
138**
See also DLB 107

Wordsworth, William 1770-1850 .. **NCLC 12,
38, 111; PC 4, 67; WLC**
See also BRW 4; BRWC 1; CDBLB 1789-
1832; DA; DA3; DAB; DAC; DAM MST,
POET; DLB 93, 107; EXPP; LATS 1:1;
LMFS 1; PAB; PFS 2; RGEL 2; TEA;
WLIT 3; WP

Wotton, Sir Henry 1568-1639 .... **LC 68**
See also DLB 121; RGEL 2

Wouk, Herman 1915- .... **CLC 1, 9, 38**
See also BPFB 2, 3; CA 5-8R; CANR 6,
33, 67, 146; CDALBS; CN 1, 2, 3, 4, 5,
6; CPW; DA3; DAM NOV; DLBY 1982;
INT CANR-6; LAIT 4; MAL 5; MTCW 1, 2;
MTFW 2005; NFS 7; TUS

Wright, Charles (Penzel, Jr.) 1935- .. **CLC 6,
13, 28, 119, 146**
See also AMWS 5; CA 29-32R; CAAS 7;
CANR 23, 36, 62, 88, 135; CP 3, 4, 5, 6,
7; DLB 165; DLBY 1982; EWL 3;
MTCW 1, 2; MTFW 2005; PFS 10

Wright, Charles Stevenson 1932- ..... **BLC 3;
CLC 49**
See also BW 1; CA 9-12R; CANR 26; CN
1, 2, 3, 4, 5, 6, 7; DAM MULT, POET;
DLB 33

Wright, Frances 1795-1852 .... **NCLC 74**
See also DLB 73

Wright, Frank Lloyd 1867-1959 .... **TCLC 95**
See also AAYA 33; CA 174

Wright, Jack R.
See Harris, Mark

Literary Criticism Series
Cumulative Topic Index

This index lists all topic entries in Thompson Gale's *Children's Literature Review* (CLR), *Classical and Medieval Literature Criticism* (CMLC), *Contemporary Literary Criticism* (CLC), *Drama Criticism* (DC), *Literature Criticism from 1400 to 1800* (LC), *Nineteenth-Century Literature Criticism* (NCLC), *Short Story Criticism* (SSC), and *Twentieth-Century Literary Criticism* (TCLC). The index also lists topic entries in the Gale Critical Companion Collection, which includes the following publications: *The Beat Generation* (BG), *Feminism in Literature* (FL), *Gothic Literature* (GL), and *Harlem Renaissance* (HR).

Topic Index

LC Cumulative Nationality Index

AFGHAN

Babur **18**

AMERICAN

Bache, Benjamin Franklin **74**
Belknap, Jeremy **115**
Bradford, William **64**
Bradstreet, Anne **4, 30**
Brown, William Hill **93**
Byrd, William, II **112**
Edwards, Jonathan **7, 54**
Edwards, Sarah Pierpont **87**
Eliot, John **5**
Franklin, Benjamin **25**
Hathorne, John **38**
Henry, Patrick **25**
Hopkinson, Francis **25**
Knight, Sarah Kemble **7**
Mather, Cotton **38**
Mather, Increase **38**
Morton, Thomas **72**
Munford, Robert **5**
Occom, Samson **60**
Penn, William **25**
Rowlandson, Mary **66**
Sewall, Samuel **38**
Stoughton, William **38**
Taylor, Edward **11**
Washington, George **25**
Wheatley (Peters), Phillis **3, 50**
Wigglesworth, Michael **106**
Winthrop, John **31, 107**

BENINESE

Equiano, Olaudah **16**

CANADIAN

Hearne, Samuel **95**
Marie de l'Incarnation **10**

CHINESE

Lo Kuan-chung **12**
P'u Sung-ling **3, 49**
Ts'ao Hsueh-ch'in **1**
Wu Ch'eng-en **7**
Wu Ching-tzu **2**

DANISH

Holberg, Ludvig **6**
Wessel, Johan Herman **7**

DUTCH

Erasmus, Desiderius **16, 93**
Huygens, Constantijn **114**
Lipsius, Justus **16**
Spinoza, Benedictus de **9, 58**

ENGLISH

Addison, Joseph **18**
Alabaster, William **90**
Amory, Thomas **48**
Andrewes, Lancelot **5**
Arbuthnot, John **1**
Ascham, Roger **101**
Askew, Anne **81**
Astell, Mary **68**
Aubin, Penelope **9**
Bacon, Francis **18, 32**
Baldwin, William **113**
Bale, John **62**
Barker, Jane **42, 82**
Beaumont, Francis **33**
Behn, Aphra **1, 30, 42**
Boswell, James **4, 50**
Bradstreet, Anne **4, 30**
Brome, Richard **61**
Brooke, Frances **6, 48**
Browne, Thomas **111**
Bunyan, John **4, 69**
Burke, Edmund **7, 36**
Burton, Robert **74**
Butler, Samuel **16, 43**
Camden, William **77**
Campion, Thomas **78**
Carew, Thomas **13**
Cary, Elizabeth, Lady Falkland **30**
Cavendish, Margaret Lucas **30**
Caxton, William **17**
Centlivre, Susanna **65**
Chapman, George **22, 116**
Charles I **13**
Chatterton, Thomas **3, 54**
Chaucer, Geoffrey **17, 56**
Chettle, Henry **112**
Churchill, Charles **3**
Cibber, Colley **66**
Cleland, John **2, 48**
Cleveland, John **106**
Clifford, Anne **76**
Collier, Jeremy **6**
Collier, Mary **86**
Collins, William **4, 40**
Colman the Elder, George **98**
Congreve, William **5, 21**
Cooper, Anthony Ashley **107**
Coventry, Francis **46**
Coverdale, Myles **77**
Cranmer, Thomas **95**
Crashaw, Richard **24**
Crowne, John **104**
Daniel, Samuel **24**
Davenant, William **13**
Davies, John **85**
Davys, Mary **1, 46**
Day, John **70**
Day, Thomas **1**
Dee, John **20**
Defoe, Daniel **1, 42, 105**
Dekker, Thomas **22**

Delany, Mary (Granville Pendarves) **12**
Deloney, Thomas **41**
Denham, John **73**
Dennis, John **11**
Devenant, William **13**
Dodsley, Robert **97**
Donne, John **10, 24, 91**
Drayton, Michael **8**
Dryden, John **3, 21, 115**
Durfey, Thomas **94**
Elizabeth I **118**
Elyot, Thomas **11**
Equiano, Olaudah **16**
Etherege, George **78**
Fanshawe, Ann **11**
Farquhar, George **21**
Felltham, Owen **92**
Fielding, Henry **1, 46, 85**
Fielding, Sarah **1, 44**
Finch, Anne **3**
Fletcher, John **33**
Foote, Samuel **106**
Ford, John **68**
Foxe, John **14**
Fuller, Thomas **111**
Garrick, David **15**
Gascoigne, George **108**
Gay, John **49**
Gibbon, Edward **97**
Golding, Arthur **101**
Googe, Barnabe **94**
Gower, John **76**
Gray, Thomas **4, 40**
Greene, Robert **41**
Greville, Fulke **79**
Grey, Lady Jane **93**
Hakluyt, Richard **31**
Hall, Joseph **91**
Harvey, Gabriel **88**
Hawes, Stephen **17**
Haywood, Eliza (Fowler) **1, 44**
Henry VIII **10**
Herbert, George **24, 121**
Herrick, Robert **13**
Heywood, John **65**
Heywood, Thomas **111**
Hobbes, Thomas **36**
Hoccleve, Thomas **75**
Hogarth, William **112**
Holinshed, Raphael **69**
Hooker, Richard **95**
Howell, James **13**
Hunter, Robert **7**
Johnson, Samuel **15, 52**
Jonson, Ben(jamin) **6, 33, 110**
Julian of Norwich **6, 52**
Kempe, Margery **6, 56**
Killigrew, Anne **4, 73**
Killigrew, Thomas **57**
Kyd, Thomas **22, 125**
Langland, William **19, 120**
Lanyer, Aemilia **10, 30, 83**
Lawes, Henry **113**

Nationality Index

LC-125 Title Index

ISBN 0-7876-8742-1